SOCIETIES, NETWORKS, AND TRANSITIONS

A GLOBAL HISTORY

SOCIETIES, NETWORKS, AND TRANSITIONS

A GLOBAL HISTORY

VOLUME II: SINCE 1450

CRAIG A. LOCKARD

University of Wisconsin—Green Bay

HOUGHTON MIFFLIN COMPANY   Boston   New York

Senior sponsoring editor: Nancy Blaine
Senior development editor: Julie Swasey
Senior project editor: Carol Newman
Associate project editor: Deborah Berkman
Senior art and design coordinator: Jill Haber
Senior photo researcher: Jennifer Meyer Dare
Composition buyer: Chuck Dutton
Associate manufacturing buyer: Brian Pieragostini
Senior marketing manager for history: Katherine Bates

Cover image: Wat Yai Chai Mongkon, Ayuthaya. Pce de Phra Nakhon si Ayuthya, Thailand, 1357. Robert Harding.

Text Credits: Ch. 22, pp. 669–670: Rabindranath Tagore, *Gitanjali* Visva-Bharati Publishing Department of Visva-Bharati University. Ch. 24, p. 733: "Pastures of Plenty," words and music by Woody Guthrie TRO. © Copyright 1960. (Renewed) 1963. (Renewed) Ludlow Music, Inc. New York. Used by permission. Ch. 25, p. 77: By kind permission of the trustees of the will of the late Dame Margery Perham. Ch. 29, p. 913: "The Times They Are a Changin'." Copyright © 1963 by Warmer Bros. Inc. Copyright renewed 1991 by Special Rider Music. All rights reserved. International copyright secured. Reprinted by permission. Ch. 29, p. 922: Johnny Clegg and Savuka, "Berlin Wall," *Third World Child.* Lyrics by Johnny Clegg and Savuka. Copyright © 1987. Reprinted with permission. Ch. 30, p. 956: "Conflict" by Mabel Segun. Copyright © 1962 by Mable Segun. From *Reflections: Nigerian Prose and Verse,* edited by Frances Ademola, published by African Universities Press. Reprinted by permission of the author.

Printed in the U.S.A.

Library of Congress Catalog Card Number: 2006928173

ISBN 13: 978-0-547-04791-1
ISBN 10: 0-547-04791-6

1 2 3 4 5 6 7 8 9-DOW-11 10 09 08 07

BRIEF CONTENTS

CONTENTS

MAPS

FEATURES

Awareness of the need for a universal view of history—for a history which transcends national and regional boundaries and comprehends the entire globe—is one of the marks of the present. Our past [is] the past of the world, our history is the first to be world history.[1]

British historian Geoffrey Barraclough wrote these words over two decades ago, yet historians are still grappling with what it means to write world history, and why it is crucial to do so. Twenty-first-century students, more than any generation before them, live in multicultural countries and an interconnected world. The world's interdependence calls for teaching a wider vision, which is the goal of this text. My intention is to create a meaningful, coherent, and stimulating presentation that conveys to students the incredible diversity of societies from earliest times to the present, as well as the ways they have been increasingly connected to other societies and shaped by these relationships. History may happen "as one darn thing after another," but the job of historians is to make it something more than facts, names, and dates. A text should provide a readable narrative, supplying a content base while also posing larger questions. The writing is as clear and thorough in its explanation of events and concepts as I can make it. No text can or should teach the course, but I hope that this text provides enough of a baseline of regional and global coverage to allow each instructor to bring her or his own talents, understandings, and particular interests to the process.

I became involved in teaching, debating, and writing world history as a result of my personal and academic experiences. My interest in other cultures was first awakened in the multicultural southern California city where I grew up. Many of my classmates or their parents had come from Asia, Latin America, or the Middle East. There was also a substantial African American community. A curious person did not have to search far to hear music, sample foods, or encounter ideas from many different cultures. I remember being enchanted by the Chinese landscape paintings at a local museum devoted to Asian art, and vowing to one day see some of those misty mountains for myself. Today many young people may be as interested as I was in learning about the world, since, thanks to immigration, many cities and towns all over North America have taken on a cosmopolitan flavor similar to my hometown.

While experiences growing up sparked my interest in other cultures, it was my schooling that pointed the way to a career in teaching world history. When I entered college, all undergraduate students were required to take a two-semester course in Western Civilization as part of the general education requirement. Many colleges and universities in North America had similar classes that introduced students to Egyptian pyramids, Greek philosophy, medieval pageantry, Renaissance art, and the French Revolution, enriching our lives. Fortunately, my university expanded student horizons further by adding course components (albeit brief) on China, Japan, India, and Islam while also developing a study abroad program. I participated in both the study abroad in Salzburg, Austria, and the student exchange with a university in Hong Kong, which meant living with, rather than just sampling, different customs, outlooks, and histories.

Some teachers and academic historians had begun to realize that the emphasis in U.S. education on the histories of the United States and western Europe, to the near exclusion of the rest of the world, was not sufficient for understanding the realities of the mid-twentieth century. Young Americans were being sent thousands of miles away to fight wars in countries, such as Vietnam, that few Americans had ever heard of. Newspapers and television reported developments in places such as Japan and Indonesia, Egypt and Congo, Cuba and Brazil, which had increasing relevance for Americans. Graduate programs and scholarship directed toward Asian, African, Middle Eastern, Latin American, and eastern European and Russian history also grew out of the awareness of a widening world, broadening conceptions of history. I attended one of the new programs in Asian Studies for my M.A. degree, and then the first Ph.D. program in world history. Thanks to that program, I encountered the stimulating work of pioneering world historians from

North America such as Philip Curtin, Marshall Hodgson, William McNeill, and Leften S. Stavrianos. My own approach owes much to the global vision they offered.

To bring some coherence to the emerging world history field as well as to promote a global approach at all levels of education, several dozen of us teaching at the university, college, community college, and high school level in the United States came together in the early 1980s to form the World History Association (WHA), for which I served as founding secretary. The organization grew rapidly, encouraging the teaching, studying, and writing of world history not only in the United States but all over the world. The approaches to world history found among active WHA members vary widely, and my engagement in the ongoing discussions at conferences and in essays, often about the merits of varied textbooks, provided an excellent background for writing this text.

The Aims and Approach of the Text

Societies, Networks, and Transitions: A Global History provides an accessible, thought-provoking guide to students in their exploration of the landscape of the past, helping them to think about it in all its social diversity and interconnectedness and to see their lives with fresh understanding. It does this by combining clear writing, special learning features, current scholarship, and a comprehensive, global approach that does not omit the role and richness of particular regions.

There is a method behind these aims. For nearly thirty-five years I have written about and taught Asian, African, and world history at universities in the United States and Malaysia. A cumulative seven years of study, research, or teaching in Southeast Asia, East Asia, East Africa, and Europe gave me insights into a wide variety of cultures and historical perspectives. Finally, the WHA, its publications and conferences, and the more recent electronic listserv, H-WORLD, have provided active forums for vigorously discussing how best to teach world history.

The most effective approach to presenting world history in a text for undergraduate and advanced high school students, I have concluded, is one that combines the themes of connections and cultures. World history is very much about connections that transcend countries, cultures, and regions, and a text should discuss, for example, major long-distance trade networks such as the Silk Road, the spread of religions, maritime exploration, world wars, and transregional empires such as the Persian, Mongol, and British Empires. These connections are part of the broader global picture. Students need to understand that cultures, however unique, did not emerge and operate in a vacuum but faced similar challenges, shared many common experiences, and influenced each other.

The broader picture is drawn by means of several features in the text. To strengthen the presentation of the global overview, the text uses an innovative essay feature entitled "Societies, Networks, and Transitions." Appearing

at the end of each of the six chronological parts, this feature analyzes and synthesizes the wider trends of the era, such as the role of long-distance trade, the spread of technologies and religions, and global climate change. The objective is to amplify the wider transregional messages already developed in the part chapters and help students to think further about the global context in which societies are enmeshed. Each "Societies, Networks, and Transitions" essay also makes comparisons, for example, between the Han Chinese, Mauryan Indian, and Roman Empires, and between Chinese, Indian, and European emigration in the nineteenth century. These comparisons help to throw further light on diverse cultures and the differences and similarities between them during the era covered. Finally, each essay is meant to show how the transitions that characterize the era lead up to the era discussed in the following part. In addition, the prologues that introduce each of the six eras treated in the text also set out the broader context, including some of the major themes and patterns of wide influence as well as those for each region. Furthermore, several chapters concentrate on global developments since 1750 C.E.

However, while a broad global overview is a strongly developed feature of this text, most chapters, while acknowledging and explaining relevant linkages, focus on a particular region or several regions. Most students learn easiest by focusing on one region or culture at a time. Students also benefit from recognizing the cultural richness and intellectual creativity of specific societies. From this text students learn, for instance, about Chinese poetry, Indonesian music, Arab science, Greek philosophy, West African arts, Indian cinema, and Anglo-American political thought. As a component of this cultural richness, this text also devotes considerable attention to the enduring religious traditions, such as Buddhism, Christianity, and Islam, and to issues of gender. The cultural richness of a region and its distinctive social patterns can get lost in an approach that minimizes regional coverage. Today most people are still mostly concerned with events in their own countries, even as their lives are reshaped by transnational economies and global cultural movements.

Also a strong part of the presentation of world history in this text is its attempt to be comprehensive and inclusive. To enhance comprehensiveness, the text balances social, economic, political, and cultural and religious history, and it also devotes some attention to geographical and environmental contexts as well as to the history of ideas and technologies. At the same time, the text also highlights features within societies, such as economic production, technological innovations, and portable ideas that had widespread or enduring influence. To ensure inclusiveness, the text recognizes the contributions of many societies, including some often neglected in texts, such as sub-Saharan Africa, pre-Columbian America, and Oceania. In particular, this text offers strong coverage of the diverse Asian societies. Throughout history, as today, the great majority of the world's population have lived in Asia.

All textbook authors struggle with how to organize the material. To keep the number of chapters corresponding to the twenty-eight or thirty weeks of most academic calendars in North America, and roughly equal in length, I have often had to combine several regions into a single chapter in order to be comprehensive, sometimes making decisions for convenience sake. For example, unlike texts that may have only one chapter on sub-Saharan Africa covering the centuries from ancient times to 1500 C.E., this text discusses Africa in six chronological eras, devoting three chapters to the centuries prior to 1500 C.E. and three to the years since 1450 C.E. But this sometimes necessitated grouping Africa, depending on the era, with Europe, the Middle East, or the Americas. The material is divided into eras so that students can understand how all regions were part of world history from earliest times. I believe that a chronological structure aids students in grasping the changes over time while helping to organize the material.

Distinguishing Features

Several features of *Societies, Networks, Transitions: A Global History* will help students better understand, assimilate, and appreciate the material they are about to encounter. Those unique to this text include the following.

Introducing World History World history may be the first and possibly the only history course many undergraduates will take in college. The text opens with a short essay that introduces students to the nature of history, the special challenges posed by studying world history, and why we need to study it.

Balancing Themes Three broad themes—uniqueness, interdependence, and change—have shaped the text. They are discussed throughout in terms of three related concepts—societies, networks, and transitions. These concepts, discussed in more detail in "Introducing World History," can be summarized as follows:

- **Societies** Influenced by environmental and geographical factors, people have formed and maintained societies defined by distinctive but often changing cultures, beliefs, social forms, institutions, and material traits.
- **Networks** Over the centuries societies have generally been connected to other societies by growing networks forged by phenomena such as migration, long-distance trade, exploration, military expansion, colonization, the spread of ideas and technologies, and webs of communication. These growing networks modified individual societies, created regional systems, and eventually led to a global system.
- **Transitions** Each major historical era has been marked by one or more great transitions sparked by events or innovations, such as settled agriculture, Mongol imperialism, industrial revolution, or world war, that have had profound and enduring influences on many societies, gradually reshaping the world. At the same time, societies and regions have experienced transitions of regional rather than global scope that have generated new ways of thinking or doing things, such as the expansion of Islam into India or the European colonization of East Africa and Mexico.

Through exposure to these three ideas integrated throughout the text, students learn of the rich cultural mosaic of the world. They are also introduced to its patterns of connections and unity as well as of continuity and change.

"Societies, Networks, and Transitions" Minichapters A short feature at the end of each part assists the student in backing up from the stories of societies and regions to see the larger historical patterns of change and the wider links among distant peoples. This comparative analysis allows students to identify experiences and transitions common to several regions or the entire world and to reflect further on the text themes. These features can also help students review key developments from the preceding chapters.

Historical Controversies Since one of the common misconceptions about history is that it is about the "dead" past, included in each "Societies, Networks, and Transitions" feature is a brief account of a debate among historians over how an issue in the past should be interpreted and what it means to us today. For example, why are the major societies dominated by males, and has this always been true? Why and when did Europe begin its "great divergence" from China and other Asian societies? How do historians evaluate contemporary globalization? Reappraisal is at the heart of history, and many historical questions are never completely answered. Yet most textbooks ignore this dimension of historical study; this text is innovative in including it. The Historical Controversy essays will help show students that historical facts are anything but dead; they live and change their meaning as new questions are asked by each new generation.

Profiles It is impossible to recount the human story without using broad generalizations, but it is also difficult to understand that story without seeing historical events reflected in the lives of men and women, prominent but also ordinary people. Each chapter contains a profile that focuses on the experiences or accomplishments of a woman or man, to convey the flavor of life of the period, to embellish the chapter narrative with interesting personalities, and to integrate gender into the historical account. The profiles try to show how gender affected the individual, shaping her or his opportunities and involvement in society. Several focus questions ask the student to reflect on the profile. For instance, students will examine a historian in early China, look at the spread of Christianity as seen through the life of a pagan female philosopher in Egypt, relive the experience of a female slave in colonial Brazil, and envision modern Indian life through a sketch of a film star.

Special Coverage This text also treats often-neglected areas and subjects. For example:

- It focuses on several regions with considerable historical importance but often marginalized or even omitted in many texts, including sub-Saharan Africa, Southeast Asia, Korea, Central Asia, pre-Columbian North America, ancient South America, the Caribbean, Polynesia, Australia, Canada, and the United States.
- It includes discussions of significant groups that transcend regional boundaries, such as the caravan travelers of the Silk Road, Mongol empire builders, the Indian Ocean maritime traders, and contemporary humanitarian organizations such as Amnesty International and Doctors Without Borders.
- It features extensive coverage of the roots, rise, reshaping, and enduring influence of the great religious and philosophical traditions.
- It blends coverage of gender, particularly the experiences of women, and of social history generally, into the larger narrative.
- It devotes the first chapter of the text to the roots of human history. After a brief introduction to the shaping of our planet, human evolution, and the spread of people around the world, the chapter examines the birth of agriculture, cities, and states, which set the stage for everything to come.
- It includes strong coverage of the world since 1945, a focus of great interest to many students.

Witness to the Past Many texts incorporate excerpts from primary sources, but this text also keeps student needs in mind by using up-to-date translations and addressing a wide range of topics. Included are excerpts from important Buddhist, Hindu, Confucian, Zoroastrian, and Islamic works that helped shape great traditions. Readings such as a collection of Roman graffiti, a thirteenth-century tourist description of a Chinese city, a report on an Aztec market, and a manifesto for modern Egyptian women reveal something of people's lives and concerns. Also offered are materials that shed light on the politics of the time, such as an African king's plea to end the slave trade, Karl Marx's *Communist Manifesto*, and the recent *Arab Human Development Report*. The wide selection of document excerpts is also designed to illustrate how historians work with original documents. Unlike most texts, chapters are also enlivened by brief but numerous excerpts of statements, writings, or songs from people of the era that are effectively interspersed in the chapter narrative so that students can better see the vantage points and opinions of the people of that era.

Learning Aids

The carefully designed learning aids are meant to help faculty teach world history and students actively learn and appreciate it. A number of aids have been created, including some that distinguish this text from others in use.

Part Prologue and Map Each part opens with a prologue that previews the major themes and topics—global and regional—covered in the part chapters. An accompanying world map shows some of the key societies discussed in the part.

Chapter Outline, Primary Source Quotation, and Vignette A chapter outline shows the chapter contents at a glance. Chapter text then opens with a quotation from a primary source pertinent to chapter topics. An interest-grabbing vignette or sketch then funnels students' attention toward the chapter themes they are about to explore.

Focus Questions To prepare students for thinking about the main themes and topics of the chapter, a short list of thoughtfully prepared questions begins each chapter narrative. These questions are then repeated before each major section. The points they deal with are then revisited in the Chapter Summary.

Special Boxed Features Each chapter contains a Witness to the Past drawn from a primary source, and a Profile highlighting a man or woman from that era. The Historical Controversy boxes, which focus on issues of interpretation, are included in each "Societies, Networks, and Transitions" essay. Questions are also placed at the end of the primary source readings, historical controversies, and profiles to help students comprehend the material.

Maps and Other Visuals Maps, photos, chronologies, and tables are amply interspersed throughout the chapters, illustrating and unifying coverage and themes.

Section Summaries At the end of each major section within a chapter, a bulleted summary helps students to review the key topics.

Chapter Summary At the end of each chapter, a concise summary invites students to sum up the chapter content and review its major points.

Annotated Suggested Readings and Endnotes Short lists of annotated suggested readings, mostly recent, and websites providing additional information are also found at the end of each chapter. These lists acknowledge some of the more important works used in writing as well as sources of particular value for undergraduate students. Direct quotes in the text are attributed to their sources in endnotes, which are located at the end of the book.

Key Terms and Pronunciation Guides Important terms likely to be new to the student are boldfaced in the text and immediately defined. These key terms are also listed at the end of the chapter and then listed with their definitions at the end of the text. The pronunciation of foreign and other difficult terms is shown parenthetically where the terms are introduced to help students with the terminology.

Ancillaries

A wide array of supplements accompany this text to help students better master the material and to help instructors in teaching from the book:

- Online Study Center student website

Online Study Center

- Online Teaching Center instructor website

Online Teaching Center

- HM Testing CD-ROM (powered by Diploma)
- Online Instructor's Resource Manual
- PowerPoint maps, images, and lecture outlines
- PowerPoint questions for personal response systems
- Blackboard™ and WebCT™ course cartridges
- Eduspace™ (powered by Blackboard™)
- Interactive ebook

The *Online Study Center* is a companion website for students that features a wide array of resources to help students master the subject matter. The website, prepared by Robert Shannon Sumner of the University of West Georgia, is divided into three major sections:

- "Prepare for Class" includes material such as learning objectives, chapter outlines, and preclass quizzes for a student to consult before going to class.
- "Improve Your Grade" includes practice review material like interactive flashcards, chronological ordering exercises, audio mp3 files of chapter summaries, primary sources, and interactive map exercises.
- "ACE the Test" features our successful ACE brand of practice tests as well as other self-testing materials.

Students can also find additional text resources such as an online glossary, an audio pronunciation guide, and material on how to study more effectively in the General Resources section. Throughout the text, icons direct students to relevant exercises and self-testing material located on the *Online Study Center*. Access the *Online Study Center* for this text by visiting **college.hmco.com/pic/lockard1e.**

The *Online Teaching Center* is a companion website for instructors. It features all of the material on the student site plus additional password-protected resources that help instructors teach the course, such as an electronic version of the *Instructor's Resource Manual*, blank maps of world history, and PowerPoint slides. Access the *Online Teaching Center* for this text by visiting **college.hmco.com/pic/lockard1e.**

HM Testing (powered by *Diploma*) offers instructors a flexible and powerful tool for test generation and test management. Now supported by the Brownstone Research Group's market-leading *Diploma* software, this new version of *HM Testing* significantly improves functionality and ease of use by offering all the tools needed to create, author, deliver, and customize multiple types of tests. *Diploma* is currently in use at thousands of college and university campuses throughout the United States and Canada. The *HM Testing* content was developed by Candace Gregory-Abbott of California State University, Sacramento, and Timothy Furnish of Georgia Perimeter College and offers key term identification, multiple-choice questions (with page references to the correct responses), short-answer questions, and essay questions (with sample answers) as well as unit examination questions, for a total of approximately two thousand test items.

The *Instructor's Resource Manual*, prepared by Siamak Adhami of Saddleback Community College and Doug T. McGetchin of Florida Atlantic University, contains advice on teaching the World History course, suggestions on how to utilize the book's boxed feature program, instructional objectives, chapter outlines and summaries, lecture suggestions, suggested debate topics, writing assignments with sample answers, and cooperative learning activities.

We are pleased to offer a collection of world history PowerPoint lecture outlines, maps, and images for use in classroom presentations. Detailed lecture outlines correspond to the book's chapters and make it easier for instructors to cover the major topics in class. The art collection includes all of the photos and maps in the text, as well as numerous other images from our world history titles. PowerPoint questions and answers for use with personal response system software are also offered to adopters free of charge.

A variety of assignable homework and testing material has been developed to work with the *Blackboard*™ and *WebCT*™ course management systems, as well as with *Eduspace*™: Houghton Mifflin's online learning tool (powered by *Blackboard*™). *Eduspace*™ is a web-based online learning environment that provides instructors with a gradebook and communication capabilities such as synchronous and asynchronous chats and announcement postings. It offers access to assignments, such as over 650 gradable homework exercises, writing assignments, interactive maps with questions, primary sources, discussion questions for online discussion boards, and tests, all ready to use. Instructors can choose to use the content as is, modify it, or even add their own. *Eduspace*™ also contains an interactive ebook that contains in-text links to interactive maps, primary sources, audio pronunciation files, and review and self-testing material for students.

Formats

The text is available in a one-volume hard cover edition, a two-volume paperback edition, a three-volume paperback edition, and as an interactive ebook. *Volume 1: To 1500* includes Chapters 1–14; *Volume 2: Since 1450* includes Chapters 15–31; *Volume A: To 600* includes Chapters 1–9; *Volume B: From 600 to 1750* includes Chapters 10–18; and *Volume C: Since 1750* includes Chapters 19–31.

Acknowledgments

The author would like to thank John Tanke for his work on the Geography Overview as well as the following community of instructors who, by sharing their teaching experiences and insightful feedback, helped shape the final textbook and ancillary program:

Siamak Adhami, Saddleback Community College
Sanjam Ahluwalia, Northern Arizona University
David G. Atwill, Pennsylvania State University
Ewa K. Bacon, Lewis University
Bradford C. Brown, Bradley University
Gayle K. Brunelle, California State University–Fullerton
Rainer Buschmann, California State University, Channel Islands
Jorge Canizares-Esguerra, State University of New York–Buffalo
Bruce A. Castleman, San Diego State University
Harold B. Cline, Jr., Middle Georgia College
Simon Cordery, Monmouth College
Dale Crandall-Bear, Solano Community College
Cole Dawson, Warner Pacific College
Hilde De Weerdt, University of Tennessee, Knoxville
Anna Dronzek, University of Minnesota, Morris
James R. Evans, Southeastern Community College
Robert Fish, Japan Society of New York
Robert J. Flynn, Portland Community College
Gladys Frantz-Murphy, Regis University
Timothy Furnish, Georgia Perimeter College
James E. Genova, Ohio State University
Deborah Gerish, Emporia State University
Kurt A. Gingrich, Radford University
Candace Gregory-Abbott, California State University, Sacramento
Paul L. Hanson, California Lutheran University
A. Katie Harris, Georgia State University
Gregory M. Havrilcsak, University of Michigan–Flint
Timothy Hawkins, Indiana State University
Don Holsinger, Seattle Pacific University
Mary N. Hovanec, Cuyahoga Community College
Jonathan Judaken, University of Memphis
Thomas E. Kaiser, University of Arkansas at Little Rock
Carol Keller, San Antonio College
Patricia A. Kennedy, Leeward Community College-University of Hawaii
Jonathan Lee, San Antonio College
Thomas Lide, San Diego State University
Derek S. Linton, Hobart and William Smith Colleges
David L. Longfellow, Baylor University
Erik C. Maiershofer, Point Loma Nazarene University
Afshin Marashi, California State University, Sacramento
Robert B. McCormick, University of South Carolina Upstate
Doug T. McGetchin, Florida Atlantic University
Kerry Muhlestein, Brigham Young University–Hawaii
Peter Ngwafu, Albany State University
Monique O'Connell, Wake Forest University
Annette Palmer, Morgan State University
Nicholas C. J. Pappas, Sam Houston State University
Patricia M. Pelley, Texas Tech University
John Pesda, Camden County College
Pamela Roseman, Georgia Perimeter College
Paul Salstrom, St. Mary-of-the-Woods
Sharlene Sayegh, California State University, Long Beach
Michael Seth, James Madison University
David Simonelli, Youngstown State University
Peter Von Sivers, University of Utah
Anthony J. Steinhoff, University of Tennessee–Chattanooga
Nancy L. Stockdale, University of Central Florida
Robert Shannon Sumner, University of West Georgia
Kate Transchel, California State University, Chico
Sally N. Vaughn, University of Houston
Thomas G. Velek, Mississippi University for Women
Kenneth Wilburn, East Carolina University

The author has incurred many intellectual debts in developing his expertise in world history, as well as in preparing this text. To begin with, I cannot find words to express my gratitude to the wonderful editors and staff at Houghton Mifflin—Nancy Blaine, Julie Swasey, Carol Newman, and Jean Woy—who had enough faith in this project to tolerate my missed deadlines and sometimes grumpy responses to editorial decisions or some other crisis. I also owe an incalculable debt to my development editor, Phil Herbst, who prodded and pampered, and helped me write for a student, rather than scholarly, audience. Carole Frohlich, Jessyca Broekman, Susan Zorn, and Jake Kawatski ably handled the photos, maps, copyediting, and indexes, respectively. Sandi McGuire and Katherine Bates provided great help with marketing. I also owe a great debt to Pam Gordon, whose interest and encouragement got this project started. Ken Wolf of Murray State University prepared the initial drafts of several of the early chapters and in other ways gave me useful criticism and advice. I would also like to acknowledge the inspiring mentors who helped me at various stages of my academic preparation: Bill Goldmann, who introduced me to world history at Pasadena High School in California; Charles Hobart and David Poston, University of Redlands professors who sparked my interest in Asia; George Wong, Bart Stoodley, and especially Andrew and Margaret Roy, my mentors at Chung Chi College in Hong Kong; Walter Vella and Danny Kwok, who taught me Asian studies at Hawaii; and John Smail and Phil Curtin, under whom I studied comparative world history in the immensely exciting Ph.D. program at Wisconsin. My various sojourns in East Asia,

Southeast Asia, and East Africa allowed me to meet and learn from many inspiring and knowledgeable scholars. I have also been greatly stimulated and influenced in my approach by the writings of many fine global historians, but I would single out Phil Curtin, Marshall Hodgson, L. S. Stavrianos, William McNeill, Fernand Braudel, Eric Hobsbawm, Immanuel Wallerstein, and Peter Stearns. Curtin, Hobsbawm, and McNeill also gave me personal encouragement concerning my writing in the field, for which I am very grateful.

Colleagues at the various universities where I taught have been supportive of my explorations in world and comparative history. Most especially I acknowledge the friendship, support, and intellectual collaboration over three decades of my colleagues in the Social Change and Development Department at the University of Wisconsin–Green Bay (UWGB), especially Harvey Kaye, Tony Galt, Lynn Walter, Larry Smith, Andy Kersten, Kim Nielsen, and Andrew Austin. I have also benefited immeasurably as a world historian from the visiting lecture series sponsored by UWGB's Center for History and Social Change, directed by Harvey Kaye, which over the years has brought in dozens of outstanding scholars. My students at UWGB and elsewhere have also taught me much.

I also thank my colleagues in the World History Association, who have generously shared their knowledge, encouraged my work, and otherwise provided an exceptional opportunity for learning and an exchange of ideas. I am proud to have helped establish this organization, which incorporates world history teachers at all levels of education and in many nations. Among many others, I want to express a special thank-you to several longtime friends, early officers and members of the WHA from whom I have learned so much and with whom I have shared many wonderful meals and conversations: Ross Dunn, Lynda Shaffer, Kevin Reilly, Jerry Bentley, Heidi Roupp, Mark Gilbert, Steve Gosch, Judy Zinsser, and Anand Yang.

Finally, I need to acknowledge the loving support of my wife Kathy and our two sons, Chris and Colin, who patiently, although not always without complaint, put up for the ten years of the project with my hectic work schedule and the ever-growing piles of research materials, books, and chapter drafts scattered around our cluttered den and sometimes colonizing other space around the house. Now perhaps we shall have a chance to once again smell the roses and marvel at the sunsets without my obsessing about a chapter revision to complete, after I clear away the clutter.

About the Author

Craig A. Lockard is Ben and Joyce Rosenberg Professor of History in the Social Change and Development Department at the University of Wisconsin–Green Bay, where since 1975 he has taught courses on Asian, African, comparative, and world history. He has also taught at SUNY-Buffalo, SUNY-Stony Brook, and the University of Bridgeport, and twice served as a Fulbright-Hays professor at the University of Malaya in Malaysia. After undergraduate studies in Austria, Hong Kong, and the University of Redlands, he earned an M.A. in Asian Studies at the University of Hawaii and a Ph.D. in Comparative World and Southeast Asian History at the University of Wisconsin–Madison. His published books, articles, essays, and reviews range over a wide spectrum of topics: world history; Southeast Asian history, politics, and society; Asian emigration; the Vietnam War; and folk, popular, and world music. Among his major books are *Lands of Green, Waters of Blue: Southeast Asia in World History* (forthcoming); *Dance of Life: Popular Music and Politics in Modern Southeast Asia* (1998); and *From Kampung to City: A Social History of Kuching, Malaysia, 1820–1970* (1987). He was also part of the task force that prepared revisions to the U.S. National Standards in World History (1996). Professor Lockard has served on various editorial advisory boards, including the *Journal of World History* and *The History Teacher,* and as book review editor for the *Journal of Asian Studies* and the *World History Bulletin.* He was one of the founders of the World History Association and served as the organization's first secretary. He has lived and traveled widely in Asia, Africa, and Europe.

NOTE ON SPELLING AND USAGE

Transforming foreign words and names, especially those from non-European languages, into spellings usable for English-speaking readers presents a challenge. Sometimes, as with Chinese, Thai, and Malay/Indonesian, several romanized spelling systems have developed. Generally I have chosen user-friendly spellings that are widely used in other Western writings (such as *Aksum* for the classical Ethiopian state and *Ashoka* for the classical Indian king). For Chinese, I generally use the *pinyin* system developed in the People's Republic over the past few decades (such as *Qin* and *Qing* rather than the older *Chin* and *Ching* for these dynasties, and *Beijing* instead of *Peking*), but for a few terms and names (such as the twentieth-century political leaders *Sun Yat-sen* and *Chiang Kai-shek*) I have retained an older spelling more familiar to Western readers and easier to pronounce. The same strategy is used for some other terms or names from Afro-Asian societies, such as *Cairo* instead of *al-Cahira* (the Arabic name) for the Egyptian city, *Bombay* instead of *Mumbai* (the current Indian usage) for India's largest city, and *Burma* instead of *Myanmar*. In some cases I have favored a newer spelling widely used in a region and modern scholarship but not perhaps well known in the West. For example, in discussing Southeast Asia I follow contemporary scholarship and use *Melaka* instead of *Malacca* for the Malayan city and *Maluku* rather than *Moluccas* for the Indonesian islands. Similarly, like Africa specialists I have opted to use some newer spellings, such as *Gikuyu* rather than *Kikuyu* for the Kenyan people. To simplify things for the reader I have tried to avoid using diacritical marks within words. Sometimes their use is unavoidable, such as for the premodern Chinese city of *Chang'an;* the two syllables here are pronounced separately. I also follow the East Asian custom of rendering Chinese, Japanese, and Korean names with the surname (family name) first (e.g., *Mao Zedong, Tokugawa Ieyasu*). The reader is also referred to the opening essay, "Introducing World History," for explanations of the dating system used (such as the Common Era and the Intermediate Era) and geographical concepts (such as Eurasia for Europe and Asia, and Oceania for Australia, New Zealand, and the Pacific islands).

INTRODUCING WORLD HISTORY

A journey of a thousand miles begins with the first step.

CHINESE PROVERB

This introduction is designed to help you take the important "first step" toward understanding the scope and challenge of studying world history. By presenting the main concepts and themes of world history, it will serve as your guide in exploring the story of the world presented in the rest of the book. The introduction will also give you a foretaste of the lively ongoing debates in which historians engage as they try to make sense of the past, especially how societies change and how their contacts with one another have created the interconnected world we know today. By examining world history, you can better understand not only how this connection happened, but also why.

What Do Historians Do?

History is the study of the past that looks at all of human life, thought, and behavior and includes both a record and an interpretation of events, people, and the societies they developed. Therefore, the job of the historian is to both describe *and* interpret the past. Both tasks are important. Although beginning students generally see history as the story of "what happened," most professional historians regard the attempt to make sense of historical events as the more exciting part of their work. Two general concepts help historians in these efforts. When they look at humans in all their historical complexity, historians see both changes and continuity. The legal system in the United States, for example, is unlike any other in the world, and yet it has been shaped in part by both English and ancient Roman legal practices.

Historians face their greatest challenges in their role as interpreters of the past. Although historians agree on the need for extensive evidence to support their generalizations, they often disagree on how an event should be interpreted. Often the disagreements reflect differences in political points of view. In 1992 a widely publicized disagreement took place on the occasion of the 500-year anniversary of the first cross-Atlantic voyage of Christopher Columbus to the Western Hemisphere in 1492. Depending on their political biases, historians used the well-known records of this event in different ways. Some historians pictured Columbus as a farsighted pioneer who made possible communication between the hemispheres, while others saw him as an immoral villain who mistreated the local American peoples, beginning a pattern of exploitation by Europeans. Similar debates have raged about whether it was necessary for the United States to drop atomic bombs on Japan in 1945, a deadly decision that killed thousands of Japanese civilians but nevertheless ended World War II.

While the events of the past do not change, our understanding of them does, as historians both acquire new information and use the old information to answer new questions. Only within the past fifty years, for example, have historians studied the diaries and journals that reveal the important role of women on the home front during the American Civil War. Even more recently historians have used long neglected sources to conclude that, a millennium ago, China had the world's most dynamic economy and sophisticated technology. Similarly, historians have recently discovered, in the West African city of Timbuktu, thousands of old books written in African languages, forcing a rethinking of literacy and scholarship in West African societies hundreds of years ago.

What history "tells us" is constantly evolving. New evidence, changing interests, and the asking of new questions all add up to seeing things in a new light. As you read the text, remember that no text contains the whole or final truth. **Historical revision**, or changing understanding of the past, is at the heart of historical scholarship. This revision and the difficulties of interpretation also make history controversial. In recent years heated debates about what schools should teach about history have erupted in many countries, including Japan, India, and the United States.

Historians bridge the gap between the humanities and the social sciences. As humanists, historians study the philosophies, religions, literatures, and arts that people have generated over the ages. As social scientists, historians examine political, social, and economic patterns, though frequently asking questions different from those asked by anthropologists, economists, political scientists, and sociologists; the last three groups especially are generally more concerned with the present and often more interested in theoretical questions. Because they study people in their many roles and stations in life—the accomplishments of the rich and famous as well as the struggles and dreams of common women and men—historians must be familiar with the findings of other relevant academic disciplines.

Why Study World History?

World history is the broadest field of history. It studies the human record as a whole and the experiences of people in all the world's inhabited regions: Africa, the Americas, Asia, Europe, and the Pacific Basin. World history helps us better understand individual societies and their traditions by making it easier to look at them comparatively. Studying history on a global scale also brings out patterns of life, cultural traditions, and connections between societies that go beyond a particular region, such as the spread of long-distance trade and Buddhism, which followed the trade routes throughout southern and eastern Asia nearly two thousand years ago. World, or global, history takes us through the forest of history in which the individual societies represent the individual trees. World history helps us comprehend both the trees and the forest, allowing us to situate ourselves in a broader context.

The study of world history helps us understand our increasingly connected world. Decisions made in Washington, D.C., Paris, or Tokyo influence citizens in Argentina, Senegal, and Malaysia, just as events in Africa, the Middle East, or Latin America often affect the lives of people in Europe, North America, and Australia. World historians use the widest angle of vision possible to comprehend a world in which diverse local traditions and international trends intermingle. International trends spread from many directions. Western phenomena such as McDonald's, Hard Rock Cafes, French wines, Hollywood films, churches, the Internet, and cell phones have spread around the world. Non-Western products and ideas, however, have also gained global followings; among these are Mexican soap operas, Chinese food, Japanese cars, Indonesian arts, African rhythms, and the Islamic religion. While it is important to study the histories of individual nations, we must remember that, for all their idiosyncrasies, each nation develops in the context of a wider world.

Along with the growing interconnectedness of the world, a global perspective highlights the past achievements of all peoples. The history of science, for example, shows that key inventions—printing, sternpost rudders, the compass, the wheelbarrow, gunpowder—originated in China and that the modern system of numbering came from India, reaching Europe from the Middle East as "Arabic" numerals. Indeed, various peoples—Mesopotamians, Egyptians, Greeks, Chinese, Indians, Arabs—built the early foundation for modern science and technology, and their discoveries moved along the trade routes. The importers of technology and ideas often modified or improved on them. For example, Europeans made good use of Chinese, Indian, and Arab technologies, as well as their own inventions, in their quest to explore the world in the fifteenth and sixteenth centuries. The interdependence among and exchanges between peoples is a historical as well as a present reality.

The World History Challenge

When we study world history, we see other countries and peoples, past and present. We do not, however, always see them accurately. Nevertheless, by studying the unfamiliar, world history helps us to recognize how some of the attitudes we absorb from the particular society and era we live in shape, and may distort, our understanding of the world and of history. Coming to terms with this mental baggage means examining such things as maps and geographical concepts and acquiring intellectual tools for comprehending other cultures.

Broadening the Scope of Our Histories

During much of the twentieth century, high school and college students in English-speaking countries were often taught some version of a course, usually called Western Civilization, that emphasized the rise of western Europe and the European contributions to modern North American societies. The Western Civilization course recognized the undeniably influential role of Western nations, technologies, and ideas in the modern world, but it was also a reflection of historians' extensive acquisition of data on Europe and North America compared with the rest of the world. This approach exaggerated the role that Europe played in world history before the sixteenth century, pushing Asian, African, and Native American peoples and their accomplishments into the background while underplaying the contributions these peoples made to Europe. Students usually learned little about China, India, or Islam, and even less about Africa, Southeast Asia, or Latin America.

In the 1960s the teaching of history began to change, particularly in North America. The political independence of most African nations from Western nations and the civil rights movement in the United States, which demanded equality between blacks and whites, forced a reappraisal of African history that was less influenced by colonialism and racism. By the 1970s the academic study of not only African but also Asian, Latin American, Native American, and Pacific island history in North America and Europe had become far more sophisticated. The increased knowledge has made it easier to write a world history that takes into its scope the entire globe. As a result, world history courses, rare before the 1960s, became increasingly common in U.S. universities, colleges, and high schools by the late twentieth century and have been proliferating in several other countries, such as Australia, Canada, South Africa, China, and the Netherlands.

Revising Maps and Geography

Maps not only tell us where places are; they also create a mental image of the world, revealing how peoples perceive themselves and others. For example, Chinese maps once portrayed China as the "Middle Kingdom," the center of

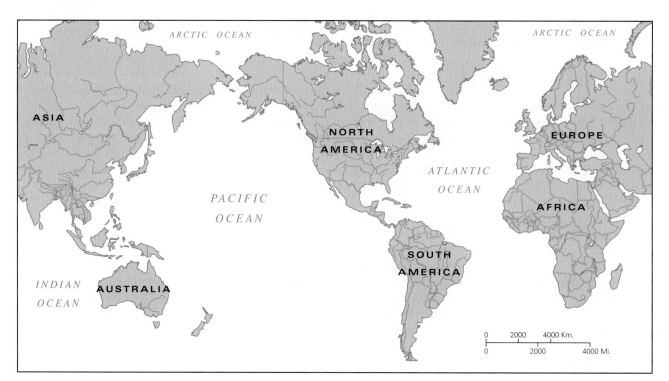

Mercator Projection

the world surrounded by "barbarians." This image reflected and deepened the Chinese sense of superiority over neighboring peoples. Similarly, 2,500 years ago, the Greeks developed a map that showed Greece at the center of the inhabited world known to them.

Even in modern times, maps can be misleading. For example, the Mercator projection (or spatial presentation), a map still used in many schools in North America and elsewhere and standard in most atlases, is based on a sixteenth-century European model that distorts the relative size of landmasses, greatly exaggerating Europe, North America, and Greenland while diminishing the lands around the equator and in the Southern Hemisphere. In this projection, Africa, India, Southeast Asia, China, and South America look much smaller than they actually are. In the United States, maps using a Mercator projection have often tellingly placed the Americas in the middle of the map, cutting Asia in half. The implicit message is that the United States, appearing larger than it actually is, plays the central role in the world.

Alternative maps have emerged that give a more accurate view of relative size. For example, the Eckert projection is an oval-shaped projection using an ellipse that shows a better balance of size and shape while minimizing distortion of continental areas. A comparison between the Mercator and Eckert world maps is shown on this page and the next.

The same shaping of mental images of geography found in maps is also seen in concepts of geographical features and divisions, such as continents, the large landmasses on which most people live. The classical Greeks

were probably the first to use the terms *Europe*, *Africa*, and *Asia* in defining their world 2,500 years ago, and later Europeans transformed these terms into the names for continents. For centuries Western peoples have taken for granted that Europe is a continent. Actually, however, Europe is not a separate landmass, and the physical barriers between it and Asia are not that significant. If mountains and other geographical barriers define a continent, one can make a better case for India (blocked off by truly formidable mountains) or Southeast Asia than for Europe. At the same time, seeing Asia as a single continent is also a problem, given its spectacular size and geographical diversity. Today world geographers and historians usually consider Europe and Asia to constitute one huge continent, Eurasia, containing several subcontinental regions, such as Europe, South Asia, and East Asia.

Popular terms such as *Near East*, *Middle East*, or *Far East* are also misleading. They were originally formulated to describe regions as Westerners saw them in relationship to Europe. Much depends on the viewer's position; Australians, for example, often label nearby Southeast and East Asia as the "Near North." But, rejecting a Europe-centered approach, few Western scholars of China or Japan today refer to the "Far East," preferring the more neutral term *East Asia*. This text considers the term *Near East*, long used for western Asia, as outdated, but it refers to Southwest Asia and North Africa, closely linked historically (especially after the rise of Islam 1,400 years ago), as the Middle East, since that term is more convenient than the alternatives. The text also uses the term *Oceania* to refer to Australia, New Zealand, and the Pacific islands.

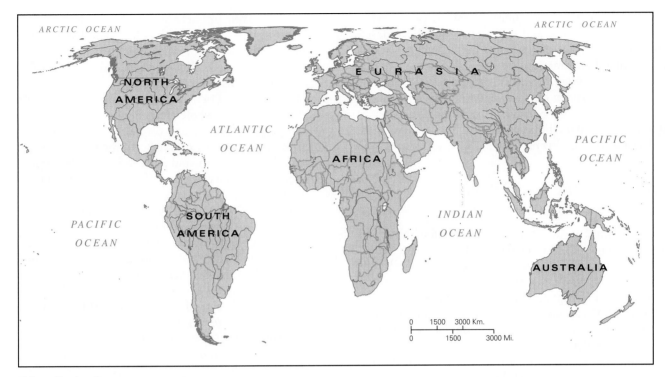

Eckert Projection

Rethinking the Dating System

A critical feature of historical study is the dating of events. World history challenges us by making us aware that all dating systems are based on the assumptions of a particular culture. Many Asian peoples saw history as moving in great cycles of birth, maturation, and decay (sometimes involving millions of years), while Westerners saw history as moving in a straight line from past to future (as can be seen in the chronologies within each chapter). Calendars were often tied to myths about the world's creation or about a people's or country's origins. Hence, the ancient Roman calendar was based on the founding of the city of Rome around 2,700 years ago, reflecting the Romans' claim to the territory in which they had recently settled.

The dating system used throughout the Western world today is based on the Gregorian Christian calendar, created by a sixteenth-century Roman Catholic pope, Gregory XIII. It uses the birth of Christianity's founder, Jesus of Nazareth, around 2,000 years ago as the turning point. Dates for events prior to the Christian era were identified as B.C. (before Christ); years in the Christian era were labeled A.D. (for the Latin *anno domini*, "in the year of the Lord"). Many history books published in Europe and North America still employ this system, which has spread around the world in recent centuries.

The notion of Christian and pre-Christian eras has no longer been satisfactory for studies of world history because it is rooted in the viewpoint of only one religious tradition, whereas there are many in the world, usually with different calendars. The Christian calendar has little relevance for the non-Christian majority of the world's people. Muslims, for example, who consider the revelations of the prophet Muhammad to be the central event in history, begin their dating system with Muhammad's journey, within Arabia, from the city of Mecca to Medina in 622 A.D. Many Buddhists use a calendar beginning with the death of Buddha around 2,500 years ago. The Chinese chronological system divides history into cycles stretching over 24 million years. The Chinese are now in the fifth millennium of the current cycle, and their system corresponds more accurately than does the Gregorian calendar to the beginning of the world's oldest cities and states, between 5,000 and 6,000 years ago. Many other alternative dating systems exist. Selecting one over the others constitutes favoritism for a particular society or cultural tradition.

Therefore, in recent years most world historians and an increasing number of specialists in Asian, African, and European history have moved toward a more secular, or nonreligious, concept, the Common Era. This system still accepts as familiar, at least to Western and Latin American readers, the dates used in the Western calendar, but it calls the period after the transition, identified by Christians with the birth of Jesus, a "common" era, since many influential, dynamic societies existed two millennia ago in various parts of the world, not only in the Judeo-Christian Holy Land. Around two millennia ago, the beginning of the Common Era, the Roman Empire in the West was at its height while Chinese and Indian empires ruled large chunks of Asia. At the beginning of the Common Era many peoples in the Eastern Hemisphere were also linked by trade and religion to a greater extent than ever before. At the same time, several African societies flourished, and states and cities had long before developed in the Americas. Hence this period makes a useful and familiar benchmark.

In the new system, events are dated as B.C.E. (before the Common Era) and as C.E. (Common Era, which begins in year 1 of the Christian calendar). This change is an attempt at a method of dating that includes all the world's people and avoids favoring any particular religious tradition.

Rethinking the Division of History into Periods

To make world history more comprehensible, historians divide long periods of time into smaller segments, such as "the ancient world" or "modern history," each marked by certain key events or turning points. Historians call this process of dividing time **periodization**. For example, scholars of European, Islamic, Chinese, Indonesian, or United States history generally agree among themselves on the major eras and turning points for the region they study, but world historians need a system that can encompass all parts of the world. Finding such a system, however, presents difficulties, since most historic events did not affect all regions of the world. For instance, developments that were key to the eastern half of Eurasia, such as the spread of Buddhism, or to western Eurasia and North Africa, such as the spread of Christianity, did not always affect southern Africa, and both the Western Hemisphere, or the Americas, and some Pacific peoples remained isolated from the Eastern Hemisphere for centuries.

Given the need for a chronological pattern that is inclusive, this book divides history into periods, each of which is notable for significant changes around the world:

1. **Ancient (100,000–600 B.C.E.)** The Ancient Era, during which the foundations for world history were built, can be divided into two distinct periods. During the long centuries known as Prehistory (ca. 100,000–4000 B.C.E.), Stone Age peoples, living in small groups, survived by hunting and gathering food. Eventually some of them began simple farming and living in villages, launching the second period, the era of agrarian societies. Between 4000 and 600 B.C.E., agriculture became more productive, the first cities and states were established in both hemispheres, and some societies invented writing, allowing historians to study their experiences and ideas.

2. **Classical (600 B.C.E.–600 C.E.)** The Classical Era is marked by the creation of more states and complex agrarian societies, the birth of major religions and philosophies, the formation of the first large empires, often encompassing entire regions, and the expansion of long-distance trade, which linked distant peoples.

3. **Intermediate (600–1500 C.E.)** The Intermediate Era comprises a long middle period of expanding horizons that modified or displaced the classical societies.

It was marked by increasing trade connections between distant peoples within the same hemisphere, the growth and spread of several older religions, the rapid rise of a new religion, Islam, and oceanic exploration by Asians and Europeans.

4. **Early Modern (1450–1750 C.E.)** During the Early Modern Era, the whole globe became intertwined as European exploration and conquests in the Americas, Africa, and southern Asia fostered the rise of a global economy, capitalism, and a trans-Atlantic slave trade; undermined American and African societies; and enriched Europe.

5. **Modern (1750–1945 C.E.)** The Modern Era was characterized by industrialization and empire building on an unprecedented scale. These centuries featured rapid technological and economic change in Europe and North America, Western colonization of many Asian and African societies, the rise of nationalism and socialism, political revolutions, world wars, and a widening gap between rich and poor societies.

6. **Contemporary (1945–present)** The Contemporary Era has been marked by a more closely interlinked world, including the global spread of commercial markets, cultures, and communications, the collapse of Western colonial empires, international organizations, new technologies, struggles by poor nations to develop economically, environmental destruction, and conflict between powerful nations.

Understanding Cultural and Historical Differences

The study of world history challenges us to understand peoples and ideas very different from our own. The past is, as one writer has put it, "a foreign country; they do things differently there."[1] As human behavior changes with the times, sometimes dramatically, so do people's beliefs. Even moral and ethical standards have changed. For example, in Asia centuries ago, Assyrians and Mongols sometimes killed everyone in cities that resisted their conquest. Some European Christians seven hundred years ago burned suspected heretics and witches at the stake and enjoyed watching blind beggars fight. Across the Atlantic, American peoples such as the Aztecs and Incas engaged in human sacrifice. None of these behaviors would be morally acceptable today in most societies.

Differences in customs complicate efforts to understand people of earlier centuries. We need not approve of empire builders and plunderers, human sacrifice and witch burning, but we should be careful about applying our current standards of behavior and thought to people who lived in different times and places. There is always the danger of **ethnocentrism**, viewing others narrowly through the lens of one's own society and its values. Historians are careful in using value-loaded words such as *primitive, barbarian, civilized,* or *progress.* Such words carry negative or positive meanings and are often matters of judgment rather than fact. For instance, soldiers facing each other on the battlefield may consider themselves civilized and their opponents barbarians. And progress, such as industrialization, often brings negative developments, such as pollution, along with the positive.

Today anthropologists use the term **cultural relativism** to remind us that, while all people have much in common, societies are diverse and unique, embodying different standards of correct behavior. For instance, cultures may have very different ideas about children's obligations to their parents, what happens to people's souls when they die, or what constitutes music pleasing to the ear. Cultural relativism still allows us to say that the Mongol empire builders in Eurasia some eight hundred years ago were brutal, or that the mid-twentieth-century Nazi German dictator, Adolph Hitler, was a murderous tyrant, or that laws in some societies today that blame and penalize women who are raped are wrong and should be protested. But cultural relativism discourages us from criticizing other cultures or ancient peoples just because they are or were different from us. Studying world history can make us more aware of our ethnocentric biases.

The Major Themes

Determining major themes is yet another challenge in presenting world history. This text uses certain themes to take maximum advantage of world history's power to illuminate both change and continuity as we move from the past to the present. Specifically, in preparing the text, the author asked himself: What do educated students today need to know about world history to understand the globalizing era in which they live?

Three broad themes help you comprehend how today's world emerged. These themes are shaped around three concepts: societies, networks, and transitions.

1. **Societies** are broad groups of people that have common traditions, institutions and organized patterns of relationships with each other. The societies that people have organized and maintained, influenced by environmental factors, were defined by distinctive but often changing cultures, beliefs, social forms, governments, economies, and ways of life.

2. **Networks** are arrangements or collections of links between different societies, such as the routes over which traders, goods, diplomats, armies, ideas, and information travel. Over the centuries societies were increasingly connected to other societies by growing networks forged by phenomena such as population movement, long-distance trade, exploration, military expansion, colonization, the diffusion of ideas and technologies, and communication links. These growing networks modified individual societies, connected societies within the same and nearby regions, and eventually led to a global system in which distant peoples came into frequent contact.

3. **Transitions** are passages, changes, events, or movements that reshape societies and regions. Each major historical era was marked by one or more great transitions that were sparked by events or innovations that had profound, enduring influences on many societies and that fostered a gradual reshaping of the world.

The first theme, based on societies, recognizes the importance in world history of the distinctiveness of societies. Cultural traditions and social patterns differed greatly. For example, societies in Eurasia fostered several influential philosophical and religious traditions, from Confucianism in eastern Asia to Christianity, born in the Middle East and nourished both there and in Europe. Historians often identify unique traditions in a society that go back hundreds or even thousands of years.

The second theme, based on networks, acknowledges the way societies have contacted and engaged with each other to create the interdependent world we know today. The spread of technologies and ideas, exploration and colonization, and the growth of global trade across Eurasia and Africa and then into the Western Hemisphere are largely responsible for setting this interlinking process in motion. Today networks such as the World Wide Web, airline routes, multinational corporations, and terrorist organizations operate on a global scale. As this list shows, many networks are welcome, but some are dangerous.

The third theme, transitions, helps to emphasize major developments that shaped world history. The most important include, roughly in chronological order, the beginning of agriculture, the rise of cities and states, the birth and spread of philosophical and religious traditions, the forming of great empires, the linking of Eurasia by the Mongols, the European seafaring explorations and conquests, the Industrial Revolution, the forging and dismantling of Western colonial empires, world wars, and the invention of electronic technologies that allow for instantaneous communication around the world.

With these themes in mind, the text constructs the rich story of world history. The intellectual experience of studying world history is exciting and will give you a clearer understanding of how the world as you know it came to be.

Online Study Center
Improve Your Grade Flashcards

Key Terms

history	cultural relativism
historical revision	societies
periodization	networks
ethnocentrism	transitions

Suggested Reading

After each chapter and essay, you will find a short list of valuable books and useful websites to help you explore history beyond the text. The general books and websites listed below will be of particular value to beginning students of world history.

Books

Bender, Thomas. *A Nation Among Nations: America's Place in World History*. New York: Hill and Wang, 2006. Looks at the history of the United States as part of modern world history.

Bentley, Jerry H. *Shapes of World History in 20th Century Scholarship*. Washington, D.C.: American Historical Association, 1996. A brief presentation of the scholarly study of world history.

Christian, David. *Maps of Time: An Introduction to Big History*. Berkeley: University of California Press, 2004. A detailed but path-breaking study mixing scientific understandings into the study of world history.

Dunn, Ross, ed. *The New World History: A Teacher's Companion*. Boston: Bedford/St. Martin's, 2000. A valuable collection of essays on various aspects of world history and how it can be studied. Useful for students as well as teachers.

Hodgson, Marshall G. S. *Rethinking World History: Essays on Europe, Islam, and World History*. Edited by Edmund Burke, III. New York: Cambridge University Press, 1993. Written by one of the most influential world historians for teachers and scholars but also offering many insights for students.

McNeill, J. R., and William H. McNeill. *The Human Web: A Bird's-Eye View of World History*. New York: W.W. Norton, 2003. A stimulating overview of world history using the concept of human webs to examine interactions between peoples.

McNeill, William H., et al., eds. *Berkshire Encyclopedia of World History*, 5 vols. Great Barrington, Mass.: Berkshire, 2005. One of the best of several fine encyclopedias, with many essays on varied aspects of world history.

Stavrianos, Leften S. *Lifelines from Our Past: A New World History*. Rev. ed. Armonk, N.Y.: M. E. Sharpe, 1997. A brief but stimulating reflection on world history by a leading scholar.

Stearns, Peter N. *Western Civilization in World History*. New York: Routledge, 2003. A brief examination of how Western civilization fits into the study of world history.

Wiesner-Hanks, Merry E. *Gender in World History*. Malden, Mass.: Blackwell, 2001. A pioneering thematic survey of a long-neglected subject.

Websites

The Encyclopedia of World History (**http://www.bartleby.com/67/**). A valuable collection of thousands of entries spanning the centuries from prehistory spanning the centuries to 2000.

Internet Global History Sourcebook (**http://www.fordham.edu/halsall/global/globalsbook.html**). An excellent set of links on world history from ancient to modern times.

Women in World History (**http://chnm.gmu.edu/wwh/**). Invaluable collection of links covering many societies and all eras.

World Civilizations (**http://www.wsu.edu/~dee/MAIN/HTM**). An internet anthology maintained at Washington State University.

World History for Us All (**http://worldhistoryforusall.sdsu.edu**). A growing site with useful essays and other materials, sponsored by San Diego State University.

World History Sources (**http://worldhistorymatters.org**). Valuable annotated links on different subjects, based at George Mason University.

Geography Overview

Maps are among the most powerful of human inventions, showing us where we are, where we have been, and where we might go in the future. They are essential tools in nearly every aspect of social life, enabling politicians to govern their people, soldiers to defend against invasions, and merchants to conduct trade and commerce. As noted in the *Introducing World History* essay, maps also create mental images of the world and, hence, help shape the way people look at the world and their place in it.

Maps are especially useful for the historian or student of history. Historical maps show us where different peoples lived and interacted, at one point in time or over long periods. Typically, they use lines, symbols, shading, and text to present a combination of physical and political information. The physical part pertains to the natural world—the shape of landmasses and bodies of water—and serves as a kind of background or screen onto which political information is projected. Categories of political information commonly featured on historical maps include the location and names of important cities and states, the changing borders of nations and empires, and the routes people traveled as they explored, migrated, traded, or fought with one another. In order to read an historical map, one must first understand its legend. The legend provides a key for interpreting the map's graphical symbols.

The first map in this overview, Map 1.3 Indo-European Migrations and Eurasian Pastoralism, uses colored shading to show that around 4000 B.C.E. a people called the Indo-Europeans lived by the Caucasus Mountains in western Asia, and blue arrows to show that over the next 3000 years various Indo-European tribes migrated into western and northern Europe, Central and southwestern Asia, and northern India. Black capital letters are used to name important regions of human settlement, such as

Anatolia and Mesopotamia, and black italic capitals for topographical features, such as mountains and desert. Red italic capitals indicate how people in different parts of Eurasia and Africa sustained themselves at this time—whether by raising livestock, farming, hunting and gathering, or some combination of these.

Every map is designed to convey only selected categories of information and, therefore, may leave certain questions about the geographical area and its inhabitants at either the same or different points in history unanswered. Thus, Map 1.3 tells us very little about the other human populations that lived in Eurasia between 4000-1000 B.C.E. The names *Sumer* and *Akkad* appear, but their status as regions where the world's first urban societies arose is something the student will only discover by reading the beginning of Chapter 2 and looking at Map 2.1 Ancient Mesopotamia. Arrows show the probable routes taken by different Indo-European tribes as they migrated from their homeland, but these tribes are not named, and the student must read the rest of Chapter 2 and all of Chapter 3 before learning that they included the Greeks in Europe and the Aryans in northern India.

To introduce you to the maps in this text, and the world history they help to illuminate, seven maps have been reproduced in this section, each provided with an analytical introduction and set of questions. Every part of the world is covered, and every historical period is represented by one map—except for the Early Modern Era, which is represented by two maps. The introductions help explain the content of each map by placing it in its broader historical context. That context includes the other maps in this text, and these are referenced whenever possible. For almost any subject about which the student would like to learn more, there are several maps that should be consulted. A list of all the maps in this text follows the table of contents. •

The Indo-European Migrations and Eurasian Pastoralism

A fter the first human communities learned to domesticate native plants and animals, between 11,500 and 7000 years ago, two types of cultures arose: farming societies in fertile river basins and pastoral societies in areas dominated by grassland, mountainous terrain, or desert (see Map 1.2). Important early farming societies include the city-states of Sumer and Akkad in Mesopotamia (see Map 2.1), the Harappan cities of the Indus Valley in India (see Map 2.2), the Egyptian and Nubian states along the Nile River in Africa (see Map 3.1), and the Shang state by the Yellow River in China (see Map 4.1). Bordering these peoples were pastoral societies who raised livestock as their main source of food and raw material and lived in smaller, dispersed groups over large areas of Eurasia, Africa, and Arabia. One such society, or collection of tribes, were the Indo-Europeans, who lived near the Caucasus Mountains around 4000 B.C.E. Over the next three thousand years, various Indo-European peoples migrated from their homeland: the Greeks settled in the eastern Mediterranean, the Hittites in central Anatolia, and the Aryans in northern India. Most European languages and many languages of southwestern Asia, Central Asia, and India are direct descendants of the prehistoric language spoken by the Indo-Europeans.

MAPS REFERENCED

MAP 1.2 The Origins of Agriculture (p. 20)

MAP 2.1 Ancient Mesopotamia (p. 34)

MAP 2.2 Harappan Culture and Aryan Migrations (p. 43)

MAP 3.1 Ancient Egypt and Nubia (p. 58)

MAP 3.3 The Ancient Eastern Mediterranean (p. 72)

MAP 4.1 Shand and Zhou China (p. 86)

Online Study Center

Students: Visit us online at **college.hmco.com/pic/lockard1e** for answers to these questions.

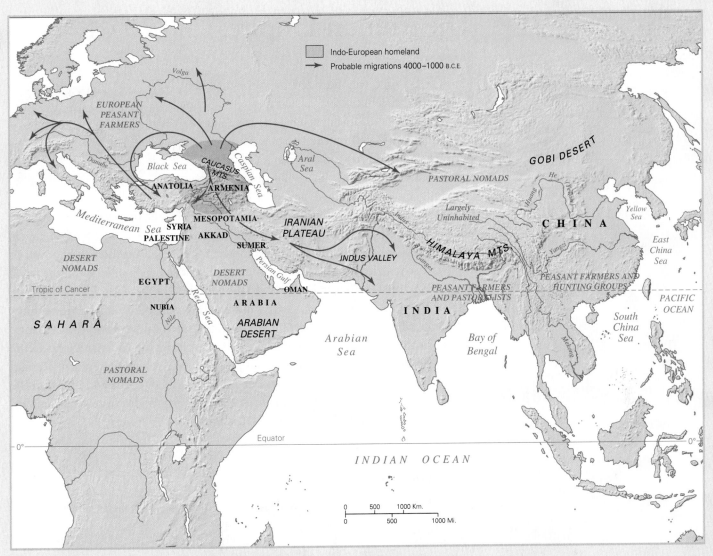

Indo-European homeland
Probable migrations 4000–1000 B.C.E.

MAP 1.3 The Indo-European Migrations and Eurasian Pastoralism   Some societies, especially in parts of Africa and Asia, adapted to environmental contexts by developing a pastoral, or animal herding, economy. One large pastoral group, the Indo-Europeans, eventually expanded from their home area into Europe, southwestern Asia, Central Asia, and India.

QUESTIONS

1. The Indo-Europeans were pastoral nomads, most of whom later became farmers. Which regions on this map are suited to pastoralism and which to farming economies?

2. The blue arrows on this map show the probable migration routes taken by various Indo-European tribes from 4000 to 1000 B.C.E. Identify the main geographical features (rivers, seas, mountain ranges, etc.) of the Indo-European homeland and the regions settled by Indo-Europeans during their migrations.

3. Why do you think some early pastoral societies were more mobile than farming societies?

4. After the period of migrations, which powerful Indo-European societies grew up in the second millennium B.C.E. (see also Maps 2.1, 2.2, and 3.3)?

The Roman Empire, ca. 120 C.E.

R ome was founded in the eighth century B.C.E. by the Latin people, a tribe of Indo-European pastoralists. In 509 B.C.E., influenced by the cultures of the neighboring Greek and Etruscan city-states (see Map 8.1), the Romans established a republic—a form of government in which political power is exercised by elected representatives of the people. The Roman Republic became a great military power, defeating the trading empire of the Carthaginians, and, by 58 B.C.E., under Julius Caesar, the Celtic tribes in Gaul (modern France). With the rise to power of Octavian, who defeated Mark Anthony and Queen Cleopatra of Egypt at the naval Battle of Actium in Greece in 31 B.C.E., the Republic became a military dictatorship. At the time of emperor Hadrian's death in 138 C.E., the Roman Empire dominated the whole of the Mediterranean basin, bounded in the west by the Atlantic Ocean, in the south by the Sahara Desert, to the north by Germanic and Celtic tribes, and to the east by the Parthian empire and the Arabian Desert. The Roman Empire was unified by a network of over 150,000 miles of roads and linked to the peoples of Africa and Asia by numerous land and sea trade routes (see map on page 258, "Great Empires and Trade Routes").

MAPS REFERENCED

MAP 8.1 Italy and the Western Mediterranean, 600-200 B.C.E. (p. 202)

SNT 2 Great Empires and Trade Routes (p. 258)

Online Study Center

Students: Visit us online at **college.hmco.com/pic/lockard1e** for answers to these questions.

MAP 8.2 The Roman Empire, ca. 120 C.E. The Romans gradually expanded until, by 120 C.E., they controlled a huge empire stretching from Britain and Spain in the west through southern and central Europe and North Africa to Egypt, Anatolia, and the lands along the eastern Mediterranean coast.

QUESTIONS

1. At the Battle of Alesia, Julius Caesar defeated a confederation of Celtic tribes, thereby completing the Roman conquest of Gaul. Where and when did this famous battle take place?

2. Which Roman emperor had a 73-mile wall built to secure the province of Britain from Celtic tribes to the north?

3. Many European cities grew up on the sites of Roman provincial settlements. What were the Roman names for Mérida in Spain, York in Great Britain, Cologne in Germany, and Vienna in Austria?

4. Which three rivers helped define the borders of the Roman Empire by the death of Augustus (Octavian) in 14 C.E.?

5. The Roman city of Pompeii, near Naples, Italy, was destroyed by the eruption of what volcano in 79 C.E.?

Dar al-Islam and Trade Routes, ca. 1500 C.E.

The rise and spread of Islam in the Intermediate Era is paralleled by that of Christianity in Europe and Buddhism in Asia (see the map on page 413, "World Religions and Trade Routes, 600-1500"). By 750 C.E. the Umayyad Caliphate had conquered Spain and North Africa in the west (see Map 10.1), and a year later Arab armies defended their conquest of Central Asia by defeating Chinese forces from the Tang Empire at the Battle of Talas (see Map 11.1). From its capital in Baghdad, the Abbasid Caliphate ruled an empire stretching from Egypt to the Indus River (see Map 10.2). Like Latin culture in Europe, Arabic literature and science flourished during this period; new long-distance trade routes enriched Arab merchants and rulers, and stimulated interest in the wider world. The confidence and curiosity of Islamic culture at this time is shown by the life and writings of the fourteenth-century Moroccan jurist and explorer Ibn Battuta. Logging more than 60,000 miles in thirty years, Ibn Battuta traveled to the far reaches of the Islamic world, from Timbuktu in the West African empire of Mali (see Map 12.1) to the Delhi Sultanate in India (see Map 13.1) and the cities of Pasai and Melaka in Southeast Asia (see Map 13.3).

MAPS REFERENCED

MAP 10.1   Expansion of Islam, to 750 C.E. (p. 277)

MAP 10.2   The Abbasid Empire, ca. 800 C.E. (p. 281)

MAP 10.4   The Ottoman Empire, 1566 (p. 293)

MAP 11.1   The Tang Empire, ca. 700 C.E. (p. 302)

MAP 12.1   Major Sub-Saharan African Kingdoms, 1200-1600 C.E. (p. 330)

MAP 13.1   India and the Delhi Sultanate, ca 1300 C.E. (p. 366)

MAP 13.3   The Spread of Islam in Island Southeast Asia (p. 379)

MAP 14.3   Europe, 1400-1500 (p. 406)

SNT 3   World Religions (p. 413)

MAP 28.3   The Dissolution of the Soviet Union (p. 892)

Online Study Center

Students: Visit us online at **college.hmco.com/pic/lockard1e** for answers to these questions.

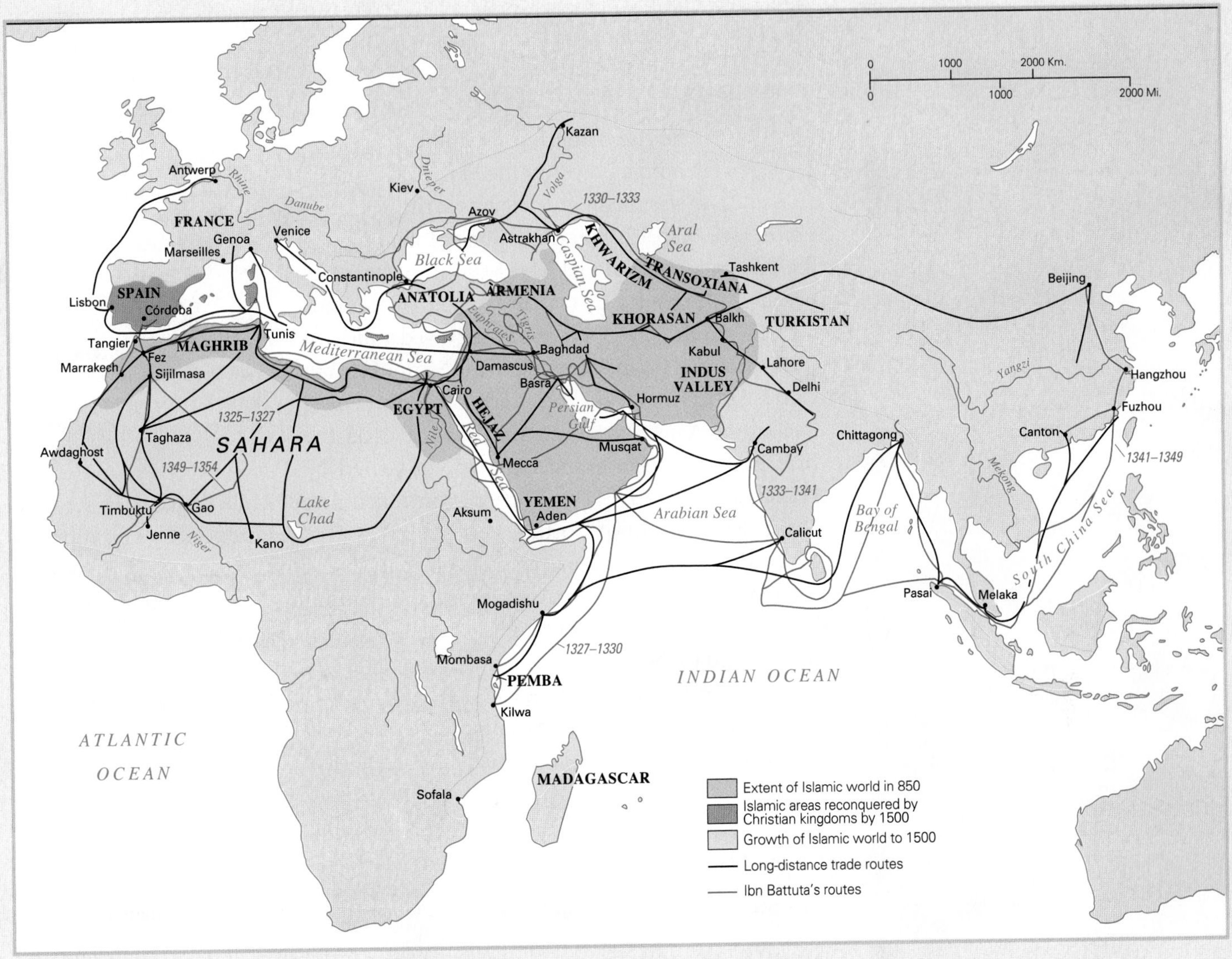

MAP 10.3 Dar al-Islam and Trade Routes, ca. 1500 C.E. By 1500 the Islamic world stretched into West Africa, East Africa, and Southeast Asia. Trade routes connected the Islamic lands and allowed Muslim traders to extend their networks to China, Russia, and Europe.

QUESTIONS

1. Ibn Battuta followed maritime trade routes to reach the Islamic cities and states of Africa and Asia. What famous overland route did he *not* take on his journey from China to West Africa in 1349 (see also Map 11.1 and the map on page 413)?

2. Which modern Central Asian nation has its capital in Tashkent and occupies the historical region known as Transoxiana? (see also Map 28.3)

3. Which European cities conducted maritime trade with Islamic societies in the Intermediate Era?

4. Islam spread to which western European land during the early Intermediate Era (see also Map 10.1)?

5. Islam spread to eastern Europe with the expansion of the Ottoman Empire in the fifteenth century. Which Balkan nations were ruled by the Ottomans in 1500 (see also Maps 10.4 and Map 14.3)?

The Atlantic Economy

T he rise of European political and economic power in the Early Modern Era was made possible by maritime exploration (see Map 15.1) and missions of conquest in the Americas (see Map 17.1). In four voyages between 1492 and 1504, Christopher Columbus crossed the Atlantic Ocean and surveyed much of the Caribbean Basin, claiming it for Spain. Hernán Cortés sailed from Cuba to eastern Mexico and conquered the Aztec Empire in 1521, and in 1535 the Inca Empire in South America was conquered by Francisco Pizarro. By 1700, Portugal controlled Brazil, while England, France, and Spain claimed most of North America (see Map 17.2). European colonization was devastating to indigenous peoples. The introduction of infectious diseases like small pox, to which Native Americans had no immunity, reduced their population by ninety percent from 1500 to 1700. Millions of West Africans were enslaved and transported to the Americas, where they mined gold and silver and produced sugar cane and tobacco on plantations (see Map 16.2). European states prospered from the development of capitalist economies, and the revenue from colonial slave labor and increased global trade put them in a position to dominate the world.

MAPS REFERENCED

MAP 15.1 European Exploration, 1450-1600 (p. 432)

MAP 16.1 African States and Trade, 1500-1700 (p. 462)

MAP 16.2 Trans-Atlantic Slave Trade 1526-1870 (p. 472)

MAP 17.1 The Americas and Early European Exploration (p. 492)

MAP 17.2 The English and French in North America, ca. 1700 (p. 498)

Online Study Center

Students: Visit us online at **college.hmco.com/pic/lockard1e** for answers to these questions.

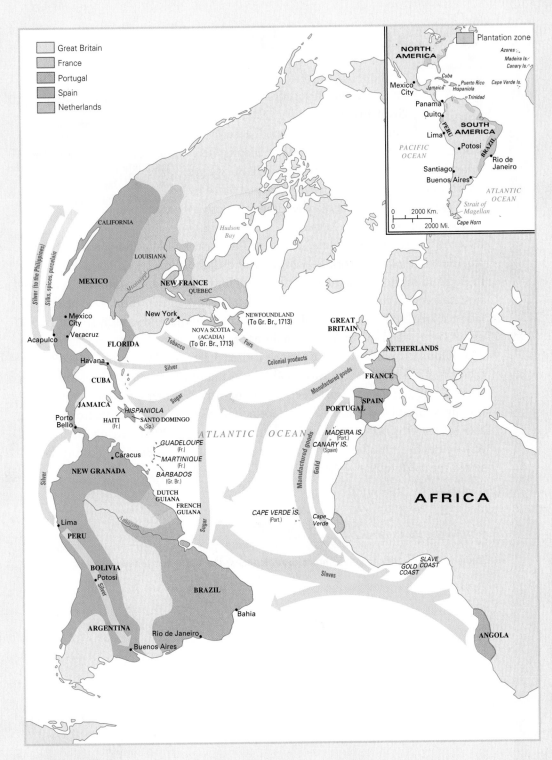

MAP 17.3 The Atlantic Economy The Atlantic economy was based on a triangular trade in which African slaves were shipped to the Americas to produce raw materials that were chiefly exported to Europe, where they were turned into manufactured goods and exported to Africa and the Americas.

QUESTIONS

1. The Treaty of Tordesillas, negotiated in 1494, allowed which country to claim Brazil and Angola as colonies (see also Map 15.1)?

2. Why are the Caribbean islands also called the West Indies (*Hint:* See page 493)?

3. Which Caribbean islands were colonized by Spain, France, and Great Britain?

4. European slave-traders seized the majority of their slaves from lands on the West African coast. What modern nations correspond to Senegambia, the Gold Coast, and Igboland (see also Map 16.2)?

5. Which Spanish American port imported silks, spices, and porcelain from Asia?

6. Settlers from which American colony exported furs to Europe?

U.S. Expansion Through 1867

The successful revolution in 1776 of Great Britain's thirteen North American colonies inaugurated a series of revolutions throughout the Western Hemisphere. Apart from Cuba and Puerto Rico, all of Spain's Latin American colonies achieved independence by 1840 (see Map 19.2). In 1783 the United States extended as far west as the Mississippi River; in 1803 its territory was doubled by the Louisiana Purchase; by 1848, after a war with Mexico, the territories of Texas, New Mexico, and California were annexed. Beginning in England in the 1770s, the Industrial Revolution had—and continues to have—far-reaching effects on the social and political history of the world. Europe's population soared, and industrial capitalism enriched nations and wealthy investors, but also impoverished and dislocated millions of people. From 1821 to 1920 more than 30 million Europeans emigrated to the United States (see Map 20.1). In 1865, after a bloody Civil War, slavery was abolished in the southern states. Only four years later, a large and diverse workforce, including African Americans and Chinese immigrants, completed the first transcontinental railroad. Immigrants from Britain also settled Oceania during the Modern Era (see Map 20.3), seizing the lands of Aborigines in Australia and Maori in New Zealand, just as European colonists had seized the lands of Native Americans two centuries before.

> **MAPS REFERENCED**
>
> **MAP 19.2** Latin American Independence, 1840 (p. 576)
>
> **MAP 20.1** European Emigration, 1820-1910 (p. 600)
>
> **MAP 20.3** Australia and New Zealand (p. 624)

Online Study Center

Students: Visit us online at **college.hmco.com/pic/lockard1e** for answers to these questions.

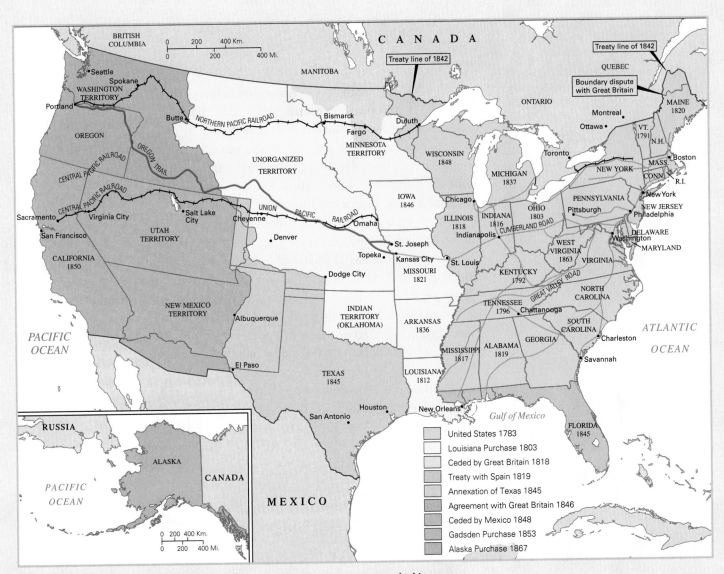

MAP 20.2 U.S. Expansion Through 1867 The United States expanded in stages after independence, gaining land from Spain, France, Britain, and Mexico until the nation stretched from the Atlantic to the Gulf and Pacific coasts by 1867. During the same period Canadians expanded westward from Quebec to British Columbia.

QUESTIONS

1. First mapped in 1811, the Oregon Trail became the primary overland route for settlers migrating to the Pacific Northwest. Which future states did it pass through?

2. What river has partly defined the United States' border with Mexico ever since the annexation of Texas in 1845 (See Map 19.2)?

3. Which cities in the western United States benefited from the California Gold Rush of 1849?

4. The first transcontinental railroad was a joint effort of the Union Pacific and Central Pacific Railroads. What two cities did it join by 1869?

5. In 1755 the British deported much of the population of Acadia (modern Nova Scotia) to the French colony of Louisiana, forming the basis for what modern French-speaking community (see pages 503–504)?

Africa in 1914

After losing their American colonies, European nations projected their power to the south and east, and by 1914 they had colonized most of Africa, India, and Southeast Asia (see Map 19.4). Numerous Africans resisted European colonization, such as the Mandinka king Samory Toure, who fought the French in West Africa, and the confederation of Shona and Ndebele peoples, who fought the British in Southern Rhodesia. Ultimately, however, a combination of deceitful diplomacy and superior firearms made the Europeans unstoppable. Belgium seized the Congo river basin, France took control of most of West Africa, and Great Britain conquered lands in a north-south band stretching from Cairo to Cape Town. The remaining African territories, with the exception of independent Ethiopia and Liberia, were colonized by Germany, Italy, and Portugal. The spread of Muslim culture beyond the Middle East and Central Asia, begun in the Intermediate Era, was unaffected by European colonialists and Christian missionaries: today Islam is the majority religion in northern Africa and Southeast Asia (see Map 26.3 and Map 30.2).

MAPS REFERENCED

MAP 19.4 The Great Powers and Their Colonial Possessions in 1913 (p. 592)

MAP 26.1 Decolonization (p. 804)

MAP 26.3 World Religions (p 826)

MAP 30.2 The Islamic World (p. 946)

Online Study Center

Students: Visit us online at **college.hmco.com/pic/lockard1e** for answers to these questions.

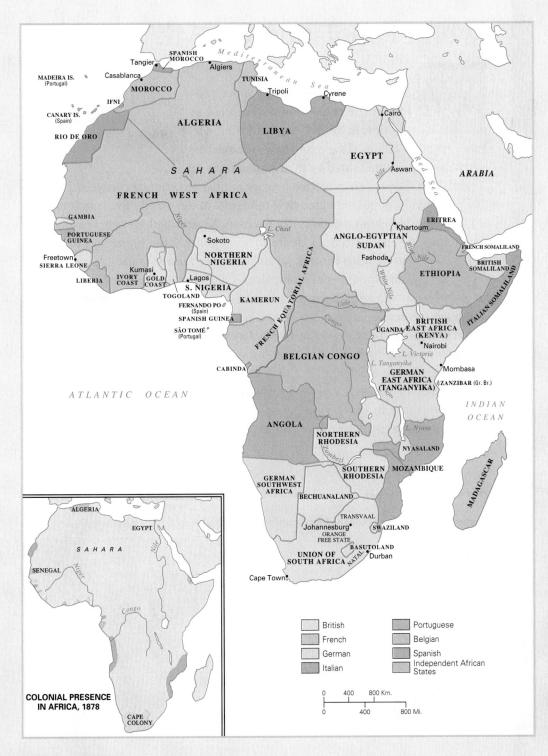

MAP 21.1 Africa in 1914
Before 1878 the European powers held only a few coastal territories in Africa, but in that year they turned to expanding their power through colonization. By 1914 the British, French, Belgians, Germans, Italians, Portuguese, and Spanish controlled all of the continent except for Ethiopia and Liberia.

COLONIAL PRESENCE IN AFRICA, 1878

Legend:
- British
- French
- German
- Italian
- Portuguese
- Belgian
- Spanish
- Independent African States

QUESTIONS

1. Which European state had a single African colony?

2. What world religions are predominant in northern and southern Africa, respectively (see also Map 26.3)?

3. Around which two African river basins did the British and French base their colonies?

4. What two West African territories were colonized by Germany in 1884 and apportioned to France and Great Britain after World War I, finally achieving their independence in 1960 (see also Map 26.1)?

5. The British imperialist Cecil Rhodes named two African territories after himself-Northern and Southern Rhodesia. What is the modern name of Southern Rhodesia, which gained its independence in 1980 (see also Map 26.1)?

World Population Growth

orld population increased more rapidly in the contemporary era than at any time in history--from 2.5 billion to more than 6.5 billion. This map shows the relative size of nations, as measured by their populations in 2002. It also shows their projected average annual growth rates between 2002 and 2015. Currently, population growth is moderate in the world's five largest nations, and higher in developing nations like Pakistan, Nigeria, and Mexico. For a number of reasons, including women's desire to work outside the home and to prevent pregnancy by using birth control, Japan and many European nations have declining birth rates and aging populations. Since 1900 there has been a massive increase in global industrial output, consumption of resources, and all forms of pollution. Although the developing nations of Asia have the largest populations, most of the world's wealth is concentrated in North America, western Europe, and Japan (see the map on page 1008, "Global Distribution of Wealth"). In 2000, over 1 billion people were desperately poor. People living in wealthier nations consume a much greater share of the earth's raw materials and cause more damage to the environment than those in developing nations. The average American consumes some twenty times the resources of the average Pakistani.

MAPS REFERENCED

SNT 6 Global Distribution of Wealth (p. 1008)

Online Study Center

Students: Visit us online at **college.hmco.com/pic/lockard1e** for answers to these questions.

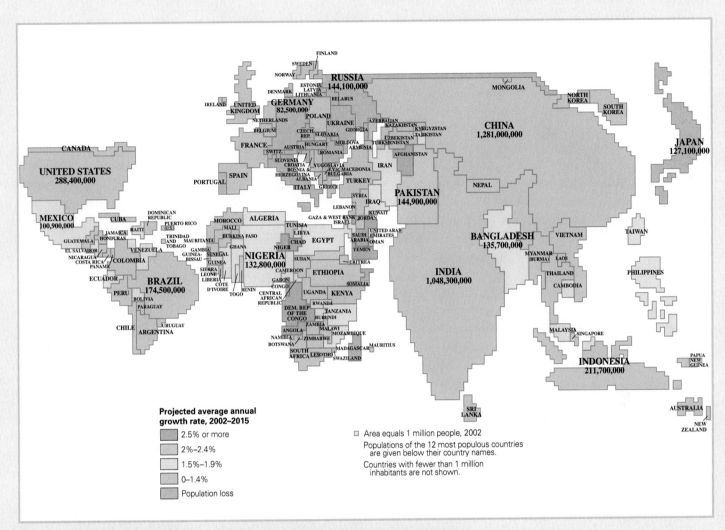

MAP 26.2 World Population Growth This map shows dramatically which nations have the largest populations: China, India, the United States, Indonesia, and Brazil. It also shows which regions experience the most rapid population growth: Africa, South Asia, and Central America.

QUESTIONS

1. In 2002, the population of India was how many times greater than that of the United States? How many times greater was the population of China?

2. Based on the same principle as this map, the map on page 1008 shows the relative wealth of nations as measured by their GDP or Gross Domestic Product (the total value of goods and services produced in a year). How much wealthier is the United States than India and China, respectively?

3. What challenges confront developing nations with large and growing populations?

4. What are some things developing nations can do to meet these challenges?

PART IV

Connecting the Globe: Forging New Networks in the Early Modern World, 1450–1750

A major theme of history is global integration, as networks were built that increasingly connected distant societies. The roots of global integration go back deep into history, to the trade routes of the Classical Era, such as the Silk Road, that spread products and ideas, expanding horizons. However, global connections increased dramatically in the Early Modern Era, between 1450 and 1750.

Europeans played a major role in building the new connections. After many centuries in which various Asian and Islamic societies had led the world in economic development, science, and effective government, western Europeans revitalized their societies, improved their military and naval technology, and honed their economies, often through their increasing contacts with the wider world. The Portuguese began maritime exploration around Africa to locate the sources of the valuable commodities, especially spices, coming into Europe from Asia. The Spanish joined the search for Asian wealth in 1492, and the expedition led by Christopher Columbus forged the first permanent link across the Atlantic to the Americas. The Dutch, English, and French soon began their own explorations. What was originally an active system of exchange and communication within an Afro-Eurasian zone became genuinely global, making it possible to speak of a world history linking all peoples. The Early Modern Era established the basic framework for the connected world we live in today.

European exploration, often followed by military conquest and colonization of other societies, affected millions of people around the world, but especially in the Americas and parts of Africa. In the Americas the Europeans encountered often prosperous societies, including the Aztec Empire of Mesoamerica and the Inca Empire of South America. Technologically stronger, Europeans established colonial governments in the Americas and built new economies based on mining, ranching, and plantations and on slave labor brought from Africa. The European and African encounters with Native Americans led in turn to the spread of diseases from Eurasia that ravaged the American population. The European quest to acquire enslaved Africans for their American colonies also transformed the political and economic

Chinese Porcelain Chinese products attracted merchants from all over Eurasia. This Chinese-made porcelain bowl from the 1700s, made for export, is decorated with a view of the major southern Chinese port city and commercial center, Guangzhou (also known as Canton). (Courtesy of the Trustees of the British Museum)

life of West and Central Africa. European activities eventually stretched into the Islamic Middle East and southern Asia, where Europeans colonized several ports and islands by 1750. The connections established between Europeans and other societies fostered the rise of a truly world economy, fueled by the new capitalist economy of Europe.

However, while historians often speak of the rise of the West in this period, it is misleading to assume that the spread of Western influences constituted the whole story. Europe's impact on large, still powerful Asian societies, such as China, India, Persia, and the Ottoman Empire, was modest at best. Despite growing European power, China and India remained key centers of the Eurasian economy, and several other Asian and some African societies enlarged their territories and remained dynamic. Some of the same political, economic, and intellectual trends that were then reshaping Europe also sprouted independently in a few Asian societies. Indeed, many Asian, African, and even American peoples were scarcely aware that European merchants, adventurers, and missionaries were seeking out wealth, power, and converts around the world. From the perspective of a Chinese mandarin official, Japanese samurai warrior, Siamese Buddhist monk, Indian peasant, Turkish architect, Arab governor, Persian artist, Ethiopian noble, or Hausa merchant, the West was chiefly a curiosity rather than a threat. By 1750 Western influence and power around the world were growing but still very incomplete.

Historians consider this period the *Early* Modern Era because, while much of the globe was now more closely linked, life was still vastly different from what it is today. Before Europeans and North Americans saw their lives transformed by industrialization in the nineteenth century, they lived more like their ancestors of 1,500 years ago than like their descendants in the twenty-first century. Much of their work, technologies, and household goods would not have astonished earlier generations. As the chapters in Part V will show, the changes since 1750, a date commonly used to mark the end of the Early Modern period, have been much more far-reaching. However, by 1750, closer contacts than ever before between the world's many societies—contacts that often widened the gap in power and wealth between Europeans and the peoples they came to dominate politically and economically—had set the stage for the modern world.

NORTH AND CENTRAL AMERICA
The bridging of the Atlantic by a Spanish expedition led by Christopher Columbus in 1492 had major consequences. In the century to follow, the Spanish conquered various Caribbean islands, Mesoamerica, and southwestern North America. The English and French established settlements and then colonies along the Atlantic coast and gradually expanded westward, at the expense of Native American societies that were devastated by diseases brought from Eurasia. In the southern colonies and the Caribbean islands, plantations worked by African slaves became the major economic activity.

SOUTH AMERICA
The arrival of the Spanish and Portuguese changed the politics, economies, and demographics of the region. The Spanish toppled the Inca Empire and colonized much of South and Central America, while the Portuguese dominated Brazil. The European colonizers established mines, ranches, and plantations. After diseases from Eurasia killed much of the Native American population, the colonizers imported African slaves as workers. As a result, European, Native American, and African peoples and cultures blended to foster unique Latin American societies.

EUROPE

Several European societies emerged as major world powers. The Portuguese and Spanish in the 1500s, followed by the Dutch, English, and French in the 1600s and 1700s, established footholds and colonies in Africa, the Americas, and Asia. The resources obtained abroad, especially the minerals and plantation crops of the Americas and Southeast Asia, brought wealth to Europe. Exposure to a wider world fostered capitalism, science, technology, and a questioning of long-standing religious doctrine, resulting in the Protestant Reformation and the Enlightenment.

WESTERN ASIA

The Ottoman Empire became the world's major Islamic power, controlling not only much of western Asia but also much of North Africa and southeastern Europe. Rivals of the major European powers, especially the Russians, the Ottoman Turks prospered by fostering learning, accommodating ethnic minorities, and importing military and technical expertise. To their east, the Persians under the Safavid dynasty dominated parts of Central Asia and flourished for several centuries.

EASTERN ASIA

While experiencing dynastic changes, China remained a major world power and the key Eurasian manufacturing center and commercial economy. China dealt with European traders and governments on its own terms, setting strict limits on trade and diplomatic relations. In both China and Japan, Western missionaries were at first tolerated and then expelled. Likewise, the Tokugawa government in Japan maintained a rigid social order and secluded the country from the West.

AFRICA

Many African societies experienced dramatic change. The need by European powers for cheap labor in their American colonies fostered the trans-Atlantic slave trade, which disrupted much of the West and Central African coast as millions of Africans were enslaved and shipped to the Americas. Although some African states, such as Ashante and Benin, flourished from the slave trade and other commerce, warfare between states became more common. The Portuguese conquered the states of Angola and Kongo and destabilized the East African coastal cities, while the Dutch established a foothold in South Africa.

SOUTHERN ASIA AND OCEANIA

India, ruled by the Islamic Mughal dynasty, was one of the world's major powers, with a flourishing economy that attracted merchants from many societies. After obtaining footholds in India, Europeans then sought wealth in nearby Southeast Asia. First the Portuguese and then other European powers gained a modest presence in Southeast Asia, the Spanish colonizing the Philippines and the Dutch parts of Indonesia. While Europeans began exploring the Pacific Basin, their impact on Oceania was slight. Nonetheless, the Spanish trade across the Pacific between the Philippines and Mexico laid a foundation for the global economy.

CHAPTER 15

Global Connections and the Remaking of Europe, 1450–1750

Online Study Center

This icon will direct you to interactive activities and study materials on the website: college.hmco.com/pic/lockard1e

Amsterdam Stock Exchange During the seventeenth century, the Dutch port city of Amsterdam was the center of European commerce and played a key role in the world economy. The Amsterdam stock market, shown here in a painting by Dutch artist Job Adriaenz, attracted merchants and financiers from all over Europe.   (Amsterdams Historisch Museum)

"O, wonder! How many goodly creatures are there here! How beauteous mankind is! O brave new world That hath such people in't!"

MIRANDA, IN *THE TEMPEST* BY WILLIAM SHAKESPEARE, 1611[1]

The European and world economy changed rapidly in the sixteenth century, and few places exemplified change more than the port city of Antwerp (AN-twuhrp), on the River Scheldt (skelt) in what is now Belgium. In 1567 an Italian diplomat and historian, Ludovico Guicciardini (loo-do-VEE-ko GWEE-char-DEE-nee), published a description of the mostly Flemish-speaking city and its fabulous Bourse (boors), a huge, multistory building in the city center that served as a combination of marketplace, not unlike a modern department store, and stock exchange. The Bourse posted a motto above its entrance: "For the service of merchants of all nations and all languages." An economic boom centered on the Bourse brought prosperity to Antwerp's merchants and bankers, as well as to the businesspeople from many lands who came to the Bourse to buy and sell. Guicciardini wrote that "all of these persons being people who are earning money, invest it not only in commerce but also in building, in buying lands and properties, and thus the city flourishes and increases marvelously."[2]

From the late 1400s until the late 1500s Antwerp was the European hub for ever-widening world networks of commerce. Every week fabulous merchandise arrived from all over the world, some delivered by wagons, some by ships. As many as 2,500 ships from different lands anchored at one time in the harbor, many laden with gold and silver from the Americas, and the Bourse became the clearinghouse for their cargo. Every day goods were put on sale, and bustling crowds of merchants, foreign visitors such as Guicciardini, and affluent local consumers thronged the rooms. They came to buy spices from Southeast Asia and India, sugar from the Americas, tin from England, Venetian glass, Spanish lace, German copper, paintings by great Flemish artists, and even the service of assassins or professional soldiers. Thus one great city linked the economies not only of Europe but also of the wider world. The Antwerp Bourse represented a postmedieval Europe shaped by the fruits of overseas exploration, conquest, and expanding commerce. The new economic thrust was one component of the changes in many areas of life and thought that the English playwright Shakespeare referred to as a "brave new world."

In 1500, as the Early Modern Era began, western Europeans were still medieval in many respects: they were dominated by the multinational Roman church, their countries had little sense of national identity, they were skeptical of science, and they were minor participants in hemispheric commerce and barely aware of distant lands. By the mid-1700s, however, Europe and parts of the wider world had undergone a profound economic, intellectual, and political transition. Europeans were conquering and settling the Americas, and various European countries had established colonies or trading networks in Asia and Africa. As a result, wealth flowed into Europe, enriching some and fostering investment in science and technology. New knowledge of, and influences from, non-European cultures reshaped European thinking and cultures. The Catholic Church faced severe challenges. In cultural and religious life, some European thinkers were influenced as much or more by secular ideas, including science, as by Christian doctrines. Although such changes were not always beneficial, often resulting in strains that produced long and bloody wars, they nevertheless remade Europe's political and social systems. By 1750 Europeans had left many of their medieval institutions and beliefs behind and were on the verge of introducing even more profound changes to the world.

FOCUS QUESTIONS

1. How did exploration, colonization, and capitalism increase Western power and wealth?

2. How did the Renaissance and Reformation mark a crucial cultural and intellectual transition?

3. What types of governments emerged in Europe in this era?

4. How did major intellectual, scientific, and social changes help to reshape the West?

◆ Transitions: Overseas Expansion and Capitalism

How did exploration, colonization, and capitalism increase Western power and wealth?

The foundations for the dramatic changes that reshaped many Early Modern European societies were established in late medieval times and embellished by developments after 1500. The European encounter with America and its riches, which began in the 1490s, the growth of a trans-Atlantic slave trade, and the opening of direct trade with Asia all increased European wealth and stimulated the development of **capitalism**, an economic system in which property, exchange, and the means of production, such as factories, are privately owned. By the 1600s huge quantities of valuable Asian spices and precious American metals and plantation crops were pouring into Europe. Inherently dynamic, capitalism gradually expanded its scale of operation to a global level. The economic revolution fostered stronger European states and reshaped the daily lives of nearly all Europeans.

capitalism An economic system in which property, exchange, and the means of production are privately owned.

Economic and Urban Roots

Some of the economic changes of the Early Modern Era simply continued trends already apparent in western Europe before 1500. During the 1400s commerce and merchants flourished, cities grew larger and more numerous, and the feudal social systems and the values that supported them broke down. Commerce, with its widening trade networks, became a part of everyday life. The ability of the middle classes to buy more luxury goods, especially fine clothes, spurred the growth of industries like textile manufacturing. However, most Europeans were still neither urban nor middle class; 80 percent were peasants who worked the soil. Their life was organized around the male-dominated household: men tilled the fields while women had responsibility for the house, barn, and gardens. Many peasants were now free or tenant farmers rather than serfs, but most farmers were still heavily burdened with taxes and service obligations to lords. They also tithed crops and livestock to the church. Only a few farm people, mostly boys, received any formal education.

Yet, despite being rooted in farming, the economy was changing, partly as a result of population growth and climate change. The European population (excluding Russia) increased from 70 to 100 million between 1500 and 1600, and then to 125 million by 1750, making for larger commercial markets. The global cooling that began around 1300 intensified, reached its height in the late 1600s, and then began to

CHRONOLOGY

	Cultural and Intellectual Changes	Political Changes
1300	**1350–1615** Renaissance	
1400		
1500	**1517–1615** Protestant Reformation	**1588** Defeat of Spanish armada
1600	**1600–1750** Scientific Revolution **1675–1800** Enlightenment	**1618–1648** Thirty Years War **1641–1645** English Civil War **1688–1689** English Glorious Revolution

thaw around 1715, finally ending in the mid-1800s. This "Little Ice Age" brought winter freezing to canals and rivers, caused poor harvests, and helped motivate overseas explorers to seek better conditions and food sources elsewhere. Importing foods from the Americas, such as corn and potatoes, helped avert mass famine.

Political and economic changes were felt more strongly by urban populations. By 1500 cities such as Paris and London had grown to over 200,000. Although this was still small by Asian standards, such cities were unique in the world for their growing political power and autonomy. Unlike Chinese or Ottoman cities, European cities existed in a politically fragmented region rather than a centralized empire. Not having to answer to centralized authorities, city leaders could bargain with kings for advantages and autonomy.

Merchants also benefited from changing conditions. More favorable attitudes toward commerce gave some European merchants a status and power that were unusual in the world. In addition, many western European societies offered an opportunity for making profit and also had institutions, such as banks, that favored economic growth. Blessed with these advantages, late medieval Europeans laid the foundation for an economic transition that, in the fifteenth and sixteenth centuries, began to fundamentally alter western European life and later spread its influences around the world.

Some western European societies developed capitalism, a dynamic system that was highly oriented to economic growth. In the 1400s cities such as Venice and Genoa in Italy, and Bruges (broozh) and Antwerp in what is today Belgium, became centers of capitalistic enterprise. Venetians and Genoese,

Antwerp Marketplace The marketplace at the center of Antwerp, in what is today Belgium, was the main hub for European trade in the 1500s, the place where goods from all over Europe and from Africa, the Americas, and Asia were bought and sold. (Musées Royaux Beaux-Arts de Belgique)

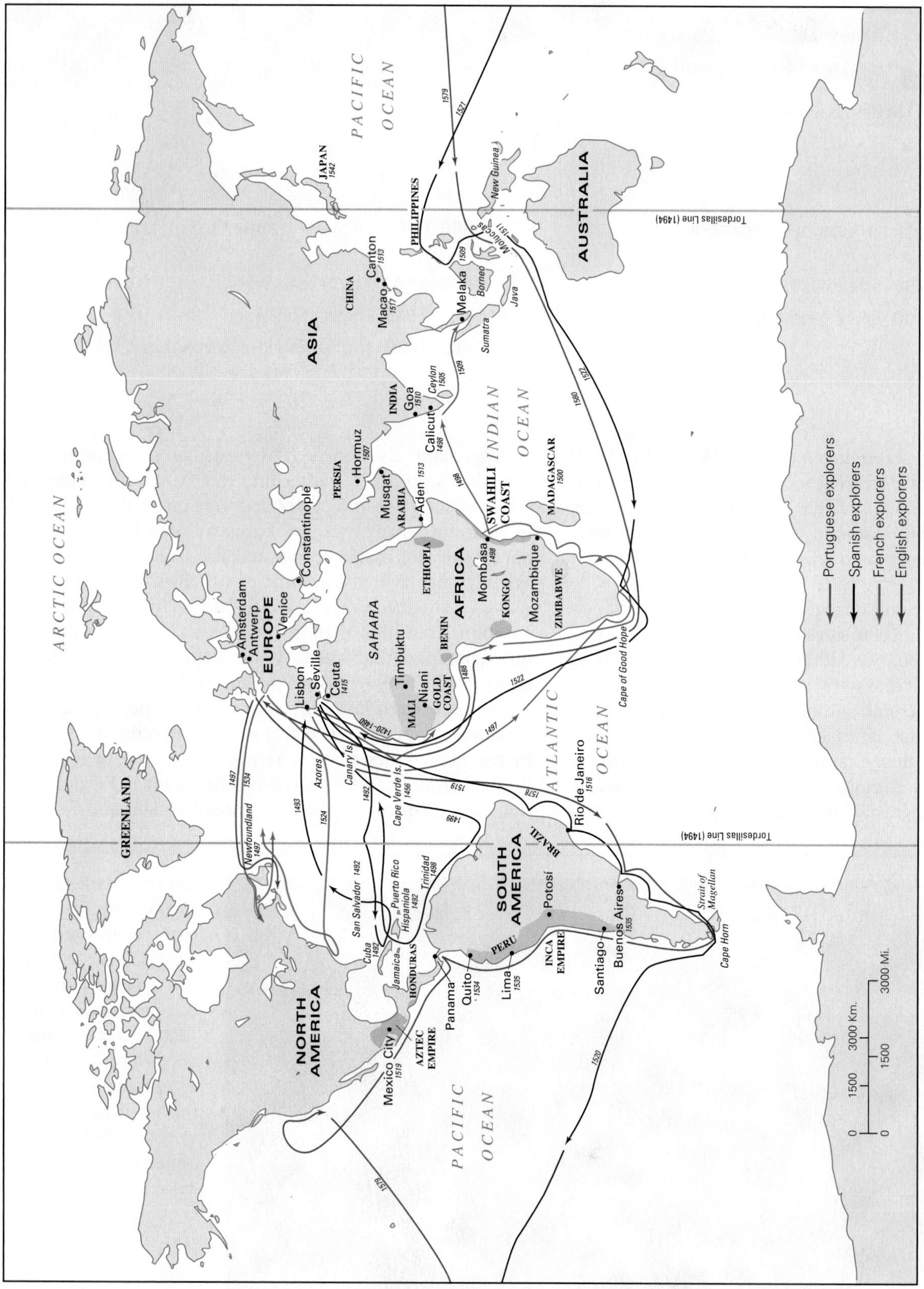

Map 15.1   European Exploration, 1450–1600

Between the early 1400s and mid-1600s explorers sponsored by Portugal, Spain, France, Holland, and England discovered the sea route around Africa to South and Southeast Asia, and crossed the Atlantic to the Americas, permanently connecting the two hemispheres. They also sailed across the Pacific Ocean from the Americas to Asia.

fierce competitors, traded all over Europe, western Asia, and North Africa. But early capitalism was limited by the Catholic Church's condemnation of usury and by cumbersome business methods. Not until after 1500 did the scope and nature of capitalism, fostered by overseas exploration and conquest, change dramatically, allowing the Antwerp merchants to build a Bourse that became a marketplace for world products.

Political, Intellectual, and Technological Roots

The political shape of western Europe also began to shift in the 1500s. After the ending of the Roman Empire in the Late Classical Era, western Europe had remained politically fragmented, and in 1500 it contained some five hundred states or ministates. Unlike in China, Ottoman Turkey, or Mughal India, which had powerful bureaucracies, no single imperial state could dominate the economy and enforce intellectual conformity. But in the 1500s some of the small states were gradually transformed into integrated monarchies, which became enriched by resources obtained by their merchants and adventurers in Africa, the Americas, and Asia. Both merchants and monarchs resented the power and independence of the landed aristocracy and cooperated to destroy their influence in a series of bloody wars. For the first time since the Roman Empire and the Carolingians, large centralized states developed in Europe, particularly in England and France. The growth of these strong but competitive states made the political system dynamic and unstable.

New intellectual currents also emerged that fostered broader horizons, especially improvements in mapmaking. In 1375 Abraham Cresques (kres-kay), a Jewish cartographer on the Spanish island of Majorca (muh-JOR-kuh), used Christian, Muslim, and Jewish traditions and the accounts of many travelers to produce a map that placed Jerusalem rather than Europe at the center of the world. Cresques also offered a much more realistic picture of northern Africa than was found in earlier maps. In the 1400s Portuguese mapmakers drew innovative maps that influenced Flemish mapmakers of the 1500s such as Gerardus Mercator (muhr-KAY-tuhr). But these maps were also misleading and, unlike Cresques' effort, did not de-center Europe. For example, Mercator's 1569 world map vastly exaggerated the size of Europe and North America while diminishing the size of Africa, India, China, and South America. In spite of these distortions, Mercator's approach, which pictures the earth as an uncurved rectangle intersected by straight lines for latitude and longitude, is still widely used.

The foundation for the reshaping of European societies also came from developments in technology and mathematics, some of them inspired by earlier Arab, Chinese, and Indian innovations. Between 1450 and 1550 Europe's technology surpassed that of the Arabs and was catching up to that of China. The major improvements came in shipbuilding, navigation, weaponry, and printing. European ships took advantage of lateen sails developed by Arabs and sternpost rudders from China, and they could also use the Chinese magnetic compass to navigate. Facing much rougher, stormier waters than the placid Mediterranean and Indian Ocean, the people along Europe's Atlantic coast also had to build sturdier ships, giving them a naval advantage over other maritime societies. Europeans also greatly improved gunpowder weapons and printing processes, both invented in China. The introduction of the European printing press in the mid-1400s made possible the dissemination of both Christian and secular knowledge to an increasingly literate audience. Some 13,000 books were published in Europe by 1500. Europeans also blended imported mathematical concepts, such as the Indian numerical system and Arab algebra, with their own insights to improve quantification. Countries that developed and marketed these new technologies and techniques increased their power, while those holding on to existing technologies fell behind.

"Gold, God, and Glory": Explorations and Conquests

During these centuries, the rise of Europe as a world power took place within a context of European overseas expansion and conquest (see Chapters 16–18). Historians use a standard shorthand, "Gold, God, and Glory," to describe European motives in going out into the world in this era. "Gold" was the search for material gain by acquiring and selling Asian spices, African slaves, American metals, and other resources. A desire to establish a direct connection to Asian trade led to the first European voyages of discovery in the 1400s. "God" refers to the militant crusading tradition of Christianity, including the rivalry with Islam and the hatred of non-Christian religions. Many Christians wanted to convert the world to what they believed to be the true faith. Reflecting this view, a missionary Catholic priest in Spanish America argued that "it is a great thing that so many souls should have been saved and that so many evils, idolatries, homicides, and great offenses against God [by Native Americans] should have been halted."[3] "Glory" describes the goals of the competing monarchies, who sought to establish their claims to newly contacted territories so as to strengthen their position in European politics. Motivated by these three aims, various western European peoples expanded overseas during the Early Modern Era, gaining control over widening segments of the globe. By the late nineteenth century Europeans dominated much of the world politically and economically.

During the 1400s the seafaring peoples of the Iberian peninsula, the Spanish and Portuguese, ventured out into the Atlantic and discovered the Azores (A-zorz), Madeira (muh-DEER-uh), and Canary island chains off northwest Africa (see Map 15.1). Several factors pushed Iberians to pioneer in overseas expeditions: a favorable geographic location facing the Atlantic Ocean and North Africa, a maritime tradition of deep-sea fishing, an aggressive Christian crusading tradition, and possession of the best ships and navigation techniques in Europe by the 1400s. The Iberians also had economic motives. For centuries gold from West Africa had passed through North Africa to southern Europe, where it was used for coins, treasuries, and jewelry and as tender (money) to buy valued Asian goods. But trade with Islamic North Africa and western Asia had stalled in the 1400s. Furthermore, the earliest Iberian exploration sought a way to circumnavigate the Venetian monopoly over the valuable trade from southern Asia through Persia and Egypt. The Iberians were also interested in finding new food sources, since Iberia did not produce enough meat and wheat to feed its growing population.

This maritime exploration and conquest required new technologies, such as a new type of ship to sail the rough Atlantic. The Portuguese invented the caravel, an easily maneuverable type of ship designed to travel long distances. However, since caravels used Chinese sternpost rudders and Arab lateen sails, they were not entirely a Portuguese invention. Some historians even argue that the caravel was modeled on the earlier Arab ship known as a carrack (KAR-uhk). Later the Iberians built larger ships such as galleons, which provided much more cargo space and room for larger crews than caravels. To chart the position of the sun and stars, Iberian sailors used the astrolabe (AS-truh-labe), invented by tenth-century Arabs. Some Europeans also learned how to mount weapons on ships, which increased their advantage at sea and enabled them to overwhelm coastal defenses and defeat lightly armed ships. The Spanish in the Americas and the Portuguese in Africa and Asia, using artillery, naval cannon, and muskets, could conquer or control large territories if the inhabitants lacked guns. By the late 1500s, the English were building the most maneuverable ships and the best iron cannon, and by the 1700s European land and sea weapons greatly outclassed those of once militarily powerful China, India, Persia, and Ottoman Turkey. Europeans now posed a threat to the great Asian states.

The intense competition between major European powers led to increased exploration, the building of trade networks, and a scramble for colonies, subject territories where Europeans could directly control primary production. In the 1400s the Portuguese began direct encounters with the peoples of coastal Africa, and by 1500 Portuguese explorers had reached East Africa and then sailed across the Indian Ocean to India. Soon, they seized key Asian ports such as Hormuz on the Persian Gulf, Goa in India, and Melaka in Malaya. Meanwhile, the Spanish discovered that a huge landmass to the west, soon to be named America, lay between Europe and East Asia. By the later 1500s the Spanish had explored large regions of the Americas and conquered many of its peoples, including the great Inca and Aztec Empires, making them the most powerful European state for some decades. Portugal, England, France, and Holland also colonized other parts of the Americas and sent emigrants to what they called "the New World." At the same time, various European states established colonies in several African locations and carried increasing numbers of enslaved Africans to the Western Hemisphere to work on plantations growing cash crops, such as sugar, cotton, and coffee, for European consumption. In the sixteenth and seventeenth centuries, the Portuguese, Dutch, and Spanish colonized several Asian port cities and various Southeast Asian islands, including the Philippines, Java, and the Spice Islands of Indonesia. American minerals, especially silver, supported a great expan-

sion of the European economy and allowed Europeans to buy into the rich Asian trade, especially from China. These conquests and economic activities enabled the transfer of vast quantities of resources to Europe, especially silver, gold, sugar, coffee, and spices, and the fortunes of leading European trading ports such as Venice, Genoa, Lisbon, Seville, Antwerp, and Amsterdam rose or fell depending on their importance in overseas trade.

During the Early Modern Era Europeans gradually brought various peoples into their economic and political sphere, laying the foundations for a system of Western dominance in the world after 1750. Several European societies benefited the most. The Portuguese and Spanish prospered in the 1500s from their overseas activities, while in the 1600s the overseas trade of the Dutch, English, and French enabled them to become the most powerful European countries. But European influence was still limited in many regions. During this era Asian and African societies such as China, Siam, Japan, and Morocco remained powerful and dynamic and were able to successfully resist or ignore European demands. Nonetheless, overseas trade and exploitation provided some European societies with valuable human labor and natural resources and contributed to the growth of capitalism.

Early Capitalism

Arising first in western Europe, capitalism has taken many forms and fostered new values around the world. Under capitalism, the drive for profit from privately owned and privately invested capital has largely determined what goods are produced and how they are distributed. Capitalism was unique when it first arose because, on a much greater scale than ever before, money in the form of investment capital was used to make profits. The various forms of capitalism that emerged as the economic system spread had certain common features: the need for constant accumulation of additional capital, economic self-interest, the profit motive, a market economy of some sort, and competition. These features shaped both economic and social relations between people. For example, individual carpenters who once shared their services with the community on a barter basis, or who belonged to a guild that operated for the benefit of all local carpenters, began to charge fees instead, competing for customers with other carpenters. By the 1800s capitalism also included private ownership of the means of production, such as factories, businesses, and farms.

Capitalism was not necessarily inevitable. The profit motive, wealth accumulation, and competition were incompatible with certain cultural values. For example, many traditional cultures had a bias against people accumulating more wealth than their neighbors or working hard for the sole purpose of maximizing income. Even today, some Asian, African, American Indian, and Latin American cultures value cooperation, religious piety, or generosity more than acquiring great wealth. For instance, many Malays in Southeast Asia respect Muslim pilgrims to Mecca more than successful businessmen and mistrust shopkeepers. In precapitalist societies governments siphoned off surplus wealth, and the elite spent their resources on conspicuous consumption of luxuries, such as the building of magnificent cathedrals, palaces, and pyramids that now impress tourists. In medieval Europe merchant and craft guilds emphasized ethics, accepting a strict regulation of economic activity for the greater good. By contrast, capitalists invested some profits in further exchange or production, always with the goal to make more money. This reinvestment fostered an economic expansion that differentiated capitalism from earlier economic systems, transforming small-scale trade into global capitalism.

While western Europe became increasingly capitalist, parts of eastern Europe discouraged capitalism. In the 1500s, as the demand for agricultural products increased while cooler climates hindered farming, eastern European nobles faced a labor shortage on their estates. Allied with the landowning aristocracy, kings in Poland, Lithuania, Prussia, and Russia mandated serfdom on the peasantries and imposed new laws forbidding people to leave the land. At the same time, by providing little support to the local merchant classes, these governments thwarted capitalist expansion and diminished the political influence of cities. As local merchants declined, foreign merchants, including Dutch, Germans, Jews, and Armenians, moved into eastern Europe, becoming the major middlemen and gradually dominating the region's commerce. As the economies became chiefly agrarian and serf-based, however, many once vibrant cities declined into sleepy provincial towns, inhabited by many foreign-born merchants or their descendants. For example, many Polish and Lithuanian cities had large populations of Jewish merchants and artisans.

The Rise of Capitalism

During the 1500s capitalism took hold in some cities and states of north and northwest Europe. Indeed, the English and the people of the Low Countries (today's Belgium and the Netherlands), especially the Flemish and Dutch, developed the most dynamic forms of capitalism, and soon they eclipsed Italy, shifting the economic balance of power in Europe from the Mediterranean to the English Channel and North Sea. Enriched by distributing American silver and controlling the Baltic grain trade, Antwerp became Europe's main financial capital until 1568, when Genoa temporarily regained dominance as a banking center. By the 1620s Amsterdam in Holland had emerged as Europe's capitalist powerhouse, dominating much European and Asian trade. This clean, orderly, and prosperous Dutch city boasted amenities rare elsewhere, such as street lamps and watch patrols to prevent crime. In 1728 the English writer Daniel Defoe concluded that "the Dutch must be understood as they really are, the Middle Persons of Trade, the Factors and Brokers of Europe. They buy to sell again, take in to send out, and the greatest part of their vast commerce consists in being supply'd from all parts of the world that they may supply the world again."[4]

Expanding capitalism fostered new economic ideas, social groups, and consumption patterns. For example, spurred by increasing trade, old concepts of investing wealth in land ownership gradually gave way to the view that capital should instead be invested in business and industry to help increase production of ships, armor, arms, and textiles. This increased production would then create more capital. Indeed, people needed more money because the import of American metals caused a rapid rise in prices. The increase in available capital began to change business methods, especially the use of credit on a large scale, which fostered banking. Society also changed. Capitalism produced a new social group known as the **bourgeoisie**, an urban-based, mostly commercial, middle class. Members of this group ranged from small-scale merchants to financiers. In addition to the bourgeoisie, many western Europeans were affected by the new materialism, which also encouraged lotteries and gambling. More people of all backgrounds purchased consumer goods, from tea, coffee, and sugar to clocks, china, and glassware.

As a new capitalist order emerged, many Europeans changed their attitudes toward charging interest for loans and seeking profit. The medieval church had denounced charging interest as usury, a mortal sin, and had also opposed commercial profit. A good Christian could not become a merchant or banker, leaving much commerce and banking to the Jewish minority. By the late 1500s, however, many rejected these church teachings and instead heeded the cynical saying that "he who takes usury goes to hell; he who doesn't goes to the poorhouse." Acceptance of interest by Christians reflected a gradual shift to an entirely different type of society in western Europe.

Jacob Fugger (FOOG-uhr) (1459–1525) of Augsburg (AUGZ-burg), a southern German city, was living proof that an ambitious commoner could prosper from the capitalist trends. The grandson of a weaver and son of a successful merchant, Fugger built a financial empire of banks, factories, silver mines, and farmlands. Earning an annual profit of 54 percent for sixteen years, Fugger became Europe's richest man, in the process loaning money to royal houses and acquiring a castle and the title of count. He wrote the epitaph for his own tomb, praising himself as "behind no one in attainment of extraordinary wealth, in generosity, purity of morals and greatness of soul."[5] His sons also published the first newsletter for merchants and bankers, which tracked political and economic developments in Europe.

Commercial Capitalism and Mercantilism

As a dynamic, flexible economic system, capitalism continually changed in character and expanded in scope. Under the form of capitalism dominant in western Europe between 1500 and 1770, **commercial capitalism**, most capital was invested in commercial enterprises such as trading companies, including the world's first joint-stock companies (see Chronology: Political, Economic, and Intellectual Developments, 1500–1750).

---

bourgeoisie The urban-based, mostly commercial, middle class that arose with capitalism in the Early Modern Era.

commercial capitalism The economic system in which most capital was invested in commercial enterprises such as trading companies, including the world's first joint-stock companies.

companies protected from competition. To attract bullion held by other nations, these governments tried to limit imports and increase exports. In the 1600s the French finance minister Jean Baptiste Colbert (kohl-BEAR), the son of a merchant, used this approach brilliantly to support French industries and industrial exports. Some of the largest joint-stock companies obtained royal charters, which granted them monopolies and the right to colonize other lands in the name of the government. In England such companies, founded by business and government leaders, financed overseas exploration and supported piracy against Spanish and French shipping. Spurred by mercantilism, during the 1500s commercial capitalism expanded out of western Europe and into Africa, Asia, and the Americas.

> ### SECTION SUMMARY
>
> ■ Europe's political decentralization allowed for the growth of cities and the development of capitalism.
>
> ■ Europeans made great strides in mapmaking and improved technologies such as shipbuilding, navigation, weaponry, and printing by borrowing and building on the work of Arabs, Chinese, and Indians.
>
> ■ Motivated by "Gold, God, and Glory," Europeans, led by the Spanish and the Portuguese, set up colonies in the Americas, Africa, and Asia.
>
> ■ Despite entrenched value systems that opposed its single-minded emphasis on accumulating wealth, capitalism took hold in western Europe, while eastern European leaders resisted it and instead mandated serfdom.
>
> ■ By the early seventeenth century, Amsterdam had established itself as the center of capitalist Europe and the medieval Christian prohibition on usury was softening.
>
> ■ Commercial capitalists, assisted by the mercantilist policies of their countries, increased their market power by pooling resources in such organizations as joint-stock companies.

To increase their efficiency and profits, these precursors of today's giant multinational corporations pooled their resources by selling shares, or stocks, to merchants and bankers. Joint-stock companies encouraged investment and mobilized great capital, and their directors were chosen for their experience. A typical company employed many cashiers, bookkeepers, couriers, and middlemen skilled in various languages, and it invested in diversified economic activities such as real estate, mining, and industry. Few Asian or African merchants could compete with this collective power.

Commercial capitalism was strongly shaped by the cooperation of the state and big business enterprises, which worked together for their mutual benefit. States practiced **mercantilism**, an economic approach based on a government policy of building a nation's wealth by expanding its reserves of precious metals. The Atlantic states of England, Holland, France, and Spain particularly pursued mercantilism. The purpose was to strengthen monarchies by amassing gold and silver bullion. Trading was controlled by semimilitary, government-backed

The Renaissance and Reformation

How did the Renaissance and Reformation mark a crucial cultural and intellectual transition?

Two major movements, the Renaissance and the Reformation, reshaped European thought and culture in the 1500s. During the Renaissance, a dramatic flowering in arts and learning that began in Italy around 1350 (see Chapter 14), new philosophical, scientific, artistic, and literary currents paved the way for more creative, secular societies. The movement reached its peak in the 1500s, when it spread throughout Europe as the large quantities of gold and silver imported from the Americas spurred economic expansion and provided more

---

mercantilism An economic approach that emerged in Early Modern Europe based on a government policy of building a nation's wealth by expanding its reserves of precious metals.

people with money to purchase art and books. It lasted until 1615 (see Chronology: The Renaissance and Reformation, 1350–1615). Although historians disagree about its impact and importance, many believe that the Renaissance, which was sparked in part by trade with Asia and North Africa, provided a bridge between medieval and modern western Europe. In the same century the **Reformation**, the movement to reform Christianity, spawned new Christian churches that provided alternatives to the Roman Catholic Church. Both movements helped to undermine the pillars of medieval society and changed western European cultural and religious life.

Renaissance Philosophy and Science

The Renaissance fostered new ideas in philosophy and science. During this spurt in knowledge, thinkers and artists rediscovered the ideas of the Classical Greeks and Romans while receiving products and ideas from the Islamic world and China through exciting exchanges between East and West. The Renaissance promoted values such as individualism, secularism, tolerance, beauty, and creativity. Renaissance philosophy, known as humanism, emphasized humanity and its creations rather than God.

Humanism also focused on problems in the church. A growing crisis of confidence in the Roman Catholic Church, with its abuses by leadership and clergy, became more serious after 1400. Some Renaissance thinkers favored gradual church reform and less rigid ideas. The Dutch philosopher Erasmus (uh-RAZ-muhs) (1466–1536), for instance, called for a more personal religion and more tolerance of diverse beliefs, arguing that Jesus commanded people nothing except to love one another. Erasmus also advocated the use of living languages rather than Latin. The French humanist writer François Rabelais (RAB-uh-lay) (ca. 1494–1553) was even more critical toward the church than Erasmus, calling monks "a rabble of counterfeit saints, hypocrites, pretended zealots, who disguise themselves like masquers to deceive the world."[6] By spurring freedom of thought and offering critical insights, humanists began to topple the authoritarian medieval attitudes that had crippled scientific investigation. But popes rejected any significant changes in doctrine or institutions.

In the area of political thought, Niccolò Machiavelli (MAK-ee-uh-VEL-ee) (1469–1527), the Florentine author of a political manual, *The Prince*, was perhaps the first European to study power as something separate from moral doctrine. In making his arguments, Machiavelli claimed to draw on the lessons of history, but he also used his experience as a diplomat. *The Prince* argued that the ruler must always keep the end in mind and apply ruthless policies, such as deception and violence, in pursuing vital national interests. But the exercise of power did not necessarily require tyranny, since the ruler must avoid being hated. Rulers ignored popular moral values at their peril. Machiavelli also argued that it was not necessary for a leader to have piety, faith, integrity, and humanity, but he must seem to have them. Machiavelli's writings became very influential as a guide for European leaders.

Online Study Center Improve Your Grade
Primary Source: The Prince: Power Politics During the Italian Renaissance

Although Greco-Roman traditions greatly influenced Renaissance thought, some thinkers developed more interest in science, often employing direct experimental methods and direct observation. For example, the Florentine Leonardo da Vinci (lay-own-AHR-doh dah VIN-chee) (1452–1519) argued that simply repeating classical traditions without verifying them placed emphasis on memory more than intelligence. A painter, sculptor, architect, scientist, mathematician, and engineer, da Vinci exemplified the versatile Renaissance personality and openness to varied influences. Being knowledgeable about Muslim science and architecture, in 1504 he even negotiated unsuccessfully with the Ottoman sultan to build a bridge in Istanbul.

Another influential scientist, Polish astronomer Nicolaus Copernicus (koh-PUR-nuh-kuhs) (1473–1543), studied the skies and Islamic scholarship on astronomy, especially the influential writings of the Arab mathematician Ibn al-Shatir (1304–1375), whose research suggested that the earth might not be the center of the universe. Copernicus then transformed astronomy and physics when he devised his revolutionary "heliocentric," or sun-centered, theory of the solar system in 1507. Copernicus refuted the traditional European idea that earth was the center of the universe, arguing that

Reformation The movement to reform Christianity that was begun by Martin Luther in the sixteenth century.

CHRONOLOGY

The Renaissance and Reformation, 1350–1615

ca. 1350–1615	Era of Renaissance
ca. 1517–1615	Protestant Reformation
1532	Formation of Church of England (Anglicans)
1534	Founding of Society of Jesus (Jesuits)
1536	Move of John Calvin to Geneva
1545–1563	Council of Trent
1558–1603	Elizabethan era in England
1562–1589	Wars of religion in France
1571	Defeat of Turks at Lepanto by "Holy League"
1588	English defeat of Spanish armada
1598	Edict of Nantes

earth and the planets revolved around the sun. He did not dare publish his findings until after his death, fearing persecution by the church. Nor was the church alone in not liking these new ideas. The English poet John Donne regretted the shattering of the old beliefs, writing in 1611: "And new Philosophy calls all in doubt, The Element of fire is quite put out; The sun is lost, and the earth, and no man's wit Can well direct him where to look for it. 'Tis all in pieces, all coherence gone."[7]

Late Renaissance Art and Literature

The Renaissance reshaped European art and spread Italian artistic influence. The art of this period was founded upon a desire to reflect the deepening knowledge of humanity by more accurately representing people and their concerns in sculpture, painting, architecture, and literature. Some of the inspiration came from the growing contacts with Islamic, Asian, and African peoples and their artistic traditions. Italians such as the Venetian painter Giovanni Bellini (ca. 1430–1516) worked in or visited Muslim cities such as Istanbul and Cairo, spreading Italian influences but also returning with new perspectives. In the early 1500s Rome replaced Florence as the new capital of Italian art. Among those who worked in Rome, the eccentric Florentine Michelangelo Buonarroti (mi-kuhl-AN-juh-loh bwawn-uh-RAW-tee) (1475–1564) became famous for his realistic sculptures, paintings, and frescoes. He paid keen attention to the attitudes and gestures of each figure he painted on the ceiling of the Vatican's Sistine Chapel. Later Venice became the main Italian art center, where rich merchants and aristocrats offered artists generous financial support. The Venetian painters produced landscapes and portraits rather than the religious artworks that had once been common. One Venetian, Titian (TISH-uhn), (ca. 1488–1576) broke with Christian tradition by painting nudes and pre-Christian fables. Some women artists gained a following. The most famous was Artemisia Gentileschi (1593–ca. 1652), who survived a rape by her art teacher, and torture to test her allegations, to paint figures, especially heroic women, from Greek mythology and the Bible.

The Renaissance spread well beyond Italy, fostering other artistic innovations. In the Low Countries, for example, Pieter Bruegel (BRU-guhl) the Elder (ca. 1525–1569) integrated Renaissance and local traditions, painting realistic landscapes and sympathetic scenes of peasant and town life. El Greco (ell GREK-oh) (1541–1614), a native of Crete who studied in Italy before settling in Spain, blended Venetian, Byzantine, and Spanish traditions.

As in art, the growing secularism and humanism had literary consequences. For example, in England during the brilliant reign of Queen Elizabeth I (r. 1558–1603), writers replaced religious concern for the hereafter with stories of human passions. The Elizabethans also celebrated both the individual person and their nation, concerns reflected in the plays of William Shakespeare (1564–1616). The son of a prosperous businessman, Shakespeare moved to London to act in the theater and eventually began writing histories, comedies, and tragedies that many literary scholars have believed transcend time and place. His contemporary playwright Ben Jonson

Bruegel's *Peasant Wedding* Painted around 1567, Pieter Bruegel's, *The Peasant Wedding,* celebrates the rituals of peasant life, in this case a wedding dinner for a village. The Flemish artist may also have intended the painting of the feasting villagers as a satire on self-indulgence. The bride, composed and radiant, presides over the feast under a canopy. (Musée de la Ville de Paris, Musée Carnavalet/The Bridgeman Art Library International)

wrote that Shakespeare was not of an age, but for eternity. Yet, his work was shaped by his milieu, and some of his plays, such as *Henry V* and *Julius Caesar*, addressed English or ancient history. Other plays, such as *Othello*, *Hamlet*, and *The Merchant of Venice*, commented on the world beyond England. Shakespeare often profiled strong individuals, and one of his best-known characters, Hamlet, voiced Renaissance exuberance: "What [a] piece of work is a man, how noble in reason, how infinite in faculties…"[8]

In Spain in 1615, Miguel de Cervantes (suhr-VAN-teez) Saavedra (1547–1616) published one of the era's great novels, *Don Quixote* (kee-HO-tee). Cervantes was well qualified to examine society: he had worked as a steward and soldier, had been enslaved in Algiers, and then had become a purchasing agent who was eventually imprisoned for debt. His book painted a vast panorama of society at the end of Spain's golden age. The main character, Don Quixote, sets out to battle dragons and evil men, right injustice, defend the oppressed, and protect the innocent, but he mainly makes a grand nuisance of himself. Don Quixote dreams of an ideal past when love and friendship replaced greed. Cervantes reflected Renaissance attitudes by dignifying the human spirit but also, like some classical Greek playwrights, making fun of its plight.

Growing knowledge about other cultures forced some Europeans to reconsider their assumptions about the world, and their new ideas helped reshape literature and social thought. For example, the new information gained from exploration stimulated debate about the nature of Native American society. In *Utopia*, published in 1516, the English author Thomas More (1478–1535) portrays Native Americans as living in a paradise and views European society with disgust, saying that it is filled with poverty, injustice, hatred, and war. Similarly, the French writer Michel Eyquem de Montaigne (mon-TANE) (1533–1592) idealized Native American societies, popularizing the notion of a "Noble Savage" uncorrupted by "civilization." Shakespeare took up the theme in his 1611 play *The Tempest*, where he mocked the idea of the Noble Savage. In the play he creates a contrast between the civilized Prospero and the savage Caliban (KAL-uh-ban) (an anagram for *cannibal*). His Caliban is fierce and brutal, a far cry from the Noble Savage. Some observers see the play as a comment on the often hostile encounter between English settlers and Native Americans in Virginia.

The Reformation and Religious Change

Changing societies and a questioning of the old order also spawned the Reformation. For centuries the Roman church had dominated Europe. But to critics, it had become corrupt and complacent, often led by incompetent popes who intervened too rashly in secular political affairs. Moreover, some church leaders and clergy blatantly violated priestly requirements for celibacy and poverty. In addition, the spread of literacy and printed books inspired some individuals to examine and interpret Christian writings for themselves. These trends generated divisions within the church, and throughout the 1500s various groups sought church reform. Some, later called

Protestants, eventually broke completely with the Roman Catholic Church. The Reformation (1517–1615) transformed the religious makeup of Europe and profoundly reshaped Western thought (see Map 15.2). By 1600 almost 40 percent of non-Orthodox Europeans, mostly in the north, had renounced the Catholic faith and adopted some form of Protestantism, such as Lutheranism, Calvinism, and Anglicanism. From Europe, Protestant faiths were carried across the Atlantic by English and Dutch settlers in North America. Eventually dozens of differing Protestant churches competed with each other and with Catholics for influence in western Europe and North America.

Martin Luther (1483–1546), a German, launched the movement that ended the unity of Western Christianity. Germany provided fertile ground for such a movement. The power of the Holy Roman Emperor was weakening as conflicts with German princes and cities produced widespread discontent among peasants and craftsmen. Many German Christians also resented the pope and the bishops for leading luxurious lives. Luther studied law, then became an Augustinian monk, and later earned a doctorate in theology, after which he taught at the University of Wittenberg (WIT-n-burg). Eventually he concluded that nothing in scripture justified papal power and elaborate church rituals. Tormented by religious doubts, he came to believe that, contrary to Catholic teachings, only faith, not good works, could wipe away a person's sin and ensure salvation.

Luther's break with the church was prompted by the lucrative church practice of selling indulgences, clerical statements that canceled punishment due for sins in exchange for cash contributions to the church. In 1517 Luther, hoping to start a debate, distributed a paper containing ninety-five statements in Latin attacking indulgences. Soon Luther's statements, translated into German and printed, became the talk of the country. Pope Leo X excommunicated Luther in 1520 for refusing, as ordered, to retract his views and burn his books. Luther then translated the Bible into German and developed his religious doctrines, condemning Rome as "the greatest thief and robber that has ever appeared on earth or ever will. Poor Germans, we have been deceived."[9] Lutherans formed a church rooted in the Augsburg Confession, a doctrinal statement issued in 1530 that argued for the Bible as the only source of faith, stated that every believer had the freedom to interpret scripture, and attacked the cults of the Virgin Mary and the saints, priestly celibacy, and the monastic orders.

Luther's break gained him support but generated unrest and divided Western Christianity. Lutheranism spread widely in northern Germany, Scandinavia, and the eastern Baltic coast. In the 1520s many German city officials, princes, priests, professors, and common people threw their support to Luther and the reform cause. But in 1524 a major conflict split the reform movement when peasants, inspired by Luther's challenge to Catholic Church power, revolted against the lords and church leaders who owned the land. Luther, opposed to mixing religion and social protest, unsuccessfully mediated between

Protestants Groups that broke completely with the Roman Catholic Church as the result of the Reformation.

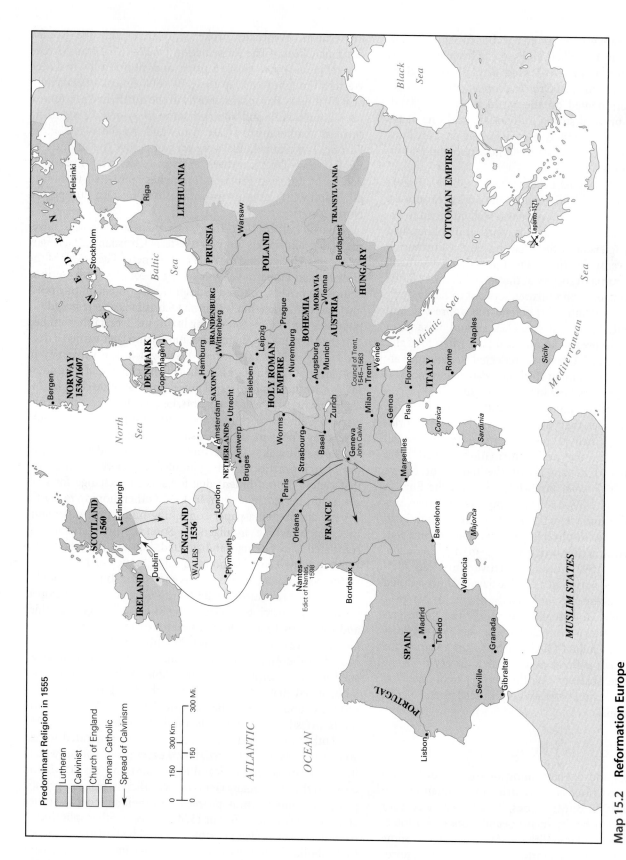

Map 15.2 Reformation Europe

The Protestant Reformation reshaped Europe's religious landscape in the 1500s and early 1600s. By the mid-1550s some form of Protestantism had become dominant in much of northern Europe, England, and Scotland. Catholicism remained predominant in the southern half of western Europe and parts of eastern Europe.

the sides and then supported the nobles, who crushed the up-risings. The result was over 100,000 deaths. The Lutheran Church became closely linked to governments, and many German princes became Lutheran, while their overlord, the Holy Roman Emperor, remained staunchly Catholic.

Non-Germans were also inspired by Luther's example, founding Protestant movements. In Switzerland the theologian, priest, and humanist Ulrich Zwingli (ZWING-lee) (1484–1531) preached similar ideas. But Luther and Zwingli soon disagreed. Whereas Luther interpreted the Bible literally, Zwingli was more open-minded and applied reason to religious doctrine. Zwingli's activities sparked a civil war among Swiss Catholics and Protestants that resulted in Zwingli's death. Another Protestant movement, Calvinism, was more radical than Lutheranism in rejecting Catholic doctrine. Its founder, John Calvin (1509–1564), was forced to leave France for supporting Luther's ideas and settled in Geneva (juh-NEE-vuh), Switzerland. Like Luther, Calvin emphasized reading the Bible, practicing charity, and never questioning God. However, unlike Luther, Calvin believed not in human free will but in predestination, the doctrine that an individual's salvation or damnation was already determined at birth by God. Since good behavior and faith could not guarantee reaching Heaven, the authorities must enforce morality to maintain order. Under Calvin, Geneva became a theocratic society, ruled by church leaders with growing intolerance of other views. Some dissenters were even burned at the stake. Calvin demanded strict morality and attacked worldly pleasures. For example, inns had to forbid behavior such as swearing, dancing, dice, playing cards, indecent songs, or staying up after nine at night. Calvinism spread rapidly in Switzerland, England, and Holland and also developed centers of strength elsewhere. In 1561, for instance, the Calvinist John Knox founded the Presbyterian Church in Scotland, where it became the dominant church.

In England, unlike Germany and Switzerland, the initiative for religious change came from the king, Henry VIII (r. 1509–1547), who was then a Catholic. Henry had no male heir with his wife, Catherine of Aragon, a Spanish princess. To preserve his dynasty, he asked the pope to annul his marriage so that he could marry Anne Boleyn (1501–1536), the much-courted daughter of English aristocrats who had rebuffed Henry's invitations to become his mistress. When Rome refused the annulment, Henry chose to break with the church in 1532, rejecting papal supremacy. He announced his divorce, married Anne Boleyn, and arranged to be made head of the Church of England, later known as the Anglican Church, newly formed by his allies. Henry quickly moved to suppress both Calvinism and the Catholic Church. He closed the English monasteries and distributed their lands to his allies among nobles and businessmen. However, the Anglicans largely retained Catholic dogma. Ironically, Henry grew disenchanted with Anne Boleyn, who also bore him no sons, and had her beheaded in 1536 for alleged treason and adultery. Henry married four more times.

Henry's moves generated religious strife in England. His only male heir, the sickly Edward VI (r. 1547–1553), came to the throne at age ten but died at sixteen of tuberculosis. The Catholic reaction was led by Edward's successor, Henry's daughter by Catherine of Aragon, Queen Mary Tudor (TOO-duhr) (r. 1553–1558), who suppressed the Anglican Church. But she was succeeded by Elizabeth I (1533–1603), the daughter of Henry VIII and Anne Boleyn, who restored the Anglican Church. Calvinist influences then began reshaping Anglican dogma. English Calvinists (known as Puritans) were at first tolerated by Anglicans but later persecuted by Elizabeth's successors for opposing moves toward Catholic-Anglican reconciliation. Some Puritans emigrated to Holland. From there one small Puritan group, the Pilgrims, moved to North America in 1620 to seek more religious freedom, helping plant Puritan influence in the New England colonies.

Protestantism and Capitalism

Modern historians avidly debate the relationship between the rise around the same time of both capitalism and Protestantism. While many doubt any direct connection, other scholars believe that Protestant doctrines contributed to, and supplied religious underpinnings for, capitalist values. Some forms of Protestantism were certainly congenial to the thriving new economic attitudes. In particular, Calvinists believed that citizens demonstrated their fitness for salvation by being law-abiding, industrious, thrifty, and sober, all values that supported the capitalist order. Like Calvinists and other Protestants, capitalists also favored productive labor, frugality, and accumulation of wealth as good in themselves. Many Protestant hymns warned against wasting money on frivolous pleasures. Both Protestantism and capitalism also encouraged individualism, thus undermining the medieval values that the Catholic Church defended.

The relationship between capitalism and Protestantism certainly seems to have been congenial. Although capitalism also emerged in some Catholic societies, as with the Fuggers, the wealthy entrepreneurs in southern Germany mentioned earlier, it flourished in several Protestant societies, especially Holland, England, and northern Germany. The strongest capitalist societies were also the most Protestant; they were also the most intellectually diverse and gave rise to some secularized free thinkers. Although Luther and Calvin may have been intolerant of other religious views, they opened the doors to democracy: once people had freely voiced their opinions on religion, they moved on to seeking a voice in government. Similarly, when women were encouraged to become literate so that they could read the scriptures, they also gained some new options.

The Counter Reformation and Catholic Reform

The Protestant challenge generated a reaction, the **Counter Reformation**, a movement to confront Protestantism and crush dissidents within the Catholic Church. The church used varied strategies to fight Protestantism. Pope Paul IV praised

Counter Reformation A movement to confront Protestantism and crush dissidents within the Catholic Church.

Few women have ever enjoyed the power and respect of England's Renaissance queen, Elizabeth I. Her forty-five years of rule (1558–1603) marked a brilliant period for English culture, especially in literature and theater. On her death, the admiring playwright Ben Jonson wrote her epitaph: "For wit, features, and true passion, Earth, thou hast not such another." The queen may have been, as her detractors claimed, deceptive, devious, and autocratic, but her intelligence and formidable political skills helped her maneuver successfully through the snake pit of both English and European politics. But English-Spanish relations deteriorated, prompting war. In 1588, as the powerful Spanish armada sailed toward the English coast, Elizabeth launched the English ships with a speech to her subjects that ironically played off her gender to reinforce her link with the English people. With the help of foul weather, the English defeated the Spanish, changing the fortunes of both countries.

My loving people. We have been persuaded by some that are careful for our safety, to take heed how we commit ourselves to armed multitudes, for fear of treachery, but I assure you, I do not desire to live to distrust my faithful and loving people. Let tyrants fear; I have always so behaved myself, that, under God, I have placed my chiefest strength and safeguard in the loyal hearts and good will of my subjects, and therefore I am come amongst you, as you see, at this time, not for my recreation and disport, but being resolved in the midst and heat of the battle, to live or die amongst you all, to lay down for my God, and for my kingdoms, and for my people, my honor and my blood, even in the dust.

I know I have the body of a weak and feeble woman; but I have the heart and stomach of a king, and of a king of England too; and I think foul scorn that . . . Spain, or any prince of Europe should dare to invade the borders of my realm; to which rather than any dishonor shall grow by me, I myself will take up arms, I myself will be your general, judge, and rewarder of every one of your virtues in the field.

I know already for your forwardness you have deserved rewards and crowns; and we do assure you in the word of a prince, they shall be duly paid you. In the meantime my lieutenant general shall be in my stead, than whom never prince commanded a more noble or worthy subject; no doubting but by your obedience to my general, by your concord in the camp, and your valor in the field, we shall shortly have a famous victory over those enemies of my God, of my kingdoms, and of my people.

THINKING ABOUT THE READING

1. How did Elizabeth justify the forthcoming battle with Spain?

2. What personal qualities did this Renaissance monarch suggest she could offer to her people in their time of peril?

Source: Charles W. Colby, ed., *Selections from the Sources of English History* (Harlow: Longmans, Green, 1899), pp. 158–159. Quotation in introduction from A. L. Rowse, *The Elizabethan Renaissance: The Life of the Society* (New York: Charles Scribner's, 1971), p. 59.

the Holy Inquisition, the church court formed in medieval times to combat heretical ideas (see Chapter 14), as the apple of his eye. Persecution of dissidents by the Inquisition became especially ferocious in Spain, where several thousand people believed to hold dissident ideas were burned at the stake. In addition, the pope formed a new church office, the Congregation of the Index, to censor books and decide which ones, among them Protestant writings, were to be forbidden altogether. Missionary activity also entered into the Counter Reformation. The Spanish Basque former soldier, Ignatius of Loyola (loi-OH-luh) (1491–1556), founded a new missionary order, the Society of Jesus, in 1534. The Jesuits, as they were known, boasted strict discipline. One prominent Jesuit, the Spanish Basque St. Francis Xavier (ZAY-vee-uhr) (1506–1552), became a pioneering missionary in India, Southeast Asia, and Japan.

For all their harsh punitive measures, the Inquisition and Index did not manage to suppress dissidence within the church, prompting the pope to sponsor a series of conferences, the Council of Trent (a city in northern Italy), to reconsider church doctrines in free-wheeling discussions. However, the council (1545–1563) reaffirmed most Catholic dogma, including those ideas and practices rejected by Protestants. It supported the value of both tradition and scripture, condemned Calvin's doctrine of predestination and Luther's sole reliance on faith, endorsed the church hierarchy and papal authority, and maintained priestly celibacy. But the council did bring about some reform: it imposed more papal supervision of priests and bishops, and it mandated that all clergy be trained in seminaries. The Trent reforms were continued by three reforming popes, enabling Catholicism to check its loss of believers to Protestantism and recover some lost ground. The reforms within the church and the competition with Protestants allowed the Catholic Church to survive and flourish in a modified form. The church gradually turned from confronting Protestants to converting the peoples outside of Europe.

But religious passions continued to foster intolerance. Indeed, in Europe, religious minorities, such as Jews, French Protestants, and English Catholics, faced discrimination and sometimes violence. Several popes pursued anti-Jewish policies, as did some Protestants: Luther advocated burning synagogues, arresting rabbis, and confiscating Jewish property. Throughout the Early Modern Era many Jews faced expulsion from the countries where they lived or segregation in city ghettoes. Many Jews and minority Catholics and Protestants emigrated to other European countries or to the Americas to escape religious persecution.

Religious Wars and Conflicts

Religious divisions contributed to a series of European wars and other conflicts from the late sixteenth through early eighteenth centuries, which reshaped several societies. The Spanish Empire, ruled by a branch of the Habsburg family, was particularly troubled by religious tensions. During the 1500s Spain emerged as a major European power, which, thanks to exploration and conquest, controlled a vast empire in the Americas and Southeast Asia. The Spanish Habsburgs also ruled other Europeans, including Portugal, the Low Countries, and parts of Italy. King Philip II of Spain (r. 1556–1598), known as "the most Catholic of kings," put the resources of the Spanish crown toward defending the Catholic cause in Europe while spreading the faith abroad.

Philip faced one of his biggest challenges in the Low Countries, where his suppression of Calvinism antagonized businessmen and the nobility, who demanded autonomy and freedom of worship. Inflamed Protestants attacked Catholic churches, and Spain's execution of dissident leaders spurred a general revolt in 1566, in which both Catholics and Protestants rallied behind the Calvinist leader, the Dutchman William of Nassau (NAS-au), Prince of Orange. Philip dispatched an occupation army that executed over 1,100 Protestants and, in 1576, sacked Antwerp, Europe's wealthiest city. In 1579, hoping to divide his opponents, Philip promised political liberty to the ten largely Catholic Flemish- and French-speaking southern provinces of the Low Countries, thereby forging the foundations of modern Belgium and Luxembourg.

Because of English assistance to the Low Country rebels and English attacks on Spanish shipping in the Americas, Philip II tried to invade England by sea in 1588 but faced a determined foe in Queen Elizabeth I (see Witness to the Past: Queen Elizabeth I Rallies Her People). The English ships outmaneuvered Spain's armada of 130 ships and then triumphed when a fierce storm in the English Channel devastated the Spanish fleet. This disastrous defeat of Spain's once invincible navy weakened Philip. The mostly Protestant, Dutch-speaking northern provinces of the Low Countries broke away from Spain in 1588 and became fully independent in 1609, forming the country later officially called the Netherlands, but popularly known as Holland.

Between 1562 and 1589 religious conflicts also raged across France. The French Calvinists, known as Huguenots (HYOO-guh-nauts), were led by the powerful Bourbon (BOOR-buhn) family. In 1572, after the assassination of Calvinist leaders on royal orders sparked Huguenot rioting in Paris, Catholic forces massacred 30,000 Huguenots. Religious

rivalries also became enmeshed in succession disputes for the French crown. In 1593 Henry of Bourbon (1553–1610), remarking that "Paris is well worth a mass," renounced Calvinism for Catholicism in order to become King Henry IV. Remaining a Protestant sympathizer, in 1598 he signed the Edict of Nantes (nahnt), which ended the religious conflicts by recognizing Roman Catholicism as the state church of France but giving Huguenots the right to freely practice their religion.

While Protestant-Catholic tensions in Europe were intense, Christian-Muslim conflicts also simmered, as they had for centuries, and often translated into political and military conflict. Many Europeans worried in particular about the growing power of the Muslim Ottoman Turks (see Chapter 16). The Ottomans sought to expand their empire, which already included Greece, much of the Balkans, and Bulgaria. When some people in the Balkans abandoned Christianity for Islam, Christian leaders became alarmed, and the Holy Roman Emperor Charles V marshaled allies to defeat the Turks at Vienna in 1529. Then in 1571 the so-called Holy League of Spain, Rome, and Venice used advanced naval gunnery to destroy the Turkish fleet at the Battle of Lepanto (li-PAN-toh), off Greece, ending Turkish ambitions for a while. In 1683 the Turks besieged Vienna, and Austria was saved only by Polish intervention. Finally the Austrians pushed the Turks out of Hungary. Ottoman expansion in Europe had ended, and with it the Christian fear of more conversion to Islam.

SECTION SUMMARY

- Renaissance humanists questioned the authority of the Catholic Church, while thinkers such as Machiavelli, Leonardo da Vinci, and Copernicus challenged accepted truths of morality, science, and astronomy.
- Renaissance artists such as Michelangelo aimed to represent humanity more realistically, and writers such as Shakespeare and Cervantes examined the concerns of individuals and the broad sweep of society.
- Martin Luther, who criticized the corruption of the Catholic Church, set the Reformation in motion; it was propelled by figures such as John Calvin, whose ideas were taken up by the Puritans, and King Henry VIII of England, who made England Protestant.
- While not all capitalists were Protestant, many historians see a link between the individualism and thrift of Protestants and their success in business.
- In the Counter Reformation, the Catholic Church attempted to reassert its dominance, but ultimately it focused its energy on converting non-Europeans rather than combating Protestants.
- Religion sparked several wars: Spain's attempts to keep the Low Countries Catholic led to costly conflict with England and the eventual fragmentation of the area; Catholics massacred Huguenots in France; and several battles finally ended Ottoman expansion in Europe.

✦ Changing States and Politics

What types of governments emerged in Europe in this era?

The encounters with the wider world, capitalism, Renaissance humanism, and the Protestant Reformation reshaped Europe, creating new institutions and beliefs to challenge old ones. European politics also changed. The transition from the medieval to the Early Modern order unleashed forces that threatened to consume Europe. Bloody wars drew much of Europe into conflict and produced political changes: kingdoms were torn asunder and reconfigured, old states declined, and new states gained influence. These states were probably not nations in the modern sense, since most were multiethnic entities ruled by royal families who married across national lines. Moreover, patriotic feelings of belonging to a nation, common today, were mostly restricted to the elites. Many of these states used mercantilist policies to provide them with monetary resources, and in some states, some form of royal absolutism flourished. A few other states developed representative governments with elements of democracy.

Regional Wars and National Conflicts

Various wars raged during much of this era; some were prompted by religious divisions, but others were spawned by tensions between rival states and within large multinational empires such as the Habsburg-ruled realms of Spain and the Holy Roman Empire. Even after religious tensions subsided, warfare remained a constant reality, involving most European societies at one time or another.

The major conflict was the Thirty Years War (1618–1648), a long series of bloody hostilities that claimed millions of lives and involved many countries. The Thirty Years War was a continuation of the religious wars and national rivalries of the 1500s. This complex struggle for regional power started in the Holy Roman Empire, as Czech (check) Protestants revolted against Habsburg Catholic rulers trying to limit religious freedom. Eventually the fighting also drew in German princes and two mostly Lutheran countries, Denmark and Sweden. Finally France, although a mostly Catholic country, went to war against its Habsburg rivals who ruled Austria and Spain. In 1648 the conflict ended after a four-year-long European congress in Westphalia (west-FALE-yuh), a German province. The Treaty of Westphalia reaffirmed freedom of religion but did not permanently end Protestant-Catholic conflict. The new balance of power in Europe favored France and curbed the Habsburgs, and France enjoyed unrivaled prestige after 1659 while two of its major rivals, Spain and the Holy Roman Empire, were militarily exhausted. The Holy Roman Emperor lost influence to German princes, Sweden gained territory, and the conference recognized Swiss independence from Habsburg rule. Perhaps the Dutch benefited the most, because the long struggle had weakened their longtime enemy and former ruler, Spain.

After Westphalia European warfare changed. The wars of the later 1600s and early 1700s were fought between states with well-drilled professional soldiers, large warships, and more deadly gunpowder weapons, including cannon and rifles. The most widespread conflict, the War of the Spanish Succession (1701–1714), brought together England, Holland, Austria, Denmark, Portugal, and some German states to battle France and Spain over who would inherit the Spanish throne from the

Soldiers' Return   In the early 1600s the French artist Jacques Callot made a series of moving etchings about the Thirty Years War called "Miseries of War." This etching shows a group of discharged soldiers, so impoverished and brutalized by war that they either beg for food or die alongside the road.
(Courtesy of the Trustees of the British Museum)

last Habsburg king, and how the Spanish Empire might be partitioned as a result. With deadlier weapons, the human costs of war increased. For example, in the 1709 Battle of Malpaquet 40,000 French soldiers were killed or wounded.

The War of the Spanish Succession had major political and economic consequences for Europe. The Treaty of Utrecht (YOO-trekt), which ended the war, forced Spain to transfer its territory in Belgium and Italy to Austria. The once prosperous Dutch had overextended themselves in the war, damaging their economy, and Venice became a peripheral, declining state. Now a major maritime power, England received most of the spoils of war, including the strategic Gibraltar peninsula at Spain's southern tip, which commanded the entrance to the Mediterranean Sea, as well as some French territory in eastern Canada. Utrecht resulted in a new system of European states that was governed by the idea of maintaining a balance of power between rival states. Most of Europe entered a period of calm as the threat of war finally receded.

Absolutist and Despotic Monarchies

States changed during the Early Modern Era, with many governments moving far from medieval forms. New ways of thinking as well as political, social, and religious strife set the stage for diverse patterns of government by the seventeenth century. One trend among states was the rise of **absolutism**, a system of strong monarchial authority in which all power was placed under one supreme authority, a king or queen. Supporters saw absolutism as the best way to avoid chaos. Spain, ruled by the Habsburgs and, after 1715, the Bourbon dynasty, and Habsburg-ruled Austria exercised despotic power, as did the Papal States of central Italy, governed by the Vatican, and the Turk-dominated Ottoman Empire. But the French kings and the Russian czars best represented this increasing concentration of political power.

Absolutism in France   For a time absolute monarchies dazzled Europe, with the France of King Louis XIV (r. 1661–1715) serving as the model. Other rulers admired and envied the French monarchy. French became the language of European diplomacy, while French art and architecture were imitated as far away as imperial Russia. By the mid-1600s France, with 18 million people, was western Europe's largest country, was self-sufficient in agriculture, and had some thriving industries. All groups were subordinate to the French crown. Some historians, however, question whether French absolutism was as dictatorial as is often thought, since French kings had to work within a context of legality, bureaucracies, and tradition, which limited their exercise of power.

Louis XIV believed that he was the state and that his power derived from God; thus he was a monarch by divine right. He wrote that "princes act as Ministers of God and are his lieutenants on Earth."[10] Known as "the Sun King" for the brilliant extravagance of his court, Louis enjoyed great power, demanding obedience from all at the expense of the nobility. The monarch admitted that his dominant passion was love of glory. Few French kings valued marital fidelity, and Louis had many mistresses and children, legitimate and illegitimate.

The king tried to control everything. He imposed mercantilism, fostering industries and companies subject to royal domination, and he revoked the Edict of Nantes, forbade Protestant pastors to preach, and closed Protestant schools and churches. His repression of Protestantism led 200,000 Huguenots to emigrate to England, Holland, and North America. Louis also ordered a spectacular palace built at Versailles (vuhr-SIGH), a Paris suburb. Some 5,000 servants and courtiers lived on the grounds, with 14,000 more nearby. Versailles became the center of French cultural life and was regularly visited by French nobles and foreign leaders, all of whom were spied upon by the king. Louis' finance minister, Colbert, complained that "every day is one long round of dances, comedies, music of all kinds, promenades, hunts and other entertainments."[11] The king patronized the arts and literature by giving annual allowances to a court composer and financing playwrights and ballet dancers. In gratitude, artists celebrated the king, comparing him to classical Greek and Roman leaders.

Louis XIV's search for power elsewhere in Europe caused four major wars aimed at preventing Habsburg dominance. Marrying his dreams of personal glory to his goal of state prestige, he built up an effective military force. French power reached its height around 1680, but the wars proved financially ruinous and fell short of their objectives. The War of the Spanish Succession sapped the French treasury and military and enabled Austria, England, and Holland to counterbalance French power. Although France remained a major state after 1715, it had lost some of its glory. The absolutist French monarchy collapsed in revolution in the late 1700s.

Russian Despotism and Expansion   Just as France represented a concentration of power, Russia also developed a strong and often tyrannical government led by czars, some of whom pursued bold policies. The Russians had freed themselves from Mongol domination by the late fifteenth century. Ivan (ee-VON) IV (r. 1533–1584), known as Ivan the Terrible because of his paranoia and brutality, built a centralized Russian state while fighting wars with neighboring Poland and Sweden and conquering the Tartar (or Tartar) states, founded by Mongols and Turks three centuries earlier, along the lower Volga River. With the name of God on his lips, Ivan also ordered the death or torture of many thousands of Russians whom he considered enemies. Muscovite czars after Ivan imposed a rural economy based on serfdom to gain support from the landed nobility. Just as they sold land or horses, lords could sell their serfs, making them little better than slaves. The czars imposed tight control over the Russian Orthodox Church after it broke officially from the Greek Orthodox Church in the late 1500s. They also began extending their sovereignty toward the Black and Baltic Seas. In the early 1600s Muscovite expansion reached the southeastern Baltic region, where the Russians came into conflict with the Poles and Lithuanians.

absolutism   A system of strong monarchial authority in which all power is placed in a supreme authority, a king or queen.

St. Petersburg This painting, made around 1760, shows the Winter Palace, inhabited by the Russian royal family, occupying the left side of the Neva River in St. Petersburg, a major port that attracted many trading ships. Other government buildings occupy the right bank.　(Michael Holford)

Russia gradually developed an even more powerful state, especially during the reign of Peter I the Great (r. 1682–1725), an enlightened but despotic czar who encouraged Russia's integration with the West. Nearly 7 feet tall and possessed with tremendous energy, Peter dedicated himself to transforming his backward realm into a modern state. Peter saw Russia's only hope as copying Western technology and administrative techniques. To find out about the West, he secretly toured Europe under an assumed name for eighteen months, spending time in Austria, England, and Holland. He visited factories, museums, government offices, hospitals, and universities, and even worked as a carpenter in a Dutch shipyard to view firsthand the most advanced industrial and military technology. Returning to Russia in 1698, the czar launched ambitious political, economic, military, and educational reforms and hired foreign specialists to advise him.

Peter's policies had mixed though often significant consequences. Some policies to promote western European practices were superficial and unpopular, such as banning beards, no longer fashionable in western Europe, and the traditional long coats worn by men. He increased royal power at the expense of the church and nobility and often in a harsh manner, such as by mandating compulsory military service for some nobles. With such great power, Peter expanded Russia's frontiers, established industries, strengthened autocracy and serfdom, put together a navy to protect his Baltic flank, and developed a more efficient government. Since he hated gloomy Moscow, with its medieval flavor, in 1713 he began building a new capital on the Baltic, modeled on Amsterdam and Venice, and named it St. Petersburg. For his summer place near St. Petersburg, Peter enlisted Italian architects and French garden designers.

Peter had many foreign achievements. Wanting a stronger presence on the Baltic Sea, which was mostly dominated by Sweden, in 1699 he forged a secret alliance with Sweden's rivals, Denmark and Poland. During the Great Northern War that began in 1700, Russia and its allies battled the Swedes. But Swedish power was formidable, and only in 1709 did an exhausted Sweden abandon the eastern rim of the Baltic to Russia. Russia's growing power unsettled European rivals. As one of Peter's diplomats admitted in 1721: "We know very well that the greater part of our neighbors view [us] very unfavorably. If they seek our alliance it is rather through fear and hate than through friendship."[12] Peter and other Russian czars also pursued expansion to the south and east. Anxious to forge permanent access to the warm Mediterranean Sea because it was open to shipping twelve months a year, Russian forces pushed south toward the Black Sea and the Straits of Bosporus (see Map 15.3). They also began acquiring territory in Siberia and Muslim Central Asia (see Chapter 16).

By eventually creating a huge colossus of an empire and exploiting the resources of the newly colonized areas, Russia developed a largely self-sufficient economy. It had limited trade with western Europe and attracted few merchants from that region. Despite Peter the Great's Westernization policies, most czars were wary of foreign influence. Today Russia remains the last great land empire, ruling over various non-Russian peoples.

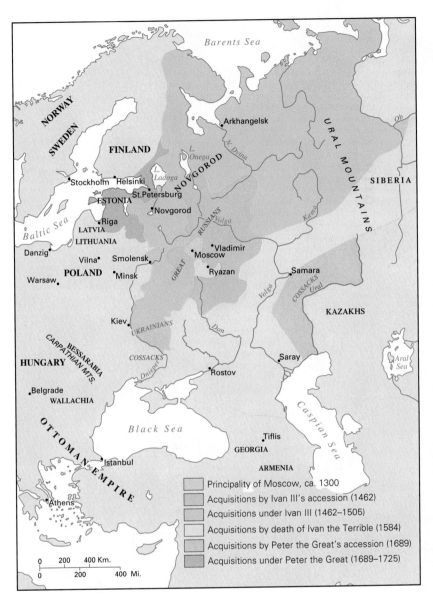

Map 15.3   Russian Expansion, 1300–1750
Beginning in the 1300s the Russians expanded from a small remote northern state, based in Moscow, into an empire. By the mid-1700s the Russians had spread over a wide area and gained political domination over western Siberia, the northern Caucasus, and part of what is today the eastern Baltic region and the Ukraine.

◗ *Online Study Center* **Improve Your Grade**
Interactive Map: Expansion of Russia to 1725

Map legend:
- Principality of Moscow, ca. 1300
- Acquisitions by Ivan III's accession (1462)
- Acquisitions under Ivan III (1462–1505)
- Acquisitions by death of Ivan the Terrible (1584)
- Acquisitions by Peter the Great's accession (1689)
- Acquisitions under Peter the Great (1689–1725)

The Rise of Representative Governments

Some European countries moved toward greater political freedom. In this era Iceland and Switzerland had the most democratic societies. Iceland enjoyed self-rule, including an elected assembly, for several centuries, while Switzerland was a multilingual, decentralized, and constitutional confederation of self-governing Catholic and Protestant districts. The Italian city-state of Venice was also a self-governing republic, although noble and merchant families dominated political life. Among the more powerful states, the Netherlands and England developed the most open and accountable governments. Both of these commercial powers were enriched by sea trade, which allowed the commercial class and many nobles to amass huge fortunes and hence play political roles. Eventually they demanded more influence. As a result, the Netherlands became a republic and England a constitutional monarchy.

The Dutch Republic   The Netherlands enjoyed a golden age during much of the 1600s. It built a colonial empire, including holdings in the Americas, South Africa, Sri Lanka, and Southeast Asia, and also dominated the Atlantic, Baltic, and Indian Ocean trade. Large Dutch joint-stock companies controlled the overseas market. The most powerful, the Dutch East India Company formed in 1602, monopolized the spice trade from Southeast Asia, making huge profits from the import of cinnamon and pepper. The company also imported other valuable Asian products, including Chinese silks and porcelain, Japanese art, Indian cotton textiles, and precious metals. These commercial activities amassed capital, some of which was invested in Dutch industry. The Netherlands became Europe's most prosperous society, with Amsterdam serving as a major hub of world trade. As an added benefit, economic prosperity fostered a market for Dutch artists.

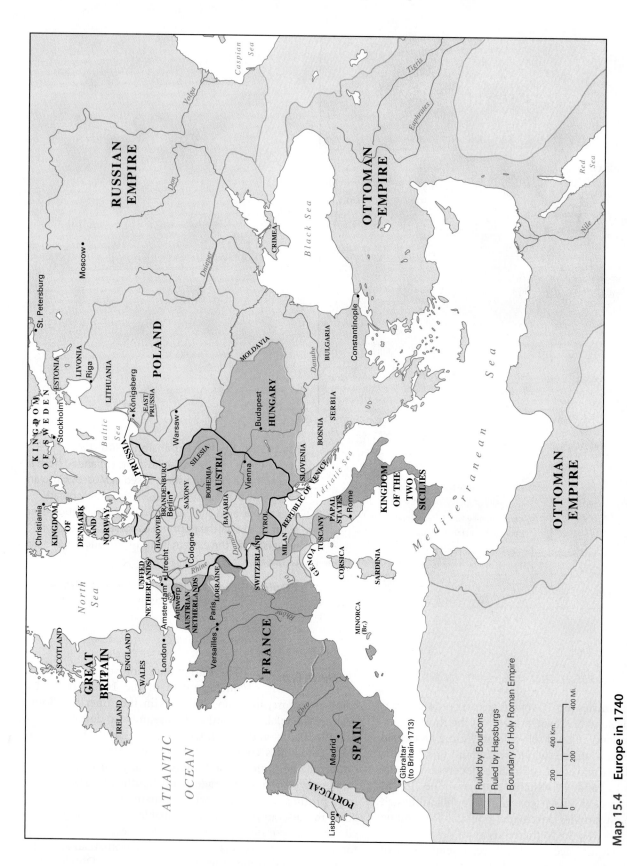

Map 15.4　Europe in 1740

By the mid-1700s France and Great Britain were the most powerful western European states. While once powerful Spain and Portugal had lost influence and the Germans and Italians remained divided, Prussia, Sweden, Russia, and Habsburg-ruled Austria were gaining strength.

The flow of wealth from overseas activities also influenced Dutch political life, fostering an innovative republican system. Holland had long enjoyed a climate of freedom and tolerance, attracting people who sought refuge from persecution, such as Portuguese Jews, or a more open intellectual atmosphere, such as French philosopher René Descartes. After breaking away from Spanish domination, the predominantly Protestant Netherlands became a republic and confederation linked by common institutions such as the assemblies of delegates. But the system encountered problems. The powerful Nassau (NAA-saw) family held the top post, that of Stadhouder General, and thus had control of the army and navy. The Nassaus' search for a more centralized authority put them at odds with the merchant elite, who favored provincial autonomy. These differences resulted in continued tensions between the two camps, and in 1619 the Stadhouder dragged the country into the Thirty Years War. Although the peace in 1648 favored the business and banking interests and diminished Stadhouder influence, a French invasion of the Netherlands in 1672, which shattered the peace, allowed the Stadhouders to regain power.

England and Parliamentary Government Over several centuries the English forged a colonial empire. England already held Ireland as a colony and sent Protestant settlers to some northern and eastern districts of that mostly Catholic island. Following the establishment of the English East India Company in 1601 to pursue commerce and conquest in Asia, England also founded a colonial empire in North America and the Caribbean. In the 1600s England adopted Dutch economic ideas, and by 1700 it overtook its rivals as major international traders. Between 1610 and 1640 English trade increased tenfold.

England also experienced profound political changes. In the 1600s, two political upheavals secured first a republic and then a constitutional monarchy. Hostile to absolutism, the English had long struggled to define the relative rights of kings and parliaments. Even one of the most effective European monarchs in history, Queen Elizabeth I, had to tolerate the appearance of parliamentary power while using her astute political and personal skills to get her way. However, the Stuarts, the Scottish royal family who became the monarchs of both Scotland and England after Elizabeth I died without an heir, had absolutist ambitions. Stuart king Charles I's decision to make Anglicanism the only recognized faith in both Scotland and England antagonized the Puritans and Presbyterians. In 1641, Parliament condemned despotic Stuart policies, prompting the English Civil War. The parliamentary troops were led by Oliver Cromwell (1599–1658), a member of the rural gentry and a zealous Puritan who was utterly convinced he was doing God's will. Cromwell's army defeated the royalist forces by 1645, and King Charles I was beheaded.

Parliament abolished the monarchy and proclaimed a republican Commonwealth (1649–1660) dominated by Cromwell. Some historians view the defeat of the royalists as a turning point, even a revolution, in which Puritans inclined toward capitalism and protecting property rights ended the last vestiges of feudalism in England. But Puritan "revolution" was not such a straightforward accomplishment. The Puritan majority in Parliament were fanatics determined to root out what they considered heresy and "godlessness" and to establish laws based solely on the biblical edicts of Moses. They had no patience with constitutional government and expelled the Presbyterians from Parliament. Eventually, to maintain order, Cromwell became dictator and imposed Puritan morality: he banned newspapers, executed dissidents, and crushed a Catholic rebellion in Ireland by burning crops and massacring many thousands of Irish resistors. On Cromwell's death Parliament restored the Stuarts to the throne after they agreed to guarantee individual freedom of religion.

However, after the Stuart restoration the Protestant-Catholic conflicts resumed and eventually led to a broad-based government with a stronger Parliament. Since Stuart king James II (r. 1685–1688) favored absolutist and pro-Catholic policies, Parliament, now dominated by Anglicans, offered the kingship to Dutch Stadhouder William of Orange (r. 1689–1702), a champion of the Protestant cause. In 1688 people in London rioted against James II with the cry of "No Popery," forcing the king to abdicate and flee to France. In what came to be known as the Glorious Revolution (1688–1689), Parliament decreed William and his wife, Mary, sovereigns after they accepted a Bill of Rights stating that the power of the laws is above the power of the king. This document recognized the right of petition and required parliamentary approval of taxes. The Toleration Act, establishing freedom of religion, followed.

After the Glorious Revolution, England moved only partway toward a democracy involving all the people. Although royal power was modified, the government represented only the factions that had political influence and wealth: the nobility, wealthy merchants, and property owners. English kings now had far less power than absolutist monarchs, and the great landed aristocratic families, elected from towns and counties, dominated Parliament. Only Parliament could vote the money for the king and his army. Certain ethnic minorities also had no representation. In 1707 England, Scotland, and Wales officially combined as the United Kingdom, often known as Great Britain. But English supremacy in the United Kingdom came at the expense of ethnic minorities. To better control them, the Scottish highlanders were cleared from their lands and forced to move to coastal cities or emigrate, and their Celtic language, Gaelic (GAY-lik), was banned. Today fewer than 1 percent of Scots can speak Gaelic. In colonized Ireland, Protestant English and Scottish settlers acquired land and Catholics became second-class citizens. Laws denied the majority Irish Catholics the right to education, property, parliamentary seats, and political office.

Rising New States, Declining Old States

The forces unleashed by capitalism, religious change, warfare, and shifting political power caused several powerful new states to emerge and several longtime powers to decline (see Map 15.4). Among those that emerged was Catholic and German-speaking Austria, which, under the Habsburg monarchs, became a major power after the Thirty Years War, outshining the German states to the west. The new centralized Austrian empire governed diverse societies: Czechs, Croats, Slovenians, most Hungarians, and some Italians, Romanians, and Serbs.

Much of Sweden, another emerging power, became independent of once mighty Denmark in 1520. Swedish society was distinctive: its peasants had never been serfs, many owned their own land, and peasant representatives served in the national assembly. The Swedish state became a hereditary but not absolutist monarchy, with an efficient administration and Lutheranism as the state religion. Soon Sweden dominated Baltic trade, but eventually lost their economic position to the Dutch. Dutch access to Baltic salt allowed them to circumvent the Spanish producers for this scarce and valuable commodity, which was used to process herring, butter, and cheese. Under King Gustavus Adolphus (r. 1611–1632), an earthy and paunchy but brilliant military strategist and creative administrator, Sweden gained control of parts of Poland and Prussia and most of the eastern Baltic societies, thereby becoming one of Europe's most influential states. By the mid-1600s the country controlled much of Poland and had regained more territory from Denmark, now reduced to a minor power even though it controlled Norway and Iceland. By 1721, however, the Swedes had lost all their possessions in the eastern Baltic except Finland to Russia or Prussia (PRUH-shuh).

A third state on the rise in Europe was Prussia, which originated as a small, mostly German-speaking state along the eastern Baltic coast, on the borderlands between the Holy Roman Empire and Poland. Long under Polish rule, the state became independent in 1660. In the mid-1700s Prussia built one of the most formidable military forces in Europe around a standing army under an authoritarian but constitutional monarchy. Under King Frederick II the Great (r. 1740–1786) Prussia rapidly expanded its territory at the expense of Poland, Austria, and the Holy Roman Empire. A brilliant leader and strategist, Frederick had many dimensions: he was warlike and ruthless but also a fine musician who enjoyed conversations with philosophers.

As some new states emerged in Europe, several older states declined. By the 1500s the Holy Roman Empire had become a political entity without much coherence, rather than a centralized state such as Austria or Prussia. The emperors, elected by leading princes, were little more than figureheads presiding symbolically over a collection of some three hundred states representing many German-speaking people as well as assorted eastern Europeans and Italians. In the mid-1700s the French writer Voltaire (vawl-TARE) mocked the entity as neither holy nor Roman nor an empire. Most people owed their allegiance to a prince or city government rather than the distant emperor. The empire was effectively swept away in 1740, when Austria and Prussia began a 130-year struggle for dominance in the region. Italians also remained divided into small states, some ruled by the pope, some under Habsburg or Holy Roman domination.

Poland and Lithuania had been major states in medieval times. In 1569 the two predominantly Catholic states combined to form a republican commonwealth, launching a golden age of economic prosperity and tolerance of religious diversity. Jewish communities in Poland and Lithuania, in contrast to the rest of Europe, enjoyed many legal rights and some self-government. Elected kings and noble-dominated national and local assemblies presided over a somewhat decentralized semidemocracy. But by the mid-1600s the commonwealth was struggling amidst rebellion and invasion. The state lost territory to the Swedes and Russians, and invasions by the latter led to the destruction of towns and the slaughter of Jews. Catholics turned on Protestants, forcing many into exile. After 1717 Poland became little more than an appendage to the expanding Russian empire, Lithuania became a Russian province, and Catholicism became crucial to Polish and Lithuanian identity.

SECTION SUMMARY

- Europeans fought a series of wars, some religiously motivated and some not; for example, in the Thirty Years War, which involved many countries, Catholic France triumphed over the Catholic Habsburgs.

- Louis XIV of France, the archetypal European monarch, lived in astounding luxury and wielded great power.

- Russian czars from Ivan the Terrible on exercised tight control while expanding Russia's territory, traditions that Peter the Great continued while pushing to modernize and Westernize his country.

- The Dutch were extremely successful colonial merchants and instituted a decentralized republican system of government that was somewhat strained by the military power held by the Nassau family.

- Through a series of struggles between Parliament and monarchs, English political power became more equally shared, though it was still held largely by a limited number of aristocrats and wealthy merchants.

- Amidst the ongoing political turmoil in Europe, Austria and Prussia became major powers, Sweden saw its fortunes rise and fall, and Poland and Lithuania came under Russian power.

 # The Transformation of Cultures and Societies

How did major intellectual, scientific, and social changes help to reshape the West?

Europeans' sixteenth- and seventeenth-century voyages of discovery and the colonization that followed altered their view of the world and its peoples, broadened their horizons, and contributed to intellectual change within Europe. In some seventeenth-century societies, most notably England,

Scotland, Switzerland, Poland-Lithuania, and especially the Netherlands a measure of religious tolerance added further to the ferment of ideas. With declining barriers to free thought and diverse religious views, science, philosophy, and technology could proceed with fewer obstacles than in the Islamic world, where governments often promoted religious uniformity and discouraged questioning of accepted wisdom. By 1750 even China and India produced less creative thought than before. Nevertheless, some European thinkers made use of Islamic and Asian ideas. New ways of perceiving the natural world fostered an emphasis on reason. At the same time, capitalism spurred by overseas expansion reshaped social patterns, creating a transition from a largely rural to an increasingly urban society.

Arts and Philosophy

The expanding horizons of thought opened by the Renaissance and Reformation led to an extravagant and, to many, shocking artistic movement in the 1600s known as the **baroque**, a term that originally meant "contorted" or "grotesque." The baroque style shocked many people because it encouraged release from restraints of thought and expression and questioned accepted ideas. Baroque artists emphasized new perspectives, including movement, tension, exaggerated lighting, intense emotions, and decoration. In Italy baroque art, such as the marble statues and fountains of the Roman architect and sculptor Gianlorenzo Bernini (buhr-NEE-nee) (1598–1680), was expressive and sensuous, rejecting restraint and emphasizing freedom.

In Holland many painters concentrated on landscapes, still lifes, and domestic scenes, a sharp break from medieval preoccupation with religious themes. Dutch painters such as Rembrandt van Rijn (see Profile: Rembrandt van Rijn, Dutch Artist) and Jan Vermeer (1632–1675), influenced by baroque approaches, conveyed an impression of emotion and immediacy in their portraits and other works. Their paintings communicated personality, the thoughts and feelings of individuals, even of ordinary people in Amsterdam. In contrast to Renaissance artists such as Michelangelo, Dutch artists saw their work as a capitalist enterprise and often produced for the wider market rather than for individual patrons.

By no means all creative people worked in the baroque spirit. For instance, some music composers created works that appealed to a wide audience. The German Lutheran composers George Frederick Handel (HAN-dl) (1685–1750) and Johann Sebastian Bach (BAHCH) (1685–1759) produced work of enduring popularity. Handel settled in London, where he wrote his famous choral work, *The Messiah*. Bach wrote pieces for both Protestant and Catholic churches and for many instruments. He also wrote a cantata about a young women so madly in love with coffee that her father feared she would never find a husband. The growing fad for coffee that Bach memorialized suggested the significance of products obtained from abroad, in this case Arabia and Indonesia.

The rise of baroque art corresponded to the greatest era of philosophical and scientific speculation in Europe since the classical Greeks. The Englishman Francis Bacon (1561–1626) built some of the foundations for this intellectual growth. Bacon had been active in English politics, but he was eventually convicted of bribery and banned from political life. He then turned to philosophy. Bacon sought to eliminate intellectual restraints on science by separating philosophy from theology and advocating the use of reason. He developed a famous maxim: "Knowledge is power." Bacon's scientific method, probably based in part on the ideas of earlier Islamic thinkers, encouraged systematically studying things that need understanding. The scientist should develop an idea, test it experimentally, and then draw conclusions. These ideas, considered, like baroque art, unsettling at the time, made him a major influence on later thinkers.

Another key thinker and the founding father of modern philosophy, René Descartes (DAY-cart) (1596–1650), promoted pure reason and a rationalist view of the world. Born in France, Descartes traveled widely and at various times served in both the Dutch and Bavarian armies. Descartes viewed people as autonomous rational beings. Human rationality, he believed, was founded on a distinction between mind and body. Reflecting the baroque spirit, he wanted to sweep away traditional learning, much of which he doubted, and establish a new system of knowledge embracing all aspects of reality. The only thing he could not doubt was his own existence, writing in his most famous passage: "While I wanted to think everything false, it was absolutely necessary that I, who was thinking thus, must be something. I think, therefore I am."[13] Just as science brought order to the physical world, Descartes intended to bring order to thought. Besides being a philosopher, he also studied mathematics, optics, physics, and physiology.

The English political thinker Thomas Hobbes (1588–1679), a friend of Descartes, believed that society was not perfectible, even with the use of reason or Christian teachings. Hobbes, a pessimist, held that, in the state of nature, with no government to control humanity's anarchic, power-seeking instincts, the life of man was "solitary, poor, nasty, brutish, and short."[14] His disturbing book, *The Leviathan*, provided a new view of the state and its relationship to the individual. Since war and conflict were inherent to human society, Hobbes believed, people needed despotic power to control them. Nature contained no truth, reason, or justice. These values, however useful, were just artificial attributes of human society created by social convention and language. People could either give in to violent, selfish human nature or erect a powerful state to ensure harmony. Many of Hobbes's contemporaries condemned his views, including his royalist slant and apparent atheism. But his idea of a social contract between citizens and rulers influenced later thinkers.

---

baroque An extravagant and, to many, shocking European artistic movement of the 1600s that encouraged release from restraints of thought and expression.

REMBRANDT VAN RIJN, DUTCH ARTIST

The bounty from Dutch commerce in the 1600s helped foster a brilliant period of painting in the Netherlands. For the first time, artists made their livelihood in a free market, and they could be found in every town. Wealthy Dutch merchants commissioned works of art to decorate their houses, town halls, and guild halls. The painters catered to this taste, offering realistic pictures of everyday life, group portraits, landscapes, and the interiors of well-appointed houses. Most art celebrated personal success, the material world, and the Protestant faith. Nearly every Dutch family of means owned at least one original piece of art.

No artist had more success meeting this demand than Rembrandt van Rijn, born in 1606 in Leiden, a city on the Rhine River where his father's mill stood. As a youth, Rembrandt enjoyed watching ships and walking in the countryside. He studied for a while at Leiden University but left to apprentice with a local artist. In 1631 he moved to Amsterdam and soon made a good living painting portraits of churchmen, poets, rich merchants, and fashionable ladies. His income enabled him to decorate his art studio and home with fabulous silks, velvets, and swords from all over the world, as well as paintings from Italian Renaissance artists. At twenty-seven the artist married Saskia van Uylenburgh, the daughter of a prominent city official, and showered her with fine jewelry. He also often painted her portrait. They had several children, but only one lived to adulthood.

Rembrandt's work took art beyond the traditions of the Renaissance and even of the baroque. The prolific artist produced many etchings (300 survive), some 2,000 drawings, and 650 paintings. For Rembrandt, influenced by baroque interest in emotions and light, the subject was usually humankind, its pain, power, and pride. He found that by manipulating the direction, distance, and intensity of light and shadow, he could reveal nuances of mood and character. He mastered light, which washes over all forms in his paintings with a special glow.

In his portraits, including sixty remarkable self-portraits, Rembrandt penetrates deeply into souls and inner feelings. In one of his most famous group portraits, the *Syndics of the Cloth Guild* (often called "The Cloth Makers"), a splendid oriental rug covers a table around which black-coated drapers discuss the guild's affairs. Perhaps Rembrandt's finest work is *The Night Watch,* painted in 1642, where he discards the conventional portrait format to portray a military company scurrying about organizing themselves for a march. The public was confounded when *Night Watch* transformed a typical group scene into a luminous baroque drama of movement and lighting filled with many mysteries. According to legend, the soldiers in shadow refused to pay their share of the commission. Rembrandt was the first major European artist to paint for himself rather than a patron, to pursue his own impulses and interpretations.

After Saskia's death from tuberculosis, Rembrandt painted little for a while and had to sell his house and furnishings to pay his debts to merchants and bankers. He proved a poor businessman and gradually became removed from his clients. When he resumed painting, he concentrated on depicting Bible stories and celebrating the humility of Jesus. His religious paintings reveal a personal piety. This final stage in Rembrandt's career, in which he sought inner truth, was the least understood. While some admirers supported his work, this more introspective art did not attract a mass audience, and he died bankrupt in 1669. Modern critics revere Rembrandt as an artist of great versatility and a unique interpreter of Protestant conceptions of biblical scripture.

THINKING ABOUT THE PROFILE

1. What does Rembrandt's life tell us about Dutch society in the 1600s?

2. Why do you think Rembrandt is considered one of the greatest artists in European history?

3. How did his work reflect the baroque tradition?

Rembrandt's *Night Watch* Rembrandt's most famous painting, *Night Watch,* completed in 1642, depicts a militia group that policed Amsterdam's streets. The masterful use of light and the portrayal of the men in action rather than just posing were artistic innovations. (Rijksmuseum)

Science and Technology

The **Scientific Revolution** (ca. 1600–1750), an era of rapid advance in knowledge, particularly in mathematics and astronomy, built on the work of thinkers like Bacon and Descartes to gain a new understanding of the natural and physical world and to create several technological innovations. By attempting to solve long-standing mysteries, European scientists also helped to demolish the medieval view of the earth's position in the cosmos, stimulated European intellectual life, and laid the groundwork for later intellectual and industrial transitions. Although offering new ideas could be dangerous in a continent full of religious conflicts and despotic monarchs, advances occurred in many areas. For example, the English physician William Harvey (1578–1657) discovered the circulation of blood and analyzed the working of the heart.

The Scientific Revolution derived in part from imported Asian and Islamic ideas and technologies. European scientists were quite familiar with the writings of earlier Muslim thinkers. They also learned from China. The Jesuits who sojourned in China in the sixteenth and seventeenth centuries sent back to Europe reports, soon published in various languages, that praised Chinese scientific traditions and inventions. Prompted by scientists, French King Louis XIV even sent a mission to China in 1685 to acquire scientific and technical knowledge. As Europeans assimilated and improved imported models while creating new ones, the general dynamism of science and technology shifted from China and the Middle East to Europe. Between the seventeenth and nineteenth centuries western Europe caught up with and then surpassed China technologically.

Astronomers made some of the most significant scientific discoveries. The German mystic Johannes Kepler (1571–1630) used mathematics to amplify the discoveries of Copernicus showing that all the planets revolved around the sun. The era's greatest astronomer, the Italian Galileo Galilei (gal-uh-LAY-oh gal-uh-LAY-ee) (1564–1642), proved experimentally that Copernicus's theories were correct. He believed that the forces of nature could be understood with human rationality, writing that "to pretend that truth is so deeply hidden and hard to distinguish from falsehood is quite preposterous."[15] By adapting spectacles, invented by the Dutch, Galileo built the first telescope in 1609. With this telescope Galileo discovered that the moon had mountains, Jupiter had four large moons, and our solar system was but a small part of a Milky Way galaxy containing thousands of stars that could not be seen with the naked eye. These findings were dangerous, especially when combined with Galileo's talent for insulting critics, mocking conventional wisdom, and arguing that the biblical view of astronomy was ignorant. In 1615 the Catholic Church summoned the scientist to Rome to be tried as a heretic, and he was forced to publicly recant his views in order to leave prison. But he continued publishing his findings. As punishment, Inquisition officials placed him under house arrest for the last decade of his life.

Scientific activity reached its height with Sir Isaac Newton (1642–1727), a mathematics professor at Cambridge University who discovered some fundamental laws of physics. Newton's work was the culmination of a century's efforts, a synthesis of Francis Bacon's methodologies, Descartes' mathematics, Galileo's discoveries, and other scientific findings. Newton's importance to the world was proclaimed in a famous epitaph by his contemporary, the poet Alexander Pope: "Nature and Nature's laws lay hidden in night; God said, 'Let Newton be!' and all was light."[16] In 1687 Newton published his *Mathematical Principles of Natural Philosophy*, which accounted for all the motions of the planets, the comets, the moon, and the sea. While Newton still held certain medieval beliefs, such as an obsession with biblical prophecy and alchemy, he had found the connection, especially the law of universal gravitation, that tied together varied parts of the physical world into an ordered whole. Newton's ideas dominated Western scientific thinking for the next two hundred years.

In the wake of scientific discoveries, and sometimes borrowing from advances made in other societies, technology improved. During the 1500s more advanced gunpowder weapons and such useful items as the watch, lead pencil, thermometer, and concrete became available. In the 1620s an English mathematician developed the first slide rule and a German mathematician invented the first mechanical calculator. These devices performed multiplication, division, and much more. The Dutch scientist Christian Huygens (HYE-guhnz) introduced a more accurate clock in 1657. Many other such advances came in England in the early 1700s. A farmer, Jethro Tull, using a two-millennia-old Chinese model, developed a drill to sow seeds, the first step toward rural mechanization. Perhaps also inspired by old Chinese models, Abraham Darby devised a modern blast furnace, and Thomas Newcomen invented the first crude steam engine for use in pumping water from mines. By the 1730s the English textile industry became more efficient with spinning machines, similar to those introduced in China in the 1200s, for making cotton products.

The Enlightenment

The **Enlightenment**, which began in 1675 and continued until 1800, was a philosophical movement based on science and reason that rejected many traditional ideas. This Age of Reason, as it was sometimes called, was perhaps the most fertile period in the history of Western philosophy. Without the earlier achievements in the study of science and human reason by scholars like Bacon, Descartes, and Newton, the Enlightenment would have been unthinkable. But the movement also owed something to growing European knowledge of egalitarian Native American societies and of Chinese thought. In 1687 the French translator of a book on the classical Chinese philosopher

---

Scientific Revolution An era of rapid European advance in knowledge, particularly in mathematics and astronomy, that occurred between 1600 and 1750.

Enlightenment A philosophical movement based on science and reason that began in Europe in the late seventeenth century and continued through the eighteenth century.

Painting of Madame Geoffrin's Salon This mid-eighteenth-century painting by French artist Lemoinnier shows a gathering of Enlightenment thinkers and artists at the elegant Paris salon operated by Madame Geoffrin, seated toward the right. These salons offered dinners and stimulating conversation that allowed for a free exchange of ideas. (Reunion des Musées Nationaux/Art Resource, NY)

Confucius wrote that the sage's "moral system is infinitely sublime, simple, sensible. Never has Reason appeared so well developed with so much power."[17] Indeed, some historians call Confucius the Enlightenment's patron saint. An intellectual attitude more than a specific set of opinions, the Enlightenment helped replace unquestioning religious faith with observed fact and suggested that objective truth could be established through reason. The scientific investigation of the natural world could now be separated from religious doctrines. In philosophy, these ideas took human destiny away from God and placed it in human free will. Many Enlightenment thinkers admired Christianity's moral authority but opposed what they considered the dogmatic attitudes of organized churches. Some adopted **deism**, the belief in a benevolent God who designed the universe but does not intercede in its affairs.

In England, France, Scotland, and elsewhere, fresh ideas emerged, including new notions of tolerance, individual rights, and the relationship between citizens and the state. Overall the Enlightenment spread a humanistic secularism, promoted critical approaches to knowledge, and aimed at increasing human happiness. It also provided a forum for addressing gender issues. Some women joined the movement, and a few wrote essays promoting women's rights. For example, in France Louise d'Epinay (1726–1783) condemned gender discrimination and negative female stereotypes, arguing that "it is the essence of humanity in general to struggle against pain, difficulties, obstacles. Men and women have the same nature."[18] Some male thinkers also favored women's education and equality in marriage. Yet,

historians debate how much the movement benefited women, some arguing that gender issues were usually marginalized and that many Enlightenment thinkers accepted the gender prejudices and stereotypes of the era.

The Englishman John Locke (1632–1704), a physician who lived for a decade in France and Holland, was one of the first major Enlightenment philosophers. Locke made experimental studies of medicine and science that led him to proclaim the value of **empiricism**, an approach that stressed relying on experience and testing propositions rather than using reason alone to acquire knowledge. Empirical approaches later became common in the social and natural sciences.

Locke became particularly influential as a political theorist, his work providing a foundation for the modern democratic state and notions of human freedom. In contrast to Thomas Hobbes, Locke condemned absolute monarchy and urged people to defend their freedom by uniting in a civil society where people cooperated for common goals but the state enjoyed only limited powers over the individual. The state, he conceded, was needed to protect popular desires but must not disregard the citizen's need to preserve self-governance and freedom. If the state transgressed these rights, people had the right to oppose it. He favored individual rights, such as the separation of church and state, but also favored some limits, such as restricting political participation to people with property. Many of Locke's ideas became influential not only in England but also among the founders of the United States, especially Thomas Jefferson. Locke's view that people were entitled to life,

---

deism Belief in a benevolent God who designed the universe but does not intercede in its affairs.

empiricism An approach that stresses experience and the testing of propositions rather than reason alone in acquiring knowledge.

liberty, and estate became enshrined in the United States Declaration of Independence in 1776, drafted by Jefferson.

The French Enlightenment was fostered by intellectuals known as **philosophes** (fill-uh-SOHF) (philosophers). In Paris, educated women such as Madame Maria-Therese Geoffrin (JOFF-rin) (1699–1777) operated salons (sa-LAW): large, elegant rooms where Enlightenment thinkers and artists gathered for conversation and polished their ideas. Some philosophes chafed at absolutist government. For example, Baron de Montesquieu (maw-tuh-SKYOO) (1689–1755) attacked arbitrary power and proposed a republican government with checks and balances, including the separation of powers between the executive, legislature, and judiciary. He also criticized religious views, suggesting that the earth was much older than the Bible indicated. His ideas, like Locke's, were widely discussed in the North American colonies.

The best-known philosophe, Voltaire (1694–1778), a poet, dramatist, and historian, believed that science and rational social behavior led people to live happier lives. He was occasionally imprisoned in France for resisting the system, and he spent many years in exile in England, Switzerland, and Prussia. Greatly influenced by the writings of Locke and Newton, Voltaire embraced empiricism. Growing European knowledge of China and Confucianism led him to view China as an admirable political model of a despotic but secular and benevolent state, in contrast to absolutist France. Although a deist, he supported tolerance toward other views. But tolerance had its limits; Voltaire and some other Enlightenment thinkers fiercely attacked established religion and also disliked the Jews for their separation, often involuntary, from mainstream society and their commitment to tradition.

Capitalism and Rural Society

Capitalism gradually reshaped rural society. In many places, a changing economy turned many peasants into a displaced labor force. England experienced this change in the 1500s, when King Henry VIII seized the lands of the Catholic Church and distributed them to his cronies, including wealthy businessmen, who began buying land as an investment. This action turned agriculture from subsistence living to a commercial venture. The new hard-hearted landowners increased demands on peasants or shifted land use from agriculture to more profitable sheep raising, ejecting peasants from the land. With a policy known as **enclosure**, landlords, claiming ownership rights, also fenced off common lands once used by the public for grazing livestock and collecting firewood. As their options dwindled, the English peasantry mostly disappeared as a class and were replaced by tenant farmers and poor farm workers working for big landlords (often London businessmen).

---

philosophes The intellectuals who fostered the French Enlightenment.

enclosure Arising in Early Modern Europe, the pattern in which landlords fenced off common lands once used by the public for grazing livestock and collecting firewood.

The transition to capitalism brought pain to English rural dwellers. Thousands of English peasants became landless. Some found jobs in towns, and some became rural craftsmen such as weavers. But many could not find steady work and became rural vagabonds, drifting around the countryside and resorting to any measures, including crime, to stay alive. The plight of these "beggars" and the negative attitudes they encountered are evident in nursery rhymes that date to that period: "Hark hark the dogs do bark, the beggars are coming to town. Some give them white bread, and some give them brown, and some give them a good horsewhip and send them out of town." This suggests a "blame the victim" mentality: if you are poor, it is your own fault. Whereas under feudalism people saw individual well-being as socially controlled, a product of the manor, under capitalism it became individually controlled: people were responsible for their own condition. Some communities imprisoned debtors and flogged the homeless.

Rural poverty in England had economic consequences. The peasants' loss of their land ruined many lives but also created a labor pool for fledgling industries, thus giving the English an advantage in competing with the French, who were reluctant to abandon feudal laws protecting peasants, and with the labor-short Dutch. Capitalism also undermined guilds as businessmen gave crafts production to displaced peasants and paid them for each item they made. In exploiting desperate peasants, businesses thus destroyed medieval concepts of economic justice. Eventually these trends reached the Low Countries and then other western European societies.

Nothing comparable to the forced poverty of the peasantry happened elsewhere in the world. The imperial power of the Chinese or Ottoman state could curb the greed of both landowners and merchants, preventing peasant ejection from the land. Contemporary travelers noted that western European peasants, many of whom heavily consumed alcohol as an escape, were far worse off than peasants in Islamic societies.

The great contrast between the few rich and the many poor, amplified by famine and the devastations of war, brought on uprisings, such as the bloody peasant revolt in Germany in 1524 mentioned earlier. In England, the suffering of the Civil War of the 1640s fostered widespread discontent and radical movements, often with a rural following, such as the Levellers, who were led by soldiers of lower-class background. The Levellers advocated equality, democracy, and complete religious freedom: "Freedom is the man who will turn the world upside down, therefore no wonder he hath enemies." In their 1648 manifesto, they pleaded, "May the pressing needs of our stomachs reach Parliament and the City [London]; may the tears of our unhappy, starving babies be preserved; may the cries of their tender mothers begging for bread to feed them be graven in metal."[19] After a Leveller revolt failed, the movement collapsed.

Life was increasingly dangerous and unhealthy for both rural and urban people. One chronicle in the 1500s reported that, in rural areas, "none goeth unarmed in public; each hath his sword by his side for any chance emergency."[20] Between wars and rebellions, bandits prowled the roads and mercenary soldiers roamed the countryside attacking merchant convoys and plundering villages. Many rural folk fled to the cities, which were overcrowded and filled with beggars. There trash-filled streets, polluted water, the stench of human waste, and disease made life deplorable for most people. In the 1600s one-third of London's children died before the age of one. Reflecting on the difficulties of coping with such misery, an observer in 1751 called gin the principle sustenance of over 100,000 Londoners. In France people said that nine-tenths of the people die of hunger, one-tenth of indigestion.

Families and Gender Relations

Family life and gender relations also changed in the Early Modern Era. For the growing middle classes of northern Europe, the nuclear family of parents and their children, rare in medieval times, increasingly became common, in contrast to southern and eastern Europe, where large extended families remained the norm. Unlike medieval times, when children were viewed as small adults, societies increasingly recognized childhood as a distinct phase of life, inventing toys and games for children and opening more schools, mostly for boys. However, half or more of children left their families by their early teens, many to become apprentices or servants with other families.

The economic roles and status of women also shifted. The growing availability of consumer goods, such as cotton clothing and bedding made from fabrics obtained in Asia, meant that European women no longer always had to produce such goods but could now purchase them. Men now often made much higher wages than women. These trends may have lowered women's social status. In contrast to medieval times, when many women never married and also worked, often from necessity, in a wide variety of occupations, western European women were now encouraged to look chiefly to marriage and motherhood; their place was in the home. Women in northwest Europe, however, married late, often not until their mid-to-late twenties, while elsewhere many women were married by their early teens. But marriage was not universal. Between 10 and 20 percent of people never married at all. The Roman Catholic church demanded celibacy for nuns and male clergy and encouraged church vocations over marriage. At the Council of Trent church leaders rejected the Protestant pattern of married clergy, denouncing the notion that "it is better and happier to be united in matrimony than to remain in virginity and celibacy."[21]

The experiences of women varied across Europe. For instance, many Dutch women enjoyed liberated lives, some becoming merchants. Elsewhere, some women also engaged in trade. The German Jewish merchant Glukel of Hameln (HAH-muhln) (1646–1724), the mother of eight, traveled widely to trade fairs and wrote her memoirs of her experiences. But in most European societies few women controlled enough financial resources to become major traders. A few educated French women achieved influence in the intellectual and cultural realms. For example, Voltaire's friend and then lover, Emilie du Chatelet (EM-ih-lee de SHA-the-lay) (1706–1749), wrote works on mathematics and natural philosophy, and analyzed the ideas of scientists such as Newton. At the opposite extreme, many Russian women were, according to a German visitor, "most miserable; for men consider no woman virtuous unless they live at home, and be so closely guarded that she go out nowhere."[22] Women's paid work and unpaid housework were increasingly devalued in much of Europe. Lower-class women faced considerable exploitation, and many could only find paid work as servants in middle- or upper-class households.

Some women faced worse problems, however. While a few male and female thinkers explored rational thinking, millions of people believed in magic, astrology, prophecy, ghosts, and witchcraft. For centuries people feared witches, thought to be capable of destroying crops and causing personal misfortunes. As wars and religious conflicts raged in the sixteenth and seventeenth centuries, official persecution of alleged witches provided a diversion. Many thousands of women, most of them single, were suspected of being witches and were executed or banished from the community. Some faced horrific ordeals. In a Polish trial, a suspected witch was stripped naked, anointed with holy oil, bound hand and foot, and suspended from the ceiling to prevent her from touching the ground and calling the Devil to her aid before she confessed.

Nonconformity to social standards faced increasing hostility. More restrictive views of sexuality led to punishment of women and men who defied convention. Often prompted by churches, governments became more concerned with regulating sexual and moral behavior, partly to encourage family life. They closed brothels while prosecuting adultery and premarital sex. Yet, many people ignored these laws, and premarital pregnancy rates ranged from 10 to 30 percent. As a result, fatherhood was often defined socially rather than biologically.

In addition, Catholic and Protestant churches condemned homosexuality, men or women engaging in homosexual behavior faced severe sanctions, including execution. Yet, laws were enforced erratically, especially in tolerant England and Scandinavia, and male homosexuals congregated in large cities. Except in Spain, where nonconformists faced being burned at the stake, antisodomy laws in Catholic countries often ignored the clergy and nobility. The Catholic Church investigated, and sometimes punished, clergy who openly advocated, as some did, same-sex relationships. Historians have identified some very influential men as possible or probable homosexuals, among them Leonardo da Vinci, Michelangelo, Francis Bacon, and several popes and kings such as Prussian king Frederick the Great. Indeed, many European kings had same sex bedmates. Fewer lesbians were public about their love life but, some historians believe, the Swedish queen Christina (1626–1689) was a notable exception. The daughter of King Gustavus Adolphus, himself rumored to have had homosexual relationships, the cosmopolitan, flamboyant Christina, an outspoken supporter of the French Enlightenment and science who spoke some ten languages, had a long affair with one of her ladies-in-waiting. Christina abdicated her crown in 1654, moving to Rome, adopting Catholicism, and becoming a patron of the arts. In Rome she maintained an irreverent attitude toward religion and an active sexual life, alarming conservatives.

- The extravagant baroque style that followed the Renaissance emphasized artistic freedom, while Dutch painters eschewed religious themes for natural ones.

- Bacon and Descartes emphasized the role of reason in science and philosophy, respectively, while Thomas Hobbes developed a pessimistic political philosophy.

- Advances in astronomy, particularly those made by Galileo, greatly antagonized Catholic officials, while Isaac Newton discovered fundamental laws of physics.

- Locke, Montesquieu, and Voltaire were among the prominent thinkers of the Enlightenment, a movement that favored reason over unquestioning faith.

- First in England and then elsewhere in western Europe, rural peasants were impoverished by landowners' greed and served as a ready source of labor for industry.

- As imported goods became more available, the economic role of women declined, as, in many cases, did their social standing.

Online Study Center ACE the Test

◆ Chapter Summary

During the Early Modern Era many agrarian, feudalistic societies in Europe were reshaped. The Portuguese and Spanish led the way in maritime exploration and flourished for a time from their conquests in the Americas, Africa, and Asia. The Dutch, English, and French also developed overseas empires that brought them considerable wealth. The growth of trade, capitalism, and mercantilism fostered a new commercial orientation and economic values while shifting economic and political power to the countries of the Atlantic seaboard. The Renaissance, which spread humanist and secular values, and then the Reformation changed Europe's philosophical and religious terrain, challenging the supremacy of the Roman church. Protestant leaders Martin Luther and John Calvin argued for biblical authority rather than church tradition and for an emphasis on faith rather than works. Their followers organized churches, and by the mid-1500s much of northern Europe had become Protestant. These challenges generated a Counter Reformation and reforms within the Catholic Church.

Wars raged during much of the era and contributed to political changes. Some states, such as France and Russia, developed absolutist and despotic monarchies, whereas England and Holland enjoyed greater political freedom. Powerful new states such as Austria and Prussia emerged while older states such as the Holy Roman Empire declined.

The discovery of new lands as well as the changing political, religious, and economic forces created a renewed interest in scientific discovery and a philosophical stress on individual rights, leading to the Enlightenment. The Scientific Revolution gave birth to such revolutionary thinkers as Newton and al-

lowed Europe to surpass China and the Middle East technologically. Capitalism made many rural peasants homeless, and family life, including the status of women, also changed.

Online Study Center **Improve Your Grade** Flashcards

Key Terms

capitalism	Protestants	Enlightenment
bourgeoisie	Counter	deism
commercial	Reformation	empiricism
capitalism	absolutism	philosophes
mercantilism	baroque	enclosure
Reformation	Scientific Revolution	

Suggested Reading

Books

Cameron, Euan, ed. *Early Modern Europe: An Oxford History*. New York: Oxford University Press, 1999. Includes excellent essays on various aspects of the era.

Davies, Norman. *Europe: A History*. New York: Oxford University Press, 1996. An interesting and valuable survey.

Hughes, Lindsey. *Russia in the Age of Peter the Great*. New Haven, Conn.: Yale University Press, 1998. A readable, detailed study.

Jacob, Margaret. *The Cultural Meaning of the Scientific Revolution*. Philadelphia: Temple University Press, 1988. Places scientific discoveries in a larger social and cultural context.

Jensen, De Lamar. *Reformation Europe: Age of Reform and Revolution*. 2nd ed. Lexington, Mass.: D.C. Heath, 1992. Places the movements in a broader social, political, and economic context.

Kamen, Henry. *Empire: How Spain Became a World Power, 1492–1763*. New York: Perennial, 2003. Provocative chronicle.

MacCulloch, Diarmaid. *The Reformation: A History*. New York: Penguin, 2005. Fascinating, readable study of the era.

Porter, Roy. *The Enlightenment*. 2nd ed. New York: Palgrave Macmillan, 2000. An up-to-date synthesis.

Schama, Simon. *Embarrassment of Riches. An Interpretation of Dutch Culture in the Seventeenth Century*. New York: Knopf, 1987. A popular study of the Netherlands during the golden age.

Weir, Alison. *The Life of Elizabeth I*. New York: Ballantine, 1999. One of the best and most readable biographies of the English ruler.

Websites

British History (http://www.british-history.com/). Contains links to short essays on various periods of British history.

Medieval, Renaissance, Reformation: Western Civilization, Act II (http://www.omnibusol.com/medieval.html). A treasure trove of links on many aspects of society in these centuries.

Modern History Sourcebook (http://www.fordham.edu/halsall/mod/modsbook.html). A very extensive online collection of historical documents and secondary materials.

Russian History Index: The World Wide Web Virtual Library (http://vlib.iue.it/hist-russia/Index.html). Contains useful essays and links on Russian history, society, and politics.

CHAPTER 16

New Challenges for Africa and the Islamic World, 1450–1750

Online Study Center

This icon will direct you to interactive activities and study materials on the website: college.hmco.com/pic/lockard1e

Glassblowers' Procession The Ottoman rulers periodically had the members of several hundred occupational guilds in Istanbul parade before them, including storytellers, taxidermists, potters, and even executioners. This painting, from an illuminated manuscript finished around 1582, shows the glassblowers, some of them on a wheeled cart demonstrating their skills.
(Topkapi Palace Museum)

Warriors will fight scribes for the control of your institutions; wild bush will conquer your roads; your soil will crack from the drought; your sons will wander in the wilds. Yes, things will fall apart.

IGBO ANCESTRAL CURSE[1]

Confirming the Igbo curse, things fell apart for many Africans in the Early Modern Era, while for others things were put together. Among the many Africans caught up in unprecedented new challenges was Ayuba Suleiman Diallo (ah-YOO-bah SOO-lay-mahn JAH-loh). In 1731 the thirty-year-old educated son of a leading family in the West African kingdom of Bondu visited the western Senegambia region, at the western tip of Africa, on a trading mission. There he was captured by enemies and sold to the British as a slave. Eventually he was shipped to Maryland, where he was put to work on a plantation growing tobacco. After an attempted escape, he was taken in by Thomas Bluett, an English entrepreneur who recognized both his talents and his connections to West African commercial life. Diallo's Islamic faith and ability to read and write Arabic reflected the influence of Islam and Arab traditions in parts of West Africa. Bluett emancipated Diallo and then took him to London and presented him at the English court. The British hoped he might help them to increase their commercial and slaving activity in the Senegambia, and he agreed to act as middleman in obtaining more slaves. Finally, after pledging friendship with the British, Diallo was able to return to Bondu and resume his life. Until his death in 1773, Diallo profited from his connection to British merchants as a trading partner. He had been both victim and beneficiary of the new economic forces of his times.

Some aspects of Ayuba Suleiman Diallo's story represent the changing Atlantic world of the Early Modern Era, when Europe, Africa, and the Americas became increasingly linked in unprecedented ways. African life changed during these years, in part because of contact with Europeans, whose presence in Africa gradually increased. The West African trading world that produced Diallo now included English, Portuguese, Dutch, and French companies seeking gold, gum, hides, ivory, and especially slaves. Goree (go-ray) Island, just off Senegambia near the present day-city of Dakar (duh-KAHR), became a major slave collection center, and several French garrisons had been established up the Senegal River near Bondu. Diallo's story is unique, partly because he gained freedom quickly and eventually returned home, and partly because he came from the mostly Muslim Fulani (foo-LAH-nee) ethnic group, a widely distributed inland people who rarely went as slaves to the Americas. But the ancient Igbo curse proved prophetic for the many other Africans who were shipped off as slaves, for they faced significant new challenges and often disaster.

Not all of Africa was affected by European activities. Like the Fulani, many Africans remained untouched by the various slave trades and other disruptive European activities and continued to pursue their ways of life as they always had, expanding and flourishing or declining and decaying from local conditions unrelated to what Europeans might be doing, often only with African agreement, along the coasts. Still, Diallo's experience illustrates the expanding influence of Europe in Africa and the Americas during the early modern centuries. Encounters with Europe reshaped parts of Africa and drew them into an emerging Atlantic world, as first the Portuguese and then other Europeans established trading posts along the West African coast. Soon these trading posts, such as Goree Island, became centers for acquiring and shipping slaves. The Portuguese and Dutch also began to conquer and settle several African regions.

The growing European power was also gradually felt in some of the Islamic lands of the Middle East (western Asia and North Africa) and Central Asia, though not to the extent that it was in certain parts of Africa. By the 1500s Islam, the monotheistic religion that had arisen in Arabia a millennium earlier, dominated a huge chunk of Afro-Eurasia, from the westernmost fringe of Africa to central Indonesia and the southern Philippines. Islamic political ideas, trade networks, and literary traditions linked many millions of people, and several large and dynamic Islamic states dominated much of the Middle East and South Asia, the successors to the great Islamic empires of earlier centuries. The powerful Ottoman Empire, which included much of western Asia, North Africa, and southeastern Europe, and a new Persian state, the Safavid Empire, had increasing connections of trade and conflict with non-Islamic societies. But while these Islamic societies experienced some changes, they also maintained long-standing traditions and remained largely in control of their own destinies.

FOCUS QUESTIONS

1. How did the larger sub-Saharan African societies and states differ from each other in the sixteenth century?
2. What were the consequences of African-European encounters in this era?
3. How did the trans-Atlantic slave trade develop and impact Africa?
4. What factors made the Ottoman Empire such a powerful force in the region?
5. How did the Persian and Central Asian experience differ from that of the Ottomans?

 # Sub-Saharan African Societies

How did the larger Early Modern Era sub-Saharan African societies and states differ from each other in the sixteenth century?

At the beginning of the Early Modern Era African societies reflected considerable political, economic, and cultural diversity, and many flourished. Some, especially in West and East Africa, had much in common with societies in western Asia, Europe, and China and formed great empires and states, engaging in extensive long-distance trade, fostering intellectual debate, and connecting with the wider Eastern Hemisphere. Many people in the Sudanic region of West Africa and along the East African coast had adopted Islam. But many other Africans had decentralized political systems based on villages and religions mixing monotheism, polytheism, and animism. Whatever their ways of life and thought, many African societies possessed valuable human and natural resources that attracted Europeans as the era progressed, posing new challenges and changing Africa's relationship to the world.

The Last Sudanic Empire: Songhai

The last of the great Sudanic empires, Songhai (song-GAH-ee), became the major power in interior West Africa during the 1400s and flourished through much of the 1500s (see Map 16.1 on page 462). From its capital of Gao (ghow) on the Niger River, Songhai built an empire stretching some 1,500 miles

CHRONOLOGY

	Sub-Saharan Africa	Middle East
1300		1300–1923 Ottoman Empire
1400	1497 Portuguese encounters with East Africa	
1500	1526–1870 Trans-Atlantic slave trade	1501–1736 Safavid Persia
		1520–1566 Suleiman the Magnificent
1600	1591 Destruction of Songhai	1554–1659 Sa'dian Morocco
	1652 Dutch settlement of Cape Town	

from east to west. The people of Songhai blended Islam with local customs. For example, in contrast to the gender segregation and female seclusion common in Arab society, the women of Songhai and some other Islamic states in the Sudan held a high social position and enjoyed considerable personal liberty, much to the shock of Arab visitors. Many women engaged in small-scale commerce, and in some Sudanic cities women were free to have lovers as they desired. Some Sudanic societies were matrilineal; the heir to the throne was not the king's son but the son of his sister.

The Songhai city of Timbuktu became a major terminus for the trans-Saharan trade that shipped to North Africa large supplies of gold and ivory as well as slaves for Arab and European markets. For nearly two centuries Timbuktu remained the greatest Islamic city in sub-Saharan Africa. It was not only a center of commerce but also a major center of Islamic scholarship, boasting schools, libraries, and several universities teaching theology, law, and literature. Its well-stocked bookstores sold books from many lands. An early sixteenth-century Arab visitor, Leo Africanus, reported that Timbuktu had "numerous judges, doctors of letters, and learned Muslims. The king greatly honors scholarship. Here too, they sell many hand-written books. More profit is had from their sale than from any other merchandise."[2] The Islamic University of Sankore at Timbuktu was modeled after the respected University of Cairo. Its faculty, which included several well-known Arab scholars, and the student body were drawn from throughout the Islamic realm. In recent years thousands of crumbling books from that era, written in Arabic and several African languages, have been found in forgotten Timbuktu storage rooms.

But Songhai did not remain a dominant state in West Africa. After several strong kings ruled the empire, Songhai's leadership deteriorated and succession struggles emerged. In 1591, when an army from Morocco seized much of the Niger River territory from Songhai, the kingdom collapsed (see Chronology: Africa and the Atlantic World, 1482–1750). One Timbuktu historian of the time wrote that everything changed, as danger, poverty, and violence replaced security, wealth, and peace. The end of Songhai marked the end of the era of huge imperial states in the western Sudan.

CHRONOLOGY

Africa and the Atlantic World, 1482–1750

1482	First Portuguese-Kongo encounter
1487	Portuguese discovery of Cape of Good Hope
1497	Vasco da Gama's first voyage to East African coast
1505	Portuguese pillage of Kilwa
1514	First African slaves to Americas
1507–1543	Rule of Alfonso I in Kongo
1526–1870	Trans-Atlantic slave trade
1562	Dutch settlement of Cape Town
1575	End of Portuguese technical assistance to Kongo
1591	Destruction of Songhai

Other West African States

Besides Songhai, several other Sudanic and Guinea Coast societies exercised regional influence and flourished from trade. The small Sudanic kingdoms formed by the Mandinka, Bambara (bahm-BAH-rah), and Mossi peoples in the upper Niger Basin after the fall of Songhai had effective, cavalry-based armies and were closely linked to the commercial networks of the Sudanic region. The Dyula (JOO-lah), a large Mandinka-speaking Muslim mercantile clan, became the most important trading group, with operations throughout West Africa. Dyula merchants moved goods such as gold and salt through the forest with caravans of porters, down the rivers in canoe fleets, and across the grasslands in donkey trains. Yet, women usually dominated the village markets. Many Sudanic and

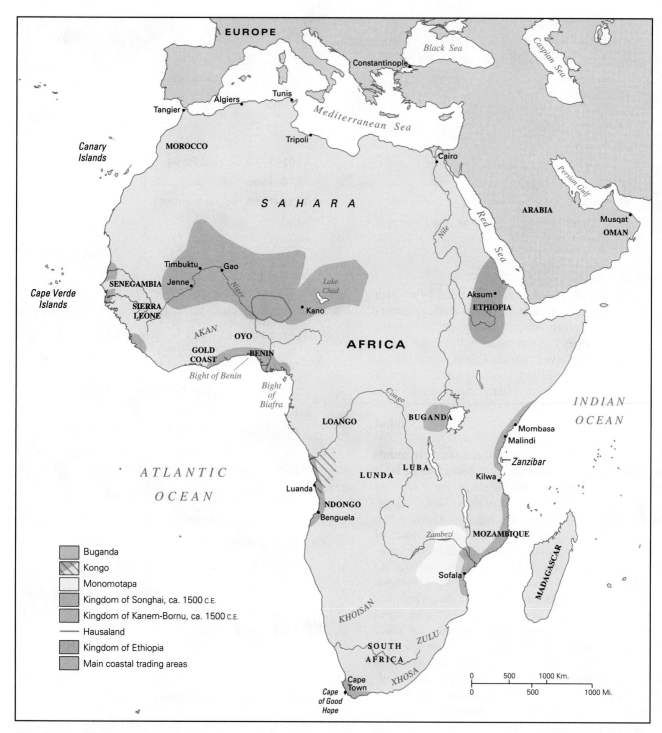

Map 16.1   African States and Trade, 1500–1700
Some African states, such as Songhai, Kanem-Bornu, Benin, Lunda, Buganda, and Ethiopia, remained
powerful in this era. West African coastal societies were increasingly drawn into world trade while the East
African coastal cities remained significant in Indian Ocean trade.

Online Study Center   **Improve Your Grade**   Interactive Map: The African Slave Trade, 1500–1800

Guinea societies were matrilineal, and some of these, as well as
a few patrilineal societies, sometimes had women chiefs or
queens. Queen mothers of kings enjoyed great power. The Igbo
people of southeastern Nigeria worshiped female deities and
some of them preferred female leaders. Africans often venerated women elders for their wisdom and closeness to the ancestors.

Several strong Islamic kingdoms and states arose to the
east of the Niger River. For example, the Islamic kingdom of
Kanem-Bornu (KAH-nuhm-BOR-noo), centered on Lake

Sankore Mosque   Built in the fourteenth century, the Sankore Mosque in the Sudanic city of Timbuktu, a center of commerce and scholarship in the Songhai Empire, symbolized the spread of Islam in the region but also the adaptation of the faith to West African traditions, reflected in the mosque's unique architecture.   (Aldona Sabalis/Photo Researchers, Inc.)

Chad, had formed in the ninth century and prospered from trans-Saharan trade, especially from trading slaves to North African Arabs for horses. The kingdom reached its height in the late 1500s and early 1600s under King Idrus Aloma (IH-dris ah-LOW-ma), who extended his territories northward deep into the Sahara and imported guns from the Ottoman Empire. A devout Muslim, Idrus Aloma reformed the easygoing local customs by imposing Islamic law. As a result, according to a contemporary, "he wiped away the disgrace [of adultery and obscenity] and the face of the age was blank with astonishment."[3] The most purely Islamic state in sub-Saharan Africa, Kanem-Bornu began to decline only in the later 1700s.

Among other flourishing West African trading states were the city-states of the Hausa (HOUSE-uh) people, of what is now northern Nigeria, eastern Niger, and southern Chad. The warriors of Hausa states were well equipped with helmets and chain-mail armor. Headed by kings, these fiercely competitive states dominated some of the trans-Saharan trade into the eighteenth century. Hausa cities were centers for manufacturing cotton cloth and leatherwork, some of which was sold as far away as Europe. Hausa merchants established trading centers around West Africa. Hausa cities such as Kano (KAH-no) and Katsina also attracted Muslim scholars in the 1400s and

1500s, and Islam gradually became the dominant faith throughout the Hausa lands. But, in contrast to women in the patriarchal Muslim societies in the Middle East, Hausa women, like those in other savannah states such as Songhai and Kanem-Bornu, continued to play vital political and social roles. For instance, Queen Amina of Zaria (ZAH-ree-uh) extended her city's power while building effective walled defenses against rival states and raiders.

Important non-Muslim states occupied the Guinea Coast from today's Ghana to eastern Nigeria. For example, the Akan (AH-kahn) peoples of the Volta (VAWL-tuh) River Basin, farmers with a matrilineal social structure, were organized into several small states that prospered from mining and trading gold to the north. In western Nigeria, the Yoruba (YORE-a-bah) peoples developed a series of states, each based on a large city ruled by a king or prince. Yet, women also exercised political influence through the position of *Iyalode* (literally, "mother of the town"), elected by women to the council of chiefs. Many Yoruba towns served as both commercial and political centers and were ruled by elaborate bureaucracies. By the late 1300s one Yoruba state, Oyo (OY-oh), had become the most powerful kingdom. Oyo, which had a feared cavalry force equipped with bows, javelins, and swords, flourished until the late 1700s under able kings.

Another great Guinea kingdom, Benin (buh-NEEN), in what is now south-central Nigeria, shared many cultural and political traditions with the Yoruba. According to Benin myths, their early kings may have been Yoruba immigrants. Beginning in the late thirteenth century, Benin established a sizeable empire. European visitors in the 1500s and 1600s admired the prosperous society they encountered, including the capital city of wide streets and large wooden houses with verandas. A Dutch merchant marveled at the palace of the Benin king, which had galleries "as big as those on the Exchange at Amsterdam [supported by] wooden pillars encased with copper where their victories are depicted."[4]

As Arab merchants did before them, the first European explorers and merchants in West Africa could tap into well-established trade networks and markets. Weekly markets had been held in various towns and villages for many centuries. For example, at Guinala (gwee-NAH-la), a Mandinka-governed district in what later became Guinea-Bissau (GIN-ee-bi-SOU), the Portuguese encountered in 1591 a huge weekly market where over 12,000 men and women gathered to trade. As one Portuguese merchant wrote, "All that is available in this land and in surrounding lands is offered for sale, that is, slaves, cloth, provisions, cows, and gold."[5] Undoubtedly some of the merchants at Guinala were Dyula and Hausa.

Bantu Trading Cities and Kingdoms

By the sixteenth century various peoples speaking closely related Bantu languages had settled much of eastern, Central, and southern Africa, and some were closely linked to the wider world. The closest ties to hemispheric networks were forged by various city-states along the East African coast, where Bantu settlers and Arab immigrants had created a Swahili (swah-HEE-lee) culture mixing African and Islamic traditions. For nearly two millennia the Indonesians, Indians, Persians, and Arabs had regular contact with East Africa, bringing ideas, products, technologies, and immigrants to enrich the African mosaic. The varied city-states, all thriving centers of trade, achieved considerable grandeur. In 1502 a Portuguese explorer was amazed at Kilwa, a major trading city off the coast of today's Tanzania. The walled city included large buildings made of stone and mortar with terraces and towers, as well as luxuriant trees and gardens that supplied vegetables, lemons, oranges, and sugar cane.

The golden age of the East African coast, with its royal court, mosques, and luxury goods, reached its peak from the twelfth through the fifteenth centuries. Ships from Arabia, Persia, and India regularly visited the coast, and Chinese voyagers explored the area in the early 1400s. East African city-states such as Kilwa and Malindi became a significant part of the great trading network around the Indian Ocean, a network generally dominated by seafaring Arabs and Indian Muslims. These Swahili ports functioned as trade centers, collecting goods from the African interior to be exchanged for Asian goods. The foreign traders brought pottery, Chinese porcelain, glass beads, and Indian cotton and traded them for iron, ivory, tortoise shell, leopard skins, gold, and slaves. This trade brought the coastal people noted prosperity. The first Portuguese visitors to Malindi in 1498 reported that the "king wore a robe of damask trimmed with green satin, and a rich turban. He was seated on two cushioned chairs of bronze, beneath a round sunshade of crimson satin attached to a pole. Two trumpets of ivory made sweet harmony."[6]

Other major Bantu states emerged in south-central Africa. On the plateau bordering the great Zambezi (zam-BEE-zee) River the Shona people flourished from gold mining, exporting gold as well as ivory to the Middle East and India through the coastal city-state of Sofala (so-FALL-a), the southernmost Swahili-speaking city. Swahili boats carried these exports from Sofala to Kilwa, where they were plugged into the international trade networks. By 1500 the once great Shona kingdom of Zimbabwe (zim-BAH-bway) had collapsed, and it was replaced by several competing Shona kingdoms.

Three Traders This bronze plaque, from the sixteenth century, shows three Benin merchants, possibly appointed by the king to negotiate with the Europeans who were then arriving in the region. The merchant in the center holds a staff signifying his royal appointment and royal authority over commerce with non-Benin people. (Courtesy of the Trustees of the British Museum)

Another Bantu people, the Ganda, who live in the fertile rolling hill country just west of Lake Victoria in what is now southeastern Uganda, established a small kingdom, Buganda (boo-GON-da), in the 1500s. Soon Buganda became the dominant state of the area, spreading Ganda culture to its neighbors, which were annexed to the kingdom. By the 1700s Buganda had a well-developed bureaucracy and a powerful military, as well as an extensive trade network with the East African coastal cities. As the kingdom grew in wealth and influence, the kings gained more power, eventually becoming the most absolute of the African monarchs. Art, poetry, dance, and philosophy all flourished at the Buganda court.

In the Congo River Basin as well, several influential Bantu states flourished. The large Kongo kingdom arose in the 1300s along the Congo River in what is today northern Angola and western Congo. Kongo became one of the first great African states to be visited by European explorers. Described by the first Portuguese visitors as powerful and having many vassals, the Kongo kingdom ruled a population of around 2.5 million people by 1500. It boasted many large towns and a royal capital containing some 30,000 residents. To the east, the Luba (LOO-buh) and Lunda kingdoms were established around 1350 and 1600, respectively, and built substantial empires in the southern Congo. In contrast to Kongo, situated near the Atlantic coast, their location far inland and their access to trade networks running through Central Africa allowed them to remain strong and independent, able to resist European power into the nineteenth century.

Various Bantu-speaking groups had been migrating into southern Africa for centuries. Most of the Bantu societies formed small states led by chiefs and combined farming with cattle herding. The largest societies, the Xhosa (KHO-sa) and Zulu, mostly lived along or near the Indian Ocean coast of what is today South Africa. Some non-Bantus also lived in the area. Around 50,000 Khoikhoi (KOI-KOI) pastoralists, also called Hottentots (HOT-n-TOTs), lived in and around the Cape of Good Hope at Africa's southern tip. They were a branch of the Khoisan (KOI-sahn) peoples, long resident in southern Africa, who also included the !Kung (Bushmen) of the Kalahari Desert.

Africa in the Hemispheric System

Africans had long played key roles in the Eastern Hemisphere economic system, but the rapid rise of European power between 1450 and 1600 soon presented them with serious challenges never before encountered, reshaping their role in the world. Millennia earlier sub-Saharan Africans had developed agriculture, metalworking, and long-distance trade, and for centuries African exports such as gold and ivory had traveled as far as China. A few East Africans even joined trading voyages to India and Southeast Asia.

Nonetheless, sub-Saharan Africans were vulnerable to European and Arab power because they did not enjoy the same environmental advantages and interregional connections that had benefited parts of Eurasia and North Africa. By 1500 various Eurasian and North African societies had invented or borrowed from each other cutting-edge technologies such as printing and gunpowder weapons, and they had also created more productive economies than those of sub-Saharan Africa. Being a long distance from the communication networks linking Eurasian and North African societies, most Africans never encountered the Chinese technology and Indian mathematics that spurred Middle Eastern and European development. In addition, much of sub-Saharan Africa had marginally fertile soils, scarce exploitable minerals, and few good harbors. Many Africans either learned to live within the ecological constraints or, like the Bantus, migrated to sparsely populated territories that were still open to farming or herding.

West and East Africans had been major suppliers of gold, ivory, and other commodities to the Middle East and Europe for centuries. Although this trade increased European interest in Africa, only a few Europeans and Africans had made direct contact with each other. During the Intermediate Era several Italian merchants braved the Sahara Desert to reach the Sudanic trading cities by camel caravan, and perhaps African merchants occasionally traveled to Muslim-ruled Spain or encountered Italians in Cairo or Algiers. The few remaining Christian Nubian kingdoms in the central Nile valley, the descendants of the Classical Era Kush society, may have maintained a few links with Christian leaders in Europe, and some Nubians may even have joined the Christian Crusades. But by the 1300s these kingdoms had been conquered by Muslims, and Christianity died out in Nubia.

Only in remote Ethiopia, where the Amharic (ahm-HAHR-ik) people had adopted a form of Christianity related to Eastern Orthodoxy early in the Common Era, did the religion flourish. Ethiopia's state, led by kings who traced their ancestry to the ancient Hebrew king Solomon, had survived 1,500 years in the highlands of Northeast Africa, where it built splendid churches, often on steep mountainsides. But the expansion of Islam cut off the Ethiopians from Europe. Because of these intermittent and mostly indirect contacts, Africans and Europeans knew little of each other.

Direct contacts between Europe and Africa only began in the early 1400s, when the Portuguese began exploring down the West African coast in search of gold, Christian allies against Islam (possibly a murky recollection of Ethiopian and Nubian Christians), and a hoped-for sea route to China and Southeast Asia, the sources of the silk and spices so valued in Europe. The Europeans' ignorance of black Africa helped create the myth of **Darkest Africa**, those areas of the African continent least known to Europeans but, in European eyes, awaiting to be "opened" to the "light of Western civilization." At the same time, Europeans also perplexed Africans. According to the traditions of Niger River Delta peoples in what is today southern Nigeria, the first appearance of white men around 1500 shocked the local fisherman who spotted them: "Panic-stricken, he raced home and told his people what he had seen; whereupon he and the rest of the town set out to purify themselves, [to] rid them-

Darkest Africa Those areas of the African continent least known to Europeans but, in European eyes, awaiting to be "opened" to the "light of Western civilization."

selves of the influence of the strange thing that had intruded into their world."[7]

Eventually, after they began establishing control in the Americas, Europeans became particularly interested in acquiring large numbers of enslaved Africans. Slavery existed in many African societies, especially the kingdoms of West and Central Africa and the East African cities, just as it had in other areas of the world. African slaves were for centuries also exported from Africa. Africans had been acquired in the Sudanic zone by Muslim merchants, usually Arabs or Berbers, and taken by caravan across the Sahara to North Africa, where they were sold to Arab or, sometimes, European owners. A similar Arab-run slave trade from East Africa sent slaves northward to Arabia and the Persian Gulf or, in much smaller numbers, to India and Persia. Over twelve centuries perhaps 10 to 15 million enslaved Africans were taken to the Middle East and beyond by Muslim slave traders.

Europeans began importing African slaves only long after slaves of European origin had been used there. For example, slaves from eastern Europe, particularly Russians and Greeks, had for centuries been dispatched, first by the Byzantines and then by the Ottomans, from the Black Sea region and Balkans to southwestern Europe, Central Asia, and the Middle East. European societies such as Spain, Portugal, Italy, and France used many European slaves in the 1500s, making them work as domestic servants, plantation laborers, and prostitutes. Thus slavery had no particular "racial" identity yet: Europeans, Central Asians, Persians, and Arabs were as happy to own white as black slaves. But the growing knowledge of Africa combined with the forging of plantation economies in the Americas focused more attention on Africa as a source of slaves. Europeans did not invent the African slave trade, but they soon transformed it.

SECTION SUMMARY

- Songhai, the last great Sudanic kingdom with its trading city Timbuktu, produced many scholars of Islam, but its society was much more open to contributions from women than was Arab society.

- West African states were extremely varied and included the strict Islamic kingdom of Kanem-Bornu, the Hausa traders, the Yoruba in western Nigeria, and the prosperous kingdom of Benin.

- In Bantu-speaking East Africa, coastal city-states such as Kilwa and Malindi grew wealthy from the sale of goods from across Africa to Arabia, Persia, and India; the Shona exported gold and ivory; Buganda traded extensively with East African coastal cities, and Kongo on the Atlantic coast was one of the first African states to be visited by Europeans.

- Enslavement of many peoples—for example, Africans by Africans, Africans by Arabs, eastern Europeans by western Europeans—was widespread when western Europeans began to obtain African slaves.

Sub-Saharan Africa and Early European Imperialism

What were the consequences of African-European encounters in this era?

As Portuguese ships began making ever-longer journeys down the West African coast in search of gold, the encounters that followed fostered trade with Africa but also conflict and destruction. By the later 1400s the Portuguese had made contact with the Kongo, located near the Atlantic coast, which they eventually colonized. Then during the 1500s the Portuguese became active in East Africa, undermining the coastal trading cities and affecting interior societies. Although chiefly interested in trade, the Dutch gained a foothold in South Africa. These European activities contributed to a new global system of trade and empire that harmed some African societies but was capitalized on by several others. By the 1700s the gulf in wealth, power, and development, once narrow, between Africa and Eurasia had grown very wide, greatly influencing the relationship between European and African peoples.

The Portuguese and Early African Encounters

The Portuguese were the first Europeans to have direct encounters with many African societies. Having the world's most advanced ships and well-armed with gunpowder weapons, the Portuguese began exploring the West African coastline in the early 1400s. They soon discovered and settled the uninhabited Azores and Madeira Islands. Meanwhile, the Spanish colonized the Canary Islands. By 1471 the Portuguese had reached as far as the modern nation of Ghana on the west coast, where they tapped into the gold trade from the Akan states, calling the region the Gold Coast. As they visited more of Africa, the Portuguese shifted from exploration to exploitation. They colonized the Cape Verde Islands and the nearby coastal region of Guinea-Bissau, and they established various trading forts to obtain gold, ivory, and slaves. Over the next century they expanded their operations in Africa.

In the 1480s the Portuguese began a long relationship with the prosperous Kongo kingdom of south-central Africa. They sent Catholic missionaries and skilled craftsmen to the Kongo, and the Kongolese king and some of the people adopted Christianity, blending it with their own religious concepts. Kongolese leaders also sent their children to Portugal for study. The Portuguese and Kongolese enjoyed similar standards of living and had similar views of government, both favoring strong monarchy.

Soon Portuguese explorers sailed even farther south and then east. In 1487 Bartolomeu Dias (ca. 1450–1500) led an expedition that sailed round the Cape of Good Hope, the southern tip of Africa, into the Indian Ocean and opened up a whole new chapter in Portuguese exploration, intensifying

Portuguese interest in both Africa and Asia. Dias believed that he had indeed discovered the best route to locate the Asian sources of the fabulous goods from eastern and southern Asia, and his discovery led the Portuguese king to rebuff Christopher Columbus when the Italian sailor sought sponsorship to sail west. Even when Columbus, leading a Spanish expedition in 1492, returned from his first voyage to the Americas and announced, incorrectly, that he had found a sea route to India, the Portuguese remained skeptical and pursued the route around Africa.

Portuguese explorations soon intensified contact with South African peoples. Their encounter with the Khoikhoi herdsmen living around the Cape of Good Hope foreshadowed the conflict to come between Europeans and Africans. After being at sea for months, Dias and his sailors needed clean water. Landing at the Cape, they helped themselves at a watering hole without asking permission, a violation of Khoikhoi customs. The Khoikhoi responded by throwing stones, and Dias retaliated by killing a herdsman with a crossbow.

More Portuguese exploration followed, eventually reshaping the hemispheric trade system. In 1497 four ships commanded by the zealous Portuguese captain Vasco da Gama (VAS-ko dah GAH-ma) (ca. 1469–1525) left Portugal. Surviving hurricanes and mutinies, da Gama and his remaining crew sailed south around the Cape and then up the East African coast, visiting the Swahili trading cities of Mozambique, Mombasa, and Malindi. Da Gama was disappointed to discover that the merchants in these cities had no interest in his meager trade goods, such as hats and cloaks of much poorer quality than Asian and Arab products. Refocusing his attention on India, da Gama then did what Europeans often had to do in Africa and Asia, turn to local expertise. Engaging a skillful pilot in Malindi, in some accounts the famous Arab captain Ahmad ibn Majid, in other accounts an Indian Muslim, da Gama sailed eastward across the Indian Ocean to southwestern India. Even though the Indians told him his merchandise was unworthy of even the poorest local merchant and could not compete with the more valuable and better-made products from India, China, Indonesia, and Persia, da Gama had located the sea route to the East. He acquired a small cargo of spices and precious stones and returned home in triumph. The European appetite was now whetted. Often using force, soon the Portuguese set up a network of trading bases around the Indian Ocean, and their warships attempted to limit the maritime commerce of their Arab, Ottoman, Persian, and Indian rivals.

Kongo, Angola, and the Portuguese

The Portuguese had their major impact in the Kongo and the surrounding region, all of which they eventually colonized. During the early sixteenth century an enlightened king and a dedicated Kongolese Christian, Alfonso I (r. 1507–1543), ruled the Kongo. He outfought rivals for power after the death of the former king and, the Portuguese claimed, credited his victory to the intercession of a Christian saint, St. James, the brother of Jesus. Historians debate the accuracy of the Portuguese account and the depth of Alfonso's Christian commitment. However, the Kongolese were open to foreign influence. A Portuguese merchant noted that "the grandees of the court began to dress like Portuguese, wearing mantles, capes, cloaks of scarlet silk, hats, and velvet and leather sandals."[8] The monarch used Portuguese weapons to expand his empire, and he clearly wanted to remodel and modernize the kingdom along Western lines with Portuguese help. He might have succeeded had the Portuguese not soon become less concerned with fostering a political alliance and far more interested in acquiring enslaved Kongolese.

The Portuguese began shipping slaves from Kongo in 1514. Slavery was traditional in Kongo, and even Alfonso, although he was opposed in principle, was willing to sell slaves to the Portuguese in exchange for goods and services he regarded as essential to his kingdom's progress. In Kongolese tradition, owners had a responsibility to treat slaves well. However, demands on Kongo for slaves multiplied as the Portuguese developed plantations, mostly to grow sugar, on the small island of Sao Tome (tuh-MAY), a few hundred miles northwest of Kongo. In the 1500s the Portuguese established a colony in Brazil, across the Atlantic from Kongo, and began setting up many more plantations to grow sugar and other tropical crops, multiplying the need for enslaved labor. Since Alfonso and his successors permitted only a modest trade in slaves, the Portuguese resorted to forceful tactics, such as armed raids, to procure the slaves they desired. Alfonso repeatedly asked the Portuguese to halt their coercive activities, which were damaging and depopulating his country (see Witness to the Past: A Kongolese King Protests the Slave Trade), but his pleas were unsuccessful. Although he died a Christian, Alfonso grew disillusioned with the rapacious Portuguese and wary of their ulterior motives. The Portuguese halted their cooperation with the Kongo government in 1575.

Eventually the Portuguese turned to conquest of the Kongo and its neighbors. After setting up a base at Luanda (loo-AHN-duh) in 1580, they began a war of conquest against a fringe state in the Kongolese sphere of influence, Ndongo (uhn-DONG-go), whose ruler was called the Ngola, hence the Portuguese name for the region, Angola (ahng-GO-luh). Like the Kongolese, the Ndongo warriors were skilled but armed only with arrows, lances, and swords against Portuguese guns, cannons, and steel swords.

During their long war the Portuguese encountered a formidable adversary in Queen Nzinga (en-ZING-a) of Ndongo (1624–1663), born a slave in the royal court, who became one of the most remarkable women in African history after seizing power in a time of turmoil. A brilliant diplomat, eloquent debater, and skilled warrior who dressed as a man, she led her own troops into battle. She also shrewdly negotiated with the Portuguese to preserve her kingdom, demanding to be treated as an equal with Europeans. Her best weapon was her charismatic personality, which rallied her people. After years of diplomacy alternating with war, and of military victories alternating with defeats, the pragmatic Nzinga recognized a lost cause and made peace, a victim of Portugal's superior arms

A Kongolese King Protests the Slave Trade

In the early sixteenth century the Kongolese king Alfonso I, who had embraced Catholicism and welcomed the Portuguese to his kingdom, wrote over twenty letters in Portuguese to the king of Portugal, creating the earliest known African commentary on European activities in Africa. Some letters complained of aggressive Portuguese activities and asked that the king halt the slavers from obtaining Kongolese citizens. They also requested educational, medical, and religious assistance from Portugal. The letters, usually polite in tone, revealed gradually diminished hopes as friendly early encounters turned into Portuguese plunder and exploitation. These are excerpts from several letters written in 1526.

Sir, Your Highness should know how our Kingdom is being lost in so many ways that it is convenient to provide the necessary remedy, since this is caused by the excessive freedom given by your factors and officials to the men and merchants who are allowed to come to the Kingdom to set up shop with goods and many things which have been prohibited by us. . . .

And we cannot reckon how great the damage is, since the mentioned merchants are taking every day our natives, sons of the land and the sons of our noblemen and vassals and our relatives, because the thieves and men of bad conscience grab them wishing to have the things and wares of this Kingdom which they are ambitious of; they grab them and get them to be sold; and so great, Sir, is the corruption and licentiousness that our country is being completely depopulated, and Your Highness should not agree with this nor accept it as in your service. And to avoid it we need from . . . [your] Kingdoms no more than some priests and a few people to teach in schools. . . . It is our will that in these Kingdoms there should not be any trade of

slaves nor outlet for them. . . . And as soon as they are taken by the white men they are immediately ironed and branded with fire. . . .

It happens that we have continuously many and different diseases which put us very often in such a weakness that we reach almost the last extreme; and the same [thing] happens to our children, relatives and natives owing to the lack in this country of physicians and surgeons who might know how to cure properly such diseases. And as we have got neither dispensaries nor drugs which might help us in this forlornness, many of those who had already been confirmed and instructed in the holy faith of Our Lord Jesus Christ perish and die; and the rest of the people in their majority cure themselves with herbs and breads and other ancient methods, so that they put all their faith in the mentioned herbs and ceremonies if they live. . . . And this is not much in the service of God. . . . We beg of you to be agreeable and kind enough to send us two physicians and two apothecaries and one surgeon, so that they may come with their drug-stores and all the necessary things to stay in our kingdoms, because we are in extreme need of them all.

THINKING ABOUT THE READING

1. What do these examples of letters tell us about Portuguese slaving activities and growing power in the Kongo?

2. What did Alfonso believe his kingdom needed from the Portuguese?

3. Why were the Portuguese unlikely to grant Alfonso's requests?

Source: Basil Davidson, ed., *African Civilization Revisited: Chronicles from Antiquity to Modern Times* (Trenton, N.J.: Africa World Press, 1991), pp. 223–226. This excerpt has been reprinted with the permission of Africa World Press in Trenton, NJ.

and ruthless quest for gold and slaves. Late in life she adopted the Christian faith and abandoned her harem of men, many of them slaves. After her death Ndongo became the foundation for the Portuguese colony of Angola, under a government run by Portugal.

In the early seventeenth century the Portuguese and groups of displaced Africans they had hired and armed began raiding southern Kongo. The Christian monarchy sent a series of moving appeals to the papacy for help. The popes pursued some of these appeals with the Portuguese government, which responded that the raiding was beyond their control. The appeals were mostly ignored. The Kongolese kings also devised other strategies, including arranging an alliance with the Dutch. But Kongo became engulfed in a long series of civil wars, which only generated more captives to be sold as slaves. During the late 1600s and early 1700s, an unusual Kongolese

woman, Dona Beatriz Kimpa Vita, led a spiritual movement combining Catholic and traditional elements. In addition to its religious underpinnings, her movement also aimed to reform Kongolese political life. Her growing popularity threatened many powerful government and church interests, however, and in 1706 Catholic missionaries had her burned at the stake. Eventually most of the old Kongolese kingdom was incorporated into Portuguese Angola. Some Kongolese remained Christians, but Christianity gradually lost support among many others. The Kongolese kings had cultivated cooperation with the Portuguese in good faith, but the Portuguese proved unworthy allies.

Made increasingly vulnerable by occasional warfare and deteriorating economic conditions, Angola and Kongo became deeply enmeshed in the trans-Atlantic slave trade, which, by the later 1600s, had grown much larger than the Arab and

Queen Nzinga This drawing by an Italian priest, Father Cavazzi, shows the formidable Queen Nzinga of Ndongo, in Angola, sitting on her throne, wearing a crown topped by a Christian cross and bracelets befitting her royal dignity while giving an order to attendants. (Courtesy, Dr. Michael Araldi)

Black Sea slave trades. Angola and Kongo were the major suppliers of slaves to Brazil—indeed, the largest single source of enslaved men and women to the Americas, accounting for some 35 to 40 percent of the total. The decline of Kongo allowed its rival, the Lunda kingdom, to expand westward and engage the Portuguese in trade, exchanging slaves and ivory for woolen cloth and guns. These guns gave the Lunda kings the power to control much of the regional trade.

The East African Coast and the Portuguese

Portuguese activity extended into the eastern side of Africa after Vasco da Gama's first voyage. In 1502 da Gama led a squadron of twenty ships to supervise an occupation of the trading ports of Mozambique and Sofala. To establish commercial control of the East African coast, Portuguese forces attacked and occupied several major Swahili trading cities, plundering them of their riches and burning some of them to the ground. Hence, in Mombasa, according to a Portuguese eyewitness, "everyone started to plunder the town and to search the houses, forcing open the doors with axes and iron bars. A large quantity of cotton cloth, rich silk and gold embroidered clothes was seized."[9] Kilwa was pillaged in 1505, and much of the population fled. Although the city revived for a while, to be dominated by Arabs from Oman, it never regained its preeminence. Today all that remain of Kilwa are stone ruins.

Their East African conquests gave the Portuguese bases from which to extend their power in the Indian Ocean, with the goal of gaining control of the Indian Ocean maritime trading network and the valuable goods it moved from South Asia, Southeast Asia, East Asia, and East Africa to the Middle East and Europe. During the next several decades the Portuguese conquered or established control of several key trading ports in the Persian Gulf, India, Malaya, Indonesia, and China, and they also seized the Spice Islands of eastern Indonesia, the main source for the priceless clove and nutmeg supplies. Using ruthless methods, such as attacking and sinking Arab, Persian, and Indian ships, they were able to gain partial control of the Indian Ocean maritime commerce.

The Portuguese became nominal masters of the East African coast, controlling key ports such as Mombasa, but they never really prospered because the city-states declined into poverty. Merchants quit coming, and many traders fled elsewhere. The fanatically Christian Portuguese suppressed the Islamic Swahili culture, burning Swahili books that contained epic poems, religious writings, and historical chronicles, destroying much of the literary heritage. The Portuguese dominated the coast and what commerce remained for a century, but they gradually lost their ability to control the Indian Ocean maritime trade. By the mid-seventeenth century their influence was waning all over the coast except in Mozambique. The power vacuum was filled by Arabs from Oman, on the northeast Arabian coast, who overran the Portuguese settlements in the late 1600s and established a sultanate on Zanzibar (ZANzuh-BAHR), an island off today's Tanzania, as their major base. The Omani Arabs gained control of most of the coastal cities and supervised the lucrative slave and ivory trade to the Middle East and India. They maintained their political and commercial position into the late 1800s.

New Challenges for the Shona States and Ethiopia

Eventually the Portuguese sought influence inland from the East African coast. In the early 1500s they built forts at the old coastal trading cities of Sofala and Mozambique as a base for locating and acquiring the rich source of gold on the plateau occupied by the Shona people. Portuguese adventurers seeking wealth began moving up the Zambezi River to the fringes of the largest Shona kingdom, then known as Monomotapa (MO-no-mo-TOP-a). The Portuguese first became vassals of the Monomotapa king while they built up their local power, and then they gradually took control of the lower Zambezi valley, which became the foundation for a Portuguese-governed colony later called Mozambique. The Portuguese now controlled a portion of the gold trade. They dispatched Catholic missionaries upstream, but these had little success in finding converts. In addition, because the Portuguese died in large numbers from tropical diseases such as malaria, the Shona were able to hold out for many years. By 1628, however, a decaying Monomotapa had become a virtual Portuguese puppet state.

But in trying to control the gold trade the Portuguese ended up destroying it. Monomotapa dwindled in size and was eventually overrun by neighboring African states, which forced the Portuguese out of the plateau. Eventually the goldfields became less productive. The Portuguese then began concentrating their efforts on coastal Mozambique. Those Portuguese who settled there, especially in the Zambezi valley, tended to marry African women and adopt many aspects of local culture and customs. The descendants of these Portuguese settlers, known as *prazeros*, owned vast estates, organized slaves into standing armies, and resisted Portuguese government control. Mozambique became a supplier of slaves to the Indian Ocean islands and to the Americas, but on a small scale relative to West and Central Africa. Only in the nineteenth century did the Portuguese gain firm control over the prazeros and other settlers and solidify their Mozambique colony.

The Portuguese also intervened briefly in Ethiopia, where a Christian culture maintained traditions forged many centuries earlier. In the 1520s the Portuguese sent a small force to help Ethiopians successfully repulse an invasion by Muslim neighbors backed by the rising Ottoman Turkish Empire. In the early 1600s the Portuguese renewed their contacts with Ethiopia, sending Jesuit missionaries in an effort to convert the king, Susenyos (soo-SEN-yos) (r. 1607–1632), from the state church to Catholicism. King Susenyos adopted the new faith and, at Portuguese urging, began an effort to reform Ethiopian society, including radically changing the Ethiopian Church. When both the church and the Amharic population resisted, civil war erupted. In the end the pro-Portuguese king abdicated, the missionaries and other Portuguese were expelled, and Ethiopia went back to its old ways and faith, but over the

next two centuries it also experienced turmoil as various princes contended for power. This episode and the Portuguese activities in Kongo were the first of various later attempts by zealous Westerners to change African society, attempts which, like these, often harmed local people.

South Africa and Dutch Colonization

European activity also affected the peoples living at the southern tip of Africa. The social, political, and economic evolution of the present country of South Africa differed greatly from that of most of the rest of Early Modern Africa. In 1652 the Dutch established a settlement, Cape Town, on the Cape of Good Hope, to provision the Dutch ships sailing between Europe and Indonesia, where the Dutch were trading and establishing bases. After a government was set up, Dutch settlers arrived in Cape Town and took up farming. At first they traded with the local Khoikhoi people for meat, but, since they had guns, they soon began seizing what they wanted. In 1659 the Khoikhoi rose against the Dutch. After crushing the poorly armed resistance, the Dutch claimed the Khoikhoi land, announcing that the Khoikhoi "could not expect to get the land back" and that it was their "intention to keep it."[10]

Eventually the Dutch enslaved or killed all the Khoikhoi living near the Cape and began imposing white supremacy rule over Africans in the lands they controlled. To obtain a labor supply for their farms and households, the Dutch imported slaves from Madagascar, Mozambique, and Indonesia. Soon enslaved Africans and Asians far outnumbered the whites as the agricultural economy developed. Masters and slaves lived close together, producing the roots of the mixed-race (known as "Colored") population of today. But whites always held a politically, legally, and economically superior status.

Continued Dutch immigration led to rapid population growth, and some Dutch, chafing at governmental rules, began looking eastward for new land to settle. The Dutch settlers, later called **Boers** ("farmers"), began a movement not unlike the Bantu migrations centuries earlier. To survive as they entered a different environment, many Boers adopted the sheep- and cattle-herding economy of the Bantus. As some Boers expanded east along the coast and into the interior in search of farmland in the 1700s, they encountered the Xhosa and later the Zulu peoples. These encounters plus Boer attempts to take over the land produced a series of bitter conflicts that lasted for nearly half a century. Thousands of Africans and some Boers died in the fighting. Nonetheless, these migrations of Boer settlers in cattle-drawn wagons, known as **trekking**, became a tradition, occurring whenever a Boer group wanted to flee government restraints. Trekking provided a safety valve for social discontent. But eventually the Dutch government extended its influence into the lands settled by Boer trekkers.

Boers Dutch farming settlers in South Africa in the eighteenth century.

trekking The migrations of Boer settlers in cattle-drawn wagons into the interior of South Africa whenever they wanted to flee government restraints.

✦ Africa and the Trans-Atlantic Slave Trade

How did the trans-Atlantic slave trade develop and impact Africa?

Modern relations between people of different groups that are commonly but misleadingly called races—categories based chiefly on social perceptions of superficial physical differences rather than scientific consensus—have their origins in the global expansion of Europe and the trade in African slaves. This expansion forged a global distribution of power and privilege along the lines of skin color. In particular, **racism**, a set of beliefs, practices, and institutions based on devaluing groups that are supposedly biologically different, can be traced to early Western relations with sub-Saharan Africa and the exploitation of Africans. The most prominent factor in these relations, the trans-Atlantic slave trade, which is usually dated from 1526, when the first large shipments began, to 1870, when it was completely abolished, fostered both commerce and cultural change in the lands bordering the Atlantic Ocean (see Map 16.2). This trade in human lives affected the millions of Africans who were captured, transported, and sold, the African states where slaves were obtained, the American societies that imported slave labor, and the European and North American merchants, shippers, and planters who profited from the trade.

The Trans-Atlantic Slave Trade

The economic growth of the American lands colonized by Europeans created a tremendous market for labor that could not be filled by free men and women, coerced Native Americans, or the small number of available European slaves. Newly opened American farms and mines badly needed labor after the massive decline of the Native American population during the first hundred years of European conquest and colonization. The available solution to the labor shortage, African slaves, provided the lowest available cost option apparent at the time and thereby created the racial basis of trans-Atlantic slavery. Had other options (such as transporting European criminals to the Americas) been profitable, they might have been employed. But Europeans may still have more easily rationalized the ruthless exploitation of Africans because of their different culture and appearance.

In the early 1600s the English, Spanish, French, Dutch, Danes, and some English colonists in North America began following the earlier Portuguese example by obtaining enslaved people in West Africa and shipping them across the Atlantic to meet the limitless demands of the new American plantation economies, especially after the introduction of sugar planting (see Chapter 17). Characteristics of the West African coastal region made it a target area for this enterprise. It was fragmented into many small states such as the Yoruba kingdoms, making resistance to European slavers difficult and enabling Europeans to manipulate rivalries between states. Furthermore, the region contained a sedentary and highly skilled population familiar with both tropical agriculture and mining, the enterprises in the Americas for which labor was needed.

Profits from the slave trade soared along with the volume of tranported Africans, and European forts to obtain, store, and ship slaves soon dotted the West African coast from Senegal down to Angola. Some merchants specialized in buying a small number of slaves at various ports and then bringing them all to one West African holding center, such as Accra (Ah-CRAW) in today's Ghana, Calabar in Nigeria, and Goree in Senegambia, for sale to slave ships, a system known as "bulking." Europeans traded cotton goods, guns, iron, rum, and tobacco for slaves, often with the cooperation of local African chiefs, but sometimes they acquired Africans directly by force, as exemplified by the Portuguese conquest of the Kongo and their ruthless activities in Angola.

Historians still debate the total number of Africans involved in the trans-Atlantic slave trade. How many Africans were originally enslaved for the trade is uncertain, but they probably added up to some 25 to 30 million people. Between a third and a half survived to be sold at auction in the Americas. Most studies conclude that between 9 and 12 million Africans were landed

---

racism   A set of beliefs, practices, and institutions based on devaluing groups that are supposedly biologically different.

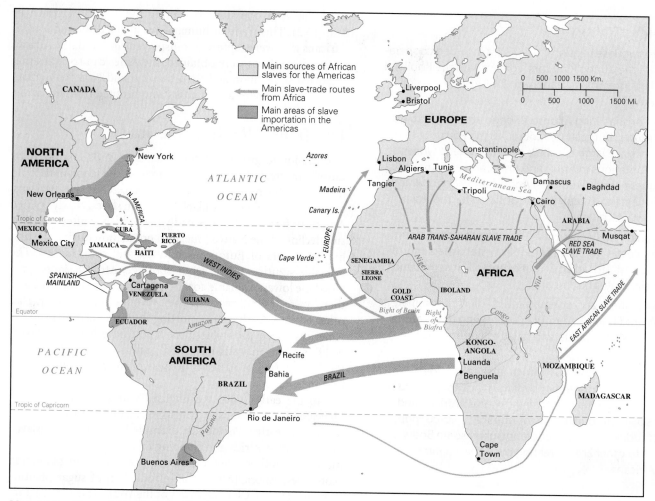

Map 16.2 Trans-Atlantic Slave Trade, 1526–1870
While the Arab-run slave trade from West and East Africa to North Africa and western Asia continued, the trans-Atlantic slave trade was far larger in scope. Millions of Africans were transported across the Atlantic, the greatest number ending up in Brazil and the West Indies. The majority of slaves came from what is today Angola, Congo, and Nigeria.

in the Americas over four centuries. Perhaps a third were women. Millions of slaves died in holding cells in West Africa or on the notorious **Middle Passage**, the slave's journey by ship from Africa to the Americas. The trans-Atlantic slave trade reached its peak between 1700 and 1800, with perhaps 100,000 Africans a year being shipped to the Americas.

The Middle Passage and Its Consequences

Both the Middle Passage and the fate of the enslaved Africans who survived the trip were horrific. Slaves were branded with the name of the company that owned them before shipment. Depending on the weather, the trip from Kongo to Brazil took one month and from West Africa to the Caribbean and North America around two months. Conditions on the notoriously

overcrowded, disease-ridden slave ships were terrible, as this description by an American observer attested:

As soon as an assortment of naked slaves were carried aboard a Guineaman, the men were shackled two by two, the right wrist and ankle of one to the left wrist and ankle of another; then they were sent below. The women—usually regarded as fair prey for the sailors—spent the night between decks, in a space partitioned off from that of the men. All the slaves were forced to sleep without covering on bare wooden floors, which were often constructed of unplanned boards. In a stormy passage the skin over their elbows might be worn away to the bare bones. Every man was allowed a space six feet long by sixteen inches wide (and usually about two feet seven inches high).[11]

The slaves on board faced harsh and cruel conditions. Olaudah Equiano (oh-LAU-duh ay-kwee-AHN-oh), an Igbo seized in Nigeria in the 1750s, described the intolerable stench of the hold, which made him ill, and of floggings on the deck for mis-

Middle Passage   The slave's journey by ship from Africa to the Americas.

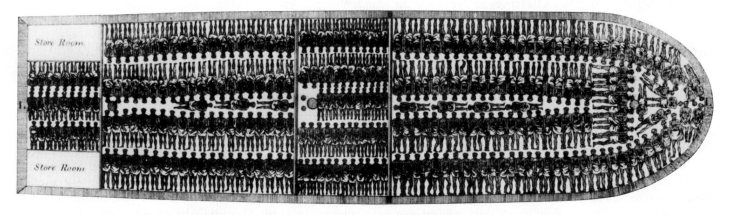

The Middle Passage   This painting from the era vividly shows the overcrowded conditions on the ships that carried African slaves, packed like sardines, on the "Middle Passage" across the Atlantic to the Americas. Such brutal conditions resulted in the deaths of many slaves and eventually prompted reformers to demand the end of the slave trade.   (From a Parliamentary Report)

conduct that sometimes resulted in death, after which the bodies were thrown overboard.

The mortality rates from deteriorating health or suicide on the voyages probably averaged around 10 to 20 percent. Slavers hotly debated whether cramming as many slaves as possible into the ships (known as "tight pack") or carrying slightly fewer slaves ("loose pack") would improve the survival rate and thus land the greater number of slaves for eventual sale. Many slaves committed suicide before reaching the Americas. Equiano recounted a case when two other Igbos, in despair, jumped overboard while chained together, and many others would have followed had the crew not ordered them all into the hold. Many crews installed nets along the sides of slave ships to catch jumpers.

There were also many mutinies, in which slaves attempted (occasionally with success) to gain control of the ship. For instance, in 1839 slaves took control of a small Spanish ship, the *Amistad,* bound from Sierra Leone to Cuba. Led by Joseph Cinque, the son of a Mande chief, the ringleaders had used a nail to pick the locks on their chains and then found a box of sugar-cane knives, which they used to kill the captain and some of the crew. After months at sea with limited cooperation from the surviving crew, and not knowing how to sail the ship home, they somehow found their way to New York. Cinque and his comrades were tried for mutiny in the United States, but the courts eventually agreed with the slaves' argument that they had been kidnapped, and freed them.

Those who survived the hardships of the Middle Passage faced a bleak future in the Americas. When they arrived they were sold without regard to personal ties. Equiano wrote of his landing in Barbados: "Without scruple, are relations and friends separated, most of them never to see each other again."[12] The majority of slaves were sold to sugar, cotton, or coffee plantations.

During the slave trade Europeans quickly developed feelings of superiority to Africans that resulted in racism. To rationalize the trade, Westerners invented the cruel fiction that Africans were subhuman savages unworthy of civilized treatment. For instance, in 1589 the English adventurer Richard Hakluyt described Africans as "a people of beastly living, without a God, law, religion, or common wealth."[13] The English

had long seen the color black as signifying "soiled, dirty, foul, malignant, deadly, sinister." Now they contrasted white and black skin color as connoting, as one observer put it, "purity and filthiness, virginity and sin, virtue and baseness, beauty and ugliness, beneficence and evil, God and the devil."[14] Western scholars at the time argued that Africans were naturally inferior to Europeans in intelligence. Slave traders and owners felt little guilt, seeing the inequality of peoples as ordained by God. Some even thought slavery helped Africans by exposing them to Western values and Christianity.

The Slave Trade and African Societies

Modern historians heatedly debate the impact of the trans-Atlantic slave trade on Africa. Clearly the harm done varied from region to region, group to group. Some coastal regions of West and Central Africa succumbed to chronic raiding and kidnapping as well as occasional warfare, in an "enslave your neighbor or be enslaved" syndrome. European guns traded for slaves made some regions dangerous, leaving plundered villages and broken families. Some societies were particularly destabilized. Some peoples, among them Kongolese, Angolans, Yorubas, Igbos, and Akans, were disproportionately transported to the Americas, and their societies were badly disrupted. Probably over three-quarters of the Africans taken to the Americas came from these groups. In Angola, European settlers later took over the land in depopulated districts. By linking parts of Africa closely to Europe and the Americas, the slave trade also created an **Atlantic System,** a large network that spanned western and Central Africa, the east coast and southern region of English North America, the Caribbean Basin, and the northern and eastern coastal zones of South America.

The slave trade fostered economic change in Africa. While their major target was slaves, Europeans also coveted gold and cloth, and Western merchants soon monopolized the African

---

Atlantic System   A large network that arose with the trans-Atlantic slave trade; the network spanned western and Central Africa, the east coast and southern region of English North America, the Caribbean Basin, and the northern and eastern coastal zones of South America.

coastal trade. But some Africans and people of mixed African and European ancestry also flourished as merchants and slave traders. For example, Gaspar Vaz, a Mandinka, became well known as a trade middleman between European and African merchants in the Sierra Leone region. Some Africans refused to cooperate in slave trading and dealt with Europeans on their own terms. Hence, until the 1700s the kings of Benin, located inland, prohibited the sale of male slaves and instead obtained the firearms needed to protect the state by trading cotton textiles, pepper, ivory, and beads. Benin women produced a cotton cloth of wide appeal and profited from its sale to Europeans.

Some states prospered by cooperating with the slave trade at the expense of their neighbors. For example, Dahomey (duh-HO-mee), which formed in the seventeenth century as a dependency of a Yoruba kingdom, grew powerful in the eighteenth century as a major supplier of slaves. Dahomey strengthened its military capabilities by recruiting women as soldiers. To the west, along the Gold Coast, the Ashante (a-SHAN-tee), a branch of the Akan peoples, had formed a small state in the seventeenth century. Their great king Osei Tutu (OH-say TOO-too), aided by a respected shaman, Anokye (a-NOK-yay), united the Ashante clans under his leadership, symbolized by a golden stool believed to contain the spirit of the entire nation. He introduced a constitution that made other chiefs members of an advisory council to the king but also gave them power in their own regions. With access to goldfields, a powerful military force, and firearms acquired from Europeans, by the mid-1700s the Ashante dominated most of the present-day nation of Ghana, trading gold northward to North Africa and slaves to the Europeans along the coast in exchange for firearms.

The most far-reaching changes were found in the coastal regions stretching from Senegambia down to Angola, sometimes reaching several hundred miles inland. Some states, such as Kongo, declined, while others, such as Ashante, rose in power. Except in the interior of Angola, most West and Central African societies far from the coast, such as Kanem-Bornu, had little direct contact with the European slavers or the coastal states. On the other hand, the Arab slave trade badly disrupted some East African regions, even reaching as far inland as the eastern Congo River Basin. The Sudan region, such as the Hausa states, remained a source of slaves for North Africa, which were transported by caravan across the Sahara.

The activities of Europeans had a long-term impact on Africa. The trans-Atlantic slave trade created economic imbalances that hindered the evolution of local industries and integrated Africa into the world economy as a supplier of human and later natural resources. The exchange was not entirely one-way. The European presence fostered the diffusion of American food crops, such as corn and peanuts, to Africa, and the slave trade spurred some African states, such as Dahomey, to develop commercially. Some African artists incorporated Western ideas and Christian symbols into their work, while some African traditions influenced Western artists. But Portuguese and Dutch colonization in southern Africa began a pattern of political control that eventually resulted in several European nations dividing up much of sub-Saharan Africa in the 1800s.

Imperialism and Africa

Slave trading fostered more intensive European activity. One of the main results of the European intrusion was **imperialism**, the control or domination, direct or indirect, of one state or people over another. Often imperialism led to **colonialism**, government by one society over another society. A few areas, such as the Cape Verde Islands, Angola, and parts of Senegambia, Mozambique, and South Africa, became Western colonies in the era of the slave trade. But the full-blown Western colonial scramble for Africa only began with rapid industrialization in Europe, which, while contributing to the end of the slave trade in the 1800s, accelerated the need for natural resources such as peanuts, palm oil, gold, timber, and cotton that could be processed into industrial or commercial products, and for new markets to consume these goods.

The heritage of racism made Africans and their descendants in the Americas a permanent underclass, treated with contempt by people of European ancestry. Racism became a pervasive ideology supporting bad treatment of particular groups. The first Europeans to encounter great African states like Benin, Kongo, and Kilwa in the late 1400s and early 1500s were awed by their prosperity and marveled at how even the poorest were treated with dignity. By the 1700s those views had changed profoundly. Europeans and North Americans came to see Africa as a continent in desperate need of Western tutelage, setting the stage for, and justifying, colonization. Meanwhile, the Islamic Middle East also encountered rising Western power but, for most societies, with less dramatic consequences.

SECTION SUMMARY
- Millions of West African slaves were shipped to North America because they were the cheapest form of labor available to work the farms and mines and because the Native American population had been decimated.
- The conditions of the Middle Passage, from West Africa to America, were horrific, and many slaves died, committed suicide, or mutinied en route.
- The slave trade led to racist views, as many Europeans justified it by claiming that Africans were inherently inferior or arguing that it benefited slaves by exposing them to Western culture and religion.
- The slave trade destabilized and harmed many African societies, but some peoples and states, such as Benin, armed themselves to resist the slave trade, while others prospered by selling neighboring peoples into slavery.
- As a result of the slave trade, European nations established imperial and colonial control over much of Africa and their impression of Africa shifted from respect to condescension.

imperialism The control or domination, direct or indirect, of one state or people over another.

colonialism Government by one society over another society.

The Ottomans and Islamic Imperial Revival

What factors made the Ottoman Empire such a powerful force in the region?

The Islamic societies of the Middle East, the large region including North Africa and western Asia, did not experience the jarring transitions felt by many Africans during the Early Modern Era. While European nations established supremacy of the seas, Islamic states remained, as they were during the Intermediate Era, major land powers. The greatest of these, the Turkish Ottoman Empire, began in 1300 and survived until 1923, eventually ruling much of southeastern Europe, the western fringe of Asia, and much of North Africa, including Egypt. The Ottomans also nearly succeeded in conquering much of eastern and central Europe before being repulsed. Ottoman government remained powerful through most of the Early Modern Era. By the 1700s, however, the Ottomans and other Middle Eastern states were suffering from chronic warfare, poor leadership, a growing rigidity, and a superiority complex in relationship to the upstart Europeans. Their decline came when Europeans were on the rise, meaning that these Islamic societies soon became targets of European imperialism.

The Ottoman Empire

From their base in central Anatolia, the Ottoman Turks gained power over much of the once great Byzantine Empire in the 1300s. The Ottoman conquest of the Byzantine capital, Constantinople, in 1453 demonstrated conclusively the power of Islamic society, as the capital of Orthodox Christianity was transformed into Muslim-ruled Istanbul. By 1512 the Ottomans controlled all of Anatolia and what is today Bulgaria, Greece, Albania, Serbia, and much of Romania. They had also invaded southern Italy in 1480, but the death of the sultan led them to withdraw before marching on Rome. Had they conquered Italy, the history of Europe might have been very different. Between 1514 and 1517, the Ottomans defeated Persian forces and added Syria, Lebanon, Palestine, and Egypt to their domains. During the sixteenth century they controlled the Mediterranean, even raiding coastal Spain and Italy.

The Ottoman golden age came under the leadership of Sultan Suleiman (SOO-lay-man) the Magnificent (r. 1520–1566), a just man famed as a lawgiver but also a merciless conqueror to his enemies who presided over military expansion and the pushing back of Christian power (see Chronology: The Middle East, 1500–1750). Under Suleiman, the Ottomans pushed north of the Danube River and into the eastern Balkans, defeated the Hungarians, and besieged Vienna. They also gained control of Egypt—according to an Ottoman historian, in the twinkling of an eye—and then the North African coast. Suleiman's forces also pushed the Portuguese from their Red Sea bases and defeated the Persians, incorporating Iraq. Suleiman's empire now stretched from Algeria to the Persian Gulf and from Hungary to

Armenia (see Map 16.3). But the Ottomans never controlled much of the Arabian peninsula, enabling independent sultanates such as Oman to extend their own power to the East African cities. Omani Arabs and other coastal Arabs remained active in the Indian Ocean trade network, enjoying a strong presence as far east as Indonesia.

Suleiman's reign revived the Islamic glory that had faded with the downfall of the Iraq-based Abbasid Empire in the 1200s. Suleiman and other Ottoman sultans claimed to have restored the caliphate, the governing system of early Islamic times that was thought to be ordained by God and that blended political and religious power. In 1538 the Ottoman ruler could boast proudly of his wide-ranging power:

> I am God's slave and sultan of this world. I am head of Muhammad's community. In Baghdad I am the shah, in Byzantine realms the Caesar, and in Egypt the sultan; who sends his fleets to the seas of Europe, the Maghrib [northwest Africa] and India. I am the sultan who took the crown and throne of Hungary and granted them to a humble slave.[15]

Suleiman's position at the center of an extensive international political system often involved him in conflicts. At various times, for example, the Ottomans allied with France or with northern European Protestants against the Habsburgs, the Catholic royal family that ruled Austria and a large area of eastern Europe bordering on Ottoman territories. But Suleiman's broad empire also gave him large commercial benefits; he controlled the overland trade routes between Europe and the Indian Ocean. Spices and other products from India, Southeast Asia, and China were shipped to the Ottoman-ruled port of Basra (BAHS-ruh), at the head of the Persian Gulf, and then transported to the Ottoman-controlled markets of Damascus, Cairo, Aleppo, and Istanbul for sale to Venetian and

CHRONOLOGY	
The Middle East, 1500–1750	
1501–1736	Safavid dynasty in Persia
1514–1517	Ottoman conquest of Syria, Egypt, and Arabia
1520–1566	Reign of Ottoman sultan Suleiman the Magnificent
1529	First Ottoman siege of Vienna
1554–1659	Sa'dian dynasty in Morocco
1682–1699	Ottoman wars with Habsburg Austria
1715	Beginning of Russian conquest of Turkestan
1722	Afghan invasion of Safavid Persia
1736–1747	Rule of Nadir Shah in Persia

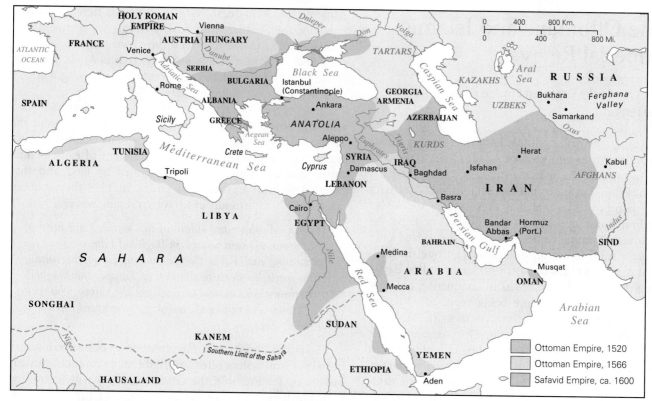

Map 16.3   The Ottoman and Safavid Empires, 1500–1750
By the later 1500s the Ottoman Empire included large parts of western Asia, southeastern Europe, southern Russia, and North Africa. Their major rivals, the Safavids, controlled Persia and parts of Iraq, the Caucasus, Afghanistan, and Central Asia.

other European merchants. Ottoman ships also controlled the Black Sea trade.

Ottoman political success owed much to military power and immigration. The Ottomans adopted gunpowder weapons, especially cannon, which were often built and operated by mercenary Hungarian Christians in Ottoman service. These weapons equaled the best of European gunnery until the late 1600s. The Ottomans also developed an effective navy, often led by Muslim refugees from Spain. These Muslims, among thousands of other emigrants, including Jews, who were expelled from or fleeing persecution in Spain in the 1400s and 1500s, settled in Ottoman territory, bringing with them valuable expertise and international connections.

Ottoman Government and Economy

Ottoman imperialism supported an effective state. For decades the Ottoman government was led by very able men. The Ottomans also chose officials based on merit, allowing Arabs and other non-Turks to serve in the government and military, often in high positions. Many European thinkers and diplomats admired the Ottoman leaders and system. For instance, a Habsburg envoy wrote in the sixteenth century: "No distinction is attached to birth among the Turks. Honors, high posts,

and judgeships are the rewards of great ability and good services."[16] The sultans governed through an imperial council headed by a prime minister. The ruling elite lived in luxury, residing in beautiful palaces with large harems of wives and concubines, children, and many servants. Sometimes favored wives or concubines had great influence over their husbands.

Christian princes remained the major landowners in Ottoman Europe, and the Ottomans especially recruited administrators and soldiers from Christian peoples. At regular intervals the sultan's agents swept through the provinces selecting Christian youth for training. Essentially becoming slaves, they were required to embrace Islam. The most talented, perhaps 10 percent of the total, were sent to the palace school to be trained for administration. There they learned to read and write Arabic, Persian, and Turkish. Many acquired power and influence; for example, prime ministers usually came from this group. The other conscripts joined the well-armed, highly disciplined, and generally effective elite military corps of infantrymen known as **janissaries** ("new troops"), who lived in barracks

janissaries ("new troops")   Well-armed, highly disciplined, and generally effective elite military corps of infantrymen in the Ottoman Empire.

and were not allowed to marry but were well paid for their loyalty. In referring to the janissary soldiers and their fortresses, an Austrian opponent in the 1700s wrote that "it is beyond all human powers of comprehension to grasp how strongly these places are built and how obstinately the Turks defend them."[17]

Under this dynamic state, the Ottoman commercial economy flourished. Istanbul and other major cities served as centers for transregional trade, where merchants from different lands bought or sold European woolens, Persian silk, Chinese porcelain, Indian spices, Arab sugar, and Anatolian iron. The Ottomans became major consumers of Indian textiles. Artisan and merchant guilds with elected leaders became central to urban life, controlling many economic activities. But the dynamic international trade mostly involved luxuries, and the empire was largely self-sufficient in necessities such as food.

Ottoman Society

The diverse Ottoman society thrived in this era. The empire's multiethnic population, about evenly divided between Christians and Muslims, was large, containing some 50 million people at its peak. This was small compared to China or India but dwarfed the largest European country of the time, France, which had less than a third of the Ottoman total. The size and diversity of the Ottoman population, including the number of religious minorities, posed administrative challenges, however. Following the pattern in most multicultural Muslim states, the sultans governed the Jewish, Greek Orthodox, and Armenian Christian communities through their own religious leaders. Each religious group had its own laws and courts. Although they faced some legal disabilities, religious minorities enjoyed a toleration rare in the world at that time.

Ottoman cities, where varied peoples mixed, were vibrant. City social life revolved around coffeehouses, public baths, and taverns. Coffeehouses became informal cultural centers where storytellers enjoyed a mass following. An Ottoman observer of one of these establishments wrote: "Some read books and fine writings, some were busy with backgammon and chess, some brought new poems and talked of literature. Pious hypocrites said: 'People have become addicts of the coffee-house; nobody comes to the mosques.'"[18]

Women had a higher status in Turkish society than in Arab tradition, and this pattern continued under the Ottomans. Women in the royal family, especially queen mothers, exercised considerable political clout. Princes were brought up in royal harems, whose women influenced their thinking while financing buildings and social service activities. Upper-class women often owned land, managed businesses, and controlled wealth. Throughout the empire women took their grievances to Islamic courts and were often treated sympathetically, the courts protecting their rights to inheritance and property. Turkish society was patriarchal but older women had control of both the young males and females in their families. Having sons provided even more security. Since men tended to die younger, women often became heads of households. Yet, women could

also be abused by men and more easily divorced, and sometimes families punished or killed women suspected of illicit sexual activity.

The Ottomans attracted many immigrants, among them European merchants and technicians, from outside the empire by exempting them from taxes and laws. Later these privileges gave the European immigrants a big commercial advantage over their local-born competitors. Many Christian peasants from southern and eastern Europe migrated into Ottoman territory or welcomed Ottoman conquest, which generally brought them a better life. Indeed, there was a saying among Balkan peasants that the turban of the Turk was better than the tiara of the pope.

Ottoman Culture and Thought

The Ottomans also stimulated literary and artistic creativity, often with royal patronage. Istanbul attracted artists and artisans from all over Europe and the Middle East. For example, the Sultan Mehmed II (1432–1481) arranged with the Venetians to have their most famous artist, Giovanni Bellini, spend two years (1479–1480) decorating his palace with paintings. Suleiman the Magnificent welcomed humanist thinkers from Italy to the capital. Ottoman poets wrote ornate verse in Persian or Turkish, and architects, such as the highly innovative Pasha Sinan, designed beautiful domed mosques and other public buildings that combined form with function (see Profile: Pasha Sinan, Ottoman Architect). Artists also produced beautiful painted tiles and pottery. In this creative environment, Ottoman and European architects and artists influenced each other. One sultan who admired Italian art even tried to woo two of the greatest talents, Michelangelo and Leonardo da Vinci, to work in Istanbul.

Although the Ottomans pursued science, by the 1700s they were falling behind some rival states. Ottoman medicine remained vibrant, and scholars published many volumes on astronomy, mathematics, and geography. Muslim geographers also produced world maps more sophisticated than those of Europe. But Ottoman intellectuals remained largely disinterested in and uninformed about scientific and technological developments in western Europe and East Asia. The emphasis on law and theology rather than science in Ottoman higher education inhibited technological innovation.

In Ottoman religious life, various mystical Sufi sects, seeking a personal experience of God, had large followings. Seyh Bedreddin (SAY beh-DREAD-en), a famous mystic who founded an order of practitioners known as dervishes, wrote about his discoveries: "Ecstasy came to me, and I remained in wonderment at God's presence. The mystic who has perceived God spreads to the whole universe; he is one with the mountains and streams. There is no here or hereafter; everything is a single moment."[19] To achieve a trancelike state, dervishes feverishly danced, whirling around faster and faster while their long skirts billowed out, creating a hypnotic effect. Although some Sufi sects operated with official approval and financial support, others, including the order founded by Seyh

Pasha Sinan,
Ottoman Architect

One of the most innovative architects in world history, Pasha Sinan (1491–1588), served as the royal architect to Ottoman sultans for fifty years and perfected the Ottoman style. Sinan's work reflected the meeting and mixing of Christian and Muslim cultures in Istanbul, the former Byzantine city of Constantinople that became the Ottoman capital. Spectacular architecture symbolized the grandiose Ottoman spirit, thanks in part to Sinan, who eventually occupied a key state office. In his long career Sinan designed over three hundred works, ranging from grand government buildings and mosques taking years to build to fountains, tombs, bridges, and baths.

Sinan was born into a Christian Greek family in central Anatolia. Selected for the Ottoman military in 1512, he was converted to Islam and then trained as a janissary warrior and fought in various military campaigns. During his military service Sinan developed a reputation for his engineering skills. For example, he figured ways to float artillery across lakes and engineered the quick building of a bridge across the Danube River. In 1538 he was appointed royal architect, based in Istanbul, by the great sultan Suleiman the Magnificent, a patron of art and architecture. In this highly visible post, Sinan developed, procured funding for, and supervised the construction of projects that would be seen by millions. To succeed, he needed the skills of a visionary, planner, administrator, and manager.

Istanbul was filled with inspiring architecture from Byzantine times, including the beautiful cathedral of Hagia Sophia, with its huge dome. Sinan was fascinated by these domed structures and concentrated on incorporating them into his own architecture. The Hagia Sophia church design, with its ascending hierarchy of sanctity ending at the altar, had reflected the Byzantine worldview and the values of the Greek Orthodox Church. Sinan sought to outdo the architects who built Hagia Sophia for the Byzantine emperor Justinian a thousand years earlier. He also wanted to adapt the dome structure to the needs of an Islamic house of worship, providing open spaces where all could face Mecca from an equal position. Sinan experimented constantly in pursuit of his vision.

During his career Sinan designed several great mosques in Istanbul in which he tried to incorporate the best features of Hagia Sophia into an Islamic setting. The Suleimaniye (SOO-lay-man-iya) mosque, for instance, finished in 1557, sits atop a high hill, dominating the city and proclaiming the triumph of Islam. A sixteenth-century English traveler, John Sanderson, exclaimed that the mosque passed "in greatness, workmanship, marble pillars, and riches all the churches of [Christian] emperors [and merited] to be matched with the 7 Wonders of the [ancient] World." The main dome is surrounded by over four hundred lesser domes. Within this huge complex were several of Istanbul's most elite schools.

Sinan's last great mosque, the Edirne (eh-DURN-a), completed in 1575, had a dome that surpassed that of Hagia Sophia. Sinan considered it his masterpiece and boasted that "architects among Christians say that no Muslim architect would be able to build such a large dome. With the help of God I erected a dome higher and wider than Hagia Sophia." In designing this mosque, Sinan tried to assert what he considered the superiority of Islam over Christianity and brought Ottoman architecture to its highest point. The mosque expressed the imperial Ottoman achievement and the splendor of Islam.

Various rich Ottomans, to show their piety and provide themselves with a burial place, endowed mosques. The women of the imperial family and the wives of wealthy Ottoman officials also financed mosques, among other good works. Sinan

Bedreddin, were suspected of political disloyalty and of modifying too many Islamic principles.

The Ottomans drew the religious establishment close to the state, which was headed by a leader who saw himself anointed by God. Some historians argue that, in the Ottoman realms and in other parts of the Middle East, Islam became more rigid during these centuries because it was too closely linked to the state. Religious leaders emphasized rote learning and memorization rather than analysis of the sacred texts, and some punished deviation from orthodoxy. Furthermore, Islamic leaders were increasingly conservative and hostile to technological innovation. Meanwhile, Christian minorities in the empire flocked to schools set up by Christian missionaries from Europe and North America, some of which taught commercial and technical subjects. Thus Christians but not Muslims were often exposed to knowledge from the wider world.

Ottoman Decline

Eventually the Ottomans faced new challenges that undermined the state and reduced the size of the empire. Well into the 1600s, however, Ottoman armies continued to effectively wage battles against European and Persian rivals. In the 1670s Ottoman forces annexed part of the Ukraine. Only in 1683, when Austria and its allies repulsed the last Ottoman attack of Vienna, did European observers begin to perceive the Ottoman decline. In the next few years the Ottomans were pushed out of much of the area north of the Danube River in eastern Europe and the Ukraine and southern Greece. By 1699 the Ottomans were forced to cede Hungary to the rival Habsburgs. Although in the early 1700s the Ottomans did reclaim some of these territories, Ottoman power was no longer feared. By 1800 European diplomats began calling the empire "the sick man of Europe."

Suleimaniye Mosque   Between 1548 and 1557 Sinan designed and supervised the building of one of Istanbul's most magnificent mosques, the Suleimaniye, honoring God and Sinan's patron, Sultan Suleiman the Magnificent, who was buried in the mosque. Overlooking the Straits of Bosporus, the mosque complex contains schools, shops, and a hospital.   (Robert Frerck/Woodfin Camp and Associates)

designed some of these mosques and also built great tombs to commemorate the powerful men and women of his day. He also designed parts of the sultan's great palace, the Topkapi Sarai (sah-RYE) (Abode of Felicity). This huge complex boasted beautiful interiors and contained a series of pavilions, gardens, courts, treasuries, reception halls, baths, kitchens, and other buildings. Begun by Sinan, it was constructed over several centuries with no particular master plan. The palace and the grand mosques remain as testimonies to Sinan's talents and the cultural vibrancy of the Ottoman Empire in the 1500s.

THINKING ABOUT THE PROFILE

1. What does Sinan's career tell us about the Ottoman system?
2. How did Sinan's architecture reflect a mixing of Islamic and Christian traditions?

Notes: Quotations from Andrew Wheatcroft, *The Ottomans* (New York: Viking, 1993), p. 143; and Aptullah Kuran, *Sinan: The Grand Old Master of Ottoman Architecture* (Washington, D.C.: Institute of Turkish Studies, 1987), pp. 168–169.

Some of the decline resulted from failing Ottoman military practices and technology. The discipline among the janissary military forces weakened, and the officers insisted on spending winters in Istanbul, thus limiting military campaigns to warm weather months. Eventually the whole training system for young men was eliminated and the sultans usually led campaigns personally, putting themselves in danger and exhausting their energy. The Ottomans' technology also fell behind. For decades, the Ottoman navy had used the most advanced technology available and capitalized on foreign immigrants. Their ships were largely designed, built, and crewed by Christian mercenaries. But by the 1600s European ships were better armed and more maneuverable, easily outclassing Ottoman galleys. The development of Ottoman weaponry, especially artillery, also stagnated just as European military technology was rapidly improving.

Problems of governing also stressed the empire. Compared to China or the emerging European states, the Ottoman state was not very centralized, and imperial control was difficult to maintain. The Ottoman sultans governed through the various religious communities or provincial leaders, allowing people to focus loyalty on their ethnic group or region rather than on the Ottoman state. In the early 1500s the Ottomans had conquered the Kurds, a Sunni Muslim ethnic group occupying a large region from what is today eastern Turkey, northern Iraq and Syria, and northwest Iran, and many Kurds increasingly resented Turkish control. At the same time, many Arabs and Balkan Christians who once welcomed Ottoman rule for providing stability and justice began to think of their own peoples as nations repressed by the empire. Ottoman citizens also disliked higher taxes, growing corruption, and a bloated bureaucracy, and many peasants fell into poverty.

Meanwhile, in Istanbul the ruling elite was able to exercise more power over a weak or incompetent sultan. Potential successors to the throne were often kept locked up in the palace as prisoners until chosen to take the throne. Some later sultans were either mentally unstable or despots. In the mid-1600s "Ibrahim the Mad," who had been imprisoned for years, proved particularly tyrannical when he took power, once ordering the drowning of 280 concubines who angered him. Nobody grieved when he was deposed and executed. With weaker male leaders, senior palace women, especially the sultan's mother, gained more influence, supporting one or another of the factions that contended for favor.

Ottoman sultans had increasing difficulty controlling restless provinces in North Africa and western Asia. Occasional rebellions were met by brute force, but during the 1600s some areas broke away from the empire. Leaders of Ottoman descent in Algeria and Tunisia became increasingly independent, although formally remaining vassals of Istanbul. In Mesopotamia, which was divided into smaller provinces, and Egypt, the Ottomans increasingly had to rule through local Arab leaders who sought more autonomy. By the mid-1700s Ottoman influence was deteriorating in large parts of the empire, and the Russians were putting pressure on Ottoman territory north of the Black Sea.

The Ottomans and the West

While beginning to deteriorate from within, the Ottomans also faced increasing economic and military challenges from western European nations, the Habsburg realm, and Russia. Indeed, the Ottomans were the first of the major Asian societies to face the rising power of the West. The increasing European role in Asian trade weakened Anatolia's historic position as a middleman, undermining economic conditions just as western Europe was growing wealthier. For example, because the Portuguese and Dutch active in Asia preferred to ship resources around Africa to Europe's Atlantic ports, the Asian-Europe trade that flowed through Ottoman ports was gradually reduced. Adding to the economic decline, Ottoman rulers gave little support to the empire's merchant class, most of whom were Greeks, Armenians, and Jews. With its own native industries growing less competitive, the once self-sufficient empire became increasingly dependent on imports from Europe.

For all these reasons, Western merchants gradually outcompeted their Ottoman rivals, gaining control over large sectors of the Ottoman economy. Large Western trading firms, armed with both great capital and better business methods and backed by their own governments, became increasingly influential in the fringe areas of the empire. Ultimately these trends reduced the Ottomans, once a hub of international commerce, to a secondary region in the emerging global trade system.

The resurgence of European power led to fierce debates in the empire. Reformers became interested in European products and customs and favored the importing of some European technology. But reformist forces struggled for influence against conservatives, who preferred the status quo, and reformers also found it difficult to overcome an Arab and Turkish superiority complex regarding the once upstart

Europeans. Many reformers looked backward to the era of Suleiman the Magnificent for inspiration. In this fashion the creaking Ottoman state limped into the 1900s.

SECTION SUMMARY

■ Under Suleiman the Magnificent, the Ottoman Empire stretched across vast areas of the Middle East, North Africa, and southeastern Europe, and it controlled the overland trade routes between Europe and the Indian Ocean.

■ Leaders of the Ottoman Empire were chosen on the basis of merit, not birth, and even Christians served as administrators and soldiers.

■ The Ottoman Empire was culturally and religiously diverse; religious minorities were allowed a measure of self-governance, and many immigrants were attracted by the empire's tolerance.

■ The Ottoman Empire attracted and encouraged a range of artists and thinkers from across Eurasia, though some believe that state influence on Islam caused it to become more rigid and close-minded.

■ Though the Ottoman Empire remained strong through much of the seventeenth century, its military discipline, weaponry, and political stability soon began a gradual decline.

■ As Europeans began to trade directly with Asia, Ottomans lost their traditional role as middlemen and became increasingly dependent on European imports.

✧ Persia, Morocco, and Central Asia

How did the Persian and Central Asian experience differ from that of the Ottomans?

Like the Ottomans, Islamic societies from Morocco to Central Asia also underwent significant changes during the Early Modern Era. East of the Ottoman Empire, in Persia, a Shi'ite dynasty known as the Safavids presided over a revival of Persian culture and became an internationally recognized power. Persian leaders, thinkers, and officials had long played a significant role in Islamic society, and Persian, widely spoken by elites from Istanbul to Delhi, India, was the closest thing to a hemispheric language. The Safavids developed a prosperous economy linked to international trade and fostered a brilliant artistic culture. In northwest Africa, Morocco became notable for its military prowess. Meanwhile, northeast of Persia, various Islamic societies in Central Asia emerged from the ashes of the Mongol Empire but struggled to maintain the ancient Silk Road trade networks. They also faced increasing pressure from the expanding Russian Empire.

The Safavid Empire

The Safavid dynasty came to power in Persia at the beginning of the sixteenth century. It was founded by a Turkish group from what is today Azerbaijan (AZ-uhr-bye-ZHAHN) in the Caucasus Mountains. Many peoples speaking Turkish languages lived in the Caucasus and in Central Asia. The Safavids belonged to a militant Sufi order that had shifted from the Sunni to the Shi'a branch of Islam. From their base in Azerbaijan, the Safavid movement grew rapidly in alliance with other Shi'ites in the region.

In 1501, the Safavids, led by a charismatic thirteen-year-old boy, Isma'il (1487–1524), invaded and conquered Persia, then a center of Sunni practice and home to a variety of small Sunni Turkish and Persian states. Isma'il, who claimed descent from Mohammad and Sassanian princes, impressed European visitors to Persia at the time. A Venetian diplomat described the youth as "of noble presence and a truly royal bearing, as in his eyes and brows there was something I know not what, so great and commanding, which plainly showed that he would some day become a great ruler. He had an elevated genius and such a lofty idea of things as seemed incredible at such a tender age."[20] Isma'il and his dedicated followers wanted to unite the region both politically and religiously. Within ten years the Turkish Safavids controlled all of Persia.

Isma'il, who thought of himself as an agent of God, mandated the conversion of the Persians to Shi'ism. Tensions between the majority Sunni and minority Shi'a had simmered since the Islamic community divided centuries earlier, and the Safavids used force when necessary on reluctant Sunni Persians, confiscating Sunni property and executing Sunni religious leaders. The shift in Persia to Shi'ism took some years, during which many Sunni families unwilling to change emigrated to India, Central Asia, or Ottoman territories. Persians, however, found the rich Shi'ite ceremonies attractive and wanted to differentiate themselves from the hated Sunni Ottomans. Eventually Persians came to view Shi'ism as central to Persian identity.

The Safavids established a strong political system. However, because they never acquired the gunpowder-based military power of their Sunni Ottoman rivals, their imperial prospects were limited. Safavid armies rode on horseback and viewed guns as both awkward and unmanly, an attitude that left them vulnerable to the gunpowder weapons possessed by their Portuguese and Ottoman enemies. The Portuguese seized and held the strategic port of Hormuz (hawr-MOOZ), on Persia's southeast coast, for decades in the 1500s. In 1514 the Ottomans drove deep into Safavid territory, acquiring Safavid lands in Armenia and Anatolia. The battle losses to the hated Ottomans demoralized Safavid military leaders, and even Isma'il, unable to cope with defeat, became an alcoholic recluse in the palace. Although the Safavids soon regained their confidence, they did not attempt to expand their empire.

The Safavids also adopted many of the governmental practices that had been common in the region for centuries. Like the Ottomans, for instance, they acquired slave boys, primarily from Christian peoples in the Caucasus such as the Armenians and Georgians, to be trained for administrative or military purposes. Over time the Safavids also adapted to local Persian customs, and the Persian element became stronger at the expense of the Turkish.

Safavid rule reached its peak under Shah (king) Abbas (ah-BAHS) I (r. 1587–1629), who consolidated his power by manipulating or executing his enemies, including leaders of powerful Sufi orders. His capital, Isfahan (is-fah-HAHN), became a beautiful, tree-shaded city of some 1 million people, filled with 160 mosques, 273 public baths, many parks, and a great bazaar that one visitor described as "the surprisingest piece of Greatness in Honor of Commerce that the world can boast of."[21] Shah Abbas planned the city with the help of Shaikh Baha al-Din Muhammad Amili, a famed Persian philosopher, judge, poet, astronomer, and engineer. The shah reserved a few special days each year, with men kept away, for the normally secluded women to visit the bazaars and promenade in the evening on Isfahan's spectacular main boulevard, a long avenue lined on both sides with gardens and pavilions and with a water channel down its center. Shah Abbas enjoyed visiting the city's teahouses, where he listened to poets and storytellers and chatted with citizens.

Abbas maintained good relations with European powers, welcoming ambassadors from a half dozen European nations and importing English advisers to help train his military forces and manufacture modern cannon and muskets, marking a change in Safavid military strategy. With these weapons, Shah Abbas waged successful wars against the invading Ottomans and Uzbeks and recaptured Hormuz from the Portuguese. For their part, Europeans sought Persia as an ally against their mutual Ottoman enemy. Tolerant in religion, he admitted Christian missionaries. To earn revenue for the government, Abbas and his successors also gradually placed more land under state control. Hence, many peasants worked on land owned by the king and received a share of the crop for their labors.

Safavid Economy and Society

Along with its strong political system, the Safavid economy flourished for several centuries. Persia remained a major exporter of silk, a trade increasingly dominated by Armenian settlers from the Caucasus, who also operated the lucrative gold and silver crafts industries. Persia was linked to networks extending all over the Eastern Hemisphere, and long-distance trade by land and sea, which had flowed through Persia since ancient times, continued during the Safavid era. Persian merchants remained active in the Indian Ocean trade; they were prominent in some Indian ports and could be found as far away as China, Southeast Asia, and East Africa. Meanwhile, foreign merchants arrived in Persia from all over, attracted by the great bazaar that developed in Isfahan, where artisans produced fine carpets, textiles, metalwork, and ceramics. Some 25,000 people worked in Isfahan's textile industry.

Armenians, who flourished from Safavid trade, also competed fiercely with Dutch, English, Portuguese, and Indian merchants in parts of Eurasia. The Armenian network radiated outward from New Julfa (JOOL-fa), a mostly Armenian city built by the Safavids near Isfahan. A central council of Armenian merchants in New Julfa coordinated local councils in the Armenian trade diaspora. Armenians could work well together because they shared a common culture and the Christian religion, and their merchants played a key role in the overland trade from India to Central Asia and the Middle East. The Armenian network eventually stretched eastward through Indian ports to Burma, Java, and China, and westward to Venice, Marseilles, Amsterdam, and London. In the 1660s New Julfa merchants also negotiated trade agreements with Russia, which allowed them to bypass the Ottoman Empire and reach northern Europe through Russia and the Baltic.

Safavid trade with Europe gradually increased. During the 1600s English, Dutch, and French merchants visited Persian ports to obtain silk, carpets, brocades, cotton, wool, and other products. English and Russian merchants were also active in northern Persia, whetting the European appetite for more extensive trade. But commerce with the West raised the question of Western intentions. In 1608 a Persian envoy to the Netherlands had warned the shah that all the Europeans' "profession of friendship were false, and that all they wanted was for the Turks and the Persians to destroy each other as well as the Muslim religion."[22] Yet, by cooperating with these traders, the Persians gained a maritime route for their exports to counteract the Ottoman control of overland routes.

Safavid society was patriarchal, with men having more rights than women, who were often restricted to the home and expected to veil themselves when they went out of the household. Yet, as in Ottoman Turkey, Persian women often had more influence than was the case among Arabs. Royal women in harems raised royal sons and also at times tried to shape government policies. As in classical Persia two millennia earlier, some women became wealthy and owned land and businesses. Even in seclusion, women could use agents to help run their enterprises and manage property or money. Poor women had no such opportunities.

Safavid Culture and Thought

The Safavids patronized art and literature as well as commerce. Like some Muslim rulers in India, the princes in Renaissance Europe, and the Chinese emperors, the Safavid shahs were often themselves artists and poets. The major cities, especially Isfahan, became centers for artists, writers, and craftsmen. Safavid artists became especially famous for miniature paintings, a style that spread to the Ottoman and Mughal Empires. Safavid painting combined the harmony of color with the rhythm of design, often to illustrate great Persian literature. In 1525 the Safavid sultan commissioned an ambitious, decade-long project to produce an illustrated version of an old epic poem recounting Persian history. The completed version contained 258 paintings by many artists. Poetry also continued to flourish. Muslim Indian courts, some of which used Persian as an official language, recruited well-known Persian poets.

This was also a golden age for crafting carpets, textiles, and ceramics, for which Persians became famous. Carpet weaving became both an art form and a national industry, with government-run factories producing a range of silks, brocades, velvets, and other fabrics. One of the most famous carpets, designed by Maqsud of Kashan (MACK-sood of KAH-shan), was woven into 15 million knots, with 340 knots per square inch, and its design portrayed the illusion of a heavenly dome with

Persian Tiles As Isfahan flourished under Shah Abbas I, wealthy Persians decorated their homes and mosques with tiles featuring scenes, often gardens, painted by local artists. This tile painting shows a woman at leisure in her garden, holding a vase while her servant offers her fruit. (Courtesy of the Trustees of the Victoria and Albert Museum)

lamps reflecting in a pool of water filled with floating lotus blossoms.

Persian Shi'ism underwent some changes. The Safavids encouraged passion plays and religious processions commemorating the tragic death of the prophet Muhammad's grandson, Husayn, in the Battle of Karbala in 680, the event that split the Islamic community. In the annual processions, hundreds of men fulfilled vows of faith by beating their bodies with chains while chanting religious dirges. Sufi influence gradually declined while religious teachers increasingly emphasized their own authority over that of the Quran and other early sacred texts. The result was increasing belief in the infallibility of Islamic leaders, who enjoyed greater power than was common elsewhere in the Islamic world. Even the shahs claimed to represent divine power, giving the state a theocratic cast. But tensions over religious power between the shahs and Shi'ite leaders, many of whom came to own vast tracts of land, continued to simmer.

Safavid Decline

By the eighteenth century the Safavid sultans had become weaker, the Shi'ite religious officials had become stronger, and the empire's economy had declined. Unable to control the clergy or trust their sons plotting for the throne, later Safavid rulers often turned to alcohol for comfort, and most were increasingly controlled by ministers and concubines. In any case, corruption grew rampant. In 1722 Afghans seized Isfahan and then repulsed Ottoman forces invading from the west. Isfahan, once one of the world's most beautiful cities and filled with splendid architecture, was nearly destroyed.

Soon a new government appeared. In 1736 a new Persian leader, Nadir Shah (1688–1747), led a force that drove out the Afghan invaders. Casting aside the remaining Safavids, he launched a vigorous new state. His armies went on the offensive, marching into Ottoman lands and north India, where his forces plundered the major city, Delhi. But Nadir Shah proved ruthless against suspected foes, antagonizing many, and economic collapse exposed millions to famine. After ill-advised efforts to reconvert the Persians from Shi'a to Sunni Islam, Nadir Shah was assassinated in 1747. His empire soon collapsed. In the decades to follow Persia was again divided into smaller states, and the early Safavid cultural dynamism became a distant memory. In this power vacuum Western pressure intensified.

Moroccan Resurgence and Expansion

While the Ottomans and Safavids dominated much of the Islamic world, the Moroccans on the far northwestern fringe of Africa forged one of the stronger Islamic states, conquered an empire, and linked themselves to various networks of exchange. Moroccan society comprised Berbers, Arabs, and an influential Jewish community. The gradual displacement of Islamic rule in Iberia resulted in many Muslims and Jews migrating across the Strait of Gibraltar to Morocco. Some Spanish Muslims joined Moroccan military forces, while Jews

invigorated commercial life. Morocco traded widely with its North African neighbors, West Africa, and Europe, and during the 1400s and 1500s ships from Venice, Genoa, and other European trading ports regularly visited Moroccan ports, exchanging metals, textiles, spices, hardware, and wine for leather, carpets, wool, grain, sugar, and African slaves.

During the later 1400s and early 1500s Moroccan encounters with the Portuguese eventually brought the Sa'dians to power. Portugal's cultivation of sugar on the Atlantic islands began undermining the Moroccan economy, which was based partly on growing sugar, and the establishment of Portuguese forts along the coast threatened the Moroccan government. In response, growing mystical Sufi movements organized tribal coalitions to resist the Portuguese. In 1554 the Sa'dians, a Moroccan family who claimed descent from the prophet Muhammad and had fought against the Portuguese forts, conquered much of Morocco with the support of Sufi and tribal leaders, launching a new era.

The Sa'dians ruled Morocco until 1659, forging a powerful military and a regime quite different from those of the Ottoman territories. The greatest Sa'dian leader, Sultan al-Mansur (man-SOOR) (r. 1578–1603), recruited mercenary soldiers from elsewhere who knew how to use firearms. By 1603 the army of 40,000 included 4,000 Europeans, 4,000 Spanish Muslims, and 1,500 Turks, armed with modern artillery. The Netherlands and England, both rivals of the Portuguese, sold Morocco ships, cannon, and gunpowder. The resulting military power allowed the Moroccans to capture the Portuguese ports along the Atlantic coast, proving the value of possessing gunpowder weapons. In 1591 Moroccan forces seized the trading city of Timbuktu in Songhai, undermining that Sudanic state, and gained control of the trans-Saharan trade linking West and North Africa.

In the later 1600s the Sa'dian system broke down, and a new Moroccan dynasty, the Alawis (uh-LAH-wees), who also claimed descent from the prophet Muhammad, came to power in 1672. This dynasty still rules Morocco today. Sufi influence continued to expand, but powerful Sufi movements sometimes clashed with the royal governments. Morocco traded even more heavily with Europe, North Africa, and the Sudan.

Central Asia and Russian Expansion

The most direct and long-lasting confrontations between Muslims and Europeans resulted from Russian imperial expansion into Central Asia and Ottoman territories. The Russians had long coveted the dry lands of Central Asia, where long-distance trade flourished and a few regions supported productive farming. Islam had a strong foothold in Central Asia, and many places had large Sufi communities where Sufi masters often gained political power. In many of the cities, including Silk Road hubs such as Bukhara (boo-CAR-ruh) and Samarkand (SAM-ar-kand), social, political, and religious patterns closely resembled those of Persians and Arabs.

As the remnants of the Mongol Empire broke up into various rival societies by the 1400s, Russia capitalized on the political vacuum to extend its own power first into Siberia and then into the Black Sea region and Central Asia. While western European nations built maritime empires, Russia, seeking resources and land for possible settlement by Russians, transformed itself into a great land-based territorial empire. The Russian eastward and southward expansion over huge distances was a saga comparable to the later westward expansion of the United States and Canada across North America. A key role in this Russian expansion was played by the **Cossacks** (KOS-aks), tough, hard-drinking adventurers and soldiers from southern Russia who were descendants of Russians, Poles, and Lithuanians fleeing serfdom, slavery, or jail. Cossacks (the Turkish word for "free men") were fierce warriors and usually defeated rival forces.

The expansion east across sparsely populated Siberia began in the 1500s and accelerated during the seventeenth and eighteenth centuries. By 1637 Russian explorers had reached the Pacific Ocean. In 1689 conflict with China forced the Russians to temporarily abandon settlements in the Amur (AH-moor) River Basin north of China (see Chapter 18), but they continued to add other Siberian territory, often after overcoming fierce resistance from local peoples. Siberia yielded the Russians furs, metals, and forest products.

Seeking direct access to maritime trade routes, the Russians also began acquiring territories on their southern fringe. Looking south, Russian leaders coveted the Black Sea and the Straits of Bosporus bisecting Istanbul, through which Russian ships could reach the warm Mediterranean. The southward thrust meant confronting the Tartars (TAHR-tuhrz), Muslim descendants of Mongols and long a threat to the Russians. In the 1400s and 1500s Tartars, Russians, Ottoman Turks, Poles, and Lithuanians fought for control of today's southern Russia. Between 1552 and 1556 the Russians seized the Tartar state of Kazan (kuh-ZAN), slaughtering many residents in the capital, and then gradually gained more land. Russian commerce benefited from Russia's new domination of the northern Caspian Sea, which made possible direct trade between the Baltic lands and Persia through Russia.

Soon the Russians turned toward Muslim Central Asia, settled largely by Turkish peoples and often known as Turkestan. By the early 1700s the Russians had gained territory occupied by the Kazakhs (kah-ZAHKS), a pastoral people who had once ruled a large area, and by 1864 they controlled all the Kazakh lands to the eastern border with China. They then targeted the Silk Road cities, those centers of Islamic learning that attracted merchants from many societies, among them Jews and Hindu Indians.

In pursuing this goal the Russians faced formidable opponents in the Uzbeks (OOZ-beks), a people of mixed Turkish, Persian, and Mongol ancestry who controlled several rival states in southern Turkestan. But the Uzbeks eventually were weakened. Uzbek sultans promoted Sunni Islam, which made them enemies of the Shi'ite Safavids. When Safavid hostility

closed Persia to Uzbek trade, the prosperity of the Silk Road cities declined, and the roads that had once brought diverse religions, cultural influences, and trade goods into Turkestan saw fewer travelers. Eventually the Uzbeks and their neighbors earned smaller revenues and their merchants lost profits. In addition, the sultans lost power to tribal chiefs. In the early 1700s the Persians gained control of some Uzbek territory and much of Afghanistan, and by the later 1800s an expanding Russia was able to conquer all of southern Turkestan.

SECTION SUMMARY

- Under the leadership of a charismatic boy named Isma'il, the Safavids, originally from Azerbaijan, conquered Persia and made the Persians convert from Sunni to Shi'a Islam.

- Under the Safavids, Persia was a major exporter of silk and remained a major conduit of trade, and its beautiful capital, built by Shah Abbas I, attracted merchants from many countries.

- The Safavid Empire patronized art and literature, and Safavid artists became famous for their miniature painting and their carpet weaving.

- Safavid religious leaders, increasingly relying on their own authority rather than that of the Quran, eventually became more influential as the power of Safavid rulers declined and then collapsed.

- Morocco, the far western outpost of Islam, absorbed many fleeing Iberian Muslims and grew into a powerful state that, under the Sa'dians, eventually defeated the Portuguese.

- With the aid of the Cossacks, Russia engaged in a large territorial expansion to create a land-based empire, an expansion that brought it into conflict with Siberian and Islamic Central Asian peoples, including the Uzbeks in Turkestan.

 *Online Study Center* ACE the Test

 # Chapter Summary

The overseas expansion of Europe during the Early Modern Era affected different regions in different ways but was only one of the forces at work in most societies. Various African societies, among them Songhai, Kanem-Bornu, the Hausa states, Benin, and Buganda, remained strong in the 1500s. Eventually, however, the arrival of Europeans set in motion forces that began to reshape parts of Africa, especially societies along the western and eastern coasts, and many Africans became linked more closely to Europe and the Americas. The Portuguese undermined Kongo, Angola, and the city-states of East Africa and ultimately established the first European colonies in sub-Saharan Africa, Angola and Mozambique. The most prominent factor in changing the course of African history was the trans-

---

Cossacks Tough adventurers and soldiers from southern Russia who were descendants of Russians, Poles, and Lithuanians fleeing serfdom, slavery, or jail.

Atlantic slave trade, which arose in the sixteenth century. Soon various Europeans began procuring slaves in West Africa and shipping them across the Atlantic to meet the limitless demands of the American plantations. This trade benefited a few African societies, such as Dahomey and Ashante, but devastated others and created chronic conflict along the West African coast.

Several Islamic societies remained powerful during the 1500s and 1600s. These included the great Islamic empires of the Ottomans and Safavids and Morocco. The Ottomans, who were Sunni Turks, built an empire over much of western Asia, North Africa, and southeastern Europe, reuniting a large part of the Islamic world for the first time in some centuries. At their zenith they had a powerful military, flourishing economy, and vibrant cultural life. The Safavids dominated part of western Asia and fostered a lively culture and economy in Persia. They also converted the Persians from Sunni to Shi'a Islam, increasing the rivalry with the Ottomans. Sa'dian Morocco repulsed the Portuguese and built a regional empire. But by the early 1700s these great Islamic states as well as Muslim societies in Central Asia experienced new challenges, some posed by Russian expansion into Muslim lands.

Online Study Center **Improve Your Grade** Flashcards

Key Terms

Darkest Africa	Middle Passage	colonialism
Boers	Atlantic System	janissaries
trekking	imperialism	Cossacks
racism		

Suggested Reading

Books

Balandier, Georges. *Daily Life in the Kingdom of the Kongo: From the Sixteenth to the Eighteenth Century.* New York: Meridian Books, 1968. A classic study of an important African kingdom.

Barendse, R. J. *The Arabian Seas: The Indian Ocean World of the Seventeenth Century.* Armonk, N.Y.: M. E. Sharpe, 2002. A lengthy but wide-ranging scholarly study of the political economy connecting Europe, Africa, India, and the Middle East.

Findley, Carter Vaughn. *The Turks in World History.* New York: Oxford University Press, 2005. A survey over many centuries.

Goldschmidt, Arthur, Jr. and Lawrence Davidson. *A Concise History of the Middle East.* 8th ed. revised and updated. Boulder, Colo.:

Westview Press, 2005. A good introduction, especially to the Ottoman and Safavid Empires.

Khodarkovsky, Michael, *Russia's Steppe Frontier: The Making of a Colonial Empire, 1500–1800.* Bloomington: Indiana University Press, 2002. A scholarly study.

Klein, Herbert S. *The Atlantic Slave Trade.* New York: Cambridge University Press, 1999. An overview that incorporates social, economic, political, and cultural history.

Northrup, David. *Africa's Discovery of Europe, 1450–1850.* New York: Oxford University Press, 2002. A sweeping survey of Africa's engagement with Europe and the varied responses.

Pearson, Michael N. *Port Cities and Intruders: The Swahili Coast, India, and Portugal in the Early Modern Era.* Baltimore: Johns Hopkins University Press, 1998. A scholarly study of the coast.

Robinson, Francis. *The Cultural Atlas of the Islamic World Since 1500.* Oxford: Stonehenge, 1992. A useful compilation of materials.

Savory, Roger. *Iran Under the Safavids.* Cambridge: Cambridge University Press, 1980. The standard survey.

Shillington, Kevin. *History of Africa,* revised 2nd ed. New York: Palgrave Macmillan, 2005. Readable survey with much on this era.

Thornton, John. *Africa and Africans in the Formation of the Atlantic World, 1400–1800.* 2nd ed. Cambridge: Cambridge University Press, 1998. An excellent examination of Africa and the diaspora.

Wheatcroft, Andrew. *The Ottomans.* New York: Viking, 1993. A readable, lively discussion with particular attention to the elites.

Websites

History and Cultures of Africa (http://www.columbia.edu/cu/lweb/indiv/africa/cuvl/cult/html). Provides valuable links to relevant websites on African history.

Internet African History Sourcebook (http://www.fordham.edu/halsall/africa/africasbook.html). This site contains useful information and documentary material.

Internet Islamic History Sourcebook (http://www.fordham.edu/halsall/islam/islamsbook.html). Useful links and source materials.

Middle East Studies Internet Resources (http://www.columbia.edu/cu/lweb/indiv/mideast/cuvlm/ancient/html). A useful collection of links.

The Trans-Atlantic Slave Trade (www.whc.neu.edu/afrintro.htm). A demographic simulation created at Northeastern University.

CHAPTER **17**

Americans, Europeans, Africans, and New Societies in the Americas, 1450–1750

Online Study Center

This icon will direct you to interactive activities and study materials on the website: college.hmco.com/pic/lockard1e

Español   3. Mestizo   2. Yndia

A Mestizo Family The intermarriage of Europeans and Indians was common in Latin America, especially in Mexico. This Mexican painting, by the eighteenth-century artist Las Castas, shows a Spanish man, his Indian wife, and their mixed-descent, or *mestizo*, son.   (Courtesy, Banco de Mexico)

Truly do we live on earth? Not forever on earth; only a little while here. Although it be jade, it will be broken. Although it is gold, it is crushed.

AZTEC POEM ON THE MEANING OF LIFE, CA. 1500[1]

In the sixteenth century Spanish colonists in Mexico trained an Aztec historian, Chimalpahin Cuahtlehuanitzin (chee-MAL-pin QUAT-al-WANT-zen), how to read and write in the Western alphabet. Using this alphabet but writing in his native Nahuatl (NAH-waht-l) language of central Mexico, the Aztec historian gave us one of the best records of the Mexican world at the threshold of the changes instigated by the coming of Europeans. He wrote, for example, of Aztec military triumphs over neighboring people and of how Aztec kings used their wealth to improve their great capital, Tenochtitlan (teh-noch-TIT-lan), constructing an aqueduct to convey fresh water and rebuilding temples to the gods. But Cuahtlehuanitzin also told of ominous developments. In particular, he recorded the reports that began to reach Tenochtitlan in 1519 of pale-skinned men in huge boats arriving on the eastern coast from the sea, where gods might come from. In fact, Aztec legends claimed that, centuries earlier, a Toltec king driven into exile by rivals had become a god, Quetzalcoatl (kate-zahl-CO-ah-tal) ("the plumed serpent"), who promised to return some day and seek revenge. These strange men on the coast seemed suspiciously godlike: they dressed in metal, had unfamiliar but lethal metal weapons, and rode on large animals as tall as the roof of a house—perhaps, Aztecs thought, some kind of deer. And they arrived around the year some believed that Quetzalcoatl would return. This was disturbing, Cuahtlehuanitzin remembered, because the god's reappearance threatened the Aztec social order.

To be sure, for all their military and cultural triumphs, the Aztecs had known challenges. Cuahtlehuanitzin wrote that, nearly three decades earlier, 13-Flint in the Aztec calendar (1492 in the Gregorian calendar) had been an unusually bad year, bringing an eclipse of the sun, volcanic eruptions, and widespread famine. The Aztec philosophy of life understood such occasional setbacks, as the poem opening the chapter suggests. But the Aztecs were not prepared for the arrival of the Europeans and the troubles they would provoke. The leader of the pale men who had arrived on the shore was the Spanish explorer Hernán Cortés. The invaders arrived in the Aztec lands, Cuahtlehuanitzin remembered, when a terrible and unknown disease, known to Europeans as smallpox, began killing off the people. And within two years, these men from afar, with horses, metal armor, and gunpowder weapons, had conquered the heart of the Aztec Empire, giving new meaning to the broken jade and crushed gold in the Aztec poem.

The first Europeans to arrive in the Americas claimed to have discovered a "new world," but it was actually an old one, long populated by a mosaic of peoples such as the Aztecs. The exploratory voyages of Christopher Columbus and the conquests of such adventurers as Cortés in Mexico often destroyed many long-existing American societies and reshaped them into new kinds of societies, in reality *creating* a "new world." In fact, the whole Western Hemisphere changed. During the 1500s the Spanish and Portuguese conquered and colonized large areas of what we now call Latin America, containing millions of people. A century later, in North America and the Caribbean, the English, French, and Dutch followed, gradually extending their power. As a result of these incursions during the Early Modern Era, with its forging of many new networks of travel and commerce around the world, few regions experienced more changes than the Americas, and the two hemispheres became closely linked. European exploration in the Americas and Southeast Asia also led to the first encounters between Europe and the diverse island societies of the Pacific Ocean.

The transitions that resulted from European encounters with Native American cultures affected both sides of the Atlantic. Among the most important consequences of European activities in the Americas was a complex global exchange of crops and animals, peoples and cultures. By the 1600s, European ships regularly crisscrossed the Atlantic, moving people, plants, animals, natural resources, and manufactured goods, while diseases carried from the Eastern Hemisphere set off a demographic disaster for Native American peoples. The societies that emerged from the European colonization of the Americas reflected diverse influences from all over the Atlantic world. Europeans, Africans, and Native Americans in Latin America and the Caribbean formed mixed cultures that differed in many respects from the societies formed in English- and French-ruled North America. Finally, in some regions of the Americas a plantation economy developed that engaged enslaved Africans and their descendants as a work force. For millions of Africans, transported across the Atlantic against their will, this consequence of Europeans' arrival meant that they now lived in conditions that were often unendurable, requiring them to develop strategies for survival.

FOCUS QUESTIONS

1. How did encounters between Europe and the Americas increase in the 1500s?

2. How did Europeans conquer and begin settling the American societies?

3. What were the major consequences of European colonization of the Americas?

4. How did the development of the American economies lead to the trans-Atlantic slave trade?

5. What impact did the emerging Atlantic System have on Europe and the American societies?

	Exploration	Latin America	North America
1400	**1492** First Columbian voyage		
1500	**1519–1521** Magellan's circumnavigation of the globe	**1521** Spanish conquest of Aztecs **1535** Spanish conquest of Incas	
1600			**1604** French settlement in Canada **1607** English settlement in Virginia **1627** Colony of New France
1700			**1759** English defeat of French in Quebec

◆ Early American-European-Pacific Encounters

How did encounters between Europe and the Americas increase in the 1500s?

American peoples developed their ways of life long before the European voyages of exploration permanently connected the two hemispheres, and a wide variety of societies, economies, and styles of governing existed in the Americas by the fifteenth century. But the Americans faced a great challenge from the coming of the Europeans. Christopher Columbus began the historic change in 1492. In the wake of the Columbian voyages, various European nations first explored and then gradually conquered, colonized, and settled the entire Western Hemisphere, drawing the Americas into commercial, travel, and religious networks centered on Europe. The exploration of the Americas also spilled over into the Pacific Ocean, though few Pacific islanders encountered the West in this era.

American Societies in 1500

In 1500 the Western Hemisphere contained many societies with distinctive institutions, customs, and survival strategies. Their differences resulted from adaptation to different environments. Those who lived by hunting, gathering, and fishing could be found particularly in the North American Great Plains, the Pacific Northwest coast, Alaska, northern Canada, and some of the tropical forest regions of Central and South America. Other peoples lived from small-scale farming, especially in eastern North America, parts of the North American desert and Amazon Basin, and southeastern Brazil.

For millennia the most complex Native American societies flourished from intensive farming in Mesoamerica (Mexico and northern Central America) and the Andes region of western South America. By 1500 the Aztecs, based in central Mexico, were the most powerful Mesoamerican society and the Incas (IN-kuhz), centered in central Peru, controlled most of the Andes region. Both the Aztecs and the Incas built states on the foundations of much older urban and farming-based societies. Like their predecessors, they worked metals and fibers for tools, decoration, and weapons.

The Aztec state, through military conquest by a strong army and a well-organized government, completed its empire building in 1428 (see Chronology: American Societies and European Discoveries, 1400–1524). Aztec warfare relied on disciplined battle formations, shrewd tactics, and deadly weapons such as bows and arrows, stone-bladed broadswords,

C H R O N O L O G Y	
American Societies and European Discoveries, 1400–1524	
1428–1521	Aztec Empire
1440–1532	Inca Empire
1492	Landing in Bahamas by Columbus
1494	Treaty of Tordesillas
1497	John Cabot's landing in North America
1500	Portuguese claim of Brazil
1513	Balboa's sighting of Pacific Ocean
1519–1521	Ferdinand Magellan's circumnavigation of globe
1524	French claim of Canada

spears, and spear-throwers. But the Aztecs only loosely controlled the various peoples in their empire, and by the early 1500s they faced mounting military confrontations with rival confederations of city-states, especially the Tlaxcalans (tlax-CALL-uns) on their eastern fringe. Cruel Aztec imperialism, including the widespread use of human sacrifice, had created enemies, some of whom were later willing to cooperate with the first European arrivals, the Spanish, to overthrow Aztec power. But Aztec society was still vigorous and expanding its influence in the early 1500s.

The Incas completed the conquest of their empire in 1440. Even more impressive than the Aztecs in material accomplishments, they formed an empire larger than the Roman or Han Chinese Empires of the Classical Era, stretching nearly 2,500 miles north to south, much of it above 8,000 feet in altitude. The Inca state was the most dynamic and integrated in all of the American states, and it was geared for conquest and paternalistic regimentation. Some Spanish colonizers admired it. For example, in the later 1500s Garcilaso de la Vega (GAHR-suh-LAH-so duh luh VAY-guh), the son of a Spanish captain and an Inca princess, wrote the most detailed study of Inca culture. While acknowledging the misery of people colonized by the Incas, he also praised the highly productive farming system, generosity, and other values of Inca society. The Incas, he concluded, "had attained to a high status of perfection. No thoughtful man can fail to admire so noble and provident a government."[2]

Probably in part due to climate change, some Native American societies had long passed their peak by 1500. By 1440 the last Maya cities and states of southern Mexico and northern Central America had collapsed. But some 5 to 6 million Mayan-speaking people, living mostly in villages, remained as examples of a once vibrant society, over 2,000 years old, whose city-states had once stretched from the northern Yucatan Peninsula southward into what is today Guatemala and Belize. In North America the mound-building and trade-oriented Mississippian culture had reached its peak in the 1100s, and the major Mississippian town, Cahokia (kuh-HOE-key-uh), had been deserted by 1250. The once vast Mississippian trading system was in steep decline by the 1400s, by which time the Anasazi (ah-nah-SAH-zee) and other societies of the southwestern desert had already abandoned their major settlements.

Flourishing Native American societies besides the Aztecs and Incas remained, however, such as the Taino (TIE-no) in the Caribbean islands and the diverse farming peoples along the Atlantic coasts of North America and Brazil. Indeed, while the first European settlers wrongly considered the Americas to be largely empty land, some regions were densely populated. By 1492 the population of the Western Hemisphere probably numbered between 60 and 75 million people, although some demographers place it at over 100 million. The majority of Americans lived in central and southern Mexico and the Andes region. The most complex agricultural and political systems

Arawak Women This woodcut, made in the sixteenth century, shows Arawak women on a Caribbean island preparing a meal of cornmeal tortillas and stew. (Courtesy of John Carter Brown Library at Brown University)

corresponded to the largest populations. Regardless of their success in mastering environments, however, because of many millennia of isolation from the Eastern Hemisphere, American peoples had no immunity to the diseases brought by Europeans and later African slaves. Hence, the coming of the West brought a terrible mortality. Native Americans also had no metal swords or firearms to resist Europeans. The vulnerability of the Western Hemisphere peoples made this the main region to suffer incursions by Europe in the Early Modern Era.

Bridging the Atlantic Barrier

The Atlantic Ocean was the major barrier between the hemispheres, but a few Europeans steadily overcame the challenge. The first known contact between Americans and Europeans did not have a long-lasting impact. In the later tenth century C.E. some Norse Vikings, whose ancestors had settled Iceland several generations earlier, sailed west and established small farming settlements in several glacier-free coastal valleys in southern Greenland. By around 1000 a few of these hardy Norse, perhaps blown off course, sighted what is now eastern Canada and explored the coast. They built a small village in Newfoundland, a large island off the coast of the Canadian region known today as Labrador, where they harvested fish and cut timber.

Largely as a result of conflicts between local Native Americans and the Norse, the Newfoundland settlement was abandoned after only a few years. The Greenland Norse, however, apparently sent occasional trading and lumbering expeditions to eastern Canada for several hundred years. A few Norse artifacts, possibly used as trade goods, have been found scattered across eastern Canada and the Arctic islands. The Greenland settlements also collapsed by 1450. There may have been factional disputes or conflicts with the native Inuit (IN-yoo-it) people of Greenland, while deforestation and colder climates made the already difficult farming impossible. But the Greenland Norse were not lost to history. Portuguese ships occasionally visited Iceland, where people knew of the Greenland and Labrador settlements, and this knowledge probably circulated in Europe.

The Norse may not have been the only people from the Western Hemisphere to spot the North American coast before 1492. The winters of the Little Ice Age in Europe brought poor harvests and reduced fish catches along Europe's Atlantic coast, pushing some desperate fishermen to venture farther from home. For many years Portuguese, Basque, Danish, English, Breton, and Moroccan fishermen had worked the waters of the North Atlantic in search of cod, whales, and sardines. Some of them probably found the fish-rich Grand Banks off Newfoundland. Perhaps a few of the fishermen also saw North America. A few scattered non-Norse European artifacts reported by early explorers in eastern North America have led some historians to suspect that some coastal people may have encountered Europeans in the later 1400s. If there were any landings they apparently went unreported in Europe. Fishermen may have kept any discoveries secret to keep rivals away from their rich fishing grounds.

Different motives, including the quest for riches, national glory, and Christian converts, encouraged other Europeans to venture out into the Atlantic on exploring expeditions (see Chapter 15). While early Portuguese expeditions concentrated on the African route to the East (see Chapters 16 and 18), others, led by Christopher Columbus, hoped to sail westward from Europe to Asia. Contrary to myth, many educated people in Europe accepted that the earth was round and hence could be circumnavigated.

Columbus's First Voyages to the Americas

The first explorers to brave the Atlantic directly from Europe with the purpose of reaching Asia came under the Spanish flag, beginning with Christopher Columbus (see Chapter 15). Columbus (1451–1506), born in the key Italian port of Genoa, had lived for many years in the Portuguese capital, Lisbon, which had a large Genoese merchant and sailing community. His connections to wealthy Genoese in Lisbon helped him court and marry Donha Felipa Moniz, the aristocratic daughter of a governor on the Portuguese-settled Atlantic island of Madeira (muh-DEER-uh). Thanks to this connection, Columbus worked in Madeira and visited the Canary and Azores (A-zorz) Islands farther out in the Atlantic. Donha Felipa died soon after giving birth to their son, Diego, but she had given Columbus social status and access to her family's navigational charts and records. Columbus had also likely sailed to Iceland and down the West African coast on Portuguese ships, and he was probably familiar with both the Norse discoveries and the tales of Portuguese fishermen.

Soon Columbus, described by a contemporary as a man of great spirit and lofty thoughts, formed grander plans of exploration. The mariner was inspired by the writings of the thirteenth-century Italian adventurer Marco Polo and owned a well-worn copy of Polo's book relating his travels in Asia and long sojourn in China. A devout Christian, Columbus claimed that he wanted to sail to China to introduce Christianity there. He also hoped to find the sea route to the silk- and spice-rich lands of China and Southeast Asia. But the inaccurate maps he acquired vastly underestimated the size of the earth and the distance to Asia.

Columbus eventually convinced the Spanish monarchs, King Ferdinand and Queen Isabella, fresh from their final triumph over the last Muslim state in southern Spain, to finance his voyages of exploration in hopes of establishing direct ties to Asia. Commanding ships far smaller than the great junks of the Chinese explorer Zheng He in the early 1400s, Columbus surveyed much of the Caribbean and some of the South American coast in four voyages over the next decade and believed that he had discovered outlying regions of Asia. When Ferdinand and Isabella realized he was wrong, they were at first disappointed. America was a heartbreaking obstacle on the route to eastern Asia.

On his first voyage in 1492, Columbus had encountered the Taino, an Arawak (AR-uh-wahk)-speaking people who lived on Caribbean islands (see Map 17.1). When Columbus and his crew sailed into the Bahamas, they were greeted by

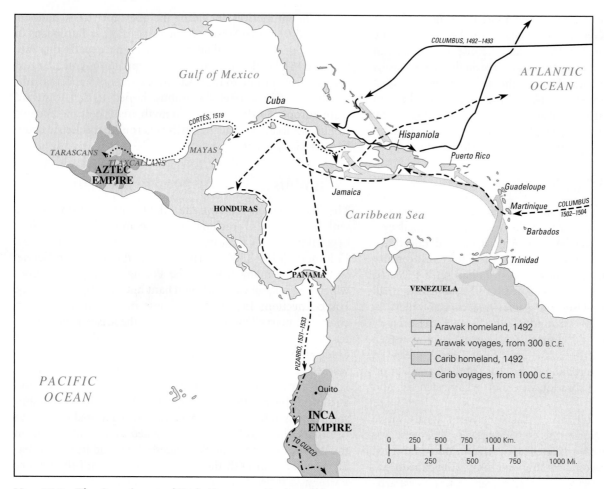

Map 17.1   The Americas and Early European Exploration
The several voyages across the Atlantic led by Columbus explored the Caribbean Basin and set the
stage for Spanish conquest of many American societies, most notably of the Aztec and Inca Empires.

curious Taino islanders. The Taino proved friendly, but the fact that they wore few clothes, a practical response to the tropical heat, shocked the straight-laced Spanish, who considered nakedness a sign of barbarism. The Taino themselves may have desired to cultivate a potential ally. Even before the arrival of the Spanish, they had often had to resist incursions by the Caribs (KAR-ibs), a more warlike Native American group that had originated in South America. By the fourteenth century Caribs were pushing Taino and other Arawaks toward more northern islands and also raiding the Yucatan coast of Mexico.

The Taino had a flourishing society; they smoked cigars, slept in hammocks, possessed a little gold, and some of them lived in sizeable towns built around Mesoamerican-style plazas and ball courts. They combined fishing with highly productive cultivation of corn (maize) and manioc, and they carried on extensive interisland trade in large canoes that were not much smaller than Columbus's ships and capable of holding up to 150 people. The women did the farming and often served as community leaders, exhibiting egalitarian gender relations that confounded the Spanish. After meeting with several communities, Columbus developed favorable views of the hospitable,

patient, and peaceable Taino, seeing them, according to the Western stereotype of certain non-Western peoples, as "noble savages," innocent children of nature: "They are a loving and uncovetous people. They love their neighbors as themselves."[3] Later, however, when Columbus encountered Taino noncooperation or armed resistance to Spanish demands, he modified his views, replacing the image of the "noble savage" with that of the "ignoble savage."

Columbus then moved on, first to the island he called Hispaniola (HIS-puhn-YO-luh), today the home of Haiti and the Dominican Republic but then dominated by six Taino chiefdoms. Leaving a small colony of Spaniards there, Columbus began his return voyage to Europe by way of Cuba, which Columbus believed might be China. There he dispatched a small party, led by a Jew who spoke Hebrew, Chaldean, and Arabic, to search the interior for, and possibly communicate with, the Chinese ruler. They returned only with some mysterious dried leaves called *tobacos*, which local people smoked. Some decades later other Europeans would take tobacco, widely consumed in the Americas, back to Europe and start a smoking fad. Columbus and his crew sailed back to Spain with six Taino Indians from the Bahamas to present at court as proof of his discoveries so that he could seek funding for a second voyage. Upon his return to Spain, Columbus was feted as a hero and promoted to admiral.

Later Columbian Voyages

Although Columbus did not find China, his discovery of the wind patterns that could push ships back and forth across the Atlantic launched a new era of exploration. He boasted that he had found the keys to open mighty ocean barriers that had long been closed with mighty chains. Spanish authorities quickly planned a second voyage and, to counteract a possible Portuguese challenge, persuaded the pope to issue an order, the Treaty of Tordesillas (tor-duh-SEE-yuhs) in 1494, that divided the newly discovered Atlantic lands into Spanish and Portuguese spheres. Ultimately the treaty gave Spain the rights to most of the Americas while the Portuguese received Africa and Brazil. Both Iberian countries promised the pope that they would evangelize and colonize the "heathen" peoples they encountered.

During his four voyages, Columbus explored much of the Caribbean region. He concentrated on Hispaniola, bringing Spanish colonists with him on his second voyage in 1493 and establishing on the island the first permanent European settlement in the Americas, called Isabella after the Spanish queen. The success of the Spanish colony depended on exploiting the Taino through forced labor and then, when that proved insufficient, slavery. As Columbus wrote, "The Indians of this island are its riches, for it is they who dig and produce the bread and other food for the [Spanish] Christians and get the gold from the mines, and perform all the services and labor of men and of draft animals."[4] Columbus also explored the coasts of Cuba and Jamaica and sighted Puerto Rico. But the Hispaniola colony he governed was a failure economically, and he returned to Spain in 1496. On his third voyage, in 1498, Columbus found Trinidad and the Venezuela coast. By now he suspected he had not reached Asia but never completely abandoned the idea. But his mismanagement of the Hispaniola colony and his failure to discover vast riches brought him disgrace, and he was ordered home under arrest in 1500.

However, Queen Isabella, her appetite now whetted for further exploration and conquest, allowed Columbus one final voyage to find a strait that might lead to India. This expedition explored the coast of Central America, from what is today Honduras to Costa Rica. Though Columbus encountered a Maya trading raft he thought might be Chinese, he also began to speak of the Caribbean islands as the "West Indies" as separate from the eagerly sought "East Indies" (India and Southeast Asia). After he and his crew were shipwrecked for a year on Jamaica, where they lived off the food obtained from local people, he returned to Spain and died in 1506, a broken man.

Eventually some Europeans began referring to the Native Americans as "Indians," a European name that confuses American peoples with those of India. Because of this, the label remains controversial among scholars, and some activists in North America prefer terms such as "Native American" or "First Nations" to Indian. The term *America* derives from an Italian merchant, Amerigo Vespucci (ves-POO-chee) (1454–1512), who claimed to have made several voyages to the Western Hemisphere. His letters to powerful European princes described two separate continents in a "new world" that was soon known as "Amerigo's land," from which we derive the name *America.*

The Continuing Search for Wealth

Columbus's encounters encouraged others to follow his example, and exploration soon became a multinational effort involving the English, French, Portuguese, and Spanish. By 1525 a series of European expeditions had explored the Atlantic and Caribbean coasts of the Americas from eastern Canada to the southern tip of South America. The explorers had diverse motives. Some sought to enrich themselves and the European monarchs who sponsored them. Others hoped to gain God's favor through Christian missionary activity.

These exploring expeditions stimulated still further European voyages and claims. Following an expedition led by another Genoese, John Cabot (KAB-uht), the English claimed the Atlantic coast of North America in 1497. This action set off a fruitless search for a northwest passage, a sea route that might lead from the Atlantic Ocean through North America to the Pacific and thus Asia, but no practical route existed. In 1500 Portugal established its claim to Brazil, which fell within the longitudes awarded to it by the pope in the Treaty of Tordesillas, and by 1502 Portuguese settlement of Brazil had begun. By 1511 the Spanish controlled Cuba, Puerto Rico, and Jamaica. Soon they also had a presence on the northern coast of South America. In 1513 a Spanish expedition led by Vasco Nunez de Balboa (bal-BOH-uh) crossed Panama and sighted the Pacific Ocean, which he claimed for Spain. The French claimed eastern Canada in 1524 with a voyage led by an Italian captain from Florence, Giovanni da Verrazano (VER-uh-ZAH-no).

The only practical sea route to Asia via the Americas was finally discovered in 1520, in a Spanish expedition led by a Portuguese captain, Ferdinand Magellan (muh-JELL-un) (1480–1521). Magellan had already visited Indonesia on Portuguese vessels by taking the route eastward across the Indian Ocean. After falling out with the Portuguese king, he gained support from the Spanish monarch, Charles V, to explore a possible Pacific route to the Spice Islands via the Americas. From Spain his ships sailed down the Atlantic and rounded the southern tip of South America; they then survived a torturous trip through the stormy strait that today bears his name and leads to the Pacific Ocean: the Strait of Magellan. Magellan continued on across the Pacific. It was a long, difficult journey during which no inhabited islands were spotted before Guam (gwahm), with the crewmen living off rat meat and boiled leather for months. Scurvy, a vitamin C deficiency caused by the scarcity of fresh vegetables, took its toll on the seamen. Eventually the expedition landed in the Philippine Islands, where Magellan was killed in a clash with local people. Magellan's one remaining ship and a small surviving crew continued on westward around Africa, limping into Europe three years after they had left Spain. Europeans now had a better idea of world geography and turned to the conquest and settlement of the Americas.

Some early explorers, greedy for quick wealth, engaged in piracy and looting. The Spanish conqueror of Aztec Mexico, Hernán Cortés, admitted that the Spanish "suffer an affliction of the heart which can only be cured by gold."[5] Sometimes they seized Native Americans as slaves. As governor of Hispaniola, Columbus supported the killing of the Taino who refused to supply gold. The harsh exploitation generated increasing Taino resistance and attacks on the Spanish, prompting Columbus to order that Taino rebels and their families be enslaved and shipped to Spain in chains. Only a few survived the journey. Later the Spanish also raided other islands for slaves. Estimates of the Taino population in the Caribbean in 1492 range from 100,000 to one million, but within thirty years all the Taino on Hispaniola, and many elsewhere, had been enslaved or killed, had died of disease or overwork, or had committed suicide because of their suffering. A Spanish priest lamented in 1518 that many Caribbean islands "were deserted as useless, by men who wished to depopulate them and to kill the Indians who lived there. They were laid to waste, and inhabited only by wild animals and birds."[6]

New Horizons and Exploration in the Pacific

Exploration of the Americas, and the continued search for a sea route to Asia, led to European exploration of the Pacific basin. Long before Europeans arrived, the Pacific islanders, scattered across many island chains, had evolved several distinctive cultural and political traditions and social systems. The Polynesian people living on mountainous islands had varied food sources from farming and fishing that supported denser settlement and states led by kings or powerful chiefs and social classes. For instance, the eight inhabited Hawaiian Islands, divided into four rival chiefdoms, had a population of perhaps 200,000. Some 100,000 to 150,000 Maori (MOW-ree), also organized into chiefdoms, lived on the two main New Zealand islands by the later 1700s. By contrast, many peoples living on small atolls only a few feet above sea level relied chiefly on resources from the sea; these societies had smaller populations and developed more egalitarian systems.

Pacific societies had many of the same experiences as peoples elsewhere in the world. Many island societies traded over vast distances and so were linked into widespread sea networks. Warfare between rival islands and states was also common. Some islanders also faced increasing destruction of their fragile environments, most famously the Polynesians who settled on remote Easter Island in the eastern Pacific. Over the centuries they recklessly deforested the small island, leaving no wood for building new boats. As a result, they were long isolated from other Polynesians, were near starvation because farmers struggled and offshore fishing became impossible, and engaged in chronic warfare for control of scarce resources. Although Easter Island was an extreme case of environmental destruction and isolation, most Pacific islanders had not been

in direct touch with Asia for millennia, making them vulnerable to Eurasian diseases later brought by Europeans.

Although Spanish ships annually sailed across the Pacific Ocean between the Philippines and Mexico beginning in 1565 (see Chapter 18), Europeans made little effort to colonize the vast Pacific region in this era. The first European expedition into the Pacific, led by Magellan in 1521, encountered no island societies before finally chancing on Guam, where they clashed with the local Chamorro (chuh-MOR-oh) people, the first of many unhappy encounters between Pacific islanders and European visitors. In the 1500s and 1600s Spanish, Portuguese, English, and Dutch expeditions discovered many islands, as well as Australia, but the islands, with few easily exploitable resources, looked unpromising for exploitation compared to Southeast Asia and the Americas.

Spain established the first successful Pacific colony in Guam in 1663, founding a Catholic mission there. But 90 percent of the Chamorros died over the next two decades, mostly from disease brought by the Spanish. In 1671 a demoralized Chamorro chief, though careful not to provoke retaliation, complained to a missionary that "the Spanish would have done better to remain in their own country. We have no need of their help to live happily. They treat us as gross barbarians."[7] Europeans did not visit some important island chains, including Hawaii, until the later 1700s, when English settlement in Australia also began.

SECTION SUMMARY

■ In 1500, many American peoples lived by hunting, gathering, and fishing, while others lived in the widespread, often repressive empires created by the Incas and the Aztecs.

■ From 1000 on, Norse from Greenland intermittently settled in Newfoundland, and other Europeans may have crossed the Atlantic in search of fish long before Columbus discovered America.

■ Beginning in 1492, Christopher Columbus explored the Caribbean and the South American coast under the impression that they were outlying areas of Asia, and his discovery of Atlantic wind patterns opened up exploration of the Americas.

■ Columbus focused on the island of Hispaniola, where he enslaved the native Taino, and gradually gave up on the idea that he had discovered an Atlantic route to Asia, which was later discovered by Magellan.

■ European nations divided up the Western Hemisphere according to the Treaty of Tordesillas, and as Europeans explored the Americas, some seeking riches and others converts, their diseases and their habit of enslaving or killing the local people decimated native populations.

■ Pacific Island societies, which ranged from the highly stratified Hawaiians and the Maori of New Zealand to subsistence atoll inhabitants, were generally not visited by Europeans in the 1500s.

◆ The European Conquest of the Americas

How did Europeans conquer and begin settling the American societies?

European explorations and the search for riches soon led to colonization in the Americas. Native Americans lacked the guns to resist the invaders and were also weakened by division into often hostile societies. Thousands of Spanish adventurers roamed the Americas seeking wealth in the 1500s. Many were soldiers engaged in armed conquest, whose leaders were known as **conquistadors** (kon-KEY-stuh-dorz). The main town established by the Spanish on Hispaniola, Santo Domingo (SAN-toe duh-MING-go), became the early Spanish base for exploration and conquest. The major Spanish conquests came in Mexico and the Andes, while the Portuguese annexed Brazil. Later, the English, French, and Dutch obtained footholds in North America, the Caribbean, and the northeast coast of South America. By 1750 many American societies were under firm colonial control by various European powers.

The Fall of the Aztec Empire

In 1519 Hernán Cortés (kor-TEZ) (1485–1547) and 550 soldiers from Spanish-controlled Cuba landed on Mexico's east coast, where they founded a settlement that later became the city of Veracruz (VER-uh-KROOZ). His major target was the rich Aztec Empire. The traditional purpose of warfare in central Mexico was to secure captives for sacrifice, not to kill opponents. Thus the Aztecs' understanding of war, along with their less deadly weapons, such as spears, put them at a disadvantage to the Spanish. First Cortés defeated and then forged an alliance with the Tlaxcalans, a people who had long resisted the Aztecs. Impressed by Spanish power, the Tlaxcalan nobles even adopted Christianity, and their soldiers joined Cortés. Marching inland, Cortés fought and defeated several other peoples on the empire's perimeter.

With hopes of conquest, Cortés and his growing force then marched through the mountains into the Valley of Mexico, the heart of the Aztec Empire. With its gleaming temples and network of canals, the Aztec capital city, Tenochtitlan (teh-noch-tit-lan), astonished the Spanish, and Cortés called it the world's most beautiful city. The Aztec leader, Moctezuma II (mock-teh-ZOO-ma), warmly greeted them. Moctezuma (r. 1502–1520) may initially have identified Cortés with Quetzalcoatl and believed the Spaniards to be gods, although he probably concluded otherwise fairly quickly. Taking advantage of the confusion, the Spanish arrested Moctezuma. With sixty Spanish soldiers supplied with horses and guns, and many Indian allies, Cortés had taken temporary control of the capital

conquistadors The leaders of Spanish soldiers engaged in armed conquest in the Americas.

of an empire of 25 million subjects. His force was soon joined by a thousand more Spanish soldiers arriving from Cuba.

But soon violence erupted, precipitating war. Spanish actions such as seizing gold and behaving arrogantly created hostility, and Aztec mobs killed or captured some Spaniards. Moctezuma, no longer a credible leader, was killed; sources differ as to whether his death came at the hand of enraged Aztecs or his Spanish captors. The Spanish had to fight their way out of the city, at great cost in Spanish life. Some fleeing Spaniards, loaded down with stolen Aztec gold, fell into the canals and drowned. According to legends, Cortés slumped under a cypress tree while watching through tear-filled eyes the bedraggled remnants of his army retreat east. Forced to return to the coast, he proceeded to make alliances with more Aztec enemies and recruited more Spanish soldiers from Cuba. His enlarged army, numbering around 1,000 Spaniards and 10,000 Tlaxcalans and other Indian allies, now laid siege to Tenochtitlan, where thousands of Aztecs resisted fiercely while a smallpox epidemic, inadvertently spread by the Spanish, ravaged their population. In 1521 the Spanish occupied the city and captured the last emperor, Moctezuma's nephew Cuauhtemoc (KWA-the-mock), while Tlaxcalans took revenge on an old enemy by massacring thousands of city residents (see Chronology: European Conquest and Settlement of the Americas, 1521–1650).

The Spanish had enjoyed significant advantages. Their huge military force had horses and was armed with deadly muskets, cannon, steel swords, and crossbows. Moreover, Aztec military leaders had underestimated the Spanish threat; they mostly wanted to push the Spanish out rather than slaughter them. In addition, as Cuahtlehuanitzin indicated in his account, smallpox accompanied the Spanish to the Americas, reaching Tenochtitlan before the final Spanish assault. Aztec poets, who for decades had written about their violent culture

CHRONOLOGY

European Conquest and Settlement of the Americas, 1521–1650

1521	Spanish conquest of Aztec Empire
1532	First permanent Portuguese settlement in Brazil
1535	Spanish conquest of Inca Empire
1587	First English colony at Roanoke
1604	First French settlement in Acadia
1607	First permanent English settlement in Virginia
1608	French settlement at Quebec City
1624	Dutch settlement at New York
1627	Colony of New France

Codex of Aztec Resistance Illustrations in a book published around 1580 revealed a local perspective on the Spanish conquest of the Aztec Empire. This illustration shows Aztec warriors besieging a Spanish force in Tenochtitlan and the difference in weapons technology. (Institut Amatller d'Art Hispanic)

in melancholy verses, now turned to bemoaning their destruction. As his people died from disease or faced demands for harsh labor, one poet lamented that "broken spears lie in the roads; we have torn our hair in our grief. The houses are roofless now, and their walls are red with blood."[8]

The Spanish now ruled the Aztec Empire, using the efficient Aztec administration to collect the tribute from the former Aztec subjects. The Spanish conquest of the Aztecs also revealed the possibilities for wealth in the Americas. From their Mexico base, Spanish conquerors pushed south to seize Central America, Panama, and, a few years later, the northern part of South America that eventually became Colombia and Venezuela. Later others moved north as far as what is now New Mexico and northern California. Hence by 1750 the Spanish empire included a third of the territory of what later would become the United States, stretching from San Francisco through Santa Fe and San Antonio all the way to St. Augustine in Florida.

The Fall of the Inca Empire

The Spanish also challenged and conquered the huge Inca Empire. From his base in Panama, the Spanish conquistador Francisco Pizarro (ca.1476–1541) began a long exploration down the west coast of South America. In 1531, as his forces marched into the Andes Mountains, he launched his campaign of conquest. As in Mexico, the first Spaniards arrived after smallpox had already wiped out millions of Incas, including much of the leadership. Indeed, the disease had killed the top Inca leader. As a result of his death, the empire was divided by civil war between two rivals for the throne. In 1532, with only

160 Spaniards but with the advantages of artillery and horses, Pizarro captured Atahualpa (AH-tuh-WAHL-puh), one of two rival claimants. In the military struggle the Spanish killed thousands of Incas, many of them unarmed. Holding the king for ransom, Pizarro demanded vast wealth in gold and silver. When that was delivered, Pizarro executed Atahualpa. Ignoring pleas from Catholic priests to treat the Incas with more leniency, Pizarro retorted that he had not come to spread Christianity but to take the Incas' gold.

The Spanish quickly expanded their territory. By 1534 the conquistadors had seized the Inca capital, Cuzco (KOOZ-ko), and had begun converting it into a Spanish settlement. Pizarro also founded the city of Lima (LEE-muh) along the Pacific coast. Over the next few years the Spanish gained control over much of what is today Peru, Ecuador, Bolivia, and Chile and brutally crushed Indian uprisings. As Cortés had done in the Aztec lands, Pizarro and his men placed themselves at the top of the efficient Inca administrative system. But the conqueror's life was dangerous, and Pizarro was later murdered in Lima by supporters of a rival Spanish leader he had executed.

The Conquest of Brazil

While the Spanish concentrated on Mexico and the Andes, the Portuguese established small trading posts along the Brazilian coast. Blessed by regular rainfall, striking natural beauty, and a benign climate, the land seemed promising. Earlier, Vespucci had called it a paradise on earth for possible settlement. The Portuguese began obtaining and shipping brazilwood, which made an excellent dye for European textiles. For some years, however, they remained more focused on exploiting the wealth of Africa and Asia than on settling in the Americas. But worried by a French effort to establish a foothold in Brazil, the Portuguese founded a permanent colony along the southern Brazilian coast in 1532 and began awarding land grants to private entrepreneurs for settlement.

Facing not the large settled societies of Mexico and the Andes but rather seminomadic food collectors and small farmers, the Portuguese viewed the Indians as potential slaves who had to be compelled to work for Portuguese enterprises. Portuguese slavers from the southern Brazilian settlement at São Paulo (sow PAU-low), and hence known as **Paulistas**, pushed deep into the interior raiding for slaves. The colonial government began to combat these activities, and expand its control in the interior, only in 1680.

The Dutch also coveted Brazil as a possible location for tropical plantations. In the seventeenth century the Dutch gained control over much of northeastern Brazil, setting up plantations that grew huge quantities of sugar for the European market. But the Portuguese eventually expelled their rivals and soon took over the profitable northeast, building a city, Salvador da Bahia, at Bahia (ba-HEE-a).

European Colonization of the Caribbean

Although the Spanish controlled several large Caribbean islands, including Cuba and Puerto Rico, and much of the Caribbean coast of Central and South America, they never established a monopoly on regional power, having to contend not only with the Portuguese but also with the Dutch, English, and French, all of whom founded settlements in the Caribbean from the later 1500s until the late 1600s. When the Portuguese expelled them from Brazil, the Dutch moved to several small Caribbean islands and also established a foothold in the northwestern South America region known as the Guianas (ghee-AHN-as), founding the colony of Dutch Guiana (now Suriname). The French seized Haiti (HAY-tee), the western half of Hispaniola, which became a center for plantations and a major source of wealth for France, as well as the islands of Guadeloupe (GWAD-e-loop) and Martinique (mahr-ten-EEK) and a portion of Guiana. Meanwhile, the English made Jamaica, Barbados (bahr-BAY-doz), British Guiana (now Guyana), and later Trinidad the linchpins for their colonial activity.

In the Caribbean, piracy by Europeans against other Europeans became a major economic activity, much of it directed at prosperous Spanish settlements or at the Spanish galleons hauling rich cargoes of silver, sugar, or imported Asian goods to Europe. For example, in 1568 the officials of a Colombian port pleaded with the Spanish king to remedy the conditions in which, they claimed, no coastal town was safe since, whenever they chose, pirates plundered the settlements. In 1670 the English pirate Sir Henry Morgan undertook a particularly brazen attack, leading a force of 1,400 men to sack Panama City, where warehouses stored wealth from Asia and

Latin America. The Spanish burned the city rather than allow it to fall to the buccaneers, leaving less treasure for Morgan and his men to divide up. Some pirates, such as the Englishmen Morgan, John Hawkins, and Sir Francis Drake, became influential and respected figures in their homelands, celebrated for the wealth they captured at the expense of rival countries. As a French buccaneer boasted in 1734, "Fortune is to be found on the sea, where one must go to collect it."[9]

One Caribbean pirate had especially ambitious plans. In 1577 Sir Francis Drake (ca. 1540–1596) set sail from England on a secret mission for Queen Elizabeth I. This journey, which eventually took him around the entire world, was not an idealistic search for knowledge but part of a strategy to outflank and plunder the Spanish empire in the Americas. Drake's fleet sailed through the Strait of Magellan and up the western coast of South America to Mexico and San Francisco Bay, looting unsuspecting Spanish settlements and treasure-laden ships along the way. Some historians think he became the first European to sail as far north as the mouth of the Columbia River and perhaps Vancouver Island. Drake then sailed across the Pacific to the Spice Islands of Indonesia and then traveled across the Indian Ocean and around Africa, arriving back in England in 1580. In the next few years he attacked more Spanish settlements in the Caribbean and then was instrumental in the English defeat of the Spanish armada sent against England in 1588, a battle that decisively shifted the power arrangements of Europe. Drake's swashbuckling career all over the world illustrated how the world had changed after 1492.

The English, French, and Indians in North America

The English and French focused their colonizing efforts on the eastern seaboard of North America, expanding their settlements at the expense of long-established Native American societies. These societies, often matrilineal and sometimes matriarchal, were mostly based on farming. Their chiefs held little power in comparison to Eurasian leaders or Inca kings. Europeans described the people as healthy, enjoying a nutritious diet. However, the Indians soon came to disdain the Europeans, viewing them as unintelligent, physically weak, and smelly—in contrast to Indians, who valued personal cleanliness, the British and French seldom bathed. Nonetheless, the Indians usually offered hospitality and eagerly traded with and sought allies among the newcomers, at least at first. Soon the newcomers had established settlements that became the basis for colonies, wearing out their welcome.

Coveting the potentially fertile land and wanting to outflank rival countries, the English planted a series of settlements up and down the Atlantic coast. In 1587 they founded a small English colony at Roanoke, in what is today North Carolina, but it did not survive. In 1607 the first successful English settlement in North America was established at Jamestown, in today's Virginia. To bolster Jamestown and other settlements, which struggled to survive in the unfamiliar land, the English began sending families from England to farm and learn about the local

Paulistas Portuguese slavers from the southern Brazilian settlement at São Paulo.

Map 17.2   The English and French in North America, ca. 1700
While the English colonized much of the Atlantic coast of North America, the French concentrated on what is today eastern Canada and the interior of North America, including the Great Lakes and the Mississippi and Ohio River Basins.

Basin. To counter English and Spanish expansion, in 1699 the French founded New Orleans, which then became the base for French activities and territorial claims in Louisiana and the Mississippi Valley (see Map 17.2).

The English colonies north of Maryland developed largely as agricultural economies of free white settlers. Settlers clung to the east coast, avoiding the frontier until the 1700s. Although most colonists were farmers, many English and French settlers also came to North America to exploit two valuable commodities, fish and fur. The seas off New England and eastern Canada teamed with cod, which became a major part of the European diet. During the Little Ice Age, cod stocks off Europe greatly diminished and fishermen began to establish bases along the North American coast. Later some English and French immigrants moved inland in search of beavers, whose fur was popular in Europe for women's and men's coats and hats. Fur remained the major Canadian export until the rise of wheat farming in the nineteenth century.

Both French and English settlement disrupted the Indian tribes (now known as "First Nations" in Canada). The French, however, generally maintained better relations with local peoples than did the English, forging alliances with tribal leaders. Nonetheless, in both French and English colonies the Native Americans died from either disease or armed conflict, were pushed north and west, or eventually were forced onto reservations. In the early 1700s various tribes, among them the Tuscarora (tus-kuh-ROR-uh) and Delaware, were forced by English colonists to abandon their coastal territories and move west of the Appalachian Mountains. These relocations foreshadowed worse treatment to come.

Some Indian groups were well organized and proved formidable opponents. The most complex political structure among North American Indians was the Iroquois (EAR-uh-coy) Confederation, a coalition formed in the 1500s to unite five once-warring tribes living between Lake Erie and the Hudson River in what is today upstate New York. These longhouse-dwelling tribes felt a shared ethnicity and a common enemy in the Huron (HYOOR-uhn) of southern Ontario, who established a rival confederation of allied groups. By the 1630s the Iroquois numbered some 16,000. Initially the Iroquois alliance was primarily a nonaggression pact among the members. Later, in the 1690s, it became a pantribal government with a council of chiefs and an oral constitution. Each member tribe had one vote, and unanimity was needed for any decision. Some scholars credit Iroquois political ideas, such as a representative congress and freedom of speech, as an influence on the later constitution of the United States. The Iroquois

environment from Native Americans. In many cases only the generosity of Native Americans, who often shared their knowledge or supplied food, enabled the colonists to survive. By the middle of the seventeenth century English settlements dotted the coast. The Dutch settlement at New York, founded in 1624, also came under English control once the sponsoring Dutch West India Company concluded it could not recruit enough settlers from Holland to offset English immigration.

The French also coveted North America. They established their first settlement in Acadia (what is today the Canadian province of Nova Scotia) in 1604, three years before Jamestown. This was followed by outposts along the St. Lawrence River in today's Quebec (ke-BEK) province, at Quebec City in 1608 and Montreal in 1642. These settlements became the major cities in New France, a colony formally established in 1627 and covering much of eastern Canada. French Jesuit missionaries (known as "Black Robes") undertook campaigns to convert the Native Americans to Catholicism and traveled widely, as far west as today's Illinois, in their pursuit of conversions. By the 1670s French leaders, seeking new resources, were encouraging exploration of the interior. Using canoes, French explorers and trappers, known as **voyageurs** (voi-uh-ZHUR), mapped and established trading outposts throughout the Great Lakes and Mississippi River

---

voyageurs   French explorers and trappers in North America.

were an effective military alliance, generally defeating rival tribes while holding off or outmaneuvering European arrivals for many years. Later the Iroquois supported the English in conflicts against the French, who were allied with their traditional rivals, the Huron and Algonquins (al-GAHN-kwinz). But eventually the Iroquois, Huron, and Algonquins, like other Native Americans, were colonized.

SECTION SUMMARY

■ The Spanish under Cortés were able to conquer the Aztecs because of their superior weaponry, their alliances with other American peoples, and a smallpox epidemic that ravaged the Aztecs.

■ From their base in Mexico, the Spanish pushed north and south, and Pizarro conquered the Incas, the Spanish proceeding to rule much of South America with great cruelty, using the Inca administrative system.

■ The Portuguese fended off attempts by the French and the Dutch to colonize Brazil and enslaved many of its Indians.

■ The Spanish, Portuguese, Dutch, French, and English all struggled for colonial control of the Americas, with pirates from each country preying on other countries' ships.

■ The English established colonies in what is now the eastern United States, while the French did so in eastern Canada, New Orleans, and the Mississippi River Basin.

■ Many North American colonies thrived on fish and fur, while others practiced agriculture, and all eventually pushed native peoples off their lands.

◆ The Consequences of American Colonization

What were the major consequences of European colonization of the Americas?

By the late sixteenth century the Spanish had explored and claimed a massive empire stretching from northern California and the Rocky Mountains southward to southern Chile and Argentina. Throughout this area they formed local governments and founded cities. While the Spanish controlled most of South and Central America and parts of the Caribbean, the English, French, and Dutch established settlements in the Caribbean region and in North America. Despite many similarities in the colonizing process, the American colonies were very different from each other. However, the results almost always came at the expense of the Native American peoples, who suffered especially from the colonists' diseases. Colonization also involved Christian missionary activity and sometimes violent repression of American resistance and culture.

The Columbian Exchange

One result of European exploration and conquest was the transfer of diseases, animals, and plants from one hemisphere to another, what historians refer to as the **Columbian Exchange**. A chief consequence was demographic: virulent microbes brought from the Eastern Hemisphere caused massive depopulation and suffering in the Americas. Of course, although often healthier than Eastern Hemisphere peoples, the Native Americans before 1492 did not live in a disease-free paradise. They suffered from such maladies as polio, hepatitis, some varieties of tuberculosis, many intestinal parasites, and syphilis. Yet, only syphilis, a sexually transmitted disease, seems to have made any serious impact when carried to Europe, although some historians think that, rather than being imported, it already existed there in medieval times. Although deadly to some Europeans, it was more an unpleasant nuisance than a mass killer.

The Native Americans had no immunity to diseases brought by Europeans and later by enslaved Africans. Diseases brought from the Eastern Hemisphere like measles, typhus, influenza, and especially smallpox claimed millions of victims. Smallpox was widespread in Europe in the 1500s and 1600s; hence, practically every ship from Europe carried the virus. Within two centuries the Native American population around the hemisphere was reduced by around 90 percent. No group remained untouched, and some were completely eliminated as the diseases spread destruction and havoc. A Maya writer reported that "great was the stench of the dead. The dogs and vultures devoured the bodies. We were born to die!"[10] Men died at higher rates than women, leaving widows to support households and young girls to grow up without the protection of fathers and male relatives.

The American population numbers began recovering as the most resistant individuals survived and as immigrants from Europe and Africa, who had developed some immunity, intermarried with Native Americans, producing less susceptible children. Eventually Native American populations grew, particularly in more isolated areas. Today the descendants of Maya, Incas, and other pre-Columbian peoples are numerous in the highlands and forests of Central and South America.

The exchange between the two hemispheres affected both sides of the Atlantic. From the one side, Europeans imported their political and social institutions as well as their religious beliefs and urban forms to the Americas. They also brought from Eurasia plants with which they were familiar, such as wheat, orange trees, and grape vines, and domesticated animals such as horses, pigs, chickens, goats, and sheep. Some imports were useful for American peoples. For example, horses brought by the Spanish enabled some of the tribes in the North American Great Plains to hunt buffalo more effectively. From the other side, many American products moved eastward across the Atlantic. Gold and silver from American mines had a

---

Columbian Exchange The transportation of diseases, animals, and plants from one hemisphere to another that resulted from European exploration and conquest between 1492 and 1750.

major impact on the Eurasian economy. American crops such as tobacco, rubber, American cotton (the basis for today's commercial version), potatoes, and maize (corn), as well as drugs such as quinine and coca, spread across the Atlantic. Some of these crops, such as potatoes and tomatoes, increased the abundance of food in Europe. Corn became a major food for Europe's domestic animals. American foods also enriched Asian diets, South American chilies became a mainstay of South and Southeast Asian cooking, making the spicy foods even hotter.

The Spanish Empire in the Americas

The conquered Americans were forced to pay the costs of the conquest. In Spanish America and Portuguese Brazil, some Europeans made great fortunes by exploiting the people, land, minerals, animals, and plants. Gold and silver from the Americas financed the building of the Spanish empire. Once in power, the Spanish and Portuguese seized all the riches they could locate, forced or persuaded the Indians to adopt Christianity, destroyed their religious centers, and murdered Indian leaders who refused to cooperate. Native American languages were discouraged or suppressed in favor of Spanish or Portuguese. While many local peoples resisted the occupying powers as best they could, these efforts were usually futile in the long run. While taking the local peoples' material wealth and disturbing the culture, the new settlers also learned from the people how to survive in these lands, and they also intermarried or had sexual relations with local women, producing people of mixed descent.

In building their American empire, the Spanish appropriated American political structures but also introduced their own institutions and ways. The Spanish colonists established settlements that became large cities, such as Havana, Buenos Aires, Lima, and Mexico City, the last-mentioned built on the site of the Aztec capital, Tenochtitlan. In the 1500s Spain divided its vast empire into two smaller divisions (viceroyalties): New Spain (governed from Mexico City) and Peru (governed from Lima). The top Spanish official in each was the viceroy, a deputy to the king who was always Spanish-born and held great power. Later two more viceroyalties were created in South America. For example, in 1739 the territory that today includes Colombia, Ecuador, Venezuela, and Panama became part of the Viceroyalty of New Granada, administered from Bogotá. Given the huge territories, each viceroyalty had to be subdivided into smaller political units known as **audiencias**, judicial tribunals with administrative functions. The Spanish reserved key political offices, from the governors down to the local mayors, for themselves. In the 1700s political and economic problems in the Americas and Spain forced some reorganization of the colonial system.

In building their empires, the Spanish and other Europeans sometimes faced considerable resistance. Maya Yucatan fell to the Spanish only in 1545 after a long, bitter military struggle. In the 1530s, many Indians rose up in rebellion in Peru. Sporadic resistance continued for two centuries, and the last major resistance by Inca descendants, a rebellion of over 10,000 led by a man calling himself Tupac Amaru II (TOO-pack ah-MAR-oo), after an Inca emperor executed by the Spanish in 1572, erupted in 1780–1781. In New Mexico resentment by some Pueblo peoples against the Spanish and the Catholic Church, which held little tolerance for Native American customs, led to several revolts. The most serious came in 1680, when a respected shaman led a force that pushed the Spanish out of the area. Although the Spanish returned in 1692 and brutally crushed the Pueblo rebels, the revolt prompted them to adopt a more cooperative, less confrontational policy.

New Latin American Societies

Gradually distinctive societies and cultures began to emerge in Spanish America and Brazil, a huge area later known as Latin America. A key group in most of these societies were the **creoles** (KREE-awl), people of Iberian ancestry who were born in Latin America. Other groups stemmed from the mixing of peoples, creating **mestizos**, a blend of white and Indian ancestry, and **mulattos**, a mix of African with white or Indian ancestry or both (see Witness to the Past: Spanish Men and Inca Women). While most creoles enjoyed positions of high status, the two mixed groups held a status between Europeans at the top of the social system and Indians and Africans at the bottom. By the 1700s the mixed groups also represented a sizeable portion of the population in many colonies. For example, Mexico and Peru developed large mestizo groups while mulattos were especially prominent in Brazil and Cuba. People born in Europe tended to view the creoles, mestizos, and mulattos with either condescension or contempt, considering them rustics. In the 1600s a scholar born in Mexico of Spanish parents complained that people in Europe "think that not only the original Indian inhabitants but also those of us who were, by chance, born in [the Americas] of Spanish parents either walk on two legs by divine dispensation or that they are hardly able to discover anything rational in us."[11]

Many writers and artists were born and educated in the Americas. Perhaps the greatest colonial American poet was the creole Mexican nun Sor (Sister) Juana Inez de la Cruz (1651–1695), who also won renown as a playwright, philosopher, and scientist. Influenced by European Enlightenment thinkers, she wrote both secular and religious works. As a young woman she mastered Latin and Aztec while studying logic, history, mathematics, and literature. To pursue her intellectual and literary interests, the well-born Sor Juana chose life in a convent over marriage, eventually collecting the largest

---

audiencias Judicial tribunals with administrative functions that served as subdivisions of viceroyalties in Spanish America.

creoles People of Iberian ancestry who were born in Latin America.

mestizos Groups in Latin America that blended white and Indian ancestry.

mulattos Groups in Latin America that blended African ancestry with white or Indian ancestry or both.

In many parts of Latin America, Spaniards married or cohabitated with Native American women, fostering a mixed, or mestizo, population. In Peru some Spaniards deliberately sought to marry Inca princesses, perhaps to establish local connections in a factionalized colonial society. In this account from the early seventeenth century by the Peruvian historian Garcilaso de la Vega, himself the product of such a match, we learn of an Inca princess who was less than enthusiastic about her Spanish suitor, a captain from a modest background. Her ambivalent response has been viewed by some historians as representing a mixed attitude common in Latin America toward the imposition of European culture: contempt for many European customs and the brutal conquest but also admiration of some European values and Europeans' military power.

... a daughter of [Inca leader] Huaina Cápac and herself ... the owner of the Indians [workers], was married to a very good soldier called Diego Hernández, a very worthy man, who was said in his youth to have been a tailor. ... [Before the marriage] the princess learned this and refused the match, saying that it was unjust to wed the daughter of Huaina Cápac with a ... tailor. Although the Bishop of Cuzco as well as ... other personages who went to attend the ceremony of betrothal, begged and pleaded with her, it was all to no purpose. They then sent to fetch her brother. ... When he came, he took his sister into a corner of the room and told her privately that it was impolitic for her to refuse the match, for by doing so she would render the whole of the [Inca] royal line odious in the eyes of the Spaniards, who would consider them mortal enemies and never accept their friendship again. She agreed, though reluctantly, to her brother's demands, and so appeared before the bishop, who wished to honor the betrothed by officiating at the ceremony.

When the bride was asked through an Indian interpreter if she consented to become the bride and spouse of the aforesaid, the interpreter said "did she want to be the man's wife?" for the Indian language had no verb for consent or for spouse, and he could therefore not have asked anything else.

The bride replied in her own tongue: ... "Maybe I will, maybe I won't." Whereupon the ceremony continued. ... They were still alive and living as man and wife when I left Cuzco.

Other marriages of this kind took place throughout the empire, and were arranged so as to give allocations of Indians to [Spanish] claimants and reward them with other people's properties. Many, however, were dissatisfied, some because their income was small and others because their wives were ugly; there is no perfect satisfaction in this world.

THINKING ABOUT THE READING

1. What does the reading tell us about social attitudes among Incas and Spaniards in colonial Peru?
2. What do we learn about the treatment of women?
3. How might the princess's attitude be seen as a form of resistance?

Source: Garcilaso de la Vega, *Royal Commentaries of the Incas and General History of Peru*, Part Two. Translated by Harold V. Livermore (Austin: University of Texas Press, 1966), pp. 1229–1230. Copyright © 1966 by the University of Texas Press. Reprinted with permission.

private library in Mexico, some 4,000 volumes. Sor Juana also struggled against patriarchal customs, arguing that "like men, do women not have a rational soul? Shall they not enjoy the privilege of the enlightenment of letters? Why is she not as able to receive as much learning and science?"[12] Another keen mind, the Mexican scholar and cleric Carlos de Siglienza y Gongora (1645–1700), was a close friend of Sor Juana who won fame as a poet, historian, mathematician, and astronomer.

Despite creative, broad-minded figures such as Sor Juana, Latin American culture remained more closely connected to the Catholic Church than was the case in western Europe, which was reshaped by the Renaissance and Enlightenment. To screen out what they considered dangerous ideas, the church had to approve all printed matter entering the colonies. The church-controlled universities, which were set up to train creole men for careers as colonial officials and priests, taught largely in Latin and employed clerics as instructors. Spanish officials also brought the ruthless, counter-reform Holy Inquisition to the colonies to root out heresy. People suspected of having secret Jewish or Protestant sympathies were tried. In particular those of *converso* background, Jews forced to convert to Christianity in Spain and their descendants, were subject to investigation, imprisonment, and sometimes gruesome executions. In the past few decades hundreds of people in the United States of Mexican and Spanish heritage have rediscovered their Jewish roots suppressed for centuries.

Latin American societies exhibited dramatic contradictions: while many of the elite looked toward Europe for inspiration, the majority of the population wanted to preserve the languages, beliefs, and ways of life from pre-Columbian times. A Spanish observer wrote of the Mexicans who remained "suspended in the middle between a lost past and a present that has not been understood."[13] Latin American writers often examined the conflicted relationship between Spain and Latin America, describing a mix of good and evil or, as one put it, sun and shadow, as in the bullfight ring. Such a mix might also describe the experiences of people in the Portuguese, English, and French colonies.

Women faced the greatest dilemmas in Latin America, often both accepting and repudiating Spanish rule. They now enjoyed new food sources, such as chickens and pigs, but they also clung to their native dress and pride. They had to be flexible and adaptive to survive. Since men had higher mortality rates, women were often heads of households. Despite patriarchal traditions, some Indians and mestizo women engaged in commerce while others worked in domestic service, tended animals, or made clothing, including carding, spinning, and weaving wool from sheep.

Christian Missions and Native Americans

Both the Spanish and the Portuguese were committed to spreading Catholicism as part of their imperial enterprise. Although they enjoyed only mixed success, missionaries were frequently militant in their faith and often had a profound influence. The mission impact on Latin American Indians came in different forms. Sometimes missionary activity altered people's settlement and even economic patterns. For example, in the eighteenth century, the Spanish Franciscan missionary Fray Junipero Serra (SER-uh) (1713–1784), known as the "walking friar" because he traveled by foot, established mission stations along the coast of California as far north as San Francisco. Not only did he convert many Indians to the faith, but Serra also encouraged and sometimes required seminomadic hunters and gatherers, like the Chumash (CHOO-mash) of the Santa Barbara area, to live in towns and cultivate crops imported from Europe. Forts were built near mission stations, allowing the Spanish to extend their control much further north.

Often the results of missionary activity were disastrous for Native Americans. In Yucatan, for instance, a few missionaries gained control over many Maya people. Although these missionaries sometimes admired Maya culture, such as the ancient writing system, they were also intolerant of non-Christian beliefs and destroyed Maya books and religious symbols, which they considered pagan. In 1562 some priests who suspected that certain converts continued to secretly worship Mayan gods launched a terrible inquisition and tortured 4,500 Indians, 158 of whom died. One witness reported that "the friars ordered great stones attached to their feet, and so they were left to hang for a space, and if they did not admit to a greater quantity of idols, they were flogged as they hung there and had burning wax splashed on their bodies."[14] The church punished the priest in charge but later made him a bishop.

As the Maya account illustrates, the missionaries often faced resistance. In the former Inca territories, for example, many women openly rejected Catholicism in the 1500s. According to a Spanish observer: "They do not confess, attend catechism classes, or go to mass. Returning to their ancient customs and idolatry, they do not want to serve God or the [Spanish] crown."[15] Native Americans could also put their stamp on Christianity. Although some historians believe the story was introduced many decades later to promote conversions, in 1531 an Aztec peasant supposedly saw a vision of the Virgin Mary at a shrine to the Aztec mother goddess. A church was later built there to honor "Our Lady of Guadalupe," and the image of the virgin as an Indian woman became a symbol of Mexican nationalism.

The Black Legend: The Spanish Treatment of Indian Peoples

Spanish actions led to the **Black Legend**, the Spanish reputation for brutality toward Native Americans, including the repression of native religions, execution of rebels, and forced labor. The Spanish were particularly zealous in persecuting homosexuals. While the Aztecs and Incas both condemned homosexuality, many Native American peoples, including the Mayas and Caribs, were tolerant of same-sex relations. The Spanish brought homosexuals before the Inquisition for punishment, or sometimes, executed them without trial, and used the charge of widespread homosexuality to justify treating Native Americans like animals. Although the Black Legend exaggerated Spanish atrocities, Spain's enemies in Europe eagerly passed along such stories. Actually, disease killed far more Indians than murder and brutality. Nor were the Spanish the only culprits; the other European settlers could be just as intolerant and forceful in their dealings with local peoples.

While many Spaniards saw the Native Americans as savages needing to be Christianized and ruled by a "superior" Spanish society, other Spaniards wanted to protect local people from exploitation. The Spanish debated the treatment of Indians, and some Catholic clerics advocated humane policies and sought to protect them. For example, the Dominican friar Bartolomé de Las Casas (lahs KAH-suhs) (1474–1566), although an ardent missionary for Catholicism, proclaimed that Indians were humans like the Spanish and bemoaned the destruction they experienced. A few observers, such as the Spanish lawyer Francisco de Vitoria in the 1500s, even questioned the whole project of Western colonization, suggesting that policies should always promote Indian welfare and interests and not only Spanish profits. In 1637 the Jesuits in what is today Uruguay (YOOR-uh-gwye) even armed the Indians to help protect them against slave raiders.

Online Study Center **Improve Your Grade**
Primary Source: A Dominican Voice in the Wilderness: Preaching Against Tyranny in Hispaniola

But the battle over how to treat Indians was won by intolerant people reflecting the values of a Europe engulfed in religious conflict between Catholics and Protestants (see Chapter 15). Most Spaniards considered the Indians justly conquered and favored exploitation of people they considered born for servitude, enhancing the Black Legend. A Spanish scholar expressed a common contempt for Indians, who, in his view, were "naturally lazy and vicious, in general a lying, shiftless people [whose] chief desire is to eat, drink, worship heathen idols, and commit bestial obscenities."[16] These harsh attitudes often affected women even more than men. In 1625, an Indian writer in Peru charged that white men exploited both women's labor and their bodies: "In the mines, Indian

Black Legend The Spanish reputation for brutality toward Native Americans, including the repression of native religions, execution of rebels, and forced labor.

Indian Slavery Spain's enemies publicized cases of Spanish brutality toward Native Americans. This sixteenth-century engraving, by the Dutch observer Theodore de Bry, portrays the misery of Native Americans subjected to slavery and forced labor. (Courtesy of John Carter Brown Library at Brown University)

their passage. Many immigrants took up farming, especially in the northern colonies. By 1730 the thirteen colonies contained around 500,000 European settlers. African slaves or their descendants, constituting 20 percent of the total colonial population, were concentrated in the South but were also found in the northern colonies such as New York.

Intellectual and religious diversity characterized English colonial life. Educated colonists were often influenced by English and French Enlightenment thinkers, such as John Locke and Baron de Montesquieu (maw-tuh-SKYOO), and espoused democratic ideals and reason. Many early English immigrants were Protestant religious dissenters seeking freedom of religion. The Puritans had an important influence on the colonial culture, especially in the north, implanting Calvinist attitudes about the value of work and commerce. In 1695 Cotton Mather, a famed Puritan preacher, stated the Puritan case vigorously: "How can you ordinarily enjoy any rest at Night, if you have not been well at work in the Day? Let your Business ingross the most of your time."[18] Puritans also maintained patriarchal attitudes. One, John Winthrop, the first governor of the Massachusetts colony, argued that women lost their reason if they gave themselves wholly to reading and writing instead of keeping their place and attending to household affairs.

Yet, to ensure survival through adaptability, colonial life also fostered change, even in gender roles. Deference to men remained deeply ingrained, and a husband had the legal right to his wife's property and wages and the couple's children. But not all women were limited to household chores. Given the labor shortage, they worked in the fields alongside men, and a few even managed farms or plantations. Partly because many women worked outside the home, most English colonists married late.

North of New York and New England, the English and French clashed for decades over control of Acadia (Nova Scotia) and New France, in what is today eastern Canada. This conflict resulted in part from a larger English-French competition for influence in Europe, the Caribbean, and southern Asia and in part over access to sources of fish and fur. Eventually England triumphed over France in North America. In 1713 the English took control of Acadia, and in 1755 they deported much of the Acadian French population to the French colony

women are made into concubines, daughters of Indian men are kidnapped. In the villages, [Spanish men convert] single women, married women, all women into prostitutes. Parish priests have concubines. There is no one who takes these women's side."[17]

This contempt, along with the economic needs of the colonies, led to the drafting of Indians to work in mines or farms. Missionaries gave them a superficial Christianity, changing local gods into Christian saints, but many Indians continued to secretly worship old gods and ancestors. After the initial violence, the church treated Indians indulgently and paternalistically, as children needing guidance. But, as a result of conquest, the Indian quality of life—health, morale, leisure, and joy—mostly declined. Demoralization and disease generated alcoholism and despair. Today many Latin American Indians remain dominated politically, socially, and economically by creoles and mestizos.

English and French Colonies in North America

The English and French competed for control in North America while expanding their settlements (see Map 17.2). By the mid-1700s the territory from New England south to Georgia was divided into thirteen separate English colonies, each administered by an appointed English governor. Immigration from Europe into the colonies increased, especially from England but also from Scotland, Ireland, Germany, and the Netherlands. Some from poor or criminal backgrounds emigrated as indentured laborers, signing contracts to work on farms or in businesses, workshops, or households to repay

Johnson Hall This grand house, built in the mid-eighteenth century by American fur trader William Johnson in what is now upstate New York, became a meeting place for Native American tribes, such as the Iroquois, allied with the British against the French. (*Johnson Hall* by Edward Lamson Henry (1841–1919), 1903. Oil on canvas 21 1/4 x 37 inches. Albany Institute of History and Art Purchase 1933.44)

of Louisiana, forming the basis for the French-speaking Cajun (KAY-juhn) community there, which today numbers nearly a million (see Chronology: The Americas, 1650–1760). In 1759 English forces defeated the French near Quebec City and in 1760 captured Montreal, gaining control over New France. French cultural influence was eventually confined chiefly to the large area of eastern Canada, once the heart of New France, now known as the province of Quebec. In 1774 the English, recognizing the tenacity of French culture, allowed the French in Quebec to hold public office, speak their language, and freely practice their religion.

The French Canadians became a permanent and rapidly growing presence in Quebec. French immigration to Canada largely ended, but the French Canadian population increased dramatically, and today it totals more than 7 million, one-fourth of Canada's population. The great majority of French Canadians live in Quebec province. Between the 1600s and mid-1900s the highly influential Catholic Church in Quebec encouraged early marriage and large families, in striking contrast to English colonists. The French Canadians always felt threatened by the more numerous and politically dominant English, a concern that may have fostered cultural conservatism. Meanwhile, both the French and the English Canadians settled down to farming, like their neighbors in New England.

At the same time, the relations between European settlers and Indian societies in North America remained complex, including both antagonism and alliance. Indians resented and often resisted the foreigners' occupation of their land, and the English and French had to deal carefully with the better-organized tribes and federations, and skirmishes between whites and Indians were common. But some Indians were inevitably drawn into the often violent English-French competition for global influence. Indians such as the Huron allied with the French; some, including the Iroquois, allied with the English; and some opposed both. Yet, because European traders acquired fur from Indians, trade was also part of the story. In fact, the Huron alliance with the French and the Iroquois alliance with the English largely reflected trading partnerships. The fur trade had an additional result. As French fur traders ventured into the interior and set up trading posts far from the cities, they tended to intermarry with Indians, producing the

CHRONOLOGY

The Americas, 1650–1760

ca. 1605–1694	Palmares maroon state
1713	English control of Acadia
1739	Stono Rebellion in South Carolina
1755	Deportation of French Acadians to Louisiana
1759	English defeat of French in Quebec

Metis (may-TEES), people of mixed French and Indian descent. Today Metis communities are scattered around Canada. In contrast, English and many French colonists tended to immigrate as families, reducing the rates of intermarriage with Indians.

The encounter with Europeans reshaped North American Indian life. Most obviously, the Europeans' seizure of Indian lands made living much more difficult for the Indians. In 1705 an English observer, Robert Beverley, noted that "they have on several accounts to lament the arrival of the English [who] have taken away great part of their country, and consequently made everything less plenty among them."[19] The Indians mistrusted the Europeans, who often broke treaties, and they were often repelled by European culture, but they also desired European trade goods, especially metal work and guns. A few tribes, like the Cherokee in the Carolinas and Georgia, who probably numbered some 30,000 in the mid-1500s, actively adopted European influences, such as new farming methods, although this often came at the expense of women, who once did most of the farming and hence enjoyed high status. Christian missionaries, whether Catholic or Protestant, had less success in North America than in Latin America. Indeed, the English devoted few resources to the missionary effort. Most missionary success came among settled farmers, and there it often fostered change. For example, among matrilineal societies like the Huron and Cherokee, missionaries undermined the traditional power and freedom of women. Imposing patriarchal Christian marriage practices increased the power of husbands by emphasizing the obedience of wives. In some tribes spousal abuse increased as men who lost their ability to support their families turned their aggression on their wives.

SECTION SUMMARY

- As a result of American colonization, huge numbers of Native Americans died from smallpox, and many animal and plant species were exchanged between Europe and the Americas, in what is called the Columbian Exchange.

- The Spanish exploited the resources of their American colonies and ruled them harshly, inspiring several rebellions and earning the label of the "Black Legend," though other countries sometimes used similar methods.

- In the Spanish American colonies, a recognizable culture developed, more rigidly Catholic than in Europe and featuring American-born Spanish (creoles) and mixed-race peoples (mestizos and mulattos).

- In their attempts to convert Native Americans to Catholicism, the Spanish and Portuguese often trampled on Native American customs and beliefs, and they crushed perceived resistance harshly. As English colonists solidified their control of the East Coast and eventually took over all of French Canada, Indian tribes were often caught between the warring powers.

Metis People in Canada of mixed French and Indian descent.

New American Economies

How did the development of the American economies lead to the trans-Atlantic slave trade?

Quite different economic and social systems emerged in Latin America and northern English America. In much of Latin America, the Caribbean, and some of the southern colonies of North America, European rule produced an inequitable economic relationship between the colonies and their colonizing countries. These colonies all produced resources for the growing world economy and were based largely on mining or plantation agriculture. The plantations depended chiefly on slave labor imported from Africa (see Chapter 16). The experience of the colonies specializing in mining and plantation agriculture, where many people lived in dire poverty, contrasted sharply with the northern English colonies in North America, which emphasized commerce and family farming and gradually moved toward economic independence.

Economic Change in Latin America

From the beginning the Latin American colonies were largely geared to export natural resources (see Map 17.3). In the Andes and Mexico the Spanish developed rich gold and silver mines. The Incas and Aztecs and the societies that preceded them had mined some silver and gold to make ceremonial objects and jewelry, but under Spain the scale of mining increased dramatically. The silver mines discovered by the Spanish in 1545 in the Andes highlands of today's Bolivia became some of the richest in the world. Drafted to labor in the mining economy, Indian mine workers in the main Andean mining center, Potosi (po-tuh-SEE), found life difficult, "working twelve hours a day, going down seven hundred feet, down to where night is perpetual, the air thick and ill smelling. When they arrive at the top out of breath, [they] find a mineowner who scolds them because they did not bring enough load."[20] By the late 1600s the mines of Mexico produced over half of the mineral wealth from the Western Hemisphere, and in the early 1700s gold mines in Brazil, mostly worked by African slaves, became increasingly valuable to the Portuguese. For much of the eighteenth century Brazil supplied over half of the world's gold.

While providing few benefits to the Native Americans, mining brought prosperity to colonial cities such as Lima, enriched merchants, filled royal treasuries, and linked the colonies to the world economy. Most of the wealth was exported, with much of the gold ultimately passing through Spain and Portugal to northern Europe as payment for manufactured goods. This transfer enriched first Flanders, then Holland, and later England. In the 1800s Brazilians mused that Brazilian gold mined by African slaves helped finance English industrialization. American silver also bought Europeans access to other world markets, especially in Asia. A large portion of American silver was shipped to China, where it purchased desirable Chinese products such as silk and tea.

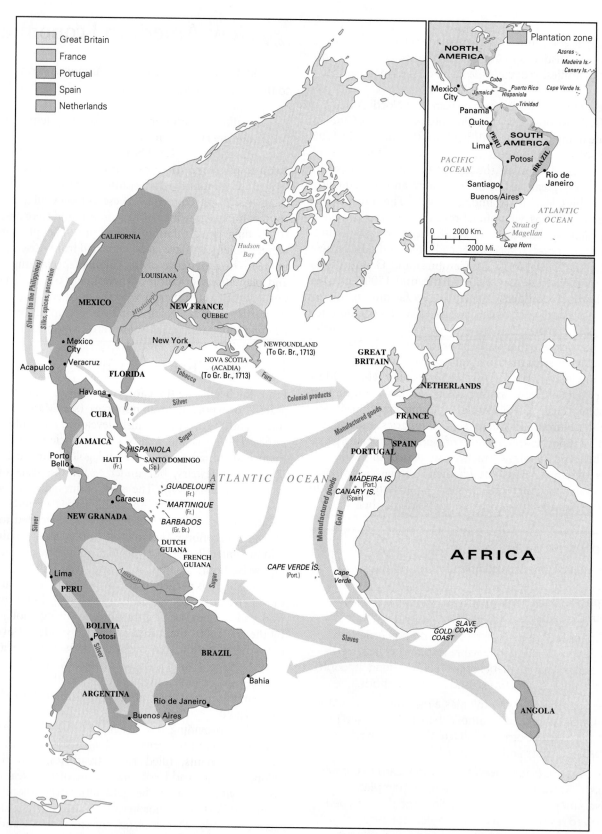

Map 17.3   The Atlantic Economy
The Atlantic economy was based on a triangular trade in which African slaves were shipped to the Americas to produce raw materials that were chiefly exported to Europe, where they were turned into manufactured goods and exported to Africa and the Americas.

While mining flourished in only a few mountainous areas, ranching became a major economic activity in many other regions. Cattle and horses brought from Europe enabled many settlers to take up ranching, especially in the vast grasslands of what is today Argentina and Venezuela. With Indian communities weak or dying, good land passed into European hands. Some of these lands were developed into vast cattle ranches, known in Spanish America as **haciendas**, that were often over 1 million acres in size. One Brazilian cattle ranch was larger than most European states. Ranching has remained a key economic activity in several countries, including Mexico, Venezuela, Argentina, Chile, and Brazil. Like the mines, the ranches provided great incomes for monarchs, merchants, and investors.

During the early 1500s, to ensure Indian labor the Spanish imposed some version of the **encomienda** ("entrustment"), the Crown's grant to a colonial Spaniard of a certain number of Indians from whom he extracted tribute. In exchange for providing labor, such as in the gold and silver mines, the Indians were instructed in Christianity by clergy. While in theory this system protected Indians, in fact it fostered many abuses. A Spanish Franciscan condemned the cruelties of the mine owners, who pursued profit at the expense of encomienda workers: "The Indian slaves who up to the present have died in these [gold] mines cannot be counted. Gold, in this land, was adored as a god."[21] Because of the abuses, Spanish monarchs sometimes sought to abandon the encomienda policy but relented in the face of revolt by Spanish colonists. By the mid-1500s the institution had been reformed considerably, but the system still allowed temporary conscription of Indian labor. Although it tolerated some abuses, the system was maintained until the later 1600s.

Despite the early Spanish and Portuguese successes in developing their colonies, Latin America eventually fell behind North America in economic development. The contrast between an increasingly stagnant Latin American economy and a vibrant North American economy became dramatic by the 1800s. At the outset, Latin America had many advantages British North America lacked: rich gold and silver mines, abundant fertile land, and a much larger population. By the 1700s Latin Americans, unlike North Americans, had built a half dozen large cities and many fine universities, and the region produced great wealth, although it was inequitably distributed. The failure of Latin American and Caribbean societies to match the economic vigor of North America resulted in part from the rise of single-product, slave-based plantations, which, like mining or ranching, fostered specialized economic production for a world market.

In the Caribbean region and parts of Latin America and North America, the plantations, like the mines and ranches, contributed to creating a system of **monoculture**, an economy dependent on the production and export of one chief commodity. Monocultures resulted in a highly specialized economic life in much of Latin America and the Caribbean islands. They were usually based on slave or coerced labor and were completely dependent on the colonizing country to buy the resource, such as sugar, silver, or beef, they produced. In return the colonizing country supplied food and other necessities to the colonized society. Plantation, mining, or ranching-based economies, however, cannot generate overall **development**, growth in a variety of economic areas that benefits the majority of people. Monoculture economies generally benefit only one segment of a population, and they prosper or decline depending on world prices for their export commodity. With few alternative forms of employment or ways to generate wealth, plantation and mining societies remained dangerously specialized, creating significant poverty. This was the condition associated with the economic stagnation of Latin America and the Caribbean as the North American economy was on the rise.

The Plantation Zone and African Slavery

At first, mines and ranches dominated the Latin American economy, but the plantation soon became the key economic institution in much of the tropical and subtropical areas of the South American mainland, the Caribbean islands, and also in southeastern North America. The first American plantations emerged in Brazil, where sugar was grown along the coast by the early 1500s. By the later 1600s, when most of the richest silver mines in the Andes and Mexico had been exhausted, plantations were flourishing in many regions, growing sugar, coffee, cotton, bananas, and sisal (a tough fiber used to make rope) for shipment to North America and Europe. The plantations depended on the labor of African slaves and their descendants.

The transition to a plantation economy created the **plantation zone**, a group of societies with economies relying on enslaved African labor and stretching from Virginia and Kentucky southward through the West Indies and the east coast of Central America to central Brazil and the Pacific coast of Colombia. The changes were particularly striking in the Caribbean islands, where sugar planting transformed whole economies. European settlers were first attracted to Caribbean islands such as Jamaica, Barbados, Hispaniola, Cuba, and Puerto Rico, and in the later 1500s and early 1600s they set up self-sufficient farms that grew diverse crops. But in the mid-1600s the growing of sugar, much more profitable than the other crops, expanded. Since sugar growing needed plentiful land and cheap labor to become profitable, white farmers were

---

haciendas   Vast ranches in Spanish America.

encomienda ("entrustment")   The Crown's grant to a colonial Spaniard in Latin America of a certain number of Indians from whom he extracted tribute.

monoculture   An economy dependent on the production and export of one chief commodity.

development   Growth in a variety of economic areas that benefits the majority of people; the opposite of monoculture.

plantation zone   A group of societies with economies that relied on enslaved African labor; the plantation zone stretched from Virginia and Kentucky southward through the West Indies and the east coast of Central America to central Brazil and the Pacific coast of Colombia.

Caribbean Sugar Mill On a West Indian plantation this windmill crushed sugar cane into juice, which was boiled down in the smoking building on the right to produce sugar granules. Such plantations were the dominant economic activity on the Caribbean islands and in parts of South America, Central America, and southeastern North America. (From William Clark, *Ten Views in the Islands of Antigua, 1823*. British Library)

gradually displaced by plantations using slave labor. In the West Indies, laws that prevented plantation owners from growing anything but sugar protected the profits of the colonial elite. Some white farmers became planters; those who could find no role in the new plantation economy often migrated to North America, while a few of the more desperate became pirates.

The growing sugar industry fostered transitions in Europe as well as the Americas. During the Intermediate Era Europeans, especially Venetians, imported sugar from the Arabs and, more rarely, from Southeast Asia, but supplies were limited. To satisfy increasing demand, in 1450 the Portuguese began growing sugar on small Atlantic islands such as Madeira. The desire to acquire more land for growing sugar boosted the European drive for empire in the Americas. With the rise of the American plantations and cheaper supplies, sugar was transformed from a rare luxury to an everyday necessity, becoming a staple of the European diet. Sugar sweetened bland foods and provided more calories for the often undernourished working classes. In England, the use of sugar in foods led to the replacement of large midday family meals with jam sandwiches and tea. Foods

and beverages containing sugar also allowed people to take their lunches with them and stay at work all day, in this way helping to foster an industrial economy in Britain.

The plantation economies of the Caribbean islands and some coastal districts in what is today Brazil, the Guianas, Venezuela, Colombia, and Mexico were essentially sugar "factories," relying on mass production of raw sugar by enslaved workers. A seventeenth-century saying noted that "without sugar, no Brazil; without slaves, no sugar; without Angola, no slaves."[22] The southern English colonies of North America differed from these Caribbean and Latin American economies only in that the crops were more varied: cotton, rice, and tobacco were grown as well as sugar. But the systems throughout the plantation zone were similar. In particular, the populations of all the plantation-based societies were composed chiefly of enslaved people of African ancestry. Slavery as a key institution stretched from the southern half of what became the United States through the Caribbean Basin and down the South American coast to central Brazil in the east and coastal Peru in the west.

The needs of the plantation economy, and the high mortality rates of enslaved labor, required the constant importation of slaves from Africa. Between 1500 and 1850 some 9 to 12 million Africans were brought into the Americas, especially to the plantation zone, as slaves. Most went to the Caribbean islands, where they became the majority population, and to Brazil, which today has the largest population of African descent in the Americas. However, African slaves were also used outside the plantation zone, in northern English colonies such as New York, New Jersey, and Massachusetts and as far south as Argentina, though on a much smaller scale. By 1850 Brazil received some 40 percent of all enslaved Africans, followed by the British Caribbean (21 percent), French Caribbean (15 percent), Spanish America (15 percent), and British North America (5 percent). About one-third of all people of African descent eventually lived in the Western Hemisphere.

As the number of transported Africans increased in the later 1600s and early 1700s, many societies in which slaves were a minority of the population were transformed into societies in which slaves constituted a majority. Given their status as enslaved workers, Africans occupied the bottom of the social ladder, where life was extremely harsh. On some sugar plantations, as many as half the slaves died within two or three years of arrival. Today the descendants of enslaved Africans constitute the large majority in Jamaica, Haiti, Barbados, the Bahamas, and most other Caribbean islands; half the population of Trinidad, Belize, Suriname, and Guyana; and substantial minorities in Brazil, Cuba, Puerto Rico, the Dominican Republic, Panama, Venezuela, Colombia, and the United States.

Economic Growth in English North America

Some English North American colonies had a different economic, and eventually political, fate than colonies with monoculture economies, such as those in the plantation zone. To explain these varied outcomes, some historians contrast the English culture, energized by capitalism and religious diversity, with the semimedieval Catholic culture of Spain and Portugal. In this view, Latin Americans were inhibited by an unwillingness to fight authority, an acceptance of poverty as God's will, and disinterest toward new or different ideas. Other historians, however, believe that colonial policies were responsible for the differences between English and Latin America: the northern English colonies enjoyed more autonomy than the Spanish colonies.

Historians also contend that, while both the cultural and colonial patterns were influential, the colonial economies and the social diversity they fostered also played a role. Conditions in the northern English colonies created economies that were strikingly different from the monocultures common elsewhere in the Americas. The northern colonies lacked mines to fill galleons with gold and silver or a large Native American labor force to exploit. Nor did they have the soil or climate for profitable tropical crops such as sugar or tobacco, or open grasslands for ranching. Slaves in the north mostly worked for farms, businesses, or households. In addition, the immigrant population was largely composed of farmers, artisans, and merchants. With these working people, the northern economies were less dependent on slave plantations and the severe social inequality they fostered.

In turn, the economic conditions contributed to differing administrative policies. In contrast to the Latin American colonial administrations, the British allowed their colonies from New Jersey north through New England considerable freedom to build diversified economies for the local market. More concerned with their more valuable Caribbean islands, such as Jamaica, the world's largest sugar producer in the 1700s, as well as plantation-dominated colonies such as South Carolina and Virginia, the British imposed fewer restrictions on New York or Massachusetts. Merchants from Boston, Providence, and New York competed with the English in the Caribbean to obtain sugar and molasses, which was converted to rum and shipped to Africa for slaves. In this way, North Americans became active in the trans-Atlantic slave trade. Some North Americans, like Europeans, amassed huge profits from the slave trade, profits that were then invested in their own broad-based economies. The northern English colonies moved toward development, while the southern English colonies, Latin America, and the Caribbean maintained largely undiversified economies.

In sum, those Latin American and Caribbean colonies with the most abundant natural and human resources to exploit had the greater short-term economic growth but less eventual development. By contrast, the northern English colonies, with fewer resources, had the opposite experience. As a result, some of the most profitable American colonies of the past, such as Haiti, Jamaica, Peru, Bolivia, and Guatemala, are now among the world's poorest countries, and northeast Brazil is one of Brazil's poorest regions, while the less profitable northern English colonies eventually became among the most developed regions in the world.

SECTION SUMMARY

- Using Indian labor imposed through the encomienda system, Spanish colonists became wealthy at first through ranching and mining gold and silver, but their economies eventually suffered from its lack of diversification.

- Plantations run with African slave labor and focused on producing a single product—sugar in Latin America and the Carribean, cotton in southeastern North America—also eventually created impoverished societies.

- As a result of the plantation system, sugar went from being a rarity to being a fundamental part of the European diet, and its use helped make the English industrial revolution possible.

- Areas of the Americas with the greatest natural resources ended up being the poorest, while those with the least natural resources, such as the northern English colonies, were forced to develop more broad-based economies and became wealthy and well developed.

CAETANA, SLAVE REBEL AGAINST PATRIARCHY

Thanks to a fascinating court case from Brazil in the 1830s, we learn about a remarkable female slave, Caetana, who challenged patriarchy. Caetana was born around 1818 on a large Rio Clara plantation owned by Captain Luis Mariano de Tolosa, in the Paraiba (par-uh-EE-buh) River Valley in south-eastern Brazil. The plantation life Caetana experienced had not changed dramatically since the 1700s. At Rio Clara about half of the slaves had been born in Africa while the other half, like Caetana, were born in Brazil. By 1835 coffee had become a major cash crop. Most of the 134 Rio Clara slaves, both men and women, planted, maintained, and harvested the 30,000 coffee bushes, often with children in tow. Some slaves raised other crops, tended cattle, or worked as artisans such as carpenters, blacksmiths, and stonemasons. The house slaves worked in Tolosa's mansion, experiencing less strenuous indoor work such as cooking, cleaning, laundering and ironing clothes, carrying water, emptying kitchen slop and human waste, delivering

Women Slaves in Brazil   This 1861 painting shows a personal maid, much like Caetana, instructing slave girls in making lace on a Brazilian plantation. Such slave girls often wore colorful skirts and, like the instructor, earrings.   (Courtesy, Fundacao Biblioteca Nacional, Rio de Janeiro)

✦ The Legacy of Slavery and the Atlantic System

What impact did the emerging Atlantic System have on Europe and the American societies?

Perhaps the major impact of the trans-Atlantic slave trade and the emergence of the American plantation zone was to forcibly link West Africa, the Americas, and Europe into a larger Atlantic System. Historians speak of a triangular trade, a vast network that saw the movement of enslaved Africans to the Americas, where they became largely plantation labor growing sugar, cotton, and tobacco for shipment to Europe. European merchants then used the lucrative proceeds from slave labor to purchase guns, rum, textiles, and other commodities for shipment to Africa to obtain more enslaved labor. As a result, enslaved Africans and their descendants reshaped the economies, social patterns, and cultures of many societies. The profits from the slave trade and the enterprises it served also influenced the development of European economies.

Slave Life and Resistance

The lives of African slaves and their unfree descendants in the Americas were governed by the imperatives of the marketplace and not by humane considerations. In contrast to the treatment of slaves in many African societies, colonial America gave enslaved people few if any legal or customary rights. They were treated simply as cost items in the production process, to be bought and sold at the whim of the owners. Since the markets for sugar and other plantation crops expanded, slave owners sought maximum profit regardless of the human consequences,

messages, nursing infants, or taking care of the older Tolosa children. In exchange for better food and medical care than was given the field hands, they were expected to be obedient and loyal.

Caetana lived in a close-knit relationship to kin, including her mother, Pulicena, and her sister, married to the free-born mulatto, Joao Ribeira da Silva, who was probably a supervisor of field hands. Caetana was also close to her aunt, the freed slave Luisa Jacinta, whose husband, Alexandre, served as Caetana's godfather and male authority figure. Caetana grew up speaking Portuguese with no direct knowledge of African ways or the terrible Middle Passage across the Atlantic. From a young age she served in the Tolosa house as a personal maid to the Tolosa women, including two daughters, and was trusted and allowed into their private quarters.

In 1835 Tolosa, without consulting her, ordered Caetana, then around seventeen, to marry Custodio, a slave in his mid-twenties, in a wedding blessed by the Catholic Church. Custodio was a master tailor who may have cut and sewn the rough cotton clothes worn by slaves and probably also made clothes for the Tolosa family. Like many slave owners, Tolosa may have believed that slave marriages fostered social stability and diminished the threat of rebellion. Perhaps he also feared that an unmarried house slave, representing unyoked female sexuality, might be a bad influence on his two daughters, twelve and two years old, and temptation for his three adolescent sons. Most adult slave women at Rio Clara were married. Caetana, however, refused Tolosa's order, saying, according to court records, that she felt "a great repugnance for the state of matrimony" and found Custodio especially distasteful. In the end she obeyed, succumbing to the pleas of her family and fearing Tolosa's threats to punish her by assigning her to field work or selling her to another plantation. But after priests performed the ceremony and the couple moved into her aunt and uncle's house, she refused to sleep with Custodio, humiliating and enraging him.

After her uncle and godfather, Alexandre, threatened to beat her if she did not submit to her husband, and with few options, Caetana fled to Tolosa's mansion and pleaded to have the marriage ended. Her rebellion was apparently not against plantation slavery as such but against male authority over her. Caetana's action against the entire system of male power—slave owner, uncle, husband, church—threw Rio Clara into turmoil. After his threats to sell Caetana or reassign her to onerous field work failed, Tolosa relented, giving her protection from her husband and asking a church court to issue an annulment. In court, Caetana complained that she was "reduced to the hard necessity of obeying solely from fear of grave punishment and lasting harm." The legal case took five years, including appeals, with the church ultimately refusing the annulment request.

We do not know why, against such long odds, she rebelled, why she despised marriage, or what ultimately happened to Caetana. Perhaps she envied unmarried free women, who were often respected, or the chaste nuns in the convents. The records do not indicate whether she continued to evade the marriage, but it seems unlikely she complied. She might have been sold to another plantation, before or after Tolosa died in 1853. What we do know is that Caetana bravely refused a demand to do something against her will.

THINKING ABOUT THE PROFILE

1. What does Caetana's experience tell us about life on a Brazilian plantation?

2. What does her rebellion tell us about the Brazilian system of patriarchy?

Note: Quotations from Sandra Lauderdale Graham, *Caetana Says No: Women's Stories from a Brazilian Slave Society* (New York: Cambridge University Press, 2002), pp. 2, 57.

---

and those consequences were often severe. Enslaved Africans experienced a high mortality rate, dying from mistreatment, disease, infant mortality, and disrupted family life. Slave women faced rape or sexual harassment by male owners and slaves.

Slaves owners organized slave labor to squeeze out profits. In Brazil, for example, while enslaved Africans and their unfree descendants labored in a wide variety of economic activities, including gold mining and cattle ranching, the great majority worked in agriculture, especially on sugar, coffee, and tobacco estates. The average Brazilian sugar plantation in the seventeenth and eighteenth centuries owned between eighty and one hundred enslaved workers. Some of them worked as mule drivers, sugar makers, household servants, or even low-level managers, but most were field hands who were each expected to produce three-quarters of a ton of sugar a year. The slave owner recovered the cost of purchasing and maintaining

slaves after about three years of such production. Brazilian slave owners earned profits from any additional years of hard work but had little incentive to maintain the health of slaves no longer able to work hard. With two men for every woman, the Brazilian population with African ancestry did not grow very rapidly and required constant replenishment from Africa. Encouraged by the Catholic Church to marry, many Brazilian slaves formed families, even though they could be broken up by sale.

Africans and their descendants often resisted the slave system. Some, like the Brazilian woman Caetana, risked severe punishment by defending their interests in a complex social system (see Profile: Caetana, Slave Rebel Against Patriarchy). Some slaves, known as **maroons** (muh-ROONS) in the English

---

maroons Slaves who escaped from plantations and set up African-type societies in the interior of several American colonies.

Caribbean, escaped from plantations and set up African-type societies in the interior of several American colonies, including Brazil, Colombia, Jamaica, Haiti, Dutch Guiana, and some of the southern colonies in North America. Maroons often recreated African cultures by mixing influences, such as religious concepts, from the various African ethnic groups involved. African women led at least two of the ten major maroon societies in Brazil. Since the colonial governments sent in military forces to recapture or control maroons, some of the maroon communities were only temporarily independent. The largest maroon community was formed in northeast Brazil, where rebellious slaves established a state around 1605, Palmares (paul-MARYS), with a government led by an African-style king and chiefs. With a population of perhaps 30,000, mostly of African ancestry, Palmares flourished, and resisted nearly annual Portuguese assaults, for nearly a century before being crushed by the Portuguese in 1694. According to legends, the last Palmares king, Zumbi, hurled himself from a cliff to avoid capture and reenslavement. Slave revolts also erupted in Haiti, Mexico, the North American colonies, and elsewhere, but they were brutally crushed and the leaders executed. For example, the 1739 Stono Rebellion in South Carolina, the deadliest of the North American uprisings, largely involved recently imported, frequently Catholic, Kongolese. The captured rebels were beheaded.

Africans and their descendants, free or unfree, became a part of local societies. Some slaves were eventually freed, a process known as *manumission*. Manumission was rare in the English colonies and more common in Latin America, especially Brazil, where women, mulattos, and local-born children were most likely to be freed. In both English and Latin America, a few slaves earned enough to buy their own freedom, and some slave owners gave favored slaves an inheritance. As a result, a slowly growing class of free blacks filled niches in Latin American life. Together the enslaved and freed people of color constituted some two-thirds of the population in parts of Brazil and Cuba. While racism—judging people based on observable physical traits such as skin color—remained influential throughout the Americas, Latin Americans tended to rank people according to their occupation and status as well as skin color, making for a flexible social order. In contrast, the English colonies rigidly divided people largely by skin color and whether they had any African ancestry.

African American Cultures

The harsh conditions of slave life notwithstanding, unique, new African American cultures emerged. Africans in the Americas and their descendants frequently mixed Western and African customs, and some created hybrid religions based on both African and Christian beliefs. For example, the ceremonies of such religions as Haitian voodoo, Cuban *santaria* (san-tuh-REE-uh), and Brazilian *candomblé* (can-dum-BLAY) involved practices derived from West Africa such as animal sacrifice and worship of African spirits and gods. Yet, many fol-lowers of these faiths also believed in the Christian God and saints. Combining African rhythms with local European and sometimes Native American musical traditions, African Americans also invented musical forms of wide appeal in the twentieth century, including North American jazz and blues; Caribbean salsa, reggae, and calypso; and Brazilian samba. A few African Americans even developed new languages, such as the Gullah (GULL-uh) dialect of the Georgia Sea Islands, which mixes English and African words.

African American cultures also influenced other ethnic groups in the Americas. For example, African words enriched the English, French, Spanish, and Portuguese spoken locally. Brazilian Portuguese, for instance, contains many words of Kongolese and Yoruba origin. In addition, many non-Africans enjoyed various folktales and traditions of African origin, such as the Brer Rabbit stories of the southern United States, and the Angolan-based *capoiera* martial arts of Brazil, which involved music as well as physical movements. Africans also introduced several crops from their homelands, including watermelons, black-eyed peas, okra, and rice, and contributed their invaluable knowledge of blacksmithing and ironworking to colonial life.

The survival of African cultural forms and values varied from place to place depending on circumstances. Survival was probably strongest in Brazil, Haiti, and a few Caribbean islands such as Cuba, Jamaica, and Trinidad. In Brazil, the Portuguese eventually learned to accept and sometimes appreciate African influences, which were brought by the thousands of Africans that arrived every year for over three centuries. Thus Brazilian culture developed as a complex mix of African and European influences. In contrast, Spanish American and North American authorities tried to repress African music and religion, with some success. Today cultural leaders in the Americas often disdain Africa-influenced cultural forms and hold up European and North American culture as the model.

The Americas and the Atlantic System

As already mentioned (see Chapter 16), trans-Atlantic migration, voluntary and forced, and increasingly close economic ties between Europe, Africa, and the Americas created an Atlantic System by which cargoes of plantation crops were shipped east across the Atlantic to Europe while cargoes of slaves moved west to the Americas. The Atlantic System comprised a large network that spanned western and Central Africa, the east coast and southern region of English North America, the Caribbean Basin, and the northern and eastern coastal zones of South America. Plantations, slavery, and the numerical prominence of Africans and their descendants in the Americas defined this system. Ultimately, this system of economic activities helped spur major developments in modern world history, including the rise of European capitalism and wealth.

As key economic activities in the Atlantic System, the slave trade and plantation economies provided enormous capital to

Europeans and North Americans. Slave trading became a hugely profitable enterprise that was operated on a sophisticated business basis and attracted large amounts of capital, which allowed for rapid expansion of the trade. The prosperity of eighteenth-century European cities such as Bristol and Liverpool in England, and of North American cities such as Boston, Providence, Charleston, Savannah, and New Orleans, depended heavily on the slave trade. Since the slavers, the cooperating African chiefs and merchants, the plantation owners, the shipbuilders, and the other groups linked directly or indirectly to the trade were all reluctant to abandon a lucrative activity, the trade endured for four hundred years, finally coming to an end only in the 1870s.

The Atlantic System also contributed to European industrialization and colonialism. Some of the profits from the slave trade and American plantations were invested in enterprises and technology in England, the Netherlands, France, and North America, helping to bring economic development to these societies and later spurring rapid industrialization in England. Some of the investment capital for inventing industrial technologies came from individuals and companies linked to the slave trade and plantations. For example, Glasgow merchants known as the "tobacco lords" because of their ties to North American tobacco plantations set up industries in Britain, such as printing companies, tanneries, and ironworks, and also invested in cotton textile plants and coal mines.

Colonial Wealth and Europe

Some Europeans made wiser use of American profits than others. However vast the profits earned from overseas commerce—the slave trade, plantation agriculture, and mining—these profits did not always result in substantial economic development in European countries. Mercantilist economic strategies could not necessarily convert the incoming wealth into a growing domestic economy. While Spain and Portugal largely squandered opportunities, by 1750 becoming poor countries within Europe, the Dutch and English pursued wiser investment policies.

Spain, the most powerful European country for most of the 1500s, had reaped vast riches from the silver mines of the Americas and the galleons that brought from the Philippines Chinese goods and tropical products. But they did not ultimately use this wealth in ways that promoted their own economic improvement. In fact, much of the exploitation of the Americas hurt Spain. For example, the flood of American bullion into Spain caused severe inflation, resulting in the need to import lower-priced products from other European countries. In addition, the thousands of Spaniards who went to the Americas and Asia created a labor shortage at home. Furthermore, the large investments in the colonies were obtained in part by heavily taxing peasants and merchants in Spain. Spanish investment also did not spur capitalism. Since most Spanish merchants were or hoped to be large landowners in Spain, they used their prof-

its to buy land rather than investing in trade or industry. By 1600 Spain was bankrupt, and a Spanish official charged that the country had wasted its wealth on frivolous spending rather than manufacturing, arguing that "the cause of [our] ruin is that riches ride on the wind, instead of [producing] goods that bear fruit. Spain is poor because she is rich [in gold and silver]."[23] Much of the silver ended up elsewhere in Europe or in China. The wealth also tempted the monarchy to pursue expensive and ultimately futile wars of expansion in Europe.

The Portuguese were second only to the English in the volume of slave trading. Their colony in Brazil was also the world's largest exporter of gold, diamonds, and sugar and a major producer of coffee and cotton. But the Portuguese squandered their colonial wealth through nonproductive investments, such as building magnificent churches and monasteries rather than financing local industry. As a small country with a small population and a weak local resource base, Portugal had a tiny domestic market and hence little incentive to build its local industries. Investment in Brazil was more profitable.

The Dutch did much better investing their profits than the Spanish and Portuguese. Enriched by its strong trade position in northern Europe, the Netherlands became a major banking center and also boasted the world's largest commercial fleet. During the 1600s, the Dutch earned vast profits from selling Indonesian coffee and spices to other Europeans, and they invested much of these profits in their domestic economy. In addition, a large share of Portuguese and Spanish wealth ended up in the Netherlands. The Dutch were the strongest European power for most of the seventeenth century until they were finally eclipsed by England.

The English enjoyed the most long-term success. Profits from the Americas and India greatly benefited England, which had replaced the Netherlands as the dominant European power by the end of the 1600s. In the 1700s England held the most powerful position in the Atlantic System, with large amounts of wealth flowing into cities such as Liverpool, Glasgow, and Bristol from the slave, tobacco, and sugar trades. The colonial wealth enriched businessmen and bankers, who could now easily mobilize capital for investment in trade, technology, and manufacturing. These factors gave England unique advantages that it fully exploited in the 1700s and 1800s.

During the Early Modern Era, the Americas were transformed and linked to the rest of the globe, and these two outcomes reshaped world history. The conquest and exploitation of Native Americans and the acquisition of American resources gave some Europeans a decided economic advantage over other Eurasian powers, such as China, India, and the Ottoman Empire. The profits from American metals, often mined by Native Americans, and American crops, chiefly grown by African slaves, enriched Europe and shifted economic power in the world. Ultimately, this economic power also added to European political and military strength. By the late 1700s or early 1800s several European countries, especially Britain, had surpassed a declining China in wealth, living standards, and power.

SECTION SUMMARY

- African slaves in the Americas were treated as commodities, and resistance to slavery was rarely successful, though freed slaves had somewhat more success in Latin America than they did in North America.

- Elements of African religion, music, language, and agriculture all found their way into American culture, though they were accepted more readily by the Portuguese than by other European colonists.

- The slave trade and plantation economies helped spur European capitalism and were extremely profitable to Europeans and North American colonists.

- Spain and Portugal wasted the wealth they derived from their colonies, but the Dutch and the English invested it wisely and, as a result, gained an advantage over other world powers.

Online Study Center **ACE the Test**

◆ Chapter Summary

After Columbus first landed in the Americas in 1492, powerful forces were unleashed around the Atlantic Ocean that generated a great historical transition. During the Early Modern Era, European explorers seeking a route to Asia, beginning with Columbus, and then conquerors seeking wealth brought the Americas and their peoples into a permanent relationship with the Eastern Hemisphere. The Spanish, Portuguese, English, and French built vast colonial empires in the Americas, using their superior military power to subjugate American peoples. The majority of Native American people perished from disease and other causes; American societies, including the great Aztec and Inca Empires, were destroyed and placed under European colonial control; and the survivors saw their lives changed enormously. The encounters created new worlds for the surviving Native Americans as well as for the African slaves and Europeans who moved to the Americas. The Native American and mixed-descent peoples had to adjust to colonial rule, Africans to the trauma of servitude, and the European colonizers and settlers to cultural resistance.

Some of the main changes derived from economic activities. The economic evolution of the Americas, especially mining and plantation agriculture, created a tremendous market for labor. Mine owners conscripted Native American workers, and planters exploited enslaved Africans and their descendants. The slave trade linked the Americas closely to the larger world, and the emerging Atlantic System closely connected Europe, West Africa, and the Americas, mostly to the benefit of Europe and European colonists. Gradually American colonies became connected to the emerging world economy as producers of raw materials, usually metals or cash crops, and as consumers of European goods. Some colonists in English North America built more diversified economies, in contrast to the

monocultures of the Caribbean and Latin America. The Spanish and Portuguese initially prospered from their conquests but later squandered the resources they obtained, while the English and Dutch capitalized on their activities to achieve greater wealth and power. American history was thus not only a dynamic saga of indigenous development but also, beginning in the late fifteenth century, the story of increasing integration into larger global processes.

Online Study Center **Improve Your Grade** Flashcards

Key Terms

conquistadors	mestizos	monoculture
Paulistas	mulattos	development
voyageurs	Black Legend	plantation zone
Columbian Exchange	Metis	maroons
audiencias	haciendas	
creoles	encomienda	

Suggested Reading

Books

Altman, Ida, et al. *The Early History of Greater Mexico.* Upper Saddle River, N.J.: Prentice-Hall, 2003. An excellent survey of Mexico in this era.

Brown, Jonathan C. *Latin America: A Social History of the Colonial Period.* 2nd ed. Belmont, Calif.: Wadsworth, 2004. A detailed survey on Europeans, Indians, and Africans.

Captive Passage: The Transatlantic Slave Trade and the Making of the Americas. Washington, D.C.: Smithsonian Institution Press, 2002. Excellent collection of essays for the general reader.

Conniff, Michael L., and Thomas J. Davis. *Africans in the Americas: A History of the Black Diaspora.* New York: The Blackburn Press, 2002. An introduction to the slave trade and the African heritage in the Americas.

Cook, Noble David. *Born to Die: Disease and New World Conquest, 1492–1650.* New York: Cambridge University Press, 1998. One of the best scholarly introductions to the topic.

Crosby, Alfred W. *The Columbian Exchange: Biological and Cultural Consequences of 1492.* 30th anniversary ed. New York: Praeger, 2002. A pioneering study of the exchange of plants, animals, diseases, and foods.

Curtin, Philip D. *The Rise and Fall of the Plantation Complex: Essays in Atlantic History.* Cambridge: Cambridge University Press, 1990. One of the best studies of the plantation zone in the Americas.

Fischer, Steven R. *A History of the Pacific Islands.* New York: Palgrave, 2002. Provides coverage of these centuries.

Fuentes, Carlos. *The Buried Mirror: Reflections on Spain and the New World.* Boston: Mariner Books, 1999. A readable overview by a Mexican scholar of the interaction of peoples and cultures.

Hoffer, Peter C. *The Brave New World: A History of Early America.* Boston: Houghton Mifflin, 2000. A lively, comprehensive portrait of North America in this era.

Kicza, John E. *Resilient Cultures: America's Native Peoples Confront European Colonization, 1500–1800.* Upper Saddle River, N.J.: Prentice-Hall, 2003. A brief survey of the encounters throughout the Americas.

Martin, Cheryl E. and Mark Wasserman. *Latin America and its People.* New York: Longman, 2005. A readable survey text.

Mattoso, Katia M. de Queiros. *To Be a Slave in Brazil, 1550–1888.* Translated by Arthur Goldhammer. New Brunswick: Rutgers University Press, 1986. An in-depth look at the context of Brazilian slavery and the slave experience.

Mintz, Sidney W. *Sweetness and Power: The Place of Sugar in Modern History.* Reprint ed. New York: Penguin, 1995. The best introduction to the role of sugar and sugar planting in this era.

Thornton, John. *Africa and Africans in the Formation of the Atlantic World, 1400–1800.* 2nd ed. Cambridge: Cambridge University Press, 1998. A provocative examination of Africa and the African diaspora in the Atlantic world.

Viola, Herman J. and Carolyn Margolis, eds. *Seeds of Change: Five Hundred Years Since Columbus.* Washington, D.C.: Smithsonian Institution Press, 1991. Excellent collection of readable essays on the changes fostered by European exploration and conquest.

Websites

Africans in America: America's Journey Through Slavery (http://www.pbs.org/wgbh/aia/home.html). A useful website offering materials relevant to a documentary series broadcast on Public Television.

The Columbian Exchange (http://www.nhc.rtp.nc.us:8080/tserve/nattrans/ntecoindian/essays/columbian.htm). A useful set of essays compiled by Alfred Crosby.

Early America (http://earlyamerica.com/earlyamerica/index.html). Offers primary sources on the thirteen North American colonies in the eighteenth century.

Internet Resources for Latin America (http://lib.nmsu.edu/subject/bord/laguia/). An outstanding site with links to many resources.

1492: An Ongoing Voyage (http://metalab.unc.edu/expo/1492.exhibit/Intro.html). An electronic exhibit from the Library of Congress on pre- and post-Columbian Europe, Africa, and the Americas.

Pictorial Images of the Transatlantic Slave Trade: A Media Database (http://hitchcock.itc.virginia.edu/SlaveTrade/). A searchable collection of three hundred images on the experiences of enslaved Africans.

CHAPTER 18

South Asia, Southeast Asia, and East Asia: Triumphs and Challenges, 1450–1750

CHAPTER OUTLINE
- Mughal India, South Asia, and New Encounters
- Southeast Asia and Global Connections
- Early Modern China and New Challenges
- Continuity and Change in Korea and Japan

■ PROFILE
Akbar, Mughal Ruler

■ WITNESS TO THE PAST
A Mandarin's Critique of Chinese Merchants

Online Study Center

This icon will direct you to interactive activities and study materials on the website: college.hmco.com/pic/lockard1e

"Southern Barbarians" This painting on a sixteenth-century Japanese screen, decorated with gold leaf, depicts a Portuguese sea captain, shaded by a parasol carried by his black servant, being greeted by black-robed Jesuit missionaries in the port of Nagasaki. His porters carry gifts for the Japanese merchants.   (Michael Holford)

The Portuguese saw that Melaka was magnificent, and its port exceedingly crowded. The people gathered around to see what the Portuguese looked like, and they were all surprised by their appearance. [But] these [Portuguese] know nothing of manners.

Sultan Mahmud Shah (MA-mood Shah) (r. 1488–1511), the Malay ruler of the great trading state of Melaka (muh-LAH-kuh), on the southwest coast of the Malay Peninsula, had a problem. In 1509 five unknown but well-armed ships, each with a banner bearing a cross and full of menacing pale-skinned men, lowered anchor off his great port city and capital. This exploratory visit by the Portuguese was prompted by Melaka's fame as a treasure-trove of Asian luxury goods, such as the Indonesian spices that fetched huge profits in Europe. Portuguese intentions were unclear to the sultan. They did not act like the peaceful Asian merchants who arrived regularly in trading ships, nor did they bring the customary valuable gifts for the sultan and his officials. Initially, as the Malay chronicles reported, curious Melakans gathered around a Portuguese envoy who came ashore, twisting his beard, taking off his hat, and grasping his hand. However, this initial encounter quickly became strained. The ill-mannered Portuguese violated local customs, antagonized Melaka officials, and alarmed influential local Indian traders, who feared competition, while the Portuguese considered Sultan Mahmud Shah arrogant and treacherous. As tensions rose, fighting between Portuguese sailors and Malay visitors to their ship broke out. After the Melakans arrested fifteen or twenty Portuguese sailors shopping in town, the remaining Portuguese force, unprepared for a full-scale assault on the heavily defended city, sailed away, vowing revenge.

Two years later, in 1511, a Portuguese fleet of some forty ships, mounted with cannon and carrying hundreds of soldiers armed with deadly muskets, sailed back to Melaka to capture the city. The sultan led the defense mounted on his elephant. As the Portuguese gained the upper hand after a bloody month-long assault, their commander, Admiral Affonso de Albuquerque (Al-ba-KER-kee), told his soldiers to cast the "Moors" (Muslims) out of the country, and his men slaughtered much of the population and looted the city. Melaka became the first Southeast Asian society severely disrupted by European power. This episode was a preview of both the conflicts and the connections forged between Europeans and Asians that followed over the next four centuries.

Many eastern and southern Asians had better success than the Melakans in deflecting the Europeans, who were beginning to arrive in the 1500s to compete with each other and Asians for markets and resources. The Portuguese in the

1500s, the Dutch in the 1600s, and the English in the 1700s established some degree of control over the Indian Ocean maritime network and colonized a few areas, such as Melaka. But, for all their deadly gunpowder weapons, the Europeans did not yet have a clear military and economic advantage over the stronger Asian states, and as a result their influence in these regions was modest. Various Asian leaders manipulated the rival Europeans and sometimes forced them to leave. Asian countries were also protected by distance, since they could be reached only by long and dangerous voyages from Europe. As a result of this freedom to run their own affairs, most Asian societies did not undergo the transitions that were reshaping the Americas and parts of Africa in this era.

Some Asian states also remained politically and economically strong. A Muslim kingdom dominated much of India, many Southeast Asian states flourished from trade, China was still a major power, able to deal with Europeans on Chinese terms, and Japanese fiercely defended their interests. As in western Eurasia, connections to networks of exchange stretching around the world helped various Asian states grow commercially. As late as 1750 China and India together still accounted for over half of world manufacturing. Trade between Asia and Europe largely involved luxuries such as Chinese tea and silk, Indonesian spices, Indian textiles, and European silver and gold. Yet, in spite of spirited resistance to European incursions, by the mid-1700s most of the great Asian states were under stress or collapsing from a combination of internal problems and destabilizing Western activities, leaving a vacuum for further European penetration.

FOCUS QUESTIONS

1. What were the major achievements and failures of the Mughal Empire?
2. How did Southeast Asia become more fully integrated into the world economy?
3. What factors enabled China to remain one of the world's strongest and most dynamic societies?
4. How did Korea and Japan change during this era?

◆ Mughal India, South Asia, and New Encounters

What were the major achievements and failures of the Mughal Empire?

During its long history, India had developed a culture linked with and shaped by the Hindu religion. During the Intermediate Era, however, Muslims had become politically influential and had introduced major changes. During the Early Modern Era, a powerful Muslim dynasty, the Mughals (MOO-guhlz), Central Asians of mixed Mongol-Turkish descent, ruled much of India and the Hindu majority. At their height in the later 1500s and early 1600s, the Mughals presided over one of the world's most creative societies, fostering artistic and religious innovations. They also fashioned a prosperous economy that allowed many Indians, both Muslims and Hindus, to flourish. Many Indians participated in international trade. In the early 1700s, however, the Mughal system rapidly declined and began to collapse, just as pressures from various European societies were mounting.

The Mughal Empire

In 1526 Babur (BAH-bur) (1483–1530), a Muslim descendant of Genghis Khan and Tamerlane, led 12,000 troops from Afghanistan and conquered much of north India to form a new ruling dynasty called the Mughal, a corruption of *Mongol* (see Map 18.1 on page 520). Babur was a learned man, a gifted poet in the Persian language, but he was also an ambitious and powerful man whose new dynasty restored the imperial grandeur of India. Indeed, at the height of their power, the Mughals created one of most magnificent societies in the world. The wealth displayed at the imperial court prompted a

CHRONOLOGY

	India	Southeast Asia	China	Japan and Korea
1300		**1350–1767** Ayuthia	**1368–1644** Ming dynasty	**1392–1573** Ashikaga Shogunate **1392–1910** Yi dynasty in Korea
1400				
1500	**1526–1761** Mughal India **1556–1605** Reign of Akbar	**1511** Portuguese conquest of Melaka **1565** Spanish conquest of Philippines		
1600			**1644–1912** Qing dynasty **1689** Treaty of Nerchinsk	**1603** Tokugawa Shogunate founded

French visitor to wonder whether any other monarch possessed more gold, silver, and jewels, and it inspired the English to use the term *mogul* to mean someone of extreme wealth. Mughal India had few rivals in military strength, government efficiency, economic power, and royal patronage of the arts.

The Mughals, like earlier Indian governments, had to manage a highly diverse society. The majority of people shared many traditions and practiced Hinduism, a religion of varied beliefs and customs. However, since the ninth century a succession of Muslim states had ruled parts of the subcontinent, and perhaps a quarter of the Indian population embraced Islam. Polytheistic Hinduism and monotheistic Islam offered starkly different visions of the cosmic and social order. As a result, Hindus and Muslims often disagreed and competed for influence in Indian society. Yet at the village level Hindus and Muslims lived side by side, sharing many customs of the larger culture. By 1500 Buddhism, which had thrived for centuries, had nearly died out in India, but the majority of people in Tibet and on the island of Sri Lanka (Ceylon) remained Buddhists. Indian society was also fragmented by caste divisions and hundreds of different regional languages, such as Bengali in the northeast and Tamil in the southeast.

While proud of their Central Asian origins and influenced by Persian culture, the Mughals adapted to Indian conditions. For example, they used **Urdu**, a mix of Hindi, Arabic, and Persian written in the Persian script, as their language of administration. Urdu had developed in earlier centuries as a common language among many Indian Muslims.

Akbar (AK-bahr) (r. 1556–1605), a grandson of Babur, pursued innovative policies and became the most outstanding

Mughal ruler (see Profile: Akbar, Mughal Ruler on page 521). Historians often consider Akbar's India to have been the best-managed state of that era in the world. Akbar, whose name means "Very Great," expanded Babur's empire over all of north India, including Bengal, and deep into south India. In part this success resulted from his winning the support of various Hindu groups, including some of the Hindu warrior caste, the Rajputs (RAHJ-putz). To ensure stability and defuse opposition, Akbar gave Hindus high positions in the government and removed the extra taxes earlier Muslim rulers in India had imposed on non-Muslims, policies that brought him wide popularity. He also reformed the government and promoted religious toleration and compromise between communities. Peace and prosperity prevailed during Akbar's reign.

Akbar earned his reputation as a reformer by having bribery and corruption strictly checked and seeing that the law was justly administered. He tried with only limited success to abolish what he considered the most pernicious social customs, such as *sati* (burning the wife on the husband's funeral pyre), child marriage, and trial by ordeal, but he did end the enslavement of prisoners of war. Akbar's India also enjoyed an enlightened criminal code for the era, and all citizens had the right of appeal to the ruler if they believed themselves wrongly convicted of a crime or mistreated in the courts.

Akbar presided over a golden age, but many of his successors had less of his tolerance and wisdom. The Mughals never worked out a stable pattern of succession. Moreover, Muslim rulers in India had many wives and concubines, producing numerous male heirs to the throne who often plotted against their father and each other. Akbar was poisoned by a rebellious son, who then occupied the throne as Jahangir (ja-HAN-gear) ("World Seizer"). Royal Mughal women had considerable power at court, and Jahangir was strongly influenced by his Persian wife, Nur Jahan (nur ja-HAN), who often defied gender

Urdu A language developed in Mughal India that mixed Hindi, Arabic, and Persian and was written in the Persian script.

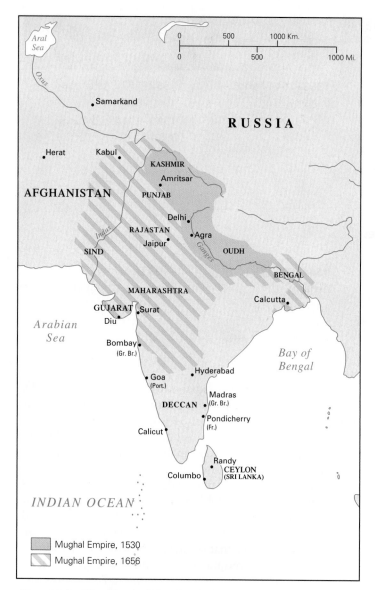

Map 18.1   The Mughal Empire, 1526–1761
By the mid-1600s the Mughals, a Muslim dynasty based in North India, controlled much of the Indian subcontinent. However, some ports fell under European rule. The Portuguese had a colony at Goa and, by the early 1700s, the British had established outposts at Bombay, Calcutta, and Madras, and the French-occupied Pondicherry.

roles by joining him on hunting expeditions. Jahangir wrote that he had handed government business over to Nur Jahan, and that he only needed wine and meat to be happy. While Jahangir generally pursued Akbar's wise public policies, his son, Shah Jahan (r. 1628–1658), abandoned the idea of a tolerant India that respected diverse traditions; instead he promoted Islam and destroyed several Hindu temples. He also took extravagant living to new heights, assembling a harem of 5,000 concubines. Sitting on his splendid jewel-encrusted Peacock Throne in Delhi, Shah Jahan doubled the tax bills, and even then his extensive building projects virtually bankrupted the state. Unsuccessful military campaigns in Afghanistan and Central Asia

added to the problems. Eventually Shah Jahan was imprisoned by his ambitious, even more intolerant son, Aurangzeb (ow-rang-ZEB) (r. 1658–1707), who greatly expanded the empire in the south but also set in motion the forces that began to undermine the Mughal state and its revenues.

Indian Economy and Society

The Indian economy and society grew and India flourished, as it had for centuries, from industry, farming, and trade. Thanks to manufacturing, especially of textiles, India had long been one of the world's most industrialized societies. During the Early Modern Era demand continued for Indian textiles all over Eurasia. India also boasted an iron industry that produced high-quality steel and cannon. By 1750 India still accounted for one-quarter of the world's industrial output, and it remained the largest producer of textiles. Its highly efficient farming, which benefited from investments in reservoirs and irrigation, produced large yields of wheat and rice. Cash crops, including cotton, indigo, pepper, sugar, and opium, found a ready market at home or abroad. The productive Indian economy and agriculture supported a doubling of the population between 1500 and 1750.

Foreign trade spurred the economy, and the bullion it brought to India benefited the Mughal treasury. India had, for much of recorded history, been a major core of the Afro-Eurasian trading networks. Beginning in the Classical Era, it had traded fine fabrics such as cashmere and gingham to Europe and the Middle East for gold and silver, and Indian merchants had traveled east to China and Southeast Asia and west to East Africa and the Middle East. In the 1600s an influx of American silver, used by European merchants to obtain textiles and other products, stimulated a tripling of the money supply. Revenues from commerce and industry allowed the Mughals to build a vast network of imperial roads linking different regions of the empire, support a luxurious court life, and fund ambitious building projects.

Indian merchants and bankers maintained and even expanded some of the largest commercial networks in the Early Modern world over vast distances. By the 1400s the Indian maritime trade diaspora stretched from Arabia, Persia, northeast Africa, and the Red Sea to Melaka, Sumatra, Siam, and China. For example, Hindu and Muslim merchant networks based in the Gujerat (goo-juh-RAHT) region of northwest India had a strong position in trade and finance around the Indian Ocean, including Melaka. Although the Portuguese cut into their Indian Ocean trade in the 1500s, the Gujeratis remained active in the 1700s. Thousands of Indians also traded across Central Asia from the 1500s through the 1800s. They were part of an overland network of Indian merchants in Afghanistan, Tibet, Persia, the Caucasus states, and Russia. As a result, Indians were the dominant commercial group at the Russian trading port of Astrakhan (AS-truh-kan) on the Caspian Sea.

The Indian merchant networks enjoyed vast amounts of capital, sophisticated credit and financing arrangements, and reputations for shrewdness. Heavily capitalized family- and caste-run firms competed successfully against European and Asian

AKBAR,
MUGHAL RULER

During the early Mughal period in the sixteenth century, Akbar, one of the most respected political leaders of history, ruled India, coming to power at the age of thirteen after his father died. A contemporary of Queen Elizabeth I of England and Shah Abbas of Persia, he was also a possible epileptic (like Julius Caesar and Napoleon) and subject to bouts of depression. His military conquests, in which he could be ruthless against his enemies, were not the source of his reputation for greatness. Rather, his greatness lay in his skills as an administrator and his ability to respect and blend the diverse traditions of India. Always seeing himself as an Indian rather than a foreign ruler, he worked hard to blend all the strands of Indian culture and religion into a unified country. Although raised a Muslim, he married a Christian and two Hindu princesses, winning non-Muslim support. The marriages symbolized acceptance of India's religious diversity.

Foreign visitors were charmed by Akbar. A Jesuit missionary who visited India in the early 1580s wrote that he was

of a stature and type of countenance well suited to his royal dignity, so that one could easily recognize even at first glance that he is the king. He creates an opportunity almost every day for any of the common people or of the nobles to see him and converse with him. It is remarkable how great an effect this courtesy and affability has in attaching to him the minds of his subjects.

Visionary, energetic, and versatile, Akbar lived to the fullest, becoming a skilled metalworker, draftsmen, polo player, and musician. Although himself illiterate, he had an insatiable love of learning and had books of all kinds read to him. His personal library included 24,000 volumes. He also patronized poets, musicians, painters, and architects, even honoring his architects and artisans by having them build a new capital at Fatepuhr Sikri near Agra, where he then lived. Akbar took a particular interest in the lovely gardens constructed around Mughal buildings in the capital and elsewhere, which featured shade trees, fountains, and pools. To show his respect to Hindus, he encouraged Hindi literature and even appointed a Hindi court poet. In response to orthodox Muslims who criticized his support of Hindu court painters, some of whose subject matter violated Islamic prejudices against human images, he argued that God loved all beauty.

Although the Mughals were officially Muslims, Akbar espoused complete freedom of religion. This was not just a political expediency but rather a reflection of an enlightened man with a restless, inquiring mind. Investigation of the mysteries of creation, he claimed, should be done according to the light of reason. He believed that all faiths had something truthful to offer and that all religions were untrue when they denied other religions' sincerity of purpose. Once a week, representatives of all religions held debates in the palace at his invitation; when Jesuit missionaries arrived from the West, they stayed with

Akbar   The great Mughal emperor, Akbar, enjoyed pomp and circumstance. This miniature painting shows him entertaining guests at a reception in his palace.   (Private Collection/The Bridgeman Art Library International)

Akbar for several years and joined in the spirited debates. Indeed, Akbar had the Christian gospels translated into Persian and even attended the occasional mass out of curiosity.

Akbar never completely bought into any religion totally, believing that no one faith had a monopoly on truth. He remained skeptical and found some beliefs in all of them that he thought contradicted reason. Later in life he adopted the Hindu custom of vegetarianism and gave up his favorite sport of hunting. Influenced by the inclusive spirit of Sufi mysticism, in the end he created his own religion, incorporating what he saw as the best features of all religions. But, since he would not impose his views on others, Akbar's religion found few takers and died with him.

THINKING ABOUT THE PROFILE

1. How did Akbar foster Indian cultural life?

2. How could Akbar afford to show so much tolerance of other religions?

Note: Quotation from Rhoads Murphey, *A History of Asia,* 4th ed. (New York: HarperCollins, 2003), p. 178.

rivals. Some merchants in Surat (SOO-raht), the main Gujerat port, were among the world's richest entrepreneurs. Other ports also had successful merchants. A Dutch diplomat wrote that the merchants of Bengal were "exceptionally quick and experienced. They are always sober, modest, thrifty, and cunning in identifying the source for their profit."[2] Dutch merchants found a commerce in the Indian ports that closely resembled the pattern of Amsterdam: maritime traders, secondhand merchants, export dealers, and many hawkers selling their wares on the streets.

The Indian traders came from a society divided by caste and gender divisions. Most of the Hindu merchants belonged to various subcastes (*jati*) of the larger caste grouping known as the *vaisya*, who ranked below the priests (*brahmans*) and warriors in a caste system that had been evolving for over two thousand years. Caste remained dynamic and subcastes moved up or down in the system. Nor did caste necessarily correspond to wealth since many traders were affluent.

Women's influence depended on their caste and family situation. Women's status had been declining for centuries, especially in north India, where both Muslim and Hindu women were often kept in seclusion, and they were expected to be chaste and obedient to fathers and husbands in a patriarchal, patrilineal society. Yet, as noted earlier, some women in the Mughal court exercised influence. For instance, Khanzada Begum (1478–1545), Babur's oldest sister, successfully interceded with rebellious brothers to end a family split and keep Babur's son, Humayun, on the throne, avoiding bloodshed. Emperor Jahangir's Hindu mother, Jodhabai, is credited with fostering his religious tolerance. The Mughal women had financial resources, which they often devoted to endow mosques and support religious scholars. Such activities helped establish the Mughal reputation for piety.

Indian Religion and Arts

The coming of Islam in the centuries before 1500 dramatically changed India's religious and cultural environment. Unlike earlier invaders into India, Muslims resisted assimilation into the Hindu fold and remained religiously distinct, often disdainful of Hindus and of the caste system. Hindus often lived side by side with them, but the two groups never united to form a single people. Nonetheless, Muslim customs, such as veiling and secluding women, influenced upper-class Hindus in north India. The early Mughals, especially Akbar, mostly left the Hindus free to practice their own faith and customs. However, in later years, less tolerant policies emerged that helped deepen the religious divide.

Mysticism became increasingly popular among both Muslims and Hindus. Sufi influences grew in the Islamic communities beginning in the 1300s, when Muslim rulers welcomed Sufi masters, some of them renowned poets, to their courts. The Sufi masters composed songs, poems, and sermons to lead their followers to communion with God. Some masters were Muslim Indians who had studied in the Middle East, while others were of Arab or Persian origin. Akbar and Jahangir were particularly sympathetic to Sufism and Sufi movements, horri-

fying Muslim dogmatists, who regarded the mystics as heretics. Sufis argued that a personal bond existed between each believer and God, and they denied that either religious or political institutions could replace that bond. As a result, some Sufi movements, such as the Chishtiya (CHIS-tee-ya), avoided association with secular powers. The Indian Chishti saint Nizam al-Din Awliya (KNEE-zam al-DIN aw-LEE-ya) wrote that "my room has two doors. If the sultan comes through one door, I will leave through the other."[3]

Meanwhile, many Hindus, particularly from lower castes, had gravitated toward the mystical bhakti (BUK-tee) devotional movement, which had first emerged in the Intermediate Era. Some bhakti groups challenged accepted wisdom by opposing the caste system, ignoring the high-caste brahmans and their traditional ritual practices, and sympathizing with the poor. Bhakti worship often involved dances, poems, and songs, as in Sufism, and focused on commitment to a particular Hindu god, such as Shiva or Vishnu. Like their Sufi counterparts, some bhakti poets achieved lasting fame and became saints to their followers.

Mysticism helped forge a gradual accommodation between some Muslims and Hindus but appealed more to women than to men. The barriers between the contrasting mystical approaches blurred, and many Muslims and Hindus venerated both Sufi and bhakti saints, making pilgrimages to their tombs. Many bhakti poets were women. The most famous, Mirabai (MEERA-buy) (ca. 1498–ca. 1546), a Rajput who was widowed at a young age, refused the pleas of her in-laws to commit sati and spent the rest of her life writing praises to Vishnu. Mirabai's life showed that women could become saints and that bhakti sometimes allowed women to defy social convention. Some historians view her life as a partly successful struggle against the patriarchal system and the brahmans (Hindu priests). Muslim women were more likely than men to honor and visit the graves of Sufi sheiks.

While many Sufi and bhakti mystics found common ground, other Indians tried to blend or transcend Hinduism and Islam by forming new sects. The largest of these sects, the **Sikhs** ("Disciples"), adopted elements, including mysticism, from both Hinduism and Islam while creating a new religion. Eventually the Sikhs numbered several million people, mostly living in the Punjab region of northwest India. The religion was founded by Guru Nanak (GOO-roo NAN-ak) (1469–1539), born a Hindu, who had been strongly influenced by Hindu bhakti movements. But he argued that devotion was not enough and that people were saved by their deeds alone: "God will not ask a man his tribe or sect, but what he has done. There is no Hindu and no Muslim. All are children of God." Nanak was followed by nine spiritual leaders who refined the faith during Mughal times. Arjan (1563–1606), the fifth leader, established the holy scripture, which announced: "I do not keep the Hindu fast, nor the Muslim Ramadan. I have broken with the Hindu and Muslim. I shall put my heart at the feet of

---

Sikhs ("Disciples") An Indian religion founded in the Early Modern Era that adopted elements from both Hinduism and Islam, including mysticism.

one Supreme Being."[4] Akbar respected the faith and granted Sikhs land for a great temple in Amritsar (uhm-RIT-suhr) in the Punjab.

Sikhs shared numerous beliefs and a mystical approach with other faiths but also had distinctive customs. Like Muslims, for example, they worshiped one universal and loving God, rejected the caste system and priests, promoted egalitarianism, forbade alcohol and tobacco, and stressed discipline, hard work, and charity for the needy. Like Hindus, they offered devotional hymns to their god. But Sikhs also differed in significant ways from Hindus and Muslims. Observant Sikh men adopted a look very different from that of Hindus or Muslims, sporting a beard, wearing a steel bracelet, and carrying a dagger or sword at all times. Prohibited from cutting their hair, many men wore a turban on their head. Sikh women enjoyed great freedom compared to Hindus and Muslims and were never secluded as were many north Indian Hindu and Muslim women. Persistent persecution by Mughal leaders after Akbar led Sikhs, once pacifists, to become militaristic. They developed a reputation as excellent soldiers and are well represented in modern India's military and police forces. The Sikhs also became skilled and practical farmers, able to make the most of their land.

Early Modern Indians also made significant achievements in the arts. For example, based on Persian models, the distinctive Mughal school of miniature painting flourished under royal patronage. This painting represented a synthesis between Islamic and Hindu cultures. The Mughals were also great builders of tombs, mosques, forts, and palaces. Their architectural style, known as Indo-Islamic, blended Indian and Persian influences and made lavish use of mosaics, domes, and gateways. The Mughal elite lived in large houses with courtyards, trees, gardens, water basins, and handsome subterranean apartments furnished with large fans where people escaped the heat of the day. In his capital, Delhi, Shah Jahan sponsored construction of a huge palace, fort, and mosque. In the audience hall of his spectacular Delhi palace, the ruler had inscribed: "If on earth be an Eden of bliss, it is this, it is this, it is this!"[5] East of Delhi, at Agra (AH-gruh), Shah Jahan left another legacy, the Taj Mahal (tahzh muh-HAHL). Often considered the world's most beautiful building, the Taj—a marble mausoleum with pools, archways, domes, and minarets—took 22,000 workers twenty-two years to complete. It was the final resting place for Shah Jahan's beloved favorite wife and close political adviser, Mumtaz Mahal (MOOM-taz muh-HAHL), who died while giving birth to her thirteenth child, and may also have reflected the devout Muslim ruler's concept of heaven.

The Decline of the Mughals

Eventually the Mughals' endless wars of expansion and extravagant royal spending drained state coffers, reducing their ability to maintain power. Before the eighteenth century the military strength of the Mughal state had been sufficient to keep Europeans and other enemies at bay. Although the state lacked the naval power to control the nearby oceans, the Mughal army, numbering some 1 million soldiers, was equipped with gunpowder weapons such as muskets and field artillery that rivaled European arms, and it had thousands of elephants to ride into battle and large cavalry units. By the early 1700s, however, the once vaunted Mughal military machine was faltering and the Mughals lacked the money to match European military capabilities. Furthermore, increasing tax demands on both merchants and peasants impoverished many of them and, combined with growing hatred toward Aurangzeb, sparked increasing opposition to Mughal rule.

Aurangzeb's ruthless and intolerant policies alienated both Muslims and non-Muslims who had once supported Mughal rule. A man with a more dogmatic view of Islam and less generous viewpoints than his predecessors toward non-Muslims, Aurangzeb placed higher taxes on non-Muslims and persecuted—sometimes even executed—Hindu and Sikh leaders he saw as a threat to his power. His cruelty toward opponents and toleration of corruption also alienated many pious and tolerant Muslims, one of whom wrote that "bribery is everywhere; mean people have become governors, and the Islamic judge himself is called a thief. May God damn the tyrant! In this world he is an infidel; in the next he is in hell."[6]

Revolt undermined Aurangzeb's later years, eventually leading to the dismantling of the Mughal state as regions broke away. To expand his empire and counter threats from other Indian states, Aurangzeb had, at great expense, significantly increased the size of his already huge army, creating logistical problems in supplying the troops just as anti-Mughal forces became bolder. The Marathas (muh-RAH-tuhz), a Hindu group from western India who had long resisted Mughal power, began raiding into the empire in the later 1600s and cutting Mughal supply lines. Some Hindu merchants, disenchanted with Mughal corruption, provided the Marathas with guns. When Safavid Iran conquered much of the Mughal-controlled areas of Afghanistan in the early seventeenth century, Mughal leaders were too busy plotting against each other to respond. Increasingly unable to control their remaining domains, the Mughal rulers were finally defeated in 1761 by Hindu and Sikh insurgents.

The decline and demise of the powerful Mughal state left India open to penetration and eventually conquest by Europeans. The anti-Mughal forces could not unite, leaving India fragmented and vulnerable. The division between Muslims and Hindus, a split intensified by the intolerance of later Mughal rulers, played a critical role in the gradual establishment of European domination. After they began annexing parts of India in the 1700s, the English encouraged the Hindu-Muslim division as a way to fragment opposition, but they also had trouble subduing the Sikhs, who dreamed of their own nation. The religious divide greatly affected twentieth-century South Asia, which became divided into rival Hindu and Muslim nations.

South Asia and the Portuguese

The Mughals were the last great precolonial Indian rulers, and with their collapse Europeans filled the power vacuum. European activity in South Asia had begun even before the Mughals

CHRONOLOGY

South Asia, 1450–1750

1498	Arrival of Vasco da Gama in India
1510	Portuguese conquest of Goa
1515	Portuguese occupation of western Ceylon
1526–1761	Mughal India
1556–1605	Reign of Akbar
1600	Founding of British East India Company
1640s	Dutch conquests in Ceylon
1717	British settlement in Calcutta and Madras

came to power. Europeans had long been interested in southern Asia as a source of spices and textiles, and this interest spurred the Portuguese to seek a sea route around Africa and the Spanish to sponsor the Columbian voyages westward across the Atlantic in search of "the Indies." The Portuguese explorers and adventurers came from a country with superior naval technology, missionary zeal, and a compelling appetite for wealth but a standard of living little if any higher than that enjoyed by many Indians, Southeast Asians, and Chinese.

The Portuguese were the first Europeans to arrive in India directly from Europe by sea around Africa. Following the Indian Ocean maritime trade route from East Africa, the pioneer Portuguese explorer, Vasco da Gama (ca. 1469–1525), reached the southwestern Indian port of Calicut in 1498 with the help of a pilot, probably a Muslim Gujerati, hired in East Africa (see Chronology: South Asia, 1450–1750). At Calicut Da Gama encountered merchants from as far away as northwest Africa. He quickly realized the economic potential of Asia and also understood that the European goods he carried had little appeal or value. Da Gama had one military advantage over the Indians—mounted cannon on his ships—but he was able without force to obtain a cargo of spices, especially pepper, which he sold in Europe at 3,000 percent profit. In 1500 a second Portuguese fleet returned to Calicut, and, after fighting broke out ashore between the Portuguese and some Arabs and local people, with some deaths on both sides, the Portuguese used their cannon to bombard Calicut, blasting the city to rubble and destroying bigger but less maneuverable Indian and Arab ships that were helping defend the city.

Like all the European powers that followed them to Asia, the Portuguese resorted to violence when they believed it necessary to enforce their power and acquire wealth, as they demonstrated in bombarding Calicut. Seeking to control the trade from Asia to the West, the Portuguese established forti-fied settlements at strategic locations around the Indian Ocean in the early 1500s. These included Hormuz (hor-MOOZ) at the entrance to the Persian Gulf, Mombasa in East Africa, Diu (dee-YOU) in northwest India, Goa on India's southwestern coast, and Melaka in Malaya. In 1515 they also occupied Colombo (kuh-LUM-bow) in western Sri Lanka, a source of cinnamon. Soon the Portuguese used their warships to exercise partial control over the maritime trade of the western Indian Ocean, extorting payments from Ottoman, Arab, Indian, and Indonesian merchant ships. Sometimes they used terrorism. For example, in 1502, just to take revenge for the Portuguese killed earlier in Calicut, Vasco da Gama attacked, plundered, and burned an Arab passenger ship bound for Calicut carrying over three hundred people, including several of Calicut's richest merchants and many women and children, killing all the people aboard.

Although their country was small, the Portuguese had huge ambitions for a grand trade empire in Asia. But, despite devoting vast resources, including some eight hundred ships, to the effort, and despite controlling several key ports, the Portuguese never completely dominated the Indian Ocean commerce. Asian merchants often found ways to outmaneuver or evade Portuguese ships, and Asian states resisted Portuguese demands. For instance, the Mughals destroyed a Portuguese base in Bengal. The long-term significance of the Portuguese presence for India was also mostly insignificant. The Portuguese mostly purchased or seized trade goods for export to Europe but still had to compete for Asian goods with Asian merchants. But the Portuguese made a lasting contribution to South and Southeast Asian cooking by introducing chilies from the Americas, making the spicy food even hotter. Before chilies, the heat in Indian dishes came from black or red peppers. In Goa the Portuguese and local Indians created a fiery hot dish, known as *vindaloo*, that combined European vinegar, American potatoes, chilies, and local ingredients and became a fixture of South Asian cuisine. Although they later lost all their other South and West Asian footholds, the Portuguese retained Goa as a colony until 1961, when India assumed control.

Although chiefly interested in trade, the Portuguese were also zealous missionary Christians. Da Gama had told Calicut leaders that the Portuguese sought "Christians and spices," a useful shorthand for understanding their motives. Hostility to Islam was a cornerstone of Portuguese policy, sometimes leading to persecution of Islamic institutions and repression of believers in Portuguese-held territories. Portuguese men settled in Goa and Colombo, marrying local women and fostering mixed-descent, Portuguese-speaking Catholic communities whose descendants still exist in these cities. The Portuguese also brought rigid gender roles to their Asian colonies. For example, they limited the role of mixed-descent women, as a Dutch visitor to Goa observed in the late 1500s: "The [Portuguese] women are little seen abroad, but for the most part sit still within the house, unless it be to church, or to visit their friends, which is likewise but very little."[7]

A Goa Market   A Dutch traveler, Jan Huygen Van Linschoten, made this plate while living in the Portuguese-ruled port city of Goa in the 1580s. It shows a street scene, including market stalls and, on the far right, a Portuguese woman walking with two Indian maids. Some Indians, wearing crosses, have become Christians.   (Cadbury Collection, Birmingham Central Library and City Archives)

South Asia's New Challenges

Before the mid-1700s European influence on India remained relatively modest. The European component of India's trade was small. For example, only some 10 percent of the silk and other cloth produced in Bengal in 1750 ended up in Europe. The internal dynamics of Indian politics, economic affairs, and religion still had more effect on the lives of most Indians than did the Europeans. But the Portuguese activity foreshadowed an increasingly active European presence. The Dutch, French, and English followed the Portuguese to Asia, and all attempted to impose their influence on parts of South Asia. The overextended Portuguese were hard-pressed to sustain their power against these European rivals, who had larger populations and were developing better ships and gunpowder weapons.

The Dutch challenged the Portuguese for domination of the Indian Ocean trade in the early 1600s, eventually destroying their power in South and Southeast Asia and gaining partial control over the Indian Ocean commerce. In 1602 Dutch merchants in Amsterdam, with the goal of tapping into the Asian trade, formed the well-financed Dutch East India Company, a private company with government backing that had its own armed fleet and operated in conjunction with other Dutch activities. In South Asia the Dutch concentrated their attention on Sri Lanka, gaining control of some of the coastal regions from the Portuguese in the 1640s. They remained in Sri Lanka, often intermarrying with local people, until they were ousted by the British in the early 1800s. Neither the Dutch nor the Portuguese before them were able to defeat and occupy the main kingdom of Kandy (KAN-dee) in central Sri Lanka. Only in 1815 did Kandy fall to the British.

Soon the French joined the competition, forming their own East India Company in 1664. In the later 1600s and early 1700s the French established a trading presence at Surat and Calcutta, and they built a military and commercial base at the southeast coast town of Pondicherry (pondir-CHEH-ree). The vigorous French competition for Indian merchandise generated tensions with the English. The two countries were also bitter rivals in Europe, and the resulting antagonisms sometimes spilled over into conflict in India. For example, in 1746 the English and French fought fierce battles for dominance in southeast India that also involved local Indian states and destabilized the region's politics.

The English, with a rapidly growing commercial economy, became the main threat to the Mughals, Dutch, and French in Asia. In 1600 British investors formed the British East India Company in London, and English traders working for the company visited various ports. But they also built a fort at Madras (muh-DRAS) (today known as Chennai) on the southeast Indian coast and established a stable commercial base at Surat in northwest India, with Mughal permission. At Surat the English forged a commercial alliance with the Parsis (PAHR-seez), the Zoroastrian descendants of Persian refugees who were leading traders in India.

By the late 1600s the English were increasing their presence in India and, in 1717, they established bases at Bombay (today called Mumbai) and Calcutta, both then sparsely populated backwaters, for collecting and exporting textiles, indigo, and saltpeter (an ingredient for gunpowder). Soon they controlled these towns. When Surat rapidly declined after a Mughal governor imprisoned the port's leading merchant, to whom he was deeply in debt, many Parsis left Surat for better prospects in Bombay, again working closely with the English for their mutual benefit. But outside of Bombay, Calcutta, and Madras, English officials still had to negotiate with the Mughals or local princes for trading privileges. When piracy and banditry grew rapidly as Mughal authority collapsed, the law and order in the three English-run towns, secured by an increasing English military presence, attracted Indian settlers. English and Indian merchants in the three English bases prospered. The growing English presence in India also had consequences in England, where competition from Indian textile imports spurred local textile manufacturers to cut costs, helping stimulate English industrialization.

By the mid-eighteenth century the English were strong enough to treat local rulers with less deference and expand their control from their three bases into the surrounding regions. When local Indian governments resisted this encroachment, the English resorted to military force. By the 1750s this had resulted in a war in Bengal, where, from their Calcutta base, the English now began their long period of military conquest in South Asia. Eventually they controlled nearly all of South Asia except for a few small enclaves, such as Portuguese Goa and French Pondicherry. The English conquest and its momentous impact recalled age-old patterns in South Asia, which had often been conquered by outsiders, including people, such as the Mughals, of different cultural and religious backgrounds. But now, with the English, India faced a major new challenge.

SECTION SUMMARY

- The Muslim Mughal Empire attained great riches and, especially under Akbar, maintained an enlightened rule over religiously diverse India, but it began to decline after the fall of Akbar.

- The Indian economy, already strong, expanded greatly as extensive foreign trade brought an influx of silver and enriched entrepreneurs.

- Tensions existed between Indian Muslims and Hindus, though some were able to bridge the gap through mysticism and others joined sects such as the Sikhs that blended or transcended the dominant religions.

- The Mughal decline hastened under Aurangzeb, a harsh and corrupt ruler who was particularly resented by non-Muslims, whom he persecuted and taxed at high rates.

- As a result of their military prowess, Portuguese traders gained a significant share of trade with India, though they never completely controlled it.

- The Dutch, French, and English all competed with each other and with the Portuguese for dominance of trade with India, with the English growing increasingly strong by the mid-eighteenth century.

Southeast Asia and Global Connections

How did Southeast Asia become more fully integrated into the world economy?

Southeast Asia, the region south of China and east of India, had long been a cosmopolitan center where peoples, religions, ideas, and products met. Southeast Asians participated in the wider hemispheric trade and most adopted Theravada Buddhism, Confucianism, or Islam. The Portuguese arrival at Melaka inaugurated a new era of transregional contacts during which European adventurers, traders, missionaries, and soldiers were active in the region. Several areas were influenced by the West before 1750, particularly Malaya, the Philippine Islands, and parts of Indonesia. However, in most parts of Southeast Asia, including strong kingdoms such as Siam, Burma, and Vietnam, Western influence remained weak until the nineteenth century.

Southeast Asian Transitions

European activity was only one aspect of the Early Modern Era in Southeast Asia. The region was undergoing a transition that included commercial growth, political change, increasingly productive agriculture, and expansion of Islam and Buddhism. Partly because of increasing connections with European, Chinese, Arab, and Indian merchants, commerce increased between the 1400s and 1700s, and Southeast Asia remained an essential hub in the maritime trade network linking East Asia with India and the Middle East. Sailing ships still stopped in the region's ports to exchange goods or wait for the monsoon winds to shift. The growing regional trade attracted merchants from afar. For example, in 1650 the capital city of Arakan (AIR-ah-kan), a coastal kingdom in today's western Burma, attracted many traders from the Middle East, Central Asia, Africa, and India. Among the region's maritime traders were the Indonesians, who for centuries had even visited the north coast of Australia to obtain items such as ornamental shells and pearls.

Increased trade encouraged political centralization, the growth of cities, and the spread of world religions. Larger, more centralized states absorbed neighboring smaller states: on the mainland some twenty states in the fourteenth century had been reduced to less than a dozen by the early eighteenth century, with Siam, Vietnam, and Burma being the most influential. Economic dynamism enhanced the value of regional ports such as Melaka, Ayuthia (ah-YUT-uh-yuh) in Siam, Pegu (Peh-GOO) in Burma's Irrawaddy Delta, and Banten (BAN-ten) in West Java. Thanks to the increased amounts of products being obtained and transported, and the wealth this created, urban merchants became a powerful group in local politics. Revenue from trade became more crucial than agricultural taxes in many states. However, agriculture remained a major activity, and new crops and varieties of rice spurred population growth. At the same

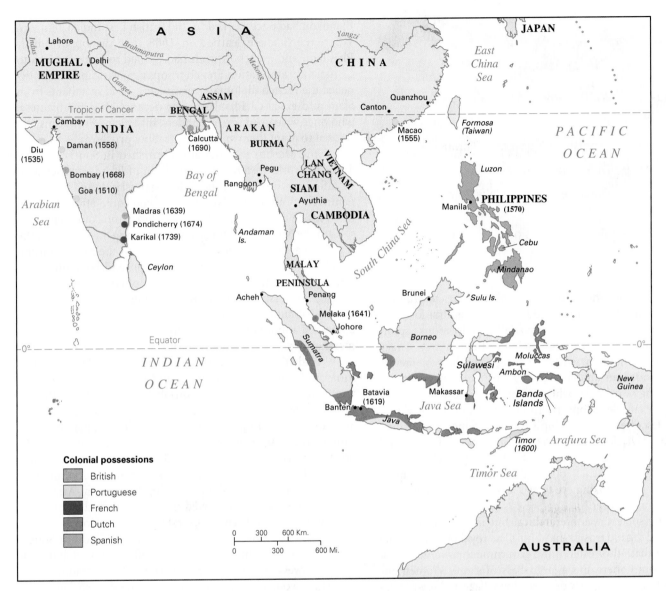

Map 18.2 Southeast Asia in the Early Modern Era
Much of Southeast Asia remained independent, able to deflect European ambitions, but the Portuguese
had captured the port of Melaka, Timor, and the Moluccas (Maluku), and the Spanish had colonized the
Philippines. In the 1600s the Dutch displaced the Portuguese from Melaka and the Moluccas, and ruled
part of Java from Batavia.

time, Theravada Buddhism dug deeper roots on the Southeast
Asian mainland, and Islam continued to spread throughout the
Malay Peninsula and the islands of Indonesia and the southern
Philippines. As a result of increased trade and exposure to new
religions, cultures were opened to the outside world.

Buddhist and Islamic Societies

Various Southeast Asian societies remained vigorous in this
era, in both the Buddhist and Islamic realms (see Map 18.2).
Among the strongest states with a mostly Theravada Buddhist
population was Siam, governed from 1350 to 1767 by kings
based at Ayuthia (see Chronology: Southeast Asia, 1450–1750).
Siam was involved in maritime trade and developed a regional

empire, extending its influence into Cambodia and some of
the small Lao (laow) states along the Mekong River. Its competition with the Burmese, Vietnamese, and the largest Lao state,
Lan Xang (lan chang), for regional dominance occasionally led
to war. Indeed, in the 1560s a Burmese army ravaged Siam and
sacked Ayuthia, carrying back to Burma thousands of Siamese
prisoners and their families. In Burma, the sophistication of
Siam's society was reflected in the occupational skills of these
Siamese captives: actor, actress, architect, artist, blacksmith,
carpenter, coiffeur, cook, coppersmith, goldsmith, lacquer-
ware maker, painter, perfume maker, silversmith, stone carver,
wood carver, and veterinarian.

Siam eventually recovered from Burma's conquest and
flourished. For example, during the reign of King Narai (na-RY)

CHRONOLOGY

Southeast Asia, 1450–1750

1350–1767	Ayuthia kingdom in Siam
1511	Portuguese conquest of Melaka
1565	Spanish conquest of Philippines
1619	Dutch base at Batavia
1641	Dutch seizure of Melaka from Portuguese
1688	Siamese expulsion of French

(r. 1656–1688), the king used some of his revenues to promote literature and art, often with a Buddhist emphasis, thus fostering a cultural renaissance. Since Theravada Buddhist monks sponsored many village schools, Siam had one of the highest literacy rates in the premodern world. The high numbers of literate readers provided an audience for writers, some of whom focused on religious themes while others addressed more earthly affairs. For example, a long poem by Sri Mahosot (shree ma-HO-sut) describes the courtship rituals of young people along the Ayuthia riverside during the evening hours: "O beautiful night! Excited voices on the riverbank. Couples closely embraced they stare at each other. There is smiling, touching, singing in chorus, looking eye to eye. There is excitement, craving and longing forever."[8]

Siamese society was hierarchical but liberal and tolerant by the world's standards at that time. The royal family and the aristocracy that administered the government remained aloof from the commoners and a large class of slaves. Women enjoyed rights, including that of operating village and town markets. Most of the ruling elite, including the king, were ardent Buddhists, and Theravada Buddhism encouraged tolerance toward other faiths. In 1636 a Dutch trader contrasted the tolerance of Siamese Buddhists with the zealous proselytizing of Christians and Muslims in that era. He observed that the Siamese did not condemn any "opinions, but believe that all, though of differing tenets, living virtuously, may be saved, all services which are performed with zeal being acceptable to the great God. And the Christians [and Muslims] are both permitted the free exercise of their religions."[9] Ayuthia's openness to merchants and creative people from all over Eurasia made it a vibrant crossroads of exchange and influence.

However, while open to the outside world, Siam had to contend with increasing European activity. English, French, and Dutch traders all established operations in Ayuthia. King Narai, who had regularly sent missions to Persia, India, and China, sent three diplomatic missions to the French court of Louis XIV to obtain Western maps and scientific knowledge. Narai employed several foreigners as officials, including a Persian Muslim as prime minister and a Greek merchant, Constantine Phaulkon (FALL-kin), as superintendent of foreign trade.

Phaulkon had once worked for the British East India Company. When the Siamese learned in 1688 that the opportunistic Phaulkon and French officials had plotted to convert Narai to Christianity and station French troops near the capital, they expelled the French diplomats, missionaries, and merchants from Siam and executed Phaulkon. For decades after, the Siamese, who once welcomed foreign traders, mistrusted Europeans and refused to grant them any special trading privileges.

Some Muslim societies also flourished in Southeast Asia. Trade networks fostered the expansion of Islam and increased its influence throughout the Indonesian islands and the Malay Peninsula. Southeast Asian Muslims who could afford to do so often made the long pilgrimage to Mecca and some sent their sons to the Middle East for study, reinforcing links between the regions. Various societies adapted Islam to their own cultural traditions. The Javanese often superimposed Islam, often with a Sufi flavor, on the existing foundation of Hinduism and mystical animism (spirit worship), producing an eclectic and tolerant mix of faiths. Some other peoples, including most Malays, embraced a more orthodox version of Islam. As more Muslim merchants called at ports with Muslim rulers, the strengthening of trade ties enriched states. The mixing of Islam and maritime trade encouraged mobility and thus connections to the wider world. For example, Hamzah Fansuri (HOM-sah fan-SIR-ee), a Sufi poet from west Sumatra famed for his mystical and romantic writings, lived for a time in Ayuthia and for a time in Baghdad. Fansuri was a follower of an earlier Spain-born mystic, Ibn al-Arabi (1165–1240), who taught, like Vedanta Hinduism, that all reality is one and everything that exists is part of the divine. By implication, al-Arabi and Fansuri's approach downplayed ritual and law and emphasized dreams, visions, and achieving ecstasy to know God.

Islam also changed gender relations. As in most of Southeast Asia, women in Indonesia had often enjoyed independence. However, Islam, rooted in patriarchal Arab traditions, diminished women's rights in some Indonesian societies. For instance, in Acheh (AH-cheh) in northern Sumatra, where four successive women had ruled in the later 1600s, women were eventually prohibited from holding royal power. But elsewhere women often continued to play key roles. Muslim courts on Java and other islands were often filled with hundreds, sometimes thousands, of women. Some were wives and concubines, but most were attendants, guards, or textile workers. By the 1600s, if not earlier, *batik*, the beautiful cloth produced in Java by a wax and dying process, had appeared. The time-consuming work of making fine batik was mostly done by women in the courts and villages. Batik arts later spread throughout the world.

Southeast Asian Trade and the European Challenge

Southeast Asia's wealth and resources, especially spices such as cloves, nutmeg, and pepper, attracted European merchants and conquerors to the region. The Portuguese who occupied Melaka were the forerunners of a powerful and destabilizing European presence that transformed Southeast Asia between

1500 and 1900. By controlling Melaka, the Portuguese now had an advantage against their European and Malay rivals and had reshaped world trade, as the victorious admiral Albuquerque boasted: "Melaka is the source of all the spices and drugs which the [Muslims] carry every year to [the Middle East]. Cairo and Mecca will be entirely ruined, and Venice will receive no spices unless her merchants go and buy them in Portugal."[10] A few years later the Portuguese brutally conquered the Spice Islands, known as Maluku (muh-LOO-ku) (Moluccas), in northeast Indonesia, thus gaining nearly total control of the valuable spice trade to Europe.

But, as in India, Portuguese power in Southeast Asia proved short-lived. Like the East African ports they occupied earlier, Melaka languished under Portuguese control, since fewer Muslim merchants chose to endure the higher taxes and Portuguese intolerance of Islam. The Portuguese effort to convert subject peoples to Christianity made them unwelcome, and they also faced constant challenge from various neighboring states. In dealing with these challenges, Portuguese policies often involved brutal force. The Jesuit missionary St. Francis Xavier, a Spaniard, described Portuguese behavior in the Spice Islands as little more than discovering new ways of conjugating the verb *to steal*. Although the Dutch replaced the Portuguese in Melaka in 1641, a small Catholic, Portuguese-speaking community still lives in the city of Melaka. Furthermore, for several centuries Portuguese became a language of trade and commerce in some coastal regions of Asia, from Basra in Iraq to ports in Vietnam.

Portuguese activities spurred the Spanish, Dutch, English, and French to compete for markets, resources, Christian converts, and power in Southeast Asia. The Spanish conquered the Philippines, and the Dutch gained some control of the Indian Ocean maritime trade by force and conquered Java and the Spice Islands. Preoccupied with India and the Americas, the English mainly sought only trade relations in this era. The French became involved in Vietnam beginning in 1615. The French sought trade but also dispatched Catholic missionaries, who recruited a small following of Vietnamese. The Vietnamese used the Chinese writing system, and to undercut Confucian influence on Vietnamese culture, French missionaries created a romanized Vietnamese alphabet, which in the twentieth century became the official Vietnamese writing system. But European power had its limits. Southeast Asian states such as Siam, Vietnam, Burma, and Acheh were strong enough to resist over three hundred years of persistent effort by Westerners to gain complete political, social, and economic domination, which they achieved only by 1900.

The Philippines Under Spanish Colonization

The greatest Western impact in Southeast Asia before 1800 came in the Philippine Islands, which were conquered by Spain. For over nearly three centuries of its colonial rule, beginning in 1565, Spain imposed the Catholic religion and many aspects of Spanish culture on the people with a policy known as **Hispanization**. However, the Filipinos managed to develop a diversity of cultures by mixing their indigenous customs with the Spanish influences. Under Spanish rule, the Philippines became a key participant in the new world economy.

Spanish Colonization Spanish interest in the Philippines was a result of their activities in the Americas and their quest for a sea route to Asia. The first Spanish ships to reach the islands in 1521, commanded by Ferdinand Magellan, were part of the first successful effort to circumnavigate the world, though Magellan himself did not complete the voyage. Magellan pressured the Filipinos he encountered to adopt Christianity. He ordered a local chief to burn all his peoples' religious figures and replace them with a cross, which every villager should worship every day on their knees. Magellan's arrogant demands inspired opposition, and he was killed in a skirmish with hostile Filipinos. Today, on the beach on Cebu Island where Magellan died, a memorial honors Lapulapu (LAH-pu-LAH-pu), the chief who led the attack, as the first Filipino to repel European aggression. When, after visiting the Spice Islands, Magellan's ships returned to Spain, they had proved that Columbus was correct that Asia could be reached by sailing west from Europe (see Chapter 17).

Magellan had chanced upon an island group inhabited by some 1 to 2 million people divided into many distinct ethnic groups and speaking over a hundred Malay languages. The population was scattered across 7,000 islands, although the majority lived on the two largest islands, Luzon (loo-ZON) and Mindanao (min-duh-NOW). Muslims occupied the southernmost islands, and Islam was slowly spreading northward, but most Filipinos mixed belief in one supreme being with animism, for which the Spanish labeled them immoral devil worshipers. Remote from the mainland and western Indonesia, the islands had historically received relatively little cultural influence from India or China. Nonetheless, they were not completely isolated. A few hundred Chinese traders lived in the major towns, and some Filipinos traveled as far as Melaka and Burma as maritime traders. Many Filipinos used a simple writing system. Unlike the kingdoms of Java or Siam, the largest Filipino political units were villages led by chiefs.

When, four decades after Magellan's death, the Spaniards returned to conquer and evangelize, they renamed the islands the Philippines after their monarch, Philip II, known as "the most Catholic of kings." Given the ethnic divisions and lack of a dominant Philippine state, the militarily superior Spanish had little trouble conquering the islands and co-opting local chiefs. But the Muslims in the south, called **Moros** by the Spanish, were never completely pacified, and Spanish authority there remained mostly nominal. Today some southern Muslims seek independence from the Christian-dominated country. The Spanish set up their colonial government in

Hispanization The process by which, over nearly three centuries of Spanish colonial rule beginning in 1565, the Catholic religion and Spanish culture were imposed on the Philippine people.

Moros The Spanish term for the Muslim peoples of the southern Philippines.

Manila (muh-NIL-uh), located on a fine natural harbor, which they also hoped to use as a base for trade with China.

The Catholic Church took a major role in the colonial Philippine enterprise. The church governed various regions outside of Manila and acquired great wealth. In many districts priests collected taxes and sold the crops, such as sugar, grown by Filipino parishioners. Catholic friars, accompanying the soldiers, began the process of conversion, and several religious orders competed to gain the most converts. Indeed, the Spanish colonial regime gave the missionaries special authority, and the Spanish crown financed the conversion efforts. Missionaries concentrated on the children of village leaders but, to better control and evangelize the Filipinos, they also required people to move into towns. Few schools were opened outside Manila, and what education existed was in church hands and emphasized religious doctrine. To control competing ideas, the Spanish destroyed nearly all of the pre-Spanish writings, which they considered pagan. The effort to spread Christianity took at least eighty years. Eventually around 85 percent of the Filipinos adopted Roman Catholicism.

However, Filipinos accepted Christianity on their own terms and incorporated their own animist traditions into the religion, to the disgust of the Spanish. Friendly spirits became Christian saints, and miracles attributed to Jesus or the Virgin Mary became the new form of magic. Some Filipinos even used religious festivals to subtly express opposition to Spanish rule. For example, the Spanish introduced passion plays on the life and death of Jesus as a way to spread Christian devotion and morality. But Filipinos wrote their own plays that expressed their anticolonial sentiments, such as by presenting Jesus as a social activist of humble background who was tormented by a corrupt ruling class. Since the Spanish conquerors had contempt for the common people, few Filipinos were able to rise in the church hierarchy or in government. Reflecting these biases, one Spanish observer mocked the Filipino priest as "a caricature of everybody. He is a patchwork of many things and is nothing. He is an enemy of Spain."[11]

Colonial Economy and Society

Inequality was not limited to government and the church; it also showed up in economic and social patterns. The colonial economy forged a rural society based on plantation agriculture and tenant farming, implanting a permanent gap between the extraordinarily rich landowners and the impoverished peasants. Traditionally the Filipinos had grown rice for themselves and some sugar to sell to foreign merchants. The Spanish encouraged a much stronger emphasis on lucrative cash crops, such as sugar and hemp, for sale on the world market. The religious orders, Spanish corporations, the Spanish crown, and the families of pro-Spanish chiefs owned most of the farmland. Peasants expressed their dissatisfaction by revolting against local landlords or the corrupt Spanish system. The Filipinos, once masters of the land, mostly became tenants working for a few powerful landowning families or the church. Priests and landowners told them their religious duty was to labor hard for others—they would get their just rewards later in heaven.

Although the Spanish created a country and expanded the economy, they did not construct a cohesive society. Regional and ethnic loyalties remained dominant. In fact, by their decentralized government, the Spanish encouraged regionalism. The Spaniards occupied the top spots, controlling the government and church. The great majority of Spanish lived in Manila, often in luxury, and few outside the church ever learned to speak local languages. Below them were mixed-descent people, known as mestizos, who resulted from intermarriage and cohabitation of Spanish men with Filipinas, and a few Filipino families who descended from chiefs. Below them were Chinese immigrants, who worked as merchants and craftsmen. Some Chinese became rich, but most remained middle class, especially those who opened small shops in rural towns. The Chinese often became Catholic, and Chinese men often married Filipinas, forming the basis for a Chinese mestizo community. Leaders of the Philippines today are frequently of Chinese or Spanish mestizo ancestry. But while the Spanish needed the Chinese as middlemen, they also despised, persecuted, and sometimes expelled them. On occasion, when

Chinese Mestizo Couple   This painting by a French artist shows two wealthy, well-dressed Chinese mestizos riding in Manila. Chinese mestizos, products of marriages between Chinese immigrants and Filipino or Spanish women, played a key role in colonial life.   [From Edgar Wickberg, *The Chinese in Philippine Life 1850-1898* (New Haven and London: Yale University Press, 1965)]

their resentment of Chinese wealth or concern with growing Chinese numbers became intense, Spanish forces slaughtered the residents of Manila's large Chinatown.

The lowest social status was held by the vast majority of Filipinos, whom the Spanish called **Indios** (Indies people). They faced many legal restrictions; for example, they were prohibited from dressing like Spaniards. The Filipinos retained their traditionally strong communal orientation, including powerful kinship networks and their close family ties. However, since the Spanish culture and church devalued women, Filipinas lost the high position they had enjoyed in pre-Spanish society and now faced restrictions on their activities. For instance, the female priestesses integral to Filipino animism were pushed to the margins of society by male Catholic priests, one of whom described the priestesses as "loathsome creatures, foul, obscene, truly damnable. My task [is] to reduce them to order."[12] Despite male prejudice and a narrowing of gender roles, Filipinas continued to control family finances and engage in small-scale trade.

Indonesia and the Dutch

In the seventeenth century the Dutch arrived, displacing the Portuguese from most of their bases and becoming the dominant European power in Southeast Asia. The Dutch gradually expanded their influence from the Spice Islands to other islands, notably Java. Since they built their empire in the Indies over a period of three hundred years, their impact varied widely over time. The Dutch sought wealth but, unlike the Portuguese and Spanish, cared little about spreading their culture and religion. Nonetheless, they fostered a unique colonial society.

The Rise of Dutch Power The Dutch became Europe's most prosperous society during the 1600s, in large part because of their trade and conquests in Asia, especially Indonesia. Dutch ships had long carried spices from Portugal to northern Europe. In 1595 a Dutch fleet visited the Spice Islands of Maluku and brought back spices to Holland. Over the next several decades the Dutch, after bloody battles, dislodged the Portuguese from most of their scattered outposts, including Maluku. Finally, they captured the Portuguese-controlled port of Melaka in 1641. But although they tried to revive Melaka as a trade entrepôt, the city never recovered its earlier glory.

Over the next several centuries the Dutch gradually gained control of the islands of Indonesia, except for the Portuguese-ruled eastern half of the island of Timor. They eliminated all competition, often by military force, and quickly became hated for their ruthlessness. For example, in 1623 the Dutch massacred the English residents of a base on Ambon (am-BOHN) Island. As Dutch forces attacked and occupied the prosperous trading city of Makassar (muh-KAS-uhr), in southeast Sulawesi (SOO-la-WAY-see), in 1659, the city's sultan asked: "Do you believe that God has preserved for your trade alone islands which lie so distant from your homeland?" The sultan's secretary, Amin, wrote a long poetic account about the disaster: "Listen, sir, to my advice; never make friends with the Dutch. No country can call itself safe when they are around."[13] Both sides sparked conflict, but with their superior military power, the Dutch often slaughtered their Indonesian opponents by the thousands.

The Dutch were also well-organized, resourceful, and shrewd diplomats, allying themselves with one state against a rival state. While exploiting local conflicts, however, they sometimes were drawn into civil wars or were faced with stiff resistance. For example, Shaikh Yusuf (ca. 1624–1699) from Sulawesi had studied Islamic knowledge in Acheh and Arabia and had become a spiritual adviser to the sultan of Banten, a small trading state in western Java. Becoming enraged by Dutch practices that threatened Islamic morality, such as the toleration of gambling, opium smoking, and cock fighting, in 1683 he led 2,000 followers into a holy war against the Dutch. It failed, however, and Yusuf was exiled to Dutch-ruled South Africa, where he died.

With trade as their major goal, for several centuries the Dutch left administration of their Indonesian bases to the Dutch East India Company, which had great capital and large resources for pursuing profit. Since Holland was ten months away by boat, there was little guidance and few restraints on the company's power, and it used its goal of gaining a monopoly of trade in Southeast Asia to justify ruthless policies. If the people of a Spice Island grew restless, Dutch forces might exterminate them or carry them off as slaves to Java, Ceylon, or South Africa. For instance, in 1621 the entire population of the spice-producing Banda (BAN-duh) Islands—some 15,000 people—were killed, taken away as slaves, or left to starve. To increase demand and reduce supply, the Dutch sometimes chopped down spice-growing trees and bushes en masse, leaving the population with no source of income.

The Dutch-Javan Encounter Eventually the Dutch concentrated on the rich island of Java, which had a flourishing mercantile economy tied to maritime trade and several competing sultanates. In the 1600s Java boasted at least two cities with over 100,000 people, and their population was a cosmopolitan mix drawn from throughout Asia. Javan artisans were noted for fine craftsmanship. For example, the island's smiths made perhaps the finest steel swords in the world. The commercial prowess of the Javanese, the main ethnic group on the island, was renowned in the region. Javanese women were prominent in business alongside the men, as an English observer noted: "It is usual for a husband to entrust his pecuniary affairs entirely to his wife. The women alone attend the markets, and conduct all the buying and selling."[14] Thus the Dutch did not come into an underdeveloped society, but one with living standards comparable to those in western Europe.

Capitalizing on Java's political instability and divisions, the Dutch slowly extended their power across the island after establishing a military and commercial base at a village they renamed Batavia, on the northwestern coast, in 1619. Batavia

Indios ("Indies peoples") The Filipinos at the bottom of the Spanish colonial social structure, who faced many legal restrictions.

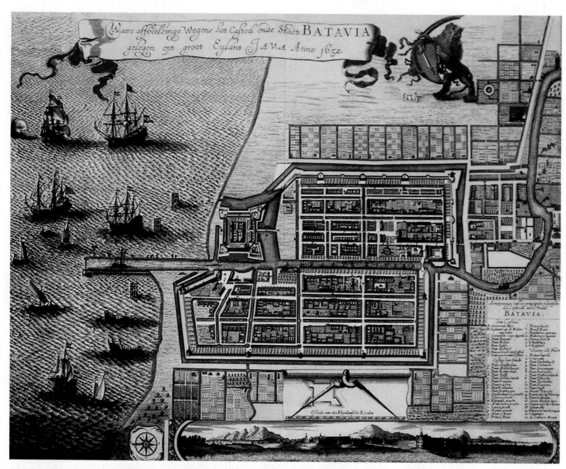

Batavia The Dutch built a port they called Batavia on the northwest coast of Java. Batavia, shown on this map from 1652, grew rapidly as the political and commercial center of the Dutch empire in Southeast Asia. (Royal Institute of Linguistics and Anthropology, Leiden)

later grew into a city, today known as Jakarta. Most of Java came under direct or indirect Dutch control by the end of the eighteenth century. The Dutch became preoccupied with consolidating their position in Java and the Spice Islands, especially after Batavia became a flourishing trading city. They co-opted the local elites and governed some districts through local rulers. Admiring the Chinese traders, who had operated in Java for centuries, the Dutch invited more Chinese to come in as middlemen. Dutch and Chinese entrepreneurs slowly displaced the Javanese merchant class, once major players in the world economy.

Soon the Dutch concentrated on making Java a source of wealth. The burden of economic change fell on the peasantry, most of whom grew rice. In the highlands of west Java, and later in Sumatra, peasants were forced to grow coffee for export through a system of annual quotas. Coffee, domesticated centuries earlier in Ethiopia and then grown in southern Arabia, had become a popular beverage in both the Middle East and Europe. The Dutch earned huge sums from this process, enough to finance much of Holland's industrialization in the nineteenth century. Coffee soon came to be called "java" in the West. Between 1726 and 1878 Holland controlled 50 to 75 percent of the world's coffee trade.

Through their political and economic activities, the Dutch gradually transformed Javan society and life. As in other colonies and pre-Dutch Java, inequality characterized the society. Europeans occupied the top rung, followed by those of mixed-descent, known as Eurasians, and the co-opted local aristocracy. Javanese now became even more preoccupied with social status, and the peasants were encouraged to treat the aristocratic officials with great awe and respect. The middle class was mostly Chinese. Like the Spanish in the Philippines, the Dutch came to fear the growing Chinese community, a fear that sometimes led to a massacre of Chinese in Batavia. The lower class included not only the peasants but also Javanese merchants. Denied real power, the Javanese royal courts turned inward to refine the traditional culture. As a result, the royal dances became fantastically fluid, graceful, and stylized; the batik fabrics produced by women at the courts more splendid and intricate.

Gradually the Dutch colonists, most of them men, became part of Javan society. Many Dutch found Javanese culture seductive and took local wives, owned slaves, dressed in Javanese clothes, and indulged in the delicious spicy curries, now enriched by American chilies. Other Dutch, however, criticized this behavior. Whatever their attitude toward local customs, most

Dutch lived in Batavia, which was built to resemble a city in the Netherlands. Its close-packed, stuffy houses and stagnant canals were poorly suited to the tropics, and the puritanical Dutch wore heavy woolen clothes in the tropical heat but bathed only once a week. The children of Dutch men and Javan women often grew up speaking Malay, the most common language in Batavia. Like many Southeast Asian cities, Batavia had a highly mixed, multiethnic society. The Dutch, who recognized religious freedom at home, spent little money on Christian missions.

Southeast Asians and the World Economy

The major changes experienced by Southeast Asians during the Early Modern Era reshaped global commerce. With the Portuguese, Dutch, and Spanish exporting luxury items such as Indonesian spices but also bulk products such as tin, sugar, and rice from their newly colonized possessions, the region became an even more crucial part of the developing world economy. Some historians trace the birth of a truly world economy to the founding of the Philippine city of Manila in 1571, which became the first hub linking Asia and the Americas across the Pacific. Each year Philippine crops and other Asian products, including Chinese silk and porcelain, were brought to Manila for export to Mexico. From there some products were shipped on to Europe. These Spanish galleons symbolized the new global reality. The galleons returned to Manila with European goods, mail, personnel, and vast amounts of silver to pay for Asian goods, draining Spanish imperial coffers and enriching Asian treasuries. Over half the silver mined in the Americas ended up in China. The American silver gave the Asian economy a great push, encouraging increased production of Philippine sugar, Chinese tea, and Indian textiles.

The Manila galleon trade was highly speculative, since Spanish businessmen bet their fortunes that the galleons would arrive in Mexico safely. Pirates, storms, and other obstacles made the voyages dangerous. For example, on a crossing in 1604, the *Espiritu Santo* became grounded on a shoal leaving Manila Bay, encountered a storm off California that destroyed much of its rigging, and was struck by lightning, which killed three crewman, before limping into the port of Acapulco two months late. Sometimes the galleons never completed their voyages. Thus, while investors could reap huge profits, they sometimes incurred huge losses. The unpredictable galleon trade fostered a "get rich quick" mentality rather than a long-term strategy to bring prosperity to the Philippines.

In spite of all the economic changes, Southeast Asians retained considerable continuity with the past. The West was not yet dominant in either political or economic spheres, except in a few widely scattered outposts such as Melaka, the Spice Islands, and the Philippines. The European interlopers had to compete with Chinese, Arab, Indian, and Southeast Asian merchants. Nor were Europeans the only growing political power. The Vietnamese, continuing their long expansion down the Vietnamese coast, had annexed the Mekong Delta by the late 1600s, and the Siamese forced the French to leave. In brief, the European powers had entered a wealthy, open, and dynamic region. Only by the eighteenth century did the Southeast Asian commercial society begin to collapse under the weight of accelerating Western military and economic activity, combined with internal strife and increasingly expensive government structures.

SECTION SUMMARY

- Increased trade in Southeast Asia led to greater political centralization and increased the influence of major world religions such as Islam and Buddhism.
- Theravada Buddhism thrived in Siam, which was highly literate and cultured, while Islam flourished on the Malay Peninsula, where an orthodox form took hold, and in the Indonesian archipelago, where it blended with local traditions.
- Europeans, beginning with the violent Portuguese and later including the Spanish, Dutch, English, and French, were attracted by Southeast Asia's riches and resources.
- The Spanish conquered the Philippine Islands and eventually succeeded in converting local people to Christianity, though the Filipinos shaped Christianity to their own ends.
- The militaristic Dutch came to dominate Southeast Asia, particularly Java, which they turned into a highly profitable coffee exporter, but whose culture they did not attempt to transform.
- As a result of European colonization, Southeast Asia entered the world economy, though European speculators often focused on making quick money rather than strengthening the region's economy for the long term.

Early Modern China and New Challenges

What factors enabled China to remain one of the world's strongest and most dynamic societies?

Two dynasties, the Ming followed by the Qing (ching), ruled China for more than half a millennium, between the overthrow of the Mongols and the advent of a republic in 1912 (see Map 18.3). These centuries make up one of the great eras of orderly government and social stability in history. Like western Europeans at this time, the Chinese enjoyed widening market networks and more cultivation of cash crops. China still remained one of the strongest, most industrialized societies through the eighteenth century, boasting a vibrant culture and economy. Because of its continuing strength and its location on the eastern fringe of Asia, European influence and pressure were relatively slight in the Early Modern Era. Although encounters with Europeans indicated the challenges ahead just as China began to experience political and technological decay, no other country could match the size, wealth, and power of Early Modern China.

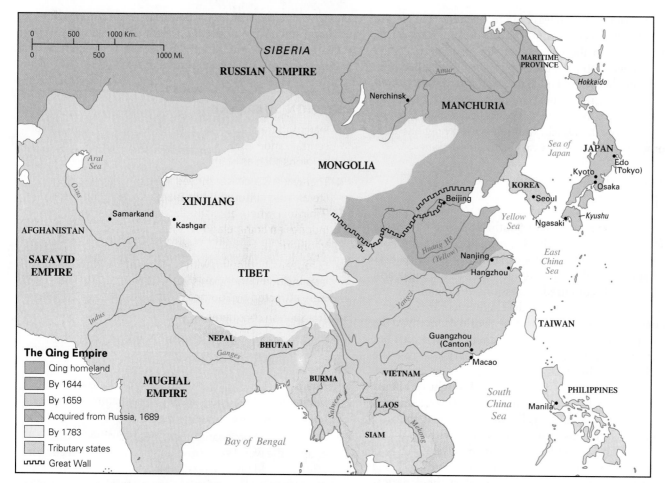

Map 18.3 Qing China and East Asia in the Early Modern Era
Qing China remained the colossus of eastern Eurasia, controlling a huge empire that included Tibet, Xinjiang, and Mongolia. Korea and Vietnam remained tributary states of China, but the Russians expanded into eastern Siberia. The Japanese partly secluded themselves from the outside world.

Online Study Center **Improve Your Grade** Interactive Map: The Qing Empire, 1644–1753

The Later Ming Dynasty

China under the Ming (1368–1644) remained strong and dynamic (see Chronology: China, 1450–1750). The imperial political system administered by the mandarins was supported by a highly productive agriculture and the world's largest, most diversified commercial economy. Although heavily regulated, commercial activity provided the people with numerous products and services, and the Mings' rebuilding of the transportation network centered on the Grand Canal made it easier to ship goods and hence stimulated manufacturing. Cotton fields in North China supplied a growing textile industry. Along with silk and tea, these textiles were exported to Japan and Southeast Asia for silver and spices.

For centuries China had been among the world leaders in scientific thought and technological invention. This inventiveness continued: late Ming and early Qing Chinese developed color woodblock printing and introduced new equipment into the textile industry. Better cotton gins, spinning wheels, and

other technologies for textile and silk production fostered growth and the employment of many more workers. Chinese also continued to publish scientific books.

At the same time, however, Ming China turned somewhat inward, concentrating on home affairs and the defense of the northern borders. Always self-sufficient and self-centered, China became increasingly ethnocentric, even antiforeign; the great maritime voyages of the early fifteenth century had ended, and the Ming court increasingly viewed foreign states as merely tribute providers. Although some foreign merchants continued to come to China, and Chinese merchants still went to Southeast Asia, the Ming launched a period of increased isolation, in contrast to the cosmopolitanism of the earlier Tang, Song, and Yuan periods. The Chinese, having turned inward, were not patrolling the Indian Ocean in their great junks when the first Portuguese ships arrived.

Misrule and other mounting problems helped undercut the Ming and led to dynastic change. During the later 1500s, crop failures, which caused famine, and a terrible plague killed

CHRONOLOGY

China, 1450–1750

1368–1644	Ming dynasty
1557	Portuguese base at Macao
1610	Death of Matteo Ricci in Beijing
1644–1912	Qing dynasty
1689	Treaty of Nerchinsk

millions in north China. In the 1590s the Ming had to dispatch soldiers and a large naval force to defend their Korean vassal from the Japanese, at a huge cost to the treasury. Adding to the pressure, Japanese pirates ravaged the southern coast and peasant revolts broke out. These problems opened the doors to the Manchus (MAN-chooz), a seminomadic pastoral people from Manchuria just northeast of China, who were angry at the migration of Chinese settlers into their homeland. United under a strong chief, the Manchus found collaborators among Chinese tired of the Ming failures. While peasant rebellions rocked the country, Manchu forces swept into China on horseback, routing the Ming. However, it took several decades to occupy and pacify the country, and Ming loyalists held out in the south and on the large offshore island of Taiwan for several decades.

Qing Empire and Society

The new Manchu rulers installed the Qing dynasty, which ruled from 1644 to 1912. The first Qing rulers were exceptionally competent overseers, governing from Beijing through the Chinese bureaucracy and patronizing Confucianism much like their Chinese predecessors. Although they retained their ethnic identity, forbidding Manchu intermarriage with Chinese, the Manchus knew that to be successful they would have to adopt Chinese institutions and culture to win the support of the Chinese people. Hence, like most earlier foreign rulers, the Manchus underwent voluntary assimilation to Chinese ways. Chinese served in high offices, and many villagers scarcely knew China had foreign rulers. Like earlier dynasties, the Qing relied on the mandarins, scholars educated in the Confucian classics, for administration.

Some Qing emperors were outstanding managers and hard workers, aware of their awesome responsibility and willing to temper arbitrary power. The most admired Qing ruler, the reflective Kangzi (kang-shee) (r. 1661–1722), wrote that "giving life to the people and killing people—these are the powers that an emperor has. He knows that administrative errors in government bureaus can be rectified, but that a criminal who is executed cannot be brought back to life any more than a chopped string can be joined together again."[15] Kangzi loved to tour the provinces inspecting public works and joining hunting expeditions. Like other emperors, he was also a

noted writer and painter, exemplifying the Confucian ideal of the virtuous ruler. His son and successor, Yongzheng (youngcheng) (r. 1723–1735), tried to improve social conditions. For example, he ordered that anyone held in hereditary servile status anywhere in the empire be freed. The law was aimed at groups in remote regions who still practiced forms of slavery.

The Manchus created the greatest Eurasian land empire since the Mongols, making China one of the world's major political powers. Qing armies reasserted Chinese control of the western and northern frontier, annexing Xinjiang (shinchang) ("New Dominions"), a desert region largely inhabited by Turkish-speaking Muslims, and Mongolia. For the first time in Chinese history, peace prevailed along the northern and western borderlands. Tibet, long a tributary state to China, was brought into the Manchu fold. While Tibetans shared with Manchus and Mongols the same mystical and magical version of Buddhism known as Lamaism (LAH-muh-iz-uhm), the Tibetans were ethnically and culturally different from Chinese. The Qing also incorporated Taiwan, off the east coast. This large, fertile island's original inhabitants were Malay peoples, but Chinese began immigrating there in large numbers in the 1600s.

Ming and Qing China owed their political and social stability in part to the Chinese gentry, whose power was based on their combined possession of land and office in an agrarian-based bureaucratic empire. As landlords and moneylenders, the gentry had dominated economic life in villages since the Tang dynasty. Natural disasters brought them even more land from bankruptcies. Because they owned land and could afford tutors, the gentry men also received a formal education and held scholarly degrees. The mid-Qing novel, *The Story of the Stone*, revealed the expectations for sons in gentry families: "A boy's proper business is to read books in order to gain an understanding of things, so that when he grows up he can play his part in governing the country."[16]

Under the Ming, a close relationship had developed between the local gentry and the imperial bureaucracy, a relationship that continued under the Qing. Most of the gentry made their peace with the Manchus and served the Qing, and together the Chinese gentry and the Manchu rulers sought to preserve the status quo. However, some of the gentry could not successfully negotiate the dynastic change. For example, the celebrated essayist, poet, and historian Zhang Dai (chang die) (1597–1680) lived a comfortable life during the late Ming, in part because the three generations of Zhang men before him had been high-ranking mandarins and he himself passed the rigorous civil service exams. His privileged status and wealth allowed him to support a wife and several consorts, by whom he had eight or ten children. As a rich man Zhang had ample leisure time, which he chiefly spent at a lakeside villa in Hangzhou (hahng choh), visiting tourist sites, collecting handcrafted lanterns, playing the lute, and getting together with a crab-eating club. However, in the 1640s the Zhangs ran afoul of changing political winds during the dangerous transition between the Ming and Qing dynasties, and they were reduced to poverty. Zhang Dai spent the remainder of his life writing about his family history, trying to recreate and memorialize the

Emperor Kangxi The Qing emperor Kangxi had one of the longest reigns in Chinese history, and his birthdays were given lavish public celebrations. In this print of Beijing, a crowd gathers around the royal dais while women observe the festivities from courtyards (foreground) and shopkeepers look on from their businesses. (Laurie Platt Winfrey, Inc)

Ming world in which the Zhangs had prospered.

Women had a complex status in the patriarchal society of Qing China. The education of women was frequently debated among the elite and was encouraged by some intellectuals. Some women from gentry and merchant families were educated informally, reading and even writing literature. Zhang Dai credited the Zhang women with keeping his extended family organized and with influencing major family decisions. However, elite women also had limited physical mobility because of footbinding, a custom introduced half a millennium earlier but which only became widespread during the Ming. Peasant women were usually illiterate but nonetheless played a key economic role. For example, women improved and promoted spinning and weaving tools. In the cloth industry, the men planted the cotton but the women picked the crop, processed it into yarn, and wove the finished product for sale. An eighteenth-century government report observed that "whole peasant families assemble, young and old; the mother-in-law leads her son's wives, the mother supervises her daughters; when the wicker lantern is lit and the starlight and moonlight come slanting down, still the click-clack of the spindle-wheels comes from the house."[17] But in many districts peasant women were gradually marginalized as their menfolk or large commercial farmers took over their livelihood in search of greater profits.

Chinese attitudes toward homosexuality fluctuated. The European traders and missionaries who visited in China in the sixteenth and seventeenth centuries were shocked at the Chinese tolerance toward homosexuality, fiercely punished in much of Europe. One Catholic missionary lamented that homosexual relations were neither forbidden in Chinese law nor considered shameful. However, some Chinese scholars blamed the downfall of the Ming on lax morality and convinced the Qing to penalize unconventional behavior, including homosexuality. Yet, by Europeans' standards, the Qing punishments were mild and the repression gradually ebbed. At least half of the Qing emperors are thought to have had same-sex bed-mates. These relationships did not preclude marriage and family, and one Qing emperor with a male lover also fathered 27 children with his wives and concubines.

Thought and Culture

Along with social conditions and steady leadership, philosophy also contributed to the stability of the Ming and Qing period. Most Chinese remained comfortable with the eclectic philosophical and religious mix of Confucianism, Buddhism, and Daoism that had evolved in the Classical Era. Nonetheless, a renaissance of Confucian thought flourished during the Ming and early Qing, when changing times seemed to call for something more than mere memorization of Confucian classics written in the Classical Era. In response to these changes, some scholars developed an interpretation of Confucianism, known as neo-Confucianism, that incorporated elements of Buddhism and Daoism, stressed rational thinking, and reemphasized the natural goodness of people.

Like their contemporaries, the thinkers of the European Renaissance and Enlightenment, Ming and Qing philosophers sought knowledge for knowledge sake whether or not it conformed to religious doctrine. Some offered ideas similar to those of such European philosophers as Sir Francis Bacon, René Descartes, and John Locke. Like Bacon, the neo-Confucian Wang Yang-Ming (1472–1529) pondered the unity of knowledge and conduct, concluding that the first necessarily required the second. Like Descartes, Wang wondered how people know the external world and concluded that "whatever we see, feel, hear, or in any wise conceive or understand is as real as ever."[18] Like Bacon and Locke, many scholars espoused the idea that the mind is reason. Others turned to the critical study of the past, emphasizing historical linguistics and archaeology. Like Enlightenment thinkers, a few Chinese scholars studied knowledge from other societies. For example, the philosopher and poet Tai Chen, a merchant's son, made comparative studies of Chinese and Western mathematics.

However, as neo-Confucianism became more influential, it turned into a new orthodoxy, limiting Chinese interest in alternative ideas. Some Qing scholars wrote that no more writing was needed because the truth had been made clear by ancient thinkers: all that was left was to practice their teachings. By the 1700s, fewer Chinese intellectuals showed much interest in practical inquiry or technological development. Neo-Confucianism reinforced a growing social rigidity, including increasing male dominance over women. Thus, although it contributed to the unparalleled continuity of Chinese society, it did so at considerable cost: intellectual conformity was hostile to originality or ideas from outside.

While intellectual inquiry began to stagnate, China's art and literature, in contrast, remained creative. As they had for centuries, artists painted landscapes featuring misty distances, soaring mountains, and angular pine trees. However, many innovative painters drew on Daoist mysticism to create fanciful scenes at odds with tradition. For example, Zhu Da (ca. 1626–1705), famous for his eccentric personality, painted bizarre conceptions of nature: huge lotuses in ponds, birds with wise-looking eyes, and surging landscapes. Qing authors wrote some of China's greatest fiction. Some scholars who had failed the civil service examinations became writers, and their experience fostered a critical detachment from traditional society. For example, in the early 1700s the novel *The Scholars,* by Wu Jingzi (woo ching-see), satirized the examination system and revealed the foibles of the pompous and the ignorant.

Likewise, *The Story of the Stone,* by Cao Xueqin (tsao swee-chin), used a large and declining gentry family to discuss, and sometimes satirize, Qing life. Often considered China's greatest novel, *The Story* contains 120 chapters and runs to some 1,300 pages. An even longer work was the world's greatest encyclopedia, 5,000 volumes long, which Qing scholars compiled under imperial patronage.

China and the World Economy

China in the later Ming and early Qing had commercial vitality, flourishing industrial production, and extensive foreign trade. Indeed, the Chinese, whose goods often sold hundreds of miles from where they were produced, enjoyed the world's largest and best-integrated commercial economy (see Witness to the Past: A Mandarin's Critique of Chinese Merchants). Government taxation policies encouraged both agriculture and industry. A Chinese official wrote in 1637 that there was at least one cotton loom in every ten houses. Gradually the fertile lower Yangzi (yahng-zeh) Basin, linked by the Yangzi River and Grand Canal to west and north China, became China's industrial heartland, commercial hub, and most prosperous region. Throughout the 1700s the people of the Yangzi Basin enjoyed living standards comparable to those of the world's other wealthiest regions, England and the Netherlands, both enriched by overseas colonization. A French visitor in the early 1700s, amazed that China's internal trade vastly exceeded the commerce of all Europe, identified some of the factors promoting economic success, writing that the Chinese put "merit ceaselessly in competition with merit, diligence with diligence, and work with work. The whole country is like a perpetual fair."[19]

Ming and early Qing China remained a major force in an international economy. China exported such products and resources as porcelain, cotton textiles, silk, tea, quicksilver, and zinc, and was a market for and source of valuable products, it

Chinese Porcelain
Like other peoples around Eurasia, people in southwestern Asia prized Chinese porcelain. This Turkish miniature painting shows several valued pieces of Chinese porcelain, probably part of a bride's dowry, being carried in a decorated cart for display during a wedding procession.
(Topkapi Palace Museum)

A Mandarin's Critique of Chinese Merchants

In the late sixteenth century, a Ming official, Zhang Han (Chang Han) (1511–1593), wrote an essay criticizing merchants. Himself from a wealthy merchant family, Zhang had the ambivalent attitude toward merchants that was typical of the Confucian elite of the day. He asserted that merchants were greedy, self-serving, arrogant, and pampered. However, he also admired the products provided by commerce and the efficiency with which they were distributed throughout the empire. And he suggested that China could benefit from lower taxes on mercantile activity.

Money and profit are of great importance to men. They seek profit, then suffer by it, yet they cannot forget it. They exhaust their bodies and spirits, run day and night, yet they still regard what they have gained as insufficient. Those who become merchants eat fine food and wear elegant clothes. . . . Opportunistic persons attracted by their wealth offer to serve them. Pretty girls in beautiful long-sleeved dresses and delicate slippers play stringed and wind instruments for them and compete to please them. Merchants boast that their wisdom and ability are such as to give them a free hand in affairs. They believe that they know all the possible transformations in the universe and therefore can calculate all the changes in the human world, and that the rise and fall of prices are under their command. They are confident that they will not make one mistake in a hundred in their calculations. These merchants do not know how insignificant their wisdom and ability really are. As [the *Chuang Tzu,* an ancient Daoist text] says: "Great understanding is broad and unhurried; little understanding is cramped and busy."

Because I have traveled to many places during my career as an official, I am familiar with commercial activities and business conditions in various places. . . . Those who engage in commerce, including the foot peddler, the cart peddler, and the shopkeeper, display not only clothing and fresh foods from the fields but also numerous luxury items such as priceless jade from [K'un-lun], pearls from the [southern] island of Hainan, gold from Yunnan (in southwest China), and corals from Vietnam. These precious items, coming from the mountains or the sea, are not found in central China. But people in remote areas and in other countries, unafraid of the dangers and difficulties of travel, transport these items step by step to the capital, making it the most prosperous place in the empire. . . . The profits from the tea and salt trades are especially great, but only large-scale merchants can undertake these businesses. Furthermore, there are government regulations on their distribution. . . .

Turning to the taxes levied on Chinese merchants, though these taxes are needed to fill the national treasury, excessive exploitation should be prohibited. . . . But today's merchants are often stopped on the road [at checkpoints] for additional payments and also suffer extortions from the [marketplace] clerks. Such exploitation is hard and bitter enough but, in addition, the merchants are taxed twice. How can they avoid becoming more and more impoverished? . . . Levying taxes on merchants is a bad policy. We should tax people according to their degree of wealth or poverty.

THINKING ABOUT THE READING

1. What criticisms does Zhang make of merchants?
2. In Zhang's view, what benefits does China gain from merchant activity?
3. How does Zhang believe merchant activity could be stimulated?

Source: Patricia Buckley Ebrey, ed., *Chinese Civilization and Society: A Sourcebook,* 2nd ed. rev. (New York: The Free Press, 1993), pp. 216–218. Reprinted with permission of the Free Press, a division of Simon and Schuster Adult Publishing Group. Copyright © 1993 by Patricia Buckley Ebrey.

influenced economic decisions made in Southeast Asia, the Middle East, Europe, and the Americas. As Europeans shipped silver to China to pay for Chinese products, Chinese production increased in response. Chinese population growth was also due to China's link to the international economy, a result of the introduction by Spanish merchants of new crops from the Americas such as corn, sweet potatoes, and peanuts, as well as Chinese development of a new fast-growing rice. The thriving economy served a population that numbered some 100 million in 1500 and reached 250 or 300 million by 1750, a quarter of the world total. Several major cities had over a million residents, including Nanjing (nahn-JING), Beijing, and Guangzhou (gwong-joe) (known in the West as Canton).

However, despite Ming and Qing China's economic dynamism, full-scale capitalism and industrialization did not develop, a result that has puzzled historians. The commercial revolution and technological advances of the Tang, Song, and Ming failed to bring about in China the revolutionary changes that transformed western European feudalism into capitalism. One reason was that, unlike the English and Dutch, the Chinese lacked an overseas empire that could be exploited to acquire capital for investment. Another basic difference from Europe was the continuity of Chinese traditions. The Han pattern was continued in essentials by the Sui, the Sui by the Tang, and so on in unbroken succession until 1912. The traditional bureaucracy-gentry, often contemptuous of merchants and their values, could absorb the effects of economic growth, keeping merchants politically weak, whereas in Europe economic growth undermined the old system. In addition, with a fast-growing population, China had no labor shortage and hence no great spur for technological innovation. Its economy met its basic needs well.

The relations between the imperial government and the merchants may also have been a factor in preventing full-scale capitalism. The imperial system heavily restricted and taxed the merchant class, a major difference from early modern Europe, where big business enterprises and the commercial middle class had a growing influence in politics. In China a large and wealthy merchant class existed and the laws encouraged markets. But the government feared that if merchants became too rich and powerful they might pose a threat to the regime, and hence their activities had to be kept in check. For example, Chinese industrialists and merchants customarily organized themselves into guilds, but the guilds were certified by the government and responsible for the behavior of their members. This made the guilds subject to government interference. During the Song commercial revolution, many mandarins came from merchant backgrounds and tended to protect their family's enterprises as well as business generally. By the Qing this was no longer true. The government also deprived the merchants of valuable goods, and ultimately inhibited capitalism, by maintaining monopolies over the production and distribution of essential commodities, including arms, textiles, pottery, salt, iron, and wine.

Indeed, few opportunities for unrestricted entrepreneurship existed in Ming and Qing China. Government policies reflected China's priorities as a centralized, agriculture-based empire. Hence, in the fifteenth century, the Ming emperor, with little opposition, stopped Zheng He's overseas voyages and ordered Chinese merchants to return home. Of course, that edict did not stop Chinese merchants from going abroad. Those from Fujian (fu-JEN) province, on the southeast coast, remained prominent in Asian trade throughout the Early Modern Era, especially in Southeast Asia. Many had no other options, since their home province offered poor conditions for farming. A Chinese official commented that Fujian men, of necessity, made fields from the sea. But, unlike their European rivals, they received no official support and often had to pay bribes to local officials when they returned home. These fundamental differences from European patterns deflected Chinese energies inward at a fateful turning point in world history, leaving the world's oceans open to Western enterprise.

China's Encounter with Portugal and Christianity

Although it turned inward, China did not cut itself off completely from the outside world. In the 1500s and 1600s European ships seeking to acquire silk, tea, porcelain, lacquer ware, and other products reached Chinese shores. The Portuguese landed on the China coast in 1514 and began a troubled relationship with China by failing to request permission from imperial officials to trade. They soon wore out their welcome, earning reputations as pirates and religious fanatics. With their naval forces spread thinly around Asia and Africa, the Portuguese were no match for Chinese armed junks. In 1557, to stop the piracy, the emperor allowed the Portuguese to estab-lish a trading base at a small unpopulated peninsula, Macao (muh-cow), near Guangzhou on the southeast coast. By the 1580s Macao had a population of 10,000, including some 500 Portuguese (many with Chinese wives), several hundred African slaves, and Chinese and Japanese merchants. When the Qing declined in the 1800s, the Portuguese transformed Macao from a trading base into the first Western colony on Chinese soil.

Christian missionaries from Europe, especially Jesuits, also became active in the late Ming and early Qing. The most influential Jesuit missionary, the Italian Matteo Ricci (ma-TAY-o REE-chee) (1552–1610), was a brilliant scholar and linguist who was trained in law, mathematics, and geography. In 1583 he entered China from Macao to study the Confucian classics and foster an interest in Christianity among Confucian scholars. Ricci impressed Chinese officials with his forceful personality and great learning, and he began training young scholars for the civil service exams. Eventually the emperor allowed Ricci and his Jesuit colleagues to settle in Beijing. Armed with his knowledge of European Renaissance science, Ricci became a scientific adviser to the imperial court, helping improve clocks, calendars, and astronomical observations. On Ricci's death the Chinese buried him with honors in Beijing. Despite earning Chinese respect, Ricci attracted only a few converts to his faith.

Online Study Center Improve Your Grade
Primary Source: Journals of Matteo Ricci

The encounter between the Jesuits and the Chinese expanded the horizons of both parties. Some Chinese leaders, in particular the emperor Kangzi, became interested in Western scientific knowledge. Kangzi wrote:

> In the 1690s I often worked several hours a day with [the Jesuits]. I had examined each stage of the forging of a cannon. I worked on clocks and mechanics. [Father] Pereira taught me to play a tune on the harpsichord and the structure of the eight-note scale. I also learned to calculate the weight and volume of spheres, cubes, and cones, and to measure distance and the angles of riverbanks.[20]

A few Chinese even visited Europe. One of them, the Christian convert Michael Alphonsus Shen, demonstrated chopstick techniques for French king Louis XIV and catalogued Chinese books in the Oxford University library.

For their part, the Jesuits, chiefly well-educated Italians, were much impressed with a China that seemed to have more wealth and a more impressive technology than did Europe. Jesuit letters home described Chinese ideas and advanced technology, knowledge that circulated widely in Europe. Enjoying their status, the Jesuits lived like mandarins and wore Chinese clothing. Their admiration of Chinese traditions led them to attempt to harmonize Christianity with Chinese philosophy and ethics as a way of attracting support from Chinese scholars. But they avoided discussing those aspects of Christian theology incompatible with Confucianism.

The efforts of Ricci and his colleagues laid some groundwork for introducing Roman Christianity to China, and by the end of the seventeenth century, some 100,000 Chinese had become Catholics. But this was a tiny percentage of the vast population, and the less tolerant Catholic missionaries who followed the early Jesuits made even less progress. After the pope prohibited any attempt at mixing Christianity and Confucianism, the faith had less appeal. Furthermore, the rival Catholic orders squabbled. Many neo-Confucian thinkers already considered Christianity intellectually false and resented the missionary enterprise for its arrogance. The emperor Yongzheng (young cheng) asked the missionaries: "What would you say if I sent a troop of Buddhist monks into your country to preach their doctrines? You want all Chinese to become Christians. Shall we become subjects of your king? You will listen to no other voices but yours."[21] In the early 1700s the Qing banned Christianity for undermining such Chinese traditions as ancestor worship, persecuted converts, and expelled missionaries.

China Confronts the Western Challenge

New challenges from the Western countries faced China in the 1600s. Before 1800 Europeans could be rebuffed because China was militarily and economically strong. But relations with the Dutch and Russians suggested changes to come. The Dutch had established a base on Taiwan in 1624 but were expelled in 1662 by the militarily stronger Ming resistance forces that had moved to the island. In 1683 the Qing took control of Taiwan, but the Dutch remained active in the China trade. In the late 1600s Russian expeditions crossed Siberia, seeking trade with China as well as sable fur. Over time they consolidated control of the sparsely populated regions north of Xinjiang and Mongolia. They coveted the Amur River valley, in eastern Siberia north of the Manchu homeland and under loose Qing suzerainty, as a gateway to the Pacific and China. In the late 1600s Russian and Chinese forces fought several battles in Siberia. The Chinese won these conflicts but granted Russians commercial privileges in the Treaty of Nerchinsk of 1689, the first treaty between China and a European power and a symbol of things to come. From this relationship the Russians obtained tea, which became popular in Russia. Furthermore, Russia maintained its ambitions in eastern Siberia, occasionally testing Qing resolve and power.

Needing little from outside, China still had considerable control of the relations with European powers before the 1800s. The Qing minimized contacts by restricting foreign trade to a few border outposts and southern ports, especially Guangzhou (Canton), and politely but firmly refused diplomatic relations on an equal basis with the Western nations. The Chinese were willing to absorb useful technologies to improve mapmaking and astronomy, as reflected in the fruitful relationship between Emperor Kangzi and the early Jesuits, but they were less interested in foreign ideas like Christianity. By the mid-Qing, China was also increasingly self-centered and complacent, underestimating the Western challenge.

China's internal problems, such as overpopulation, mounted just as Western economic, industrial, and military power increased and foreign pressures on China intensified in the later 1700s. The sequel was that China, despite full confidence in the superiority of its culture, was eclipsed within a few decades by the West. Having lived under foreign rulers such as the Mongols and Manchus, the Chinese understood political subjugation but could not comprehend that foreign forces might force them to rethink their cultural traditions, which they wanted to preserve at all costs. In late imperial China, culture and nation were one, but during the later 1800s the 2,000-year-old imperial system declined rapidly.

SECTION SUMMARY

- During the Ming dynasty, China maintained its economic power, but it turned increasingly inward and antiforeign and was ultimately undermined by plague, famine, and pressures from Japan.

- The Qing dynasty was established by foreign Manchus, who assimilated to many Chinese ways, amassed the greatest Eurasian land empire since the Mongols, and added Taiwan to China's holdings.

- Chinese neo-Confucians incorporated elements of Buddhism and Daoism in their thinking and, like their European contemporaries, emphasized reason, but over time neo-Confucianism hardened into a new orthodoxy and discouraged the growth of new ideas.

- China's economy remained extremely strong but never developed full-scale capitalism or industrialization, perhaps because it lacked an exploitable overseas empire, and perhaps because the government failed to encourage entrepreneurship.

- China had fitful encounters with Europeans, including Portuguese traders who irked Chinese authorities and established a colony at Macao, and missionaries who had little success and were ultimately banned for undermining Chinese traditions.

- Over time, China faced increasing pressure from the Russians, who fought for commercial privileges in the area north of China.

◈ Continuity and Change in Korea and Japan

How did Korea and Japan change during this era?

For much of the Early Modern Era Korea and Japan remained more isolated than China from the wider world, although both maintained trade relations with China. Korea faced little Western pressure, local issues and conflicts with Japan being far more important. Japanese history also largely revolved around the country's changing economic and social patterns. For a brief period Japan encountered a significant European presence, but when the experience proved destabilizing, the Japanese became aloof from the West.

Choson Korea

The Koreans had learned over the centuries how to mix Chinese influences with local traditions, adapting and modifying Chinese political models, Confucian social patterns, and Mahayana Buddhism. The Yi (YEE) dynasty, which called its state Choson, came to power in 1392 and survived until 1910, a longevity of over five centuries (see Chronology: Korea and Japan, 1450–1750). Strongly Confucian in orientation, the Yi borrowed Chinese models and maintained close relations with their powerful neighbor. The early Yi era was creative, enjoying progress in science and technology as well as in writing and literature. However, Choson began to decline in the 1500s, damaged by factional disputes and a Japanese invasion.

The Japanese invasion proved most disastrous for Korea. In 1592 a Japanese army of 160,000 attempted to conquer some of the peninsula. With superior military power, the Japanese soon captured the capital, Seoul (soul). However, the Koreans, aided by China, fought back and eventually prevailed. They owed their successful defense to their invention, in 1519, of the first ironclad naval vessels, four centuries before such vessels were developed anywhere else. The Koreans used these boats to cut Japanese supply lines and hence undermine the Japanese occupation. Forced to the peace table, the Japanese agreed to withdraw. But the Japanese invasion destroyed countless buildings, weakened the central government, and generated severe economic problems.

After these invasions, while the Yi maintained their power, Koreans abandoned or modified some customs borrowed from China. In theory the Yi government remained Confucian, but practice varied considerably. The rigid old class system was modified, with class lines becoming more open. The society also enjoyed economic development and change: agriculture became more productive, and population grew, reaching 7 million by 1750. Commerce and the merchant class also expanded. Growing dissension fostered movements for change that became stronger after the mid-1700s, laying the foundations for a new era.

CHRONOLOGY	
Korea and Japan, 1450–1750	
1338–1568	Ashikaga Shogunate
1392–1910	Yi (Choson) dynasty in Korea
1549	Beginning of Christian missions in Japan
1592–1598	Japanese invasions of Korea
1603	Founding of Tokugawa Shogunate
1637	Christian rebellion against Tokugawa
1639–1841	Japanese seclusion policy

Ashikaga Japan and the West

Japanese society, with its samurai (SAH-moo-rie) warrior class, distinctive mix of Buddhism, Confucianism, and Shinto, and long history of adapting foreign influences, differed dramatically from those of neighboring Korea and China. But by 1500, Japan under the Ashikaga (ah-shee-KAH-gah) Shogunate (1338–1568), like Yi Korea, was experiencing rapid change that strained the samurai-dominated political and social system that had emerged during the Intermediate Era. The Kyoto-based Ashikaga shoguns, military leaders who dominated the imperial family in Kyoto and the central government, never had much power beyond the capital. A long civil war, during which Western powers intruded into Japan, unsettled conditions even more.

Growth and Conflict in Ashikaga Japan During the Ashikaga years, rapid economic and population growth had major consequences for Japanese society. As technological advances improved agriculture, production per acre tripled, and Japan's population doubled from 16 million in 1500 to perhaps 30 million in 1750. The increased productivity in turn stimulated trade and the gradual development of cities and towns. By 1600 the largest city, Kyoto, may have grown to some 800,000 people. In the cities and towns merchants and craftsmen organized themselves into guilds. Guilds obtained monopoly rights to sell or make a product by paying fees to local governments, thus getting higher status and more freedom than most Japanese enjoyed.

As merchants became more active and assertive, they spurred foreign and domestic trade. Before this time few Japanese other than a few diplomats, fishermen, and Buddhist monks had ventured beyond Korea and China. Now Japanese traders and pirates began visiting Korea, China, and Southeast Asia. Japanese settlers and soldiers of fortune were especially prominent in Vietnam, Cambodia, Siam, and the Philippines. Several thousand Japanese lived in Manila, and one Japanese even became a governor in Siam. Indeed, there was a sizeable Japanese community in King Narai's Siam. Japan became a major supplier of silver, copper, swords, lacquer ware, rice wine, rice, and other goods to Asia. Japanese were showing a highly developed mercantile spirit.

If the Ashikaga economic and military expansion had continued, the Japanese might have been in a position to challenge the Portuguese and other Europeans for influence in Southeast Asia. Perhaps Japan was on the verge of developing into an expansionist and capitalistic country with a flexible social structure, as England, the Netherlands, and France did around the same time, with the gradual replacement of feudalism by market economies and overseas colonization. But growing instability turned Japan in a different direction.

Political turmoil and civil war in Japan were a factor in this shift. Political power became increasingly decentralized, as great territorial landowning magnates, called daimyo, increasingly dominated the regions outside Kyoto. At the beginning of the 1500s there were several hundred of these daimyo, each with a supporting samurai force. The most powerful hoped to one day rule Japan. However, the rise of the daimyo precipitated a civil war that raged for over a century, from the mid-1400s into the late 1500s. The military engagements during the centuries of warrior dominance were mainly matters of hand-to-hand conflict between samurai wielding long, slightly curved, two-handed swords with great efficiency, supported by commoner spearmen. In the late 1600s a famous poet visited a historic battleground and offered a retrospective on the fighters and the fleeting nature of their causes: "The summer grasses! All that is left of the warrior's dream!"[22]

During the late sixteenth and early seventeenth century, three men who successively became shogun gradually restored order. All were brutal warlords but also devotees of the refined tea ceremony and pragmatists willing to challenge powerful institutions. The first, Oda Nobunaga (OH-da no-boo-NAG-ga) (1534–1582), was so wild as a youth that a family servant committed suicide hoping this desperate act might settle the young man down. With the slogan "rule the empire by force," Oda, from a minor daimyo family, became a brilliant military strategist who once defeated an army of 25,000 with his own small force of 2,000 men. He usually performed a folk dance and then sang a delicate verse about life's transience before leading his samurai into bloody battles, where they sometimes slaughtered thousands of rival fighters. Oda deposed the last Ashikaga shogun. Hideyoshi Toyotomi (1536–1598), the second warlord and of peasant origins, had ambitions abroad. He demanded unsuccessfully that the Spanish governor of the Philippines send him tribute. In hopes of gaining land for his supporters, he also dreamed of conquering China. When the Koreans refused his request to use Korea as a staging base for the China invasion, he instead sent a large army into Korea in 1592. The fierce Korean resistance forced the Japanese to abandon the effort on Hideyoshi's death. The last of the three, Tokugawa Ieyasu (ee-yeh-YAH-soo) (1542–1616), one of Hideyoshi's chief generals, ended the warfare and became shogun in 1603.

The Japanese-European Encounter

During the civil war European traders and missionaries arrived in Japan, and their encounter with the Japanese sparked cultural exchange but also conflict. Thanks to the warfare and the absence of strong rule, Japan was now more open to borrowing from outside than it had been since the early Heian (HAY-an) era. The main imports during these decades were technological, especially Western guns, and religious, mainly Christianity. Nonetheless, Japanese leaders became alarmed by the superiority of Western military and naval technology, as well as the surprising effectiveness of Western Christian missionaries in Japan.

In 1542 the Portuguese reached Japan, starting an encounter that troubled both sides. The European arrivals caused a sensation, as we learn from a Japanese observer:

There came on a [merchant ship] a creature one couldn't put a name to, that [appeared to have] human form at first [glance], but might as well be a long-nosed goblin.

Careful inquiry [revealed] that the creature was called a "Padre." The first thing one noticed was how long the nose was! It was like a wartless conch-shell.[23]

The Europeans were equally astonished at what they found. An Italian Jesuit in the 1500s struggled with the cultural differences:

Japan is a world the reverse of Europe. Hardly in anything do their ways conform to ours. They eat and dress differently. Their methods of doing business, their manner of sitting down, their buildings, their domestic arrangements are so unlike ours as to be beyond description or understanding.[24]

But for all the mutual astonishment, the Europeans had an economic, religious, and military impact. The Portuguese traded Chinese silk for Japanese gold, and soon Spanish and Dutch merchants arrived to compete in the Japanese market. Francis Xavier (1506–1552), a Spanish Jesuit missionary, began to preach Christianity in 1549. As a result of energetic Spanish and Portuguese missionary efforts, by 1600 perhaps 300,000 Japanese were Christians, out of a total population of some 18 million. The converts included some of the daimyo on the southern island of Kyushu (KYOO-shoo), who converted to gain a closer relationship to European traders and acquire advanced military technology from the West. But many Japanese grew increasingly suspicious of the missionaries, resented their intolerance of Japanese faiths and local customs, and could not comprehend the fierce competition between Portuguese and Spanish priests, and between rival Catholic orders. Japanese leaders viewed the Christian communities, often armed by the missionaries, as posing a threat to their power.

But the Japanese adopted what was useful to them: Western technologies. Major consequences often followed. They acquired, then quickly improved, muskets from the Portuguese and Spanish. They also developed new tactics to use the firepower they now possessed. Indeed, European guns sharpened warfare and, since even nonsamurai could obtain them, contributed to the breakdown of social class lines. The increasingly common and deadly violence resulting from guns often prompted peasants to seek solace in religion, and some adopted Christianity.

The Tokugawa Shogunate: Stability and Seclusion

The civil war brought on by the rise of the daimyo, and intensified by gunpowder weapons, ended with the Tokugawa Shogunate, which ruled Japan from 1603 to 1868. Tokugawa Ieyasu was a great warrior and able administrator, but also cruel and treacherous. He subdued his rivals and established a shogunate at Tokyo, then known as Edo (ED-doe), presiding over the most centralized state in premodern Japanese history, in striking contrast to the weak Ashikaga shoguns a century earlier.

The Tokugawa leaders imposed a government mixing authoritarian centralization with the rigidly hierarchical social system that emerged in the later Intermediate Era, which resembled medieval European feudalism in some respects. Japan now had a more powerful shogunate than ever before, while the imperial family in Kyoto remained powerless. To discourage rebellion, some members of each daimyo family were required to live in Edo as hostages. The Tokugawa restored the pre–civil war social structure, with the samurais at the top. A samurai scholar instrumental in developing the code of chivalry (*bushido*) defended the special role of his class by saying that the farmers, merchants, and artisans were too busy to master the warrior ways. The samurai, he wrote, "is one who does not cultivate, manufacture, engage in trade. The business of the samurai consists in reflecting on his own station in life, in discharging loyal service to his master, in devoting himself to duty above all."[25]

To stop the conflict between the various Europeans and Catholic orders, Tokugawa eventually ordered a seclusion policy, closing off Japan from Western pressure and ordering home Japanese traders in Southeast Asia. In the process he ejected the feuding Catholic missionaries and merchants, and broke the power of the Christian communities. This led to a rebellion by Japanese Christians in 1637, to which Tokugawa responded by massacring 37,000 Japanese Christians. The shogun warned the Portuguese and Spanish that they were worthy of death and should justly be killed, but he generously spared their lives and instead ordered that they leave Japan and never return. But while Japan was closing itself to the West, trade with China, Korea, and Southeast Asia continued, with Japan paying for silk with its main mineral resource, silver.

While the Portuguese and Spanish were expelled, after 1639 a few Dutch traders were allowed to remain and set up a base on a small island, Deshima (DEH-shi-ma), in Nagasaki (nah-gah-SAH-kee) Bay. The Dutch were not interested in converting the Japanese to Christianity, only in commerce, and for the next two centuries the Dutch base served as Japan's only link to the European world. The Deshima station chief for the Dutch East Indies Company reported in 1650 that the restrictions and humiliations they endured were worth the gains, since Japan was the most profitable of all the company's operations.

Tokugawa Society and Culture

Tokugawa leaders believed that society could be frozen in a hierarchical pattern. But under the surface of the rigid Tokugawa rule new social forces simmered. For example, even though the rulers restricted travel between cities or regions, merchants found ways to evade the rules and move their wares. The Japanese population grew rapidly, straining the country's resources. Thousands of local peasant protests, riots, and uprisings reflected more dramatic discontent. Also a force for change, Tokugawa Japan boasted several large cities, with Tokyo and Osaka each over a million in population by 1800. The cities became centers of complex commercial networks, and their demands fostered agricultural productivity and economic prosperity, especially in the Edo region. Merchants and their values became more influential. By the mid-1700s Japan was a well-organized country, with rising living standards but growing tensions.

The Tokugawa tried to restrict Japanese women. European visitors in the 1500s were surprised that elite women seemed to have more independence than their European contemporaries. A Jesuit noted that, in contrast to Europe, women went where they wished during the day without informing their husbands. These European perceptions were partly accurate. In contrast to some Asian societies, Japanese women were never secluded and participated in community life. Some women were literate, and a few became noted writers. Nonetheless, like women in most societies, Japanese women had few legal or property rights, faced arranged marriages, and were encouraged to be dependent on men, all patriarchal customs reinforced during the early Tokugawa period. As a result, severe laws against adultery only punished women. Women in samurai families were raised to be courteous, conciliatory, and humble toward their husbands. The Tokugawa advised peasants that "however good looking a wife may be, if she neglects her household duties by drinking tea or sight-seeing or rambling along the hillside, she must be divorced."[26] However, gender expectations and relations among urban merchant and artisan families were less rigid.

In Tokugawa culture, distinctive new forms also emerged in the 1600s. In the major cities entertainment districts known as the "floating world" were filled with restaurants, theaters, geisha houses, and brothels. A playwright described a lively district in Osaka: "Through the thronged streets young rakes were strolling, singing folk-songs as they went, reciting fragments of puppet dramas, or imitating famous actors at their dialogues. From the upper rooms of many a teahouse floated the gay plucking of a *samisen* [lute]."[27] The writer Ihara Saikaku (ee-HAR-oo sigh-KOCK-oo), himself from a merchant family, chronicled the floating world and satirized urban merchant life in often erotic novels. The master artist Moronobu (more-oh-NOH-boo) introduced the colorful woodblock prints known as **ukiyo-e** (oo-kee-YO-ee), which celebrated the life of the floating world. Although many considered them vulgar, these prints achieved wide distribution, making famous the actors, geishas, and courtesans who were portrayed. Later, landscapes, such as views of Mt. Fuji, became popular themes for woodcuts. By the 1800s many European artists collected and were influenced by these prints.

New theater forms also appeared, such as the **bunraku** puppet theater and the racy **kabuki** drama, the favored entertainment of the urban population. Aimed particularly at the merchant class, kabuki featured gorgeous costumes, beautiful scenery, and scripts filled with violent passion. Men played all the roles. Professional female impersonators were highly honored and spent years mastering the voice, gestures, and other aspects of femininity.

ukiyo-e Colorful Japanese woodblock prints that celebrated the life of the "floating world," the urban entertainment districts.

bunraku The puppet theater of Tokugawa Japan.

kabuki The all-male and racy drama that became the favored entertainment of the urban population in Tokugawa Japan.

Kabuki Theater   The urban middle classes, especially the merchants and samurais, enjoyed kabuki drama. This eighteenth-century print by one of the most acclaimed artists, Moronobu, shows the audience enjoying a play about a vendetta involving two brothers.
(Tokyo National Museum/DNP Archives)

A new literary device, the seventeen-syllable **haiku** poem, also became popular. Haiku proved an excellent vehicle for discussing the passage of time or briefly summarizing some action or scene through a series of images, such as the famous presentation by the samurai turned wanderer and greatest haiku poet, Matsuo Basho (BAH-show) (1644–1694), of a sudden event on a quiet pond: "An old pond. Frog jumps in. Sound of water." Another Basho poem commented on the change of seasons and human emotions: "No blossoms and no moon, and he is drinking *sake* [rice wine], all alone."[28] Japanese did not need to be lonely on a dark winter's night, as portrayed in the poem, to appreciate Basho's delicate word art.

haiku   The seventeen-syllable poem that proved an excellent vehicle for discussing the passage of time and the change of seasons in Early Modern Japan.

Tokugawa Stability and Its Costs

Tokugawa Japan largely enjoyed security, stability, and peace for 250 years, a pattern many other societies would envy. But it came at a price. Although commerce thrived, Japan, like China, experienced no political transformation or social rejuvenation, since Tokugawa policies preserved rigid class and gender divisions and shielded the people from outside influence. The lack of political and social dynamism left the Tokugawa vulnerable to a later return of Western power, as several Western nations rapidly acquired wealth and resources and improved their technology between 1500 and 1850. The Tokugawa had merely papered over the cracks, pushing social tensions, such as between samurai and merchants and between daimyo and shoguns, below the surface.

When the West intruded in the mid-nineteenth century, the latent tensions boiled over and the Tokugawa lost their grip on power, but Japan, unlike China, was able to respond creatively. Whereas Chinese feared cultural change more than political conquest, the Japanese were more afraid of conquest and more accepting of change. Japan's history of borrowing from abroad made it uniquely prepared to make the necessary adjustments, and the Japanese could assimilate Western techniques and customs to Japanese traditions, as they had done with Chinese and Western imports in earlier eras. These differences meant that China and Japan eventually met the challenge from the West in very different ways.

SECTION SUMMARY

- The Chinese helped Korea to rebuff a 1592 Japanese invasion, but as a result Korean culture began to liberalize and shed some customs borrowed from China.

- Ashikaga Japan saw tremendous economic and population growth, but it was undermined by a lengthy civil war, during which European merchants made incursions and introduced guns and Christianity, upsetting Japan's social order.

- The Tokugawa Shogunate ended Japan's civil war, restored strict order, and expelled European missionaries and traders, with the exception of a small group of Dutch traders who were uninterested in missionary work.

- Despite the Tokugawa leaders' attempt to halt change, the Japanese economy grew rapidly, tensions in Japanese society increased, and Japan's culture flourished in the urban "floating world" and in new theatrical and literary forms.

- Tokugawa Japan was quite stable, but its rigidity hampered its growth and made it vulnerable to overthrow when Western powers returned in the mid-nineteenth century.

Online Study Center ACE the Test

 Chapter Summary

In the Early Modern Period communication between distant peoples intensified. European expansion at that time had much less impact in most of southern and eastern Asia than it had in the Americas and Africa. Many Asian societies remained strong and militarily powerful, able to manipulate or deflect the Europeans who came in search of valuable trade resources and products. Muslim-ruled Mughal India, especially under the tolerant Akbar, developed creative art and architecture and a prosperous export economy. By the 1700s, however, the Mughals weakened from overspending and religious intolerance as new challenges mounted. While various Southeast Asian states, among them Siam, remained strong, the Portuguese and then the Dutch successively captured Melaka and the Spice Islands, and the Dutch gradually conquered Java. The Spanish

carved out a colony in the Philippines and began exporting Asian goods from Manila to the Americas, helping build a world economy. Increasing commerce, fostered partly by European activity, more closely tied Southeast Asia to the growing world economy.

China during the late Ming and early Qing remained among the world's most powerful and prosperous countries, with several outstanding leaders, extensive industry, and the world's largest commercial economy. China traded with other countries on Chinese terms. However, while it remained creative in arts and philosophy, overpopulation and declining support for merchants eventually hindered China just as European pressures increased. Both Japan and Korea imposed policies of partial seclusion. After welcoming Western traders and missionaries, Japan restricted their access. The Tokugawa Shogunate maintained a rigid social and political system but also fostered a creative culture. Hence, European activity was only one of many factors influencing Asian societies.

Online Study Center Improve Your Grade Flashcards

Key Terms

Urdu	Moros	bunraku
Sikhs	Indios	kabuki
Hispanization	ukiyo-e	haiku

Suggested Reading

Books

Brook, Timothy. *The Confusions of Pleasure: Commerce and Culture in Ming China.* Berkeley: University of California Press, 1998. A readable exploration of Ming China, including the lives of China's people.

Chaudhuri, K. N. *Trade and Civilization in the Indian Ocean: An Economic History from the Rise of Islam to 1750.* Cambridge: Cambridge University Press, 1985. A scholarly study of trade and Islam, focusing on India and Southeast Asia.

Cohen, Warren. *East Asia at the Center: Four Thousand Years of Engagement with the World.* New York: Columbia University Press, 2000. A good summary of China, Korea, Japan, and Southeast Asia in Eurasian history.

Crossley, Pamela Kyle. *The Manchus.* Cambridge, Mass.: Blackwell, 1997. An excellent study of Manchu history and culture.

Ebrey, Patricia Buckley, Anne Walthall, and James D. Palais. *East Asia: A Cultural, Social, and Political History.* Boston: Houghton Mifflin, 2006. A readable, comprehensive survey.

Matsunosuke, Nishiyama. *Edo Culture: Daily Life and Diversions in Urban Japan, 1600–1868.* Honolulu: University of Hawaii Press, 1997. A detailed look at popular culture and ways of life during the Tokugawa era.

Mungello, D. E. *The Great Encounter of China and the West, 1500–1800.* 2nd ed. Lanham, Md.: Rowman and Littlefield, 2005. A readable account of the meeting of Chinese and European societies in the Early Modern Era.

Phelan, John L. *The Hispanization of the Philippines: Spanish Aims and Filipino Responses, 1565–1700.* Madison: University of Wisconsin Press, 1959. Dated but still the best general study of the topic.

Prakash, Om. *European Commercial Enterprise in Pre-Colonial India.* New York: Cambridge University Press, 1998. A valuable scholarly study.

Reid, Anthony. *Southeast Asia in the Age of Commerce, 1450–1680.* 2 vols. New Haven: Yale University Press, 1988 and 1993. A major scholarly source on the Southeast Asian societies and their interaction with the wider world.

Richards, John F. *The Mughal Empire.* Cambridge: Cambridge University Press, 1993. The major scholarly study of Mughal India.

Schimmel, Annemarie. *The Empire of the Great Mighals: History, Art and Culture.* New York: Oxford University Press, 2005. Well-illustrated survey emphasizing social and cultural history.

Spence, Jonathan D. *Emperor of China: Self-Portrait of Kang-Hsi.* New York: Vintage, 1974. A fascinating study of an important Qing emperor.

Statler, Oliver. *Japanese Inn.* Honolulu: University of Hawaii Press, 1981. A reprint of one of the best portrayals of life in Early Modern Japan.

Subrahmanyan, Sanjay. *The Portuguese Empire in Asia, 1500–1700: A Political and Economic History.* New York: Longman, 1993. An overview of the Portuguese and their impacts.

Taylor, Jean Gelman. *Indonesia: Peoples and Histories.* New Haven: Yale University Press, 2003. Highly readable survey with much on this era.

Websites

Internet East Asian History Sourcebook (http://www.fordham.edu/halsall/eastasia/eastasiasbook.html). An invaluable collection of sources and links on China, Japan, and Korea from ancient to modern times.

Internet Guide for China Studies (http://www.sino.uni-heidelberg.de/igcs/). A good collection of links maintained at Germany's Heidelberg University.

Internet Indian History Sourcebook (http://www.fordham.edu/halsall/india/indiasbook.html). An invaluable collection of sources and links on India from ancient to modern times.

East and Southeast Asia: An Annotated Directory of Internet Resources (http://newton.uor.edu/Departments&Programs/AsianStudiesDept/general.html). This site, prepared at the University of Redlands, offers many links on history, culture, and politics, with much on this era.

Nakasendo Highway: A Journey to the Heart of Japan (http://hkuhist2.hku.hk/nakasendo/). This website, hosted at Hong Kong University, uses a famous highway to introduce Tokugawa Japan.

A Visual Sourcebook of Chinese Civilization (http://depts.washington.edu/chinaciv/). A wonderful collection of essays, illustrations, and other useful material on Chinese history.

WWW Southeast Asia Guide (http://www.library.wisc.edu/guides/SEAsia/). An impressive, easy-to-use site from the University of Wisconsin-Madison.

WWW Virtual Library: South Asia (http://www.columbia.edu/cu/libraries/indiv/area/sarai/). This Columbia University site offers many useful resources.

Connecting the Early Modern World, 1450–1750

In 1552 a Spanish historian called the landing in the Americas by a naval expedition led by Christopher Columbus "the greatest event since the creation of the world."[1] It was a claim that ignored many previous achievements, yet the permanent connecting of the hemispheres that followed Columbus in fact reshaped the world, helping to make the Early Modern Era vastly different from the Intermediate Era that preceded it. History was now painted on a larger canvas and peoples' horizons around the world rapidly expanded. In this new global age, greatly increased communication and mobility resulted in encounters, some friendly others hostile, between societies once remote from each other. Travel and exploration revealed the resources of the inhabited world. As a result of this discovery, the exchange among societies of people, diseases, ideas, technologies, capital, resources, and products occurred on a greater scale than ever before. Europeans forged a new world economy, while disrupting, changing, and sometimes destroying the societies they encountered, especially in the Americas and parts of Africa and Southeast Asia. Because of the growing contacts spanning the two hemispheres, for the first time in history an interconnected world became a reality.

But the encounters between Europeans and peoples they could reach only after long sea voyages were only part of the story. The world had many political and economic centers between 1450 and 1750. In the Afro-Eurasian zone, Morocco, the Ottoman Empire, several western European societies, Safavid Persia, Mughal India, China, and a few Southeast Asian societies such as Siam were wealthy, populous, and linked to each other by trade networks and diplomatic ties. They all enjoyed military prowess, had effective states, and fostered creative thinkers. Some African kingdoms, such as Ashante and Buganda, also enjoyed influence and connections to hemispheric trade. No single country or region dominated world politics or the world economy. Yet, the links forged during the Early Modern Era laid a foundation for the building, often by force, of an even more integrated global system, encompassing even the most remote peoples, in the Modern Era.

NEW EMPIRES AND MILITARY POWER

From the dawn of recorded history some peoples have used military power to impose their will on others and create empires. As a result, people often think of history in terms of great empires such as Assyria, Rome, Tang China, the Inca, and, the largest of all, the Mongol. Increasing wealth and power, as well as more deadly weapons, led some Early Modern Era societies to build large empires. Some, such as Safavid Persia, Mughal India, Qing China, and Russia, ruled land empires. In contrast to these empires, which annexed nearby and often sparsely populated territories, the Ottoman Turks controlled large areas of southeastern Europe, western Asia, and North Africa, and the Omani Arabs established footholds in East Africa. The Portuguese, Spanish, Dutch, English, and French empires were even more ambitious, incorporating distant peoples in Africa, Asia, and the Americas. These conquests created empires on a geographical scale never imagined before, even by the Mongols. But empire also had limits, and many peoples were able to resist the imperial designs of the major powers.

Gunpowder Empires

Historians characterize most Early Modern empires as "gunpowder empires" because they depended on bigger and better gunpowder weapons, including cannon mounted on ships, field artillery, and guns used by individual soldiers. Gunpowder empires dominated Eurasia and the Americas. Various Asian and European societies sought to acquire resources and markets in neighboring societies by building empires rather than relying chiefly on trade. Only a few European countries, however, had the means, including sea power, to envision dominating very distant societies, and those countries sought resources and then territory in Africa, the Americas, Asia, and the Pacific. Only those few European countries also had the incentive: the quest for "gold, god, and glory." The worldwide exploration, trade, missionary activity, and conquest that took place during this era resulted from the transformation of various European societies by various forces—the rise of capitalism, powerful merchants, and competitive, centralizing states, as well as by rivalry between Christian churches actively seeking converts—while improved military and maritime technology provided the means for all this activity.

Europeans took advantage of their economic growth and military expansion to improve their position in the world and to compete more effectively for resources in the East, where Islamic societies, India, and China had long enjoyed the most political, economic, and cultural power. Advanced naval and military technology, including gunpowder weapons unknown in the Americas and in much of Africa and Southeast Asia, allowed the Portuguese to seize various African and Asian trading ports, and the Spanish to construct a huge empire in the Americas. The Dutch, English, and French soon followed, establishing footholds in North America, the Caribbean, coastal Africa, and southern Asia. The European powers used some of their weapons against each other. For example, the Dutch and Portuguese were bitter rivals for influence and territory in Southeast Asia, Sri Lanka, and Brazil. Europeans controlled Atlantic shipping and also gained considerable power over Indian Ocean trade, which brought them great wealth. As the English adventurer Sir Walter Raleigh recognized in 1608, "Who so commands the sea commands the trade of the world; who so commands the trade of the world commands the riches of the world."[2]

Dutch Diplomats In this print, a Dutch delegation, eager to make an alliance with the Kongolese against the Portuguese, prostrate themselves before the Kongolese king, sitting on his throne under an imported chandelier, in 1642. (From Olfert Dapper, *Beschreibung von Africa*, Amsterdam, 1670)

A Polycentric World

Despite the growth of empires, the Early Modern world had varied centers of political and economic power, a situation known as polycentrism. No one country could dominate all other rivals. Despite their weaponry, Europeans did not become dominant all over the world during this era. European power was limited in Asia, the Middle East, and parts of Africa and South America, and much of North America and the Pacific remained untouched by European exploration. For much of the era, the Ottomans, Mughals, and Chinese were more politically, economically, and culturally influential in Eurasia than European societies. For example, many Muslims admired Mughal India, which became a destination for merchants, writers, and religious scholars. A Persian poet proclaimed: "Great is India, the Mecca of all in need. A journey to India is of essence to any man made worthy by knowledge and skill."[3] The major Asian states also collected far larger tax revenues than did any European government. Societies in Eurasia, from China to England, and in Africa, from Buganda to Songhai (song-GAH-ee), extended their power into nearby territories, centralized their governments, fostered commerce, and worked to integrate ethnic minorities into the broader society.

The era was dynamic for many peoples. Across Eurasia varied societies experienced economic innovation, free markets, industrialization, and rising living standards. For example, cities such as Amsterdam in Holland, Isfahan (is-fah-HAHN) in Persia, and Ayuthia (uh-YUT-uh-yuh) in Siam were bustling trade crossroads, attracting merchants from all over Eurasia. A Jesuit who visited Surat (SOO-rat) in northwest India in 1663 found countless foreign ships and thousands of foreign merchants, among them traders from over a dozen European societies, including Swedes and Hungarians, as well as many Asians, from Turks to Chinese. Foreign merchants, such as the Dutch and Persians at Ayuthia or at Surat, had to adapt to local customs to succeed. Sometimes, as in Siam, Tokugawa Japan, and Morocco, Europeans who disregarded local customs or threatened local governments were expelled.

The encounters between peoples fostered compromises and information exchange. Many Asians and Africans adapted ideas from other cultures to meet their own needs. Among other leaders, the Chinese emperor Kangzi (KANG-see), the Siamese king Narai (na-RY), the Mughal sultan Akbar (AK-bahr), and the Kongo king Alfonso I showed a keen interest in Western ideas and technologies. Kangzi, for instance, studied Western science with Italian Jesuits, and Alfonso asked the Portuguese for technical assistance. But Europe was not the only source of knowledge. For example, Narai also borrowed architectural styles and medical knowledge from the Persians and Chinese.

The main European advantage had been in acquiring the resources of the Americas for exploitation, often using enslaved African labor. But the large-scale trans-Atlantic slave trade became possible because the kings or chiefs of some

African states, such as Ashante (ah-SHAN-tee) and Dahomey (da-ho-MAY), profited by collaborating with it. Similarly, Spanish rule in the Americas survived only because the conquerors ultimately made compromises with Indian societies. For example, in Peru, well-placed Spaniards intermarried with the Inca elite and Spanish officials adopted some Inca administrative traditions. In the Spanish empire, as well as in other empires of the era such as the Ottoman and Mughal, laws recognized local customs, and different groups often maintained their own legal codes.

Innovative thought reflected the vigor of many societies. Science and technology remained creative all over Eurasia. The Chinese and British, for example, published important scientific books and invented new technologies, especially for the textile industry. New astronomical observatories were built in China, India, and the Middle East, although Europeans had by now developed a much keener interest than Asians in clocks and mathematics. Japan's fostering of schools gave it the world's highest literacy rate and an audience for a publishing industry. Siam and Burma also enjoyed high rates of literacy, though it was chiefly restricted to males. Leaders of the European Renaissance, Reformation, and Enlightenment, Sufi mystics in the Ottoman and Mughal Empires, the Hindu bhakti (BUK-tee) movement in India, and some Chinese thinkers challenged accepted wisdom. Various European and Chinese philosophers emphasized reason, as did some Latin Americans such as the Mexican nun and scientist Sor Juana Ines de la Cruz. Indeed, some participants in the European Enlightenment were inspired by their growing knowledge of secular China, which was ruled by emperors who dabbled in philosophy. A French ambassador in 1688 praised Qing China for promoting "virtue, wisdom, prudence, good faith, sincerity, charity, gentleness, honesty [and] civility."[4]

European achievement of global power was not inevitable. In this era China as well as several western European societies had sizeable empires and the potential for great economic and political success (see Historical Controversy: The Great Divergence Between Europe and Asia). Early Modern China, boasting the world's largest commercialized economy, remained the engine of the Eurasian economy. Not only Europe but also China experienced commercial growth, increases in cash cropping, growing industrial production, and widening marketing networks.

The maritime expansion of Europe, however, contrasted sharply with that of the Chinese. Just as western Europeans turned outward and developed a naval technology to match that of the Chinese, the Chinese pulled back from their grand maritime expeditions of the early 1400s and turned inward, although some Chinese merchants continued to venture out to trade. China enjoyed huge budget surpluses until the late 1700s and did not need colonies or foreign trade to prosper. Unlike western European states, the Chinese government did not depend on rich merchants for economic and political support. Chinese rulers feared that if merchants gained more wealth and influence, they could threaten the state and undermine Confucian values. In contrast, western European merchants had the support of their mercantilist governments, especially in England, the Netherlands, Spain, and France. The resulting political competition between European states fostered exploration and colonization.

Gunpowder and Warfare

Gunpowder weapons were not new. The Chinese invented gunpowder and then made the first true guns in the tenth century C.E., primarily for defensive purposes. The Mongols improved these Chinese weapons into a more effective offensive force, to blow open city gates. By 1241 these weapons had reached Europe. Early Modern Europeans, Turks, Mughals, and Chinese owed their strength in part to improvements in gunpowder weaponry. Combined with better military organization and seagoing capability, advanced weaponry inevitably affected political and social systems.

As they spread around Eurasia and North Africa, gunpowder weapons changed warfare. Europeans learned how to make particularly deadly weapons, improving the technology in part because they had easier access to metals. In Europe—full of competitive, often hostile states—no ruler had a monopoly on weapons, such as siege cannon. Hence rulers had an incentive to constantly improve their armaments, such as handheld muskets, to maintain the balance of power. As a result, the wars in Europe became far more deadly. Indeed, even in Asia and the Americas, Europeans often used the weapons more against each other than against the local people. The French writer Voltaire wrote that after 1500 all the pepper from Calicut came dyed red with blood, and a Portuguese poet lamented that the spices of the Indies were bought with Portuguese blood. The Portuguese, Dutch, and English slaughtered each other in Southeast Asia, and the English and French fought long wars in North America. A similar increase in battlefield casualties came in Japan in the civil war era of the 1500s, when Japanese swordsmiths learned how to replicate Portuguese and Spanish guns and cannon. Japanese small arms soon proved superior to European rifles. In contrast, the Ottomans did not create a class of Turkish and Arab craftsmen and instead relied heavily on hiring European craftsmen to manufacture their military and naval technology. Ashante and Dahomey achieved military success in West Africa because they had large armies equipped with muskets acquired from European slave traders.

But Asians took the development of their gunpowder arsenals only so far. With gunpowder weapons, the Qing greatly expanded China's land frontier deep into Central Asia and Tibet, thereby stabilizing their border regions. After that, secure in their power, the Manchu emperors had little need to increase their offensive capability, while the land-oriented Mughals saw little gain in developing naval armaments. The Chinese, Japanese, and Koreans all had some naval power but no interest in challenging the Europeans in the Indian Ocean. When Chinese came into contact with foreign firearms in 1500s, they found them superior to their own. A Chinese military manual published in 1644 concluded that "nothing has more range than the Ottoman musket. The next best is the European one."[5] Nonetheless, Chinese firearms were adequate for ejecting the

The Great Divergence Between Europe and Asia

In recent years historians have debated the roots of Europe's rise to world leadership, power, and wealth while other societies, especially in Asia, lost the political and economic leadership they once enjoyed—what some call "the great divergence." To many historians the surprising rise of Europe during the Early Modern Era needs explaining. It was not inevitable; history could have turned out very differently.

THE PROBLEM

How, why, and when Europe rather than a major Asian society like China came to dominate the world remain some of the principal questions of modern world history. If several Asian societies had an edge in power and wealth over other societies during most of the Intermediate Era, then why was the world so very different by 1800? Some western European societies, especially Britain, moved toward an unprecedented level of industrialization while once influential Asian societies, including China, increasingly faced challenges from the West. And when did western Europe begin to diverge from other dynamic, commercialized economies, especially China's? The debate divides into several schools of thought.

THE DEBATE

Many historians argue that the great divergence began in the Intermediate Era, when western Europe developed unique advantages that intensified after 1500. They contend that social, cultural, and political factors gave Europeans an advantage. David Landes believes Europe enjoyed a superior social heritage because its values and institutions promoted economic growth. In his view, European countries prospered because they were vital and open, valuing both hard work and knowledge, and these values led to increased economic productivity and positive attitudes toward change. Rodney Stark emphasizes what he considers a tradition unique to Christianity of stressing reason and progress. Offering another explanation, scholars such as E. L. Jones and Nathan Rosenberg stress the political pluralism represented by fiercely competing states. The chronic warfare between states stimulated a quest for increased revenues and more effective weapons. Furthermore, the flexibility of Western institutions, including the shift toward more representative government in England and Holland, made it easier to take advantage of overseas discoveries. In contrast to dynamic Europe, Landes and Jones argue, the rest of the world was static. China, in their view, had by 1700 reached an economic, political, and intellectual dead end, possessing wealth and power but introducing few inventions leading to any breakthroughs.

Other historians reject the notion of European social and cultural superiority. James Blaut and Andre Gunder Frank contend that the key to Europe's rise was not a unique culture but European countries' acquisition of wealth, especially in precious metals, from their conquests in the Americas. Between 1500 and 1800 the colonized Americas supplied 85 percent of the world's silver and 70 percent of the gold, a huge windfall to European merchants and governments, who were selling much of it to China in exchange for tea, silk, porcelain, and other valuable Chinese exports. The rise of the slavery-based plantation economy in the Americas in the 1600s produced additional profits for the Western colonizers. The sale of profitable American minerals and cash crops such as sugar not only stimulated European capitalism but also gave Europeans new advantages as they tapped into the lucrative Asian market. Blaut also believes that Europe benefited from being much closer than was Asia to the Americas.

Many who dispute the claim that Western social and cultural traditions or the pluralistic state system were an advantage agree that Europeans capitalized on events, such as the American conquests and the acquisition of Asian and Middle Eastern technology, to foster economic growth. Scholars such as John Hobson, Alan Smith, L. S. Stavrianos, and Eric Wolf have shown that western European economies were rapidly commercializing from late medieval times and produced a full-blown commercial capitalism between 1450 and 1800 that helped generate a more widespread and powerful world economy. Nonetheless, while Europeans developed better weaponry and business organization, some historians conclude that Europe had no real advantage over China until the late eighteenth or early nineteenth centuries, when industrialization gave the British and later some other western Europeans a vastly superior technology.

Many historians disagree that China was at a dead end and in economic decline. They argue that China's commercial economy dwarfed all others, making China a major player in world trade. In 1800 China still produced a third of all the world's manufactured goods. China also imported over half of all the silver mined in the Americas. Chinese in the commercialized core regions may have enjoyed as high, if not higher, standards of living, per capita incomes, and long life spans as northwest Europeans before 1800. Chinese merchants and craftsmen were intensely competitive, hardly constrained by the Ming and Qing state. Indeed, China's commercial economy grew rapidly from the early Ming to the mid-1700s, producing abundant export products which were eagerly sought by merchants from all over Afro-Eurasia.

Scholars also question whether other Asian societies, including India, were in decline, even though their states were clearly weakening. By 1800 India could not match China's economy but still produced around a quarter of the world's industry, about the same as Europe. With their many exports and imports, China and India remained the engines for the Eastern Hemisphere trading system well into the 1700s. In the early Mughal era India enjoyed a far larger, more productive economy than England. Although the Mughal state was collapsing by the early 1700s, Indian manufactured goods still attracted a vigorous international trade. R. Bin Wong, Kenneth Pomeranz, and Andre Gunder Frank suggest that eighteenth-century China, India, western Europe, and perhaps Japan had comparable levels of economic development. The Indian scholar Amiya Kumar Bagchi agrees, stressing that western Europeans enjoyed no decisive advantage over China and India in economic production, consumption, and growth before Britain's Industrial Revolution, and that China only fell behind in the 1850s. Furthermore, he argues, most Europeans saw little improvement in their lives until the late nineteenth century.

In asking why sustained economic growth began first in northwestern Europe rather than in eastern Asia, Pomeranz argues that the densely populated Yangzi River Delta of China, Japan's Tokyo region, and possibly even India's Gujerat region were similar in many respects to the northwest European core regions, England and the Netherlands, in the seventeenth and eighteenth centuries, and that all these regions were facing similar ecological and demographic stress, such as overpopulation. The great divergence came in the 1800s, he suggests, when one country, England, developed fossil fuels, especially its coal industry, for power while increasingly reaping the benefits of cheap, often slavery-produced resources from the Americas. China had used coal many centuries before Europe, but its remaining coal reserves were remote from the major population centers. The availability of slave-produced American wealth and easily tapped coal reserves, Pomeranz suggests, put first England and then northwestern Europe on a completely new development path unavailable to China, Japan, and India, changing world history.

EVALUATING THE DEBATE

This debate will likely thrive for years, making thoughtful arguments on all sides. Some scholars see the rise of the West as inevitable, a result of certain advantageous trends building for centuries, while others argue that things could have turned out differently had Western nations not been able to exploit American resources and China had sustained its dynamism. The Industrial Revolution in Europe, beginning in the late 1700s, which gave Europeans the technology and wealth to achieve global dominance, may have been the product of long-standing and unique European attitudes, or it may have resulted from a late shift in global economic power, fueled by American resources, that favored Europe and undermined China and India. Whether or not Europe was exceptionally enterprising or simply lucky in finding useful resources, the new, expanded world economy that emerged between 1500 and 1800 benefited primarily western Europe and later North America, but it eventually touched everyone, bringing about changes in many aspects of life around the world.

Tea-Packing Factory in China This painting from the 1700s shows a tea-packing factory in China's major trading port, Guangzhou (Canton) in southern China. A European merchant negotiates with a Chinese manager while Chinese workers prepare tea for export. (Courtesy of the Trustees of the Victoria & Albert Museum)

THINKING ABOUT THE CONTROVERSY

1. Why do some historians believe the great divergence between Asia and the West did not come until after 1750?
2. How did Western expansion into the Americas give some European countries an advantage over Asian countries in the global economy?

EXPLORING THE CONTROVERSY

Historians emphasizing Europe's social, cultural, and political advantages include David S. Landes, *The Wealth and Power of Nations: Why Some Are So Rich and Some Are So Poor* (New York: Norton, 1998), Rodney Stark, *The Victory of Reason: How Christianity Led to Freedom, Capitalism, and Western Success* (New York: Random House, 2005); E. L. Jones, *The European Miracle: Environments, Economies and Geopolitics in the History of Europe and Asia*, 3rd ed. (Cambridge: Cambridge University Press, 2003); and Nathan Rosenberg and L. E. Birdzell, Jr., *How the West Grew Rich* (New York: Basic Books, 1986). On the rise of the European-dominated world economy, see Alan K. Smith, *Creating a World Economy: Merchant Capital, Colonialism, and World Trade, 1400–1825* (Boulder, Colo.: Westview Press, 1991); L. S. Stavrianos, *Global Rift: The Third World Comes of Age* (New York: William Morrow, 1981); and Eric Wolf, *Europe and the Peoples Without History* (Berkeley: University of California Press, 1983). Scholars dubious of innate European advantages include Andre Gunder Frank, *ReORIENT: Global Economy in the Asian Age* (Berkeley: University of California Press, 1998); James Blaut, *The Colonizer's Model of the World: Geographical Diffusionism and Eurocentric History* (New York: Guilford Press, 1993); Amiya Kumar Bagchi, *Perilous Passage: Mankind and the Global Ascendancy of Capital* (Lanham, M.D.: Rowman and Littlefield, 2005); and John M. Hobson, *The Eastern Origins of Western Civilization* (New York: Cambridge University Press, 2004). On China's continuing strength, see Kenneth Pomeranz, *The Great Divergence: China, Europe, and the Making of the Modern World Economy* (Princeton: Princeton University Press, 2000); and R. Bin Wong, *China Transformed: Historical Change and the Limits of European Experience* (Ithaca, N.Y.: Cornell University Press, 1997). For an excellent discussion of the great divergence debate and related issues, see David D. Buck, "Was It Pluck or Luck That Made the West Grow Rich?" *Journal of World History*, 10/2 (Fall, 1999), pp. 413–430.

Dutch from Taiwan and the Russians from the Amur Valley in the 1600s. But two centuries later, European military technology far surpassed that of Asian powers, dramatically changing the hemispheric balance of power.

THE EMERGING WORLD ECONOMY

With the opening of the Atlantic and Pacific Oceans to regular sea travel, connections spanning not just hemispheres but the entire world were forged during the Early Modern Era. Western Europeans gradually created a global network of economic and political relationships that increasingly shaped the destinies of people around the world. Rather than the luxuries of earlier times, such as silks and spices, long-distance trade increasingly moved bulk items: essential natural resources, such as sugar and silver from the Americas, and manufactured goods, such as textiles from Europe and Asia. Traders moved commodities and capital faster and more cheaply over greater distances than ever before. These trends wove together different societies in a world economy. European merchants were actually only a small part of global commerce; some Asian and African merchant groups also flourished, and some Asian states, particularly China and Siam, benefited from the increasing trade. Nonetheless, western Europeans usually benefited more, and it was Europeans who laid the foundations for a new global system to emerge after 1750.

The New Trading System

Europeans became the main beneficiaries of the increased communication and travel that shaped a gradual globalization of trade. The capitalist market economy that gradually developed was increasingly centered on northwestern Europe, especially England and the Netherlands, but a half dozen other European countries were also enriched by trade (see map). For example, the Portuguese as well as the Dutch established regular maritime trade routes between Europe and Asia around Africa that allowed Europeans to avoid the overland routes through the Middle East while harming their Muslim rivals by diminishing Persian and Ottoman commerce. The Spanish conquest of the Americas provided huge quantities of silver from Peru, Bolivia, and Mexico, which financed expansion of the European economy and, since Asian governments valued silver, enabled Europeans to gain access to Asian markets. The Spanish establishment of a base at Manila in 1571 provided an essential economic link between eastern Eurasia and the Americas, forging a major foundation for a truly world economy. European exploration and settlement in the Americas brought access to resources such as timber, marine mammals, fish, and wildlife (particularly furbearing beavers) only lightly exploited before by local peoples.

Growing commercial activity stimulated production for the market, in mining and manufacturing but especially in tropical agriculture. The highly profitable plantations that sprung up around the Caribbean Basin, along the Atlantic coast of North and South America, and on the Atlantic and Indian Ocean islands and the Philippines reflected the expansion of production. A growing trans-Atlantic slave trade provided cheap labor to the American plantations, enabling them to produce inexpensive calories for Europe in the form of sugar and, after 1700, abundant cotton for English mills. Thousands of slaves obtained in eastern Europe, East Africa, Sri Lanka, and Indonesia also labored for European and Muslim enterprises in the Middle East, South Africa, and Southeast Asia.

As a result of the growing commercial activity, including the slave trades, by 1750 millions of people worked thousands of miles from their place of birth or otherwise experienced lives very different from those of their ancestors. For example, Chinese merchants lived on Java, Persians served in the Siamese government, Turkish soldiers fought for the sultans of Acheh (AH-cheh) in Sumatra, Portuguese settled in Mozambique, Kongolese labored in Brazil, and French traders explored the Mississippi Basin. Some merchants flourished by having operations in many lands. One of the most successful was the German commercial agent Ferdinand Cron in the late sixteenth and early seventeenth century. Born in Augsburg and then based in Portuguese-ruled Goa on India's west coast, Cron supervised a network of couriers who collected information on markets and prices from Europe in the West to Melaka and Macao in the East and then used that information to make lucrative investments.

Asia and Europe in the New World Economy

The transition to a European-dominated trading system took place over several centuries in Asia. Before the 1800s, when the transition was completed, Asia boasted the bulk of world economic activity. Asians produced some 80 percent of goods as late as 1775, and this production had probably increased since 1500. The industries of China and India remained the twin pillars of Asian commerce well into the 1700s. Indian textiles such as cashmere and cotton cloth were so popular in Asia, Africa, and Europe that they almost constituted a form of currency. Handicraft industries also flourished in the Ottoman Empire, Persia, Sri Lanka, Burma, Siam, and Java during the sixteenth and seventeenth centuries. These societies imported raw materials from India (including raw cotton), China (especially silk), and Japan (copper) for production into exportable consumer goods. For example, Javanese women used beeswax and dying to transform Indian cloth into beautiful batik clothing. The economies of India and China dwarfed those of any other country. The most economically developed regions within China, Japan, India, and northwestern Europe may have enjoyed roughly comparable standards of living, including health and income levels.

Asian merchants, enjoying lower overhead and shrewd business skills, could often outcompete those from Europe. After 1670 Indian merchants even took the Indonesian textile market away from the Dutch. Like Europeans, Asians also traded over long distances. In the 1600s, for example, Arab and Persian traders remained influential at the main Mughal port, Surat, while north Indian merchants were found all over the Persian Gulf. Many wealthy Asian trading magnates had huge capital resources. The trader Virji Vohra (VEER-gee VOOR-ah) in Surat was as rich as Europe's wealthiest merchant family, the

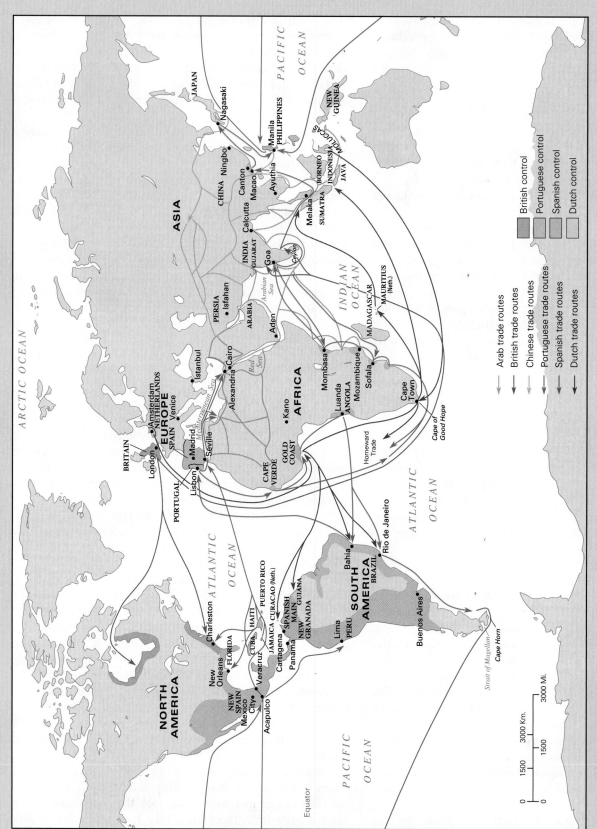

Early Modern Trade Routes

Between 1500 and 1700 the world economy developed and new trade routes proliferated. Major maritime routes linked Asia and the Americas across the Pacific; Europe, Asia, and the Americas across the Atlantic; and eastern and southern Asia with Africa and Europe across the Indian Ocean.

Fuggers in Germany. A European visitor to Goa in 1510 was amazed at the competition provided by fabulously rich Arab and Indian merchants: "We [Europeans] believe ourselves to be the most astute men that one can encounter, and the people here surpass us in everything. And they can do better calculations by memory than we can do with the pen."[6] European merchants competed best when they were, like the Dutch East Indies Company traders, supported by military force.

European-Asian trade relations often favored Asians. Since Asians had little interest in European manufactured goods such as clothing, which they considered inferior in quality to their own goods, Europeans bought Asian goods and resources with American silver and gold. For example, since Europeans traded with China for products such as tea, vast amounts of American silver ended up in China, where it served as the basis of the monetary system and promoted economic growth. The Ottoman, Safavid, and Mughal Empires also needed an expanding money supply to meet the investment needs of their expanding economies and were, like the Chinese, ready to trade goods for silver.

Asian goods found a ready market around the world. Europeans shipped bullion to Persia for silk, and Persia shipped bullion to India for cotton textiles. Chinese goods transported from the Philippines were so much cheaper than Spanish ones in Peru that the Spanish viceroy complained it was "impossible to choke off the trade since a man can clothe his wife in Chinese silks for 25 pesos, whereas he could not provide her with clothing of Spanish silks with 200 pesos."[7] While European ships carried a growing amount of seaborne trade, European merchants accounted for only a small proportion of trade from India and China. Mughal India traded far more with Central Asians and Ottomans than with the Dutch or English. Asian exports to Europe grew slowly; intra-Asian trade was far larger.

Expanding Trade Networks

The growth of long-distance trade corresponded to the expansion of trade networks operated by different commercial communities. The rise of European power allowed Dutch, English, and French merchants to establish themselves in India, Southeast Asia, West Africa, eastern Europe, Russia, and the Caribbean Basin. At the same time, Sephardic Jews, originally from Iberia, spread their trading networks throughout western Europe, flourishing particularly in Antwerp, Amsterdam, Seville, and Geneva. Eventually, Jews also became active as merchants in parts of South America, the Caribbean, and the Indian Ocean. Some entered the Asian spice trade, developing ties as far east as Melaka. The Mendes family, for instance, expelled from Spain in 1492 and eventually based in Istanbul, had business connections in several European cities and, with their banks, helped finance the gem and spice trades across Asia, Europe, and Africa.

Groups specializing in trade were prominent in many lands. Chinese remained active all over Southeast Asia, establishing permanent settlements in many cities and towns. For example, the Spanish in the Philippines depended on the Chinese merchant class to supply many consumer goods. A Spanish friar observed in the mid-1600s that although Manila "is small, and the Spaniards are few, nevertheless, they require the services of thousands of Chinese."[8] Traders of French or mixed French and Indian descent traveled deep into the North American continent contacting local peoples. In East Africa, it was the Omani Arabs who had a leading role. In West Africa, Hausa (HOUSE-uh) merchants increasingly dominated the trade networks of the Sudan by the 1600s. This trade domination brought prosperity to walled cities like Kano (KAH-no), famous for its cloth manufacturers, and Katsina. Hausa merchants became influential in the Niger Basin as far west as the Ashante kingdom and supplied resources such as kola nuts to the far-reaching trans-Saharan trade, which still flourished despite growing European trade along the west coast. In far western Africa the Dyula (JOO-lah), Mandinka Muslims, held the leading commercial position.

Similarly, some Asian merchants, especially Indians and Armenians, maintained and even expanded commercial networks over vast distances. The Indian maritime trade network stretched from Arabia, Persia, northeast Africa, and the Red Sea to Melaka, Sumatra, Siam, and China. Although the Portuguese cut into the Indians' power in the Indian Ocean, Indians remained active in the 1700s. Meanwhile, Indian overland trade networks extended across Central Asia, Afghanistan, Tibet, Persia, the Caucasus states, and much of Russia. Armenian merchants based in Safavid Persia flourished in the overland trade from India to Central Asia and the Middle East, and from Persia to Russia, England, and the Baltic. Some Armenians traveled widely. Hovannes Ter-Davtian (tur-DAHV-ti-an) left Isfahan in 1692, traded on the western and eastern coasts of India, and then spent seven years in Tibet before arriving in Calcutta in 1693 with a cargo of Chinese porcelain, gold, and musk that earned him a handsome profit. Growing Eurasian trade clearly involved, and often benefited, varied groups.

ENVIRONMENTAL CHANGES

Human activity reshaped the natural world and was influenced by it in turn. As they had for millennia, people tapped the Earth for underground resources, such as coal and iron ore, but large-scale manufacturing, which often pollutes the environment, was found in only a few widely scattered countries, mostly in Eurasia. For farming and light industries, Early Modern economies relied chiefly on traditional power sources, such as people, animals, water, and wind. For example, windmills were common in the Middle East and Europe, and spinning wheels, often operated by women, were widespread in Eurasia and North Africa. Nonetheless, natural systems came under more stress as the global population nearly doubled, putting severe pressure on land and resources. Expanding settlements and farming in frontier regions displaced woodlands, grasslands, and wetlands and reduced the variety of plant and animal life. More spectacularly, the exchange of diseases, plants, and animals across the Atlantic altered entire environments and resulted in huge population losses in the Americas.

Climate Change and Population Growth

Between 1300 and 1850 much of the world experienced a fluctuating "Little Ice Age," probably caused by a dimming sun and increased volcanic activity, that had significant consequences for many societies. In North America and Eurasia, this period brought cool temperatures, shorter growing seasons, and famine. The coldest years came between 1570 and 1730, and then through the early 1800s. For example, in the 1600s China often received either too much rain, which caused widespread flooding, or too little rain and late springs, which produced drought and reduced the growing season to allow for only one crop of rice rather than two. The lands bordering the North Atlantic saw much colder and wetter conditions, which diminished agricultural production and resulting in widespread starvation in much of Europe. Indeed, harsh weather conditions, combined with occasional outbreaks of bubonic plague, may have been one of the factors that spurred Europeans to seek new lands abroad. Climate change also affected topical regions. For example, West Africa had abundant rain until 1700, when rainfall began diminishing, allowing desert to claim much of the Sahel and pushing savannah farming southward by several hundred miles.

Nonetheless, despite the poor weather, the distribution of new food sources and other resources was widening. For instance, western European societies obtained more food, particularly grain, from eastern Europe, and thus became more linked to that region. Seaborne trade, especially from the Americas, also provided valuable resources, especially to coastal maritime states such as the Netherlands and Britain. The increased diffusion of resources fostered population growth. Indeed, American crops such as the potato helped Europe stave off even worse climate-related famines. To the east, the Mughals cleared the forests and wetlands of Bengal to create a large area for rice growing, which allowed them to feed more people. Around the world the expansion of farming to sustain more people came at the expense of shifting cultivators, pastoralists, and food collectors. Some peoples, such as the pastoral Khoikhoi (KOI-KOI) in South Africa, died off or were enslaved or killed.

Partly because of the spread of food crops, especially from the Americas to Afro-Eurasia, world population increased significantly. In 1500 the earth contained between 400 and 500 million people. Perhaps 60 percent lived in Asia, with China and India each accounting for nearly a quarter of the world total. By 1750 the world population had grown to between 700 and 750 million, probably 80 percent of them peasants living on the land. China and India together, totaling perhaps 400 million, still accounted for over half, while Europe held perhaps 20 percent and Africa 10 percent of the world total.

The Exchange of Diseases, Animals, and Crops

In this era people, chiefly Europeans and Africans, moved voluntarily or involuntarily to distant lands, deliberately or accidentally carrying with them species of animals, insects, bacteria, and plants that reshaped local ecosystems. These biological invasions, what historians have termed the Columbian Exchange, particularly accompanied the encounter between Eurasia and the Americas. The European settlers in the Americas brought with them horses and food animals: pigs, chickens, sheep, and cattle. To raise beef cattle, Europeans introduced ranching. Ships returning to Europe carried with them American turkeys, which enriched Eurasian diets.

The exchange of diseases between the Eastern and Western Hemispheres was not one-way, but it had a greater impact on the Americas than on Eurasia and Africa. Native Americans had never experienced, and hence had developed no immunities to, Afro-Eurasian diseases such as smallpox, diphtheria, measles, chicken pox, whooping cough, malaria, bubonic plague, yellow fever, cholera, typhoid fever, and influenza. These diseases devastated the Americas. Smallpox brought the greatest known demographic catastrophe in world history, killing off around 90 percent of the peoples of the Americas. This was a much greater percentage of population than that destroyed by the terrible Black Death, which ravaged much of Eurasia and North Africa in the 1300s. The demographic disaster for the Americas emptied productive land and hence paved the way for Europeans to settle the Americas and to import captive Africans to labor in mining and agriculture. Only in the highlands, such as the Andes Mountains in South America, where European diseases had a smaller impact, did substantial concentrations of Native Americans survive. In contrast, only a few American diseases, especially syphilis, brought suffering to people in Europe and Africa.

Crop exchanges also proved momentous. Eurasian and African crops transformed some American regions, and required the introduction of new agricultural practices. Most Native Americans had grown crops such as corn (maize) and potatoes on small plots, but settlers found that Afro-Eurasian crops such as wheat, rice, coffee, barley, and sugar were most successfully grown on large farms or estates. Among these imported crops, sugar had the most impact on the Americas, and vast acreage was devoted to its growth, mostly on plantations worked by African slaves and their descendants. Much of the sugar was exported to Europe for use to sweeten foods such as jam and breads, and beverages such as tea and coffee.

American crops spread widely in the Eastern Hemisphere, where people adopted them to enhance their lives or resolve some of their own food problems. Tobacco, for instance, gained popularity in China and Europe, generating both avid devotees (some of whom considered it medicinal) and opponents who considered it unhealthy or immoral. Many imports, such as tomatoes, made the once bland European meals more varied. Potatoes became a mainstay of the European diet and the major crop grown in several societies, including Ireland and Scotland. Maize (corn) could be grown on marginal land and proved a boon in Africa, southwest Asia, and China, where it was planted on unused hillsides. Corn also fed livestock, and the stalks could be used to make huts and sheds. American chilies, hotter than Asian black peppers, proved hugely popular in South and Southeast Asian cooking, adding a sharp bite to curries and other foods. Peanuts became a key crop in West

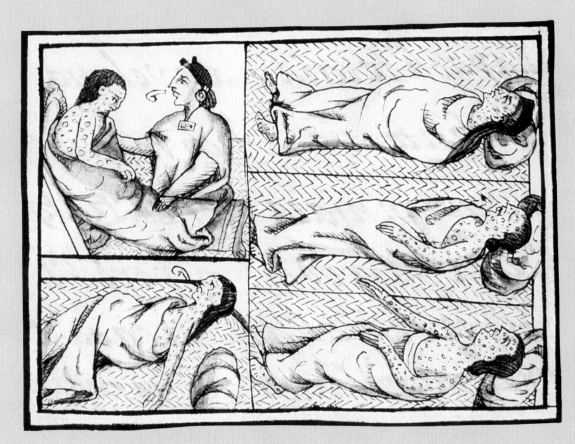

Smallpox Victims in the Americas Eurasian diseases accompanied the Europeans to the Americas, causing a catastrophic loss of life for the Native Americans, who had no immunity. As shown in this print from the 1500s, millions of people sickened and died from smallpox. (Biblioteca Medicea Laurenziana)

Africa. The new foods offered not only a more varied diet but also a healthier one. By 1750 a diner in many cities in the world could enjoy a fruit salad mixing pieces of Southeast Asian bananas and mangos, Chinese peaches, Southwest Asian pears, African watermelons, Mesoamerican papayas, South American pineapples, and Mediterranean grapes.

European expansion and colonization owed much to the spread of the Eurasian biota, a distinct package of plants, animals, and germs that overwhelmed the rest of the world, especially the Americas and, later, Oceania. Eurasian plants, such as wheat and apple trees, and animals, such as cattle, often replaced indigenous ones in the temperate zones of the Americas and, after 1800, Australia and New Zealand. These changes occurred in part because Europeans viewed animals, plants, and land largely as commodities, to be exploited for their own benefit. The English scientist Sir Francis Bacon expressed these attitudes well: "The world is made for man, not man for the world."[9]

SOCIAL AND CULTURAL CHANGE

During the Early Modern Era, the growing networks of trade, information, and technology fostered changes in societies all over the world. Some changes resulted from the increasing migration of peoples, voluntarily or by force. Intermarriage or sexual contact between people from different ethnic groups produced new peoples with mixed cultural backgrounds. Other contributing factors were changing economic systems, the growth of international trade, and the exchange of ideas.

Encounters with other ways of living and thinking stimulated curiosity and fostered rethinking. Several religions expanded their boundaries and sought converts, challenging the ancient faiths of the Americas and parts of Asia.

Migration and Hybrid Groups

Improved maritime technology made it possible for people to cross vast oceans and to do so in larger numbers than ever before. The resulting contacts between peoples reshaped societies. A new system of global migration brought people with very different customs and values together, not always happily. The largest population movement involved Europeans settling in the Americas and bringing with them enslaved Africans but few European women. Women comprised perhaps only a fifth of the Spanish and Portuguese who went to the Americas; men thus frequently sought partners among Native American and African women.

Intermarriage and sexual relations across social boundaries led to the creation of American societies that contained many mixed-descent people. By 1750 in Latin America and in French colonies such as Haiti and Louisiana a large part of the population blended European and Native American backgrounds, creating mestizos, or European and African ancestries, fostering mulattos. For example, many people in Mexico City were mestizo, while in New Orleans blacks and mulattos predominated. In turn, these groups' cultures often mixed the varying social influences, as in northeast Brazil, where people blended African religions and Catholic traditions. Unlike

English North America, where any African ancestry usually meant classification as black, in much of Latin America a complex hierarchy of social categories developed based on gradations of skin color.

Migration and intermarriage also occurred in the Eastern Hemisphere. Dutch and Portuguese adventurers and merchants, most of them men, settled in southern Africa and the port cities of South and Southeast Asia, often taking wives from the local population. Some of the Russians who moved into Siberia and the Black Sea region mixed with local peoples. As had been true for centuries, Arab and Indian traders relocated to distant lands in Africa and Eurasia, often settling permanently and sometimes taking local wives. Many Chinese also migrated, usually with their families, and moved into nearby territories such as Taiwan, and male merchants settled in Southeast Asia, where they often intermarried. For example, several thousand Chinese lived in the major Siamese city, Ayuthia; one of them wrote in the early 1600s that "Siam is really friendly to the Chinese."[10] Many of the Chinese married Ayuthia women and stayed permanently, their descendants mixing Chinese and Siamese culture. More Chinese also arrived, and by 1735 some 20,000 lived in the kingdom.

Groups of mixed European and Asian ancestry appeared in European colonies in Asia. For instance, the Portuguese men who settled in Goa, Colombo, and Melaka married local women and raised their children as Portuguese-speaking Catholics. But their descendants adopted many local customs. Hence, in Melaka today, while Catholic churches, schools, and festivals remain at the heart of Portuguese community life, the local Portuguese language contains many Malay words, the cuisine has borrowed extensively from Malay and Chinese cooking, and, unlike their merchant, sailor, and soldier ancestors, most men work as fishermen. Throughout the era Portuguese was the lingua franca of maritime Asia, spoken in many ports, and some of its words were incorporated into local languages such as Malay.

In Africa too—South Africa, Mozambique, Angola, and along the West African coast—the mixing of Europeans and Africans led to hybrid social groups. The offspring of relations between Dutch men and African or Asian women were so common in South Africa that they became a distinct racial group, known as the Coloreds. Prominent slave-trading and merchant families of West Africa often descended from Portuguese men who married women from local chiefly or royal families. Like Brazilian mulattos and many Asian mestizos, African mulattos often spoke a version of Portuguese, the first language with a global reach.

Changing Gender Relations

Although men, voluntarily or involuntarily, were much more likely than women to join overseas ventures or cross oceans, women were also affected by the changes of the era. In the Americas many European men sought Indian women, often by force. One-third of enslaved Africans taken to the Americas were women, some of whom were brought into close contact with slave-owning men, mostly white, who exercised control over their lives. The result was forced sexual activity and mixed-descent children. Since slave couples were often separated by sale, women held together many slave households, a social pattern that continued among many African Americans after the abolition of slavery. Christian missionaries working among North American Indians often pursued policies that marginalized women in once egalitarian cultures such as the Algonquians of eastern Canada and the Iroquois of New York.

Gender patterns were modified around the world, including in Africa. For instance, in the parts of Africa most affected by slave trading, the absence of men in their productive years encouraged the remaining men to take multiple wives, a practice that may or may not have made life easier for women. The traditional role of West African women in local commerce, however, also meant that, along the coast, some became active as slave traders. A few of these, such as Senhora Philippa, who in the 1630s controlled the trading center of Rufisque (ROO-feesk) in today's Senegal, became immensely wealthy and owned trading ships and magnificent houses. Women also played powerful roles in some of the newer kingdoms fostered by the trans-Atlantic slave trade, where they controlled access to the kings. For example, in Dahomey queen mothers wielded extraordinary power in a palace occupied by a few men and thousands of women, many of them wives and concubines of the king. Dahomey women also served as soldiers and bodyguards. A Portuguese missionary to one Senegambia kingdom described a powerful woman, the king's aunt, who was "so respected and obeyed that nothing of importance took place in the kingdom without her knowledge."[11] Of course, most African women, whether slave or free, enjoyed much less wealth and power in their communities than these merchants and royal women.

In much of Eurasia women experienced increasing subordination by men. Hence, women generally became more restricted in Mughal India, China, and Japan as patriarchal attitudes strengthened, largely as a result of internal factors. For example, Qing leaders turned more socially conservative, imposing harsher laws against behavior considered deviant, such as homosexuality, and stressing the purity of women, which meant less freedom for women to leave home. Adopting the idea of the "chaste widow," more Chinese widows than ever before, forever faithful to their late husbands, frequently refused to remarry. In addition, Western missionaries and officials often sought to impose their own patriarchal prejudices on Asians. Hence, in Southeast Asia, the Spanish and Portuguese were often appalled at the relative freedom of women. Spanish officials criticized Filipinos for tolerating adultery and premarital sex, and they punished those who engaged in these activities.

But there were exceptions to the growing restrictions on women. The Mughal emperor Akbar ordered that no woman could be forced by family or community pressures to immolate herself on her husband's funeral pyre, arguing that "it is a strange commentary on the magnanimity of men that they seek their own salvation by means of the self-sacrifice of their wives."[12] Many Qing women from elite families published essays and poetry that were widely read and admired. One Chinese poet recalled how her father nurtured her talent: "Understanding that I was quite intelligent, He taught his daughters as he taught his sons, [advising us to] Develop together, support, and do not impede each other."[13]

Missionaries and Religious Change

The encounters between widely differing cultures around the world also had a religious dimension, forcing people to confront different belief systems while widening or sparking divisions in established faiths. Some of the major conflicts came in Europe. Tensions simmering for several centuries finally fragmented Western Christianity into Catholic and diverse Protestant churches in the 1500s, spurring religious wars, militancy, and hostility toward non-Christians. Dissenters were punished by those in the majority. Scientists such as the Italian astronomer Galileo Galilei and the Flemish biologist Andreas Vesalius, (an-DRAY-us ve-SAL-yus) who produced the first reference manual on human anatomy, were tried by the Holy Inquisition, a Catholic Church institution organized to root out heresy.

Meanwhile, other religious traditions also dealt with tensions and divisions. Mystical Sufi orders became more influential in Islamic societies from Indonesia to West Africa. For example, the early Mughal emperors Babur (BAH-bur) and Akbar were fervent Sufis. Babur wrote in a poem that "I am their follower in heart and soul. I am a king, but yet a slave [follower] of the Dervishes [mystics]."[14] But the Sufis' popularity distressed dogmatists, fostering debate on Sufism's role and value among Ottoman, Mughal, and Central Asian Muslims. Islamic division hardened in Persia, too. Ordered by their Safavid rulers, Persians shifted from the Sunni to the Shi'a branch of Islam, causing many Sunnis to emigrate. But tensions sometimes led to secular approaches rather than to religious zeal. One such movement, neo-Confucianism, became a strong influence in China, helping secular values to triumph there while Buddhism lost influence among the elites. To comprehend a world charged with diverse and changing ideas, Chinese thinkers, European Enlightenment philosophers, and several Mughal emperors questioned religious dogmas and sought to broaden intellectual horizons.

In contrast to those who explored new ideas, many were religious militants and engaged in missionary activity. Christians actively sought converts in the Americas, Africa, and Asia. Christian missionaries were often intolerant of local traditions and scornful toward the people they were trying to reach. One prominent Spanish clergyman strongly supported conquest and evangelization as a way of "civilizing" Native Americans, whom he described as "these pitiful men, in whom you will scarcely find any vestiges of humanness. They were born for servitude. How are we to doubt that these people, so uncultivated, so barbarous, and so contaminated with such impiety and lewdness, have not been so justly conquered."[15] Catholicism eventually triumphed in Latin America, Kongo, and the Philippines, and it found a few thousand converts in East Asia. Protestant missionaries mostly concentrated on Catholic Europe, Southeast Asia, and North America, where they particularly targeted Native Americans and slaves.

At the same time, the Christian missionary enterprise faced challenges, including stiff resistance. To gain acceptance, missionaries often had to blend Christianity with local traditions, often against the opposition of church leaders. The intolerance of many Christian missionaries toward other faiths led to their expulsion from Japan and China. East Asians assimilated some useful Western technical and scientific knowledge from the missionaries, such as clock-making and mapmaking, but most rejected Christianity. Christian missionary efforts had little success among Muslims, Theravada Buddhists, and Hindus. Indeed, missionary activity sometimes prompted non-Christians to solidify support for traditional ways, as was the case in China and Japan.

Christianity was not the only missionary religion: millions of Europeans, Africans, and Asians embraced Islam. Islam spread into the Balkan societies under Ottoman control, and many Serbs, Albanians, and Bulgarians adopted the faith, forging a permanent divide between Christians and Muslims in the region. Islam continued to gain strength in sub-Saharan Africa, Mughal India, and Island Southeast Asia. Unlike Christianity, Islam was not identified with unpopular Western conquest, and it continued to link distant societies. For instance, in the 1600s Nuruddin al-Raniri, (new-ROOD-in al-RAN-eer-ee) from Gujerat in India, studied in Mecca and then traveled widely, finally settling in Acheh, Sumatra, and becoming an adviser to the king. Under Nuruddin's influence, the sultan promoted the more vigorous practice of Islamic customs, such as fasting, strict dietary laws, and alms-giving.

Some trends promoted accommodation between divergent faiths. For example, in India the Mughal emperor Akbar preached tolerance and cultural diversity. Indeed, in some respects Akbar and his ancient Indian predecessor, the Mauryan emperor Asoka, were global pioneers in promoting respect for different traditions. Akbar's more zealously Islamic successors, however, repressed Hinduism, reviving a long conflict between the two faiths. Theravada Buddhists generally respected all religions. Hence, when the French king, Louis XIV, sent a mission to King Narai of Ayuthia requesting that he and his people adopt Roman Catholicism, the Siamese monarch sent a letter back, arguing that God rejoiced not in religious uniformity but in theological diversities, preferring to be honored by different worships and ceremonies. Meanwhile, Muslims and animists lived side by side without conflict in parts of Africa. Similarly, in some European societies, notably the Netherlands and Poland, Protestants and Catholics learned to live in peace. And growing European knowledge of Chinese society, including Confucianism, led some leaders of the European Enlightenment, such as Voltaire, to view China as an admirable, secular alternative model to the religious divisions and orthodoxies of Europe. In this way Asian ideas influenced some Europeans just as European ideas spread to some non-European peoples, a testament to an increasingly connected world.

Suggested Reading

Books

Adas, Michael, ed. *Islamic and European Expansion: The Forging of a Global Order*. Philadelphia: Temple University Press, 1993. Contains excellent essays by William McNeill, Alfred Crosby, and Philip Curtin on major developments in this era.

Black, Jeremy. *War in the World: Military Power and the Fate of Continents, 1450–2000*. New Haven: Yale University Press, 1998. A global history of land and sea warfare and its contexts.

Brandon, William. *New Worlds for Old: Reports from the New World and Their Effect on the Development of Social Thought in Europe, 1500–1800*. Athens: Ohio University Press, 1986. Examines the impact on Europe of the American discoveries and cultures.

Crosby, Alfred W. *Ecological Imperialism: The Biological Expansion of Europe, 900–1900*. Cambridge: Cambridge University Press, 1993. A pioneering exploration of the environmental changes in the past millennium.

Curtin, Philip D. *The World and the West: The European Challenge and the Overseas Response in the Age of Empire*. Cambridge: Cambridge University Press, 2000. Explores relevant themes in world history since 1500.

Eltis, David. *The Rise of African Slavery in the Americas*. New York: Cambridge University Press, 2000. Overview of slavery and the Atlantic system.

Gunn, Geoffrey C. *First Globalization: The Eurasian Exchange*. Lanham, Md.: Rowman and Littlefield, 2003. An idiosyncratic but absorbing study of East-West encounters.

Hobhouse, Henry. *Seeds of Change: Five Plants That Transformed Mankind*. New York: Harper and Row, 1985. A fascinating study of how quinine, sugar, tea, cotton, and the potato changed the world.

Marks, Robert B. *The Origins of the Modern World: A Global and Ecological Narrative*. Lanham, Md.: Rowman and Littlefield, 2002. A stimulating, readable, and concise account of how the modern world emerged.

Pacey, Arnold. *Technology in World Civilization*. Cambridge: MIT Press, 1990. Provides a global overview of technological change in this era.

Pilcher, Jeffrey M. *Food in World History*. New York: Routledge, 2006. Examines changing food cultures around the world.

Pomeranz, Kenneth and Steven Topic. *The World That Trade Created: Society, Culture, and the World Economy, 1400 to the Present*, 2nd ed., Armonk, N.Y.: M. E. Sharpe, 2006. Contains dozens of brief esasys written for the general public.

Richards, John F. *The Unending Frontier: An Environmental History of the Early Modern World*. Berkeley: University of California Press, 2003. A detailed but stimulating study of environmental change, with many case studies.

Smith, Alan K. *Creating a World Economy: Merchant Capital, Colonialism, and World Trade, 1400–1825*. Boulder, Colo.: Westview Press, 1991. A valuable survey of the world economy in this era.

Wiesner-Hanks, Merry E. *Christianity and Sexuality in the Early Modern World: Regulating Desire, Reforming Practice*. New York: Routledge, 2000. A wide-ranging study of the impact of spreading Christianity on sexual practices.

Wills, John E. *1688: A Global History*. New York: W.W. Norton, 2001. A very readable and informative exploration of various peoples and societies around the world in the late seventeenth century.

WEBSITES

The Columbian Exchange
(http://www.nhc.rtp.nc.us:8080/tserve/nattrans/ntecoindian/essays/columbian/htm).　Contains varied materials on the Columbian Exchange.

Columbus and the Age of Discovery
(http://muweb.millersville.edu/_columbus/main/html).
This site, maintained by Millersville University, offers many sources related to the linking of the hemispheres during this era.

Early Modern Resources
(http://www.earlymodernwrb.org.uk/emr/).　A useful British site offering many links to essays and sources.

Internet Global History Sourcebook
(http://www.fordham.edu/halsall/global/globalsbook.html).
An excellent set of links on world history from ancient to modern times.

Internet Modern History Sourcebook
(http://www.fordham.edu/halsall/).　An extensive online collection of historical documents and secondary materials.

PART V

Global Imbalances: Industry, Empire, and the Making of the Modern World, 1750–1945

The Early Modern Era from the mid-1400s to the mid-1700s, discussed in Part IV, constituted a key stage in the building of today's world. During that era European overseas expansion established permanent communication between the Eastern and Western Hemispheres, building ever closer political and economic ties between Europe, the Americas, the West and East African coasts, and some Asian societies. These ties in turn fostered a global economy while dramatically altering the lives, for better or worse, of many people.

The next key stage in creating the world we live in today came during the Modern Era, between around 1750 and 1945, which was marked by revolutions in political, intellectual, economic, and social life around the world. In countries such as France, Britain, the United States, and Japan, political revolutions or major reforms replaced old governments with more democratic or progressive governments, inspiring other peoples to seek similar changes. Latin Americans became independent from Spanish and Portuguese colonialism. In many countries political change went hand in hand with new ideas about the relationship between citizens and governments, new visions of a better life, and more skeptical attitudes toward organized religions. At the same time, Western nations transformed world politics by asserting their power in Asia, Africa, and Latin America, a few of them establishing huge colonial empires. The peoples they colonized, however, often resisted Western rule. Meanwhile, in the economic realm, the Industrial Revolution, which produced unprecedented goods and fostered technological advances, reshaped Western economic life. In some societies assertive workers', peasants', and women's movements challenged old aristocratic social orders. Overall, great progress was made toward improving social and economic conditions, especially in providing material goods. But the progress was purchased at a high cost in the dislocation of human lives, the suppression of colonized peoples, the ravaging of the natural environment, growing antagonism toward the powerful Western nations, and the deadliest wars in history.

The increasing military, political, and economic domination of the rest of the world by several

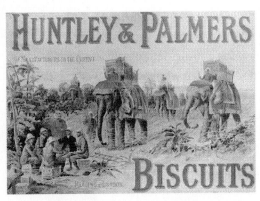

Colonial Advertisement As imperialism became a part of European life, advertisers capitalized on the interest in the colonial realm. This nineteenth-century advertisement for a British biscuit company shows a scene of the British in India. (The Robert Opie Collection)

European nations, soon joined by the United States, was a major trend in the nineteenth and early twentieth centuries. While Western peoples controlled some 35 percent of the world's land surface in 1800, they controlled over 84 percent by 1914. This domination encouraged European emigration and helped to spread capitalism, Western languages, and Western ideas such as Christianity and Marxism. It also contributed to huge changes in the world economy. Strongly shaped by Western activity, the world economy reshuffled natural resources, so that rubber, for example, a plant native to Brazil, became a major cash crop in Southeast Asia, often grown by Indian or Chinese immigrants. Around the world men and women now often worked for wages to produce goods primarily for sale in distant markets rather than the local community.

But Western expansion and domination also created imbalances. The major imbalance was a growing gap by the early 1900s between rich nations and poor societies. Rich nations enjoyed industrialization and, in some cases, imperial expansion. The poor societies, by contrast, were usually colonies of Western nations, economically subordinate to the West, or, like China and Latin America, subject to informal Western power. Most Asian societies powerful in the Early Modern Era, including China and India, declined. The West, including North America, increasingly exported industrial and consumer goods while people elsewhere largely exported raw materials. Six hundred years ago many Chinese and Southeast Asians and some Native Americans lived longer and healthier lives than did most Europeans. By the early twentieth century, however, the balance had changed and most societies in western Europe and North America were far richer and healthier, and had far more influence on the world, than other peoples.

By the first decade of the twentieth century Western imperialism had generated global integration, the increasing connections between societies. Sparked partly by these connections, major changes came to the world during the first half of the twentieth century, some of them creating widespread misery. The hopes for a more democratic, equitable world were undermined by two ruinous world wars, the decade-long collapse of the world economy, and some of history's most brutal, despotic governments. Meanwhile, people in Asia, Africa, and Latin America increasingly challenged Western power and unpopular local governments. These developments set the stage for a new world order to emerge after 1945.

NORTH AND CENTRAL AMERICA
In the later 1700s, the thirteen British colonies along the Atlantic coast revolted and established a new democratic nation, the United States, that gradually expanded across the continent. After a civil war ended slavery, the United States rapidly industrialized; as it became the world's major political and economic power in the later 1800s, it attracted immigrants. U.S. military power proved decisive in World Wars I and II. Meanwhile, Canada spread west to the Pacific and achieved self-government. After overthrowing Spanish rule, Mexico was reshaped by liberalism, dictatorship, and revolution.

SOUTH AMERICA
During the early 1800s the Latin American societies overthrew colonialism by force and became independent nations, but they also retained close economic links to Europe, reinforcing their natural resources-based economies and limiting industrialization. The struggles between liberal reformers and conservatives often led to military dictatorship. As European and Asian immigrants reshaped Latin American societies, Latin Americans created distinctive cultures by combining imported and local traditions.

EUROPE

The Industrial Revolution, which began in Britain in the later 1700s, sparked dramatic economic, social, and political change. The French Revolution and the rise of parliamentary democracy in nations such as Britain benefited the middle classes and fostered new national loyalties. Russia conquered Siberia and Central Asia. Britain, France, and Germany renewed imperialism in the later 1800s, forging large empires in Asia and Africa. After 1914 Europe was reshaped by World War I, communist revolution in Russia, economic collapse, the rise of fascism, and World War II.

WESTERN ASIA

Although gradually losing its grip on southeastern Europe and North Africa, the Ottoman Empire maintained control of much of western Asia until after World War I, when Britain and France acquired the Arab territories and the Ottomans collapsed, replaced by a modernizing Turkish state. Persia attempted reforms but still fell under Western domination. Arab nationalism challenged Western power, while secular reformers and pro- and antimodern Muslims struggled for influence throughout the region.

EASTERN ASIA

China remained strong until the early 1800s, when, unable to reform and thwart Western ambitions, it lost several wars to the West and experienced rebellions. After a revolution ended the imperial system in the early 1900s, China lapsed into warlordism and then civil war, opening the door for Japanese invasion. Fearing Western power, the Japanese had rapidly industrialized and modernized their society in the later 1800s but, ravaged by economic depression, came under military rule in the 1930s, which eventually led to their defeat in World War II.

AFRICA

Although some African states, such as Ashante, Buganda, and Egypt, remained strong into the 1800s and instituted reforms, they could not halt increasing Western power. The ending of the trans-Atlantic slave trade by the mid-1800s opened the door to Western colonization of the entire continent. The British and French built large empires in both sub-Saharan Africa and North Africa. Western imperialism created artificial countries, undermined traditional societies, and drained Africa of resources. After World War I African and Arab nationalist movements struggled against Western domination.

SOUTHERN ASIA AND OCEANIA

Overcoming local resistance, the British gradually conquered India, and their rule exploited India's resources, reshaped Indian life, and generated opposition from Indian nationalists seeking independence. Dynamic Southeast Asian states repulsed the West until the mid-1800s, when the British, French, and Dutch colonized all of these resource-rich societies, except Thailand, often against fierce resistance, and the United States replaced Spanish rule in the Philippines, crushing a local independence movement. To the east, Western powers colonized the Pacific islands and Europeans settled in Australia and New Zealand.

ARCTIC OCEAN

RUSSIA

BRITAIN
GERMANY
EUROPE
FRANCE
Danubes
ITALY
TURKEY
ASIA
JAPAN
PERSIA
CHINA
EGYPT
HIMALAYAS
Nile
Ganges R.
INDIA
Mekong R.
VIETNAM
AFRICA
THAILAND
Niger R.
NIGERIA
Congo R.
ASHANTE
BUGANDA
CONGO
INDONESIA
ATLANTIC
OCEAN
INDIAN OCEAN
SOUTH
AFRICA
AUSTRALIA

CHAPTER 19

Modern Transitions: Revolutions, Industries, Ideologies, Empires, 1750–1914

Online Study Center

This icon will direct you to interactive activities and study materials on the website: college.hmco.com/pic/lockard1e

Crystal Palace Exposition of 1851   Attracting more than six million visitors, the Great Exhibition, held at the Crystal Palace in London in 1851, showcased industrial products and the companies that produced them from all over the world but especially from Europe.
(British Museum/Laurie Platt Winfrey, Inc.)

From this foul drain the greatest stream of human industry flows out to fertilize the whole world. From this filthy sewer pure gold flows. Here humanity attains its most complete development and its most brutish.

FRENCH WRITER ALEXIS DE TOCQUEVILLE ON MANCHESTER, ENGLAND, 1835[1]

On a spring day in 1851 the people of London prepared to celebrate the technological achievements of their era. People of all social classes, from bankers and nobles to sailors, day laborers, and barmaids, crowded the city streets, heading for the spectacular new Crystal Palace in Hyde Park to see the official opening, led by Queen Victoria herself, of the Great Exhibition. The less affluent walked while the wealthy rode in horse-drawn carriages or steam-powered buses. Some people had come by railroad from other British cities or by steamships from France and Belgium. All shared in the excitement of an exhibition designed to celebrate "The Works of Industry of All Nations," with Progress as the organizing theme.

The first "world's fair," the Great Exhibition was dazzling. Some 14,000 firms participated in the displays, showcasing British industrial leadership in particular. Some exhibits featured the mineral basis for British industry: coal, iron ore, gypsum, granite, and agates. The hall of machinery contained power textile looms, hydraulic presses, printing presses, marine engines, and locomotives: inventions that had revolutionized British life. Some locomotives, for example, had attained the before unimaginable speed of 60 miles per hour. Another hall lavishly presented industrial products that British merchants sold all over the world, including fine textiles made from wool, cotton, linen, and silk. Many of these products were made in Manchester, the city condemned as a "foul drain" in the opening quote but praised for fostering development. Nearly half of the exhibitors represented other countries of Europe and North America, illustrating the spread of industrialization.

The Great Exhibition of 1851 celebrated the industrialization that had begun three-quarters of a century earlier and was already dramatically transforming the social and physical landscapes in Britain and in parts of Europe. The age of the machine had arrived. The British, enamored with the idea of progress, saw in modern industry, a growing economy, and creative science humanity's triumph over the natural world. Industrialization gave Britain and other European and North American countries the economic and military power to increase their influence around the world.

Along with industrialization, political revolutions and new ideologies were also defining developments in Europe and the Americas between 1750 and 1914. Historians refer to an age of revolutions, violent conflicts that spurred the rise of modern European, North American, and Latin American nations. In turn, the economic and political changes resulting from industrialization and revolutions fostered new ideas about politics and government and about the relationship of citizens to the state. Great Britain, France, Germany, and Russia emerged as the main powers in Europe while the United States became the strongest American country. But the industrial and political trends yielded mixed blessings. The British writer Charles Dickens, commenting on the French Revolution, summed up the era: "It was the best of times, it was the worst of times. It was the age of wisdom, it was the age of foolishness, it was the season of light, it was the season of darkness, it was the spring of hope, it was the winter of despair."[2] By the later 1800s these trends had also sparked a renewal of the imperialism, begun in the 1500s, that resulted in various European nations acquiring or expanding empires in Asia and Africa.

FOCUS QUESTIONS

1. What were the major consequences of the American and French Revolutions?
2. How did the Caribbean and Latin American revolutions compare with those in North America and Europe?
3. How did industrialization reshape economic and social life?
4. How did nationalism, liberalism, and socialism differ from each other?
5. What factors spurred the Western imperialism of the later 1800s?

◈ The Age of Revolution: North America and Europe

What were the major consequences of the American and French Revolutions?

Some historians use the phrase "the **Age of Revolution**" to refer to the period from the 1770s through the 1840s, when revolutions rocked North America, Europe, the Caribbean, and Latin America (see Chronology: The North American and European Revolutions, 1770–1815). During these years revolutionaries employed armed violence to seize power and forge fundamental changes. Two types of revolutions emerged in modern times. Political revolutions changed the personnel and structure of government, while social revolutions transformed both the political and social order. The American Revolution was the most influential political revolution in this era because it ended British colonial rule, led to a new democratic form of government, and ushered in the Age of Revolution in Europe and the rest of the Americas. The French Revolution was the major social revolution, overthrowing a discredited old order of royalty and aristocratic privilege. The revolutionary tradition and values spawned in France remained a major influence

on modern Europe and also inspired other peoples to seek radical change. For the next two centuries revolutions transformed states, ideologies, and class structures, especially in Europe, Latin America, and Asia.

Modern Revolutions

Revolutions such as those in British North America and France have been momentous events in modern world history, erupting on every inhabited continent except Australia. While most revolutions have been local in impact, some have influenced other societies. In the late 1700s Europeans and Latin Americans watched fascinated as the disaffected citizens in the thirteen British colonies in North America struggled to overthrow British rule and then established an independent federation that soon became the United States. The American revolutionary leaders proclaimed Enlightenment political theories formulated in Europe, such as democracy and personal freedom, and then sought to apply these theories to their new representative government. The French Revolution electrified Europe by violently replacing the monarchy with a republic and spreading new values that stressed liberty and social equality. But the French Revolution also generated terrible violence, the rise of despotic leaders, and long years of war. The new political dialogue created by the French Revolution and the shock waves it generated strongly shaped nineteenth-century Europe.

Whether in North America, France, Latin America, or elsewhere, revolutions usually had much in common. Revolution-

Age of Revolution The period from the 1770s through the 1840s when revolutions rocked North America, Europe, the Caribbean, and Latin America.

CHRONOLOGY

	Europe	The Americas
1750	**1770s–1870s** First Industrial Revolution **1789–1815** French Revolution	**1775–1783** American Revolution **1791–1804** Haitian Revolution
1800	**1815** Congress of Vienna	**1810–1826** Spanish-American wars of independence
1850	**1859–1870** Unification of Italy **1862–1871** Unification of Germany **1870–1914** Second Industrial Revolution	

ary leaders were often, like those in North America, France, and South America, well educated and from middle-class or upper-class backgrounds. Yet, in many cases, they mobilized followers from among disenchanted peasants and urban workers. Many revolutions, including the French, moved from moderate to more extreme actions such as purging dissidents, rivals, or opponents. Most revolutions were also destructive and brutal, but many of them replaced incompetent or repressive governments and inequitable social systems. However, few satisfied the demands of their people. In some cases, as in France, revolutionaries also had to battle outside powers seek-

ing to restore the old order. The majority of these revolutions were sparked by one or more causes, most commonly hunger, poverty, war, overpopulation, the spread of destabilizing capitalism, or, as in British North America, the desire for more personal freedom and self-government.

British Colonialism and the American Revolution

The successful political revolution in British North America resulted from resentments that had festered for decades between British colonists and the imperial government. Britain had forged a foothold on the eastern seaboard of North America in the 1600s, establishing a presence in Canada and in thirteen colonies stretching from New Hampshire south to Georgia. Since each colony had unique institutions and economies, there was little cooperation between them. The southern colonies depended largely on plantation slavery while the northern colonies combined commerce and manufacturing with farming, a more balanced mix of economic activities. Only 2 million persons lived in the colonies in the 1760s, and the largest town, Boston, had only 20,000 residents. A fifth of the colonial population was African American. They were concentrated in the southern plantation zone—slaves accounted for nearly half of Virginia's population in the mid-1800s—but were also a factor in the northern economy. For instance, slaves constituted about a fifth of the 13,000 residents of New York in 1746. Some outspoken free blacks, such as Frederick Douglas and Sojourner Truth, demanded equal rights and the abolition of slavery.

Given these conditions, the white colonists seemed to have little to rebel against. Except for enslaved African-Americans, the American colonists were generally prosperous and enjoyed considerable self-government and religious toleration. The majority of adult white males, if they owned sufficient property, could vote for local assemblies and mayors. The colonists also faced much lighter taxes than did people in Britain. Most colonists eagerly consumed British culture, including books, religious values, educational methods, dress, games, and commercial practices. By the mid-1700s the British hold on these colonies seemed strong.

CHRONOLOGY

The North American and European Revolutions, 1770–1815

1770s–1840s	Age of Revolution
1773	Boston Tea Party
1776	American Declaration of Independence
1783	Britain's recognition of United States independence
1787	United States constitutional convention; Northwest Ordinance for forming new states
1789–1815	French Revolution
1791–1792	Constitutional state in Poland-Lithuania
1804	Crowning of Napoleon as emperor of France
1810–1811	Height of Napoleon's empire
1815	Defeat of Napoleon at Battle of Waterloo; Congress of Vienna

But tensions increased between the British, who staffed the highest political offices such as governor, and the colonists. Many colonists, claiming for themselves the label of Americans, felt divorced from Britain and increasingly resented British policies. The colonists disliked being taxed without enjoying representation in the British Parliament. In addition, the British placed more restrictions than before on local American manufacturing of items such as woven cloth, beaver hats, and iron. Clumsy British attempts to raise taxes, enforce long-ignored laws, and reserve the coveted land west of the Appalachians for Indians angered many colonists, some of whom began tarring and feathering tax collectors. Both men and women also mounted boycotts of British goods. In 1773, to protest a higher tax on tea, outraged colonists, dressed as Indians, raided three British ships in Boston harbor and dumped their cargo of tea overboard, an event known as the Boston Tea Party. Colonists favoring independence, known as Patriots, and those opposed, called Loyalists, increasingly clashed. Most of the Patriot and Loyalist leaders represented wealth, property, and education, enjoying careers as lawyers, physicians, journalists, merchants, and landowners.

The Patriot supporters of independence admired progressive European thought. Deeply influenced by European Enlightenment thinkers such as John Locke in England and Baron de Montesquieu in France, they favored democracy and a republic. The Patriots were also stirred by the writings of the antiroyalist Englishman and artisan's son Tom Paine (1737–1809), a sailor and teacher turned journalist who settled in Philadelphia and promoted independence, separation of church and state, social equality, women's rights, abolition of slavery, and other ideas then considered radical. Paine's passionate pamphlet *Common Sense*, which urged Americans to oppose tyranny and free themselves by force in order to "begin the world over again," helped galvanize public opinion against colonialism. The colonies' many competing churches and schools of thought fostered intellectual diversity. Some of the Patriots were devout Protestants or Catholics; others, including Paine, Thomas Jefferson, James Madison, Benjamin Franklin, and George Washington, were deists, believing in an impersonal creator who left humanity alone, and were often suspicious of organized churches. In one way or another, Patriot leaders also reflected their times: they owned slaves, smuggled, took mistresses, had illegitimate children, and, like many other male colonists, drank heavily.

The conflicts sparked a move for independence from Britain after preliminary American-British skirmishes in 1775. Delegates from the thirteen colonies met and declared that the colonies ought to be free and independent states, with no allegiance to the British crown. On July 4, 1776, the delegates approved the Declaration of Independence, written largely by the Enlightenment thinker Thomas Jefferson (1743–1826), a Virginia planter, which stated, "We hold these truths to be self-evident, that all men are created equal, that they are endowed by their Creator with certain inalienable Rights, that among these are Life, Liberty and the pursuit of Happiness."[3] The revolution was not sought by everyone, however. Perhaps a third of the colonists remained Loyalists, and many others, especially less affluent white colonists, were neutral or apathetic.

With conflict unavoidable, a revolutionary army organized and commanded by George Washington (1732–1799) then fought the British and their allies for six bitter years, famously described by Tom Paine as "the times that try men's souls." Washington was a wealthy and respected Virginia farmer and decorated veteran of earlier wars against France and its Indian allies. The revolutionary effort also reached to the grassroots. For example, women aided the Patriot cause by raising funds for the army, serving as cooks and nurses in army camps, and engaging in sabotage and spying. A few women disguised themselves as men to join the combat. Deborah Sampson (1760–1827) of Massachusetts served for seventeen months until her gender was discovered and she was discharged. After her death her husband received a pension as a "widow" of a revolutionary soldier. Britain's rivals, France and Spain, aided the Patriot cause. The British enjoyed support from many Indians, who resented the colonists for aggressively occupying Indian lands in defiance of British attempts to restrain them, and from some black slaves, who were promised their freedom by a British general if they helped the Loyalist cause. Some Loyalists and British officials accused the Patriots of hypocrisy, wanting freedom for themselves while maintaining slavery for non-whites.

The American defeat of British forces at Yorktown, Virginia, in 1781 proved decisive, and, after negotiations, Britain recognized the independence of the thirteen colonies in 1783. Despite their democratic values, the Patriots treated the Loyalists harshly, confiscating their land and jailing them. Ultimately 100,000 Loyalists were expelled or fled to Canada, and many others left for England.

The Legacy of the American Revolution

After the successful war of independence, the thirteen colonies joined to form an independent federation, the United States of America. For several years the new country's founders debated the relative powers of the states that replaced the colonies and of a national government that could unite them. The first confederation, which required the unanimous consent of every state for major political changes, proved unworkable. Seeking a stronger central government, in 1787 delegates from each state met in convention in Philadelphia and approved a constitution for a national government that was mostly written by James Madison (1751–1836), a shy, well-educated Virginian. The constitution called for an elected president and congress presiding over a federal system that granted many powers to the states. The delegates then elected the war hero George Washington (g. 1789–1797) as the first president of the republic. Unlike Jefferson and Madison, Washington was not a talented speaker or writer, but Americans admired the general's integrity and managerial skills, and they considered him a man of deeds rather than words, traits that they saw as embodying American virtues. The first elected congress approved ten constitutional amendments, known as the Bill of Rights, which enshrined Enlightenment values such as freedom of speech, assembly, press, and religion.

The American Revolution had mainly political consequences, since the Patriot founders of the new republic made no effort to transform the American social order. As a result, despite their rhetoric of liberty and equality, they did not challenge slavery, recognize Native American claims to land, or expand voting rights beyond white men. Blacks who fought for Britain faced retribution. Some were executed or reenslaved; others left with other Loyalists for exile in Canada. Some Patriots, including Washington, freed their slaves, and most northern states gradually abolished slavery, but the institution was maintained in most of the south. Indians could only watch bitterly as the new national government, ignoring Indian rights, claimed most of the land east of the Mississippi River and made plans to survey and settle it. In 1787 the U.S. Congress approved the Northwest Ordinance, which allowed frontier settlers to organize governments and petition to join the United States. Nor did the nation's founders give women equal rights with men, even though women too had sacrificed to win independence and had also broadened gender role expectations by managing their absent husbands' shops, businesses, and farms during the war. However, women did gain some legal rights. For example, new laws made it somewhat easier for women to obtain a divorce, a right long enjoyed by men.

Americans also believed they had formed a society unique to history. This idea of a distinctive character and history, known as American "exceptionalism," was intensified after the Revolution. On the last day of the constitutional convention a leading founder, Benjamin Franklin (1706–1790), pointed to an image of the sun painted on the back of the chair used by the convention convener, George Washington, and reported happily that the sun was rising rather than falling, a good omen for the new country. Americans viewed themselves as distinctive: the most democratic, individualistic, enterprising, prosperous, technological, and self-determining society on earth. The new country seemed unhindered by the burdens of history that held down other peoples. But, in contradiction to this uniqueness, Americans also argued that their ideas and institutions were relevant for the whole world. For example, in 1630 the Puritan Massachusetts governor, John Winthrop, claimed that his new society constituted a "City upon a Hill, [with] the eyes of all people upon us."[4] A century and a half later, with the overthrow of British tyranny, these sentiments had intensified, and Thomas Jefferson declared that America was a standing monument and example for the world. These attitudes have remained powerful in American thought.

The French Revolution

The French Revolution was perhaps the world's first true social revolution, traumatic but also inspiring in its message of "liberty, equality, and fraternity." With fair distribution of wealth as a popular principle, the French middle classes took over the government in the name of the common people. But the Revolution also plunged Europe into a prolonged crisis that consumed an entire generation and resulted in a series of wars between France and its European rivals, who feared the spread of radical ideas such as social equality and sought to restore royal government to France. Ironically, these wars actually helped to spread French revolutionary ideas to other European societies.

Ending the Old Regime

The Revolution had many causes. France's participation in the American War of Independence, aiding the Patriot's anti-British cause, worsened the government's long-standing financial problems. Included in these problems was an unjust economic system that badly needed reform. For example, the Roman Catholic clergy and the privileged nobility were exempt from most direct taxes, and thus the entire burden was put on artisans and peasants. Several bad harvests increased the common peoples' hunger and misery. To calm rising passions, King Louis XVI (1754–1793), a member of the long-ruling Bourbon family, called the Estates General, a long-dormant consultative body that included the clergy, the nobility, and finally a Third Estate comprising the middle classes and peasants. Every town debated political issues, drew up lists of complaints, and then elected delegates to the Estates General. High prices, food shortages, and high unemployment spurred resentment of the government and privileged classes. The difficulty the poor had in buying bread led Marie-Antoinette, the king's wife, to contemptuously remark: "Let them eat cake."

The leaders of the Third Estate, who represented over 90 percent of the French population, demanded influence in the Estates General that reflected their numbers. Many middle-class men and women had read the works of Enlightenment thinkers such as Voltaire and had found the American Revolution inspirational. One of them described the nobility and clergy as a malignant disease preying on a sick society. Stalemated in the Estates General, the Third Estate delegates formed a rival national assembly and began writing a new French constitution. In response, the king called in the army to restore order and fired a popular reformist official. These actions provoked anger and violence as common people attacked places where arms and grain were stored.

The Revolution erupted in Paris in 1789 after armed crowds stormed the Bastille, the royal prison and a hated symbol of tyranny, to release the prisoners and seize gunpowder and cannon. The Bastille attack, which resulted in many deaths on both sides, proved so inspirational that the date (July 14) later became France's national holiday. Both men and women took up arms to oppose royal power. As unrest spread through France, the terrified nobility fled. Members of the Third Estate formed a new Constituent Assembly, which voted to destroy the social order dominated by the monarchy and inherited aristocracy. Soon the Assembly adopted the Declaration of the Rights of Man and of the Citizen, a document strongly influenced by the English Bill of Rights of 1689 and the new United States constitution. The Declaration announced that all people everywhere had a natural right to liberty, property, equality, security, religious toleration, and freedom of expression, press, and association. A new constitution preserved the monarchy

Storming the Bastille   This painting celebrates the taking of the Bastille, a castle prison in Paris that symbolized hated royal rule, by armed citizens and soldiers. The governor and his officials are led out and will soon be executed.   (Kunsthistorisches Museum Vienna/The Bridgeman Art Library International)

but made the king bound by laws and subject to an elected assembly. The leaders also outlawed slavery and weakened the church, confiscating the vast wealth of the higher clergy and reorganizing the church structure to limit papal influence.

The French example inspired other Europeans to adopt political reform. For example, in 1791 reformers in Poland-Lithuania reshaped the state and expanded voting rights. But a year later Russia, supported by the Polish nobility, invaded Poland-Lithuania and crushed the reformist government.

The Struggle for France   Counterrevolution supported by rival countries soon embroiled France in a long series of wars. France's neighbors, fearing the radicalism that the Revolution unleashed, sought a restoration of royal power in France. To preempt an invasion, French leaders declared war in 1792. With many aristocratic officers gone, the army recruited volunteers, identifying the defense of France with the defense of revolutionary ideals and proclaiming that "young men shall go forth in battle, married men shall forge weapons, women shall make tents and clothing, and shall serve in hospitals."[5] A national convention, elected by universal male suffrage, now made France a republic, ending the monarchy. In the name of all the world's people, the French began a revolutionary crusade for self-determination and the end of absolute

monarchies in Europe. Most European states declared war on France and its revolutionary zeal, but poor leadership on both sides prevented any decisive victory. With patriotic enthusiasm the French public rallied behind the revolutionary government, singing a song, the *Marseillaise* (mar-sye-EZ), that was written as a call to oppose tyranny and that is now France's national anthem. In 1793 the revolutionaries executed King Louis XVI for treason.

As military conflict intensified, so did dissension in France. The country faced not only foreign enemies but also internal dissent and worsening economic problems. Some leaders had emphasized preserving the Revolution's libertarian principles, such as freedom of speech and assembly. However, a more radical faction known as **Jacobins** (JAK-uh-binz), who believed these rights had to be set aside in the crisis, had taken control of the state and imposed a dictatorship to promote internal security. The Jacobins set up the Committee of Public Safety, which used terror against real or imagined opponents by ordering mass executions, often cutting off their victims' heads in public using the gruesome guillotine. Perhaps 40,000

Jacobins   A radical faction in the French Revolution that believed civil rights had to be set aside in a crisis and that executed thousands of French citizens.

French citizens, mostly rebellious peasants and provincial leaders, were executed, and tens of thousands more were arrested, often on flimsy evidence, to restore internal order. Some Jacobin leaders themselves were executed in factional disputes. The terror abated when the Jacobins lost power in 1795, but several constructive Jacobin policies endured down to today, including innovative laws guaranteeing the right to public education for all children and to public welfare for the poor.

The Legacy of the French Revolution

Although not all its accomplishments proved long-lasting, the French Revolution showed that an old regime could be destroyed and a new order created by its own people, providing both a model and an inspiration for generations of revolutionaries to come. The Revolution not only installed the middle class in power in France but also ultimately constructed a state much more powerful than that of the Bourbon kings. During these years much of the vocabulary of modern politics emerged, including terms such as *conservative* and *right-wing*, referring to those who favored retaining the status quo or restoring the past, and *liberal* and *left-wing*, meaning progressives wanting faster change. Revolutionary France also transformed warfare by introducing conscription and promotion through the ranks and by expanding the country's borders. The countries occupied or conquered by France, such as Belgium and some western German states, were turned into "sister republics," where new revolutionary governments promoted human rights.

But the terrible violence of the French Revolution dampened its appeal as the Jacobins' terror undermined personal liberty. The British-born American thinker Tom Paine, who had fervently admired the French Revolution and its assertion of the "Rights of Man," wrote that he despaired of seeing European liberty accomplished. Indeed, the French trauma and terror turned North Americans against revolutions, which they now feared too often degenerated into anarchy and then despotism, destabilizing societies and threatening property rights.

Observers also debated whether the French "Rights of Man" were intended to include women. Some women who today would be called feminists promoted women's rights. For example, Olympe de Gouges (1748–1793), a French butcher's daughter, published a manifesto complaining that women were excluded from decision making and tried to organize a female militia to fight for France, arguing that needles and spindles were not the only weapons women knew how to handle. For her efforts she was executed. A British campaigner for women's rights, Mary Wollstonecraft (1759–1797), whose outrage was spurred by watching her merchant father abuse her mother, moved to Paris and wrote the *Vindication of the Rights of Women* in 1792, calling for equal opportunities for women in education and society. The unconventional Wollstonecraft shocked polite society by having two children out of wedlock. But despite the efforts of reformers such as de Gouges and Wollstonecraft, women remained excluded from citizenship in France and nearly everywhere else.

The Napoleonic Era and Its Aftermath

Although the republican system had inspired many within and outside of France, the end result in France was a military dictatorship. The terror and the shifting fortunes of war led to a resurgence of pro-monarchy feelings in France and prompted antiroyalists to turn to the ambitious General Napoleon Bonaparte (BOW-nuh-pahrt) (1769–1821), a lawyer's son and a brilliant military strategist from the French-ruled island of Corsica. Bonaparte's ambitions and deeds would shake up the politics of France and Europe.

The Rise of Bonaparte Bonaparte's rise to power was astounding. In 1795 he was a lowly artillery officer just released from prison for alleged Jacobin ties. Through political connections and his forceful personality, he rapidly rose through the ranks to command major military victories in France, Italy, Austria, and Egypt, becoming the most influential French leader of his day. In 1799 Bonaparte gained the most powerful political office in revolutionary France, that of First Consul. His military victories led to a treaty with rival nations in 1801, temporarily ending conflict.

In 1804, responding to a widespread belief that only a dictator could provide stability, Bonaparte crowned himself emperor in a regal coronation, attended by the pope, that harked back a millennium to the crowning of Charlemagne. Bonaparte then quickly began to promote reconciliation within France and to restore French economic prosperity. He also standardized revolutionary laws, including the equality of all citizens before the law, thus making permanent the Revolution's core values. However, the Corsican's general dictatorial tendencies betrayed French liberty, and he also developed a taste for the trappings of royal power. Wanting an heir, he divorced his childless wife, the popular Empress Josephine, and married an eighteen-year-old Austrian princess, Marie-Louise.

Rival nations still feared Bonaparte and the wars soon began again, upsetting the entire European state system. In 1805 Britain, the world's dominant sea power and longtime rival of France, forged a coalition with Austria, Prussia, and Russia to defeat France. In the following years France won most of the land battles, enabling it to occupy much of western Europe. By 1810, Bonaparte's family ruled Spain, Naples, and some German states. But Napoleonic power eventually waned. Armed resistance in Spain and the German states, a costly French invasion of Russia resulting in humiliating retreat, and an invasion of France by rival powers all sapped Bonaparte's military strength. In 1814 allied armies entered Paris, and Bonaparte abdicated and was imprisoned on an Italian island. He escaped and regrouped his forces, but he was finally overcome by British and Prussian armies at Waterloo, a Belgian village, in 1815. While the Bourbon family reclaimed the French throne, Bonaparte, for a decade the most powerful man in Europe, spent his remaining years in exile on St. Helena, a remote, British-ruled South Atlantic island.

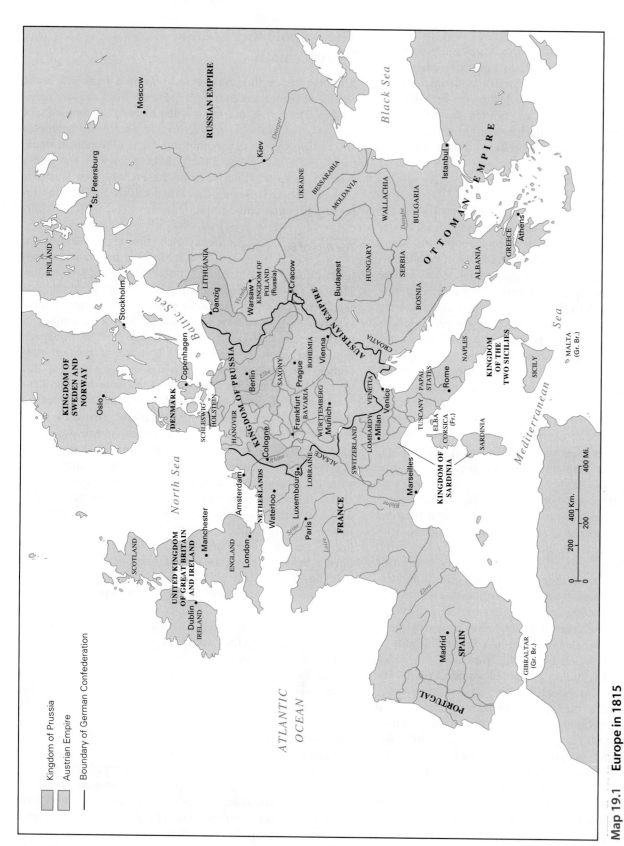

Map 19.1 Europe in 1815
With the Napoleonic wars ended, the Congress of Vienna redrew the map of Europe. France, Austria, Spain, Britain, and a growing Prussia were the dominant states, but the Ottoman Turks still ruled a large area of southeastern Europe.

A new European Politics The demise of revolutionary France and the dismantling of Napoleon's empire allowed for a partial return to the political status quo in Europe. The victorious allies met in 1815 at the Congress of Vienna to remold the European state system (see Map 19.1). Europeans who preferred monarchy and church-state alliance rejoiced at French defeat. The men who overthrew French control in Naples sang, "Naples won't stay a republic. Here's an end to equality. Here's an end to liberty. Long live God and his Majesty."[6] Dominated by Austria, Britain, Russia, and the revived royalist government of France, the Congress reaffirmed pre-Napoleonic borders and restored most of the former rulers displaced by revolutionaries and reformers. It also fostered some changes. For example, thirty-nine German states began moving toward national unity by forming the German Confederation. But some societies faced disappointment. Russia invaded Poland-Lithuania, destroying the constitutional government and partitioning the nation between Russia and Prussia. Wars and violent outbreaks also remained frequent in Europe between 1815 and 1914, many of them involving France.

Once the revolutionary genie generated by the French and American Revolutions was out of the bottle, however, all the best efforts of the established order could not put it back again. Revolutionary ideas combined with popular discontent continued to unsettle Europe, and various revolutions broke out in 1830–1831 because of discontent with despotic political systems. The French overthrew the increasingly despotic Bourbon king, Charles X, and installed his more progressive cousin and former Jacobin, Louis-Philippe (1773–1850), as a constitutional monarch who recognized democratic liberties. Uprisings in several German and Italian states and in Poland sought voting rights, and a peasant rebellion caused by poverty and unemployment rocked Britain.

Even more turbulent European revolts erupted in 1848, a result of poor harvests, rampant disease, trade slumps, rising unemployment, massive poverty, and a desire for representative government. These upheavals began in France, forcing the increasingly unpopular King Louis-Philippe to abdicate, and soon spread to Austria, Hungary, and many German and Italian states. For example, in German cities students inspired by the events in Paris met in city marketplaces to organize movements demanding elected parliaments and civil liberties such as free speech and a free press. But around Europe conservative regimes crushed the dissident movements, which had no central coordination, within a few months, often causing great bloodshed. A French observer said that "nothing was lacking" in the repression in Paris, "not grapeshot, nor bullets, nor demolished houses, nor martial law, nor the ferocity of the soldiery, nor the insults to the dead."[7] Still, the uprisings helped further spread democratic ideas, and monarchies lost ground as parliamentary power increased in countries such as Denmark and the Netherlands. To prevent revolutionary outbursts, many European governments also began to consider social and economic reforms, such as higher wages, to improve people's lives.

SECTION SUMMARY

■ Many people in the North American colonies chafed against British rule and, inspired by Enlightenment thinkers, pushed for independence, while others, including many Indians and black slaves, sided with the British.

■ After a first failed attempt at confederation, the thirteen American colonies agreed upon a system that balanced federal and state powers, but the American Revolution did little to change the social order and did not extend equal rights to blacks, women, and Indians.

■ The French Revolution, which aimed to wrest control from the nobility and the clergy, achieved some of its progressive goals and was an inspiration to some societies, but it led to a period of war and widespread terror, and its excesses turned others away from revolution.

■ In the tumultuous aftermath of the French Revolution, Napoleon Bonaparte seized power, implemented some of the Revolution's egalitarian ideals in law, and waged a series of overly ambitious wars that eventually led to his defeat and the Congress of Vienna, at which many pre-Revolution boundaries were restored. Throughout the first half of the nineteenth century, other revolutions against despotic regimes rose up and were usually crushed, but nevertheless democratic ideals made gradual progress.

The Age of Revolution: The Caribbean and Latin America

How did the Caribbean and Latin American revolutions compare with those in Europe and North America?

The Age of Revolution was not confined to North America and Europe. Just as in British North America, dissatisfaction with colonialism was common in the Caribbean and Spanish America, and it led to revolutions and wars of independence in these regions in the early 1800s. The first successful movement to overthrow colonialism came in Haiti, where slaves of African ancestry fought their way to power. Most of the American colonies of Spain eventually fought for and won their independence by the 1820s. During the same period Mexico and Brazil became independent without warfare.

Spanish and Portuguese America's Colonial Heritage

The Spanish and Portuguese ruled much larger American empires than did the British. By 1810 some 18 million people, many times the population of British North America, lived under Spanish rule from California in the north to the southern tip of South America. This population included 4 million people of European ancestry, 8 million Indians, 1 million blacks, and 5 million people of mixed descent. The empire was divided into four administrative units based in Mexico, Colombia, Peru, and Argentina, each supervised by Spanish governors. Corruption ran deep in the colonial system, but the planters, ranchers, mine owners, bureaucrats, and church officials who benefited from Spanish rule or profited from exploiting the economic resources opposed any major change. They preferred a system that sent raw materials, such as silver and beef, to Spain rather than one that developed domestic institutions or markets.

The Spanish fostered American societies with many problems and conflicts. They ruled their colonies differently than did the British in North America, allowing little self-government, maintaining economic monocultures that relied on the export of a single agricultural or mineral resource, and imposing one dominant religion: Roman Catholicism. Only a small minority of people, mostly those of European ancestry, shared in the wealth produced by the mines, plantations, and ranches. Latin American social conditions did not promote unity or equality. The creoles, whites born in the Americas, resented the influential newcomers from Spain, but they were also more cautious than the North American Patriots, fearing that resistance against Spain might get out of control and threaten their position. The great majority of the population, a dispossessed underclass of Indians, enslaved Africans, and mixed-descent people, faced growing unemployment and perhaps the world's most inequitable distribution of wealth.

In contrast to British America, Latin America, dominated by a rigid Catholic Church wary of dissent, enjoyed little intellectual diversity. The Inquisition denounced as seditious any literature espousing equality and liberty for all people and punished people it considered to be heretics. Local critics accused the government and church of "placing the strongest fetters on Enlightenment and [keeping] thought in chains."[8] Yet some thinkers sidestepped the repression. For example, the Mexican creole Jose Antonio Alzate y Ramirez (1738–1799) published a magazine that promoted science and Enlightenment rationalism.

Given the political and social inequalities, various revolts punctuated Spanish colonial rule. For instance, Mexico experienced some 142 village revolts between 1700 and 1820, including a major upheaval in 1761 when the Mayas revolted against high taxes and church repression of Maya customs, leading to Spanish reprisals. The largest revolt in Spanish America, a mass uprising led by Tupac Amaru II (1740–1781), the wealthy, well-educated mestizo who claimed to be a descendant of an Inca king, spread over large areas of Peru in the 1780s. Tupac had been stirred by historical accounts of his Inca ancestors and memories of the many earlier anti-Spanish revolts in the Andes regions. Tupac and Michaela Bastidas, his wife and a brilliant strategist, organized a broad-based coalition of groups that quickly overran much of central and southern Peru, where they hoped to establish an independent state, with Tupac as king, and where Indians, mestizos, and creoles would live in harmony. But many of Tupac's peasant followers went further, reviving the Inca religion and attacking Catholic churches and clergy. The better-armed Spanish defeated the rebel bands and

executed Tupac and his family. The Tupac Amaru revolt paved the way for larger upheavals across South America several decades later.

Portuguese Brazil also experienced dissension. By the late 1700s Brazil was the wealthiest part of the Portuguese colonial realm, but only a small minority, especially white plantation and gold mine owners, benefited from the prosperity derived from exporting the raw materials chiefly produced by slaves of African ancestry. Since Brazil was the major importer of slaves, accounting for a quarter to a third of all Africans arriving in the Americas, blacks vastly outnumbered Native Americans in Brazil, in contrast to Spanish-ruled Mexico and South America. Disgruntled Afro-Brazilians demanded a better life, but they faced many setbacks. For example, in 1799 a revolt seeking social equality and political freedom was crushed in the northeastern state of Bahia (buh-HEE-uh).

Caribbean Societies and the Haitian Revolution

Most of the small Caribbean islands and the Guianas in northeast South America were colonies of Britain, France, or the Netherlands and were inhabited chiefly by African slaves and their descendants, most of whom worked on sugar plantations. The Afro-Caribbean peoples appropriated European cultural forms and languages, welding them with retained African forms. In British-colonized islands such as Jamaica, Barbados, and Antigua, for example, most slaves adopted Christianity and Anglo-Saxon names. The African influences that shaped slave life included African musical influences, such as drumming, improvisation, and varied rhythms.

Slave revolts were common throughout the colonial era, but only one, the Haitian Revolution, overthrew a regime. In 1791 some 100,000 Afro-Haitian slaves, inspired by the French Revolution and its slogans of liberty and equality, rose up against the oppressive society presided over by French planters, thus beginning years of war and bloodshed (see Chronology: The Caribbean and Latin American Revolutions, 1750–1840). Toussaint L'Ouverture (too-SAN loo-ver-CHORE) (1746–1803), a freed slave with a vision of a republic composed of free people, became the insurgent leader. Toussaint had status on the plantation because his father came from a chiefly family in Africa. Raised a Catholic, Toussaint learned French and Latin from an older slave.

The Haitian revolution went from triumph to tragedy. For a decade the Afro-Haitians, led by Toussaint, fought the French military and, at times, anti-French British and Spanish forces hoping to capitalize on the turmoil. By 1801 Toussaint's forces had gained control over Haiti and freed the slaves. But Napoleon Bonaparte sent in a larger French force to restore order, and in 1803 French soldiers captured Toussaint, who soon died in a French prison. In 1804 Afro-Haitians defeated Napoleon's army and established the second independent nation in the Western Hemisphere after the United States. Elsewhere in the Americas the Haitian Revolution cheered slaves and those favoring abolition of slavery but alarmed planters, who became more determined to preserve slavery. Reflecting

CHRONOLOGY

The Caribbean and Latin American Revolutions, 1750–1840

1791–1804	Haitian Revolution
1808	Move of Portuguese royal family to Brazil
1810–1826	Wars of independence in Spanish America
1810–1811	First Mexican revolution
1816	Argentine independence
1819	Founding of Colombian republic by Bolivar
1822	Mexican independence; Dom Pedro emperor of Brazil
1830	Independence of Colombia, Venezuela, and Ecuador
1839	Division of Central American states

white fears of slave revolt, the United States, still a slave-owning nation, withheld diplomatic recognition of the black Haitian republic. In Haiti, French planters were either killed or fled, and the ex-slaves took over sugar production. The promise of a better life for Haiti's people proved short-lived, however. Toussaint's successor as revolutionary leader, the Africa-born Jean Jacques Dessalines (de-sah-LEEN) (1758–1806), became emperor and ruled despotically, beginning two centuries of tyranny.

South American Independence Wars

As in North America and Haiti, dissatisfaction in Spanish-ruled South America exploded into wars of national independence. In 1800 the Spanish colonial hold on its empire seemed secure, but, as in British North America, resentments simmered, especially among creoles, fostering anticolonial movements. Creole merchants and ranchers criticized Spain for its commercial monopoly, its increasing taxes, and the colonial government's favoritism toward those born in Spain. They also wanted a role in government. Creoles also often felt more loyalty to their American region than to distant Spain, and some were influenced by the Enlightenment and the American and French Revolutions. The British, who were pressuring the Spanish and Portuguese to open Latin American markets to British goods, also secretly aided anticolonial groups. At the same time, Spain was experiencing political problems at home, including French occupation during the Napoleonic wars, which weakened the country's ability to suppress unrest in Latin America.

Since Spain refused to make serious political concessions, creole revolutionaries of middle-class backgrounds waged wars of independence between 1810 and 1826, forming new countries. Two separate independence movements began in 1810–1811 in Venezuela and Argentina, and they soon came under the leadership of Simon Bolivar (bow-LEE-vahr) in the north and Jose de San Martin (san mahr-TEEN) in the south. Bolivar became the symbol of the liberation struggle. Born into a wealthy Caracas family that owned slaves, land, and mines, Bolivar (1783–1830) had studied law in Spain, was a free thinker who admired rationalist Enlightenment thought, and had a magnetic personality that inspired loyalty. He offered an inclusive view of his Latin American people: "We are a microcosm of the human race, a world apart, neither Indian nor Europeans, but a part of each."[9] Bolivar also spent time in Haiti and Jamaica, where he gained sympathy for blacks. In

Simon Bolivar The main leader of the anti-Spanish war of independence in northern South America, Bolivar came to be known as "the Liberator," a symbol of Latin American nationalism and the struggle for political freedom.
(Courtesy, Archivo CENIDIAP-INBA, Mexico City. Collection, Fernando Leal Audirac)

Map 19.2   Latin American Independence, 1840

By 1840 all of Latin America except for Cuba and Puerto Rico, still Spanish colonies, had become independent, with Brazil and Mexico the largest countries. Later the Central American provinces and Gran Colombia would fragment into smaller nations, and Argentina would annex Patagonia.

Online Study Center   Improve Your Grade   Interactive Map: Latin America in 1830

1812 he formed an army to liberate northern South America, offering freedom to slaves who aided his cause. After many setbacks, Bolivar's forces liberated the north in 1824. San Martin (1778–1850), a former colonel in the Spanish army, led the southern forces against Spain and its royalist allies, helping Argentina gain independence in 1816 and Chile in 1818. In 1824 San Martin and Bolivar cooperated to liberate Peru, where royalist sympathies were strongest.

Online Study Center **Improve Your Grade**
Primary Source: The Jamaican Letter

But these victories over the colonial regimes did not always meet the expectations of the liberated or the liberators. The wars damaged economies and caused people to flee the fighting. In addition, the creoles who now governed these countries often forgot the promises made to the Indians, mestizos, mulattos, and blacks who had often provided the bulk of the revolutionary armies. And although some slaves were freed, slavery was not abolished. Women also experienced disappointment. Some enthusiastically served the revolution as soldiers and nurses. For example, Policarpa Salavarrieta helped Bolivar as a spy until she was captured by the Spanish. Before she was executed in Bogota's main plaza, she exclaimed: "Although I am a woman and young, I have more than enough courage to suffer this death and a thousand more."[10] But women soon found that they still lived in patriarchal societies that offered them few new legal or political rights. Finally, unlike the founders of the United States, Latin America's new leaders were largely unable to form representative and democratic governments. Simon Bolivar could not hold his own country together, and in 1830 it broke into Colombia, Ecuador, and Venezuela. Meanwhile, Uruguay and Paraguay split off from Argentina, and Bolivia separated from Peru. Disillusioned, Bolivar concluded that Latin America was ungovernable.

Independence Movements in Mexico and Brazil

Political change also came to Mexico and Brazil (see Map 19.2). In 1810 two progressive Mexican Catholic priests, the creole Manuel Hidalgo (ee-DAHL-go) and the mestizo Jose Maria Morelos (hoe-SAY mah-REE-ah moh-RAY-los), mobilized peasants and miners and launched a revolt promoting independence, the abolition of slavery, and social reform to uplift the mestizos and Indians. Creole conservatives and royalists suppressed that revolt and executed Hidalgo and Morelos. But a compromise between various factions brought Mexico independence in 1822 under a creole general, Agustin de Iturbide (ah-goos-TEEN deh ee-tur-BEE-deh) (1783–1824), who proclaimed himself emperor. However, although initially the anti-Spanish struggle had united creoles, mestizos, and Indians against a common enemy, the alliance unraveled and a republican revolt soon ousted Iturbide. The Central American peoples split off from Mexico and, after several attempts at unity, by 1839 had splintered into five states.

Brazil escaped many of the conflicts bedeviling Spanish America, enjoying a nearly bloodless transition to independence. In 1808 the Portuguese royal family and government sought refuge in Brazil to escape the Napoleonic wars, and in the following years Brazilians increasingly viewed themselves as separate from Portugal. When the Portuguese government tried to reclaim the territory, a member of the royal family still in Brazil, Dom Pedro (1798–1834), severed ties with Portugal in 1822 and became emperor of Brazil as Pedro I, Latin America's only constitutional monarch. However, although a parliament was set up and elections were held, most Brazilians had no vote and Pedro I governed autocratically. Politics involved a small group of merchants, landowners, and the royal family.

SECTION SUMMARY

- Spain controlled its American colonies extremely tightly, leaving little room for intellectual freedom or economic mobility, and put down many revolts through the end of the eighteenth century.

- After over a decade of revolutionary struggle, the Afro-Haitian slaves won their freedom from the French, but they soon fell under the control of an African-born despot.

- Rising dissatisfaction among South Americans, particularly creoles, led to successful independence movements throughout the continent, though the newly free nations had trouble forming representative and democratic governments.

- After Mexico obtained its independence, the coalition that had opposed the Spanish fell apart, while members of the Portuguese royal family who fled to Brazil helped it to obtain its independence peacefully.

◆ The Industrial Revolution and Economic Growth

How did industrialization reshape economic and social life?

Along with political and social revolutions, the **Industrial Revolution**, a dramatic transformation in the production and transportation of goods, was a major force reshaping the economic, political, and social patterns of Europe and later of North America and Japan. For the first time in history, the shackles were taken off the productive power of societies and people could now manipulate nature for their own purposes. Henceforth, they became capable of the rapid, constant, and seemingly limitless increase of goods and services. This revolution was perhaps the greatest transformation in society since

Industrial Revolution A dramatic transformation in the production and transportation of goods.

settled farming, urbanization, and the first states arose thousands of years ago. Although the intellectual and economic roots of industrialization were laid in the Early Modern Era, it was in the late 1700s that breakthroughs in productivity were made. The transition began in Britain and then spread across the English Channel to western Europe, then across the Atlantic to North America, eventually helping transform the limited European power of 1750 into Western domination over much of the world by 1914.

The Roots of the Industrial Revolution

The Industrial Revolution and the changes it generated had deep roots in Early Modern Europe. The Renaissance, Reformation, and Enlightenment had generated new ways of thought, including the expanded quest to understand the natural and physical world reflected in the Scientific Revolution. The discovery of new lands, plants, peoples, cultural traditions, and animals stimulated curiosity about the world. In addition, the commercial capitalism that arose in the 1500s and 1600s generated trade and conquest overseas, forming political and economic links between the Americas, the African coast, some Asian societies, and western Europe by 1750. These connections allowed Europeans to acquire natural resources and great wealth overseas, which provided capital for investment in new technologies and incentives for producing more commodities for the world market.

Great Britain benefited more than other countries from these changes, becoming the world's leading trading nation by the 1700s. British inventors experimented with steam power, and by the 1730s spinning machines were making the English textile industry more efficient. The demands of the world market for textiles spurred Britain to replace India as the main supplier of cotton textiles. Britain had many advantages over rival countries, including an open intellectual atmosphere with diverse views and a reasonably democratic political system that included the middle classes in government. Britain also had the most productive economy, favorable terrain on which to build transportation networks, abundant raw materials like coal and iron, and many water sources to run machines. By contrast, the lack of minerals and water sources in the Netherlands explains why that prosperous and tolerant country did not initiate an industrial revolution. Between the 1780s and 1830s Britain dominated European industrialization.

Because of its earlier overseas activities in the Americas and Asia, Britain acquired one of the prerequisites for industrialization: adequate capital. Profits from the British-controlled Caribbean islands and from several colonies in North America, which produced huge amounts of sugar and tobacco, and from British trading posts in India were particularly crucial in funding the Industrial Revolution. Some British companies made

vast fortunes from the trans-Atlantic slave trade and the slavery plantations in the Americas. Although historians debate the exact connection between profits from slavery and the establishment of British industries, they tend to agree that companies owning sugar, cotton, and tobacco plantations in the Americas often invested their excess capital in new British industries. Most factories were built in the hinterland of great slave trade ports such as Liverpool. In this way the English region east of Liverpool and northern Wales known as the Midlands, near rich coal and iron ore fields, became the center of British industry (see Map 19.3). Concentrating production in large factories in or near cities such as Birmingham and Manchester in the Midlands lowered transport costs and tapped a ready labor supply.

The Age of Machines

The Industrial Revolution introduced an era in which machines produced the goods used by people and increasingly performed more human tasks, reshaping peoples' lives. Instead of making things by hand with the aid of simple tools, workers now used increasingly complicated machines and chemical processes. These machines were moved by energy derived from steam and other inanimate sources rather than human or animal sources. People were also increasingly able to tap the resources of the earth's crust and turn them into commodities. As a result, the Industrial Revolution created great material richness. Between the 1770s and 1914 a Europe of peasant

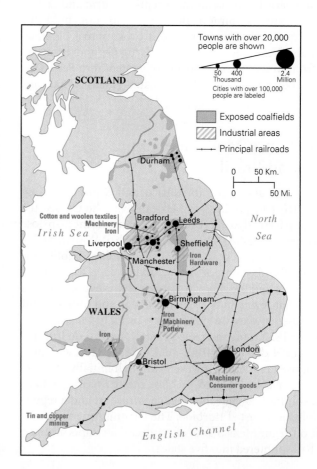

Map 19.3 Industrial Transformation in England
British industrialization mostly occurred near coalfields and iron ore deposits, spurring the rise of cities such as Birmingham, Leeds, Liverpool, and Manchester.

holdings, country estates, and domestic workshops became a Europe of sprawling and polluted industrial cities such as Manchester, with a wide gap between the few rich and the many poor (see Chronology: European Politics and Economy, 1750–1914).

In the past 250 years the material culture of the world, and particularly of Europe and North America, changed more than it did in the previous 750 years. Europeans in 1750 lived much more like Europeans in 1000 than like Western peoples in 1900. Today citizens of industrialized nations use transportation, wear fabrics, and employ building materials inconceivable in 1750. As one measure of how the world changed, one need only consider some of the words that first appeared in the English language between 1780 and 1850: *industry, factory, middle class, working class, engineer, crisis, statistics, strike,* and *pauper.*

The Industrial Revolution triggered continual technological innovations and a corresponding increase in economic activity. Inventions in one industry stimulated inventions in others. The cotton industry mechanized first. New cotton machines created a demand for more plentiful and reliable power than could be provided by traditional water wheels and horses. The steam pump invented by the Englishman Thomas Newcomen in 1712, possibly based on an earlier Chinese model and used mostly for pumping water out of mines, was innovative but inefficient. Seeking a more efficient power source, James Watt (1736–1819), a Scottish inventor who gained financial support from a wealthy merchant, Matthew Boulton, produced the first successful rotary steam engine in 1774. Watt transformed Newcomen's machine from a simple pump into a more versatile mover of energy that was useful in many types of industrial activities. Steam engines provided power not only for the textile mills but also for the iron furnaces, flour mills, and mines. When used in railroads and steamships, steam power conquered time and space, bringing the world much closer together. Watt's backer, Boulton, understood that profit required large sales, arguing that he had to sell steam engines to all the world to make money.

Technological innovations continued. The new cotton machines and steam engines required increased supplies of iron, steel, and coal. Mining and metalworking improved in response, creating a need for improved transportation facilities to move the coal and ore. After a while technological and economic growth came to be accepted as normal, provoking admiration and wonder. The British novelist William Thackeray celebrated the changes in 1860: "It is only yesterday, but what a gulf between now and then! *Then* was the old world. Stagecoaches, riding horses, pack-horses, knights in armor, Norman invaders, Roman legions—all these belong to the old period. But your railroad starts a new era."[11] In others, however, mechanization provoked fear, causing them to turn against industrialization. Between 1815 and 1830 anti-industrialization activists in Britain known as **Luddites**, mostly skilled textile

---

Luddites Anti-industrialization activists in Britain who destroyed machines in a mass protest against the effects of mechanization.

CHRONOLOGY

European Politics and Economy, 1750–1914

1770s	Beginning of Industrial Revolution in England
1774	James Watt's first rotary steam engine
1776	Adam Smith's *The Wealth of Nations*
1800	British Act of Union
1821–1830	Greek war of independence
1830–1831	Wave of revolutions across Europe
1831	Formation of Young Italy movement by Mazzini
1845–1846	Irish potato famine
1848	Wave of revolts across Europe; *The Communist Manifesto* by Marx and Engels
1851	Great Exhibition in London
1859–1870	Unification of Italy
1862–1871	Unification of Germany
1870s–1914	Second Industrial Revolution

workers, invaded factories and, with guns, hatchets, and pikes, destroyed machines in a mass protest against the effects of mechanization. Ultimately the Luddite cause proved futile. The British government sent in 12,000 troops to stop the destruction and made the wrecking of machines a crime punishable by death.

The Spread of Industrialization

For decades Britain was the world's richest, most competitive nation, with a reputation as the workshop of the world. The new factories and machines mass-produced goods of better quality and lower price than traditional handicrafts, helping the British to overcome the old problem of finding commodities to trade to the world. They now had marketable goods and a powerful need to sell them to recoup their heavy investments in machinery and materials. By the mid-1800s Britain produced two-thirds of the world's coal, half the iron, and half the cotton cloth and other manufactured goods. A British poet boasted that "England's a perfect World, hath Indies, too, Correct your Maps, Newcastle [a center of the coal industry] is [silver rich] Peru."[12] The British enjoyed political, military, and economic supremacy in Europe and significant power in other regions of the world. No other state could substantially threaten Britain's economic and political position.

Industrial Sheffield   This painting of one of the key British industrial cities, Sheffield, in 1858 shows the factories, many specializing in producing steel and metal goods, that dominated the landscape. (Courtesy, Sheffield Archives and Local Studies Library.)

However, the British invested some of their huge profits in western Europe, spreading the Industrial Revolution across the English Channel between the 1830s and 1870s. As iron-smelting technology improved, industrial operations became concentrated in regions rich in coal and iron ore. Capitalizing on its reserves of these resources, prosperous trading cities, and a strategic location between France, Holland, and Germany, Belgium industrialized in the early 1800s. By 1850 the Belgians had tripled their coal production and increased the number of steam engines from 354 to 2,300. Belgium also capitalized on the transportation revolution, building an ambitious railroad system to transport coal, iron, and manufactured goods and connecting it to neighboring countries. By the 1830s France had also begun constructing a national railroad network. In contrast to Britain and Belgium, France had to import coal, and, since it had fewer rich merchants than Britain, the government helped fund industrial activity. In the German states, political fragmentation before 1870 discouraged industrialization, except in several coal-rich regions such as the Ruhr Valley in western Germany and Silesia in Prussia. Some countries, including Portugal, Spain, and Austria-Hungary, remained largely agricultural. By 1914, however, industrialization was widespread around Europe and had also taken root in North America and Japan, and large numbers of people lived in cities and worked in factories.

Industrial Capitalism and Its Advocates

Beginning around 1770, industrialization and the vast increase in manufactured goods transformed commercial capitalism, dominated by large trading companies, into industrial capitalism, a system centered around manufacturing. During this era European industrial firms made and exported manufactured goods to other countries and in return imported raw materials, such as iron ore, to make more goods. The Industrial Revolution gave businesses marketable products and a powerful compulsion to market them in ever-increasing quantities. Because of the heavy investments in machines, success depended on a large and steady turnover of goods. Advertising developed to create demand, and banking and financial institutions expanded their operations to better serve business and industry. The industrialists, bankers, and financiers were also supported by political leaders who pursued policies of maximizing private wealth.

As economic and government efforts were made to support industrial capitalism, some thinkers felt the need to justify it. Economic philosophers emerged to praise British-style capitalism. The most influential, the Scottish professor Adam Smith (1723–1790), was a friend and supporter of Enlightenment thinkers. In his book *The Wealth of Nations* (1776), Smith helped formulate modern economics theory, known as neoclassical economics. In examining the consequences of economic freedom, Smith concluded that the market should be left alone. He advocated **laissez faire**, the restriction of government interference in the marketplace, such as laws regulating business and profits. Smith believed in self-interest, arguing that the "invisible hand" of the marketplace would turn the individual greed of the entrepreneur into a rising standard of living for all. Smith also introduced the new idea of a permanently growing economy, reinforcing the long-standing Western view of progress and of ever-increasing wealth as time went on. History was going somewhere. The popularity of Smith's writing shows how much things had changed since medieval times, when Christian leaders condemned mercantile activity. Smith's free trade ideas helped end the mercantilism of the Early Modern Era, when several European states worked closely with large commercial enterprises to accumulate wealth. The free traders like Smith believed that Britain should serve as the world's industrial center, into which flowed raw materials and out of which flowed manufactured goods.

But Smith saw the potential for both good and evil in industrial capitalism. He championed free trade but also found areas where government regulation might be useful and even essential. Smith acknowledged that free enterprise did not necessarily generate prosperity for all, since the interests of the manufacturers were not necessarily those of society or even of the broader economy. To ensure these larger interests, he encouraged businesses to pay their employees high wages, writing that "no society can surely be flourishing and happy of which the far greater part of its members are poor and miserable. [They should be] well fed, clothed and lodged."[13]

The Second Industrial Revolution

Beginning about 1870, what some historians call the Second Industrial Revolution, characterized by technological change, mass production, and specialization, got under way, continuing to 1914. The increasing application of science to industry spurred expansion and improvement in the electrical, chemical, optical, and automotive industries and brought new inventions such as electricity grids, radio, the internal combustion engine, gasoline, and the flush toilet. The United States and Germany led in implementing these changes, and by 1900 Germany was Europe's main producer of electrical goods and chemicals. By the early 1900s factory production was often done on the assembly line. Work was increasingly broken down into separate specialized tasks; for example, a worker in an automobile assembly line might only install wheels, leaving other tasks in building the automobile to others.

The Second Industrial Revolution promoted a shift to a form of capitalism in which giant monopolies, led by tycoons with unprecedented wealth, replaced the more competitive economy of industrial capitalism. The concentration of capital in what became known as "big business" gave a few businessmen and bankers, such as the Krupp family in Germany and the Rockefellers in the United States, vast economic power and control over many industries. For instance, Alfred Krupp (1812–1887) became Europe's leading manufacturer of arms and also owned steel mills and mines. His son Freidrich Krupp (1854–1902), who expanded the family empire to incorporate shipbuilding, was so influential that Germany's emperor and most top government officials attended his daughter's lavish wedding in 1906. The monopolies emerged because the huge capital investment needed for new factories eliminated many of the small businesses. Moreover, new industries producing such useful innovations as aluminum and electrical power required a heavy capital investment to start. A long depression in the late 1800s undermined competition, encouraging businesses to merge or cooperate and to moderate slumps, which hurt their profits, by fixing prices. The result was economic change that reshaped government policies and generated a drive to colonize more of the world to ensure access to resources and markets.

Industry and Social Change

The Industrial Revolution reshaped patterns of life in the industrializing countries, affecting both men and women and all social and economic classes (see Chapter 20). In 1800 Europe remained mainly agricultural. A century later many changes had occurred: a greater division of labor, growing social problems, most people living in cities, and the replacement of human workers by machines. The factory system compelled the migration of millions of people from the countryside into cities, where life was often difficult.

The cities of western Europe and North America in the 1800s were overcrowded and unhealthy, with high rates of alcoholism, prostitution, and crime. In the early industrial years city people crowded into festering slums, worked long hours for low wages, and learned new lifestyles. French writer Alexis de Tocqueville (TOKE-vill) described the atmosphere of Manchester in 1835:

> The footsteps of a busy crowd, the crunching wheels of machinery, the shriek of steam from boilers, the regular beat of the looms, the heavy rumble of carts, these are the noises from which you can never escape in the somber half-light of these streets. Crowds are ever hurrying this way and that, but their footsteps are brisk, their looks preoccupied, and their appearance somber and harsh.[14]

Factories, mines, and cities reshaped European life. Factory workers included highly skilled and experienced artisans but also millions of less skilled people who worked fourteen- and sometimes eighteen-hour days in a system of rigid discipline and punishments, including flogging, with no insurance provided in case of accidents, ill health, or old age. Many children worked seven days a week in mines or factories. In one reported case from 1887, a Scottish manufacturer on his trotting horse forced a sixteen-year-old, who had left work without permission, to run back to the factory alongside him while whipping the boy the entire way. In the English cotton mills during the 1830s and 1840s, about one-quarter of workers were adult men, over half were women and girls, and the rest

---

laissez faire Restriction of government interference in the marketplace, such as laws regulating business and profits.

TOMMY ARMSTRONG, BARD OF THE ENGLISH COAL MINES

Tommy Armstrong (1849–1919) was one of the most famous song-makers who came out of the new industrial working class of Britain. From a poor family and with little formal schooling, Armstrong began working in the mine pits around Durham in the Northumbrian region of north England at age nine. Since the youngster was born with crooked legs, his older brother William carried him to work on his back. Tommy worked first as a trapper-boy, opening the ventilation doors for coal and miners to pass through. Later he went on to more demanding jobs in the pits.

In the later nineteenth century many miners in Durham and elsewhere composed rhymes and songs. Armstrong was already writing song lyrics at age twelve. Eventually he married, but miners' wages barely covered expenses for his large family—his overworked wife and fourteen children—prompting Armstrong to seek additional money by writing songs and having them printed. Single sheets, known as broadsides, containing lyrics were then sold in pubs to raise money for his family but also to buy beer for himself. The balladeer of Tyneside, as he was known, referring to the nearby Tyne River, developed a legendary thirst. His son claimed, "Me dad's Muse was a mug of beer." Armstrong engaged in song duels with rival songwriters and even made up verses about the people in the houses he passed on his way home from work or pub. His songs usually had a strong sense of social class and social criticism. One of them encouraged educating the young, in part to avoid trouble with the law: "Send your bairns [children] to school, Learn them all you can. Make scholarship your faithful friend, and you'll never see the school-board man [truant officer]." He set his songs to folk and music-hall tunes as well as to Irish melodies brought by the thousands of Irish immigrants to the mines.

Armstrong became renowned for writing songs reflecting the miner's increasingly radical views and ballads to memorialize mining disasters, usually to raise money for union funds or the relief of orphans and widows. For example, in 1882, after an explosion killed seventy-four miners, Armstrong produced a song commemorating the lost men: "Oh, let's not think of tomorrow lest we disappointed be. Our joys may turn to sorrow as we all may daily see. God protect the lonely widow and raise each dropping head; Be a father to the orphans, never let them cry for bread." Conscious of his responsibility, he claimed that "when you're the Pitman's [coal miner's] Poet and looked up for it, if a disaster or a strike goes by without a song from you, they say: What's with Tommy Armstrong? Has someone let out all the inspiration?"

Armstrong was especially productive in the last two decades of the 1800s when strikes were common and the Miners' Union grew rapidly from 36,000 to over 200,000 members. As the struggles between miners and mine owners became more bitter, the union grew more assertive and organized. Armstrong wrote strike songs to give information and courage to miners, but also to collect money for hungry families of strikers. Some of the worst conflicts erupted in 1892, when the Durham miners were asked to take a large pay cut. When the union refused, the workers were locked out of their workplaces, prompting one of Armstrong's most famous songs: "In our Durham County I am sorry for to say, That hunger and starvation is increasing every day. For want of food and coals, we know not what to do, But with your kind assistance, we will stand the battle through. Our work is taken from us now, they care not if we die, For they [the mine owners] can eat the best of food, and drink the best when dry." After months of labor strife, the union pragmatically agreed to a lower pay reduction. The songs of Tommy Armstrong and other industrial balladeers provide a chronicle of the Industrial Revolution and the ways it shaped the lives of millions of people.

THINKING ABOUT THE PROFILE

1. How did Armstrong's life reflect the working conditions and often hardships imposed on workers by the Industrial Revolution?

2. What did the songs of industrial balladeers like Armstrong tell us about how working-class people confronted the realities of industrial society?

Note: Quotations from A. L. Lloyd, *Folk Song in England* (New York: International Publishers, 1967), pp. 359–361, 378, 380–381. Copyright © 1967 by International Publishers. Reprinted with permission.

Tommy Armstrong Known as the "Pitman's (coalminer's) Poet," Armstrong worked in the coalfields around Durham, in England, and wrote many songs celebrating the miners' struggles for a better life. (Courtesy, Northern Recording Company, UK)

were boys younger than eighteen. In these difficult conditions, workers such as the English coal miner Tommy Armstrong sometimes used cultural expression, such as songs, to express their solidarity with each other and resentment of those they worked for (see Profile: Tommy Armstrong, Bard of the English Coal Mines).

Gradually many people, especially in the cities, began to think of themselves as members in a social and economic class that had interests of its own in opposition to other classes. The working classes, such as the coal miners and factory workers, were the largest group. The middle classes included businesspeople, professionals, and prosperous farmers. A salaried labor force, today known as "white-collar" workers, emerged to handle sales and paperwork. For example, some 90,000 women worked as secretaries in Britain by 1901. The middle class prided itself on a keen work ethic and attributed poverty to poor work habits and lack of initiative. The rise of the middle class posed a challenge to the legal and social status of the beleaguered aristocrats, who struggled to maintain their dominance over the governments and churches in many countries. Crime increased as the gap between the haves and the have-nots became more apparent. In 1845 the British writer and politician Benjamin Disraeli described these two groups as inhabitants of different planets, between which there is no sympathy and no discourse.

SECTION SUMMARY

■ The Industrial Revolution began in England, which had great stores of capital derived from overseas trade, an openness to new ideas, and abundant natural resources, and the revolution gradually spread throughout western Europe and North America.

■ As technology played an increasingly important role in the economy and in people's lives, with machines constantly evolving and being put to new uses, some people marveled at the technological change while others, such as the Luddites, resisted it.

■ Commercial capitalism was changed into industrial capitalism centered on manufacturing, and economic philosophers such as Adam Smith advocated laissez faire, the idea that the market, if left alone, would improve everyone's standard of living and create ever-increasing wealth and progress.

■ The Second Industrial Revolution ushered in an age of specialization and mass production, and it favored monopolistic corporations that could afford enormous investments in new technology.

■ The Industrial Revolution brought many people from the countryside to cities, where they encountered crowding, noise, new social problems, and hard labor conditions.

■ As a result of the revolution, new classes arose—the working class; the middle classes, including a new secretarial force; and the aristocrats—and the gap between the haves and the have-nots widened.

 # Nationalism, Liberalism, and Socialism

How did nationalism, liberalism, and socialism differ from each other?

Besides the political and economic revolutions, the Modern Era also produced three new ideologies—nationalism, liberalism, and socialism—that influenced the European and American political order and that continue to shape our world. An **ideology** is a secular faith or philosophy: a coherent, widely shared system of ideas about the nature of the social, political, and economic realm. In the Modern Era, nationalism fostered unified countries, liberalism encouraged democratic parliamentary governments in various nations, and socialism sparked movements to counteract the power of industrial capitalism and the social dislocations generated by industrialization.

Nations and Nationalism

Between 1750 and 1914 many societies in Europe and North America formed, or aspired to form, nations, communities of people united by a common language and culture and organized into independent states. The ideology that sparked this transition was **nationalism**, a primary loyalty to, and identity with, a nation bound by a common culture, government, and shared territory. Nationalists insisted that support for country transcended loyalty to family, village, church, region, social class, monarch, or ethnic group. Many peoples had a growing sense of belonging to a nation, such as France or Italy, that must be independent, have its own government, and share a common identity separate from that of other nations. For example, a Swiss newspaper proclaimed in 1848 that the "nation [Switzerland] stands before us as an undeniable reality with her own voice and equipped with extensive powers. The Swiss of different cantons [small self-governing states] will henceforth be perceived and act as members of a single nation."[15] Some historians conceive of the nation as an "imagined community" that grew in the minds of people living in the same society. Nationalism provided a cement that bonded all citizens to the state. But it also fostered wars with rival nations.

The ideology of nationalism converted older ethnic identities and traditions into political beliefs and solidarity. With its vision of uniting people who shared many traditions and a sense of common destiny, nationalism became a popular, explosive force in modern Europe and the Americas, and then in Asia and Africa. It particularly appealed to the rising middle classes and intellectuals struggling to gain more political power. They claimed that the nation included not just the monarchs and aristocrats but all the people, regardless of social

ideology A coherent, widely shared system of ideas about the nature of the social, political, and economic realm.

nationalism A primary loyalty to, and identity with, a nation bound by a common culture, government, and shared territory.

status, and that the nation's people were better than those in other nations. This perception of collective identity and the special nature of the nation was captured by the India-born English poet Rudyard Kipling: "If England was what England seems, An' not the England of our dreams, But only putty, brass an' paint, 'Ow quick we'd drop 'er! But she ain't!"[16]

Most historians credit the birth of modern nationalism to France and Great Britain in the late eighteenth and early nineteenth centuries. The French revolutionaries, in "The Declaration of the Rights of Man," proclaimed that all sovereignty emanated from the nation, rather than from individuals or groups, and the Jacobins identified themselves as custodians of French nationhood. The British also began to conceive of themselves as one nation composed of several peoples. England and Wales had united in 1536 under English monarchs, but by 1700 there was no Britain, and the peoples who shared the island identified themselves as English, Scottish, or Welsh. Even after England and Scotland were combined under one monarchy in 1707, the Scottish resented English domination. But the spread of English power led to the deliberate suffocation of the Scottish and Welsh cultures and languages in the 1800s. Although some people in Wales and Scotland remained wary of England, eventually most of the English, Scots, and Welsh accepted the reality of being part of Great Britain.

Nationalism transformed Europe's political landscape. In 1750 large parts of Europe were dominated by multinational states that had ethnically diverse populations. For instance, one royal family, the Vienna-based Habsburgs, ruled Austria, Hungary, the Czech lands, Belgium, and parts of Italy. Sweden ruled Finland, and Denmark ruled Norway. But during the 1800s nationalism fostered the emergence of **nation-states**, politically centralized countries with defined territorial boundaries, such as Italy, Belgium, and Norway. By 1914 only the Russian and Habsburg-ruled Austro-Hungarian empires remained major multinational states in Europe.

Unified Nations, Frustrated Nations

In the 1800s some of the most dramatic efforts to create unified nations were made in Greece, Italy, and Germany. The Greeks, long a part of the Turkish-dominated Ottoman Empire, were one of the first modern European peoples to claim nationhood through violence. Many Greeks served in the Ottoman government, and Greek merchants dominated commerce in Ottoman-ruled western Asia. Nonetheless, some Greek merchants sent their sons to western Europe to study, where they picked up nationalist ideas. Returning home, they organized a secret society that began an uprising for independence in 1821, killing many Turks. The Ottomans responded by massacring Greek villages, pillaging churches, and hanging the leader of the Greek Orthodox Church in Istanbul, acts that inflamed western European opinion. In 1827 the intervention of Britain, France, and Russia on the Greek side led to the de-

struction of the Turkish fleet. In 1830 Greece became independent, and in 1843 a rebellion against Greek royal absolutism resulted in a parliamentary government. Greek nationalism inspired other restless Ottoman subjects, and in 1862 Romania also became independent.

While the Greeks wanted independence, Italians wanted to realize a long-held dream of unity. The Italian speakers were divided into many small states, some of them part of the Habsburg and Holy Roman Empires, some ruled by the pope. In 1831 Giuseppi Mazzini (jew-SEP-pay mots-EE-nee) (1805–1872), a fiery Genoese exiled to France for membership in a nationalist secret society, founded the Young Italy movement as a brotherhood of Italians who believed that Italy was destined to become one nation. A political philosopher as well as an activist, Mazzini envisioned free nation-states eventually joining together to form a united Europe. He also promoted a republican form of government and women's rights, radical ideas in Italy. Mazzini's example inspired nationalists and democrats elsewhere in Europe, who formed imitative organizations such as Young Germany and Young Poland. In 1859 various nationalists, including Mazzini and Giuseppi Garibaldi (gar-uh-BOWL-dee) (1807–1882), who had nurtured his passion for Italy during years of exile in South America, began an armed struggle for Italian unity and drove the Habsburg forces out of the north. By 1861 Mazzini had lost influence, but Garibaldi helped create the kingdom of Italy, which included all the states except papal-dominated Rome. In 1870 Italian troops entered Rome, reuniting Italy for the first time since the Roman Empire. Thus the nation-state of Italy had been forged, but, as one leader told parliament, the job of creating Italians, people who shared a common national vision, would take longer.

German reunification also came in stages. In 1862 Otto von Bismarck (BIZ-mahrk) (1815–1898), the prime minister of Prussia, brought together many northern German states under Prussian domination. Bismarck came from the landed nobility and had spent his youth gambling and womanizing. But after marrying a devout Lutheran he changed his ways and began a rapid political ascent to Prussian leadership. Bismarck shared with the Prussian king William I a dislike of business and professional leaders, who favored expanding democratic political rights. Instead Bismarck looked to uniting the Germans through warfare, a policy he characterized as "blood and iron." War with Denmark in 1864 added Schleswig (SHLES-wig) and Holstein (HOLE-stine) to Prussian territory. Prussia quickly followed up with the defeat of Austria in 1866, driving the Habsburgs out of their last German holdings. A war with France in 1870 then brought southern Germany and the Alsace-Lorraine border region between France and Germany into the Prussian orbit. In 1871 King William I of Prussia was declared *kaiser* (emperor) of a united Germany, by now one of Europe's major powers.

Unlike the Greeks, Italians, and Germans, some peoples were unable to satisfy their nationalist aspirations. For example, the Poles frequently but unsuccessfully rebelled against the Russians and Germans who controlled Poland. The Jewish

---

nation-states Politically centralized countries with defined territorial boundaries.

Battle of Langhada The Greek war for independence from the Ottoman Turks gained strong support from liberals and nationalists all over Europe. This painting, by the Greek artist Panagiotis Zographos, uses Byzantine art traditions to show Greek soldiers riding to fight the Turks in the Battle of Langhada. (Gennadeion Library, Athens/Visual Connection Archive)

minorities faced even more difficult barriers, scattered as they were around Europe and often having little in common. Many Jews, especially in Russia, Poland, and Lithuania, had been restricted to all-Jewish villages and urban neighborhoods known as ghettoes, and they often maintained conservative cultural and religious traditions and avoided political activity. Other Jews, especially in Germany, France, and Britain, often adopted a more secular approach and moved toward assimilation with the dominant culture. Although often facing discrimination, they identified with the nations in which they lived. Reacting against widespread anti-Semitism, other Jews gravitated to revolutionary groups or to **Zionism** (ZYE-uh-niz-uhm), a movement founded by Hungarian-born journalist Theodor Herzl (HERT-suhl) (1860–1904) that sought a Jewish homeland. No Jewish state was possible in Europe, but in 1948 the Zionists formed the state of Israel in Palestine.

Zionism A movement that sought a Jewish homeland.

The Irish were particularly frustrated in their desire for their own nation. Ireland had been a colony of England for centuries, and Irish opposition to harsh English rule simmered, sometimes erupting in violence. The English attempted to destroy the language, religion, poetry, literature, dress, and music of the Irish people. As an Irish folk song from 1798 protested, "She's the most distressful country that ever yet was seen. [The English] are hanging men and women for the wearing of the green [Ireland's unofficial national color]."[17] Much of the best farming land in Ireland came under the control of rich English landlords. Conditions worsened after 1800, when English domination intensified. The English mounted even more severe laws to restrict Irish rights, deporting thousands who resisted to Australia. Many Irish men, with few job prospects, were recruited into the British army, to fight in England's colonial wars abroad. As a result, Irish ballads are filled with men going out to fight, of mothers or wives greeting their wounded men when they returned, or of grieving for those who would never return. Then during the 1840s the potato crop failed for several successive years because of a fungus blight. One and a half million Irish died from starvation while English landlords ejected Irish peasants from the land so that they could replace subsistence food growing with more profitable sheep raising. Millions of Irish people sought escape from poverty and repression by emigrating to the Americas and Australia.

But the Irish, not to be defeated, rebelled against British rule every few years. In the mid-1800s resistance became more organized, led by the Fenians (FEE-nians), a secret society dedicated to Irish independence. After experiencing many failures, by 1905 the Fenians were transformed into Sinn Fein (shin FANE) (Gaelic for "Ourselves Alone"), which first favored peaceful protest and then turned to violence against English targets. Sinn Fein extremists formed the Irish Republican Army, which organized a rebellion on Easter Monday, 1916, in which some 1,500 volunteers seized key buildings in Dublin, including the General Post Office, and proclaimed a republic in Ireland. The English quickly crushed the rising, shot the ringleaders, and jailed 2,000 of the participants, but Sinn Fein, the IRA, and acts of terrorism continued to bedevil the English colonizers.

Liberalism and Parliamentary Democracy

While nationalism reshaped states, another ideology emerged to offer a vision of democracy and individual freedom, including representative and inclusive government institutions. Influenced by Enlightenment thinkers such as John Locke and Baron de Montesquieu, **liberalism** favored emancipating the individual from all restraints, whether governmental, economic, or religious. Liberals, mainly from middle-class backgrounds, favored the sovereignty of the people, representative government, the right to vote, and basic civil liberties such as freedom of speech, religion, assembly, and the press. The liberal Scottish philosopher John Stuart Mill (1806–1873) offered the most eloquent defense of individual liberty and free expression, writing that no one should restrict what arguments a legislature or executive should be allowed to hear. Liberal politicians fought against slavery, advocated religious toleration, and worked for more popular participation in government.

Liberal ideas found their political and institutional expression in modern democracy, which involves choice and competition, usually between contending political parties and policies, within a constitutional framework that allows free choice for the electorate. Liberalism proved particularly popular in Britain and the United States, and it provided the bedrock for the United States Constitution and Bill of Rights. To protect against tyranny, the nation's founders mandated a separation of executive, legislative, and judicial powers.

Democratic decision making is an old and widespread idea. Village democracies that allowed many residents to voice their opinions and shape decisions had long existed in various tribal and other stateless societies of Asia, Africa, and the Americas. For example, the Tiv, Gikuyu, and Tswana (SWAN-a) peoples in Africa had village councils composed of elders from each family. The classical Greeks and Romans had also introduced democratic institutions, such as the mass public assemblies in Athens that selected leaders, but political rights were restricted to a small minority of male citizens. Representative institutions later appeared in England, the Netherlands, Switzerland, Iceland, and Poland. But in the nineteenth century more fully democratic and participatory systems, inspired in part by liberalism, emerged in parts of Europe. For some nations this meant evolution toward **parliamentary democracy**, government by representatives elected by the people.

Britain became the most successful parliamentary democracy in Europe. Democracy had gradually grown in Britain as royal power declined over several centuries and then flowered in the 1800s. The popular Queen Victoria (r. 1837–1901) reigned over Britain for sixty-four years after becoming queen at eighteen, and Victoria and her German-born husband, Prince Albert, provided a model of morality and stability. But by the 1800s the British monarch, even one as respected and shrewd as Queen Victoria, was no longer very powerful, exercising influence mostly behind the scenes. Instead prime ministers, elected by the majority of Parliament members, had become the major power holders. The base of democracy gradually widened as the elected House of Commons exercised more power than the appointed and hereditary House of Lords. Both houses offered extensive possibilities for dialogue and debate between political parties.

But democracy remained somewhat limited in Britain, whose leaders struggled with issues of democratic access. Throughout the 1800s British reformers wanted average people to have more voice in the electoral system. The Reform Act of 1832 increased the number of voters to about 650,000, all upper- and middle-class males, but this left out many men and all women. The major protest movement, Chartism, was based in the working class and called for universal adult male suffrage, a secret ballot, and paying members of Parliament so that people without wealth could run for office. Although the Chartists did not call for women's suffrage, many women supported the movement, founding political clubs and organizing boycotts of unsympathetic merchants. Some Chartists, led by Elizabeth Neesom, advocated the rights of women to participate in government. Chartists used demonstrations, strikes, and riots to support their demands, without much success. Fearing that radical ideas such as wealth redistribution might be proposed, Englishmen with property refused to allow the working class to have a say in government.

---

liberalism An ideology that favored emancipating the individual from all restraints, whether governmental, economic, or religious.

parliamentary democracy Government by representatives elected by the people.

Socialism and Marxist Thought

While liberals tended to favor preservation of wealth and property rights and therefore feared radical popular movements, a third ideology did encourage protest. In contrast to liberalism's promotion of individual liberty, **socialism** offered a vision of social equality and the common, or public, ownership of economic institutions such as factories. Socialism grew out of the painful social disruption that accompanied the Industrial Revolution.

The Rise of Socialism In the eighteenth and nineteenth centuries utopian socialists in Britain, France, and North America, many influenced by Christian ideals of a community based on faith and cooperation, offered visions of perfect societies shaped by the common good. A few even founded communal villages based on ideas such as service to the community and renunciation of personal wealth. For example, the British industrialist Robert Owen (1771–1858) set up a model factory town around his cotton mill, where workers put in ten hours a day on the job rather than the seventeen hours common elsewhere, and children attended school instead of working in the mill. Owen later moved to the United States and founded a model socialist community, New Harmony, in Indiana. Some proponents of women's rights, such as Emma Martin (1812–1851) in Britain and Flora Tristan (1801–1844) in France, promoted socialism as the solution to end female oppression. These views stirred controversy. For example, clergymen opposed to feminism and socialism urged their congregations to disrupt Martin's speeches, and sometimes outraged mobs chased and stoned her.

Karl Marx (1818–1883) had the most long-lasting influence on socialist thought, and his ideas, known as Marxism, became one of the major intellectual and political influences around the world. Marx, a German Jew with a passion for justice, came from a wealthy family, studied philosophy at the University of Berlin, and then worked as a journalist in several European cities before settling in London. Marx wrote his classic works in the middle and late 1800s. In England he worked closely with his German friend, Friedrich Engels (1820–1895), who had moved to England to manage his father's cotton factory. Engels, who collaborated in writing and editing some of Marx's books, introduced Marx to the degraded condition of English industrial workers. Marx called himself a communist to differentiate himself from earlier socialists such as Robert Owen, whom he dismissed as naive utopians divorced from working-class life.

In *The Communist Manifesto* (1848), Marx developed a vision of social change in which the downtrodden could redress the wrongs inflicted upon them by rising up in a violent socialist revolution, seizing power from the capitalists,

socialism An ideology offering a vision of social equality and the common, or public, ownership of economic institutions such as factories.

and creating a new society (see Witness to the Past: The Communist View of Past, Present, and Future). Marx wrote that violence was the midwife of every old society, which is pregnant with the new. He argued that, through revolution, peoples can change their conditions and alter the inequitable political, social, and economic patterns inherited from the past. He also opposed nationalism, writing that working people had no country, only common interests, and needed to cooperate across borders. In 1864 Marx helped form the International Workingmen's Association to work toward those goals.

Marx was a product of his scientific age and considered his socialist ideas as laws of history. In his most influential work, the three-volume *Capital*, Marx argued that historical change resulted from class struggle, in which the confrontation between antagonistic social classes produced change. All social and economic systems, he suggested, contain contradictions that doom them to conflict, which generates a higher stage of development. For example, feudalism was undermined by the confrontation between nobles, merchants, and serfs, leading to capitalism. Eventually, Marx predicted, this process would replace capitalism with socialism, where all would share in owning the means of production and the state would serve the interests of the masses rather than the privileged classes. Finally would come communism, where the state would wither away and all would share the wealth, free to realize their human potential without exploitation by capitalists or governments. A revolutionary new society, Marx claimed, could create an equitable distribution of wealth and power. Such a vision of change proved attractive to many disgruntled people in Europe and later around the world.

The Marxist Legacy Marx offered some astute ideas that economists and historians have debated ever since. He believed that history was shaped by material conditions, that the nature of the economic system and technology determined all aspects of society, including religious values, social relations, government, and laws. Hence, in each type of system, such as feudalism or capitalism, the ways in which land and labor were allocated to production, work was organized (such as on medieval manors or in capitalist factories), and products were distributed, as well as the tools used, determined such patterns as family relationships, the gods people worshiped, and the ideas that emerged. Marx also argued that religion was the "opiate of the people," encouraging people to fatalistically accept their lot in this life in hopes of earning a better afterlife rather than protesting or rebelling. He criticized capitalism for creating extremes of wealth and poverty and for separating workers from ownership and management of the means of production—the farms, mines, factories, and businesses where they labored—to furnish wealth to the owners and managers as well as to the urban-based, mostly commercial, middle class that Marx called the bourgeoisie. Under capitalism, workers had become tenants and employees rather than self-employed farmers and craftsmen. Marx observed that the industrial working

The Communist View of Past, Present, and Future

In 1848 Karl Marx and Friedrich Engels published *The Communist Manifesto* as a statement of beliefs and goals for the Communist League, an organization they had founded. In this excerpt Marx and Engels outlined their view of history as founded on class struggle, stressed the formation of the new world economy, and offered communism as the alternative to an oppressive capitalist system. They ended their summary of the problems of contemporary society by inviting the working class to take its future into its own hands through unity and revolution.

A specter is haunting Europe—the specter of communism. All the powers of old Europe have entered into a holy alliance to excise this specter.... Where is the party in opposition that has not been decried as communistic by its opponents in power? ... The history of all hitherto existing society is the history of class struggles. ... Oppressor and oppressed stood in constant opposition to one another, carried on in an uninterrupted, now hidden, now open fight, a fight that each time ended, either in a revolutionary reconstitution of society at large, or in the common ruin of the contending classes.

In the earlier epochs of history, we find almost everywhere a complicated arrangement of society into various orders, a manifold gradation of social rank. In ancient Rome we have patricians, knights, plebeians, slaves; in the Middle Ages, feudal lords, vassals, guild-masters, journeymen, apprentices, serfs; in almost all these classes, again, subordinate gradations. The modern bourgeois [middle class] society that has sprouted from the ruins of feudal society has not done away with class antagonisms. It has but established new classes, new conditions of oppression, new forms of struggle in place of the old ones.

Our epoch, the epoch of the bourgeoisie, possesses, however, this distinctive feature: it has simplified the class antagonisms. Society as a whole is more and more splitting up into two great hostile camps, into two great classes directly facing each other: bourgeoisie and proletariat (working class).... The discovery of America, the rounding of the Cape [of Good Hope], opened up fresh ground for the rising bourgeoisie. The East Indian and Chinese markets, the colonization of America, trade with the colonies, the increase in the means of exchange and in commodities generally, gave to commerce, to navigation, to industry, an impulse never before known, and, thereby, a rapid development to the revolutionary element in the tottering feudal society.... Meantime the markets kept ever growing, the demand ever rising. Even manufacture no longer sufficed. Thereupon, steam and machinery revolutionized industrial production. The place of manufacture was taken by the giant, modern industry, the place of the industrial middle class, by industrial millionaires....

Modern industry has established the world market, for which the discovery of America paved the way. ... The bourgeoisie, by the rapid improvement of all instruments of production, by the immensely facilitated means of communication, draws all, even the most barbarian, nations into civilization. The cheap prices of its commodities are the heavy artillery with which it batters down all Chinese walls.... It compels all nations, on pain of extinction, to adopt the bourgeois mode of production.... It creates a world after its own image....

[The Communists] have no interests separate from those of the proletariat as a whole. ... The immediate aim of the Communists is ... the formation of the proletariat into a class; the overthrow of the bourgeois supremacy; and the conquest of political power by the proletariat.... The Communists disdain to conceal their views and aims. They openly declare that their ends can be attained only by the forcible overthrow of all existing social conditions. Let the ruling classes tremble at a Communistic revolution. The proletarians have nothing to lose but their chains. They have a world to win. WORKING MEN OF ALL COUNTRIES, UNITE!

THINKING ABOUT THE READING

1. What did Marx and Engels identify as the opposing classes in European history?
2. What developments aided the rise of the bourgeoisie to power?
3. What is the goal of the Communists?

Source: From *The Communist Manifesto,* trans. 1880. http://www.anv.edu.au/polisci/marx/classics/manifesto.html.

class, the **proletariat**, grew more miserable as wealth became concentrated in giant monopolies in the later 1800s.

Marxist ideas attracted a wide following, first in Europe and later in various American, Asian, and African countries. In Europe they stimulated unrest. For example, in 1871, in the aftermath of a disastrous French war with Germany and the election of a conservative French government, a people's government comprising Marxists, other socialists, republicans, and other groups briefly gained control of the Paris city government, with the moderate goal of ensuring that all sectors of the population were represented in politics. The Paris Commune, as this government was called, experimented with some socialist programs such as better wages and working conditions, and thus led Karl Marx to believe that the end of capitalism was at hand. To suppress the Commune, the French government attacked Paris with ruthless force, and in response

proletariat The industrial working class.

the Commune supporters, known as Communards, burned public buildings and killed the Catholic archbishop of Paris. The brutality of the French government troops prompted a horrified British reporter to conclude that "Paris the beautiful is Paris the ghastly, the battered, the burning, the blood-splattered."[18] When the dust had cleared, 38,000 Communards had been arrested, 20,000 executed, and 7,500 deported to the South Pacific. Not discouraged, later rebels across Europe would hoist the Marxist banner for radical redistribution of power and privilege.

With its promise of a more equitable society, Marxism became a major world force. Socialist parties were formed all over Europe in the late 1800s and early 1900s, and, in some cases, more radical socialists soon split off to establish parties that called themselves communist. Marxism also influenced the founding of labor unions in the late nineteenth and early twentieth centuries in Europe and North America. But not all poor people or industrial workers in Europe gravitated to Marxism. While many envied the rich and thought life unfair, they were also inhibited by family, religion, and social connections from joining radical movements or risking their lives in a rebellion that might fail. An English pub toast from the 1800s reflected the desires of people for more immediate pleasures: "If life was a thing that money could buy, the rich would live and the poor might die. Here's oceans of wine, rivers of beer, a nice little wife and ten thousand a year."[19] North Americans had a weaker sense of social class, and Marxism never became as influential in the United States as in parts of Europe. Furthermore, Marx mistakenly believed that socialist revolution would first occur in leading capitalist nations such as Britain and Germany. Instead the first successful socialist revolution came, over three decades after Marx had died, in Russia.

Social Democracy and Social Reform

Eventually a more evolutionary version of socialist thought gained influence in many European societies. In contrast to the call by radical Marxists for revolution, some Marxists and other socialists favored a more gradual, evolutionary approach of working within constitutional governments. These socialists established the foundation for social democracy, a system mixing capitalism and socialism within a parliamentary framework. The first Social Democratic Party was formed in Germany in 1875. Soon other Social Democratic parties emerged in other western and eastern European countries. Criticizing Marxist revolutionaries, a German Social Democratic leader, Eduard Bernstein (1850–1932), argued that socialists should work less for the better future and more for the better present. Social Democrats and other socialists often felt a kinship with people of shared views and class backgrounds in other countries. This feeling of solidarity and the memory of the earlier International Workingmen's Association led in 1889 to the founding of the Second International Workingmen's Association by nonrevolutionary socialist parties, with the goal of working for world peace, justice, and social reform.

Social Democrats, Marxists, and other socialists actively supported labor unions and strikes to promote worker demands. Skilled workers were the first to organize unions. Although most employers were opposed, unions gradually gained recognition as representatives of the work force. Between 1870 and 1900 unions gained legal status in many nations, and in Britain, France, Germany, the Netherlands, and Sweden, trade unions and labor parties acquired enough political influence to force governments to legislate better working conditions.

In the later 1800s governments implemented social reforms to address the ills of the Industrial Revolution, laying the foundation for welfare states. This era saw the rise of the interventionist, bureaucratic state with state-run welfare systems. Many European nations passed laws regulating the length of the working day, laws regarding working conditions, and safety rules. Reformers pushed for nationalizing landed property, state inspections of housing, town planning, and slum clearance. To tackle the problem of poverty, Germany and Britain passed social legislation introducing health and unemployment insurance and creating old age pensions. Contrary to Marx's expectations, life for many European workers improved considerably by the early 1900s. But many people still worked in dangerous and unhealthy conditions or faced a ten-hour working day, and child labor continued.

SECTION SUMMARY

■ With the rise of nationalism, the inhabitants of a given country came to identify with each other as distinct from, and often better than, the inhabitants of other countries.

■ Greece attained nationhood through revolution, Italy through a unification movement, and Germany through collective war against others, while the Poles, the Irish, and the Jews struggled unsuccessfully to form nations.

■ Liberalism, which favored maximizing individual liberty, was particularly influential in Britain and the United States of America.

■ Socialism aimed to achieve economic equality through common ownership of industry, and its major proponent, Karl Marx, argued that history is driven by class struggle and that capitalism would inevitably give way to a communist society.

■ Marx's ideas exerted a strong influence on the Paris Communards and the founders of labor unions, but the first successful Marxist revolution took place not in an industrialized country as Marx had predicted, but in Russia.

■ Social Democrats, who rejected Marx's revolutionary ideas and instead favored working to better the lot of workers within a capitalist democracy, managed to greatly improve working conditions by the early 1900s.

◆ The Resurgence of Western Imperialism

What factors spurred the Western imperialism of the later 1800s?

The Industrial Revolution provided economic incentives, and nationalism provided political incentives, for European merchants and states to exploit the natural and human resources of other lands in order to enrich their own nations and thwart the ambitions of rival nations. Initially the British were most successful in dominating the growing world economy. But economic, political, and ideological factors in the West eventually fostered a resurgence of imperialism, leading European nations to colonize and dominate much of Asia and Africa. The explosion of imperialism reshaped the global system. By virtue of imperialism, industrial capitalism became a genuine world economy. With the entire world connected by economic and political networks, history from now on transcended regions and became truly world history.

British Trade and Empire

The quest for colonies diminished somewhat in the first phase of the Industrial Revolution, even for the strongest European power, Great Britain. From the later 1700s through the mid-1800s, the British feared no competitor in world trade because they had none. The free traders who influenced the British government, wanting neither economic nor political barriers to their operations, viewed the acquisition of more colonies as too expensive. Adam Smith argued that colonialism actually impoverished the homeland. In any case, Britain already controlled or had gained access to valuable territories in the Americas, Africa, Asia, and the Pacific. While Britain lost its thirteen North American colonies, it took control of French Canada and Australia. Furthermore, Britain's Spanish and Portuguese rivals suffered even graver losses. The collapse of Spain and Portugal during the Napoleonic wars led to most of their Latin American colonies becoming independent in the 1820s, opening doors for British commercial activity.

British merchants also benefited from new technologies that enabled them to compete all over the world. Steam power meant that sailors were no longer dependent on trade winds. This revolution in transportation improved maritime shipping, allowing British ships to reach distant shores faster. The first exclusively steam-powered ships appeared in 1813 and took 113 days to travel from England around Africa to India, in contrast to eight or nine months by sailing ships. Then in 1869 the completion of the Suez Canal linking the Mediterranean Sea and the Red Sea dramatically cut the travel time between the Indian Ocean and Europe to several weeks. Britain, the canal's major shareholder, now found it easier to extend its influence to East Africa and Southeast Asia. By 1900 the England-India trip took less than twenty-five days, making for more efficient transport of resources and goods.

Despite a pragmatic preference for peaceful commerce, Britain did obtain some colonies between 1750 and 1870. The British took over territories or fought wars when local governments refused to trade or could not protect British commerce by establishing law and order. For example, as states in India grew weaker and banditry increased, the British began expanding the territory under their control in the subcontinent. Hence, during the later eighteenth and early nineteenth centuries the British gradually gained direct control or indirect power over most of India and also established footholds in Malaya, Burma, China, and South Africa. But the British preferred to undercut the power of their rivals. For example, British merchants were successful in gaining economic influence in some South American countries such as Argentina, Brazil, and Chile. Because of their economic power, the British could flood a society with cheap manufactured goods. In this way, by the late 1800s they had greatly diminished the crafts and industries of India for their own benefit. To protect their own position, British industrialists and merchants opposed any attempts to foster rival enterprises, such as textile mills, in Asian and African states, among them China, Burma, and Egypt.

However, the British economic advantage in world markets gradually diminished as economic leadership in the world changed during the later 1800s. The British invested many of the profits that they earned from India and their Caribbean colonies in other nations, much of it in the United States, Canada, and Australia, all countries settled by European, particularly British, immigrants. This investment helped develop these countries' economies, and the United States soon became a serious competitor. British investment also benefited some European nations, including Germany, and increasingly the United States and Germany were able to gain on Britain. Because British investors found it more profitable to invest abroad rather than at home, British industrial plants became increasingly obsolete. In 1860 Britain had been the leading economic power, with France a distant second followed by the United States and Germany. By 1900, however, the hierarchy had changed: the United States was now at the top, followed by Germany and then a fading Britain and France. Some British officials predicted accurately that the United States would soon dwarf Britain and other European countries economically.

Industrialization and Imperialism

As they industrialized, Germany, France, and the United States became more competitive with Britain, and the growing economic and political competition between the leading powers renewed the quest for colonies abroad. The shift to domestic economies dominated by large monopolies was a major factor in the new push for colonies in Africa and Asia. The monopolies stimulated empire building by piling up huge profits and hence excess capital that needed investment outlets abroad to keep growing. Furthermore, by the 1880s some of the wealth generated by the industrial economy began to filter down to the European working classes, stimulating new consumer interests in tropical products such as chocolate, tea, soap, and rubber for bicycle tires. To satisfy the need for resources and markets, businessmen in Britain, Germany, Italy, France, Belgium, and the United States looked for new opportunities to exploit in Africa, Asia, and the Pacific and then pressured their governments to pursue colonization to assist their efforts.

National rivalries also motivated imperialism. Nations often seized colonies to prevent competing nations from gaining opportunities. For example, the British sometimes occupied an African territory to block the French from doing so, and vice versa. While expanding British control in southern Africa, the British imperialist Cecil Rhodes (1853–1902) was moved by the words of his Oxford University professor, the philosopher and art critic John Ruskin: "This is what England must either do, or perish: found colonies as fast and as far as [it] is able, seizing every piece of waste ground [it] can get [its] foot on."[20] The national rivalries and the intense competition for colonies also planted the roots of conflict in Europe. By the early 1900s Germany and Austria-Hungary had forged an alliance, and this prompted Britain, France, and Russia to do likewise, setting the stage for future wars.

The conflicts between European powers led to a resurgence of Western imperialism between 1870 and 1914. Often this resulted in colonialism, or direct political control of another society, though Western imperialism also sometimes led to neocolonialism, or strong influence over another country's government and economy. Seizure of colonies not only brought profits for business interests but also strengthened a nation's power in competition with rival nations. The result was the greatest land grab in world history: a handful of European powers dividing up the globe between themselves.

The Scramble for Empire

With the resurgent Western imperialism, millions of people in Africa, Asia, and the Pacific Islands were conquered or impacted by Western nations and thus brought into the Western-dominated world economic system. These operations were bloody and costly for both sides. Many peoples fiercely resisted conquest. The Vietnamese, Burmese, and various Indonesian and African societies held off militarily superior European armies for decades, and even after conquest guerrilla forces often continued to attack European colonizers. For instance, in Vietnam, for fifteen years after the French annexed the country, anticolonial fighters refused to surrender, preferring to fight to the death. Countless revolts punctuated colonial rule, from West Africa to the Philippines, and Western ambitions were sometimes frustrated. In Africa, Ethiopians defeated an Italian invasion force bent on conquest. A few Asians maintained their independence by using creative strategies. The Japanese prevented Western political domination by modernizing their own government and economy, and the Siamese (Thai) used skillful diplomacy and selective modernization to deflect Western power.

Lipton Tea   European imperial expansion brought many new products to European consumers. Tea, grown in British-ruled India, Sri Lanka (Ceylon), and Malaya, became a popular drink, advertised here in a London weekly magazine.   (The Illustrated London News Library)

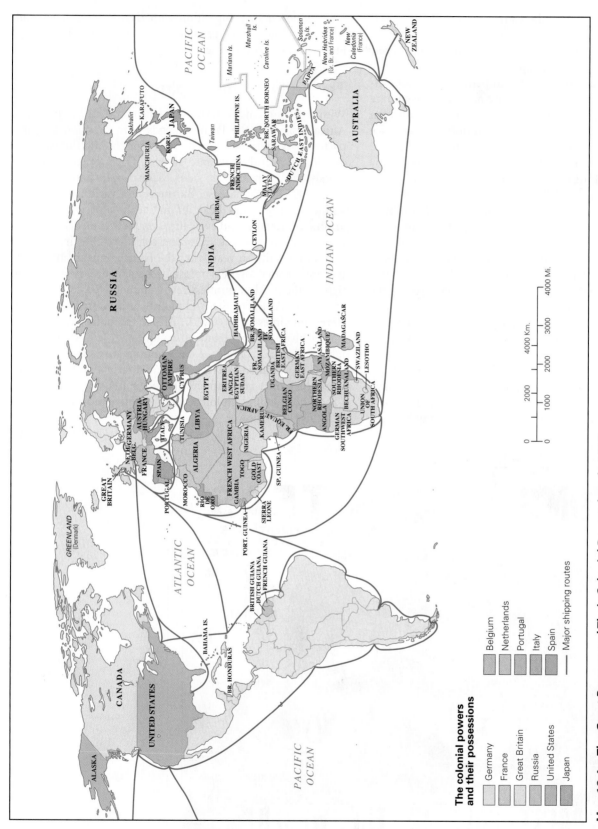

Map 19.4   The Great Powers and Their Colonial Possessions in 1913

By 1913 the British and French controlled huge empires, with colonies in Africa, southern Asia, the Caribbean zone, and the Pacific Basin. Russia ruled much of northern Eurasia while the United States, Japan, and a half dozen European nations controlled smaller empires.

New technologies permitted and stimulated imperial expansion. The Industrial Revolution gave Europeans better weapons, including the repeating rifle and the machine gun, such as the lightweight, quick-firing Maxim Gun invented in 1884, to enforce their will. A British writer boasted: "Whatever happens we have got the Maxim Gun, and they have not."[21] These weapons gave Europeans a huge advantage against Asians and Africans, and the discovery of quinine to treat malaria enabled European colonists and officials to survive in tropical Africa and Southeast Asia. Later, better communication and transportation networks, such as steamship lines, colonial railroads, and undersea telegraph cables, also helped consolidate Western control. They also more closely connected the world. In 1866 a speaker at a banquet honoring Cyrus Field, the American most responsible for building the transatlantic cable linking Europe and North America, one of the greatest engineering feats of the 1800s, noted that on the statue of Christopher Columbus in Genoa, Italy, was the inscription: "There was one world; let there be two." Now, with the cable, the speaker boasted, "There were two worlds and [now] they [are] one."[22]

As the scramble continued, old European empires grew and new ones were founded (see Map 19.4). By 1900 Western colonial powers controlled 90 percent of Africa, 99 percent of Polynesia, and 57 percent of Asia. By 1914 the British Empire, the world's largest, included fifty-five colonies containing 400 million people, ten times Britain's population, inspiring the boast that "the sun never sets on the British Empire." British leaders were proud of their empire, and some even compared it favorably to the Roman Empire. France acquired the next largest empire of twenty-nine colonies. Germany, Spain, Belgium, and Italy joined in the grab for African colonies. Between 1898 and 1902 the United States took over Hawaii, Samoa, Puerto Rico, and the Philippines. Russia also continued its expansion in Eurasia, which began in the Early Modern Era (see Chapter 23).

Western imperialism forged networks of interlinked social, economic, and political relationships spanning the globe. Hence, decisions made by a government or business in London or Paris soon affected people in faraway Malaya or Madagascar, and silk spun in China was turned into dresses worn by fashionable women in Chicago and Munich. Westerners had the strongest position in this network, ruling many subject peoples and enjoying advantageous trade relations with or strong influence over neocolonies such as China, Siam, Persia, and Argentina. Yet various Asian, African, and Caribbean peoples also mounted nationalist movements to challenge the colonial regimes and cultural movements to assert their own traditions (see Chapters 21, 22, and 25). For example, South African blacks, risking prison, demanded equality with whites, and South Asians reaffirmed the value of their Hindu, Muslim, and Buddhist beliefs.

The scope of Western imperialism changed world power arrangements. In 1750 China and the Ottoman Empire remained among the world's strongest countries, but by 1914 they could not match Western military and economic power.

In 1500 the wealth gap between the more economically developed and the less developed Eurasian and African societies was small, and China and India dominated world trade and manufacturing. By 1914 the gap in total wealth and personal income between industrialized societies, whether in Europe or North America, and most other societies, including China and India, had grown very wide.

Social Darwinism and Imperial Ideology

By the late 1800s, a new ideology, known as Social Darwinism, supported the revival of imperialism and colonialism. Supporters of imperialism used the ideas about the natural world developed by the British scientist Charles Darwin, who described a struggle for existence among species (see Chapter 20). This idea led other thinkers to conclude that this struggle led to the survival of the fittest, a notion that they then applied to the human world of social classes and nations. The industrialized peoples considered themselves the most fit and saw the poor or exploited as less fit. A German naval officer wrote in 1898 that "the struggle for life exists among individuals, provinces, parties and states. The latter wage it either by the use of arms or in the economic field. Those who don't want to, will perish."[23] Social Darwinists stereotyped the Asian and African societies as "backward" and held their own nations up as "superior" peoples who had the right to rule. Accepting Social Darwinism, most Westerners took the innate inequality of peoples for granted, and this ideology in fact created a relationship of inequality.

As a result of this ideology, Western racism and arrogance toward other peoples increased. For example, in the 1600s and 1700s many Western observers had admired the Chinese, and Enlightenment thinkers saw China as a model of secular and efficient government. But by the 1800s Europeans and North Americans had developed scorn for "John Chinaman" and the "heathen Chinee," as Europeans stereotyped them. Most Western peoples accepted these stereotypes, which were even popularized by intellectual and political leaders. The British imperialist Cecil Rhodes boasted, "I contend that we British are the finest race in the world, and that the more of the world we inhabit the better it is for the human race."[24]

This self-proclaimed superiority legitimized the effort to "improve" other people by bringing them Western culture and religion. The French proclaimed their "civilizing mission" in Africa and Indochina, the British in India claimed that they were "taking up the white man's burden," and the Americans colonized the Philippines claiming condescendingly to "uplift" their "little brown brothers." Western defenders argued that colonialism, despite much that was shameful, gave so-called stagnating non-Western societies better government and drew them out of isolation into the world market. A British newspaper in 1896 claimed that "the advance of the Union Jack means protection for weaker races, justice for the oppressed, liberty for the down-trodden."[25] This rationale also preserved the status quo favoring the European colonizers. However, most people in Asia, Africa, and the Pacific opposed colonialism, seeing it only for the terrible toll it took on their lives. The Indian nationalist leader Mohandas Gandhi, educated in Britain, reflected the resentment. When asked what he thought about "Western civilization," he replied that civilizing the West would be a good idea.

SECTION SUMMARY

■ Even after losing thirteen of its North American colonies, Britain continued to dominate the world economy through its other holdings and its technological advantages, but it gradually lost ground, especially to the United States.

■ As Germany, France, and the United States became more competitive with Britain, the powers competed for colonies that could provide natural resources for their industries and power over their rivals.

■ In the renewed scramble for colonial domination, many African, Asian, and Pacific peoples struggled for their independence, but the technological advantage of Western nations often proved insurmountable.

■ Westerners rationalized imperialism and colonization as good for the colonized, who were offered the fruits of Western culture in exchange for their independence.

 **Online Study Center**   ACE the Test

✦ Chapter Summary

The years between 1750 and 1914 were an age of revolutions that reshaped economies, governments, and social systems in Europe and the Americas. Political and social revolutions generated major changes. Colonists in North America overthrew British rule and established a republic that included democratic institutions such as an elected president and congress. The French Revolution ended the French monarchy and brought France's middle classes to power. Although the Revolution was consumed in violence and then modified by Napoleon Bonaparte's dictatorship, the shock waves of the upheaval in France reverberated around Europe, carrying with them new ideas about liberty and equality. The American and French Revolutions also inspired peoples in the Caribbean and Latin America. Haitians ended slavery and forced out the French colonial regime and planters, and in South America creoles waged successful wars of independence against Spanish rule.

People in North America and Europe also experienced other dramatic changes. The Industrial Revolution, which began in Britain in the late 1700s, transformed societies as profoundly as agriculture had transformed ancient societies millennia earlier, reorienting life to cities and factories and producing goods in unparalleled abundance. Until the 1850s Britain enjoyed unchallenged economic power. With the

spread of industrialization, however, positions of world economic leadership began to change. In the meantime, however, new ideologies contributed to the creation of new states and government structures. Appealing to hearts and minds, nationalism introduced new ideas of the nation and provided a glue to bind people within the same nation. Another ideology, liberalism, promoted increasing freedom and democracy. A third, socialism, addressed the dislocations industrialization created and sought to improve life for the new working classes by forging a system of collective ownership of economic property. Capitalism, industrialization, and interstate rivalries also generated in the West a worldwide scramble for colonies and neocolonies in the later 1800s, allowing Western businesses to seek resources and markets abroad. This imperialism brought many more societies into a global system largely dominated by the West.

 **Online Study Center**   **Improve Your Grade**   Flashcards

Key Terms

Age of Revolution	laissez faire	liberalism
Jacobins	ideology	parliamentary
Industrial	nationalism	democracy
Revolution	nation-states	socialism
Luddites	Zionism	proletariat

Suggested Reading

Books

Anderson, Benedict. *Imagined Communities: Reflections on the Origin and Spread of Nationalism.* Rev. ed. London: Verso, 1991. An influential scholarly examination of the rise of nationalism.

Anderson, M. S. *The Ascendancy of Europe, 1815–1914.* 3rd ed. Harlow, U.K.: Pearson, 2003. A good overview of the era by a British historian.

Baumgart, Winfried. *Imperialism: The Idea and Reality of British and French Colonial Expansion, 1880–1914.* New York: Oxford University Press, 1986. A readable analysis of the imperial quest.

Connelly, Owen, and Fred Hembree. *The French Revolution.* Wheeling, Ill.: Harland Davidson, 1993. A thoughtful, brief survey emphasizing the Revolution's long-term consequences.

Countryman, Edward. *The American Revolution.* Rev. ed. New York: Hill and Wang, 2003. An excellent treatment of the conflict and its context.

Grosby, Steven. *Nationalism: A Very Short Introduction.* New York: Oxford University Press, 2005. Highlights social, historical, and philosophical perspectives.

Headrick, Daniel R. *The Tools of Empire: Technology and European Imperialism in the Nineteenth Century.* New York: Oxford University Press, 1981. A pathbreaking study of the role of technology in European expansion.

Heilbroner, Robert L. *The Worldly Philosophers: The Lives, Times and Ideas of the Great Economic Thinkers.* 7th ed. New York: Simon and Schuster, 1999. A classic and readable introduction to these thinkers.

Hobsbawm, Eric. *The Age of Revolution, 1789–1848; The Age of Capital, 1848–1875; The Age of Empire, 1875–1914.* New York: Vintage, 1996. This outstanding trilogy by an esteemed British historian remains the standard survey of the period.

Martin, Cheryl E. and Mark Wasserman. *Latin America and Its People.* New York: Longman, 2005. An introductory survey, especially strong on this era.

Samson, Jane. *Race and Empire.* New York: Longman, 2005. Examines the relationship of racism and imperialism.

Sperber, Jonathan. *Revolutionary Europe, 1780–1850.* Harlow, U.K.: Pearson, 2000. A good overview of these turbulent decades.

Stearns, Peter N. *The Industrial Revolution in World History.* Boulder: Westview Press, 1993. An overview from a global perspective.

Wesseling, H. L. *The European Colonial Empires, 1815–1919.* Harlow, U.K.: Pearson, 2004. A useful overview of the entire colonial enterprise by a Dutch scholar.

Websites

The American Revolution (http://revolution.h-net.msu.edu/intro.html). An excellent collection of links, essays, and other resources.

BBC Outline: History (http://www.bbc.co.uk/history/). Offers valuable information by topic and time.

British History (http://www.british-history.com/). Contains links to short essays on various periods of British history.

Internet Resources for Latin America (http://lib.nmsu.edu/subject/bord/laguia/). An outstanding site with links to many resources.

Modern History Sourcebook (http://www.fordham.edu/halsall/). An extensive online collection of historical documents and secondary materials.

CHAPTER **20**

Changing Societies in Europe, the Americas, and Oceania, 1750–1914

Online Study Center

This icon will direct you to interactive activities and study materials on the website: college.hmco. com/pic/lockard1e

Australian Gold Rush The discovery of gold in southeastern Australia set off a gold rush in the 1850s. Hoping to strike it rich, miners, often from other countries, among them Chinese, flocked to the goldfields, and immigration to Australia boomed.   (The Art Archive)

Of course, some day we [Americans] shall step in. We are bound to. We shall be giving the word for every-thing: industry, trade, law, journalism, art, politics, and religion. We shall run the world's business whether the world likes it or not. The world can't help it, and neither can we, I guess.

AMERICAN MILLIONAIRE IN JOSEPH CONRAD'S NOVEL *Nostromo* (1904)[1]

In 1871 a thirty-three-year-old Japanese samurai and Confucian scholar, Kume Kunitake (1839–1931), boarded an American steamship at Yokohama and began a three-week voyage to San Francisco as a member of an official information-gathering delegation sent from Japan to the United States and then Europe. Hoping to avoid domination or conquest by the West, the government had asked Kume's group to assess the factors behind the growing Western power in the world. Upon reaching San Francisco, Kume's delegation toured California and then traveled across the country, visiting factories, museums, schools, churches, public parks, and scenic mountains. Kume proved a perceptive observer, faithfully recording his impressions of Western life but also filtering them through the cultural lens of Japan. He concluded that "the customs and characteristics of East and West are invariably different." Kume admired U.S. democracy but also saw its potential for disorder, since Americans were "careless about official authority, each person insisting on his own rights." Kume recorded the Americans' friendliness and kindness but also their brashness, ambition, and sense of destiny, attitudes frequently noted by foreign visitors and satirized four decades later by the Polish-born British novelist Joseph Conrad through the words of his fictional American millionaire quoted at the chapter opening.

After leaving the United States, Kume's delegation traveled around Europe. Kume was delighted to see how Europeans treasured and even imitated Japanese art. He loved the cafes, theaters, and art museums of Paris. But, as an ardent Confucian rationalist, he disliked Christianity, which he saw as irrational, and considered the Christian Bible full of "absurd tales." Kume contrasted the splendor of the churches with the poverty of the people. He also criticized what he saw as the "unbounded greed" of Western rulers and merchants. But Kume preferred Europe's constitutional monarchies to the untidy U.S. republic and saw rapidly industrializing Germany as Japan's natural model.

Finally, returning by ship to Japan, Kume's delegation saw the Western imperial world, passing through colonies such as Ceylon, Singapore, and Hong Kong. Kume wrote of his encounters with European colonizers: "Ever since the Europeans began to travel to distant places, the weak countries of the tropics have all been fought over and devoured, and their abundant products taken. They treated the natives with arrogance and cruelty."[2] The journals of Kume, who later became a distinguished professor of history at Tokyo University, convey an outsider's view of nineteenth-century American and European societies while also informing us about the Modern Era, especially its imbalances in wealth and power.

Between 1750 and 1914 the European, American, and Oceanic societies experienced profound changes. Spurred by revolutions, industrialization, nation-building, and overseas imperialism, Europeans reshaped their social, cultural, and intellectual patterns. Most American societies achieved independence from European rule. By 1914 the United States, Canada, and Mexico occupied all of North America, while Latin America was divided into many countries large and small. Some Caribbean societies were independent, but many remained colonies of European nations. In the Pacific Ocean Basin, the Europeans had also settled the region known today as Oceania, which comprises Australia and the two large islands of New Zealand, while colonizing the smaller Pacific islands.

Although Europe, the Americas, and Oceania were separated from each other by vast distances and had unique characteristics, the societies of these regions were shaped by similar patterns of capitalism, migration, and nation-building. The United States, Canada, Australia, and New Zealand, but also Latin American countries such as Argentina, Uruguay, Brazil, and Chile, all developed as settler societies that were colonized chiefly by European immigrants who planted European institutions and ideas after the indigenous populations were largely dispossessed by conquest or killed by disease. Europeanization also occurred in societies such as Mexico, Cuba, Venezuela, and Peru, where nonwhite and mixed-descent peoples were a larger percentage of the population. European traditions and institutions remained influential in American and Oceanic settler societies but were modified by time, circumstances, and the cultures of ethnic minorities, either indigenous peoples, such as Native Americans and New Zealand Maori, or imported societies, such as Afro-Brazilians and Afro-Cubans.

In the Americas, the United States and Canada gradually diverged from the Latin American and Caribbean societies in their economic and social patterns and cultures. As Kume observed and Conrad's fictional American millionaire boasted, the people of the United States saw themselves as the country of the future, with vast expectations for global influence and wealth. By expanding its frontiers and rapidly industrializing in the 1800s, the United States became the colossus of North America and a world power, often extending its political and economic influence into Latin America and the Caribbean.

FOCUS QUESTIONS

1. How and why did European social, cultural, and intellectual patterns change during this era?
2. What impact did westward expansion have on American society?
3. How did immigration and industrialization reshape U.S. society?
4. What political, economic, and social patterns shaped Latin America after independence?
5. Why did the foundations for nationhood differ in Canada and Oceania?

CHRONOLOGY

	United States	Latin America	Canada and Oceania
1800	**1803** Louisiana Purchase **1846–1848** U.S.-Mexican War	**1823–1889** Abolition of slavery	**1840s–1890** Colonization of Pacific islands
1850	**1861–1865** Civil War **1898–1902** Spanish-American War	**1889** Brazilian republic	**1850** Treaty of Waitangi **1867** Canadian Confederation
1900		**1910–1920** Mexican Revolution **1914** Panama Canal	**1901** Australian Commonwealth

❖ The Reshaping of European Societies

How and why did European social, cultural, and intellectual patterns change during this era?

Thanks to destabilizing revolutions in political and economic life (see Chapter 19), modern Europeans lived in a world very different from that of their ancestors, a world of cities, new forms of work, and temptations to abandon home villages for visions of a better life in faraway lands. The European population grew rapidly, prompting millions of people to migrate to industrialized regions in Europe or to emigrate to the Americas, southern Africa, and Oceania in search of work and a better life. Industrialization led to changing social structures and family systems. The world of thought, the arts, and science reflected and also shaped the new Europe that emerged in the Modern Era, and the resulting innovations influenced peoples around the world.

Population Growth, Emigration, and Urbanization

Expanding economies, better public health, and the introduction of new crops such as potatoes from the Americas lowered Europe's mortality rate and fostered population growth. In England and Wales, for example, life expectancy rose from thirty-five in 1780 to forty in 1840 as a result of improved public health. People married earlier, increasing the birthrate, and more people married than in Early Modern times. Europe's population (including Russia) grew from 100 million in 1650 to 190 million in 1800 and to 420 million in 1900, one of the world's highest growth rates at that time.

Rapid population growth created new problems, however. Thomas Malthus, an English clergyman and economist, argued in 1798 that population growth was checked by poverty, disease, war, and famine, but if these problems were eliminated, the gains in human security would soon disappear as the world's population outgrew its means of subsistence. As Malthus feared, overpopulation did indeed bring bleak poverty and underemployment to many areas of Europe, and this impoverishment was accelerated by the replacement of small family farms by large farms that needed fewer workers. But the growth of cities and industries also alleviated some of the problems of a growing population by providing new employment opportunities.

Population growth and the poverty it produced led to migration within Europe and emigration overseas. Many Poles, for example, moved to the mines of northern France and western Germany, and Irish immigrants built railroads, canals, and roads in England. Emigration cut Ireland's population by half between 1841 and 1911. Jews, too, migrated as the tensions caused by competition for scarce resources increased. As an identifiable, non-Christian minority, the Jews were often turned into public scapegoats for unresolved problems and sometimes subjected to violent, usually coordinated mob attacks known as *pogroms* (from the Russian word meaning "round-up"). Particularly common in Russian-ruled territories such as Ukraine and Poland, pogroms prompted Jews to seek better lives in western Europe and the Americas, especially the United States. Some 45 million Europeans emigrated to the Americas, Australia, New Zealand, Algeria, and South Africa to escape poverty (see Map 20.1).

Europeans also moved from rural areas to cities. The earliest areas to be industrialized became the most urbanized. For example, the population of Manchester, the British center of the cotton industry, grew tenfold between 1800 and 1900. By 1900 Britain had the world's most urban society, with 90 percent of its people living in towns and cities. The larger European cities grew spectacularly between 1800 and 1900. London increased from 900,000 to 4.7 million, Paris from 600,000 to 3.6 million, and Berlin from 170,000 to 2.7 million. But in many countries the majority of people still lived in the countryside.

Urbanization increased social problems. Rapidly expanding cities lacked social services such as sanitation, street cleaning, and water distribution. Among the sanitary nuisances were overflowing privies and littered streets. Huge numbers of people lived in poverty, crammed into overcrowded housing with high disease rates. Millions lived in crime-ridden slums. As the English poet William Blake wrote: "Every night and

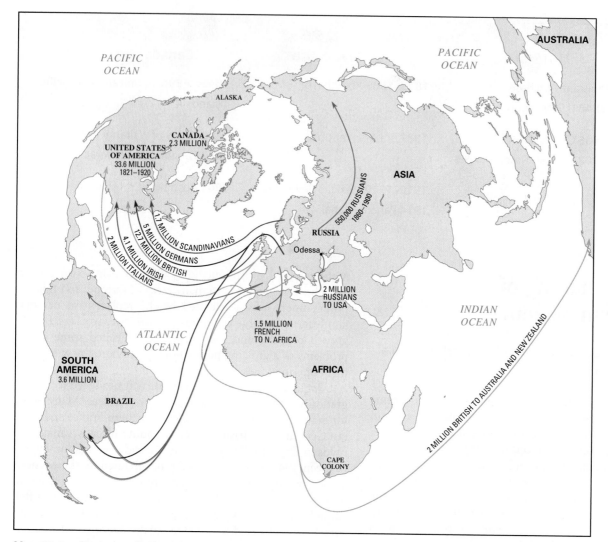

Map 20.1 European Emigration, 1820–1910

Pushed by rapid population growth and poverty, millions of Europeans left their homes to settle in the Americas (especially the United States), North and South Africa, Siberia, Australia, and New Zealand. The British and Irish accounted for the largest numbers of emigrants, nearly 17 million combined. (Adapted from Map 20.1 European Migrations, 1820–1910, *The Times Atlas of World History, 3rd ed.* Reprinted by permission of HarperCollins Publishers, Ltd. Copyright HarperCollins Publishers Ltd. Some data from Eric Hobsbawm, *The Age of Empire, 1875–1914* (New York: Pantheon, 1987).

every morn, some to misery are born." For instance, over half the residents of Paris lived in dire poverty in 1830. Critics saw these cities and their terrible slums and pollution as symptoms of the destruction of traditional society. The standard of living did not rise much for most Europeans until the 1880s, when incomes began to improve and several countries, including Britain and Germany, began building a social safety net for their citizens. By 1900 British and French workers were earning nearly twice the wages of workers in 1850.

While cities grew dramatically, western European rural life also changed. Rural social forms with deep roots in history fell by the wayside. Agricultural technology and practices developed rapidly, resulting in better yields, more mechanization, and improved animal breeding. Market agriculture largely displaced the subsistence production of earlier times. But even with improved farming methods, peasants often earned low wages, and many small farmers frequently lost their land to more highly capitalized and mechanized operations. Occa-

sional famines also occurred, notably in Ireland and Russia, but by the 1850s such disasters were rare except as a result of war. In contrast to rural life in western Europe, some feudal traditions remained influential in eastern Europe, especially in Russia and Poland, where the landed gentry retained authority over peasant lives.

Social Life and Family Patterns

Population movement and urbanization were only two manifestations of much broader changes resulting from industrialization, including the reshaping of social life. Europeans enjoyed wider horizons than their ancestors. After 1870 the rise of mass-distribution newspapers, organized football (soccer) leagues, more widespread vacation travel, and other activities connected peoples within and between nations. The world's first cinema opened in Paris in 1896, launching a film industry that would produce one of the most popular entertainments in

Europe and then the world. People enjoyed a growing range of options in areas of life once fixed by tradition, such as where to live, work, or go to church and whom to marry. Choice brought more personal freedom than Western societies had ever known, but also more social instability. Some observers viewed these changes as liberation, while others concluded that they fostered anxious uncertainty.

Industrialization also spurred a rethinking of sexual attitudes, particularly in Britain. The middle class increasingly discouraged sexual activity before marriage and limited sexual intercourse within marriage. Middle-class people considered unbridled passion a sign of bad character. In contrast, the working classes experienced higher rates of illegitimacy and more frequent sexual relations than ever before. In the many troubled families of the urban slums, marital infidelity became common. This behavior became part of middle-class stereotypes of the poor. Thus, a British factory girl in 1909 complained, "I wanted no one to know that I was a factory girl because I was ashamed at my position. I was always hearing people say that factory girls were loose-living and corrupt."[3] Thanks to improved diets, children of all classes reached sexual maturity at a younger age, making it more difficult to maintain boys' choirs as male voices changed earlier.

Families still provided the framework of social life, but home life and families underwent changes. During the Early Modern Era some people in northern Europe, especially England and the Low Countries, began to marry later and live in nuclear families, which were smaller than extended families since they usually included just parents and their several children. During the 1800s the nuclear pattern became common in most of northern Europe, especially among the middle classes, while large extended families remained the norm in southern and eastern Europe. But everywhere family feeling was strong, and families included fewer nonrelated members, such as servants and apprentices, than had been usual in earlier centuries. In the 1700s western Europeans began to adopt the notion that people should have the freedom to choose their partner and marry for love rather than to meet family demands or economic need. By the 1800s many people married for love, but critics argued that love matches would lead to marital instability and divorce when romance faded. Furthermore, married men and women were often closer to, and spent more time with, their same-sex friends than their spouses, and sometimes the line between these friendships and homosexual relationships was murky.

The industrial economy was hard on families, particularly on women and children. Most Europeans assumed that women were not breadwinners and hence should be paid less than men. Women typically earned only 25 percent of men's wages. Single mothers found it especially difficult to earn a living, and some were forced to turn to prostitution for survival. Women and children also often did hard manual labor in cotton mills and mines. In 1838 a liberal member of the British parliament reported: "I saw a cotton mill, a sight that froze my blood, full of women, young, all of them, some large with child, and obliged to stand twelve hours each day. The heat was excessive in some of the rooms, the stink pestiferous. I nearly fainted."[4] By 1850 in France about 40 percent of cotton workers were women, and another 12 percent were children under sixteen. By the early 1900s, when machines did more of the factory work, fewer women and far fewer children worked full-time in the industrial sector.

People also began to redefine family life. By the later 1800s some men and women criticized marriage as stifling and old-fashioned. Prominent people in the artistic and political worlds, such as the popular French actress Sarah Bernhardt and the fiery German socialist Rosa Luxemburg, lived openly with same-sex partners out of wedlock. A few homosexual men and women argued in essays that heterosexual marriage was not the only avenue for achieving happiness. Homosexuals could be found at all levels of society, but they often faced discrimination and persecution, as did the Irish poet, novelist, and playwright Oscar Wilde (1854–1900), the married father of two, who was tried and imprisoned in 1895 for engaging in homosexual relationships, known as sodomy. The increasing attention to homosexuality and the first scientific studies of it sparked heated and ongoing debates as to whether the behavior was rooted in nature or perversion.

Gender Relations

The Industrial Revolution reshaped life for both European women and men. Increasingly industrialization put men and women into separate work worlds and lowered the status of women by increasing their dependence on men. Some historians see the Industrial Revolution as increasing men's power over their wives as the workplace moved from the home to the factory. As they were no longer needed in economic production such as textile weaving, middle-class women lost their roles as direct producers, becoming instead home managers ("housewives") charged with keeping the house clean. Middle-class men often assumed that women belonged at home as submissive helpmates and encouraged them to cultivate their beauty and social graces to please their menfolk. An influential German author portrayed the home as a haven where a man could escape the storms in the outside world and be soothed by his wife's kindness and goodness.

As a result of these attitudes, men remained dominant in the political, social, economic, and religious spheres, and women's roles were increasingly restricted to marriage, motherhood, and child rearing. Moreover, often women had no legal standing and could not divorce their husbands. Women struggled to adapt to the changing circumstances. Upper- and middle-class women practiced artificial birth control and had fewer children than in earlier eras. Some of them also treated their health and personal problems with opium-based drugs, even drugging their babies with opium elixirs to keep them quiet. By 1900, however, women enjoyed longer life expectancies and devoted fewer years to childbearing and rearing.

In the later 1800s European women gained more legal rights and economic opportunities, and British women even gained property rights. Some European women took new jobs as secretaries, telephone operators, or department store sales clerks. Although the job qualifications women acquired were

CHRONOLOGY	
European Society and Culture, 1750–1914	
1859	Publication of Charles Darwin's *On the Origin of Species*
1860s	Beginning of impressionist artistic movement in France
1896	Women's suffrage in Finland
1905	Publication of Albert Einstein's general theory of relativity

"Convicts and Lunatics" The movement for women's right to vote, or suffrage, was particularly strong in Britain. This poster, "Convicts and Lunatics," designed by the artist Emily Harding Andrews for the Artist's Suffrage League around 1908, shows a woman graduate, deprived of basic political rights, treated similarly to a convict and a mentally disturbed woman. (Library of Congress)

not typically for high-status or high-paying positions, there were occasional doors open to professional jobs. For example, the Netherlands had Europe's first woman physician in 1870, and France the first woman lawyer in 1903. Leading professional women such as the Italian educator Maria Montessori (mon-ti-SAWR-ee) (1870–1952), who devised innovative schools allowing children to develop at their own pace; the Polish-born French scientist Marie Curie (1867–1934), who won a Nobel Prize in Physics in 1903; the influential German composer and pianist Clara Schumann (1819–1896); and the British nurse Florence Nightingale (1820–1910), who revolutionized nursing practices, provided role models. Schools for girls grew in number. In 1867 the University of Zurich in Switzerland became the first university to admit women, and it was soon followed by universities in France, Sweden, and Finland.

In quest of more rights, some women began movements promoting what later became known as **feminism**, a philosophy promoting political, social, and economic equality for women with men. One leader of the British movement, Harriett Taylor, wrote bitterly that "all that has been said respecting the social condition of women goes on the assumption of their [innate] inferiority. People do not complain of [women's] state being degraded at all."[5] Inspired by pioneers such as Mary Wollstonecraft in the late 1700s, the first feminist movements emerged in Britain and Scandinavia, with some women, later known as **suffragettes**, pressing for the same voting rights as men. In 1896 Finland became the first European nation to accept female suffrage (see Chronology: European Society and Culture, 1750–1914). In Britain suffragettes led by Emily Pankhurst (1858–1928) campaigned for the right to vote by giving speeches, writing slogans on pavement, canvassing door-to-door, and demonstrating. French suffragettes also organized, but their natural political allies, the socialists, thought liberating the working classes took precedence over expanding women's rights. In other countries, especially in southern and eastern Europe, feminists had only a small following.

feminism A philosophy promoting political, social, and economic equality for women with men.

suffragettes Women who press for the same voting rights as men.

Thought and Religion

The industrial and political revolutions, and the social changes they sparked, fostered new directions in European thought. Philosophers such as the Germans Immanuel Kant (KAHNT) (1724–1804) and Friedrich Nietzsche (NEE-chuh) (1844–1890) debated the values of the Enlightenment, a movement based on reason that began in the 1600s and continued through the 1700s. A major Enlightenment figure, Kant greatly influenced modern Western philosophy. He believed that experience alone was inadequate for understanding because the perceptions it fosters are ultimately shaped by the mind, which imposes a structure on the sensations we see and converts these sensations into knowledge. Kant doubted that a perfect society could ever be achieved, arguing that "man wishes concord, but nature, knowing better what is good for his species, wishes discord."[6]

Nietzsche was the most prominent thinker to reject the Enlightenment notions of progress. Nietzsche perceived a growing decadence in European culture, which he blamed on Christian values and democratic ideas. To Nietzsche, there was no funda-mental truth, including moral and scientific truth, as the Enlight-enment philosophers had thought, but rather misconceptions developed by each culture as its members tried to understand the world. With no absolute truth, absolute good and evil cannot exist. In the twentieth century extreme nationalists and racists dis-torted Nietzsche's ideas to persecute ethnic minorities. Nietzsche's notion that truth is relative influenced many European and North American intellectuals in the later twentieth century to argue that knowledge was culturally constructed.

For many Europeans, religion also changed with the times. Gradually Protestants and Catholics learned to tolerate each other, but religious passions did not diminish. In the later 1700s and early 1800s a religious revival inspired many Euro-pean Protestants to cross the Atlantic to the United States. Evangelicals, especially numerous among English Anglicans and Baptists, stressed personal relations with God, favored missionary activity, and condemned behavior they considered sinful, such as social dancing and drinking. Soon new churches appeared. The charismatic British Anglican preacher John Wesley (1703–1791), seeking a more emotional faith, founded the Methodist movement, which appealed particularly to min-ers and factory workers. Eventually the Methodists left Angli-canism to form their own church. Another church, the Society of Friends, better known as Quakers, had been formed in the 1650s and now became influential supporters of social reform and humanitarian causes. Believing in nonviolence, human dignity, and individual conscience, the Quakers fought against slavery and for social and political freedom.

In contrast to evangelical movements, some Europeans embraced secular approaches. Many middle-class Protestants sought a liberalized faith stressing social tolerance rather than the hellfire and damnation preached by some evangelicals. The relevance of religion declined for many Europeans. Thus, by 1851 only half of the English population attended church. The divide between the more liberal and the more devout resulted in public debates across Europe about the role of religion in society. For instance, in Britain evangelicals sought to impose their values on the increasingly secular society by trying to ban alcohol and gambling and requiring all businesses to close on Sunday, moves fiercely opposed by many Protestants and Catholics.

The Roman Catholic and Greek Orthodox Churches also faced challenges. Spurred by the French Revolution, the Catholic clergy in France and Belgium lost the privileged sta-tus they had enjoyed for centuries, such as control of educa-tion and exemption from taxes. France opened a public school system in the 1890s and mandated state neutrality toward re-ligion in 1905. At the same time, however, the Catholic Church generally strengthened church dogma and organiza-tion. Popes reasserted their theological infallibility and an-nounced new doctrines such as the Immaculate Conception of the Virgin Mary. The church also remained a major spiri-tual force and landowner in Austria, southern Germany, Poland, Spain, Portugal, and Italy. The Greek Orthodox world fragmented into national churches in Greece, Serbia, Roma-nia, and Bulgaria.

Culture

Literature and the arts also reflected the changing times. The growth of a literate public eager and able to consume cultural products liberated writers, composers, and artists from de-pendence on wealthy patrons, but they now had to satisfy the new commercial world of a consuming public. Inspired by the political revolutions of the late 1700s and early 1800s, some thinkers and artists adopted **romanticism**, a philosophical, lit-erary, artistic, and musical movement that questioned the En-lightenment's rationalist values and instead glorified emotions, individual imagination, and heroism. Some romantics were apolitical, some celebrated great figures such as Napoleon Bonaparte, and others detested all existing governments. In contrast to romanticism, writers and artists embracing another movement, realism, portrayed a grimy industrial world filled with uncertainty and conflict. For example, the liberal Spanish painter Francisco de Goya (GOI-uh) (1746–1828) produced a moving series on the Napoleonic invasion of Spain that portrayed not warfare's glory and heroism but its horrors: or-phans, pain, rape, blood, and despair.

Many writers were inspired by romanticism or realism. For instance, the German Friedrich Schiller (1759–1805), a former soldier, offered intense romantic images with a nationalist tinge, such as a poem that turned the story of William Tell, a legendary hero of Swiss resistance against foreign invasion, into a mani-festo for German political freedom. Other writers turned to real-ism to portray the world around them. The British novelist and former factory worker Charles Dickens (1812–1870) revealed the hardships of industrial life, the injustices of capitalism, and the miseries of the poor. Some writers fit into no particular trend. One of these, Jane Austen (1775–1817) in Britain, wrote novels of keen wit that offered subtle observations on society. Although dealing largely with love and marriage, her novels also confronted women's status in a male-dominated society. Austen's works remain popular today and have been turned into successful feature films by a film-maker born in India.

Imbibing various movements, European classical music enjoyed a golden age, and the compositions of this era are still enjoyed by audiences around the world. Influenced by the Enlightenment, the Austrian Wolfgang Amadeus Mozart (MOTE-sahrt) (1756–1791) wrote thirty-five symphonies, eight operas, and many concertos. Romanticism inspired many later composers, most famously the German Ludvig von Beethoven (BAY-toe-vuhn) (1770–1827), whose much ad-mired Ninth Symphony set Schiller's poem, "Ode to Joy," to music. Nationalism also influenced composers. One of the early operas of the Italian Giuseppi Verdi (VER-dee) (1813–1901) begins with the refrain: "Long live Italy!"

Between 1880 and 1914 Europe was swept by a quite dif-ferent movement, **modernism**, a cultural trend that openly

romanticism A philosophical, literary, artistic, and musical move-ment that questioned the Enlightenment's rationalist values and instead glorified emotions, individual imagination, and heroism.

modernism A cultural trend that openly broke with romanticism and other traditions by embracing progress and welcoming the future.

broke with romanticism, realism, and other traditions by welcoming the future and new ideas. Modernism derived from confident, enterprising, and adaptable societies. Several significant movements influenced by modernism shaped the visual arts in the later 1800s, sparked in part by the increasingly connected world. The movements lacked the political thrust of romanticism and realism but reflected influences from Asian, African, and Pacific art. Realistic landscape paintings, the appearance of photography, and the introduction of Japanese prints, whose popularity in Europe had surprised Kume Kunitake, contributed to the rise in France of **impressionism**, an artistic movement that sought to express the immediate impression aroused in momentary scenes, bathed in changing light and color. French impressionists painters such as Claude Monet (moe-NAY) (1840–1926) and Pierre Renoir (ren-WAH) (1841–1919) achieved worldwide fame.

Combining their own genius with artistic influences from around the world, in the 1880s some French artists rebelled against impressionism, experimenting with a return to familiar shapes and compositions. The most influential included Paul Cezanne (say-ZAN) (1839–1906), famous for his landscapes and portraits; the prolific Dutch-born Vincent Van Gogh (van GO) (1853–1890), who introduced intense primary colors and thick brushstrokes; and Paul Gauguin (go-GAN) (1848–1903), a former stockbroker whose intense paintings reflected many years living in Peru, the Caribbean, and Polynesia. Gauguin's richly colored paintings often featured idyllic scenes of Polynesian life, stimulating European interest in the wider world. By the early 1900s Pablo Picasso (pi-KAH-so) (1881–1973), a young Spaniard who settled in Paris, was already revolutionizing Western art with new approaches such as integrating ideas from African sculpture and masks. By then, and thanks in part to international influences, European art bore little resemblance to medieval European art.

Science and Technology

The Modern Era saw spectacular achievements in science and technology, which were produced by men and women all over Europe. Some major breakthroughs came in medicine and public health. For example, physicians introduced the first effective vaccines against deadly diseases such as smallpox that had ravaged the world for centuries, and they also discovered that different diseases were caused by different bacteria and viruses. Other medical technologies improved, as well as drugs. In 1895 the German physicist Wilhelm Rontgen (RUNT-guhn) (1845–1923) discovered x-rays, spurring progress in diagnosis and surgery. Medical advances and improved sanitation led to better public health and the prevention of many diseases. For example, thanks to cleaner water, by 1874 cholera had been eradicated from Europe's industrial cities.

Scientists also made major contributions to the understanding of nature. In particular the British naturalist Charles Darwin (1809–1882), after years spent traveling around the world studying plants, animals, and fossils in many lands, formulated the theory of evolution emphasizing the natural selection of species. In his book, *On the Origin of Species*, Darwin argued that all existing species of plants and animals, including humans, had evolved into their present forms over millions of years. Species either adapted to their environment over time or died out. Eventually evolution became the foundation for the modern biological sciences, confirmed by many studies and accepted by most scientists, but generated opposition from many churches, whose leaders saw Darwin's evolutionary ideas as a degradation of humans and a negation of religious faith.

The German-born Jewish physicist Albert Einstein (1879–1955) ranks with Galileo, Newton, and Darwin as a pathbreaking European scientist. His papers on the theory of relativity, published in the early 1900s when he worked as a clerk in the Swiss patent office, provided the basis for modern physics, our understanding of the universe, and the atomic age. Einstein offered a new view of space and time, showing that distances and durations are not, as Newton thought, absolute but are affected by one's motion. He also proved that matter can be converted into energy and that everything is composed of atoms, insights that provided the basis for atomic energy. Einstein also argued that physics cannot make definite predictions on any physical action but can offer only probable rather than certain outcomes, a troubling idea that physicists still debate. His papers electrified the scientific world. Einstein taught in Swiss, Czech, and German universities before immigrating to the United States in 1934.

New and rapid technological discoveries all over Europe characterized the age, improving people's lives. In the early 1800s electric batteries, motors, and generators emerged as new sources of power. In the 1890s the Italian Guglielmo Marconi (mahr-KO-nee) (1874–1937) introduced wireless telegraphy, and in 1901 he used his invention to communicate between England and Canada, opening another network connecting the world. Various inventors worked on building internal combustion engines, and two Germans, Gottlieb Daimler and Karl Benz, became the "fathers of the automobile," producing the first petroleum-powered vehicle in the 1880s.

Meanwhile, some scientists worried about the effects of industrial pollution on the environment. The observation that carbon dioxide emissions from coal-burning factories heated the atmosphere led the Swedish scientist Svante Arrhenius to speak of a "greenhouse effect" that potentially threatened modern societies. Scientific studies over the next century confirmed his fears. The world still struggles with the promise but also the perils of the technologies and industrial processes developed in this era.

---

impressionism An artistic movement that sought to express the immediate impression aroused by momentary scenes that were bathed in light and color.

◈ The Rise of the United States

What impact did westward expansion have on American society?

After the American Revolution, in which the thirteen colonies successfully overthrew British control, the former colonists turned to building their new nation. The United States became an ongoing experiment as Americans learned how to balance regionalism and national unity, freedom and control, individualism and social obligation, popular representation and special interests, and national uniqueness and world leadership. During the early republic Americans established new forms of government, reshaped economic patterns, fostered a new culture, and began the movement westward, conquering Native Americans, acquiring Mexican territory, and becoming involved in the wider world.

Government and Economy

The new American republic, weak and small and surrounded by hostile neighbors in British Canada and the Spanish American Empire, found nation-building a challenge. Unity was fragile. In erecting a distinctive new system of representative government, Americans faced the daunting task of establishing principles to unite the diverse states and erecting a legal system. Ultimately they forged a new form of democracy and constructed an economic framework to preserve independence and encourage free enterprise capitalism.

American leaders were divided over many issues, including the power of a national government and the relative autonomy of the separate states. The Constitution and Bill of Rights, approved in 1787, established a relatively powerful central government, elected by voters in each state, within a system, known as federalism, that ensured the sovereignty and recognized the lawmaking powers of each member state (see Chronology: The United States and the World, 1750–1914). White Americans gained many civil liberties, and white adult males were granted the right to vote, but the government maintained slavery and excluded Native Americans and women from political activity. Professing a love for freedom, Americans ever since independence have had to constantly redefine—in political debates, legislative bodies, the workplace, schools, and the bedroom—the balance between the rights of the state and the individual, and of the majority and the minority.

The U.S. political system reflected a mix of liberalism, which underpinned the Bill of Rights, and fear of disorder. Inspired by a liberal hatred of despotic government in Europe, the founders made tyranny difficult through the separation of powers into executive and legislative branches and an independent judiciary, with each institution having defined roles. But wary of potential radicalism and shocked by the excesses of the French Revolution, the nation's leaders also discouraged attacks on the interests of the upper classes by limiting voting rights. For example, states imposed property and literacy qualifications for voting. The indirect election for the presidency through the Electoral College, in which each state chose electors to cast their votes, also reduced popular sovereignty and produced results that did not always reflect the choice of the majority of citizens.

American leaders also had to establish a sound economic foundation for the new nation. The southern plantation interests favored free trade to market their crops abroad without obstacles, especially cotton, tobacco, and sugar. But many founders insisted that economic independence was necessary to safeguard political independence and thus favored self-reliance and **protectionism**, the use of trade barriers to shield local industries from foreign competition. This strategy, they hoped, would be the first step toward fostering an Industrial Revolution like Britain's. The first treasury secretary, the West Indian–born Alexander Hamilton (1757–1804), laid the basis by establishing a national bank, favoring tariffs to exclude competitive foreign goods, and providing government support for manufacturing. A controversial figure, brilliant but arrogant, Hamilton later died in a duel with a political rival.

Hamilton's policies and protectionism encouraged manufacturing. Continued conflicts with Britain brought about a U.S. decision in 1807 to temporarily embargo all foreign trade, which stimulated domestic manufacturing to offset the lost imports. Conflicts between Britain and the U.S. over trade, U.S.-Canada border tensions, and other issues led to

protectionism Use of trade barriers to shield local industries from foreign competition.

CHRONOLOGY

The United States and the World, 1750–1914

1787	U.S. Constitution
1803	Louisiana Purchase
1812–1814	U.S.-British War of 1812
1823	Monroe Doctrine
1825	Completion of Erie Canal
1846–1848	U.S.-Mexican War
1848	U.S. acquisition of Texas, California, and New Mexico
1849	California gold rush
1861–1865	Civil War
1862	Lincoln's Emancipation Proclamation
1867	U.S. purchase of Alaska from Russia
1869	Completion of transcontinental railroad
1898	U.S. incorporation of Hawaii
1898–1902	Spanish-American War
1902	U.S. colonization of Philippines
1903	First powered flight by Wright Brothers

the War of 1812 (1812–1814). The British captured Washington, burning down the White House, and repulsed a U.S. invasion of Canada but, after some U.S. victories, the two sides negotiated peace. Industrialization proceeded in the U.S. northeast and, in 1813 the first large textile mills to convert raw cotton into finished cloth opened in New England. The northern industrialists who favored protectionist policies soon prevailed over the southern planters who wanted free trade. Meanwhile, to move resources and products, Americans also built over 3,300 miles of canals by 1840. The Erie Canal, completed across New York State in 1825, connected the Hudson River at Albany to Lake Erie, linking the markets and resources of the Midwest and Mississippi Basin to the port of New York City.

Society and Culture

Gradually Americans forged a society distinct from Britain's. The French writer Alexis de Tocqueville (TOKE-vill) (1805–1859), who visited the United States in the early 1830s, noted the American commitment to democracy and individualism, the "blending of social ranks," and Americans' "unbounded desire for riches."[7] But he also considered slavery and racial prejudice a dark blot on American claims to equality, and he feared that too much individualism and greed for riches undermined

community. De Tocqueville was fascinated by America's gender relations, which differed from those in Europe. For instance, he admired the independence of single American women, the tendency to view marriage as a voluntary contract between loving equals, and the resulting influence of married women in the family, which gave them more responsibility for child rearing than in Europe, where fathers made most of the decisions about children's upbringing. Nonetheless, he noted, unmarried women and many wives were still under the strong control of fathers and other men, who believed that women's place was centered on the home.

Slavery shaped the society of the southern states. Enslaved African Americans, mostly plantation workers, were the majority in many southern districts, constantly replenished by new arrivals from Africa. They created music, including spirituals, which were based in part on African rhythms and song styles and used Christian images to indirectly protest slavery and to express a longing for freedom. In "Go Down Moses," for example, the refrain emphasized "let my people go," a clear call for emancipation, just as, in the biblical account, the Hebrews in Egypt were led to freedom by Moses. Many white Americans also wanted to eliminate slavery and other social ills. One abolitionist musical group, the Hutchinson Family, toured the country with songs that attacked slavery and the mistreatment of Native Americans, favored women's suffrage, and opposed smoking. The abolitionist Sojourner Truth (c. 1797–1883), a former slave, also eloquently advocated gender equality. Sarah Grimke (1792–1873), a Quaker from a South Carolina slaveholding family, became an active abolitionist and one of the first American feminists. She rejected the notion of different male and female natures and roles (see Witness to the Past: Protesting Sexism and Slavery). Discovering that their deceased brother had fathered two sons with one of his slaves, Sarah and her sister Angelina flouted custom and state laws by raising and educating their nephews, who both became active in the equal rights cause.

This period also saw the development of distinctively American religious and cultural beliefs. For example, Americans often ignored rigid doctrines and dogmatic church leaders. Like some of the nation's founding leaders, many Americans embraced secular values, such as tolerance for diverse ideas and indifference to organized religion. Others actively sought a personal and intense religious experience. Religious dissenters, such as Quakers and Methodists, had long flocked to North America, and Protestant denominations there multiplied, a pattern reinforced by the religious revivals that periodically swept the country, sometimes inspired by evangelical movements in Britain. At the same time, Puritan and Calvinist values remained influential, promoting a dedication to hard work at the expense of leisure and leading some Americans to criticize activities such as music, dancing, and reading for pleasure.

Manifest Destiny and Westward Expansion

The nation's boundaries gradually expanded westward, providing a counterpart to European imperialism in Asia and Africa (see Chapter 19) and allowing the acquisition of

Protesting Sexism and Slavery

Sarah Grimke and her younger sister, Angelina, were the daughters of a wealthy slaveholding family in Charleston, South Carolina. Adopting the Quaker faith, which emphasized human dignity, and rejecting their positions as members of the state's elite, they dedicated their lives to advocating women's rights and the abolition of slavery. In 1837 they moved north and began giving lectures before large audiences. Because they spoke out so publicly, they were often criticized by churches for violating gender expectations. Sarah Grimke responded in 1838 by writing letters to her critics that often used Christian arguments to defend women's right and obligation to voice their views. When the letters were published together in one volume, they became the first American feminist treatise on women's rights. The following excerpts convey some of Grimke's arguments.

Here then I plant myself. God created us equal; he created us free agents; he is our Lawgiver, our King and our Judge, and to him alone is woman bound to be in subjection, and to him alone is she accountable for the use of those talents with which her Heavenly Father has entrusted her. . . . As I am unable to learn from sacred writ when woman was deprived by God of her equality with man, I shall touch upon a few points in the Scriptures, which demonstrate that no supremacy was granted to man. . . . [In the Bible] we find the commands of God invariably the same to man and woman; and not the slightest intimation is given in a single passage, that God designed woman to point to man as her instructor. . . .

I hope that the principles I have asserted will claim the attention of some of my sex, who may be able to bring into view, more thoroughly than I have done, the situation and degradation of women. . . . During the early part of my life, my lot was cast among the butterflies of the *fashionable* world; and of this class of women, I am constrained to say, both from experience and observation, that their education is miserably deficient; that they are taught to regard marriage as the one thing needful, the only notice of distinction; hence to attract the notice and win the attentions of men, by their external charms, is the chief business of fashionable girls. They seldom think that men will be allured by intellectual acquirements, because they find, that where any mental superiority exists, a woman is generally shunned and regarded as stepping out of her "appropriate sphere," which, in their view, is to dress, to dance, to set out to the best possible advantage her person. . . . To be married is too often held up to the view of girls as [necessary for] human happiness and human existence. For this purpose . . . the majority of girls are trained. . . . [In education] the improvement of their intellectual capacities is only a secondary consideration. . . . Our education consists almost exclusively of culinary and other manual operations. . . .

There is another class of women in this country, to whom I cannot refer, without feelings of the deepest shame and sorrow. I allude to our female slaves. . . . The virtue of female slaves is wholly at the mercy of irresponsible tyrants, and women are bought and sold in our slave markets, to gratify the brutal lust of those who bear the name of Christians. . . . If she dares resist her seducer, her life by the laws of some of the slave States may be . . . sacrificed to the fury of disappointed passion. . . . The female slaves suffer every species of degradation and cruelty, which the most wanton barbarity can inflict; they are indecently divested of their clothing, sometimes tied up and severely whipped. . . . Can any American woman look at these scenes of shocking . . . cruelty, and fold her hands in apathy, and say, "I have nothing to do with slavery"? *She cannot and be guiltless.*

THINKING ABOUT THE READING

1. What do the letters tell us about the social expectations and education for white women from affluent families?

2. In what way do Grimke's letters address the issue of slavery?

Source: Sarah M. Grimke, *Letters on the Equality of the Sexes, and the Condition of Woman* (Boston: Issac Knapp, 1838).

---

abundant fertile land and rich mineral deposits. In the later 1700s American pioneers began moving across the Appalachian Mountains in search of new economic opportunities. As they expanded westward, Americans developed the potent notion of their **Manifest Destiny**, the conviction that their country's institutions and culture, which they regarded as unmatched, gave them a God-given right to take over the land, by force if necessary. Manifest Destiny offered a religious sanction for U.S. nationalism and the thrust outward, and American leaders promoted this view. In 1823 Secretary of State John Quincy Adams set a goal of transforming the United States into "a nation, coextensive with the North American continent, destined by God and nature to be the most populous and powerful people ever combined under one social compact."[8]

Expansion to the Pacific coast was achieved during the 1800s. After acquiring the Ohio territory, in 1787 the new nation extended from the Atlantic to the Mississippi River, and it was further enlarged in three expansionist waves. In the first, President Thomas Jefferson (g. 1800–1809) astutely bought from France, in the Louisiana Purchase (1803), a huge section

---

Manifest Destiny Americans' conviction that their country's institutions and culture, regarded as unmatched, gave them a God-given right to take over the land.

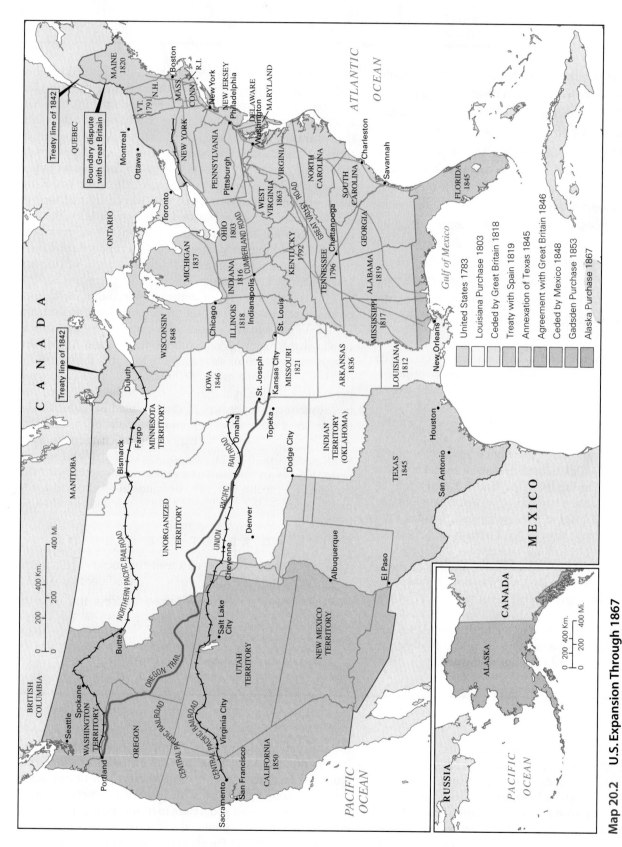

Map 20.2 U.S. Expansion Through 1867
The United States expanded in stages after independence, gaining land from Spain, France, Britain, and Mexico until the nation stretched from the Atlantic to the Gulf and Pacific coasts by 1867. During the same period Canadians expanded westward from Quebec to British Columbia.

American Progress   This 1893 painting by the American artist John Gast extols progress and shows Americans, guided by divine providence, expanding across, and bringing civilization to, the forests and prairies of the Midwest and West. The painting reflects views held by many Americans of their destiny and special role in the world.   (Library of Congress)

of the Midwest and South that doubled the size of the country. In the second wave, the United States acquired Florida and the Pacific Northwest from Spain. Many Americans moved into the Midwest, and others continued on to Oregon by wagon train, crossing vast prairies, deserts, and mountains. In the third wave, the United States obtained from Mexico in 1848 Texas, California, and New Mexico as a result of the U.S.-Mexican War. The discovery of gold near what is today Sacramento in 1849 prompted over 100,000 Americans, known as "49ers," to board sailing ships or covered wagons and head for California from the distant east, hoping to strike it rich. In California the "49ers" sometimes clashed with the long-settled Mexicans and newcomers, such as immigrant Chinese, who were also seeking a better life. The 1867 purchase of Alaska from Russia eliminated all European rivals from North America (see Map 20.2). By 1913 the United States had grown to forty-eight states.

The gradual migration west shaped a pioneer society different from that on the eastern seaboard. The vast North American frontier offered conditions where settlers could develop new ways of life and ideas. For example, the rise of ranching, especially of cattle, on the Great Plains fostered the growth of a new occupation, that of the cowboy. Cowboys on horseback were needed to guide herds of several thousand cattle on long, lonely drives, sometimes hundreds of miles, to railroad towns

for shipment east. These cowboys—whites, Mexicans, African Americans, and men of mixed descent—often learned survival skills and knowledge of horses from Native Americans. Some historians argue that the frontier helped democratize the United States as individualists sought adventure, social equality, and a better life. But life on the frontier was often hard, especially on women. An Illinois farm wife, Sara Price, lamented her hardship in poetry, writing that "life is a toil and love is a trouble. Beauty will fade and riches will flee. Pleasures will dwindle and prices they double, And nothing is as I would wish it to be."[9]

Westward expansion came at the expense of the people already there, including Mexicans, Spaniards, and especially Native Americans. Indians saw whites as invaders in their territory and often resisted violently. To whites, Indians represented an alien way of living and thinking and needed to be controlled, that is, restricted to reservations. The U.S. Supreme Court ruled in 1831 that the Indians' "relation to the United States resembles that of a ward to his guardian."[10] Over time many Indians were removed from their native lands. Even tribes who lived in peace with whites and had adopted aspects of European culture were not spared. For example, the Cherokee, farmers who had developed their own written language, published a newspaper, and had a written constitution, had long cultivated good relations with their white neighbors. Yet, after gold was discovered on their land, 15,000 Cherokee from Georgia were forced into concentration camps and then in 1838 sent on a forced march of 1,200 miles, the "Trail of Tears," to Oklahoma. Four thousand Cherokee died from starvation or exposure on the journey. Other tribes were broken up in coerced relocations. For instance, the Delaware, who once controlled a vast mid-Atlantic territory, were scattered from Canada to Texas. Some tribes also resisted removal. The Seminole (SEM-uh-nole) in Florida, led by Chief Osceola (os-ee-OH-luh) (ca. 1804–1838), fought two wars with the U.S. army, attacking with guerrilla tactics and then retreating into the Everglades swamps. Fifteen hundred American soldiers died in the long conflict. Finally Osceola was captured, after which the Seminole resistance faded and many of the tribe were exiled to Oklahoma.

The United States, Latin America, and Asia

Although Americans avoided interference in European affairs until World War I, the belief that they had God's favor, along with the quest for resources and markets, led ultimately to territorial expansion into Latin America and the formation of a new kind of empire. In 1823 James Monroe (1758–1831), the fifth president of the United States, delivered a message to Congress that became one of the major principles of U.S. foreign policy. The Monroe Doctrine was a unilateral statement warning European nations against interfering in the Western Hemisphere and affirming U.S. commitment to shape the Latin American political future after the overthrow of Spanish colonialism. The doctrine claimed that the United States enjoyed a special political and economic status in the Americas, and it effectively marked off Latin America as an American **sphere of interest**, an area in which one great power assumes exclusive responsibility for maintaining peace and attempts to monopolize the resources of that area. Nearly a century after the Monroe Doctrine, Secretary of State Robert Lansing reaffirmed this pattern, claiming that the United States "considers its own interests. The integrity of other American nations is an incident, not an end."[11] As a result, the Monroe Doctrine forged complex links between the United States and the rest of the Americas, often provoking hostility in Latin America, and it set the stage for the rise of the United States as a world power.

As a result of the U.S.-Mexican War of 1846–1848, the United States more than doubled its national domain by seizing territory at the expense of a Latin American nation. Some 35,000 Americans and their slaves had settled in the Mexican province of Texas. Chafing at Mexican rule and its antislavery policies, the Americans rebelled and, despite a defeat at the Alamo, a fort in San Antonio, pushed the Mexican forces out and declared themselves an independent republic in 1836. Soon the Texans sought annexation to the United States, a move favored by the proslavery southern states and opposed

by the antislavery northern states. As antislavery forces stalled the annexation in the United States Congress, Texans talked of alliance with Britain, alarming U.S. leaders. In 1844 the U.S. president and Congress moved to admit Texas to statehood, provoking the pride of Mexicans, who had never recognized Texan independence and now reasserted their claims.

The war that followed stirred politically divisive and passionate debate among politicians and the media in the United States, where many people opposed the conflict. After President James Polk (1795–1849) ordered military action, the United States Congress went along, but some members were troubled that Polk evaded the constitutional mandate that only the Congress could declare war. The war badly divided Americans. A Massachusetts legislative resolution proclaimed "that such a war of conquest, so hateful, unjust and unconstitutional in its origin and character, must be regarded as a war against freedom, against humanity, against justice, against the Union."[12] The war ended when 14,000 U.S. troops invaded Mexico and captured Mexico City. This victory allowed the United States to annex Mexican territories from Texas to California. However, the conflict had killed 13,000 Americans and 50,000 Mexicans, and it had also fostered an enduring Mexican distrust of the United States.

Many Americans supported the extension of Manifest Destiny to Latin America and Asia, some citing economic factors. Polk wanted to seize California and its harbors from Mexico as a way of increasing the profitable commerce with China. In 1853 Senator William Seward placed expansion in global perspective, advising Americans: "You are already the great continental power. But does that content you? I trust that it does not. You want the commerce of the world. The nation that draws the most from the earth and fabricates most, and sells the most to foreign nations, must be and will be the great power of the earth."[13] Americans soon eyed trade opportunities across the Pacific. By the early 1800s traders were participating in the lucrative China trade, including opium smuggling. Meanwhile, the U.S. navy led the way in opening up reclusive Japan. American traders, missionaries, adventurers, diplomats, and soldiers flocked to Asia (see Chapters 22–23).

Many historians argue that during the nineteenth century the United States began to build a new kind of empire, not a territorial one like the British, French, Spanish, and Russian Empires, but chiefly an "informal" one based on using financial controls and military operations to extend U.S. power rather than gain formal political control. Hence, American naval forces intervened in Southeast Asia almost annually from the 1830s through the 1860s, often arrogantly. For example, in 1832 a U.S. naval expedition bombarded a port on the Indonesian island of Sumatra, whose officials had seized a private U.S. ship for illegal activities, and U.S. officials boasted that the demolition of the port had "struck terror" into the Sumatrans, forcing them to release the ship. Some American leaders advocated military action to gain trade agreements, an aggressive attitude that increasingly influenced U.S. policies during the century. Various presidents also sought to obtain nearby Cuba from Spain or helped to finance Cuban revolts to overthrow Spanish rule.

---

sphere of interest An area in which one great power assumes exclusive responsibility for maintaining peace and attempts to monopolize the area's resources.

SECTION SUMMARY

- Politically, the United States balanced individual liberty with systems designed to check disorder; economically, it balanced protectionist and free-market interests.

- Americans were more individualistic and offered more independence to women than Europeans, and a struggle raged between supporters and opponents of slavery.

- Americans gradually pushed toward the West Coast, taking advantage of abundant natural resources and inflicting great suffering on Native Americans.

- The Monroe Doctrine announced that the United States saw Latin America as its own sphere of interest, off limits to European powers.

- The bloody and divisive U.S.-Mexican War brought a large chunk of Mexican territory under American control.

✦ An Industrial United States and Global Power

How did immigration and industrialization reshape U.S. society?

Between 1860 and 1914 the United States changed dramatically. The Civil War, which began in 1861 and lasted four years, maintained the territorial unity of the nation, ended slavery, and led to the increased centralization of the federal government at the expense of state and regional interests. This centralization, combined with economic protectionism, allowed the United States to duplicate the economic and political growth that was spurred by mercantilism in Early Modern western Europe. Industrialization created more wealth, supported U.S. power, and reshaped American social patterns. By 1900 the United States was rapidly changing as immigrants poured into the country. The country had a larger population than all but one European nation, boasted the world's most productive economy, owned half a continent, and enjoyed a powerful, stable, democratic government, all sustained by an abundance of natural resources. The nation also increasingly exercised its power abroad to extend its political and economic influence.

The Civil War, Slavery Abolition, and Social Change

The Civil War (1861–1865), a major transition for the United States, reshaped U.S. society by ending slavery. Like Sarah Grimke, many Americans had believed that slavery mocked liberal democracy. Slavery had largely disappeared from northern states by the early 1800s, and the U.S. government outlawed the slave trade in 1810, although it continued elsewhere. Thousands of free blacks occupied a precarious position in the southern states. The Civil War was a last gasp for the slavery-based southern society, which desperately tried to break free from the forces of urbanization, industrialization, and social change percolating in the northern states. Economic disparities exacerbated the North-South conflict. By 1860, the North was the home of industry, banks, and great ports such as New York, Boston, and Philadelphia. By contrast, the South was largely a monocultural plantation economy supported by 350,000 white families and 3 million black slaves. The northern leaders mostly favored high customs tariffs to protect their industries but this policy threatened the South, which depended on exports to survive.

In 1860–1861 eleven southern states seceded from the union, forming the proslavery Confederate States of America. President Abraham Lincoln (1809–1865), a lawyer from Illinois who wanted to end slavery and preserve the union, mobilized the military forces of the remaining states to resist the secession. In 1862 he issued the Emancipation Proclamation, freeing all slaves. After four years of war the North defeated the South, mainly because the North's dynamic economy better mobilized resources for war and the North also had a population advantage of nearly 4 to 1.

The Civil War was in many respects a social and political revolution. Not only did it end slavery, but it also ultimately displaced the southern planters and their plantation system: it crushed the southern struggle for self-determination, destroyed the South's economic link to Britain, firmly established protectionism as economic policy, and fostered a much stronger federal government. The war resulted in more deaths than all other wars combined that were fought by Americans before or since, killing 360,000 Union and 258,000 Confederate troops, and it devastated the southern countryside. The South began to enjoy balanced economic development only with the growth of industry in the mid-twentieth century, largely paid for by northern investors.

The Civil War emancipated African Americans from slavery but did not eliminate the disadvantages faced by them and other ethnic minorities. Determined to overcome barriers, many former slaves taught themselves to read—usually forbidden under slavery—and some opened schools to expand opportunities for young blacks. Many African Americans left the plantations to find work elsewhere, but their prospects were chiefly limited to sharecropping such as growing cotton, or physical labor, such as mining or longshoreman work. Long after slavery ended, African Americans faced discrimination reflected in laws restricting their rights and were often prevented from voting. The southern states and some northern states had rigid laws against intermarriage and, unlike Latin America, little separate recognition for people of mixed ancestry, who were lumped with African Americans and treated as such. Yet, many African Americans had some European ancestry. Classifications based on skin color and presumed ancestry were often codified in state laws. Any trace of African ancestry meant automatic relegation to inferior status. Skin color became the major determinant of social class, and segregation based on this physical feature remained the norm in the South until the 1960s. African Americans attended separate schools, were largely confined to their own neighborhoods, and could not use public facilities, such as parks, restaurants, and drinking fountains, reserved for whites. Those who violated these laws and customs faced jail, beatings, or even executions (some 235 in 1892 alone) by white vigilantes. The journalist Ida B. Wells (1862–1931), born into slavery, sparked a long movement to end mob violence, including hangings (known as "lynchings").

Native Americans also continued to suffer. In the aftermath of the Civil War, as peace brought a resumption of westward American expansion into central and western North America, more Native Americans lost control of their destinies. After 1865 whites subdued the Great Plains and its people with new technology, including the six-shooter, the steel plough, and the barbed-wire fence. Settlers, railroad builders, and fur traders massacred 15 million bison, the chief source of subsistence for Indian tribes on the Great Plains, while farmers and ranchers reshaped the environment of the prairies and northern woodlands, rendering the territory unfit for Indian survival. Indians resisted but eventually faced defeat. In 1886 the Apache of Arizona, under their chief, Geronimo (juh-RON-uh-moe) (1829–1909), finally surrendered after years of fighting. In 1890, the United States Army's massacre of three hundred Lakota Sioux followers of the Ghost Dance, an Indian spiritual revival movement, at Wounded Knee in South Dakota marked the triumph of U.S. colonization of the west. Defeated by the army, decimated by epidemics, and reduced to poverty, Indians were put on reservations controlled by the federal government. Their children, prohibited from speaking their native languages or practicing tribal traditions in boarding and public schools, were thereby stripped of their cultural heritage. Indians experienced the American dream in reverse, as democracy became tyranny and liberty became confinement.

Industrialization

The northern victory in the Civil War and economic policies of protectionism spurred the great industrial growth in the later 1800s, which fostered a better material life but also generated changes in American class structure and ways of living. These decades saw the rise of the food processing, textile, iron, and steel industries and the growth in coal, mineral, and oil production. The industrial economy in the United States resembled those in Europe but became more productive. In 1860 the United States ranked fourth among industrial nations, but by 1894 it ranked first; in addition, American exports had tripled, and the nation was second only to Britain as a world trader.

A surge in technological innovation changed economic life. Electricity as a power source, combined with improved factory production methods, turned out goods faster, more cheaply, and in greater quantities than ever before, increasing U.S. competitiveness in the world. New inventions by Americans such as the typewriter, cash register, adding machine, telegraph, and telephone increased business productivity, while American and European inventions such as water-tube boilers, steam-powered forging hammers, portable steam engines, and the internal combustion engine revolutionized industry. U.S. factories tripled their output between 1877 and 1892. Thomas Edison (1847–1931) benefited the public as well as industry by perfecting the light bulb.

American life and population patterns were also shaped by an improved transportation and communication network. The transcontinental railroad, completed in 1869, opened western lands for settlement, and by 1890 the U.S. railroad network was larger than all European railroad systems combined. Railroad construction owed much to ethnic minorities and

Women Textile Workers
In both Europe and North America women became the largest part of the workforce in the textile industry. These women, working in a New England spinning mill around 1850, endured harsh work conditions and the boring, often dangerous, job of tending machines.
(George Eastman House)

immigrants, since many of the workers who drove the spikes and blasted the passages through rocks and mountains were African Americans, Chinese, or Irish. The transportation revolution continued when Henry Ford (1863–1947) started a motor company in 1903 and began turning out the first affordable cars and refining the mass-production assembly line. In another transportation breakthrough, Orville and Wilber Wright became the first men to achieve powered flight in 1903, launching the age of aviation.

But industrialization also led to monopoly capitalism, a concentration of industrial and financial resources similar to Europe's that worsened the inequitable distribution of wealth. A few fabulously wealthy tycoons such as John D. Rockefeller and J. P. Morgan, known to their critics as the Robber Barons, had great influence over politicians, controlled much of the economy, and expected workers to labor at subsistence wages. Using Social Darwinist thinking (see Chapter 19), Rockefeller claimed that "the growth of large business is merely survival of the fittest and a law of God."[14] The wealthy flaunted their success and financed political allies, and many less affluent Americans also valued and hoped to acquire wealth, believing that the United States was a land of opportunity where anyone could succeed with hard work regardless of social background.

Industrialization reshaped the American social structure by creating new classes of workers. Although many Americans prospered, industrial workers often experienced a hard life. For example, in the coal mines of the southern Appalachians and Ohio River Valley, the work was dangerous, the hours long, and the wages low. Children worked alongside their parents, and miners often died young from breathing coal dust. Textile workers also faced hardship. Before the Civil War the textile industry, centered in New England, was based on exploitation of women and children. Companies recruited teenage girls from poor rural families to work in dark, hot mill rooms filled with cotton dust. They labored six days a week from 5 A.M. to 7 P.M. and were housed in company dormitories, six to eight girls per room. By the 1880s the textile industry had abandoned New England and moved south, to Virginia and the Carolinas, where wages were lower and people even more desperate for jobs. The mill town became a feature of southern life, with poor rural females the major labor force.

Immigration, Urbanization, and Social Movements

This era was also marked by social change, including the influx of millions of immigrants. Some 25 million Europeans immigrated to the United States between 1870 and 1916, and by 1900 over a million Europeans entered the nation each year in search of a better life. At first they came largely from northwestern Europe, especially English, Irish, Germans, and Scandinavians. Later many arrived from southern and eastern Europe, including Italians, Greeks, Serbs, and Poles. The population of European ancestry in the United States increased from 2.5 million in 1770 to 32 million in 1860 and 92 million by 1910. For example, many Jews fleeing persecution in Europe saw the United States as the Promised Land. In 1870 the number of Jews, mostly from Germany, that were living in the United States was 250,000, and by 1927 immigrants from Russia and eastern Europe had swelled this total to 4 million. Meanwhile, thousands of Chinese and Japanese immigrants landed on the Pacific Coast in the later 1800s, followed by Filipinos after 1900. Most of these newcomers, both European and Asian, typically faced discrimination. For instance, some businesses posted signs saying, "No Irish need apply." Chinese and Japanese immigrants, mostly living in the western states, faced even harsher restrictions and sometimes violence.

In less than a century the United States went from a mostly rural nation along the Atlantic coast to a transcontinental powerhouse. The federal government encouraged migration westward by passing liberal land laws such as the 1862 Homestead Act, which allotted 160 acres in parts of the Midwest to every pioneer family free of charge. Farming became dominant in the Midwest, pushing cattle ranching westward. Frontier territories became states within the Union. During this time the United States also became urbanized, with half of the people living in cities, including metropolises such as New York and Chicago.

The decades between 1865 and 1914 were also marked by movements seeking economic and social change. Since factories poured out more goods than Americans could consume, by the 1890s the nation was in turmoil. Economic depression, panics, and bloody labor conflicts fostered working-class radicalism, which threatened the wealthy and the middle class. Farmers and workers resented the wealth of the Robber Barons and the power of large corporations and railroads. Even while increased agricultural output made the United States the world's leading agricultural producer, many farmers went bankrupt, losing their land to banks. Political leaders worried that an inflamed public mood would spark a revolution.

Popular movements, some led by women and others by men, fought those with power and privilege. Labor unions had first appeared in the 1820s. Two decades later mill girls, led by Sarah Bagley, campaigned for better conditions and a shorter workday in the textile mills of Lowell, Massachusetts. In 1860 female strikers in the textile mills of nearby Lynn chanted, "American ladies will not be slaves." Eugene Debs (1855–1926), the socialist leader of the railway union, explained in 1893 that "the capitalists refer to you as mill hands, farm hands, factory hands. The trouble is he owns your head and your hands."[15] By the early 1900s the radical, Marxist-influenced International Workers of the World (better known as the Wobblies) were gaining influence among industrial workers, miners, and longshoremen. Employers and their political allies disparaged union members as communists and fought their demands, eventually destroying the Wobblies as a mass movement.

Women also struggled for their civil rights. The republic excluded more than half of the population from democracy for the first 150 years. During the 1800s, although large numbers of women worked in factories, shops, and offices, they also managed their homes. Despite their increasing economic roles, women were also urged by religious leaders to be more pious, self-sacrificing, and obedient to men. They wore stiff, uncomfortable whalebone corsets that constrained movement and accentuated their figure, a symbol of their submission to male taste and expectations. Many women wanted more options; the banners carried by striking factory workers in 1912 read, "We want bread and roses too."

Women gained basic privileges more on a par with men only after a long, nonviolent effort. The suffrage movement for the vote was born in 1848, when women meeting in Seneca Falls, New York, declared, in a reference to the U.S. Declaration of Independence, that "all men and women are created equal." They opposed a system in which women had no rights to property or even to their own children in case of divorce. After seven decades of marching, publicizing their cause, and lobbying male politicians, suffragettes convinced Congress to give women the right to vote in 1920.

Thought, Religion, and Culture

While some Americans, especially on the East Coast, still looked to Europe for cultural inspiration, the nation increasingly created its own distinctive literary and intellectual traditions. Later-nineteenth-century writers such as Walt Whitman and Mark Twain helped forge a uniquely American literature that examined society and its problems. Whitman (1819–1892), a journalist influenced by European romanticism, celebrated democracy, the working class, and both heterosexual and homosexual affection while addressing the transformations of the Industrial Revolution. In 1855 Whitman described his ethnically diverse and dynamic nation as "a newer garden of creation, dense, joyous, modern, populous millions, cities and farms. By all the world contributed."[16] Twain (1835–1910), a former printer and riverboat pilot from Missouri turned journalist, was inspired by European realism and sought material for his essays, short stories, and novels all over the country and the world. Unlike the optimistic Whitman, Twain emphasized the underside of American life and character, was skeptical about technology's value, and opposed the increasing U.S. imperial thrust in the world.

American philosophy and religion also went in new directions. In a constantly changing world, some thinkers concluded, eternal ideas were harder to justify. The leading American philosophers, such as William James and John Dewey, broke with the European tradition by claiming that ideas had little value unless they enlarged people's concrete knowledge of reality, an approach known as pragmatism. While many Americans embraced secular and humanist views, many others took a different view, seeking truth in religion. The Protestant missionary impulse, inherited from the first settlers and augmented by the growth of evangelical churches, fostered religious and moral fervor. As a result, Americans became active as Christian missionaries around the world. At the same time, the nation itself became more religiously diverse. In 1776 most Americans were Protestant, often Calvinist. By 1914 the United States contained followers of many faiths, including some Buddhist and Muslim immigrants from Asia.

Americans also produced unique music, largely the result of the mixing of black and white traditions. In the South, especially the states along the Mississippi River, new forms of music developed in the early 1900s out of African American culture. One of these, the blues, grew out of the plantation economy. Sung mainly by blacks on street corners or in saloons, the blues detailed personal woes in a world of harsh reality and racism. Bluesmen sang of lost love, the brutality of police, jail, joblessness, and oppression. The blending of black blues with white folk music and popular music provided a foundation for several forms of American popular music in the twentieth century, including jazz, rock, rhythm and blues, and soul, which spread around the world.

American Capitalism and Empire

As in Europe, industrial capitalism fostered imperialism and warfare. A series of economic depressions from the 1870s through the 1890s spurred public demand for foreign markets and for extending Manifest Destiny to other parts of the world. As a result, by the later 1800s many American businessmen, farmers, and workers favored acquiring territories overseas to improve national economic prospects. Others hoped to spread American conceptions of freedom, which they increasingly equated with individualism, private property, and a capitalist marketplace economy. Since domestic problems, such as the wide gap between the very rich and very poor, were not easily resolved, many argued, only the imposition of direct or indirect control over other societies, in order to acquire resources and markets, could generate enough wealth to avoid domestic turmoil.

These pressures led to military interventions. The United States sent military forces to at least twenty-seven countries and territories between 1833 and 1898 to protect the economic interests of American businesses during insurrections or civil strife or to suppress the piracy that threatened U.S. shipping. Troops were dispatched at various times to nearly a dozen Latin American nations, China, Indonesia, Korea, North Africa, and Hawaii. For example, for decades U.S. gunships patrolled several of China's rivers to protect American businessmen and missionaries from Chinese who resented Western imperialism.

U.S. forces also brought the Hawaiian Islands, a Polynesian kingdom where Americans had long settled as traders, whalers, planters, and missionaries, into the U.S. empire. The growing American population in Hawaii, led by sugar planters, resented the Hawaiian monarchy. In 1891 Liliuokalani (luh-lee-uh-oh-kuh-LAH-nee) (1838–1917), a Hawaiian nationalist who wanted to restrict settler political influence, became queen. She was strong and resolute, spoke excellent English, and was beloved by her people as a songwriter, but she faced economic disaster when the United States Congress abandoned preferential treatment for Hawaiian sugar imports.

Hoping to reestablish close ties to the United States, in 1893 American settlers, aided by 150 U.S. troops, overthrew the monarchy, formed a provisional government, and announced that they would seek affiliation with the U.S. Americans already dominating the island economy, effectively making Hawaii a neocolony. A heated debate in the United States on the advantages and disadvantages of direct colonization as opposed to informal control delayed annexation of the islands as a territory until 1898. The end of the monarchy transformed the islands not only politically but also socially, as thousands of Japanese, Chinese, Korean, and Filipino immigrants become the main labor force, mostly working on plantations owned by American settlers and companies. By the 1930s, Asians constituted the large majority of Hawaii's population.

The major conflict involving the United States was the Spanish-American War (1898–1902), which pitted American against Spanish forces in several Spanish colonies. The war was a watershed in U.S. foreign affairs that helped make the United States a major world power and empire. On the eve of the war, President William McKinley (1843–1901) argued for the necessity for obtaining foreign markets for America's surplus production, linking expanding markets with the maintenance of prosperity. In what Secretary of State John Hay called "that splendid little war," the United States fought with Spain over that country's remaining, restless colonies: Cuba, Puerto Rico, Guam, and the Philippines. The war unleashed American nationalist fervor. One observer described patriotism as oozing out of every boy old enough to feed the pigs.

The United States quickly triumphed against the hopelessly outmatched Spanish. However, 5,500 Americans died in Cuba, largely because of malaria and yellow fever rather than enemy gunfire. A surgeon who labored among the disease-ridden survivors wrote of pale faces, sunken eyes, staggering gaits, and emaciated forms, which marked these veterans as wrecks for life. The war also changed Americans' outlook on the world. A future president, Woodrow Wilson, boasted about America's emergence as a major power in the global system: "No war ever transformed us quite as the war with Spain. No previous years ever ran with so swift a change as the years since 1898. We have witnessed a new revolution, the transformation of America completed."[17] However, to colonize the Philippines, the United States had to brutally suppress a fierce nationalist resistance by Filipinos opposed to U.S. occupation (see Chapter 22). The U.S. struggle against Filipinos seeking independence and democracy after three and a half centuries of unpopular Spanish rule, while ultimately successful, resulted in the deaths of thousands of Filipinos and Americans and indicated the challenges and costs of exercising power in the world. The colonization of the Philippines, Puerto Rico, and Guam, and economic and political domination over nominally independent Cuba, also transformed the United States from an informal into a territorial empire much like the Netherlands and Portugal.

SECTION SUMMARY

- The Civil War killed hundreds of thousands, did tremendous damage to the South's economy, and freed the slaves, though discrimination and segregation continued for at least another century.

- American industry advanced rapidly, producing immense wealth for a small number of tycoons, helping others to prosper, and creating difficult, hazardous work for many.

- Millions of immigrants poured into the United States, seeking opportunity and often finding discrimination, while social movements seeking better treatment for workers and greater rights for women came into being.

- A distinctive American culture developed that celebrated democracy and practicality and that reflected the diverse origins of the American people.

- In the interests of promoting and protecting American business interests, the U.S. military intervened in the affairs of many foreign countries and territories, most notably in the Spanish-American War, which brought the United States its first formal colonies.

◆ Latin America and the Caribbean in the Global System

What political, economic, and social patterns shaped Latin America after independence?

Brazil and most of Spain's Latin American colonies won their independence in the early 1800s, although the Caribbean islands mostly remained colonies (see Chapter 19). But the new Latin American states did not forge the enduring democracy of their northern neighbors or foster significant social and economic change. Most Latin Americans experienced considerable turmoil, including political instability, economic decline, and regional conflicts. However, by the 1870s conditions stabilized somewhat. Expanding European markets by then had created a greater demand for Latin American exports and stimulated economic growth, though free-trade policies also deepened the Latin American and Caribbean monocultures. Black slaves gained their freedom, and waves of European immigrants poured into some nations, changing the social landscape. Latin American and Caribbean societies also forged new cultural forms, and the United States increasingly exercised power in the region.

Latin American Nations

After winning their independence from Spain and Portugal, Latin Americans faced new challenges. Some countries, such as Argentina, Brazil, and Mexico, were large and unwieldy, while others, such as El Salvador and the Dominican Republic, were small and had limited resources. Except for Brazil, which was governed by an emperor, the new countries were republics. Creating stable political systems proved to be a struggle. Despite efforts to forge national identities and unity, the new governments did not always win the allegiance of all the people within the country. Civil wars for dominance continued some places into the 1860s, often pitting those favoring federalism and regionalism against partisans of a strong centralized government. In addition, various frontier disputes fostered occasional wars. For example, Chile fought Peru and Bolivia in 1837 and again in 1879–1884, acquiring territory from those two countries as a result (see Chronology: Latin America and the Caribbean, 1750–1914).

Political instability dominated Latin American politics in the decades to follow, often leading to military dictatorships and wars. Unlike England, Spain and Portugal had never fostered democratic conditions at home or in their colonies. Most of the Latin American countries adopted U.S.-style constitutions, but their provisions were often ignored in the authoritarian political systems. Many nations had regular elections but enjoyed little democracy. Furthermore, tensions between central governments and remote regions became chronic. For example, the Argentine government did not impose its authority on remote provinces until the 1870s.

Although the Latin Americans achieved political independence, most leaders did not favor dramatic social and economic change. The wealthy upper class largely consisted of creoles who owned large businesses, plantations, and haciendas or had seized them from the departing Spaniards. The small middle class of shopkeepers, teachers, and skilled artisans was mainly composed of mestizos and mulattos. Over half of the population, including most Indians and blacks, remained at the bottom of the social structure. Whether in North America, the Caribbean, or Latin America, economies based chiefly on plantation agriculture or mining had similar, highly unequal social structures. These societies offered limited education for the workers because little alternative employment was available.

In Latin American countries politics usually remained chiefly an affair among planters, ranchers, mine owners, merchants, and military officers, and political and economic leaders often restricted the political participation of the poor nonwhite majority. To contain or prevent unrest resulting from the severe gap between rich and poor, military strongmen, known as **caudillos**, who acquired and maintained power through force, gained control of many Latin American countries. Some of these, such as the dictator Juan Manuel de Rosas (huan man-WELL deh ROH-sas) (1793–1877) in Argentina, were tyrants. To defend the interests of the big ranchers and merchants, Rosas's police and thugs beat up, tortured, or murdered opponents, often poor peasants. For their armies, caudillos and regional leaders sometimes recruited local cowboys, known as **gauchos** in Argentina and Uruguay, who worked on large ranches and were skilled horsemen and fighters. Like North American cowboys, the gauchos were European, Indian, black, or of mixed descent.

Most Latin American nations established some stability by the 1850s, although politics remained highly contentious. Many countries sought both "progress and order," which often led to caudillo rule. But a few fostered multiparty systems in which competing parties sought access to national power in order to

caudillos Latin American military strongmen who acquired and maintained power through force.

gauchos Cowboys in Argentina and Uruguay who worked on large ranches and were skilled horsemen and fighters.

CHRONOLOGY

Latin America and the Caribbean, 1750–1914

1861–1872	Benito Juarez president of Mexico
1876–1911	Diaz dictatorship in Mexico
1842	End of trans-Atlantic slave trade by most nations
1862–1867	French occupation of Mexico
1886	Abolition of slavery in Cuba
1889	Abolition of slavery in Brazil
1889	Brazilian republic
1879–1884	War between Chile and Peru-Bolivia
1885–1898	Cuban revolt against Spain
1898–1902	Spanish-American War
1901	Platt Amendment to Cuban constitution
1910–1920	Mexican Revolution
1912	U.S. intervention in Nicaragua
1914	Completion of Panama Canal

reward supporters. The political elite often disagreed on policies. Liberals generally favored federalism, free trade, and the separation of church and state. Often irreligious or anticlerical, they viewed the institutional power of the Catholic Church as being opposed to individual liberty. Conservatives sought centralization, trade protectionism, and maintenance of church power. Conflicts between these groups were sometimes violent.

Brazil was the only Latin American nation to maintain a monarchy rather than a republic. By the 1880s Brazilians had begun debating the legitimacy of the monarchy, which seemed unwilling to consider popular aspirations. Many Brazilians favored abolishing slavery, the source of growing social conflict, and forming a republic. As tensions simmered, the army seized power in 1889, exiled Emperor Dom Pedro II, and replaced the monarchy with a republic. However, although a federal system on the U.S. model emerged, suffrage was highly restricted, the majority of Brazilians gained neither property nor civil rights, and many remained desperately poor. In the end Brazil maintained an authoritarian tradition, but rebellions and regionalism constantly challenged the government.

Revolution in Mexico and Cuba

Social and economic inequalities in Latin American countries often led to reforms and sometimes to revolutions. Revolution was most notable in Mexico; however, the birth of the Mexican republic in 1824 did not bring stability to the vast country, which stretched from northern deserts to southern rain forests and was difficult to administer effectively. Between 1833 and 1855 a caudillo, General Antonio Lopez de Santa Anna (SAN-tuh AN-uh) (1797–1876), led a series of dictatorships punctuated by civil war. By leading his country into the disastrous U.S.-Mexican War (1846–1848), Santa Anna also lost half of Mexico's territory, including Texas and California, to the United States, a humiliation that is still felt by Mexicans today.

Santa Anna's misadventures and growing social problems sparked upheaval. In 1861 Mexican liberals led by Benito Juarez (WAHR-ez) (1806–1872), a pragmatic lawyer and Zapotec Indian, defeated the conservatives and suspended repayment of the foreign debt. In 1862 this provoked a short-lived occupation by France, whose ruler, Napoleon III, dreamed of renewed American empire. The French made a member of the Habsburg family, Maximilian of Austria (1832–1867), emperor of Mexico. However, under pressure from Mexican liberals and the United States, France withdrew its troops, and Maximilian's regime collapsed in 1867. Juarez again served as president from 1867 until his death in 1872, seeking social justice, fighting corruption and the privileged classes, and subordinating the church to the secular state. Juarez sold church lands and dissolved Indian communes, assigning individual properties to their tenants in order to create free peasants. His reformist policies and his Indian ancestry—his admirers called him the "man of bronze" because of his dark skin—made Juarez Mexico's most honored leader and a symbol of the nation.

In 1876 Mexico came under the dictatorship of Porfirio Diaz (DEE-ahs) (1830–1915), a caudillo of mestizo ancestry who ruled until 1911. Diaz brought stability and economic progress, allowing the country's population to grow from 9 million in 1874 to 15 million in 1910. But Diaz also allowed foreign business interests and investors to take over much of Mexico's economy, and he did little to help the growing mass of impoverished people. Under Diaz and his free enterprise policies many Indians sold their land to pay off debts, and much of it became owned by large haciendas and land companies. Women such as Dolores Jimenez (hee-MEH-nes), who led a working-class organization advocating women's empowerment, were among those opposed to Diaz.

Although Diaz brought some development to Mexico, he did so at the expense of most Mexicans, and his rule ended in civil war and revolution. In 1910 various forces coalesced to fight the unpopular Diaz regime in the Mexican Revolution (1910–1920). One faction was led by political liberals such as the creole Francisco Madero (muh-DER-oh) (1873–1913), a landowner's son who was also a spiritualist and vegetarian and who was educated in France and the United States. Another rebel leader, Pancho Villa (VEE-uh) (1877–1923), a field laborer's son and former cowboy, attracted support chiefly from ranchers in northern Mexico. In the south, the mestizo Emiliano Zapata (zeh-PAH-teh) (1879–1919), a charismatic former peasant, organized a peasant army that seized haciendas and fought the federal army. With the defeat of Diaz, largely by Zapata's forces, the idealistic Madero was elected president but proved a weak leader, unable to hold the revolutionary movement together, and was murdered by a rival. Madero's death

Women Revolutionaries in Mexico   Women joined men in fighting, and sometimes dying, for one or another faction during the Mexican Revolution. Many women hoped that the revolution would bring social change and a greater emphasis on improving women's political and economic rights.   (Archivo General de la Nación, Mexico, courtesy of Martha Davidson)

generated a free-for-all for power between the armies of Madero, Villa, Zapata, and other leaders. For years Mexico was engulfed in sporadic violence, all factions used ruthless tactics, and alliances formed and collapsed, often confusing Mexicans. A novel of the period concluded that "thinkers prepare the Revolution; bandits carry it out. At the moment no one can say with any assurance: 'So-and-so is a revolutionary and What's-his-name is a bandit.' Tomorrow, perhaps, it will be clearer."[18] Zapata was assassinated by a rival in 1919, but his reputation lived on in death, making him the most celebrated revolutionary hero.

The fighting had raised expectations for social change and fostered a yearning for peace. For example, hoping to gain more rights and influence, women played a critical revolutionary role. They cooked and commanded troops, served as spies and couriers, shot carbines and pistols, and fought disguised as men. Some of their hopes seem realized in a constitution introduced in 1917, which set forth progressive goals such as an eight-hour work day and paid maternity leave. But the constitution ignored other goals set out by liberal women, such as women's suffrage. In 1920 the revolutionary conflict wound down after claiming 1 million lives. While most Mexicans remained impoverished, a new party led by former revolutionaries formed a government and brought political stability while also opening some space for women to enter the business world and state governments.

In the Caribbean, Cuba also experienced revolt. The Spanish retained a tight control of Cuba and its valuable sugar plantations, but by the later 1800s an independence movement had developed. Its major spokesman, the journalist Jose Marti (mahr-TEE) (1853–1895), was a true citizen of the world who had travelled and lived in Europe, the United States, and various Latin American nations. Marti wrote innovative poetry and essays promoting freedom, social justice, and equitable distribution of wealth, and his writings helped inspire a Cuban revolt in 1895. Marti welcomed Afro-Cubans and women, who became the backbone of the struggle. However, Marti was killed in the fighting, and eventually the revolution was sidetracked by U.S. intervention during the Spanish-American War, which turned Cuba into a U.S. neocolony, Americans dominating the economy and having strong influence over the Cuban government.

Latin American Economic Patterns

Like North Americans, Latin Americans debated the benefits of free trade as opposed to protectionism, of heavy involvement in the world economy as opposed to self-sufficiency. After the destructive wars of independence, Latin American exports and investments declined. However, in contrast to the protectionist United States, this decline did not prompt Latin American leaders to move toward economic independence. Instead, they largely pursued free trade and maintained the monoculture based on plantations, mines, and ranches, concentrating on the export, mainly to the United States and Europe, of raw materials such as Ecuadorian cocoa, Brazilian coffee, Argentine beef, Cuban sugar, and Bolivian and Chilean ores.

The decision to concentrate on exporting natural resources left Latin American societies economically vulnerable. Around the region, earnings from minerals and cash crops ebbed and flowed with the fall or rise of world commodity prices. For instance, the "boom-and-bust" pattern for Brazil's coffee and rubber made sustained growth difficult and created regional pockets of alternating prosperity and decline. By the twentieth century the fate of Brazil and other Latin American countries became closely tied to fluctuating world prices for those countries' exports. Reflecting this fact, the politically unstable Central American countries, whose economies depended on tropical agriculture, were derisively called "banana republics." Unbalanced development had its hazards. For example, when silver deposits were exhausted at Potosi in Bolivia, the once famed mining city that had supplied so much wealth to Spain rapidly declined to a sleepy Andean town offering few jobs. In addition, because Latin American economic policies fostered growth but not development, the majority of people saw few benefits and the gap between the rich and the poor widened.

Some countries may have had few viable alternatives to free trade. The impoverished state of most Indians and blacks, in contrast to prosperous white North Americans, gave them little purchasing power to support any local industries that might be developed. And attempts to foster economic change often failed. Efforts to industrialize in Brazil, Colombia, and Mexico in the 1830s and 1840s failed because of competition from European imports. Only Argentina had some success fostering modest manufacturing in the later 1800s.

Investment by North Americans and Europeans in mines and plantations drew Latin America more firmly into the global market, exposing the region's peoples to continued exploitation by outsiders. Independence opened Latin America to North American, French, and especially British merchants and financiers, who used their economic power to dominate banking and the import trade for industrial goods such as cotton textiles and who also invested in mines and plantations. Brazil became heavily dependent on Europe and North America for loans, investment, technology, and markets. By the mid-1800s British businessmen and bankers controlled the imports and exports of both Brazil and Argentina. Argentina was sometimes called an informal member of the British Empire, and in 1895 an Argentine nationalist complained that "English capital has done what English armies could not do. Today our country is tributary to England."[19] After 1890 the United States also became a powerful economic influence in Latin America.

Foreign investment and domination had several consequences for Latin Americans. First, foreign corporations increasingly owned the plantations and mines. For example, the U.S.-based United Fruit Company dominated Central American banana growing. Such companies sent their profits to the United States or Europe rather than investing further in Latin America. Second, Latin America became a major contributor to world commodity markets, producing some 62 percent of the world's coffee, 38 percent of the sugar, and 25 percent of the rubber by World War I. Third, by the later 1800s, increased communication and transportation, as well as growing U.S. demand for markets and raw materials, fostered economic expansion in many countries. Despite this growth, however, inequalities grew. In some rural areas of Brazil, for example, powerful landed families maintained the peasantry in what was essentially bondage through private armies and gunmen. Throughout Latin America powerful families or foreign corporations increasingly owned the usable land, creating social and economic imbalances that produced political unrest in the twentieth century.

Slavery, Abolition, and Social Change

The abolition of slavery opened the door to social change in Latin America. Some of the leaders who overthrew Spanish rule, such as Simon Bolivar and Jose de San Martin, had favored emancipation and freed slaves who fought in the wars of independence. The emancipation movement continued. Between

1823 and 1854 slavery was legally abolished in most of Latin America and the Caribbean. Most European and American countries outlawed the trans-Atlantic slave trade by 1842 although the smuggling of African slaves to the Americas continued on a gradually diminishing scale through the 1870s. By the 1880s only Cuba and Brazil still maintained legal slavery. The Spanish rulers finally granted Cuban slaves their freedom in 1886, and abolitionists became more outspoken in Brazil, where slavery remained common in the sugar and coffee industries. Their most fiery spokesman, Joaquim Aurelio Nabuco de Araujo (wah-KEEM na-BOO-ko day ah-RAO) (1849–1910), a diplomat and the son of a rich landowner, denounced slavery for corrupting everything and robbing workers of their virtues. Increasing resistance by slaves, growing opposition by educated Brazilians, and the desire to promote European immigration led finally to abolition in 1889.

However, as in the United States, emancipation brought Latin American and Caribbean blacks freedom but did not dramatically improve their economic conditions. Many blacks shifted from being slaves to sharecroppers, tenant farmers, and laborers, experiencing little change in their low social status. As a popular Brazilian verse lamented: "Everything in this world changes; Only the life of the Negro [black] remains the same. He works to die of hunger."[20]

While life for most blacks changed little, the immigration of millions of Europeans and Asians reshaped many Latin American societies. European immigrants, especially Italians, Spaniards, Germans, Russians, and Irish, sought better economic prospects in new lands, particularly in Argentina, Brazil, Chile, Uruguay, and Venezuela. European arrivals most strongly shaped Argentina and Uruguay. The majority of people in Buenos Aires today trace their roots to Italy. The continued immigration encouraged Latin Americans to emulate European fashions, which generated a long-term market for European products. Owing in part to immigration, Latin America's population doubled between 1850 and 1900 to over 60 million.

Seeking, like Europeans, a better life, people from overcrowded lands in Asia and the Middle East also immigrated to the Americas in the later 1800s and early 1900s. In Trinidad, British Guiana, and Dutch Guiana, the abolition of slavery prompted labor-short planters to import workers in large numbers from India, and Indians eventually accounted for around half of the population in these colonies. Japanese settled in Brazil, Peru, and Paraguay as farmers and traders. Arab immigrants from Lebanon and Syria developed trade diasporas throughout Latin America, and Indonesians moved to Dutch Guiana as plantation workers. Chinese flocked to Peru and Cuba and, in smaller numbers, to Jamaica, Trinidad, and the Guianas. As different peoples came together, cultural mixing occurred. For example, an Afro-Trinidadian might have a Spanish surname, belong to the Presbyterian Church, possess a Hindu love charm, enjoy English literature, and favor Chinese food. People of Asian or Middle Eastern ancestry have sometimes headed Latin American or Caribbean governments.

Despite the newcomers, Latin America remained more conservative than North America in social structure. The creole elite dominated most countries while European and Asian immigrants and mixed-descent people constituted the middle class. Many mulattos and most blacks and Indians remained in the lower class. Indians in countries such as Mexico, Guatemala, Peru, Bolivia, and Colombia often withdrew into their village communities and limited contact with the national society. In 1865 a Mexican described the wide gap between whites and Indians: "The white is the proprietor; the Indian the worker. The white is rich; the Indian poor and miserable."[21]

Because of its large populations of European, African, and mixed-descent people, Brazil developed a society and culture different from those of other Latin Americans countries. Brazilians wrote of their nation's unique, multiracial society, which they considered to be less obsessed by skin color than other countries. Unlike in the United States, economic class and skin color did not always coincide, and marriage and cultural mixing between members of different groups was common. For instance, millions of Brazilians of all backgrounds blended African religions with Catholicism, creating new sects. Yet blacks were also more likely than whites to experience prejudice and to be poor, a fact reflected in Rio de Janeiro's largely black hillside shantytowns.

Latin American and Caribbean Cultures

Latin American and Caribbean societies created diverse forms of culture. Latin Americans struggled to reconcile indigenous with imported cultural traditions and debated how much to look to Europe for inspiration. Rejecting European models, novelists focused on social themes. For example, Euclides da Cunha (KOO-nyuh) (1866–1909) helped create a modern, realistic Brazilian literature concerned with describing the life of the country's poor (see Profile: Euclides da Cunha, Brazilian Writer). The Chilean essayist Francisco Bilbao was even more radical, praising freedom and rationalism and denouncing slavery, Catholicism, and the expansionism of the United States. In contrast, the cosmopolitan, well-traveled Nicaraguan poet Ruben Dario (1867–1916) rejected the expression of ideas in art in favor of escapist and fantastic images and a stress on beauty as an end in itself. But he also expressed unease at growing U.S. political and economic power in the region.

Especially creative cultural innovations came in music and dance. For example, the sensuous dance called the tango emerged in the bars and clubs of poor neighborhoods in Buenos Aires, which had over 1,600,000 people by 1914, and it became the most popular music in Argentina and Uruguay. The tango reflected a mixing of African and European traditions, since the music was based partly on rhythms derived from the drumming of African slaves and featured the accordion-like *bandoneon*, invented in Germany and carried to Argentina by Italian immigrants. The tango became a symbol of lower-class identity, as much a philosophy of life as an entertainment. By the early 1900s it had become popular in the ballrooms and nightclubs of Europe.

Brazil's unique music blended European melody and African rhythms. The abolition of slavery and the migration of Afro-Brazilians from Bahia State in the northeast to Rio de

EUCLIDES DA CUNHA, BRAZILIAN WRITER

Euclides da Cunha   Euclides da Cunha was one of the major writers and social critics of late nineteenth-century Brazil.   (Courtesy, Fundacao Biblioteca Nacional, Rio de Janeiro)

Euclides da Cunha (1866–1909) was one of Latin America's greatest writers, respected for his prose style, and the spokesman for a rising Brazilian nationalism. Born near Rio de Janeiro to a family originally from Bahia in the northeast, Cunha grew up at a time of great social change and political turmoil, when Brazilians abolished slavery and the Brazilian empire became a republic. He attended a military college to study engineering but rebelled against the rigid discipline. After angrily hurling down his sword in front of the Minister of War, he left the college before graduating to work as a journalist. Cunha was also a scientist interested in geography and a sociologist interested in people. A man of many skills, later in life he worked as a sanitary engineer and surveyor as well as a professor of logic. He lived most of his life in Rio de Janeiro and São Paulo.

Cunha's generation of urban Brazilian intellectuals, influenced by European writers, sought political democracy, national unity, and an end to violence and racial prejudice. A voracious reader, Cunha came to passionately share these progressive views. Cunha also wanted Brazilians to free themselves from slavish imitation of European philosophical and intellectual trends and make Brazil rather than Europe their spiritual home. Perhaps because of his unhappy military school experience, he became antimilitarist, writing that war is "a monstrous thing, utterly illogical." Nonetheless, Cunha rejoined the army for a while to defend the new republican government that had replaced the conservative imperial state. But the republic's inability to maintain democracy proved demoralizing, and he left the army to work as a civil engineer before returning to writing.

Cunha's greatest literary contribution was his book *Rebellion in the Backlands*, published in 1902, which is often called the bible of Brazilian nationality and a major work of world literature. Cunha's book challenged the nation's conscience and stimulated other authors to question accepted political wisdom. The book examined a rebellion, the Canudos War of 1896–1897, in an impoverished and parched rural region of Bahia State in the northeast, where most people worked on cattle ranches. Cunha's somber book recounted the powerful story of a rural mystic, Antonio Conselheiro, who, preaching a primitive Christianity that rejected private property, gathered a fanatic group, numbering in the thousands, to oppose Brazil's republican government. Federal officials responded with force, brutally crushing the uprising and killing most of the rebels. The book was a sociological analysis that reads like fiction.

Cunha called his searing account of the struggle a "cry of protest" against an "act of madness" by the government, an attack on the barbarity of the "civilized" against the weak. He portrayed sympathetically the mestizo backwoods people, detailing their customs, occupations, joys, diversions, and sorrows. For example, he described their "multitude of extravagant" beliefs, a mix of Christian and African traditions, and their ceremonies to revere the dead: "It is a charming sight to see a backwoods family at nightfall kneeling before their rude altar, by the dim light of oil lamps, praying for the souls of their loved ones who have died or seeking courage against the storms of this life."

Few urbanites knew anything about the northeast backlands people, who were alien to urban Brazilians. "It was not an ocean which separates us from them," Cunha wrote, "but three whole centuries." Cunha portrayed the confrontation between two cultures, the coast and interior, a theme that became popular in Latin American literature. The deeply religious backlanders could not comprehend the antireligious, rationalist ideas popular in the major cities, while the urbanites could not understand why rural people did not want the modern vision of political and social progress offered them. Cunha admired the rural men who had thrown off European culture and desired to be left alone, finding in the northeastern cowboy "the very core of our nationality." He believed that mestizos, blacks, and Indians were all part of the nation but that bringing the urban and rural people together in one nation would take many years.

Cunha's writing laid the groundwork for artists, writers, and scholars in Brazil and the rest of Latin America to explore new topics. Sadly, Cunha himself would not live to see his influence spread. In 1909 he was a victim of the violence he deplored. Discovering that his wife was having an affair with an army officer, Cunha rashly confronted the rival and was mortally wounded in the ensuing exchange of gunfire.

THINKING ABOUT THE PROFILE

1. How did Cunha's ideas reflect the Brazil of his era?

2. How did he view the backlanders and their role in the Brazilian nation?

Note: Quotations from Euclides da Cunha, *Rebellion in the Backlands*, translated by Samuel Putnam (Chicago: University of Chicago Press, 1957) pp. xiii, v, iii, 112, 161, xvi.

Janeiro gave rise to **samba**, a popular music and dance developed by Bahian women, known as the *tias,* or "aunts," who settled in Rio's hillside shantytowns. The tias mixed the African traditions of Bahia with the popular music styles favored by Rio's whites. The result, samba, became an integral part of Carnival, the three-day celebration before the long Christian period of fasting and penitence known as Lent, which was first organized in Rio de Janeiro in the 1890s. Samba emerged as the soul of Brazil, popular with all classes.

Like Brazilians, Caribbean peoples also mixed African and European influences to produce distinctive cultures, but often in defiance of colonial restrictions. On Trinidad, the British colonial officials, who feared the black majority, passed laws to prohibit African-based musical forms, but they found them difficult to enforce. Two traditions emerged to reflect Afro-Trinidadian identity and defiance of British rule. The first was **calypso**, a song style that often featured lyrics addressing daily life and topical subjects and that eventually became the major popular music in the English-speaking islands of the eastern Caribbean. The second tradition was the pre-Lent Carnival, which, as in Brazil, became a major festival and assumed great social significance for average people while providing a forum for calypso. Calypso songs performed during Carnival often questioned colonial policies. A song in the 1880s protested colonial restrictions on music during Carnival: "Can't beat my drum, In my own native land. Can't have Carnival, In my native land."[22] Informal calypso presentations in makeshift theaters evolved by the 1920s into elaborate, heavily rehearsed shows. Nationalists adopted calypso and carnival in their anticolonial struggle.

The United States in Latin America

Latin Americans faced challenges from the increasingly powerful United States, a nation they both envied and feared, whose citizens and military forces occasionally intervened in Central America and the Caribbean. For example, in 1856 William Walker, an American adventurer financed by influential U.S. businessmen interested in acquiring natural resources and markets, invaded Nicaragua with a well-armed mercenary force of three hundred Americans and temporarily seized the country. Walker proclaimed himself president, and, despite opposition by Central American leaders, the United States granted his government diplomatic recognition. Walker introduced slavery and tried to make English the official language before being forced out in 1857, becoming a hated symbol in Central America of what Latin Americans often called Yankee imperialism.

The Spanish-American War led to U.S. domination in Cuba, which became a U.S. neocolony. The Platt Amendment to the Cuban constitution, imposed by the United States in 1901, integrated the Cuban and U.S. economies and required that the United States Congress approve any treaties negotiated by Cuban leaders. The American military governor summarized the consequences of the Platt Amendment: "There is little

samba A Brazilian popular music and dance.

calypso A song style in Trinidad that often featured lyrics addressing daily life and topical subjects.

or no real independence left to Cuba. She is absolutely in our hands, a practical dependency of the United States."[23] U.S. businessmen soon owned much of Cuba's economy, including railroads, banks, and mills, and the United States acquired a naval base at Guantanamo (gwahn-TAH-nuh-moe) Bay. Later Cuban nationalists blamed Cuba's squalid condition not on the often despotic Cuban governments but on the United States. The Platt Amendment was finally repealed in 1934.

In the early 1900s the United States became more deeply involved in Central America and the Caribbean. To build a canal across Central America linking the Pacific and Atlantic Oceans, the United States helped Panama secede from Colombia in 1903. Now essentially a U.S. protectorate, Panama leased a 10-mile-wide zone across the isthmus in perpetuity to the United States for the canal. Several thousand workers from Panama and various Caribbean islands died in the ten arduous years of construction. In 1914 the Panama Canal, 51-miles long, was completed, one of the great engineering feats of history and a boon to maritime commerce and travel. U.S. and other ships could now sail between the Atlantic and Pacific Oceans safely and conveniently.

Americans also intervened elsewhere. In 1912 the United States overthrew the president of Nicaragua, who was suspected of inviting the British to build a rival canal across his country. But the unrest that followed prompted the United States to send in a military force, which remained until 1933. U.S. soldiers also occupied Haiti (1915–1933) and the Dominican Republic (1916–1924) to quell unrest or maintain friendly governments. These interventions set the stage for a more active U.S. imperial policy in Latin America and the Caribbean.

SECTION SUMMARY

- After gaining independence from Spain, Latin American nations were plagued by instability, undemocratic governments, and socioeconomic inequality along racial lines.
- After a disastrous period as a republic, a brief occupation by the French, and a probusiness dictatorship, a long, violent revolution finally led to political stability in Mexico.
- Latin American economies tended to focus on the export of one or two natural resources, which created instability and made them susceptible to foreign domination.
- The abolition of slavery in Latin America did not greatly improve the economic conditions of former slaves, and millions of immigrants from Europe, India, Japan, and elsewhere flowed into Latin American countries.
- The tango developed in lower-class Buenos Aires, and samba was a result of cultural mixing in Rio de Janiero, while Caribbean calypso was a legacy of resistance to British efforts to stamp out African-based music on Trinidad.
- The United States repeatedly intervened in Latin American affairs, most directly in Cuba, whose diplomatic affairs it dominated for three decades, and Panama, through which it built the Panama Canal.

❖ New Societies in Canada and the Pacific Basin

Why did the foundations for nationhood differ in Canada and Oceania?

The United States became the most powerful and, in this era, most prosperous of the societies founded in the Americas and Oceania by European settlers, but it was not the only one to build a democratic nation and foster growing economies. To the north of the United States, Canada also expanded across the continent to the Pacific and formed a federation of states. During this era Western nations also located and colonized the island societies scattered around the Pacific Basin. Meanwhile, in Australia and New Zealand, Britain established settler colonies, the British immigrants bringing with them their political institutions, ways of earning a living, and cultural traditions, which helped to transform these South Pacific territories.

Making a Canadian Nation

France originally colonized most of what is today eastern Canada, but by 1763 the British had defeated the French forces and gained control of this large region, including the main French colony, Quebec (see Chronology: Canada and the Pacific Basin, 1750–1914). The victorious British now had to forge a stable relationship with 80,000 French-speaking people, most of them in Quebec, who resisted assimilation into British culture and instead maintained their language, culture, and identity. By 1774 the British pragmatically recognized the influential role of the Catholic Church and French civil law in Quebec. Meanwhile, British colonists settled chiefly in the Atlantic coastal region, known today as the Maritimes, as well as west of Quebec in what became Ontario. Although the British governed Quebec and the largely English-speaking regions separately until 1841, relations between British and French Canadians, with different cultures and languages, remained uneasy, causing a British official in the 1830s to conclude that Canada was "two nations warring in the bosom of a single state."[24] The influence of France in North America ended in 1803, when the United States acquired the vast Louisiana territory, including the Mississippi River Basin long coveted by Americans.

Whatever their ethnic backgrounds, Canada's peoples had to deal with the ambitions of the United States, whose leaders hoped that Canada might eventually join the Union. In a U.S.-British treaty in 1783, the United States recognized British control north of the Great Lakes and the Saint Lawrence River. After the American Revolution, many Loyalists, who had supported continued British rule, moved north to Canada, increasing the English-speaking population substantially, especially in what became Ontario. Although Loyalists opposed the United States republic, they nevertheless imported its democratic ideals to Canada, promoting democratic reforms and representative assemblies.

The relations between the United States and British-ruled Canada remained tense for years. Americans feared that their northern neighbors were aiding the Native Americans who resisted U.S. expansion in the Ohio region. For example, Americans suspected that, from their Canada base, the British supported the powerful and charismatic Shawnee chief Tecumseh (teh-CUM-sah) (1768–1813), who gathered a large alliance of tribes to drive the white settlers out of Ohio and reinvigorate Indian ways. Tecumseh's forces repeatedly fought the United States Army. When conflict between the United States and Britain led to the War of 1812, Tecumseh served with the British. During the war Americans repeatedly invaded Canada with hopes of annexing the territory but were repulsed. The war ended U.S. attempts to expand north and also stimulated a sense of distinctiveness among Canadians, laying the seeds for a national identity separate from the United States and Britain. In 1846 another treaty fixed the U.S.-Canada boundary in the west.

Canadians could now turn to building a diverse society and democratic nation in peace while working to modify British control. Canada welcomed 800,000 British immigrants between 1815 and 1850, many of whom settled in Ontario. Growing popular sentiment prompted the British to consider reforms that eventually brought a unified Canada and an elected national parliament, and British influence over the Canadian government waned. But Canadians rejected complete

CHRONOLOGY

Canada and the Pacific Basin, 1750–1914

1763	British defeat of French forces in Canada
1774	British recognition of French culture and laws in Quebec
1770s	Cook expeditions to Polynesia, New Zealand, and Australia
1788	First British penal colony in Australia
1792	First British settlers in New Zealand
1812–1814	U.S.-British War of 1812
1840s–1900s	Western colonization of Pacific islands
1850	Treaty of Waitangi
1851	Discovery of gold in Australia
1867	Canadian Confederation
1885	Canadian transcontinental railroad
1901	Formation of Australian Commonwealth
1907	New Zealand self-government

Along the Canadian Pacific Railroad During the late nineteenth century both native-born Canadians and immigrants from many lands—British, Dutch, Germans, Poles, Russians, Scandinavians—followed the Canadian Pacific Railroad to settle the newly opened lands of the midwestern prairies and western mountains. Some people set up temporary tent villages by railroad stops before taking up farming, mining, logging, trade, or fishing. (Library and Archives Canada, #PA 38667)

independence in favor of self-rule within the British Empire as a strategy to help Canada maintain stability, settle the west, foster economic development, and resist U.S. power. In 1858 Canadians built a national capital at Ottawa, safely located well north of the U.S. border along the Ontario-Quebec boundary. In 1867 leaders from Ontario, Quebec, and New Brunswick and Nova Scotia in the Maritimes negotiated a Canadian Confederation that was largely independent of Britain in domestic affairs and that guaranteed strong provincial rights and preservation of the French language wherever it was spoken. Under this arrangement Canada became a **dominion**, a country having autonomy but owing allegiance to the British crown.

The confederation soon faced new challenges. Expansion of white settlement and political power to the west fired resentment among Indians and people of mixed descent, the French-speaking Metis (may-TEES), which sometimes led to violence. The combative Metis leader, Louis Riel (ree-EL) (1844–1885), who had once studied to be a Catholic priest, led two rebellions before being executed for treason, thus becoming a martyr to those who opposed domination by English Canadians. Eventually, however, Manitoba and British Columbia joined the confederation and the federal government promised to build a transcontinental railroad. Canada's first prime minister and Riel's chief opponent, Scottish-born John MacDonald (g. 1867–1873, 1878–1891), hoped the railroad would transform the 4 million Canadians into a unified nation. Crossing over 2,000 miles of forests, prairies, and high mountains, the railroad was completed in 1885. The government negotiated treaties with Native Americans, allocating reservations to many of them. Although they faced some resistance from Indians, white settlers increasingly moved to the

western provinces, and towns sprung up along the railroad. By 1905 Canada included all the present provinces except Newfoundland.

The Canadian economy and ethnic structure were transformed between the 1860s and 1914. Beaver fur and fish had been the major exports of Canada since the 1600s, but now wheat grown in the Great Plains surpassed fur as the major export. Gold strikes in the Yukon and the offering of free land in western Canada attracted immigrants from many lands, including the United States. From 1896 until 1911 over 2 million British and other European immigrants arrived, often settling in the west, where many built sod houses and grew wheat. Immigrants from eastern and southern Europe as well as newcomers from China and Japan enriched the ethnic mosaic. Increasingly critical of British imperialism in the world, by 1911 Canadians took control of their own foreign affairs and diplomacy. Over the next several decades Canada fostered increased industrialization and established warmer relations with the United States while maintaining the British monarch as symbolic head of state.

Exploration and Colonization of the Pacific Islands

The peoples who lived on the small mountainous islands and flat atolls scattered across thousands of miles in the vast Pacific Ocean Basin were the last to experience European expansion, but when it came, the impact was significant. The Spanish colonized Guam, in the Marianas, in 1663 but otherwise there had been little European contact with Pacific islanders during the Early Modern Era. By the mid-1700s the British and French had begun a race to explore what they considered the last frontier, the Pacific Ocean. Eventually these two countries, along with Spain, Germany, Russia, and the United States, had colonized all the inhabited islands.

dominion A country having autonomy but owing allegiance to the British crown.

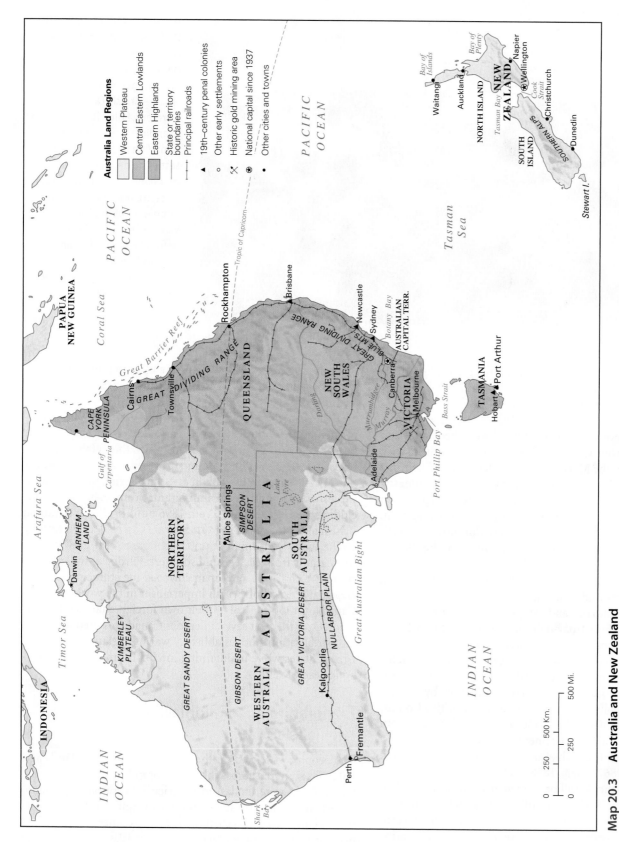

Map 20.3   Australia and New Zealand
The British colonized and gradually settled Australia and New Zealand between the late 1700s and 1914.
In 1901 the six Australian colonies became a federation, with a capital eventually built in Canberra.

The English captain James Cook (1728–1779), the self-made son of an agricultural laborer, led some of the most extensive explorations, greatly aided by the learned Polynesian high priest, Tupaia (ca. 1725–1771). Cook reached the eastern Polynesian island of Tahiti in 1769, where he recruited Tupaia, who came from a family that had been sailing around Polynesia for generations and whose skills as a navigator and speaker of several Polynesian languages greatly aided the expedition. A scientist with Cook concluded that Tupaia knew more of Polynesia's geography, produce, religion, laws, and customs than anyone else. Tupaia drew up the charts that helped Cook map Polynesia, including New Zealand, and the coast of Australia, but then died on Java of fever. Cook made two more expeditions to the Pacific in the 1770s; after becoming the first known person to circumnavigate Antarctica, he located the Hawaiian Islands in 1778 and then sailed to Alaska. His early reports created an image of the South Sea islands as paradise, a "Garden of Eden" with amiable people, an image that still survives in popular culture, but Cook himself was killed in Hawaii after antagonizing local leaders, and some explorers who encountered hostility developed negative views of the Pacific islanders.

European explorations eventually led to economic exploitation and Christian missionary activity. In the late 1700s the Russians established a foothold in Alaska and the Aleutian Islands as a base for hunting seals and sea otters for their fur. By the 1850s both animals had been hunted to near extinction, and thousands of Aleuts had died from exposure to European diseases. Deep-sea whaling lasted longer, attracting Western sailors, especially British and Americans, as well as Polynesians in search of sperm whales. Western traders also visited the Pacific islands, seeking resources such as sandalwood, greatly valued in Asia for building furniture. It took only ten years to cut and export all of Fiji's sandalwood. Meanwhile, Protestant and Catholic missionaries went to the islands seeking converts, with varied results. The Samoans welcomed the missionaries, often adopting Christianity. Fijians initially rejected missionaries but later, desiring trade with the West, tolerated them. Fijian converts often pragmatically mixed Christianity with their own traditions. One chief, Ratu Tui Levuka, reportedly said that his right hand was Methodist, his left hand Catholic, and his body heathen. Some peoples were hostile to outside influences. For instance, the New Hebrides people killed the first missionaries who reached the islands.

Traders and missionaries opened the way for colonization, and between the 1840s and 1900 Western powers colonized all of the Pacific societies. Between the 1840s and 1870s the French gained domination over many island chains, such as the Society Islands, which included Tahiti, and the Marquesas, while the British colonized various others, among them the Fijian archipelago. By 1898 the Germans and Americans had divided up Samoa, and the British imposed a protectorate over the kingdom of Tonga. By 1900 the Germans had acquired most of Micronesia, and Britain and France controlled much of Melanesia. Hawaii's experiences with the West mirrored those of other Pacific societies. Hawaii was home to some 150,000 Polynesians in 1778. By 1875 the smallpox, measles, and venereal diseases introduced by Western visitors and settlers had reduced it to 50,000. The Western arrivals gradually gained economic power and political influence, but Hawaii remained a Polynesian kingdom until 1893, when American settlers seized control.

The Rise of Australia and New Zealand

The British colonized the continent they named Australia and the two large islands they called New Zealand, landmasses in the western Pacific whose human histories long predated the arrival of Europeans (see Map 20.3 and Chapter 9). European settlement in Australia began when the British began transporting convicts, often Irish, from overcrowded British jails to a penal colony they founded at Botany Bay on the southeast coast in 1788. Eventually more penal colonies were founded in fertile southeastern and southwestern Australia. Settlements formed around the fine harbor at Sydney, just north of Botany Bay, and eventually former convicts and discharged soldiers began settling the land. Agriculture, ranching, and mining became the basis for the modern economy. The British divided the continent into six colonies, with New South Wales and Victoria in the southeast having the largest populations.

British colonization came at the expense of the Aborigines, peoples completely different from the Pacific islanders in language, culture, and ways of life. The Aborigines' ancestors had lived on the continent for thousands of years. Divided into hundreds of scattered tribes and numbering somewhere between 500,000 and 3 million in 1750, Aborigines lived chiefly by fishing and nomadic hunting and gathering. The European settlers considered the Aborigines to be an inferior people with a primitive way of life. Adding to these negative feelings, many Aborigines resisted encroachments on their land by raiding British settlements. In the early 1800s the British settlers killed as many as 20,000 Aborigines. As was the case for Native Americans and Pacific islanders, diseases brought by Europeans such as smallpox and influenza were responsible for killing the majority of the Aboriginal population. By 1875 only 150,000 Aborigines remained, and many were further destabilized by having their land forcibly settled by white newcomers. Eventually, to survive, many Aborigines had little choice but to move to cities, where they faced unfamiliar ways of life, or to work on European cattle and sheep ranches. However, large numbers remained on tribal reservations, mostly in the interior and along the northern coast, where they maintained many of their traditions and beliefs.

Creating a common Australian identity and nationhood took over a century. Throughout the 1800s Europeans clung to the coastal regions suitable for farming and ranching and avoided the desert interior, which to them was inhospitable because, unlike the Aborigines, they lacked the skills to exploit it. The discovery of gold in southeastern Australia in 1851 attracted settlers from Europe, and by the 1860s over a million whites lived in Australia. Gold mining also prompted Chinese and other Asians to seek their fortunes in Australia, creating resentments among the Europeans. In 1899 one European leader charged that Asians "will soon be eating the heart's blood out of the white population."[25] Violence between Europeans and Asians, especially in the mining camps, led to laws restricting Asian immigration, which ended only in the later twentieth century. Tensions between Europeans, Asians, and Aborigines were not the only social challenge, however. White women struggled for influence in the male-dominated Australian society. By the 1880s white women's movements were pressing for moral reform and suffrage, and white women gained the right to vote in 1902, but women still enjoyed little political power at the local or national level. Aborigines only gained the right to vote in 1962.

Gradually Australia became a nation. By 1890 Britain had turned all six of its Australian colonies into self-governing states (see Map 20.3). Worried that disunity threatened their long-term security, the states formed the Commonwealth of Australia in 1901, with the British monarch remaining symbolic head of state. Like Canada, Australia became a self-governing, democratic dominion and maintained close political links with Britain, but it gradually formed its own identity. A transcontinental railroad system, completed in 1917, connected the vast country. Even with the railroad, however, the white population of the interior remained small; the majority of the 4 million Australians lived in or near five coastal cities. In 1908 Canberra, midway between the two largest cities, Sydney and Melbourne, became the nation's capital. Distance from European supplies fostered some local manufacturing, including steel production, and white Australians enjoyed prosperity.

The British also colonized the two large mountainous islands of New Zealand, 1,200 miles east of Australia, at the expense of the Polynesian Maori people. The Maori had lived on the islands, which they called Aotearoa, for a millennium, gradually dividing into sometimes warring tribes headed by chiefs and surviving by hunting, fishing, and horticulture. In 1792, when the first British settlers arrived, the Maori numbered around 100,000. Some Maori took advantage of the British newcomers for their own purposes. For example, one Maori chief, Hongi Hika (ca. 1772–1828), befriended a Protestant missionary, who took him to England. Returning to New Zealand with guns, Hongi and his warriors raided rival tribes, who soon began acquiring their own firearms from the British. Maori intertribal warfare became more deadly, killing many thousands by 1850, and made it harder for the rival tribes to cooperate against the British.

As more British settlers came, territorial disputes with the Maori increased. The Treaty of Waitangi in 1850 between the British and five hundred Maori chiefs seemingly confirmed the Maori's right to their land while acknowledging British sovereignty. But the Maori were unaware that the English-language and Maori-language versions of the treaty differed. Maori chiefs thought they still had authority over their lands and people, while the British asserted the treaty gave them political and legal power. Disagreement over the treaty provisions and the occupation of more Maori land by British settlers led to a series of wars that ended only in the 1870s and resulted in an even sharper decline in the Maori population. The British skillfully exploited Maori tribal rivalries and had the military advantage of heavy artillery and armored steamships. Eventually Maori resistance subsided, leading to an 1881 peace agreement that accorded Maori control over some districts.

Gradually the European identity in New Zealand grew stronger. The discovery of gold in 1861 stimulated European immigration, mostly from Britain, so that by 1881 the Maori accounted for only 10 percent of the half-million population. Immigrants were attracted by higher living standards than they enjoyed in Europe, to a colonial economy based on farming and sheep raising, and to a growing government welfare system. New Zealand prospered after 1882, when steamships acquired refrigerated holds to carry lamb and dairy products from the islands to Europe. A parliamentary government including Maori representatives was formed in 1852, and by 1893 both men and women of all communities enjoyed universal suffrage. New Zealand gained self-government as a British dominion in 1907, but it continued a close alliance with Britain as a guarantee of security and proudly remained an outpost of the British Empire well into the twentieth century.

SECTION SUMMARY

- Canada had to contend with the challenge of forming a unified country that included French and English speakers, as well as with the threat of the neighboring United States.

- Over time, Canada became increasingly independent of Britain and stretched across the continent, and wheat eventually surpassed beaver fur as the country's top export.

- Western nations, starting with Britain and France but later including Russia, the United States, and Germany, colonized the Pacific islands and exploited their natural resources.

- Starting as penal colonies, British settlements in Australia expanded and pushed the native Aborigines off their land and then clashed with Asians who came to mine gold.

- British colonizers of New Zealand clashed repeatedly with the native Maori, ultimately deceiving them into signing away the rights to their land in the Treaty of Waitangi, which led to a series of wars that ended only in the late nineteenth century.

Online Study Center　ACE the Test

◆ Chapter Summary

During the Modern Era European societies and cultures were reshaped by industrialization, revolutions, and new ideologies such as nationalism and socialism. Populations grew and millions of people migrated within Europe or emigrated to the Americas and Oceania. More people lived in cities, where social problems and poverty increased. The industrial system influenced the relations between men and women, as family life changed and European women lost status, fostering feminist movements. Reacting to political and social turbulence, some European thinkers abandoned Enlightenment ideas, and writers and artists addressed the explosive forces around them with new styles. The pace of scientific and technological innovation also increased.

Across the Atlantic, the new democratic republic in the United States gradually became a regional and then world power with a diversified economy and distinctive culture. The United States expanded westward toward the Pacific, eventually incorporating large sections of North America, some of it acquired after war with Mexico. As Americans moved west and settled the frontier, they subdued Native Americans and fostered new social patterns. The Civil War temporarily divided the nation and abolished slavery. In the aftermath, economic growth and industrialization spurred massive immigration from Europe and social movements to improve the lives of workers and women. Industrial capitalism also motivated Americans to increase their influence in the wider world, eventually leading to the Spanish-American War. The U.S. victory in that conflict made the United States a world power.

Other new nations arose in the Americas and Oceania during the Modern Era. By the 1820s most of Latin America had gained independence from Spain and Portugal, but the new republics remained authoritarian and fostered little economic or social change. Latin American and Caribbean economies remained monocultures geared to the export of raw materials and under foreign domination. While millions of European immigrants arrived, most blacks and Indians remained poor. Social inequalities produced tensions and, in Mexico, a revolution. Latin American and Caribbean societies created unique cultures that reflected the mix of peoples from around the world. The United States also played an increasing role in the region, fostering resentments that have lingered into the present. Despite a division between French and English speakers, Canada expanded to the Pacific and became a nation with a self-governing democracy. Meanwhile European powers colonized the Pacific islands. Europeans settled in Australia and New Zealand and, like Canadians, elected to remain tied to Britain even while developing their own democratic nations.

Online Study Center **Improve Your Grade** Flashcards

Key Terms

feminism	protectionism	gauchos
suffragettes	Manifest Destiny	samba
romanticism	sphere of interest	calypso
modernism	caudillos	dominion
impressionism		

Suggested Reading

Books

Christensen, Carol and Thomas. *The U.S.-Mexican War*. San Francisco: Bay Books, 1998. Well-illustrated survey for the general public.

Costa, Emilia Viotti da. *The Brazilian Empire: Myths and Histories.* Chicago: The Dorsey Press, 1985. A study of the nineteenth century by a Brazilian historian.

Dubofsky, Melvyn. *Industrialization and the American Worker, 1865–1920.* 3rd ed. Wheeling, Ill.: Harlan Davidson, 1996. A good summary of the Industrial Revolution and its impact.

Fischer, Steven R. *A History of the Pacific Islands.* New York: Palgrave, 2002. A recent overview including New Zealand.

Foner, Eric. *The Story of American Freedom.* New York: W. W. Norton, 1998. A provocative examination of how Americans have pursued the dream of a free society.

Keen, Benjamin, and Keith Haynes. *A History of Latin America.* 7th ed. Boston: Houghton Mifflin, 2004. A good general survey.

Knight, Alan. *The Mexican Revolution.* Cambridge: Cambridge University Press, 1986. A readable synthesis of this major uprising.

Kraut, Alan M. *The Huddled Masses: The Immigrant in American Society, 1840–1921,* 2nd ed. Wheeling, I.L.: Harlan Davidson, 2001. Brief survey.

Longley, Lester D. *The Americas in the Modern Age.* New Haven: Yale University Press, 2004. Relates recent relationships to developments around the hemisphere since the mid-1800s.

Nile, Richard, and Christian Clerk. *Cultural Atlas of Australia, New Zealand, and the South Pacific.* New York: Facts on File, 1996. A comprehensive and readable overview of history and cultures.

Paterson, Thomas G. et al. *American Foreign Relations: A History.* 6th ed. Boston: Houghton Mifflin, 2005. A fine survey.

Riendeau, Roger E. *A Brief History of Canada.* Toronto: Fitzhenry and Whiteside, 2000. A short work covering 400 years of Canadian development.

Smith, Bonnie G. *Changing Lives: Women in European History Since 1700.* Lexington, Mass.: D.C. Heath, 1989. A comprehensive study of women's lives and their roles in public life.

Stearns, Peter N., and Herrick Chapman. *European Society in Upheaval: Social History Since 1750.* 3rd ed. New York: St. Martin's, 1991. A readable survey with lively material.

Stephanson, Anders. *Manifest Destiny: American Expansion and the Empire of Right.* New York: Hill and Wang, 1995. A readable brief analysis of this important American doctrine and its consequences.

Websites

WWW-VL: History: United States (http://vlib.iue.it/history/USA/). A virtual library that contains links to hundreds of sites.

Internet Resources for Latin America (http://lib.nmsu.edu/subject/bord/laguia/). An outstanding site with links to many resources.

Latin American Resources (http://www.oberlin.edu/faculty/svolk/latinam/htm). An excellent collection of resources and links on history, politics, and culture.

Modern History Sourcebook (http://www.fordham.edu/halsall/mod/modsbook.html). A very extensive online collection of historical documents and secondary materials.

The World of 1898: The Spanish-American War (http://www.loc.gov/rr/hispanic/1898). A Library of Congress site that provides excellent documents and resources.

CHAPTER **21**

Africa, the Middle East, and Imperialism, 1750–1914

Online Study Center

This icon will direct you to interactive activities and study materials on the website: college.hmco.com/pic/lockard1e

Tomb of Muhammad Ahmad in Khartoum Muhammad Ahmad ibn 'Abd Allah, known to history as the Mahdi ("Divinely Guided One"), used Islamic appeals to recruit a large army and lead opposition to the joint British and Egyptian rule in Sudan. He died soon after routing the British forces in 1885, but his tomb remains a popular place of pilgrimage and a symbol of Muslim resistance to Western power. (Tim Beddow/Eye Ubiquitous)

The power of these Europeans has advanced to a shocking degree and has manifested itself in an unparalleled manner. Indeed, we are on the brink of a time of [complete] corruption. As for knowing what tomorrow holds, I am blind.

MOROCCAN HISTORIAN AHMAD IBN KHALID AL-NASRI, 1860s[1]

Fresh from his victories in Italy and Austria, in 1798 the French general Napoleon Bonaparte vowed to add his name to the list of illustrious European conquerors who had achieved glory and riches before him in the Middle East, the region encompassing North Africa and western Asia. In the fourth century B.C.E. Alexander the Great had conquered Egypt and Persia, and later Roman and Byzantine emperors had controlled the eastern Mediterranean and the lucrative trade routes that passed through it. Medieval Christian crusaders had also established temporary footholds in western Asia. A student of history, Bonaparte admired the earlier military commanders and coveted the rich lands they had gained. In his mind, Europe was a mere "molehill," hardly a match for his talents when the rich, Muslim-dominated lands of the Middle East beckoned. First he planned to invade Egypt, and then he intended to reduce the Ottoman Turks and Persians to French vassals. Eventually he hoped to reach India and found a new religion.

With an armada of four hundred ships carrying 50,000 soldiers, Bonaparte quickly established control over northern Egypt. He also took with him some five hundred French scholars to gather valuable information on Egyptian history, society, language, and environment. Near a town in the Nile River Delta they discovered the Rosetta stone, a tablet made in 196 B.C.E. that contained writings in several languages. Since one of those languages was Greek, scholars for the first time could translate ancient Egyptian hieroglyphics into Western languages. This development sparked the beginning of Egyptology as a field of study.

Bonaparte acted like a Muslim ruler and even hinted that he might embrace Islam. In a bid for popular support, the French general confidently announced: "People of Egypt, I come to restore your rights; I respect God, His Prophet and the Quran. We are friends of all true Muslims. Happiness to the People!"[2] He also claimed to have liberated the people from Egypt's repressive Mamluk (MAM-look) rulers, and he organized representative councils to promote self-government. Indeed, the Mamluks were widely disliked despots, but Bonaparte's policies soon alienated Egyptians, who came to see the French as even worse. Conquest soon proved a burden. The French army, small and ill-equipped, withered in the desert heat. An attempt to conquer Syria having failed, Bonaparte left

629

for Paris in 1799, becoming just another example of a western society unsuccessfully attempting to control Muslim peoples.

Although unsuccessful, the French invasion of Egypt provided a harbinger of more invasions of the kind feared by the Moroccan historian Ahmad ibn Khalid al-Nasri, through which Europe would extend its domination in the world. Although the French were soon chased away, Bonaparte's expedition was a turning point in Western relations with sub-Saharan Africa and the Middle East, the cutting edge of a European thrust that also overwhelmed India, Southeast Asia, and the Pacific islands. The Industrial Revolution and capitalism in Europe had greatly accelerated Europe's need for natural resources that could be processed into industrial and commercial products, as well as for new markets to consume these goods. These economic factors combined with European political rivalries and a powerful industrial and military technology to launch a ruthless policy of incorporating territories in sub-Saharan Africa and the Middle East.

For sub-Saharan Africans and the Arabs and Berbers of North Africa, the most common form of Western imperialism was colonialism, political control of another country. This colonialism generally lasted for only a century or less, during which time sub-Saharan and North Africans often resisted Western power. Some scholars argue that this era was too short to permanently transform societies with rich histories and traditions. Yet the power of Western governments, technologies, and ideas reshaped African societies and their economies, cultures, and political systems. Colonialism also linked these regions more closely to a European-dominated world economy. Western Asian societies experienced less disruption than the peoples of Africa, but the Ottomans lost their North African and European territories, and the Ottoman and Persian states struggled to meet the challenges posed by increased European power.

FOCUS QUESTIONS

1. How did various Western nations obtain colonies in sub-Saharan Africa?
2. How did white supremacy shape South Africa?
3. What were some of the major consequences of colonialism in Africa?
4. What political and economic impact did Europe have on the Middle East?
5. How did Middle Eastern thought and culture respond to the Western challenge?

◆ The Colonization of Sub-Saharan Africa

How did various Western nations obtain colonies in sub-Saharan Africa?

During the nineteenth century various Western nations colonized most of sub-Saharan Africa. Although Europeans had established a few small, scattered outposts in West Africa and colonized coastal regions of Angola, Mozambique, and South Africa in the sixteenth and seventeenth centuries, the full-blown quest for colonies began only with the end of the trans-Atlantic slave trade and the spread of the Industrial Revolution in Europe in the mid-1800s. At this time European imperial ambitions fostered what a British newspaper called the "scramble for Africa," during which the European powers divided up the African continent among themselves, often against fierce resistance, and commenced the full-scale economic penetration of Africa. By 1914, when World War I began, the colonization process was complete.

C H R O N O L O G Y

	Sub-Saharan Africa	The Middle East
1800		**1805–1848** Rule of Muhammad Ali in Egypt
		1840 French colonization of Algeria
1850	**1870** Ending of trans-Atlantic slave trade	**1859–1869** Building of Suez Canal
	1874–1901 British-Ashante wars	**1882** British colonization of Egypt
	1884–1885 Berlin Conference on colonialism	
	1899–1902 Boer War	

The End of the Slave Trade

For over three centuries the trans-Atlantic slave trade (1520–1870) dominated relations between Africa, Europe, and the Americas, but growing opposition in all three regions eventually brought it to an end. Humanitarian as well as economic concerns spurred the abolition movement. In the West, especially in Britain, abolitionists hoped to open Africa to both Christian missionaries and free trade in commodities other than slaves. Many abolitionists were prompted largely by religious and moral outrage at slavery, and Protestant churches were active in the movement. Other abolitionists were influenced by the Enlightenment vision of human equality. One sympathizer wrote that people "are not objects. Everyone has his rights, property, dignity. Africa will have its day."[3]

Africans and African Americans also struggled against slavery. For example, Olaudah Equiano (oh-LAU-duh ay-kwee-AHN-oh) (1745–1797), an Igbo captured by slave raiders in Nigeria at the age of ten and taken to Barbados and then Virginia, eventually purchased his freedom and then actively campaigned in Europe for abolition. Equiano published a best-selling book in the 1780s that chronicled his own horrific experiences as he was shifted from owner to owner. In this book he pointed out the contradiction in self-proclaimed devout Christians mistreating and devaluing the humanity of their slaves. Slave revolts in the Americas, including the successful revolution in Haiti (see Chapter 19), as well as attempts by slaves to seize control of slave ships conveying them to the Americas, indicated the willingness of many slaves to risk their lives for freedom and also forced many Europeans to rethink their views on slavery. The British abolitionist movement was spurred by the tragic experience of Henry Williams, a slave who was badly beaten in Jamaica in 1829 for trying to assert his equality by attending a white church on the island. American and European opposition to slavery was also fueled by the widely read poetry and Christian writings of Phyllis Wheatley (ca. 1753–1785), a Senegal-born slave in Boston who learned Latin and Greek and eventually won her freedom. Her published writings, and those of others, undermined the notion widespread among whites that people of African ancestry were incapable of sophisticated thought.

Another force working against slavery was the Industrial Revolution, which made slavery uneconomical. Overseas markets for factory-made goods became more desirable than cheap labor for plantations. Furthermore, so many colonies produced sugar that the market was flooded and the price fell, making the plantations less profitable at the same time that African states were charging more to provide slaves. By 1800 British bankers could make more money investing in manufacturing than in plantations and the slave trade.

As a result of this combination of moral and economic factors, the slave trade from Africa to the Americas and the slavery era came to an end in the Atlantic world in the nineteenth century. The slave trade was first outlawed in Denmark in 1804, then in Britain in 1807, and then in all British-controlled territories, including their plantation-rich Caribbean colonies, in 1833 (see Chronology: Sub-Saharan Africa, 1750–1914). The British government declared war on the slave traders, intercepting slave ships in the Atlantic and returning the slaves to Africa. Many Latin American nations and Haiti outlawed slavery in the early 1800s, forcing planters to shift to free labor. By 1842 most European and American countries had made it illegal to transport slaves across the Atlantic, although some illicit trafficking continued until 1870. The Civil War ended slavery in the United States in 1865, and in the later 1880s Brazil and Cuba also finally outlawed slavery.

The East African trade that sent slaves to the Middle East and the Indian Ocean islands, run chiefly by Arabs from the eastern Arabian state of Oman, continued longer than the trans-Atlantic trade. In 1835 the Omani leader, Sayyid Sa'id (SIGH-id SIGH-eed) (r. 1806–1856), moved his capital to Zanzibar, an island just off the coast of modern Tanzania, and built a commercial empire that flourished for forty years procuring and shipping ivory to India, China, and Europe and shipping slaves to India, the Persian Gulf, and South Arabia. During the 1860s East African ports such as Zanzibar exported some 70,000 slaves a year. The Omanis also profited from growing Indonesian cloves on slave plantations on Zanzibar.

To obtain slaves and ivory, Omani and Swahili merchants opened or expanded overland trade routes through Tanzania into the eastern Congo River Basin. In 1873 the British convinced the Zanzibar sultan to close the island's slave market, and as compensation Britain imported vast amounts of ivory, which the British used for making piano keys, billiard balls, and cutlery handles. While fewer slaves were now exported from the coast, slavers still raided African villages to acquire the labor needed

CHRONOLOGY

Sub-Saharan Africa, 1750–1914

1804	Launching of Fulani jihads by Uthman dan Fodio
1804	Abolition of slave trade by Denmark
1806	British seizure of Cape region from Dutch
1807–1833	Abolition of slave trade in Britain and its territories
1816	Beginning of Shaka's Zulu Empire
1838	Great Trek by South African Boers
1842	Ending of trans-Atlantic slave trade by most European nations
1847	First American freed slave settlement in Liberia
1874–1901	British-Ashante wars
1878	Belgian colonization in Congo
1884–1885	Berlin Conference
1886	Discovery of gold in South Africa
1898	French defeat of Samory Toure
1899–1902	Boer (South African) War
1905	Maji Maji Rebellion in Tanganyika
1912	Founding of African National Congress in South Africa

to carry the huge ivory tusks to the coast for export, often in well-armed caravans of up to a thousand people. The British gained control of Zanzibar in 1890, but some slave trading continued on a modest scale in parts of East and Central Africa until the early 1900s.

Freed Slaves, Adventurers, and Traders

Between the later 1700s and later 1800s the diminishing importance and then ending of the trans-Atlantic slave trade gradually changed the relationship between Africans and Europeans, fostering several new African societies, exploration of Africa by Western adventurers, and increased commerce between Europeans and Africans. The Western impact on Africa had been uneven during the slave trade, which had integrated Africa into the world economy chiefly as a supplier of human beings. While it lasted, the slave trade had impeded most other trade between Europeans and Africans. The willingness of some African states to sell slaves for transport to the Americas also reduced the European appetite for territorial con-

quest to obtain this resource. But, as the demand for slaves waned, Europeans became more interested in acquiring African agricultural and mineral resources.

New African Societies Even before slavery was abolished in the Americas, freed slaves there who chose, or were pressured, to return to Africa from the Americas had established several West African states and port cities. The black founders of these states, and the whites who helped finance them, had both humanitarian aims and commercial goals, wanting to give the freed slaves opportunities to run their own lives while also setting up new centers of Western trade. Thousands of freed slaves also settled in coastal towns of the Gold Coast (modern Ghana), Nigeria, and Dahomey, where some became merchants engaged in trade with the Americas.

The two largest settlements of freed slaves emerged in Sierra Leone and Liberia. Spurred by abolitionists such as Olaudah Equiano, in 1787 the British settled four hundred former slaves around the fort at Freetown, which became the core of their colony of Sierra Leone. Over the next few decades the British shipped more former slaves to Freetown. Some came from the West Indian colonies, while others came from British-ruled Canada, where they had settled to escape retaliation for supporting the Loyalist cause during the American Revolution. Freed slaves from the United States were first shipped to Liberia in 1847, and they were joined by others after the Civil War. Although Liberia remained an independent state governed by the descendants of former slaves, its economy was dominated by U.S.-owned rubber plantations. In both Sierra Leone and Liberia, the local Africans often resented the freed slave settlers from the Americas, who were mostly English-speaking Christians, because they occupied valuable land, often dominated commerce, and held political power. In recent decades conflicts between the two groups have torn apart both countries.

Both Sierra Leone and Liberia produced reformers, such as West Indian-born Edward Blyden (1832–1912), one of the first African nationalists. Denied admission to universities in the United States because he was black, he emigrated to Liberia. Blyden believed that, given the racism in the Americas and Europe, people of African ancestry could realize their potential only in Africa. But he encouraged Africans to blend their traditions, such as the emphasis on the community rather than the individual, with Western ideas, such as Christianity and science.

Explorations and Encounters The decline of the trans-Atlantic slave trade, which had caused turmoil and made travel dangerous in parts of Africa, also made Africa more accessible to Western explorers. Europeans wanted to discover whether the great African rivers such as the Nile and the Niger were navigable for commercial purposes. The Scottish explorer Mungo Park (1771–1806), a doctor for an English trading company in West Africa who traveled along the Niger, hoped to open to British "ambition and industry new sources of wealth, and new channels of commerce."[4] Adventurers were obsessed with finding the source of Africa's greatest river, the Nile, and they finally located Lake Victoria in 1860. The most famous explorer, David Livingstone (1813–1873), a Scottish cotton mill worker turned medical missionary, spent over two decades traveling in eastern Africa, where he collected information and opened the region to Christian missionary activity and trade with the West.

Park, Livingstone, and other European adventurers claimed to have "discovered" inland African societies and geographical features, but these European explorers discovered little that Africans and Arabs did not already know, and they usually followed long established trading routes and used local guides. The ethnocentric stereotype of intrepid white explorers struggling in hardship through virgin territories is a myth, but it shaped Western views. Explorers publicized their findings and spread the notion of "Darkest Africa," which was seen as awaiting salvation by Christian missionaries and Western traders.

With Africa more open in the 1800s, European traders began to obtain various raw materials needed by the West, such as peanuts, palm oil, gold, timber, and cotton. In pursuing this goal they had to contend with dynamic West African merchants who, with the end of the slave trade, had set up cash crop plantations, many of which grew the trees that produced palm oil, the main lubricant for industrial machinery in Europe before the development of petroleum. For example, the Efik (EF-ik) and Ijo (EE-joe) merchants of coastal Nigeria, who had been active slave traders, now prospered from providing palm oil. To avoid these middlemen, British traders traveled up Nigeria's rivers to buy palm oil directly from the producers, especially the Igbo (EE-boh) people. With superior financial resources and the support of their governments, European companies eventually gained the upper hand over West African merchants, undermining states that were reluctant to grant trade concessions to Europeans and outcompeting their African rivals. As a result, by 1890 in the trading port of Lagos, once a center of African commerce, only one rich African merchant was still able to compete with British merchants.

African Muslim Warrior While Western pressure on coastal societies increased, several Muslim peoples expanded their influence in the West African interior. Some military forces, having acquired Western arms in exchange for slaves and gold, conquered regional empires that flourished for a century or more. [From John H. Hanson, *Migration, Jihad, and Muslim Authority in West Africa* (Bloomington and Indianapolis: Indiana University Press)]

Islamic Resurgence

Some major developments within Africa in this era derived largely from forces within African societies rather than from relations with the West. Among these forces were tensions within the Islamic societies of the Sudan that fostered militancy and political expansion. The most notable example, the Fulani jihad (holy war), was part of a larger religious ferment in West Africa that had begun in the Intermediate Era when expanding Islam encountered African traditions. Many West Africans had embraced Islam, but they also often blended the religion with their own customs and sometimes animist beliefs. Conflicts between those who wanted to purge Islamic practice of pre-Islamic customs and those who mixed Muslim and African traditions broke out sporadically in parts of West Africa in the seventeenth and eighteenth centuries. Often these conflicts involved the Fulani, a pastoral and trading people who lived in communities scattered across the western and

central Sudan from Senegal east to Chad. Some Fulani were devout Muslims, some nominal Muslims, and some animists.

By the 1790s the religious conflicts had spread to the Fulani in the prosperous Hausa states of northern Nigeria. One of these Fulani, Uthman dan Fodio (AHTH-mun dahn FOH-dee-oh) (1754–1817), a respected Muslim scholar and ardent follower of Sufi mysticism, criticized the tolerant attitude of many Hausa rulers toward religion, called for the conversion of non-Muslim Fulani, and proclaimed the goal of making Islam and the Quran central to Sudanic life. His magnetic personality and Islamic zeal soon attracted a Fulani and Hausa following. A follower said: "people trusted him. He spread knowledge and dispelled perplexity."[5] Uthman's attacks on high taxes and social injustice, and his promise to build a government that would spread Islam and purify it of animist beliefs, alarmed Hausa rulers, who feared the unrest he was causing and tried to restrict his activities. After an attempt was made on his life, Uthman mobilized his followers and launched a jihad in 1804. After conquering the Hausa states and then nearby territories, he created the Sokoto (SOH-kuh-toh) Caliphate, based in the city of Sokoto, and ruled much of what is today northern Nigeria. Uthman divided his empire into small, Fulani-led states led by governors, known as *emirs*, who were subordinate to Sokoto.

Uthman's jihad, and the vision of a purified Islam he offered, sparked others to take up his cause, and during the early 1800s several other jihadist states, often led by Fulani religious scholars turned state builders, formed in the Sudan. The Islamic revival sparked by the jihads, which continued into the 1880s, allowed a more orthodox Islam to spread widely. As a result, just as Western influence was increasing in some parts of Africa, the Sudan was becoming even more Islamic. But by the later 1800s, as leaders entrenched their powers and forgot Uthman's reformist vision, the Fulani states declined and Sokoto's power waned. A Hausa poet complained that the Fulani rulers forcibly seized possessions from the peasants and left them with nothing except the sweat of their brows. The Fulani resisted French and British expansion but eventually were unable to stop it. Nevertheless, Islam remained a vital cultural and political force in the Sudanic zone, and it still is today.

European Conquest

European interest in African resources accelerated in the late 1800s, when Britain, France, Germany, Spain, Belgium, and Italy all acquired African colonies, often by intimidating African leaders through warfare or the threat of force (see Map 21.1). Several factors propelled and made possible the Europeans' conquest. First, Western companies sought government help to compete with African traders and to pressure states to admit Western merchants. Second, advances in tropical medicine, especially the use of quinine for malaria, freed Europeans from high tropical mortality rates. Third, the invention of more powerful weapons gave Europeans a huge military advantage over African forces, which were armed only with rifles or spears. When possible, Europeans achieved conquest peacefully by using deceptive treaties, offering bribes, dividing up states, and convincing African leaders that resistance was futile. When faced with resistance, however, Europeans used ruthless force.

King Leopold of Belgium took the lead in colonization. In 1878 he hired Henry Stanley (1841–1904), a Welsh-born American and former Confederate soldier and journalist. As a journalist working for a New York newspaper, Stanley had earlier searched successfully in East Africa to find David Livingstone, who had lost touch with Europe, and then explored the Congo River Basin, which King Leopold now commissioned Stanley to acquire for Belgium.

Soon other European powers joined the scramble to obtain colonies. In 1884–1885 the colonizing nations held a conference in Berlin to set the ground rules for colonization. For a claim to be recognized, the colonizer had to first give notice to the other Western powers of its intent and then occupy the territory with a military presence. Agents of European governments, such as Stanley working for Belgium, asked African chiefs, most of whom knew no Western languages, to sign treaties of friendship in these languages, but the treaties actually gave the land to European countries. African chiefs usually had no right to sign over land, since it was owned by the people. To Africans the Westerners' concept of private ownership was alien, making it easy for European agents to manipulate them. If chiefs refused to sign, they were threatened with war. Fearing a slaughter and hoping to manipulate conditions for their own benefit, many chiefs signed. The king of Buganda reflected the Africans' distress when he concluded that, in his view, the Europeans were coming to eat his country. A Nigerian writer lamented in 1891 that the slavers' forcible possession of Africa's people had only been replaced by the European governments' forcible possession of Africa's land.

Europeans achieved domination for several reasons. First, the colonial scramble came at a time of famine when rains failed, and also when epidemics of smallpox and cholera were killing millions, especially in eastern Africa. One French missionary reflected the despair: "wars, drought, famine, pestilence, locusts, cattle-plague! Why so many calamities in succession? Why?"[6] For most Africans these were bitter years indeed.

The military disparity in weapons and tactics also played a role. For example, the British had the Gatling gun, which could fire 3,000 rounds per minute, and the Maxim gun, a totally automatic machine gun invented in 1884, while rifles were the most effective weapons available to Africans. Using these and other powerful weapons, Westerners willingly slaughtered thousands. Some of the worst atrocities occurred in Southwest Africa (today's Namibia), where the Germans killed all but 15,000 of the 80,000 Herero (hair-AIR-oh) people after a rebellion in 1904. In Kenya, British military expeditions attacked villages for chasing away tax collectors or for ambushing Western military patrols that were sent as a show of force to intimidate potential resisters. A British officer in Kenya wrote home in 1902 about punishing a Gikuyu village containing several hundred people because an Englishman had been killed nearby. The officer boasted about giving orders that every living thing, except children, should be killed without mercy. As a result, every adult villager was either shot or bayoneted, and the British burned all the huts and then razed the banana farms to the ground. The British called their policy of establishing law and order from the Kenya coast to Uganda, often by force, the "Pax Britannica," or British peace.

Finally, after centuries of rivalries and slave wars, Africans could not unite for common defense, and Europeans took advantage of the political instability and rivalries between societies, pitting state against state and ethnic group against ethnic group. For example, for many centuries the region that became Nigeria had been the home of various independent kingdoms, such as those of the predominantly animist Yoruba and the Muslim Hausa-Fulani, as well as village-based stateless societies such as the Igbo. Some of these societies were already unstable by the mid-1800s, and, partly because of conflicts generated by the trans-Atlantic slave trade, the Yoruba had engaged in a bitter civil war for much of the century. Capitalizing on these divisions, between 1887 and 1903 the British conquered or otherwise annexed these diverse societies, creating the artificial political unit they called Nigeria because it occupied both sides of the lower Niger River.

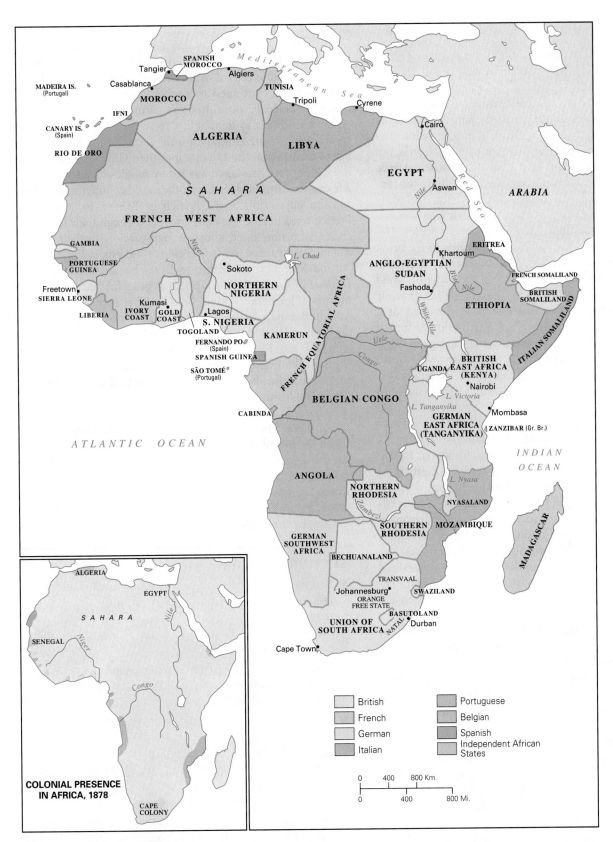

Map 21.1 Africa in 1914

Before 1878 the European powers held only a few coastal territories in Africa, but in that year they turned to expanding their power through colonization. By 1914 the British, French, Belgians, Germans, Italians, Portuguese, and Spanish controlled all of the continent except for Ethiopia and Liberia.

Partition and Resistance

The conquest of Africa resulted in its partition. By 1914 European powers, by drawing boundaries and staking claims, had divided up the entire continent except for Ethiopia and Liberia. The French empire was concentrated in North, West, and Central Africa and extended across the Sahara from Senegal in the west to Lake Chad in North-Central Africa. The British had four colonies in West Africa, including Nigeria, but they built most of their empire in eastern and southern Africa. The four German colonies were scattered, while Italy concentrated on the Horn region of Northeast Africa, including Somalia and Eritrea, and on Libya in North Africa.

European nations competed fiercely for territories. Despite the Berlin Conference, sometimes they came to the brink of war over rival claims, which had to be arbitrated. Britain wanted to control the whole region from the Cape of Good Hope at the southern tip of Africa to Cairo in the north, while the German chancellor, Otto von Bismarck, dreamed of a German empire in Central Africa. German colonization of Tanganyika inspired Britain to move into Kenya, Uganda, and Zanzibar, partly to block Germany. In South Africa, the brash British imperialist Cecil Rhodes (1853–1902), a clergyman's son who had made millions in the South African diamond mining industry, wanted to push British power north, outflanking the Portuguese and Germans. Rhodes was largely responsible for extending British influence into the territory he arrogantly named Northern and Southern Rhodesia. British settlers migrated to Southern Rhodesia (today's Zimbabwe) and Kenya, solidifying the British hold on the region.

While many Africans had little hope of repulsing the well-armed Europeans, others offered spirited resistance to European conquest and occupation. As a result, it took decades for Europeans to conquer and occupy some territories. For example, the Mandinka leader Samory Toure, in the western Sudan, resisted for decades (see Profile: Samory Toure, Mandinka King and Resistance Leader). Similarly, the British had to conquer each Yao village in today's Malawi one by one, and many people in Sokoto, the Fulani state founded by Uthman dan Fodio, chose to join their leaders and die in battle against the British in 1903 rather than surrender. Ethiopia, fortified in high mountains difficult to penetrate, was not conquered until the 1930s. In 1896 Emperor Menelik (MEN-uh-lik) II (1844–1914), a reformer, easily defeated an invasion force of 10,000 Italian troops with a French-trained army of 80,000 men.

In the West African region known as the Gold Coast (today's Ghana), the Ashante kingdom offered particularly strong political and military resistance. The Ashante, like many African states, expanded in the early 1800s. The British, seeking to protect their coastal forts, repeatedly clashed with the prosperous, powerful Ashante during this time, with both sides claiming some victories. In 1874, after more British-Ashante conflict over the coastal settlements, the British dispatched a large force against Ashante and secured control of the coastal zone. However, effective Ashante resistance prevented the British from pushing very deep into the interior. The British then deliberately fomented a civil war in the remaining Ashante territories to undermine the state, but the Ashante king continued to refuse British ultimatums to surrender. In 1896 three thousand well-armed British troops finally occupied the Ashante capital, Kumasi, and exiled the king. However, resistance continued after rebels captured the British governor, who had committed an unpardonable offense to Ashante tradition by demanding to sit on the golden stool reserved for Ashante kings. Not until 1901 did the British manage to incorporate the Ashante into their Gold Coast colony.

Sometimes resistance was led by religious leaders. In West Africa, the mystical Sufi brotherhoods sometimes rallied Muslim opposition to the French or British. In Senegal the French tried to rule the Wolof people through their kings and chiefs, who now faced a loss of legitimacy with their people. Many Wolof turned to Muslim clerics and especially to Amadu Bamba Mbacke (AH-mah-doo BOM-ba um-BACK-ee) (ca. 1853–1927), who had founded a peaceful Sufi order, the *Murids* ("learners seeking God"). The French considered Amadu Bamba a threat, exiling him for many years. Eventually they realized that they could only rule Senegal with the cooperation of the Murids and reached a compromise: Amadu Bamba acknowledged French administration but was free to expand the Murids, which remain a powerful influence among Senegalese Muslims. Religion also sparked resistance in southern Africa. The Shona and Ndebele (EN-deh-BAY-lee) people in Southern Rhodesia, although historic enemies, both resented the loss of their land and cattle to the British and joined to rally around Mlimu, an animist spirit who they believed spoke through a human medium. Believing that Mlimu had ordered a mass uprising, the Shona and Ndebele rose up in 1896–1897, killing many British. But the result was bloody repression by the British.

SECTION SUMMARY

- Opposed by many Europeans on humanitarian and religious grounds, African slavery became less profitable than manufacturing as the Industrial Revolution gained momentum, and it was phased out by the end of the nineteenth century.

- With the end of the slave trade, Europeans began to explore Africa's interior and to take advantage of its vast store of natural resources.

- At the same time, tensions increased between purist and moderate West African Muslims, and Uthman dan Fodio, who led the Fulani jihads, established the Sokoto Caliphate, which became a strong presence in the Sudan.

- European nations rapidly colonized Africa by engaging in deceptive negotiations, by threatening and often carrying out acts of violence, and by exploiting existing rivalries among groups of Africans.

- By 1914, all but a small portion of Africa had been divided up among the European powers, which sometimes feuded over control of various territories and sometimes met fierce resistance from Africans such as the Ashante.

SAMORY TOURE, MANDINKA KING AND RESISTANCE LEADER

Samory Toure Samory Toure, the ruler of a Mandinka state, led a military force that resisted French incursion into their West African region in the late nineteenth century, but was eventually captured by the French. This photo shows him (front, left) in custody. (Roger-Viollett/Getty Images)

Samory Toure (1830–1900) was an effective resistance leader in West Africa and a powerful empire builder. He grew up an animist in a Mandinka village in what is today Guinea. Samory's mother was an animist Mandinka, and his father was a farmer descended from the Dyula, a Muslim merchant caste with branches throughout West Africa. His father's family had earlier abandoned Islam, but their connections to the Dyula trading world gave Samory links to a broader community and an understanding of both merchant and farmer concerns. The growing Atlantic trade brought prosperity to the Dyula and firearms to the interior, at a time when regional Islamic movements were energizing Muslims and fomenting conflict between varied Muslim and animist groups.

Samory began his career as a foot soldier and eventually became an inspirational military commander. By 1870 he had recruited a large, well-armed, well-trained, and intensely loyal force from many Mandinka groups. Skillfully exploiting divisions among his opponents while maintaining connections to both Muslims and animists, Samory built a large state, Kankan, in the Guinea highlands and western Niger River basin. He personally adopted Islam, perhaps chiefly for political reasons, and earned Dyula support by keeping open the trade routes. Islamic revivalism in West Africa influenced Samory to view Islam as a unifying force that could hold his ethnically diverse empire together, and in 1884 he transformed the kingdom into an Islamic state. However, the required conversion of animists led to rebellion. In a pragmatic move that showed his willingness to ignore Islamic scruples to further his political goals and personal ambitions, Samory abolished the theocracy and replaced it with a state based not on Islam but on personal loyalty and national unity.

A political rather than a religious figure, Samory was aware of the traditions of Mandinka empires going back to the great Mali Empire founded by Sundiata in the thirteenth century, and he became the architect of a revived Mandinka Empire modeled on Mali. His later admirers viewed him as an early nationalist trying to maintain a Mandinka state. Samory recruited friends and relatives to form an advisory council, and its members became ministers responsible for specialized tasks such as supervising the treasury, the system of justice, religious affairs, and relations with Europeans. At the same time, Samory also respected the authority of local chiefs. In addition, he gained merchant support by seeking a stable and crime-free order where, as he said, "a woman alone should be able to travel as far as Freetown" in Sierra Leone without facing assaults or robberies.

Samory spent his last ten years defending his state against the French. He had long avoided conflict with Europeans, but his state posed a barrier to French expansion into the interior, and in the 1880s French forces began to move into the gold-rich area. After being defeated by Samory's army, they sent a larger force but again faced stiff resistance and were forced to negotiate a truce. During the 1890s the two sides fought a war for seven years. To oppose the French effort, the British in Sierra Leone gave Samory firearms in exchange for slaves and gold, and Samory built workshops to maintain and make muskets and rifles. His army of 30,000 men included mostly foot soldiers and an elite core of cavalry. A clever military strategist who made good use of guerrilla tactics, Samory also developed an effective system of intelligence throughout the villages to detect French movements. Asked how he repeatedly discovered French movements without giving away his own, he replied, "It is because I eat alone" (thus keeping his secrets).

But the French had more and better weapons, including heavy artillery and machine guns. Samory was also disadvantaged by not being able to unite with rival African states after years of conflict. The French gradually pushed Samory eastward, where he forged a new empire in today's northern Ivory Coast and Ghana. As they retreated into the interior, Samory's forces carried out a scorched earth policy that devastated the inhabitants and cost him popular support. In 1898 the French finally defeated Samory's brave but exhausted and hungry army, captured the ruler, and exiled him to the new French colony of Gabon in south-central Africa, where he died.

THINKING ABOUT THE PROFILE

1. What does Samory's career tell us about Sudanic politics in this era?

2. How was Samory able to resist the French for decades?

Note: Quotations from *The Horizon History of Africa* (New York: American Heritage, 1971), p. 431; and Robert W. July, *A History of the African People,* 5th ed. (Prospect Heights, Ill.: Waveland, 1998), p. 207.

◆ The Making of Settler Societies

How did white supremacy shape South Africa?

While this era saw Europeans advancing in both Asia and Africa, only in Africa did Europeans take over large tracts of land as settlers. The largest settler colony, South Africa, experienced an unusual history: over three centuries of white supremacy introduced by the Dutch colonizers and perpetuated by the British. The first Dutch settlement, Cape Town, was established at the Cape of Good Hope in 1652. Over the next two centuries Dutch control gradually expanded along the coast and into the interior at the expense of the indigenous Bantu-speaking African peoples, who strongly resisted. South Africa's political, social, and economic system reshaped life for both Europeans and Africans. European immigrants also settled in British East Africa, the Rhodesias, and the Portuguese colonies. Asian migrants joined them, often as traders.

Europeans and South Africans

From the beginning, South Africa was shaped by conflicts between European settlers and the African peoples whose ancestors had lived in the region for centuries. The Dutch settlers, known as Boers (Dutch for "farmers"), established a system in South Africa based on white rule over nonwhites that enforced as much physical separation of the groups in all areas of life as possible. The system of white supremacy became even more rigid among those Boers who boarded wagon trains and migrated east along the coast and into the interior, a journey they called trekking, to find good farming land and to escape government policies they saw as inhibiting their freedom of action.

Trekking led to chronic conflict between the migrating Boers and the Bantu-speaking Xhosa (KHO-sa) people, farmers and pastoralists who already lived in the eastern Cape region. The two groups collided in the late 1700s and fought for nearly half a century. Many thousands died, mostly Xhosa. When fearing attack, trekkers pulled their wagons into a circle, known as a **laager**, a tradition that symbolized Boer resistance to new ideas and their desire for separation from other peoples.

The trek became the common way for Boers to flee restraints by any government. In 1806 the British annexed the Cape Colony, giving the Boers even more reason to migrate into the interior. The Boers and the British spoke different languages and shared few values. Boers viewed white supremacy as sanctioned by their strict, puritanical Calvinist Christian beliefs, and the system also ensured them a cheap labor supply for their farms and ranches. By ending South African slavery,

---

laager   A defensive arrangement of wagons in a circle. Used by the Boers in South Africa in the eighteenth and nineteenth centuries to guard against attacks by native Africans.

---

the British harmed the Boer economy, which depended on thousands of slaves of African and Asian origin. Later, the British granted the right to vote and hold office to Africans and mixed-descent people, known as coloreds, privileges that the Boers considered heresy.

While the Boers at the Cape had to deal with the British, the migrating Boers had to contend with the largest Bantu-speaking South African group, the Zulus. In the early 1800s some Zulu peoples began a military expansion under an ambitious military genius, Shaka (ca. 1787–1828), who overcame the disadvantage of being born out of wedlock in a minor Zulu clan to gain fame as a courageous warrior. His exploits in war allowed him to become a powerful chief. Planning to gain dominance over the whole region, he united various Zulu clans in Natal (nuh-TALL), the region along South Africa's Indian Ocean coast, into a powerful nation. Shaka organized a disciplined army of some 40,000 warriors and invented effective new military tactics, such as dividing his troops into regiments armed with short, stabbing spears. In 1816, to build his empire, he began invading other groups' territories, and the resulting wars killed thousands of Africans, both Zulus and non-Zulus, and wreaked widespread disruption. A French missionary reported the "desolate countryside. On every hand we saw human bones whitening in the sun and rain."[7] After conquering much of the interior plateau, Shaka grew more despotic and was assassinated by his brother. This event undermined Zulu military effectiveness, and eventually the Zulu empire fell to the Boers.

Historians still debate Shaka's wars. Some suspect that the scale of fighting and the number of victims were exaggerated by Zulu enemies, both the Africans who fought the Zulus and the Boers who coveted the land being contested. Estimates of the dead vary widely. Soil exhaustion, severe drought, population growth in the region, and fears of potential Boer migration may all have been factors provoking Zulu expansion. Ironically, by depopulating large areas of the mineral-rich interior plateau, the wars made it easier for the Boers to later move in.

Some leaders of Bantu-speaking groups found effective ways to avoid conquest by the Zulus and Boers. Perhaps the most successful was Moshoeshoe (MOE-shoo-shoo) (b. ca. 1786), who created a kingdom for his branch of the Sotho (SOO-too) people. With the region in turmoil from warfare because of the Zulu and Boer expansion, Moshoeshoe moved his people to an easily defended flat-top mountain in 1824. There he strengthened his community by taking in African refugees regardless of their ethnic origin and integrating them into his people. The king emphasized not only military defense but also diplomacy, preferring peaceful negotiation to warfare; for example, he offered tribute, such as cattle, to his African rivals. Moshoeshoe also skillfully cultivated friendship with the British as a counterweight to the Boers. To gain British sympathy, he invited Christian missionaries to his state and used them to acquire guns and horses. While neighboring Africans fell under Boer rule, British support for Moshoeshoe allowed his Sotho kingdom to remain independent until 1871, when it was absorbed into the British-ruled Cape Colony.

British-Boer Conflict and White Supremacy

In the decades after British annexation of the Cape, conflict between the Boers and the British intensified, eventually leading to political change in South Africa. In 1838 about one-fifth of all the Boers, alienated by British policies in the Cape Colony, began what they called the Great Trek, boarding their wagons and, with their sheep and cattle, heading in well-armed caravans of several hundred families north into the interior. After many hardships, including fighting with Zulus, they moved into the high plateau of what is now northern South Africa and created two independent Boer republics, Transvaal (TRANS-vahl) and the Orange Free State. Although the Bantu peoples battled the Boers for decades, Boer military superiority ultimately prevailed. After conquering the Africans, the Boers seized their cattle and forced them to work on Boer farms.

As the Boers consolidated control over Bantu societies and their lands, their ideas of keeping themselves separate from Africans and upholding what one Boer leader called the proper relations between white "master" and African "servant" grew stronger. The evolving Boer ideology considered black Africans an "inferior race" unable to benefit from modernity and hostile to European values. Devaluing Africans and despising the British, the Boers committed themselves to maintaining their identity and culture whatever the cost.

However, the discovery in the Boer republics of diamonds in 1867 and gold in the 1880s spurred the British to seek control over Boer territories, and their attempts to annex the Boer republics led to the South African War (1899–1902), often called the Boer War. The war culminated in British victory but also created chronic Boer resentment of the British. During the war, the Boers employed guerrilla tactics, acting as civilians by day and raiding British targets at night. To eradicate local support for the Boer commandos, the British burned Boer farms, destroyed towns, and interned thousands of Boers, including women and children, in concentration camps, where 26,000 died of disease and starvation. These brutalities discredited the war in Britain. Moreover, the British relied on African troops for victory, and thousands of Africans died fighting the Boers in hopes that the British would be less oppressive. But, when the war ended, Africans found they had merely exchanged one set of white masters for another.

After the Boer War, British and Boer leaders worked out a compromise in which the South African government became essentially a collaboration between the two groups, restoring Boer rights and strengthening white supremacy policies. To win Boer cooperation, the British extended discriminatory Boer laws, restricting African civil and political rights and putting many Africans on reserves, rural lands with few resources from which workers desperate for jobs could be recruited while their families stayed behind. Africans were valued chiefly as cheap unskilled labor for the white-owned economy. The British instituted laws to limit Africans' movement and conduct and reserved the more desirable neighborhoods and jobs only for whites. These policies became a constant source of humiliation and tension for Africans. Continued African resistance gradually led the British to build a police state to enforce their racial policies. Furthermore, despite the political compromises they had made, British-Boer tensions simmered as thousands of British settlers arrived, eventually becoming a third of the white population. Asserting their long-established position in the country, the Boers began to style themselves Afrikaners (people of Africa) and their Dutch-derived language Afrikaans.

The Great Trek Many Boers migrated into the South African interior in wagon trains. These migrants, known as Trekkers, endured hardships but also eventually subjugated the local African peoples, taking their land for farming, pasturing, and mining. (MuseuMAfricA Johannesburg/ISOKO Museums)

South African Cultural Resistance

Domination by the Boers and the British reshaped South African life and culture in the later 1800s and early 1900s. Africans were recruited into the white-owned economy and often became Christian. Thousands of Africans moved to cities, especially the Transvaal mining center of Johannesburg, thus becoming temporarily or permanently removed from their farming villages and transformed into salaried workers. They experienced dreadful work conditions on white-owned factories and farms, but nowhere were conditions as bad as in the mines. There, where safety regulations were few, hundreds of miners died each year. The Zulu poet B. W. Vilakezi described the miner's life in the early 1900s:

> Roar, without rest, machines of the mines,
> Roar from dawn till darkness falls.
> To black men groaning as they labor,
> Tortured by their aching muscles,
> Gasping in the fetid air,
> Reeking from the dirt and sweat.
> The earth will swallow us who burrow.
> And, if I die there, underground,
> What does it matter?
> All round me, every day,
> I see men stumble, fall and die.[8]

Africans often resisted Western domination by adapting their cultural forms to changing conditions. For example, Zulu warriors reworked dance tunes and turned them into songs to protest white military incursion. The Sotho people gradually transformed their tradition of poetry praising influential people and ancestors into songs expressing the fears and experiences of male migrants working in the mines and the women left behind in the villages.

Educated urban Africans, who formed a middle class of professionals and traders, also found ways to oppose white supremacy. One of these, the Johannesburg lawyer Pixley ka Isaka Seme, a graduate of Columbia University in New York, helped found the African National Congress in 1912 to promote African rights and spur Africa's cultural regeneration. Some Bantu composers creatively mixed Christian hymns with traditional Xhosa or Zulu choral music. The African National Congress adopted one such hymn, "God Bless Africa," as their official anthem. Later the song, with its uplifting message of hope, became the anthem of black empowerment:

> Bless the youth, that they may carry the land with patience. Bless the wives and young girls. Bless agriculture and stock raising. Banish all famine and diseases. Fill the land with good health. Bless our effort, of union and self-uplift, of education and mutual understanding.[9]

European Settlers and Asian Traders

Like South Africa, several other colonies restricted African civil and economic rights, particularly Portuguese-ruled Angola and British-ruled Kenya and Southern Rhodesia. These colonial governments reserved for immigrant white farmers not only the best land, such as the fertile Kenyan highlands once dominated by the Gikuyu people, but also the most lucrative crops. For example, in Kenya coffee could be grown only on white-owned farms. African farmers also faced barriers in obtaining bank loans to compete with white farmers. The whites in these colonies participated in government, perpetuating their supremacy by preventing Africans from gaining any political power. The settler colonies erected rigid color bars to limit contact between whites and Africans except as employers and hired workers.

Asian minorities also became part of colonial societies. Beginning in the 1890s Indians arrived to build railroads, work on sugar plantations, or become middle-level retail traders. Indians became the commercial middle class of East Africa and occupied a key economic niche in South Africa, the Rhodesias, Mozambique, and Madagascar. Cities such as Nairobi in Kenya, Kampala in Uganda, and Durban in South Africa had substantial Indian populations, and their downtowns were dominated by Indian stores and Hindu temples. Indians also operated shops and restaurants in the towns of these colonies. In West and Central Africa, Lebanese occupied the middle levels of the economy as shopkeepers in cities and towns. The growing influence and wealth of the Asian immigrants, resented by black Africans, led after independence to many governments restricting Asian economic power. However, while the Europeans themselves disliked the Asians, they also recognized their value in perpetuating divide and rule since Africans often focused their resentment on the Asian traders they dealt with directly rather than the more remote European officials.

SECTION SUMMARY

- Dutch settlers of South Africa, called Boers, pursued a policy of white supremacy in spite of more liberal British policies.

- South Africa was also shaped by the conquests of Shaka, a Zulu leader.

- The Boers fled inland to escape British control, but when diamonds and gold were discovered in the Boer republics, the British instigated and won the South African War, after which they agreed to enforce white supremacist policies in order to gain Boer cooperation.

- Blacks suffered greatly in white-dominated South Africa, but many resisted through poetry, music, dance, and political organizations such as the African National Congress.

- Whites dominated other African colonies as well, reserving the best resources and all political power for themselves, while Indians came to form the middle class in many African societies.

The Colonial Reshaping of Sub-Saharan Africa

What were some of the major consequences of colonialism in Africa?

The experience of living under Western colonial domination from the 1880s to the 1960s reshaped sub-Saharan Africans' politics, society, culture, and economy. The trans-Atlantic and East African slave trades had devastated parts of Africa for four centuries, but the colonial conquests that began in 1884 undermined the autonomy of all African societies. Colonialism created artificial states and transformed Africans into subject peoples who enjoyed few political rights. It also allowed Western business interests to penetrate the continent and integrate Africa into the global system as a supplier of valuable raw materials.

Colonial Governments

The colonial policies devised in London, Paris, Berlin, Lisbon, and Brussels introduced new kinds of governments in Africa, as each colonizing power sought the best way to achieve maximum control at minimum expense. The French grouped their colonies into large federations such as French West Africa that were headed by one governor, while the British preferred to handle each colony, such as the Gold Coast and Nigeria, separately. While the types of government varied, Europeans usually supervised administration and always held ultimate political authority. Africans had to abide by decisions made by European bureaucrats who often had little understanding of or interest in African culture.

The colonizers practiced two broad types of administration, direct rule and indirect rule. Under **direct rule** the administration was largely European, even down to the local level, and chiefs or kings were reduced to symbolic roles. Under **indirect rule** the Europeans gave the traditional leaders of a district, the kings or chiefs, considerable local power but kept them subject to colonial officials. In general, indirect rule, which left much of the original society intact, caused less disruption than direct rule. But even under indirect rule African leaders faced restrictions and were required to consult with the local European adviser on many matters. The advisers enforced colonial law and order, collected taxes, and supervised public works. Since Europeans lacked enough officials to administer a large colony such as Nigeria or Tanganyika, this form of rule was inspired by pragmatism. However, it did not

benefit African society. In order to work with local leaders, Europeans sometimes strengthened weak chiefs or appointed chiefs where none previously existed, undermining village democracy.

Nigeria, an unwieldy colony that contained some 250 distinct African ethnic groups, provided an example of both kinds of administration. Indirect rule was taken to its fullest extent in northern Nigeria. As the British struggled to keep the largely Muslim north pacified, they needed the collaboration of the region's Hausa and Fulani rulers. Lord Lugard, the British governor, proclaimed that every ruler "will rule over the people as of old time but will obey the laws of the [British] Governor."[10] Under this system the British left the traditional Hausa-Fulani courts and social structure largely undisturbed.

By contrast, the British governed southern Nigeria chiefly through direct rule, with the result that greater change occurred in the south, including the introduction of Christian missions and cash crop farming. Peoples such as the Igbo and Yoruba successfully adapted to these changes that transformed their regions. The Igbo, who were particularly receptive to culture change and Christianity, became prominent in Nigeria's educated middle class. The Yoruba successfully blended aspects of their indigenous culture, such as a rich artistic tradition and polytheism, with imported cultural traditions, such as English literature and Christianity, maintaining a high degree of tolerance for divergent views. They described their culture as a river that is never at rest, caught up within swift-moving currents that can either run deep and quietly or be turbulent and overpowering. Rejecting fate and helplessness, the Yoruba emphasized the obligation to make one's life meaningful by drawing upon creative capacities.

However, many changes were aimed at politically handicapping the Africans. Supporters of colonialism defended Western rule as providing "a school for democracy," but the rationale clearly differed from reality. By 1945 fewer than 1 percent of Africans enjoyed political rights or access to democratic institutions. Such access for Africans was largely limited to a few urban merchants and professionals in British Nigeria and the Gold Coast who could vote for and serve on city councils, and to males in French Senegal, who elected the members of the colonial council and a representative to the French parliament. Meanwhile, even the traditional African leaders, the chiefs and kings, served European interests if they wanted to keep their positions. They were expected to remain loyal to colonial rule and help implement such policies as cash crop agriculture, as well as recruit people for labor and war. Africans often viewed these privileged and wealthy leaders as little better than paid agents of colonialism.

Colonial States and African Societies

The boundaries that European colonizers drew up to partition Africa into colonies created artificial countries that often ignored traditional ethnic relationships. Modern countries such as Nigeria, Ghana (the former Gold Coast), Congo, and Mozambique were colonial creations, not nations built on shared culture and

direct rule A method of ruling colonies whereby a largely European colonial administration supervised all activity, even down to the local level, and native chiefs or kings were reduced to symbolic roles.

indirect rule A method of ruling colonies whereby districts were administered by traditional (native) leaders, who had considerable local power but were subject to European officials.

identity. Colonizers ignored the interests of local people, sometimes dividing ethnic groups between two or more colonial systems. For example, the Kongolese, once masters of a major African kingdom, were split between Portuguese Angola and the Belgian and French Congos. At the same time, rival societies were sometimes joined, creating a basis for later political instability. For instance, in Nigeria the tensions between ethnic groups, including the Igbo, Yoruba, and Hausa-Fulani, have fostered chronic conflict, including a civil war, since the end of British rule. Other countries have also experienced ethnic conflicts that have sometimes led to violence.

To maintain their privileged position, Europeans also imposed a color bar that kept Africans out of clubs, schools, and jobs reserved for Europeans. Europeans typically considered African culture irrational and static, having no history of achievement. An ethnocentric British scholar argued in 1920 that "the chief distinction between the backward and forward peoples is that the former are of colored skin."[11] This prejudice translated into the demeaning and self-serving idea that Africans were unfit to rule themselves and badly in need of Western leadership. Such views ignored several thousand years of African governments, ranging from centralized kingdoms to village democracies, as well as participation in Eastern Hemisphere trade networks from ancient times. Racist ideology spawned the French and Belgian idea of the "civilizing mission," which viewed Africans as children who could attain adulthood only by adopting French language, religion, and culture.

The colonizers often misunderstood African societies and ethnic complexities. For example, to simplify administration and census data, the British tended to identify people of similar culture and language as "tribes," such as the Yoruba of Nigeria and Gikuyu of Kenya, even though these peoples were actually collections of subgroups without much historical unity. Despite loose cultural homogeneity, the Yoruba were traditionally divided into several competing states, each with its own king, while the Gikuyu had few political structures higher than the village. In reality, African peoples such as the Yoruba, Gikuyu, Igbo, Xhosa, and Mandinka were ethnic groups, not unlike the politically divided Italians, Irish, and Poles of early-nineteenth-century Europe or the Javanese and Malays of Southeast Asia.

Christian Missions and African Culture

Christian missionaries, whose primary goal was to reshape African culture and religious life, played a key role in colonial Africa. Christian missions established most of Africa's modern hospitals and schools. Both institutions helped Africans but also reflected Western views. Mission doctors practiced Western medicine and denounced African folk medicine. Mission schools taught new agricultural methods, simple mathematics, reading, writing, and Western languages, thus giving a small group of educated Africans the skills they could use in the colonial economy and administration. Critics complained that the mission schools taught not only Western values but also European history, ignoring African history, and held up European culture as superior while deriding African beliefs as su-

perstition. Some African nationalists, themselves products of mission schools, charged that these schools, as an Igbo writer put it, "miseducated" and "de-Africanized" them, perpetuating their status as "hewers of wood and haulers of water"[12] who were unable to challenge their subservience to Europeans. Furthermore, the Africans who attended mission schools and adopted Western ways often became divorced from their village societies. The individualism encouraged in mission schools conflicted with traditional African community, loosening the social glue of African societies.

Despite the mission schools, modern education reached only a small minority of Africans. Before 1945 only 5 percent of children attended any government or mission school. The schools typically produced clerks in governments and businesses or cash crop farmers, although a few graduates became teachers, doctors, lawyers, and journalists. The first modern African college was established in Sierra Leone in 1827. But before 1940 the few Africans who could attend a university had to do so usually in Europe or the United States.

Millions of Africans adopted Christianity, but Christian beliefs and practices varied widely. Some Africans became devout Catholics or Protestants, while others only partially embraced Christianity, adopting those beliefs they liked while rejecting others. For instance, Africans often emphasized Bible passages that seemed to call for justice and the equality of all people. In 1908 Elliott Kamwana in British Nyasaland (now Malawi) founded the Watchtower Sect, preaching that Jesus would soon return to liberate Africa from colonization. These views led to his arrest by alarmed colonial officials. Some African churches combined Christian doctrines with African practices and beliefs. Hence, in 1901 some Nigerians left the Anglican Church to form their own church, which condoned men having more than one wife. Yorubas, tolerant of diverse religious beliefs, often just added the Christian and Muslim gods to their polytheistic pantheon.

Christianity impacted women's lives. It marginalized the female dieties and shamans who had been common and influential, reducing women's religious roles. Promoting monogamy, Christian leaders sometimes asked men to give up multiple wives, leaving these women without support or their children. Yet, women often welcomed monogamy and favored Christian social values such as promoting education for girls.

Africans in the World Economy

The transformation of African economic life was at least as significant as the political reorganization. Extracting wealth from a colony required tying its economy more closely to that of the colonizer. For this reason, businessmen from colonizing countries came to control the top level of the economy, including the banks, import-export companies, mines, and plantations. In addition, colonial economic policies tended to undermine African societies. For example, colonial taxation forced changes on farmers and prompted others to migrate.

Colonial governments also imposed economic policies to transform Africans into producers for the world market, hence rejecting the subsistence agriculture that, while having sustained Africans for centuries, now could not produce enough revenues for the government or investors. Requiring taxes to be paid in cash promoted a shift from food cultivation to growing cash crops such as cotton, cocoa, rubber, and palm oil or mining copper, gold, oil, chrome, cobalt, and diamonds. If taxation did not work to induce Africans to shift from subsistence farming, authorities sometimes resorted to forced labor, most notoriously in the Belgian Congo, where much of the African population was reduced to near slavery and required to grow rubber for Belgian planters. If Congolese failed to cooperate, they were shot or mutilated. An American missionary reported in 1895 that the Belgian policies "reduced the people to a state of utter despair. Each town is forced to bring a certain quality [of rubber]. The soldiers drive the people into the bush. If they will not go they are shot down, and their left hands cut off. The soldiers often shoot poor helpless women and harmless children."[13] Over half of the Congo's population died from overwork or brutality over a twenty-year period.

Through such measures as these, colonial Africa became linked to the West and the world economy, but often this global economy left Africans vulnerable. For example, African livelihoods became subject to the fluctuations in the world price for the commodities they produced, a price determined largely by the whims of Western consumers and corporations. Colonies also became markets for Western industrial products, which displaced village handicrafts. Many Africans lost their economic self-sufficiency, becoming exporters of cash crops they did not consume, such as cocoa and rubber, and importers of goods they did not produce. Even many of the major cash crops that dominated African lives had been introduced from outside. For example, peanuts and rubber were brought from South America, and cocoa was brought from Mexico. With the growth of an automobile culture in the West, an oil-drilling industry also emerged along the West African coast from southern Nigeria to northern Angola, making these societies dependent on oil exports. In all such ventures, Western businesses and planters exercised considerable influence over governments.

Colonies often became economic monocultures dependent on the export of one or two major commodities, such as copper from Northern Rhodesia (now Zambia), cocoa from the Gold Coast, peanuts from Senegal, and cotton from Sudan. The dependence of Ghanaians on growing and selling cocoa was well described in a local popular song from the 1960s: "If you want to send your children to school, build your house, marry, buy cloth [or] a truck, it is cocoa. Whatever you want to do in this world, it is with cocoa money that you do it."[14] Many colonial policies made it difficult for Africans to diversify their economies.

The opportunities and demands of the colonial economy touched nearly everyone in some way, profoundly affecting the lives of both men and women. As men were frequently recruited or forced to migrate to other districts or colonies for mining or industrial labor, a permanent pattern of labor migration became established. For example, the white-owned farms and mines of South Africa recruited thousands of workers from Mozambique and British Central Africa on renewable one-year contracts, and men from the Sahel migrated to the cocoa estates of the Ivory Coast and Gold Coast. This migration

IN THE RUBBER COILS.

Rubber Coils in Belgian Congo The Belgians colonized the Congo hoping to exploit its resources. This critical cartoon, published in the British satirical magazine *Punch* in 1906, shows a Congolese ensnared in the rubber coils of the Belgian king Leopold in the guise of a serpent. Rubber was the major cash crop, introduced by the Belgians to generate profits. (Punch Cartoon Library & Archive)

disrupted family and village life, helping to further destabilize African society. The male migrants often lived in crowded dormitories or huts that offered little privacy, enjoyed few amenities other than drinking beer in makeshift bars, and were able to visit their families back home for only a few days a year.

African women faced a different combination of hardship and opportunities. In many African societies women had long enjoyed considerable autonomy, playing a major role as traders and farmers. Now, however, as men migrated for work or took up cash crop farming, women were left with all food production, which was less lucrative than the men's work and which increased their workload. For example, the agricultural workweek for women in the German-ruled Cameroons went from forty-five to seventy hours. The Baule women of Ivory Coast, who had long profited from growing cotton and spinning it into thread, lost their position to Baule men when cotton became a cash crop and textiles an export item. Many women traders who had dominated town markets now faced competition from Indians or Lebanese. Some women responded with self-help organizations. Ashante market women in Kumasi organized themselves under elected leaders later known as market queens to promote cooperation and settle disputes among themselves. Thanks to education, self-help, and ambition, some African women gained skills to support themselves as teachers, nurses, and merchants, lessening their dependence on men. But many poor women were overwhelmed by the challenges of trying to preserve their families while fulfilling their new responsibilities.

African Adaptiveness and Resistance

Africans responded to colonialism in various ways. The Igbos of Nigeria capitalized on change by taking up lucrative cash crop farming or using education to forge careers as professionals or clerks. Other Africans dealt with change by enriching traditional ways. The imaginative Yoruba artist Olowe of Ise (oh-LO-way of ee-SAY) (ca. 1875–1938), while emphasizing Yoruba themes and ideals in the woodcarvings, elaborately carved doors, and other objects he sculpted for Yoruba kings, also expressed his personal style by creating richly textured surfaces and the illusion of movement in his art. Some Africans negotiated change by mixing Western and African ideas. The Black Zion movement in South Africa had Christian overtones, as in the belief that Jesus was African, but it also promoted African pride and traditions such as faith healing.

Many Africans, however, chose noncooperation. Tax evasion and other forms of passive protest were rampant, especially in rural areas, while other Africans chose a more activist strategy and formed labor unions. Although unions were usually illegal in colonial systems that protected Western-owned businesses, strikes were common, especially among mine workers, who protested unsafe working conditions or long hours. The strike leaders were arrested and added to the growing number of political prisoners rotting away in colonial prisons.

Africans also used their traditional cultural forms both to protest colonialism and to address problems within their own societies. For example, in Nigeria, Igbo women used a unique combination of dance and theater to exercise influence in their individualistic but also patriarchal society, dancing and singing their grievances. In a strategy known as "sitting on a man," the dance performances were sometimes used to encourage noncooperation with colonial demands, such as increased taxes, or with excessive male Igbo chauvinism. The dances served to move people toward social action. When local leaders ignored the dance messages of dissatisfaction, the women were prepared to take stronger action, including rioting.

Sometimes distress and anger led to more drastic resistance. Rebellions sparked by unpopular policies, such as new taxes or forced labor, punctuated colonial rule. The Maji Maji Rebellion, for example, broke out in German-ruled Tanganyika in 1905 and was suppressed only after a bitter two-year struggle. Maji Maji began as a peasant protest against a new cotton-growing scheme that worked poorly because the people forced to work in the cotton fields earned only 35 cents a month. The disenchanted Africans preferred to be subsistence farmers and grow their own food rather than be commercial farmers. These feelings led to a new religious cult known as Maji Maji ("water medicine"), which used magic water in hopes of better crops. Maji Maji sparked a rebellion involving thousands. The rebels occupied some towns and sprinkled their bodies with magic water in hopes it would make them immune from bullets, but the Germans, using machine guns against rebels armed only with spears, soon regained the towns. Finally in 1907 the Maji Maji were defeated, at the cost of 26,000 African lives; however, the resistance caused the Germans to end forced labor.

The Legacy of Colonialism for Africans

Whether colonialism stimulated modern development or retarded and distorted it is one of the central questions of modern African history. Some historians contend that colonialism increased the productive capacity of the land, built cities and transportation networks, brought advances in technology, stimulated Africans to produce more wealth than they ever had before, and created rich opportunities for beneficial trade with the outside world. Other historians, however, question the purpose and beneficiaries of the globalization of the African economies in this era. They argue that colonial rulers stole land, exploited labor, gained profitable access to raw materials, shifted profits back to Europe, limited Africa's economic growth, and created artificial, unstable countries.

Although economic growth occurred, colonial Africa enjoyed little development or balanced growth that benefited the majority of the people. One observer in the early 1900s noted that in Portuguese-ruled Mozambique a man "works . . . all his life under horrible conditions to buy scanty clothing for his wife and daughters. The men and boys can rarely afford proper clothing."[15] Moreover, while any benefits brought to Africa by colonialism may be debated, it is clear that colonialism imposed an economic system that discouraged diversified growth, with the result that many of the former colonies are economically vulnerable today. Some of the profits from plantations and mines supported European industrialization and enriched European businesses, but the African peoples supplying the resources benefited little. For example, seventy-five years of Belgian colonialism in the Congo failed to build any paved road system linking the major cities or to establish more than a handful of schools and medical clinics for the millions of Congo's people. As a result of such policies transferring wealth from Africa to Europe, sub-Saharan Africa was the most impoverished region of the world at the end of the colonial era, a legacy difficult to overcome.

SECTION SUMMARY

◼ African colonial governments served the interests of the colonizers, though the colonizers' involvement in local affairs varied between forms of direct and indirect rule.

◼ Colonizers divided Africa into countries with artificial boundaries, sometimes splitting an ethnic group into more than one country and sometimes throwing rival groups into a single country, thus creating lasting tensions.

- Christian missionary schools provided a small minority of Africans with skills they could use in the white world but largely ignored and often damaged the native African culture.

- As African economies came to depend on a single commodity desired by Europeans, colonized Africans lost their subsistence skills, were sometimes forced into near slavery, and were often forced to work far from home.

- Some Africans took advantage of opportunities offered by colonization, others enriched their traditional ways, and a few, such as the Maji Maji, openly rebelled, though never successfully.

- While some historians think that colonization brought beneficial development to Africans, economic growth benefited mainly the colonizers, did little to materially improve African lives, and prevented Africans from building diversified and strong economies.

✦ Imperialism, Reform, and the Middle Eastern Societies

What political and economic impact did Europe have on the Middle East?

Between 1750 and 1914 most Muslim societies suffered repeated challenges from the growing power of western Europe and Russia. The Ottoman Empire remained the only significant Muslim power and, despite a remarkable ability to rejuvenate itself, fell behind the industrializing West. Expanding European empires ate at the fringes of Persia and the shrinking Ottoman domain, and European economic penetration and cultural influences reshaped Middle Eastern life. The response of Muslims to these changes differed from society to society.

Challenges to the Ottoman Empire

For a thousand years Islamic influence had spread throughout much of Afro-Eurasia. Muslims dominated the trade routes connecting sub-Saharan Africa, southern Asia, and the Mediterranean world until the 1500s, and they still played key roles in interregional trade in the 1800s. During the Early Modern Era large Islamic states stretched from Morocco to Indonesia. The Ottoman Turks forged a huge empire in southeastern Europe and western Asia, as well as gaining a strong influence across North Africa, while Safavid Persia and Mughal India also exercised regional power. Since many Muslims viewed the Ottoman sultan as the caliph, the successor to the Prophet and leader of the Islamic community, Ottoman leaders had enormous prestige in the Muslim world. But the rising influence of western Europeans posed a threat to the Islamic states. By 1750, as a result of both Western pressure and internal problems, the Ottoman power had diminished, the Safavids had fallen, the Mughals had lost most of India, and the Dutch ruled much of Indonesia. After 1750 the Islamic world faced new challenges. However brief, Napoleon Bonaparte's conquest of Egypt, discussed in the chapter opening, sent shock waves through the Middle East and suggested dangers ahead.

In the nineteenth century rising pressure from European nations, especially Russia, undermined the Ottoman Empire and its more than 60 million people (see Map 21.2). Since the 1500s the Russians had been slowly expanding south toward the Black Sea, and in 1768 they defeated Ottoman forces and gained control over part of the northern Black Sea coast. Between 1792 and 1812 they extended this control to include the Crimean peninsula, and in 1829 they took over the largely Christian Caucasus state of Georgia (see Chronology: The Middle East, 1750–1914). In 1853 Czar Nicholas I characterized the weakening Ottoman Empire as "the sick man of Europe," a reputation that would stick.

Perceiving Ottoman decline, the major European powers schemed to outflank each other while building up their influence in the weakening empire. With European support, the

C H R O N O L O G Y	
The Middle East, 1750–1914	
1792–1812	Russian control of northern Black Sea lands
1794–1925	Qajar dynasty in Persia
1798–1799	French occupation of Egypt
1805–1848	Rule of Muhammad Ali in Egypt
1829	Greek independence from Ottoman Empire
1840	French colonization of Algeria
1859–1869	Building of Suez Canal
1882	British colonization of Egypt
1890s–1915	Turkish genocide against Armenians
1897	First Zionist conference
1899	British protectorate over Kuwait
1905–1911	Constitutional revolution in Persia
1908	Young Turk government in Ottoman Turkey
1907–1921	Russian and British spheres of influence in Persia
1908	Discovery of oil in Persia
1911–1912	Colonization of Libya and Morocco

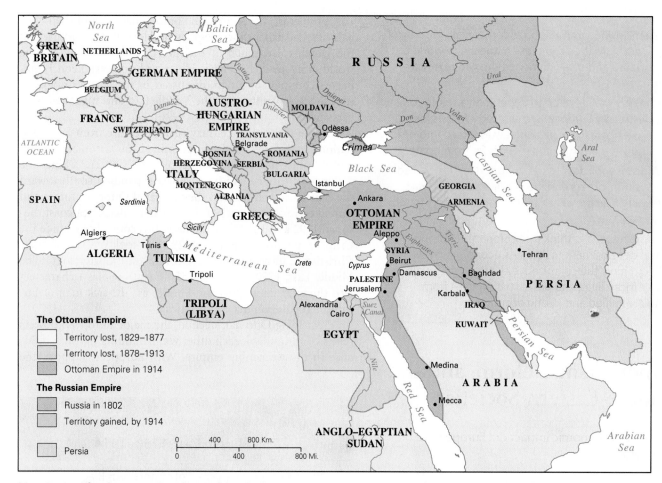

Map 21.2 The Ottoman Empire and Persia, 1914
The Ottoman Empire once included much of southeastern Europe, western Asia, and North Africa.
By 1914, after losing most of its European, Caucasian, and North African territories, it was restricted
largely to parts of western Asia.

Greeks, Serbs, Romanians, and Bulgarians rebelled and threw off Ottoman power in the 1800s. The Greek revolt, which enjoyed support from Britain, France, and Russia, revealed Ottoman weaknesses (see Chapter 19). A combined Ottoman-Egyptian force had nearly defeated the Greeks when an Anglo-French fleet and the Russian army intervened, shifting the military balance. The 1829 treaty that ended the war recognized Greek independence and gave autonomy to the Ottoman territories of Serbia and Moldavia.

Along with military setbacks, the Ottoman state also faced growing internal problems. Weakened by military losses, the central government had more difficulty satisfying the desires of the empire's multiethnic population. The Turks had long benefited from the empire's ethnic diversity, using the varied peoples to enrich their state. Non-Muslim minorities played major roles in Ottoman commerce, the professions, and government. Moreover, the Ottomans had generally been tolerant of ethnic and religious minorities such as Kurds (mostly Sunni Muslims), Jews, and Arab Christians. To respect minority cultures and keep the minorities from combining politically, the Ottomans allowed each group to basically rule itself through

its own religious establishment, such as the Greek Orthodox Church. Christians and Jews felt particularly secure in the major Ottoman cities, which commonly had large minority communities, and Jews in much of the empire enjoyed more security and prosperity than they did in Europe. Multiethnic Istanbul was described in 1873 as "a city not of one nation but of many. Eight or nine languages are constantly spoken in the streets and five or six appear on the shop fronts."[16] Various small religious sects also settled in the Lebanon mountains, where they maintained their traditions.

But in spite of the accommodation to ethnic diversity, some ethnic minorities became restless. Deteriorating Turkish relations with the Christian Armenians in eastern Turkey and the Caucasus led to a conflict between the two groups. Armenians had generally remained loyal Ottoman subjects, and some held high positions in the government. But during the 1800s the nationalist and socialist ideas percolating in Europe filtered into the Armenian communities and influenced some Armenians to want their own state where they could make their own laws. Acting on these nationalistic feelings, Armenians founded their own schools, colleges, libraries, hospitals, presses, and charitable organizations and looked to Europe and North America for financial and moral support.

Armenian-Ottoman conflict intensified, with deadly consequences for the Armenians. In the 1890s and early 1900s the Ottoman government responded to increasing Armenian assertiveness, including terrorist attacks on Ottoman targets, by seizing Armenian property, killing over 100,000 Armenians, and exiling thousands more. Many Armenians moved to North America to escape the persecution. In 1915, during World War I, the Ottoman government charged Armenians with supporting Russia and used the charge of treason to begin removing Armenians from eastern Anatolia, where in response Armenian nationalists declared a republic. During the turmoil the Ottoman army, aided by local Turks and Kurds, killed around a million Armenians. Many historians consider the violent assault a genocide, the singling out of one group for mass killing, but Turkish nationalists view it as an incidental side effect of war. The mass killings still complicate Armenian-Turkish relations. The surviving Armenians formed a small republic in the Caucasus, Armenia, that was absorbed by Russia in 1920.

Ottoman Reform and Modernization

Growing internal problems, combined with military setbacks, spurred Ottoman efforts to reform and modernize in order to match Western power. To survive, Ottoman sultans tried hard to build a strong, modern, and more secular government. They believed this required renewed centralization; however, because many interest groups benefited from weak central authority, this was no easy task. The various groups included the Islamic religious leaders, the privileged military force known as Janissaries, local officials in Anatolia, and governors of distant Arab provinces, who were virtually independent.

Gradually the system changed as Ottoman leaders and thinkers recognized the need to obtain knowledge and aid from the Christian West. One of the first reformist sultans, Mahmud II (MACH-mood) (r. 1808–1839), tried to reestablish central authority over local leaders. He also had to eliminate the Janissaries, who had once been an effective fighting force but who resisted change and had become a costly and ineffective burden. Mahmud recruited a new military force that attacked and crushed the Janissaries, and then he slowly built a modern state and an army trained by Prussian officers. His successors set up new schools that taught European learning and languages, and by 1900 the University of Istanbul had become the Muslim world's first modern institution of higher education. The Ottomans also replaced many older Islam-based laws with laws based on the French codes introduced during the French Revolution. Increasingly the Ottoman rulers marginalized Islam and treated Islamic knowledge as irrelevant, and Islamic leaders and institutions lost standing, demoralizing conservatives.

The growth of a more centralized government and a modern, secular Ottoman nationality continued through the 1800s, aided by the introduction of railroads and telegraphs. To foster a national identity, in 1846 Ottoman rulers declared all citizens equal before the law regardless of their ethnicity and religion, announcing that "the differences of religion and sect among the subjects is something not affecting their rights of citizenship. It is wrong to make discriminations among us."[17]

But attempts to involve the people in government largely failed, and the reforms proved inadequate, instead fostering rebellion and eventually the dissolution of the Ottoman Empire. In the 1880s a modernizing group known as the **Young Turks** emerged in the military and the universities. Their goal was to make Turkey a modern nation with a liberal constitution, and by 1908, when the Young Turks led a military coup that deposed the old sultan, Islam had faded as a political influence. The Young Turks espoused Turkish nationalism, and hoped to spread the Turkish language into Arab provinces, and unite all Turkish peoples in western and central Asia. Under the facade of parliamentary government, they ruled as autocrats and military modernizers. During World War I, as an ally of Germany and Austria-Hungary, the Young Turks embraced a Turkish ethnic identity, secularization, and closer ties to the Western world at the expense of Islamic connections. After their defeat in World War I, the Ottoman Empire was dissolved and the Arab peoples once ruled by the Ottomans fell under British or French rule. By 1920 the Turks were struggling to hold on to their Anatolian heartland.

Egypt: Modernization and Occupation

The most extensive effort to deflect Western pressure through modernization came in Egypt, but only after Ottoman influence was minimized. The Ottomans, who occupied Egypt in 1517, had governed the province through the Mamluks, a Muslim caste of Turkish origin, but by the later 1700s Egyptians considered the Mamluks corrupt, oppressive, and unable to deal with the repeated famines and epidemics that killed millions of Egyptians. Mamluk misrule gave French general Napoleon Bonaparte an excuse to invade the country. While claiming to liberate the Egyptians, Bonaparte hoped to revitalize Egypt's usually productive agriculture to provide grain for France. When Bonaparte abandoned his Egyptian adventure in 1801, Egypt came under the rule of Muhammad Ali (r. 1805–1848), a Turkish-speaking Albanian who had led the Ottoman forces that helped eject the French. Muhammad Ali encouraged innovations but ultimately these did not succeed in staving off British colonization.

Muhammad Ali's Egypt After being appointed viceroy by the Ottoman sultan, Muhammad Ali moved to centralize his power in what was effectively now an independent country. However, he was forced by the European powers, who feared his ambitions, to officially remain loosely bound to the weakening Ottoman state. The charming sultan impressed Europeans with his talents: "If ever a man had an eye that denoted genius, [he] was the person. Never dead nor quiescent, it was fascinating like that of a gazelle; or, in the hour of storm, fierce as an eagle's."[18]

Young Turks A modernizing group in Ottoman Turkey that promoted a national identity and that gained power in the early twentieth century.

Muhammad Ali Meets European Representatives Muhammad Ali, the Egyptian sultan who tried to modernize his state, cultivated ties with Western nations. This painting shows the sultan in 1839 meeting with representatives from several European governments. (Mary Evans Picture Library)

Muhammad Ali introduced ambitious reforms to transform Egypt into a European-style state with an effective army. He increased trade and moved to foster an industrial revolution by using government revenues from increased agricultural exports to establish textile, sugar, and glass factories, as well as foundries and shipyards. The Egyptian leader established a conscript army trained by Western instructors, formed a navy, and created an arms industry. He also replaced Islamic with French legal codes, as the Ottoman sultans had done, sent Egyptians to study technical subjects in Europe, encouraged the establishment of the first Arab newspapers, and laid the foundation for a Western-influenced state educational system to train people for the military and bureaucracy. These changes have led historians to credit Muhammad Ali with founding Egypt as a modern nation-state.

However, while Muhammad Ali's programs added to Egypt's power and wealth, they did not ultimately protect Egyptian independence and foster development, a failure that in time invited British interference. Some hurdles could not be overcome. For example, unlike European nations, Egypt lacked iron and coal, and the work force, not used to industrial regimentation, failed to care for their machines. In addition, as Muhammad Ali and his successors welcomed Western investment, the Egyptian economy became more shackled to European finance. In 1838 the British obtained free trade within Ottoman domains. The resulting influx of cheap British commodities stifled Egypt's textile industry and its cottage handicraft manufacturing. Although the Egyptian cotton industry was stimulated in the 1860s by the American Civil War, which cut exports from the United States to Europe, Europeans were more interested in procuring Egyptian raw cotton for processing in their own mills than they were in buying finished textiles.

Following the European model, Muhammad Ali turned to seeking resources and markets through the conquest of neighboring societies. Egyptian armies moved south into Nubia and the eastern Sudanic lands along the Nile River, which they made into an Egyptian colony, and also into the Ottoman territories of Arabia, Palestine, Syria, and Greece. But a northern thrust alarmed the European powers, and they intervened to push the Egyptians back. The British sought to destroy Egypt as a rival in order to have more influence in the region and to gain control of the Suez Canal, which was built as a French-Egyptian collaboration between 1859 and 1869. The 100-mile-long canal, a magnificent technological achievement whose construction had cost the lives of thousands of Egyptian workers, linked the Mediterranean and Red Seas, greatly decreasing the shipping time between Europe and Asia. British merchant and naval ships became the canal's major users, and in the end Britain also gained control of the canal by capitalizing on the failure of Muhammad Ali and his successors to transform Egypt. In 1875 Egypt's sultan Ismail, Muhammad Ali's grandson, was forced by his country's skyrocketing national debt to sell Egypt's large share in canal ownership to the British government.

The British in Egypt Eventually, to preempt the ambitions of other European powers, the British decided to seize Egypt using military force. By the 1870s Egypt was bankrupt and deeply in debt to European financiers and governments. In addition, the country's political and commercial elite, including many Coptic Christians, were oriented toward Western ideas and committed to modernization; indeed, many Copts, fearing Muslim nationalism and familiar with Western sciences and languages, welcomed the British. But most Egyptians, being chiefly influenced by conservative Islamic ideas and leaders, opposed the growing Western influence. In 1882 increasing local unrest and threats to European residents provided an excuse for the British to bombard Egypt's major port, Alexandria, and then invade the country. Thus, several decades after Muhammad Ali's death, Egypt became part of Britain's growing worldwide empire.

Soon after gaining control of Egypt, the British had to deal with a challenge coming from the Sudanic region straddling the Nile River to Egypt's south (today the nation of Sudan), which the Egyptians had seized between the 1820s and 1860s. In 1881 a militant Arab Muslim in the Sudan, Muhammad Ahmad (1846–1885), the son of a shipbuilder, declared that he was the Mahdi (MAH-dee) ("the Guided One") and pledged to restore Islam's purity and destroy the Egyptian-imposed government, which he accused of corruption, lax morality, and subservience to European advisers. He recruited an army that defeated the Egyptian forces and their British officers, after which he formed an Islamic state. However, the Mahdist government wasted money in wars with neighbors, and in 1898 British and Egyptian forces defeated the Mahdists and formed a new state known as the Anglo-Egyptian Sudan, which was effectively a British colony.

Persia: Challenges and Reforms

Persia, increasingly known as Iran, had long played a central role in the Islamic world, but in the 1700s it faced new problems. After the Safavid collapse in 1736 and the following decades of turmoil, in 1794 one Persian tribe, the Qajars (KAH-jars), established control over much of Persia from their base in Tehran and ruled uneasily until 1925. The Qajars took over an impoverished country that suffered from deserted villages, desolated cities, and much reduced trade after years of civil war and anarchy. The early Qajar rulers, presiding over a weak central government, were unable to resolve most of Persia's problems and became noted instead for greed, corruption, and lavish living. One particularly extravagant shah married 158 wives, fathering nearly 100 children, and was survived by some 600 grandchildren.

Under the Qajars, Persia was more a diverse collection of tribes, ethnic groups, and religious sects than a nation, a condition that fostered conflict. The majority of Persia's people, including the Qajar rulers, were Shi'ites, but the population also included Christian Armenians, Jews, Zoroastrians, and Sunni Kurds, all of whom sought to increase their autonomy. Shi'ite clerics, however, exercised great influence, controlling education, law, and welfare and enjoying vast wealth from landholdings and tithes. Independent of any government, the top Shi'ite clerics engaged in power struggles with the Qajar shahs, arguing that a virtuous and learned Shi'ite scholar should rule Persia and that few Qajar rulers fit that description. Meanwhile, Shi'ites persecuted as heretical the **Bahai** (buh-HI) religion. Founded in 1867 by the Persian Bahaullah (bah-hah-oo-LAH)

(1817–1892) as an offshoot of Persian Shi'ism, Bahai called for universal peace, the unity of all religions, and service to others. Shi'ites killed many Bahais and forced their leaders into exile.

Persia also faced continuous pressure from Russia and Britain. By the 1870s Russia had gained territory on both sides of the Caspian Sea, including the Caucasus, and between 1907 and 1921 it asserted a sphere of influence in northern Persia. Meanwhile, capitalizing on the Suez Canal, British power steadily grew in the Persian Gulf and along Arabia's Indian Ocean coast. The British, who wanted a strong Persia to keep the Russians away from the Persian Gulf and India, asserted a sphere of influence in southeastern Persia, which gave them a foothold at the entrance to the Persian Gulf. British entrepreneurs controlled a monopoly on Persian railroad construction, banking, and oil. The Anglo-Iranian Oil Company (later British Petroleum), which struck oil in 1908, became Persia's dominant economic enterprise, but profits went chiefly to Britain. Persians disliked the powerful British economic role, which they considered a humiliation.

The weakness of the central government, combined with foreign pressure, led to political reforms. Some Qajar shahs provided an opening for change when they attempted to restore central government power. In the later 1800s they rebuilt an army, set up a Western-style college, introduced a telegraph system, and gave Christian missionaries the right to establish schools and hospitals. Some celebrated the changes. The Persian writer Mirza Malkum (1834–1898) marveled in 1891 that all manner of new ideas were astir to shake a society needing change. However, these Qajar reforms also threatened the conservative Shi'ite clergy, who hoped to thwart modernization.

From 1905 to 1911 Persia enjoyed a constitutional revolution, unique in the Middle East, that fostered a brief period of democracy. The more liberal Shi'ite clergy, allied with merchants in the capital, Tehran, Armenians, and Western-educated radicals, imposed a democratic constitution that sought to curb royal power by setting up a parliament elected by several major groups and granting freedom of the press. Soon over four hundred newspapers were published. When a conservative, pro-Russian shah took power in 1907 and attempted to weaken the parliament, liberal newspapers, writers, and musicians lampooned him and his allies. Troubadours sang songs about the love of country, democracy, freedom, justice, and equality.

The progressive direction did not last, however. Britain and Russia formed an alliance and increased pressure on Persia to grant them more influence, straining the progressive leadership. As a result, the constitutionalist forces soon split into pro-Western nationalists seeking separation of religious and civil power, land reform, and universal education, and Shi'ite clerics and nobles who favored slower change. Many clergy had become alarmed at the secular direction. As violence increased in 1911, the conservative royal government closed down the parliament and ended the democratic experiment. Aref Qazvini, a popular pro-revolution songwriter, lamented the setback: "O let not Iran thus be lost, if ye be men of truth."[19] By then, however, Britain and Russia, stationing troops in southern and northern Persia, respectively, had reduced Persia's political and economic independence.

Bahai An offshoot of Persian Shi'ism that was founded in 1867; Bahai preached universal peace, the unity of all religions, and service to others.

Ottoman Syria, Lebanon, and Iraq

Declining Ottoman power, combined with growing Western activity, eventually had an impact on the Arab provinces of the eastern Ottoman Empire. Syria and Lebanon, which the Ottomans governed as one province, were particularly affected. Despite their diverse ethnic and religious mosaic, which included Arab and Armenian Christians, Sunni and Shi'ite Arabs, and Sunni Kurds, the peoples of these two adjacent territories had mostly lived in peace under Ottoman rule. By recognizing the autonomy of each community, the Ottoman government had promoted some degree of religious tolerance. A British writer commented on the generally stable conditions and social harmony in the late 1700s, writing that in Lebanon "every man lives in a perfect security of life and property. The peasant is not richer than in other countries, but he is free."[20]

However, in the 1850s poverty and a stagnant economy began to foster occasional conflicts in Syria and Lebanon, and as a result the densely populated region around Mount Lebanon came under the influence of several Western powers. For example, the French developed a special relationship with the Maronites (MAR-uh-nite), Arab Christians who sought a closer connection with the Roman Catholic Church, and American Protestant missionaries established a college in the main Lebanese city, Beirut, in 1866 that spread modern ideas. By the later 1800s the weak economy had also encouraged emigration from Syria and Lebanon. The majority of emigrants were Lebanese Christians, who often left as families for the United States. Other Lebanese Christians and Muslims moved to other parts of the Middle East or to West Africa, Latin America, or the Caribbean. By 1914 perhaps 350,000 Arabs from Syria and Lebanon had emigrated to the Americas.

Change also came to Ottoman-ruled Iraq, the heart of ancient Mesopotamia, which had spawned the first cities and states and had later become the center of a great Islamic empire. Under Ottoman rule, however, Iraq lacked political unity and had not prospered. The Ottomans divided Iraq into three provinces: a largely Sunni Arab and Kurdish north, a chiefly Sunni Arab center, and a Shi'ite Arab–dominated south. The Ottomans had difficulty collecting taxes in the south. Iraqis suffered from major floods and repeated epidemics of plague and cholera. A British official described Iraq as "a country of extremes, either dying of thirst or of being drowned."[21] Iraq also lacked order, foreign capital, and a transportation system such as railroads or steamships on the rivers. Pirates attacked shipping in the Persian Gulf, and Bedouin tribes raided land caravans. Although gradually more schools were founded in the later 1800s, the literacy rate remained extremely low.

Although the challenges were daunting, Western interest in this Ottoman backwater grew. European travelers were unanimous that Iraq had great economic potential: navigable rivers, fertile land, a strategic location, access to the Persian Gulf, and minerals. To gain a foothold in the region, in 1899 the British established a protectorate over the small neighboring kingdom of Kuwait (koo-WAIT) at the west end of the Persian Gulf. This relationship preserved the royal government but allowed the British to station troops and agents. But Iraq remained of more interest, particularly as both the British and Germans came to believe that it might have considerable oil, and in the early 1900s the Ottomans and foreign investors poured money into Iraq. However, World War I temporarily halted Western efforts to discover Iraqi oil.

European Colonization in Northwest Africa

Northwest Africa also experienced European colonization. The Arabic-speaking societies along Africa's Mediterranean coast from Libya to Algeria had never been under firm Ottoman control, and their proximity to Europe made them natural targets for colonization. In 1840 the French embarked on full-scale colonization of Algeria, in part to divert the French public from an unpopular home government. Abd al-Qadir (AB dul-KA-deer), an energetic Algerian Muslim cleric, used Islamic appeals to unite Arab and Berber opposition to the French. His resourceful followers quickly learned how to make guns. The French captured Abd al-Qadir in 1847, but the fighting continued for years. Facing determined resistance, the French attempted to demoralize the Algerians by driving peasants off the best land and selling it to European settlers. To diffuse opposition, they also relocated and broke up tribes. Yet various anti-French revolts, often spurred by appeals to Islamic traditions, erupted until the 1880s. The ruthless French conquest and suppression of rebellions cost tens of thousands of French and hundreds of thousands of Algerian lives.

French policy reshaped Algerian society. The French intended, as an official wrote in 1862, to impose French culture, settlers, and economic priorities on the Arabs. General Bugeaud, the conqueror of Algeria, conceded in 1849 that "the Arabs with great insight understand very well the cruel revolution we have brought them; it is as radical for them as socialism would be for us."[22] Between the 1840s and 1914 over a million immigrants from France, Italy, and Spain poured into Algeria, erecting a racist society similar to South Africa. The European settlers eventually elected representatives to the French parliament as Algeria was incorporated into the French state. The mainstay of the settler economy, vineyard cultivation and wine production, displaced food crops and pasture, an economic change that mocked Islamic values prohibiting alcoholic beverages.

Gradually European power in Northwest Africa increased. In Morocco, a coastal country west of Algeria, Sultan Mawlay Hassan (r. 1873–1895) skillfully worked to preserve the country's independence by playing the rival European powers off against each other. However, the French and Spanish, attracted by Morocco's economic potential and strategic position, by 1912 had divided the country between them. Tunisia, just east of Algeria, had long enjoyed considerable autonomy under Ottoman rule, and the port city of Tunis prospered as a center of trade and piracy. Coveting this trade, in 1881 France sent in troops to occupy Tunisia. Libya, a sparsely populated, mostly desert land between Tunisia and Egypt, was conquered by the

Italians in 1911 and 1912. The country's Islamic orders led repeated resistance efforts, and the resulting conflicts killed one-third of Libya's people. European colonialism now dominated the whole of North Africa.

SECTION SUMMARY

- After 1750, the Ottoman Empire's power began to wane under pressure from Russia and western Europe and also from the Armenians, who exerted pressure from within the empire for greater autonomy.

- The Ottomans modernized their army, adopted French-style laws, and became increasingly secular, but their decline continued until the empire was broken apart in World War I.

- After Napoleon left Egypt, an Ottoman-appointed governor, Muhammad Ali, attempted an ambitious and somewhat successful program of modernization; ultimately, however, Britain gained control of the Suez Canal and made Egypt a colony.

- Persia, fragmented under the rule of the Qajars, came to be dominated economically by Britain, and interference by both Britain and Russia helped to end a brief period of progressive rule.

- Westerners became increasingly influential in Syria and Lebanon, as well as in Iraq, which was backward and undeveloped but attracted Western attention because of its abundant resources, particularly oil.

- Europeans colonized Northwest Africa: first Algeria, where settlers established a racist society; then Morocco, which was shared by France and Spain; and finally Tunisia and Libya.

✦ Middle Eastern Thought and Culture

How did Middle Eastern thought and culture respond to the Western challenge?

West Asian and North African societies responded to the challenges facing them in three ways. One response was to form vibrant Islamic revivalist movements that promoted a purer version of Islamic practice rooted in early Muslim tradition. The second response involved reform movements that attempted to combine Islam with modernization and secularization. The early stirrings of Arab nationalism constituted a third response. While governments stagnated or struggled, revivalist, reform, and nationalist movements pumped fresh vitality into Islamic culture and religious life, influencing social and cultural patterns. But none of these movements offered an effective resistance to Western economic and military power.

Islamic Revivalism

Political crises in the Middle East helped spark influential movements of **Islamic revivalism**, which sought to purify Islamic practices by reviving what their supporters considered to be a purer vision of Islamic society than the existing one. Revivalists wanted to return to the earliest form of Islam for guidance and embraced what they regarded as God's word in the Quran and the sayings of the Prophet Muhammad. They also reaffirmed the ideal of the theocratic state of the early caliphs in Mecca, which blended religion and government.

The revivalists rejected what they considered the corruption of true Islam, criticizing the scholarly and mystical additions that had resulted from encounters with Persian, Hindu, Indonesian, African, and European cultures over the centuries. For example, in many African and Southeast Asian societies, Muslims still consulted shamans skilled in magic and healing, revered Sufi saints, and permitted women to engage in trade and reject veiling. Muslim revivalists despised Sufism and its mystical practices, such as music and dance, which had developed centuries after the founding of Islam. Heeding this criticism, several Sufi brotherhoods eventually moved away from mystical beliefs toward an emphasis on the original teachings of the Prophet Muhammad.

While political leaders lost prestige and authority, religious leaders allied to merchant and tribal groups seized the initiative to spread revivalist thought. Groups seeking to impose revivalist goals on others sometimes used violence, interpreting the early Muslim idea of jihad, or struggle for the faith, as a call to wage holy war against those Muslims who blended Islamic and local traditions. The Fulani jihads in West Africa led by Othman dan Fodio and the Mahdist army in Sudan, both discussed earlier in the chapter, were notable examples of Muslims waging war on other Muslims because of disagreements over faith.

Carried by scholars, merchants, and missionaries, revivalist Islam spread from the Middle East to societies in every other part of the Islamic world, fostering debates over the role of Islam and how to meet the Western threat. Many sub-Saharan African, Indian, and Southeast Asian Muslims visited, studied, or sojourned in the Middle East, often embracing the revivalist ideas. During the 1800s revivalist movements stiffened resistance against French colonization in Algeria and West Africa, British colonization in Sudan, and Dutch colonization in Indonesia.

The Rise of the Wahhabis

Revivalism had its greatest impact in Arabia, where it spurred a militant movement in the 1700s known as **Wahhabism** (wah-HAH-bi-zuhm). The movement's founder, Muhammad Abd

Islamic revivalism Arab movements beginning in the eighteenth century that sought to purify Islamic practices by reviving what their supporters considered to be a purer vision of Islamic society.

Wahhabism A militant Islamic revivalist movement founded in Arabia in the eighteenth century.

al-Wahhab (al-wah-HAHB) (1703–1792), led a long campaign to purify Arabian Islam. Al-Wahhab had left his home in central Arabia to study Islamic theology in Medina and Iraq, where he adopted a strict interpretation of Islamic law. Returning home, he preached against those who were lax in their religious practice and promoted intolerance toward all alternative views, such as Sufism and Shi'ism. In 1744 his campaign gained a key ally, Muhammad Ibn Saud (sah-OOD), a tribal chief who took an oath to help al-Wahhab spread his views. Together al-Wahhab and Ibn Saud put together a fighting force to expand their influence.

Wahhabi power ebbed and flowed. During the later 1700s the Wahhabis used military force to take over parts of Arabia and then advanced into Syria and Iraq, where they occupied the Iraqi city of Karbala (KAHR-buh-luh), the major Shi'ite holy site; to demoralize the Shi'ites, they destroyed much of the site. By 1805 the Wahhabis controlled Mecca and Medina, Islam's two holiest cities, where they horrified non-Wahhabi Muslims by massacring the residents and trying to destroy all sacred tombs in order to prevent saint worship. Their actions represented a major threat to conventional Islam. In response, Muhammad Ali, the governor of Egypt, used his European-style army and modern weapons to push the Wahhabis back from the holy cities. Despite these setbacks, however, Wahhabi ideas, puritanism, and zeal spread widely during the 1800s as Western power undermined Middle Eastern governments. Yet many Muslims condemned Wahhabi intolerance, extremism, and such practices as the forced veiling of women.

In 1902 the still-allied descendants of al-Wahhab and Ibn Saud launched a second great expansion. The head of the Saud family, Abdul Aziz Ibn Saud (1880–1953), sent Wahhabi clergy among the Bedouins to convince them to abandon their nomadic ways and join self-sufficient farming communities that mixed military and missionary goals. The Wahhabi Bedouin communities adopted extreme asceticism and a literal interpretation of the Islamic legal code, the Shari'a, expecting everyone to conform to their strict beliefs. For example, Wahhabi clergy beat men for arriving late for prayers, and Wahhabi

men pledged to die fighting for their beliefs. In 1925 the Saud family established Saudi Arabia, a state based on the Shari'a, and discovery of oil in 1938 gave the Saud family and their Wahhabi allies the wealth to maintain their control.

Online Study Center **Improve Your Grade**
Primary Source: The History and Doctrines of Wahhabis

Modernist Islamic Thought

Islamic revivalism as reflected in the Wahhabi movement was only one of several strands of Islamic thought that emerged during the Modern Era. Some Muslim thinkers, rejecting a rigid, backward-looking vision of Islam such as Wahhabism, promoted modernization as a strategy for transforming Islamic society in response to the challenges of rising Western power and weakening Muslim governments. While Wahhabis were rejecting the modern world, modernist ideas grew stronger among Muslim intellectuals, who argued that Muslims should reject blind faith and reconcile Islam with modernization by welcoming fresh ideas, social change, and religious moderation.

Modernists detested many conservative Muslim traditions, including the restricted role of women. For example, Qasim Amin (KA-sim AH-mean), a French-educated Egyptian lawyer, argued in 1898 that the liberation of women was essential to the liberation of Egypt, that acquiring their "share of intellectual and moral development, happiness, and authority would prove to be the most significant development in Egyptian history." Women reformers such as Bahithat al-Badiya (buh-TEE-that al-buh-DEE-ya) echoed these sentiments (see Witness to the Past: Egyptian Women and Their Rights). A few modernist men and women were even more radical on gender issues. The male Iraqi poet Jamil Sidqi az-Zahawi, like some other liberal intellectuals, identified the veil as the symbol of female exclusion, imploring women to "unveil yourself for life needs transformation. Tear it away, burn it, do not hesitate. It has only given you false protection!"[23]

Muslim modernists believed that introducing change would be a straightforward process. Leaders such as Muhammad Ali in Egypt thought that all they had to do was translate the technologies and institutions that made Europe strong to their own societies. They believed that by buying weapons and machines they could strengthen their armies and industries to deflect Western pressure, enrich their countries, and avoid domestic unrest. But

Cairo Opera House Hoping to demonstrate modernization, Egyptian leaders built an opera house in Cairo in the 1860s. One of the first pieces staged was an opera by Italian composer Giuseppe Verdi to celebrate the opening of the Suez Canal in 1869. *(Hulton/Getty Images)*

Egyptian Women and Their Rights

One of the leading women writers and thinkers in early twentieth-century Egypt, Bahithat al-Badiya (buh-TEE-that al-buh-DEE-ya) (1886–1918), advocated greater economic and educational rights for women in a rapidly changing society. She wrote at a time when Egyptian nationalists were demanding independence from Britain and a modern state and intellectuals were debating the merits of modernity as opposed to tradition. In 1909, in a lecture to an Egyptian women's club associated with a nationalist organization, Bahithat offered a program for improving women's lives. Struggling against male and Islamic opposition to women's rights, she sought a middle ground between Islamic conservatism and European secular liberalization.

Ladies, I greet you as a sister who feels what you feel, suffers what you suffer, and rejoices in what you rejoice. . . . Complaints about both men and women are rife. . . . This mutual blame which has deepened the antagonism between the sexes is something to be regretted and feared. God did not create man and women to hate each other but to love each other and to live together so the world would be populated. . . . Men say when we become educated we shall push them out of work and abandon the role for which God has created us. But isn't it rather men who have pushed women out of work? Before, women used to spin and to weave cloth for clothes, . . . but men invented machines for spinning and weaving. . . . In the past, women sewed clothes . . . but men invented the sewing machine. . . . Women . . . [made bread] with their own hands. Then men invented bakeries employing men. . . . I do not mean to denigrate these useful inventions which do a lot of our work. . . . Since male inventors and workers have taken away our work should we waste our time in idleness or seek other work to occupy us? Of course, we should do the latter. . . .

Men say to us categorically, "You women have been created for the house and we have been created to be breadwinners." Is this a God-given dictate? . . . No holy book has spelled it out. . . . Women in villages . . . help their men till the land and plant crops. Some women do the fertilizing, haul crops, lead animals, draw water for irrigation, and other chores. . . . Specialized work for each sex is a matter of convention, . . . not mandatory. . . . Women may not have to their credit great inventions but women have excelled in learning and the arts and politics. . . . Nothing irritates me more than when men claim they do not wish us to work because they wish to spare us the burden. We do not want condescension, we want respect. . . .

If we had been raised from childhood to go unveiled and if our men were ready for it I would approve of unveiling those who want it. But the nation is not ready for it now. . . . The imprisonment in the home of the Egyptian woman of the past is detrimental while the current freedom of the European is excessive. I cannot find a better model [than] today's Turkish woman. She falls between the two extremes and does not violate what Islam prescribes. She is a good example of decorum and modesty. . . . We should get a sound education, not merely acquire the trappings of a foreign language and rudiments of music. Our education should also include home management, health care, and childcare. . . . We shall advance when we give up idleness.

THINKING ABOUT THE READING

1. How does Bahithat evaluate women's roles and gender relations in Egypt?
2. What does her moderate advice to Egyptian women suggest about Egyptian society and the power of patriarchy?

Source: Bahithat al-Badiya, "A Lecture in the Club of the Umma Party, 1909," trans. by Ali Badran and Margot Badran, in *Opening the Gate: A Century of Arab Feminist Writing,* ed. by Margot Badran and Miriam Cooke, (Bloomington: Indiana University Press, 1990), pp. 228–238. Copyright © 1990 by Indiana University Press. Reprinted with permission of the publisher Indiana University Press.

---

their dreams proved impractical. The visionaries were ahead of their largely conservative populations.

By the later 1800s the challenges increased as Western technical and economic capabilities grew. Like European Enlightenment thinkers they often admired, some Muslim modernists struggled with how to reconcile faith and reason. They worried that the reforms needed to spur modernization required adopting Western philosophical and scientific theories, which were often contrary to Islamic beliefs about society, God, and nature. For example, capitalism undermined the Quranic prohibition against charging interest on loans, and the concept of human rights challenged slavery, still widespread in the nineteenth century Muslim world. Belief in equality contradicted the low status of Muslim women, and the Western notions of popular sovereignty and the nation troubled those who believed that only God could make laws or establish standards, which the state must then administer. Some reformers doubted whether Islam, with its universalistic idea of a multiethnic community guided by God, was compatible with nationalism, which emphasized the unity of one group of people defined by a common state. An Indian Muslim poet warned that, in the West, politics had dethroned religion. The Moroccan historian Ahmad ibn Khalid al-Nasri, quoted at the beginning of the chapter, feared that Western ideas tainted reforms. Writing of military cadets being trained in Western weapons and tactics, he worried that "they want to learn to fight to protect the faith, but they lose the faith in the process of learning how."[24] What role, the modernizers wondered, could clerics and the Shari'a have in a world of machines and nations?

Egypt-based thinkers took the lead in arguing the compatibility of Islam with modernization. The Persia-born activist and teacher Jamal al-Din al-Afghani (1838–1895), for example, preached innovative concepts of Islam. Al-Afghani favored modern knowledge and believed that reason and science were not contrary to Islam. In his view, rigid interpretations of Islam combined with the weight of local traditions contributed to Arab backwardness and stifled science. He lamented that, partly because of intolerance to new ideas, "the Arab world still remains buried in profound darkness."[25] Rational interpretations of Islam, he argued, would free Islamic societies for positive change in all areas of life. But al-Afghani also promoted resistance to Western power. His strong criticisms of British activity in Egypt and Persia as well as of Arab leaders he viewed as puppets led to his exile to Paris, where he published a weekly newspaper that promoted his views.

Another major modernist thinker, Muhammad Abduh (AHB-doo) (1849–1905), wanted to reform his native Egypt, to which he returned after some years in Beirut and Paris, and rejuvenate Islam. Although opposed to wholesale Westernization, Abduh admired major European thinkers; since Islam was reasonable, he argued, no knowledge, whatever its origin, was incompatible with the faith. In 1899 he was appointed to a top Islamic legal position, from which he promoted modernist Islam at Al-Azhar University, the most influential institution of higher education in the Middle East.

The Roots of Arab Nationalism

During the 1800s an Arab national consciousness developed in response to foreign domination by the Ottoman Turks and then by the British and French. There was even talk of a pan-Arab movement that would unite Arabs from Morocco to Iraq in a common struggle for political and cultural independence. But Arab identity was murky, divided by differences in religious and group affiliation. Arabs were predominantly Sunni Muslims, but some, particularly in the Persian Gulf and southern Iraq, were Shi'ites, and others, especially numerous in Egypt, Lebanon, and Syria, were Christians. They did not all have the same agenda or face the same problems. Even within the same society, Arabs were often divided into feuding patriarchal tribes that sometimes disliked rival tribes as much as they disliked Ottoman or European overlords, and some tribal leaders collaborated with such overlords to protect their own group. Indeed, many Arabs remained loyal to Ottoman rule. Furthermore, in 1876, hoping to defuse ethnic nationalism, the Ottomans introduced a new constitution and gave the Arabs seats in the legislature based on their large population in the empire. Thus a pan-Arab or pan-Muslim movement remained unrealistic.

Yet, some thoughtful Arabs began to envision self-governing Arab nations free of Ottoman or Western domination. Arab nationalism emerged from a literary and cultural movement in Syria in the later 1800s. Some of the pioneering writers were Lebanese Christians, one of whom published a poem calling on Arabs to "arise and awake." The writings of modernist Muslim scholars were also influential, although they posed a conflict between a pan-Islamic approach and a stress on Arab identity and language. Arab nationalist groups formed all over the Ottoman Empire in response to Ottoman centralization. For example, Abd-al-Rahman al-Kawabiki

(1849–1903), a Syrian who had studied in Egypt and Mecca, wrote witty books that criticized Ottoman despotism as contrary to Islam and suggested that Arabs should take leadership of their societies. Known for his hatred of intolerance and injustice and for making friends with Christians and Jews, al-Kawabiki had a pan-Arabist position. But before World War I the nationalist groups were small and had little public influence.

The Zionist Quest

While Middle Eastern societies struggled to respond to the Western challenge, the Zionist movement (see Chapter 19) introduced another challenge. In the Jewish ghettoes of eastern Europe, especially Poland and Russia, some thinkers began a quest for a homeland for their long persecuted people, who had been living in a diaspora scattered around the world since being forced by the Romans to leave Palestine nearly two millennia earlier. Prayers in Jewish synagogues for worshiping "next year in Jerusalem," the ancient Hebrew capital in Palestine, had endured for centuries. In fact, few European Jews spoke Hebrew, and many rejected Zionism, identifying instead with the country where they lived. But for others, Zionism functioned like nationalism, offering promises of a Jewish state. Looking deep into history, the first Zionist conference, held in Basel, Switzerland, in 1897, identified Palestine, then under Ottoman rule, as the potential Jewish homeland. For centuries some Jews had visited or settled in Palestine, and perhaps 20,000 lived there in 1870, but the Ottomans refused Zionist leaders permission to organize a massive settlement of Jews because many would likely come from the Ottomans' bitter enemy, Russia. This setback prompted the Zionist leader, the Hungarian-born journalist Theodor Herzl (1860–1904) to propose accepting a British offer for a temporary home in East Africa, but this plan was rejected by Russian Zionists.

Soon militant Zionists began promoting Jewish migration to Palestine without Ottoman permission or the support of European governments. By 1914 some 85,000 Jews, most of them newcomers from Russia and Poland, lived in Palestine alongside some 700,000 Arabs. Committed to creating a socialist society, the immigrants established dozens of Jewish collective farms, each known as a **kibbutz**, whose members shared their wealth and promoted Hebrew rather than a language such as the German-based Yiddish widely spoken by central and east European Jews. Immigrants also built the first largely Jewish city, Tel Aviv. Settlement in Palestine was funded by several international Zionist organizations, who bought land from absentee Arab and Turkish landowners. The Zionists had a flag, an anthem, and an active Jewish press. However, since Jewish aims and institutions had no legal recognition in Palestine, the stage was set for future conflict with Palestinian Arabs, who resented the newcomers and their plans to acquire more land for a Jewish state.

---

kibbutz A Jewish collective farm in Palestine that stressed the sharing of wealth.

SECTION SUMMARY

- One response to European pressure was Islamic revivalism, which advocated a pure form of Islam, favored a theocratic state, and sometimes used violence.

- Revivalism was most influential in Arabia, where militant followers of al-Wahhab and Ibn Saud took over a number of cities and eventually formed Saudi Arabia.

- Some intellectuals tried to modernize their religion, but modern European ideas such as equality continued to clash with Islamic practices such as slavery and the subjugation of women, and Western nationalism was at odds with the idea of a universal brotherhood under God.

- Some tried to inspire Arab nationalism, but religious divisions and rivalries made this a difficult task.

- Muslims were also challenged by European Zionists, who moved to Palestine in spite of Ottoman objections and also in spite of the Palestinian Arabs, setting the stage for future conflict.

 **ACE the Test**

◆ Chapter Summary

Both sub-Saharan Africa and the Middle East underwent extensive change between 1750 and 1914. The ending of the trans-Atlantic slave trade opened Africa to exploration and trade by Europeans, and industrial Europe's need for resources and markets fostered a "scramble for Africa" as various Western nations colonized African societies, sometimes by military force against protracted resistance. The French colonized a vast area of West and Central Africa; Britain forged a large empire in West, Central, and East Africa; and the Germans, Belgians, and Italians also acquired African colonies. European settlers flocked to colonies in southern and eastern Africa, most notably South Africa, where they established white supremacist societies that exploited the African population. Colonialism created artificial, multiethnic countries. It also replaced subsistence agriculture with cash crop farming, plantations, and mineral exploitation while enmeshing Africa in the world economy as a supplier of natural resources. Africans mounted strikes and rebellions against colonial enterprises and governments, but all such efforts were eventually defeated.

The Middle East also experienced European imperialism. The Ottoman Empire attempted to stall its decline with Western-style reforms, but it still lost territory and influence over some provinces. Egypt attempted an ambitious modernization program, but it proved inadequate to prevent British colonization. In Persia, Western economic and political influence sparked reforms that were later rejected by Persian conservatives. After suppressing resistance, France and Italy colonized North Africa, and French settlers displaced Algerians from valuable land. In response to these changes, some Muslims, most notably the Wahhabis, pursued a revivalist strategy to

purify the religion and reject Western influence, while modernist reformers sought to adapt secular Western ideas to Islam in order to energize Muslim societies. Arab nationalist movements also arose but remained weak before World War I. Finally, Jewish Zionists posed a threat to Palestinian Arabs by beginning to settle in Palestine, where they hoped to build a Jewish state.

Online Study Center **Improve Your Grade** Flashcards

Key Terms

laager	Young Turks	Wahhabism
direct rule	Bahai	kibbutz
indirect rule	Islamic revivalism	

Suggested Reading

Books

Cleveland, William L. *A History of the Modern Middle East*, 2nd ed. Boulder: Westview, 2000. One of the best surveys of the era.

Hochschild, Adam. *King Leopold's Ghost: A Story of Greed, Terror, and Heroism in Colonial Africa*. Boston: Houghton Mifflin, 1998. A study of the Belgian Congo.

MacKinnon, Aran S. *The Making of South Africa: Culture and Politics*. Upper Saddle River, N.J.: Prentice-Hall, 2003. A comprehensive, readable survey.

Marsot, Afaf Lufti al-Sayyid. *Egypt in the Reign of Muhammad Ali*. New York: Cambridge University Press, 1984. An excellent study.

Northrup, David. *Africa's Discovery of Europe, 1450–1850*. New York: Oxford University Press, 2002. A sweeping survey.

Palmer, Alan. *The Decline and Fall of the Ottoman Empire*. New York: Barnes and Noble, 1992. A readable narrative.

Robinson, Francis. *The Cultural Atlas of the Islamic World Since 1500*. Oxford: Stonehenge, 1992. A useful compilation of materials.

Rodney, Walter. *How Europe Underdeveloped Africa*. Washington, D.C.: Howard University Press, 1982. Influential and controversial critique of the West in Africa by a Guyanese scholar.

Shillington, Kevin. *History of Africa*, rev. 2nd ed. New York: Palgrave Macmillan, 2005. A standard text with good coverage of this era.

Wheatcroft, Andrew. *The Ottomans*. New York: Viking, 1993. A lively discussion with particular attention to the governing elites.

Websites

Africa South of the Sahara (http://www-sul.stanford.edu/depts/ssrg/africa/). A valuable site that contains links relevant to African history.

History and Cultures of Africa (http://www.columbia.edu/cu/lweb/indiv/africa/cuvl/cult/html). Provides valuable links to relevant websites on African history.

Internet African History Sourcebook (http://www.fordham.edu/halsall/africa/africasbook.html). Contains useful information and documentary material on Africa.

Internet Islamic History Sourcebook (http://www.fordham.edu/halsall/islam/islamsbook.html). A comprehensive examination of Islamic history and culture.

Middle East Studies Internet Resources (http://www.columbia.edu/cu/lweb/indiv/mideast/cuvlm/index.html). A useful collection of links.

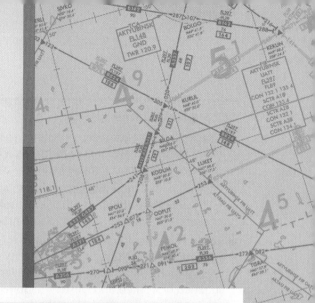

CHAPTER 22

South Asia, Southeast Asia, and Colonization, 1750–1914

CHAPTER OUTLINE

- Forming British India
- The Reshaping of Indian Society
- Southeast Asia and Colonization
- The Reshaping of Southeast Asia

PROFILE
Kartini, Indonesian Feminist and Teacher

WITNESS TO THE PAST
Challenging British Imperialism with Spiritual Virtues

Online Study Center

This icon will direct you to interactive activities and study materials on the website: college.hmco. com/pic/lockard1e

Dipenegara This painting shows Prince Dipenegara, a Javanese aristocrat who led a revolt against the Dutch colonizers in the 1820s, reading, with several attendants at hand.
(Universiteits-Bibliotheek, Leiden. Snouk Hurgronje Collection, Codex Orientales 7398)

Rice fields are littered with our battle-killed; blood flows or lies in pools, stains hills and streams. [French] Troops bluster on and grab our land, our towns, roaring and stirring dust to dim the skies. A scholar with no talent and no power, could I redress a world turned upside down?

PROTEST BY VIETNAMESE POET NGUYEN DINH CHIEU AGAINST FRENCH CONQUEST, LATE NINETEENTH CENTURY[1]

Frustrated by the Vietnamese emperor's refusal to liberalize trade relations with Western nations and protect Christian missionaries, the French, seeking to expand their empire in Asia, attacked Vietnam with military force in 1858 and over the next three decades conquered the country against determined resistance. A blind Vietnamese poet, Nguyen Dinh Chieu (NEW-yin dinh chew) (1822–1888), became a symbol of the Vietnamese resistance to the French when he wrote an oration honoring the fallen Vietnamese soldiers after a heroic defense in a battle in 1862: "You preferred to die fighting the enemy, and return to our ancestors in glory rather than survive in submission to the [Westerners] and share your miserable life with barbarians." The French retaliated by seizing Chieu's land and property. The poet remained unbowed, refusing to use Western products such as soap powder and forbidding his children to learn the romanized Vietnamese alphabet developed by French Catholic missionaries. In verse spread by word of mouth and painstakingly copied manuscripts distributed throughout the land, Chieu rallied opposition. He heaped scorn on his countrymen who collaborated with the French occupiers and advised them to maintain the struggle for independence: "I had rather face unending darkness, Than see the country tortured. Everyone will rejoice in seeing the West wind [colonialism], Vanish from [Vietnam's] mountains and rivers."[2]

Chieu had the talents and background to rally the Vietnamese against a French occupation. The son of a mandarin in southern Vietnam, he overcame the handicaps of blindness to become a physician, scholar, teacher, and renowned writer and bard, famous for his epic poems sung in the streets. These poems extolled the love of country, friendship, marital fidelity, family loyalty, scholarship, and the military arts. Chieu earned admiration for his loyalty to family, king, and country even if his blindness prevented him from taking up arms. He rejected the French offer of a financial subsidy and the return of his family land if he would rally to their cause. Today the Vietnamese continue to revere the stirring poems Chieu composed to aid the resistance to the French.

By providing deadly new weapons and increasing the need for resources and markets, the Industrial Revolution in Europe and North America (see Chapters 19–20) set in motion an intensive Western penetration of other regions, including India (the major society of South Asia) and Southeast Asia. With enhanced military, economic, and technological power to assert their will, a few Western nations brought all southern and eastern Asia under direct colonial or indirect neocolonial control, with the single exception of Japan. Western domination destroyed traditional Asian political systems, reoriented Asian economies, and posed challenges for societies and their world-views, including the Vietnamese whom Nguyen Dinh Chieu attempted to rally.

Between 1750 and 1914 the principal colonizers in Asia were Britain, France, the Netherlands, and the United States, following the Portuguese and Spanish, who had established footholds in the Early Modern Era. The British, expanding their influence around the world, had by 1850 completed their conquest of India, and during the 1800s Britain, France, and other Western powers, after scrambling for colonies in Southeast Asia, eventually ruled all the societies except for Siam (Thailand). Since Western domination occurred while Western Europeans were at the high point of their military and industrial development and at the peak of their cultural arrogance, colonialism proved a transforming experience. It linked these regions more closely than ever to a European-dominated world economy and transmitted to the colonies the ideas and technologies of Western life. In turn, Asian workers produced resources that spurred Western economic growth.

Asians struggled with some success to reshape their relationship with the West. The unyielding resistance to imperialism exemplified by Nguyen Dinh Chieu gave hope to colonized people in Africa and the Middle East. Furthermore, the exchange of ideas was not all one way: Asian religions and arts attracted interest in the West and even developed a small following there. While European power was too great to be overthrown in this period, resentment against colonialism simmered for decades, and eventually the Indians, Vietnamese, and Filipinos, among others, used the Western concept of nationalism to assert the rights of their peoples for self-determination. After World War II the colonial systems finally ended, and the peoples of South and Southeast Asia regained their independence.

FOCUS QUESTIONS

1. How and why did Britain extend its control throughout India?

2. How did colonialism transform the Indian economy and foster new ideas in India?

3. How did the Western nations expand their control of Southeast Asia?

4. What were the major political, economic, and social consequences of colonialism in Southeast Asia?

 Forming British India

How and why did Britain extend its control throughout India?

By the early 1700s the Muslim Mughals who ruled much of India (see Chapter 18) were in steep decline, challenged by both Indians and Europeans. In the sixteenth and seventeenth centuries the splendor of the Mughal court and India's valuable exports had attracted the Portuguese, Dutch, and British. As the Mughals lost power, the British took advantage of a fragmented India and began their conquest of the subcontinent in the mid-1700s, thus beginning the era of Western dominance throughout Asia. By the mid-1800s Britain controlled both India and the island of Sri Lanka. British conquest was in keeping with the history of South Asia, which had often

CHRONOLOGY

	South Asia	Southeast Asia
1750	**1757** Battle of Plassey	**1788–1802** Tayson rule in Vietnam
1800	**1802** British colonization of Sri Lanka	**1819** British colony in Singapore
		1824–1886 Anglo-Burman Wars
1850	**1850** Completion of British India	**1858–1884** French conquest of Vietnam
	1857–1858 Indian Rebellion	**1898–1902** United States conquest of Philippines
	1885 Indian National Congress	
1900		

been conquered by outsiders from Western and Central Asia. But unlike the Asian invaders, who often became assimilated into Indian society by adopting Hinduism or Buddhism or spreading Islam, the British maintained their own separate identity and cultural traditions.

Indian Trade, the West, and Mughal Decline

Europeans had long coveted South Asia for its spices and textiles, which had been a part of regional commerce for millennia. Even today, small, single-masted sailing barges ply the coastline between western India, the Persian Gulf, and East Africa, continuing the ancient exchange of merchandise with the coming and going of monsoon winds. The Portuguese were the first Europeans to trade directly with India. In 1498 they established a base at Goa (GO-uh), and for a century they sought to control the trade from India and Southeast Asia to the West.

Soon other European traders arrived, and between 1500 and 1750 European powers controlled some of the Indian Ocean maritime trade; however, they conquered or gained control of only a few scattered outposts in South Asia. The Dutch challenged the Portuguese for domination of regional trade and eventually destroyed Portuguese power in South and Southeast Asia, although Goa remained a Portuguese colony until 1961. The Dutch concentrated on Sri Lanka and, farther east, Indonesia. The British also became active in South Asia. By 1696 the British East India Company possessed three fortified trading stations in India: at the towns of Calcutta in Bengal, Madras (today known as Chennai) on the southeastern coast, and Bombay (today called Mumbai) on the west coast. Meanwhile, the French formed a small colony in Pondicherry, a town near the British base at Madras, and became involved in regional politics.

Europeans encountered a fragmenting India. By 1750 the Mughals were corrupt and weak since many Indians had already broken away from Mughal control. Emperors might sit on the spectacular Peacock Throne in Delhi's Red Fort—a huge complex of royal apartments, government offices, factories, and military barracks and home to thousands of officials, servants, royal concubines, and royal family members—but the Mughal rulers had little actual power, often consoling themselves with the large royal harem or smoking opium. During the later 1700s Mughal factions quarreled and different rivals claimed the throne, but the Mughal government controlled little beyond Delhi, and the countryside became increasingly disorderly. Without a powerful imperial state to control it, Indian society, with its diverse cultures, castes, languages, regions, and religions, lacked strong national cohesion and was unable to effectively resist European encroachments.

With the Mughals losing their grip, groups like the **Marathas** (muh-RAH-tuhs) and the Sikhs built powerful new states. The Marathas were a loosely knit confederacy led by Hindu warriors from west-central India, and the Sikhs were a religious minority in northwest India; both of these groups competed with new Muslim states that were often set up by Mughal governors whose allegiance to the Mughal emperor was nominal. By 1800 the Marathas ruled much of western India, and the Sikhs, under their leader, the dynamic Ranjit Singh (RUN-ji SING) (1780–1839), had conquered the Punjab and Kashmir in the northwest. Mounted on sturdy ponies, the Marathas developed an appetite for plunder and became feared for their quick raids deep into central India against helpless Mughal armies. The various Indian states employed Europeans to train and lead their armies. In southern India, the Mughal collapse left a power vacuum that both Britain and France attempted to fill by supporting their respective Indian allies in the struggle for regional advantage. Ultimately, however, none of the rising Indian states, including the Marathas and Sikhs, gained enough power, acquired enough weapons, or forged enough cooperation to repulse the West.

Marathas A loosely knit confederacy led by Hindu warriors from west-central India; one of several groups that challenged British domination after the decline of the Mughals.

The Founding of British India

The British posed the gravest challenge to India, especially in Bengal, India's richest and most populous region. Bengal was ruled by Muslim governors who mostly ignored the Mughal government in Delhi. When local Indian governments resisted an expansion of the British presence into their lands, the British resorted to military force. In the mid-1700s the Bengali ruler, Aliverdi Khan (r. 1740–1756), had left British trade unmolested. But his successor, Siraja Dowlah (see-RAH-ja DOW-luh) (ca. 1732–1757), considered the British bothersome leeches on his land's riches. Soon after becoming ruler, Dowlah alienated Western merchants and even his own more cautious officials, and in 1757 he rashly attacked British trading stations. After capturing the main station, Calcutta, Dowlah's forces placed 146 captured British men, women, and children in a crowded jail known as the **Black Hole of Calcutta**. The next day only 23 staggered out, the rest having died from suffocation and dehydration. Siraja Dowlah was blamed for the atrocity, though he may not have been personally responsible for it.

Their rage and determination now fired, the British dispatched a force under Robert Clive (1725–1774) to regain Britain's holdings. A former clerk turned into a daring war strategist, the ambitious Clive and his 3,200 soldiers defeated some 50,000 Bengali troops at the Battle of Plassey in 1757 and recaptured Calcutta, marking the dawn of the British epic in India (see Chronology: South Asia, 1750–1914). Clive allied with Hindu bankers and Muslim nobles unhappy with Siraja Dowlah, who was executed, and by 1764 he controlled Bengal.

The British government, following a policy of mercantilism to acquire wealth for the state, allowed the British East India Company (often known as "the Company") to govern Bengal and other parts of India, as they were acquired, and to exploit the inhabitants while sharing the profits with the British government. The British showed a lust for riches equal to that of the Spanish conquistadors in the 1500s. As governor of Bengal (1758–1760, 1764–1767) for the Company, Clive launched an era of organized plunder, allowing British merchants and officials gradually to drain Bengal of its wealth while Company officials, including Clive, lived like kings in Calcutta. Praised by British political leaders and celebrated in the press and schoolboy stories, Clive became the idol of every young Englishman who dreamed of marching to glory and wealth via India's battlefields and bazaars. After 1760 the cry of "Go East," inspired by Clive's rags-to-riches story, fueled British imperialist ambitions. As they expanded their control of more Indian territory, the British became a new high caste, and, much like the former Mughal rulers, expected the Indians to serve them. Eventually the British Parliament accused Clive

Black Hole of Calcutta   A crowded jail in India where over a hundred British prisoners of a hostile Bengali ruler died from suffocation and dehydration in 1757. This event precipitated the beginning of British use of force in India.

CHRONOLOGY

South Asia, 1750–1914

1744–1761	Anglo-French struggle for Coromandel coast
1757	Battle of Plassey
1764	British acquisition of Bengal
1774–1778	Warren Hastings governor of Bengal
1793	New land policy in Bengal
1799	British defeat of Mysore
1802	British colonization of Sri Lanka
1816	British protectorate over Nepal
1819	British occupation of all Maratha lands
1820s	Beginning of British Westernization policy
1839–1842	First Anglo-Afghan War
1849	British defeat of Sikhs in Punjab
1850	Completion of British India
1857–1858	Indian rebellion
1858	Introduction of colonial system in India
1877	Founding of Muslim college at Aligarh
1878–1880	Second Anglo-Afghan War
1885	Formation of Indian National Congress
1903	British invasion of Tibet
1906	Formation of Indian Muslim League

of corruption and fraud. Although cleared of the charges, a depressed Clive committed suicide at the age of forty-nine.

To transform the economic chaos left by Clive into a more profitable order and to consolidate the British position, the Company appointed Warren Hastings to serve as governor-general (1774–1778) of Bengal. Hastings redesigned the revenue system, made treaty alliances, and also pursued outright annexations to safeguard the British bases. A scholarly man who was influenced by Enlightenment thought, he also had sympathy for India. Hastings saw his task as a holding operation of limited ambitions, arguing that he hoped to never see the whole of India colonized. In contrast to other British officials, Hastings respected the people he governed, advising one of his successors that, like the English, many Indians had a strong intellect, a sound integrity, and honorable feelings and should be treated as participants in society, enjoying the same equal rights as the English colonizers. His successors, however, often disregarded his advice.

Clive Meets Indian Leaders
In this painting, Robert Clive meets the new Bengali official, Mir Jafir, after the British victory in the 1757 Battle of Plassey. Clive supported Mir Jafir's seizure of power from the anti-British leader, Siraja Dowlah.
(National Portrait Gallery, London)

Expanding British India

Success in Bengal fueled further British expansion in the subcontinent. In 1773 the British government gave the Company authority to administer all British-controlled Indian territories. Nonetheless, the Company still saw its role as mainly commercial. In 1794 the British Parliament forbade further annexation and declared territorial expansion to be repugnant to the honor and the policy of the nation. But despite the ban, governor-generals after Hastings continued to authorize the occupation of more areas of India, often against opposition, to prevent trade disruption or to counteract rival European nations. Some imperialists talked about Britain's sacred trust to reshape the world, viewing the extension of British authority—and with it British culture, Christianity, and free trade policies—as a great blessing for Asians.

The reality, however, was often something other than a blessing. In acquiring more Indian territory, the British mixed military force, extortion, bribery, and manipulation. Because India contained much political, linguistic, and religious diversity, British agents and merchants could play off one region against another, Hindu against Muslim. The British were aided by Indian collaborators, especially businessmen eager to increase their connections to the world market. Employing superior weapons and disciplined military forces, the British placed the resistance, however spirited, at a huge disadvantage. From India's warrior and peasant castes, mostly Hindus but also some Muslims, they recruited mercenary soldiers, known as **sepoys**, under the command of British officers. By 1857 there were nearly 200,000 sepoy troops in the Company military force, greatly outnumbering the 10,000 British officers and soldiers.

The French initially provided the major European roadblock to British expansion in India. European wars involving the British and French were extended into an imperial contest for India that focused on India's southeastern Coromandel coast from 1744 to 1761. Victory there over the French soon led the British into actions against Indian states outside their control. One of the most formidable foes was Mysore (my-SORE), a mostly Hindu state in south-central India. Mysore gained prominence under Haidar Ali Khan (r. 1761–1782), a devout Muslim and French ally who modeled his army on Western lines. A brilliant military strategist of guerrilla war, Haidar warned the British, "I will march your troops until their legs swell to the size of their bodies. You shall not have a blade of grass, nor a drop of water."[3] Only in 1799, after twenty years of bloody wars, was Mysore defeated.

During the late 1700s and early 1800s the British imposed their control over much of western, central, and northern India. The Maratha confederacy, which controlled much of western and central India, was divided by rivalries. In 1805 the

---

sepoys Mercenary soldiers recruited among the warrior and peasant castes by the British in India.

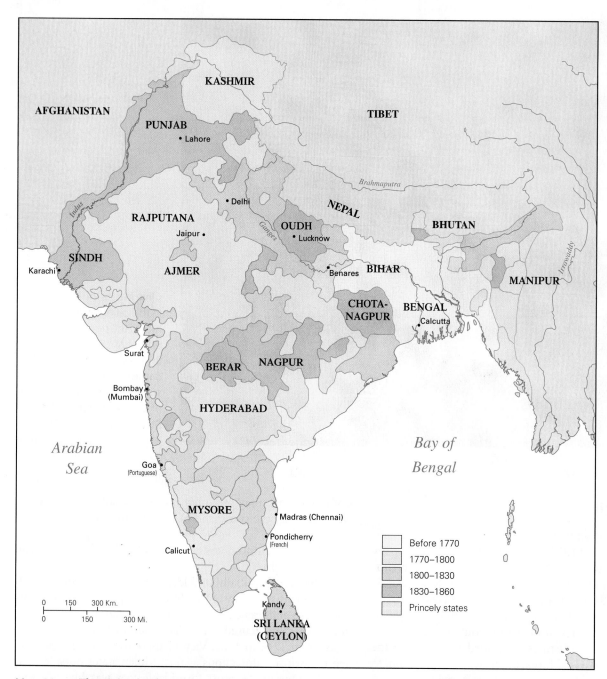

Map 22.1   The Growth of British India, 1750–1860
Gradually expanding control from their bases at Calcutta, Madras, and Bombay, the British completed
their military conquest of the final holdout states by the 1850s.

Online Study Center **Improve Your Grade** Interactive Map: India, 1707–1805

British occupied the Marathas' northern territories and entered Delhi, where they deposed the aged and powerless
Mughal emperor. They took the remaining Maratha lands in
1819. They then turned their attention to the states of northwest India, which were dominated by Rajputs (RAHJ-putz) and
Sikhs. The Rajputs, a Hindu warrior caste, were no longer the
feared fighters they had been in earlier centuries and now
signed treaties giving Britain claims on their lands. Only the

Sikhs remained a threat to the British. But the death of the Sikh
leader, Ranjit Singh, in 1839 shattered the Sikhs' unity and undermined their powerful military state. In 1849, after a series of
bloody British-Sikh wars, Britain finally triumphed. Britain
then stationed troops in the many small independent princi-
palities scattered around India, thus turning them into de-
pendencies. By 1850, the British ruled all Indians directly or
through princes who collaborated with them (see Map 22.1).

Britain and India's Neighbors

British expansion in India eventually led to interventions in neighboring societies, including Sri Lanka, the large, fertile island just south of India that the British called Ceylon. Fearing that the French might establish a base there, the British pursued a more aggressive policy in Sri Lanka. In 1796 they acquired the territory the Dutch had held since the 1630s, and in 1802 they declared their Sri Lankan holdings a crown colony. However, they only controlled the entire island after conquering the last remaining Sri Lankan kingdom, Kandy, in 1815. The British transformed Sri Lanka, seizing rice-growing land from peasants to set up coffee, tea, and rubber plantations and recruiting Tamil-speaking workers from southeast India as laborers. Cultivating crops such as rubber and tea was enormously time-consuming, and the Tamil workers on the Sri Lankan estates were poorly paid and enjoyed little time for leisure. By 1911 the Tamil laborers and their families made up 11 percent of the Sri Lankan population. Largely isolated on plantations, the Tamils maintained their own customs, language, and Hindu religion and had little contact with Sri Lanka's majority population, the Buddhist Sinhalese. By the end of the 1800s some educated Sinhalese, having turned to nationalism, considered both the British and the Tamils unwanted aliens. Sinhalese-Tamil tensions simmered and, after independence, led to a long civil war in Sri Lanka.

Fearing that the Russians, who were conquering Muslim Central Asia, intended to expand into South Asia by land, the British also attempted to secure India's land borders. First they turned to Nepal, a kingdom just north of India in the Himalayan Mountains. Nepal's Hindu ruling caste, the Gurkhas (GORE-kuhz), were fierce fighters who had sometimes invaded north India. British victory over the Gurkhas in 1814–1816 turned Nepal into a British protectorate, in which the British served as advisers to the government while the Gurkha monarchy remained in power. Soldiers recruited from Nepal, also known as gurkhas, became a special military force for Britain and were employed on battlefields around the world in support of British objectives.

Afghanistan, a mountainous region just west of India, seemed the most vulnerable to Russian expansion. An ethnically diverse region that had enjoyed only short periods of political unity, Afghanistan seemed an unlikely candidate to become a viable independent state. However, Afghans, among them the devoutly Islamic Pashtun tribes in the south, possessed the fighting skills to oppose Europeans bent on conquest. To establish some political influence, the British twice invaded Afghanistan and occupied the major eastern city, Kabul, but they faltered against fierce resistance by Pashtun fighters. In the first Afghan War (1839–1842), Pashtuns massacred most of the 12,000 retreating British and Sepoy troops and the British civilians, including women and children, who had accompanied them on what they naively thought would be a long-term occupation. Undeterred, the British fought the second Afghan War (1878–1880) and replaced a Pashtun leader who favored the Russians with one who was pro-British and who gave Britain control of Afghanistan's foreign affairs. With an ally as ruler, the British concluded that Afghanistan could not be annexed by military force.

India Under the East India Company

The British East India Company gradually tightened its control of India and began to impose Western values on Indians. After Hastings, the Company shifted from sharing government with local rulers to becoming the sole power and administering India through British officials. In typically arrogant colonial language that ignored centuries of Indian achievements, Sir Thomas Munro, governor of Madras from 1820 to 1827, explained the imperial mission to nurture a new India. He claimed that the British must maintain their rule until the

British East India Company Court
This painted wood model shows an Indian court presided over by an official of the British East India Company. (Courtesy of the Trustees of the Victoria & Albert Museum)

Indians, sometime in the distant future, abandoned their "superstitions" and became "enlightened" enough to govern themselves. Reflecting these views, the Company promoted a policy of **Westernization**, a deliberate attempt to spread Western culture and ideas, which led to some challenges to Indian culture and imposed economic policies that affected rural society.

Westernization   The Company policy of Westernization to change India began in the 1820s. Protestant movements were especially influential in Britain in this era, and Christian evangelism influenced the reform ideas proposed for India. One devout Company director argued that Britain must diffuse Christian teachings among Indians, whom he described as sunk in darkness and misery. British officials, often disregarding Indian religious and cultural sensitivities, encouraged Christian missions and tried to ban customs they disliked. Many Indians rejoiced when they banned *sati*, the northern custom of widows throwing themselves on their husband's funeral pyre. But there was less Indian enthusiasm for British attempts to tinker with Muslim and Hindu law codes that were rooted in religious beliefs.

The British also established schools that taught in English rather than an Indian language. This policy was spurred by Lord Macaulay (1800–1859), a reformer and firm believer in Western cultural superiority who considered it pointless to teach Indian languages, declaring in 1832 that "a single shelf of a good European library is worth the whole native literature of India and Arabia." Consequently, Macaulay, reflecting racist views then current in the West, proposed creating "a class of persons Indian in blood and color but English in taste, opinions, morals and intellect."[4] Indians often criticized the insistence on English as the language of education and considered it a threat to both Hindu and Muslim customs. Yet some Indians welcomed the English-medium schools because they opened Indian students to a wider world, and it was Indians themselves who formed the first English-medium institution of higher education, the Hindu College in Calcutta, in 1818.

Not all the British in India found Indian culture to be backward. Some British admirers of Indian culture, reflecting what came to be called **Orientalism**, showed a scholarly interest in India and its history and attempted to gain further knowledge about the Hindu classical age. Warren Hastings, for example, encouraged the study of Indian culture, languages, and literature. A scholar as well as an administrator and soldier, he preferred reading the European and Asian languages he had mastered—Greek, Latin, Persian, and Urdu—to pursuing his official duties. One of his officials, William Jones (1746–1794), who mastered Arabic, Persian, and Sanskrit, became the most influential Orientalist scholar, but his views,

Westernization   A deliberate attempt to spread Western culture and ideas.

Orientalism   A scholarly interest among British officials in India and its history that prompted some to rediscover the Hindu classical age.

however respectful of India, often reflected an attempt to fit India into Western concepts of history and religion. Knowing that Christians and Jews considered the Bible to reflect historical truth, Jones treated Vedic texts from ancient times as an accurate historical record rather than as religious teachings and argued that Sanskrit was the original source for other Indo-European languages. He also claimed that the classical Greeks, such as the mathematician Pythagoras and the philosopher Plato, derived their theories from the same ancient source as the classical Indian sages. Jones's ideas shaped European scholarly understanding of Indian history for generations. In addition, several religious movements based on Hindu concepts, such as reincarnation, gained a small following in the West, especially in Britain. Yet by the later 1800s Orientalist cosmopolitanism and respect had largely been replaced by British nationalism and intolerance.

The encounter between India and the West, as well as the British reforms, also fostered a Hindu social reform movement and philosophical renaissance under the brilliant leadership of the Bengali scholar Ram Mohan Roy (1772–1833). After seeing his sister burn to death on a funeral pyre, and concerned about what he saw as the harmful side of customs such as *sati* and caste divisions, Roy began a British-Indian dialogue in hopes of adopting certain Western ways to reform and strengthen Hinduism. To better understand the world by studying non-Hindu religions, Roy mastered their source languages—Hebrew and Greek for Christianity, Arabic and Persian for Islam—and thus became the world's first modern scholar of comparative religion. Roy and his followers attempted to create a synthesis of the best in Hinduism and Christianity. Roy also founded secondary schools, newspapers, and an organization working for reform of Hindu society and beliefs. Viewing the British positively as promoters of knowledge and liberty, Roy wanted Britain to promote modernization while also seeking Indian advice.

British Land Policy   In order to make India more profitable, the British East India Company built roads, railroads, and irrigation systems; most significantly for rural Indians, they revised the land revenue collection, the principal source of public finance, a change that reshaped peasant society. The British viewed Indian rural society as stagnant, unable to provide the tax revenues needed to support British administration. In precolonial times, most Indians, living in self-sufficient villages that were governed by the family and caste, had enjoyed a measure of social stability. Despite high taxes, bandits, and sometimes warfare, Indian villages generally provided psychological and some economic security by promoting cooperation among their residents. Land belonged to the royal families, but peasants had the hereditary right to use it. British observers recognized the village system as self-sufficient and stable over time. One wrote that "the village communities [have] everything they want within themselves. They seem to last when nothing else lasts. Dynasty after dynasty tumbles down; but the village communities remain the same."[5]

Indian Railroad Train   The railroads built during British rule carried both resources and passengers. This lithograph shows a Sikh signalman at the station and a train conveying Indian women and a European.   (Courtesy of the Trustees of the Victoria & Albert Museum)

Yet, while admiring this stability, Company officials decided that a different form of land ownership would provide the easiest way to gain revenues. They therefore began collecting taxes from farmers in money rather than, as had been common for centuries, a portion of the crop. In 1793 British officials in Bengal, inspired by the propertied aristocracy that once owned much of England's land, converted the Mughal revenue collectors, or **zamindars**, into landlords, who, in addition to their other tax obligations, were given the rights to buy and sell land on the understanding that they paid additional high taxes whenever they did so. Under this system, peasant farmers became tenants to landlords and were denied their hereditary rights to use the land. Many landlords sold their land rights at a good profit to businessmen, often city dwellers, who became absentee landlords and grew rich from the crops grown by the peasants. In Madras, however, a somewhat different system appeared. The Madras governor, Sir Thomas Munro, mistakenly believed that the peasants were or could be converted into profit-seeking individualists like English farmers. In his system the peasant farmer dealt directly with the government but had to pay tax in cash and could be evicted for nonpayment.

Under both systems, the village economy was changed from a barter economy, in which villagers such as barbers, carpenters, and farmers agreed to exchange their services or products with each other for their mutual benefit, to a money economy. Since some villagers earned more money, the cash-based system sacrificed a large measure of the stability and security peasants had once enjoyed. The emphasis on money benefited a moneylender caste that came to control much of the land. The Company also encouraged a switch from food crops to cash crops such as opium, coffee, rubber, tea, and cotton, often grown on plantations rather than peasant farms.

zamindars   Mughal revenue collectors that the British turned into landlords who were given the rights to buy and sell land.

Resistance: The 1857 Revolt

In spite of Indian reform movements such as Roy's, Indians usually resented the British East India Company's Westernization and its associated economic policies. Many once prosperous families had lost land or become indebted as a result of British land policies and the courts that enforced laws based on British traditions, and these losses fueled hostility. Even some British officials recognized that land sales and the revenue system were destroying the peasant class. As a result of such grievances, local revolts punctuated British rule. Furthermore, Sepoys increasingly resented the aggressive attempts of British officers to convert them to Christianity. The sepoys stationed in Bengal were particularly offended by new army rifle cartridges, which had to be bitten off with the teeth before being rammed down the gun barrel. What outraged the soldiers was the rumor, probably true, that the cartridges were greased with beef and pork fat, violating the religious dietary prohibitions of both cow-revering Hindus and pork-avoiding Muslims.

In 1857 one revolt, sparked by Sepoy outrage, spread rapidly and offered a serious challenge to British authority. The British called it the Indian Mutiny, and Indian nationalists later termed it the first War of Independence. The revolt began among sepoys in the army and was soon supported by peasant and Muslim uprisings. A few members of Hindu and Muslim princely families also joined the rebel cause. Among them was the widow of the Maratha ruler of Jhansi, a small state recently annexed by the British. The Rani (queen) of Jhansi led her troops into battle dressed as a man. Historians still debate whether the revolt was truly "national," since it was confined largely to north and northeast India. Because no rebel leaders envisioned a unified Indian nation, British observers argued that the rebels had limited and selfish goals. But broad groups of the population had perceived their customs and religions threatened by British policies. Some rebel leaders attempted to unite Hindus and Muslims by calling for a joint defense of their religions against their common British enemy.

The rebels captured Delhi and besieged several cities, but they could not hold them for long. The desperate struggle involved ruthless tactics; both sides committed massacres. For example, rebels murdered a thousand British residents when they occupied the city of Kanpur. On the other side, when British troops recaptured Delhi, they became berserk and engaged in widespread raping, pillaging, and killing. The Muslim poet Ghalib mourned: "Here is a vast ocean of blood before me. Thousands of my friends are dead. Perhaps none is left even to shed tears upon my death."[6] The rebellion had also attracted some conservatives who hoped to restore the old Mughal order. The anti-British sentiment was not widespread enough, however, to overcome the rebels' problems: inadequate arms, weak communications, and lack of a unified command structure. In addition, the rebels received no support from people in other parts of India, and they had no strategy for a national revolt. Linguistic, religious, cultural, and regional fragmentation made a united Indian opposition impossible. When the British captured the last rebel fort, held by the Rani of Jhansi, in 1858, she was killed and the rebellion collapsed, although a few small rebel groups fought skirmishes with the British until 1860.

SECTION SUMMARY

- Fragmented after the decline of the Mughals, India was unable to resist encroachment by the Portuguese, Dutch, British, and French.

- In reaction to the Black Hole of Calcutta, the British under Robert Clive took over Bengal and proceeded to plunder its riches; though his successor, Warren Hastings, was more respectful, many governor-generals disregarded Indians' rights.

- Though initially opposed by the French, the British East India Company gradually expanded its control over India by employing local collaborators and playing groups off against each other, and by 1850 Britain controlled all of India.

- The British expanded into Sri Lanka, where they imported Tamils to work on the tea plantations; into Nepal, where they recruited effective soldiers; and into Afghanistan, where they met fierce resistance but ultimately installed a friendly ruler.

- Many British tried to make Indians more Western by abolishing customs they considered backward, while others became interested in studying traditional Indian teachings.

- By having peasants pay their taxes in cash rather than in crops, the British began to shift India from a barter economy to a money economy, a change that undermined centuries of rural stability.

- Though some Indians supported Westernization, periodic revolts occurred, and in 1857 the sepoys began a large rebellion that led to much bloodshed and eventually Indian defeat.

The Reshaping of Indian Society

How did colonialism transform the Indian economy and foster new ideas in India?

The 1857 revolt prompted the British to replace the British East India Company government with direct colonial rule. The British felt betrayed by the rebels, but some officials understood the causes of the revolt, viewing the troubles as symptoms of deeper discontents that needed to be addressed. To move in that direction, the 1858 Government of India Act transferred sovereignty to the British monarch. In 1876 Queen Victoria was proclaimed Empress of India, head of the government known as the British *Raj*, named for the ancient title of Hindu kings. India became the brightest "jewel in the imperial crown," a source of fabulous wealth. The policies pursued by the British Raj reshaped Indian society, sparking new economic, intellectual, and social patterns and eventually inspiring movements reflecting a new sense of the Indian nation.

Colonial Government and Education

The British Raj bore many similarities to the Mughal system it had replaced. The top British officials, the viceroys, lived, like Mughal emperors, in splendor in Delhi. The British made efforts to win Indian support by pomp and circumstance, including Mughal-style ceremonies and building a new capital at New Delhi, next to the old Mughal capital of Delhi, with gigantic architecture dwarfing even the monuments of the Mughals. The British built palatial mansions, museums, schools, universities, and city halls. Yet, while they usually lived well, many British residents also faced health problems from the tropical heat and from diseases such as malaria. After 1857 British officials mistrusted Indians but, like the Mughals before them, also viewed the traditional princes, both Hindu and Muslim, as sources of support whose positions had to be preserved. The princes were allowed to keep their privileges and palaces in exchange for promoting acceptance of British policies.

Borrowing Mughal practices, the British ruled through a mix of good communications, exploitation of Hindu-Muslim rivalries, and military force. The British connected India with a network of roads, bridges, and railways, and by 1900 India had over 25,000 miles of track, the fourth largest rail system in the world. The British also deliberately pitted the Hindu majority against the Muslim minority by favoring one or the other group in law, language, and custom. For example, Hindus protested that the main Muslim language, Urdu, was used in many North Indian courts and that Muslim butchers were allowed to kill cows, considered sacred animals by Hindus. The British divide-and-rule policy helped maintain British power but also exacerbated hatreds that remain today. Local revenue supported a huge army of 200,000 men, mostly Indian volunteers, who were needed to keep the peace in India and fight British battles abroad.

In their efforts to rule, the British also introduced policies at variance with Mughal practice, among them discrimination against Indians. The British typically believed that Western colonialism improved Asian and African societies. Rudyard Kipling (1865–1936), a Bombay-born, Britain-educated English poet and novelist, reflected this view in his writings: "Take up the White Man's burden—Send forth the best ye breed— Go, bind your sons in exile. To serve your captives' need."[7] Some policies reflected racism. Much like colonized Africans, Indians were excluded from European-only clubs and parks as well as high positions in the bureaucracy, and enjoyed no real power or influence. Recognizing the pervasive discrimination, the Raj announced but did not always implement reforms.

Colonial Britain also concerned itself with border security and Russian ambitions. Frontier policy often relied on diplomacy but sometimes involved military aggression. For example, as part of what Kipling called the "Great Game" of strategic rivalry with Russia, Britain invaded Tibet in 1903, prompting Tibetan leaders to agree not to concede territory to Russia or any other foreign power. Lord Curzon (viceroy from 1899 to 1905) remarked that "we do not want their country. It would be madness for us to cross the Himalayas and to occupy it. But it is important that no one else should seize it, and that it should be turned into a sort of buffer state between the Russian and Indian Empires."[8]

The Raj continued the Westernization policy of the British East India Company, promoting British and often Christian values through an expanded English-medium education system. Thanks to these schools, English became the common language for educated Indians. However, only a privileged minority, mostly drawn from higher-caste Hindus, could afford to send their children, mostly boys, to the English schools. By 1911 only 11 percent of men and 1 percent of women were literate in any language.

Nonetheless, the schools fostered change by introducing new ideas. A small minority of Indians (less than 2 percent) had converted to Christianity by 1911. More importantly, an English-educated middle class emerged, with a taste for European products and ideas. These Indians sent their sons and a few daughters to British universities, where their children often studied, for the first time, Indian history and also learned about the ideas of Western political liberalism. Notions like "freedom" and "self-determination of peoples" learned in European universities stood in sharp contrast to conditions in India. The returning students asked why the British did not practice such ideas in their colony. As a result, British educational and political institutions fostered an Indian nationalist movement. The growing British-educated professional class organized social, professional, and political bodies concerned with improving Indian life and acquiring more influence in government.

Economic Transformation

The British also transformed the Indian economy. Before 1700 Mughal India had been an economic powerhouse and manufacturing center, and the world leader in producing cotton textiles. India still produced a quarter of all world manufactured goods in 1750. The disparity between urban and rural wealth was narrower than in most societies. However, two centuries later, conditions had changed. Many historians believe that British policies, which were designed to drain India of its wealth to benefit Britain, harmed the Indian economy. In their view, British land policies commercialized agriculture while tax and tariff policies diminished the existing manufacturing.

As already mentioned, British land policies greatly affected the rural economy and peasant life. The land tax system first introduced by the British East India Company in parts of India exploited the peasantry. By turning once self-sufficient peasants into tenants, the British planted the roots of one of contemporary India's greatest dilemmas, inequitable land distribution. As peasants lost their land rights and came to depend on the whims of landlords, they often fell hopelessly into debt. Furthermore, required now (as in Africa) to pay taxes in cash, peasants had to grow cash crops such as cotton, jute, pepper, or opium rather than food. As a result, famine became more common, killing millions as food supplies and distribution became more uncertain.

Other changes also affected rural life. The introduction of steamships freed shipping routes and schedules from the vagaries of monsoon winds, and the opening of the Suez Canal in 1869 made it easier and much faster to ship raw materials from India to Europe, increasing the demand for these resources. The return ships brought to India cheap machine goods, which undermined the role of village craftsmen such as weavers and tinkers. As imported goods displaced artisans and farmers shifted to cash crops, the village economy came to be based not, as it had been for millennia, on a symbiotic exchange of goods and services but on cash transactions. The quest for revenues and the priorities of commerce, which included felling forests and ploughing grassland to grow more cash crops, also placed massive pressure on the physical environment.

Some historians argue that the decline of Indian manufacturing was another key result of British rule. Hoping to find new markets abroad for Britain's industrial products, especially textiles, the British parliament denied India tariff protection for its more expensive handmade products and excluded Indian manufactured goods from Britain. The British also discouraged Indian manufacturing by taxing Indian-made goods passing between Indian states and by prohibiting the import of industrial machinery. Meanwhile, as often occurred in colonial Africa and Southeast Asia, British products flooded the country, destroying the livelihood of many skilled craftsmen. For example, textile imports increased sixfold in value between 1854 and 1913, ruining millions of Indian weavers. They, along with metalworkers and glass blowers, had little choice but to become farm laborers. A British report in 1909 stated that the only way for the Indian weavers to compete with British goods was to lower the price of their products, but this strategy left insufficient income for maintaining families.

Industrial activity did not disappear from India between 1815 and 1914, and, despite many barriers, a few Indians found ways to prosper. British entrepreneurs established the world's largest jute-manufacturing industry while Indians continued to compete with British imports by manufacturing cotton textiles and initiated a modern iron and steel sector. For example, the Gujerati industrialist Jamsetji N. Tata (1839–1904) built cotton mills, while his son, Sir Dorabji Tata (1859–1932), founded the Indian steel industry in 1907. Unable to get British funding, they raised money among Indian investors. They used their wealth to promote scientific education and found technical colleges.

By the late 1800s the limits on India's industries became a subject of heated controversy. Indian critics of British policies alleged that tariffs protected British industries while strangling Indian industries that might have competed with them. While the British claimed that their rule improved India, the gap between British and Indian wealth grew. By 1895 the per capita income in Britain was fourteen to fifteen times higher than India's, a much greater gap than existed two hundred years earlier. Indian scholars attacked what one called "The Drain" of wealth and argued that British policies gave India "peace but not prosperity; the manufacturers lost their industries; the cultivators were ground down by a heavy and variable taxation; the revenues were to a large extent diverted to England."[9] Defenders of British policies replied that British rule brought investment, imported goods, railroads, and law and order. But critics questioned whether these innovations benefited most Indians and fostered overall development or rather resulted in more systematic exploitation by increasingly prosperous British merchants and industrialists, as well as the Indian businessmen and landlords who cooperated with them. Whatever the merits of the arguments on both sides, by 1948, after two centuries of British rule, most Indians remained poor.

Population Growth and Indian Emigration

The plight of the peasant was worsened by population growth. Despite the deadly famines, under British rule the Indian population rose from perhaps 100 million in 1700 to 300 million by 1920. The British removed the traditional restraints on population growth posed by war and disease by imposing peace and improving sanitation and health; in addition, by encouraging agricultural productivity, they provided economic incentives to have more children to help in the fields. A similar population increase occurred in Europe at the same time, although for different reasons, but growing numbers of Europeans could be absorbed by industrialization or emigration to the Americas and Australia. Unlike Europe, India enjoyed neither an industrial revolution nor an increase in farm productivity. Indian landlords had a stake in the cash crop system and wanted no innovations that might threaten their dominance. As a result, the number of people far outstripped the amount of available food and land, creating dire poverty and widespread hunger.

As these problems mounted, millions of desperately poor Indians were recruited to emigrate to other lands. After the abolition of slavery in the Americas, African American workers often left the plantations. The need to replace them created a market for Indian labor in Trinidad, British Guiana (today's Guyana), and Dutch Guiana (now Suriname). Plantations in Sri Lanka, Malaya, Fiji, the Indian Ocean island of Mauritius,

and South Africa also wanted Indian labor. Many Indians saw no alternative to leaving, but travel was hazardous. For example, in 1884 a family of low-caste landless laborers, who faced starvation in the north Indian state of Bihar, boarded a sailing ship at Calcutta bound for the distant Fiji Islands in the South Pacific. The family was led by Somerea, a fifty-year-old widow, and included her two sons, a daughter-in-law, and four grandchildren ranging from ten years to fourteen months in age. The ship they boarded carried 497 adults and children. After three months of travel the ship arrived in the islands but, thanks to cases of cholera, dysentery, and typhoid and a shipwreck in Fijian waters, 56 passengers had died during the trip. Somerea's family apparently survived the journey, but their fate in Fiji is unknown.

Indian emigrants fell into several categories. Most, including Somerea's family, were destined for plantations growing cash crops such as sugar, tea, or rubber and were indentured, meaning they had signed contracts that obligated them to work for a period of years (usually three to five) in order to repay their passage. Somerea's family probably worked on a sugar plantation. The indenture contracts also stipulated the number of days per week (six) and hours per day (usually nine to ten) that must be worked. In addition to indentured workers, many Indian merchants, moneylenders, and laborers also emigrated, flocking to British Burma, Singapore, Malaya, and East Africa. Between 1880 and 1930 around a quarter million people a year, both men and women, left India. Few returned. The mortality rates for the indentured workers were so high and the indenture terms so unfavorable that critics considered the system another form of slavery. The pay was so low—a few pennies a day—and loss of income due to illness so common, that many Indians could never pay off their contracts.

The resulting diaspora made Indians one of the most recognizable global societies. Cities such as Nairobi in Kenya, Rangoon in Burma, and Port of Spain in Trinidad had large Indian neighborhoods. Indians now had key economic roles in many countries. Indian trade networks, usually based on family or caste ties, reached around the Indian Ocean and Pacific Rim. The future leader of the Indian nationalist movement, Mohandas Gandhi (GAHN-dee), then a young law school graduate, experimented with his ideas of nonviolent resistance to illegitimate power while working among Indians in South Africa. Today people of Indian ancestry make up half or more of the populations of Mauritius, Trinidad, Guyana, Suriname, and Fiji and are substantial minorities in Sri Lanka, Malaysia, Singapore, Burma, Kenya, and South Africa. However, although many Indian emigrants succeeded in business or the professions, large numbers in Southeast Asia, Sri Lanka, South Africa, Fiji, and the Caribbean still labor on plantations growing cocoa, rubber, tea, or sugar.

Indian Thought and Literature

In the later 1800s Indian intellectuals responded to British rule and ideas in several ways. A small group of well-educated Indians, in the tradition of Ram Mohan Roy during the early 1800s, wanted to combine the best of East and West. They sought reforms of customs, such as the ban on widow remarriage, that they saw as corruptions of Hinduism. But their influence waned after 1900. Another group, hostile to Western ways, sought to revive Hindu culture, calling attention to the glories of the past and arguing that India needed nothing from the West.

One thinker, Swami Vivekananda (SWAH-me VIH-vee-keh-NAHN-da) (1863–1902), was particularly influential in his concern for ending both British cultural and political domination: "O India, this is your terrible danger. The spell of imitating the West is getting such a strong hold upon you. Be proud that thou art an Indian, and proudly proclaim: 'I am an Indian, every Indian is my brother.'"[10] Swami Vivekananda was a reformer, condemning the oppression of untouchables and inspiring devotion to the needs of the poor. For inspiration, he turned to the traditions of popular Hinduism. His writings and lectures gave Indians great pride in their own culture.

Swami Vivekananda also became involved in the spread of Hindu thought to the West. In 1893, on a visit to New York, he formed the Vedanta Society, which promoted a philosophical view of Hinduism based on the ancient *Upanishads*. Vedanta thought portrayed the Hindu holy books, the Vedas, compiled over 2,500 years ago, as the supreme source of religious knowledge, although not necessarily authored by either God or humans. Even earlier, in the 1870s, Vedanta ideas had contributed to another North American and European movement, **Theosophy**, that attracted some Western followers by blending Hindu ideas with Western spiritualist and scientific ideas. Founded by Ukrainian-born Helena Blavatsky (1831–1891), Theosophy promoted the idea that India was more spiritual than other societies.

Like Hindus, Muslims were forced to rethink their values and prospects, and several currents of thought emerged. The British left many Muslim institutions, including the schools, untouched. But Muslims resented Christian missionaries setting up schools and trying to make converts, an effort that was supported by British officials openly critical of Islam. To Muslims, India seemed increasingly dominated by European and Hindu values and ideas. In response, some Muslims traveled to the Middle East in pursuit of Islamic knowledge and came home with Islamic revivalist ideas. The most dogmatic and militant form of Islamic revivalism, Wahhabism (see Chapter 21), became popular in the northwest frontier and Bengal. Opposed to modernization, especially progressive ideas such as women's rights, the revivalists clashed with other Muslims, Christians, Sikhs, and Hindus. Some revivalists opened schools to spread their version of Islam.

In contrast to revivalists, Muslim modernists, led by the cosmopolitan Sayyid Ahmad Khan (1817–1898), wanted Muslims to gain strength to achieve power. Khan argued that "the more worldly progress we make, the more glory Islam gains." He wanted to show that Islam was compatible with modern science, and in 1877 he founded a college at Aligarh (AL-ee-

GAHR) that offered Western learning within a Muslim context. Trained for jobs in government service and politics, Aligarh students studied many subjects in English, and graduates, often not devout, typically learned how to play the British game of cricket and then went on to study at top British universities. A satirist observed the secular atmosphere at Aligarh, whose leaders "neither believe in God, nor yet in prayer. They say they do, but it is plain to see, What they believe in is the powers that be."[11] Aligarh graduates dominated Muslim political activity in India until independence.

Indian literature during this period included some with a nationalist bent. For example, the Tagore family, Hindus from Calcutta, were pioneers in the movement to awaken national pride and find literary outlets for self-expression. The most significant writer of the era, Rabindranath Tagore (RAH-bin-drah-NATH ta-GORE) (1861–1941), was a poet, educator, patriot, and internationalist whose writings won him the Nobel Prize for literature in 1913 (see Witness to the Past: Challenging British Imperialism with Spiritual Virtues). Writing of the romantic patriotism of his wealthy family in the 1870s, he recalled that they adopted foreign customs but also nurtured a pride in the Indian nation. Tagore sought a new and freer India, "where the mind is without fear and the head is held high; Where knowledge is free; where the clear stream of reason has not lost its way into the dreary desert sand of dead habit; Into that heaven of freedom, let my country awake."[12]

Social Life and Gender Relations

British policies also affected Indian social patterns, including the caste system. Some historians argue that caste has for centuries been an active, continually changing part of Indian life, providing a structure to separate people of higher status from those of lower status, especially untouchables. Others question whether the elaborate caste system of modern times was common in earlier centuries, arguing that the modern system reflected the views of colonial era officials seeking to classify Indians for administrative and census purposes. A case can be made for this argument. Before the colonial era, Hindus in Bengal, Punjab, and south India generally saw the formal differences among varied castes as of only moderate importance for groups and individuals. From the early 1800s, however, and owing partly to British attempts to win support from high-caste Hindus by emphasizing their elite status in the caste hierarchy, the caste system became more rigid. British policies sharpened caste identities, classifying people largely through their caste affiliations. Furthermore, as different Indians increasingly came into contact with one another, causing confusion about status, some Indians sought firmer social and moral boundaries by further dividing castes from each other. In the nineteenth century, much of India became more caste-conscious than ever before, with upper castes stressing their uniqueness and lower castes wanting to emulate the upper castes to improve their social status.

By the early 1900s caste had acquired even more meaning in the lives of Indians, but, as in precolonial times, it remained fluid and diverse, differing from region to region. Envying the highest

Theosophy A nineteenth-century North American and European movement that blended Hindu thought with Western spiritualist and scientific ideas.

On the last day of the nineteenth century Rabindranath Tagore wrote a poem in Bengali protesting the brutal imperialism of the war Britain was waging against the Boers in South Africa, driven, Tagore believed, by British nationalism. The poem suggested that the patient cultivation of the "spiritual virtues" of India and the East would become a force in the world after the reckless power of Western imperialism, sparked by nationalism, had lost its control over humankind. In this, he echoed the views of many Hindu nationalists and reformers that Hinduism and India had a special devotion to peace and spiritual insights that could benefit the Western world. For this poem and other influential writings, Tagore won the Noble Prize for literature in 1913.

> The last sun of the century sets amidst the blood-red clouds of the West and the whirlwind of hatred.
>
> The naked passion of self-love of Nations, in its drunken delirium of greed, is dancing to the clash of steel and the howling verses of vengeance.
>
> The hungry self of the Nation shall burst in a violence of fury from its own shameless feeding, for it has made the world its food.
>
> And licking it, crunching it, and swallowing it in big morsels, It swells and swells,
>
> Till in the midst of its unholy feast descends the sudden shaft of heaven piercing its heart of grossness.
>
> The crimson glow of light on the horizon is not the light of thy dawn of peace, my Motherland.

> It is the glimmer of the funeral pyre burning to ashes the vast flesh—the self- love of the Nation—dead under its own excess.
>
> The morning waits behind the patient dark of the East, Meek and silent.
>
> Keep watch, India.
>
> Bring your offerings of worship for that sacred sunrise.
>
> Let the first hymn of its welcome sound in your voice and sing.
>
> "Come, Peace, thou daughter of God's own great suffering. Come with thy treasure of contentment, the sword of fortitude, And meekness crowning thy forehead."
>
> Be not ashamed, my brothers, to stand before the proud and the powerful, With your white robe of simpleness.
>
> Let your crown be of humility, your freedom the freedom of the soul.
>
> Build God's throne daily upon the ample barrenness of your poverty.
>
> And know that what is huge is not great and pride is not everlasting.

THINKING ABOUT THE READING

1. How does Tagore perceive nationalism?
2. How does he believe India should respond to Western power?

Source: William Theodore De Bary, ed., *Sources of Indian Tradition*, vol. 2 (New York: Columbia University Press, 1958), pp. 234–235 © Copyright 1958 Columbia University Press. Reprinted with permission of the publisher.

caste, brahmans (priests), other castes adopted brahman rituals and ideas, such as vegetarianism. For example, some untouchable leather workers, at the bottom of the social hierarchy, joined a movement that opposed the caste system but, like Brahmans, respected cows and avoided eating meat. In response to attempts by lower castes to improve their status, higher castes hoped to preserve their privileged positions by demanding that members of lower castes be excluded from government jobs. Hindu thinkers were divided about the caste system. Some social reformers called for abolishing caste, while defenders of Hindu culture praised the ideals of conduct and morality embedded in the caste system. Still others, such as Swami Vivekananda, took a middle ground, arguing that caste had its bad side but that its benefits outweighed its disadvantages.

Gender relations also changed during colonial times. Traditionally women and men had performed separate but interdependent roles within a household governed by men. Ploughing was men's work; transplanting and weeding were shared duties; and women did the house and garden. But both men and women in farming families faced a loss of work as

land came under the control of absentee landlords who emphasized growing cash crops rather than food. Lower-caste men in north India who sought to emulate the upper castes often placed more restrictions on their women, including forcing some into purdah, or seclusion. At the same time, however, new opportunities arose for other women. More girls attended school, and many became teachers, nurses, and midwives. The first women doctors graduated in the 1880s. By the 1870s women were publishing biographies of their experiences and struggles as women. Like boys, some girls now enjoyed social gatherings separate from their families. For centuries girls had been married early and had little choice in the matter. Now Indians began to speak of the "new women," a small minority in Indian cities who led more independent lives than had their mothers and married later, in their twenties or thirties, or sometimes did not marry at all.

Indian men and women also debated changes in gender relations, some taking strong positions. Indian and British reformers sought to improve the lives of Indian women and foster greater equality between the genders. A new marriage act in 1872 provoked controversy by providing for both civil marriage and marriage across caste lines. The British tried incremental reforms, such as banning sati, allowing widow remarriage, and raising the age of female consent from ten to twelve. Both British and Indian reformers tended to support the idea of marriage as based on love but also encouraged wives to show their husbands and children self-sacrificing devotion. This was not enough progress for some women, however. The first Indian feminist, Pandita Ramabai (1858–1922), whose writings urged women to take control of their lives, came from a prominent brahman family. Her father, a noted social reformer, declined to marry her off as a child. Her knowledge of Sanskrit won her the reputation of *Saraswati*, after the Hindu goddess of wisdom. She married a lawyer of low-caste background, a shocking move for a brahman woman, and then traveled to England, where she became a Christian. Upon returning to India, Ramabai opened a school for girls, especially child widows, and later a refuge for female famine victims. She also invited controversy by supporting girls who refused to enter arranged marriages.

The Rise of Nationalism

British rule inevitably produced a nationalist reaction. The Western idea of the "nation," defined by a feeling of inclusiveness among people living within the same state (see Chapter 19), was new for Indians, who tended to think of themselves as joined by a common Hindu or Muslim culture rather than a centralized state. Nonetheless, by establishing political unity in India under the Raj, educating Indians in European ideas, including nationalism, but then largely excluding Indians from administration, Britain fostered national feelings and bitterness. Furthermore, by 1900, Indians were publishing six hundred newspapers in various languages, which reported on world events such as the Irish struggle for independence from England, the Japanese defeat of Russia in war, and the U.S. conquest of the Philippines, all of which inspired Indians to oppose British rule.

Nationalist activity blossomed. In 1885 nationalists formed the Indian National Congress, which worked for peaceful progress toward self-government. But the Congress, as it came to be known, mostly attracted well-educated professionals and merchants, especially Bengalis, of brahman backgrounds and had few working class or peasant members. British officials were scornful of the Congress, doubting the possibility of Indian unity in such a diverse society. Constitutional reforms in 1909 brought a measure of representative government, but Indians still lacked true legislative and financial power.

Growing frustrations led impatient members to form a more aggressive nationalist faction within the Congress. By 1907 this radical group, led by a former journalist of Maratha background, Bal Gangadhar Tilak (1856–1920), transformed the Congress from a gentleman's pressure group into the spearhead of an active independence movement. A fierce opponent of Western influences, Tilak defended Hindu orthodoxy and custom, using religion as a vitalizing force for the nationalist movement. But many politically aware Indians disliked Tilak and remained wary of the Congress. Some feared that democratic values threatened their aristocratic privileges.

Muslims perceived the Hindu-dominated Congress, particularly radical leaders like Tilak, as anti-Muslim. As Hindu-Muslim tensions increased, new Muslim organizations were formed. In 1906 the All-India Muslim League was founded with the goal of uniting a population scattered in pockets all over the country. Hindus constituted 80 percent of India's population; Muslims were a majority only in eastern Bengal, Sind, north Punjab, and the mountain districts west of the Indus Valley. The Muslims' minority status led the influential Muslim reformer and educator Sayyid Ahmad Khan to oppose majority rule in 1887, arguing that "it would be like a game of dice, in which one man has four dice and the other only one."[13] The Muslim League's first great victory came in 1909, when British reforms guaranteed some seats in representative councils to Muslims, setting a precedence for minority representation. The Congress was enraged, charging divide and rule. Hindu-Muslim rivalries continued to complicate the nationalist movement throughout the twentieth century, eventually leading to separate Hindu- and Muslim-majority nations, India and Pakistan, in 1949.

SECTION SUMMARY

- After 1857, the British monarchy ruled India through the British Raj, which built palatial buildings, a large railroad system, and an expanded English-language school system, thereby educating Indians about Western ideals such as nationalism and sowing the seeds for an Indian revolution against Britain.

- Britain stifled Indian industry by using India as a market for British industrial products, and it turned Indian peasants into tenants who had to grow cash crops for Britain rather than their own food, thus destroying the centuries-old village economy and exacerbating famine and poverty.

- As the Indian population increased, many poor Indians were driven to work all over the world in indentured servitude, while other Indians emigrated to work as laborers, merchants, and moneylenders.

- While some Hindus wanted to combine the best in British and Indian culture, others, such as Vivekananda and Tagore, sought to revive more traditional Hindu traditions, while a Muslim college at Aligarh trained Muslims in English government and science.

- The caste system became more rigid under British rule, with lower castes imitating upper castes, upper castes trying to strengthen their privileges, and women facing greater restrictions in some cases and expanded opportunity in others.

- As Indian nationalists began to unite in their opposition to the British, the Hindu majority formed the Indian National Congress in 1885, but it was opposed by some aristocrats who feared losing their privileges and by Muslims, who formed the All-India Muslim League in 1906.

◈ Southeast Asia and Colonization

How did the Western nations expand their control of Southeast Asia?

Like Indians, Southeast Asians also had colonization imposed on them by Western military force. Arising on the Asian mainland and islands east of India and south of China, Southeast Asian societies had long flourished from trade and had formed strong, often dynamic, states, but by the 1700s most faced increasing political and economic challenges from Western powers. During the 1800s the challenges became more threatening, and by 1914 all the major Southeast Asian societies except the Siamese had come under Western colonial control. The major changes came in Indonesia, Vietnam, and Burma, where the Dutch, French, and British, respectively, increased their power, and in the Philippines, which by the end of the 1800s was controlled by the United States. Thus Southeast Asian societies became tied, more than ever before, to the larger world but lost their political and economic independence.

Dutch Colonialism in Indonesia

Between 1750 and 1914 the Dutch expanded their power in the Indonesian archipelago. They already controlled the Spice Islands (Maluku) of northeast Indonesia and the large island of Java, territories that supplied them with great wealth. In 1799 the Dutch government abolished the Dutch East Indies Company, which had governed the Dutch holdings, because of debts and corruption and replaced it with a formal colonial government charged with reenergizing the administration of the scattered Dutch-controlled territories and making Java even more profitable (see Chronology: Southeast Asia, 1750–1914). The Dutch colonial regime concentrated its economic exploitation in Java and Sumatra.

In 1830 Dutch administrators introduced the **cultivation system**, an agricultural policy that forced farmers on Java to grow sugar on their rice land. The government profited by setting a low fixed price to pay peasants for sugar, even when world prices were high. The cultivation system enriched the Dutch but ultimately impoverished many peasants. A Dutch critic of the system described the results: "If anyone should ask whether the man who grows the products receives a reward proportionate to the yields, the answer must be in the negative. The Government compels him to grow on *his* land what pleases *it*; it punishes him when he sells the crop to anyone else but *it*."[14] Dutch-owned plantations growing sugar and other cash crops replaced the cultivation system in the 1870s.

In the later 1800s the Dutch turned their attention to gaining control, and exploiting the resources, of the Indonesian islands they had not already conquered, such as Borneo and

cultivation system An agricultural policy imposed by the Dutch in Java that forced Javanese farmers to grow sugar on rice land.

CHRONOLOGY	
Southeast Asia, 1750–1914	
1786	British base at Penang Island
1799	Abolition of Dutch East Indies Company
1788–1802	Tayson rule in Vietnam
1802	Nguyen dynasty in Vietnam
1819	British base at Singapore
1823–1826	First Anglo-Burman War
1830–1870	Cultivation system in Java
1851–1852	Second Anglo-Burman War
1858–1884	French conquest of Vietnam
1868–1910	Kingship of Chulalongkorn in Siam
1869	Opening of Suez Canal
1885–1886	Completion of British conquest of Burma
1897	Formation of Federation of Indochina
1898–1902	U.S. conquest of Philippines
1908	Dutch defeat of last Balinese kingdom

Sulawesi (see Map 22.2). In some areas the Dutch resorted to violence to impose their rule and suppress resistance. For example, they sent in armed forces between 1906 and 1908 to crush the small kingdoms on Bali, an island just east of Java. After the valiant Balinese resistance failed, the royal family of the largest Balinese kingdom committed collective suicide, walking into the guns of the Dutch forces rather than surrendering, shaming the Dutch and depriving them of any sense of victory. The Dutch created Indonesia as a country by uniting the thousands of scattered societies and dozens of states of this vast, diverse archipelago into the Dutch East Indies. But the colony, governed from Batavia (now Jakarta) on Java, promoted little common national feeling and remained a collection of peoples with diverse languages and distinctive cultures. Later this diversity made it difficult to build an Indonesian nation with a common identity.

The Making of British Malaya

At the same time as the Dutch were expanding their power, the British became more politically and economically active in the southern part of the Malay Peninsula, later known as Malaya, and eventually they subjugated the varied Malay states. British Malaya originated in coastal port cities. Seeking a naval base in the eastern Indian Ocean, the British East India Company purchased Penang (puh-NANG) Island, off Malaya's northwest

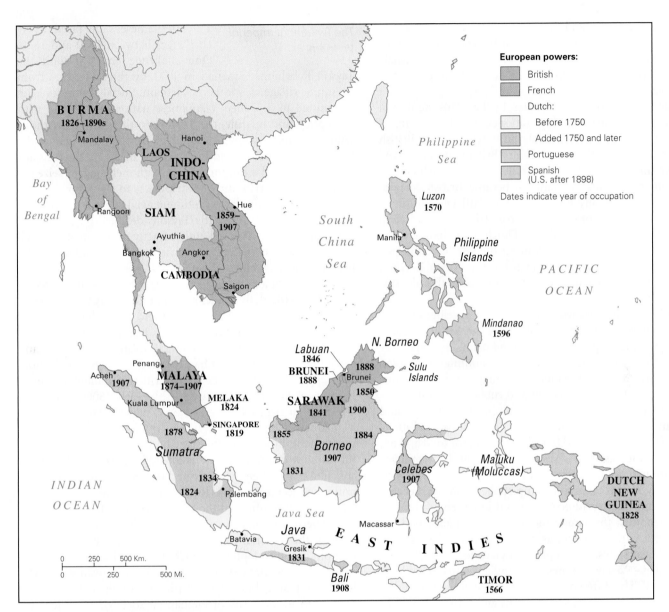

Map 22.2   The Colonization of Southeast Asia
Between 1800 and 1914 the European powers gradually conquered or gained control over the Southeast Asian societies that had not been colonized in the Early Modern Era. Only Siam remained independent.

coast, from a cash-strapped Malay sultan in 1786. This action marked the first stage in creating a regional British sphere of influence. In 1819 a visionary British agent of the British East India Company, Jamaican-born Thomas Stamford Raffles (1781–1826), capitalized on local political unrest to acquire sparsely populated Singapore Island, at the tip of the Malay Peninsula. A fine harbor and strategic location at the southern end of the Straits of Melaka, the midpoint for shipping between China and India, made Singapore the base for Britain's regional thrust and a great source of profit to both British businessmen and government treasuries. The British founded a town and welcomed Chinese immigrants, making Singapore the major hub for Chinese economic activity and networks in Southeast Asia. By the 1860s the city built on Singapore, with a

mostly Chinese population, had become the key China-India trade link and crossroads of Southeast Asian commerce. After obtaining the port city of Melaka from the Dutch in 1824, Britain now governed the three Malayan ports as one colony, known as the Straits Settlements.

From their coastal ports the British extended their influence into the Malay states. British merchants in the Straits Settlements, for whom European markets, thanks to the opening of the Suez Canal in 1869, were now much more accessible, pressured British authorities to intervene in the Malay states to acquire resources and markets. Adding to these challenges for the British was the steady immigration of Chinese to western Malaya, where they contracted with local Malay rulers to mine tin and gold. Demand for metals in industrializing Europe increased dramatically, and British merchants, competitors of the Chinese, wanted to gain control of the gold and tin mining. Chinese settlers also established towns such as Kuala Lumpur (KWAH-luh loom-POOR), which later grew into major cities.

To facilitate access to these states, by the 1870s the British used order and security as their rationale for threatening or forcing the sultans of various Malayan states to accept British advisers and then British domination. Britain soon achieved formal or informal control over nine sultanates, which, together with the Straits Settlements, became British Malaya. These actions eventually resulted in the artificial division of the historical Malay world into two countries, British Malaya (now part of Malaysia) and the Dutch East Indies (now Indonesia). The British also colonized the northern third of Borneo, creating the states of Sabah (British North Borneo) and Sarawak and imposing a protectorate over the old sultanate of Brunei.

British rule changed Malaya. Economic development occurred largely along the west coast, where the British encouraged the planting of pepper, tobacco, oil palm, and especially rubber. As thousands of Chinese and Indian immigrants settled there to work, Malaya developed a mining- and plantation-based economy that produced tin and rubber for Western resource and market needs. Tin was shipped to Europe and North America to be used in manufacturing household utensils and to make tin cans and barrels for storage of food and oil, which made life easier for Western families and for military forces stationed far from home. In addition, Malay villagers, pressured by British taxes to take up rubber planting, became integrated into the world economy and lost their traditional self-sufficiency. At the same time, the British maintained the Malay sultans and aristocracy as symbolic and privileged leaders of the Malay states. Thus a **plural society** developed, a medley of peoples—Malays, Chinese, and Indians—that mixed but did not blend. The different groups maintained their own cultures, religions, languages, and customs and related mainly to their own members, as a Malay proverb said: "raven with raven, sparrow with sparrow."

Vietnam: Colonization and Resistance

For centuries a major power in Southeast Asia, Vietnam fell to French colonialism after a bitter struggle. In the 1700s Vietnam was beset by growing problems, including civil war and rebellion. While a new dynasty reestablished some stability, it was unable to thwart the aggressive actions of the French, who colonized Vietnam against stiff resistance. The unpopular French regime changed Vietnamese society by introducing competitive capitalism into once cooperative communities, linking the Vietnamese to the uncertainties of the world economy, undermining traditional politics, and otherwise exploiting the Vietnamese people.

The Twilight of Imperial Vietnam

The Vietnamese state faced many challenges between 1750 and 1850. One challenge emerged with the Tayson Rebellion, launched in 1771 by three brothers from Tayson, a village in southern Vietnam. Social revolutionaries committed to a unified Vietnamese nation and fed up with corruption and misrule, the Tayson brothers and their thousands of armed followers fought for thirty years against the Vietnamese emperors and their French allies. The Taysons appealed for radical economic change with their slogan "seize the property of the rich and redistribute it to the poor."[15] They also skillfully manipulated sentiment against foreign assistance to the emperors. In 1788 the Taysons defeated their foes and reestablished the national unity fractured in the long civil wars. They also sponsored economic expansion and rallied the people against a Chinese invasion.

A little over a decade later, in 1802, Nguyen Anh (NEW-yin ahn) (1761–1820), the leader of a princely family based in Hue, led a force that defeated the Taysons and established a new imperial dynasty with French assistance, but the Nguyen dynasty he founded was unpopular and unable to address the social and economic inequalities that had inspired the Tayson Rebellion. *The Tale of Kieu*, a 3,300-line poem written by diplomat Nguyen Du (no relation to the dynasty) in the early 1800s, reflected a growing criticism of the greed and hypocrisy of upper-class Vietnamese. The poem, cherished by Vietnamese even today, sympathetically narrates the story of an intelligent and beautiful young woman, Kieu, who is forced by poverty to become a concubine and then a prostitute but who keeps her sense of honor and secretly remains loyal to her true love. To many Vietnamese, Kieu symbolized the Vietnamese people mistreated by the upper-class Vietnamese and their French allies. Another critic of the imperial court and of Confucianism, the patriarchal philosophy adopted from China centuries earlier, was the outspoken woman poet Ho Xuan Huong (ho swan wan), who had been a concubine to several high officials. Using wit and sarcasm to attack the ills of Vietnamese society, she wrote freely about sex, championed women's rights, and attacked polygamy: "One wife gets quilts, the other wife must freeze. To share a husband . . . what a fate! I labor as a wageless maid."[16]

The internal challenges facing the Nguyen were soon eclipsed when the French conquered Vietnam. In 1858 the militarily powerful French, hoping to gain more commerce by controlling the Mekong and Red River trade routes to China, began what they arrogantly called a "civilizing mission" to spread French culture and Christianity and launched a bloody campaign of conquest against a determined but badly outgunned imperial Vietnamese resistance. In a quarter century of conflict the French first conquered the south and then moved north, facing Vietnamese opposition the whole way.

Vietnam and the French

By 1884 the French had conquered Vietnam but still had to consolidate their gains before they could impose their goals on the country. Consolidation proved more difficult than expected, as they faced prolonged resistance. It took the French another fifteen years to suppress the heroic efforts of thousands of poorly

plural society   A medley of peoples who mix but do not blend, maintaining their own cultures, religions, languages, and customs.

Bastille Day Parade in Vietnam This painting, by an unknown Vietnamese scholar, subtly criticizes the unpopular French colonization by satirizing the annual French holiday. A French man is shown with his arm around a Vietnamese woman while unarmed Vietnamese lantern-bearers are being commanded by a French official. (Courtesy of l'Ecole d'Extreme Orient, Paris)

armed rebel groups known as the **can vuong** (kan voo-AHN) ("aid-the-king"), who waged guerrilla warfare throughout the country, just as their ancestors had resisted the Chinese and Mongol invaders, often against hopeless odds. One of the rebel leaders, the mandarin Nguyen Quang Bich, rejected any compromise with the French: "Please do not mention the word *surrender* any more. You cannot give any good counsel to a man who is determined to die." As a French witness admitted, the Vietnamese resisted fiercely: "We have had enormous difficulties in imposing our authority. Rebel bands disturb the country everywhere, appear from nowhere, arrive in large numbers, destroy everything, and then disappear into nowhere."[17]

The can vuong rebels became powerful symbols of resistance for later generations of Vietnamese fighting colonialism and foreign invasion. In waging their guerrilla warfare, the rebels enjoyed strong support, including food and shelter, from the local population. The rebels ruled the night, the French the day. In suppressing the can vuong struggle, the French massacred thousands, including surrendered or captured rebels, who were routinely executed.

In 1897 the French created the Federation of Indochina, so named because their Southeast Asian colonies were located between India and China. The federation was an artificial unit linking Vietnam, which the French broke into three separate territories, with newly acquired Cambodia and the diverse societies the French combined to create the colony of Laos. Both Cambodia and Laos had very different social, cultural, political, and historical legacies from those of Vietnam and relatively little in common with each other.

The French maintained their rule by force while allowing French commercial interests and settlers to exploit natural resources and markets. Following the pattern of European colonization elsewhere, the colonial regime destroyed the traditional autonomy of the Vietnamese villages by appointing leaders, often from outside, rather than allowing villages to select their own leaders, the traditional system, and by greatly increasing the tax burden to finance colonial administrative costs. Powerful French enterprises prospered even if French Indochina proved a financial drain for the French government. Under French rural policies many peasants lost their land or access to communal lands, and perhaps half of the cultivated land was turned over to private landowners, investors, and rubber planters, mostly French. France also made rice a major export crop, but the expanded production favored large landowners rather than peasants.

Burma and the British

As they expanded their power in India, the British coveted Burma's rich lands and worried about Burmese claims to border regions. In three wars between 1824 and 1886, the British conquered Burma (today Myanmar). After the first two wars, in which both sides suffered huge casualties, the British controlled much of southern Burma, leaving the Burman kings in control of only the north. As with the French in Vietnam, it took decades to colonize the country and overcome resistance. Vastly differing cultures and clashing strategic interests produced violent British-Burmese conflict.

The gradual loss of independence disrupted traditional society and proved devastating to the Burmans, the country's majority ethnic group. As they lost territory in the first two military defeats, Burmans began to feel an impending doom. Fear for the future was expressed in a frenzied cultural activity, including drama, love poetry, and music. For instance, Myawaddy (mee-ya-WAH-dee) (1761–1853), a government minister, soldier, scholar, and musician from a prominent noble family, tried to salvage Burman traditions by writing plays set in villages and collecting folk songs from the Burmans and other ethnic groups in the kingdom. But the desire to preserve Burman culture did not preclude interest in foreign ideas that might aid the country's survival. Myawaddy, for example, appreciated Siamese music and culture, learned some Hindi (the major language of north India), and hired a Spaniard to

---

can vuong ("aid-the-king") Rebel groups who waged guerrilla warfare for fifteen years against the French occupation of Vietnam.

translate English-language newspapers from India. The court, fearing that the Burmese heritage might disappear if the British triumphed, also compiled *The Glass Palace Chronicle*, a history of Burma from earliest times.

Between 1853 and 1878 a new Burmese king, the idealistic Mindon, tried to salvage his country's prospects by pursuing modernization and cultural renewal and seeking good relations with the British. However, worried that he might succeed in strengthening Burma, the British tried to humiliate Mindon and his government; Mindon in turn attempted to break down barriers between the court and the Burmese people. Also during his rule, the introduction of cheap printing presses spurred a literary revival. For example, the multitalented Lady Hlaing, a member of an aristocratic family, wrote long, romantic plays on the love lives of princes and princesses and introduced a new kind of song that combined dignity with melancholy.

As the Burmans had feared, in 1886 the British completed their conquest, taking control of the government and exiling the royal family. When some Burmese resisted British rule, the British, in what they called "pacification," retaliated by destroying whole villages and executing rebel leaders. The Burman aristocracy and the royal system they had administered were destroyed, and Burma became a province of British India, a humiliating fate for this proud people. For the next fifty years the British undermined Burmese Buddhism and cultural values by removing government patronage from Buddhist institutions, establishing Christian mission schools, and recruiting non-Burman hill peoples into the government and army.

Siamese Modernization

Burma's traditional enemies to the east, the Siamese (today known as the Thai), were the only Southeast Asian country that retained their independence, a success that resulted from certain favorable conditions and wise leadership. In the early 1800s, when the British began pressuring Burma, Siam was a strong, flexible state under the vigorous new Bangkok-based Chakri dynasty, founded in 1767. Seeing Burma's dilemma, able Chakri kings mounted a successful strategy to resist Western pressures. Geography also played a role in Siamese success. Burma, on Siam's western flank, bordered British India and had been engulfed in conflict with European ambitions even before the British had completed their conquest of India. To Siam's east, the French were concentrating on Indochina. With Britain and France, who both coveted Siam, preoccupied with controlling neighboring societies, Siamese leaders had time to counter a possible Western threat by strengthening government institutions, improving their economic infrastructure, and broadening their popular support in their diverse kingdom. The Western nations were also reluctant to attack Siam because they wanted closer trade relations with Siam's ally, China.

The farsighted Siamese kings who ruled during the late nineteenth and early twentieth centuries understood the changes in Southeast Asian politics and the rise of Western power, and they promoted a modernization policy designed to ensure political independence and economic growth: they yielded to the West when necessary and consolidated what remained. The price of political independence for Siam was giving up its claims over Laos and transferring northern Malaya to Britain. Siamese leaders also agreed to commercial agreements that opened the country to Western businesses. Nonetheless, the Siamese retained some control over their future. Recognizing Siamese determination and pressed to maintain their control of Burma and Indochina in the face of these countries' continuing resistance, Britain and France decided that conquering Siam would be too costly and would possibly increase British-French rivalries. To minimize conflict with each other, they left Siam as a buffer between British Burma and French Indochina.

Two kings and their advisers were most responsible for Siam's success in avoiding colonization and modernizing the kingdom. The first, the scholarly, peace loving King Mongkut (NAHN-kut) (r. 1851–1868), who had served as a Buddhist monk and teacher for several decades, was probably the most perceptive leader of his time in Southeast Asia. An outspoken man who had studied science and had learned to read Latin, Mongkut calculated that if many Western nations obtained rights in Siam, they would fight each other first. Rather than inviting invasion, therefore, he signed treaties with various Western powers, often with terms unfavorable for Siam, and invited Western aid to modernize his kingdom. To foster goodwill and provide his heirs with an understanding of the West, Mongkut hired the wives of Christian missionaries to teach English to his wives and sons.

The second king, Mongkut's son, Chulalongkorn (CHOO-lah-LONG-corn) (r. 1868–1910), who had traveled in Asia, built on his father's foundation by emphasizing diplomacy and modernization. Chulalongkorn started a broad reform program that included abolishing slavery, centralizing government services, strengthening the bureaucracy, and establishing a Western-style government education system. Along with introducing gradual social changes, he also stimulated economic growth by encouraging the immigration of Chinese merchants and opening new land for rice production; as a result, Siam became one of the world's leading rice exporters. By strengthening the government and economy, these measures helped Siam successfully resist the colonizing intentions of the Western powers. Siam's economic development generally kept pace with that of its colonized neighbors but under Siamese rather than colonial direction. When Chulalongkorn died in 1910, Siam (today called Thailand) was still independent, and the Western appetite for new colonies had waned. Nevertheless, Western economic pressures kept Siam in a neocolonial situation, allowing Western businessmen to enjoy numerous advantages.

The Philippines, Spain, and the United States

The Spanish had colonized the Philippines much earlier than the Dutch, French, and British had acquired territory in Southeast Asia (see Chapter 18). However, by the 1870s Spanish rule had decayed and local resentment had grown. Philippine nationalism sprouted in the struggle against the Spanish, eventually generating an armed revolution that inspired other colonized Asian peoples. But the Filipino nationalists soon faced a more powerful foe, the United States. The military intervention of the United States during the revolution had momentous consequences, as the Americans helped defeat Spain but then crushed the revolutionary movement, replacing Spain as the colonial power.

The Philippine Struggle Against Spain

As happened in the Spanish colonies in Latin America (see Chapter 19), hostility toward the corrupt, repressive, and economically stagnant rule of Spain had simmered for decades in the Philippines. Educated, local-born Filipinos of Spanish, indigenous, and mixed descent (mestizo) background resented colonial power, the privileged immigrants from Spain, and the domination of the Catholic Church. Anti-Spanish feeling was particularly significant among writers such as the poet and novelist Jose Rizal (ri-ZAHL) (1861–1896). Rizal, partly Chinese in ancestry, had lived for a time in Spain and Germany, thus illustrating how the world had become more interconnected in this era. Rizal's novels, which satirized the government and the church, earned him condemnation by top officials as a subversive, antipatriotic heretic, and he was publicly executed for alleged treason against the colonial government in 1896. Rizal had earlier prophesied that "the day the Spanish inflict martyrdom [on me] farewell Spanish government."[18] Indeed, Rizal's death united varied opposition groups.

The Philippine nationalist movement arose to bring together all the diverse societies of the islands and to oppose continued Spanish domination. Gradually resentment of Spain turned nationalists toward revolution, which broke out in 1896. One dissident, Emilio Aguinaldo (AH-gee-NAHL-doe) (1870–1964), a small-town mayor of Chinese mestizo background, called on the Filipinos to rebel: "Filipinos! Open your eyes! Lovers of their native land, rise up in arms, to proclaim their liberty and independence." The revolutionaries welcomed women into their movement, even while they maintained conventional gender attitudes, viewing a woman as, in the words of one leader, a "helper and partner in the hardships of life."[19] Yet women managed to play active roles in the movement, serving as soldiers, couriers, spies, and nurses. Gregoria de Jesus, the wife of a major revolutionary leader, fought alongside her husband, and Melchora Aquino, the eighty-four-year-old wife of a mayor, fed and nursed revolutionary fighters. Despite the revolutionary's heroic efforts, however, by 1897 the Spanish had contained the revolution, though they failed to capture all the leaders or to crush scattered resistance.

The situation changed dramatically in 1898 when the U.S. fleet, commanded by Admiral George Dewey, sailed into Manila Bay and destroyed the Spanish navy, causing thousands of Spaniards to flee Manila. Americans had engaged in occasional naval skirmishes in Southeast Asia throughout the 1800s, and the American intervention in the Philippines reflected decades of American activity in Southeast Asia as Americans sought resources and markets. But not until the Spanish-American War in 1898 did the United States assert its military power on a large scale in the region. The fighting between U.S. and Spanish forces began in the Caribbean and led to the U.S. occupation of Cuba and Puerto Rico (see Chapter 20). It was as part of this conflict that the United States intervened in the Philippines, thereby beginning the first of four ground wars that it would fight in East and Southeast Asia over the next eight decades. The U.S. attack on Manila rejuvenated the revolutionaries led by Aguinaldo, who received initial American support and soon controlled much of the country. The revolutionaries declared independence and established a republican government with a semidemocratic constitution. But the revolutionary leaders, divided into factions, disagreed in their objectives and on how an independent nation would be structured. In any case, U.S. leaders had other plans for the country.

The Philippine-American War

The decision by the United States to remain in the Philippines as a colonizer after helping defeat the Spanish led to its suppression of the nationalist revolution. Taking up Rudyard Kipling's call to assume world responsibilities and "the white man's burden," U.S. President William McKinley's order for colonization reflected the American idea of Manifest Destiny, the notion that God supported U.S. expansion, while ignoring centuries of Filipino history and the deep Filipino desire for independence. McKinley proclaimed: "It is our duty to uplift and civilize and Christianize and by God's Will do our very best by [the Filipinos]."[20] McKinley, who admitted he could not locate the Philippines on a world map, underestimated the Filipino opposition to the U.S. occupation. Some 125,000 American troops fought during the four-year Philippine-American War, and over 5,000 Americans and some 16,000 Filipinos died in battle. Another 200,000 Filipinos died either in guarded compounds the Americans set up to keep villagers from helping the revolutionaries or from famine and disease generated by the conflict.

Americans faced a determined foe and were forced to fight for every town. In many districts, Filipino soldiers enjoyed the active support of most of the local population. With peasant help, the elusive revolutionaries lived off the land and practiced a harassing form of guerrilla warfare that demoralized the American soldiers, who had expected a quick victory. Americans controlled the towns and revolutionaries the countryside. Both sides committed atrocities, including torture. Americans destroyed whole villages and looted Catholic churches while Filipinos killed captured Americans. Angered by American deaths there, U.S. General Jacob Smith ordered his men to turn Samar Island into a "howling wilderness," to "kill and burn. The more you kill and burn the better you will please me."[21]

Americans at home became deeply split on the war. Strong supporters, especially in the business community, coveted Philippine resources and markets, and U.S. newspapers urged the slaughter of all Filipinos who resisted. Other Americans, however, organized a protest movement opposing the war and the crushing of the Filipino republic. The writer Mark Twain satirized American economic motives for the war in his 1900 rewriting of "The Battle Hymn of the Republic": "Mine eyes have seen the orgy of the launching of the Sword; He is searching out the hoardings where the strangers' wealth is stored; He hath loosed his fateful lightnings, and with woe and death has scored; His lust is marching on." American critics also rejected the imperialism: "We've taken up the white man's burden, of ebony and brown; Now will you tell us, Rudyard [Kipling], how we may put it down."[22]

By 1902, after the revolutionaries were defeated and many wealthy Filipinos, to protect their interests, had decided to support U.S. rule, the United States declared the Philippines an American colony. The Americans attempted to reshape the society of those they paternalistically called "our little brown brothers," using the United States as the preferred model. They established an elected legislature filled mostly by Filipinos, but its decisions had to be approved by U.S. officials. In contrast to most Western colonies, the American colonial government fostered education, literacy, and modern health care, and the schools produced a large number of Filipinos fluent in English. But American rule generally ignored peasant needs while perpetuating the power of the Filipino landowners, who supported U.S. rule. These landowners controlled the lives of millions of impoverished peasant tenants. The Americans also locked the colony even further into a cash crop economy now closely linked not to Spanish but to American economic needs.

SECTION SUMMARY

- As the Dutch expanded their control over the Indonesian archipelago, they joined together vastly disparate cultures and disrupted the traditional economy, such as by forcing Javanese farmers to grow sugar on rice land and to sell it at unfairly low prices.

- The British expanded control over the Malay Peninsula, which they used to supply raw materials such as tin and rubber, and Singapore, which became a key crossroads of Southeast Asian and India-China trade.

- After conquering Vietnam, the French faced fierce resistance from can vuong rebels, but they ultimately conquered the rebels and opened the country to exploitation by French commercial interests.

- As the British gradually conquered Burma, native Burmans attempted to preserve their culture, but after the British victory in 1886 the Burmese traditions were largely undermined.

- Unlike the rest of Southeast Asia, Siam (now Thailand) avoided colonization because of its fortunate geographical location and its farseeing leaders, who gave in to some Western demands and consolidated popular support.

- After defeating the Spanish in the Philippines and supporting local rebels, the U.S. government turned against the Filipinos and, after a bloody struggle, established a colony geared toward American economic needs.

 # The Reshaping of Southeast Asia

What were the major political, economic, and social consequences of colonialism in Southeast Asia?

Colonialism in Southeast Asia had many parallels to that in India and Africa. Although some Southeast Asians benefited, many others experienced worsening living conditions. A chant popular among Vietnamese peasants lamented the seizure of Vietnamese resources by the French: "Ill fortune, indeed, for power has been seized by the French invaders. It's criminal to set out the food tray and find that one has nothing but roots and greens to eat."[23] From a global perspective, colonialism linked Southeast Asia more firmly to a Western-dominated world economy. But colonial policies also affected local political, social, intellectual, and cultural life. Like Indians, Southeast Asians responded to the challenges of colonialism in creative ways.

Colonial Governments

Colonialism proved a shattering experience, destroying the political autonomy of Southeast Asians. The only colony with much self-government was the U.S.-ruled Philippines, which had an elected legislature. The British did allow Malayans some participation in city or state government and, in 1935, formed a legislature in Burma that included both elected and appointed members. France and the Netherlands, however, although democracies themselves, allowed little democracy in their colonies. Colonialism often meant government by stodgy, autocratic European bureaucrats. In a few cases local democracies were ended. For example, Chinese who began immigrating to western Borneo in the later 1700s to mine gold had established several small republics with general assemblies and executive councils, which even Dutch observers conceded were extremely democratic governments. But the Dutch crushed the republics when they colonized the region in the 1850s.

Colonial governments varied widely, although Europeans always held ultimate political authority. As in sub-Saharan Africa (see Chapter 21), Europeans introduced either direct or indirect rule. Direct rule removed traditional leaders, such as the Burmese kings, or made them symbolic only, as with the Vietnamese emperors. Direct rule was used in Burma, the Philippines, Vietnam, and parts of Indonesia. By contrast, in Malaya, Cambodia, Laos, and some parts of Indonesia, Europeans applied indirect rule, governing a district through the traditional leaders, such as Malay sultans, Cambodian kings, or Javanese aristocrats. If their positions were protected, the traditional leaders frequently supported colonial rule and enjoyed considerable local power. But whether governing directly or indirectly, the colonial authorities played off one ethnic group or one region against another, in the process creating problems that persisted after independence and made national unity difficult. As was true in Africa, where European colonization often formed countries with little ethnic or cultural unity, colonial boundaries in Southeast Asia ignored traditional ethnic relationships and rivalries, laying a basis for political instability. Countries such as Burma, Indonesia, and Laos were artificial creations of European colonialism rather than organic unities with more or less culturally similar populations.

Southeast Asia in the World Economy

As in India, the transformation of economic life, which linked Southeast Asian societies tighter to the world economy, was at least as significant as that of conquest and political reorganization. Southeast Asians had long participated in world trade as exporters of valuable resources, from spices and sugar to tin and gold. Southeast Asian resources helped spur the European quest for a sea route to the East in the 1400s and 1500s. Colonialism now further reshaped economic life. Since subsistence food farming could not produce enough revenues for colonial governments or investors, it was replaced by cash crop farming, and the age of the cash crop farmer, plantation worker, and miner replaced the earlier age of commerce. Extracting mineral or agricultural wealth required tying the colony's economy more closely to that of the colonizer and reorienting trade to Europe or North America. Western businessmen controlled the top level of the economy, including the banks, import-export companies, mines, wells and plantations. Gradually, as Southeast Asia came to be integrated into the world economy as a producer of raw materials and consumer of Western food and manufactured goods, it became one of the world's most valuable economic areas.

The quest for revenues fostered colonial taxation policies that encouraged people to grow cash crops, such as rubber, pepper, sugar, coffee, tea, opium, and palm oil; cut timber; mine gold and tin; and drill oil. Some of the cash crops that now dominated Southeast Asian lives came from abroad. For example, rubber was brought from Brazil and coffee from the Middle East. Many colonies developed monoculture economies that were dependent on the export of one or two major commodities, such as rubber and tin from Malaya, rice from Burma, or rubber and rice from Vietnam. The world price for these exports fluctuated with unstable global demand, fostering a local economy that prospered or floundered depending on decisions made in Europe or North America. These economic activities also had an impact on the natural environment, as forests were cleared for plantations or logged for timber to be shipped out of the region.

For many Southeast Asians, rubber growing became the key factor in shaping their lives. The invention of the first bicycles and then automobiles opened up vast markets for rubber tires. To meet this need, the British introduced rubber to Malaya, where it became the dominant cash crop in the 1890s. Rubber growing then spread to Sumatra, Borneo, southern Thailand, Vietnam, and Cambodia. Thousands of acres of forest were cleared for rubber growing, mostly on European-owned plantations. Malaya became the world's greatest exporter of natural rubber, supplying over half of the world supply by 1920. To produce rubber, plantation workers suffered long hours, strict discipline, monotonous routine, and poor food. On most plantations, workers, including children, arose before dawn to tend the rubber trees and replace the buckets that collected the sap, trying to finish their labor before the blazing tropical sun made hard physical work unhealthy. A Vietnamese writer, on witnessing a French-owned rubber estate, said that "every day one was worn down a bit more, cheeks sunken, eyes hollow. Everyone appeared almost dead."[24]

Economic growth had major consequences for everyone but did not benefit all equally. For some, especially the European colonizers and the local officials and merchants who cooperated with them, it brought wealth. For example, the Dutch and Javanese aristocrats who carried out the policy prospered from requiring the Javanese peasants to grow sugar, which the Dutch could then sell on the world market. For most Southeast Asians, however, the results of economic growth were mixed. For instance, the Javanese peasants who grew the sugar initially earned new income, and some took advantage of improved irrigation facilities to grow more rice as well as the required sugar. But costs also rose faster than the compensation earned, forcing the peasants to grow more sugar and work longer hours to earn the same profit as before.

Java Coffee Plantation This painting from the nineteenth century shows a European manager supervising barefoot laborers who are raking and drying coffee beans, a major Javan cash crop. (British Library)

With sugar enjoying an ever-expanding world market, the peasants came to depend on sugar profits for survival but often became impoverished because of the rising costs. By 1900 some Dutch officials admitted that colonial rule had reduced many Javanese to complete poverty. Peasants faced disaster when world prices for sugar and coffee declined and then, in the 1930s, collapsed altogether.

In addition to exploiting resources and developing economic monocultures, colonial policies, as in India, also sparked rapid population growth. In 1600 perhaps 20 to 25 million people lived in Southeast Asia. By 1800 this number had grown to 30 or 35 million, and by the late 1930s it was around 140 or 150 million. The greatest increases came on Java, creating a burden for contemporary Indonesia. In 1800 some 10 million people lived on Java, and this figure grew to 30 million by 1900 and 48 million by 1940. Dutch policies contributed to population growth directly or indirectly by fostering better health care and largely maintaining social order. As a result, people lived longer. Economic incentives also encouraged larger families to provide more labor for the fields. However, women on Java faced not only more hours working in the fields but also increased expectations for bearing more children. These stressful demands may have reduced the period women were able to breastfeed babies, making mothers fertile for a longer time. Fast-growing populations, especially in Java, Vietnam, and the Philippines, resulted in smaller farm plots and more landless people.

Chinese and Indian Immigration

Between 1800 and 1941 millions of Chinese and smaller numbers of Indians immigrated to Southeast Asia to work as laborers, miners, planters, and merchants. The Chinese chiefly came from poor, overcrowded coastal provinces in southeast China. Although some Chinese arrived to establish businesses or join relatives, the majority immigrated under the indenture system, which obligated them to pay off their passage by working for years in mines, plantations, or enterprises. Chinese immigrants typically were males whose goal was to make enough money to return to their native village wealthy and respected. While some did achieve this goal and many eventually opened shops in Southeast Asia with their earnings, others remained too poor to return to China and spent their lives as laborers, miners, or plantation workers. For example, the poorly paid men who pulled the rickshaws in the streets of steamy Singapore, an exhausting job that damaged health, often died young.

Many Chinese prospered as merchants, planters, and mine owners, but, instead of returning to China, decided to remain in Southeast Asia. Through enterprise, cooperation, and organization, they dominated retail trade. Chinese become the commercial middle class in every colony except Burma, operating general stores, specialty shops, and restaurants in every town. Some cities, such as Kuala Lumpur and Singapore, were largely Chinese in population; other cities also had substantial Chinese communities. The Chinese who settled permanently married local women or brought families from China. The descendants of Chinese immigrants often adopted aspects of local culture and language. By adjusting to local conditions, the Chinese became a permanent presence in Southeast Asian life.

British Malaya attracted Indian settlers as well as Chinese, creating a more complex ethnic configuration. Indian immigrants had come to the Straits Settlements cities for decades as traders, craftsmen, and workers. Beginning in the 1880s people from the Tamil-speaking region of southeast India were imported to work on Malayan rubber plantations, where they experienced the harshness of plantation life. The Chinese and Indians together eventually outnumbered the Malays, sparking Malay fears of being overwhelmed by immigrants. The British, to maintain their control, skillfully used divide-and-rule tactics, governing the various communities through their own leaders: Malay chiefs, Chinese merchants, and urban Indian traders. But this strategy maintained the political separation of the three groups and discouraged cooperation between them.

Social Change: Gender Relations and City Life

Colonial policies altered the lives of men and women, whether rural or urban, immigrant or local-born, in Southeast Asia. Economic changes reshaped gender relations, especially among peasants, and stimulated movements by women to address the challenges they faced. Colonialism also fostered the growth and ethnic diversity of cities.

The changes during the colonial era particularly affected women, who had traditionally played a major economic role in local society as farmers, traders, and weavers and often enjoyed considerable independence from men. Now, as men took up cash crop farming, which brought in much of the family income, the responsibility for growing the family's food was often largely left to women, increasing their workload. Economic change also robbed many women of their key role as small traders in the local marketplace, decreasing their status as income earners for the family. Increasingly men, especially Chinese, Indians, and sometimes Arabs, took over small-scale trade in towns, leaving women to the less profitable village markets.

The expansion of textile imports also affected women's status. Traditionally women had dominated weaving, spinning, and dying, often even growing the fibers. Weaving was hard work, even drudgery, but women could do it at home with friends and relatives while caring for children. But after 1850, when inexpensive industry-made textiles began pouring in from Europe, people began to switch from using local handwoven cloth to imported goods, slowly forcing women out of the business. A Javanese noblewoman wrote in a 1909 essay that "little by little [women] feel that their life is no longer of such value, considered by men only as ornaments as they are no longer contributing to the household coffers."[25] Poor families were hit especially hard, since they not only lost income but also could not afford to buy imported textiles. Women had to find other income sources, but devoting more time and energies to food farming or trade often took them away from the home and children.

Women did not face their problems passively, however. Some joined movements to assert their rights. The European feminist movement had some influence in Southeast Asia in the late nineteenth and early twentieth centuries. Siamese feminists opposed polygamy and supported girls' education. An inspirational Javanese woman, Raden Adjeng Kartini, represented a new form of social consciousness in Southeast Asia (see Profile: Kartini, Indonesian Feminist and Teacher). Although she died young, the schools for girls she founded in 1900 multiplied and fostered Indonesian women's awareness of their situation. Today many Indonesians honor Kartini as a heroine whose writings and life influenced the rise of Indonesian feminism and nationalism. Like Kartini, other women struggled to cope with the changing world.

Southeast Asia already had large cities, but the coming of Western rule encouraged more rapid urbanization. Cities such as Manila, Jakarta, Rangoon (today known as Yangon), Singapore, Kuala Lumpur, and Saigon (today Ho Chi Minh City) grew in prominence as colonial capitals. Cities attracted immigrant populations from other societies, such as the Chinese, and migrants from nearby districts. Ethnic variety characterized colonial towns and cities, which offered a diverse assortment of food stalls and restaurants, private schools that catered to different ethnic groups, and buildings erected by different religious sects. Nearly every city contained Muslim mosques, Buddhist, Hindu, and Chinese temples, and Christian churches. Despite a tendency for people to remain attached to their own culture, however, not everyone observed the ethnic barriers. Some descendants of Chinese and Indian immigrants assimilated into the surrounding culture; friendships and even marriages crossed ethnic lines. For example, much of Thailand's political and economic leadership today has some mix of Chinese and Siamese ancestry, a result of cultural assimilation or intermarriage.

Cultural Change

Colonial governments differed in their commitment to educating the people and fostering indigenous cultures. Most colonies left education to the Christian missions. As a result of the influence of mission schools, some Vietnamese, Indonesians, and Chinese became Christian, and hill peoples frequently did so, though few Theravada Buddhists or Muslims abandoned their faiths. A few colonies set up government schools. The U.S.-ruled Philippines had the best educational record, spending 25 percent of the total budget on public education and enrolling 75 percent of children in elementary school. Independent Siam also opened public schools that made education widely available for both boys and girls. At the other extreme was French Vietnam, which spent little public money on schools. In general, in both the mission and government schools, the Western emphasis on individualism conflicted with traditional community values and loosened the social fabric.

Some communities developed alternatives to Western education. Buddhist and Muslim groups, which had sponsored schools for centuries, expanded their schools to enroll more students and teach them from a non-Western perspective. Other schools mixed Eastern and Western ideas. For example, in 1922 a mystical Javanese religious organization established schools that provided an alternative to both Islamic and Christian instruction. These schools emphasized Indonesian arts such as music and dance but also used Western ideas; for example, they encouraged students to express their own ideas and stressed social equality and the psychological development of their students. Many graduates became nationalist leaders.

Southeast Asians also expressed their sentiments in new cultural forms. For instance, on Java, musicians mixed European string instruments with the rhythms of the largely percussion Javanese gamelan orchestra to create a romantic new popular music, *kronchong*, which became widely popular on the island. In the 1800s the music was particularly favored by Indonesian sailors and soldiers, as well as by disreputable young Javanese men, known as kronchong crocodiles, who dressed flamboyantly, gambled, and drank heavily. By the early 1900s kronchong came to be considered respectable, and eventually it was embraced by Indonesian nationalists as an artistic weapon against the Dutch. Kronchong musicians offered not only sentimental songs but also songs on topical and nationalist themes that expressed a loyalty to Indonesia and its people. The cultural exchange was not one-way. For example, during the early twentieth century Western composers who observed performances by Javanese and Balinese gamelan orchestras while visiting Indonesia, or who saw gamelan orchestras that toured the West, incorporated gamelan influences into their music.

In most colonies, a modern literature developed that reflected both alienation from colonial rule and an awareness of rapid social and cultural change. But its criticism of the colonial regime was suppressed, forcing authors to make their points indirectly. For example, Vietnamese writers used historical themes from precolonial times or critiques of Vietnamese society to discuss contemporary conditions. This evasion was necessary to avoid censorship or even arrest for dissent. Since they could not openly discuss politics, Indonesian writers focused on psychological problems, exploring characters experiencing despair and disorientation because of the colonial system. Southeast Asian writers, placing their own views in the mouths of their fictional characters, discovered the novel as a force for education and change.

SECTION SUMMARY

■ Colonized Southeast Asian peoples were allowed varying degrees of autonomy, though in general they had very little and were frequently joined into countries with little ethnic or cultural unity.

■ Economic life in colonies was reshaped to serve Western nations' needs for raw materials, especially rubber, and for markets for their goods, and in many cases it led to destruction of the natural environment and the impoverishment of native Indonesians.

■ Millions of Chinese immigrated to Southeast Asia, where many prospered as merchants and retailers, while a

KARTINI, INDONESIAN FEMINIST AND TEACHER

The inspirational social activist and teacher Raden Adjeng Kartini (RAH-den AH-jeng KAR-teen-ee) (1879–1905), usually known to Indonesians simply as Kartini, represented a feminist consciousness new to Indonesia. In her life, she shared the problems and faced the prejudices Indonesian women encountered in the colonial system and their own societies. The daughter of a Javanese aristocrat, she chafed against the confined lives of her social class, which expected young women to obey men, especially their fathers, without question, stay home, and train for marriage. However, Kartini's parents were unusually liberal, subscribing to Dutch-language newspapers and hiring Dutch tutors for their sons and daughters. Kartini's progressive father sent her and her siblings to a Dutch-language primary school. Her brothers later moved on to a Dutch-language high school, and one even attended a university in Holland. A good student, Kartini also keenly wanted to complete high school and then study in Holland. But attending high school or a Dutch university would have required her to leave home. Since Javanese customs discouraged aristocratic women from traveling without their families, her father would not permit it. In conformity with aristocratic custom, at puberty Kartini was restricted to the family's house and ordered to prepare herself for an arranged marriage by learning domestic skills.

But Kartini had larger ambitions. From her experience in Dutch-language school and friendships with Dutch women, she drew a model of personal freedom contrary to that of her Javanese society, including a commitment to educate Javanese women in order to give them more options in life. Eventually Kartini bowed to her parents' demands and entered an arranged marriage with a man she scarcely knew who already had two other wives, but who agreed to support her plan to open a school for girls. Kartini sent a memorandum to the colonial government entitled "Educate the Javanese," and then, at twenty, she opened Indonesia's first girls' school, which combined Javanese and Western values.

Kartini wrote a series of fascinating letters to Dutch friends in Java and Holland that reveal much about her thinking. Her correspondents were often nonconformist career women with socialist leanings, known in Holland as "modern girls," who encouraged Kartini's educational plans and thirst for knowledge. In 1899 she told a pen-friend, the radical feminist Stella Zeehandelaar: "I have been longing to make the acquaintance of a 'modern girl,' that proud independent girl who has

Raden Adjeng Kartini This painting, completed decades after Kartini's death, honors the young Javanese woman who founded girls' schools. (Courtesy, Photo Gallery, Indonesian Embassy, London)

all my sympathy." Mixing her Dutch friends' ideas with her own, Kartini's letters asserted women's right to education and freedom from polygamy and child marriage.

Like European feminists, in her letters Kartini criticized the constraints of marriage, family, and society. She had serious doubts about the advantages of marriage in her own society: "But we must marry, must, must. Not to marry is the greatest sin which the Muslim women can commit. And marriage among us? Miserable is too feeble an expression for it. How can it be otherwise, when the laws have made everything for the man and nothing for the woman. When law and convention both are for the man; when everything is allowed to him." She thought women repressed: "The ideal Javanese girl is silent and expressionless as a wooden doll, speaking only when it is necessary." She also condemned religious prejudice, whether by Muslims or Christians: "We feel that the kernel of all religion is right living, and that all religion is good and beautiful. But, o ye peoples, what have you made of it?" But she had hope for change: "I glow with enthusiasm toward the new time which has come. My thoughts and sympathies are with my sisters who are struggling forward in the distant West."

Kartini died in childbirth at age twenty-five. Her Dutch friends, such as Zeehandelaar, later published Kartini's letters, ensuring her fame. Thanks partly to the royalties from her published letters, the schools Kartini founded multiplied after her death, educating thousands of Indonesian girls in the twentieth century. But Kartini left a controversial legacy for Indonesians. Her schools filled a great need, for which many Indonesians are grateful. Although Kartini had criticized Javanese culture and admired Western ideals, in 1964 the Indonesian president named her a national heroine and honored her as the nation's *ibu*, or "mother." But conservatives accused her of abandoning Islam and Javanese culture. Because of her close ties to Dutch friends, her detractors labeled Kartini an apologist for colonialism. Some contrasted her unfavorably to Rahma El-Yunusiah, a devout Muslim woman from Sumatra who taught Arabic and the Quran and who refused any contact with the Dutch. Nonetheless, today Kartini is honored as a proponent of Indonesian women's rights and a precursor of Indonesian nationalist sentiment.

THINKING ABOUT THE PROFILE

1. What does Kartini's life tell us about the challenges that faced Javanese women of her day?

2. How do Kartini's thoughts reflect the meeting of East and West?

Note: Quotations from Raden Adjeng Kartini, *Letters of a Javanese Princess*, edited with an introduction by Hildred Geertz (New York: W. W. Norton, 1964), pp. 31, 34, 42, 45, 73.

smaller number of Indians came to work in Malayan rubber plantations.

■ Economic changes due to colonization forced women to grow food for their families and eliminated the market for their handmade textiles, thus taking away their traditional ability to earn an income.

■ Education in colonies included both Western-style and more traditional schools, and cultural and artistic interchange between Westerners and colonized peoples produced new cultural forms, such as kronchong music.

Online Study Center ACE the Test

◆ Chapter Summary

Change was more obvious than continuity in South and Southeast Asia during the decades between 1750 and 1914. Gradually Britain extended its control over the Indian subcontinent, using military force but also outmaneuvering rivals, forging alliances, and intimidating small states into accepting British domination. By 1850 the British East India Company controlled all of India directly or indirectly. The Company introduced policies to reshape India's economy and culture, including a Westernizing education system. The rebellion in 1857, suppressed with great difficulty, shocked the British into replacing the Company with colonial government rule. The new British Raj allowed little Indian participation in government. British policies transformed the Indian economy by favoring landlords at the expense of peasants and by suffocating traditional industries to benefit British manufactures. Population growth and poverty fostered emigration. The encounter with the West also prompted Indian thinkers to reassess their cultural traditions. Some Indians adopted Western influences, some rejected them, and others tried to mix East and West. Unpopular British policies generated a nationalist movement that challenged British rule.

While the British were consolidating control of India during the nineteenth century, they and other European powers finished colonizing Southeast Asia. Using military force or threats, the Dutch became dominant throughout the Indonesian archipelago, reaping its wealth in part by compelling Javanese to grow cash crops. Britain gained control of Burma through warfare but needed less force in Malaya, which proved profitable as a source of minerals and cash crops. Against strong resistance the French occupied Vietnam, exploiting and reshaping rural Vietnamese society. The Americans displaced the Spanish as the colonial power in the Philippines after suppressing a nationalist revolution. The Americans maintained the cash crop economic system in the Philippines but also fostered some political participation. Only Siam, led by perceptive kings, avoided colonization. Colonialism reshaped social patterns, undermining the economic activities of women, fostering urbanization, and promoting the immigration of Chinese, who later became the commercial class. Southeast Asians responded by forming creative schools and unique cultural activities.

Online Study Center Improve Your Grade Flashcards

Key Terms

Marathas
Black Hole of Calcutta
sepoys
Westernization
Orientalism
zamindars
Theosophy
cultivation system
plural society
can vuong

Suggested Reading

Books

Bayly, C. A. *Indian Society and the Making of the British Empire*. New York: Cambridge University Press, 1988. A masterly scholarly synthesis of research on the Company era.

Bayly, Susan. *Caste, Society and Politics in India from the Eighteenth Century to the Modern Age*. New York: Cambridge University Press, 1999. A major scholarly study.

Bose, Sugata, and Ayesha Jalal. *Modern South Asia: History, Culture, Political Economy*, 2nd ed. New York: Routledge, 2004. A recent brief survey text.

Brown, Ian. *Economic History in South-East Asia, c. 1830–1980*. Kuala Lumpur: Oxford University Press, 1997. A detailed but readable scholarly assessment.

Brown, Judith M. *Modern India: The Origins of an Asian Democracy*, 2nd ed. New York: Oxford University Press, 1994. A detailed study of India since 1750, especially strong on politics.

Forbes, Geraldine. *Women in Modern India*, rev. ed. New York: Cambridge University Press, 1999. A scholarly study since 1750.

Karnow, Stanley. *In Our Image: America's Empire in the Philippines*. New York: Ballantine, 1989. A readable survey.

Marr, David G. *Vietnamese Anticolonialism, 1885–1925*. Berkeley: University of California Press, 1971. A scholarly examination of the resistance to French colonization.

Owen, Norman G., et al. *The Emergence of Modern Southeast Asia: A New History*. Honolulu: University of Hawaii Press, 2005. The best survey, comprehensive and readable.

Tandon, Prakash. *Punjabi Century, 1857–1947*. Berkeley: University of California Press, 1968. A personal view of a century of change.

Tarling, Nicholas, ed. *The Cambridge History of Southeast Asia*, vol. 2. New York: Cambridge University Press, 1992. Contains interpretive essays on varied topics by major scholars.

Wyatt, David K. *Thailand: A Short History*, 2nd ed. New Haven: Yale University Press, 2003. The best general survey.

Websites

Asian Studies (http://coombs.anu.edu.au/WWWVL-AsianStudies.html). A vast Australian metasite.

East and Southeast Asia: An Annotated Directory of Internet Resources (http://newton.uor.edu/Departments&Programs/AsianStudiesDept/general.html). This site offers many links.

Internet Indian History Sourcebook (http://www.fordham.edu/halsall/india/indiasbook.html). An invaluable collection.

Virtual Library: South Asia (http://www.columbia.edu/cu/libraries/indiv/area/sarai/). A major site on India.

WWW Southeast Asia Guide (http://www.library.wisc.edu/guides/SEAsia/). An easy-to-use site.

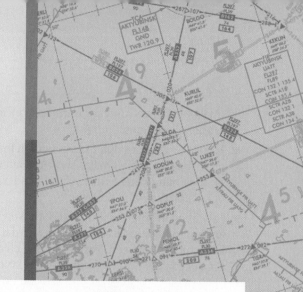

CHAPTER 23

East Asia and the Russian Empire Face New Challenges, 1750–1914

Online Study Center

This icon will direct you to interactive activities and study materials on the website: college.hmco.com/pic/lockard1e

Treaty Between Japan and China After an industrializing Japan defeated a declining China in a war over Japanese encroachments in Korea (1894–1895), diplomats from both nations met to negotiate a peace treaty. This painting shows the Chinese and Japanese representatives, easily identified by their different clothing styles, discussing the terms. (Visual Connection Archive)

The sacred traditions of our ancestors have fallen into oblivion. Those who watch attentively the march of events feel a dark and wonderful presentiment. We are on the eve of an immense revolution. But will the impulse come from within or without?

A Chinese official, 1846[1]

In 1820 Li Ruzhen (LEE Ju-Chen) (1763–1830) published a satiric novel that boldly attacked Chinese social conditions, knowing that it would expose him to criticism from conservatives who favored the status quo. Set in the Tang dynasty a millennium earlier, *Flowers in the Mirror* was a complex novel that explored, among other themes, a sensitive topic that had been only superficially discussed by earlier male Chinese writers: the relationship between the sexes. In one section of *Flowers*, Li describes a trip by three men to a country in which all the gender roles followed in China for centuries have been reversed. In this country, it is men who suffer the pain of ear piercing and footbinding and who endure hours every day putting on makeup, all to please the women who run the country. One of the men, Merchant Lin, is conscripted as a court "lady" by the female "king":

> *In due course, his [bound] feet lost much of their original shape. Blood and flesh were squeezed into a pulp and then little remained of feet but dry bones and skin, shrunk to a dainty size. Responding to daily anointing [with oil], his hair became shiny and smooth. His eyebrows were plucked to resemble a new moon. With blood-red lipstick, and powder adorning his face, and jade and pearl adorning his coiffure and ears, Merchant Lin assumed, at last, a not unappealing appearance.*[2]

Li seemed an unlikely man to address so starkly and sympathetically the low social status and daily challenges faced by women. A conventionally educated Confucian scholar who had failed the civil service examinations and never qualified for a government position as a mandarin, Li became a writer on various nonfiction subjects, including language, political philosophy, mathematics, and astrology. But because Li's China was now awash in problems, he no longer felt bound to continue treating these more traditional subjects. Growing Western pressure to open China's borders to foreign trade, unchecked population growth, domestic unrest, political corruption, and growing opium addiction spurred Chinese scholars such as Li to reassess the relevance of Chinese traditions, such as outmoded civil service examinations, the inequality of wealth, and women's footbinding, for a changing world. In *Flowers* Li addressed the social inequities that he believed kept women from actively participating in China's regeneration. The growing dissatisfaction with China's practices that Li's provocative book represented, combined with Western intervention in China, set the stage for the immense revolution, predicted by the official in the chapter opening quote, that would eventually transform this ancient society.

A major world society for over two millennia, China was still powerful in the late 1700s. But in the 1800s, Western military, economic, and political pressure on China to open its doors to Western trade, combined with mounting domestic problems, contributed to three military defeats, a devastating rebellion, and increasing poverty for millions of Chinese. In response, the imperial government supported some reforms, but these did not foster the modernization, especially of military technology and government, that China needed to control foreign influence or to prevent the rise of revolutionary movements. Eventually these movements overthrew the imperial system.

Like the Chinese, the Japanese also faced challenges, even before Western ships forced the nation open in the 1850s. Soon the old system fell, and in the 1870s Japan's new leaders began an all-out program of modernization in an effort to prevent Western domination. By 1900 the Japanese had heavy industry, a modern military, and a comprehensive educational system. Emulating the Western imperialist countries, they also sought their own resources and markets abroad and soon colonized their neighbor, Korea, which had not modernized.

Although historically linked more closely to Europe than to Asia, Russia also became a factor in Asian politics after it expanded across Siberia to the Pacific. Perched on the borders of Europe, East Asia, and the Islamic Middle East and Central Asia, Russia engaged with societies in each of these regions through trade, warfare, and conquest. After it became dominant in parts of eastern Europe, pushed its borders southward into Ottoman territories, and conquered the Central Asian states, Russia was the largest territorial power in Eurasia.

FOCUS QUESTIONS

1. What were the causes and consequences of the Opium War?
2. Why did Chinese efforts at modernization fail?
3. What factors aided Japan in the quest for modernization?
4. How did the Meiji government transform Japan and Korea?
5. What factors explain the expansion of the Russian Empire?

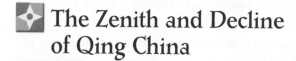 The Zenith and Decline of Qing China

What were the causes and consequences of the Opium War?

Established by the Manchus, pastoralist invaders from Manchuria, the Qing (ching) (1644–1912) was the last dynasty in China's long history, the final phase of China's 2000-year-old imperial system (see Chronology: China, 1750–1915). After reaching its zenith in the eighteenth century, Qing China experienced decay in the nineteenth. The challenges facing the Qing in the early and mid-1800s were particularly severe. Several catastrophic wars resulted in unequal treaties with the West that increased Western penetration, and dynastic decline fostered major rebellions. Meanwhile, China's economy underwent changes, Christian missionaries posed a challenge to Chinese culture, and increasing poverty prompted millions of Chinese to seek their fortunes abroad. Although the Qing survived into the early 1900s, it had lost much of its strength. This decline in world standing had as much to do with Europe's rise as with China's failures.

Qing China in the 1700s

In the eighteenth century, Qing China was still one of the world's largest, most powerful, most prosperous, and most technologically sophisticated societies, largely self-sufficient

CHRONOLOGY

	China	Japan and Korea	Russia and Central Asia
1800	**1839–1842** Opium War		
1850	**1850–1864** Taiping Rebellion	**1853** Opening of Japan by Perry **1867–1868** Meiji Restoration	**1800–1870s** Russian conquest of Turkestan and Caucasus
1900	**1911** Chinese Revolution	**1910** Japanese colonization of Korea and Taiwan	**1905** First Russian Revolution

and very self-centered. But troubling signs of decay developed. Although the Manchus had followed the political example of earlier Chinese dynasties, they were more despotic. Manchus dominated the top government positions and forbade intermarriage with the Chinese. While the Chinese accepted Manchu rule, as they had tolerated alien rule in the past, they resented the ethnic discrimination. There were other problems as well. Like various earlier dynasties, the Qing had built a great empire by occupying predominantly Muslim Xinjiang (shin-jee-yahng), a mostly desert region just west of China; conquering the Mongols; annexing Tibet; and adding to the empire the fertile island of Taiwan (tie-WAN), to which thousands of Chinese migrated. Although this expansion consolidated China's borders, it also stretched Qing military power and proved economically costly.

Despite the challenges, the Qing generally maintained domestic prosperity and a growing economy for nearly two centuries. Chinese opened new lands for settlement. Taking advantage of trade with the West, they also introduced crops from the Americas that provided additional food sources, such as corn, sweet potatoes, and peanuts. Cash cropping of cotton and tea, both traditional crops, and of tobacco from the Americas expanded, although this agricultural growth also led to a growing concentration of land ownership. The volume of domestic trade grew in the 1700s, spurred by new textile factories, increased copper mining, and more money in circulation in the world's largest commercial economy. In 1830 China still accounted for a third of world manufacturing, and in the 1850s a British observer called the Chinese the world's greatest manufacturing people. Some historians suggest that the mid-Qing economic trends, such as a highly commercialized economy, resembled the patterns that sparked economic change in western Europe in the Early Modern Era.

As a result of its prosperity and agricultural growth, China's population doubled from 150 million in 1700 to 300 million by 1800, and then rose to 432 million by 1850. Peasants responded to population pressure by finding additional marginal land to farm and expanding their use of irrigation and fertilizer. But population growth still outstripped the growth of the food supply, straining resources and fostering corruption, which increased Chinese resentment of the Qing government. Although in the 1700s living standards in the more developed regions of China were probably comparable to those of the more affluent parts of western Europe, in the 1800s they deteriorated, partly because of overpopulation.

While the economy thrived, Chinese culture and society became more conservative. In 1783 the Qing government prohibited books and plays that it considered treasonable to the Manchu state or subversive to traditional Chinese values. Some scholars, considering these works immoral and arguing that moral laxness caused the fall of dynasties, applauded the crackdown. They worried particularly about fiction and other creative forms composed by both men and women, such as sung poetry, which often had an erotic, sometimes homosexual, focus. The Qing introduced harsher laws against unconventional behavior, such as homosexuality, which Chinese governments had generally tolerated for centuries, and increased social pressures on women to conform to such gender expectations as refusing to remarry after they became widows.

The Qing mandated that public meetings be held every month in which an imperial edict be read out. It emphasized

CHRONOLOGY

China, 1750–1915

1644–1912	Qing dynasty
1839–1842	Opium War
1842	Treaty of Nanjing
1856–1860	Arrow War
1850–1864	Taiping Rebellion
1894–1895	Sino-Japanese War
1898	100 Days of Reform
1900	Boxer Rebellion
1911	Chinese Revolution
1912	Formation of Chinese Republic
1915	Japan's 21 Demands on China

Confucian notions of moral virtue, heaping honor on filial sons, loyal officials, philanthropists, and faithful wives. Since increasing numbers of women were literate, the government published instructional books containing historical writings, some of them over two millennia old, on female obligations. Women were advised not to look around when walking, laugh aloud, talk loudly, or sway their skirts when standing. Yet, women also read and probably enjoyed popular literature, such as the satirical novel *Flowers in a Mirror*, discussed in the opening vignette. And, in a few districts in central China, peasant women wrote their observations and communications in a secret script, *nuxu* (noo-shoe), that may have been first developed by and for women centuries earlier.

Qing China in an Imperial World

China's problems during the later Qing can be traced to both internal decay and foreign pressure. Internally, by 1800 the Qing began to show clear signs of dynastic decline, such as increasing poverty and administrative corruption. For example, greedy officials in the court as well as in remote towns took bribes to allow the smuggling and sale of narcotic drugs, and sometimes they even participated in these illegal activities. Local rebellions against the Qing were suppressed, but the costs of defeating them added to increasingly severe economic problems.

As political, economic, and social conditions deteriorated at home, European nations exerted pressure on the Qing government to grant them more privileges. China had experienced pressure from Western adventurers and traders already in the sixteenth and seventeenth centuries. The Portuguese had established a base at Macao on the southern coast in 1557 and gradually turned it into a colony. The Russians, too, forged direct contacts as they expanded their influence in eastern Siberia and established trading posts along the Amur River separating Siberia from Manchuria. In the 1700s Dutch and English traders were granted permission to trade at the southern port of Guangzhou (gwahng-jo) (known to the British as Canton). Britain had become the most powerful European nation in the 1700s. Westerners wanted increased access, including freedom to travel inside China.

The Chinese debated how much contact with the West to allow. Chinese merchants in coastal cities, who had long traded with Southeast Asia, often supported contact because they could make fortunes by trading with the Europeans. From the early 1700s to the mid-1800s some merchants benefited from **Chinoiserie**, a Western vogue for Chinese artistic products such as ceramics, painting, lacquer ware, and decorative furniture. This trend grew after Europeans found themselves unable to produce porcelain duplicating the quality of China's. Western merchants and diplomats commissioned Chinese artists in

Guangzhou to paint Chinese people, costumes, and city scenes using Western artistic techniques, especially watercolor. In the early 1800s a merchant's guild called the **Co-hong** had a monopoly on Guangzhou's trade with the West, and its head, Howqua (How-kwah) (1769–1843), became one of the world's richest men. Howqua was famous in China for his spectacular pleasure garden and lavish mansion, which employed a staff of five hundred servants.

Nevertheless, being largely self-sufficient in food and resources, China did not need foreign trade, and Qing emperors were unwilling to make concessions to the more open trade system desired by the Europeans. Before 1800 the Qing restricted trade to a few ports such as Guangzhou and Siberian outposts, and they refused diplomatic relations on an equal basis with the West. In the 1600s Catholic missionaries were expelled for their bickering and intolerance toward Chinese traditions, and thereafter Christian missionaries were prohibited from working in China. The Chinese knew little of the Western world and were confused by the diverse nationalities of the European peoples, whom they disparagingly called "foreign devils." Chinese leaders viewed European merchants as barbarians bearing tribute, and they required visiting diplomats to perform the humiliating custom of *kotow*, in which they prostrated themselves before the emperor.

Chinese and European world-views were also incompatible. The British righteously saw themselves as benefiting China by opening the country to free trade. A British official wrote in 1821 that governments should let the stream of commerce flow as it will. The Chinese differed. China's attitude toward foreign trade and the outside world was well exemplified in a letter written by the Qing emperor Qianlong (chee-YEN-loong) (r. 1736–1795) to King George III of Britain following a British trade mission in 1793 requesting more access. The emperor denied Britain permission to establish an embassy but commended the king for his respectful spirit of submission and humility in sending tribute: "Our dynasty's majestic virtue has penetrated into every country under heaven. Our celestial empire possesses all things in prolific abundance. It behooves you, O king, to display ever greater devotion and loyalty in the future, so that by perpetual submission to our throne, you may secure peace and prosperity for your country hereafter."[3]

The Opium Trade and War

Half a century after Emperor Qianlong blithely dismissed the British request with these words, the tables were turned. Two wars in the mid-1800s, in which Qing China suffered humiliating defeats, forcibly jarred the Chinese from their complacency and made clear that the world was changing. The first war, resulting from an increasing trade in opium centered in Guangzhou, granted new rights to the West, while the second expanded those rights. These wars forced China to open its doors and to rethink traditional values and institutions.

Chinoiserie   An eighteenth- and nineteenth-century Western vogue for artistic products of China such as painting, ceramics, lacquer ware, and decorative furniture.

Co-hong   A nineteenth-century Chinese merchant's guild that had a monopoly on Guangzhou's trade with the West.

Guangzhou   During the eighteenth century, the Western traders in China were restricted to one riverside district in Guangzhou (Canton), where they built their warehouses, businesses, and homes in European style.   (Photograph Courtesy Peabody Essex Museum, E79708 View of Guangzhou ca. 1800)

The Opium Trade   In the late 1700s the British, taking the lead in the China trade, badly wanted more Chinese silk and tea, which had become valued revenue sources for British merchants. But China, desiring little from the West, accepted only precious gold and silver bullion as payment. Between the 1760s and 1780s the import of silver into China increased over 500 percent, presenting a serious balance of payments problem for Western economies. Seeking a marketable product that would solve this unfavorable trade disparity, the British found it in opium, an addictive drug that was grown in India and the Middle East. European sailors had first introduced opium into China in the 1600s, and it was first used as a painkiller. In the 1720s, however, the Chinese discovered that they could smoke opium for pleasure by mixing it in a pipe with tobacco. By the later 1700s businesses known as opium dens, where people could buy and use opium, began to appear. The drug gave users a dreamy, relaxed experience that temporarily relieved boredom, stress, physical pain, and depression. Opium appealed to bored officials, wealthy women cooped up at home, busy clerks, anxious merchants, nervous soldiers, and overworked peasants. A highly addictive drug, it produced severe withdrawal symptoms such as cramps and nausea.

The British, who began to grow opium as a cash crop in the Bengal region of India in the 1700s, soon found foreign markets around Asia, and British enterprises such as the British East India Company were greatly enriched by this trade. In fact, the sale of opium, chiefly obtained from the British, became an important revenue source for all the European colonial governments in Southeast Asia. U.S. traders also participated, shipping opium from Ottoman Turkey to East Asia. Eventually British and American traders began smuggling opium into China. The Western drug smugglers and the governments that supported them, being concerned only with profits, were indifferent to the terrible moral and social consequences of their enterprise. Between 1800 and 1838 opium imports to China increased sixfold, and by 1838 there were 5 to 10 million Chinese addicts. The opium trade undermined the country's social fiber and impoverished thousands of families. One Chinese official concluded that "opium is nothing else but a flowing poison [which] utterly ruins the minds and morals of the people, a dreadful calamity."[4] Another argued in 1838 that opium smokers should be strangled and the pushers and producers beheaded.

The corrupt opium trade system at Guangzhou fostered conflict. China outlawed the opium trade in 1729, and the emperor issued decrees forbidding the marketing, smuggling, and consumption of the drug. British, American, and other Western traders were then forced officially to trade through the Co-hong merchant's guild, but this restriction did not limit the opium trade; the British found that officials could be bribed to overlook opium smuggling. To continue bringing in their huge profits from this trade, during the 1830s the British doubled opium imports while also pressing for reform of the trading system.

Chinese leaders responded by further isolating the Western traders and mounting an attack on the opium trade. The emperor appointed the mandarin Lin Zezu (lin tsay-shoe) (1785–1850) to go to Guangzhou as commissioner and end the opium trade. Lin, an incorruptible Confucian moralist, concluded that if the opium traffic was not stopped, China would become poorer and its people weaker. He wrote to Britain's Queen Victoria: "Suppose there were people from another country who carried opium for sale to England and seduced your people into buying and smoking it. Certainly you would be bitterly aroused."[5] Lin ordered his officials to raid the Western warehouses, where they seized and destroyed 20,000 chests of opium worth millions of dollars.

Online Study Center **Improve Your Grade**
Primary Source: Letter to Queen Victoria, 1839

The Opium War Lin's seizure of opium outraged Western traders, and Britain declared war. In the following Opium War (1839–1842), as the British called it, Western military power proved disastrous for China. The British fleet raided up and down the Chinese coast, blockading and bombarding ports, including Guangzhou. The Chinese fought back, often resisting against hopeless odds, but they lacked the weapons to triumph. Although China had one of the world's most formidable military forces in 1600, since then Europeans had greatly surpassed China in naval and military technology. The British won most of the battles of the war.

With defeat certain, dozens of Qing officers committed suicide. The lost battles also forced the Chinese to assess the Western threat. A few alarmed officials were concerned with the inadequacy of Chinese technology. Commissioner Lin wrote to a friend that China badly needed ships and guns like the British had, but he did not broadcast his views fearing the hostile reaction from his more conservative government colleagues. Unlike Lin, most officials and other educated Chinese rejected such ideas and remained scornful of all things Western. One official wrote to the emperor that "the English barbarians are a detestable people, trusting entirely to their strong ships and large guns." Average Chinese reacted with rage. One placard in Canton in 1841 was addressed to "rebellious barbarian dogs. If we do not completely exterminate you we will not be manly Chinese able to support the sky over our heads. We are definitely going to kill you, cut your heads off, and burn your bodies in the trash."[6]

In 1841, when the British made preparations to blow down the walls of the major city of Nanjing, along the Yangzi River in central China, the Qing were forced to negotiate for peace. In 1842 they signed the Treaty of Nanjing, the first of a series of humiliating unequal treaties that nibbled away at Chinese sovereignty. The treaty gave Britain permanent possession of Hong Kong, a sparsely populated coastal island downriver from Guangzhou; opened five ports to British trade; abolished the Co-hong and its trade monopoly; set fixed tariffs so that China no longer controlled its economic policy; and gave the British **extraterritoriality**, or freedom from local laws. The Chinese were also forced to pay Britain the war costs. Soon other Western countries signed treaties with China that gave them the same rights as the British. Each successive treaty expanded foreign privileges.

The Treaty System

The Opium War became to the Chinese a permanent symbol of Western imperialism. The debacle of the Opium War soon led to other wars and a treaty system that opened China to the West. After the Opium War, Westerners, especially the British, remained dissatisfied with the amount of trade, and the Chinese sought to evade their obligations. These factors ensured that another conflict would develop, and the one that did is often known as the Arrow War (1856–1860). China had imprisoned some Chinese sailors for suspected piracy aboard a Chinese ship, *The Arrow*, registered in Hong Kong, which the British were building into a key trading port, and Britain used this event as a pretext to attack China. France also entered the war, using the mysterious murder of a French priest as an excuse. Facing two formidable powers, China was again defeated and forced to sign new treaties that favored the West. This treaty opened more ports on the coast and along interior rivers to Western traders, established foreign embassies in Beijing, and permitted Christian missionaries to enter the Chinese interior. Again forced to pay the war costs, China fell deeper into debt. The Arrow War also undermined China's position as a regional power. China was forced to give up its claim to Vietnam, a longtime vassal state being colonized by France, and to acquiesce in the Russian takeover of eastern Siberia.

By restricting China's control of its economy and limiting Chinese power to make rules for Western residents, the treaty system deprived China of some of its autonomy. It also led to the formation of **international settlements**, zones in major Chinese cities set aside for foreigners in which no Chinese were allowed. They were in effect foreign cities with foreign governments in major ports such as Guangzhou and Shanghai. For example, a small island on the riverfront adjacent to downtown Guangzhou, and accessible only by a footbridge, became the home of Western merchants, officials, and missionaries. It boasted mansions, warehouses, clubs, and churches built by and serving the largely British, American, and French population. Some historians question whether the popular notion that signs in the international settlement in Shanghai warning "no dogs or Chinese allowed" really existed, but Chinese were clearly unwelcome except as servants.

The Opium and Arrow Wars and the treaty system they fostered forced the Chinese to debate how best to respond to the new dangers the country faced. Some Chinese officials and other scholars understood the need for China to learn from the West, to examine Western books and build modern ships and guns in order to meet the Western challenge. A few scholars argued that the Chinese should seriously study science, mathematics, and foreign languages. These views influenced the provincial official and reformer Zeng Guofan (zung gwoh-FAN) (1811–1872), who recommended making modern weapons and steamships. But, failing to see the magnitude of the challenges, few mandarins showed interest. One conservative mandarin rejected

---

extraterritoriality Freedom from local laws for foreign subjects.

international settlements Special zones in major Chinese cities set aside for foreigners, where no Chinese were allowed; arose as a result of China's defeat in the Opium and Arrow Wars.

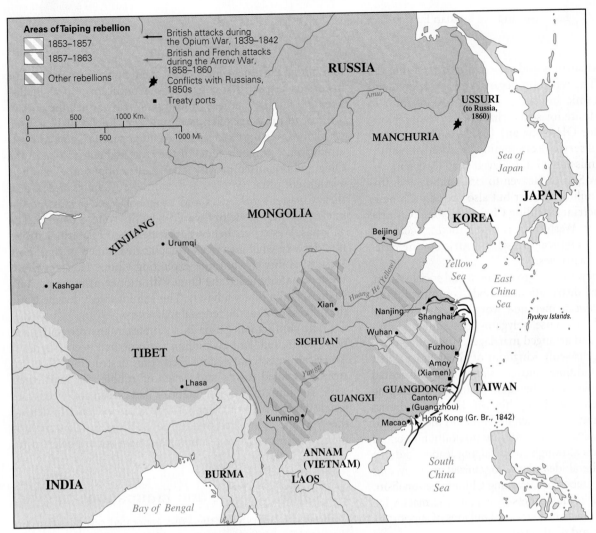

Map 23.1 Conflicts in Qing China, 1839–1870

During the mid-1800s Qing China experienced repeated unrest, including several major rebellions. The largest and most destructive, the Taiping Rebellion, engulfed a large part of southern and central China between 1850 and 1864.

Online Study Center Improve Your Grade Interactive Map: Conflicts in the Qing China, 1839–1870

Western knowledge because, he argued, Western sciences were based largely on earlier Chinese discoveries. In fact, Chinese discoveries had contributed to Western science and technology for centuries, but by the 1800s the West held the creative edge.

While scholars debated, China's problems multiplied, especially in the coastal provinces. To pay for the wars, the government had to raise taxes, causing many peasants to lose their land. The dispossessed often turned to begging or banditry. Natural disasters further demoralized the country. Between 1800 and 1850 the Yellow River flooded twenty times and then changed course, wiping out hundreds of towns and villages.

As a result of the treaty system, Western cultural influence—to Chinese critics just another form of imperialism—increased. Much of this influence spread through Christian missionaries from the United States and Britain. The missionaries opened most of China's Western-type schools and hospitals, providing educational and health benefits to those Chinese who had access to them. By the 1920s there were 2,500 American missionaries in China, some of them attached to the thirteen American-operated and funded colleges. However, Christian

missionaries posed a challenge to Chinese religions and provoked negative opinions. The Chinese knew that missionaries often lived well and were protected by Western military power. The missionaries and other Western residents, often ethnocentric and seeing themselves as the cutting edge of what they considered to be a superior Western and Christian civilization, tended to view the Chinese as depraved heathens and mocked their culture. Chinese generally distrusted not only the Christian missionaries but also the several hundred thousand Chinese who became Christian.

The Taiping Rebellion

Deteriorating conditions, government corruption, and the increasing Western presence eventually generated the Taiping Rebellion (1850–1864), the most critical of several midcentury upheavals against the Qing (see Map 23.1). Guangdong (GWAHNG-dong) province, on the southeast coast, experienced particularly severe social and economic dislocations that increased popular unrest. Officials reported that peasant families had no food surplus and were reduced to eating the chaff of the wheat. The rebellion began in a remote area and was fueled by economic insecurity, famine, loss of faith in government, and a desire for social change. The leader, Hong Xiuquan (hoong shee-OH-chew-an) (1813–1864), who had failed to pass the civil service examinations and had also studied with Christian missionaries, believed that God had appointed him the new Son of Heaven to exterminate evil. Impressed by Western military power but also proudly Chinese, Hong preached a doctrine blending Christianity and Chinese thought, a response to Western disruption, mixing local and Western ideas, that was typical in Asia and Africa in the nineteenth and twentieth centuries.

Hong wanted a new form of government and social system. He promoted an equal distribution of goods, communal property, and equality between men and women. The puritanical Hong also prohibited opium use, polygamy, footbinding, prostitution, concubinage, and arranged marriages. Hong established a sect, the Taipings (Heavenly Kingdom of Great Peace), that rejected Confucian traditions and envisioned a God-oriented utopia where all people would be equal. Many of the Taiping men and women were, like Hong himself, Hakkas, a dialect group in south China whose women never bound their feet and were raised to be assertive. These traditions no doubt influenced Taiping gender policies although male Taiping leaders did not always follow these liberal ideas. Hong organized an army, and in 1850 he launched a rebellion, invoking Chinese nationalism: "We raise the army of righteousness to liberate the masses for the sake of China."[7] Soon he had attracted millions of supporters from among the poor and disaffected.

The Taipings enjoyed early success, but ultimately their efforts failed and weakened China. Taiping armies conquered large parts of central and southern China, but the Taipings suffered from conflicts within their leadership, and their hostility to traditional Chinese culture cost them popular support. Some historians suspect that conservative Confucians especially disliked the Taiping espousal of women's rights, which they saw as a threat to the patriarchal family system. Intellectuals accused them of subverting Chinese society and opening China to Westernization. Ultimately most of the educated elite rallied to the Qing and organized provincial armies to oppose the Taipings. Westerners often sympathized with the Taipings because of their Christian influences and progressive social message but knew that a Qing victory would benefit Western nations. The Taipings, Westerners believed, threatened to establish a strong new dynasty, whereas a weak Manchu government meant more Western ability to continue exploiting China. Hence, various Western nations aided the Qing with money, arms, mercenary soldiers, and military advisers. The Taipings were defeated, and the process of dynastic renewal was aborted.

The conflict left China in shambles. Many provinces had been devastated, and 20 million Chinese had been killed. An American missionary described the destruction: "Ruined cities, desolated towns and heaps of rubble still mark their path. The hum of busy populations had ceased and weeds and jungle cover the land."[8] The Qing were now deeper in debt to the West and compelled to adopt even more conciliatory attitudes. The imperial government also lost some power to regional leaders.

Economic Change and Emigration

China's encounters with the West generated several economic changes. The extension of Western businesses into the interior stimulated the growth of the Chinese merchant class and small-scale Chinese-owned industries, such as match factories and flour mills. The Chinese merchants, however, disliked Western economic domination and the Qing government, which offered

Rattan Factory in Guangzhou This photo, taken around 1875, shows Chinese men and women workers, mostly of peasant background, in a factory making rattan, along with the factory's European owners. (Courtesy, Daniel Wolf Collection, NY)

little resistance to Western imperialism. Gradually a new working class, including women, labored in mines, factories, railways, and docks. The gulf between peasants in the interior and the merchants and workers in the coastal cities was vast.

The unequal treaties enabled Western economic penetration into China, increasing the incorporation of China into a world economy dominated by the West, and China's economy became increasingly geared to Western rather than Chinese needs. Westerners often ran Qing government agencies, banks, railroads, factories, and mines and guarded them with Western police. Western goods, entrepreneurs, and capital came into China. By 1920 foreign companies controlled most of China's iron ore, coal, railroads, and steamships, and Western businessmen became inspired by the notion of the vast China market. One U.S. firm launched an advertising campaign to put a cigarette in the mouth of every Chinese man, woman, and child. As happened in Southeast Asia, imported British textiles frequently displaced Chinese women from textile production, which peasant women had done for centuries to supplement family incomes. Local spinning was eliminated, and although women continued to weave, they earned lower incomes than before.

Historians debate whether this foreign economic penetration helped or hindered China's own economic development. Some scholars view economic imperialism as a spur to the growth of China's domestic economy. Others argue that Western competition ruined Chinese industries such as cotton spinning and iron and steel production, hurting China's ability to compete with the West. Western businesses had the advantages of greater capital and the support of Western governments and military power. Standard Oil's kerosene from the United States, for instance, replaced locally produced vegetable oil in the lamps of China. China's traditional exports also declined because of competition with other Asian countries. By 1900 India and Sri Lanka had become the world's largest producers of tea and Japan the largest producer of silk. The Qing, already deeply in debt to Western governments and banks, had little money left for building China's economic institutions.

Deteriorating economic, social, and political conditions in hard-hit coastal provinces, combined with natural disasters, prompted millions of Chinese to emigrate between the 1840s and 1920s, usually to places where Western colonialism and capitalism were opening new economic opportunities. Emigration accelerated in the later 1800s. Between 1880 and 1920 several hundred thousand people a year left from southern ports, usually headed for Southeast Asia but also, in many cases, bound for Pacific islands such as Hawaii and Tahiti or for Australia, Peru, Cuba, North America, and South Africa (see Chapters 20 and 22). The Chinese who emigrated to join relatives in their business enterprises, or to establish new ones, formed the basis for local middle-class Chinese business communities. The majority left China as part of the notorious "coolie trade," a labor system known as such because Westerners called the emigrant workers, whether Chinese or Indian, "coolies," a derogatory term. Under this system, desperate Chinese, usually peasants, were recruited or coerced to become indentured workers in faraway places, signing contracts that required them to labor for years on plantations or in mines, or to

work building railroads to repay their passage. Those laborers who survived the difficult voyages in crowded ships faced discrimination and harsh working conditions in alien lands.

Chinese had migrated to Southeast Asia for centuries, but the increased emigration now greatly enlarged the Chinese diaspora to a global scale. The societies where Chinese settled, especially in Southeast Asia, became more closely connected to China through economic and social networks than ever before. For example, Chinese businesses in Southeast Asia often had branches and labor recruitment offices in China, and families in China maintained ties to family members or their descendants living abroad. Chinese emigrants often returned to their native villages with wealth earned abroad, but others remained poor, never earning enough money to return to China as they originally hoped. Others who saved enough after years of hard work to establish small businesses often settled permanently abroad. Most emigrants were men, who sometimes supported wives and children in China or brought family members to their overseas homes. Chinese men also married local women, often non-Chinese. The emigrants and their descendants, while often sustaining Chinese culture and language, also mixed Chinese and local customs. Today some 30 million people of Chinese ancestry live outside of China, the large majority of them in Southeast Asia. They constitute a major source of investment capital for China, helping to finance businesses, industries, and educational institutions in their ancestral homeland.

SECTION SUMMARY

- In the eighteenth century, Qing China was still thriving on the strength of its agriculture, trade, and manufacturing, but its rapidly growing population began to produce internal problems such as poverty and corruption.

- In the nineteenth century, China faced increasing problems as well as pressure from Westerners for greater trade opportunities, but the Qing refused to allow an open trading system, thus creating a severe trade imbalance between the West and the East.

- To solve this imbalance, the British began smuggling opium into China, and when China resisted the British defeated China in the Opium War and forced the Chinese to agree to highly unfavorable terms that allowed the British to trade in China.

- After another war, China was forced to set aside special areas exclusively for Westerners, called international settlements, and to also allow Christian missionaries into the country.

- Economic insecurity, famine, and Western interference eventually led to the Taiping Rebellion, a widespread and devastating revolt that was ultimately put down by the Qing with help from Western powers.

- China's economy was increasingly penetrated and transformed by Western powers, and millions of Chinese emigrated throughout the world, some to be indentured workers and others to go into business.

From Imperial to Republican China

Why did Chinese efforts at modernization fail?

The rebellions, government stagnation, poverty, and growing Western demands brought about a crisis for the Qing. Some Chinese still concluded that China should reaffirm its traditional ways and reject the West. But other Chinese increasingly recognized the need to evaluate Western technologies and assess the severity of the Western challenge. For centuries China had absorbed invaders to survive, and a growing number of reformers now wanted to also adapt useful Western technologies to Chinese ways. As challenges mounted and China lost a war with Japan, some gave up on reform and organized revolutionary movements. In the early 1900s, revolutionaries overthrew the imperial system to form a republic, but these developments did not solve China's problems.

Conservatives and Liberals

China's educated elite divided over how much China should modernize its society: conservatives argued against borrowing Western models, while liberals wanted moderate reforms. The conservatives, who dominated the bureaucracy, advised that China hold fast to traditions, protecting itself with Confucian moral conduct. Believing China could learn nothing from Westerners, they opposed railroads, underground mines, and other innovations because these disrupted the harmony between humanity and nature, disturbed the graves of the ancestors, and put boatmen and cart drivers out of work. One conservative wrote that it was "better to see the nation die than its way of life change."[9] Conservatives asked how the Chinese could change some aspects of their life without changing others, since new technologies undermined social, economic, and even political values.

Liberals, believing China had to adopt certain Western ideas to survive, sponsored impressive government innovations. They streamlined central and regional governments, set up a foreign ministry, formed a college to train diplomats, and sent some students to schools in the West, especially to the United States. Several provincial governments established industries. A few bold reformers argued that Confucius had supported the idea of democratic government and favored reforms, and they questioned customs that exalted the ruler and demeaned his subjects and that favored the male over the female. Few liberals, however, wanted radical transformation, preferring to protect the core of Chinese tradition by simply grafting on some technological innovations. As one noted, "China should acquire the West's superiority in arms and machinery, but retain China's superiority in Confucian virtue."[10] Perhaps naively, liberals believed they could adopt Western tools while rejecting Western ideas and institutions. To them, Western ideas such as political democracy and nationalism were too foreign to easily adapt to China's family-centered society, which was defined in cultural rather than political terms.

Liberals also sought to modernize military forces. Chinese leaders perceived Western strength as essentially one of ships and guns, not of the dynamic and aggressive Western culture. Military reformers in the provinces, calling themselves "self-strengtheners," aimed to strengthen China to protect it. In the late nineteenth century these self-strengtheners built arsenals and shipyards. By 1894 China had a better-trained army and sixty-five warships. But this was still insufficient against a fully industrialized enemy.

The reforms failed to save the Qing because the technological innovations themselves generated new problems. The Chinese built warships but then needed coal to make steam to power them, which meant they needed improved coal-mining technology. Railroads had to be built to move the coal, and they in turn required telegraphs to communicate train movements. Technical schools were needed to train workers for these new enterprises. In addition, the new working class hired by the companies and factories did not fit into Confucian social categories, which divided society into scholars, peasants, artisans, and merchants. China also employed Western advisers to help set up and run the new industries, and it developed government departments such as the post office and maritime customs. But the new enterprises were often poorly run. The innovations were also expensive, further complicating the economic problems of a Chinese government forced to pay war reparations and to finance a growing debt to Western nations and banks.

China's problems grew less manageable. China was too large and overpopulated, its surplus wealth was too small for investment, and it was too saddled with a poorly led, bureaucratic, and overly conservative government to make any radical changes. From 1861 to 1908 the imperial government was dominated by the Empress Dowager Ci Xi (zoo shee) (1835–1908), a concubine of the old emperor; on his death Ci Xi had become the regent of the child emperor who replaced him. Forceful and intelligent, she was also covetous and irresponsible. For example, she diverted money intended to build a modern navy, spending it instead on constructing the magnificent Summer Palace, just outside Beijing, for her imperial retreat. Some historians identify the ineptitude and selfish policies of Manchu leaders such as Ci Xi as a major factor in China's failure to rapidly modernize. China's inability to deflect the growing challenges fostered escapism among many thoughtful Chinese, expressed by a poet official: "I'll drink myself merry, Thrash out a wild song from my lute, And let the storms rage at will."[11]

Foreign Pressures on Late Qing China

Historians have often emphasized external rather than internal factors in China's decline. They view late Qing modernization as impressive but thwarted by foreign economic and political domination that placed constraints on what China could accomplish. The foreign pressures, these historians argue, put Chinese leaders into a siege mentality. Indeed, by the late 1800s

Chinese Study Maxim Gun After the Taiping Rebellion, the Qing emperor sent two Chinese mandarins to England to examine and purchase new weapons. In this photo, they examine a Maxim gun, one of the first machine guns that gave Western nations a great military advantage. (Peter Newark's Military Pictures)

China lacked full autonomy: Western gunboats patrolled its rivers, international settlements existed in the major cities, Christian missionaries challenged Chinese values, and Westerners exerted influence on the imperial government, and also had partial control of the economy. Some foreign powers dominated particular regions as spheres of influence, such as Britain in Guangdong and the Germans in Shandong, acquiring resources, establishing enterprises, and manipulating local governments.

The United States, Britain, France, and Germany exercised their power over China through **gunboat diplomacy**, the use of superior firepower to impose a country's will on local populations and governments. The term comes from the use of Western gunboats to patrol some of China's rivers and seacoasts in the late 1800s and early 1900s, interceding to protect Western businessmen, missionaries, and diplomats whose activities generated Chinese hostility. The most notorious was a U.S. naval force known as the Yangzi Patrol, a group of shallow-draft gunboats, often supplemented by a half-dozen destroyers and cruisers, that patrolled the hundreds of miles of the Yangzi River between Shanghai and central Sichuan province between 1890 and World War I. According to a patrol commander, the mission of the Yangzi Patrol was "to make every American feel perfectly safe in coming into the valley to

live or to transact business, until such time as the Chinese themselves are able to afford these guarantees."[12] Sovereign Chinese rights and the people's outrage at foreign intrusion counted for little. But gunboats were only part of the story. Americans also promoted free trade, generously funded Christian missionaries, and donated to humanitarian causes such as flood relief and orphanages.

Despite the limits on its autonomy, China never became a full Western colony such as India or Vietnam, perhaps because too many foreign powers were involved. The United States, which had become one of the most powerful and prosperous Western nations in the late 1800s, discouraged full colonization by promoting what it termed an "Open Door" policy that allowed equal access by all the foreign powers to China's vast markets and resources. The Open Door enabled the Western nations and, eventually, Japan to avoid conflict among themselves and to acquire the economic fruits of empire without the high political and military costs of conquering and governing China.

Late Qing Reforms and Wars

Between 1890 and 1916 the growing foreign challenge now included Japan, which was rapidly industrializing. In search of resources and markets to exploit, in the 1890s Japan began intervening in Korea, long a vassal state of China. The Koreans sent pleas for help to China, and the resulting Sino-Japanese War (1894–1895) ended in a humiliating defeat for China. In

---

gunboat diplomacy The Western countries' use of superior firepower to impose their will on local populations and governments in the nineteenth century.

the treaty ending hostilities, China was forced to pay an indemnity and to recognize Korean independence, and in 1910 Korea became a Japanese colony. The Qing were also forced to cede the large island of Taiwan, populated largely by Chinese, to Japan, the island becoming a Japanese colony in 1910, and to acknowledge Japanese control of the Ryukyu (ree-OO-kyoo) Islands, between Japan and Taiwan, whose Japanese-speaking people had an independent state and a long-standing tributary relationship with China. The Manchus had already lost influence over other tributary states, such as Vietnam (to France) and Burma (to Britain). The defeat by Japan proved a blow to Chinese pride and to the credibility of the Qing rulers.

These crises brought a group of progressive reformers to the attention of the young Manchu emperor, Guangxu, and, in 1898, under their influence, he called for dramatic changes, later known as the 100 Days of Reform, which included a crash program of economic modernization. But the Empress Dowager Xi Ci and her conservative allies blocked the proposals, arrested the reformers, and placed the emperor under house arrest. Xi Ci and the reactionaries reclaimed power, promoted an antiforeign atmosphere, and encouraged the Chinese to organize antiforeign militias.

The ensuing tensions led to the Boxer Rebellion, a popular movement in 1900 that aimed at driving the foreigners out of China but that resulted in an even stronger Western presence. The Qing gave strong backing to the Boxers ("Righteous Harmony Fists"), an anti-Western, anti-Christian secret society comprising mostly poor peasants. To spread their cause, the Boxers wrote jingles promising that when all the foreigners were expelled from China, the Qing would bring peace to the land. The Boxers attacked foreigners in north China, occupied Beijing, and besieged the foreign embassies. The Qing declared war on all the foreign powers with which it had been forced to sign unequal treaties. In response, the British, Americans, French, and other powers put aside their differences and organized an international force that routed the Boxers, occupied Beijing, and forced the Qing to pay another huge indemnity and to permit foreign military forces to stay in China. The Europeans talked openly of dismantling China, and the Russians used the rebellion as an excuse to occupy Manchuria.

The string of defeats generated final frantic efforts at reform and modernization, setting the stage for more dramatic transitions. Fearing China might soon be divided into colonies, the chastened Manchus now began more serious reform efforts, looking to Japan for models. The Qing abolished the Confucian examination system, established two millennia earlier, set up modern, Western-style schools, and sent 10,000 students to Japan. By 1911 some 57,000 state schools enrolled 1,600,000 students, though this was in fact only a fraction of China's school-age children. The Qing also formed new government departments, allocated more money to the military, and strengthened provincial and local governments. Reformist ideas also sparked movements among women. Some women studying in Japan formed the Encompassing Love Society, with the goal of uplifting Chinese women and making them full participants in society. Other women, including some Chris-

tians, strived to raise female literacy and expand economic opportunities. The feminist Zhang Zhuzhun encouraged Chinese women to emulate Western women role models such as the British nurse Florence Nightingale and the American antislavery crusader Harriett Beecher Stowe.

Liberals who had criticized the Qing reformers for going too slowly now became more influential. Many reformers had read and even translated European literature and scholarship, including that of Enlightenment writers, and were deeply impressed by Japan's modernization in the later 1800s. The leading liberal reformer, Liang Qichao (1871–1929), represented change within tradition. A scholar and journalist, Liang promoted a modernization that blended Confucian values and Western learning. He also believed China should industrialize, form a constitutional government, and focus on the idea of nation instead of culture. Liang's colleague and teacher, Kang Youwei (1858–1928), envisioned a world government, the end of nationalist strife and gender discrimination, and a welfare state to nurture humanity. Both men promoted women's education, and Kang founded the anti-footbinding movement to stop the longtime Chinese practice of forcing women to compress their feet to please men's taste. Footbinding severely hampered women; as a song passed among illiterate women put it, "Your body is so heavy a burden for your feet that you fear you may stumble in the wind."[13]

Chinese Nationalism and Revolutionary Movements

For some Chinese inspired by nationalism, most importantly Sun Zhong Shan, better known as Sun Yat-Sen (soon yot-SEN), the fiasco of the Boxer Rebellion showed the futility of trying to change China by reform from above and prompted them to organize a revolution from below that could sweep the Manchus from power. Inspired by the Taipings, Meiji Japan (see next section), and the West, Sun (1866–1925) mixed tradition and modernity. Unlike the liberal reformers such as Liang and Kang, Sun did not come from an upper-class mandarin background. He knew little of the Confucian classics and had no commitment to the traditional system. He identified with the poor and downtrodden, writing that he was a coolie and the son of a coolie. Born near Guangzhou to a peasant family that had supported the Taipings, Sun moved to Hawaii at age thirteen to join an elder brother. There he studied in an Anglican high school and became a semi-Christian. He then received a medical degree in British-ruled Hong Kong. Influenced by Western thought, he began dressing in Western clothes and visited England, where he learned that Westerners often criticized their own systems and sometimes favored socialism. Convinced that the Qing system was hopeless, Sun decided to devote his life to politics and became the chief architect of the Chinese Revolution.

In 1895 Sun founded an anti-Manchu secret society dedicated to replacing the imperial system with a Western-style republic, and branches were set up in China, Japan, and Hawaii (see Witness to the Past: Planning a Revolutionary New

Planning a Revolutionary New China

In 1905 various radical Chinese groups met in Japan and merged into one revolutionary organization, the *Tongmen Hui* (Chinese Alliance Association), led by Sun Yat-Sen, then based in Tokyo. Most of the members were drawn from among the 10,000 Chinese students enrolled in Japanese universities. Unhappy with the Qing government and impressed by modernizing Japan, they sought to change China through revolution. In their founding proclamation, which was influenced by Western thought, they set out their agenda, visionary but vague, for a three-stage passage from military to constitutional government and a more equitable society.

Since the beginning of China as a nation, we Chinese have governed our own country despite occasional interruptions. When China was occasionally occupied by a foreign race, our ancestors could always . . . drive these foreigners out . . . and preserve China for future generations. . . . There is a difference, however, between our revolution and the revolutions of our ancestors. The purpose of past revolutions . . . was to restore China to the Chinese, and nothing else. We, on the other hand, strive not only to expel the ruling aliens [Manchus] . . . but also to change basically the political and economic structure of our country. . . . The revolutions of yesterday were revolutions by and for the heroes; our revolution, on the other hand, is a revolution by and for the people. . . . everyone who believes in the principles of liberty, equality, and fraternity has an obligation to participate in it. . . .

At this juncture we wish to express candidly and fully how to make our revolution today and how to govern the country tomorrow.

1. Expulsion of the Manchus from China. . . . We shall quickly overthrow the Manchu government so as to restore the sovereignty of China to the Chinese.
2. Restoration of China to the Chinese. China belongs to the Chinese who have the right to govern themselves. . . .
3. Establishment of a Republic. Since one of the principles of our revolution is equality, we intend to establish a republic. . . . all citizens will have the right to participate in the government, the president of the republic will be elected by the people, and the parliament will have deputies elected by and responsible to their respective constituencies. . . .
4. Equalization of land ownership. The social and economic structure of China must be so reconstructed that the fruits of labor will be shared by all Chinese on an equal basis. . . .

To attain the four goals . . . , we propose a procedure of three stages. The first . . . is that of military rule . . . [in which] the Military Government, in cooperation with the people, will eradicate all the abuses of the past; with the arrival of the second stage the Military Government will hand over local administration to the people while reserving for itself the right of jurisdiction over all matters that concern the nation as a whole; during the . . . final stage the Military Government will cease to exist and all governmental power will be invested in organs as prescribed in a national constitution. This orderly procedure is necessary because our people need time to acquaint themselves with the idea of liberty and equality . . . , the basis on which the republic of China rests. . . . On . . . restoring China to her own people, we urge everyone to step forward and to do the best he can. . . . Whatever our station in society is, rich or poor, we are all equal in our determination to safeguard the security of China as a nation and to preserve the Chinese people.

THINKING ABOUT THE READING

1. How does the proclamation use Western revolutionary and nationalist ideas?
2. How will revolution build a new China?

Source: Pei-Kai Cheng and Michael Lestz with Jonathan D. Spence, eds., *The Search for Modern China: A Documentary Collection* (New York: W. W. Norton, 1999), pp. 202–206.

China). Facing arrest in China for treason, Sun traveled extensively, recruiting financial support and membership among Chinese merchants in Southeast Asia and North America, Chinese businessmen in the treaty ports, Chinese students in Japan, and sympathetic military officers. Sun and his followers thought of themselves as nationalists, more interested in China as a nation than as a culture. The cause of dramatic change also attracted feminists such as Qin Jin (Chin Chin) (1877–1907), who left her arranged marriage for study in Japan and then started a women's magazine and pursued political activity. Later she was executed as a revolutionary. She wrote in a poem, "Our women's world is sunk so deep, who can help us? Unbinding my feet I clear out a thousand years of poison."[14] She expressed the hope that one day China would see free women "blooming like fields of flowers."

Sun also began to develop his program, which he termed the "Three Principles of the People." The first principle, nationalism, involved overthrowing the Manchus, restoring ethnic Chinese to power, and reclaiming China's historical greatness. For his second principle, he favored republicanism, a constitutional democracy with an elected representative government rather than the constitutional monarchy sought by the liberal reformers. The third principle, people's livelihood, envisioned an equitable economic status for all. Sun was vague on the details but favored partial state control of the economy, the transformation of the peasants into a literate, property-owning class, and the reshaping of China into a modern, wealthy, powerful nation. In pursuing a national, democratic, and social revolution, Sun did not necessarily want to imitate Europe and the United States, writing that, while the Western powers were strong, their people remained poor. Eventually the day would come, he hoped, when the Chinese could look over their shoulder and find the West lagging far behind.

Revolution: The End of Imperial China

Sun was traveling in the United States raising money for his cause when, on October 10, 1911, some Chinese influenced by Sun's ideas began the uprising. Soldiers in the Yangzi River city of Wuhan (WOO-HAHN) in central China mutinied against the Qing government and were soon joined by sympathizers in other cities. Within two months the revolutionary soldiers controlled provinces in central and southern China. As the authority of the Qing government quickly crumbled outside their power base in the north. Sun returned to China for the first time in sixteen years. From their capital in Beijing, the Manchus hesitated, then asked an ambitious general, Yuan Shikai (yoo-AHN shee-KAI) (1859–1916), to deal with the revolutionaries. In control of a large army and in touch with both sides, Yuan decided to replace the dynasty with his own rule. To improve his position, he actively played the Manchus off against the revolutionaries.

The revolution had wide popular support, since many Chinese hated the Manchus. Sun's nationalist message spread rapidly, and the Chinese felt a new sense of social solidarity through their loyalty to the nation. Nationalist sentiments were especially strong among students, military officers, and Chinese in the treaty ports. Sun now reorganized his anti-Manchu secret society into a political party, the Guomindang (gwo-min-dong) (Chinese Nationalist Party), which gathered varied nationalists and liberal reformers into the fold. However, although widely respected, Sun was not a forceful leader, and the revolutionaries could agree only on opposing the Manchus.

Two centers of power now existed. General Yuan Shikai held the dominant position in the north and considerable influence over the Qing leaders in Beijing. The revolutionaries controlled the Yangzi Valley and parts of south China, and they made plans to establish a provisional republican government. Worrying about Yuan's military might, Sun sought a compromise to save China from civil war. Sun offered to make Yuan president of the republic if Yuan arranged for the abdication of the five-year-old Qing emperor. Yuan agreed, and in February 1912 the Qing dynasty, and with it the 2,000-year-old imperial system, was ended. In March 1912 a republic was established in Nanjing, on the Yangzi River in east-central China. In a move symbolizing a change of direction for China, the new government adopted the Western calendar. But Sun had underestimated Yuan's ambitions. While a modernizer, Yuan was no republican and hoped to restore an autocratic system with himself at the top. Yuan soon moved the capital back to Beijing in the north.

The Early Republican Era

The new republic began with some signs of liberal accomplishment. During the first year, the republic's leaders established liberal institutions, including a constitution written by Sun that provided for a two-chamber parliament and a president. In early 1913 a restricted electorate chose a national assembly and provincial assemblies in the first and most open general election in China's long history. Sun's Guomindang, identified with nationalist revolution, won a majority of seats but lacked a consensus about the directions of change. A new women's suffrage movement, influenced by its counterparts in Europe, pressed for equal rights for women and their inclusion in politics.

In part because of Yuan Shikai's ambitions, however, the republican system failed to bring stability and liberty, dashing the hopes of Sun and his colleagues. Convinced that China needed a strong leader and government, Yuan considered Sun and the Guomindang formidable obstacles. He had Guomindang leaders assassinated, bought off, or, in the case of Sun, forced into exile. Yuan soon outlawed the Guomindang, suspended parliament, and banned the women's suffrage movement. He enjoyed the support of much of the army, the imperial bureaucracy, and the foreign powers, who preferred a strongman to the democratic uncertainties of Sun. Sun and his closest followers moved to Japan, embittered and demoralized. Having eliminated the liberal institutions, Yuan became increasingly autocratic and announced plans to found a new dynasty.

Yuan's plans, however, were put on hold by current problems in China, including constant pressure from foreign powers and the secession of regions occupied largely by non-Chinese. Although growing nationalism made concessions to foreign powers unpopular, China was bankrupt, and Yuan was forced to borrow heavily from foreign governments to keep the country afloat. Much of Mongolia declared independence in 1911, and it later became allied with Russia. Tibet, formerly a Qing province, also expelled the Chinese administration. In 1915 China also faced diplomatic challenges. During World War I China remained neutral, but Japan, allied with Britain, occupied the German sphere of influence in the Shandong peninsula on China's east coast. Japan then presented Yuan with 21 Demands, including control of Shandong, more rights in Manchuria, and the appointment of Japanese advisers to the Chinese government. The 21 Demands set off huge Chinese protests and boycotts against Japan and Yuan's inability to protect China's interests.

His imperial restoration plans aborted, a humiliated Yuan died in 1916. The liberal reformer Liang Qiqao concluded scornfully that Yuan, by assuming that everything could be bought with gold and intimidated by the sword, caused his own downfall while ruining China. Yuan's years in power had wrecked the republican institutions, and his submission to Japan's 21 Demands suggested that China was even weaker than before. After Yuan's death, China fell into the abyss of prolonged civil war.

SECTION SUMMARY

- In the debate over what China should do next, conservatives thought China should stick to its traditions, while liberals tried to modernize China, but their reforms failed to bring it to the technological and military level of the West.

- By the late 1800s, China's autonomy had been all but eliminated by gunboat diplomacy, under which Western powers ensured the safety of Westerners in China through the use of force.

- After China lost its influence over Korea in the Sino-Japanese War and the Boxer Rebellion failed to rid China of foreigners, liberals moved to modernize and Westernize Chinese education and culture.

- Sun Yat-Sen, born to Chinese peasants but educated in Western schools, formed a secret society devoted to replacing imperial rule with a Western-style republic and set out three principles: nationalism, republicanism, and economic equality.

- A revolution inspired by Sun Yat-Sen succeeded in toppling the Qing dynasty with the assistance of General Yuan Shikai.

- Yuan seized power after Sun Yat-Sen's party won the republic's first election, but he was weakened by Japanese encroachment and the loss of influence over areas such as Mongolia and Tibet, and after his death China entered a period of civil war.

✦ Japan and Korea Under Challenge

What factors aided Japan in the quest for modernization?

In the second half of the nineteenth century Japan met the Western challenge more successfully than China, rapidly transforming itself into a powerful industrialized nation. Although it had serious internal problems, Japan also possessed significant strengths that allowed it to achieve success. The shoguns, military dictators from the Tokugawa family ruling in the name of the emperor, had governed Japan since 1600 and had kept a tight hold on Japanese society (see Chronology: Japan and Korea, 1750–1914). When the first Western ships arrived demanding to open Japan, the Japanese, largely shut off by policies of seclusion from the outside world, were just as far behind the West in military and industrial technology as China, India, and other Asian societies had been. Across the straits, Korea had also chosen a seclusion policy, and it, too, faced severe challenges in the early 1800s.

CHRONOLOGY

Japan and Korea, 1750–1914

1392–1910	Yi dynasty in Korea
1600–1867	Tokugawa Shogunate
1853	Opening of Japan by Perry
1854	Treaty of Kanagawa
1867–1868	Meiji Restoration
1894–1895	Sino-Japanese War
1904–1905	Russo-Japanese War
1910	Japanese colonization of Korea and Taiwan

Tokugawa Japan and Qing China

Like China, Japan faced foreign pressures that led to change, but Japan successfully met the challenge of the Western intrusion while China, failing to rally, gradually lost some of its autonomy. The differences between these two ancient neighbors, historians argue, help explain the different outcomes. Geography played a role. Japan, being compact and linguistically homogeneous, had a strong sense of national unity and of loyalty to the emperor as a national symbol, whereas China's vastness created difficulties in communications and linguistically divided the country. In China, sentiments of loyalty were restricted largely to the family. While new ideas, such as Buddhism, reached China over the centuries, their assimilation was a slow process, whereas Japan had a long tradition of readily borrowing from outside, as exemplified in the ancient Japanese slogan "Chinese learning, Japanese spirit." As a result, Japanese leaders could more easily make a conscious decision to import and adopt new ideas, technologies, and institutions.

The two neighbors also differed in the influence of their merchants and in their political and military systems. The Japanese merchant class was assertive and influential and was rapidly expanding its scope and power, whereas in China the commercial energies had reached their height centuries earlier, only to be contained and restricted by the government. Furthermore, in contrast to China's centralized empire, the Japanese government was pluralistic; the Tokugawa shogun, based in Edo (today's Tokyo), had to balance the interests of the various daimyo, the influential leaders of regional landowning families, while keeping the Kyoto-based emperor powerless. The Japanese also respected military endeavors more than did the Chinese. Although the samurai had lost their fighting edge under the long enforced Tokugawa peace, they still held a respected position in Japanese society.

In the face of challenges from the outside world, the Japanese and Chinese also valued different aspects of their own

ANDO HIROSHIGE,
JAPANESE ARTIST

The nineteenth-century Japanese artist Ando Hiroshige (1797–1858) gained a worldwide reputation for work that reflected a distinctly Japanese vision of landscape and urban life. His work, along with that of his four-decades-older contemporary, Katsushika Hokusai, portrayed old Japan on the eve of dramatic change, a Japan of rice fields, small shops, traveling peddlers, sedan chairs, samurai warriors, and dirt roads rather than the later Japan of factories, conglomerates, railroads, and steamships. By portraying scenery and diverse urban scenes, Hiroshige and Hokusai carried printmaking far beyond the early Tokugawa tradition, which emphasized life in the restaurants, teahouses, theaters, and bordellos of the "Floating World" entertainment districts.

Hiroshige was born into a samurai family in Edo (Tokyo) in 1797. His father was a member of the fire brigade, and the family lived at the fire station. As a child, Hiroshige learned to read, write, and master martial arts, and he also developed a talent for poetry. Like other young samurai, he probably visited the Floating World to enjoy kabuki theater and to patronize courtesans. In 1809 the twelve-year-old youngster succeeded to his father's position as a fireman. Underpaid and enjoying art more than firefighting, he began studying with several famous artists. From this time on he used the name Utagawa Hiroshige, a tribute to the Utagawa school of art in which he had been trained. Dutch traders at Nagasaki had introduced Western art to Japan, and Hiroshige probably assimilated ideas from imported Dutch etchings. Inspired by mountains, rivers, rocks, and trees, the young artist gained a working knowledge of different modes and the techniques to use in depicting them. Influenced by Hokusai's pioneering work, Hiroshige began favoring rural landscapes and Edo scenes. At the age of twenty-seven he passed on his fire brigade post to his son and pursued art full time.

Although having much in common, Hokusai and Hiroshige had different outlooks. Hokusai's landscapes divided attention between the setting and the people in it, usually workers such as weavers, carpenters, and spinners. By contrast, Hiroshige subordinated everything to the setting, especially to the mood established by weather, season, time of day, and angle of view. Influenced by Chinese art, Hiroshige portrayed the insignificance of humans against the vastness of nature. His rain and snow scenes are marvels of mood, showing mastery of light and subtle harmony, mixing fact with imagination.

Hiroshige's art often reflected his personal experiences. In 1832, while accompanying an embassy of the Tokugawa shogun to the imperial court in Kyoto, Hiroshige gathered material for his famous work, *The 53 Stations of the Tokaido*, which depicts scenes of villages, inns, and lakes along the Tokaido (Eastern Sea Route) highway connecting Tokyo and Kyoto. Hiroshige immortalized the highway, which skirted the Pacific coast of Honshu Island, where mountains sweep down to the sea, and then traversed inland through majestic snow-capped mountains and past beautiful Lake Biwa. A continued stream of people—daimyo and their processions, couriers, monks, pilgrims, merchants, adventurers, entertainers—traveled the well-maintained Tokaido to and from the shogun's court. Stations with inns, restaurants, brothels, and bathhouses flourished as rest stops for the bustling traffic.

Since many Japanese had money to indulge in art, Hiroshige's later collections of prints sold thousands of copies, and he remained a very popular artist. Townspeople loved this art reflecting daily life or the worldly dreams of the merchant

societies. Never having been successfully invaded, the Japanese felt vulnerable when they encountered the well-armed Westerners. They prized political independence far more than cultural purity, having radically changed their culture several times in the past. The Chinese, however, were used to foreign rule and prized their Confucian traditions more than political independence. Thus Japanese leaders, after first learning of Western intentions and capabilities through the only Westerners allowed in Japan, the Dutch traders at the southern port of Nagasaki, were far more sensitive to the Western threat than the Chinese elite.

Late Tokugawa Society and Culture

Japan also benefited from the energy and openness to new ideas of late Tokugawa society. Its many schools resulted in high literacy rates, and several schools specialized in so-called Dutch learning acquired from Dutch traders. This Western knowledge included sciences such as medicine, physics, and chemistry. One reformer argued that "Dutch [Western] learning is not perfect, but if we choose the good points, what harm could come? What is more ridiculous than to refuse to discuss its merits?"[15] Even some Japanese women who, as in China, generally suffered a low status, gained an education. For example, the poet and painter Ema Saiko (1787–1861) compared her reading with her father's: "My father deciphers Dutch books; His daughter reads Chinese poetry. Divided by a single lamp, We each follow our own course."[16] Whatever their status and occupation, the Japanese demonstrated a pattern of hard work, thrift, saving, and cooperation—attributes that lent themselves to modernization.

Tokugawa Japan enjoyed a thriving city life. Cities such as Edo and Osaka, already among the world's largest, offered a flourishing commerce and diverse entertainments. A description of a carnival in Edo in 1865 recorded the following amusements, services, and vendors: kabuki theater, archery booths, fortunetellers, wandering balladeers, massage healers, barbershops, and peddlers of chilled water, sushi (raw fish), confectionery, stuffed fritters, dumplings, fried eel livers, toys, and lanterns.

class. Hiroshige produced some 5,500 different prints, sold individually or in collections such as the *53 Stations of the Tokaido* and *One Hundred Views of Famous Places in Edo*. However, his personal life was often troubled. Hiroshige never prospered financially and was often pressed to finance his beloved nightly cup of rice wine. He married several times and sired several children. His eldest daughter's husband, known as Hiroshige II (1826–1869), continued Hiroshige's artistic tradition. At the age of sixty Hiroshige became a Buddhist monk, not an unusual step for aging Japanese men. He died at age sixty-two in 1858 of cholera during a great epidemic. On his deathbed, he discouraged his family from holding a lavish funeral by reciting an old verse: "When I die, Cremate me not nor bury me. Just lay me in the fields, to fill the belly of some starving dog."

Hiroshige was the last of the major Japanese print masters. Shortly after he died, Westerners opened up Japan, ending the secluded world that had nourished the woodblock prints and the artists who produced them. But Hiroshige prints continued to be traded around the world, giving foreigners their most vivid impressions of Japan. When Europeans imported the pictures in the late 1800s, they proved a revelation to artists looking for new ways to portray landscapes. Hence woodblock prints, born of isolation, became one of the first major cultural links between Japan and the outside world.

THINKING ABOUT THE PROFILE

1. How did Hokusai and Hiroshige's prints differ from earlier Japanese prints?

2. What do Hiroshige's life and art tell us about late Tokugawa Japan?

Note: Quotation from Julian Bicknell, *Hiroshige in Tokyo: The Floating World of Edo* (San Francisco: Pomegranate Artbooks, 1994), p. 50.

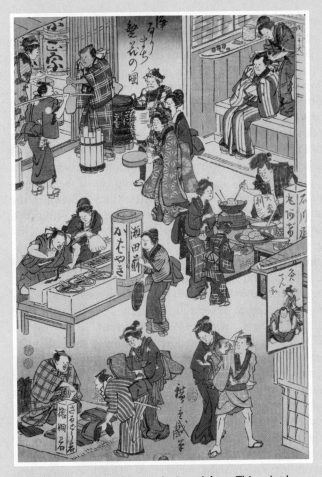

Street Stalls and Tradesmen in Joruricho This print by Hiroshige portraying the street life in Edo reveals the artist's sympathy for common people, such as the peddlers, barbers, and food-sellers shown at work and their customers.
(Courtesy of the Trustees of the Victoria & Albert Museum)

Tokugawa arts were also vigorous, producing creations that achieved renown worldwide. Japanese artistic products that were prized in the West, such as ceramics, jewelry, and furniture, enriched the Dutch traders at Nagasaki who controlled the export trade. The late 1700s and early 1800s was a great age for painting and woodblock prints, some of it influenced by Western ideas. The two greatest artists blended Japanese and imported art styles. Katsushika Hokusai (HO-koo-sie) (1760–1849) produced tens of thousands of paintings and drawings, but he was most famous for landscape prints such as the *Thirty-six Views of Mount Fuji*. He strove to improve his craft, predicting that "by ninety I will surely have penetrated the mystery of life. At one hundred, I will have attained a magnificent level and at one hundred and ten, each dot of my work will vibrate with life."[17] Ando Hiroshige (1797–1858) concentrated on Tokyo scenes and landscapes emphasizing nature (see Profile: Ando Hiroshige, Japanese Artist). The treatment of atmosphere and light in Japanese color prints influenced the French impressionist painters of the later 1800s, who empha-

sized the effect of light and color in momentary scenes (see Chapter 20). Both Japanese prints and French impressionism asked the viewer to look at an everyday scene in a new way. The influential European artist Vincent Van Gogh admitted that he strove to emulate Japanese landscape painting.

Growing Problems and Reform

Despite these advantages, by the early 1800s some Japanese sensed internal decay. Japanese of all classes increasingly blamed the Tokugawa for the nation's growing domestic problems: inflation, increasing taxes, and social disorder. In addition, there was the gradual impoverishment of the samurai. Over the years the daimyo families, burdened with heavy expenses, had cut the salaries of the samurai, who were trained as warriors but often worked as bureaucrats in daimyo domains. With their income declining, and finding it harder to support their families, the samurai borrowed money and became indebted to merchants. In the 1830s Japan was also experiencing widespread famine and starvation. The growing social tensions and resentments reached a breaking point, fostering urban riots, peasant revolts, and various plots to depose the Tokugawa shogun.

While worried about domestic unrest, Japanese officials were more concerned about the growing Western presence in the region, which they correctly perceived would impact Japan. They knew that Russians had been active in Siberia and the North Pacific since the 1700s and that British ships had sailed along Japan's coast. In 1825 the shogun ordered that whenever a foreign ship was sighted approaching the coast, the samurai should fire on it and drive it away. After China's defeat in the Opium War, Japan's shocked leaders encouraged the samurai to develop new, more effective weapons and contemplated starting a navy. The Japanese considered the Westerners money-grasping barbarians who did not understand the proper rules of social behavior and who would contaminate the national spirit. As the samurai vowed to fight to the death to resist Western invasion, this feeling of nationalism grew, putting pressure on the shogun to deal firmly with the Western threat.

Japanese leaders responded with reforms to strengthen the country. The Tokugawa reforms implemented at the national level, such as breaking up merchant monopolies, establishing a bureau to translate Western books, and reducing the number of government officials to save money, were largely unsuccessful in energizing the system. But some provincial governments, especially in the southwest, attempted more daring and creative changes. They recruited men of talent to their local administrations, emphasized mastery of "Dutch studies," and even sponsored industrial experiments, including the construction of an electric steam engine in the 1850s. Samurai in several of these domains learned how to cast better guns and to produce iron suitable for making modern cannon.

The Opening of Japan

The need for change was made urgent by external forces that arose in the 1850s. Spanish and Portuguese merchants and missionaries had introduced Western influence into Japan in the 1500s, but their aggressive behavior and antagonizing of Japanese leaders had caused the Tokugawa to end the cultural and economic exchange. The Dutch presence at Nagasaki, which benefited both the Dutch and the Japanese, was the legacy of Japan's earlier encounter with the West. By the 1850s, however, Japan faced a new threat to its seclusion policy.

The most dramatic attempt to break down Japanese seclusion came from the Americans. American ships had occasionally visited the Dutch base at Nagasaki to trade, and by the early 1800s, besides trade, U.S. leaders also wanted Japan to protect shipwrecked sailors and provide fresh water and coal to ships making the long trip between California and China. In 1853 a fleet of eleven U.S. warships commanded by Commodore Matthew Perry sailed into Tokyo Bay and delivered a letter from the U.S. president, Millard Fillmore, to the shogun. The letter demanded that the Japanese sign a treaty opening the country or face war when Perry returned the following year. The three U.S. steamships with the expedition, known as

the "black ships," shocked the Japanese with their ability to move against the wind and tide. The shogun, remembering the Opium War and more realistic than his critics, granted Perry's demands in the Treaty of Kanagawa (1854) and then accepted the blame for the nation's humiliation. The treaty opened two ports to U.S. trade and allowed for the stationing of a U.S. consul. By 1856 American diplomats demanded a stronger commercial treaty, the opening of more ports, extraterritoriality, and the admission of Christian missionaries. The shogun reluctantly agreed; he soon signed similar treaties with the Dutch, British, French, and Russians.

Like China, Japan experienced a forcible intrusion from the West that held the seeds of potential colonization. Although the changes still limited the Westerners' movement in Japan, most Japanese leaders saw that Japan was the loser in these dealings. Western merchants soon arrived, flooding the nation with cheap industrial goods to create a market and destroy the native industries, as they had done earlier in China and India. International settlements restricted to foreigners were established in Japan's major port cities. Westerners enjoyed ever increasing economic and legal privileges, and escalating domestic disunity held the potential for enhancing Western power.

The Tokugawa Government in Crisis

Western encroachment provoked a crisis for the Tokugawa government and a national debate about how Japan should respond to its challenges. Some Japanese believed accommodation was preferable to war and favored either a complete or a limited opening to the West. One prominent Westernizer, Fukuzawa Yukichi (1835–1901), traveled in the West and became a strong proponent of Western liberalism, rationalism, and political freedom. Another group advocated complete defiance and the use of force to expel the intruders. One such advocate wrote that the Americans had dishonored Japan and that every Japanese needed to help stop the nation from becoming enslaved by other nations. Turning against the ineffective Tokugawa shoguns but not the powerless emperor who symbolized the nation, one faction proclaimed, "Revere the Emperor, Expel the Barbarians."

Shaken by the Western presence, the Tokugawa government launched efforts at modernization. It established a shipbuilding industry, promoted manufacturing, hired two hundred Western teachers, sent a few Japanese students abroad, established an institute of Western studies, and expanded the study of foreign languages. The Japanese who had already become interested in Western science and technology, however, saw these innovations as too little and too late.

Despite the reforms, the Tokugawa shogun was now widely perceived as weak. Aware of Japan's military disadvantage, the shogun always chose negotiation rather than defiance, even when the Westerners badly misused their power and retaliated for any attacks on Western residents. The shogun's strategy of avoiding confrontation led a respected poet to complain angrily: "You, whose ancestors in the mighty days, Roared at the skies and swept the earth, Stand now helpless to drive off wrangling foreigners—How empty your title, 'Queller of the Barbarians.'"[18] Furthermore, the Western powers continually made new demands. By the 1860s the Japanese seemed to be repeating the experience of China, gradually losing control of their political and economic future.

Challenges to the Korean Kingdom

Like Tokugawa Japan, Korea, though faced with growing problems in this era, had also chosen relative isolation. From ancient times the peoples of the mountainous Korean peninsula had been shaped by their location between powerful China and Japan. Over the centuries Koreans had mixed China's religions, political structure, and writing system with their own customs. Still, the Koreans maintained a strong national identity and learned how to balance close links to China with their political independence. Like China, Korea became a unified state presided over by a series of family dynasties ruling with a Confucian ideology.

The last of the Korean dynasties, the Yi (YEE) (1392–1910), ruled the state they called Choson (choh-SAN) for over five centuries, favoring powerful landlord families. By officially closing off Korea from the outside world after the Manchus invaded and pillaged the capital in the early 1600s, the Yi earned Choson the label of "the Hermit Kingdom." However, as in Tokugawa Japan, seclusion from the outside was not absolute. Korea still traded with China. Better irrigation technologies and new strains of rice from China increased agricultural productivity. Korean scholars also visited China and on their return some wrote books favorably contrasting Chinese society with what they considered Korea's overly rigid and inequitable social system. A few Koreans met Westerners in China and found their philosophies, political ideas, and technologies of interest.

Korean seclusion did not result in cultural stagnation. Several strong kings in the 1700s fostered a renewed culture of learning, including the printing of encyclopedias and historical records. Knowledge of writing in Korean spread more widely. Educated aristocratic women wrote memoirs, diaries, and stories of court life, and even some commoners wrote stories and novels. Literature, philosophy, painting, and ceramics flourished. Some thinkers, to promote justice, examined social conditions by studying the peasants.

However, by the early 1800s Choson, like Qing China and Tokugawa Japan, began to succumb to stress. As in Japan, the rigid social structure crumbled as the economy grew. Korea's population doubled to some 9 million between 1669 and 1800, increasing pressure on the land. With Buddhism losing influence, some Koreans turned to Christianity. Although officially prohibited, a few French and Chinese Christian missionaries nevertheless illegally entered Korea and spread their message. During the 1800s Korea also experienced recurrent famines and increased political instability, including peasant uprisings. The Choson government blamed and hence persecuted Christians and Western missionaries for undermining society and causing turmoil. One official told the French missionaries he was expelling that they had no right to tell Koreans to abandon their ancient teachings and accept those of alien cultures.

The challenges to Korea and its neighbors caused Koreans to reflect on and deal with the threats. As in China and Japan, Korean intellectuals debated the value of Western learning, and some pushed for reforms of the traditional political and social system. With the Yi refusing direct commercial negotiations with the West, Korean military forces drove away French and American ships seeking to open Korea to Western trade, and in 1871 they repulsed a U.S. naval force. The Yi also worried about Russian expansion to the north, in eastern Siberia. By the later 1800s Korea seemed in need of rejuvenation.

SECTION SUMMARY

- Japan was better able than China to deal with foreign pressures because of its compactness and homogeneity, its openness to outside ideas, its balance of power between groups of elites, its strong merchant class, and its sensitivity to the threat posed by foreigners.

- Late Tokugawa Japanese culture was vigorous, open to Western learning, and marked by thriving urban centers and ambitious artists.

- Internal decay in Japan led to riots and revolts, but officials, more concerned with external threats, embarked on reforms designed to strengthen the country and enable it to withstand pressure from Westerners. However, when faced with a choice between war and opening Japan to American trade, the Japanese shogun chose trade, which led to trade agreements with other Western nations, a flood of cheap manufactured goods, and special privileges for Westerners in Japan.

- For hundreds of years, the Yi dynasty had closed Korea off from the rest of the world, earning for itself the label "the Hermit Kingdom," and when Korea experienced famine and instability in the 1800s, its leaders blamed the influence of Christian missionaries.

 # The Remaking of Japan and Korea

How did the Meiji government transform Japan and Korea?

The ultimate Japanese response to Western intrusion was radically different from China's, allowing Japan to avoid the shackles of colonialism and become the only non-Western nation to successfully industrialize and achieve Western standards of living before World War II. This transition owed much to a revolution that ended Tokugawa rule in 1868 and created a new government that fostered dramatic reforms that helped Japan resist the West. By the early 1900s a powerful Japan had increased its influence in the wider world. Meanwhile, Korea was forced to abandon several centuries of isolation and eventually became a Japanese colony.

Tokugawa Defeat and the Meiji Restoration

By the 1860s the deteriorating situation in Japan led to a revolution against the Tokugawa shogunate, known as the **Meiji Restoration** (1867–1868) because it was carried out in the name of the emperor, whose reign name was Meiji (MAY-gee). The revolution that overthrew the Tokugawa resulted from a conspiracy by regional leaders, especially the progressive daimyo and younger samurai from the southwestern part of Japan. The anti-Tokugawa leaders, united mostly by their hatred of the status quo, had varied goals and perspectives. Some were avid Westernizers, others extreme nationalists. Most were ambitious outsiders of samurai background who were alienated from the Tokugawa power structure. Although they came from privileged families, they were unafraid to ally with commoners, especially merchants. They were generally pragmatic men who understood that protecting Japan from foreign domination required radical change.

As public respect for the shogun faded, Japanese dissidents turned to the relatively powerless Meiji emperor as an alternative. While the shoguns had exercised power from Edo, the imperial family had lived in seclusion in Kyoto two hundred miles to the south. In 1868 anti-Tokugawa leaders, backed by military force, seized the imperial palace in Kyoto and convinced the emperor to dismiss the shogun and decree the restoration of his own rule. The decree ousted the Tokugawa family from their land and positions, opened the government to men of talent, appointed the rebels as advisers to the emperor, and announced that "all matters shall be decided by public discussion" and "the evil customs of the past shall be broken off. Knowledge shall be sought throughout the world."[19] The Tokugawa family and their supporters fought back, sparking a bitter one-year civil war that cost many lives. Ultimately, however, the rebel forces prevailed and crushed all armed resistance.

The new regime took shape early. Among the major changes introduced by the new leaders, Japan joined the world community and agreed to honor all treaties. As a symbolic attack on centuries of tradition and an affirmation of a new beginning, the imperial residence was moved from Kyoto to Tokyo (formerly Edo), a much larger and more dynamic city. Perceiving change as a necessary evil, the Meiji leaders had no master plan but pragmatically sought ways to achieve national unity, wealth, defense, and equality with the West.

Meiji Government and the Military

The Meiji regime's crash program of modernization lasted for thirty years. Although influenced by Western political and economic models, Meiji reformers also incorporated Japanese traditions in building a distinctive form of industrial society, in the process defusing the threat of colonialism and neocolonialism. Despite its flaws, the system introduced by the Meiji proved both productive for Japan and, in recent decades, an attractive model for the rapidly industrializing nations in East and Southeast Asia.

Meiji Restoration A revolution against the Tokugawa shogunate in Japan in 1867–1868, carried out in the name of the Meiji emperor; led to the successful modernization of Japan.

Meiji leaders needed to establish an effective governmental structure and secure the loyalty of the population. One of their first acts was to form a State Council to advise and control the emperor. They then moved to defuse potential opposition by recruiting both samurais and commoners into the new bureaucracy while convincing the regional daimyo families to give up control of their land, and the peasants living on it, in exchange for appointment as regional governors with guaranteed salaries. Freeing the peasants made it easier for them to move to cities in search of manufacturing or service work, something illegal under the Tokugawa. The government employed thousands of Western advisers, teachers, and even workers, who gave advice but were required to train Japanese assistants to replace them when their contracts expired. Because it financed these programs through tax revenues, Meiji Japan did not need foreign loans, hence avoiding the debt trap that ensnared most Latin American and Middle Eastern societies as well as China.

The new political system had democratic trappings, but reformers were divided on how much democracy to foster. The Japanese had no tradition of political freedom and had to invent a new word for the concept. A small group of leaders made most of the key decisions until after the turn of the century. Nonetheless, responding to a growing movement for more popular participation in decision making, in 1889 the Meiji leaders wrote the first constitution in Japanese history and formed a constitutional monarchy symbolically headed by the emperor. The constitution introduced an independent judiciary and a two-house parliament that was elected by the 450,000 men who were tax-paying property holders. Parliament chose members for the cabinet, which made policy and supervised the government apparatus. The first political parties, led mostly by former samurai, were formed in the 1880s, but they remained factionalized and weak as a political force.

Using the slogan "rich country, strong army," the government stressed industrial development and enhanced communications by building railroads and telegraphs, in part to aid the construction of a modern military force to protect the nation. Anxious about Western imperialism in Asia, the Japanese concluded that military power was necessary to assert national interest in the modern world. To build up the armed forces, including a modern navy, Meiji leaders drafted commoners as soldiers, once a profession limited to samurai. By breaking down the former distinction between samurai, merchant, and peasant, the military draft promoted social leveling. Furthermore, military service fostered literacy and nationalism among the peasants who joined.

Compared with China, the Meiji leaders enjoyed more freedom of action to reshape their society to strengthen the nation. Since pressure from the West gradually diminished, Japan had time to improve its military. Japan was also a much less inviting target for the West than China or Southeast Asia, since it had few natural resources that could be profitably exploited. Westerners viewed Japan as a market for their goods, but China had many more potential consumers. The various Western powers, largely preoccupied elsewhere, saw Japan mainly as a potential ally against each other.

First Commercial Bank in Edo
During the Meiji era the banking industry grew. This bank, built in Western style in Edo, was owned by the Mitsui family, which also owned large stores, breweries, factories, coal mines, and other enterprises. Mitsui was one of the major business conglomerates in Japan, with branches all over Asia. (Laurie Platt Winfrey, Inc.)

Economic and Social Consequences of Meiji Policies

Meiji policies fostered a modern economy and society. In building an economic foundation, the Japanese created a new model of political economy, **state capitalism**, an economic system in which the state takes a leading role in supporting business and industrial enterprises and then regulates and closely monitors the economy once it is privatized. The state subsidized or purchased stock in light industries such as textiles and in heavy industries such as mines and steel mills. Sometimes the state also formed new corporations that, once operating, were sold at low prices to a few families and companies with political connections. An example was Mitsui (MIT-soo-ee), a family-owned company whose business interests dated back to Tokugawa times. The most powerful corporations, the **zaibatsu**, dominated the national economy and maintained especially close ties to the government. They believed economic independence from the West to be patriotic: "The foreigners did not come to our country out of friendship [but] to seek profits through trade. If we allow them to monopolize our foreign trade, we are betraying our duty."[20]

State capitalism and the growth of industry often favored city people over the rural peasantry. Capital for industrialization was obtained by squeezing the peasants through the land tax. In exchange, however, the government spurred agricultural productivity by providing new seeds, improving land use, and supplying better irrigation. However, public investment favored the cities, prompting one liberal scholar to complain that "steel bridges glisten in the capital, and horse-drawn carriages run on the streets, but in the country the wooden bridges are so rotten one cannot cross them. We must cease making Tokyo richer and concentrate on rural districts."[21]

The new economic structure perpetuated the traditional group orientation and social controls of Japanese society. Most Japanese identified closely with the company that employed them, and the economy flourished by exploiting Japanese workers. The government kept wages deliberately low so that scarce capital could be devoted to building factories, shipyards, and railroads. Ultimately the sacrifices paid off by creating new jobs and fostering national wealth, but life in the Meiji era was not easy for most Japanese. For example, as in the United States and Europe, the textile mills mainly employed women, half of them below the age of twenty and 15 percent younger than fourteen, chiefly recruited from rural villages. The young factory women, paid half the salary of male workers, lived regimented lives; they were housed in crowded, often locked dormitories and commonly worked twelve-hour shifts, interrupted only by one half-hour meal break. Mill workers experienced high death rates from overwork, physical abuse from supervisors, and diseases such as tuberculosis caused by crowded working conditions.

Meiji reforms also fostered social change by attacking the rigid Tokugawa class system. New laws allowed people, regardless of background, to change occupations and travel or move freely. They also stripped the samurai of their privileges. Losing their monopoly on military occupations, some samurai adapted by becoming lawyers, teachers, or journalists. Disgruntled samurai joined opposition movements, becoming perennial political dissenters. To involve Japanese of all backgrounds in modernization, the regime placed a high priority on mass education and constructed a universal school system paid for by both taxes and tuition. The Meiji adopted the strict, examination-based educa-

state capitalism An economic system in which the state takes a leading role in supporting business and industrial enterprises; introduced by the Meiji government in Japan.

zaibatsu The most powerful Japanese corporations that dominated the national economy beginning during the Meiji regime and maintained an especially close relationship to the government.

tional system of European nations such as Germany, opened technical schools and universities, and dispatched students to Europe and the United States. By 1900 Japan was training its own scientists, engineers, and technicians.

Meiji policies stimulated debate about the value of various social patterns. Some reformers blamed the traditional family, ruled firmly by senior men, for discouraging personal independence, while conservatives worried that the individual was taking the place of the family. Generally the Meiji sought to preserve gender roles. Confucian books popular in Japan claimed that the lifelong duty of woman was obedience, while men made decisions for the family and supported it. Adopting these views, Meiji policies promoted the idea of "Good Wife, Wise Mother" to strengthen families by having mothers stay at home with their children. Married women, with little income, had a low social status. While many women may have been satisfied with their restricted lives, others struggled to improve their position in a patriarchal society that ignored women's opinions and problems. For example, Fukuda Hideko founded a magazine in 1907 to promote feminist and socialist thought, writing that "virtually everything [for women] is coercive and oppressive, making it imperative that we women rise up and develop our own social movement."[22] Fukuda rejected the model of "Good Wife, Wise Mother."

It proved difficult to completely eradicate old social prejudices. For instance, the **Burakumin** (boo-ROCK-uh-min), or "hamlet people," a despised subgroup traditionally restricted to poor neighborhoods who performed jobs considered unclean and undignified, such as meat processing and leatherworking, remained subject to discrimination. Despite Meiji laws giving the Burakumin legal equality, Japanese maintained Tokugawa practices, such as forbidding intermarriage with Burakumin and banning them from temples and shrines.

Westernization and Expansion

During the Meiji era the Japanese became acquainted with Western philosophy, social theory, economic thought, literature, and fashions, all of which influenced Japanese society. The peak of Westernization came in the 1870s. In these years the Japanese adopted the Western calendar, added European words to the Japanese language, became familiar with chairs and couches, began eating more meat, wore leather shoes, attended fancy dress balls, carried umbrellas, sported watches, wore trousers, shook hands rather than bowing, and often married in the Western style. Many Japanese equated all of this with progress. The Meiji ended the Tokugawa prohibition on Christianity, though missionaries never converted more than a few thousand Japanese. Writers found that Western literary styles such as realism and romanticism were liberating and allowed them freer expression. Indeed, Western influence stimulated all the arts. For example, Futabatei Shimei (1864–1909) wrote the first modern Japanese novels, strongly influenced by

Russian writers and Western realism, in colloquial language rather than the highly formal language that had long been expected of Japanese writers.

Observers, foreign and Japanese, debated the impact of the Meiji reforms. Many Westerners were amazed at the dramatic transformation in Japan. A German doctor wrote that he felt lucky to be an eyewitness to the interesting experiment as Japan tried to make, in one great leap, the changes toward industrial society that took Europeans five centuries to complete. But Japanese literature reflected the difficulty of life in a transitional era. In 1911 a Japanese novelist worried about a "nervous collapse" that would devastate the society as a result of the cultural confusion. Japan seemed neither traditional nor Western.

By the later 1880s the mania for Western fads had abated. Understanding the need to keep Westernization from overwhelming Japan, the Meiji leaders carefully fostered a synthesis of old and new. By the 1890s there was a renewed emphasis on traditional values, including the ancient myths about the Japanese people arising from the gods and the divinity of the emperor. The Japanese were never slavish imitators of the West or alienated from their own traditions. In the Meiji view, a new culture combining East and West could be produced and taught to the people, just as had been done in earlier centuries with Korean and Chinese influences.

The dramatic changes Japan experienced, however, created tensions within Japanese society and between Japan and other nations that ultimately fostered a more imperialistic foreign policy. Throughout the Meiji era some samurai, unable to find a new purpose, had advocated an invasion of Korea as a way for them to serve their nation in glory. But the Meiji leaders, fearful of antagonizing the Western powers, tried to follow a cautious foreign policy. Nonetheless, they sponsored a vast colonization of the large northern island of Hokkaido (ho-KIE-do) to protect the country from potential Russian aggression.

Eventually Meiji Japan fought two wars (see Map 23.2). China and Japan battled each other in the Sino-Japanese War (1894–1895) over their competing influence in Korea, which Japan had long coveted for its fertile land but now also viewed as a market for Japanese products. One influential imperialist argued that Japan needed to colonize Korea so it could take a proud place alongside the expansionist Western powers. The war resulted in a smashing Japanese military victory and consequent dominance in Korea as well as in the Chinese island of Taiwan, both of which the Japanese transformed into outright colonies in 1910. Impressed by Japanese military capabilities, Britain forged an alliance with Japan that endured through the Meiji era. Britain's rival, Russia, also had ambitions in Korea. Furthermore, Russia had acquired a foothold in resource-rich Manchuria, a nearby Chinese-controlled region Japan wanted to exploit. The rising tensions led to the Russo-Japanese War (1904–1905). During the conflict the Japanese seized a Russian-held Manchurian port and then destroyed the Russian fleet sent out from Europe.

The Japanese victory electrified the world. For the first time a non-Western nation had defeated a major European power, giving hope to societies under Western domination. The war contributed to the great awakening of Asian national-

---

Burakumin ("Hamlet people")　A despised Japanese subgroup who traditionally were restricted to poor neighborhoods and performed jobs considered unclean and undignified.

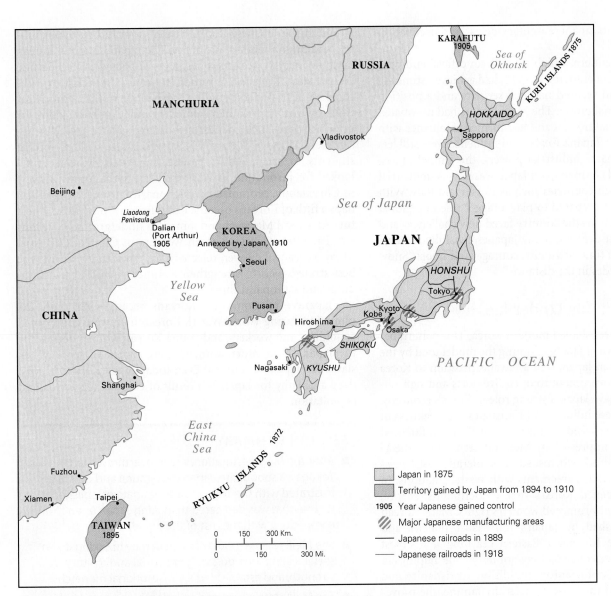

Map 23.2   Japanese Modernization and Expansion, 1868–1913
Japan undertook a crash modernization in the later 1800s. By 1910 its military power had increased, and it had won a war with Russia and colonized Korea, Taiwan, and Sakhalin (then known as Karafutu).

ism that struggled against Western colonialism and neocolonialism. The triumph in the war further enhanced the pride of the Japanese people in their nation and confirmed that Japan had, in three decades, become a world power. Among the fruits of victory was the transfer to Japan of some Russian holdings in Manchuria and control of the southern half of Sakhalin island, off the Siberian coast.

The Meiji Legacy

The changes imposed on Japanese society during the Meiji era have provoked debate. Some historians view the Meiji policies as having fostered a transformation so radical that it qualifies as a political and social revolution, not unlike the French Revolution in its uprooting of the old society. Others link the

changes to the longtime Japanese willingness to modify culture in order to strengthen the country. The Japanese themselves have been ambivalent, viewing the Meiji with a mixture of pride for its accomplishments and regret for the traditions that were abandoned. At the time some Japanese found the changes shattering, while others took them in stride. Still others were enthusiastic, one proclaiming Japan's "marvelous fortune. I feel as though in a dream and can only weep tears of joy." Another enthusiast wrote that "we are no longer ashamed to stand before the world as Japanese, known by the world."[23] But concerned that the growing military power would corrupt his country, one writer predicted disaster, calling on his people to awake and open their eyes to the dangers ahead. His fears were realized three decades later in World War II, when Japan's conquest of an Asian and Pacific empire provoked U.S. retaliation, ultimately leading to Japanese military defeat and occupation by U.S. forces.

In sum, the Meiji era, which came to an official end with the death of the Meiji emperor in 1916, had achieved stunning successes. Japan had secured national security and a position as a powerful regional power. The Meiji leaders had negotiated an end to the unequal treaties and had formed an alliance with the powerful British. Japan's wealth and influence were still less than that of the major industrial powers: the United States, Britain, France, and Germany; but Japan was now an industrial nation, on a par with countries such as Russia and Italy. With 50 million people, it prepared to play a bigger role in regional and world affairs. But as the country faced new challenges and setbacks in the next decades, many Japanese wisfully remembered the Meiji as a time of vitality, courage, and hope: "Snow is falling, Meiji recedes in the distance."

Korean Transitions Under Japan

Rising Japanese power shaped modern Korea. This pattern began in 1876, when Meiji Japan, adopting the model used by the United States to open Japan, sent a naval expedition to Korea that forced the Yi government to open five ports and sign unequal treaties that gave Japan a strong role in Korea's economy. The growing Japanese influence in Korea and the weakness of the Yi government sparked changes within Korea. Influenced by Korean officials impressed by Meiji modernization, the Yi government introduced reforms, such as toleration of Christianity, and signed trade agreements with Western nations. In 1886 Christians opened Korea's first modern girls' school, whose graduates later promoted women's rights. Many Korean peasants, impoverished by Japan's imperialist policies and drought, joined the Tonghak ("Eastern Learning"), a protest movement with an eclectic ideology not unlike the Taipings in China, that mixed Confucianism, Buddhism, Christianity, and hatred of Japan and the West. Spurred by famine, the movement grew into the nationwide Tonghak Rebellion against the Yi government in 1894. When Korea's longtime ally, China, sent in troops to help the Yi government repress the rebellion, China's rival, Japan, responded by also sending in a force and capturing the Korean capital, Seoul, holding the Yi royal family hostage to gain influence over the Korean government.

The desire of both China and Japan to capitalize on Yi weakness and on the Tonghak Rebellion led to the Sino-Japanese War (1894–1895), which resulted in a humiliating Chinese withdrawal and a stronger presence on the part of the Japanese after they stamped out Korean resistance. Some 18,000 Koreans, mostly peasants who rallied to the Yi government, died in fighting the Japanese. Japan forcibly annexed Korea in 1910, transforming it from the "hermit kingdom" into a Japanese colony and ending the decrepit Yi dynasty. One resistance leader expressed the widespread Korean despair: "I was unable to repel our nation's enemies, or hold back our 4000 year long civilization from falling to the ground."[24]

Between 1910 and 1945 Korea was a heavily exploited, harshly ruled Japanese colony. It endured Japanese racism and brutal suppression of Korean nationalism and culture, although the Japanese also increased educational opportunities and built a modern economy. The Japanese seized Korean land for Japanese companies and restricted civil liberties. Nonetheless, Koreans continued to protest and resist. In 1919 the Japanese police brutally crushed peaceful demonstrations by men and women calling for independence, killing or injuring some 24,000 demonstrators and arresting 47,000. Resentment simmered as repressive measures, such as forcing students to speak only Japanese, increased. Koreans often looked for inspiration in Western ideas. Some found answers in Christianity, promoted by missionaries from the West. Perhaps a fifth of Koreans became Catholics or Protestants. Others turned toward Marxism and joined an underground Communist Party founded by Korean workers in China and Russia. Many Koreans, however, rejected Western ideas, believing the best strategy was to strengthen Confucianism. There was no dominant nationalist thread.

Japanese relations with Koreans became even more exploitative during World War II. Korean men were conscripted as soldiers and workers, and young Korean women, termed by the Japanese "comfort women," were forced to serve as sex slaves for Japanese soldiers. Even today many Koreans have a deep antipathy for Japan as a result of colonial repression and exploitation.

SECTION SUMMARY

■ After the Meiji Restoration, which overthrew the Tokugawa shogunate, Japanese samurai and others frustrated with the Tokugawa shogunate established a regime that was dedicated to making Japan open to and competitive with the rest of the world.

■ The Meiji regime modernized Japan by breaking down social distinctions, pursuing industrial and military strength, and establishing a constitutional monarchy.

■ The Meiji state supported and closely regulated industry, gave workers new rights to change occupation and travel freely but kept wages deliberately low, stripped samurai of their traditional privileges, and attempted to preserve traditional gender roles.

■ In the late 1800s, Meiji leaders worked to balance traditional practices with newly adopted Western ones and, while there was debate over how to conduct foreign policy, Japan fought successful wars against both China and Russia.

■ Historians debate whether the Meiji era was a fundamental transformation or a continuation of Japan's ability to change with the times, and Japanese were torn between pride in Meiji successes and regret over traditions they abandoned.

■ Meiji Japan forced Korea to accept unequal trade agreements and, after defeating China in the Sino-Japanese War, turned Korea into a colony and ruled it extremely harshly, brutally suppressing dissent and exploiting its men and women during World War II.

Russia's Eurasian Empire

What factors explain the expansion of the Russian Empire?

Between 1750 and 1914 Russia built a vast Eurasian empire stretching 3,200 miles from the Baltic Sea to the Bering Straits, in the process creating more intensive ties to Asian societies. During the Early Modern Era Russians crossed Siberia seeking trade with China and pushed their frontiers into Central Asia and south toward the Black Sea. The expansion continued through the 1800s, making Russia a hemispheric power controlling vast amounts of land. Located on the fringe of Europe, Central Asia, and the Middle East, Russia was influenced by all three regions. Russian society was characterized by autocratic governments led by czars and czarinas, alternating periods of reform and reaction, a rural system with some resemblance to medieval feudalism, and chronic discontent. During this era Russia played an increasingly critical role in both Asian and European politics.

Europeanization and Czarist Despotism

Russians had long debated whether they belonged to the European tradition or had a unique heritage, and these debates were reflected in Russian politics. Influence from western Europe was particularly strong during the long reign of Catherine the Great (r. 1762–1796), who carried on Peter the Great's campaign of Europeanization (see Chronology: Russia and Central Asia, 1750–1914). Influenced by the Enlightenment, Catherine denounced slavery and hailed liberty and, like western European monarchs, patronized the arts and literature. She also presided over a golden age of opulence for the nobility, called by a contemporary the happiest period in all Russian history. Wearing sumptuous gowns, the czarina gave elegant private parties and masked balls. Also, like many European kings, Catherine had a series of lovers, some twenty-one in all. The Russian elite copied royal France and learned

CHRONOLOGY	
Russia and Central Asia, 1750–1914	
1762–1796	Reign of Catherine the Great
1861	Emancipation of Russian serfs
1800–1870s	Russian conquest of Caucasus and Turkestan
1891–1915	Building of Trans-Siberian Railroad
1904–1905	Russo-Japanese War
1905	First Russian Revolution

French, increasing the already huge gulf between them and the peasant masses, who were bound to estates as serfs.

Catherine's policies led to worsening social ills and imperialist expansion. Despite her liberal views, she could not encourage freedom among the common people, especially the disgruntled peasantry, because she needed support from the landed aristocracy. To gain the aristocracy's favor, she extended serfdom to Ukraine and denounced the French Revolution, which abolished the monarchy and aristocracy, as irreligious and immoral, the enemy of God. Continuing the expansionism of her predecessors, Catherine's energetic foreign policy added Poland and Finland to Russia's realm and, pursuing a goal long sought by czars, extended the empire south to the Black Sea, annexing the Crimean peninsula in 1783, where Russia built a major naval base.

To maintain order and their own position, the czars who followed Catherine, whether Westernizers or not, often relied on the brutal despotism common in Russian history. Despotism flourished particularly under Czar Nicholas I (r. 1825–1855), who earned the hatred of the liberal intelligentsia. Alarmed by the social changes in western Europe, the aristocracy opposed

Catherine the Great
Resplendent in her royal robes, Catherine the Great triumphantly enters one of the ports of the Crimean peninsula recently captured from the Turks. Catherine presided over an expansion of the Russian Empire and efforts at modernization. (Giraudon/The Bridgeman Art Library International)

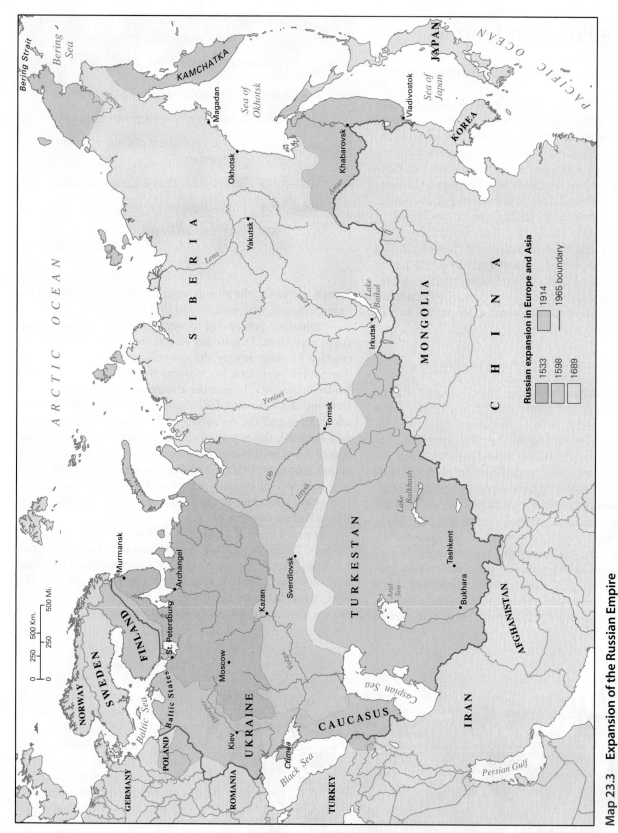

Map 23.3   Expansion of the Russian Empire

Between the 1500s and 1914 Russia gradually gained control of Siberia, Turkestan, the Caucasus, Ukraine, Poland, the Baltic states, and Finland, becoming the world's largest contiguous territorial empire.

industrialization, which they worried might upset serfdom and undermine their rural power. Although a police official warned the czar that serfdom was a powder keg under the state, Nicholas feared alienating the aristocracy and instead suppressed the restless Poles and formed a secret police force with wide powers to harass, imprison, or eliminate opponents.

Nicholas also expanded the empire further by invading Hungary and seeking dominance over the Ottomans to secure access for transport of Russia's grain exports through the Black Sea to the Mediterranean. His attempts to absorb the Ottoman-held Balkan societies by encouraging Slavic rebellion and occupying several Ottoman provinces provoked Britain and France and led to the Crimean War of 1854, which pitted Russia against a British-French-Ottoman alliance. Some 250,000 soldiers on all sides died in the war. Armies of conscripted Russian serfs were no match for modern British and French forces, and Russia was defeated and had to withdraw from Ottoman territory.

Nicholas's successor, Czar Alexander II (r. 1855–1881), was more oriented to western Europe and followed a reformist domestic policy, emancipating the serfs in 1861 and decentralizing government. But many serfs were unable, as required by the new law, to pay the landowners for the lands they wanted to use, and discontent grew through the later 1800s.

Russian Expansion in Asia

During this era the Russians became more engaged with Asia, expanding their power in Siberia, the Caucasus, and Central Asia to form the largest contiguous land empire in the world (see Map 23.3). In search of imperial glory, markets, and resources such as sable fur, Russia had been expanding eastward across Siberia since the 1500s and had reached the Pacific coast in the 1600s. Russia's attempt to seize the fertile Amur River Basin separating Manchuria from Siberia ended in Chinese defeat of Russian military forces. By the early 1800s the Russians were anxious to counter British and French expansion in Asia and the Pacific. With Qing China in decline, Russians occupied the Amur Basin and in 1860 gained official Chinese recognition of their claims in exchange for helping negotiate the end of the Arrow War pitting China against Britain and France. They also acquired a coastal zone that allowed them to satisfy their long-held goal for an ice-free port on Siberia's Pacific shore, to be used as a base for Russian commercial and military activity in the Pacific Basin. There the Russians built the city of Vladivostok ("Ruler of the East").

For several centuries the Russians had also expanded around the Black Sea, seeking an outlet to the Mediterranean Sea and its maritime trade routes. Between 1800 and the 1870s the Russians expanded their control south through the mountainous Caucasus on the east of the Black Sea, absorbing Armenia and Georgia, both largely Christian, as well as Muslim Azerbaijan (az-uhr-bye-JAHN). Sometimes they faced fierce resistance in the Caucasus: they needed four decades to conquer the strongly Islamic Chechens (CHECH-uhnz). Led by Shamyl (1797–1871), the charismatic leader of an austere Muslim revivalist movement, Chechen men and women fought a relent-

less guerrilla war. The Russians triumphed in 1859 by ravaging Chechen lands, herds, and crops and beheading their captives. These atrocities fostered a Chechen hatred of Russian rule.

The Russians also colonized Muslim Central Asia, the first step in gaining direct access to the Indian Ocean trade and preventing Britain from establishing influence in the region from their base in India. By 1864 the Russians controlled all the lands of the Kazakh (KAH-zahk) people, east of the Caspian Sea, and looked south to the old Silk Road cities of Turkestan. Although they remained vigorous centers of Islamic learning and Sufism, diminished overland trade and warfare with Persians, Russians, and rival states had caused economic decline in these Central Asian states, except for Bukhara (boo-CAR-ruh), a strong Uzbek (OOZ-bek)–dominated state that maintained a thriving trade. By the 1870s Russia's military capabilities had enabled it to dominate Turkestan. Russia now coveted Afghanistan, to the south of Turkestan, as a gateway to the Indian Ocean, but the forbidding mountain and desert terrain and formidable reputation of Afghan warriors discouraged occupation. Eventually Afghanistan became a buffer between British India and Russian Central Asia.

Czarist policy in Central Asia and the Caucasus promoted changes that chiefly benefited Russians. Some Central Asian land proved suitable for growing the cotton needed by the Russian textile industry; this land was given to several hundred thousand Russian farmers. Central Asian economies were now open to Russian food imports and industrial products. The czars also gradually introduced a policy of **Russification**, the promotion of Russian language and culture for the non-Russian peoples. This policy sparked resentment and spiritual revival among many Muslims.

Russian expansion brought problems along with the gains: the seemingly mighty empire had weaknesses. Its sheer size hindered governance, fostered corruption, and prevented the ready exploitation of the vast resources. In addition, colonization of non-Russian lands made Russian leaders permanently fear rebellion, and they needed a huge army to maintain security in the colonized territories. The world's longest railroad, the Trans-Siberian, built between 1891 and 1915, fostered Russian settlement of eastern Siberia and helped Russian traders penetrate Manchuria and Korea. But this expansion brought conflict with Japan, generating the Russo-Japanese War (1904–1905). Russia's defeat in that war humiliated the country and its last czar, Nicholas II (r. 1894–1917).

Russian Economy, Society, and Culture

Territorial expansion and political developments such as reform or repression created changes in other areas of Russian life. This was particularly true of the economy. Spurred by the acquisition of the Caucasus and Central Asian markets, the Russian economy grew and new factories fostered an industrial proletariat in the cities. Russia enjoyed increased industrialization during the

---

Russification A czarist policy in the nineteenth century that promoted Russian language and culture for non-Russian peoples; created resentment among many Muslims.

later 1800s, financed largely by western European capital and by local bankers and businessmen of German or Jewish origin. By 1914 Russia ranked fifth in the world as an industrial power. With this came worker discontent. The factory workers, who increased in number fivefold between 1860 and 1914, often resented the exploitation they faced. For instance, textile workers were often housed in crowded dormitories and usually labored thirteen hours a day. The lives of male workers, like their counterparts in British and German cities, often revolved around the factory whistle and late-night tavern. However, the majority of Russia's people still lived in villages, dominated by the local nobility.

Like women in western European societies, North America, China, and Japan, some Russian women sought reform to improve their status. While noblewomen frequently were educated and enjoyed some public influence, most commoner women had less power over their lives. While many enjoyed happy marriages, others were beaten and abused by husbands, since the laws gave men the power to control their wives and children. Sometimes villagers forced reluctant girls to marry. Peasant women and men often spent their entire lives in the village where they were born. In contrast, some elite women became scholars and writers. Yet, they still had fewer rights and options than men. By the 1830s a few female writers published fiction that addressed the repression of women. By the mid-nineteenth century a women's movement had emerged, led chiefly by women of noble birth, that emphasized access to higher education. Thanks to these efforts, by the 1870s a few courses of study became available and more women were able to earn their living as doctors, midwives, and teachers.

Political and economic reformers were often influenced by western European ideas, but the appeal of these ideas caused Russian thinkers to torment themselves over their national identity and goals. Many educated Russians were Westernizers who admired the efforts of rulers such as Catherine the Great to foster modernization. Some of this group also wanted to abolish serfdom and the nobility. The work of some Russian writers, such as Russia's beloved poet Alexander Pushkin (POOSH-kin) (1799–1837), reflected familiarity with western European literature and thought. Opposed to the Westernizers were the **Slavophiles**, who rejected what they saw as decadent Western models and defended Russian culture, such as respect for the Russian Orthodox Church. The church remained a dominant force in Russian society, revered by conservatives and many liberals. Slavophiles often advocated that Russians unite with other Slavs in eastern Europe and the Balkans to confront the West. One proponent of pan-Slavism wrote in 1871 that Russia was never an integral part of Europe, having different and, in his view, superior traditions.

Whether reformers or conservatives, Westernizers or Slavophiles, Russians were proud of their rich literary and artistic tradition. Literature often reflected Russian life. For instance, the novels of Fyodor Dostoyevsky (dos-tuh-YEF-skee) (1821–1881) reflected his experiences as an exile in Siberia for revolutionary activities and his travels in Europe. His major books were steeped in dark themes shaped by his awareness of poverty and the troubled human soul. Another celebrated Russian novelist, Leo Tolstoy (tuhl-STOI) (1828–1910), master of the psychological novel, fought in the Crimean War. His epic novel, *War and Peace* (1869), which profiled two noble families during war, portrayed humans as mere victims of chance. One of Russia's most honored composers, Pyotr Tchaikovsky (chi-KOF-skee) (1840–1893), traveled widely in Europe and was criticized by Russian nationalists for his cosmopolitan approach to music and by conservatives for his homosexuality. He wrote operas as well as ballets of enduring popularity around the world, especially *Swan Lake* and *The Nutcracker*.

Russian Unrest and Revolution

Discontent with the autocratic system and the rising costs of empire building increased through the 1800s, resulting in violent resistance. To crush opposition, over the decades the czars sent thousands of dissidents to remote Siberian prison camps, where many died of illness, starvation, overwork, or the harsh climate. Repression fueled resentment of the government. Some anticzar Russians joined the illegal Socialist Revolutionary Party, founded in 1898, that used terror to strike against the regime. After assassinating a minister of state, the party proclaimed that "the crack of the bullet is the only possible means to talk with our ministers, until they listen to the voice of the country."[25]

In 1905 discontent, intensified by the sacrifices imposed on common people by the Russo-Japanese War, sparked a major socialist-led revolutionary movement involving both men and women and widespread violence. The unrest began when 100,000 factory workers in the capital, St. Petersburg, who were required to work longer hours to produce war supplies, went on strike and then mounted a protest march demanding equality before the law, freedom of speech, an eight-hour workday, social insurance, and other progressive goals. Russian troops opened fire on the peaceful marchers, killing some 200 and wounding hundreds more. The violence shattered public support for the czar and fueled increasing revolutionary activity, which soon spread to the armed forces. The revolutionaries were split in their goals, a division that enabled the government to crush the uprising, executing thousands of rebels and burning prorebel villages. But the czar bowed to public demands and allowed an elected national assembly with limited powers. In defeat, the socialist movement fractured into hostile factions. However, conflicts among Russians simmered, and in 1917 they produced the greatest upheaval in Russia's history, which ended the czarist system (see Chapter 24).

SECTION SUMMARY

■ The Russian leader Catherine the Great paid lip service to Enlightenment values, but she presided over an era of royal opulence, territorial expansion, and expanded serfdom, and she was followed by the despotic Nicholas I, who led the nation to defeat in the Crimean War.

Slavophiles Nineteenth-century Russians who emphasized Russia's unique culture and rejected Western models.

- Russian expansion brought it control of eastern Siberia, Muslim Central Asia, and the Caucasus states, although some peoples, such as the Chechens, fiercely resisted.
- Russia's economy expanded along with its territory, creating a discontented proletariat while many Russian thinkers embraced Western ideals, the Slavophiles argued for the superiority of traditional Russian culture.
- Russians increasingly discontented with the demands of empire-building and autocratic rulers joined terrorist groups and supported a revolution in 1905, which, while put down, led to reforms

Online Study Center ACE the Test

◆ Chapter Summary

Between 1750 and 1914 China faced daunting challenges from the Western powers. Qing China had long been able to rebuff Western demands for more trade, but the government and economy were declining by the early 1800s. China's attempts to halt British opium smuggling led to the Opium War, and its defeat in that war resulted in an unequal treaty system that gave Western nations greater access to China and its resources. Increasing poverty and rebellions further undermined Qing power. Attempts at modernization failed because of China's vast size, conservative opposition, and fears of radical culture change. In 1911 revolution ended the imperial system, but the new republic soon collapsed in civil war.

While the Western challenges progressively undermined China, they prompted Japan to transform its society. Tokugawa Japan faced increasing problems by the early 1800s. The arrival of American ships demanding that Japan open itself to the West forced the issue and undermined the shogunate, which gave in to Western demands. The shogunate then lost power in the 1868 Meiji Restoration, a short revolution led by progressive daimyo and younger samurai. Capitalizing on dynamic merchants, high literacy rates, a tradition of cultural borrowing, and national loyalties, the Meiji government launched a crash program to modernize Japan's government, military, economy, and social patterns, importing Western ideas and institutions. By 1900 the Meiji had industrialized Japan, deflected Western ambitions, and turned Japan into a world power. This power allowed Japan to defeat China and Russia in two wars and to colonize Korea.

Russian expansion into Asian power brought it into conflict with China and Japan, but Russia was shaped more by its proximity to Europe and Muslim Asia. Despotic Russian leaders pushed Russian control across Siberia and into eastern Europe and colonized Central Asia and the Caucasus. By the later 1800s Russia dominated large parts of Eurasia, forming the world's largest contiguous land empire. But maintaining an empire against restless colonized societies strained Russian capabilities. Russia also industrialized and promoted social change, but repression of the Russian peasants ultimately brought dissent and revolutionary movements.

Online Study Center **Improve Your Grade** Flashcards

Key Terms

Chinoiserie
Co-hong
extraterritoriality
international settlements
gunboat diplomacy
Meiji Restoration
state capitalism
zaibatsu
Burakumin
Russification
Slavophiles

Suggested Reading

Books

Allworth, Edward, ed. *Central Asia: 130 Years of Russian Rule*, 2nd ed. Durham, N.C.: Duke University Press, 1994. A collection of essays.

Chang, Hsin-Pao. *Commissioner Lin and the Opium War*. New York: W. W. Norton, 1964. The classic account.

Ebrey, Patricia Buckley, Anne Walthall, and James B. Palais. *East Asia: A Cultural, Social, and Political History*. Boston: Houghton Mifflin, 2006. A recent, balanced survey.

Evtuhov, Catherine, et al. *A History of Russia: Peoples, Legends, Events, Forces*. Boston: Houghton Mifflin, 2004. A detailed survey.

Fahr-Becker, Gabriele, ed. *Japanese Prints*. New York: Barnes and Noble, 2003. A well-illustrated introduction to this wonderful art.

Madariaga, Isabel de. *Russia in the Age of Catherine the Great*. London: Phoenix Press, 1981. Reprint of a well-balanced and panoramic examination of Catherine and her era.

Matsunosuke, Nishiyama. *Edo Culture: Daily Life and Diversions in Urban Japan, 1600–1868*. Honolulu: University of Hawaii Press, 1997. A fascinating look at popular culture during the Tokugawa era.

McClain, James L. *Japan: A Modern History*. New York: W. W. Norton, 2002. An excellent survey of events since 1600.

Schirokauer, Conrad, and Donald N. Clark. *Modern East Asia: A Brief History*. Belmont, Calif.: Thomson/Wadsworth, 2004. A survey of China, Japan, and Korea in this era.

Smith, Richard J. *China's Cultural Heritage: The Ch'ing Dynasty, 1644–1913*, 2nd ed. Boulder, Colo.: Westview Press, 1994. A readable and comprehensive study.

Spence, Jonathan D. *The Search for Modern China*, 2nd ed. New York: W. W. Norton, 1999. A provocative examination.

Websites

East and Southeast Asia: An Annotated Directory of Internet Resources (http://newton.uor.edu/Departments&Programs/AsianStudies-Dept/general.html). Links on history, culture, and politics.

The Floating World of Ukiyo-e: Shadow, Dreams, and Substance (http://www.loc.gov/exhibits/ukiyo-e/). Introduces the Japanese prints at the Library of Congress.

Internet Guide to Chinese Studies (http://www.sino.uni-heidelberg.de/igcs/). An excellent collection of links, maintained by a German university.

Internet East Asian History Sourcebook (http://www.fordham.edu/halsall/eastasia/eastasiasbook.html). Sources and links on China, Japan, and Korea.

Russian History Index: The World Wide Web Virtual Library (http://vlib.iue.it/hist-russia/Index.html). Useful links.

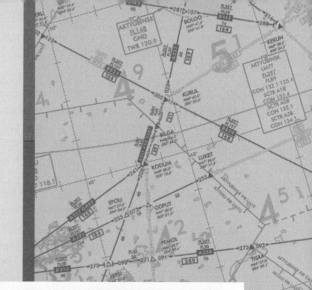

CHAPTER 24

World Wars, European Revolutions, and Global Depression, 1914–1945

Online Study Center

This icon will direct you to interactive activities and study materials on the website: college.hmco. com/pic/lockard1e

Global Communism The communist leaders of the Soviet Union hoped that their revolution in Russia in 1917 would inspire similar revolutions around the world, ending capitalism and imperialism. This poster reflects the dream of a triumphant communism.   (Museum of the Revolution, Moscow/The Bridgeman Art Library International)

My beautiful, pitiful era. With an insane smile you look back, cruel and weak, like an animal past its prime, at the prints of your own paws.

OSIP MANDELSTAM, RUSSIAN POET[1]

By April 1917 the French army had been fighting the Germans for over two and a half years. World War I was creating growing casualty lists and inflicting tremendous hardship on soldiers on both sides. The French officers were divided between those who favored a more aggressive strategy, likely to result in many more deaths, and those who wanted a more defensive approach. The latter group included a new French commander, General Philippe Pétain (peh-TANH) (1856–1951), who implemented a strategy to minimize French casualties. A peasant's son with the demeanor of an aristocrat, Pétain was noted for his sweeping white moustache and his passion for romance, including many love affairs with other men's wives. Pétain regarded his soldiers as more than cannon fodder, a view that made him popular with the fighting men.

At first Pétain was overruled, and the French launched another frontal assault on the well-fortified German lines. The result was a military disaster that caused perhaps 120,000 deaths and broke the fighting spirit of the French troops. Mutinies broke out in the units, ranging from minor infractions of code to violent disturbances. Some soldiers even proposed a protest march on Paris, and 20,000 deserted. Most mutineers were loyal to their nation, but they protested the slaughter resulting from a futile military strategy of suicidal assaults. The army executed about 50 mutineers but also made concessions to the frontline troops, granting them more leave, better food, and more generous rations of wine. Mutinies and an overwhelming war-weariness occurred among all the combatant nations. Pétain muttered that France should immediately consider peace negotiations. He emerged from World War I as a French hero, but he later lost his hero status when he served as the nominal head of the French government under hated Nazi occupation in World War II. Pétain died in prison, a broken man looking back on three tumultuous decades that had brought so much distress and destruction to the world.

Those three decades between 1914 and 1945 included not only two great military struggles involving many nations, but also a mighty revolution in Russia, a terrible economic depression with worldwide consequences, and the rise of new ideologies. The Russian Jewish poet Osip Mandelstam, reflecting on the turbulent decades beginning with World War I—an era full of achievements and atrocities, heroism and hardship—aptly described them as a "beautiful, pitiful era."

In the years before World War I some Europeans had believed that the world was poised for a new age in which the ideals of Western democracy might be achieved throughout the world and the horrors of war would be ended forever, bringing an era of international cooperation. Liberals even hoped World War I would be the war to end all wars, a goal it spectacularly failed to achieve. Indeed, the hopes of the idealists were dashed by two world wars, fought partly in Europe, that challenged the Western world-view of liberalism and rationalism that had captured the European imagination since the Enlightenment; and the faith in progress was shattered by dictatorship in Russia, economic collapse, and organized slaughter. The disarray in Europe, combined with the spread of new ideologies and technologies, helped undermine Western political influence in the world, except for that of the rising Western power, the United States.

FOCUS QUESTIONS

1. What was the impact of World War I on the Western world?
2. How did communism prevail in Russia and transform that country?
3. How did the Great Depression reshape world politics and economies?
4. What were the main ideas and impacts of fascism?
5. What were the costs and consequences of World War II?

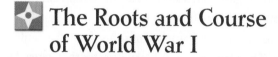

The Roots and Course of World War I

What was the impact of World War I on the Western world?

In August 1914, war broke out between the major powers of Europe. As the fighting began, the British foreign secretary remarked, "The lights are going out all over Europe. We shall not see them again in our lifetime."[2] The conflict pitted two alliances. Britain, France, and Russia formed the Triple Entente, which later included Serbia, Japan, Italy, Portugal, Romania, Greece, and eventually the United States. These nations, also known as the Allies, faced the Central Powers: Germany, Austria-Hungary, the Ottoman Empire, and Bulgaria. Although most of the military action took place in and around Europe, the leaders of the countries involved saw the conflict as nothing short of a struggle to control the global system, with its industrial economies and colonial empires. The Great War, as many Europeans called it, was history's first total war, an armed conflict between industrialized powers that lasted four terrible years. The war brought down empires and dynasties, made the United States a world power, and weakened western Europe's hold over the colonial world. And the end of the conflict made a second major war almost inevitable.

European Societies in the Early 1900s

In the early 1900s, before World War I began, Europeans enjoyed affluence, social stability, and growing democracy; there were few signs of a major war involving the key European powers. The productive European economies benefited from their links to each other and their access to resources and markets in other parts of the world. Some thinkers of the time believed nations tied by interlocking transnational economies and commercial interdependence would never wage war against each other. European nations cooperated in many things besides trade. For example, they agreed on treaties binding their nations to protect the right of workers to pensions and health insurance while restricting child labor. Furthermore, culture often transcended borders. Whatever their nationality, educated Europeans shared a love for the music of the eighteenth-century Austrian composer Wolfgang Amadeus Mozart and the novels of the nineteenth-century Russian writer Leo Tolstoy. Europeans frequently spoke two or three languages, traveled in other countries, and were often citizens of countries whose royal families had intermarried. In 1899 European nations met in the Netherlands and agreed to limit armaments and create the International Court to settle disputes between nations. Although submitting disputes was voluntary and the court was seldom invoked, these European nations hoped it would discourage a sudden outburst of war.

Europeans looked to the future with confidence, felt superior to the rest of the world, and enjoyed their prosperity. Thanks in part to imperial expansion, which had acquired resources in colonized Africa and Asia, Europeans now consumed new products such as chocolate and rubber tires, and rising populations expanded markets. Between 1880 and 1910 the population grew 43 percent in Germany, 26 percent in Britain, and over 50 percent in Russia. European emigration to the Americas and Australia increased markets there for European goods, and improved transportation, such as automobiles and large ships, made it easier to move people, natural resources and manufactured products over long distances. European capital financed South African gold and diamond mines, Malayan rubber plantations, Australian sheep stations, Russian railways, and Canadian wheat fields, not to mention every sector of the growing U.S. economy.

CHRONOLOGY

	World War I and Aftermath	Era of Great Depression	World War II
1910	**1914–1918** World War I **1917** Russian Revolution		
1920	**1926** Fascist state in Italy	**1929–1941** Great Depression	
1930		**1933** Nazi triumph in Germany **1937** Japanese invasion of China	**1939–1945** World War II
1940			**1941** Japanese attack on Pearl Harbor **1944** Bretton Woods Conference

The Preludes to War

World War I was rooted in the European and global economic and political configurations of the early 1900s. The prosperity, interdependence, and idealism of the era had their limits, and other conditions also worked against them to breed tensions and resentments. Particularly unconducive to unity among European nations was the quest for imperial glory, which increased the competition between the major European powers for economic and political influence outside of Europe. Britain, France, and Germany were the wealthiest, most powerful nations and fierce rivals with large overseas empires in Africa, Asia, the Pacific, and the Caribbean. Most Europeans still considered wars necessary struggles rather than terrible evils; they also stood by their national interests. Each nation felt threatened in some way, pushed to settle scores with competitors. By 1911 leaders began to plan for war. The chief of the German General Staff told the German chancellor, "I hold war to be inevitable, and the sooner the better. Everyone is preparing for the great war, which they all expect."[3]

Britain, France, and Germany's fierce economic rivalry, in particular, had stoked the fires of war during the scramble for colonies in the late 1800s. Because they began empire building later than Britain and France, the Germans resented those nations' political control of much of the world and the resources and markets it gave them access to. Germany rapidly industrialized and challenged Britain for economic dominance in overseas markets. The two nations bolstered their military strength against the perceived threat of the other. Britain, which had commanded the seas for a century, became concerned in 1900 when Germany began building a naval fleet. The growing rivalries meant stepping up the manufacture or acquisition of heavier weapons and drafting more young men into the military.

As economic and military rivalries grew, alliances began to form. France and Russia shared with Britain hostility toward an increasingly aggressive Germany, which in turn felt encircled by these three hostile powers. Austria-Hungary, Germany's most

loyal ally, and the Ottoman Empire shared German dislike of Russia. The growing nationalist agitation for self-determination by the many ethnic minorities within the multinational German, Russian, Austro-Hungarian, and Ottoman Empires added to the combustible mix.

Austria-Hungary faced a particularly difficult challenge in governing the restless Czech, Slovak, and Balkan peoples within its empire. Conflict in the Balkans, the mountainous region in southeastern Europe, was fostered by the rivalries between nations and tensions between Balkan ethnic groups. The Balkans were coveted by the Ottomans (who lost most of their Balkan territory between 1908 and 1913), Russia, and Austria-Hungary. In 1908 Austria-Hungary annexed Bosnia-Herzegovina (boz-nee-uh-HERT-suh-go-vee-nuh), a Balkan territory containing three often feuding Slavic peoples—Croats, Serbs, and Muslims—and also coveted by the neighboring country of Serbia (see Chronology: World War I, 1914–1919). If their ally

CHRONOLOGY

World War I, 1914–1919

1908	Austria-Hungarian annexation of Bosnia-Herzegovina
1914	Outbreak of conflict
1916	Battle of Verdun
April 1917	U.S. intervention
March 1917	Fall of czarist government in Russia
March 1918	Brest-Litovsk Treaty
November 1918	End of conflict
1919	Paris Peace Conference

Map 24.1 World War I

World War I pitted the Triple Entente of Britain, France, and Russia, and its allies, against the Central Powers: Germany, Austria-Hungary, and the Ottoman Empire. The worst fighting occurred along the western front and in eastern Europe and Russia. The intervention of the United States in 1917 against the Central Powers proved decisive.

Germany could restrain the major Serbian ally, Russia, the leaders of Austria-Hungary thought war with Serbia over their conflicting Balkan claims might salvage their decaying empire, which once ruled large parts of Europe.

Whether World War I could have been prevented is a controversial question among historians. Historians often blame the conflict on failures of diplomacy, breakdowns in communication among nations, and the personal ambitions of leaders and mistrust among them. The German monarch, Kaiser Wilhelm II (r. 1888–1918), who saw himself as a king with divine rights and answerable only to God, deserves some share of blame. Although a grandson of Britain's Queen Victoria, Wilhelm grew to envy British power. Wilhelm and other political and military leaders underestimated the human costs and long-term consequences of conflict. Although overstating the case, a key British leader later conceded that "the nations slithered over the brink into the boiling cauldron of war without a trace of apprehension or dismay."[4]

Whatever the leadership failures, other issues also paved the road to war. Some scholars suggest that a few governments hoped war might divert public attention from festering domestic problems, such as Irish resistance to English policies and growing German social ills. In any case, while the general public did not pressure its governments for war, it did not try to restrain them. Feminists and socialists opposed war on principle, but, when war came, they often closed ranks and accepted the inevitable. A British diplomat reported from the Austrian capital, Vienna, on vast crowds who paraded through the streets singing patriotic songs through the night. Yet, people also worried. A German writer wrote that his people expected a nightmare. Meanwhile leaders, although believing war was preferable to maintaining a fragile peace, also feared their people would tire of it.

The Course of the European War

The tensions led to war in 1914. The pretext for war was a political dispute between Austria-Hungary and Serbia over the assassination of the Austrian archduke Franz Ferdinand (1863–1914), the heir to the Habsburg throne, and his wife, Sophie, while they rode in a motorcade through the crowded streets of Sarajevo (sar-uh-YAY-vo), the capital city of Bosnia-Herzegovina, during an official visit. Although he advocated a conciliatory policy toward the Slavic minorities in the empire, the archduke symbolized to Serbs, especially Serb nationalists in Bosnia, continuing Austro-Hungarian domination. The group behind the assassination, the Black Hand, were Bosnian Serbs who wanted to end Austrian rule in their land and merge Bosnia with Serbia. Pushed by anti-Slav hardliners in the government, Austria-Hungary responded to the assassination by declaring war on Serbia, whose leaders they suspected of aiding the assassination. Germany followed suit to support Austria-Hungary, its militarily weaker ally, and Britain, France, and Russia entered the conflict against Germany. Several months later Ottoman Turkey, long a rival of Russia, joined the Central Powers, closing off British and French access to the Black Sea. Concerned with fighting a two-front war, Germany

planned a quick knockout blow against France, hoping that this would allow most troops to then be sent east to face Russia. These plans were thwarted.

European leaders expected a short war, lasting perhaps six months; instead they got a long, brutal conflict, the most devastating war in history to that point, and the first to be fought in three dimensions: air, sea, and land. It became a war of attrition requiring huge investments to sustain big armies. This was the first fully industrialized war, as whole economies geared for war and modern military technology invented more efficient and indiscriminate ways of killing, including long-range artillery, poison gas, flamethrowers, and aerial bombing. The war massacred a generation of men, doomed youth cut down by shrapnel that tore flesh to pieces, high explosives that pulverized bone, and gas that seared the lungs. The German soldier turned writer Erich Maria Remarque remembered the "great brotherhood [caused by] the desperate loyalty to one another of men condemned to die." On the other side, the British poet Wilfred Owen wrote: "By his dead [comrade's] smile I knew we stood in hell."[5] The surviving soldiers were often maimed mentally or physically. Thousands suffered from shellshock, a horrific nervous condition which made normal life difficult or impossible. The war also generated disease and starvation among civilians.

Online Study Center **Improve Your Grade**
Primary Source: Mud and Khaki: Memoirs of an Incomplete Soldier

The war on the western front in Belgium and northern France was largely one of soldiers huddling in muddy trenches, gas masks at hand, and using artillery and machine guns to pound the enemy troops in their trenches. In hopes of a breakthrough, one or another general ordered attacks across the barbed wire–filled ground, known as "No Man's Land," between the opposing trenches, which resulted in countless casualties. But for all the sacrifices required of soldiers, the front lines moved little in four years. The cataclysmic Battle of Verdun (vuhr-DUN), a fortress in northeastern France, in February 1916 symbolized the senseless slaughter of the war on the western front. The Germans launched a surprise offensive, firing up to a million shells a day at the French positions. The French stopped the German assault, but the Battle of Verdun claimed nearly a million French and German casualties. More soldiers may have been killed per square yard at Verdun than in any other battle in history. But despite the carnage, and the courage of the soldiers on both sides, Verdun had little impact on the war itself. By 1917 more effective offensive tactics using armored tanks put more pressure on the German lines. The British invented the first armored tank, "Big Willie," that was equipped with large guns and ran on belted treads, known as caterpillar tracks, and could cross over No Man's Land and German trenches.

The war had several fronts (see Map 24.1). In the east, Germany and its allies quickly overran Serbia and Romania and pushed deep into western Russia against poorly organized Russian armies. By 1917 Russian morale was cracking. The war had killed or wounded over 7 million Russians and caused hun-

John Nash, *Over the Top* This painting, by the British artist John Nash, shows the trench warfare common on the western front during World War I. Here Allied soldiers leave their trenches to attack across "no man's land" on a snowy day. (Imperial War Museum/The Bridgeman Art Library International)

dreds of thousands of Russian peasants to flee eastward, only to face hunger, disease, and homelessness far from home. Originally a German ally, Italy switched sides in 1915 but lost heavily in several unsuccessful battles. In the Middle East fighting took place over a wide area. Initially the Ottomans took a heavy toll on the Allied troops that were sent to invade Turkey, which included many soldiers from Australia and New Zealand killed or wounded while trying to occupy the Gallipoli Peninsula, the gateway to Istanbul. But an Arab uprising begun in 1916 and a British invasion of Ottoman-controlled Iraq forced the Ottoman forces to fight in western Asia and eventually to retreat from that area. Some fighting also broke out in East Africa, as the British and South Africans invaded the German colony of Tanganyika. On the other side of the world, Japan, a British ally, occupied German-held territory in China and the Pacific.

Although the Germans won more battles than they lost, eventually the tide turned against them. Over time the economic power of the Allies proved decisive. The Allies had superior wealth, better weapons, and more troops. The use of sea power was also crucial in determining the course of the war. Britain and Germany possessed the world's two most powerful navies, with gigantic battleships known as dreadnoughts, and they engaged each other in the North Sea and the eastern Mediterranean. Eventually, responding to growing public uneasiness over mounting casualties and economic hardships, the Germans used their submarines to break Allied supply lines. Their attacks on British and U.S. shipping carrying supplies to Britain, however, brought a reluctant United States into the war.

U.S. Intervention: The End of the War

Two fateful developments in 1917—the Russian Revolution, discussed later in this chapter, and the intervention of the United States—altered the conflict. The Russian Revolution overthrew the czarist government and took Russia out of the war in early 1918. Freed from the eastern front, German armies made breakthroughs against the British and French forces in the west. But the U.S. intervention on the Allied side, the first major U.S. interference in European affairs, eventually offset German success. For the first three years of the war the United States had remained neutral. But, as a German victory seemed more likely, U.S. military leaders, munitions makers, politicians, and businessmen all pressed for intervention. U.S. companies and banks had a big stake in an Allied victory because Allied defeat might have prevented payment on orders for American products and investments in the British and French economies. Americans were also enraged by German submarine attacks on U.S. merchant ships. With public support, President Woodrow Wilson committed the United States to war, linking the military commitment to idealistic American values when he told Congress that "the world must be made safe for democracy. We are the champions of the rights of mankind."[6]

The U.S. intervention proved decisive in securing an Allied victory. Beginning in April 17 1917, some 300,000 American troops poured into Europe and were warmly welcomed in Allied nations. Most of the young men, often from rural backgrounds, had never been to a foreign country and struggled to comprehend European ways; some American troops, however, developed a taste for European culture and a fondness for European cities steeped in history, such as London and Paris. Supported by the United States, the Allies blockaded German ports, creating severe economic problems. As U.S. troops and resources arrived, an Allied offensive pushed the German forces back. Soon Germany's allies began surrendering. The deteriorating conditions demoralized Germans. For example, a German workers' group, claiming their children were starving, begged the state to bring relief to common people. Its overextended army in disarray, and suffering food and fuel shortages at home, Germany was forced to agree to peace in November 1918. Kaiser Wilhelm II and the Austro-Hungarian emperor both abdicated, ending two long-standing European monarchies. The Allies dictated the peace terms.

Consequences of World War I

World War I undermined the power of Germany and shifted more influence to the victors: Britain, France, and the United States. It reshaped Europe politically and rearranged the colonial empires. World War I and its aftermath also affected the societies of Asia and Africa, destroying their hopes for achieving independence or self-rule. Although powerful Western nations still dominated world politics and the world economy, the war also changed the old global order and began a new one.

A New Europe The Paris Peace Conference of 1919, held in the former royal palace in the Paris suburb of Versailles (vuhr-SIGH), reshaped Europe and resulted in the Treaty of Versailles. The U.S. president, Woodrow Wilson, went to Paris hoping to use his prestige and his nation's growing power to sell an agenda, known as the Fourteen Points, to skeptical British and French leaders. Favoring political freedom and stability, Wilson also proposed conciliatory treatment of Germany because he worried that a humiliated, crippled Germany would become chaotic and seek revenge. However, Wilson had to compromise with the hardline French, who wanted to divide Germany. Although the final treaty did not divide Germany, it required Germany to partly dismantle its military; abandon its Asian, African, and Pacific colonies; and shift land to its European neighbors, leaving 3 million ethnic Germans outside of Germany in countries such as Czechoslovakia and Poland. The Treaty of Versailles also forced Germany to pay huge annual payments, known as reparations, to the Allies to compensate for their war costs. In short, Germany was left virtually disarmed and bankrupt. Ultimately the treaty failed to create a lasting settlement, instead planting the roots for future problems, as Wilson had feared. The new German leader, Fridrich Ebert, had a foreboding about Germany's troubled future: "The armistice will not produce a just peace. The sacrifices imposed on us must lead to our people's doom."[7]

The war had taken an appalling human toll on both sides, causing Europeans to reflect on what had happened. Altogether 9 to 10 million soldiers died, including 2 million Russians, 2 million Germans, 1.5 million French, and 75,000 Americans. Since some 10 million civilians died, the total killed was around 20 million. The war also had a social and political impact on Europe. The brutality and waste radicalized many workers and peasants, especially in eastern Europe. Leftist political parties—Socialists and Communists—gained strength. In 1914 Europeans had gone to war with patriotic enthusiasm, but by 1918 some philosophers and writers feared that the initial enthusiasm for war meant the rejection of Enlightenment rationality, and they concluded that the slaughter had destroyed the Western claim to moral leadership in the world. Pacifist, antiwar sentiments grew. The French writer

Henri Barbusse, a soldier himself, reflected these sentiments in these words: "The work of the future will be to wipe out the present. Shame on military glory, shame on armies, shame on the soldier's calling that changes men by turns into stupid victims and ignoble brutes."[8]

The war destroyed several old states and created new ones. The fall of centuries-old imperial houses brought political instability that worsened the social and economic dislocations. Four empires—the Russian, Ottoman, Austro-Hungarian, and German—collapsed. As a result of the Russian Revolution of 1917, Communists gained power in Russia, launching a new political and economic system. Elsewhere, Wilson, believing that ethnically homogeneous nation-states could prevent nationalist rivalries, promoted the self-determination of peoples in Europe. Wilson's efforts proved persuasive: the Paris Peace Conference redrew national boundaries to give ethnic minorities their own states. In eastern Europe, Poland, Czechoslovakia, Yugoslavia, and Finland were carved out of the ruins of the German, Austro-Hungarian, and Russian Empires. These countries later became pawns in the struggle for influence between Germany and Russia that helped launch World War II. But most of the new states placed various ethnic groups within arbitrary boundaries. For example, the country that became Yugoslavia included varied peoples—Orthodox Serbs, Catholic Croats and Slovenes, and Muslim Slavs and Albanians—who had fought each other for centuries and did not share a common national identity. The sacrifices of war, and the appeal of national independence, also led to changes within the British Empire. Britain faced uprisings and civil war in its longtime colony, Ireland, and in 1921 it was forced to grant most of the island special status within the British Empire as the self-governing Irish Free State. In 1937 Ireland became completely independent of the British crown, finally realizing the centuries-old dream of Irish nationalists.

Global Consequences The victorious powers ignored the principle of self-determination for their colonies. Woodrow Wilson advocated democracy and human rights, but in seeking to strengthen the main U.S. allies, Britain and France, he decided to support the preservation of their colonies in Asia, Africa, the Pacific, and the Caribbean. The peace settlement transferred Germany's African colonies to Britain, France, Belgium, and South Africa and its Asian and Pacific territories to Britain, France, Australia, New Zealand, and Japan. Furthermore, Britain and France also gained control of the Middle Eastern societies formerly ruled by Ottoman Turkey. The peace settlements of World War I, by ignoring the political struggles of colonized peoples, thus spurred opposition to the West in Asia and Africa. The death of thousands of Asian and African colonial subjects conscripted or recruited to fight for Britain, France, or Germany in World War I sparked even deeper resentments. Thus World War I was one of the key factors in the rise of nationalism, the desire to form politically independent nations, in the colonies between 1918 and 1941 (see Chapter 25).

The global system shaped by colonial empires and Western economic power survived, but European prestige and influence weakened. The war undermined European economies, allowing the United States to leap ahead of Europe. Like British leaders in the nineteenth century, Wilson, now president of the world's largest, most productive economy, wanted free trade and an open world economy in which American industry could assert its supremacy. Since European nations had borrowed money from the United States to finance the war, they now owed the United States $7 billion. This war debt allowed the United States, long a debtor nation, to become a creditor nation. By 1919 it was producing 42 percent of all the world's industrial output, more than all of Europe combined, and had replaced Britain as the banker and workshop of the world.

Wilson also proposed and helped form a League of Nations, the first organization of independent nations to work for peace and humanitarian concerns. But Wilson could not persuade the U.S. Congress, controlled by the largely isolationist Republican opposition, to approve U.S. membership in the league. Hence, the only nation with the power and stature to make the league work stayed outside, leaving Britain and France alone to deal with European and global issues.

SECTION SUMMARY

- The early 1900s in Europe were marked by great affluence and stability, expanding markets, and shared notions of culture, justice, and human rights.

- Many factors contributed to the start of World War I, including Germany's resentment of British and French colonial holdings, which led to a military buildup on both sides; competing claims on Bosnia-Herzegovina; and a few governments' desire to divert attention from domestic problems.

- Sparked by the assassination of Austrian archduke Franz Ferdinand in Sarajevo, the war soon involved Austro-Hungary, Germany, Britain, France, and Turkey, all of which employed unprecedented military technology that caused millions of deaths.

- In 1917, Russia left the war and Germany seemed on the verge of victory when the United States entered the fighting, in part because of pressure by business interests that provided goods to France and Britain and in part because of outrage over German submarine attacks on U.S. ships.

- The United States helped the French and British win the war, but U.S. president Woodrow Wilson could not prevent the French from dictating harsh settlement terms that required Germany to partially dismantle its military, abandon its colonies, give up some of its territory, and pay heavy reparations.

- The horrors of World War I led to the radicalization of many Europeans; a growth of antiwar sentiment; the breakup of the Ottoman and German Empires, much of which were colonized by Britain and France; the breakup of much of the Russian and Austro-Hungarian Empires, which were carved into new countries; and the world dominance of the United States.

✦ The Revolutionary Path to Soviet Communism

How did communism prevail in Russia and transform that country?

The Russian Revolution, a major consequence of World War I, was a formative event of the twentieth century, shaping European and world history, politics, and beliefs. In the wake of the revolution, Russia provided a testing ground for a radical new ideology, communism, which fostered a powerful state that reshaped Russian society and provided an alternative to the capitalist democracy dominant in North America and western Europe.

The Roots of Revolution

The Russian Revolution had deep roots in Russian society and its history under the czars, the hereditary rulers (see Chapter 23). Controlling a huge Eurasian empire, Russia had enjoyed some industrialization under the despotic czarist governments. However, vested interests, including the powerful and wealthy landed aristocracy, opposed further industrialization. Socially and economically, Russia was still a somewhat feudalistic country. Although serfdom had been legally abolished in the nineteenth century, peasants often remained subject to the dictates of landowners and enjoyed little social mobility or wealth. Only revolution could forge a decisive change in Russian society.

Growing discontent among intellectuals, the floundering middle class, underpaid industrial workers, and peasants who wanted more control over their lives fomented radical movements. All of these groups hated the autocratic czarist system and the privileges enjoyed by the hereditary aristocracy. In 1905 a revolution broke out, only to be brutally crushed by the government, but it left a revolutionary heritage for the **Bolsheviks**, the most radical of Russia's antigovernment groups, who transformed the revolutionary socialist views promoted by Karl Marx in the mid-1800s into a dogmatic communist ideology. The Bolsheviks started as one faction of a broader socialist movement that split into several rival parties in 1903. The founder and leader of the Bolsheviks, Vladimir Lenin (LEN-in) (1870–1924), who was born into a middle-class family and trained as a lawyer, was humorless and uncompromising but a clever political strategist who recruited supporters with his passionate beliefs and persuasive speeches. Lenin's mission in life changed after reading the works of Karl Marx. He was further radicalized when the government executed his older brother for having joined an assassination plot against the czar. Most of the Bolshevik leaders, including Lenin, had spent time as political prisoners in harsh Siberian labor camps for opposing the gov-

Bolsheviks The most radical of Russia's antigovernment groups at the turn of the twentieth century, who embraced a dogmatic form of Marxism.

Lenin The Bolshevik leader Vladimir Lenin stirred crowds with his fiery revolutionary rhetoric, helping to spread the communist message among Russians fed up with ineffective government, war, and poverty. (Sovfoto)

The Bolshevik Seizure of Power

By 1917 the Russian people were sick of war and seeking change, sparking two revolutions. The first revolution, which came in March, toppled the czar, imprisoned the imperial family, and set up a provisional government (see Chronology: Russia, 1917–1938). The unplanned March revolution erupted while riots and strikes caused by food shortages and other problems were paralyzing the cities. Working women had begun the protests by swarming the streets of the capital, St. Petersburg, demanding relief and food, and they soon gained support from the soldiers sent to control them. The new provisional government leaders, such as the teacher's son and lawyer Aleksandr Kerensky (kuh-REN-skee) (1881–1970), who had often defended political dissidents in court, were well-meaning urban liberals who wanted reform and Western-style democracy, but they had no roots among the mass of the population. They failed because they refused to provide the two things most Russians wanted: peace and land. Because of their commitments to the Allies, they vowed to continue fighting the highly unpopular war. They also declined to redistribute land from the old aristocracy to the peasantry until the war ended and elections could be held for a planned Constituent Assembly to form a new, more representative, Russian government.

The political situation became chaotic. While the increasingly discredited provisional government asked for

ernment, and they were embittered toward the czarist system. To avoid another arrest Lenin had lived in exile elsewhere in Europe since 1907, organizing his movement.

The Bolsheviks, inspired by the Marxist vision of a revolution that would bring about a transition to a classless communist society, espoused a goal of helping the downtrodden workers and peasants redress the wrongs inflicted upon them by the rich and privileged. A new society, forged by revolutionary violence, could bring about, Bolsheviks claimed, a more equitable distribution of wealth and power throughout the society. In his book *What Is to Be Done* (1902), Lenin advocated organizing a professional core of activists to lead the revolution. The Bolsheviks favored a small, disciplined revolutionary organization that would work for workers' interests but would include only full-time revolutionaries. All members had to abide by the decisions made by the leaders, a system known as the party line.

When World War I broke out, the Russian people and even most opposition political parties rallied around the unpopular czarist government, seeing it as a patriotic war of defense against the hated Germans, the longtime rivals for dominion in eastern Europe. Only the Bolsheviks opposed the war, which they saw, with some justice, as an imperialistic struggle over markets and colonies. But the war soon lost its allure as Russian military forces collapsed in the face of German armies. Russia lacked the economic power and military and political leadership to compete in the war.

CHRONOLOGY	
Russia, 1917–1938	
1917	March revolution
1917	October revolution
March 1918	Brest-Litovsk Treaty
1918–1921	Russian Civil War
1922	Formation of Soviet Union
1924	Death of Lenin
1928	Beginning of Five-Year Plans
1929–1953	Stalin's dictatorship
1936–1938	Stalin's Great Purge

time, radicals organized **soviets**, local action councils that enlisted workers and soldiers to fight the factory owners and military officers. The soviets represented a grassroots movement for change that undermined government authority. The strongest soviet, in the capital, St. Petersburg, had between 2,000 and 3,000 members and was headed by an executive committee. As the soviets and the government jockeyed for control of St. Petersburg, the Germans, hoping to undermine the Russian provisional government, helped Lenin, in exile in Switzerland, to secretly return to Russia hidden in a railroad box car. Using the slogans of "peace, bread, and land" and "all power to the soviets," Lenin rapidly built up Bolshevik influence in the soviets. The provisional government, increasingly discredited, tried to prevent leftist extremism, such as the peasants seizing land, but government control was weak.

In October 1917, the Bolsheviks and their 240,000 party members staged an uprising and grabbed power from Kerensky's crumbling provisional government. Aided by the soviets, the Bolsheviks seized key government buildings in St. Petersburg, including the czar's Winter Palace. With a fragile hold on power, the Bolsheviks had to allow diverse parties to freely contest elections for an assembly, which met in January 1918. After the assembly refused to support a Bolshevik bid for leadership, however, the Bolsheviks used troops to disperse the assembly and take over the national and city governments, pushing other parties aside and terrorizing or executing opponents. The Bolshevik's rivals, the moderate, prodemocracy Socialists, some of whom had served in the provisional government, were consigned, in the words of a Bolshevik leader, to the dustbin of history. Lenin claimed his goal for Russia was to transfer power from the capitalists to the working class. Defending the violence, he asserted that chefs cannot make an omelet without breaking eggs. The Bolsheviks renamed themselves the Communist Party. In one of its first moves, the communists gained popular support by pulling Russia out of the war. In the Treaty of Brest-Litovsk, negotiated with Germany in March, 1918, Russia gave up some of its empire in the west to Germany, abandoning the Ukraine, eastern Poland, the Baltic states, and Finland. They also moved the capital from St. Petersburg, which they renamed Leningrad, to Moscow.

Communist International and Civil War

Once in power, the communist regime had to develop a strategy for dealing with the wider world. In 1919, Lenin, hoping to protect Russia's revolution by promoting world revolution, organized the Communist International, often known as the Comintern, a collection of communist parties from around the world. It would battle the U.S. vision, articulated by Woodrow Wilson, of promoting capitalism and democracy. Before World War II, however, the United States had the greater success in spreading its influence, partly because it

helped stabilize postwar Europe with economic, political, and food assistance to promote procapitalist, anti-communist governments. The prospect of world revolution that would foster the spread of communism soon faded.

The Russian Revolution sparked the Russian Civil War (1918–1921) (see Map 24.2). The conservative, anti-communist forces, who called themselves White Russians in contrast to the communists' military force, the Red Army, included the czarist aristocracy (among them large landowners), generals who were angry at losing their dominance, and a few pro-Western liberals favoring democracy. Heavily funded and armed by Western nations, which were alarmed by the Revolution, the White Russian armies fought the communist forces in the fringe areas of the Russian Empire in the three years following World War I. In mounting their defense, the communists capitalized on the disunity among White Russian leaders and their Western backers. The cohesion and leadership of the Communist Party and the brilliant military leadership of the Red Army also helped. Most crucially, the communists received growing support from the working class and the peasants, who feared the return of the hated landowners with a White Russian victory. Although the communists initially looked vulnerable, they eventually gained the advantage, defeating the White Russians and even reclaiming some of the territory lost in the Brest-Litovsk Treaty, including the Ukraine.

The outside intervention added an international flavor to the Russian Civil War. This intervention had come chiefly from Japan, Britain, France, and the United States. Japan, which concentrated on eastern Siberia, and Britain sent the largest number of troops into Russia—60,000 and 40,000, respectively. The possibility of a permanent communist government in Russia also worried the liberal idealist Wilson, who sent two separate American military forces to Russia in 1918 to roll back the communist regime and, he claimed, spread democratic values. Five thousand American troops went to northern Russia to battle the Red Army for control of two port cities. But the episode proved disastrous for Americans: brutal winter weather, poor provisions, and 500 American casualties drove the U.S. troops to near mutiny. Another contingent of 10,000 Americans entered eastern Siberia. Soon recognizing the whole intervention effort as a quagmire, Wilson lamented that it was harder to get out than it was to go in. U.S. and other Western troops were finally removed in 1920, in some cases after soldiers mutinied. The Western intervention helped to solidify the communist government, which was widely seen by Russians as fighting a nationalist war against foreign powers seeking to restore the old discredited czarist order.

Lenin and a New Society

By 1922 the Communist Party controlled much of the old Russian Empire, but it faced severe challenges. The civil war had left the country devastated and its people starving, as well as making good relations with the capitalist democracies impossible. The civil war had also reinforced the paranoid, authoritarian, and militaristic attitudes of the communists. Crediting

---

soviets Local action councils formed by Russian radicals before the 1917 Russian Revolution that enlisted workers and soldiers to fight the factory owners and military officers.

Map 24.2 Civil War in Revolutionary Russia (1918–1921)
The communist seizure of power in Russia in 1917 sparked a counteroffensive, backed by varied Western nations and Japan, to reverse the Russian Revolution. The communists successfully defended the Russian heartland while pushing back the conservative offensive.

Karl Marx as the key inspiration, the party had forged the world's first state based on communist ideas; committed to world revolution, it inspired the growth of communist groups in other countries. Russia's leaders renamed their nation the Union of Soviet Socialist Republics (USSR), in theory a federation of all the empire's diverse peoples—such as Kazakhs, Uzbeks, Armenians, and Ukrainians—but in actuality largely controlled by Russians, and hence, to opponents, essentially a continuation of the Russian Empire built by the czars. Soon the USSR turned from world revolution to building what the leaders termed "socialism in one country"—the USSR—using coercion against reluctant citizens if necessary. Yet party leaders did not yet have a blueprint for transforming Russian society.

Since they had no model of a communist state, the Soviet leaders experimented while using their secret police to eliminate opponents, including those they called enemies of the working class, among them liberals and moderate socialists. The basis for Soviet communism was **Marxism-Leninism**, a mix of socialism (collective ownership of the economy) and **Leninism**, a political system in which one party holds a monopoly on power. Lenin initially favored centralization and nationalization of all economic activity, but he was forced by peasant opposition to adopt the **New Economic Policy** (NEP), a pragmatic approach that mixed capitalism and socialism. The NEP brought economic recovery and included limited capitalism in agriculture, allowing peasants to sell their produce on the open market. However, since the economy produced few consumer goods, the peasants had no incentive to sell their produce for profit because there was little to buy with the money they earned.

Lenin was dissatisfied with the results of the revolution, which he called socialist in appearance but not substance: "czarism slightly anointed with Soviet oil."[9] He criticized the bloated bureaucracy and warned, accurately, that his probable successor, Joseph Stalin (STAH-lin) (1879–1953), had dictatorial tendencies. Decades later Lenin's assessment of his government's failures remained accurate, since the USSR never became the egalitarian communist society envisioned by Karl Marx. Lenin himself, who combined ruthless authoritarianism with concern for the poor and exploited, deserves some of the blame. While Lenin and other Soviet rulers constructed myths about the mass nature of their revolution and what they termed the "dictatorship of the proletariat," led by the Communist Party, the ties between the political leaders and the Soviet masses remained weak. The instability and divisions caused by World War I and the Russian Civil War made the communist leaders even less willing to trust the people or allow dissent, which they feared would provoke unrest.

The long Russian tradition of authoritarian, bureaucratic government under the czars and an obedient population provided a foundation for communist dictatorship. The communists were a small party, and most party leaders were, like Lenin, intellectuals from urban middle-class backgrounds who knew little of Russia's largest social class, the peasants. To regenerate the economy, they eventually adopted not popular control of farms and enterprises by workers and peasants but a top-down managerial system staffed by officials chiefly of middle-class origin. Peasants and workers became just employees, not partners. Increasingly the Communist Party and state became bureaucratic. The middle class was now largely composed of state employees, managers, and bureaucrats with salaries and privileges that were denied the masses and dedicated not to fostering social change but to maintaining their own power. They made policies without consulting the people. Lenin hoped to reform the party but died in 1924.

Stalinism, Industrialization, and One-Man Rule

Lenin's successor was a master bureaucrat, Joseph Stalin (1879–1953), who reshaped Soviet communism and Russia. Born in the Caucasus province of Georgia, the son of a shoemaker, he studied to be a Russian Orthodox priest before being expelled from the seminary. After joining the Bolsheviks, he adopted the name Stalin ("Man of Steel"). Aided by his control of the Communist Party apparatus, Stalin outmaneuvered his party rivals to succeed Lenin. Stalin came to power as the peasants increasingly turned away from the Communist Party because they no longer feared the return of the landlords. Viewing the peasants as self-indulgent, Stalin urged a hard line against those who resisted state policies, eliminated all his competition in the party, and became a dictator. The system he imposed, known today as **Stalinism**, included state ownership of all property, such as lands and businesses, a planned economy, and one-man rule.

In 1928 Stalin ended Lenin's NEP and introduced an economic policy based on an annual series of plans for future production, known as Five-Year Plans, formulated by state bureaucrats. The Five-Year Plans produced basic industrial goods, such as steel and coal, but few consumer goods. Stalin also launched a massive crash industrialization program and withdrew the country from the global political and economic system. Under Stalin, the Soviet Union mobilized its own resources, refusing foreign investment. In order to introduce machines, such as tractors and harvesters, to increase farm production, Stalin strengthened the party's grip on the rural sector by collectivizing the land and turning private farms into commonly owned enterprises, in the process destroying the wealthier small farmers, the *kulaks*, as a class. Peasants who refused to join the collective farms were often exiled to Siberia.

Marxism-Leninism   The basis for Soviet communism, a mix of socialism (collective ownership of the economy) and Leninism.

Leninism   A political system in which one party holds a monopoly on power, excluding other parties from participation.

New Economic Policy (NEP)   Lenin's pragmatic approach to economic development, which mixed capitalism and socialism.

Stalinism   Joseph Stalin's system of government, which included state ownership of all property, such as lands and businesses, a planned economy, and one-man rule.

The 1930s and 1940s were hard years for the Soviet people, filled with terror. Stalin's rule was marked by purges, or campaigns to eliminate actual or potential opponents; forced-labor camps for suspected dissidents; and the widespread use of the secret police (known as the KGB), which spied on and sometimes terrorized the people. For example, when the collectivization of farming provoked a widespread famine, the growing dissent among the common people and some party members led to the Great Purge of 1936–1938, which was marked by well-publicized trials of some party leaders as traitors.

Stalin also deported millions of people to the harsh forced-labor camps in Siberia known as **gulags** (Russian shorthand for State Camp Administration). Some 4 to 5 million people were arrested and half a million executed for alleged subversion. From 1929 until 1953 some 18 million people passed through the massive gulag system, and about 4.5 million of these never returned home. Gulag inmates toiled, starved, and died building railroads, cutting timber, or digging canals. Not even beloved artists were spared the repression, especially, given Stalin's embrace of long-standing Russian anti-Semitism, if they were Jewish. One of Russia's most revered poets, Osip Mandelstam (MAHN-duhl-stuhm) (1891–1938), a Jew whose comment on the era begins this chapter, died in the gulag in 1938. By the early 1950s the dead and jailed from Stalin's policies numbered around 40 million people, casualties of twenty-five years of repression. The Russian poet Anna Akhmatova (uhk-MAH-tuh-vuh) (1889–1966), in her requiem for a lost generation, summarized the horror: "Madness has already covered, Half my soul with its wing. And gives to drink of a fiery wine, And beckons into the dark valley."[10]

The repression also came at a high economic cost. Peasants often destroyed their equipment and livestock as a protest against forced collectivization, and agriculture suffered from these losses for decades. Peasants adopted a stance of passive resistance, doing just the minimum to survive. Russia's annual food production between 1928 and 1980 was less than in 1924. Since agriculture stagnated, the government could not use the surplus to finance industrialization. Instead, it squeezed the urban workers, who were forced to labor long hours for low wages and few consumer goods. Like the peasants, workers became alienated and passively resisted, voicing their feelings in the common expression: "The government pretends they are paying us so we pretend we are working." The economic system was hurt by a lack of initiative and creativity, as well as by high rates of alcoholism and theft.

Reshaping Russian Society

Even as the agricultural economy stagnated and the terror continued, however, the communists were reshaping Russian society by introducing modern ideas. The crash industrialization raised national economic power and the gross national product (GNP), the annual total of all economic activities, to second in the world by 1932. The Five-Year Plans successfully mobilized the population for industrialization, aided by government; as with Meiji Japan, the state, rather than private capital, was the main agent for change. The work force that was engaged in industrial production nearly tripled between 1928 and 1937. Mass education raised the literacy rate from 28 percent in 1900 to over 90 percent by the 1980s. Better medical care raised life expectancy from thirty-two in 1914 to seventy in 1960. The transformation in one decade, due in part to the nation's abundant natural resources, was impressive.

Communism also reshaped social patterns. Lenin had wanted to promote social equality by breaking up traditional institutions, including the family. In 1918 the Soviet official and feminist Alexandra Kollontai (1872–1952) wrote that the old patriarchal family had seen its day. Kollontai argued that the state should fund child care and domestic work, and envisioned public kitchens, laundries, and nurseries so that women could work outside the home. Lenin made divorce easier, legalized homosexuality, sanctioned free love and abortion, and, in Muslim areas, forbade women from wearing the veil and men from having multiple wives. Later, however, Stalin, whose social attitudes were less liberal than Lenin's, reversed Lenin's policies: he restored the family, made divorce more difficult, banned abortion, and promoted a strict sexual code that persecuted homosexuals. Kollontai, whose outspokenness on women's freedom, sexuality and empowerment antagonized party leaders, later became the Soviet ambassador to Sweden, the world's first female ambassador. Unlike the atheistic Lenin, who considered religion a form of spiritual oppression by promoting a belief in a better life after death, Stalin, a former seminarian, moderated official atheism and pragmatically reached some accommodation with the Russian Orthodox Church, ending overt persecution but keeping it weak and subject to state control. While many Soviet citizens professed atheism, at least half identified themselves as religious in the 1936 census. Stalin also ordered literary and artistic works to depict Soviet life from a revolutionary perspective, a style known as **socialist realism**.

The USSR was the first society to leave the capitalist world order, industrialize rapidly under direct state control, and establish a new, socialist society. This model held the promise of catching up to the West in a short time and to do so without capitalism, although it came at a high cost in human rights and lives. The USSR's pervasive system of political repression and state control, which was far greater even than that of the czars, limited its appeal to other societies. Historians debate how much of the Soviet political and economic system was due to communism and how much to a long-established autocratic Russian tradition that despised merchants and promoted deference to state power. The USSR can be seen as a combination of Marxist ideology and czarist despotism, driven in turn by the missionary impulse derived from Christianity. The latter gave Soviet leaders the notion of spreading their "true faith" to the world.

---

gulags   Harsh forced-labor camps in Siberia.

socialist realism   Literary and artistic works that depicted life from a revolutionary perspective, a style first introduced in Stalin's Russia.

SECTION SUMMARY

- The Bolsheviks, a group of Marxist revolutionaries led by Vladimir Lenin, were energized by the unsuccessful 1905 Russian revolution and organized a core of professional activists devoted to violent revolution and more equitable distribution of wealth and power.

- In March 1917, a spontaneous revolution overthrew the czar, but its urban liberal leaders could not satisfy the people's demand for reform and an end to the war, so radical soviets, allied with the Bolsheviks, organized and in October seized power, after which they removed Russia from the war.

- In the interest of spreading the revolution, Lenin founded the Communist International, but he was soon fighting the Russian Civil War against the White Russians, who included defenders of the aristocracy and were funded and armed by Western nations disturbed by the Bolshevik revolution.

- After winning the civil war, the Bolsheviks focused on establishing Marxism-Leninism in the USSR, a brand of socialism achieved through one-party rule that treated opponents ruthlessly and failed to achieve a true connection between the masses and the government.

- Lenin's successor, Joseph Stalin, sent millions to forced-labor camps called gulags and imposed state ownership of all property and a planned economy, which led to decreased harvests and widespread misery.

- Rapid industrialization made the USSR the second largest world economy by 1932, and other advances greatly increased the literacy rate and life expectancy, but at the cost of many lives and limitations of human rights even more severe than under the czars.

◆ The Interwar Years and the Great Depression

How did the Great Depression reshape world politics and economies?

In Europe after World War I, peace had brought a great questioning of the old order. By the early 1920s, western Europe had stabilized and much of the European continent had come under democratically elected governments. Meanwhile, the United States, though suffering severe economic inequalities, enjoyed widespread prosperity. Western affluence, however, was dramatically undermined by the significant event of the 1930s, the **Great Depression**, a collapse of the world economy that lasted in varying degrees of severity through the 1930s.

Great Depression   A collapse of the world economy that lasted in varying degrees of severity through the 1930s.

The global extent of the Depression, rooted in developments in Europe and North America after World War I, illustrated the economic interdependence of the world's societies. The distress caused by the Depression, which affected both industrialized nations and those countries and colonies supplying raw materials, in turn fostered radical political movements.

Postwar Europe and Japan

The 1920s was a decade of political, economic, and social change throughout western Europe and Japan. Governments struggled to maintain stability, economic fortunes rose and fell, and people challenged long-standing social customs. Like much of western Europe, Japan, which had rapidly industrialized in the late 1800s and established a constitutional monarchy, enjoyed elected governments and increasing influence for the urban middle class.

A New Europe   Europe's very slow and painful recovery from the war fostered political opposition movements that placed conservatives on the defensive as they tried to uphold the old ways. Many European governments were weakened by political infighting between political factions. Where these governments were under conservative leaders from the middle and upper classes, the demands of workers for better conditions or unions were usually crushed. The resentment resulting from this repression, however, caused socialist and social democratic parties, such as the British Labor Party, to grow stronger; these parties worked to extend the rights and protections of workers through legislation.

For various reasons, some countries remained politically and economically unstable. For instance, under a new democratic government, the Weimar (VIE-mahr) Republic, Germany struggled with high unemployment and a devastated economy. A German politician declared that the economy determined his nation's fate, noting that a healthy one could overcome social and political problems. In 1923 France occupied the industrialized Ruhr district of western Germany to enforce reparations payments. The costly reparations caused hyperinflation in Germany, which in turn stimulated the growth of extremist political groups. Since German prosperity was essential to spur the European economy, the Allies reduced reparations and the United States extended loans, but the Weimar regime continued to face domestic challenges. Meanwhile, certain multiethnic, eastern European countries, such as Poland, with its large German, Russian, and Ukrainian minorities, and a Czechoslovakia that mixed Czechs and Slovaks with Germans, Poles, Hungarians, and Ukrainians, experienced ethnic tensions that created political problems.

Some western European countries enjoyed a degree of economic recovery that curbed inflation and unemployment. To stimulate their economies, Europeans borrowed U.S. mass production processes, including the assembly lines pioneered at Ford Motor Company in Detroit. With growing middle-class prosperity, more Europeans could afford the improved versions of earlier inventions such as cars, radios, refrigerators, vacuum cleaners, and central heating. Labor unions also gained strength, helping certain workers achieve an eight-hour day. The center of gravity shifted to the cities and a fast-growing new white-collar class that tended to oppose the socialism popular with the working class. Yet Europe's economies were more and more bound up with the world economy, in which they lost ground to the United States and Japan. Between 1913 and 1928 Europe's share of world exports fell from 53 to 45 percent, a drop that spurred competition for world markets among European nations.

Various forces fostered European unity to safeguard peace. To promote a shared sense of identity among European nations, some leaders pointed to their common roots in classical Greece, Rome, and Christianity. The French foreign minister, Aristide Briand (bree-AHND) (1862–1932), an active visionary, led the effort to officially renounce war among European nations. In 1930 Briand proposed a European federal union and common market, arguing that the task of uniting Europe was urgently necessary. His vision only came to fruition two decades later, with the formation of the European Common Market.

Social change also marked the 1920s, especially in the cities. Europeans developed new patterns of leisure and consumption. In European cities, affluent people found entertainment at nightclubs, cabarets, and dancehalls and shopped at large department stores. Consumers also discovered U.S. culture, especially jazz, which became widely popular. Religious convictions also changed at this time. Religious observance declined because some Europeans felt abandoned by God on the battlefields or rejected Christianity as a patriarchal faith out of tune with the changing times.

Gender patterns showed signs of change, too. The new fashion for women emphasized short hair and a boyish figure, while the "new woman," as the popular designation made her, also sought financial independence through paid work. The war had killed millions of young men, leaving fewer men to marry or hire. To fill this gap, women moved into office jobs, and the female secretary replaced the male clerk. More women also became lawyers, physicians, and even members of parliaments. In many countries, women fought for and often achieved legislation guaranteeing women's suffrage and other rights. Before the war only Norway and Finland had women's suffrage. Denmark gave women the vote in 1915 and Germany in 1919, while Britain extended it to women over thirty in 1918 and to all women over eighteen in 1928. But many countries, including France and Italy, ignored the demands for women's suffrage.

As gender standards changed, once shocking attitudes became common, including an openness about sexuality and rejection of traditional marriage. Even a leading British bishop conceded in 1922 that marriage laws needed to be liberalized because society's dramatic changes were reshaping social morality. Once attired in long dresses that covered the body, women now wore clothes that showed off their figure and beauty contests featured women in revealing swimsuits that would have been considered scandalous in earlier eras.

Official attitudes toward homosexuality also shifted, chiefly toward repression. In the nineteenth century Europeans had not thought much about homosexuality, male or female, and, despite antisodomy laws on the books, courts usually dismissed charges of homosexual relations. Europeans understood that some men and women had same-sex relations or emotional ties, a pattern particularly known among men in naval forces. By the early 1900s, however, the media had identified homosexuals as essentially different in attitudes and life experiences from heterosexuals. Believing that same-sex love challenged mainstream values, British officials prosecuted the award-winning British writer Radclyffe Hall (1883–1943) for obscenity after the banning of her 1928 novel, *The Well of Loneliness*, about lesbian identity. While gay men and lesbians lived openly in cities such as Paris and Berlin in the 1920s, they were often watched and suffered police raids on their clubs. Although Soviet Russia and Weimar Germany legalized homosexuality, these tolerant policies were later reversed. In 1934 Stalin defined homosexuality as a crime against the state, and in 1935 Nazi Germany prosecuted 50,000 men for homosexual activity. In the 1930s a return to traditional female roles in European nations brought bans on abortion and birth control.

A New Japan As in Europe, industrialization, democratic politics, and liberalization reshaped Japan during the 1920s, generating prosperity and new possibilities for the growing middle class. However, the prosperity was not shared by all. Japan's population tripled between 1860 and 1940 to 60 million, but lack of land forced many rural people to move to cities or emigrate to the Americas to find work. Cheap labor in factories helped to gain foreign markets for the consumer goods the Japanese produced, especially textiles. Powerful business interests dominated the democratic system formed only a few years earlier. The resulting corrupt and volatile politics disillusioned many Japanese of all social classes.

Internationally, Japan played a visible role in the world. Even before World War I, Japan had colonized Taiwan and Korea, where it ruthlessly repressed nationalist protests, and had gained footholds in northern China, leading some Japanese to dream of further colonial expansion in China and Southeast Asia. As a British ally in World War I, Japan had also gained control of the German colonies in the Pacific and had taken over the German sphere of influence in eastern China. Japan's assertive role in the world, however, also created enemies. Tensions with the United States increased, fostered in part by Japanese bitterness toward the blatant racist discrimination against Japanese immigrants in the United States, which passed laws restricting their entry and rights, and by U.S. hostility to Japanese ambitions in Asia and the Pacific.

As in the 1870s, Japan was open to the world, and a wave of Western influence permeated the cities. Urban middle-class Japanese were influenced by popular culture from the United States, and baseball became a popular Japanese sport. In Tokyo, young men and women, known as the "modern boy" and "modern girl," wore the latest imported styles while enjoying jazz, beer halls, and Western films. Young women, both housewives and those in the workforce, became avid readers of mass women's magazines and many questioned the Japanese tradition of the submissive female and dominant male. Many young

YOSHIYA NOBUKO, JAPANESE WRITER AND GENDER REBEL

Yoshiya Nobuko
A prominent Japanese writer for popular audiences, especially for girls and young women, Yoshiya Nobuko represented the modern girl. She wore her hair short and usually dressed in a mannish style that defied gender expectations. (Kyoto News Photos)

Yoshiya Nobuko (1896–1973) was a popular, gender-bending writer who lived through major transitions as Japan moved from a parochial society through imperial power and world war to become an industrial powerhouse. She was born in the northern Honshu city of Niigata just after the Japanese victory over China in the Sino-Japanese War (1894–1895). Her middle-class, culturally conservative parents trained her for the "good wife, wise mother" role expected of women in Meiji Japan. Yoshiya observed that her mother encouraged her to adopt traditional roles of female domesticity and obedience to men while she herself remained in a loveless arranged marriage to Yoshiya's father.

Yoshiya, who began writing as a child, published her first short stories at age twelve. In 1915 she moved to Tokyo, where she began to diverge from Japanese society's career and gender expectations. Rising Japanese literacy was opening doors to literature aimed at a popular audience, allowing writers such as Yoshiya to make a living from their work. Between 1916 and 1924 Yoshiya's short stories were serialized in a popular magazine, *Girl's Illustrated*, aimed at young, chiefly female readers. The stories she published inspired a generation of women writers and made Yoshiya famous. They appealed to schoolgirls and to the growing group of women not yet committed to marriage and children. According to tradition, women were supposed to be married by age twenty-four, but many young women now worked in the public sector as clerks, cafe hostesses, ticket sellers, schoolteachers, typists, and telephone operators. Yoshiya's core audience came from this group, especially the so-called modern girl, a Westernized urban woman who avoided or postponed marriage. Critics accused these women of being un-Japanese and manly.

In her writing and life, the very modern Yoshiya took advantage of the new public sphere opened to women for redefining relations between them. She challenged the conventions of family life, openly avowing her lesbianism. Japanese had traditionally tolerated homosexuality, including public displays of affection by people of the same gender. Now more openly passionate friendships between females were becoming common among students, educators, civil servants, and actresses. Japanese society viewed female homosexuality as spiritual, in contrast to the popular image of the carnal male version. Gradually lesbianism developed from a phase of life among girls to an adult subculture. Despite laws requiring women to have long hair, Yoshiya was one of the first Japanese women to emulate Western fashion in the 1920s by cutting her hair short, symbolizing her maverick persona. In 1923 Yoshiya met her life partner, Monma Chiyo, a mathematics teacher at a Tokyo girls' school. They remained inseparable and openly lived together as a couple, writing steamy, often erotic, love letters to each other even when together. In 1957 Yoshiya adopted Monma, the only legal way for homosexual couples to share property and make medical decisions for each other. Yoshiya also flouted gender expectations in

other ways. She designed her own house, was one of the first Japanese to own a car, and was the first Japanese woman to own a racehorse.

Yoshiya became one of Japan's most successful and highest-paid writers. A literary critic wrote in 1935 that "there isn't a [Japanese] woman alive who hasn't heard of Yoshiya." Her Japanese readership included many middle-class men and women, gay and straight, single and married. She published girls' fiction, social commentary, and autobiographical essays. Some literary critics criticized Yoshiya for seeking a mass audience, but her defenders argued that Yoshiya's writing broadened minds. She and Monma spent 1929 traveling in Russia, Europe, and the United States, where she was impressed by what she considered America's liberated women. After the trip, she vowed to no longer write about women "who cried a lot and simply endured their miserable lot in life."

While an ardent feminist, Yoshiya mistrusted political parties and never became active in the organized Japanese feminist movement. Yoshiya also disliked the militaristic turn of the 1930s, which brought more censorship. To avoid political harassment or imprisonment, she joined a government writers' group that toured Southeast Asia and China during World War II and wrote stories and reports praising Japanese imperial ambitions. After the war she continued to publish fiction and nonfiction, winning numerous awards. She began to write historical novels to redress female stereotypes in male fiction, such as the dutiful wife, and to restore the voice of women to Japanese history. She died at home at age seventy-seven, holding Monma's hand. Yoshiya's writings remain popular in Japan today.

THINKING ABOUT THE PROFILE

1. How did Yoshiya's life reflect the social changes of the era in Japan?

2. Why might her writing have attracted a large audience?

Note: Quotations from Jennifer Robertson, "Yoshiya Nobuko: Out and Outspoken in Practice and Prose," in Anne Walthall, ed., *The Human Tradition in Modern Japan* (Wilmington, Del.: SR Books, 2002), pp. 156, 167.

people also sought freedom to choose their own marriage partners. To conservatives, these young people and their styles posed the threat of sexual liberation and redefined gender roles. For them, nontraditional Japanese such as the openly lesbian writer Yoshiya Nobuko (yo-SHE-ya no-BOO-ko), whose work had a large following among youth (see Profile: Yoshiya Nobuko: Japanese Writer and Gender Rebel), were leading Japan in the wrong direction. Conservatives also disliked the emerging women's movement, celebrated by the feminist poet Yosano Akiko: "All the sleeping women, Are now awake and moving."[11] A leading feminist, Kato Shidzue (KAH-to shid-ZOO-ee) (1897–2001), became a strong proponent of family planning after having sojourned in the United States and later turned to socialism and promotion of equal political rights for women.

Perplexed by the divide between traditional and modern values, Japanese thinkers and artists pondered national and cultural identity. For example, the writer Akutagawa Ryunosuke (1892–1927) combined Western and Japanese traditions by adding psychological dimensions to ancient folk tales. His influential short story *Rashoman* tells of a rape and murder from several eyewitness perceptions. In spite of renewed interest in Western thought, including Marxism, among the educated elite, the working classes and rural population were alienated from the Westernized culture of the cities. They saw little benefit in either the liberalization of social customs or the individualistic ideals promoted by Western thought. Nor did they share in the economic prosperity.

U.S. Society and Politics

In the United States, change occurred in a context of social restlessness and political unrest, including a new political repression. Anticommunism prompted by the Russian Revolution and growing middle-class prosperity aided the triumph of conservative forces. While western Europeans often feared socialism, Americans developed a powerful hostility for socialism of any kind and especially for the most extreme form, the communist ideology. Hatred of Germans during World War I was now replaced by hatred of Russians and communism. The ensuing anticommunist fervor had enormous domestic costs. In 1919–1920 widespread public fear of communism, known as the "Red Scare," generated the first in a series of government crackdowns on dissidents, including suppression of strikes, harassment of labor unions, arrests of political radicals, and deportation of foreigners, in each case trampling civil liberties (see Chronology: Europe, North America, and Japan, 1919–1940). The Red Scare froze attitudes toward the Soviet Union and communist movements for generations, as the United States pursued a long-term policy of isolating the USSR from international contact. A U.S. senator and critic of this policy concluded in 1925, "So long as you have a hundred and fifty million people [in the U.S.S.R.] outlawed, it necessarily follows that you cannot have peace."[12] Not until 1933 would the United States soften its policy of isolation toward the Soviet Union by extending diplomatic recognition.

The Red Scare was prompted partly by growing domestic unrest. Strikes for better wages by desperate workers, many of

CHRONOLOGY	
Europe, North America, and Japan, 1919–1940	
1919–1920	First Red Scare in United States
1921	Irish Free State
1921	Formation of Italian fascist movement
1926	Formation of fascist state in Italy
1929–1941	Great Depression
1931	Japanese occupation of Manchuria
1933–1945	Presidency of Franklin D. Roosevelt
1933	Nazi electoral victory in Germany
1933–1938	Anti-Jewish legislation in Germany
1935–1936	Italian conquest of Ethiopia
1936	Start of fascist government in Japan
October 1936	Hitler-Mussolini alliance
1936–1939	Spanish Civil War
1937	Japanese invasion of China
March 1938	Austrian merger with Germany
1938	German annexation of western Czechoslovakia
August 1939	Nazi-Soviet pact
September 1939	German invasion of Poland
1940	Tripartite Pact between Germany, Italy, and Japan

whom had joined leftwing unions, proliferated. Union militants such as Mary Harris ("Mother") Jones (1830–1930), an Irish immigrant who called herself a hellraiser and organized coal miners and railroad workers, fought against the power of "big business." These activities frightened federal, state, and local governments, which all helped employers fight labor unions in the Appalachian coal fields, Detroit auto plants, and South Atlantic textile mills. The police broke up strikes and often arrested union organizers. Another source of tension was the widespread resentment of the United States Congress for passing Prohibition, which outlawed alcohol production and made it harder to obtain liquor, especially for the less affluent. In addition, World War I veterans protested when they found that the government was slow in providing their back pay and they had trouble finding jobs.

Federal government policies often increased unhappiness by making life worse for the less affluent, and political leaders ignored terrorism, including lynchings, by white racists against African Americans in the South. To escape mistreatment and limited economic prospects, several million African Americans, in what was later called the Great Migration, moved from southern states to the north and west in the 1920s, doubling the black populations of cities such as Chicago, Detroit, and New York. Dominating the federal government, the Republicans, oriented toward big business, also frustrated some Americans by neglecting the country's natural and human resources, thereby contributing to eroded croplands and fouled rivers.

In contrast to the less affluent, for the top half of the U.S. population, these years were the "Roarin' 20s," the hedonistic era when high society let down its inhibitions. The growing middle class enjoyed increasing prosperity. Affluent whites found it easy to evade Prohibition by buying illegally produced liquor. Gatsby, a character in a 1925 novel by the popular writer and famed playboy F. Scott Fitzgerald (1896–1940), exemplified the optimistic and hedonistic American values of the time: "Gatsby believed in the green light, the future that year by year recedes before us. It eluded us then, but that's no matter—tomorrow we will run faster, stretch out our arms farther, and one fine morning..."[13]

Other changes, unrelated to hedonism, affected all Americans. For example, jazz music, rooted in southern black culture, provided employment for black musicians and became part of the mainstream, enjoyed by all classes. Jazz became so popular that the era was often known as "the Jazz Age." Women, who had been active in labor unions, social reform movements, and religious organizations for decades, finally won the vote in 1920, and this success allowed more of them to enjoy a larger public role. Americans of all backgrounds celebrated the first nonstop flight between North America and Europe, made by Charles Lindbergh (1902–1974) in 1927. Lindbergh's brave and lonely feat demonstrated both heroism and advances in technology.

In contrast to Woodrow Wilson's idealistic globalism, American leaders in the 1920s proclaimed an isolationist U.S. foreign policy, touting the benefits of avoiding interference in other nations' affairs; but despite the rhetoric, interventionism was often practiced. Always pushing outward, restless American citizens sought new Christian converts, commercial markets, and business investments. Energetic expansionism reflected the optimistic, unsettled character of American society, which emphasized free enterprise and the belief that other societies should emulate the successful American political and economic model. In 1904 President Theodore Roosevelt had proclaimed that the goal of the United States was to ensure that its neighbors were orderly and that America should intervene as an international police power whenever a country, in his estimation, committed chronic wrongdoing. This view, adopted by later U.S. presidents, justified numerous military interventions to punish opponents and reward allies, especially in Latin

America. U.S. Marines remained in Nicaragua for decades (1909–1933), and El Salvador, Haiti, Mexico, and the Dominican Republic all experienced major U.S. military incursions between 1914 and 1940.

Economic Collapse

The major spur to change in the interwar years was the Great Depression. The crisis began in the United States in the fall of 1929, when prices on the New York Stock Exchange fell dramatically, ruining many investors. This crash ultimately precipitated a worldwide economic disaster unprecedented in intensity, longevity, and spread, affecting industrial and agricultural economies alike. The Depression lasted until 1941.

Global factors helped foster the Great Depression. The flow of wealth into the United States intensified existing imbalances in the world economy in trade and investment. Since the United States was generally self-sufficient, it was less dependent on world trade than Britain had been when it was the world's leading economic power. Unlike the British, who had typically invested profits abroad, Americans hoarded the wealth, mostly investing and spending at home to satisfy a self-indulgent society. The U.S. government also imposed stiff tariff barriers against European manufactured goods, hurting European economies. The nation had maintained protectionist policies since the U.S. Civil War, refusing to shift to an aggressive free trade position until well into the 1930s. Furthermore, the world banking and credit structure was very unstable, partly because, unlike Britain in the 1800s, the United States did not use its unmatched economic power to make sure the world economy worked efficiently. Yet U.S. banks, too anxious for profits, became overextended in loans to Britain, France, and Germany.

Conditions within the United States also played a role in generating the Great Depression. A "get-rich-quick" philosophy, common among both the public and the business community, led to reckless financial practices, such as risky loans and investments. Income was increasingly distributed unevenly: by 1929 the top 20 percent of American families earned 54 percent of the income while the bottom 40 percent earned 12.5 percent. As more wealth gravitated to fewer hands and more people fell into poverty, purchasing power declined while more consumer products became available, causing a glut. Many manufacturers could not sell enough products at home or abroad to stay in business or avoid layoffs. These problems led to the stock market crash, followed by bank failures. As U.S. banks faced ruin, they called in their debts from western European banks, triggering a chain reaction of bank failures in North America and Europe. In the United States the GNP fell by one-half in four years, industrial output fell by 50 percent, and unemployment rose from 3 to 25 percent of the labor force by 1932. All areas of the U.S. economy were hurt, and the misery was widespread.

The global consequences were also severe. Things were even worse in European nations than in the United States. Some 30 percent of Germans were out of work by 1932, and German industrial output declined by half. A French politician

WORLD'S HIGHEST STANDARD OF LIVING

There's no way like the American Way

Depression Breadline During the Depression, breadlines, such as this one in New York City, were common in the United States as millions of unemployed and desperate people sought food from social service providers, including religious groups. (Time Life Pictures/Getty Images)

summed up the disaster in his nation: "The oceans were deserted, the ships laid up in the silent ports, the factory smokestacks dead, long lines of workless in the towns, poverty throughout the countryside. Nations were economically cut off from one another, but they shared the common lot of poverty."[14] Societies in Asia, Africa, Latin America, and the Caribbean were devastated as demand for, and hence the price of, raw materials such as rubber, tin, and sugar plummeted. Only the USSR avoided major pain, since it was largely outside the world economy and hence insulated from the dislocations.

Depression and Liberal Reform in the United States

The Great Depression brought severe economic distress to the wealthiest industrialized nation, the United States. The trauma was so great that one influential legal scholar suggested that, henceforth, the terms B.C. and A.D. should refer to "Before Crash" and "After Depression." Homeowners and farmers saw banks foreclose on their property. Migrant workers moved around in a futile search for jobs. Hungry Americans flocked to breadlines and soup kitchens for food and milk supplied by charitable organizations. Vendors, who shared the city streets with panhandlers, hoped to make a few pennies selling apples or other needed items. Shantytowns sprang up on the edges of cities to house the unemployed and dispossessed.

Parts of the Midwest and Southwest became a **Dust Bowl**, as terrible drought and disappearing topsoil, caused by erosion and government neglect, put agriculture badly out of balance.

Dust Bowl Parts of the U.S. Midwest and Southwest during the 1930s where disappearing topsoil and severe drought threw agriculture badly out of balance.

Farm income dropped 50 percent between 1929 and 1933, causing 3 to 4 million people, mostly former farmers, to head to the West Coast, especially California, after selling or losing their land. A witness in 1932 told a congressional committee: "The roads of the West and Southwest teem with hungry hitchhikers. The campfires of the homeless are seen along every railroad track. I saw men, women, and children walking along the hard roads."[15] The experiences of these impoverished migrants, often known as "Okies" because so many came from Oklahoma, were chronicled in the novels of John Steinbeck (1902–1968), such as *The Grapes of Wrath*, and by the leftwing Oklahoma-born folksinger, Woody Guthrie (1912–1967), in songs such as "Pastures of Plenty": "I've worked in your orchards of peaches and prunes, Slept on the ground in the light of the moon, On the edge of your city you've seen us and then, We come with the dust and we go with the wind."[16]

Panic, despair, and disillusionment seized the country. A top official suggested that the U.S. currency should have pictures of lines of people at factory gates or standing in relief lines under dark skies, and of distraught farmers fearful of losing their lands. Unlike some western Europeans, Americans had no social security, unemployment insurance, or welfare system to turn to. In 1932 ragged World War I veterans marched in Washington, D.C., demanding payment of the bonuses once promised them. Congress rejected their demands and President Herbert Hoover ordered federal troops to disperse the unarmed protesters at gunpoint. The union movement grew rapidly, as did leftwing political parties such as the communists. Labor militancy and strikes led to confrontations between workers and the police, who supported the employers. Women in families evicted from their homes had to stay with their children in tent cities while their husbands looked for work. Jobless men lost status, and often turned to drink, as their wives asserted more influence in the family and found ways to prevent pregnancies. Meanwhile, the Depression intensified the poverty of African Americans, whose unemployment rate approached 70 percent.

The Depression caused a turnaround in U.S. government policy and economic theory, as well as a change of leadership. Discontent against government inaction drove the Republicans from office in 1933 and brought in a new president, Democrat Franklin Delano Roosevelt 1882–1945. Roosevelt expressed optimism, telling the nation that they had nothing to fear but fear itself, but they needed to act quickly. He introduced the **New Deal**, a new government policy of liberal reform within a democratic framework to alleviate the suffering caused by the Great Depression. Roosevelt proposed that the nation should guarantee what he called the "four freedoms"— freedom of speech and worship and freedom from want and fear. His reforms included regulations on banks and stock exchanges to prevent future depressions and public welfare programs, such as public works jobs and social security, that guaranteed retirement income for workers. For the first time in U.S. history, the federal government took responsibility for providing pensions and other supportive help to citizens. Roosevelt also legalized strikes and supported the organizing of workers to fight for better working conditions.

The direct involvement of the federal government in helping alleviate social and economic problems altered the United States. Although it did not end the Depression, the New Deal made government popular and modified the pain enough that radicalism began to wane. By defusing the appeal of socialism and communism, the New Deal reforms, many historians conclude, probably saved U.S. capitalism. In the later 1930s, when the recovery faltered, Roosevelt used the ideas of the British economist John Maynard Keynes (1883–1946), who advocated deficit spending by governments to spur economic growth, a policy known as Keynesian economics. However, it was the mobilization of military forces and manufacturing during World War II that finally ended the Depression.

Depression in Europe and Japan

By devastating the economies of Europe and Japan, the Depression shattered the illusion of stability and challenged the weaker, less entrenched democratic systems. In most European countries a quarter to a third of people were jobless. Germans often faced malnutrition, and hunger marches became common in Britain. A French observer described Paris as an "abyss of misery, suffering, and disorder, the theaters nearly empty, factories shut, businesses bankrupt; grey faces and bad news everywhere."[17] Countries developed public works programs to create jobs and also discouraged imports, further reducing international trade. Even Britain ended a century of free trade.

Some nations, among them Weimar Germany, lacked the resources of the United States for a New Deal type of reform. Germany, whose democracy was fragile, had an enormous debt, and to pay the World War I reparations it had been forced to borrow heavily, especially from the United States. The German government had no way to repay the loans.

A few nations discovered remedies to gradually relieve the distress. Although British heavy industry recovered only modestly, newer industries such as motor and aircraft production and electronics showed rapid growth, and increased consumer demand for these products gradually turned around the British economy. The Scandinavian nations of Denmark, Norway, and Sweden had the most success by pursuing what came to be known as "the Middle Way," a combination of undogmatic socialist economics with long-established democratic traditions based on community action. Social democratic parties, which favored a mix of free markets and a welfare state within a democratic political framework, had come to power in the Scandinavian nations in the 1920s, but the Depression gave them dominance. By increasing government intervention in the economy, the social democrats ensured full employment and protected people from hardship.

The Depression hit Japan even harder than Europe and the United States, making clear its near total dependence on foreign trade. As the world economy collapsed, many foreign markets closed and unemployment skyrocketed. Japan's foreign trade was cut in half in two years, forcing Japan's 100 million people to dramatically reduce consumption not only of luxuries but also of necessities, such as food and fuel. Unlike Britain, France, and the United States, Japan had no access to the resource-rich Western colonies in Southeast Asia. To resolve the nation's problems, Japanese leaders, becoming more authoritarian, turned to radical solutions, including expansion abroad and building a heavy arms industry at home.

Western Cultures, Thought, and Science

Tempered by the trauma of war and then by the Depression, Western culture went in new directions during the interwar years. One major trend was the rise of mass culture, popular entertainments attuned to the tastes of a wide segment of the population and disseminated by the new mass media of radio and motion pictures. During the 1920s radio stations appeared and the recording industry grew. By 1930, 40 percent of U.S. families owned a radio; by 1940, 86 percent did. The number of radios in Britain increased fivefold between 1926 and 1939.

The United States took the lead in developing and exporting this mass culture. In North America and Europe the urban white middle class found solace especially in popular music. American jazz musicians such as Louis Armstrong, Duke Ellington, and Billie Holiday had an international following. Songs written by New York City–based writers, known collectively as Tin Pan Alley, reached millions around the world through radios, records, movies, and musical theater. The romantic songs of American songwriters like Richard Rodgers

New Deal A new U.S. government program of liberal reform within a democratic framework introduced by President Franklin Roosevelt to alleviate suffering caused by the Great Depression.

and Lorenz Hart, George and Ira Gershwin, Irving Berlin, Jerome Kern, and Cole Porter buoyed the spirits of people in North America and Europe. Porter's song, "Anything Goes" (1934), chronicled changing fashions: "In olden days a bit of [women's] stocking, was looked on as something shocking. Now, heaven knows, anything goes." By contrast, other popular songs of the 1930s, such as "The Boulevard of Broken Dreams" and "Brother, Can You Spare a Dime?," addressed harsh reality.

Cultural vistas expanded in other ways. Painters, poets, and novelists settled in a few run-down Paris neighborhoods and produced work that brought them fame. The best painters, vigorously breaking from older traditions, enlarged the world's sensibility. The innovative and versatile Pablo Picasso (pi-KAH-so) (1881–1973), a Spaniard who settled in Paris, shifted his style in the early twentieth century as he helped invent **cubism**, a form of painting that rejected visual reality and emphasized instead geometric shapes and forms that often suggested movement. Critics accused the Cubists of promoting revolutionary politics and contempt for tradition. Soon Picasso, who later joined the Communist Party, abandoned representational art entirely and sought visual experience as transformed by the artist in his mind. At the same time, literature explored the inner world of thought and feelings. For example, the Irishman James Joyce (1882–1941), who had enjoyed no formal education but became close to many of the nation's leading thinkers and writers, broke traditional rules of grammar, and his books were often banned for using obscenity. In England Virginia Woolf (1882–1941) converted the novel from a narrative story into a pattern of internal monologues, a succession of images, thoughts, and emotions known as stream of consciousness. Her 1929 novel, *A Room of One's Own*, championed women's growing economic independence.

The social and natural sciences also developed during the first half of the twentieth century, allowing for a greater understanding of human behavior and the physical world. Sigmund Freud (FROID) (1856–1939), an Austrian Jewish physician, developed the field of psychoanalysis, a combination of medical science and psychology, and shocked the world by arguing that sex was of great subconscious importance in shaping people's behavior. In physics, Albert Einstein (1879–1955) radically modified the Newtonian vision of physical nature and rejected the absolutes of space and time. Time, he argued, depended on the relative motion of the measurer and the thing measured. Einstein had fled the anti-Jewish atmosphere of Nazi Germany for the United States, where he helped convince President Roosevelt to sponsor research on atomic weapons that eventually produced atomic bombs. Einstein spent the rest of his life seeking a unifying theory to explain every physical process in the universe. He failed, but some of the ideas he developed contributed to ongoing attempts by physicists to explain the universe.

SECTION SUMMARY

- After the war Germany experienced rapid inflation because of its postwar debt, Europe lost economic ground to the United States and Japan, and women entered the work force and the political sphere.

- Many Japanese benefited from postwar economic growth, though some rural Japanese had to move to cities or emigrate, while Japan played a larger role in world affairs and clashed with the United States over its treatment of Japanese immigrants and Japanese ambitions in Asia.

- American fear of communism led to the "Red Scare," a harsh crackdown on dissidents and union organizers, while the split widened between the poor, who suffered under government policies, and the affluent, who enjoyed the "Roarin' 20s."

- Among the factors contributing to the Great Depression were America hoarding its profits, American tariffs against European imports, risky investment practices (which helped cause the stock market crash of 1929), and uneven distribution of income.

- With millions of Americans jobless, homeless, and hungry, radical movements grew in power and President Franklin Delano Roosevelt instituted the New Deal, a sweeping series of programs that put people to work, provided pensions, and protected against future depressions.

- The Great Depression hit Europe and Japan even harder than the United States, rendering Germany unable to pay its heavy debts and causing Japan to become more authoritarian and expansionist, while Scandinavian nations emerged in better condition by combining socialism and democracy.

- The United States took the lead in developing the new mass media of radio and motion pictures, painters such as Picasso broke radically with earlier forms, and Freud and Einstein did pioneering work in psychoanalysis and physics.

◆ The Rise of Fascism and the Renewal of Conflict

What were the main ideas and impacts of fascism?

By devastating the economies of Germany and Japan, the Great Depression helped spread a new ideology in these countries. Although its form varied from country to country, this ideology, **fascism**, typically involved extreme nationalism, hatred of ethnic minorities, ruthless repression of opposition

---

cubism A form of painting that rejected visual reality and emphasized instead geometric shapes and forms that often suggested movement.

fascism An ideology that typically involved extreme nationalism, hatred of ethnic minorities, ruthless repression of opposition groups, violent anticommunism, and authoritarian government.

The Doctrine of Fascism

Benito Mussolini gradually developed an ideology for his movement that appealed to the Italian people's nationalistic emotions. The following excerpt comes from an essay under Mussolini's name that was published in an Italian encyclopedia in 1932. In fact, the true author was a Mussolini confidant, the philosopher Giovanni Gentile. The essay reflected Mussolini's vision of fascism as the wave of the future, in which the individual would subordinate her or his desires to the needs of the state.

Fascism, the more it considers and observes the future and the development of humanity quite apart from political considerations of the moment, believes neither in the possibility nor the utility of perpetual peace. It thus repudiates the doctrine of Pacifism—born of the renunciation of the struggle and an act of cowardice in the face of sacrifice. War alone brings up to its highest tension all human energy and puts the stamp of nobility upon the peoples who have the courage to meet it. . . . Fascism [is] the complete opposite of . . . Marxian Socialism, the materialist conception of history. . . . Above all Fascism denies that class-war can be the preponderant force in the transformation of society. . . .

After Socialism, Fascism combats the whole complex system of democratic ideology, and repudiates it, whether in its theoretical premises or in its practical application. Fascism denies that the majority, by the simple fact that it is a majority, can direct human society; it denies that numbers alone can govern by means of periodic consultation. . . . The democratic regime . . . [gives] the illusion of sovereignty, while the real effective sovereignty lies in the hands of other concealed and irresponsible forces. . . .

But the Fascist negation of Socialism, Democracy, and Liberalism must not be taken to mean that Fascism desires to lead the world back to the state of affairs before 1789 [the French Revolution]. . . . Given that the nineteenth century was

the century of Socialism, of Liberalism, and of Democracy, it does not . . . follow that the twentieth century must also be the century of Socialism, Liberalism, and Democracy: political doctrines pass, but humanity remains. . . .

The foundation of Fascism is the conception of the State, its character, its duty, and its aim. Fascism conceives of the State as an absolute, in comparison with which all individuals or groups are relative, only to be conceived of in their relation to the State. . . . The Fascist state is itself conscious, and has itself a will and a personality. . . . The Fascist state is an embodied will to power and government, the Roman tradition is here an ideal of force in action. . . . Government is not so much a thing to be expressed in territorial or military terms as in terms of morality and the spirit. It must be thought of as an Empire— . . . a nation which directly or indirectly rules other nations. . . . For Fascism the growth of Empire, . . . the expansion of the nation, is an essential manifestation of vitality, and its opposite a sign of decadence. . . . But Empire demands discipline, the co-ordination of all forces and a deeply felt sense of duty and sacrifice; this fact explains many aspects of the practical working of the regime, the character of many forces in the State, and the necessarily severe measures which must be taken against those who would oppose this spontaneous and inevitable movement of Italy in the twentieth century, and would oppose it by recalling the outworn ideology of the nineteenth century.

THINKING ABOUT THE READING

1. Why does fascism reject pacifism, socialism, and liberal democracy?

2. What role does the state play under fascism?

Source: B. Mussolini, "The Political and Social Doctrine of Fascism," *Political Quarterly*, IV (July–September, 1933), pp. 341–356. Copyright © 1993 by Blackwell Publishing. Reprinted with permission by Blackwell Publishing.

---

groups, violent anticommunism, and authoritarian government. Fascist movements also often included a party with a large membership, such as the Nazis (National Socialist German Workers), that was headed by a charismatic leader and that supported military expansion. Fascism was an assault on the liberal values and rational thinking of the Enlightenment. It came to power in Italy, Germany, and Japan and also influenced China and several eastern European and Latin American nations.

Roots of Fascism

First emerging in Italy in 1921 in the aftermath of World War I, fascism was a response to the inadequacies, corruption, and instability of democratic politics there, as well as to the economic

problems caused by World War I. Domestic unrest increased as Italy's peasants sought a more just society, workers demanded the right to form unions, and the economy slumped. Fascism arose from a pragmatic alliance of upper-class conservatives in the military, bureaucracy, and industry with discouraged members of the middle class who faced economic hardships. Both groups feared the possibility of Communist revolution. The middle class chiefly furnished the mass support for fascism. Benito Mussolini (MOO-suh-LEE-nee) (1883–1945), a blacksmith's son, one-time teacher and journalist, and former socialist and World War I veteran, founded the Italian fascist movement, which advocated national unity and strong government.

Mussolini and his movement soon forged a new Italy. A spellbinding orator, Mussolini had a talent for arousing mass enthusiasm by promising a vigorous and disciplined Italy. He especially attracted war veterans with his nationalistic rhetoric, accusing socialists of being unpatriotic and using an ancient Roman symbol, the *fasces*, a bundle of sticks wrapped around an ax handle and blade, to symbolize the unity and power he wanted to bring Italy. Landowners and industrialists funded his movement because it battered labor and peasant organizations. The upper classes viewed Mussolini as a bulwark against the radical workers. Mussolini also won the support of the Italian king, the Catholic Church, and the lower middle class, from which the fascists organized a uniform-wearing paramilitary group, the Blackshirts, who violently attacked and intimidated opponents, assaulting socialists and striking workers and murdering antifascist politicians. In 1922 the king asked Mussolini to form a government. By 1926 Mussolini had killed, arrested, or cowed his opponents, turned Italy into a one-party state with restricted civil liberties, and created a cult of personality around himself. He also began to formalize his concept of fascism (see Witness to the Past: The Doctrine of Fascism). Despite the brutality, many Italians believed Mussolini was restoring social order. Furthermore, they appreciated that the government was efficient; for example, the trains ran on time, a rare experience under democratic Italian regimes.

Nazi Germany

Fascism became dominant in Germany after the Depression undermined the moderate, democratic Weimar Republic. Since the country had lost its empire after World War I, Germany had no colonies to tap for resources and markets that might aid recovery. The liberal Weimar leaders could not solve the severe problems. Even before the Great Depression, some Germans had advocated wars of territorial expansion against other Europeans to help the economy. The German people, who had an authoritarian political tradition and an economy in shambles, also shared a widespread resentment of the penalties imposed after World War I, especially the reparation payments, which drained the treasury. Many Germans, preferring security to freedom, were willing to listen to a charismatic leader who offered simplistic answers to complex problems. As in Italy, the German upper and middle classes feared working-class socialism.

The Nazi Party, led by Adolph Hitler (1889–1945), offered a strategy for regaining political and economic strength and efficiency and for keeping workers under control. Hitler was an Austrian-born social misfit and frustrated artist of modest origins who had made a precarious living painting signs and doing other odd jobs before joining the German army in World War I. Already at this time Hitler nurtured a hatred of Jews, or extreme anti-Semitism, and labor unions. After the war he became involved in rightwing German politics and, in 1920, helped form the Nazi Party, which promised to halt the unpopular reparations payments imposed by the Treaty of Versailles.

Hitler and the Nazis capitalized on the Great Depression to increase their strength. With economic collapse, the industrial workers moved left toward the communists while the middle classes moved right toward the growing Nazi movement, financed by big industrialists. Germany was becoming a polarized society, with a shrinking political center. Many Germans were willing to believe, as Hitler claimed, that Germany's problems could be blamed on unpopular minorities, especially the Jews, and foreign powers. Hitler understood propaganda and how to use a few basic ideas, such as anti-Semitism, and he made up "facts" to gain support. In his book

Hitler's Motorcade In this photo from 1938, Adolph Hitler, standing stiffly in his car, salutes members of a paramilitary Nazi group, the Brownshirts, who parade before him at a Nazi rally in Nuremburg. (Time Life Pictures/Getty Images)

Mein Kampf (My Struggle), written in 1924, he argued that "all effective propaganda has to limit itself to a very few points and to use them like slogans. A political leader must not fear to speak a lie if this might be effective."[18] Hitler developed a catchy slogan: "one people, one government, one leader."

The Nazis won the largest number of seats in the 1932 elections, garnering nearly 14 million votes, and, with support from non-Nazi conservatives, Hitler became Chancellor (the equivalent of prime minister) in January, 1933. Even though the Nazis won only 44 percent of the vote in the 1933 elections, Hitler tightened his grip on power and moved immediately to impose dramatic changes. His goals included a thorough purging of the educational system, theater, cinema, literature, and press so that his government could use them for its own purposes. The Nazis outlawed leftist parties, suspended civil liberties, imposed ideological conformity and heavy censorship, mobilized youth, told women to stay at home and take care of their husbands and children, and expanded the army. They also regeared the economy toward rearmament, thus solving the terrible unemployment problem. Massive government work-creation schemes eradicated unemployment by 1936. By 1939 Germany's GNP was 50 percent higher than it had been in 1929, mainly because of the manufacture of heavy machinery and armaments.

Beginning in 1933 Hitler introduced laws to reshape Germany. The Nazi myth about maintaining a pure German people—what Hitler termed the Aryan race, after the ancient Indo-Europeans who settled Europe, Persia, and India—led to anti-Semitic laws between 1933 and 1938. Hitler banned marriage and sexual relations between Jews and so-called Aryan Germans. He also excluded the half million Jews, many of them assimilated into German culture, from the civil service and varied occupations, pushing them back into the Jewish ghettos of German cities, where they could be watched. New laws also deprived the Jews of citizenship. The Nazis also enacted harsh laws against homosexuals and the Romany, or Gypsies, another unpopular, vulnerable minority.

Japanese Militarism and Expansion

During the 1930s Japan and Germany came to resemble each other fairly closely, even if their forms of fascism were very different. Although Japan never developed a mass-based Fascist Party like the Nazis, Japanese politics turned increasingly nationalistic and imperialistic. Japanese leaders often blamed foreign nations, especially the United States and the USSR, for Japan's problems. As in Nazi Germany, big business supported military expansion to gain resources and markets for exploitation. Groups of military officers assassinated liberal politicians and also fomented violence in the Chinese province of Manchuria to increase Japanese influence there. Manchuria, controlled only loosely by the Chinese government, was rich in natural resources, especially minerals such as coal and iron, and had open land on which to settle Japanese not needed at home.

Soon Japan turned more aggressive and authoritarian. In 1931 it invaded and gained control of Manchuria. The League of Nations imposed no stiff penalties on Japan, a failure that helped to discredit that organization. The Japanese military, in alliance with big business and bureaucratic interests, now played a key role in the Japanese government. By 1936 the military controlled Japan and, as in Nazi Germany, imposed a fascist government that promoted labor control, censorship, the glorification of war, police repression, and hatred of foreign powers (the West). The schools and media indoctrinated the population in obedience, patriarchy, and the sacred origins of the Japanese people while attacking Western values such as individualism and democracy. In 1937 a military skirmish outside Beijing provided an excuse for Japan to launch a full-scale invasion of China, which prompted the United States to impose an oil embargo on Japan. By 1938 Japan controlled most of eastern China. When Japan signed a pact with Germany and Italy in 1940, the United States and Britain introduced stronger economic sanctions, including an oil embargo. Japan now faced economic collapse or war.

The Road to War

During the later 1930s the European nations moved toward war, and various alliances formed. The United States, Britain, and France, known as the Allies, led a group of western European democracies that wanted to preserve the European state structure, the global economy, and the Western colonial system in Asia and Africa. The fascist countries, led by Germany, Italy, and Japan, known as the Axis Powers, sought to change the political map of Europe and Asia and gain dominance in the world economy. The prelude to another world war was also marked, as it had been for World War I, by diplomatic problems caused in part by a massive arms buildup all over Europe.

The big problem for the Allies was dealing with the imperialism of the Axis nations. Hitler pursued an aggressive foreign policy to dominate eastern Europe, arguing that Germany needed living space and colonies in order to prosper again. By doing this, Hitler sought to unite the several million ethnic Germans living in eastern and southeastern Europe, the legacy of centuries of migration and shifting state boundaries. In 1936 Hitler's troops occupied the Rhineland, German territory west of the Rhine River demilitarized after World War I. Demonstrating how fascism had made Italy a strong power, in 1935 Italy invaded and brutally conquered the last independent African kingdom, Ethiopia. The League of Nations voted ineffective sanctions against Italy. Hitler and Mussolini forged a close alliance in 1936, but the later Tripartite Pact of 1940, linking Germany and Italy with Japan for mutual defense, was a marriage of necessity, strained and wary. The Japanese did not view their interests as identical with those of the European fascists and pursued the pact partly to warn the United States that opposing Japanese aggression in Asia also meant facing the Germans and Italians.

Civil war in Spain heightened European tensions by drawing in foreign intervention and pitting competing ideologies against each other. Liberals and conservatives had struggled for two centuries to shape Spanish politics, and by the 1930s Spain was polarized between left and right. During the 1936 elections, Spain's Republicans, a leftwing coalition of liberals, socialists, and communists promising reforms, edged out the National Front of conservatives, monarchists, and staunch Catholics. British observer George Orwell wrote of the Republicans that they felt they had "suddenly emerged into an era of equality and freedom, not as cogs in the capitalist machine."[19] Alarmed, the right rallied around the fascist military forces led by General Francisco Franco (1892–1975), launching the Spanish Civil War (1936–1939). The Loyalist government forces, aided by the USSR, ultimately lost to Franco's fascists at a huge cost in lives on both sides. The war had an international flavor. Germany and Italy helped the Spanish fascists with weapons and advice, and several thousand volunteers from North America and varied European nations fought for the Loyalist cause. But the governments of the Western Allies refused to support the Loyalists, whom they viewed as too radical. The German bombing of Guernica (GWAR-ni-kuh), a village in northern Spain inhabited largely by Basque people, caused an international outcry and prompted Pablo Picasso to paint a celebrated testament to the atrocity. Spain endured Franco's fascist dictatorship until 1975.

In the late 1930s the Allies led by Britain followed a policy of appeasement toward fascist aggression. They were not yet prepared for war, and the catastrophe of World War I, in which several million young British and French men had died, had hung over the succeeding decades. Many in the Allied nations saw another war as too terrible to contemplate, even, as one British leader believed, the end of civilization. Some historians have considered the appeasement policy and the concessions it made realistic, the best of the available options, especially since public opinion in most countries opposed war,

while others view it as a shameful betrayal that only whetted fascist appetites and postponed the inevitable conflict.

War became inevitable. In 1938 Hitler turned his attention to eastern Europe. He succeeded through threats in merging Austria, a German-speaking nation with many pro-Nazi citizens, into Germany and then stimulated riots by German minorities in western Czechoslovakia and launched a claim to the territory. Czechoslovakia was handed over and occupied by German troops. As the war clouds approached, Hitler declared: "We shall not capitulate—no never! We may be destroyed, but if we are, we shall drag a world with us—a world in flames."[20] In August, 1939 Hitler and Stalin signed the Nazi-Soviet Pact, a nonaggression agreement. In September, with the Soviet threat temporarily removed, Hitler launched an invasion of Poland, forcing France and Britain to declare war against Germany (see Chronology: World War II, 1939–1945).

SECTION SUMMARY

- The Italian fascists, led by Benito Mussolini, appealed to those upset by instability, corruption, and economic problems and viciously fought communists and any others who opposed them.

- A new ideology, fascism, that developed out of economic collapse, stressed extreme nationalism, an authoritarian state, and hatred of minorities and leftists.

- Suffering from the Depression, resentful of post–World War I reparations, and fearful of socialism, many Germans supported Adolph Hitler's Nazi Party, which blamed problems on minorities such as the Jews and revived the economy through a military buildup.

- Japan became increasingly nationalistic and imperialistic, blamed its problems on foreigners, took over most of eastern China, and signed a pact with Germany and Italy.

- Tensions rose as Italy invaded Ethiopia, Fascists took over Spain, and Germany took over Austria and Czechoslovakia; France and Britain declared war after Germany signed a nonaggression pact with the Soviet Union and invaded Poland.

CHRONOLOGY

World War II, 1939–1945

1939	Beginning of war in Europe
June 1941	German invasion of Soviet Union
December 1941	Japanese bombing of Pearl Harbor; invasion of Southeast Asia
1942	Battle of Midway
1944	Allied landing at Normandy
July 1944	Bretton Woods Conference
February 1945	Yalta Conference
April 1945	Allied invasion of Germany
August 1945	U.S. bombing of Hiroshima and Nagasaki

 World War II: A Global Transition

What were the costs and consequences of World War II?

Historians have sometimes viewed the years from 1914 to 1945 as one continuum, with World War II a continuation and amplification of World War I. Both wars shared some of the same causes, including nationalist rivalries, threats to the European balance of power, and a struggle to control the global economic system. But there were differences, too. For one, World War II also involved a three-way ideological contest

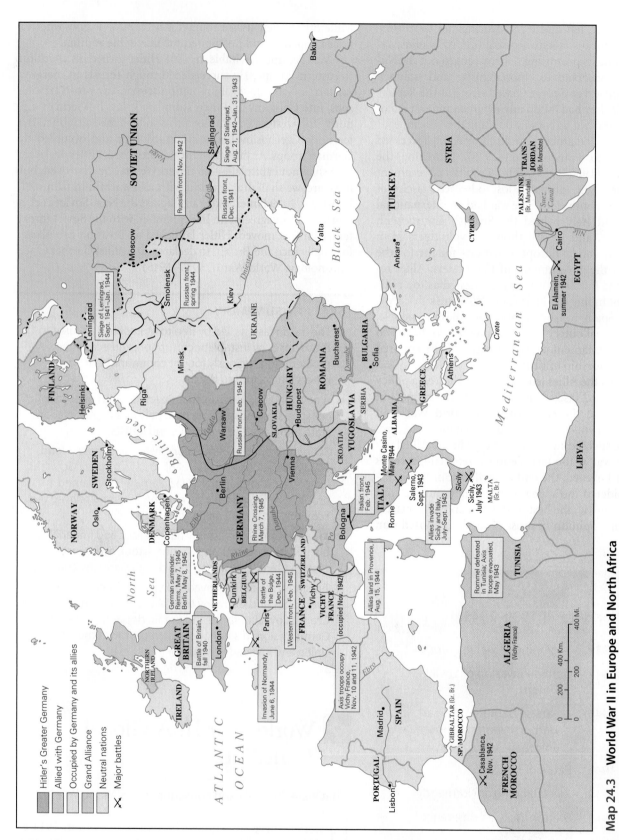

Map 24.3 World War II in Europe and North Africa
The Axis Powers, led by Germany and Italy, initially occupied much of Europe, and in 1941 they invaded the Soviet Union, but they were unable to hold their gains against the counteroffensive of the United States, Britain, the Soviet Union, and the Free French forces.

between democracy, fascism, and communism. For another, the trench warfare and modest aerial bombing of World War I was superseded by the far more widespread aerial bombing and mobile armies used in World War II, with civilians now fair game.

World War II began as a European conflict, and for the first two years, major battles were confined largely to Europe, the North Atlantic, and North Africa. The firestorm soon became global, however, creating almost a separate war fought in East and Southeast Asia and the western Pacific. The conflict became the most costly war in world history, bringing staggering misery and ultimately killing some 50 million people. The war resulted in some of history's worst genocides and the use of the deadliest weapons ever known. It marked a major transition that reshaped world politics and international relations.

Cataclysmic War and Holocaust

In September 1939, Europe plunged into armed struggle, and in the next year Germany and its allies overran nearly all of Europe except for valiant Britain and neutral Switzerland and Sweden (see Map 24.3). Germany imposed puppet regimes in the conquered territories, including the Vichy (VISH-ee) government in France headed by World War I hero, General Philippe Pétain, described in the chapter-opening vignette. The purpose of German occupation of all the conquered countries was economic exploitation: the occupied countries had to send raw materials and food to Germany. Millions of civilians were enslaved to work on German farms and in factories.

But Germany failed to achieve all of its strategic objectives. An heroic British resistance deserved some of the credit. Britain withstood a blitz of aerial bombing in 1940, prompting Prime Minister Winston Churchill (1874–1965) to boast that it was Britain's finest hour. German submarines tried but failed to sever Britain's maritime link with North America. Italian efforts to carve out a Mediterranean empire faltered, as Greece pushed the Italians back and the British seized parts of Italian North Africa and destroyed Italy's naval forces. Italian failures compelled the Germans to divert military resources in order to confront British power in North Africa and Greece. Also frustrating Nazi goals, underground movements emerged all over Europe to fight the Nazis. One of the major resistance heroes was the Swedish diplomat Raoul Wallenberg (1912–1947?), stationed in occupied Hungary, who risked death to save some 100,000 Jews by giving them Swedish passports and smuggling many out to safety.

In June 1941 the conflict expanded eastward. Germany broke its nonaggression pact and invaded Russia, driving deeply into the country. Top German officers opposed the invasion, but Hitler wanted the rich resources and open lands of Ukraine and western Russia for German colonization. Hitler believed himself to be a military genius, smarter than his generals, and took control of all military operations, which proved a mistake, since he made many strategic blunders. Hitler also had an obsessive fear of communism, which he believed to

have been a Jewish plot. This invasion relieved pressure on Britain, since two-thirds of the German army was now committed to the eastern front.

After misjudging German intentions and reeling from the invasion, the Soviet leader, Joseph Stalin, joined the anti-Axis alliance and received aid from the United States and Britain that helped the USSR resist. It was an alliance of convenience, since the Western leaders and Stalin mistrusted each other. Indeed, Western leaders still despised the Soviet system and expected Russia to remain a long-term threat to their interests. By winter 1941, German forces had reached the outskirts of Moscow and encircled another major city, Stalingrad. But although Germany had superior military forces, it ultimately failed to capture the major Russian cities because the Red Army began an effective counterattack. Soon the German high command realized the folly of the invasion, one officer writing that they had badly underestimated the Russian colossus. The turning point came in February 1943, as the Soviet Red Army stopped the Germans at Stalingrad (today Volgograd). By the summer German forces, like the French army of Napoleon Bonaparte a century and a half earlier, began a long, humiliating retreat from Russia.

German racist nationalism led to horrific campaigns of extermination against unpopular minorities and conquered peoples. Hitler ordered what he called the "final solution" of the "Jewish Question." The term **Holocaust** came to be used for the Nazis' deliberate murder of Jews and Romany (Gypsies), one of the worst genocides, or deliberate mass killings of a target group, in history. Ultimately some three-quarters of Europe's Jews were killed in the Holocaust. During 1942 the Germans had erected death camps, such as Bergen-Belsen (BUR-guhn-BEL-suhn) in western Germany and Auschwitz (OUSH-vits) in western Poland, targeting especially the large Jewish populations of Germany, Poland, and Ukraine. For instance, some 200,000 Jews living in the Polish city of Lvov, a third of the city's population, were murdered. But Jews everywhere in Nazi-occupied Europe—Vichy France, the Netherlands, Hungary, Russia—were rounded up and put in death camps, where they were killed in gas chambers, starved, or worked to death. In addition to the 6 million Jews and half a million Romany (Gypsies) murdered in the Holocaust, the Nazis were responsible for the deaths of 11 million Slavs (including over 3 million Poles) and a half million other Europeans, including German communists, socialists, anti-Nazi Christians, homosexuals, and children deemed physically or mentally unfit to serve the German nation. The Germans also deliberately killed many prisoners of war through starvation or overwork.

Historians differ in their thinking about how complicit the German people were in the Nazi government's genocide. Some historians blame the grip of a terrorist dictatorship that suppressed information. The Nazis did not publicize the gas chambers, and Nazi police chief Heinrich Himmler (HIM-luhr) told

Holocaust The Nazis' deliberate murder of Jews and Romany (Gypsies), one of the worst genocides in world history.

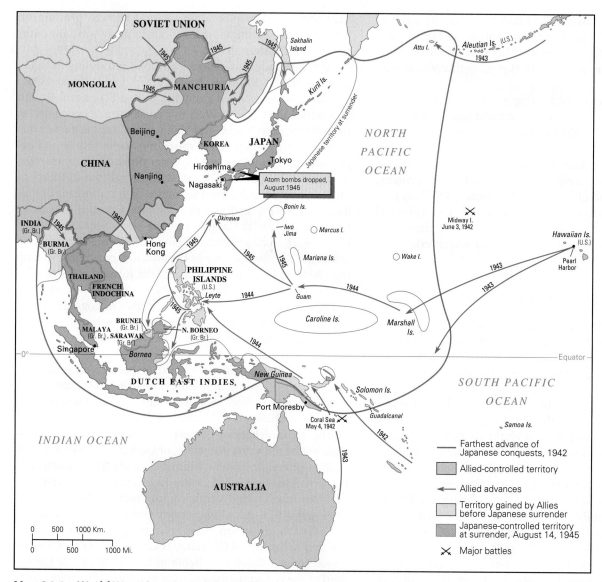

Map 24.4 World War II in Asia and the Pacific

After invading China in 1937, Japan disabled the U.S. fleet at Pearl Harbor in 1941 and in 1941–1942 occupied most of Southeast Asia and the western Pacific. The United States and its allies pushed back the Japanese forces from their bases in the Pacific and bombed Japan from those bases, but Japan did not surrender until 1945, when the United States dropped atomic bombs on Hiroshima and Nagasaki.

Online Study Center **Improve Your Grade** Interactive Map: World War II in the Pacific

the murderous special force, the SS, that "among ourselves, we can speak openly about it [the Holocaust], though we can never speak of it in public. That is a page of glory in our history that never can be written."[21] Other historians, however, spread responsibility to the German people, many of whom broadly shared Hitler's anti-Semitic views. Only a few brave Germans dared to resist or subvert Nazi policies and actions. Those who did, such as the Lutheran theologian Dietrich Bonhoeffer (BON-ho-fuhr) (1906–1945), a strong critic of Nazism and anti-Semitism who supported the underground German resistance, faced retribution. The Nazis sent Bonhoeffer to a concentration camp in 1943 and hanged him in 1945.

Globalization of the War

Conflict between Japan and the United States eventually globalized the war (see Map 24.4). On December 7, 1941, what President Franklin D. Roosevelt called "a date which will live in infamy," Japanese navy ships and planes attacked the U.S. naval base at Pearl Harbor, Hawaii, destroying a considerable portion of the U.S. Pacific fleet, killing 2,400 Americans, and ending U.S. neutrality. Japanese leaders had a plan for a new economic order in the East led by Japan, and they knew that to achieve this goal they had to eliminate not only the Western colonial powers but also the threat from the United States, a country they had quarreled with for some years. At the same time they were attacking Pearl Harbor, Japanese military forces launched an invasion of Southeast Asia. Within several months they controlled most of the region, having forced the United States out of the Philippines and jailed the British and Dutch residents of their respective colonies. For its industrial economy, Japan badly needed the resources of Southeast Asia, especially the oil and rubber of the Dutch East Indies (Indonesia). The Japanese already controlled eastern China after their invasion of 1937. Preoccupied with war in Europe, the Western powers were unable to resist the Japanese advance.

Japanese leaders disagreed about challenging U.S. power in the Pacific. Some top military officers argued against the Pearl Harbor attack, knowing that the superior U.S. military and economic power could defeat Japan if Americans geared up to do so. But other leaders, impressed by Hitler's quick victories in Europe, thought that they could duplicate that success in the Pacific. A strike at Pearl Harbor might immobilize or destroy the U.S. fleet and allow time for Japan to consolidate control of Asia and the Pacific. If Germany kept the United States focused on Europe, they thought Roosevelt might sue for peace with Japan rather than fight a costly war in Asia. Top Japanese leaders also assumed that Americans, addicted to creature comforts, lacked the will to mobilize. But the surprise Pearl Harbor attack proved a strategic disaster for Japan, since it united Americans in support for war. Admiral Isoruku Yamamoto (EE-so-ROO-koo YAH-muh-MO-toe), the former university student in the United States and brilliant strategist who planned the attack, somberly told colleagues: "I fear all we have done is to awaken a sleeping giant and fill him with a terrible resolve."[22]

The Pearl Harbor attack outraged Americans once reluctant to go to war. Roosevelt had been looking for ways to turn U.S. public opinion toward war against the Axis Powers and end his nation's isolationism, and Pearl Harbor served that purpose well. Historians remain divided about how much U.S. officials, including Roosevelt, knew about the forthcoming attack and whether they let it happen to shock the U.S. public into supporting the war. While U.S. officials anticipated a military conflict with Japan, they may not have expected an assault on Hawaii, where Japanese Americans constituted over half of the population. Whatever the case, the United States quickly mobilized and regeared the economy for war. A patriotic wave swept the country as America entered the war on both fronts, with early efforts aimed at defeating the Nazis in Europe.

The war affected American society, especially women and ethnic minorities, in various ways. Fifteen million Americans moved, often to find work. Six million women joined the work force, replacing the men going off to fight. Although husbands, business organizations, and union leaders often objected to the trend, by 1943 the government encouraged women as their "patriotic duty" to take up jobs once considered unladylike, such as on factory assembly lines. A popular song celebrated "Rosie the Riveter" who was "making history working for victory." The song could have described Sybil Lewis, an African American from Oklahoma, who originally moved to Los Angeles to work as a waitress, became instead a riveter making airplane gas tanks for Lockheed Aircraft, and then worked as a shipyard welder. Anxious for workers, companies often ignored racism to hire African Americans like Sybil Lewis, thus posing a challenge to prevailing racial attitudes. Some 5 million blacks left southern rural areas in the 1930s and 1940s and often found jobs in northern and western cities. When the war ended in 1945, over 19 million American women, like Sybil Lewis, had full-time paid jobs, and the black population of many American cities had doubled. After defeating fascism abroad, more white Americans were sympathetic to the demands of black organizations that they now wanted democracy in the United States, especially in the segregated South.

But racism aimed at 110,000 Japanese Americans fueled one of the greatest invasions of civil liberties in U.S. history. Many of these Americans were U.S.-born or naturalized citizens living in western states. Suspecting that some of these Japanese Americans might have been spies or supported the Japanese war effort, though they produced little evidence to support these charges, the U.S. government rounded them up, seized their property, and sent them to sparse internment camps in remote areas of the western and southern states, such as Manzanar in the harsh California desert, for the duration of the conflict. Their property was never returned. With a few exceptions, German and Italian-Americans faced no similar harassment or imprisonment. Most of them, like Japanese Americans, opposed fascism. Many Japanese Americans, especially from Hawaii, joined U.S. military units to fight in Europe.

The End of the War in Europe

The U.S. entry in the war on the Allied side changed the shape of the conflict. The Axis forces had been triumphant through 1942, as Germany dominated much of Europe and North Africa, and Japan controlled most of Asia east of India and large areas of the western Pacific. Only in the Balkans and France did armed resistance cause the Germans much trouble. In 1943, however, the tide began to turn. The Germans were defeated in North Africa, and Allied landings in Italy knocked that country out of the war. In June 1944, British and American forces landed on five beaches at Normandy, on the Atlantic coast of France. But German defenses did not collapse, forcing the Allies to fight every step of the way, suffering huge casualties. Finally the Allies, including the anti-Vichy Free French forces under General Charles DeGaulle (duh GAWL) (1890–1970), began pushing the Germans back in France.

The Axis forces were now on the defensive in Europe, but Germany was defeated only by massive Allied ground offensives and aerial bombardment, which stopped German armed forces and demoralized the civilian German population. The British firebombed several German cities; for example, 30,000 civilians were killed in a firestorm in Hamburg. The Soviet Red Army pushed the Germans back in the east, while U.S. and British forces retook Italy, France, and other Nazi-occupied countries. By December 1944, Allied forces had pushed the battered German army back to Germany. The Allies gained command of the skies when Germany could not obtain enough oil for its air force. Through the winter the German war economy collapsed. As the losses mounted, Hitler lost touch with reality, giving orders to nonexistent army divisions. In spring 1945, as British and U.S. armies moved into Germany from the west and the Soviet Red Army from the east, Hitler and his mistress, Eva Braun, went through a marriage ceremony and then committed suicide in their underground bunker in Berlin. Germany surrendered. Soon newsreels of the liberation of the concentration camps revealed to the whole world the full extent of Nazi atrocities.

A major reason for the Nazi defeat was Hitler's racist and imperialistic policies. Hitler believed that Germans were racially superior to all other peoples, including the conquered Slavic peoples of eastern Europe. The occupied eastern areas were brutally exploited to feed and supply Germany. Had the Germans patronized the east Europeans and Russians, they might have won their support, since the old governments in these countries were often unpopular. Indeed, some Ukrainians, Russians, Lithuanians, and Latvians worked with the Nazis because they hated the communists more. Among their own people, however, they came to be hated as collaborators with the German occupiers.

The End of the War in Asia

The Japanese defeat was more dramatic than that of the Nazis in Europe. In June 1942, the United States stopped the Japanese Pacific advance at the battle of Midway Island, west of Hawaii, and began an offensive to isolate the Japanese bases in the Pacific. By mid-1944 it had pushed the Japanese out of most of the western Pacific islands, from which it launched bombing raids on Japan. By early 1945 U.S. forces, aided by the Australians and British, started to retake Southeast Asia and China from Japanese forces. The invasion of the small Japanese island of Okinawa (oh-kee-NAH-wah), in the Ryukyus just south of Japan, cost the lives of 10,000 American troops and 80,000 Japanese civilians, suggesting to U.S. officials what an invasion of the main Japanese islands might entail. Devastating as the war had been for both sides, however, U.S. and Japanese leaders could not agree on negotiations for peace. Japan resisted American demands for total surrender.

In August 1945, the United States forced the issue, forever changing the potential of warfare by dropping an atomic bomb on the Japanese city of Hiroshima. The bomb demolished most of the city and killed 80,000 people; thousands more were maimed or died later from injuries or radiation. The Japanese cabinet was divided on surrender, debating whether the United States had more than one bomb. Three days later, an American plane dropped a second bomb on Nagasaki, killing another 60,000 Japanese civilians. The Japanese emperor, Hirohito (HEAR-oh-HEE-toe) (1901–1989), opted for surrender on August 15. He went on the radio to ask his people to "suffer the insufferable, endure the unendurable," and cooperate with the U.S. occupation. For the first time in its long history, Japan had been defeated and successfully invaded. Disgraced, more than five hundred military officers committed suicide. One vice admiral wrote a farewell poem in his own blood as he lay dying: "Refreshed and clear, the moon now

shines, After the fearful storm." But a long imprisoned Japanese leftist celebrated the defeat: "Ah, such happiness, At somehow living long enough, To see this rare day, When the fighting has ceased."[23] World War II had come to an end.

Historians differ on whether it was necessary militarily to drop the atomic bombs on Japan, causing so many civilian deaths. Many contend that the Japanese would have fiercely resisted an American invasion and hence the bombs ultimately saved many American and Japanese lives. Others argue that Japan was near surrender but U.S. leaders misread their intentions. Some scholars conclude that the United States rushed to defeat Japan because the Soviet Union, anxious to expand its power in East Asia, was going to join the struggle against Japan and would demand territory or a role in the postwar occupation of Japan. Indeed, Soviet troops had moved into Manchuria as Japanese resistance collapsed. In this view, the bomb was a warning to the Soviet Union about U.S. capabilities, intended to dissuade Stalin from any expansionist ideas. Some who defend the Hiroshima bombing, however, also doubt that the Nagasaki bombing was justified. The debates may never be resolved.

Japan lost the war primarily because it overstretched its forces and failed to convert Southeast Asian resources into military and industrial products fast enough to defeat the larger, wealthier United States. In addition, like the Germans, Japan imposed increasingly authoritarian, brutal policies on its subject peoples. For example, Japanese troops, upon capturing China's capital in 1937, killed thousands of Chinese and looted the city in an orgy of destruction that became known as "the Rape of Nanjing." As a result of such acts, in most cases the Japan military alienated the Chinese and Southeast Asians, seldom gaining their cooperation. After a while, most Southeast Asians looked on the Japanese as perhaps even worse than the Western colonizers they had replaced.

The Costs and Consequences of Global War

World War II had heavy costs and large-scale consequences. It took a terrible toll in lives: approximately 15 million military and 35 million civilian deaths. Soviet Russia, which lost over 20 million people, or 10 percent of its population, now had one more bitter memory in a long history of threats and, as with Napoleonic France and Kaiser Wilhelm's Germany, invasions by countries to the west. Poland and Yugoslavia both lost over 10 percent of their people. Britain lost 375,000 people and France 600,000 respectively. Strategic bombing blasted parts of every major German city to rubble. In Asia, over 2 million Japanese military personnel and probably a million Japanese civilians died, and 7 million Chinese were killed or wounded. Fighting on both fronts, some 300,000 American military personnel died. The European and Asian countries involved were economically devastated.

The war cleared the way for new global economic arrangements. In 1944 U.S. president Roosevelt summoned representatives of forty-four countries to a conference held in Bretton

Bombing of Nagasaki
This photo shows the awesome power of the atomic bomb dropped by the United States on the Japanese city of Nagasaki in August, 1945, three days after the atomic bombing of Hiroshima. Some 60,000 Japanese died in the Nagasaki bombing. (Courtesy of the Trustees of the Imperial War Museum)

years, while Germany was temporarily divided into sectors controlled by Russia, Britain, France, and the United States. But the Allies gave the defeated nations massive aid and guidance to speed economic recovery. The war also fostered political changes in Asia. Chinese, Korean, and Vietnamese communists took advantage of Japanese occupation to gain support for their movements, and Western colonial rule was undermined throughout Southeast Asia, the Japanese having displaced the West in power. Furthermore, Indian nationalists who had been jailed because they opposed the British use of Indian troops in the war were even more embittered against British rule (see Chapter 25).

Allied leaders also developed new political institutions and links for the postwar world. In February 1945, Roosevelt, Churchill, and Stalin met at a conference at Yalta (YAWL-tuh), in Russia's Crimean peninsula, to determine the postwar political order. The conference agreed to set up a world organization, the United Nations, and proposed goals, an institutional structure, and a voting system for the new organization. The Yalta Conference also divided Europe into anti-communist and communist spheres of interest. Western leaders, drained by war and seeking postwar stability in Europe, reluctantly agreed to Stalin's demand that the Soviet Union be allowed to dominate eastern Europe by stationing troops there and influencing its governments.

The aftermath of war also fostered a new rivalry between the two emerging superpowers, the United States and the USSR, that complicated the new global political order. The United States, which had not fought on its own soil, emerged from the war not only much less devastated than any other major combatant but also politically and economically stronger, becoming the dominant world power. As a result, the United States took the lead in protecting a global system in which it held the strongest cards. But the USSR emerged from the war as a military power with imperial ambitions. U.S.

Woods, New Hampshire, to establish the postwar world economic order, including a system of international monetary cooperation to prevent the financial crises that caused the Great Depression. The Bretton Woods Conference set up the International Monetary Fund and the World Bank, both dominated by the United States, to provide credit to states requiring financial investment for major economic projects. Bretton Woods also fixed currency exchange rates and encouraged trade liberalization, both policies that benefited the United States most.

World War II also transformed world politics. It removed the twin threats of German Nazism and Japanese militarism. In contrast to World War I, the victorious Allies were more generous toward the vanquished. Germany, Italy, and Japan lost their colonies and were required to adopt democratic forms of government. U.S. forces occupied Japan for several

leaders realized their nation would have to help reconstruct Europe and Japan to restore political stability and thwart Soviet ambitions there.

The political history of the world between 1945 and 1989 revolved around the conflict between these two competing superpowers, which had very different governments and economies. Rapidly rebuilding after the war, the USSR replaced Germany as the dominant power in eastern Europe and installed communist governments, including one in the eastern part of Germany under Soviet occupation. Indeed, World War II increased the appeal of communism worldwide and led to the establishment of communist regimes in Yugoslavia and North Korea. Both Soviet and U.S. leaders tended to look at the world through the lens of their World War II experience. For the USSR that meant paranoia about any threat from the West and the need for military power. Americans tended to find a repeat of Hitler's aggression anywhere in the world they experienced a political threat, such as a nationalist or communist-inspired revolution in Asia or Latin America; and they often sought to assert their power to reshape the world. The U.S.-Soviet rivalry created a world very different from that existing before World War II.

SECTION SUMMARY

- Germany rapidly took over most of Europe and used it as a source of raw materials, but the British withstood extended bombing and Germany wasted valuable resources on an ultimately unsuccessful invasion of the Soviet Union.

- Nazi Germany deliberately killed 6 million Jews and a half million Gypsies in death camps, along with millions of others; historians are divided on how much the German people knew about the death camps and how responsible they were for them.

- After Japan attacked Pearl Harbor, the United States entered the war in both Asia and Europe, and many women and blacks found work in professions that had until then been closed to them, while Japanese Americans were put in internment camps.

- After the United States entered the war, the Allies slowly began to win the war in Europe, and in the spring of 1945, with U.S. forces advancing from the west and the Soviets from the east, Hitler committed suicide and Germany surrendered.

- After Japan refused to agree to a total surrender despite serious setbacks, the United States dropped atomic bombs on Hiroshima and Nagasaki, killing, injuring, and sickening scores of thousands; historians still debate whether these bombs were necessary.

- World War II killed 50 million military personnel and civilians, but in its aftermath, Germany, Italy, and Japan were aided rather than punished, and the United States and Soviet Union emerged as the world's dominant powers.

Online Study Center **ACE the Test**

 # Chapter Summary

The years between 1914 and 1929 in the industrialized Western nations were dominated by war and its aftermath. Growing tensions between European powers led to World War I, in which industrial technology produced new weapons that killed millions of civilians and soldiers alike. The terrible losses fostered widespread disillusionment and brought major political changes to Europe and the wider world. New nations were carved out of the German, Russian, Austro-Hungarian, and Russian Empires, while the United States emerged as a major world power. During the war the communist Bolsheviks seized power in Russia and created the Soviet Union. Lenin forged a one-party state, and his successor, Stalin, imposed a brutal dictatorship under which he collectivized the economy, used Five-Year Plans to encourage industrialization, and modernized the society.

During the 1920s much of Europe, the United States, and Japan experienced liberal democracy and middle-class prosperity. However, Europe changed dramatically in the 1930s. The Great Depression brought economic collapse, a sharp decline in world trade, and millions of unemployed workers. A few wealthy nations, especially the United States, pursued recovery through liberal reform and government spending, sustaining democracy despite the economic hardship. But for Germany, Italy, and Japan, economic disaster fostered fascism, an ideology that favored an authoritarian state, extreme nationalism, and repression of minorities. The increasing aggression of the fascist nations, in search of lands to exploit for their resources and markets, led to World War II. During the war, Nazi brutality led to genocide against the Jews and other minorities. Germany initially dominated eastern Europe and occupied much of western Europe, while Japan invaded China and Southeast Asia. With the entry of the United States into the war, however, the Allies eventually won. The war cost 50 million lives and devastated Europe and much of Asia. The United States emerged as the world's major superpower, with the Soviet Union as its major rival.

Online Study Center **Improve Your Grade** Flashcards

Key Terms

Bolsheviks	gulags	cubism
soviets	socialist realism	fascism
Marxism-Leninism	Great Depression	Holocaust
New Economic Policy	Dust Bowl	
Stalinism	New Deal	

Suggested Reading

Brendon, Piers. *The Dark Valley: A Panorama of the 1930s.* New York: Alfred A. Knopf, 2000. A readable account of this decade in both Europe and North America.

Doughty, Robert A., et al. *World War II: Total Warfare Around the Globe.* Lexington, Mass.: D.C. Heath, 1996. A brief account emphasizing military history.

Dower, John. *War Without Mercy: Race and Power in the Pacific War.* New York: Pantheon, 1986. Provocative look at the U.S.-Japan conflict.

Fitzpatrick, Sheila. *The Russian Revolution*, 2nd ed. New York: Oxford University Press, 2001. A provocative, concise, and readable account of developments from 1917 through the 1930s.

James, Harold. *Europe Reborn: A History, 1914–2000.* New York: Longman, 2003. An excellent survey of the period.

Kitchen, Martin. *A World in Flames: A Short History of the Second World War in Europe and Asia, 1939–1945.* New York: Longman, 1990. A readable narrative.

Lee, Stephen J. *European Dictatorships, 1918–1945*, 2nd ed. New York: Routledge, 2000. An interesting study of the major dictatorships and their leaders.

Lewin, Moshe. *The Soviet Century.* New York: Verso, 2005. Provocative and critical overview of the Soviet Union and Soviet Communism.

Lyons, Michael J. *World War I: A Short History*, 2nd ed. Upper Saddle River, N.J.: Prentice-Hall, 2000. A readable and comprehensive overview.

Mann, Michael. *Fascists.* New York: Cambridge University Press, 2004. Detailed but readable study of European fascism in this era.

Martin, Russell. *Picasso's War: The Destruction of Guernica and the Masterpiece That Changed the World.* New York: Plume, 2002. Examines the era through the artist and his most famous painting.

McClain, James L. *Japan: A Modern History.* New York: W. W. Norton, 2000. A very readable recent account with good coverage of these decades.

Moss, George Donelson. *America in the Twentieth Century*, 5th ed. Upper Saddle River, N.J.: Prentice-Hall, 2003. A readable survey of the United States in this period.

Neiberg, Michael S. *Fighting the Great War: A Global History.* Cambridge: Harvard University Press, 2005. A scholarly analysis of the conflict.

Parrish, Michael E. *Anxious Decades: America in Prosperity and Depression, 1920–1941.* New York: W.W. Norton, 1992. An examination of this era in the United States.

Sato, Barbara. *The New Japanese Women: Modernity, Media, and Women in Interwar Japan.* Durham: Duke University Press, 2003. A fascinating scholarly study.

Wilkenson, James, and H. Stuart Hughes. *Contemporary Europe: A History*, 10th ed. Upper Saddle River, N.J.: Prentice-Hall, 2004. A comprehensive general survey.

Websites

The Great War
(http://www.pitt.edu/~pugachev/greatwar/ww1.html). A useful site on World War I with many essays and links.

WWW-VL: History: United States
(http://vlib.iue.it/history/USA/). A virtual library, maintained at the University of Kansas, that contains links to hundreds of sites.

Russian History Index: The World Wide Web Virtual Library
(http://vlib.iue.it/hist-russia/Index.html). Contains useful essays and links on Russian history, society, and politics.

Modern History Sourcebook
(http://www.fordham.edu/halsall/mod/modsbook.html). A very extensive online collection of historical documents and secondary materials.

CHAPTER 25

Imperialism and Nationalism in Asia, Africa, and Latin America, 1914–1945

Online Study Center

This icon will direct you to interactive activities and study materials on the website: college.hmco.com/pic/lockard1e

The Arsenal This portion of a famous mural, painted by Mexican artist Diego Rivera on a courtyard wall at the Ministry of Education in Mexico City in 1928, celebrates average Mexicans gathering weapons at an arsenal during the Mexican Revolution. (Reproduced with permission of Instituto Nacional de Bellas Artes, Mexico City. Courtesy, Banco de Mexico.)

What unhappiness strikes the poor, Who wear a single worn-out, torn cloth. Oh heaven, why are you not just? Some have abundance while others are in want.

PEASANT FOLK SONG PROTESTING COLONIALISM IN VIETNAM[1]

In 1911 Nguyen Tat Thanh, a young man from an impoverished village in French-ruled Vietnam, signed on as a merchant seaman on a French ship; he would not return to his homeland for another thirty years. Nguyen hated colonialism and was dreaming of an independent nation of Vietnam. While a seaman he visited various ports in North Africa and the United States, and while touring several U.S. cities he developed both a distaste for America's white racism and an admiration for its freedom, which was born of revolution. After working as a cook in London, Nguyen moved to Paris and worked chiefly as a photo retoucher, all the while seeking to develop an anticolonial movement among the Vietnamese exiles in France. Adopting a new alias, Nguyen Ai Quoc ("Nguyen the Patriot"), he spent his free time reading books on politics and working with Asian nationalists and French socialists to oppose colonialism, especially in Vietnam but also wherever imperialism had imposed direct or indirect power over weaker countries.

Nguyen Ai Quoc became famous among Vietnamese exiles in Europe for his efforts to address the delegates at the Paris Peace Conference after World War I about the self-determination of peoples. Determined to force the issue of independence for colonized peoples, he attempted to enter the meetings and to present a moderate eight-point plan for changes in France's treatment of its Southeast Asian colonies, through which he hoped to gain personal basic freedoms, representation in government, and release of political prisoners. But the major Western powers, unwilling to consider any change in their colonial domains, refused to permit his entry. Becoming disillusioned with Western democracy, the Vietnamese exile helped found the French Communist Party, which promised to abolish the French colonial system. He then moved to the Soviet Union and later, under a new name, Ho Chi Minh ("He Who Enlightens"), the former seaman led the communist forces in Vietnam in their long struggle against French colonialism and then against the Americans seeking to reshape the country. While nationalists and communists did not necessarily share the same goals, Ho concluded that communism was the most effective strategy for promoting nationalism. Ho became a worldwide symbol of national assertion, opposition to Western imperialism, and sympathy for the plight of peasants, who were often negatively affected by colonial policies in Vietnam and elsewhere.

Between 1914 and 1945 nationalistic Asians such as Ho Chi Minh challenged the imperialism that had reshaped Asian and African politics and economies in the late nineteenth and early twentieth centuries. Rapid, often destabilizing

749

change sparked political and cultural nationalism aimed at escaping Western domination or control, especially after World War I weakened the European powers. In response to economic dislocations and colonial repression, nationalist forces were awakened in colonies from Indonesia to Egypt to Senegal, becoming especially strong in India and Vietnam. Similar trends were also at work in independent countries such as Siam (now Thailand), Persia (now Iran), and particularly China. The Great Depression and World War II unsettled the world even more. In some societies in these regions, those seeking to overturn the status quo, such as Ho Chi Minh, mobilized large followings from discontented people. Despite frequent uprisings and protests against them, the Western powers were able to retain their empires until after World War II. During and after that war, however, nationalist movements became even stronger, making a return to the world of the 1930s impossible.

FOCUS QUESTIONS

1. What circumstances fostered nationalism in Asia, Africa, and Latin America?
2. How and why did the Communist movement grow in China?
3. What were the main contributions of Mohandas Gandhi to the Indian struggle?
4. How did nationalism differ in Southeast Asia and sub-Saharan Africa?
5. What factors promoted change in the Middle East and Latin America?

Western Imperialism and Its Challengers

What circumstances fostered nationalism in Asia, Africa, and Latin America?

The events that rocked the industrialized nations between 1914 and 1945—two world wars, the Russian Revolution, and the Great Depression—also affected the nonindustrialized societies of Asia, Africa, and Latin America, who enjoyed little power in the global system. But the developments in the nonindustrialized societies also owed much to local dynamics. In particular, some of the local social and economic changes resulting from colonialism proved destabilizing. Many disenchanted Asians and Africans adopted nationalism and Marxism to struggle for power in their own societies and against Western colonizers.

The Impact of Colonialism

The colonialism imposed by Western nations on most Asians, Africans, and West Indians between 1500 and 1914 had a major impact on these peoples. World War I, for instance, fought chiefly among Western nations, had indirect effects in the colonies. The slaughter of millions of people during the war undermined Western credibility and whatever moral authority

Western peoples claimed to possess. Adding to the resentment was the death of thousands of colonial subjects conscripted in Asia and Africa as soldiers and workers to support the colonial powers in the war effort. Both France and Germany drafted men, often through harsh and arbitrary methods similar to forced labor, from their African colonies, while Britain sent Africans and Indians. Some 46,000 Kenyans died fighting for Britain, and at least 25,000 West Africans perished helping France on the front lines. British and French officials had muted African resistance to the draft by promising democratic reforms and special treatment for war veterans, but these promises were not carried out. Few of the families of dead African soldiers ever received any compensation for their loss.

Colonialism also reshaped societies, often with harmful political, economic, and social results. As discussed in Chapters 21 and 22, colonization had resulted in the creation of artificial states that often ignored the ethnic composition of the territory or the historical configuration and economic bases of states in the region. As a result, colonies such as Dutch-ruled Indonesia, British Nigeria, and the Belgian Congo incorporated diverse and often rival ethnic groups who had little sense of national unity.

To cover the costs of managing the colonies, the colonial governments used a variety of methods that increased resentment, including higher taxes and forced labor. Forced labor was common in the African colonies. For instance, in Portuguese-ruled Mozambique, men and women who had no cash to pay the required taxes were assigned to work on plantations or in

CHRONOLOGY

	Asia	The Middle East and Africa	Latin America
1910	**1916–1927** Warlord Era in China		
1920	**1928–1937** Republic of China	**1920–1922** Nationalist unrest in Kenya **1922** Formation of Turkish republic **1925–1979** Pahlavi dynasty in Iran	
1930	**1930** Indochinese Communist Party **1935–1936** Chinese Communist Long March		**1930–1945** Estado Novo in Brazil **1934–1940** Cardenas presidency in Mexico
1940	**1941–1945** Japanese occupation of Southeast Asia **1942** Gandhi's Quit India campaign		

mines in a system not unlike slavery. After months of labor they often received little more than a receipt saying they had met their tax obligation for the year. Among the worst abuses by colonial regimes in Southeast Asia were their opium and alcohol monopolies, which provided revenues for governments. For example, in French-ruled Vietnam all villages were required to purchase designated amounts of these products to enrich government coffers. By 1918 opium sales accounted for one-third of all colonial revenues in Vietnam, and some Vietnamese became addicted to opium. Moreover, villages that bought too little alcohol or were discovered making their own illicit alcoholic beverages were fined, even though Vietnamese peasants had made their own rice wine for many generations.

Another problem was that rising birth rates and declining death rates, abetted by colonial economic policies and, in some cases, improved health and sanitation, fostered rapid population growth in colonies such as India, Indonesia, the Philippines, and Vietnam. This population growth outstripped economic resources, exacerbating poverty and, for Indians and Indonesians, stimulating emigration. Furthermore, most of the colonies developed economies that locked them into the almost exclusive production and export of one or two primary commodities, such as rice and rubber from Vietnam, sugar from Barbados and Fiji, copper from Northern Rhodesia, and oil from Trinidad and Iraq. These economic limitations put a brake on later economic diversification, as many Latin American nations had discovered after gaining independence in the early 1800s.

Colonized peoples also disliked the arrogance of the Western colonizers. Europeans and North Americans assumed that their societies were superior, above those of other peoples of the world. This ethnocentric, often racist attitude was enshrined in the Covenant for the

Exporting Resources from Indonesia Small boats brought cash crops grown in eastern Java, part of the Dutch East Indies, to the port of Surabaya, from where they were shipped to Europe. (Royal Commonwealth Society Collection, Cambridge University Library Y30333/A9)

new League of Nations formed after World War I, which considered the colonized peoples not yet able to govern themselves in the modern world. Exploiting their unequal power, the Western officials, businessmen, and planters in the colonies commonly lived in luxury—with mansions, servants, and private clubs—while many local people lived in dire poverty, often underfed and malnourished.

At the same time, colonial governments built a modern communications and economic infrastructure that often spurred economic growth. The governments of British India, Dutch Indonesia, and British East Africa financed railroads that facilitated the movement of goods and people. Colonialism also fostered the growth of cities. For example, in 1890, to service their new East African Railroad from the Kenyan coast to Uganda, the British opened a settlement with a hotel and bar at Nairobi, a Gikuyu village in the Kenyan highlands. The British later made Nairobi, with its cool climate, the colonial capital. By 1944 Nairobi had grown to over 100,000 people. Port cities founded by Western colonizers, such as Hong Kong on the China coast, Jakarta in Indonesia, Singapore at the tip of Malaya, Bombay (today's Mumbai) in India, and Cape Town in South Africa, became key hubs of world trade. However, while defenders of colonialism boasted of their contributions, critics questioned how much they benefited Asians and Africans.

Capitalism

The capitalism introduced by the West also spurred resentment and anticolonial nationalism. Some non-European merchants, such as the Chinese in Southeast Asia and the Lebanese in West Africa, did profit from the growing economic opportunities. But colonial social and economic policies that promoted the spread of the capitalist market, expanded communications, and eroded traditional political authority also destabilized rural villages, fomenting opposition to these policies. The disruptions of capitalism also laid the groundwork for the rise of revolutionary responses in countries like Vietnam.

A radical innovation for many societies, capitalism reshaped rural life. The commercialization of agriculture transformed traditional, often communal, landowning arrangements into money-based private property systems. Rural societies were disrupted by the introduction by colonial officials or Western traders of competitive attitudes and policies that converted land into a commodity to be exploited on the free market. In many colonies, among them British India, French Vietnam, and Portuguese Angola, a powerful landlord class flourished at the expense of once self-sufficient peasant farmers. Even if peasant farmers held on to their land, they had no control over the constantly fluctuating prices paid for their crops. Lacking the money or connections to influential people to compete, many peasants fell into dire poverty. A Vietnamese peasant later recalled the bitter years of hardship under French colonization: "My father was very poor. He and my mother, and all of my brothers and sisters, had to pull the plow. In the old days, people did the work of water buffalo."[2]

The Great Depression of the 1930s brought economic catastrophe to many nonindustrialized societies as demand for their resources in the industrialized nations plummeted. The damage was widespread. For example, collapsing prices for rubber, sugar, and coffee crops harmed Southeast Asians. In Latin America, Argentina saw the livestock and wheat prices collapse, and Cuba was staggered by falling sugar prices. The Brazilians threw their nearly worthless sacks of coffee beans into the sea. To deal with the economic collapse while protecting Western investors, international agreements restricted rubber growing to large plantations, causing distress to many small farmers, rubber workers, and the shopkeepers who serviced them in colonies such as Malaya, Sri Lanka, and the Belgian Congo. As the marketing of the main exports declined, colonial revenues also fell. For instance, because rubber and tin provided the bulk of tax revenues in British Malaya, the price collapse in these commodities necessitated huge budget cuts, which in turn undermined such activities as education and road building.

Unequal landowning, growing mass poverty, limited economic opportunities for displaced peasants, and foreign control of the economy produced political unrest and activism. For example, the economic devastation of the Caribbean island of Trinidad, a British colony, by the Great Depression led to strikes, labor unrest, and increased efforts to organize opposition. The calypso singer Growling Tiger asked the colonial government in song not to ignore human suffering: "The authorities should deal much more leniently with the many unemployed in the colony; work is nowhere to be found but there is rent to pay while the money circulation decreases by the day."[3] But most colonial regimes, including Trinidad's, harassed and jailed protest leaders.

Nationalism and Marxism

As a result of these hardships, ideologies of resistance, including nationalism and Marxism, grew in influence in the colonized world. In time movements for change became movements for independence. Since colonial governments repressed nationalism and jailed or exiled the leaders, nationalists had to organize underground. Nationalism became especially popular among the educated middle class—lawyers, teachers, merchants, and military officers—who faced white racism and often found the doors to higher education closed to them. University and secondary school students were also drawn to nationalist movements. Colonial powers set up few universities, but those that existed offered a venue for nationalist-government conflicts and campus protests. In British Burma (today's Myanmar) during the 1920s and 1930s, for instance, nationalist students, both men and women, at the University of Rangoon repeatedly went on strike to protest British policies. After a major strike in 1936, student leaders were expelled, but the administration also met some student demands, such as introducing scholarships for poor students and allowing student representation on the university board.

To anticolonial leaders, nationalism promoted a sense of belonging to a nation, such as Indonesia or Nigeria, that transcended parochial differences such as social class and religion. But the "nation" sometimes existed only in people's imagination: in the multiethnic colonies of Africa, Southeast Asia, and the Caribbean, it was difficult to overcome ethnic antagonism and rivalries to create a feeling of nationhood. Nationalism also seemed a vehicle for addressing social problems. Whereas colonialism had uprooted people from their villages, families, customs, and traditions, nationalists sought to foster stability and help the poor. A main concern was capitalism, which was identified with foreign control.

Whether colonized or not, some Asians, Africans, and Latin Americans who sought radical change, such as Ho Chi Minh, mixed nationalism with Marxism, the ideas of socialism and revolution advocated by the nineteenth-century German Karl Marx. For them, Marxist ideas provided an alternative vision to colonialism, capitalism, and discredited local traditions and leaders. Young Asians, Africans, and West Indians studying in Europe and North America often adopted Marxism after facing bleak employment prospects and political repression back at home. Some of them gravitated to the most dogmatic form of Marxism, the communism imposed on and practiced in the Soviet Union by the Bolsheviks (see Chapter 24), which offered a dynamic approach to addressing social inequality and political powerlessness under the leadership of a centralized revolutionary party.

Radical nationalists, especially in Asia, also adopted revolutionary ideas developed by the Russian communist leader, Vladimir Lenin. Lenin blamed the poverty of the colonial and neocolonial societies on the industrialized nations that had imposed a capitalist system on subject peoples. He saw the world as divided between imperial countries (the exploiters) and dominated countries (the exploited). Lenin's view appealed to radical nationalists who sought to make sense of their subjugation to the West. For example, an Indian nationalist observed in the 1930s that younger Indian men and women who used to read about, and admire, Western democracies now read about socialism and communism and found inspiration in Soviet Russia. Although communist nations, among them the Soviet Union, also proved capable of blatantly imperialistic policies, during the first four decades of the twentieth century Lenin's theory of capitalism-based imperialism seemed to offer validity.

Lengthening the Imperial Reach

At the same time that anti-imperialist feelings were rising between 1900 and 1945, powerful nations were expanding their imperial reach and continuing to intervene in less powerful nations. For example, after World War I and the defeat of Germany and its Ottoman ally, Britain and France took control of the former Ottoman colonies in western Asia and the German colonies in Africa. Some of these societies, such as oil-rich Iraq, had valuable resources. Likewise, Australia and Japan occupied the German-ruled Pacific islands. Supported by colonial governments, Europeans continued to settle in Algeria, Angola, Kenya, South Africa, and Southern Rhodesia and to dispossess local people from their land. Moreover, while the war had ended, Western military conquests in Africa had not. In 1935–1936 Italy invaded and brutally conquered the last independent African state, Ethiopia, killing some 200,000 Ethiopians. The Ethiopian forces faced a fully mechanized and mobile Italian army, and, despite their spirited defense of the mountainous terrain, they succumbed to superior Italian aerial bombing and firepower. Italy's fascist dictator, Benito Mus-

solini, argued that it was a war to spread "civilization" and "liberate Africans"; in fact, he hoped to settle Italians in Ethiopia.

Meanwhile, the major Western power after World War I, the United States, continued to exercise influence in the Americas. For example, President Woodrow Wilson sent thousands of U.S. troops into Mexico during the Mexican Revolution to restore order and thereby protect large U.S. investments. Americans owned a large share of the Mexican economy, including most of the oil industry. American attitudes favoring the spread of democracy and capitalism in the world also played a role in the interventions, with Wilson arguing that he would teach the Latin American republics to elect good leaders. The longest U.S. intervention came in Nicaragua, where the U.S. Marines overthrew a government hostile to the United States and then remained there from 1909 to 1933, often fighting an anti-U.S. peasant resistance led by Agusto César Sandino (san-DEE-no) (1895–1934), who became a hero to nationalist Central Americans. The United States' desire to protect U.S. investments by maintaining stability in Central America meant supporting the governments led by landowners and generals, such as the notoriously corrupt Nicaraguan president, Anastasio Somoza (1896–1956). President Franklin D. Roosevelt defended the U.S. government's long relationship with Latin American dictators by maintaining that "they may be SOBs, but they're our SOBs."[4] Repeated U.S. interventions in the region left an aftertaste of local resentment against what Central Americans called "Yankee imperialism."

SECTION SUMMARY

■ World War I affected colonies in Asia, Africa, and the Caribbean as thousands of colonial subjects were forced to fight and die for France, Germany, and Britain, and promises of democratic reforms and special treatment for war veterans were not carried out.

■ Colonial governments imposed heavy taxes and hard labor on the colonial peoples, who often lived in poverty while their Western counterparts lived in luxury, a state of affairs that was defended by the Western idea that the colonial peoples could not yet govern themselves.

■ Western capitalism disrupted traditional rural life in many colonies, placing formerly self-sufficient farmers at the mercy of landowners and the world economy, which led to misery, political unrest, and activism during the Great Depression.

■ Nationalism appealed to many frustrated colonial subjects, though many multiethnic colonies struggled to develop a sense of nationhood, and Marxism appealed to many, such as Vietnam's Ho Chi Minh, as an alternative to exploitative capitalism.

■ Despite local opposition, Western nations expanded their colonial reach between 1900 and 1945: Italy brutally conquered Ethiopia, France and Britain took over former Ottoman colonies, and the United States continued to meddle in Central America.

✦ Nationalism and Communism in China

How and why did the communist movement grow in China?

The Chinese Revolution of 1911–1912, which ended the 2,000-year-old imperial system (see Chapter 23), had led to a republic that Chinese hoped would give the nation renewed strength in the world, but these hopes were soon dashed (see Chronology: China, 1911–1945). China lapsed into warlordism and civil war, with a central government in name only, nominally independent but nonetheless subject to pressure from the West and Japan. Alarm at China's domestic failures and continuing Western imperialism sparked movements that fostered a resurgent nationalism that was more influential than in most nonindustrialized countries, as well as the formation of a communist party and China's eventual reunification.

Warlords, New Cultures, and Nationalism

During the demoralizing Warlord Era (1916–1927), China was divided into territories controlled by rival **warlords**, local political leaders that had their own armies. The warlords extracted revenue as their armies terrorized the local population. They were a mixed lot. Some called themselves nationalists and reformers and were interested in promoting education and industry. A few social reformers prohibited prostitution, gambling, and opium in their domains. Still others took bribes to carry out policies favoring merchants or foreign governments. Meanwhile, high taxes, inflation, famine, accelerating social tensions, and banditry made life difficult for most Chinese.

Radical new currents arose out of the people's despair. Cities became enclaves of revolutionary ideas, fostering new intellectual, social, cultural, and economic thought that helped set new agendas for China. New schools and universities opened, though students were frustrated at China's failure. Schools for girls became more common. Between 1910 and 1919 the number of these schools increased from 40,000 to 134,000, and the enrollments from 1.6 million to 4.5 million girls, although vastly more boys enjoyed access to formal education. Thanks to the schools, by the 1920s many women worked as nurses, teachers, and civil servants, especially in cities, but few rural women became literate or enjoyed these new opportunities. Exposure to Western ideas in universities, especially those run by Western Christian groups, led some Chinese students to question their own cultural traditions. For instance, women activists and sympathetic men campaigned successfully against footbinding, which largely disappeared except in remote rural areas by 1930. New social and economic groups, including industrialists and a working class, formed chambers of commerce and labor unions.

CHRONOLOGY	
China, 1911–1945	
1911–1912	Chinese Revolution
1915	Beginning of New Culture Movement
1916–1927	Warlord Era
1919	May Fourth Movement
1926–1928	Northern Expedition to reunify China
1927	Guomindang suppression of communists
1927–1934	Mao Zedong's Jiangxi Soviet
1928–1937	Republic of China in Nanjing
1931	Japanese occupation of Manchuria
1935–1936	Long March by Chinese communists
1937–1945	Japanese invasion of China

During this time Chinese intellectuals supported the **New Culture Movement**, which sought to wash away the discredited past and sprout a literary revival. The movement originated in 1915 at Beijing University, China's intellectual mecca that dared to hire radical professors, some of them educated in Europe or Japan, and that encouraged a mixing of Chinese and Western thought. There a group of professors began publishing the literary magazine *New Youth,* which became the chief vehicle for attacking China's traditions, including Confucianism, which they believed were irrelevant to the modern world and kept China backward by promoting conformity and discouraging critical thinking. Seeking answers for China's problems, the magazine's editor, Chen Duxiu (chen too-shoe) (1879–1942), wanted a new culture based on republican government and science. Contributors to the magazine, while detesting Western imperialism, admired the liberal, open intellectual atmosphere in Western nations and viewed modern science as liberation from superstition. Essays asked youth to destroy the old society, derided the traditional Chinese family system as contrary to individual rights and ambitions, and advised women to seek equality with men. *New Youth* and similar progressive magazines were popular among both young men and women.

Chinese rage against Western and Japanese imperialism increased in the aftermath of World War I. During that war China had remained neutral, but Japan, allied with Britain, had occupied the German sphere of influence in the Shandong peninsula of eastern China. In 1919, with the war over, Japan

---

warlords Local political leaders with their own armies.

New Culture Movement A movement of Chinese intellectuals started in 1915 that sought to wash away the discredited past and sprout a literary revival.

presented China with 21 Demands, including control of Shandong, increased rights in Manchuria, and appointment of Japanese advisers to the Chinese government. The 21 Demands and the decision by the Western allies to allow Japan to take over Shandong provoked a radical nationalist resurgence, known as the **May Fourth Movement**, that opposed imperialism and the ineffective, warlord-controlled Chinese government. The students and workers, many of them women, supporting the movement mounted mass demonstrations, strikes, and boycotts of Japanese goods. Shouting that China's territory could not be given away, the protestors also decried social injustice and government inaction. Merchants closed their businesses in sympathy. Capitulating to the protests, the Chinese government refused to sign the Versailles treaty that followed World War I. The new communist government running the Soviet Union openly sided with China and renounced the special privileges that had been obtained by the czars in the 1800s, winning admiration among the Chinese.

Some Chinese also began studying communism, finding in it new promise for organizing change. In 1921 professors and students at Beijing University, many of whom had been active in the New Culture and May Fourth Movements, organized the Chinese Communist Party (CCP). Some of the party founders, such as the first secretary general, the *New Youth* editor, Chen Duxiu, were European- or Japanese-educated reformers who admired Western science and culture. Others were nationalists who despised Western models and believed the Chinese people, including the peasantry, had the ability to liberate China from imperialism if they were mobilized for revolution. Soviet advisers encouraged the party to organize among the urban working class but otherwise largely neglected the Chinese communists as unlikely to become influential. The communists recruited support by forming peasant associations, labor unions, women's groups, and youth clubs, and the party grew slowly; by 1927 it had enrolled some 60,000 members.

The Communist Party was only one strand of a resurgent nationalism that sparked new attempts to end the political drift and reunify China. Sun Zhongshan, better known as Sun Yat-sen (soon yot-SEN) (1866–1925), who had led the revolutionary movement that overthrew the Qing dynasty but had then been forced into exile (see Chapter 23), began to rebuild his nationalist forces, the Guomindang (gwo-min-dong), or Nationalist Party. Receiving no help from the Western nations, who benefited from China's disarray, Sun forged closer ties to the Soviet Union, which sent advisers and military aid. In the mid-1920s Sun's Guomindang and the Chinese communists worked together, in an alliance known as the United Front, to defeat warlordism and prevent foreign encroachment. However, Sun's ideology grew less democratic and more authoritarian, and he came to believe that China's 400 million people—in his view just "loose sand"—were not ready for democracy. Sun died in 1925, and the new Guomindang leader, Sun's brother-in-law, Jiang Jieshi (better known in the West as Chiang Kai-

shek) (1887–1975), was more conservative. Chiang, who came from a wealthy landowning family, was a pro-business soldier and a patriot but indifferent to social change. He began developing a close relationship with the United States while building a modern military force.

The Republic of China

Between 1926 and 1928 the Guomindang forces and their communist allies reunified China with a military drive known as the Northern Expedition, during which they defeated or co-opted the warlords. Thus in 1928 one national government finally replaced the series of warlord regimes, which had been impotent in the international community. The foreign powers recognized Chiang's new Republic of China. However, during the drive, tensions had grown between leftwing and rightwing political factions, which had different goals. Whereas communist and leftist Guomindang leaders sought social change and mobilization of workers, the right wing, led by Chiang, was allied with the antiprogressive Shanghai business community. Chiang expelled the communists from the United Front in 1927, even before the nation's reunification had been completed, and began a reign of terror against the leftists, killing thousands of them; those who survived went into hiding or fled into the rural interior or abroad.

From 1928 to 1937 Chiang's Republic of China, based at Nanjing (nahn-JING) along the Yangzi River in east-central China, launched a program to modernize China. The Republic's leaders, many of them Western-educated Christians, fostered economic development and forged a modern state. They built railroads, factories, a banking system, and a modern army, streamlined the government, fostered public health and education, and adopted new legal codes. New laws promoted monogamy and equal inheritance rights for women, though Chiang's government had little power to carry them out. The regime also negotiated an end to most of the unequal international treaties imposed by the Western nations and Japan in the 1800s. The U.S. government, closely allied with Chiang's regime, and private Americans provided generous political and financial support for Chiang's modernization efforts. Spurred by the idealistic desire to help the Chinese by reshaping them along American lines, Americans felt a paternalistic responsibility for China and funded schools, hospitals, orphanages, and Christian missionary activity. In 1940 a prominent U.S. senator, reflecting the notion that Americans could enrich and Westernize China, proclaimed: "We [Americans] will lift Shanghai up, ever up, until it is just like Kansas City."[5]

Yet the Republic faced domestic challenges. While the urban elite in big coastal cities prospered, Chiang was unable or unwilling to deal with the growing poverty of the peasantry. Commercialization of agriculture gradually shifted more land to landlords, and by 1930 about half of China's peasants lacked enough land to support their families. Adding to the problems, Chiang also tolerated government corruption and rewarded his financial backers in the merchant and banking sector. As unhappiness with the government grew, Chiang, influenced by European fascism, expanded the repression used against the

May Fourth Movement   A radical nationalist resurgence in China in 1919 that opposed imperialism and the ineffective, warlord-controlled Chinese government.

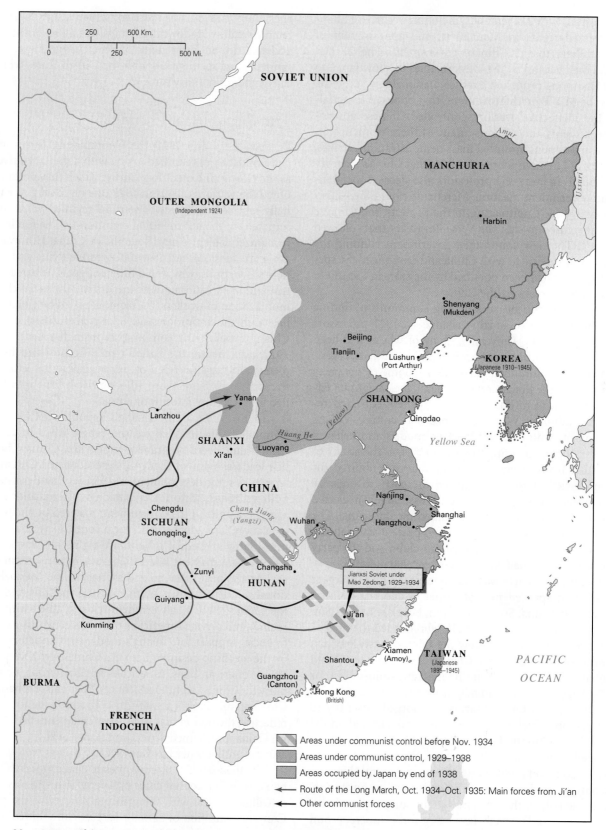

Map 25.1   Chinese Communist Movement and Chinese-Japanese War
Japan occupied much of northern and eastern China by 1939. In 1935–1936 the Chinese communists made the famous 6,000-mile Long March from their base in Jiangxi in southern China to Yan'an in northwest China.

communists and built an authoritarian police state that brutally repressed all dissent.

China also faced problems with Japan. In 1931 Japanese forces seized Manchuria, the large northeastern region rich in mineral resources and fertile farmland, and set up a puppet government under the last Manchu emperor, Henry Pu Yi (1906–1967) (see Map 25.1). Japan gradually extended its military and political influence southwest toward the Great Wall that separated Manchuria from northern China. Unable to match Japanese military power, Chiang was forced to follow a policy of appeasement. His attempts to strengthen the Chinese military diverted scarce resources from economic development, and his reluctance to fight Japan left him open to charges that he was unpatriotic.

During the years of warlordism and then the Republic, the challenges facing China were reflected in cultural life. Disillusioned by China's weakness in the world and continued political despotism, many intellectuals lost faith in both Chiang's regime and Chinese traditions. For example, the writer Lu Xun (LOO Shun) (1881–1936) had expanded his horizons by studying in Japan and becoming proficient in several foreign languages. On his return to China, he published satires on what he considered the failures of Chinese to grasp the challenges of the modern world. Lu Xun later formed a leftist writers' group and supported the communists, but he never joined the Communist Party. In criticizing both imperialism and greedy Chinese leaders, he argued, "Our vaunted Chinese civilization is only a feast of human flesh prepared for the rich and mighty, and China is only a kitchen where these feasts are prepared."[6]

Ding Ling (1904–1985) was one of China's first feminist writers. She had fled her native village to avoid an arranged marriage, had participated in the May Fourth Movement, and lived a liberated city life. Her early novels and short stories focused on women's issues and featured passionate, independent modern women unable to find emotional or sexual satisfaction. Ding became alienated from the Republic when the Guomindang killed her politically activist husband. After this she dedicated her writing to the revolutionary cause, but she was later persecuted by the communists for the feminism in her writing and her reluctance to follow the party line.

Chinese Communism and Mao Zedong

As the communists who survived Chiang's terror worked to rebuild their movement, one of the younger party leaders, Mao Zedong (maow dzuh-dong) (1893–1976), pursued his own strategy to mount the revolution he now saw as necessary to replace the Chiang regime and reshape China. From a peasant family led by a domineering father who badly abused Mao's mother, Mao had run away from home to attend high school. In 1918 he moved to Beijing to work in the Beijing University Library, where he came to embrace communism. Over the next decade he edited a radical magazine, became an elementary school principal, and organized workers and peasants. In 1927, as Chiang attempted to eliminate communists,

Mao fled to the rugged mountains of Jiangxi (kee-ON-see) province in south-central China, where he set up a revolutionary base, known as the **Jiangxi Soviet** after the political action groups of early twentieth-century Russia (see Chapter 24). There he organized a guerrilla force to fight the Guomindang. Rejecting the advice of Soviet advisers to depend on support from the urban working class, as the communists had done in Russia in 1917, Mao opted instead to rely on China's huge peasantry, arguing that without the peasants no revolution could succeed.

In Jiangxi, Mao built an army out of peasants, bandits, and former Guomindang soldiers and mobilized the local population to provision and feed the army. Mao believed that violence was necessary to oppose Chiang, having earlier written that "a revolution is not a dinner party, or writing an essay, or painting a picture, or doing embroidery; it cannot be so refined, so leisurely and gentle. A revolution is an act of violence by which one class overthrows another."[7] Between 1928 and 1934 Mao expanded the Jiangxi Soviet by setting up communist-led local governments and redistributing land from the rich to the poor. He got little help from the Soviet Union, however. As Chiang's repression intensified, top Chinese Communist Party leaders, who had once scorned Mao, moved to the Jiangxi Soviet. Increasingly alarmed by Mao's growing base and communist inroads in other parts of China, Chiang had his army blockade the Jiangxi Soviet to keep out essential supplies. This move forced Mao to reluctantly abandon his base.

In 1935 Mao and 100,000 soldiers and followers broke through the blockade and, in search of a safer base, began the **Long March**, an epic journey, full of hardship, in which Mao's Red Army fought their way 6,000 miles on foot and horseback through eleven provinces. During the one-year venture, the communists crossed eighteen mountain ranges, forded twenty-four rivers, and slogged through swamps, averaging seventeen miles a day; they lost 90 percent of their people to death or desertion. Finally in late 1936 the ragtag survivors arrived in a poor northwestern province, where they moved into cavelike homes carved into the hills around the dusty city of Yan'an (YEH-nan). The Long March saved the communists from elimination by Chiang, making Mao the unchallenged party leader. Mao celebrated the achievement: "The Long March is the first of its kind in the annals of history [and has] proclaimed that the Red Army is an army of heroes."[8] But the communists were still vulnerable to Chiang's larger, better-equipped forces.

The communists would be saved by the decision of the Japanese to invade China in 1937. This decision, which was motivated by the desire for more resources to survive in the Great Depression, forced Chiang to shift his military priorities

Jiangxi Soviet A revolutionary base, established in 1927 in south-central China, where Mao Zedong organized a guerrilla force to fight the Guomindang.

Long March An epic journey, full of hardship, in which Mao Zedong's Red Army fought their way 6,000 miles on foot and horseback through eleven Chinese provinces to establish a safe base.

The Long March This painting glorifies the crossing, over an old iron chain bridge, of the Dadu River in western Sichuan province by the communist Red Army during the Long March. This successful crossing, against fierce attacks by Guomindang forces, was a key event in the communists' successful journey to northwest China. (Private Collection)

from attacking the communists at Yan'an to fighting the Japanese. These developments gave the communists an opportunity to regroup and spread their message of change against a weakened Chiang in wartime China.

Japanese Invasion and Communist Revolution

The Japanese invasion of China in 1937 and the disastrous Chinese-Japanese war that followed altered China's politics as Chiang had to divert money from modernization to the military. Mao captured the patriotic mood of the country by proposing a united front against Japan and Chiang had little choice but to agree, relieving pressure on Mao's Yan'an base. The Japanese soon occupied the major cities of north China and the coast, and by the end of 1938 Japanese forces had swept over most of the eastern seaboard and controlled the best farmland and the industrial cities. War and occupation affected the rival Chinese parties in opposite ways: it undermined Chiang's government, and it allowed the communists to recruit support for their revolution, thus setting the stage for major changes in Chinese politics in the later 1940s.

The Republican Decline The Japanese invasion forced Chiang's government to relocate inland to Chongqing (CHUNG-king), a city protected by high mountains on the Yangzi River in west-central China. This move was followed by a mass migration of Chinese fleeing the Japanese. Unlike the modern, cosmopolitan coastal cities, Chongqing was a city with no bright lights or French restaurants and a depressing climate of fog and humidity. Fatigue, cynicism, and inflation discouraged the Guomindang and its followers. Virtually broke, Chiang's government had to squeeze

the peasants in the areas they still controlled for tax revenues to support an army of 4 to 5 million men.

Gradually many Chinese lost faith in the Republic. Militarily ineffective, politically repressive, and economically corrupt, Chiang's government offered limited resistance to the Japanese, killed and imprisoned opponents of Guomindang rule, and put the personal gain of its leaders above the economic well-being of China's people. The United States supported Chiang as an ally in the struggle against imperial Japan, but it was able to supply the Guomindang-held areas only by difficult, mountainous routes from Burma and India. Chiang often ignored U.S. advice in military and political matters. As the war wore on, Chiang, unable to push the Japanese out of China, also lost some of his popular support.

Yan'an Communism Although facing challenges, the communists at Yan'an were able to improve their prospects. Used to poverty, they had a more disciplined army than Chiang's with a higher morale. While Chiang's much larger forces had the main responsibility to fight the Japanese, the communists concentrated on mobilizing the people behind their revolution by forging a close relationship with the peasantry in north China and by mounting guerrilla bands, mostly peasants, to harass the Japanese. These guerrillas engaged in an unconventional struggle, which Mao called **"people's war,"** that combined military action and political recruitment. In Mao's strategy of guerrilla war, "the enemy advances, we retreat; the enemy halts, we harass; the enemy retreats, we pursue."[9] On the political side of "people's war,"

---

people's war An unconventional struggle combining military action and political recruitment, formulated by Mao Zedong in China.

communist activists set up village governments and peasant associations and encouraged women's rights, punishing abusive husbands. The communist message of social revolution, now blended with nationalism, offered hope for a better life to the downtrodden. Thousands of Chinese, including students, intellectuals, writers such as Ding Ling, and workers, flocked to Yan'an to join the communist cause. By 1945 the party had 1.2 million members.

The experiences of the communist leaders at Yan'an, marked by war and popular mobilization to support revolution, fostered the development of what later came to be known as **Maoism**, an ideology promoted by Mao that mixed ideas from Chinese tradition with Marxist-Leninist ideas from the Soviet Union. Mao emphasized the subordination of the individual to the needs of the group (a traditional Chinese notion), the superiority of political values over technical and artistic ones, and belief in the human will as a social force. Mao also contended that political power grows out of the barrel of a gun (the military) and that the Communist Party must command the gun. To combat elitism, Mao introduced mass campaigns in which everyone engaged in physical labor that benefited villages, such as building dams and roads. As part of this effort, the communists sent intellectuals into villages to teach literacy and also to learn from the peasants. Mao expressed faith that the Chinese people, armed with political understanding, had the collective power and creativity to triumph over nature, poverty, and exploitation to build a new society.

During the Japanese occupation Mao's communists built the foundation for revolution by gaining domination over much of rural north China, where Mao's ideas on new forms of community, social change, and economic justice had gained popular support. Hence, when the war ended in 1945, the Chinese communists had improved their prospects for fostering revolution while Chiang's Guomindang, although still a superior military force, was beset with problems resulting from its inability to defeat the Japanese and maintain popular support. As a result, the communists were able to succeed in their revolutionary efforts: in the late 1940s they won a bitter civil war, and in 1949 they established a communist government.

SECTION SUMMARY

- After the end of the imperial system, rival warlords controlled China during a period of civil war, and intellectuals formed the New Culture Movement, which called for a modernized China that fostered individualism and equality rather than traditions such as Confucianism.

- Japan's aggressive demands after World War I enraged the Chinese, and some were attracted to communism but Sun Yat-sen's successor, the pro-business Chiang Kai-shek, allied the nationalist movement with the United States.

- Chiang Kai-shek's Republic of China launched a modernization program, but it was hampered by a split with the communists, persistent rural poverty, and the Japanese seizure of Manchuria.

- Mao Zedong organized peasants into a communist revolutionary army and then led them on the punishing Long March in search of safety from Chiang Kai-shek's far stronger army, which might have triumphed had it not been diverted by a 1937 Japanese invasion.

- The Chinese people lost faith in Chiang's government as it squeezed them for taxes to support a failing war against Japan, while Mao's communists instilled hope through guerrilla attacks on the Japanese and a promise of equality and progress through shared sacrifice.

◈ British Colonialism and the Indian Response

What were the main contributions of Mohandas Gandhi to the Indian struggle?

In India, as in China, resentment of Western imperialism, despotic government, and an inequitable social order sparked a powerful nationalist movement. Like the Chinese, Indians did not benefit from the reshaping of world political arrangements following World War I. Those who hoped that war would bring them self-determination could see that the British rhetoric about democracy and freedom did not apply to India. Growing organized opposition to British colonialism, spurred by the Indian National Congress formed in the later 1800s, led to unrest that forced the British to modify some of their colonial policies. At the same time, growing nationalism set the stage for the turmoil that eventually created separate Hindu and Muslim nations after World War II.

British Policies and the Nationalist Upsurge

Nationalist opposition to the British Raj, which had been building for decades, was spurred by the severe dislocations caused by World War I. To pay for the war, the British raised taxes and customs duties on Indians, policies that sparked several armed uprisings. In addition, over 1 million Indian soldiers fought for Britain in France and the Middle East, and 60,000 of these were killed. Many Indians expected a better future because of the sacrifices they had made in a war they did not start or want—a reward of self-government similar to that of Australia and Canada, former colonies where the British political presence was now largely symbolic. But the British dashed all hopes of major political change by declaring in 1917 that they would maintain India as an integral part of the British Empire. However, British prestige suffered from the losses incurred by war; by war's end, Britain, whose power was

---

Maoism An ideology promoted by Mao Zedong that mixed ideas from Chinese tradition with Marxist-Leninist ideas from the Soviet Union.

MOHANDAS GANDHI, INDIAN NATIONALIST

Few individuals have had as much impact on history as Mohandas Gandhi (1869–1948), who became the leading figure of Indian nationalism in the 1920s by formulating ideas of nonviolent opposition to repressive colonial rule that influenced millions both inside and outside India. Gandhi was born into a well-to-do family of the vaisya caste in the western state of Gujerat; although vaisyas were commonly involved in commerce, his father was a government official. His parents maintained traditional attitudes, and his mother was a devout Hindu. Like many Hindu families, they arranged for him to marry young. The thirteen-year-old Mohandas married Kasturbai Kapada (KAST-er-by ka-PO-da) (1869–1948), the daughter of a rich merchant. Kasturbai proved a courageous helpmate in his later political activities.

Gandhi wanted to study law in London, but his family feared he would be corrupted there because his young wife, now with a son, had to stay in India. To gain their approval, he vowed to live a celibate life in England and never to touch meat or wine. In England he expanded his knowledge by reading Indian works such as the *Bhagavad Gita* and Western books such as the Christian Bible. His three years in London also gave him contact with Western nationalism and democracy, as well as a law degree.

At first unable to find a suitable position back in India, in 1893 Gandhi was hired by a large Indian law firm to work in South Africa, where the racist government and white minority mistreated not only Africans but also the thousands of Indians who had been recruited as laborers and plantation workers. With his wife's encouragement, he turned to helping the local Indians assert their rights, for which he was jailed, beaten by mobs, and almost killed by angry opponents, both white and Indian. The British who ruled South Africa raised taxes on Indians, shut down Indian gatherings, and refused official recognition of Hindu marriages. In response, and influenced by Kasturbai's advocacy of justice and nonviolence, Gandhi began developing his strategy of nonviolent resistance against oppressive rule, ideas that later inspired admirers throughout the world and that were used by Dr. Martin Luther King, Jr., in the U.S. civil rights movement of the 1950s and 1960s.

Between 1906 and 1914 Gandhi carried on his fight for justice for Indians in South Africa, spreading ideas of nonviolence. He led hunger strikes, public demonstrations, and mass marches, in which thousands of Indians resisted oppression by willingly risking beating or arrest for their cause. In 1914 the colonial regime bowed to the constant pressure and lifted the worst legal injustices against the Indians. Gandhi was forty-five years old when the triumph in South Africa earned him fame and the respected title of *Mahatma* (Great Soul) among Indians in South Africa and at home.

With the outbreak of World War I in Europe, Gandhi, Kasturbai, and their four children left South Africa to return to India. In 1915 he established a spiritual center near the Gujerat capital, Ahmedebad, where he trained followers in his ideas of nonviolence. Though Gandhi was deeply religious, he also believed that everyone had to reach truth in his or her own way, writing that "there are innumerable definitions of God, because His manifestations are innumerable. But I worship God as Truth only. I have not yet found Him, but I am seeking after Him." Moved by the poverty and suffering of the Indian masses, he also took up their cause. To identify with their plight, the high-caste Gandhi adopted the dress of the simple peasant and always traveled third class.

The British massacre of Indian protesters at Amritsar in 1919 shook Gandhi's faith in British justice. In 1920 he became the leader of India's major nationalist organization, the Indian National Congress, and over the next three decades he was at times a religious figure and at other times the consummate politician, crafty and practical. Needing mass support to build a policy of massive noncooperation, he launched three great campaigns of civil disobedience, in 1920, 1930, and 1942. Each time the British jailed him for long periods. His self-discipline was reflected in his practice of fasting to protest oppression, which added to his saintly image.

In his personal life, Gandhi was also troubled. His wife, Kasturbai, aided in his campaigns, but Gandhi was gone for long periods, neglecting her and their four children. One embittered

once believed unchallengeable, was no longer the imperial giant it had formerly seemed.

Growing problems, including a severe economic slump after the war, heightened Indian discontent and alarmed the British, causing them to clamp down on dissent and political activity and to maintain the laws that had been imposed during the war. The repression reached its height in 1919. In the Punjab city of Amritsar, British officers, fearing a mass uprising, ordered their soldiers, without warning, to open fire on an unarmed crowd at an unauthorized rally held in a walled field where escape was difficult (see Chronology: South Asia, 1914–1945). The attack killed 400 protesters and wounded 1,000, including women and children. The shooting stopped only when the troops ran out of ammunition. Throughout India, the Amritsar massacre was greeted with outrage. The anger intensified when the British hailed the officer in command, General Dyer, as a national hero. Dyer further enraged Indians by defending his action as the least amount of firing that would produce the necessary effect of intimidating potential Indian resistance. Prominent Indians, many once pro-British, were appalled at the cruelty, which shook their faith in British rule. The Nobel Prize–winning writer Rabindranath Tagore (tuh-GAWR) (1861–1941) wrote, "The enormity of the measures taken up for quelling some local disturbances had, with a rude shock, revealed to our minds the helplessness of our position as British subjects in India."[10]

Gandhi Addressing Calcutta Meeting
Mohandas Gandhi addressed some of his followers—many women as well as men—on a lawn following a meeting with British officials in Calcutta in 1931.
(Bettman/Corbis)

son rejected his father entirely. When Gandhi took a lifelong vow of chastity in 1906, Kasturbai did also. Both kept their vows. Although both were born into affluent families, the Gandhis agreed to live simply. Critics accused Gandhi of sometimes humiliating his wife by, for example, asking her to do menial tasks such as cleaning toilets. Arrested during Gandhi's "Quit India" campaign, Kasturbai, in failing health, died in her husband's lap in prison in 1944. Before she passed away, she noted that they had shared many joys and sorrows and asked that she be cremated in a sari (dress) made from yarn he had spun.

Gandhi helped lead India to independence from Britain. Shortly thereafter, when trying to end accelerating Hindu-Muslim violence in 1948, he was assassinated by a Hindu fanatic who opposed Gandhi's tolerant approach (see Chapter 31). India's first prime minister, Jawaharlal Nehru, called Gandhi's death the loss of India's soul: "The light has gone out of our lives and there is darkness everywhere."

THINKING ABOUT THE PROFILE

1. How did Gandhi's South African experiences shape his political strategies?

2. How did Gandhi's ideas and activities have a great influence in the world?

Note: Quotations from Judith M. Brown, *Modern India: The Origins of an Asian Democracy,* 2nd ed. (New York: Oxford University Press, 1994), p. 211; and Rhoads Murphey, *A History of Asia,* 4th ed. (New York: Longman, 2003), p. 437.

CHRONOLOGY

South Asia, 1914–1945

1919	Amritsar massacre
1930	Gandhi's Great Salt March
1931	London Conference
1935	Government of India Act
1937	Provincial elections
1942	Gandhi's Quit India campaign

Gandhi: Nonviolent Resistance and Mass Politics

The unrest brought to the fore new Indian nationalist leaders, the most outstanding of whom was Mohandas K. Gandhi (GAHN-dee) (1869–1948). Gandhi developed unique ideas and exhibited eccentric personal behavior that generated bitter opponents and sometimes frustrated even his devoted allies (see Profile: Mohandas Gandhi, Indian Nationalist). After getting his law degree in Britain, Gandhi lived for twenty-two years in South Africa, where the British colonial regime practiced racial segregation and white supremacy (see Chapter 21). To assert the rights of the Indian immigrants in South Africa, Gandhi developed tactics of **nonviolent resistance**, noncooperation with unjust laws and peaceful confrontation with illegitimate authority. After returning to India, in 1920 he became the president of the main nationalist organization, the Indian National Congress. Gandhi's message of resisting the colonial regime nonviolently led him to mount mass campaigns against British political and economic institutions. Inspired by his example, huge numbers of ordinary people—factory workers, peasants, estate laborers—joined his movement, shaking the foundations of British colonial rule.

Gandhi's Ideology Influenced by his pacifist wife, Kasturbai, Gandhi developed a doctrine of nonviolence based on ideas against taking life that had been introduced 2,500 years earlier by the Jains and Buddhists, two of India's religious groups, and that were also promoted by the Quakers, a pacifist Christian movement Gandhi had encountered in England. Nonviolence—Gandhi often called it passive resistance—was, he wrote, "a method of securing rights by personal suffering; it is the reverse of resistance by arms."[11] Gandhi believed that violence, embodying hate and irrationality, was never justified. The enemy was to be met with reason, and if he responded with violence, this had to be endured in good spirit. Gandhi's approach required severe self-discipline.

Gandhi made mass civil disobedience, involving such tactics as marches, sit-ins, and boycotts, the most effective expression of nonviolence. He perfected the tactics of the boycott of British government institutions and businesses. Disobedience also involved hunger strikes, peaceful violation of law, and refusal to pay taxes. Gandhi's Congress colleague, Jawaharlal Nehru (JAH-wa HAR-lahl NAY-roo), placed Gandhi's strategy in perspective: "Gandhi was like a powerful current of fresh air that made us stretch ourselves and take deep breaths, like a Whirlwind that upset many things but most of all the working of people's minds."[12]

At the same time, some of Gandhi's ideas were outside the mainstream of nationalist thought, confounding allies. For instance, Gandhi opposed the global economic system because it was marked by competitive capitalism and trade between societies with unequal power and wealth. To escape that economy, he believed that India should reject Western capitalist models and return to the self-sufficient, village-based economy of precolonial times, where everyone could spin their own cloth. He called industrialization "a machinery which has impoverished India. India's salvation consists in unlearning what she has learned during the past fifty years. The railways, telegraphs, hospitals, [and] lawyers have all to go."[13] Critics considered Gandhi's ideal of a nation of self-sufficient villages living in simplicity a utopian fantasy, out of touch with the modern world, that prevented the development of more practical policies to improve people's lives.

Gandhi had other controversial views. He insisted that Indian society's lowest social group, the untouchables, be included in political actions, much to the distress of high-caste Hindus. Gandhi considered untouchability a religious and moral rather than a social and economic problem. He coined the term *harijans* (children of God) as a more dignified label to replace *pariahs,* the centuries-old name for untouchables. Gandhi did not entirely reject the caste system as a way of organizing society, but he wanted all people to enjoy the same dignity. In his conception, harijan toilet cleaners would have the same status as brahmans, members of the priestly caste, but would go on cleaning toilets. Even untouchable leaders often considered Gandhi's views unrealistic and patronizing.

Mass Campaigns Thanks to Gandhi's efforts, during the 1920s the Congress developed a mass base that was supported by people from all of India's cultures, religions, regions, and social backgrounds. The Congress sponsored strikes by factory workers, walkouts of workers on tea estates, and tax boycotts by peasants. Gandhi compared massive civil disobedience to an earthquake that could shut down a government. His tactics bewildered the British, who, while claiming to uphold law, order, and Christian values, clubbed hunger strikers, used horses to trample nonviolent protesters, and arrested Gandhi and other leaders. One of Gandhi's Indian critics told British officials in 1930 that the Congress "has undoubtedly acquired a great hold on the popular imagination. On roadside stations where until a few months ago I could hardly have suspected that people had any politics, I have seen demonstrations and heard Congress slogans."[14] Each campaign led to British concessions and a growing realization that Britain could not hold India forever.

The Great Depression that began in 1929 and lasted around the globe through the 1930s lowered the standard of living for most Indians, intensifying the nationalist unrest. The prices earned for India's major cash crops were cut in half, and this collapse, combined with a collapse of rural credit, caused distress and suffering. The suffering led to a new Gandhi-led campaign in 1930, beginning with what Gandhi called the Great Salt March. During this event, Gandhi and several dozen followers marched to the west coast, where they produced salt from the Indian Ocean seawater. In so doing they broke British laws, since salt production was a lucrative government monopoly. Gandhi's action and arrest caught the popular imagination, setting off a wave of demonstrations, strikes, and boycotts against British interests. In quelling the unrest, the British killed 103, injured 420, and imprisoned 60,000 resisters. They released Gandhi a few months later, and he agreed to halt civil disobedience campaigns if the British would promote Indian-made goods and hold a conference to discuss India's political future.

Hindu-Muslim Division

While these events were proceeding, a growing Hindu-Muslim division posed a problem for Indian nationalism. Although some Muslims supported the Indian National Congress, the fact that it was mainly Hindu sparked concerns among Muslims and other minorities about their role in India. While

---

nonviolent resistance Noncooperation with unjust laws and peaceful confrontation with illegitimate authority, pursued by Mohandas Gandhi in India.

Gandhi respected all religions and welcomed Muslim support, Muslim leaders, fearing that India's independence would mean Hindu domination, mounted their own nationalist organizations, separate from the Congress, to work for a potential Muslim country of their own. In 1930 student activists in Britain called their proposed Muslim nation Pakistan, meaning "Land of the Pure" in the Urdu language spoken by many Indian Muslims. Accounting for some 20 percent of British India's population and largely concentrated in the northwest and Bengal, Muslims occupied all niches of society but were divided themselves by social status, ancestry, language, and sect. The great majority were Sunni but some were Shi'a.

While Muslim leaders often focused on the need for a state that enshrined their religious values, Congress leaders were chiefly Western-oriented Hindu intellectuals who wanted a secular state that was neutral toward religion and, in contrast with Gandhi, a modern India. The forty-year-old Jawaharlal Nehru (1889–1964), who succeeded Gandhi as Congress leader in 1929, was the strongest advocate of a secular, modern India. Born into a wealthy brahman family and endowed with unusual charisma and rare public speaking skills, Nehru was an aristocratic, Marxist-influenced product of an elite Western education with a passion for the welfare of the common people. Nehru, like Gandhi, demanded complete freedom from British domination. But while Gandhi wanted to reshape colonial society, Nehru and other Congress leaders focused more on political independence. Few of the Indian nationalists, whether Hindu or Muslim, shared the Chinese Communist goal of radical social transformation as a necessary part of economic development.

By the 1930s the main rival to the Congress was the Muslim League, led by the Western-educated Bombay lawyer Muhammed Ali Jinnah (jee-NAH) (1876–1948), a dapper figure in his tailored suits who always spoke English and never learned Urdu. Jinnah promoted a Two Nations Theory, arguing that Islam and Hinduism were different social orders and that it was a naive Congress dream that the two groups could ever forge a common nationality. Jinnah developed the Muslim League into a mass political movement in competition with the Congress. His claim to speak for all Muslims outraged the Congress, which had over a hundred thousand Muslim members—some secular, some devout—and saw itself as a national party representing all religions and castes. But it faced a skilled foe in Jinnah, who cultivated good relations with the British and convinced regional Muslim leaders, some once pro-Congress, to support the Muslim League. The Congress tried to marginalize the Muslim League and refused to form a coalition with it, which proved to be a mistake in the long run.

The competing visions of the Congress and the Muslim League complicated British efforts to introduce representative government institutions. The two rival organizations clashed in 1931, when, as a result of Gandhi's agreement to suspend civil disobedience, Indian leaders and British officials met in London to discuss expanded elections. Represen-tatives of various minorities, including Muslims, Sikhs, and untouchables, demanded separate electorates to ensure that their groups gained representation. Seeing this as a tactic that would allow the British to divide and rule, Congress objected, but the minorities won electoral rights in India's many provinces.

The electoral agreement also did not end anticolonial unrest and counterviolence by the British. However, in 1935, their power in retreat, the British introduced a new constitution that allowed some 35 million Indians who owned property, including 6 million women, to vote for newly formed provincial legislatures. In the first provincial elections, in 1937, the Congress won 70 percent of the popular vote and the majority of seats, defeating the Muslim League even for seats reserved for Muslims. More Indians also rose to leadership positions in the army, police, and civil service. However, British officials argued that the communal divisions necessitated the continuation of British rule to maintain order, and Jinnah, battered but not broken by the disappointing Muslim League electoral performance, redoubled his efforts to unite Muslims against the Congress.

Social Change: Caste and Gender Relations

Nationalist politics, economic dislocations, and the stresses posed by rapid population growth also had an effect on India's social structure. India's population grew from 255 million in 1871 to 390 million in 1940. The trends that had reshaped the caste system beginning in the 1800s continued, including the adoption by lower castes, anxious to improve their status, of high-caste practices such as vegetarianism, and more awareness of caste identities than had existed in earlier centuries. These caste trends affected the untouchables, the most disadvantaged and powerless group in Hindu society and perhaps a fifth of India's population. Although Gandhi, a high-caste Hindu, urged fair treatment for all groups, increasing attention to caste identities often resulted in more discrimination against untouchables, which encouraged untouchable leaders to mount movements promoting the rights of their community.

The largest such movement was led by Dr. Bhimrao Ramji Ambedkar (BIM-rao RAM-jee am-BED-car) (1893–1956). Ambedkar rose from one of the lowest groups, the sweepers who cleaned village streets, to earn a Ph.D. and a law degree from major U.S. and British universities. On his return to India he started schools, newspapers, and political parties. Ambedkar rejected Gandhi's policies as patronizing and inadequate for real change. He successfully lobbied the government to promote upward mobility for the untouchables by offering them government jobs and scholarships for higher education. Later in life, believing untouchables could never flourish within Hinduism, Ambedkar led thousands of followers to abandon Hinduism and adopt Buddhism, which by then had only a small following in India.

Attitudes toward women were also changing. Hindus increasingly favored widow remarriage, once forbidden, to help offset what they believed to be the higher Muslim birthrate.

The trends, however, including greater emphasis on what traditionalists considered proper female conduct, largely favored male authority. Yet, while the feminist movement remained weak and had little support among Muslim and peasant women, many women joined the Congress and some demanded a vote equal to men for representative institutions, such as provincial legislatures. With British assent, all the legislatures granted women the franchise between 1923 and 1930. Educated women published magazines. Some were daring in challenging male authority. For example, Rokeya Hossain (1880–1932), a Bengali Muslim raised in seclusion who had opened girls' schools and campaigned for equal rights, published, with her liberal husband's support, a utopian short story, "Sultana's Dream," that portrayed men confined to seclusion because of their uncontrolled sexual desires while women governed. Gandhi's views on women were mixed. He advocated social equality between men and women and encouraged women's participation in politics and the rest of public life. He also urged women to abandon seclusion and join the nationalist cause in a women's corps known as "servants of the nation." But, once involved in the women's corps, women were usually offered the more menial tasks such as picketing and cooking. Gandhi himself, unable to escape patriarchal attitudes, promoted women's traditional roles as wives, mothers, and supporters of men. Impressed by his wife Kasturbai's advocacy of nonviolence, Gandhi believed women were especially suited to passive resistance. He wrote paternalistically that women were nobler than men, the embodiment of humility, sacrifice, and silent suffering. But some women with a more militant vision of change joined men in terrorist organizations aimed at undermining colonialism. For example, Pritilata Waddedar (1911–1932), a brilliant Bengali university graduate, led and died in an armed raid on a British club that reportedly boasted a sign: "Dogs and Indians not allowed."

Towards Two Nations

World War II was the deciding event in the path to Indian independence, but it also reshaped the nationalist dialogue by increasing the Hindu-Muslim divide. The British committed Indian troops to the war without consulting Congress leaders, who protested that cooperation must be between equal partners and by mutual consent. In 1942 Gandhi, fearing that the British had no intention of ending their colonial rule, mounted a campaign calling on the British to "Quit India." In response, the British arrested Ghandi, Nehru, and the entire Congress leadership and 60,000 party activists, jailing many of them for the duration of the war. World War II harmed the rural poor and urban workers, as prices for essential goods soared. At the same time, famine in Bengal killed 3 million to 4 million people. In response to these hardships, Nehru's main rival for Congress leadership, the militant Bengali Marxist Subhas Chandra Bose (1895–1945), allied with imperial Japan, Britain's fascist enemy along with Nazi Germany. With Japanese backing, Bose organized an Indian National Army, recruited largely from among Indian soldiers in the British Indian army and Indian emigrants in Southeast Asia. His army invaded India from Japan-held Burma to attack the British. The invasion failed, but many Indians saw Bose and other Indian National Army leaders as national heroes.

Meanwhile, the arrest of Congress leaders had left a vacuum that allowed for Jinnah to completely sever his Muslim League from the Congress. Seeking Indian support, the British cultivated Jinnah, who joined the government and consolidated the power of the Muslim League. Jinnah demanded the creation of a separate Muslim state, Pakistan, based on the provinces where Muslims were the majority. Rejecting Muslim separatism, the jailed Gandhi urged Muslims to resist what he termed the suicide of partition. But Gandhi's plea was futile, and British efforts to bring the factions together also failed. After World War II, the struggle between Indian nationalists and the British, and between Hindus and Muslims, resumed, leading to the end of British rule and the creation of two separate independent nations, predominantly Hindu India and a chiefly Muslim Pakistan carved out of the Muslim majority areas of British India.

SECTION SUMMARY

- In the aftermath of World War I, in which tens of thousands of their people died, Indians were angry that Britain denied them greater autonomy and imposed higher taxes to pay for the war, and resentment peaked with the massacre of hundreds of peaceful protesters at Amritsar.

- Mohandas Gandhi, the foremost Indian nationalist leader, promoted nonviolent resistance to British rule, including strikes, boycotts, and refusal to pay taxes, and won a massive popular following for the Indian National Congress.

- While even his Indian supporters considered some of Gandhi's ideas naive and utopian, campaigns such as the Great Salt March were highly effective in winning concessions from the British.

- Feeling threatened by the predominantly Hindu National Congress, the Muslim League, led by Jinnah, argued that Indian Muslims should have a country of their own, which they called Pakistan.

- Leaders of the untouchables, the lowest Hindu caste, pushed for and obtained greater opportunities, and women were allowed somewhat more freedom, though many Indian men, including Gandhi, did not see them as entirely equal to men.

- The British jailed tens of thousands of Indian National Congress activists after Gandhi objected to Indian troops being forced to fight in World War II, a Bengali Marxist led a failed invasion of India, the Muslim League grew increasingly independent, and eventually, after the end of World War II, both Pakistan and India gained independence from Britain.

Nationalist Stirrings in Southeast Asia and Sub-Saharan Africa

How did nationalism differ in Southeast Asia and sub-Saharan Africa?

As in India, the challenges posed by European colonialism were also being addressed by nationalist movements and protests in Southeast Asia and sub-Saharan Africa, though few of them were as influential as the Indian National Congress. In 1930 the Indonesian Nationalist Party, struggling against Dutch colonialism, urged Indonesians to be zealous in the cause of national freedom and building a new nation. The plea symbolized the nationalist response in several other Southeast Asian colonies, especially French-ruled Vietnam. Although in sub-Saharan Africa organized nationalist movements, often based on ethnicity, were weaker than comparable movements in India or Southeast Asia, African nationalism was strongly expressed in cultural developments.

Changing Southeast Asia

Nationalism proved as influential a force in parts of Southeast Asia as in China and India, and stronger than in Africa, during this era. The first stirrings of Southeast Asian nationalism came in the Philippines in the late 1800s, but the revolution was thwarted by first Spain and then the United States. In the Philippines the U.S. promise of eventual independence and the co-optation of nationalist leaders into the colonial administration tended to reduce radical sentiments. By 1941 nationalism also had a large following in Vietnam, British Burma, and parts of Indonesia, all places that had suffered particularly oppressive colonial rule and where independence would come only through revolutionary war or the threat of armed force. Compared to these colonies, nationalism was weaker in French-ruled Cambodia and Laos and in British Malaya, all colonies that had experienced less social, economic, and political disruption.

One of the stronger nationalist movements arose in Burma (today's Myanmar). Despite limited self-government by the 1930s, including an elected legislature, the colony's majority ethnic group, the Burmans, viewed British rule as oppressive and resented British favoritism toward ethnic minorities who became Christian. They also resented the large, often wealthy Indian community, which had immigrated to Burma when the British combined the colony with British India and who dominated the economy. These resentments fostered the rise of nationalism among university students and graduates. The colony's schools, whether run by the government or by Christian missions, encouraged their students to adopt Western ways, including Western clothing styles, and devalued Buddhist traditions. The nationalists used Theravada

Buddhism, the faith of most Burmese, as a rallying cry to press for reform, and some favored women's rights. When the Japanese invaded Burma in 1941, many Burmans welcomed them as liberators.

Although Siam (today's Thailand) was not a colony, nationalism grew there out of tensions between the aristocratic elite and the rising middle class of civil servants, military officers, and professionals; the latter groups wanted more influence in a political system dominated by the royal family and other aristocrats. This middle-class discontent was further fueled by the Great Depression, which forced salary and budget cuts. In 1932 military officers of middle-class background, who called themselves nationalists, took power in a coup against the royal government (see Chronology: Southeast Asia and Africa, 1912–1945). The Siamese king, whose family had ruled the country since the late 1700s, agreed under pressure to become a constitutional, mostly symbolic monarch. Military leaders then ran the government through the 1930s, pursuing nationalist policies, renaming the country Thailand ("Land of Free People"), and urging the Thai people to live modern lives, including dressing in a modern Western fashion, with hats and shoes. During the late 1930s Thailand forged an alliance with the rising Asian power, imperial Japan, and introduced features of a fascist regime, militarizing the schools and suppressing dissent.

CHRONOLOGY

Southeast Asia and Africa, 1912–1945

1912	Formation of African National Congress in South Africa
1912	Formation of Islamic Union in Indonesia
1920	Formation of Indonesian Communist Party
1920–1922	Nationalist unrest in Kenya
1926–1927	Communist uprising in Indonesia
1927	Formation of Indonesian Nationalist Party
1928–1931	Peasant rebellions in the Congo region
1930	Founding of Indochinese Communist Party
1932	Nationalist coup in Thailand
1935–1936	Conquest of Ethiopia by Italy
1941	Formation of Viet Minh in Vietnam by Ho Chi Minh
1941–1945	Japanese occupation of Southeast Asia

Vietnamese Nationalism and Resistance

The most powerful nationalist movement in Southeast Asia emerged in Vietnam as a result of its destabilization during French colonial rule, when peasant lands were seized. The earliest nationalists seeking an end to French rule were led by the passionately revolutionary Phan Boi Chau (FAN boy chow) (1867–1940). Phan was born into a family of mandarins who had served the Vietnamese emperors as officials for generations, and he was educated in Confucian learning, like his paternal ancestors in a society strongly influenced by Chinese thought. By the time of his death in a French prison, Phan had inspired Vietnamese patriotism and resistance. As he wrote in his prison diaries, "It has been but a yearning to purchase my freedom even at the cost of spilling my blood, to exchange my fate of slavery for the right of self-determination."[15]

But the older Confucian scholars, such as Phan, gradually lost their nationalist leadership to the younger, urban, French-educated intellectuals of the Vietnamese Nationalist Party, which, against the well-armed French, had few options other than terrorism: they assassinated colonial officials and bombed French buildings. A premature uprising sparked by the group in 1930 brought about a French reign of terror against all dissidents. French repression destroyed the major nationalist groups except for the Vietnamese communists and, by eliminating noncommunist nationalist movements, unwittingly became a turning point in Vietnamese history.

The rise of Vietnamese communism during the repression owed much to Ho Chi Minh, a mandarin's son and former sailor turned leftwing political activist, as described at the start of the chapter. Ho had spent many years organizing the communist movement among Vietnamese exiles in Thailand and China. Ho came to believe that revolution, not reform, was the answer to economic exploitation, cultural stagnation, and political repression in Vietnam. Ho also favored equality for women and improving the lives of the peasants and plantation workers. Marxism provided an alternative to the discredited imperial system, an unjust society, and French rule. In 1930 Ho and his colleagues established the Indochinese Communist Party, which united anticolonial radicals from Vietnam, Cambodia, and Laos.

Vietnamese Marxists linked themselves to the patriotic traditions of the earlier Vietnamese rebels, who for 2,000 years had led resistance first to Chinese conquerors and then to the French. One of Ho Chi Minh's best-known poems examined the long history of Vietnam and praised the men and women who struggled against foreign aggression and for an equitable society. Another Vietnamese Marxist, writing in 1943, exemplified the links with the past: "And, so it seems we are not lost after all. Behind us we have the immense history of our people. There [are] still spiritual cords attaching us."[16] Remembering Vietnam's long history of resistance to foreign occupation, Vietnamese communism took on a strongly nationalist flavor. During the 1930s the Indochinese Communist Party, led by Ho, brought together all nationalist forces in a Marxist-led united front that worked toward revolution and independence.

In 1941 Ho established the **Viet Minh**, or Vietnamese Independence League, a coalition of anti-French groups that waged war against both the French colonizers and the Japanese, who occupied Vietnam during World War II.

Indonesian Nationalism

Southeast Asian nationalist activity emerged in the Dutch East Indies in the early twentieth century. Diverse organizations sought freedom from Dutch control while seeking ways to unite the diverse population, which included hundreds of ethnic groups with distinct languages. One strategy was to adopt a unifying language. Malay was the mother tongue for many peoples in the western Indonesian islands, while elsewhere in the archipelago it served as a trading language in the marketplace. Its wide use in trade made Malay a **lingua franca**, a language widely used as a common tongue among diverse groups that also had their own languages. Nationalist intellectuals began using Malay as a unifying national language and called it Indonesian, which gradually became the language of magazines, newspapers, books, and education.

Nationalist ideas competed with and sometimes reshaped Indonesian religious traditions. For example, some Muslims, impressed with but also resenting Western economic and military power, sought to reform and purify their faith by purging it of practices based on older pre-Islamic influences, such as mysticism and the sharp division between aristocrats and commoners, which they believed held Indonesians back by promoting cultural and social conservatism. *Muhammadiyah* ("Way of Muhammad") and its allied women's organization, *Aisyah,* criticized local customs and promoted the goal of an Islamic state. The organizations stressed the five pillars of Islam, devalued the writings of religious scholars after Muhammad, and favored the segregation of men and women in public, a custom long ignored by most Indonesians. In 1912 Javanese batik merchants who mixed these reformist religious ideas with nationalism established the colony's first true political movement, the Islamic Union, which by 1919 had recruited 2 million members.

As Marxism became an influence in Indonesia after the Russian Revolution, some Indonesians began working with Dutch communists living in Indonesia. The colonial government responded by arresting Marxists. The more radical Marxists, bent on revolution, established the Indonesian Communist Party in 1920, which grew rapidly by attracting support chiefly from nondevout Muslim peasants and labor union members in Java. Overestimating their strength, the communists sparked a poorly planned uprising in 1926. The government crushed the uprising with massive force and executed the communist leaders.

Viet Minh The Vietnamese Independence League, a coalition of anti-French groups established by Ho Chi Minh in 1941 that waged war against both the French and the Japanese.

lingua franca A language widely used as a common tongue among diverse groups with different languages.

Sukarno Indicts Dutch Colonialism

Sukarno, the fiery Indonesian nationalist, was skilled at articulating his criticisms of colonialism. A splendid orator, he attracted a large following through his use of Indonesian, especially Javanese, religious and cultural symbols and frequent historical references in his speeches. Arrested by the Dutch in 1930, Sukarno delivered a passionate defense speech, known as "Indonesia Accuses," at his trial that became one of the most inspiring documents of Indonesian nationalism. Sukarno stressed the greatness of Indonesia's past as a building block for the future.

The word "imperialism" . . . designates a . . . tendency . . . to dominate or influence the affairs of another nation, . . . a system . . . of economic control. . . . As long as a nation does not wield political power in its own country, part of its potential, economic, social or political, will be used for interests which are not its interests, but contrary to them. . . . A colonial nation is a nation that cannot be itself, a nation that in almost all its branches, in all of its life, bears the mark of imperialism. There is no community of interests between the subject and the object of imperialism. Between the two there is only a contrast of interests and a conflict of needs. All interests of imperialism, social, economic, political, or cultural, are opposed to the interests of the Indonesian people. The imperialists desire the continuation of imperialism, the Indonesians desire its abolition. . . .

What are the roads to promote Indonesian nationalism? . . . First: we point out to the people that they have had a great past. Second: we reinforce the consciousness of the people that the present is dark. Third: we show the people the pure and brightly shining light of the future and the roads which lead to this future so full of promises. . . . The P.N.I. [Indonesian Nationalist Party] awakens and reinforces the people's consciousness of its "grandiose past," its "dark present" and the promises of a shining, beckoning future.

Our grandiose past? Oh, what Indonesian does not feel his heart shrink with sorrow when he hears the stories about the beautiful past, does not regret the disappearance of that departed glory! What Indonesian does not feel his national heart beat with joy when he hears about the greatness of the [Intermediate Era] empires of Melayu and Srivijaya, about the greatness of the empire of Mataram and Madjapahit. . . . A nation with such a grandiose past must surely have sufficient natural aptitude to have a beautiful future. . . . Among the people . . . again conscious of their great past, national feeling is revived, and the fire of hope blazes in their hearts.

THINKING ABOUT THE READING

1. What is Sukarno's evaluation of imperialism?
2. How does he think Indonesians should capitalize on their past?

Source: Harry J. Benda and John A. Larkin, eds., *The World of Southeast Asia: Selected Historical Readings* (New York: Harper and Row, 1967), pp. 190–193. Copyright © 1967 Harper and Row. Reprinted with permission of John A. Larkin.

The destruction of the communists left an opening for other nationalists. For example, organized women's groups arose originally with the goal of improving Indonesian women's lives, and in 1928 the Congress of Indonesian Women began openly advocating independence. More influential politically, the Indonesian Nationalist Party, led mostly by Javanese aristocrats who rejected Islamic reform ideas, was established in 1927. This party promoted a new national identity. Sukarno (soo-KAHR-no) (1902–1970), the key founder, was born into a wealthy aristocratic Javanese family. After studying engineering, he dedicated his life to politics and to achieving a free Indonesia. Sukarno loved the shadow puppet stories, often based on Hindu epics from India, that had been popular on Java for centuries, in which the same characters might be heroes and villains at the same time. Like the characters in those stories, Sukarno (who had no first name) had a way of bringing together ideas that might appear contradictory, such as Islamic faith and atheistic Marxism. The mass popularizer of Indonesian nationalism, he created a slogan: "one nation—Indonesia, one people—Indonesian, one language—Indonesian." He even designed a flag and wrote the national anthem for the independent Indonesia he favored. The Dutch authorities arrested Sukarno in 1929 and exiled him to a remote island prison for the next decade, making him a nationalist symbol and increasing his popularity (see Witness to the Past: Sukarno Indicts Dutch Colonialism). With the best-known nationalist leader, Sukarno, in jail, the Indonesian Nationalist Party and the nationalist vision grew slowly throughout the 1930s.

Japanese Occupation: The Remaking of Southeast Asia

The occupation of Southeast Asia by Japanese forces during World War II from 1941 to 1945 boosted nationalism and weakened colonialism. Before 1941 colonial authority had remained strong. Only Vietnamese nationalism enjoyed widespread popular support and posed a serious threat to colonial rule. Then, in a few weeks in late 1941 and early 1942, everything changed. Japan had already bullied Thailand and the French colonial regime in Vietnam, which now took orders from the pro-Nazi Vichy government in France (see Chapter 24), to allow the stationing of Japanese troops. Then the bombing of Pearl Harbor in 1941 was quickly followed by a rapid Japanese invasion of Southeast Asia. With superior naval and air strength, the Japanese easily overwhelmed the colonial forces. Within four months they controlled major cities and heavily populated regions, shattering the mystique of Western invincibility. As an Indonesian writer later remembered, the Japanese occupation "destroyed a whole set of illusions and left man as naked as when he was created."[17] European and American officials, businessmen, planters, and missionaries were either in retreat or confined in prison camps. The Japanese talked of "Asia for the Asians," and some Japanese officers with anticolonial sentiments sympathized with Southeast Asian nationalists. But this rhetoric also masked the Japanese desire for resources, especially the rubber, oil, and timber of Indonesia, British Borneo, and Malaya. Japanese rule, whose impact varied from place to place, did not endure.

The Impact of Occupation

Japanese domination was brief, less than four years, yet it led to significant changes. For example, in many places, conflicts between ethnic groups increased because of selective repression. In Malaya, Japanese policy that favored the majority Malays allowed Malay government officials to keep their jobs while members of the Chinese minority often faced property seizures and arrest, creating antagonism between Malays and Chinese that persisted long after the war. By destroying the link to the world economy, the occupation also caused economic hardship. Western companies closed, causing unemployment, while Japanese forces seized natural resources and food. By 1944 living standards, crippled by severe shortages of essential goods such as food and clothing, were in steep decline. Southeast Asians suffered also from harassment by the Japanese police, who treated even minor violators of occupation regulations, such as breaking curfews or hoarding food, with brutality. In addition, the Japanese forcibly conscripted thousands of Southeast Asians: Javanese men became slave laborers and Filipinas, called "comfort women" by the Japanese, served the sexual needs of Japanese soldiers. As their war effort against the United States faltered, the desperate Japanese resorted to even more repressive policies to keep order and acquire resources.

Although often harsh for local people, Japanese rule also offered some political benefits for Southeast Asians. For instance, since they needed experienced local help, the Japanese promoted Southeast Asians into government positions once reserved for Westerners. These Indonesians or Burmese were often better educated and more able than the Europeans they replaced. In addition, the Japanese, seeking to purge the area of Western cultural influences, closed Christian mission schools, encouraged Islamic or Buddhist leaders, and fostered a renaissance of indigenous culture and an outpouring of literature, especially fiction that examined life under Japanese rule.

The Japanese also promoted Southeast Asian nationalism, at least indirectly, because of their recruitment of Southeast Asian leaders to lend legitimacy to their rule. Under colonialism most nationalists had been in jail or exile and hence powerless. The Japanese freed nationalist leaders such as Sukarno from jail and gave them official positions, if little actual power. The nationalists enjoyed a new role in public life and used the Japanese-controlled radio and newspapers to foster nationalist beliefs. The Japanese also recruited young people into armed paramilitary forces, and these became the basis for later nationalist armies in Indonesia and Burma that resisted the return of Western colonialism after World War II.

Japanese Defeat and Political Change

Some Southeast Asians dared to actively oppose Japanese rule, especially in Vietnam. Vietnamese communism might never have achieved power so quickly had it not been for the Japanese occupation, which marginalized and therefore discredited the French administration and imposed great hardship on most of the population, a fact that the communists used to advantage. The Viet Minh, led by Ho Chi Minh, were now armed and trained by American advisers, who, after the United States entered the war and needed local allies, had been sent to help anti-Japanese forces. In 1944 the Viet Minh moved out of their bases along the Chinese border and expanded their influence in northern Vietnam, attracting thousands of poor peasants to the anti-French nationalist cause while attacking the Japanese occupiers with guerrilla tactics. The Viet Minh rapidly gained popular support and recruits, thanks partly to a 1945 Japanese policy that exported scarce food to Japan while a famine killed 2 million Vietnamese. To establish a political presence, the Viet Minh organized local village administrations led by peasants who sympathized with their movement.

Japanese fortunes waned as the United States gained the upper hand in the war, opening the way for political change in Southeast Asia. U.S. bombing of Japanese installations in Southeast Asia alerted local people that the regional balance of power was changing. Fearing the return of Western power in Asia, the Japanese encouraged Southeast Asians to resist Western attempts to reestablish colonial control. In Indonesia, Japanese officials helped set up a committee of nationalists to prepare for Indonesian independence, and Sukarno told the members that together the united Indonesian people would renew their struggle to end forever Dutch colonialism. Japanese officials allowed Burmese nationalists to establish a government. As Japanese power diminished, some Southeast Asian nationalists began secretly working with the Western Allies. Changing sides, the Burmese nationalist army helped push Japanese forces out of Burma.

Tired of economic deprivation and repression, few Southeast Asians regretted Japan's defeat, and some, especially in Malaya, British Borneo, and the Philippines, even welcomed the return of Western forces. Before World War II the United States had promised to grant independence to the Philippines and did so in 1946, turning the country over to pro-U.S. leaders. But often the returning Westerners faced growing political volatility. The end of war set the stage for dramatic political change in Vietnam, Indonesia, and Burma, as nationalist forces resisted any return to the prewar status quo and successfully struggled for independence in the late 1940s and early 1950s.

Nationalism in Colonial Africa

The roots of the African nationalist struggle had been planted in the decades before World War II, although nationalist protests were less disruptive in Africa than in Southeast Asia and India, and African nationalist organizations also lacked the mass base of the Vietnamese and Indian nationalists. African nationalists tried with only limited success to overcome a major barrier to fostering widespread popular support: the creation by colonial powers of artificial national boundaries that enclosed ethnically diverse, often rival groups within a common administrative structure. Another obstacle was that usually imperial regimes did not prepare their colonies for political and economic independence by permitting African participation in government or opening enough schools to produce a large educated class that could assume the responsibilities and burdens of nationhood.

The artificial division of Africa was a major hindrance to nationalist organizing. All over Africa the colonial regimes, by using divide-and-rule strategies to govern the diverse ethnic groups, had made it difficult to create viable national identities. Without a national identity, an anticolonial nationalist movement that would unite all people within a colony against Western rule faced an uphill struggle. For example, Nigeria, in West Africa, was an artificial creation, the result of the late-nineteenth-century British colonization of diverse and often rival ethnic groups. While some Pan-Nigerian nationalists sought unity, most of the Nigerian nationalist organizations found their greatest support only among particular regions or ethnic groups within Nigeria. In the 1940s a prominent leader of one of the major ethnic groups, the Yoruba, expressed the common fear that no Nigerian nation was really possible:

> Nigeria is not a nation [but] a mere geographical expression. There are no "Nigerians" in the same sense as there are "English" or "French." The word "Nigerian" merely distinguish[es] those who live within the boundaries of Nigeria from those who do not.[18]

West African nationalist currents were strongest in the growing, usually multiethnic cities, such as Lagos in Nigeria, Accra in the Gold Coast, and Dakar in Senegal. These became the breeding grounds of new ideas. City life, which offered a wide range of economic activities, also encouraged the growth of trade union movements, which sponsored occasional strikes to protest colonial policies or economic exploitation. Hence, market women in Lagos, Nigeria, protested taxation, zealously protected their control of the local markets, and demanded the right to vote. During World War II they refused to cooperate with price controls, forcing the British to back down. However, rural people, especially farmers, also asserted their rights. For example, during the 1930s cocoa growers in the British-ruled Gold Coast held back their crops from the government to protest low prices.

African nationalism was sparked by World War I and the unfulfilled expectations for better lives in its aftermath. During the war the British, French, and Germans had all drafted or recruited men from their African colonies to fight on European battlefields, where thousands died. When the survivors returned home, the promises the colonial powers had made to them about land or jobs proved empty. Africans were further embittered when taxes were raised. For example, Kenyan soldiers came back from the war to find that British settlers had seized their land. In response Harry Thuku (THOO-koo) (ca. 1895–1970), a middle-class Kenyan and member of Kenya's largest ethnic group, the Gikuyu, created an alliance of diverse Kenyan ethnic groups in 1920 to confront the British. When the British arrested Thuku in 1922, rioting broke out led by Gikuyu women and the British fired on the rioters, killing over twenty of them. Anticolonial protests were common in the Belgian Congo too, where they led to rebellions by peasant farmers upset at Belgian demands that they undertake unpaid labor. Women were often in the forefront of resistance. During World War II, for instance, Aline Sitoe Diatta (1920–1944) led an uprising in Senegal when the French conscripted her village's rice supplies. She was exiled and later executed. In Nigeria in 1929, tens of thousands of Igbo women, particularly the local palm oil traders, rioted to protest taxes on them. When the rioters attacked a district office, the British opened fire, killing thirty-two of them. The protests escalated and it took months to restore order.

Inspired in part by Harry Thuku's movement, organized nationalist organizations developed in various colonies in the 1920s and met with occasional success, especially in West Africa. These urban-based organizations were formed in part to press for more African participation in local government. They were led by Western-educated Africans who sought democracy and eventual political freedom. Among these was J. E. Casely Hayford (1866–1930), a lawyer and journalist in the British Gold Coast (today's Ghana) who was influenced by Gandhi. Some Africans, including Casely Hayford, favored a Pan-African approach and sought support across colonial borders; they did not view colonial boundaries as the basis for nations. Both nationalists and Pan-Africanists were unable to overcome the divide among rival ethnic groups within each colony and, unlike the Indian and Vietnamese nationalist leaders, the gap between the cities and the villages. Hayford, for example, had little understanding of rural life and criticized the traditional chiefs who often exercised considerable power outside the cities. Furthermore, some African merchants, chiefs, and kings profited from their links to the colonizers and discouraged protests. For all these reasons, the urban nationalists were unable to capitalize on unpopular Western actions, such as the brutal Italian invasion and occupation of Africa's last independent country, Ethiopia, in 1935–1936, and had little influence before World War II, and most African states would not achieve their independence until the 1960s.

Though Africans did not mount an organized resistance to the Western powers, colonial rule generated new cultural trends that allowed people to express their views, often critical, about colonial African life. For instance, during the 1930s a musical style arose in the Gold Coast and soon spread into other British West African colonies. It was carried chiefly by guitar-playing sailors, including Africans who had visited the Americas and West Indians who regularly crossed the Atlantic.

African Jazz Band Jazz from the United States had a wide following in the world in the 1920s, 1930s, and 1940s. Jazz especially influenced the music of black South Africans, some of whom formed jazz groups such as the Harmony Kings. (Courtesy, National Library of South Africa)

This widely popular new style, **highlife**, was an urban-based mix of Christian hymns, West Indian calypso songs, and African dance rhythms. Later West African musicians added musical influences from Cuba, Brazil, and the United States, especially jazz, indicating the continuing cultural links between West Africa and the Americas. Although the music was closely tied to dance bands and parties, some highlife musicians began addressing social and political issues, and this trend grew with nationalism. The very term *highlife* signified both an envy and disapproval of the Western colonizers and rich Africans, who lived in luxury in mansions staffed by servants. Highlife songs dealt with the problems of everyday life, such as work, poverty, marital distress, and death. Many highlife songs were sung in **pidgin English**, the form of broken English that developed during the colonial era. This language, a mix of African and English words and grammar, spread throughout British West Africa as a marketplace lingua franca among ethnically diverse urban populations.

South African Nationalism and Resistance

The racial inequality and white supremacy established by the Dutch in South Africa and largely maintained by the British remained in place during most of the twentieth century, sparking nationalism that led some to resist oppression. The early South African nationalists, such as the founders of the African National Congress (usually known as the ANC, established in 1912), came from the urban middle class. The ANC encouraged education and preached African independence from white rule but did not directly confront the government until the 1950s. However, more militant African resistance also flourished, especially in the mining industry, where strikes

were endemic throughout the twentieth century despite severe government repression.

Given a white supremacist government anxious to suppress dissent, resistance was often subtle, involving noncooperation with the authorities or affirmation of African cultural forms. Protest was often expressed in music, although usually veiled to avoid arrest. Even hymns in African churches had a protest element, since they were sung using African rather than Western vocal traditions. Knowing that few whites understood lyrics sung in African languages, African workers filled the mining camps and labor movements with political music, offering messages such as "we demand freedom" and "workers unite." Many work songs bemoaned the ills of white rule. For decades, road gangs worked to songs such as "We Say: Oh, the White Man's Bad." Zulu and Swazi workers blended their own traditions with Western influences to create new dances performed by men. Virile, stamping dancers laced their performances with provocative songs: "Who has taken our land from us? Come out! Let us fight! The land was ours. Now it is taken. Fight! Fight!"[19]

In the cities jazz became a form of resistance to the South African regime. A potent vehicle for protest, this music, adapted from African Americans, reflected the African rejection of the culture of the conservative and racist Afrikaners, the descendants of Dutch settlers and the largest white ethnic group in South Africa. African American musicians such as the trumpeter Louis Armstrong (1901–1971) and the pianist Duke Ellington (1898–1974), who led a famed big band, were particularly popular in the 1930s and influenced the formation of South African jazz bands and new jazz-based musical styles. Educated urban Africans who loved jazz envisioned a modern African culture and sometimes rejected African traditions, as one Johannesburg resident proclaimed:

Tribal music! Chiefs! We don't care about chiefs! Give us jazz and film stars, man! We want Ellington, Satchmo [Louis Armstrong], and hot dames! Yes, brother, anything American. You can cut out this junk about [rural home-

---

highlife An urban-based West African musical style mixing Christian hymns, West Indian calypso songs, and African dance rhythms.

pidgin English The form of broken English that developed in Africa during the colonial era.

steads] and folk-tales—forget it! You're just trying to keep us backward![20]

The preferred music of the small, educated black professional and business class, jazz ultimately became a symbol of black nationalism in South Africa.

SECTION SUMMARY

■ Southeast Asian nationalism was strong in places such as Burma, which experienced harsh colonial rule, and even emerged as a rallying cry in Siam, which was never colonized but where a military coup of middle-class background overthrew the royal government.

■ Vietnamese resistance to French rule dated back to the late nineteenth century and was continued by the terrorist Vietnamese Nationalist Party, which the French harshly repressed, and the Viet Minh, a coalition led by the communist Ho Chi Minh.

■ A variety of groups representing Muslims, women, and communists worked toward independence for the Dutch East Indies, and of these the Indonesian Nationalist Party, which was led by Sukarno and incorporated both Islam and Marxism, was most influential.

■ Southeast Asians suffered greatly under Japanese occupation, but Japanese control of Southeast Asia during World War II also showed that Westerners could be defeated and primed the colonized peoples to resist recolonization by Westerners after the war was over.

■ Although African nationalist movements were hampered by the existence of rival ethnic groups within artificial colonies, anger over the poor treatment of Africans who had fought in World War I inspired many, especially in cities, to work for independence.

■ In South Africa, nationalists opposed the repressive white supremacist government through education, strikes, and, most pervasively, music.

◆ Remaking the Middle East and Latin America

What factors promoted change in the Middle East and Latin America?

The peoples of both the Middle East (the chiefly Muslim societies of North Africa and western Asia) and of Latin America, while having different histories, cultures, and political systems, were influenced by nationalism between 1914 and 1945. While North Africans, like sub-Saharan Africans and Southeast Asians, experienced Western colonial rule, Arabs in much of western Asia had been controlled for five hundred years by the Ottoman Turks, and under their rule the region was stagnating economically by the 1800s. European influence intensified after World War I, when the Ottoman colonies in western Asia were transferred to Britain and France, sparking nationalist resentment among the western Asian Arabs. Latin Americans, mostly Christians, achieved their independence in the nineteenth century and shared few recent experiences with colonized Arabs, Africans, and Southeast Asians, but two world wars and the Great Depression in the twentieth century caused turmoil, fostered dictatorships, and, as in other regions, spurred feelings of nationalism.

The Ottoman Territories

World War I was a watershed for Middle Eastern societies because it dismantled the region's major state, the Turkish-dominated Ottoman Empire, and reshaped Arab politics. In the war the Turks favored their longtime ally Germany because it shared their hatred of Russia, which had long hoped to control the narrow body of water that bisected the Ottoman capital city, Istanbul (formerly Constantinople), and provided access between the Black and Mediterranean Seas. The Ottoman Turks also dreamed of liberating Russian-controlled lands in the Caucasus and Central Asia that were inhabited largely by Turkish-speaking peoples. However, the Ottomans and their European allies lost the war, and the resulting breakup of the Ottoman Empire led to the emergence of a new, very different Turkish nation.

The Fall of the Ottoman Empire The hardships during World War I spurred Arab nationalism against Ottoman rule. Unrest in Syria brought on fierce Ottoman repression, as the Ottomans sent nationalist dissidents into exile and hanged others for treason. The most serious challenge to Ottoman rule came in Arabia, where Sharif Hussein ibn Ali (1856–1931), the Arab ruler of the Hejaz, the western Arabia region that included the Muslim holy cities of Mecca and Medina, shifted his loyalties in the war from the Ottomans to the British, who promised to support independence for the Arabs in Ottoman territory. In 1916, at British urging, Sharif Hussein launched an Arab revolt against the Turks (see Chronology: The Middle East, 1914–1945). British officers, including the flamboyant Lt. T. E. Lawrence (famous as "Lawrence of Arabia"), advised Sharif Hussein's tribal forces, which attacked Ottoman bases and communications. The British invaded and occupied southern Iraq, an Ottoman province, which had a strategic position between Arabia, Syria, and Iran and was thought to have oil.

The end of World War I brought crushed dreams and turmoil to the Middle East. The Arab nationalists such as Sharif Hussein did not know that during the war the eventually victorious European Allies—Britain, France, and Russia—had made secret agreements for dismantling the Ottoman Empire that ignored Arab interests. The czarist Russians had planned after the war to incorporate Istanbul and nearby territories into their empire while Britain and France agreed to partition the Ottoman provinces in western Asia between them, despite British promises to Sharif Hussein about Arab independence. The Russian plans had to be modified after the communists

CHRONOLOGY

The Middle East, 1914–1945

1916	Arab revolt against the Turks
1917	Balfour Declaration
1919	British withdrawal from Iran
1919–1922	Turkish Revolution by Ataturk
1921	Formation of Iranian republic by Reza Khan
1922	Formation of Turkish republic
1922	End of British protectorate in Egypt
1925	Formation of Pahlavi dynasty by Reza Khan
1928	Formation of Muslim Brotherhood in Egypt
1930	Independence for Iraq
1932	Formation of Saudi Arabia
1935	Discovery of oil in Saudi Arabia
1936	Britain-Egypt alliance
1936–1939	Civil war in Palestine

took power in Russia in 1917 and signed a peace treaty with Germany that allowed the Caucasus region, once under Ottoman rule but occupied by the Russians in the 1800s, to be returned to Germany's Ottoman ally. When the war ended, British troops occupied much of Iraq and Palestine, and French troops controlled the Syrian coast.

World War I caused great suffering to diverse Ottoman societies. The Caucasus peoples, especially the Christian Armenians, desired independence. Suspecting them of aiding Russia, the Turks turned on the Armenians living in eastern Anatolia (see Chapter 21). More than a million Armenians were deported, chiefly to Syria and Iraq, while perhaps another million died of thirst, starvation, or systematic slaughter by the Ottoman army. These sufferings created a permanent Turkish-Armenian hostility. After the war the Russians regained control of the Caucasus, including Armenia. In a different context, hunger and disease also affected millions of Arabs in the Ottoman Empire, with 200,000 dying in Syria alone during the war.

The Versailles treaty that ended World War I brought major political change, including dismemberment of the Ottoman Empire (see Map 25.2). Turkey's neighbors—the Greeks, Italians, and Armenians—made claims on Anatolia and adjacent islands, and European Zionists asked for a Jewish national home in Palestine (see Chapter 21). The Allies ended Ottoman control of Arab territories and gave autonomy and the option

of eventual independence to the Kurds, a Sunni Muslim people, distinct from both Arabs and Turks, who inhabited a large, mountainous region of Western Asia and were also the dominant ethnic group in southeast Turkey. Both Syria and Iraq declared their independence from the Ottoman Empire. However, the League of Nations, dominated by Western countries, awarded France control over Syria and Lebanon, and Britain control over Iraq, Palestine, and Transjordan (today Jordan), under what the League called mandates. In theory mandates were less onerous for local people than colonies because they allowed for administrative assistance for a limited time.

Instead of mandates, which they viewed as a new form of colonialism, Arabs often wanted to build their own governments and shape new social systems. Arab nationalists in Syria proposed a democratic government, and some favored granting women the vote, a daring idea; indeed, few Western nations had granted women voting rights. Ignoring Syrian Arab views, French forces quickly occupied Syria and, after facing armed but futile resistance, exiled nationalist leaders. The Allies also ignored the desire of the Kurdish people for their own nation. Despite British proposals for such a change, the Kurds remained divided between Turkey, Persia (Iran), Iraq, and Syria, thus becoming the world's largest ethnic group without their own state.

A New Turkey While all the former Ottoman territories experienced change after World War I, the heart of the empire, Turkey, saw the most revolutionary changes. The disastrous defeat in the war and the humiliating agreements that followed left the Turks helpless and bitter, as well as facing a Greek invasion and Arab secession. But under the leadership of the daring war hero and ardent nationalist later known as Kemal Ataturk (kuh-MAHL AT-uh-turk) (1881–1938), the Turks enjoyed a spectacular resurgence. In 1919 Ataturk began mobilizing military forces in eastern Anatolia into a revolutionary organization to oppose the Ottoman sultan, who was discredited by defeats, and to restore dignity to the Turks. Ataturk accepted the loss of Arab lands but wanted to preserve the Turkish majority areas and the eastern Anatolia districts inhabited chiefly by Kurds.

After establishing a rival Turkish government in the central Anatolia city of Ankara, Ataturk led his forces in fighting both the sultan's government in Istanbul and the foreign occupiers, especially the Greek forces that had moved deep into Anatolia. He finally pushed the Greeks back to the Aegean Sea, and eventually Turkey and Greece agreed to a population transfer in which many Greeks living in Turkish territory moved to Greece and the Turks dwelling in Greek lands moved to Turkey. In 1922 Ataturk deposed the Ottoman sultan and set up a republic with himself as president.

Ataturk was a controversial figure among Turks. He violated Muslim customs by pursuing sexual promiscuity and drinking heavily in public; devout Muslims also suspected his morality because of his agnostic stance. In addition, being a Turkish nationalist who glorified the pre-Islamic Turkish past, Ataturk dismissed Islamic culture as an inferior mix of age-old

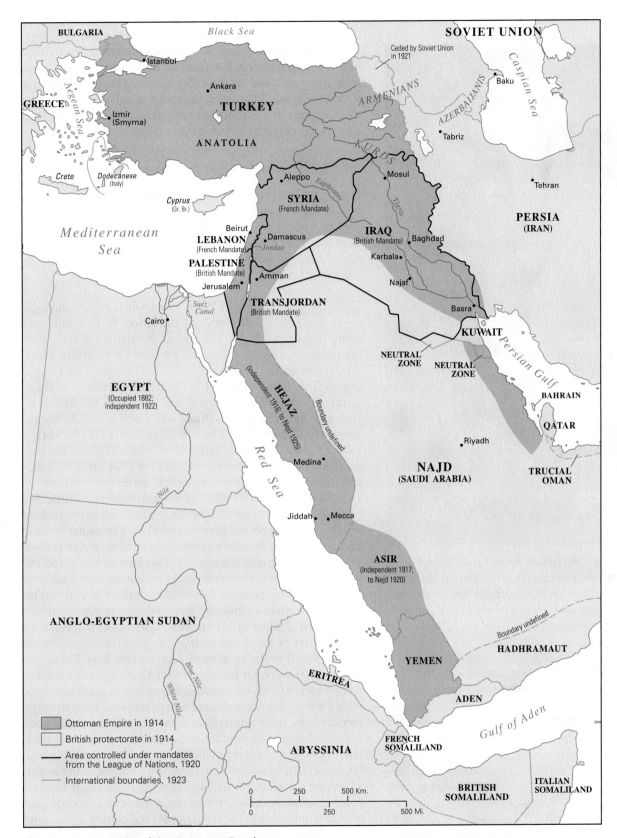

Map 25.2 Partition of the Ottoman Empire

Before 1914 the Ottoman Turks controlled much of western Asia, including western Arabia. After World War II the League of Nations awarded Iraq, Transjordan, and Palestine to Britain. Syria and Lebanon were given to France, and western Arabia was ruled by Arabs. Eventually the Saudi family, rulers of the Najd, expanded their rule into western Arabia and created Saudi Arabia.

Online Study Center Improve Your Grade
Interactive Map: The Disintegration of the Ottoman Empire, 1829–1914

Ataturk Wedding Dance The Turkish leader Kemal Ataturk promoted and adopted Western fashions while defying Muslim customs. In this photo from around 1925, Ataturk dances with his daughter at her Western-style wedding. (Hulton Archive/Getty Images)

nority by suppressing their language and culture. Ataturk left a deeply changed nation, but many of the reforms he introduced were never adopted in the villages, where Islam remained a strong influence. However, Ataturk's secular approach remained popular with Turkish nationalists, including military officers, influencing Turkish politics today.

Modern Iran, Egypt, and Iraq

During this era major changes also occurred in the other major Middle Eastern countries. Like Turkey, Persia, later known as Iran, moved toward modernization, though with fewer permanent changes, and Egyptians and Iraqis turned toward nationalism in response to British attempts to maintain power in those countries.

Modernizing Iran Before World War I, when Britain and Russia exercised influence, Persian independence had been limited. The end of the war left Britain with the power to impose a protectorate over Persia under which the Persian government was maintained but was forced to accept British loans, financial controls, advisers, and military forces. Growing Persian opposition prompted the British to withdraw their troops in 1919 and seek a new approach. Britain supported General Reza Khan (REE-za kahn) (1877–1944), a soldier from a modest background who wanted to end the corrupt, ineffective royal dynasty, installed in 1794, establish a secular republic, and address economic underdevelopment. In 1921 Reza Khan took control of the government with British backing, ending the monarchy. Reza Khan was supported by secular Shi'ites, who had long struggled for a more democratic and open society. In 1924 an influential local magazine praised Reza Khan for freeing the country from having a king and expressed the hope that soon it would escape the domination of the powerful Shi'ite clergy. But in 1925, at the urging of Shi'ite clerics, Reza Khan abandoned the republican government and formed the Pahlavi (PAH-lah-vee) dynasty, with himself as king (known in Persia as a shah).

Although restoring a royal government, Reza Khan, like Ataturk in Turkey, set his country on a path toward modernization and, in 1935, renamed his nation Iran, a symbolic break with the past. The shah created a large national army through conscription, built railroads and roads, and established government factories to produce textiles, sugar, cement, and steel. He spurred the economy by taking control over the oil industry, an act that improved Iran's political standing in the world. The regime also made social changes that outraged Muslim conservatives, such as introducing a Western law code and encouraging men to wear Western hats and clothes. It also outlawed the veiling of women in public, which had the unintended effect of forcing women who wanted to wear the veil to stay home. But while the modernists, merchants, and middle class supported Reza Khan's policies, there was little improvement for poor Iranians, who mostly despised the government. Reza Khan expanded the landlord class at peasant expense.

The shah admired Ataturk's reforms but, lacking Ataturk's charisma and education, had less success in transforming Iran.

mentalities. He favored modernization, announcing that "our eyes are turned westward. We shall transplant Western institutions to Asiatic soil. We wish to be a modern nation with our mind open, and yet to remain ourselves."[21] Ataturk claimed that secularization and the emancipation of women were the Turkish tradition.

In the 1920s these ideas were put in action through a dazzling series of reforms that challenged Muslim traditions. They included revamping the legal system along Western lines, replacing Arabic-based script with a Western alphabet, prohibiting polygamy, and granting women equal rights in divorce, child custody, and inheritance. Ataturk abolished Islamic religious schools and courts, and he removed reference to Islam as the state religion from the constitution. He also pushed Western-style clothing and banned the brimless hats popular with Muslim men, such as the *fez*, turban, and skullcap. His government resembled a parliamentary democracy, but he exercised near dictatorial power and alienated the Kurdish mi-

During World War II Reza Shah favored Germany. This position prompted an Anglo-Russian occupation of Iran, which the Allies needed as a supply route. Humiliated by the foreign intervention, Reza Shah abdicated in favor of his twenty-two-year-old son, Muhammad Reza Pahlavi (REH-zah PAH-lah-vee) (1919–1980), and went into exile. The son ruled until 1979.

Egypt, Iraq, and the British British control of Egypt and Iraq and Arab resistance to that control fostered nationalist feeling in those countries. In Egypt during World War I the British had imposed martial law and drafted peasants to build roads and railroads and dig trenches in war zones. Egyptians resented these policies and the thousands of British soldiers stationed in their country during the war. A peasant song of the period castigated British officials for carrying off the peasants' corn, camels, and cattle and pleaded to be left alone. After the war nationalists unsuccessfully sought an end to British domination. The leading nationalist party, the *Wafd*, was led by Saad Zaghlul (sod ZOG-lool) (ca. 1857–1927), who had studied theology under Islamic modernists and then earned a French law degree. The Wafd was a secular movement seeking independence, representative government, civil liberties, and curtailed powers for the pro-British monarchy.

British missteps led to political change. In 1919 the British arrested Zaghlul and other Wafd leaders. Enraged Egyptians responded with strikes, student demonstrations, sabotage of railroads, and the murder of British soldiers. The anti-British movement united rich and poor, Muslims and Coptic Christians, men and women. The turmoil forced the British to release Zaghlul, who then went to the Paris Peace Conference to plead for national self-determination but, like Vietnam's Ho Chi Minh, was ignored. Upon returning to Egypt, Zaghlul was arrested again, but the resulting unrest forced Britain to grant Egypt limited independence in 1922, which nationalists saw as a sham, since Britain still controlled Egypt's defense and foreign affairs. In 1936 Britain officially ended its occupation and established an alliance with Egypt. But Britain still kept thousands of troops along the Suez Canal, which connected the Mediterranean and Red Seas through northeast Egypt, and it also shared with Egypt the administration of Sudan, the territory bordering Egypt on the south. Resentment of the continuing British presence increased during World War II.

The British also struggled to control Iraq, an artificial creation that united three Ottoman provinces, each dominated by a different group: Sunni Kurds, Sunni Arabs, and Shi'ite Arabs. Describing their occupation as a "liberation," the British promised to bestow on the Iraqis an efficient administration, honest finance, impartial justice, and security; in reality they planned to discourage self-government. To give the appearance of popular support, they held a plebiscite, but they manipulated the results to suggest pro-British sympathies. British occupation soon embittered many Iraqis. In 1920 Shi'ite clerics seeking an Islamic state proclaimed a holy war against the British, prompting various Shi'a and Sunni tribes to rise in rebellion. The British suppressed the rebellion, but at a great cost in money and lives: some 10,000 Iraqi and 400 British died in the fighting. The British kept their own casualty lists low by relying heavily on aerial bombing, which flattened whole villages.

Shaken by the fierce resistance, the British changed direction in Iraq. They introduced limited self-government that allowed Iraqi participation in an appointed Council of State. The skilled diplomacy of a pro-Arab British archaeologist, writer, and diplomat, Lady Gertrude Bell (1868–1926), defused tensions. Seeking a king for Iraq who would be content to "reign but not govern," as Bell put it, in 1921 Britain installed a member of the Hashemite (HASH-uh-mite) royal family of Mecca, Sharif Hussein's son Faisal (1885–1935). In 1930 Faisal convinced Britain to grant Iraq independence, but only after he agreed to accept continued British military bases and government advisers. By then the British had found oil in Iraq, making them unwilling to cut their ties. Many Arabs considered Faisal and his Hashemite successors to be British clients serving British interests, but Iraqi politics after 1930 was shaped by a series of Sunni Arab military strongmen, autocrats who dominated the kings and strongly influenced government policies, more than the kings themselves.

Islam and Zionism

The stranglehold of European power and Western culture remained concerns of most Middle Eastern societies during the era. Although various colonized peoples struggled to free themselves, nationalist success came slowly. Some movements tried, with limited success, to unite Arabs or Muslims across national borders. In the absence of political success, religion became a focus of attention. Arabs debated the merits of Westernization, the role of Islam in their societies, and the challenge posed by Zionism, an encounter that fostered a long-term hostility between Muslims and Jews.

Struggles over Westernization and Islam Middle Eastern leaders and thinkers debated how or whether to emulate the powerful Western nations. They envied Western economic development, such as industrialization and a wealth of consumer goods, but disagreed about how many Western cultural, political, and social patterns, such as freethinking, parliamentary democracy, and women's rights, should be adopted. Some sought wholesale transformation; some favored Islamic tradition; and still others sought a middle path between the two, such as mixing Western and Islamic laws. Between 1923 and 1930 Western-style constitutions, which provided for civil liberties and an elected parliament, were adopted in Egypt, Iraq, Lebanon, Transjordan, and Syria. But these parliaments were limited in their duties and unrepresentative. Real power usually remained in the hands of European officials or powerful kings, and most Arab politicians had little respect for civil liberties. Inspired by Western ideals of modernity, Arabs made progress in education, public health, industrialization, and communications, but change came slowly. The Egyptian literacy rate rose from 9 percent in 1917 to only 15 percent in 1937.

Some women also asserted their rights and sought social change. One of these was the Egyptian Huda Shaarawi (HOO-da sha-RAH-we) (1879–1947). From a wealthy Cairo family, Huda had been married off at age thirteen to a much older cousin. Finding the marriage confining, Huda organized nonviolent anti-British demonstrations by women after World War I and then publicly removed her veil in 1923, shocking Egyptians. She founded and led the Egyptian feminist movement, which succeeded in raising the minimum marriage age for girls to sixteen and increasing educational opportunities for women.

The debates over Westernization fostered new intellectual currents in the Islamic world, some pro-Western, others anti-Western. Representing the former approach, a blind Egyptian, Taha Husayn (1889–1973), educated in traditional Islamic schools but also at the Sorbonne in Paris, became the key figure of Egyptian literature in the era. In his writings he challenged orthodox Islam and, in 1938, proclaimed that Westernizing Arab culture, which he favored, would fit with Egypt's traditions, which he described as a mix of Pharaonic, Arab, and Western cultures. "I want," he wrote, "our new life to harmonize with our ancient glory." In contrast, the popular reaction against Westernization came with a new Egyptian religious movement, the **Muslim Brotherhood**, founded in 1928 by schoolteacher Hasan al-Banna (1906–1949). Al-Banna despised Western values, arguing that it "would be inexcusable for us to turn aside from the path of truth—Islam—and so follow the path of fleshly desires and vanities—the path of Europe."[22] The Brotherhood followed a strict interpretation of the Quran and the hadiths, though it also accepted modern technology and was open to a more active public role for women. Expressing a widespread resentment against Western influence, such as films, bars, and modern, figure-revealing women's fashions, the Brotherhood soon developed a following in Sudan and western Asia.

The most extreme anti-Western reaction was that of the puritanical Wahhabi movement, which eventually dominated Arabia. The Wahhabis sought a return to a supposedly pristine version of Islam uncorrupted by centuries of change. They were opposed to shaving beards, smoking tobacco, and drinking alcohol. Wahhabi influence grew with the success of a tribal chief, Abdul Aziz Ibn Saud (sah-OOD) (1902–1969), who expanded the power of the Saudi family, which ruled much of central and eastern Arabia (a region known as Najd) (see Chapter 21). By 1932 his forces had taken western Arabia and the Islamic holy cities of Mecca and Medina from the Hashemites and formed the country of Saudi Arabia. As king, Abdul Aziz began strictly enforcing Islamic law by establishing Committees for the Commendation of Virtue and the Condemnation of Vice to police personal behavior. Policemen used long canes to enforce attendance at the five daily prayers, punish alcohol use and listening to music, and harass unveiled women. At the same time, the Saudis welcomed material innovations from the West, such as automobiles, medicine, and telephones. In 1935 oil was discovered in Saudi Arabia, which contained the world's richest oil reserves. The oil wealth chiefly benefited the royal family and their allies, the Wahhabi clergy.

Zionism and Palestine

The roots of a long-term problem for Arab nationalists were planted in Palestine. Before World War I Palestine was part of Ottoman-ruled Syria and had a largely Arab population. The British took over Palestine from the Ottomans after World War I. Meanwhile, the Zionist movement, which sought a Jewish homeland for the Jewish people, had been formed in the Jewish ghettoes of Europe (see Chapters 19 and 21). The Zionist slogan—"a land without a people for a people without a land"—offered a compelling vision: take the long persecuted Jewish minorities and return them to the homeland in Palestine from which they had been expelled by the Romans two millennia earlier. Zionist leaders cultivated the British government, which in 1917 issued the **Balfour Declaration**, a letter from the British foreign minister to Zionist leaders giving British support for the establishment of Palestine as a national home for the Jewish people. But the Zionist slogan had a flaw: Palestine was not a land without a people. Palestinian Arabs had lived there for many centuries, building cities, cultivating orchards, and herding livestock. A Zionist leader later conceded that Jewish settlers, under the impression that the land was largely uninhabited, were surprised to find people there. In Arab eyes, Jewish immigrants were European colonizers planning to dispossess them.

In the 1920s and 1930s, thousands of European Jews migrated to Palestine with British support, some of them fleeing Nazi Germany. By 1939 the Palestine population of 1.5 million was one-third Jewish. Although Jewish settlers established businesses, industries, and productive farms that contributed greatly to Palestine's economic development, Arabs did not see many benefits and feared they would become a vulnerable numerical minority in what they considered their own land. Land became a contentious issue. Zionist organizations began buying up the best land from absentee Arab landlords who disregarded the customary rights of villagers to use it, uprooting thousands of Arab peasants.

As tensions increased, violence spread, bewildering the British. Sometimes hundreds of Arabs and Jews were killed in armed clashes. In 1936 a major Arab rebellion fostered a three-year civil war. All Arab factions united to demand an end to Jewish immigration and land sales to Jews and to oppose plans for establishing an independent Palestine. Concluding that the Arab-Jewish divide was unbridgeable, Britain proposed a partition into two states and the removal of thousands of Arabs from the Jewish side. Both groups rejected the proposal. In 1939, worried about alienating Egypt and Iraq as Europeans prepared for World War II, Britain placed a limit on Jewish immigration and banned land transfers. But the Holocaust against the Jews in Europe during World War II spurred a more militant Zionism, reinforcing the Jewish desire for a homeland where they could govern themselves.

Muslim Brotherhood　An Egyptian religious movement founded in 1928 that expressed popular Arab reaction to Westernization.

Balfour Declaration　A letter from the British foreign minister to Zionist leaders in 1917 giving British support for the establishment of Palestine as a national home for the Jewish people.

Politics and Modernization in Latin America

While Islamic societies grappled with colonialism and the encounter with the West, Latin America, with economies reliant on a few natural resource exports such as beef, copper, coffee, and sugar, became more vulnerable to global political and economic crises. Sometimes this resulted in foreign interventions and domination, as when military forces from the United States occupied Nicaragua from 1909 to 1933 and Haiti from 1915 to 1934. Latin Americans paid a price for their openness to the world economy as foreign investment fell and foreign markets closed during the Great Depression in the 1930s, cutting the foreign trade of some countries by 90 percent. By 1932 Latin America as a whole was exporting 65 percent less than it had in 1929. Economic downturns led to political instability, which paved the way for governments led by military dictators, known as caudillos.

During the Great Depression dictators came to power all over the region (see Map 25.3). In 1930–1931 armed forces overthrew governments, among them elected ones, in a dozen Latin American nations, including large countries such as Peru, Argentina, and Brazil (see Chronology: Latin America and the Caribbean, 1909–1945). Some of the new governments, such as those in Argentina and Brazil, were influenced by European fascism. In Argentina one fascist military leader who took power announced boldly that there were no more political parties, only the Argentine people. Dictators often increased their governments' role in the economy, such as by beginning industries to provide products normally imported. They also used their power to amass huge fortunes for themselves and to repress dissent. In El Salvador, for example, President Maximiliano Hernandez Martinez massacred 30,000 protesting Indian peasants. He put a "positive spin" on poverty by saying that people who went barefoot could better receive the "beneficial vibrations" of the earth than those with shoes. Some dictatorships continued for years. For instance, Cubans suffered under brutal dictatorships for most of the era. The repressive Cuban rightwinger Gerardo Machado (r. 1925–1933) was forced out of office when the collapse of sugar prices generated a massive strike, temporarily bringing less autocratic leftwing nationalists and Socialists to power. But the United States disliked the new government, which challenged the U.S. claim of special privileges in Cuba and implemented labor and social reforms that hurt influential American and Cuban business interests. In 1934 the United States encouraged a coup by Sgt. Fulgencio Batista (fool-HEN-see-o bah-TEES-ta) (1901–1973), who dominated Cuba for the next twenty-five years as a rightwing dictator.

The challenges of the era also affected Chile, one of the most stable and open Latin American nations. Chileans typically accepted participatory government, claiming that Chile was "the England of Latin America." Although the military had occasionally seized power for short periods, Chile had generally enjoyed elected democratic governments and highly competitive elections involving several parties. The dislocations of the Great Depression helped the more reformist political par-

CHRONOLOGY

Latin America and the Caribbean, 1909–1945

1909–1933	U.S. military force in Nicaragua
1930–1931	Military governments throughout Latin America
1934	Fulgencio Batista Cuban dictator
1930–1945	Estado Novo in Brazil
1934–1940	Presidency of Lazaro Cardenas in Mexico

ties and social movements to gain support, and the squabbling leftist and centrist parties, all of which supported democratic processes, united in a Popular Front that came to power in the 1939 elections. Their reformist government, supported by labor unions, sponsored industrialization.

During the 1930s a growing women's movement that was allied with Chile's political left brought once forbidden ideas into the political debates of patriarchal, strongly Catholic Chile. Demanding respect for Chilean women and an end to what one organization called "compulsory motherhood," they lobbied for prenatal health care, child-care subsidies, and family planning, including birth control and the right to abortion, which was illegal but widely practiced. But while women won some basic legal rights, they still struggled for voting rights and could not get most of their social agenda, including abortion rights, approved, in part because of opposition by conservative Chilean women.

As elsewhere in Latin America, Brazil experienced political change that was often tinged with nationalism. In the 1920s middle-class reformers challenged domination by a corrupt ruling class that they felt did not listen to the common people or assert Brazil's national interests in the world. The reformers sought economic transformation. Their proposals for a more liberal society included official recognition of labor unions, a minimum wage, restraints in child labor, land reform, universal suffrage, and expansion of education to poor children. Worker unrest aided the growth of labor unions, but a chronic labor surplus limited the rise in organized labor's power.

Eventually the Great Depression reshaped Brazilian politics, prompting a civilian-military coup by Getulio Vargas (jay-TOO-lee-oh VAR-gus) (1883–1954) in 1930. A former soldier, lawyer, and government minister, Vargas launched the **Estado Novo** ("New State"), a fascist-influenced, modernizing dictatorship that ruled until 1945. A businessman who opposed Vargas described him as "intelligent, extremely perceptive, but also a demagogue who knew how to manipulate the masses."[23] Vargas's fascism was reflected in his use of torture and censorship

Estado Novo ("New State") A fascist-influenced and modernizing dictatorship in Brazil led by Getulio Vargas between 1930 and 1945.

Map 25.3   South and Central America in 1930
By 1930 Latin America had achieved its present political configuration, except that Britain, France, and Holland still had colonies in the Guianas region of South America, and Britain controlled British Honduras (today's Belize) in Central America.

to repress opponents. But the Estado Novo also sponsored modernizing reforms that made Vargas widely popular with the lower classes. He nationalized the banks, financed industrialization, introduced the vote for literate eighteen-year-olds and working women, and also introduced social security, an eight-hour workday, a minimum wage, and the right to strike. Gradually the dictator became more populist and nationalist. He was deposed by the army in 1945 after he had begun moving to the left. Acute tensions between rightwing and leftwing Brazilians remained.

Mexico After the Revolution

As in Chile and Brazil, strongly progressive and nationalist ideas emerged in Mexico. After the turmoil of the decade-long Mexican Revolution (see Chapter 20), which ended only in 1920, Mexico badly needed funds for reconstruction but faced sharply reduced export earnings and a deepening economic slump. A popular song from 1920 noted the hardship on common Mexican men and women: "The scramble to be president is one of our oldest haunts. But to eat a peaceful tortilla is all the poor man wants."[24] President Plutarcho Elias Calles (KAH-yays) (r. 1924–1928) put the political system on a solid footing by creating a new party that brought together various factions. Yet many Mexicans saw little improvement in their lives. For example, despite their sacrifices during the Mexican Revolution, women remained largely excluded from public life and were viewed by men as unfit to manage their own lives, let alone assume public positions of responsibility.

In 1934 Mexicans launched a new era by electing Lazaro Cardenas (car-DAYN-es) (r. 1934–1940), an army officer with socialist leanings, as president. Peasants had grown cynical about the promises by leaders during the Mexican Revolution to supply them with land. Cardenas fulfilled this promise by assigning land ownership to the *ejidos* (eh-HEE-dos), the traditional agricultural cooperatives, who now apportioned land to their members. As a result, some 800,000 people realized their dream. Cardenas hoped the ejidos would build schools and hospitals and supply credit to farmers, uplifting Mexico's poorest social class. But agricultural production for the market fell, and the money and services the government had promised never materialized.

Cardenas also introduced reforms that made him wildly popular with other Mexicans. Wooing the urban workers, he encouraged the formation of a large labor confederation. With this organization, the working class enjoyed a higher standard of living and more dignity. Cardenas also followed a nationalist economic policy. U.S. firms owned much of the oil industry, which was one of the world's largest. After these companies ignored a Mexican Supreme Court order to improve worker pay, Cardenas nationalized the industry, spurring celebrations in Mexico and outraging U.S. leaders. Workers gained a role in managing both the oil industry and the railroads. The president also supported women's rights, arguing that working women had the same right as men to participate in electoral struggles. In addition, Cardenas reorganized the ruling Party of Revolutionary Institutions around four functional groups: peasants, organized labor, the military, and the middle class. Organizing these groups allowed for more government control. Cardenas gave the Mexican Revolution new life, while the wealthy Mexican landowners and merchants, as well as U.S. political and business leaders, hated him.

Online Study Center Improve Your Grade
Primary Source: Speech to the Nation

Cardenas was followed by more moderate leaders who reversed support for the ejidos, favoring instead individual farmers, and ignored women's rights. Mexican women could not vote until 1953. These leaders also cooperated with the United States on immigration issues. Poor Mexicans had moved to the United States for decades. During World War II Mexico and the United States signed an agreement to send more Mexican workers north to fill the job positions in industry, agriculture, and the service sector left vacant by drafted American men. The flow northward of poor Mexicans, legal and illegal, became a floodtide after the war.

Cultural Nationalism in Latin America and the Caribbean

Cultural nationalism greatly affected Latin American and Caribbean societies. For example, a Brazilian literary trend known as Modernism sought to define a distinct national expression by exploring the country's rich cultural heritage. Rather than emulating European literary trends, modernist writers used forms and ideas reflecting Brazil's uniqueness. For instance, the poet, novelist, and critic Mario de Andrade (1893–1945) mixed words from various regional dialects and Native American, African, and Portuguese folklore into his work. Some modernists had a more internationalist outlook. Oswald de Andrade (1890–1954) saw Brazil as a creative consumer of world culture. He argued that Brazilians should mix ideas from all over the world and turn them into something distinctively Brazilian.

Nationalism, including the use of folk traditions, shaped Brazilian music. The prolific and unconventional composer Heitor Villa-Lobos (vee-luh-LO-bose) (1890–1959) developed a music to express the national character that was inspired by Afro-Brazilian and Indian religious rites and urban popular music. The popular music and dance known as *samba* became not only a world symbol of Brazilian society but also a way for the otherwise voiceless Afro-Brazilian lower classes to express themselves. Samba began as a street music and dance associated with the annual pre-Lenten carnival, a raucous celebration, in Rio de Janeiro. In 1928 professional samba groups organized into diverse schools that competed for prizes awarded by a jury, thus making samba a major social activity of the city's shantytowns. Samba infused the annual carnival processions, which grew increasingly extravagant, featuring elaborate floats, flamboyant costumes, and intricate group choreography.

The progressive spirit of the times also spurred literary and artistic movements throughout Latin America. In Chile writers combined radical politics with cultural renaissance. For example, the work of Marxist-influenced Chilean writers such as the poet Pablo Neruda (ne-ROO-duh) (1904–1973) bristled with anger over economic inequalities. Sometimes governments retaliated against dissident artists; Neruda wrote some of his greatest poetry while in hiding or exile. Meanwhile, Mexican culture reflected the currents of the revolution as it glorified the country's mixed-descent, or mestizo, heritage and addressed the poverty and powerlessness of the remaining Native American communities. Mexico produced several great artists who painted, usually on walls of public buildings, magnificent murals, showing the life of Mexico's people. Among them was Diego Rivera (rih-VEER-a) (1885–1957), a Marxist, who became one of the most famous artists in the Western Hemisphere. His huge, realistic murals depicted the common people, especially peasants and workers, struggling for dignity. Some of his murals depicting Mexican history emphasized the conflicts between the indigenous peoples and the Spanish colonizers. His wife, Frida Kahlo (KAH-lo) (1907–1954), the daughter of a German Jewish immigrant, specialized in vivid, even shocking paintings that often expressed the physical and psychological pain suffered by women, thus reflecting her own

stormy personal relationships and lifelong struggle against illness.

A cultural renaissance also occurred in the Caribbean, where intellectuals sought to create an authentic West Indian identity. In part this involved overcoming the negative attitudes, especially those held among the political and economic elite, toward acknowledging influences from Africa, the ancestral home of most West Indians. Adopting British and French racist stereotypes, West Indians had often associated Africa with the uncivilized. In contrast, Afro-Caribbean intellectuals such as the Trinidadian Marxist C. L. R. James (1901–1989) sought to rebuild Afro-Caribbean pride by celebrating African roots, which he argued were a major contributor to the distinctive West Indian culture. James also wanted to link cultural nationalism with political nationalism by using literature, art, and music to challenge Western colonialism. James was a well-traveled historian, prolific writer, political theorist, critic, skillful cricket player, and activist in Trinidad politics who was equally at home in the Caribbean, Europe, Africa, and North America. His ability to combine Afro-Caribbean nationalism with an internationalist perspective inspired intellectuals around the world.

Diego Rivera, *Sugar Cane* Diego Rivera, the greatest of the Mexican mural painters, was noted for art with an historical and political focus, often showing political leaders, cruel overlords, and suffering peasants and workers. This painting, *Sugar Cane,* pictures a Spanish overseer ordering black and Indian workers to cut, bind, and carry the sugar cane. [Diego Rivera, *Sugar Cane,* 1931. Philadelphia Museum of Art, Gift of Mr. and Mrs. Herbert Cameron Morris (1943-46-21)]

SECTION SUMMARY

- In the post–World War I breakup of the Ottoman Empire, lands such as Iraq, Syria, and Lebanon that sought freedom were instead colonized by Britain and France, but Turkey revived under the leadership of Ataturk, who modernized the country and minimized the role of Islam.

- Reza Khan, the British-supported shah of Persia, attempted to modernize his country as Ataturk had Turkey, though with less success, while Britain, in reaction to violent opposition, granted Egypt and Iraq increasing measures of autonomy and independence.

- Arab leaders debated how to balance modernization with Islam; the most puritanical form of Islam, Wahhabism, came to dominate Saudi Arabia; and the return of Jews to Palestine caused great tensions with the Arabs who had lived there for centuries.

- Vulnerable Latin American economies were greatly damaged during the Great Depression, which led to instability and the rise of military dictators in many countries, while in Chile, instability led to a progressive, prolabor government.

- Impoverished and frustrated after a long revolution, many Mexicans were pleased by the rule of Lazaro Cardenas, who gave land to agricultural cooperatives, nationalized industries, and supported women's rights, but who was followed by less progressive leaders.

- Latin American and Caribbean artists, musicians, and writers worked to produce art that expressed their unique cultural perspectives.

Online Study Center **ACE the Test**

 # Chapter Summary

During this era, in the face of major world changes, nationalism became a strong force in the Western colonies and other dominated societies of Asia, Africa, and Latin America. The global transitions of two world wars and the Great Depression had destabilized local economies, capitalism had reshaped rural life for millions of peasants, and many Asians and Africans resented the activities of the Western powers. In response, nationalism, often blended with Marxism, gained support as a strategy to oppose Western domination.

Nationalism became particularly influential in China and India. Nationalists reunified China after two decades of fragmentation and warlord violence but could not improve rural life or halt Japanese expansion, providing an opening for the Chinese communists under Mao Zedong to gain support by offering a program to transform society. In India, nationalism in response to repressive British colonialism gained a mass following. Mohandas Gandhi mounted massive, nonviolent campaigns of civil disobedience, which undermined British rule.

But Gandhi and other nationalist leaders, mostly Hindus, could not prevent the minority Muslims from seeking a separate nation.

Nationalism had an uneven history in Southeast Asia, sub-Saharan Africa, and the Middle East. In Vietnam, Ho Chi Minh organized an effective communist resistance to the French, while in Indonesia, Sukarno led opposition to Dutch rule. During World War II nationalists in Vietnam, Indonesia, and Burma organized to oppose a resumption of Western colonialism when the war ended. While political nationalist organizations developed in Africa and black South Africans resisted white domination, nationalism was often more influential as a cultural force, especially in music. World War I left the Middle East in turmoil, as Britain and France extended their power into Arab societies once ruled by the Ottoman Empire. But the Turks, led by Kemal Ataturk, and Iran developed modern states open to Western influences. Muslim intellectuals debated whether to adopt Western ideas or maintain Islamic traditions. Arab conservatives, including the Wahhabis, used Islam to oppose any social or cultural changes. The rise of Zionist immigration to Palestine posed another challenge to the Arabs. In many Latin American nations, while progressive social and literary movements proliferated, economic problems intensified and dictators gained power. Some Latin American governments, especially in Mexico and Brazil, tried to help the poor. Nationalism permeated literary, musical, and artistic expression in both Latin America and the Caribbean.

Online Study Center **Improve Your Grade** Flashcards

Key Terms

warlords	people's war	pidgin English
New Culture Movement	Maoism	Muslim Brotherhood
May Fourth Movement	nonviolent resistance	Balfour Declaration
Jiangxi Soviet	Viet Minh	Estado Novo
Long March	lingua franca	
	highlife	

Suggested Reading

Books

Bogle, Emory C. *The Modern Middle East: From Imperialism to Freedom, 1800–1958.* Upper Saddle River, N.J.: Prentice-Hall, 1996. An overview of the region during this era.

Brown, Judith M. *Gandhi: Prisoner of Hope.* New Haven: Yale University Press, 1989. One of the key studies of this seminal nationalist leader and thinker.

Brown, Judith M. *Modern India: The Origins of an Asian Democracy,* 2nd ed. New York: Oxford University Press, 1995. A strong introduction to modern Indian history.

Cleveland, William L. *A History of the Modern Middle East,* 2nd ed. Boulder: Westview Press, 2000. One of the best surveys.

Erlmann, Veit. *African Stars: Studies in Black South African Performance.* Chicago: University of Chicago Press, 1991. Essays on South African music and nationalism in this era.

Findley, Carter Vaughn, and John A. M. Rothney. *Twentieth Century World*, 6th ed. Boston: Houghton Mifflin, 2006. A comprehensive survey of this era.

Freund, Bill. *The Making of Contemporary Africa: The Development of African Society Since 1800*, 2nd ed. Bloomington: Indiana University Press, 1999. An excellent discussion of the colonial era and the changes it brought.

Huynh Kim Khanh. *Vietnamese Communism, 1925–1945*. Ithaca: Cornell University Press, 1982. A valuable scholarly study of this topic.

Keen, Benjamin, and Keith Haynes. *A History of Latin America*, 7th ed. Boston: Houghton Mifflin, 2004. A comprehensive account with considerable coverage of these decades.

Marlay, Ross, and Clark Neher. *Patriots and Tyrants: Ten Asian Leaders*. Lanham, Md.: Rowman and Littlefield, 1999. Sketches of Asian nationalists such as Gandhi, Nehru, Ho, Mao, and Sukarno.

Martin, Cheryl E. and Mark Wasserman. *Latin America and its People*. New York: Longman, 2005. A readable introduction with much on this era.

Owen, Norman G., et al. *The Emergence of Modern Southeast Asia: A New History*. Honolulu: University of Hawai'i Press, 2005. The best survey of modern Southeast Asian history, comprehensive and readable.

Sheridan James E. *China in Disintegration: The Republican Era in Chinese History, 1912–1949*. New York: Free Press, 1975. Dated but still the standard work on this period in China.

Spence, Jonathan D. *The Gate of Heavenly Peace: The Chinese and Their Revolution, 1895–1980*. New York: Penguin, 1982. A masterful account of China in this era through the eyes of artists, thinkers, and writers.

Stavrianos, Leften S. *Global Rift: The Third World Comes of Age*. New York: William Morrow, 1971. A provocative, innovative, and readable study that provides a global context.

Wolf, Eric R. *Peasant Wars of the Twentieth Century*. New York: Harper and Row, 1969. A pathbreaking study of the revolutions in China, Vietnam, Algeria, Cuba, and Mexico.

Websites

History of the Middle East Database (http://www.nmhschool.org/tthornton/mehistorydatabase/mideastindex.htm). A useful site on history, politics, and culture.

Internet African History Sourcebook (http://www.fordham.edu/halsall/africa/africasbook.html). This site contains useful information and documentary material on Africa.

Internet East Asian History Sourcebook (http://www.fordham.edu/halsall/eastasia/eastasiasbook.html). An invaluable collection of sources and links on China, Japan, and Korea from ancient to modern times.

Internet Indian History Sourcebook (http://www.fordham.edu/halsall/india/indiasbook.html). An invaluable collection of sources and links on India from ancient to modern times.

Internet Islamic History Sourcebook (http://www.fordham.edu/halsall/islam/islamsbook.html). A comprehensive examination of Islamic societies and their long history, with many useful links and source materials.

Internet Modern History Sourcebook (http://www.fordham.edu/halsall/mod/modsbook.html). An extensive online collection of historical documents and secondary materials.

Latin American Resources (http://www.oberlin.edu/faculty/svolk/latinam.htm). An excellent collection of resources and links on history, politics, and culture.

WWW Southeast Asia Guide (http://www.library.wisc.edu/guides/SEAsia/). An easy-to-use site.

Global Imbalances in the Modern World, 1750–1945

Aworld traveler in the nineteenth century could not help but notice the imbalances in wealth and power between the world's societies, imbalances that became even wider in the early twentieth century. One of these travelers, the American writer Mark Twain, author of beloved novels about Tom Sawyer and Huckleberry Finn, became a critic of the imperialism that increased these imbalances. Returning to the United States after lengthy travels in the South Pacific, Asia, Africa, and Europe, Twain blasted U.S. policies in Asia, including the costly military occupation of the Philippines as part of the Spanish-American War, writing in 1900 that "I left these [American] shores a red-hot imperialist. I wanted the American eagle to go screaming into the Pacific. But I have thought more, since then. [Now] I am opposed to having the eagle put its talons on any other hand."[1] His travels had convinced him that, despite Western stereotypes, most peoples, including Filipinos, were capable of governing themselves and that efforts to impose U.S. models on others were doomed to failure.

The imbalances that Twain had observed in his travels or gleaned from news accounts were part of the modern world, which was shaped in part by revolutions and innovations in western Europe and North America. In these Western societies, capitalism and industrialization fostered wealth and inspired new technologies, such as the steamships and railroads that conveyed travelers like Twain, resources, and products over great distances. But the new technologies also included deadly new weapons, such as repeating rifles and machine guns, that enabled the Western conquest of Asian and African societies, reshaping the world's political and economic configuration. Just as Spain and Portugal controlled Latin America until the early 1800s, a half-dozen Western nations ruled, or influenced the governments of, most Asian, African, and Caribbean peoples by 1914. Western domination of the global economy fostered investment but also facilitated a transfer of vast wealth to the West.

While several Western societies exercised disproportionate power in this era, other societies were not passive actors, simply responding to the West. In whatever part of the world they lived, people were linked to a global system that, however imbalanced in terms of political and economic power, promoted often useful exchanges between distant societies. Societies borrowed ideas, institutions, and technologies from each other, though redefining them to meet their own needs. Societies such as Siam (later Thailand), Persia (later Iran), Turkey, and, most spectacularly, Japan successfully resisted colonialism and, borrowing Western models, introduced some modernization. In fact, resistance to Western power was endemic in the global system. Even in colonized societies such as Vietnam, Indonesia, India, and South Africa, local peoples actively resisted domination and asserted their own interests. The movement of products, thought, and people, on a larger scale than ever before,

transcended political boundaries, connecting distant societies. Europeans avidly imported Asian arts, Africans embraced Christianity, and peasants from India settled in the South Pacific and the West Indies. By the 1930s people around the world, often using borrowed Western ideas such as nationalism and Marxism, were challenging Western political and economic power.

IMPERIALISM, STATES, AND THE GLOBAL SYSTEM

The world's governments changed greatly during the Modern Era, fostering new types of empires and states. A more integrated international order, dominated by a few Western nations and, eventually, also by Japan, was built on the foundation of the varied Western and Asian empires that had been the main power centers during the Early Modern Era. Societies worldwide grappled with the global political trends that affected people's well-being and livelihoods.

Global Empires

Powerful societies had formed empires since ancient times, but over the centuries successive empires grew larger and more complex. In the mid-1700s over two-thirds of the world's people lived in one of several large, multiethnic empires whose economies were based largely on peasant agriculture. These empires stretched across the Eastern Hemisphere from Qing China and the Western colonies in Southeast Asia, such as Dutch Java and the Spanish Philippines, to the Ottoman, Russian, and Habsburg Empires. In the Americas the huge Spanish Empire, Portuguese Brazil, and British North America all resembled the Eurasian empires in their multiethnic populations and agrarian base, although much of the agriculture was done by unfree

Queen Victoria as Seen by a Nigerian Carver This wood effigy of the British monarch was made by a Yoruba artist in just-colonized Nigeria in the late nineteenth century. (Pitt Rivers Museum, Oxford University)

labor. In addition to empires but smaller, there were also strong states such as Tokugawa Japan, Siam, and the Ashante kingdom in West Africa. All empires and states depended on a command of military power, especially gunpowder weapons. Great Britain and the Netherlands differed from the other strong states mainly in their greater reliance on world trade.

Many of the empires of the mid-1700s had crumbled by the early twentieth century. The Spanish, Portuguese, and British lost most of their territories in the Americas, and the Habsburg and Ottoman Empires were dismantled after World War I. In their place, modern empires had emerged. Between 1870 and 1914, Britain and France established overseas empires on a grander scale than ever before in history, ruling colonies in Africa, Asia and the Pacific, and Russia now controlled a vast expanse of Eurasia. On a smaller scale, Germany, Japan, and the United States also forged territorial empires. A huge portion of the globe, divided up into colonies or spheres of influence by the West, was incorporated into a Western-dominated world economic system. The influential British imperialist and author Rudyard Kipling summarized the rationale for exercising imperial power: "That they should take who have the power, And they should keep who can."[2]

Like empires throughout history, modern imperial states, whatever their democratic forms at home, punished dissent in their colonies. Sometimes protests, such as those led by Mohandas Gandhi in India, forced Western colonizers to modify their policies; more commonly, protest leaders, such as Gandhi, Harry Thuku in Kenya, and Sukarno in Indonesia, were jailed or exiled. Some observers recognized the failure of democratic countries to encourage democracy in their own colonies. For example, British critics condemned the repressive colonial policies of their government, especially the harsh treatment designed to discourage rebellion in Ireland against Britain. A nineteenth-century English wit charged that "the moment the very name of Ireland is mentioned, the English seem to bid adieu to common feelings, common prudence and common sense, and to act with the barbarity of tyrants and the fatuity of idiots."[3]

Nations and Nationalisms

Whether parts of empires or not, all over the world societies struggled to become nations, enjoying self-government and a common identity. But Western peoples formed the most powerful nations. Many European nations were formidable forces because of their strong government structures and democratic practices that fostered debate; they also enjoyed economic dynamism, possessed advanced weapons, and engaged in fierce rivalries with each other. Across the Atlantic most Latin American nations struggled to achieve prosperity and internal unity, but the United States matched European capabilities and shared similar imperial ambitions by the later 1800s, much to the disgust of anti-imperialists such as Mark Twain. Americans believed in the tenets of Manifest Destiny, articulated by an influential U.S. politician: "God has marked the American people as his chosen nation to finally lead in the regeneration of the world."[4] By contrast, few people in the colonies shared any sense of common identity, let alone a national mission; colo-

nial governments were unpopular and usually viewed by the colonized as illegitimate. By drawing up arbitrary colonial borders, often without regard to ethnic connections or economic networks, the British created Nigeria, the Dutch created Indonesia, the French created Laos, and the Belgians created the Congo, all colonies lacking any national cohesion. The ethnic diversity of most colonies—Indonesia and the Congo each contained several hundred ethnic groups—inhibited nationalist feeling and thus the formation of nationalist movements.

Still, despite the barriers, nationalism spread, often encouraged by travel, exile, or education. Giuseppi Garibaldi (gee-you-SEP-ee gare-a-BALL-dee) (1807–1882), for instance, who helped unify Italy, was born in France of Italian parents and nursed a love for his ancestral homeland during his years living in South America and then the United States before he returned to Italy. The Venezuelan Simon Bolivar, the Filipino Jose Rizal (rih-ZALL) (1861–1896), and the Vietnamese Ho Chi Minh (1890–1969), all disenchanted with colonial restrictions, embraced a nationalist agenda while living in Europe. Indian students discovered the writings of the English-born American revolutionary and exponent of liberty Tom Paine and wondered why their British rulers had ignored Paine's "rights of man" in India. Yan Fu, a Chinese student living in England in the 1870s, recalled spending "whole days and nights discussing differences and similarities in Chinese and Western thought and political institutions."[5] He perceived how Europeans became powerful by combining military aggression, well-defined national states, growing commerce, and a culture approving of political and religious debate. Back in China, Yan Fu translated the work of liberal British thinkers and used it to spread nationalism and other Western ideas in China. But nationalists seeking to confront Western power did not all look to the West for inspiration. By 1900 Japan was a role model of nationalism and modernization for many Asians, and the Vietnamese anticolonial leader Phan Boi Chau (fan boy-CHOW) (1867–1940) advised his countrymen to look east to Japan.

But nationalism was not always an imported sentiment. Many Asians had a sense of identity similar to nationalism long before the nineteenth century. People in Korea, Japan, and Vietnam, for example, had long enjoyed some national feeling based on shared religion, a common language, bureaucratic government, and the perception of one or more common enemies. African kingdoms such as Ashante (ah-SHAN-tee), Oyo (OH-yo), and Buganda (boo-GONE-da) enjoyed some attributes of nationhood. Reflecting such national feeling, in 1898, Hawaii's last monarch, Queen Liliuokalani (luh-lee-uh-oh-kuh-LAH-nee), pleaded with the United States not to colonize the islands, since her people's "form of government is as dear to them as yours is precious to you. Quite as warmly as you love your country, so they love theirs."[6] U.S. leaders ignored her pleas and annexed Hawaii. To protect their position, colonizers labored hard to crush these traditions and to counter anticolonial nationalism through the use of divide-and-rule strategies, such as the British encouragement of the Hindu-Muslim divide in India. Formerly well-defined states, such as Ashante and Buganda in Africa, lost their traditional cohesion as they now became parts of larger colonies. To resist colonial strategies, nationalists sought ways to regain the initiative and achieve sovereignty. The Indian nationalist Jawaharlal Nehru expressed the search for a successful anticolonial strategy: "What could we do? How could we pull India out of this quagmire of poverty and defeatism, which sucked her in?"[7]

Nationhood Through Revolutions

Some societies needed major rebellions and revolutions to transform old discredited orders and create new nations. The American and French Revolutions of the later 1700s began an Age of Revolution and inspired people elsewhere to take up arms against unjust or outdated governments. In the U.S. case, disgruntled colonists overthrew British rule, and key American revolutionaries, such as Thomas Jefferson and English-born Tom Paine, became known around the world as exponents of political freedom. During the mid-nineteenth century the Taiping (TIE-ping) Rebellion against China's Qing dynasty and the Indian Rebellion against the British East India Company, although they ultimately failed, provided fierce challenges to established governments in the world's two most populous societies. Like these upheavals, the rebellion by the southern states of the United States against the federal government, which resulted in some 600,000 deaths during the American Civil War did not succeed. Nonetheless, the struggle reshaped American society by allowing President Abraham Lincoln to abolish slavery and forge a stronger national government. Early in the twentieth century, other revolutions overturned old governments and built nations in Mexico, Turkey, and China; the Chinese revolution ended 2,000 years of imperial control and established the foundation for a modern republic. The Russian Revolution of 1917 installed the world's first communist government, inspiring communist movements and revolutionary nationalists around the world.

The aftermath of World War I brought new revolutionary upheavals and ideologies. Old states collapsed in eastern Europe, fascism spread in Germany and Japan in the economic shambles caused by the Great Depression, and Spain erupted in civil war. In 1914 Marxism, the revolutionary socialist vision developed by Karl Marx (1818–1883), had relatively little influence outside of Germany and Russia, but by 1945 the ideology had mass support in many societies. Communist revolutionary movements percolated in China, Korea, Indonesia, and Vietnam. Karl Marx had supplied the critique of the old society, which he saw as shaped by class struggle and capitalism. Now the Russian leader, Vladimir Lenin (1870–1924), forged a revolutionary party and strategy to overthrow that society, and the Chinese communist leader Mao Zedong (maow dzuh-dong) (1893–1976) contributed a vision of a new, unselfish socialist society. Unlike Lenin, Mao believed that revolutionaries must work closely with the local people, writing that "the people are the sea, we [communists] are the fish, so long as we can swim in that sea, we will survive."[8] By combining communism with nationalism, the Vietnamese revolutionary Ho Chi Minh provided a workable model to overthrow colonialism. The ideas of Lenin, Mao, and Ho made Marxism a major vehicle for change after World War II.

Change in the Global System

During the Modern Era the global system expanded and changed as Western influence increased. Networks of trade and communication linking distant societies grew in number and extent. However, because some Western nations came to enjoy more political and military power than other societies, they benefited more from their exchanges with the rest of the world. Aided by this power, Western culture dominated local traditions, especially in Western colonies. For example, textbooks in French colonial schools, where the students were of African, Afro-Caribbean, Asian, or Pacific islander descent, celebrated the history of the French—"our ancestors the Gauls"—while children in the U.S.-ruled Philippines, a tropical and predominantly Catholic land, learned English from books showing American youngsters throwing snowballs, playing baseball, and attending Protestant church services. In some cases this deliberate Westernization reshaped beliefs and ways of life, as occurred among the Filipinos and the Igbos of southern Nigeria. However, Western cultural influence was weak in other colonized societies, especially Muslim ones such as Egypt, the Hausa of northern Nigeria, and the Achehnese of Indonesia.

Countries gained or lost power in the global system, depending on their wealth, type of government, and access to military power (see Historical Controversy: Modernization or World-System?). In 1750, Western overseas expansion, including military conquests, had already reshaped the Americas and some regions of Africa and southern Asia. Chinese, Indians, and western Europeans were the richest peoples at this time, the Chinese accounting for a third and India and western Europe each accounting for a fourth of the world's total economic production. Collectively they accounted for 70 percent of all the world's economic activity and 80 percent of its manufacturing. China remained the greatest engine of the world economy. Britain was the rising political and economic European power, but it faced challenges from France, Russia, Spain, and the Ottoman Empire. The more economically developed districts and the major cities within the two wealthiest countries, Britain and China, apparently enjoyed similar living standards, such as abundant food and long life spans, until at least 1800. As late as the 1830s British observers reported that residents of Britain's capital, London, and the key Chinese trading city of Guangzhou had a roughly comparable material life.

By 1914, however, after a century and a half of Western industrialization, imperial expansion, and colonization, the global system had become more divided than ever before into rich and poor societies. India was now among the poorer countries, and China had succumbed to Western military and economic influence, falling well behind the West. Meanwhile, a few Western nation-states—especially Great Britain, the United States, Germany, and France—had grown rich and powerful, enjoying substantial influence around the world and over the global economy. Because of their unparalleled military power, all four of these nations ruled colonial empires, from which they extracted valuable resources; played a leading role in world trade; and tried to spread, with some success, their cultures and ideas. Also among the richest nations, but having less international power, were a few other western European countries,

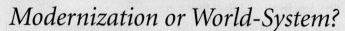

Modernization or World-System?

Historians and social scientists in the West have vigorously debated which theories best explain the modern world, especially how it became interconnected. One influential approach uses the concept of modernization and focuses on individual societies. The other approach, world-system analysis, emphasizes the links between societies. This second approach has often interested world historians.

THE PROBLEM

Historians and historically-oriented social scientists have sought to understand societies and their changes over time. These efforts have spawned new intellectual approaches in the past several decades. Scholars have asked why some societies in the modern world, such as the United States, Britain, and Japan, became rich and powerful while others, such as Mozambique, Haiti, and Laos, remained poor and weak. Have societies developed as they did because of their own traditions or because of their connections to the larger world? Should we study societies as separate units, as the modernization approach advocates? Or should societies be examined as part of a larger system of exchange and power, or a world-system? Or are both of these approaches inadequate?

THE DEBATE

During the 1950s and 1960s modernization theory was developed in the United States by scholars such as C. E. Black and W. W. Rostow. In their classification, most societies were traditional, retaining centuries-old political and economic institutions and social and cultural values. These societies had despotic governments, extended family systems, and fatalistic attitudes. In contrast, a few dynamic societies became modern by adopting liberal democracy, secularism, flexible social systems, high-consumption lifestyles, and free market capitalism. This modernization began in Europe between 1500 and 1750 and reached its fullest development in the United States by the mid-twentieth century. All societies, these theorists asserted, were moving, rapidly or slowly, in the same direction toward U.S.-style modernization—some enthusiastically, others reluctantly—and this modernization was desirable.

Modernization theory was influential in the United States for several decades, but by the 1970s it began losing considerable support among historians. While the notion of modernity seemed helpful, critics found many flaws in the theory of modernization. They argued that it centered history on the West as the dynamic nursery of modernization and neglected other politically and economically successful societies, such as Qing China, Tokugawa Japan, Siam (today's Thailand), Ottoman Turkey, Morocco, and the Ashante kingdom in Africa. Although these societies had all either collapsed or struggled against Western imperialism during the nineteenth century, they had once flourished and fostered economic growth despite having few of the characteristics associated with moder-

nity. Furthermore, by emphasizing the individual trees (societies) at the expense of the larger forest (the global context), the theory failed to explain the interconnections of societies through various international networks and processes that created global imbalances, such as the transfer of wealth and resources—Indonesian coffee, Iraqi oil, West African cocoa, Latin American silver, Caribbean sugar—from colonies to colonizers.

Modernization theory generally reflects the views of scholars who believe that U.S.-style individualism, democratic government, and free enterprise capitalism are the best strategies to promote personal freedom and economic growth, and who want to export these ideas to the world. Modernization theorists such as Rostow have considered challenges to U.S. influence and to capitalism, from Marxists and radical nationalists, to be diversions leading to despotic governments and an economic dead end. While agreeing that political and economic freedom were valuable ideas that generally benefited Western peoples, critics doubt these are the foundation of modernity or applicable everywhere. By characterizing traditional societies as "backward" and blaming them for being this way, modernization theory, critics contend, reflects Western prejudices about the world, such as the French "civilizing mission" and the U.S. notion of "Manifest Destiny," and supports the expansion of Western political power and economic investment into Asia and Africa on the grounds that it fosters "progress." Furthermore, critics argue, most societies are a mix of "traditional" and "modern" traits. For example, the "modern" United States has been a highly religious society from its beginning, arguably less secular than "traditional" China. Nor have Asians and Africans always found Western social and cultural models, such as nuclear families and Christianity, to be more appealing or useful than their own traditions; some, often inspired by Western ideas, have hoped to reform Muslim, Hindu, Confucian, or Buddhist traditions, but most continued to find meaning in the beliefs and customs of their ancestors.

Challenging modernization theory's neglect of connections, scholars led by the American sociologist Immanuel Wallerstein developed the concept of the "world-system," a network of interlinked economic, political, and social relationships spanning the globe. To Wallerstein the world-system, originating in Europe in the 1400s and based on a capitalist world economy, rival European states, and imperialism, explains growing Western global dominance after 1500. By 1914 Western military expansion, colonialism, and industrialization had enriched Europe and brought other societies into the modern world-system. An Africa specialist, Wallerstein views the modern world-system as more widely spread than the more limited networks, such as those of the Mongols and Arabs, that linked Afro-Eurasian societies prior to the 1400s.

In this view, modernization involves not only changes within societies but also their changing relationship to the dominant political powers and the world economy. For example, the Ashante kingdom became a West African power in the 1700s by trading slaves to the West, but, in the late 1800s, it was conquered and absorbed into the British colony of the Gold Coast (modern Ghana). Under British rule, the Ashante chiefly grew cocoa for export and thus were dependent on the fluctuations of the world price for cocoa. To understand modern Ghana, then, requires knowledge of the Ashante relations to both British colonialism and the world economy.

To describe the world political and economic structure, Wallerstein divided the world-system into three broad zones, or categories of countries: the *core*, *semiperiphery*, and *periphery*. In 1914 the core included the rich and powerful nations such as Britain, France, and the United States, which all benefited from industrialization, growing middle classes, democracy, a strong sense of nationhood, and political stability. They sometimes used their armies and financial clout to assert power over other societies, even independent ones such as China, where Western powers established spheres of interest patrolled by their gunboats. By 1914 Wallerstein's middle category, the semiperiphery, included countries such as Japan, Russia, and Italy, which were partially industrialized, politically independent nation-states but less prosperous and powerful than the core nations. Finally, the largest group in 1914, the periphery, comprised the colonized societies, such as French Vietnam, British Nigeria, and the U.S.-ruled Philippines, and the neocolonies such as Brazil, Thailand (Siam), and Iran (Persia). These societies were burdened with export economies based on natural resources, little or no industrialization, massive poverty, little democracy, and domination by more powerful core nations. Colonialism transferred wealth from the periphery to the core, which used the wealth for its own economic development. As Wallerstein acknowledges, the world-system is not rigid, and a few societies shifted categories over the centuries. For example, the United States was semiperipheral in 1800, but by 1900 industrialization and territorial expansion had propelled it into the core. By contrast, once powerful China fell into peripheral status after 1800. But even with some movement up or down, Wallerstein argues, the core-semiperiphery-periphery structure still characterizes the world-system today.

If modernization theory predicts an increasing standardization around the world toward a Western-influenced pattern, world-system analysis suggests that the core and periphery, serving different functions in the world economy, have moved in opposite directions, toward wealth on the one hand and poverty on the other. Since the economic exchange between them was unequal, the periphery became dependent on the core for goods, services, investment, and resource markets, giving core societies, which exploited the resources of the periphery, great influence. For example, the Gold Coast's cocoa growers needed British markets, and British companies provided consumer goods to the shopkeepers, often Lebanese immigrants, who served these communities. The wealth and power of a country, then, reflect its political and economic position in the world-system.

Like modernization theory, world-system analysis has provoked controversy. Some scholars embrace a world-system approach but disagree with Wallerstein's version. Whereas Waller-

A Japanese View of America This Japanese print records the impression of the United States and its wealth and power by a Japanese trade mission in 1860. It shows an American man and woman posing with symbols of modern technology, a pocket watch and a sewing machine. (Private Collection)

stein believes a world-system began only around 1500, Christopher Chase-Dunn and Thomas Hall emphasize a longer history with diverse intersocietal networks that can be called world-systems beginning in ancient times. Andre Gunder Frank and Barry Gills identify one single world-system existing for 5,000 years, since, they argue, some form of capitalism began with the earliest states, such as Sumeria, in Afro-Eurasia. Some critics accuse Wallerstein, like the modernization theorists, of overemphasizing the West and underestimating the key roles played by Asians in the Afro-Eurasian economy.

Other critics are harsher. Some charge that Wallerstein's stress on exchange between countries downplays inequitable economies and class structures within countries—such as rapacious landowners, privileged aristocrats, tyrannical chiefs, and greedy merchants—hence shifting the blame for poverty to the world economy. Others, such as Daniel Chirot, question whether exploitation of the periphery explains the economic growth of the core. Critics also wonder whether terms such as *core* and *periphery* constitute a more sophisticated version of "modernity" and "tradition," marginalizing and perhaps demeaning poor societies. Finally, some think Wallerstein's focus on economic factors neglects politics and cultures, including religion, and places so much stress on the forest that it misses the trees.

EVALUATING THE DEBATE

The modernization and world-system theorists launched an ongoing debate about how world history can be understood, but neither approach fully explains modern history. World historians widely agree that the once dominant modernization theory is inadequate for understanding the world as a whole. Some are attracted to one or another version of world-system analysis. While many details of Wallerstein's approach are open to challenge, the general concept of a global system, divided into several categories of countries each with common features, helps understand relations between societies and the exchanges within the world economy. Situating societies within an interlinked world helps explain the impact of colonialism, the background to military interventions by more powerful countries, and the political turbulence of the poorer states today. While each society has unique characteristics that shape its history, perceiving some sort of global system or systems that rise and fall over time helps us understand large-scale, long-term change and explains how thousands of small hunting and gathering bands 12,000 years ago became the contemporary global community of nation-states.

THINKING ABOUT THE CONTROVERSY

1. How do modernization and world-system approaches explain the modern world and its diverse societies differently?

2. What are the major advantages and problems of each of the two approaches?

EXPLORING THE CONTROVERSY

Among the major works of modernization theory are C. E. Black, *The Dynamics of Modernization: A Study in Comparative History* (New York: Harper and Row, 1966); and W. W. Rostow, *The Stages of Economic Growth: A Non-Communist Manifesto* (Cambridge: Cambridge University Press, 1960). Immanuel Wallerstein has summarized his ideas in *The Capitalist World-Economy* (New York: Cambridge University Press, 1979) and *World-Systems Analysis: An Introduction* (Durham, N.C.: Duke University Press, 2004). Alternative versions of the world-system concept include Christopher Chase-Dunn and Thomas D. Hall, *Rise and Demise: Comparing World-Systems* (Boulder, Colo.: Westview Press, 1997); and Andre Gunder Frank and Barry K. Gills, eds., *The World System: Five Hundred Years or Five Thousand?* (New York: Routledge, 1996). Daniel Chirot takes issue with world-system analysis on many issues in *Social Change in the Modern Era* (New York: Harcourt Brace Jovanovich, 1986). Excellent summaries and critiques of world-system analysis and competing ideas can be found in Thomas R. Shannon, *An Introduction to the World-System Perspective* (Boulder, Colo.: Westview Press, 1989); Alvin Y. So, *Social Change and Development: Modernization, Dependency, and World-System Theories* (Newbury Park, Calif.: Sage, 1990); Stephen K. Sanderson, ed., *Civilizations and World Systems: Studying World-Historical Change* (Walnut Creek, C.A.: AltaMira Press, 1995); and Thomas D. Hall, ed. *A World-Systems Reader: New Perspectives on Gender, Urbanism, Cultures, Indigenous Peoples, and Ecology* (Lanham, M.D.: Rowman and Littlfield, 2000). For a provocative critique of these debates and the rise of the world economy by an Indian scholar, see Amiya Kumar Bagchi, *Perilous Passage: Mankind and the Global Ascendancy of Capital* (Lanham, M.D.: Rowman and Littlefield, 2005).

including the Netherlands, Belgium, and Switzerland. A middle category of countries—Canada, Japan, and European nations such as Russia, Italy, Portugal, and Spain—had a weaker economic base and less military power than those of the richest nations, but they still enjoyed economic and political autonomy. A third category of countries were those that were economically poor and militarily weak, either ruled directly as Western colonies, such as India, Indonesia, Nigeria, or Jamaica, or under strong political and economic influence as neocolonies, such as China, Thailand, and Iran. Economically, Latin American countries, relative to the rich North American and western European nations, were also poor.

Living conditions and governments in the rich countries differed dramatically in 1914 from those in the poor societies. Capitalism fostered growth in Europe and North America, although it took many decades for the benefits to reach the common people. The rich countries, such as Britain and the United States, were highly industrialized and enjoyed well-diversified economies and large middle classes. Many of their people lived in cities and, owing to mass education systems, became literate. These countries also boasted efficient, well-financed, constitutional governments. Rich countries were typically democratic, with their governments being chosen by voters (though usually only men) through regular elections. These governments generally tolerated an independent mass media, including newspapers and magazines, and diverse political opinions, such as those represented by socialist and feminist movements. These patterns were also common in the less powerful Western nations and in Japan.

By contrast, the poor societies, especially Western colonies in Asia and Africa, where many people worked the lands owned by foreign landlords or planters, were not industrialized and people earned meager wages. Economic growth was often determined by foreign investment and markets rather than by local needs. For example, rather than growing food for the local community, farmers in Honduras, in Central America, grew bananas for the U.S. market while farmers in French-ruled Senegal, in West Africa, raised peanuts for export. Politically, a small upper class—African chiefs, Indian princes, Javanese aristocrats—played a political role by cooperating with Western rulers. Only a small minority of people had access to formal education. A tiny middle class and low rates of literacy made democracy difficult, even if it had been allowed, but most Western colonies also prohibited or limited voting or officeholding by anyone who was not white and European.

Their general poverty and lack of economic and political options did not mean that people in poor societies were always miserable. For many generations, and through successive governments, they had learned how to make the best of poverty. Celebrating their survival skills in the early 1900s, the Indian writer and thinker Rabindranath Tagore (rah-BIN-dra-NATH TUH-gore) (1861–1941) found both triumphs and tragedies in Indian peasant life through the ages, which "with its everyday contentment and misery, has always been there in the peasants' fields and village festivals, manifesting their very simple and abiding humanity across all of history—sometimes under Mughal rule, sometimes under British rule."[9]

In the colonies, heavy Western cultural influence, such as the policies the French called their "civilizing mission" in Vietnam and West Africa, by which they tried to impose French ways on people they regarded as culturally inferior, was combined with psychological trauma as once proud peoples succumbed to foreign rule and its racist restrictions. An anti-imperialist African organization complained in 1927 that colonialism had abruptly cut short "the development of the African people. These nations were later declared pagan and savage, an inferior race."[10] Although Western Christian missionaries often found eager converts, as in Vietnam, Nigeria, and Uganda, nationalists frequently criticized the well-funded Christian missions, accusing them of undermining traditional beliefs. Western domination, however, did not preclude cultural and scientific achievements by colonized people. For example, although their country was a British colony, various Indian mathematicians, biochemists, and astrophysicists won international renown. In Calcutta the experiments of Sir Chandrasekhara Raman (CHAHN-dra-SEE-ker-ah RAH-man) (1888–1970) led to significant advances in the theory of the diffusion of light, for which he won the Noble Prize for physics in 1930.

Between 1914 and 1945 the global system underwent further changes. Wars were now sometimes world wars, fought on a greater scale than ever before and on battlefields thousands of miles apart. The United States became the world's richest, most powerful nation. Because of its military defeat in World War I, Germany temporarily lost wealth and power. Germany, Italy, and Japan—all middle-ranking nations by the 1930s—challenged the rich nations—Britain, France, and the United States—during World War II. Several Latin American nations and Turkey enjoyed enough economic growth and stability of government to move into the middle-ranking category by the 1940s. Yet most of the societies of Asia, Africa, Latin America, and the Caribbean remained poor colonies or neocolonies, exercising little diplomatic and economic influence in the global system.

THE WORLD ECONOMY

Even before the Western overseas expansion that occurred between 1500 and 1914, trade had taken place over vast distances. Chinese, Indian, Arab, and Armenian merchants had long dominated the vigorous Asian trade, and for centuries Chinese silks and porcelains and Southeast Asian and Indian spices had reached Europe, the Middle East, and parts of sub-Saharan Africa. European explorers wished to locate the source of these riches, and after 1500 the Portuguese, Dutch, and British played key roles in this trade, beginning the rise of the world economy. European influence on the world economy increased in the 1700s and 1800s when Western traders, supported by their governments, sought new natural resources and markets in the tropical world, thereby creating a truly global economic exchange. By 1914 the entire world was enmeshed in a vast economic exchange that particularly benefited the more powerful nations. People often produced resources or manufactured goods—Middle Eastern oil, Indonesian coffee, British textiles—for markets thousands of miles away. Europe's Industrial Revolution, which provided manufactured goods to trade for resources, dramatically reshaped the Western economies in the 1800s but only slowly spread to other regions.

The Inequality of Global Economic Exchange

Economic exchange between societies within the world economy did not proceed on an even playing field. As had been the case for empires throughout history—Assyrian, Roman, Chinese, Inca, Spanish, Dutch—imperialism and colonialism remained the means for transferring wealth to the imperial nations, which used that wealth to finance their own development. The imperial powers, seeking to enhance the value of their colonial economies, also used their control of world trade to shift cash crops indigenous to one part of the world to another. For example, Europeans introduced South American peanuts and rubber to colonized Africa, and coffee from Arabia became a major cash crop in Brazil and Indonesia. This transfer benefited colonial treasuries and plantation owners but also sometimes earned income for the small farmers who started growing these crops.

Gearing economic growth chiefly to the needs of the imperial powers impeded economic development that might have benefited everyone. Many colonies developed economies that produced and exported only one or two primary resources, such as rice and rubber from French Vietnam, sugar from Spanish Cuba, and cocoa from the British Gold Coast. Most of these resource exports were transformed into consumer goods, such as rubber tires and chocolate candies, and sold in stores in Western nations, to the profit of their merchants. For instance, chocolate, whose use for over two millennia was confined to elites in Mexico, became popular among wealthy Europeans after 1500. During the nineteenth century European chemists figured out how to produce chocolate bars, and soon chocolate products gained an eager market among all classes throughout the Western world. Meanwhile, the Western manufactured goods exchanged for these resources, especially textiles, found markets in Africa, Asia, and Latin America. Although much of this exchange was largely at the expense of the colonized peoples, some of them, including a few women, managed to capitalize on it. For example, Omu Okwei (OH-moo AWK-way) (1872–1943), an Igbo, made a fortune trading palm oil for European imported goods, which she distributed widely in Nigeria through a vast network of women traders.

Societies specializing in producing one or two natural resources were especially vulnerable to a changing world economy. To take one case, British Malaya was a major rubber exporter, but most of its rubber plantations, worked chiefly by poorly paid Indian immigrants, were British-owned, and Malayans had little influence over the world price of rubber, which was determined largely by demand in the West. And the prices of agricultural and mineral exports fluctuated more than the prices for industrial goods, which were produced largely in the West. Furthermore, the rise and fall of rubber prices affected not only the rubber tappers and their families but also the shops, often owned by Chinese immigrants, who sold them goods or extended credit to them. Thus the livelihoods of people all over the world increasingly became subject to chronic fluctuations in the world prices of the resources they grew or mined. These prices rose or fell depending on the whims of Western consumers and decisions by the corporations who controlled the international trade.

The world economy widened the wealth gap between societies. In 1500 the differences in per capita income and living standards between people in the richer regions—China, Japan, Southeast Asia, India, Ottoman Turkey, and western Europe—had probably been minor. And these peoples were roughly only two to three times better off materially than the farmers and city folk of the world's poorest farming societies. By 1750, however, while China, western Europe, and British North America enjoyed similar levels of economic production, the wealth gap between them and others was increasing. By 1900 the wealth gap between the richest and poorest societies had grown to about 10 to 1. This trend accelerated throughout the twentieth century, in part because the wealth produced in Western colonies seldom contributed to local development. For example, by the 1950s, after seventy-five years of Belgian colonialism that produced vast wealth for Belgian corporations, mine owners, and rubber planters, the Belgian Congo still lacked all-weather roads linking the major cities and had only a few schools and health clinics for its millions of people.

Unequal economic exchange also fostered conflict. Wars erupted as one country threatened another's access to markets and resources. For example, British free trade policies caused the Opium War with China in the mid-1800s. The Qing government worked to end both the legal and illegal opium trade, but, as the leading opium supplier, Britain needed to protect the opium exports to China from British India, which earned 20 percent of its colonial revenues from charging duty on opium. Britain's defeat of China hastened Chinese decline. In the first half of the twentieth century, World War I was at least partly caused by the bitter competition between European nations for resources in Asia and Africa.

The Spread of Industrialization

The Industrial Revolution, which began in Britain in the late 1700s, was not just a Western development. China and India had once been the world's leading manufacturing countries, and knowledge of Chinese mechanical devices probably stimulated several British inventions. Between 1750 and 1850, however, Britain took the lead in industrialization, and by the mid-1800s it produced about half of the world's manufactured goods while China and India fell behind. Various other European nations, the United States, and Japan industrialized in the later 1800s. Only these few nations increased their resources and weapons as a result of industrialization, and hence only a few became world powers. Some of the profits from colonialism and other overseas activities stimulated or furthered European industrialization. For instance, the Dutch based some of their industrial and transportation growth on profits earned from selling coffee and sugar grown by peasants in their Indonesian colony. But even in Europe agriculture and other nonindustrial activities, such as trade, remained economically important. By 1881 only 44 percent of the British, 36 percent of the German, and 20 percent of the American labor force were employed in industrial or industry-related occupations.

Industrialization gradually spread beyond Europe and North America, but it was highly uneven in its impact and pace. Western policies commonly discouraged other societies, especially colonies, from maintaining or opening industries that might compete with Western manufacturers. For instance, India had been the world's greatest textile manufacturer for centuries, but British colonization gradually diminished the industry through tax and tariff policies, opening the way for British-made textiles to dominate the Indian market. The British saw India not only as a market for their goods but also as a source of cash crops, such as jute and opium. Hence, in 1840 a British official boasted that his nation had "succeeded in converting India from a manufacturing country into a country exporting raw materials."[11] The once flourishing Indian textile center of Calcutta lost two-thirds of its population between 1750 and 1850 as its manufacturing declined.

Several nations sought to foster development by setting up manufacturing operations. China, Persia, Egypt, the Ottoman Empire, and Mexico introduced textile industries in the nineteenth century. However, the British, nominally proponents of free trade, used tariffs, or stiff duties on imports to Britain, to stifle many of these industries, thereby opening doors for the export of British fabrics and clothing to these countries. Between 1900 and 1945 there was resurgence of efforts at industrialization in various nations—China, Argentina, Brazil, and Australia—but agriculture remained the economic foundation for most of their population.

Before 1880 few industrial cities had emerged outside of northwestern Europe and North America, but, in a global economy, several cities far from factories had grown dependent on the Industrial Revolution for their livelihood, becoming hubs for the distribution of imported industrial products. For example, Shanghai thrived as the commercial gateway to central China's interior, Singapore served as the economic hub for much of Southeast Asia, and Alexandria was the import-export center for Egypt and the upper Nile basin.

FRONTIERS AND MIGRATIONS

People have always been pushed to relocate by necessity or drawn to new lands by opportunity. But the rise of a modern world economy, and its constant quest for resources, markets, and labor, accelerated migration. Modern transportation networks, linked by larger and faster ships and later airplanes, facilitated the movement not only of commodities but also of people. Rapid population growth also spurred migration. Between 1800 and 1900 the world population grew from 900 million to 1,500 million, with two-thirds of these people living in Asia. While some people escaped poverty and overcrowding by moving into nearby frontier regions, many others, more than 100 million between 1830 and 1914, left for distant lands. Some, such as enslaved Africans transported to the Americas, were taken from their homes unwillingly. In contrast, millions of Europeans and Asians sought, and often found, a better life in other countries.

Settling Frontiers

From ancient times people left overcrowded lands to move into sparsely settled frontiers. Bantu-speaking Africans, for instance, took their ironworking and farming technologies from West Africa into the sparsely populated grasslands and forests of central, eastern, and southern Africa, and Chinese expanded from north China into central and south China. Similar movements continued in modern times. For example, millions of Russians migrated east into Siberia and Turkestan to settle what they wrongly considered virgin lands. White Americans and Canadians moved westward across the North American continent, subduing, marginalizing, and killing off the Native American peoples and seizing their land. In Australia, New Zealand, and South Africa, European colonists also settled the land at the expense of local peoples. In South America, Brazilians moved from the Atlantic coast westward into the rain forests and grasslands, setting up farms or ranches after pushing out or killing local Indians, and Argentines settled the vast interior grasslands they called the Pampas. Generally the frontier settlers thought they were bringing "progress" to a "wild" area. An influential leader in the United States, Benjamin Franklin, ignoring the native peoples who still inhabited America, wrote in 1784 about the "vast quantity of forest land we have yet to clear, and put in order for civilization."[12]

Remote from central government controls and traditional social structures, the frontier fostered innovations. Frontier social conditions were often freer and more fluid and flexible, promoting new ideas and offering new opportunities. Cultures met and mixed, and people of different groups intermarried, such as white backwoods hunters, trappers, and itinerant traders with Native Americans. Cultural blending produced hybrid social groups such as the Russian Cossacks, western American cowboys, and Argentine gauchos. The cowboys and gauchos, who chiefly herded cattle for ranchers, combined European and self-sufficient Native American customs, and many were themselves of mixed white and Native American ancestry. Eventually, however, as farmers, ranchers, towns, and states gradually replaced the frontier pioneers, the nearby states incorporated the frontier territories. In this way, for example, the settlers in frontier territories, such as Kentucky, Kansas, and Oregon, were gradually absorbed into the larger U.S. society, and the prairie provinces and British Columbia joined Canada.

African and European Population Movements

The largest population movements of the era involved the involuntary transport of African slaves across the Atlantic to the Americas and the chiefly voluntary migration of European emigrants to the Americas, southern Africa, Australia, and New Zealand. The Africans, shipped in chains and filth, were forced to work for whoever purchased them in the Americas. They typically faced lives shortened by harsh conditions. In contrast, most of the Europeans chose to leave their homelands to seek a better life, and often succeeded.

The major movement of Africans resulted from the trans-Atlantic slave trade, which reached its height between 1760 and 1800. During these years over 70,000 people a year were herded onto crowded slave ships and shipped from Africa. Between

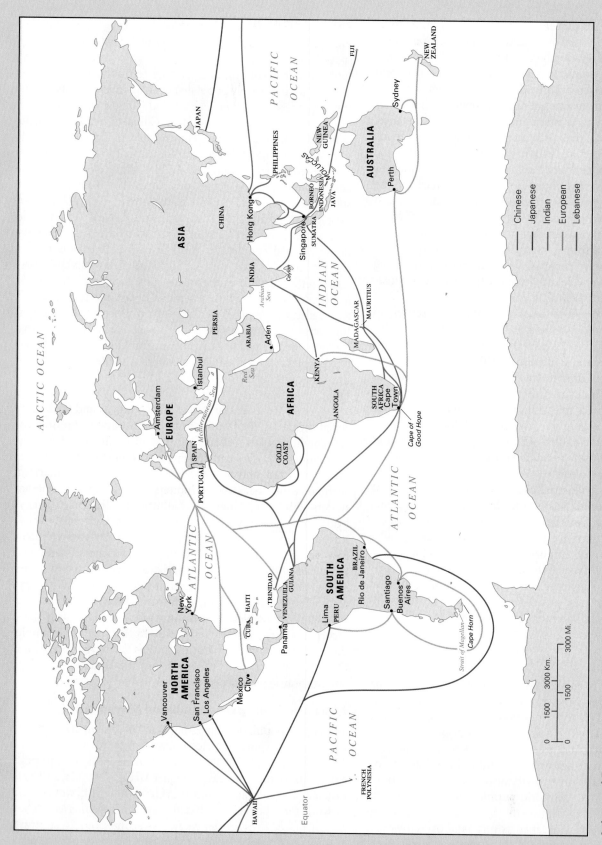

Asian and European Migration, 1750–1940 During this era millions of Europeans emigrated to the Americas, South Africa, Australia, and New Zealand. Millions of Asians, especially Chinese and Indians, left their homes to work or settle in Southeast Asia, Africa, the Pacific islands, and the Americas.

1800 and 1850 the annual export of Africans to the Americas ranged between 36,000 and 66,000. The great majority of Africans were landed in Brazil and the Caribbean islands, where people of African ancestry today account for a large part of the population. But the gradual abolition of slavery in the Americas eroded the trade. Between 1851 and 1867 the flow of human cargo dropped dramatically. However, the longtime slave trade from East and Central Africa to the Middle East continued until the end of the nineteenth century. By the early 1900s slavery had declined significantly or been abolished in Africa, the Middle East, and Southeast Asia. Abolition resulted in part from the efforts of Western colonial governments, often prompted by humanitarian organizations and Christian missionaries, and both Western and local abolitionists. Some had themselves been slaves, such as Mary Prince, a slave from the British West Indies who was taken to London, freed, and became an active abolitionist, arguing eloquently in 1831: "All slaves want to be free. They work night and day, sick or well, till we are quite done up."[13] The end of plantation slavery in the Americas opened the doors to recruitment of impoverished workers from Asia, who chiefly came voluntarily but under restrictive contracts that limited their rights by requiring them to work for years under harsh conditions.

During the Modern Era the European migration across oceans to the Americas and the South Pacific dwarfed other population movements (see map). Unlike the African slaves, many European emigrants were escaping poverty or political repression and expected to improve their lives abroad. While the ships carrying the emigrants were often crowded and unhealthy and the emigrants sometimes struggled to find jobs that could support their families, Europeans did not arrive in chains, with no possibility of freedom. Some of them received free land upon arrival. The emigrants represented Europe's ethnic diversity but came largely from the British Isles, Germany, Italy, Spain, Poland, and Russia.

Between 1500 and 1940 some 68 million people left Europe, creating new societies in the Americas, Australia, New Zealand, and southern Africa. The largest movement came in the nineteenth and early twentieth centuries. For example, between 1820 and 1930 some 32 million Europeans moved to the United States, the major destination. In the same period another 20 million shipped off to Argentina, Canada, Brazil, and Australia. Not all movement was by ship, however; some 14 million Russians moved overland to the Asian regions of their empire. The result of this large population movement was a Europeanization of societies, as European cultures were implanted far from their ancestral homes. The tendency to look toward Europe for inspiration was especially strong in Argentina, Chile, Canada, Australia, and New Zealand. In these societies many immigrants and their descendants tended to maintain their native languages, churches, and social customs and to identify with their homeland. As a result, the numerous Italians in Argentina's capital, Buenos Aires, often spoke Italian, while Anglo-Argentines sent their children to private English-medium schools. Similarly, Canadians, Australians, and New Zealanders commonly revered the British crown. Immigrants contributed much to their new lands. For example, in the United States, the Scottish-born Andrew Carnegie (1835–1919) helped build the iron and steel industry and with his philanthropy sponsored libraries. Others found different ways to improve their new societies, such as working for social change. The controversial Lithuanian-born leftwing activist Emma Goldman (1869–1940) was one of these individuals. Goldman had moved with her family to Russia and then to Germany fleeing anti-Semitism. She finally reached the United States in 1885, where she was later arrested and deported for being an advocate for slum-dwellers and for opposing U.S. entry into World War I.

Asian Migrations

During this era, peoples from eastern and southern Asia also emigrated in large numbers, usually by ship to distant shores. They went in response to the demand among Western colonies and American nations for a labor force for the mines and plantations that supplied their wealth. As a result, Chinese mined tin in Southeast Asia and gold in California and Australia, while Indians worked on rubber plantations in British Malaya and sugar plantations in South Africa, Fiji in the South Pacific, and the Guianas in South America. Immigrants often died from overwork or ill health and, as happened with Chinese in California, sometimes suffered from violent attacks by local people who resented their presence. Yet, many Asians survived to raise families in their new homes. Today approximately 40 to 45 million Asians live outside, and often thousands of miles away from, their ancestral homelands. Chinese and Indians constituted the great majority of Asian migrants, settling in Southeast Asia while also establishing communities, often large, in the Americas, the Pacific islands, and parts of Africa. Their descendants became a vital presence in the world economy as merchants, miners, and plantation workers.

Although most moved as poor contract laborers, Asian emigrants often found success abroad, chiefly as merchants. Through hard work, organization, and cooperation many Chinese in Southeast Asia became part of a prosperous, urban middle class that controlled retail trade, operating everything from small general stores and coffee shops to large import-export firms and banks. Today the majority of Chinese in Southeast Asia, the South Pacific and Indian Ocean islands, the Caribbean, and Latin America are engaged in commerce. A Chinese man who settled in New Zealand in the 1920s recalled the hard work that brought him success: "My generation really worked for a living. We had to open the shop at 7 A.M. and we closed [at] 1 A.M. Then we had to clean the shop. It was seldom before 2 A.M. before we got to bed."[14] The descendants of Chinese immigrants have constituted the most dynamic economic sector in Southeast Asia, with their money and initiative spurring the dynamic economic growth since 1970. Indian merchants also prospered in the diaspora. Many were linked to Indian trade networks that moved capital and products around the Indian Ocean and Pacific Rim as well as into Central Asia and Russia. Lebanese and Syrians became merchants in the Americas and West Africa.

Singapore's Chinatown
By the early 1900s Singapore, a major Southeast Asian port and commercial crossroads, was predominantly Chinese in population. The bustling streets were lined by shops, workers' quarters, theaters, and brothels.
(Courtesy, Singapore History Museum)

Pushed by poverty, overpopulation, or war, people also emigrated from Northeast and Southeast Asia, forming cohesive communities in new lands. Numerous Japanese and Koreans left their homelands between 1850 and 1940. Some settled in Hawaii to work on pineapple plantations or in the canning industry. Many Japanese migrated to the Pacific Coast of the United States and Canada, some taking up farming. In response to growing local prejudice against all Asian immigrants, the United States and Canada restricted Japanese immigration in the early 1900s. As a result, the Japanese emigrant flow turned to Latin America, especially Peru and Brazil. Southeast Asians also departed from their homelands to live abroad. Between 1875 and 1940 Indonesians, mostly Javanese, were recruited to work on plantations in Malaya and British North Borneo but also in Dutch Guiana (today's Suriname), in South America, and on the French-ruled South Pacific island of New Caledonia. Some 50,000 Javanese today live in Suriname. After the United States colonized the Philippines, Filipinos began migrating to Hawaii and the U.S. Pacific coast as factory workers or farm laborers. Today one and a half million Filipinos live in the United States.

THE SPREAD OF TECHNOLOGY AND MASS CULTURE

The modern global system owed much to innovations in technology. Improved methods of communication and transportation allowed people, ideas, and products to travel farther and faster than ever before, enhancing networks of power and exchange. More effective military technologies enabled a few societies to gain control of other societies and to combat rival powers. Finally, the increasing connections around the world enabled cultural ideas and products to spread across national and regional borders.

Communication and Transportation

For much of history, communication over long distances had been slow, depending largely on beasts of burden carrying riders or pulling wagons, and later on sailing ships. In 500 B.C.E. a message carried by successive riders on horses could travel the 1,800-mile length of the Persian Empire in nine days. Two millennia later, in the 1600s, it took Dutch ships some nine months to sail from Amsterdam to Dutch-ruled Java to deliver news and orders. Then in the nineteenth century, thanks to the Industrial Revolution, communications changed dramatically. In 1844 the first telegraph messages were exchanged between Washington and Baltimore. By 1861 submarine telegraph cables linked Britain to North America, prompting a poet to write: "Two mighty lands have shaken hands, Across the deep blue sea; the world looks forward with new hope, Of better times to be."[15] By 1870 the cables had reached from Britain to India. The invention of the telephone in 1876 and radio in 1895 further increased the potential for communications. In 1906 a Canadian scientist, Reginald Fessenden, broadcast the first experimental entertainment program on radio, featuring Christmas carols and speeches. As the possibilities and advantages of broadcasting over great distances became apparent, the New Zealand premier proposed in 1911 that Britain build an empirewide radio network because of "the great importance of radio for social, commercial, and defensive purposes."[16] World War I postponed the scheme, but radio technology improved. By the 1920s radio transmissions had become commonplace in industrial nations and British broadcasts could reach Canada, South Africa, India, and Australia.

Some technologies conveyed people and commodities as well as messages, transforming peoples' lives around the world. Railroads were built all over the world to carry goods and passengers, and as trains reached stations, telegraph messages smoothed their journeys by passing on traffic and weather information. By 1869 railroads connected the Pacific and Atlantic coasts of North America, and by 1903 anyone determined to make the long journey could ride the 9,000 miles between Paris and Siberia's Pacific coast. While railroads extended land networks, shipping lines that employed steamships linked the world. The opening of the 105-mile-long Suez Canal in 1869 and the 51-mile Panama Canal in 1914, both of which cost the lives of thousands of workers during their construction, greatly reduced travel times for many sea journeys and also made it easier and cheaper to ship resources from Asia and Latin America to Europe and North America. Now it only took a few weeks to sail from China or Singapore to New York or London. Political and economic leaders took advantage of the new travel opportunities. For instance, seeking to forge diplomatic alliances and recruit laborers for his islands' plantations, in 1880–1881 Hawaii's king, David Kalakaua (KAH-la-COW-ah) (r. 1874–1891), sailed around the world by steamship and in the course of his journey met the Japanese emperor, the Siamese king, the pope, and Britain's Queen Victoria, among other dignitaries. In Japan, he signed an agreement to import thousands of Japanese laborers to his kingdom.

In the early 1900s motor cars and buses continued the revolution in land transportation begun by railroads, allowing people to more easily commute to city jobs and downtown stores or to travel between cities. After World War I thousands of middle-class Europeans and North Americans owned their own cars, and in the 1930s the first commercial air flights began, making long-distance journeys even faster. Transportation depended increasingly on fossil fuels, first coal and then oil. The use of vehicles fueled by oil increased the strategic importance of oil-rich regions such as the Middle East, Indonesia, Mexico, and the Gulf Coast of the United States.

Technologies of Warfare

New technologies included those devoted to warfare that made it easier to kill more people and at a greater distance. Most of these weapons remained largely a monopoly of Western nations and Japan during this era, and thus contributed to the imbalances in global power. White adventurers and settlers used the rifle invented by the American Philo Remington (1816–1889), which was effective at 1,500 yards, to defeat, and seize the lands of, the Native Americans and the Australian Aborigines. In 1878 an Argentinean observed that the Remington rifle has left "the land strewn with the bodies of those [local Indians] who dared to oppose it."[17] Effective rifles also proved devastating in Africa against warriors armed only with spears and arrows. The British-born American explorer Henry Morton Stanley boasted of his use of repeating rifles and terrorism to destroy a hostile Congo village that had greeted him with spears and arrows: "I skirmish in their streets, drive them pell-mell into the woods beyond; with frantic haste I fire the huts, and end the scene by towing their canoes into midstream and setting them adrift."[18]

Military weaponry quickly improved, including more powerful repeating guns. In 1861 an American doctor, Richard Gatling (1818–1903), invented what quickly came to be known as the Gatling gun, which could fire up to 3,000 rounds of ammunition a minute. The Gatling gun was quickly adopted by Western armies. The first totally automatic machine gun, spitting out 11 bullets a second, was invented in 1884 by Hiram Maxim (1840–1916), an American working in Britain, and gave the British an unparalleled military advantage. The Western powers used the Maxim gun and similar repeating weapons to subdue resistance to colonialism in Africa and Asia. During World War I, since most Western armies had an array of repeating weapons and field artillery, the two rival alliances in that war inflicted terrible casualties on each other. The Western nations had also by this time developed the first armored tanks and increasingly relied on battleships at sea. Air power was introduced to combat in World War I but did not become central to wars until the Spanish Civil War and World War II. The methods of warfare were now more indiscriminate in their targets and lethal than ever before in history. In 1945 the United States used the most deadly weapon in history, the atomic bomb, to force Japanese surrender and end World War II.

The Spread of Mass Cultures

The revolution in communications and transportation technologies contributed to the creation and spread of mass cultures, popular entertainments appealing to a large audience that often crossed class divisions and national borders. People were increasingly exposed to cultural products, such as films and music, and pastimes, such as sports, that were common in other regions of their countries or imported from abroad. Mass cultures percolated into and spread outward from the major cities, where the emerging mass media, such as newspapers and radio, were centered. These media disseminated mass culture, reporting on film stars and sports events or playing popular music. The influence of Paris on the rest of France, Berlin on Germany, Tokyo on Japan, Istanbul on Turkey, Buenos Aires on Argentina, and New York City on the United States grew. As literacy rates rose, the print media gained particular influence. Between 1828 and 1900 the number of newspapers published around the world grew from 3,100 to 31,000, making available news and opinions in hundreds of languages. India alone supported 600 different newspapers in several dozen languages in 1900. Popular books, from Arab detective novels to romances written in South Africa's Xhosa (KHO-sa) language, competed with classic works of philosophy and religion for the hearts and minds of readers.

By spreading cultural influences into other societies, mass communications and increased travel sometimes fostered Westernization. Reflecting Westernization, orchestras playing Western classical music appeared in various Asian societies, including India, China, and Japan, by the early 1900s. Like Europeans, many educated Asians enjoyed the music of Beethoven, Bach, and Mozart. Films and popular music from the United States had an even larger international audience. American film stars such as Charlie Chaplin, born in Britain, became known throughout the world, and U.S.-born jazz musicians often made a living playing the nightclubs of Europe and Asia, where they inspired local musicians to take up jazz. Many societies adopted and excelled in Western sports. For example, Indians became skilled in British cricket; India's Prince Ranjitsinhji

(RAHN-jeet-SING-jee) (1872–1933) became one of the world's best players. India's field hockey team remained unbeaten in the Olympics from 1932 through 1960. European football, also known as soccer, became an international sport that was played and watched all over the world.

But Westernization was only part of the story. Influences from non-Western cultures also spread, contributing to a creative cultural mixing. For example, in the eighteenth and nineteenth centuries the growing Western interest in Chinese painting, Japanese prints, Indonesian gamelan music, and African woodcarvings influenced Western arts. Later, in the 1930s, Indian films and Indian popular music became popular in Southeast Asia and the Middle East, and Cuban music, a mix of African and Western traditions, developed a large following in West and Central Africa, where it blended with local styles. Hawaiian music, which mixed Polynesian and Western influences, became popular in the continental United States in the 1920s and later developed a following in Southeast Asia. People found ways to combine imported ideas, whatever their source, with their own traditions. For instance, in his lyrical suite, *Bachianas Brasileiras*, of 1930, the Brazilian composer Heitor Villa-Lobos (HAY-tore VEE-ya LOW-bos) (1887–1959) adapted the Baroque influences of German composer Johann Sebastian Bach (1685–1750) to Brazilian folk and popular music.

The reach of organizations and social movements expanded, as did awareness of the world. Some organizations developed a global focus. For example, the Red Cross, a Christian organization formed in nineteenth-century Switzerland to alleviate human suffering by helping war victims, eventually became an international movement devoted to humanitarian aid around the globe. Its global reach encouraged it to adapt to non-Christian cultures; in the Islamic world it became the Red Crescent. Social movements also crossed borders. For instance, women in China, Japan, Indonesia, Egypt, and Chile, inspired in part by feminist movements in Europe and North America, sought to adapt the notions of women's rights and education to their own societies. The winning of women's suffrage resulted from the efforts of women worldwide. Thus, in the United States, Susan B. Anthony (1820–1906) began campaigning at age seventeen for equal pay for female teachers and later cofounded the key national and international organizations working for women's suffrage. Across the Pacific, Ichikawa Fusae (ITCH-ee-KAH-wa foo-SIGH) (1893–1918) fought for the rights of women to attend political meetings and, in 1924, formed the major women's suffrage group in Japan, which won the right to vote in 1945.

Global crises now became more widely known, and people followed world events in newspapers and radio newscasts. An avid news follower, the Trinidad calypso singer who humorously called himself Atilla the Hun, appraised the devastation in the world of the later 1930s:

> All we can hear is of unrest, riots, revolutions; There is war in Spain and China. Man using all his skill and ingenuity making weapons to destroy humanity. In the [Italian invasion of Ethiopia] it is said, over six hundred thousand maimed and dead. The grim reaper has taken a gigantic toll. Why all the bloodshed and devastation, Decimating the earth's population? Why can't this warfare cease? All that the tortured world needs is peace.[19]

Soon after Atilla's plea, World War II raised the level of violence even further, providing a fitting end to a turbulent, violent era during which the world's people had become more closely linked into a common global system.

SUGGESTED READING

BOOKS

Bayly, C. A. *The Birth of the Modern World, 1780–1914*. Malden, Mass.: Blackwell, 2004. A brilliant, detailed study.

Cohen, Robin. *Global Diasporas: An Introduction*. Seattle: University of Washington Press, 1997. A brief, valuable survey.

Cook, Scott B. *Colonial Encounters in the Age of High Imperialism*. New York: Longman, 1996. Examines Western imperialism.

Curtin, Philip D. *The World and the West: The European Challenge and the Overseas Response in the Age of Empire*. New York: Cambridge University Press, 2000. An interesting study of reactions to European imperialism.

Hobsbawm, Eric. *The Age of Extremes: A History of the World, 1914–1991*. New York: Pantheon, 1994. A masterful overview, especially strong on social and cultural history.

Hoerder, Dirk. *Cultures in Contact: World Migrations in the Second Millennium*. Durham, N.C.: Duke University Press, 2003. A comprehensive, detailed summary of migrations and diasporas.

Marks, Robert B. *The Origins of the Modern World: A Global and Ecological Narrative*. Lanham, Md.: Rowman and Littlefield, 2002. A concise, readable examination of some major themes.

Neiberg, Michael S. *Warfare in World History*. New York: Routledge, 2001. Good coverage of this era.

Ponting, Clive. *The Twentieth Century: A World History*. New York: Henry Holt and Company, 1998. Thematic study.

Stavrianos, Leften S. *Global Rift: The Third World Comes of Age*. New York: William Morrow, 1971. A provocative, innovative study.

Wesseling, H. L. *The European Colonial Empires, 1815–1919*. Harlow, United Kingdom: Pearson, 2004. A useful overview of the entire colonial enterprise by a Dutch scholar.

Wolf, Eric R. *Europe and the People Without History*. Berkeley: University of California Press, 1982. A thought-provoking analysis of the Western impact on the wider world from 1400 to 1914.

WEBSITES

Modern History Sourcebook (http://www.fordham.edu/halsall/). An extensive online collection of historical documents and secondary materials.

Modern World History Links (http://www.loeser.us/mhist.html). Quirky site with links to various useful information sources.

Modern World History Resources (http://www.historesearch.com/modworld.html). Has links to sites on many topics and regions.

PART VI

Global System: Interdependence and Conflict in the Contemporary World, Since 1945

The key events of the first half of the twentieth century, including the rise of communism in Russia, the growth of anti-Western nationalism in Africa and Asia, the economic disaster of the Great Depression, and the traumas of World Wars I and II, laid a foundation for a new global system. Yet the world of today has also been shaped by the trends marking the decades since World War II, what historians often term the Contemporary Era. During this era, political and economic power in the world passed from huge Western colonial empires to Russia, Japan, China, and especially the United States. Meanwhile, the world's nations became more closely linked through trade, cooperation, and worldwide movements.

A key feature of world politics until the end of the 1980s was the conflict known as the Cold War. Marking this conflict was a competition for influence between the United States and its allies and the Soviet Union and its allies. Another major political trend was the ending of Western colonial control in Asia, Africa, and most of the Caribbean and Pacific islands by the 1970s. Nationalist movements in these colonized areas demanded and gained political independence but sometimes achieved their goals only through violent resistance, including revolutions in countries such as Indonesia, Algeria, and Mozambique. While the Soviet Union imposed communism on eastern Europe, communist-led movements came to power through revolution in countries such as China, Vietnam, and Cuba. Despite fierce competition between the major powers, new international organizations, among them the United Nations, fostered cooperation among nations on issues of common concern, such as women's rights, proliferating nuclear weapons, and threats to public health.

The world has also seen significant economic change since 1945. Western Europe and Japan recovered quickly from World War II, regaining prosperity. Economic links between nations became much stronger, greatly enlarging the world economy. A trend known as globalization spread, facilitating the flow of investment, jobs, resources, and products, not to mention information and ideas, around the world. New or improved technologies, from home appliances and automobiles to cell phones and computers, made life more convenient while fostering economic change.

"Handle with Care" As science revealed more about the natural systems that sustain life on earth, many observers became alarmed about the fate of the planet as people used up resources, fouled the environment, altered the climate, and developed weapons capable of destroying life on a massive scale. This poster reflects these concerns. (Corbis)

Capitalizing on globalization, several industrializing Asian nations, including India, South Korea, Malaysia, and especially China, grew economically, reshaping world trade. But Japan and the Western nations, led by the United States, have controlled much of the world's wealth and have had the most productive economies. The gap between these industrialized countries and the world's poorest countries has grown even wider.

Furthermore, economic growth has come at a huge cost in environmental destruction, from the cutting down of forests to the polluting of the world's air, land, and water. Skyrocketing population growth has harmed the environment, diminished natural resources, and fostered poverty. While people in several dozen nations have enjoyed unprecedented affluence and longer, healthier lives, a fifth of the world's people live in desperate poverty, unable to meet their basic needs for food and shelter.

Social and cultural change has also characterized recent decades. Spurred by war or the quest for a better life, for example, people have left their homelands to settle in other lands. As a result, millions of Africans, Arabs, Turks, and South Asians live in Europe while Latin Americans and Asians have moved to North America. In many countries women have gained better job opportunities and political rights, and ethnic minorities have struggled for social equality. Popular culture products, such as Hollywood films Caribbean reggae music, and Japanese video games, have spread around the world. Although secular thought has enjoyed increasing influence, especially in western Europe and East Asia, Christianity and Islam have rapidly gained followers and influence in many lands. These social and cultural changes, however, are balanced by continuities. While people often enjoy the latest entertainments and gadgets, in many ways they remain like their ancestors, devoted to their families, faiths, and customs. Most societies are a mix of old and new, the traditional and the contemporary.

Since the collapse of European communist regimes and the Soviet Union at the end of the 1980s, which left the United States as the sole global superpower, the world's nations have faced other challenges. These include international terrorism, deadly diseases, food and energy shortages, weapons of mass destruction, global warming, unstable nations engulfed in conflict, and the growing inequality between rich and poor countries. How nations, working together, deal with these and other problems will determine the shape of the future.

NORTH AND CENTRAL AMERICA
The United States became the world's richest nation and greatest political, economic, and military power. It led the Western alliance against the Soviet Union, fighting major wars in Korea and Vietnam and intervening in other nations. After 1990 the United States had no major rival but confronted international terrorism, which prompted it to send military forces into Afghanistan and Iraq. Mexico's economic growth lagged, fostering emigration to the United States, while the Cuban Revolution brought communists to power, provoking U.S. hostility.

SOUTH AMERICA
The South American nations, often troubled by tensions between the political left and right, struggled to achieve political stability and economic growth. Some nations, such as Brazil, Argentina, and Chile, alternated between democratic, reformist regimes and brutal military dictatorships. U.S. intervention helped overthrow several leftist governments. After 1990 Argentina faced economic collapse; Brazil and Chile, mixing capitalism and socialism, enjoyed growth; and Venezuela turned to the left.

EUROPE

Although western Europe recovered quickly from World War II, the imperial Western states were unable to maintain control of their colonies. The western European nations forged stable welfare states, providing a social safety net, and moved toward close cooperation and economic unity among themselves. The Soviet Union became a global superpower, controlling eastern Europe, but at the end of the 1980s it and its communist satellites collapsed. Germany, divided after World War II, was reunified, and Russia sought a new role in the world.

WESTERN ASIA

Nationalists gained control of the western Asian nations but faced new challenges. Israel, a new Jewish state in Palestine, won wars against Arab neighbors, and Arab-Israeli hostilities have remained a source of tension. Some nations, such as Turkey, pursued modernization. An Islamic revolution reshaped oil-rich Iran, which fought oil-rich Iraq in the 1980s. Saudi Arabia and several Persian Gulf states flourished from oil wealth. After 2001 U.S.-led forces invaded and occupied Afghanistan and Iraq but, while removing despotic governments, struggled to restore stability.

EASTERN ASIA

Coming to power through revolution in 1949, communists transformed China, creating a socialist society and fighting the United States during the Korean War. After 1978 new communist leaders mixed free markets with socialism and fostered modernization, turning China into an economic powerhouse. Japan recovered rapidly from World War II, embracing democracy and becoming an economic giant. Borrowing Japanese models, South Korea and Taiwan industrialized. North Korea remained a repressive communist state.

ARCTIC OCEAN

RUSSIA

BRITAIN
GERMANY
EUROPE
FRANCE
Danube
ITALY

ASIA

TURKEY

KOREA JAPAN

IRAQ IRAN
CHINA

ALGERIA
Nile
PAKISTAN
Ganges R.
HIMALAYAS

SAUDI
ARABIA
TAIWAN

Niger R.
INDIA

AFRICA
VIETNAM
Mekong R.
THAILAND

NIGERIA
BANGLADESH

Congo R.
MALAYSIA

ATLANTIC
OCEAN
INDONESIA

INDIAN OCEAN

ANGOLA

AUSTRALIA

SOUTH
AFRICA

NEW ZEALAND

AFRICA

As Arab and African nationalism grew stronger, colonies became independent nations, sometimes, as in Algeria and Angola, through revolution. In North Africa, Egypt promoted Arab nationalism and became a regional power but faced economic problems. Most of the new sub-Saharan African nations, which were artificial creations of colonialism, struggled to maintain political stability and foster economic development, but South Africans finally achieved black majority rule.

SOUTHERN ASIA AND OCEANIA

Britain granted independence to predominantly Hindu India but also to largely Muslim Pakistan, which eventually split when Bangladesh seceded. India enjoyed democracy and economic progress, but Pakistan and Bangladesh often fell under military rule. In Southeast Asia, the U.S. and British colonies gained independence peacefully while Indonesians triumphed through revolution. Vietnamese communists first defeated the French and then the United States. Malaysia, Singapore, and Thailand developed economically. Australia and New Zealand established closer links to Asia, and most of the Pacific islands gained independence from Western colonialism.

CHAPTER 26

The Remaking of the Global System, Since 1945

CHAPTER OUTLINE
- Decolonization, New States, and the Global System
- Cold War, Hot Wars, and World Politics
- Globalizing Economies, Underdevelopment, and Environmental Change
- New Global Networks and Their Consequences

■ PROFILE
Wangari Maathai, Kenyan Environmental Activist

■ WITNESS TO THE PAST
An Agenda for the New Millennium

Online Study Center

This icon will direct you to interactive activities and study materials on the website: college.hmco.com/pic/lockard1e

"Our World Is not for Sale" In 2004 tens of thousands of activists from all over the world, under the banner of "Our World Is not for Sale," marched on the streets of Mumbai (formerly Bombay), India's largest city, to protest economic globalization, racial and caste oppression, and the United States-led war in Iraq. The march reflected the globalization of social movements and political protests in the contemporary world. (AP/Wide World Photos)

One heart, one destiny. Peace and love for all mankind. And Africa for Africans.

BOB MARLEY, REGGAE SUPERSTAR[1]

In April 1980, when the new African nation of Zimbabwe (zim-BAHB-way) (formerly Southern Rhodesia) celebrated its independence from British rule, Bob Marley, a reggae music star from Jamaica and a symbol of black empowerment, performed at Zimbabwe's national stadium. Marley's experience there reflected many of the politcal and cultural trends of the later-twentieth-century world. Marley had been invited to appear in part because his songs, such as "Catch a Fire," "Stir it Up," and "Get Up Stand Up," often dealt with issues such as poverty, racial prejudice, and asserting one's rights, realities for thousands of Zimbabweans in the audience, who had lived for decades under an uncaring British colonial and then white minority government. But Marley's concert was disrupted by the local police, mostly whites who had enjoyed a privileged position under British rule. Fearing a riot and vandalism against white-owned property, they used tear gas to disperse thousands of black Zimbabweans who gathered outside the overcrowded stadium. The next night Marley ignored threats of violence against him by local white racists, who opposed Zimbabwe's rapid shift from white to black rule, and gave a free concert for 40,000 Zimbabweans, many of them unemployed. Although the free concert encountered no major problems, the violence of the previous night and the threats to his life had shown Marley that the social ills and ethnic hatreds he knew in Jamaica occurred elsewhere in the world as well. In Zimbabwe, where these ills ran particularly deep, they would not be solved by the nation's newly won independence under a black majority government.

An eloquent advocate of political and cultural freedom whose music was enjoyed by millions of fans around the world, Marley was an obvious choice to entertain people who had suffered through decades of white minority rule. Although he came from the slums of a small island of barely 2 million people, Marley and his music touched hearts and minds across racial, political, religious, class, and cultural barriers. Reggae itself was a truly world music, an intoxicating mix of African, Caribbean, and North American traditions. To the world, Marley personified reggae's progressive politics and spiritual quest. As Judy Mowatt, another reggae star, noted: "His music has caused people all over the universe to be enlightened, happy, dancing. His spirit is really touching all nationalities."[2] However, Marley failed to convince the racists among Zimbabwe's white minority to accept blacks as their equals.

Marley's career reflected a world interconnected as never before in history and, largely because of that connectedness, in great flux. Some 2,500 years ago ancient thinkers such as the Buddha in India, Daoists in China, and the Greek philosopher Heraclitus had argued that nothing was permanent except change; the world was in perpetual transition. Never, it seemed, was this more true than in the second half of the twentieth century. Since World War II the pace of change quickened and the global economy grew dramatically. Economic and cultural networks linked societies ever more closely while ideas, technologies, and products flowed across porous borders, affecting the lives of people everywhere. World politics were turbulent, reflecting the conflict between the United States and the Soviet Union (USSR), the world's two most powerful nations, and the struggle of African, Asian, and Latin American countries for decolonization and development. Since 1989, when the Soviet bloc collapsed, the world has groped toward a new political configuration while dealing with mounting economic and environmental problems and combating international terrorism.

FOCUS QUESTIONS

1. How did decolonization change the global system?
2. What roles did the Cold War and superpower rivalry play in world politics?
3. What were some of the main consequences of a globalizing world economy?
4. How did growing networks linking societies influence social, political, and economic life?

◆ Decolonization, New States, and the Global System

How did decolonization change the global system?

The contemporary world derived both from Western imperialism in the five centuries before 1945 and from the resistance waged against it. After World War II Asia, Africa, and Latin America became the major battlegrounds between the United States and the Soviet Union; these two nations had so much military, political, and economic might in comparison to other countries that they were known as superpowers. The struggle of Asian, African, and Latin American societies to end domination by Western nations and to develop economically also shaped the postwar era. Nationalist movements proliferated, some seeking deep changes through social revolution. In some cases these nationalist and revolutionary struggles led to interventions by Western powers or the USSR anxious to preserve their political and economic influence. The former colonies also became part of a dynamic global system marked by continued imbalances in wealth and power.

Nationalism and Decolonization

The nationalism that spread through Europe and the Americas in the 1800s became a powerful force in the colonized world in the 1900s (see Chapter 19). Three basic types of nationalist movements developed between the early 1900s and the 1960s. In the first type, which occurred in most colonized societies, the nationalist goal was the end of colonial rule but not necessarily major social and economic change. Colonial powers were often willing to grant political independence where nationalist leaders, in countries such as Nigeria, Uganda, and the Philippines, accepted continued Western control of mines, plantations, and other resources. The second type of nationalist movement, mounted by social revolutionaries inspired by Marxism, wanted not only political independence but also a new social order free of Western economic domination. In China, for example, the communist movement led by Mao Zedong sought to reorganize Chinese society while limiting contact with the world economy and the United States. Making up a third type were the nationalist movements by long repressed nonwhite majorities in white settler colonies such as Algeria and Zimbabwe. Struggling against domination by the minority whites, who owned most of the land and resources, they faced stiff

C H R O N O L O G Y

	International	Eurasia	The Americas
1940	**1945** Formation of the United Nations **1946–1975** Decolonization in Asia, Africa, and Caribbean **1946–1989** Cold War	**1950–1953** Korean War **1959–1975** U.S.-Vietnam War	
1960	**1968** Widespread political protests		**1962** Cuban Missile Crisis
1980		**1989–1991** Dismantling of Soviet bloc and Soviet Union	
2000			**2001** Al Qaeda attack on United States

resistance. Whatever the type of nationalist movement, the dislocations caused by the Great Depression and World War II intensified anti-Western and anticolonial feelings.

Colonialism gradually crumbled, often after confronting nationalist resistance led by charismatic figures such as Mohandas Gandhi in India and Sukarno in Indonesia, in the three decades after World War II. By the 1950s most of the Western colonizers realized that the increased military force required to maintain their political control against growing nationalist protests, strikes, and peasant unrest was too expensive. In 1946 the United States began the decolonization trend by granting independence to the Philippines (see Chronology: Global Politics, 1945–1989). Weary of suppressing nationalist resistance, in the later 1940s the British gave up their rule in India and Burma, and the Dutch abandoned Indonesia. Whatever the nationalist strategy, either peacefully or through the treat of violence, between 1946 and 1975 most of the Western colonies in Asia, Africa, and the Caribbean achieved independence (see Map 26.1).

Some colonizers accepted decolonization only after attempts to quell nationalist uprisings had failed. The Dutch intended to regain their control of Indonesia, a source of immense wealth, after World War II but faced a violent resistance by a nationalist army. In 1950, after losing many soldiers and anticipating more violence ahead, the Dutch granted Indonesia independence. Similarly, the French had no plans to abandon their profitable colonies in Vietnam and Algeria, but uprisings by revolutionaries in these colonies forced them to leave. In Vietnam, the communist forces led by Ho Chi Minh fiercely resisted French power, and heavy U.S. aid to the French could not prevent a humiliating French defeat in 1954. The ultimately successful anticolonial struggles by the Indonesian, Vietnamese, and Algerian nationalists had electrifying global effects, giving hope to colonized peoples elsewhere that they could also overthrow Western domination and warning the Western powers that they would pay a heavy cost for opposing decolonization.

Both superpowers sought to capitalize on the nationalist surge. The Soviet Union generally supported nationalist movements, sometimes supplying arms to revolutionaries. The Soviets also offered economic aid and diplomatic support to Asian and African countries that achieved independence and had strategic value because of their size or location, such as India and Egypt, or valuable resources, such as oil-rich Iran and Indonesia. The most powerful Western nation, the United States, followed a mixed policy on decolonization. Wanting access to trade and outlets for investment in Asia and Africa, the

C H R O N O L O G Y

Global Politics, 1945–1989

1945	Formation of United Nations
1946–1975	Decolonization in Asia, Africa, Caribbean
1946–1989	Cold War
1949	Communist victory in China
1950–1953	Korean War
1954	Vietnamese defeat of French
1955	Bandung Conference
1959–1975	U.S.-Vietnam War
1959	Communist victory in Cuba
1962	Cuban Missile Crisis
1968	Widespread political protests
1975	End of Portuguese Empire

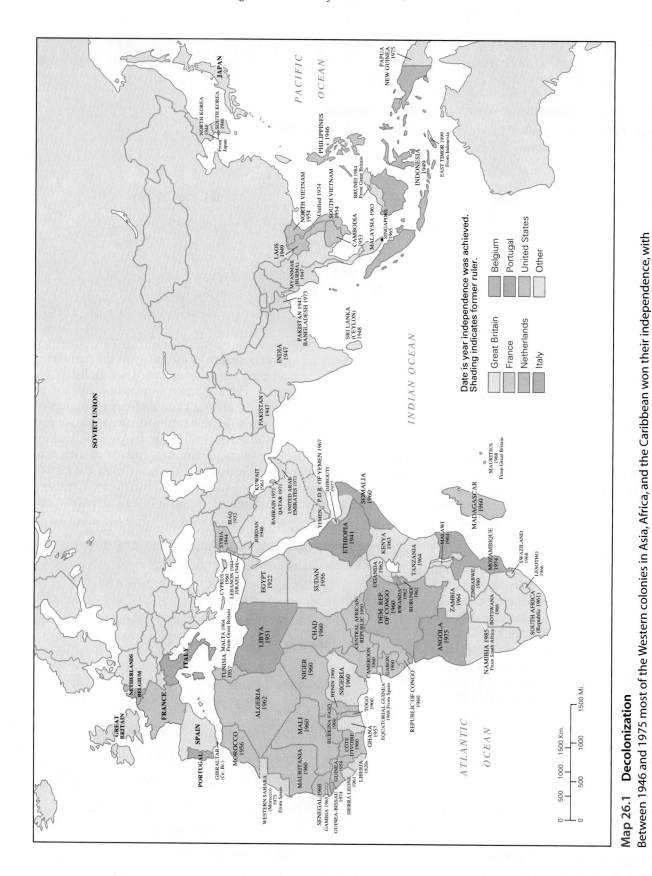

Map 26.1 Decolonization

Between 1946 and 1975 most of the Western colonies in Asia, Africa, and the Caribbean won their independence, with the greatest number achieving independence in the 1960s. The decolonization reshaped the political map, particularly of Africa, South Asia, and Southeast Asia.

Online Study Center **Improve Your Grade** Interactive Map: Decolonization and Independence, 1947 to 1997

United States encouraged the Dutch to leave Indonesia and urged independence for some British colonies in Africa. But Americans also opposed communism and the spread of Soviet influence. Consequently, where nationalism was led by communists or had a leftist orientation, as in French-ruled Vietnam and Portuguese-ruled Mozambique, the United States supported continued colonial power, no matter how unpopular among the colonized people, and helped finance the French and Portuguese military efforts to suppress the revolutionaries. With U.S. aid, Portugal stubbornly resisted decolonization until festering African rebellions, growing demoralization at home, and the toppling of its fascist dictator forced it to abandon its African empire in 1975.

Colonialism did not completely disappear. By the 1980s one major territorial empire, the USSR, remained, and it strained to repress the nationalist demands of the Baltic, Caucasus, and Central Asian peoples it ruled. The Soviet Empire was largely dismantled between 1989 and 1991, when the Soviet Union's communist system collapsed, although Russians still controlled some unwilling subjects, such as the Chechens, a Muslim people in southern Russia. At the beginning of the twenty-first century Britain, France, and the United States controlled small empires. Britain and France, who once ruled huge empires, retained direct control of a few islands, mostly in the South Pacific, South Atlantic, and the Caribbean, and some outposts, notably British Gibraltar, a strategically valuable naval base on the Spanish coast at the entrance to the Mediterranean Sea, and French Guiana, on the northeast coast of South America. The territories, mostly self-governing, linked to the United States included Puerto Rico and the Virgin Islands in the Caribbean and a few Pacific islands such as American Samoa and Guam.

Decolonization often resulted in neocolonialism, a continuing strong political and economic influence by the former colonizers. This happened in the Philippines, where Americans maintained a major role in the economy, Philippine governments loyally supported U.S. foreign policies, and Filipinos avidly consumed American products and popular culture such as music, films, and fashions. Similarly, the French controlled much of the economy and advised the government in the African nation of Cote d'Ivoire (COAT dee-VWAHR) (better known as Ivory Coast), and many Ivoirians favored French cuisine, literature, and language. A West Indian–born writer offered a radical nationalist view of why most former colonies accepted neocolonialism: "The colonial power says, 'Since you want independence, take it and starve' [after economic aid ends]. Other countries refuse to undergo this ordeal and agree to [accept] the conditions of the former guardian power."[3] This view simplified complex relationships but was often shared by Asian and African nationalists. Disenchantment with the continuing strong Western presence prompted some Asian and African intellectuals to advocate "decolonizing the mind," to escape what Bob Marley called a "mental slavery" that kept formerly colonized people in awe of Western power, wealth, and culture. Instead he offered "songs of freedom." "Decolonizing the mind" sometimes meant building a nationalist culture reflecting local traditions or abandoning the use of

African Independence In 1961 the British monarch, Queen Elizabeth II, made an official visit to newly independent Ghana, the former British colony of the Gold Coast. Here she walks under a ceremonial umbrella with the Ghanaian president, Kwame Nkrumah. (UPI/Bettmann/Corbis)

Western languages in people's writing. For example, the Kenyan novelist Ngugi wa Thiongo switched from writing in English to writing in his native Gikuyu.

Social Revolutionary States

During the twentieth century, revolutionary activity erupted in Asia, Africa, and Latin America, intensified by the drive to end colonialism and other forms of Western domination. In most cases this revolutionary activity engaged peasants, who were often impoverished by the loss of their lands or the declining prices for the cash crops they grew. Revolutionary intellectuals, often spurred by a Marxist vision, capitalized on this unhappiness to mobilize support, although those who joined their movements did not always embrace the more radical ideas. Understanding this, Amilcar Cabral (AM-ill-car ka-BRAWL) (1924–1973), the revolutionary leader in Portugal's West African colony of Guinea Bissau (GIN-ee bi-SOU), advised his Marxist colleagues to "always bear in mind that the people are not fighting for ideas, for the things in anyone's head. They are fighting to win material benefits, to live better, and in peace, to see their lives go forward, to guarantee the future of their children."[4] Between

1949 and 1980 social revolutionary regimes came to power through force of arms not only in Algeria and Vietnam but also in several other countries, such as China, Cuba, and Mozambique. Opposed by the United States and often mistrusted by western European regimes, these states necessarily looked to the USSR for political, economic, and military support. Revolutionary movements with some popular support were also active, although ultimately frustrated, in a dozen other countries, mostly in Latin America and Southeast Asia.

The fruits of revolution were subject to debate. Thinkers and activists around the world, such as the West Indian–born psychiatrist and writer Frantz Fanon (1925–1961), who joined the anti-French movement while working in colonial Algeria, often romanticized the revolutionaries' promise to create more just societies. Yet scholars of politics disagreed as to whether revolutions ultimately achieved their stated goals of improving life and righting injustice or instead fostered tyranny and economic stagnation. While social revolutionary governments often substantially raised living standards for the poor and gave them more influence in their communities, they also commonly became bureaucratic, despotic, and intolerant of dissent, and they frequently compiled poor human rights records. But although often disappointed in the new society, most people in these revolutionary societies welcomed the end of the uncaring, often repressive governments the revolutions replaced.

Social revolutionary states had uneven relations with the world economy and the capitalist nations. Influenced by Stalinism, which fostered state-directed economic growth in the USSR in the 1930s, these states usually chose to withdraw from the world economy, partially or completely, in order to limit outside interference, renounce foreign debts, and assume control of their economic direction. They created planned economies in which economic decisions, such as allocation of food and investment capital, were made centrally, by governments, rather than through free markets, as in capitalist societies.

Social revolutionary approaches brought mixed results. Some countries saw their goals sidetracked by civil wars or by rebellions supported by Western powers. For example, in Angola, a country in southwest Africa, South Africa and the United States provided financial and military support to rebels who fought the Marxist-dominated government for over two decades. The civil war cost over 200,000 lives, ruined much of the country, and forced the Angolan government to devote most of its resources to the military rather than to improving people lives with schools and clinics. After the fighting ended in the late 1990s, the Marxists still held power, but the country's people were poorer than ever: half of the nation's children suffered from malnutrition. In contrast to Angola's woes, between 1949 and 1978 communist-run China was able to increase its economic potential and reduce social problems, but at a heavy cost in repressing dissent and limiting personal freedom. After 1978 China dramatically modified its socialist economy with market forces, such as by allowing foreign investment and free enterprise, which sparked even more rapid growth. The shift of China, followed by Vietnam, toward market economies and greater participation in the world economy

in the 1980s suggested that revolution may have helped nations to gain control of their resources but was ultimately insufficient to raise living standards to the levels of the richer nations. Yet, China and Vietnam also found that capitalism and free markets could create more wealth than socialism but did not necessarily lead to an equitable distribution of wealth, fostering explosive social tensions.

A New Global System

A new global system, differing in many respects from that of the 1930s, formed after 1945. The prewar world had been dominated by a few great Western powers, led by Britain and France, ruling over vast empires encompassing large parts of Asia, Africa, and the Caribbean, but decolonization, the rise of the United States and Soviet Union to superpower status, and other trends modified this pattern. During the later twentieth century, observers often divided the world into three categories of countries, each one having a different level of economic development. One category, the **First World**, comprised the industrialized democracies of western Europe, North America, Australia-New Zealand, and Japan. The **Second World** referred to the communist nations, led by the USSR and China. The **Third World** was made up of most societies in Asia, Africa, Latin America, and the Caribbean that were marked by mass poverty and a legacy of Western colonization or neocolonialism. Some experts added a fourth category, the **Fourth World**, or the poorest societies, which had very small economies and few exploitable resources, such as Laos, Bangladesh, Haiti, and Mali.

The notion of different worlds of economic development helped bring to light the roles played by different countries in global politics and economics between 1945 and the late 1980s, when the Western nations and the communist bloc, both wealthy and powerful compared to other societies, competed for influence in the rest of the world. However, critics argued that lumping the world's societies—with their very different histories, cultures, and global connections—into a few categories was highly misleading. Furthermore, during the 1980s and 1990s the global system was changing, complicating attempts to categorize nations. Countries such as Malaysia, South Korea, Dubai (doo-BYE), and Chile, once grouped with the Third World, achieved rapid economic growth, and the communist systems that had defined the Second World often collapsed.

At the economically developed end of the global system, most Western nations and Japan enjoyed new heights of prosperity from the 1960s through the 1980s. After World War II the dominant and wealthiest world power, the United States,

---

First World The industrialized democracies of western Europe, North America, Australia-New Zealand, and Japan.

Second World The communist nations, led by the USSR and China.

Third World Societies in Asia, Africa, Latin America, and the Caribbean, which were shaped by mass poverty and a legacy of colonization or neocolonialism.

Fourth World The poorest societies, with very small economies and few exploitable resources.

offered generous aid to its allies; this aid promoted further economic growth in industrialized countries that already had literate, skilled, and mostly urban populations, well-funded governments, and diversified economies. U.S. aid and investment also helped western Europe and Japan recover from the ashes of World War II and stabilize and prosper. Japan's economy increased fivefold between 1953 and 1973, the fastest economic growth in world history. As Western and Japanese businesses invested heavily around the world, international trade soared. Japan and West Germany became the second and third largest capitalist economies. By the 1970s several Western nations, such as West Germany, Sweden, Canada, and Australia, had standards of living similar to those in the United States. In addition, most of these nations had far less inequality in the distribution of wealth and income than did the United States.

Although economic growth rates often slowed after 1990, Western prosperity relative to the rest of the world continued. By 2004, the Human Development Report, an annual study by the United Nations that rates the quality of life of the world's 177 nations by examining per capita income, health, and literacy, ranked, in order, Norway, Sweden, Australia, Canada, and the Netherlands as the most livable nations; following these were Belgium, Iceland, the United States, Japan, and Ireland. A hundred years earlier Norway, Sweden, and Ireland had been among the poorest European countries. Now Sweden achieved the world's lowest poverty rate (7 percent). Swedish poverty decreased largely because the Swedish state provided each citizen with free education, subsidized health care, and other welfare benefits, and the Swedish economy grew steadily. The report ranked thirty-six nations, mostly in sub-Saharan Africa, as having a low quality of life—massive poverty, inadequate health care, and low rates of literacy—even though their people may have enjoyed rich cultures and rewarding social relationships. Tanzanian president Julius Nyerere (nye-RE-re) put the gap between rich and poor nations in perspective: "While the United States is trying to reach the moon, Tanzania is trying to reach its villages."[5]

Some nations had more resources and advantages to secure their citizens' lives. The nations enjoying a higher quality of life boasted not only wealth but also political stability. Richer nations usually benefited from democracy and allowed voters to freely choose their leaders. They were also nation-states where the large majority shared a common culture and language. Some of these nations did contain restless ethnic or religious minorities. For example, the Basques in northern Spain, a people with a language and identity completely different from the Spanish majority, sought autonomy or independence from Spain. By and large, however, democratic governments controlled social tensions and generous welfare systems prevented mass poverty. Many western European states, Canada, and New Zealand adopted ambitious welfare systems, including comprehensive national health insurance. The European welfare states promoted a high degree of social justice and equality.

Poorer nations, often with highly diverse populations, small budgets, and competition among citizens for limited resources, faced greater challenges in building stable nation-states. Violence, such as the repeated ethnic conflicts in Yugoslavia in the 1990s, occurred in nations that had abandoned communism and its safety net of free or low-cost education, health care, and housing. The fighting between Yugoslav groups sometimes resulted in brutal atrocities and the forced expulsion of minorities. Only a few non-European nations, such as Sri Lanka and oil-rich Brunei and Saudi Arabia, tried to mount welfare states with free education and health care, but they struggled to pay for them.

SECTION SUMMARY

■ Between 1946 and 1975, most Western colonies achieved independence, in many cases as a result of violent opposition movements, though the United States continued to oppose communist anticolonial movements and the Soviet Union's vast colonial empire endured until 1989.

■ Western nations maintained a great deal of influence over the economy and culture of many of their former colonies, which led some intellectuals to call for "decolonizing the mind."

■ Revolutionary regimes, often inspired by Marxism, came to power in a number of Asian, African, and Latin American nations, though they met with mixed economic success and in some cases were embroiled in long-term civil war.

■ The division of the world's nations into First, Second, and Third Worlds grew blurry as some Third World nations developed First-World-level economies and the Soviet Union collapsed, though democratic countries tended to be more stable and offer more support to their citizens.

◈ Cold War, Hot Wars, and World Politics

What roles did the Cold War and superpower rivalry play in world politics?

A new global political configuration emerged after World War II: two major superpowers, the United States and the Soviet Union, each developed a system of allies in their competition for international influence, while other nations struggled to carve their own paths. The confrontation between the two superpowers fostered the **Cold War**, a conflict lasting from 1946 to 1989 in which the United States and the USSR competed for allies and engaged in occasional warfare against their rival's allies rather than with each other directly. The United States enjoyed much greater influence than the USSR in the

Cold War A conflict lasting from 1946 to 1989 in which the United States and the USSR competed for allies and engaged in occasional warfare against their rival's allies rather than each other directly.

global system and boasted more allies. While the Cold War did not lead to a military conflict in which U.S. and Soviet military forces fought each other, it produced chronic tensions between the superpowers. The rivalry also led to covert and military interventions around the world by each of the superpowers seeking to block gains by the other.

The Cold War: A Divided World

During the Cold War the world took on a bipolar political character. Nations practicing capitalism and often democracy, led by the United States, fell on one side, and often called themselves the Free World; those marked by socialist authoritarianism, led by the USSR and known as the Soviet bloc, were on the other. For over four decades U.S.-USSR relations, and the struggle of each superpower to gain an advantage over its rival, were a major factor in international affairs. While seeking to contain the spread of communism, the United States enhanced its own influence, while the USSR worked to protect its interests by spreading communism and undercutting American influence. Various other countries, in Asia, Africa, and Latin America, sought to forge a third bloc, asserting their interests while navigating the dangerous shoals of superpower demands. Leaders of nations such as Egypt, India, and Indonesia promoted nonalignment with either superpower. In 1955 leaders from twenty-nine nonaligned Asian and African countries held a conference in Bandung, Indonesia to oppose colonialism and gain recognition for what they called a Third World bloc, but they had trouble maintaining unity in the decades to follow.

Although Britain had been the world's leading economic, political, and military power in the nineteenth century, the United States became the world's most powerful nation in the twentieth, enjoying far greater wealth, military power, and cultural influence than any other nation, including the USSR. In 1945, the United States already had 1,200 warships, 3,000 bombers, and the atomic bomb; produced half of the world's industrial output; and held two-thirds of the gold. Americans seemed willing to bear a heavy financial and military burden to sustain their leading role in world affairs and to promote U.S. economic growth. U.S. President Dwight D. Eisenhower (g. 1953–1961) defended his nation's foreign policy, which included interventions against unfriendly governments, as necessary to obtain raw materials and preserve profitable markets.

Online Study Center **Improve Your Grade**
Primary Source: The Long Telegram

After World War II, U.S. concern shifted from opposing Nazi Germany and imperial Japan to countering the USSR. Americans now perceived their wartime ally as a rival for influence in the world, especially in the Western colonies that were experiencing tumultuous changes and frequent unrest. By 1948 the Soviets controlled all of eastern Europe and were allied with communist governments in Mongolia and North Korea. The U.S. policy of preventing the emergence of communist regimes, which would be probable Soviet allies, became globalized: first, Americans tried unsuccessfully to prevent commu-

nists from coming to power in China in the late 1940s; then they became involved in the Korean War (1950–1953) to fight successfully the North Korean effort to forcibly reunify the Korean peninsula. Yet, in spite of U.S. efforts, communist regimes came to power in China in 1949, North Vietnam in 1954, and Cuba in 1959. Furthermore, waging the Cold War and seeking to contain communism with military force, including a long war in Vietnam, financially burdened the United States, costing it $4 trillion or $5 trillion and some 113,000 American lives, mostly soldiers, between 1946 and 1989.

Superpower Conflict in the Cold War

The Cold War fostered misunderstandings and tensions between the superpowers. Historians debate whether the USSR actually posed a serious military threat to the United States and how much both sides misinterpreted their rival's motives and actions. Remembering centuries of invasions from the west, Soviet leaders occupied eastern Europe as a buffer zone and considered the United States and its western European allies a lethal danger; their combined military power greatly exceeded that of the USSR. American leaders mistrusted the USSR and despised communism, which excluded two of America's most treasured values, democracy and market economies. Americans viewed themselves as protecting freedom, while the Soviets claimed that they were helping the world's exploited and impoverished masses and acting as the beacon of anti-imperialism.

Some historians believe the Cold War brought a long period of peace and stability, while others point to some eighty wars, often related to superpower rivalry, between 1945 and 1989 that resulted in 20 million deaths and perhaps 20 million refugees. The Cold War rivalries also transformed world politics by dragging in emerging nations, already damaged by their long, humiliating subservience to Western colonialism and military power, and led to upheavals in some of them that bankrupted economies and devastated entire peoples. In place of a USSR-U.S. war, a series of smaller conflicts occurred involving surrogates, governments, or movements allied to one superpower and fighting the troops from the other superpower. During two of the major conflicts, in Korea and Vietnam, U.S. troops battled not Soviet armies but allied communist forces that were Soviet surrogates. In Vietnam, the Soviets sent military supplies and advisers to help the Vietnamese communists, led by Ho Chi Minh, fight first the French and then the United States, which had helped install and then supported a pro-Western government in South Vietnam after the French defeat. The communists gained control of the entire country in 1975. Americans also used surrogates, such as when they supplied Islamic groups fighting the Soviets in Afghanistan in the 1980s.

In this warfare, rebels often used low-technology weapons and military strategies if those methods provided the most practical options available. Insurgencies became common in which people resorted to unconventional warfare, such as sniping, sabotaging power plants, and planting roadside bombs, to struggle against a government or occupying force.

Insurgents fighting superpower forces often resorted to **guerrilla warfare**, an unconventional military strategy of avoiding full-scale direct confrontations in favor of small-scale skirmishes. In Vietnam, for example, communist guerrillas staged hit-and-run attacks on American patrols and field bases and planted land mines, explosives that detonated when stepped on, on trails used by American troops.

The Cold War fostered interventions—both covert and military—by both superpowers to protect their interests. The USSR sent military forces into Poland, Hungary, and Czechoslovakia to crush anti-Soviet movements and into Afghanistan to support a pro-Soviet government. Sometimes Soviet invasions proved disastrous; this was the case in Afghanistan, where the heavy Soviet losses and humiliating withdrawal in 1989 contributed to the collapse of the Soviet system. The Soviets, Chinese, and Cubans also gave aid to communist movements around the world. Communist parties and other leftist groups established a strong presence in nations such as Indonesia, India, and Chile, where they participated openly in politics, and they also launched insurgencies against governments in several countries, such as Peru, Malaysia, and the Philippines. But these communist-led insurgencies failed to mobilize enough local support and were crushed.

For its part, the United States actively sought to shape the political and economic direction of Asian, African, and Latin American societies. It often did this by giving generous U.S. aid and promoting human rights. Americans were generous in donating food, disaster and medical assistance, offering technical advice, and supporting the growth of democratic organizations. But other efforts destabilized or helped overthrow governments deemed unfriendly to U.S. business and political interests, including left-leaning but democratically elected regimes in Brazil, Chile, and Guatemala.

The earliest U.S. intervention came in 1953 in oil-rich Iran, which was governed by a nationalist but non-communist regime that had angered the Americans and British by nationalizing British- and U.S.-owned oil companies operating in Iran, companies that sent most of their huge profits abroad, paid their Iranian workers less than fifty cents a day, and offered them no health care or paid vacations. Most of the workers lived in shantytowns with no electricity. In response to the nationalization, Britain and the United States imposed an economic boycott on Iran, making it hard for Iran to sell its oil abroad. American agents recruited disaffected military officers and paid Iranians to spread rumors and spark riots that paralyzed the capital, forcing the nationalists from power and leading to a pro-U.S. but despotic government. The deposed Iranian leader argued that he faced U.S. wrath for trying to remove "the network of colonialism, and the political and economic influence of the greatest empire on earth [the U.S.] from this land."[6] For the first time ever the United States had organized the overthrow of a foreign government outside the Western Hemisphere. One result was the long-term hatred of the United States by many ordinary Iranians.

To critics, the U.S. actions and other superpower interventions constituted a new form of imperialism. The interventions often proved costly as well. In Vietnam, for example, the communist-led forces achieved a military stalemate that cost the United States vast sums of money, killed some 58,000 Americans, and forced it to negotiate for peace and withdraw, harming U.S. prestige in the world. The war also had spillover effects: it created economic problems in the United States and reduced the U.S. willingness to exercise military power for several decades. But the conflict in Vietnam also cost the lives of several million Vietnamese on all sides and required the USSR and China to spend scarce resources to supply their communist allies.

The Nuclear Arms Race and Global Militarization

The arms race between the superpowers and increasing militarization around the world became major components of the Cold War. Both superpowers developed **nuclear weapons**, explosive devices that owe their destructive power to the energy released by either splitting or fusing atoms. These weapons were the most deadly result of the technological surge that can be traced back to Albert Einstein, Sir Isaac Newton, and the scientific discoveries of the seventeenth and eighteenth centuries. A nuclear explosion produces a powerful blast, intense heat, and deadly radiation over a wide area. The nuclear weapons era began when the United States built the first atomic bombs and dropped two of these bombs from airplanes on the Japanese cities of Hiroshima and Nagasaki to end World War II. In the following decades, both the United States and the USSR developed even more deadly nuclear warheads that could be placed on the tips of missiles. The growth of nuclear arsenals was only the most dangerous part of a larger trend toward increased militarization, the expansion of war-making ability by many nations.

Both superpowers and the rest of the world feared the devastating power of nuclear weapons of mass destruction. Since 1945 the world has lived in the shadow of nuclear weapons; a small number of them could reduce whole countries to radioactive rubble. Many scientists believe that even limited use of such weapons could produce a nuclear winter, radically altering global weather patterns by producing pollution that might cool the earth. Einstein fretted that the unleashed power of the atom, which he helped foster, would change everything save peoples' ways of thinking, and he worried that leaders would create a global catastrophe by rashly using the new technologies.

Fortunately these weapons were never used after 1945, although the world was close to a nuclear confrontation on several occasions. For example, in the early 1950s, as French colonial forces were losing the fight against communist-led insurgents in Vietnam, the Eisenhower administration in the United States offered atomic bombs to the French, who wisely

guerrilla warfare An unconventional military strategy of avoiding full-scale direct confrontations in favor of small-scale skirmishes.

nuclear weapons Explosive devices that owe their destructive power to the energy released by either splitting or fusing atoms.

declined the offer. In 1962, after discovering that the USSR had secretly placed nuclear missiles in Cuba, just 90 miles from Florida, President John F. Kennedy (1917–1963) demanded they be removed but vetoed a U.S. invasion that might have sparked all-out nuclear war. Some of Kennedy's advisers recommended that he attack Cuba with nuclear weapons. Kennedy rejected this advice but his firm stance against missiles in Cuba created a tense crisis, ultimately forcing the Soviets to withdraw them. However, before that withdrawal, the confrontation had nearly turned disastrous. In response to a U.S. attack on his boat during the crisis, a Soviet submarine commander armed a missile which carried a nuclear weapon and aimed it at the United States, but he was talked out of firing it by other Soviet officers.

Nuclear weapons shaped global politics. The Cold War fostered a balance of terror, with both superpowers unwilling to use the awesome power at their command for fear the other would retaliate. Historians debate whether the nuclear arms race helped preserve the peace by discouraging an all-out U.S.-USSR military confrontation or instead unsettled international politics and wasted trillions of dollars. Various other countries, including Britain, France, China, India, and Pakistan, also constructed or acquired nuclear bombs, while countries like Iran and North Korea began programs to do the same. In 1987 the two superpowers negotiated their first treaty to reduce their nuclear arms. Nevertheless, more nations sought a nuclear capability, provoking concerns about nuclear proliferation, especially that North Korea or Pakistan could sell bombs to other countries or perhaps to terrorist groups. But some outside the West argued that the monopoly on such weapons by a few powerful nations was unfair, and Middle Eastern leaders worried about Israeli nuclear efforts; a nuclear weapon would give Israel a decisive military advantage in any regional conflict.

The proportion of total world production and spending devoted to militaries grew dramatically during the Cold War. By 1985, the world was spending some $1.2 trillion annually on military forces and weapons, more than the combined income of the poorest 50 percent of world countries. The two superpowers together, with 11 percent of the world population, accounted for 60 percent of military spending, 25 percent of the world's armed forces, and 97 percent of its nuclear weapons; both the U.S. and USSR had stockpiles of thousands of nuclear weapons. They both also sold conventional weapons to other countries with which they had friendly relations. The world's weapons, from rifles and land mines to non-nuclear bombs, were often used in the era's many wars and conflicts.

Whether or not related to Cold War rivalries, the varied wars caused enormous casualties, with civilians accounting for some three-fourths of the dead. Two million people died during the Chinese civil war (1945–1949), 800,000 during the violent partition of India (1948), 2 million during the American-Vietnamese War, 1 million during the Nigerian civil war (1967), and more than 2 million in the Cambodian violence from 1970 to 1978. Millions of these deaths resulted from genocide, the deliberate killing of whole groups because of their ethnic or religious origin. Genocide, practiced for centuries, had reached

its most organized campaign with the Nazi holocaust against the Jews during World War II (see Chapter 24). In the later twentieth century genocides continued. For example, in the 1990s members of the Hutu majority slaughtered people belonging to the Tutsi minority in Rwanda (roo-AHN-duh), a Central African country, while extremist Serb Christians, seeking to maintain their political power, killed Bosnian and Albanian Muslims in Yugoslavia, in a policy they called "ethnic cleansing." The Yugoslav killings were finally stopped when the United States and western European nations sent in troops to restore order and punish the worst violators of human rights.

Global Organizations and Activism

During the Cold War, more than ever before in history, public and private organizations emerged with a global reach and mission to promote political cooperation and address various causes. The largest attempt by most of the world's sovereign nations to cooperate for the common good, the United Nations, was founded in 1945, in the burning embers left by World War II, with fifty-one members and became a key forum for global debate and an agency for improving global conditions. The founding United Nations Charter enumerated the organization's principles: "To develop friendly relations among nations based on respect for the principle of equal rights and self-determination of peoples and to take other appropriate measures to strengthen universal peace." Furthermore, the founding members agreed that the United Nations came about to "save succeeding generations from the scourge of war, reaffirm faith in fundamental rights, and respect international law."[7] The United Nations endorsed human rights and dignity. As colonies gained independence and joined, the organization grew to over one hundred members by the mid-1960s and to nearly two hundred by 2000. Pursuing cooperation on humanitarian aims, it developed agencies, such as the World Health Organization, that monitored diseases, funded and fostered medical research, and promoted public health, as well as the United Nations Children Fund, or UNICEF, which promoted children's welfare and education around the world, especially in poor countries, earning it the Nobel Peace Prize in 1965. U.N.-sponsored health and nutrition programs helped increase average life expectancy from 45 in 1900 to 75 in 2000, and greatly reduced the risk of mothers dying in childbirth. Yet, critics believed that political differences among member states often obstructed the U.N.'s humanitarian work.

The United Nations influenced international relations by discouraging, although not preventing, states from using force whenever they desired. To gain support for a possible military action, nations often felt it necessary to make their case before, and endure criticism in, the policymaking Security Council; sometimes they received support, as when the United States led a United Nations military force to prevent a North Korean conquest of South Korea. However, nations determined to go to war often ignored widespread disapproval by the organization's members, as the United States did when it invaded Iraq in 2003.

The Security Council sometimes voted to send peacekeeping troops into troubled countries, especially in Africa. Built on the ashes of the doomed League of Nations, the United Nations gave each of the five major powers of 1945 (the United States, China, Britain, France, and the USSR) permanent seats with veto power in the Security Council. Both superpowers vetoed decisions that challenged their national interests. For instance, the United States often vetoed resolutions aimed at penalizing its ally, Israel, and also blocked, for over two decades, the Chinese Communist government from occupying China's seat in the United Nations. Western nations found it more difficult to shape United Nations policies after Afro-Asian nations became the majority in the organization.

Since World War II, groupings of nations also cooperated to improve global conditions by forging international agreements and treaties. For example, most nations ratified an agreement banning biological weapons, such as deadly diseases like anthrax, in 1972. In 1997, 132 nations signed an international treaty to ban the production, use, and export of land mines, which continued to kill and injure civilians years after the end of the conflicts for which they were intended. In 1997 most nations signed the Kyoto Protocol, pledging to begin reducing the harmful gases that contribute to global warming. In 2002 a treaty establishing an International Criminal Court went into effect, with the goal of prosecuting the perpetrators of genocide, war crimes, and crimes against humanity. But the United States and several other industrial nations impeded international cooperation by refusing to approve the modest efforts made by these agreements to reduce weapons, promote environmental stability, and establish accountability for international crimes.

Private organizations and activists, chiefly based in western Europe, also worked for issues of peace, social justice, health, refugees, famine, conflict resolution, and environmental protection. Organizations such as Doctors Without Borders, which sent medical personnel to societies facing famine or epidemics, and Amnesty International, which worked to free political prisoners, were supported chiefly by private donations. In addition, leaders from different religious faiths worked for world peace, justice, and humanitarian concerns. For example, the Dalai Lama (DAH-lie LAH-ma) (b. 1935), the highest Tibetan Buddhist spiritual leader, won the Nobel Peace Prize in 1989 for his efforts—through speeches, writings, and conferences—to promote human rights, nonviolent conflict resolution, and understanding among different religions. In 1997 the Dalai Lama pleaded, "We all have a special responsibility to create a better world. No one loses, and everyone gains by a shared universal sense of responsibility to this planet and all living things on it."[8] Similarly, the Aga Khan IV (b. 1936), the spiritual leader of a largely Indian Shi'ite Muslim sect, funded charitable activities, such as schools and clinics, all over the world. Among Christian groups, the World Council of Churches, supported by diverse Protestant and Eastern Orthodox churches, encouraged interfaith cooperation and international understanding between Christians and non-Christians. Several Catholic popes favored inter-faith dialogue but their denouncing of war, birth control, abortion, and capital punishment were more controversial.

U.N. Peacekeepers in Congo
The United Nations has regularly sent peacekeepers into troubled countries such as the Congo. This photo, from 2003, shows U.N. troops from Uruguay guarding a U.N. office while a Congolese woman and her four children, displaced from her village by factional fighting, seek U.N. help. (AP/World Wide Photos)

World Politics Since 1989

Between 1989 and 1991 the Soviet bloc disintegrated and the communist regimes in eastern Europe and the former USSR collapsed, ending the Cold War and the bipolar world it had defined (see Chronology: Global Politics Since 1989). Historians disagree as to whether any particular leaders or nations deserve credit for ending the Cold War. Many scholars concur with longtime State Department official George Kennan (KEN-uhn) (1904–2004), the architect of the U.S. policy to contain communism in the 1940s, who concluded that no country or person "won" the Cold War because it was fueled by misconceptions and nearly bankrupted both sides. Other nations, especially Japan and West Germany, both protected from potential enemies by U.S. military bases, had gained the most economically from the conflict, at least in the short term, by investing heavily in economic growth rather than their own defense. Both U.S. and Soviet leaders deescalated tensions between the two superpowers in the later 1980s. When the Cold War ended, the United States became the sole superpower. By 2001 it had a larger annual military budget than the ten next largest military spenders, including Russia, China, and Britain, combined and was the major supplier of arms to the rest of the world. Yet, U.S. power was not absolute. Some observers perceived a tripolar system in which the U.S. had to share political and economic leadership with Western Europe, whose nations now cooperated closely, and several Asian nations, especially China and Japan.

The first major post–Cold War challenge for the United States came from Iraq's brutal dictator, Saddam Hussein (sah-DAHM hoo-SANE) (b. 1937), who ordered his army to invade and occupy Iraq's small, oil-rich neighbor, Kuwait. The United States had supported Saddam and provided his military with weapons in the 1980s, when Iraq was fighting a war against Iran, whose Islamic government the United States opposed. Now the United States organized an international coalition, funded chiefly by Arab nations, and, in the Gulf War of 1991, rapidly defeated the Iraqis and pushed them out of Kuwait. In the aftermath of the quick victory over Iraq, U.S. president George H. W. Bush proclaimed a "new world order"—a new global system, led by the United States, that was based on American values and faced no powerful challenge from communism. He envisioned the United States as a world policeman, with no superpower rival to check its power.

The end of the long, costly rivalry between capitalist countries and communist societies, however, did not result in universal peace and stability or the triumph of American political values. Instead of a new world order, the 1990s saw what some observers called a new world disorder. Ethnic and nationalist conflicts exploded in massive violence in Yugoslavia, eastern Europe, and Rwanda in central Africa. States with weak or dysfunctional governments, such as Haiti in the Caribbean, Liberia and Sierra Leone in West Africa, and Somalia in Northeast Africa, also experienced chronic fighting and civil war. Rising tides of religious militancy, usually fundamentalist, or conflict between rival faiths complicated politics in countries such as India, Indonesia, Algeria, and Nigeria. Militant Islam demonstrated its potency in Iran, Sudan, and Afghanistan and led some extremists to form terrorist groups to fight moderate Islamic regimes,

CHRONOLOGY	
Global Politics Since 1989	
1989–1991	Dismantling of Soviet bloc and empire
1997	Kyoto Protocol on climate change
2001	Al Qaeda attack on United States
2003	U.S. invasion of Iraq

Israel, and Western nations. By the early 2000s Islamic radicals posed a greater challenge in Southeast Asia and the Middle East than the declining communist movements. The ambitions of aggressive dictators, such as Iraq's Saddam Hussein, and the communist regime in North Korea, which limited contact with the outside world, fostered regional tensions. The new world order promise of a peaceful world moving, with U.S. support, toward democracy foundered on the shoals of proliferating regional, nationalist, religious, and ethnic conflicts that, combined with uneven economic growth, produced a context for violence.

SECTION SUMMARY

- During the Cold War, the United States and the USSR struggled for world control, with the United States generally favoring democracy and capitalism but also seeking access to resources and foreign markets, and the USSR supporting emerging communist regimes and movements.

- Though the United States and the USSR never fought directly, they were involved in dozens of wars in other countries, such as Vietnam, Korea, and Afghanistan, in which millions died, and they intervened in countries such as Guatemala, Iran, Poland, Hungary, and Czechoslovakia.

- The United States and the USSR participated in a massive arms race, spending trillions of dollars on nuclear weapons, which led to widespread fear of mass destruction, though some argue that this fear helped prevent all-out war.

- The United Nations was formed with the goal of promoting world peace and human rights, and various agreements have been signed to ban biological weapons and land mines, to prevent global warming, and to facilitate an international justice system, though they have encountered opposition by the United States and some other industrial nations.

- When the Soviet Union collapsed, the United States was the sole superpower, with a military budget dwarfing that of other countries and dreams of a peaceful democratic world, but religious extremism and ethnic and nationalist conflicts have ensured continuing conflict.

Globalizing Economies, Underdevelopment, and Environmental Change

What were some of the main consequences of a globalizing world economy?

In the decades after 1945, the world economy was increasingly characterized by **globalization,** a pattern in which economic, political, and cultural processes reach beyond nation-state boundaries. This trend reduced barriers between countries and turned the world into a more closely integrated whole. Globalization transformed the world through worldwide commercial markets, finance, telecommunications, and the exchange of ideas. It also allowed for more collaboration between nations and the spread of new ideas. However, it came with some major problems. One was the widening inequality of nations. Another was the environmental consequences of industrialization and economic growth, including ever increasing pollution and a warming climate. In response to population growth and economic policies, people expanded agriculture into semidesert areas and cut down rain forests, causing widespread environmental deterioration.

The Transnational Economy

Globalization has increased the interconnectedness between societies; events occurring or decisions taken in one part of the world affect societies far away. For example, rising or falling prices on the Tokyo or New York stock exchanges quickly reverberate around the world, influencing stock markets elsewhere. Similarly, the decision by U.S. or British governments to sell supplies of stockpiled rubber, hence depressing world prices, affects the livelihood of rubber growers, and the businesses that supply them, in Malaysia, Sri Lanka, Brazil, and the Congo. Not all the transnational economic activity has been legal, especially the flow of narcotics. Heroin and cocaine sold in North America and Europe, creating millions of addicts, originates largely in Asia and Latin America and is smuggled by transnational criminal syndicates, some of them linked to corrupt politicians. Whatever the problems, economic globalization became a fact of contemporary life and had numerous impacts on the world's societies.

A World in Flux The roots of globalization are old: a world economy that links distant societies has been developing over the past 2,500 years. As a measure of this growth, the world's production of goods and services was 120 times higher in 2000 than it had been in 1500. Average personal income grew fourfold between 1900 and 2000. After World War II economic globalization involved the spread of

globalization A pattern in which economic, political, and cultural processes reach beyond nation-state boundaries.

market capitalism as well as flows of capital, goods, services, and people. The United States, now the axis of the world economy, has been the major proponent of globalization, with its leaders arguing that open markets and conditions favorable to investment and trade foster prosperity. By 2000 the United States produced nearly a third of the world's goods and services; Japan, with the next largest economy, accounted for around a sixth. International observers described the impact of U.S. leadership metaphorically: when the United States sneezes, the rest of the world catches cold.

In spite of the growth of the world economy, globalization has had its critics. They charge that it promises riches it does not always deliver, distributing the benefits unequally. Economic growth in a country does not, by itself, improve the living conditions of the majority of people; better conditions also require well-functioning governments, secure legal and political rights, and health and education services available to all. The visionary Indonesian diplomat Soedjatmoko (so-JAHT-mo-ko) (1922–1989) argued that economic development, as opposed to economic growth, could only be understood as part of a larger process that reshaped societies and improved people's lives.

Globalization also brought more advantages to some nations, and some people within nations, than to others. By the 1990s two nations, the United States and China, were gaining the most from the trend toward removing trade barriers and fostering competitive markets worldwide. Both sucked in investment capital, aggressively acquired natural resources from around the globe, and supplied diverse products to growing foreign markets. China became the world's third largest economy, rapidly gaining ground on the second largest, Japan. Chinese factories turned out clothing, housewares, and other consumer goods to sell in both rich and poor countries. As they expanded their global connections, the Chinese even began investing in Africa, Latin America, and the Middle East and buying U.S.-based companies. However, not all Chinese benefited. China's state-owned enterprises, established before the shift to a market economy, were less efficient than private ones and often closed down, laying off workers, while peasants protested as their farmland was bulldozed to build foreign-owned factories, private housing developments, and golf courses for affluent Chinese.

Impacts of Globalization Globalization's impact has been uneven. By the early twenty-first century a few other nations, such as India, Ireland, Singapore, and South Korea, had, like the United States and China, also capitalized on globalization, fostering economic growth and becoming centers of high technology. But not all countries enjoyed such success. By the 1990s even Japan and some European nations, such as France and Germany, struggled to compete in the globalizing economy, while many Asian, African, and Caribbean nations fell deeper into poverty. As United Nations Secretary General Kofi Annan (KO-fee AN-uhn), a Ghanaian, put it in 2002: "Our challenge today is to make globalization an engine that lifts people out of hardship and misery, not a force that holds them down."[9]

Although experiencing occasional setbacks, the Western industrial nations and Japan have generally maintained a favorable position in the global economy. They control most of the capital, markets, and institutions of international finance, such as banks, and their corporations also own assets in other nations. For example, U.S. citizens control businesses, mines, and plantations in Latin America, Japanese operate factories in Southeast Asia, and the French maintain a large economic stake in West Africa. The capitalist systems in the industrialized nations have ranged from the laissez-faire approach, featuring limited government interference, common in the United States, to the mix of free markets and welfare states in western Europe, to the closely linked government-business relationship in Japan and South Korea. These contrast with the economies in many former colonies, especially in Africa, where power holders, often closely linked to foreign or domestic business interests, preside over largely poor populations. For instance, in the former Belgian Congo, corrupt national and local leaders work to protect the interests of the Belgian-owned and local corporations who fund them.

Some once-poor countries have exploited the transnational economy to their advantage, achieving spectacular growth. If revenues are not stolen by corrupt leaders, as has happened in some countries, such as Iraq and Nigeria, possession of oil, a natural resource in high world demand, provides an economic foundation for national wealth. A few oil-rich nations, such as the Persian Gulf states of Kuwait and the United Arab Emirates, use oil revenues to improve the material lives of their citizens. Although lacking vast oil reserves, various Asian countries, much like Japan in the late 1800s, have combined capitalist market economies, cheap labor, and powerful governments to orchestrate industrialization. At the same time they have ensured political stability and attracted foreign investment by repressing political opposition and harassing or arresting dissidents. These countries have favored export-oriented growth, producing consumer goods—clothing, toys, housewares—for sale abroad, especially in the richer, consuming nations of Europe and North America. This strategy has fostered high growth rates and the import of industrial jobs from other, often Western, countries; at the same time, however, these countries have held political prisoners, exploited labor, and suppressed strikes and labor unions.

Asian countries using this development strategy improved their position in the global system. In the 1980s and 1990s China, South Korea, Taiwan, Malaysia, Thailand, and Singapore fostered the fastest-growing economies in the world and considerable prosperity, their major cities boasting well-stocked malls, freeways, diverse restaurants, and luxury condominiums. Often the growing middle class and labor leaders have demanded a larger voice in government and political liberalization. By the 1990s Indonesians, South Koreans, Taiwanese, and Thais had replaced dictatorships with democratic governments that were chosen in free elections. The Asian systems became models for successful development by mixing capitalism, which is useful for creating wealth, with socialism, which can distribute wealth equitably. The Asian economic resurgence had the potential to restore the leading role some

Asian societies had enjoyed in the world economy for many centuries before 1800. But in the late 1990s the economies of many Asian nations, except for China's, crashed, and Indonesia experienced political turmoil, posing at least a temporary setback to Asian resurgence.

International Economic Institutions

Various institutions shaped the transnational economy. The international lending agencies formed by the World War II anti-fascist allies in 1944 to aid postwar reconstruction played crucial roles, especially the World Bank, which funded development projects such as dams and agricultural schemes, and the International Monetary Fund (IMF), which regulated currency dealings and helped alleviate severe financial problems. Most Asian, African, Caribbean, and Latin American governments, dependent chiefly on exporting natural resources, did not earn enough income from selling these resources to buy food and medicine, import luxuries, or finance projects such as building dams and improving ports. To get these funds, governments, emulating consumers, took out loans, mostly from the World Bank or the IMF, both institutions closely linked to the United States. The IMF, which had the right to dictate economic policies to countries borrowing from it, favored Western investment and free markets, often at the expense of government funding for social services such as schools and health clinics. Borrowers failing to make these changes risked loss of IMF loans. Especially in Latin America and Africa, countries fell deeply into debt, often having to devote 40 to 50 percent of their foreign income just to pay the interest on their loans.

Trade agreements and trading blocs also shaped the world economy, reflecting an economic connectedness between nations unprecedented in world history. In 1947, twenty-three nations established the General Agreements on Trade and Tariffs (GATT), which set general guidelines for the conduct of world trade and rules for establishing tariffs and trade regulations (see Chronology: The Global Economy and New Technologies). The inauguration of the World Trade Organization (WTO) by 124 nations in 1995 marked a new phase in the evolution of the postwar economic system, replacing GATT. By the early twenty-first century several communist nations with market economies, including China and Vietnam, had joined the WTO. The WTO had stronger dispute-resolution capabilities than GATT, and a member country could not veto a WTO decision that declared one of its regulations, such as environmental protection, to be an unfair restriction on trade. Various regional trading blocs also formed. For example, the European Common Market (now the European Union) eventually included most European nations.

Giant business enterprises, known as **multinational corporations** because they operate all over the world, gained a leading role in the global marketplace. Some 300 to 400 companies, two-thirds of them U.S.-owned, dominated world

---

multinational corporations Giant business enterprises that operate all over the world, gaining a leading role in the global marketplace.

The Global Economy Cambodian Buddhist monks, following ancient traditions, collect their food from the devout in the capital city, Phnom Penh, while advertising for American cigarettes entices Cambodians into the global economy, despite government concerns about the health danger posed by tobacco products. (AP/World Wide Photos)

production and trade. By the early 1980s the multinationals had together become the third largest economic force in the world, exercising great influence over governments. By 2000 half of the world's 100 biggest economic entities were countries and half were multinational corporations, the largest being four U.S. companies—General Motors, Wal-Mart Stores, Exxon-Mobil, Ford Motor Company—and the Germany-based Daimler-Chrysler automobile company.

The multinational corporations set the world price for various commodities, such as coffee, copper, or oil, and could play off one country against another to get the best deal. They also could easily switch manufacturing and hence jobs from one country to another. Multinationals have created millions of jobs in poor countries. Increasingly women, willing to work for lower wages than men and less likely than men to challenge managers, have become the majority of the labor force in what economists called the global assembly line: factories producing for export. Supporters argue that moving jobs from high-wage to low-wage countries, a pattern known as outsourcing, fosters a middle class of managers and technicians and offers work to people, especially young women, with few other job prospects. Indeed, some impoverished African

nations with high unemployment would probably welcome such globalization. Critics reply that most of these jobs pay low wages, require long hours, and often offer little future. For example, the U.S.-based Nike Corporation, praised for creating needed jobs by making shoes in Vietnam, is also criticized because the Vietnamese employees, mainly women, work in unhealthy conditions, face sexual harassment from their male supervisors, and are fired if they complain.

The Spread of Industrialization

The industrialization that had transformed Europe and North America in the nineteenth century spread to other parts of the world, especially to Asia and Latin America, during the later twentieth century. Entrepreneurs or state agencies in countries such as China, India, South Korea, Brazil, and Mexico built textile mills, steel mills, and automobile plants, primarily to produce goods for local consumption and later for export. Chinese textiles, Indian steel, and South Korean cars found markets around the world. Increasing competition from Asia and Latin America challenged Western and Japanese dominance in industrial activity. For example, the U.S. share of world industrial production fell from 50 percent in 1950 to below 30 percent in the late 1980s. Americans built over 75 percent of all cars in 1950 but less than 20 percent by the early 1990s. Consumers worldwide now had more choice. Malaysian car buyers, for example, could test-drive Volvos made in Sweden, Hyundais made in South Korea, Toyotas made in Japan, and Proton Sagas manufactured locally.

Technological innovations since 1945 spurred economic growth. The so-called **Third Industrial Revolution** came

---

CHRONOLOGY

The Global Economy and New Technologies

1947	Formation of GATT
1947	Invention of transistor
1958	Invention of silicon microchips
1995	Formation of World Trade Organization

Third Industrial Revolution The creation since 1945 of unprecedented scientific knowledge of new technologies more powerful than any invented before.

about through the creation of unprecedented scientific knowledge of new technologies more powerful than any invented before. These new technologies made the creations of the first Industrial Revolution, which began in the late 1700s, and the second Industrial Revolution of the later 1800s seem obsolete. With the new innovations, traditional smokestack industries such as steel mills in industrialized nations were displaced by nuclear power, computers, automation, and robotry. The technological surge also brought rocketry, genetic engineering, silicon chips, and lasers. Space technology produced the first manned trips to the moon and unmanned crafts exploring the solar system. In 2005 a probe from one of these crafts astounded the world by landing on Saturn's large, mysterious, cloud-covered moon, Titan, and sending back photographs of the surface. The increased knowledge of the solar system, and, owing to more powerful telescopes, of the universe, including the discovery of planets circling other stars, produced insights and gave earthlings a complete glimpse of their planet for the first time. The British poet Archibald MacLeish observed that the astronauts on the space capsules circling the planet did not perceive national boundaries or international rivalries, but only oceans and lands containing people with a common planetary home: "To see the Earth as we now see it, small and blue and beautiful in that eternal silence [of space] where it floats, is to see ourselves as rulers on the Earth together."[10]

The Third Industrial Revolution has had potentially dramatic consequences for people around the world. For example, the **Green Revolution** has fostered increased agricultural output through the use of new high-yield seeds and mechanized farming, such as gasoline-powered tractors and harvesters. Farmers with the money to take advantage of these innovations can shorten the growing season, thus raising two or three crops a year. Between 1965 and 1978, one village in India, using high-yield seeds, increased its food output by 300 percent. Once poor, the village now gained a paved road, regular bus service, and electricity while its people built bigger homes. But not all farmers benefited from the Green Revolution. In countries such as India, the Philippines, and Mexico, the Green Revolution, which requires more capital for seeds and machines but fewer people to work the land, has often harmed poor peasants whose labor was no longer needed or who could not afford the investment. Agriculture, however, was not the only economic sphere to feel the impact of new technology. In many industries, such as automobile manufacturing, automation has taken over production, allowing companies to fire workers.

Industry and other economic activities have also become globalized. By the 1990s over two hundred export processing zones, industrial parks occupied largely by foreign-owned factories paying low taxes and wages, and making goods of all kinds for the global economy, had been established around the world. For example, factories in northern Mexico, usually U.S.-owned, made goods, such as clothing, largely for the U.S. market and employed nearly half a million workers, mainly women. But not all the new jobs were in factories. During the

later twentieth century, the service and information exchange industries also grew. More people worked in service enterprises, such as fast-food restaurants, while others established transnational computer networks, such as AOL and Google, to help people use the Internet for communication and knowledge acquisition. By the 1990s India, responding to these trends, was graduating each year thousands of people fluent in English and skilled in computer technology, becoming a world center for offshore information and technical services. Increasingly consumers calling North American companies for computer technical support, product information, or billing questions reached Indians working in cubicles in cities such as Bangalore and Bombay (known in India as Mumbai).

Yet, the opportunities of industrialization and its globalization have come with risks. Hoping to better compete in the world economy, businesses have moved factories to countries with low wages and costs. Some Western and Japanese businesses have shifted operations to South Korea or Taiwan, where the average worker earns in a month what a U.S. or German worker earns in a week or ten days, yet produces as much. Others have established operations in Asian, African, Latin American, or Eastern European nations where workers earn even less. As North American and western European companies have sought more profits, they have outsourced, or relocated, the jobs once held by several million workers to foreign countries with cheap labor costs and eager workers, such as India and Mexico. As an example of how outsourcing has affected some people negatively, in 1990 the U.S. clothing maker Levi Strauss closed its plant in San Antonio, Texas; laid off 1,150 workers, most of them Mexican American women; and relocated the operation to Costa Rica. Viola Casares, one of the fired workers, expressed the despair: "As long as I live I'll never forget how the white man in the suit said they had to shut us down to stay competitive."[11] Between 1981 and 1990 Levi Strauss, losing markets to lower-priced competitors, closed fifty-eight U.S. plants with over 10,000 workers while shifting half of its production overseas. While some, such as these Americans, lost jobs, other people now had better economic opportunities.

Underdevelopment

Uneven economic growth contributed to a growing gap between rich nations and poor nations, often described as underdeveloped or developing. The gap was already wide in 1945, since colonialism often did little to raise colonial people's general living standards. A Guyanese historian concluded that "the vast majority of Africans went into colonialism with a hoe and came out with a hoe."[12] Outraged that they gain little from the polluting oil wells around them, local people in Nigeria's main oil-producing region have sabotaged operations and kidnapped foreign oil workers. Many Asian, African, and Latin American economies grew rapidly in the 1950s and 1960s, when the world economy boomed. In the 1970s and 1980s, however, as the world economy soured and the world prices for many exports collapsed, the growth rates of these economies declined. Then the world economy revived for a few years, only to experience a dramatic downturn in the later 1990s and early

---

Green Revolution Increased agricultural output through the use of new high-yield seeds and mechanized farming.

2000s. Despite economic growth, some countries remained underdeveloped, while women and children in these countries often faced more problems than did men.

Growth and Development

Economic growth has not always fostered development, growth that benefited the majority of the population. With economic globalization growing, rich countries pressure or encourage other nations to open their economies to foreign corporations and investment. Some nations, especially in East and Southeast Asia, have prospered from this investment, earning money to build schools, hospitals, and highways, but elsewhere Western investment often has done little to foster locally owned businesses and instead encourages the nation to rely on exporting one or two resources. In Nigeria, for example, as in colonial times, British-owned enterprises have controlled banking, importing, and exporting, and foreign investment has gone mainly into cash crops and oil production, controlled largely by Western companies, such as Royal Dutch Shell. Furthermore, in countries like Nigeria and Congo, foreign investment and aid has often been misused to support projects favored by influential politicians or siphoned off to line the pockets of corrupt leaders, bureaucrats, and military officers.

Scholars debate how poor countries can better profit from their connections to the world economy and spur local efforts at development. One of the most influential scholars, the Indian economist Amartya Sen (b. 1933), had helped run evening schools for illiterate rural children as a youth. This experience laid a foundation for his studies of global poverty, for which he won the Nobel Prize in economics in 1998. Sen believes that the main challenges were how to use trade and technology to help the poorest people and improve their lives by addressing famine, poverty, and social and gender inequality. Influenced by his first wife, a prominent Indian writer and political activist, Sen began focusing on the role of women in development, wanting to enhance not just their well-being but also their abilities to improve their lives. Sen argues that women's literacy and employment are the best predictors of both child survival and fertility rate reduction, prerequisites for fostering development in poor villages. His views on poverty and gender inequality influenced the United Nations when, in 2000, that body developed an agenda to address the world's pressing problems, such as the kind Sen studies, by 2020 (see Witness to the Past: An Agenda for the New Millennium). However, without outside financial support, few poor countries have sufficient resources to seriously combat widespread poverty or promote women's empowerment.

While some nations have become richer, others have become poorer. Most poor nations have suffered from some combination of rapid population growth, high unemployment, illiteracy, hunger, disease, corrupt or ineffective governments, and reliance on only a few exports, chiefly natural resources. A United Nations conference on the Environment and Development in 1997 bluntly concluded: "Too many countries have seen economic conditions worsen, public services deteriorate, and the total number of people in the world living in poverty has increased."[13] By the 1990s the richest fifth of the world's people received 80 percent of the total income while the poorest fifth earned less than 2 percent. For example, in the Central American nation of Guatemala, 90 percent of people lived below the official poverty line, and nearly half had no access to health care, indoor plumbing, piped water, or formal education. A fifth of the world's people earned less than $1 per day. By 2000 the world's three richest persons owned more assets than the forty-eight poorest nations together, and 358 billionaires had a combined net worth equal to that of the bottom 45 percent of the world's population combined. Furthermore, the policies of rich countries often penalized poor countries. Despite preaching the benefits of free trade, rich nations have often blocked or restricted food and fiber exports from poor nations into their own markets while heavily subsidizing their own farmers. Hence, wheat farmers in the West African country of Mali, however industrious, cannot compete with French or U.S. wheat farmers, who can sell their crops at much lower prices because of the financial support from their governments.

Rich and Poor in Brazil The stark contrast between the wealthy and the poor in many nations can be seen in the Brazilian city of Rio de Janeiro. Seeking jobs in expanding industries, millions of migrants flock to the city, building shantytown slums and squatter settlements in view of luxury high-rise apartment and office buildings. (Stephanie Maze/Woodfin Camp & Associates)

An Agenda for the New Millennium

In 2000 the United Nations called together the 188 member states for a summit at its headquarters in New York City to discuss the issues facing the world during the new millennium. In the following document, distributed before the summit, the United Nations secretary general, Kofi Annan of Ghana (GAH-nuh), laid out his vision for the organization and the challenges it faced in a world that had changed dramatically since the organization's formation over five decades earlier.

If one word encapsulates the changes we are living through, it is "globalization." We live in a world that is interconnected as never before—one in which groups and individuals interact more and more directly across State frontiers. . . . This has its dangers, of course. Crime, narcotics, terrorism, disease, weapons—all these move back and forth faster, and in greater numbers, than in the past. People feel threatened by events far away. But the benefits of globalization are obvious too: faster growth, higher living standards, and new opportunities—not only for individuals but also for better understanding between nations, and for common action.

One problem is that, at present, these opportunities are far from equally distributed. How can we say that the half of the human race which has yet to make or receive a phone call, let alone use a computer, is taking part in globalization? We cannot, without insulting their poverty. A second problem is that, even where the global market does reach, it is not yet underpinned by rules based on shared social objectives. In the absence of such rules, globalization makes many people feel they are at the mercy of unpredictable forces. So, . . . the overarching challenge of our times is to make globalization mean more than bigger markets. To make a success of this great upheaval we must learn how to govern better, and . . . how to govern together. . . . We need to get [our nations] working together on global issues—all pulling their weight and all having their say.

What are these global issues? . . . First, freedom from want. How can we call human beings free and equal in dignity when over a billion of them are struggling to survive on less than one dollar a day, without safe drinking water, and when half of all humanity lacks adequate sanitation? Some of us are worrying about whether the stock market will crash, or struggling to master our latest computer, while more than half our fellow men and women have much more basic worries, such as

where their children's next meal is coming from. . . . I believe we can halve the population of people living in extreme poverty; ensure that all children—girls and boys alike, particularly the girls—receive a full primary education; and . . . transform the lives of one hundred million slum dwellers around the world.

The second main [issue] is freedom from fear. Wars between States are mercifully less frequent than they used to be. But in the last decade internal wars have claimed more than five million lives, and driven many times that number of people from their homes. . . . We must do more to prevent conflicts from happening. Most conflicts happen in poor countries, especially those which are badly governed or where power and wealth are very unfairly distributed between ethnic or religious groups. So the best way to prevent conflict is to promote [fair representation of all groups in government], human rights, and broad-based economic development.

The third [issue] is . . . the freedom of future generations to sustain their lives on this planet. Even now, many of us have not understood how seriously that freedom is threatened. We are plundering our children's heritage to pay for our present unsustainable practices. We must stop. We must reduce emissions of . . . "greenhouse gases," to put a stop to global warming. . . . We must face the implications of a steadily shrinking surface of cultivable land, at a time when every year brings many millions of new mouths to feed. . . . We must preserve our forests, fisheries, and the diversity of living species, all of which are close to collapsing under the pressure of human consumption and destruction. . . . We need a new ethic of stewardship to encourage environment-friendly practices. . . . Above all we need to remember the old African wisdom which I learned as a child—that the earth is not ours. It is a treasure we hold in trust for our descendants.

THINKING ABOUT THE READING

1. What does Annan see as the major global issues of the new millennium?

2. How are the problems he outlined connected to each other?

Source: United Nations, *The Millennium Report* (**http://www.un.org/ millennium/sg/report/state.htm**). Reprinted with permission of the United Nations.

Despite the challenges they have faced since World War II, the nations outside of Europe and North America can boast of achievements. Between 1960 and 2000 they reduced infant mortality by half and doubled adult literacy rates. China, Sri Lanka, Malaysia, and Tanzania have been particularly successful in providing social services, such as schools and clinics, to rural areas. Various countries have developed their own locally based development strategies. In sub-Saharan Africa, for instance, some countries, such as Burkina Faso (buhr-KEE-nuh FAH-so) and Niger (nee-jer), have moved away from big, expensive prestige projects—such as building large dams to supply hydroelectric power—to small-scale labor-intensive projects that aid the environment, such as tree-planting campaigns and hand-built dams to supply water for growing food crops in a small area. In these countries local cooperative banks have provided credit to farmers and stored grain for later consumption by villagers. However, these food supplies did not last long when severe drought caused major famine, as occurred in 2005, bringing widespread starvation.

Women and Development

Women and their children have faced the harshest problems as modern economic growth has destroyed the traditional cycles of peasant life and undermined the handicrafts that once provided incomes for women. It has also fragmented families: men sometimes have to find work in other districts or countries, leaving their wives to support and raise the children. For example, in Africa, men migrate each year from Burkina Faso to the cocoa plantations and logging camps of the Ivory Coast, and from Mozambique to the mines of South Africa. Meanwhile, migrant work is becoming more feminized. Women leave India, Sri Lanka, and the Philippines to work as domestic servants for rich Arabs in the Persian Gulf states and Saudi Arabia, some facing sexual harassment or cruel employers. Asian and Latin American women are also recruited to work in homes and businesses in North America and Europe, some of them ending up in sweatshops or brothels. Furthermore, women often face social customs that accord them little influence at home and, in case of divorce, award the children to the father. A folk song in north India expressed the bitterness of powerless village women who, after marriage, have no claim on their birth family's property: "To my brother belong your green fields, O father, while I am banished afar."[14]

Experts once assumed that schemes to foster economic development would benefit both genders. But women have generally been left behind because of their inferior social status, relative invisibility in national economic statistics, and minimized role in local decision making. According to United Nations studies, women do 60 percent of the world's work and produce 50 to 75 percent of the world's food, yet they own only 1 percent of the world's property and earn 10 percent of the world's income. While many poor women earn money from growing food, engaging in small-scale trade, or working as domestic servants, most of women's labor—food preparation, cleaning, child rearing—is unpaid and done at home. This housework is often demanding. For example, in Senegal, in West Africa, a typical rural sixteen-year-old girl, married at a young age, gets up at 5 A.M. to pound millet, the staple food, for an hour. She then walks a few hundred yards or perhaps several miles to get water from a well, makes breakfast for the family, goes to the village shop, makes the family lunch, takes food to her mother-in-law working in the fields, does laundry for six adults and a child, makes supper, and then pounds millet again before bed. Some days she also has to find wood for cooking. Older women have to combine all this with farm work.

Some nations have fostered economic development that helps women and children through bottom-up policies relying on grassroots action: the efforts of common people. The Grameen (GRAH-mean) Bank in Bangladesh, which promotes a philosophy of self-help, provides an outstanding model. The founder, the economist Muhammad Yunus (b. 1940), felt that the conventional economics taught in universities was hollow and ignored the poverty and struggles occurring in his nation's villages. He credited this insight to a chance meeting with a poor woman who told him that, after repaying the loan for the cane she wove into mats, she earned only four cents a day. Learning that conventional banks did not make loans to the poor, in 1983 Yunus opened the Grameen Bank, which makes credit available on cheap terms to peasants, especially women, for small-scale projects such as buying the tools they needed to earn a living. For example, a borrower might buy a cell phone that villagers could use to make business or personal calls, paying the borrower for each call, or purchase bamboo to make chairs and use the profits from selling the chairs to buy more bamboo. The bank eventually made loans of less than $100 to over 2 million people. Only less than 2 percent of borrowers defaulted. The newly empowered women, earning an income for their families, now enjoyed higher social status. Rather than jeopardize their income by having more children, 40 percent of the women began using contraceptives, helping lower the Bangladesh birthrate from 3 to 2 percent a year.

Population, Urbanization, and Environmental Change

Rapid population growth and overcrowded cities became manifestations of global imbalance. With too many farmers competing for too little land, rural folk often had to abandon the livelihoods that had sustained their ancestors. They often ended up in crowded cities—Jakarta in Indonesia, Calcutta in India, Cairo in Egypt, Mexico City—where they survived any way they could, often living in shantytowns or, for the even less fortunate, on the sidewalks. Population growth and the resulting expansion of settlement into marginal lands posed unprecedented environmental challenges and increased competition for limited resources, such as oil, timber, and tin. These trends and the enormous surge of economic activity fueled by the use of energy based on fossil fuels have changed the world's environment.

People and Cities

During the past fifty years the world's population has grown faster than ever before in history (see Map 26.2). Two thousand years ago the earth had between 125 and 250 million people. It took roughly 10,000 generations for the world to reach 1 billion in 1830. At the end of World War II the population had risen to 2.5 billion, and by 2006 it had more than doubled to 6.5 billion people. Some experts talked of a "population bomb" overwhelming the world's resources—water, food sources, forests, minerals—and a population of perhaps 12 billion by 2100, which the earth's resources could not support. But fertility rates began dropping in much of the world during the late twentieth century, with the biggest declines occurring in industrialized nations. The reasons for the decline were the introduction and widespread use of artificial birth control, such as contraceptive pills, which allowed women to decide if and when they wanted to become pregnant; better health care; and larger numbers of women entering the paid work force. By 1990 over half of the world's couples with

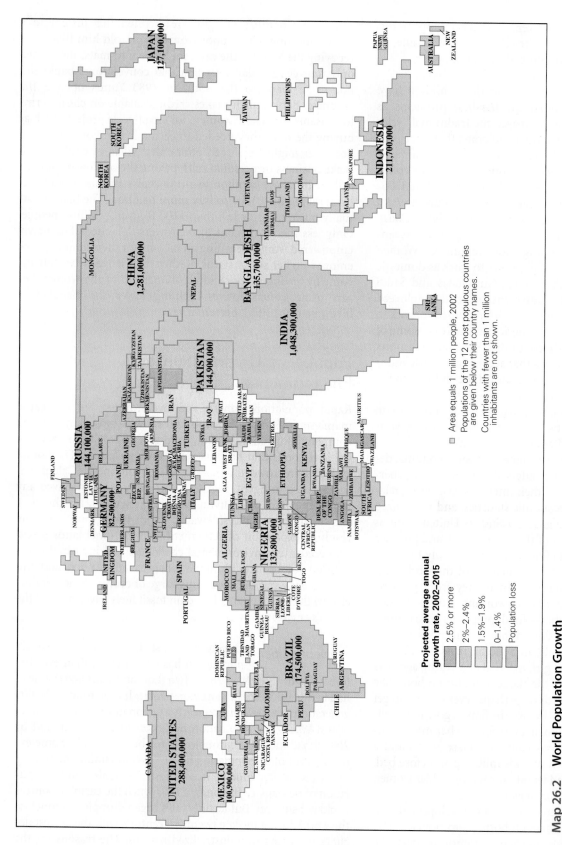

Map 26.2   World Population Growth

This map shows dramatically which nations have the largest populations: China, India, the United States, Indonesia, and Brazil. It also shows which regions experience the most rapid population growth: Africa, South Asia, and Central America.

women of reproductive age practiced some form of contraception to prevent births. Nonetheless, in the 1990s nearly 100 million people were born each year. Demographers now envision a world population of some 9 to 9.5 billion by 2050, which will still impose a heavy burden on countries to supply food and services. Some experts fear such major population growth could lead to increasingly severe social, economic, and environmental problems for the world. They argue that overpopulation, and the ensuing competition for limited resources, probably contributed to civil wars in crowded countries such as Rwanda and El Salvador in the later twentieth century.

Population growth has been more rapid in some world regions than in others. Most of it has occurred in Asia, Africa, and Latin America. By 2000, three of the five countries with the largest populations were in Asia; China and India had the highest number, with around a billion people each. While Asia has continued, as it has for millennia, to house at least 60 percent of humanity, Europe's share of population fell from a quarter in 1900 to an eighth. Because of their falling birthrates, various European nations and Japan have declining and aging populations, which put a growing burden on those of working age to produce more wealth to support elderly populations. Italy and Spain, both predominantly Roman Catholic nations that once had high birthrates, now have the world's lowest fertility rates. North American birthrates have also dropped, but the decline has been offset by immigration.

Nonetheless, the Western nations and Japan, enjoying high rates of resource consumption, have done more harm to the environment than countries with large populations but low consumption rates. For example, owing to heavy use of energy and metals-dependent innovations—air conditioners, central heating systems, gasoline-powered vehicles, refrigerators—the average American or Canadian consumes some twenty times, and the average Australian, German, or Japanese ten to fifteen times, the resources of the average Pakistani or Peruvian.

Population growth has diminished the possibility for economic development in overcrowded nations already struggling with a scarcity of food, health care, housing, and education for their people. For instance, in countries such as the Philippines, Pakistan, and Uganda, the population of school-age children has expanded faster than the resources needed to build new schools and hire teachers. By 2000, over 1 billion people around the world were desperately poor and unable to obtain basic essentials, such as adequate food. The Green Revolution, sparking dramatic increases in food production, averted mass famine, but by the 1990s harvests reached a plateau, producing only small food increases or sometimes even decreases in food supplies. Furthermore, by the 1990s fish catches were declining steeply, partly because of overfishing by Western and Japanese fleets using high-technology equipment. Feeding the new mouths has also required massive clearing of forests for new cropland. Twentieth-century advances in health and welfare could be reversed unless nations find ways to slow population growth that outstrips the ability of governments to solve social and economic problems.

The most effective tool to slow population growth, birth control, has been controversial, especially when this involves abortion, which is condemned as taking life by varied religious groups. Predominantly Islamic and Roman Catholic nations often discourage birth control as contrary to their religious beliefs, which oppose artificial curbs on pregnancy and favor large families. Prompted by these religious objections, some nations, including the United States, have opposed international family planning organizations. But other nations have pursued vigorous population control programs, thereby increasing their economic potential. For example, Thailand cut its birthrate by a fifth between 1980 and 2000. Using harsher means, overcrowded China dramatically reduced fertility, especially in the cities, through policies that promoted one child only per family; couples who flouted the laws faced stiff fines or, sometimes, forced abortions.

The most successful campaigns to limit growth have targeted women by giving them better education, health care, and a sense of dignity independent of their roles as mothers. For countless generations, many people viewed children—expected as adults to support their parents—as insurance for old age. This was true especially in societies with high infant mortality rates, where people expected that not all their children would survive into adulthood. In Mali, in West Africa, for example, the average woman had seven children, of which four survived to adulthood. Economic development, however, including better health care for women to lower infant mortality, often changed these attitudes. Most evidence suggests that increasing affluence reduces birthrates. Thus, as rural women in Bangladesh opened small businesses, which contributed to family incomes, they had fewer children.

During the twentieth century people increasingly lived in cities, where populations grew thirteenfold. In 1900 cities held some 10 percent of the world population. That figure rose to 50 percent by 2000. Cities often grew into vast metropolises. Thus Cairo, Egypt, grew from under 900,000 in 1897 to 2.8 million in 1947 and 13 million in 1995. In 1950 Western cities, headed by New York, dominated the list of the world's ten largest cities; fifty years later the rankings had changed dramatically as Asian and Latin American cities dominated the list. Tokyo, the world's largest city with 28 million people, was followed by Mexico City, Bombay (India), São Paulo (Brazil), and Shanghai (China). Huge traffic jams made driving in Bangkok, Tokyo, Mexico City, and Lagos a nightmare. Struggling to provide needed services, cities usually dumped raw sewage into bays and rivers. By the early twenty-first century cities are responsible for 75 percent of the world's resource consumption and produced 75 percent of its trash. City life has also reshaped traditional ways, to the distress of some. In a pop song from Peru in 1970, a boy who migrated to the capital city, Lima, but upheld rural values, complained that his girlfriend had abandoned these values: "You came as a country girl. Now you are in Lima you comb your hair in a city way. You even say, 'I'm going to dance the twist' [a popular dance from the United States]."[15]

Environmental Destruction Industrialization, population growth, and urbanization have also affected environments, including soils, air, waters, and plant and animal organisms, and contributed to a warmer, drier global climate. Over the twentieth century societies increased

WANGARI MAATHAI, KENYAN ENVIRONMENTAL ACTIVIST

Wangari Maathai (wahn-GAHR-ee muh-THIGH), who won the 2004 Nobel Peace Prize for her environmental activism, was born in 1940 and grew up in Nyeri, a small village in Kenya, East Africa. As a young girl, Wangari fetched water from a small stream. She grew fascinated by the creatures living in the stream and loved the lush trees and shrubs around her village. But over the years the stream dried up, silt choked nearby rivers, and the once green land grew barren. She lamented the assault on nature. Girls in rural Kenya in the 1940s and 1950s commonly spent their youth preparing for marriage and children. But a brother convinced Wangari's parents to send the inquisitive girl to the primary school he attended.

After graduating from a Roman Catholic high school, Wangari was awarded a scholarship to study in the United States, where she earned a B.A. in biology from a small Kansas college in 1964 and then completed an M.A. at the University of Pittsburgh in 1966. She credited her U.S. experience, including her observations of anti–Vietnam War protests, with encouraging her interest in democracy and free speech. Returning home, she earned a Ph.D. at Nairobi University in 1971, the first East African woman to achieve that degree, and then joined the faculty to teach biological sciences. She became a dean and joined a local organization that coordinated United Nations environmental programs.

Throughout her life Wangari has faced and overcome gender barriers, including in her marriage. Wangari married Mwangi Maathai and had three children, but their relationship soured and they divorced after he was elected to parliament in 1974. She attributed the breakup to gender prejudice: "I think my activism may have contributed to my being perceived as an [un]conventional [woman]. And that puts pressure on the man you live with, because he is then perceived as if he is not controlling you properly."

To stop the spread of desert in Kenya by planting trees, the dogged Wangari founded the Greenbelt Movement on Earth Day, 1977. She got the idea for the movement from talking to women when she served on the National Council of Women. Women told her they needed clean drinking water, nutritious food, and energy. She realized trees could provide for all these needs. Trees stop soil erosion, help water conservation, bear fruit, provide fuel and building materials, offer shade, and also enhance the beauty of the landscape. Over 10,000 Kenyans, largely women, became involved, planting and nurturing more than 30 million trees. For each tree planted, the members earned a small income. The movement showed Kenyans that the health of their forests and rivers mattered for both their immediate well-being and their future.

Realizing that logging contracts enriched leaders of corrupt governments, including Kenya's repressive regime, Wangari began to see the link between environmental health and good governance. As a result, the Greenbelt Movement launched programs of civic education, linking human rights, ecology, and individual activism and helping thousands of women gain more control of their lives. Women took on local leadership roles, running tree nurseries and planning community-based projects. Thanks to the movement, she said, "women have become aware that planting trees or fighting to save forests from being chopped down is part of a larger mission to create a society that respects democracy, the rule of law, human rights, and the rights of women."

their industrial output twentyfold and their energy use fourteenfold. Western industrial nations and Japan faced the environmental consequences, such as air and water pollution, for several generations. Once poor nations that became richer, such as China, South Korea, and Malaysia, paid the cost in noxious air, toxic waste, stripped forests, and warmer climates. Furthermore, many forests in North America and Europe have sickened or died from the acid rain produced by industrial pollution. Some environmental disasters have devastated large populations. For example, in 1957 an explosion in a nuclear waste dump in Russia killed some 10,000 people, contaminated 150 square miles of land, and forced the evacuation of 270,000 people. Meanwhile, by the 1990s scientists were reporting a massive die-off among varieties of frogs and some ocean species, a catastrophe perhaps due to pollution and ecological instability and suggesting that diverse environments are increasingly dangerous to life. Hence, sea turtle populations decreased drastically in regions as far apart as Southeast Asia, the Persian Gulf, and Central America.

Deforestation provides one sign of environmental destruction. In the twentieth century half of the world's rain forests were cut down, as commercial loggers obtained wood for housing, farmers sought to convert forests into farms, and poor people obtained firewood. This destruction continues at a furious pace today; an area larger than Hungary is cleared each year. Between 1975 and 2000 a quarter of the Central American rain forest was turned into grasslands, where beef cattle, raised chiefly to supply North American fast-food restaurants, now graze. Already most of the world's remaining tropical rain forest survives in only three nations: Brazil, Congo, and Indonesia. In tropical regions clearing the land exposes the thin topsoil to leaching of the nutrients by rains, so that often the cleared land can be farmed only for a few years before it becomes unusable desert.

Deforestation has had enormous long-term consequences, ranging from decreasing rainfall to loss of valuable pharmaceuticals, including those that might cure cancer or other illnesses. Millions of species of plants and animals have disappeared in recent decades, and by 2000 more than 11,000 species of plants and animals were threatened with extinction. Some scientists estimate that a quarter to half of all current species could disappear by 2100. The destruction of forests, which absorb the carbon dioxide that heats up the atmosphere, has contributed to the global warming, accelerating over the

Wangari Maathai Wangari Maathai, winner of the 2004 Nobel Prize for peace, plants a tree outside the United Nations headquarters in New York in 2005. Earlier that day she challenged world leaders to dirty their hands by planting trees and working to stop the destruction of forests worldwide. (AP/World Wide Photos)

Wangari and her campaign to empower and educate rural women had many critics in Kenya, including the country's dictatorial president. She was threatened by violence, harassed, sometimes severely beaten, arrested over a dozen times, and had her public appearances broken up by police. When she led protests against the building of a 62-story tower that would destroy much of Nairobi's main public park in the mid-1970s, the police killed seven of her associates. Still, she continued to protest illegal forest clearing and the Kenya government's holding of political prisoners. Wangari's efforts inspired similar Greenbelt movements in the United States, Haiti, and over thirty other African countries, and she became an international environmental spokesperson. In 2002, during the first fair elections in years, Wangari ran for the Kenyan parliament as a Green Party member and gained election by a huge majority. In 2003 a reformist president appointed her to his cabinet as an Assistant Minister for Environment, Natural Resources, and Wildlife. In awarding her the Noble Peace Prize, the Nobel committee praised Wangari for taking a comprehensive "approach to sustainable development that embraces democracy, human relations, and women's rights," saying that she "thinks globally and acts locally." She celebrated winning the Noble Prize by planting a tree on the slopes of Mount Kenya, near her childhood home, and recommitting herself to the struggle for a better world.

THINKING ABOUT THE PROFILE

1. How did Wangari's activities help Kenyan women?
2. How did Wangari's efforts to protect the environment also foster change in the political and social realms?

Note: Quotations from Friends of the Greenbelt Movement North America website (**http://gbmna.org/a.php?id**).

past century, that scientists worry will raise ocean levels, ruin good farmland, and make tropical regions unlivable.

The destruction of arable lands has arisen as another severe problem. **Desertification,** the transformation of once productive land into useless desert, has increased with government, market, and population pressure to expand agriculture onto marginal land. For example, during the past half century in Africa, some 20,000 square miles of land became desert every year, much of it between the Sahara Desert and West Africa's coastal forests. By 2000 a third of Africa's people lived in arid or semiarid environments. To combat the resulting farming failures, Africans have used more pesticides, fertilizers, and irrigation, but these too often have long-term negative consequences. Drier climates diminish water supplies. One of Africa's largest lakes, Lake Chad, has lost 90 percent of its water since 1975. Deforestation and desertification also undermine farming by causing soil erosion, since, with less vegetation to absorb water, rains wash away fertile topsoil and cause severe flooding. Drought has become a regular reality in Africa, forc-

desertification The transformation of once productive land into useless desert.

ing millions to become refugees in other lands. With less rain to feed it, the Niger River in West Africa, once the location of great trading cities, no longer supports farming on a level of five centuries ago. The problems are not confined to Africa. In Nepal, in South Asia, farmers have stripped the once lush Himalayan mountainsides for wood. The rain has then washed unimpeded down the slopes into the rivers, causing ever more destructive floods downstream in India and Bangladesh.

To counter environmental decay, movements have emerged in different nations. Some, such as the Sierra Club in the United States and the Malaysian Nature Society, appeal chiefly to middle-class people. Others, such as the Chipko tree protection movement in India and the Greenbelt movement in Kenya, bring middle-class urbanites and rural peasants together in a common cause. In 2004 the Greenbelt leader and global environmental activist, Wangari Maathai, won the Noble Peace Prize (see Profile: Wangari Maathai, Kenyan Environmental Activist). Furthermore, the United Nations established an environmental program that issues regular reports warning that environmental destruction, combined with poverty and population growth, threaten the long-term health of the planet and its people.

SECTION SUMMARY

- Globalization has boosted world economies and has reaped great rewards for countries such as the United States and China, but it has not always benefited the lives of poor people and has also led to continued foreign domination of some groups and nations by others.

- The World Bank and the International Monetary Fund have lent money to developing nations but sometimes dictate economic policies to borrowers; while multinational corporations have become so large that they exert great influence over governments and set the world prices for some commodities.

- Industrialization has spread throughout Asia and Latin America, the Third Industrial Revolution has created powerful new technologies, the Green Revolution has allowed for increased agricultural production, and the service and information industries have grown rapidly; but some globalization practices, such as outsourcing jobs to countries with cheaper labor, have produced hardships.

- Despite worldwide economic growth, some countries remain underdeveloped and the gap between the wealthiest and poorest people is striking; however, the developing world has made great improvements in infant mortality and adult literacy.

- Women have faced great problems in the modern economy as they have been drastically underpaid for their contributions, but grassroots programs such as the Grameen Bank have offered some increased economic opportunity.

- Over the past fifty years, the world population has exploded, especially in Asia, Africa, and Latin America, prompting fears that it will eventually outstrip available resources; while in more developed countries, fertility rates have dropped and populations have grown older.

- Industrialization and population growth have led to increased pollution and deforestation, which have led to massive extinction of plant and animal species, global warming, and the rise of environmental groups.

✦ New Global Networks and Their Consequences

How did growing networks linking societies influence social, political, and economic life?

During the late twentieth century the world became connected in unprecedented ways, leading to talk of a "spaceship earth" or a **global village**, an interconnected world community in which all people, regardless of nationality, share a

---

global village An interconnected world community in which all people, regardless of their nationality, share a common fate.

common fate. A study of the interconnectedness contended that "the boundaries of the 'global village' are fluid, the inhabitants are highly mobile. Each street has its own problems, but each problem impinges increasingly on the population as a whole. The 'tyranny of distance' has been overcome; isolation has been eliminated."[16] Globalization has reshaped politics and cultures as well as economic patterns, fostering not only the movement of money, products, and labor, but also of people, diseases, cultures, and religions. Increasingly the world is marked by both unity and diversity, common influences mixing with local traditions. These transitions and encounters have not always gone smoothly, but they have often been creative.

Migration and Refugee Flows

Today, many people live in nations filled with immigrants and their descendants from the four corners of the globe. For example, 40 percent of Australians are immigrants or the children of immigrants. In western Europe, which is increasingly reliant on immigrant labor, 30 million people arrived between 1945 and 1975, chiefly from North Africa, West Africa, Turkey, South Asia, and the Caribbean. Similarly, 3.5 million Colombians moved to neighboring Venezuela and 4 million Mexicans legally entered the United States, many filling low wage jobs. Immigrants have often settled in Western nations, rapidly transforming cities such as Vancouver, Los Angeles, Sydney, and Paris into internationalized hubs of world culture and commerce. So many educated people have moved to Western nations that experts have identified a "brain drain" from poor countries. For example, doctors from India and nurses from the Philippines have played key roles in North American health care. Cosmopolitanism—a blending of peoples and cultures—flavors cities closely linked to the world economy, such as Hong Kong, Singapore, São Paulo (POU-lo), London, and Dubai.

In many societies, the immigrants' presence has triggered tension and debates. Although economists argue that migrants usually make rather than take jobs, local people have often felt threatened by the newcomers and resent their continuing attachment to their own languages and cultural traditions. While the globalization of trade and jobs dissolves economic boundaries, governments increasingly impose tighter border controls in an effort to discourage illegal immigration. For example, the United States has devoted more resources to patrolling the long border with Mexico but has been unable to stop the flow of Latin Americans flocking north.

By the late twentieth century the world contained some 100 million voluntary migrants to foreign countries, and the great majority moved for economic rather than political reasons. Many migrants—some from impoverished regions such as Central America and South Asia, others from more prosperous nations such as South Korea and Taiwan—have sought better economic opportunities in the industrialized West. For example, small Indian- and Pakistani-run sundry goods and grocery stores, known as corner shops, have become a fixture in British cities. Millions of Asians and Africans have also moved to the Middle East seeking work. Filipinos are an especially mobile people, migrating for short periods to other Southeast Asian nations and the Middle East and more permanently to North America. Some 8 million Filipinos lived abroad by 2002. Moving to a faraway, alien society is often traumatic, for both the migrant and the family members left behind. A poem by a Moroccan woman whose husband worked in Europe and rarely returned home captured the distress: "Germany, Belgium, France and Netherlands, Where are you situated? I have never seen your countries, I do not speak your language. I am afraid my love forgets me in your paradise. I ask you, give him back to me."[17]

Political turbulence, wars, genocides, and government repression have created some 20 million refugees. Desperate people have fled nations engulfed in political violence, such as Sudan, Guatemala, Afghanistan, and Cambodia, and drought-plagued states such as Ethiopia and Mali. For instance, by 2006 over 2 million African Muslims from the Darfur region of Sudan had fled genocidal attacks by Arab militias—attacks that already killed 200,000 people—for refuge in Chad, an equally impoverished nation. Cubans, Chinese, Laotians (lao-OH-shuhnz), and Vietnamese, among others, have fled communist-run states that restricted their freedoms. Others, such as Haitians, Chileans, and Congolese, have escaped brutal rightwing dictatorships or corrupt despotisms. Millions of refugees have remained for decades, even generations, in squalid refugee camps, often fed and housed by international aid organizations. For example, many Palestinians who fled conflict in Israel have lived in refugee camps in neighboring Egypt, Jordan, and Lebanon (LEB-uh-nuhn)—sometimes welcomed, sometimes resented by local Arabs—for over five decades. Refugees such as the Cubans, Vietnamese, and Palestinians have nurtured resentments against the governments whose policies they escaped from or who forced them out, and citizens in countries offering refuge have often resented the refugees. Facing increasing numbers of people seeking refugee status, by the 1990s many nations, especially in Europe, became more cautious in granting political asylum.

The Global Spread of Disease

Diseases, whether confined chiefly to a local area or traveling the routes of trade and migration, have produced major pandemics, or massive disease outbreaks, throughout history. Today, although modern medicine has eliminated diseases that had long plagued humanity, such as smallpox, leprosy, and polio, other diseases, such as cholera and malaria, still bedevil people with little access to health care. Cholera, a bacterial disease that easily crosses borders, still kills several thousand people a year in poor countries, and malaria, spread by mosquitoes, debilitates millions of people in tropical regions. In the early twenty-first century experts worried about a possible global spread of several viral diseases, perhaps killing millions of people, that passed from birds and poultry to humans. Both United Nations agencies and private organizations, such as Doctors Without Borders, have worked hard to reduce health threats and treat victims. But the travel of migrants, tourists,

business people, armies, truck drivers, sailors, and others continues to spread diseases.

The most deadly contemporary scourge affecting nations rich and poor, autoimmune deficiency syndrome, better known as AIDS, is caused by a virus known as HIV. AIDS is partly spread through the increased trade and travel associated with globalization, including migrant and transportation labor. The disease spreads through sexual contact, needle sharing by drug addicts, and selling or receiving blood. Poverty, which forces many women into prostitution, is also a factor in the spread of AIDS. For instance, long-distance truck drivers who visit prostitutes along their routes often spread the infection, especially in Africa and India. By 2005 some 42 million people around the world were infected with either HIV or AIDS, and 3.1 million died annually from AIDS, about a fifth of them children and one-third adult women, who were often infected by their husbands. In some African districts parental deaths left some 30 percent of children orphans, and as much as 30 percent of the adult population of some African nations was HIV positive. By contrast, the disease is less catastrophic in countries with less poverty and better health care and communications. Only 0.2 percent of Americans were infected, and the rate was even lower in Europe. The pandemic, compared by some experts to the Black Death seven centuries earlier, has presented an obstacle to economic development and has proved to be a particular disaster in India, Southeast Asia, and east, central and southern Africa.

Because most AIDS victims are in their twenties and thirties, in the worst affected countries the disease has killed or incapacitated the most highly trained and economically active section of the population. Treating AIDS patients also puts an added stress on the limited resources available for health care. Only a few African and Asian governments, however, among them Uganda and Thailand, have mounted education campaigns to convince people to take precautions to avoid getting the disease or to seek treatment. In some heavily affected nations, such as China, India, and Zimbabwe, governments fearing bad publicity and not wanting to devote resources to the afflicted have often hid the problem from public scrutiny. AIDS victims are often rejected by their families and communities, dying alone and neglected by society.

Cultures and Religions Across Borders

The spread of cultural products and religions across national borders and the creative mixing of these with local traditions have been hallmarks of the modern world. These trends have developed within the context of a global system in which people and ideas meet. The contacts between societies have produced new forms of entertainment. In societies around the world, popular culture, commonly produced for commercial purposes and spread by the mass media, such as radio, television, and films, has become a part of everyday life for billions of people. Spurred by globalization, religions have struggled for relevance but also found new believers and adapted to new environments.

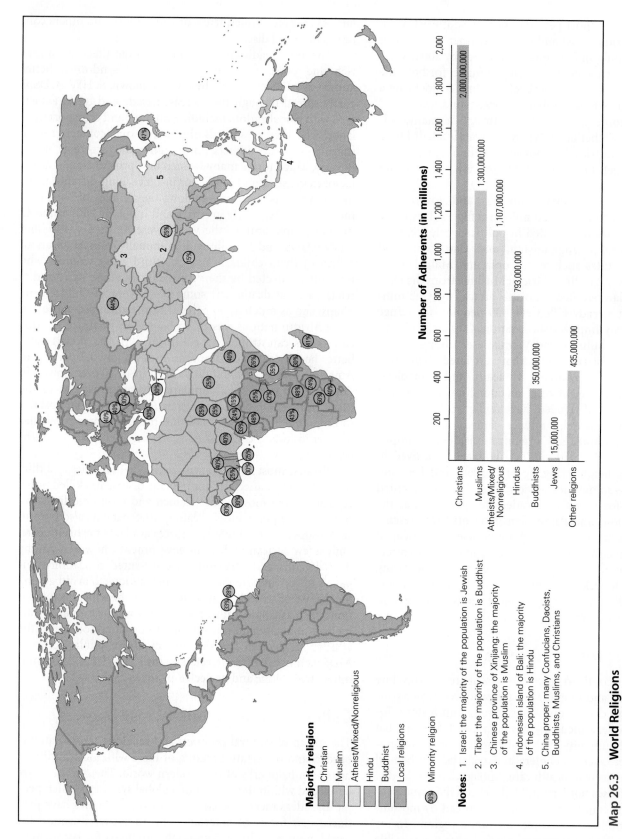

Majority religion

Christian
Muslim
Atheist/Mixed/Nonreligious
Hindu
Buddhist
Local religions

⬤ 50% Minority religion

Notes: 1. Israel: the majority of the population is Jewish
2. Tibet: the majority of the population is Buddhist
3. Chinese province of Xinjiang: the majority of the population is Muslim
4. Indonesian island of Bali: the majority of the population is Hindu
5. China proper: many Confucians, Daoists, Buddhists, Muslims, and Christians

Number of Adherents (in millions)

Religion	Adherents
Christians	2,000,000,000
Muslims	1,300,000,000
Atheists/Mixed/Nonreligious	1,107,000,000
Hindus	793,000,000
Buddhists	350,000,000
Jews	15,000,000
Other religions	435,000,000

Map 26.3   World Religions

Christianity has the most believers and is the dominant faith in the Americas, Oceania, Europe, Russia, and central and southern Africa. Most people in the northern half of Africa, western Asia, and Central Asia embrace Islam. Hindus are concentrated in India, and Buddhists in East and Southeast Asia.

Popular Cultures Societies have long exchanged cultural influences that have enriched local traditions. In the modern era, Western influences have been pervasive; yet, some of the modernization around the world that seems to reflect Westernization has remained superficial. Western videos, pop music recordings, jeans, and shopping malls that encourage consumption and present new options have attracted some youth in Asia, Africa, and Latin America, but their influence on the broader society, especially in the rural areas, is often more limited. No common world culture has emerged in this era. At the same time, Western technologies sometimes have served local needs. India, for instance, developed the world's largest film industry, producing some 1,000 films a year by 2002, three times more films than the next largest producers, the United States and Japan. And cheap, often pirated, audiocassettes in the 1970s, videocassettes in the 1980s, and DVDs in the 1990s enabled even many more poor people around the world to enjoy music and films while also enabling political or religious groups to spread their messages easily.

Modern media have reshaped people's lives, especially in cities, giving many societies a certain common denominator of experience. One observer in the 1990s noted the global popularity of television:

> Take a walk down any street, in any city or village, as the twilight fades and the darkness comes over the scene. Whether you are in London or Tokyo, Cairo or New York, Buenos Aires or Singapore, a small blue light will flicker at you from the unshuttered windows. These lights are the tiny knots in the seamless web of modern media.[18]

The mixing of cultures and the increasing role of the mass media have been reflected in popular music. Some popular musical styles, such as American jazz and Brazilian samba, emerged well before World War II, but most appeared after 1945. Anglo-American pop music styles, such as rock, jazz, and rap, all African American forms though having African roots, have found audiences all over the world. Vaclav Havel (vah-SLAV hah-VEL), the leader of the movement that overthrew Czech communism, credited the U.S. rock musician Frank Zappa with inspiring him to become an activist. Indeed, Havel had earlier in his life written songs for a Czech rock group. The South African leader, Nelson Mandela, enjoys listening to jazz, while rebellious youth in Manila and São Paulo use rap to express their feelings. Through the global reputations they often enjoy, and using the power of the mass media, Western pop stars also mount concerts to address issues such as racism, political prisoners, famine, and African poverty. Bono, the lead singer for the Irish rock band U2, uses his worldwide popularity to campaign among political leaders for causes such as debt relief for poor nations.

In the 1990s a British pop star who adopted an American Indian performance name, Apache Indian, demonstrated the creativity of transnational music by mixing West Indian reggae with American hip hop and *bhangra*, a folk music carried to Britain by immigrants from India and transformed into a distinctive pop music. Born into an Indian immigrant family in England, Apache Indian idolized both the American rocker Elvis Presley, popular in the 1950s, and the Jamaican reggae star Bob Marley. Apache Indian's often political songs express South Asian youth identity, criticize racism, and bridge tensions between blacks and South Asians in Britain. His songs also challenge caste and sexual attitudes in India. As he put it, "I want to speak on things that haven't been talked about before. I want to bring [problems] out in the open for discussion."[19]

Many forms of music have mixed indigenous and imported influences, often from outside the West. For example, Congolese popular music, which borrowed Latin American dance rhythms, gained audiences throughout Africa and Europe in the 1980s. Indian film music and Arab folk music have influenced the popular music of Southeast Asia and East Africa. Even pop music that does not cross borders can reflect a creative blending of traditions. A good case of this was *dangdut*, an Indonesian popular music that originated as a fusion of Western rock, Indian film music, and local folk music. The major dangdut star, Rhoma Irama (ROW-muh ih-RAH-muh), has sometimes faced arrest for offering political protests in songs that address poverty, human rights abuses, the struggle of the underdog, and the betrayal of the nationalist promise. Beginning in the 1970s he developed a huge following among poor rural folk and urban youth, who agree with the message of one of his more famous songs: "The rich get richer and the poor get poorer." Rhoma's music, which has a strong Islamic quality and promotes Muslim moral teachings, helped inspire the Islamic revival in Indonesia, but conservative Muslims have often condemned other dangdut singers for their erotic lyrics and suggestive performances.

Religious Dynamism Although in the modern era secular thought has become more popular than ever before in history, over three-quarters of the world's people identify with one or another universal religion with roots deep in the past. By 2000, the world contained almost 2 billion Christians, 1.3 billion Muslims, 800 million Hindus, and 350 million Buddhists. Nearly 900 million practiced a local faith, such as animism or Daoism, or professed no religion (see Map 26.3). Religion sometimes has become the basis for national identity, as in chiefly Roman Catholic Poland and Ireland and in Muslim Bangladesh and Pakistan.

Religious leaders have debated how much, if at all, their faiths need to change to better engage the contemporary world. Serious efforts at reform came, for instance, in the Catholic Church; in the 1960s Pope John XXIII (pope 1958–1963) engaged with the modern world by liberalizing church practices, such as having the mass in a vernacular language rather than Latin, and encouraged a more active dialogue with other churches and religions. Meanwhile, a movement arose among Catholic clergy and laypeople in Latin America, called liberation theology, that cooperated with socialist and communist groups to improve the lives of the poor. Catholic leaders disagreed on whether to support it. Muslim liberals and militants also confronted each other over which directions Islam should take, arguing over such issues as the role of women, relations with non-Muslims, and whether states with Muslim majorities should make Islamic law the basis of their legal systems. In sub-Saharan Africa and Southeast Asia, where Sunni Muslims are often nominal in their faith and tolerant toward other beliefs, some people have become more devout, and more men from these regions have gone to Cairo or Saudi Arabia to study religion, often returning home with more militant views.

The easy spread of ideas in the globalized world has worked to the advantage of portable creeds that are not dependent on one culture or setting. In many places, notably Africa, religions tied to local culture, usually some form of polytheism or animism, have faded while two universal religions, Christianity and Islam, fortified by missionary impulses, have gained wider followings. Protestants have evangelized and gained ground in predominantly Catholic Latin America. Protestants and Catholics have also competed with each other, and often with Muslims, for followers in Africa, Southeast Asia, and East Asia. Christian and Muslim missionaries have appealed to the downtrodden, suggesting that adopting their faith could lead not only to spiritual health but also to material wealth, and have recast their messages to recognize local cultural traditions.

At the same time, organized religion and its influence have declined in East Asia and much of the West. The communists discouraged religious observance in China while increasing numbers of Japanese found neither their traditional faiths nor imported religions relevant to their lives. Meanwhile, Christian churches in Europe, Canada, and Australia competed with widespread lack of belief. Church attendance and membership in these societies fell dramatically between 1960 and the early twenty-first century. Traditional church attitudes have also competed with changing social attitudes. Even predominantly Catholic nations in Europe have legalized abortion and moved toward equal rights for homosexuals, policies opposed by the Catholic Church. Both the Netherlands, once a center for a puritanical form of Protestantism, and Spain, before the 1970s one of the staunchest Catholic nations, have approved same-sex marriage, as did Belgium, Canada, and South Africa.

Long a source of conflict, religion has now brought new tensions between members of different faiths. Sparked by political differences and sometimes traditional hostilities, some Christians and Muslims violently attacked each other in Indonesia, the Philippines, Yugoslavia, and West Africa. For example, hundreds of people were killed or wounded in Nigeria when rival Christians and Muslims, spurred by local political rivalries and increasing religious militancy, sporadically battled for control of several cities. Meanwhile, tensions between Muslims and Hindus sparked sporadic violence in India. Catholics and Protestants opposed each other in Northern Ireland and Uganda, while Sunni and Shi'a Muslims occasionally fought in Pakistan and western Asia. Governments controlled by Sunni Muslims sometimes discriminated against or persecuted Shi'ites. In Iraq, where some 60 percent of the population is Shi'a, the Sunni dictator, Saddam Hussein, restricted Shi'ite religious holidays, executed Shi'ites who opposed his regime, and allowed few Shi'ites into the government. After his regime was toppled by the U.S. invasion, conflicts between Shi'ites and Sunnis erupted, complicating U.S. efforts to restore political stability.

Religious militancy has grown among some believers. Some Muslim militants have turned the old notion of *jihad*, or struggle within believers to strengthen their faith, into a campaign for holy war, or physical combat in God's name, against unbelievers and countries or groups they consider anti-Muslim, and for the remodeling of secular states into Islamic ones. The militants, often known as Islamists or jihadis, appeal especially to the young and poor, who are often unemployed and embittered toward their governments and the West. Many Muslims oppose market capitalism, which they view as supporting the power of large, politically well-connected corporations, and Western cultural influence. The more puritanical Muslims despise the revealing clothing styles, open romantic behavior, independent women, and rebellious youth portrayed in Western television programs and movies, fearing that exposure to these influences will corrupt their children. Some Christians, especially in the United States, Latin America, and Africa, have turned to literal interpretations of the Bible, an approach labeled as fundamentalist, and formed proselytizing churches. These churches have often opposed secular culture, rejected scientific findings they deemed incompatible with biblical accounts, and condemned leftwing political and social movements, particularly those promoting socialism, feminism, legalized abortion, and homosexual rights. Christian and Islamic militancy has sparked similar movements in Buddhism, Hinduism, and Judaism, pitting the zealous believers against those with moderate, tolerant views.

Global Communications

A worldwide communications network has been a chief engine of globalization. The introduction of radio in the early 1900s and then tape recording and television in midcentury laid the basis for this network. These were followed by the invention of the transistor by three American physicists in 1947, which allowed for the miniaturization of electronics. In 1953 portable transistor radios became available and soon reached even remote villages, opening them to the news and culture of the wider world. Even villages without electricity could use transistor radios and cassette players. For example, by the 1960s in central Borneo, a densely forested island divided between Indonesia and Malaysia, isolated villagers, few of whom understood much English, listened to radio broadcasts from the United States, Britain, and Australia, and village youth enjoyed and could often sing the songs of Western pop musicians such as the British rock group the Beatles.

Technological breakthroughs provided the foundation for more rapid and widespread communications. For decades, U.S., British, and German engineers had been gradually building a foundation for computer technology. The first general purpose computers were built in 1948. In 1958 the first silicon microchips began a computer revolution that led several decades later to the first personal computers. By 2000 the world had more than 150 million personal computers with

Internet access, 330 million Internet users, and 1.6 billion web pages, all part of a vast network often termed the information superhighway. Every minute, 10 million electronically transmitted messages, or e-mail, are dispatched via computer. E-mail allows people in different countries, however distant, such as Canada and Malaysia, to communicate instantly with each other, exchanging views, sharing jokes, and forwarding articles, essays, and other writings or even music and films. An interested reader in Hong Kong, Ghana, or Finland can access online versions of newspapers, such as the *New York Times*, *Al Ahram* in Cairo, or the *Deccan Herald* in India. Along with computers, the rise of 24-hour cable news networks able to reach worldwide audiences, such as U.S.-based CNN (Cable News Network) and the Arab-language Al Jazeera, based in the Persian Gulf state of Qatar, widened access to diverse views. These trends have enriched people's understanding of the wider world.

The rapid evolution of media and information technology has had many consequences. For one, the development of fax communications, orbiting communications satellites, portable phones, electronic mail, and the worldwide computer web means that information can be transmitted around the globe beyond the reach of governments, undermining their power to shape their citizens' thinking. Repressive states seeking to limit information flow, such as Iran and Cuba, have banned satellite dish receivers and tried to jam access to controversial websites, including those used by political dissidents, but these efforts were only partly successful. In 2006 some U.S.-based Internet providers faced criticism for helping repressive governments such as China control the information flow and identify dissidents. Another major consequence is that technologies, especially the World Wide Web, have enhanced the value of education and of English, which has gradually become a world language, like Latin in the Mediterranean zone 2,000 years ago and Arabic in the Islamic world 1,000 years ago. By 2004 some three-quarters of all websites were in English. Perhaps a quarter of the world's people know some English, and Asian countries with educated people fluent in English, such as India and Singapore, have an advantage in competing for high-technology industries. Both of these major trends have also enhanced the global exchange of scientific ideas. But in the poorest nations, only a lucky few have satellite dishes, fax machines, and networked computers, and these promising technologies have not changed the lives of peasants and low-wage workers. Furthermore, many nations resented the strong U.S. influence over the Internet, including the power to allocate web addresses and domains.

Global Movements

The increasing links between far-flung peoples have allowed for social and political movements originating in different countries and independent of governments to transcend borders and link to other movements with similar interests. A wide variety of transnational organizations has emerged to promote issues such as the treatment of political prisoners, women's rights, and antiracism. As an example, Amnesty International, based in Britain, publicizes the plight of people imprisoned solely for their political views and activities, such as the Burmese opposition leader Aung San Suu Kyi (AWNG sahn soo CHEE) and, during the Cold War, the Soviet dissident scientist Andrei Sakharov (SAH-kuh-RAWF), around the world, organizing letter writing and pressure campaigns to seek their release. Other movements have addressed globalization. For instance, the World Social Forum was formed in 2001 and has met annually in Brazil. This group brings together

Internet Cafe in Thailand In this photo, a waiter at a cyberspace café, operated by the Swiss multinational ice cream company, Häagen Dazs, in Bangkok, Thailand, helps a young Thai woman navigate one of the café's computers. (AP/Wide World Photos)

nongovernment organizations and activists who oppose globalizing free market capitalism and what they view as the imperialism of industrialized nations. They believe globalization undermines workers' rights and environmental protection.

As the world became more closely linked, social or political movements or upheavals in one nation or region sometimes spread widely. For example, during the 1960s, students, workers, and political radicals in various nations organized protests against the U.S. war in Vietnam, racism, unresponsive governments, capitalism, and other concerns. In 1968 demonstrations, marches, and strikes intensified around the world. These movements were not coordinated and addressed largely local grievances, but young protesters were often influenced by the same writers, music, and ideas. The more radical protesters revered Marxist icons, for example, wearing t-shirts celebrating Che Guevara (guh-VAHR-uh) (1928–1967), an Argentinean-born revolutionary who helped Fidel Castro take power in Cuba; Guevara became a communist martyr when he was killed while organizing a guerrilla army in Bolivia. However, other protesters looked to noncommunists or even anticommunists, such as the dissidents—often devout Catholics—who opposed the communist regime in Poland, such as the labor leader Lech Walesa (leck wa-LEN-za). To varying degrees the turbulence affected over a dozen countries, from the United States and Mexico to France, Czechoslovakia, and Japan. Not all governments, however, tolerated the activism. For instance, when thousands of demonstrators shouting "Mexico, Freedom" took to the streets of Mexico City to demand democracy and protest police brutality, the police opened fire, killing dozens of protesters. "There was a general stampede," noted one student protester, "because all hell broke loose and a hail of bullets started raining down on us from all directions."[20] In the wake of the 1968 activism, environmental, peace, workers' rights, homosexual rights, and feminist movements grew, chiefly but not only in industrialized nations.

Women have been particularly active in seeking to expand their rights. Although most women's organizations work within national boundaries, some activists have placed women's issues on the international agenda. The United Nations periodically sponsors global conferences on women's issues such as gender equality and eliminating violence against women. However, women who attend international conferences, divided by culture and by whether they come from a rich or poor country, do not always agree on goals and strategies. In the United Nation's fourth World Conference on Women, held in China in 1995, the 40,000 delegates disagreed sharply on priorities. Delegates from rich nations wanted to expand women's employment options, social freedom, and control over their bodies, while Asian, African, and Latin American delegates were often chiefly interested in making their families more healthy and economically secure. One delegate from India described the goals of U.S. delegates as irrelevant to Indian women: "They ask for abortion rights. We ask for safe drinking water and basic health care."[21] While abortion remained a controversial issue in most of the world, strongly opposed by many religious groups, it became legal in most Western and many Asian nations. In Latin America, which, despite stringent laws against it, has the world's second highest rate of abortion after eastern Europe, women's groups pushing for legalization were gaining support in several nations by the early 2000s. Women also won the right to vote in most democratic or semidemocratic nations.

Yet, despite disagreements, women have worked across borders on issues affecting all societies, such as preventing violence against women. For example, women activists and their male supporters from Muslim and Western nations fought, among other practices, the tradition common in some conservative Muslim societies of jailing or killing women for adultery while exonerating the man responsible. In 2005 Mukhtaran Bibi (MOOK-tahr-an BIH-bee), an illiterate woman from an impoverished Pakistani village without electricity, gained worldwide sympathy for her resistance to male brutality. As part of a village dispute involving her family, the tribal council had ruled that she be gang-raped to punish her family. Instead of following custom by ending the "disgrace" through suicide, however, she bravely pursued the rapists, men from another family, in court. They were convicted, and she used the money awarded her by the court to start two village schools, one for boys and one for girls. When a higher court then overturned the men's convictions, her courageous refusal to accept the verdict, a dangerous step in her patriarchal society, caused an international outcry. While the Pakistan government tried to suppress the controversy and forbade Mukhtaran from traveling abroad, men and women around the world, alerted by news accounts and Internet appeals, donated money and made her a symbol of the need for women's rights. Mukhtaran Bibi inspired millions everywhere with her courage and faith in education and justice.

Global Terrorism

Terrorism, small-scale but violent attacks aimed at undermining a government or demoralizing a population, intensified in the late twentieth and early twenty-first century, expanding to global dimensions and reshaping world politics. Terrorism, which has often targeted civilians as well as government officials and soldiers, has a long history, going back many centuries, and became common in the twentieth century. At the end of the century terrorist networks had formed which threatened the global order.

The Rise of Terrorism For centuries various groups and states used terrorism to support their goals. For example, in the 1920s Vietnamese nationalists tossed explosives and shot at the residences, offices, and police stations used by the French colonizers. After 1945 Palestinians under Israeli control, Basque nationalists in Spain, and Irish nationalists in Britain, among others, engaged in terrorism for their causes. Some states also carried out or sponsored terrorism against unfriendly governments or political movements. For example, South Africa's white minority government organized

terrorism Small-scale but violent attacks aimed at undermining a government or demoralizing a population.

or financed insurgencies that opposed the Marxist governments of Angola and Mozambique, resulting in thousands of civilian deaths. Similarly, the United States sponsored terrorism against leftist-ruled Nicaragua in the 1980s, helping form a military force, known as the *Contras,* that often attacked civilian targets, such as rural schools, day care centers, and clinics operated by the government.

While terrorism has often remained local in scope, an increasingly interconnected world has spurred some terrorist organizations to operate on a global level, forming networks that have branches in many countries. The most active of these networks, formed by militant Islamists, have exploited communication and transportation networks to operate across national borders, capitalizing on widespread Muslim anger at Israel and U.S. foreign policies. Muslim terrorist groups became increasingly active during the 1970s and 1980s in Egypt, Algeria, and Lebanon. Aiming to undermine Israel, their own secular governments, and these governments' Western backers, the terrorists attacked politicians, police, Western residents and tourists, and Israeli and U.S. targets.

As a result, terrorism became a growing threat to life in the Middle East. For example, the *Hezbollah* movement in Lebanon, formed by Shi'ite Arabs opposed to the U.S.-backed Lebanese government and to U.S. support for Israel, used suicide bombers driving explosive-filled trucks to destroy the U.S. Embassy and a Marine Corps base in Beirut, killing several hundred Americans. Later, to oppose Israeli occupation of Arab lands and demoralize Israelis, Palestinian militants strapped explosives to their bodies and detonated them in Israeli buses and businesses. Outraged by the killing and wounding of hundreds of Israeli civilians—both Jewish and Arab—the Israelis responded with force, killing or arresting Palestinians and expelling families of suspected militants from their homes, often bulldozing the houses into rubble. The poet Hanan Ashrawi (HA-non uh-SHRAH-wee), a Christian Palestinian nationalist, condemned the suicide bombings but also lamented the earlier Israeli destruction of her family's property, which had been seized and allocated to Jewish settlers: "Have you seen a stone house die? It sighs, then wraps itself around its gutted heart and lays itself to rest."[22] Divided by politics, Israelis and Palestinians have shared the bitter experience of grieving for those lost in the chronic violence, among them innocent women and children.

Terrorist Networks The Soviet military intervention in 1979 to support a pro-Soviet government in mostly Muslim Afghanistan provided the spark for forming a global network of Islamist terrorists. Islamic militants from the Middle East and Pakistan flocked to Afghanistan to assist the Muslim Afghan insurgents resisting the Soviets. In 1988 the most militant of the foreign fighters began to come together in a jihadi organization known as *Al Qaeda* ("The Base"). Al Qaeda's main leader was the Saudi Osama bin Laden (b. 1957), who came from an extremely wealthy family—his Yemen-born father had made billions in the Saudi construction industry—and had been trained as an engineer. Bin Laden used his wealth to support the Afghan rebels, mostly devout Muslims, who

were also funded and armed by the United States as part of its Cold War rivalry with the USSR. After the Soviets abandoned Afghanistan in 1989, bin Laden used his supporters among the foreign fighters to set up Al Qaeda cells in Saudi Arabia, whose government he viewed as corrupt, and to target Egypt and Iraq, whose secular regimes suppressed Islamic militants. To recruit, support, and communicate with members, Al Qaeda used the instruments of the information superhighway, publicizing their cause by setting up websites, using e-mail and satellite phones, and releasing videotapes to cable news networks of bin Laden's messages.

Eventually Al Qaeda looked beyond the Middle East for targets. In the mid-1990s the Afghanistan-based bin Laden, a ruthless man willing to kill innocent people in pursuit of his goals, began to plot terrorist efforts against his former ally in the Afghan resistance, the United States, whose military bases in Saudi Arabia, support for repressive Arab governments, and close alliance with Israel enraged many Arabs. Viewing the U.S. command of vast economic and military power as the greatest barrier to his ambition of revitalizing the Islamic world by spreading the Islamist agenda and enhancing his own power, bin Laden argued that "to kill the Americans and their allies is an individual duty for every Muslim who can do it in any country in which it is possible to do so."[23] Most Muslims rejected such violent views. Al Qaeda or related groups sponsored attacks on U.S. targets, such as the embassies in Kenya and Tanzania, causing hundreds of casualties.

On September 11, 2001, Al Qaeda members hijacked four U.S. commercial airliners and crashed them into New York's World Trade Center and the Pentagon near Washington, D.C., killing over 3,000 people, mostly civilians. The attacks shocked Americans, unused to terrorism at home, as well as people everywhere who opposed indiscriminate killing. U.S. president George W. Bush responded by declaring a war on terrorism. U.S. forces attacked Al Qaeda bases in Afghanistan, and then occupied the country, whose government, controlled by Islamists who had fought the Soviets, shielded bin Laden, but the United States failed to capture bin Laden and still faced resistance from Islamic militants.

In 2003 the United States, claiming that Saddam Hussein's Iraq was closely linked to Al Qaeda and possessed weapons of mass destruction, invaded Iraq, removed Saddam's brutal, despotic government, and imposed a U.S. military occupation. Britain provided the chief support for the U.S. effort. The U.S. troops, however, found no evidence of any Saddam ties to Al Qaeda or any weapons of mass destruction. The occupation sparked an insurgency, including suicide bombings, and unleashed sectarian divisions that hindered the U.S. efforts—supported by many Iraqis—to stabilize and rebuild Iraq. While most of the insurgents were Iraqis, mostly Sunni Muslims fearing domination by the Shi'ite majority, Islamists from other countries flocked to Iraq to attack Americans and help destabilize the country. The U.S. invasion and occupation, and the resistance to it, killed tens of thousands of Iraqi civilians, resulted in over 25,000 U.S. casualties, and kept a large U.S. military force tied down in Iraq. Whether the war in Iraq helped or harmed the U.S.-led war against terrorism remained subject to debate. The war alienated many

U.S. allies and, like the earlier U.S. conflict in Vietnam, was unpopular around the world. Meanwhile, capitalizing on anti-U.S. sentiments among Muslims, Al Qaeda spawned loosely affiliated terrorist groups, often operating without direct Al Qaeda guidance.

Terrorism by militant Muslims had direct and indirect consequences for societies around the world. Al Qaeda or related groups launched terrorist attacks on several continents, from Spain and Britain to Indonesia, Kenya, and Morocco. Nations with despotic governments, such as China, Egypt, and Uzbekistan, used the threat of terrorism as a reason to restrict civil liberties. Human rights concerns faded amid the Western obsession with terrorism. In 1993 a German historian had correctly predicted the challenges ahead in the post–Cold War world: "We are at the beginning of a new era, characterized by great insecurity, permanent crisis and the absence of any kind of *status quo*. We must realize that we find ourselves in one of those crises of world history."[24]

SECTION SUMMARY

- In the new global village, millions of people have immigrated to foreign countries seeking greater economic opportunity or an escape from insufferable conditions at home, including political repression, famine, and civil war.

- Modern medicine has eliminated many diseases, but cholera and malaria are still a serious problem, and AIDS has seriously affected India and areas of Southeast Asia and Africa.

- Western consumer culture has spread around the world, while musical forms from different cultures have mingled and musicians and performers have expressed political and often controversial views.

- The world's major religious traditions have remained numerically strong, and some have worked to adapt to the modern world; while representatives of rival religions have fought for control of various areas and many Muslims and Christians have grown more fundamentalist.

- Worldwide communication was facilitated by technologies such as radio, television, and the Internet, making a vast array of information available, even in countries such as Iran and Cuba, whose governments attempted to limit its availability.

- Increased global communication led to political movements that transcended conventional borders, such as Amnesty International, the 1968 youth protests, and women's rights movements.

- Terrorism, which had been used throughout the twentieth century by groups such as the Palestinians, the Basques, and the Irish, became more deadly, culminating in the radical Muslim group Al Qaeda's 2001 attack on the United States.

Online Study Center ACE the Test

 # Chapter Summary

The later twentieth century proved turbulent. Nationalism spread outside of Europe and the Americas, leading to decolonization. During the 1950s and 1960s most of the Western colonies gained their independence through negotiations, the threat of violence, or armed struggle, and social revolutionaries gained power in some nations. However, the West maintained a strong economic presence in many former colonies. The rivalry between the United States and the USSR also shaped the global system, generating a Cold War in which the two superpowers faced each other indirectly or through surrogates. The powerful United States had a large group of allies and sometimes intervened in Asian and Latin American nations, while the USSR occupied eastern Europe. The collapse of the Communist bloc and then the USSR allowed the United States to become the world's lone superpower.

The world was also shaped by the increasing forces of globalization, with its unprecedented flow of money, products, information, and ideas across national borders. The global economy grew rapidly but did not spread its benefits equally. As industrialization spread, most Western and some Asian and Latin American nations prospered, but poor nations struggled to escape underdevelopment and raise living standards. A billion people remained mired in deep poverty. Meanwhile millions of people migrated, social and political movements addressed local and global problems, universal religions gained new converts, and the information superhighway and other technological innovations linked millions of people in new ways. Terrorists also took advantage of globalism, as new international terrorist networks challenged governments and prompted a reshaping of world politics.

Online Study Center Improve Your Grade Flashcards

Key Terms

First World	nuclear weapons	Green Revolution
Second World	globalization	desertification
Third World	multinational	global village
Fourth World	corporations	terrorism
Cold War	Third Industrial	
guerrilla warfare	Revolution	

Suggested Reading

Books

Ali, Tariq. *The Clash of Fundamentalisms: Crusades, Jihads and Modernity*. London: Verso, 2003. A controversial but powerful examination, by a London-based Indian writer, of Western policies and Islamic movements around the world.

Axford, Barrie. *The Global System: Economics, Politics and Culture*. New York: St. Martin's, 1995. A comprehensive, thoughtful review by a British scholar of approaches to understanding the global system.

Crossley, Pamela Kyle, et al. *Global Society: The World Since 1900*. Boston: Houghton Mifflin, 2004. A comprehensive survey.

DeFronzo, James. *Revolutions and Revolutionary Movements*. Boulder, Colo.: Westview Press, 1991. Useful surveys of revolutions and the societies they made, with case studies of Russia, China, Vietnam, Cuba, Nicaragua, Iran, and South Africa.

Enloe, Cynthia. *Bananas, Beaches and Bases: Making Feminist Sense of International Relations*, 2nd ed. Berkeley: University of California Press, 2001. A provocative examination of women's experiences in global politics.

Ehrenreich, Barbara and Arlie Russell Hochschild, eds. *Global Women: Nannies, Maids, and Sex Workers in the New Economy*. Provocative look at the feminization of the migrant work force.

Hunt, Michael H. *The World Transformed, 1945 to the Present*. Boston: Bedford/St. Martin's, 2004. A readable and up-to-date survey.

Kechner, Frank J. and John Boli. *World Culture: Origins and Consequences*. Malden, M.A.: Blackwell, 2005. Examines the impact of globalization on world culture.

LaFeber, Walter. *America, Russia and the Cold War, 1945–1992*, 9th ed. New York: McGraw-Hill, 2002. An excellent examination of the Cold War around the world.

Mazlish, Bruce, and Akira Iriye, eds. *The Global History Reader*. New York: Routledge, 2005. A provocative set of essays on global trends in the twentieth century, from the information revolution and environmental change to human rights and terrorism.

McNeill, J. R. *Something New Under the Sun: An Environmental History of the Twentieth-Century World*. New York: W. W. Norton, 2000. An outstanding examination of the interface between societies and environmental change.

Ponting, Clive. *The Twentieth Century: A World History*. New York: Henry Holt, 1998. A valuable thematic examination by a British scholar.

Reynolds, David. *One World Divisible: A Global History Since 1945*. New York: W. W. Norton, 2001. A comprehensive survey.

Sen, Amartya. *Identity and Violence: The Illusion of Destiny*. New York: Norton, 2006. An influential Indian economist's views on globalization, freedom, violence, and other global issues.

Wang, Gungwu, ed. *Global History and Migrants*. Boulder: Westview, 1997. Essays on recent population movements.

Weiss, Thomas G. et al. *The United Nations and Changing World Politics*, 3rd ed. Boulder: Westview, 2001. Examines the history and roles of the United Nations.

Westad, Odd Arne. *The Global Cold War*. New York: Cambridge University Press, 2005. Provocative study by a Norwegian scholar.

Websites

Global Problems and the Culture of Capitalism
(http://faculty.plattsburgh.edu/richard.robbins/legacy/). An outstanding site, aimed at undergraduates, with a wealth of resources.

The Globalization Website
(http://www.emory.edu/SOC/globalization/). A useful site with many resources and essays on globalization.

Human Rights Watch
(http://www.hrw.org/wr2k3/introduction.html). The website of a major human rights organization that reports on the entire world.

Modern History Sourcebook
(http://www.fordham.edu/halsall/mod/modsbook.html). A very extensive online collection of historical documents and secondary materials.

United Nations Environment Program
(http://www.unep.org/geo2000/ov-e/index.htm). Provides access to United Nations reports on the world's environmental problems.

East Asian Resurgence, 1945–Present

Online Study Center

This icon will direct you to interactive activities and study materials on the website: college.hmco.com/pic/lockard1e

The China Stock Exchange The East Asian nations enjoyed an economic resurgence in this era. Since the 1980s, China has boasted the world's fastest growing economy and a booming stock exchange. (Wally McNamee/Corbis)

Once China's destiny is in the hands of the people, China, like the sun rising in the east, will illuminate every corner with a brilliant flame, and build a new, powerful and prosperous [society].

MAO ZEDONG, CHINESE COMMUNIST LEADER[1]

On October 1, 1949, after some two decades of directing brutal warfare against the Japanese invaders and the Chinese government, Mao Zedong (maow dzuh-dong) (1893–1976), the Chinese communist leader, was driven into downtown Beijing, China's capital, accompanied by a dusty band of soldiers from the communist military force, the People's Liberation Army. Mao, fifty-five years old, the son of a peasant family, had never been out of China and had spent the previous twenty-two years living in remote rural areas. Ahead of Mao's car rolled a Sherman tank, built in Detroit and originally donated by the United States to the Republic of China, the government headed by Jiang Jieshi (better known in the West as Chiang Kai-shek) (1887–1975), to help crush Mao's communist forces. But Chiang's army had lost to Mao's troops, and the president had fled to the large offshore island of Taiwan. Wearing a new suit, Mao climbed to the top of the Gate of Heavenly Peace, the entrance to the Forbidden City of the Qing emperors overlooking Beijing's spacious Tiananmen Square. Mao probably enjoyed this moment of triumph. He and his comrades had sacrificed much to reach this pinnacle of power. Millions of Chinese jammed the square to hear their new ruler announce the founding of a new communist government, called the People's Republic of China. Referring to a century of corrupt governments and humiliation and domination by Western nations and Japan, Mao thanked all those who, starting with the Opium War fought against the British in the mid-1800s, had "laid down their lives in the many struggles against domestic and foreign enemies," finally proclaiming: "The Chinese people have stood up. Nobody will insult us again."[2]

The formation of the People's Republic marked a watershed in the history of China, the rest of East Asia, and the world. The new government brought to an end a century of severe social and political instability, caused in part by the activities of foreign nations and China's inability to defend itself against imperialism. Its communist leaders were committed to the revolutionary transformation of the society while making China respected abroad once again. Given China's size and a population—1.3 billion by 2005—greater than that of North America, Europe, and Russia combined, any major transition there had global significance. By the early twenty-first century Mao was long gone and many of his policies discarded, but China, with a booming economy, had reclaimed some of the political and economic status it had lost two centuries earlier.

But Chinese were not the only East Asians to enjoy a resurgence with a global impact. In the 1980s East Asian and outside observers referred to the **Pacific Rim**, the economically dynamic Asian countries on the edge of the Pacific Basin: China, Japan, South Korea, Taiwan, and several Southeast Asian nations. These observers also predicted that the twenty-first century would be the **Pacific Century**, marked by a shift of global economic power from Europe and North America to the Pacific Rim, whose export-driven nations seemed poised to dominate a post–Cold War era where economic power outweighed military might. Reflecting this view, an Australian study concluded that the center of gravity of world economic life, for centuries located in the eastern half of Eurasia, had shifted away as Europe and the Atlantic economy rose, and then in the 1990s had moved back toward a resurgent Asia, poised to dominate the modern world economy. Economic crises, especially an Asian financial collapse in 1997, and changing world politics have challenged the Pacific Century concept, but China, Japan, and their neighbors have remained major players in the global system.

FOCUS QUESTIONS

1. How did Maoism transform Chinese society?
2. What factors explain the dramatic rise of Chinese economic power in the world since 1978?
3. How did Japan rise from the ashes of defeat in World War II to become a global economic powerhouse?
4. What policies led to the rise of the "Little Dragon" nations and their dynamic economies?

 Mao's Revolutionary China

How did Maoism transform Chinese society?

The Chinese Revolution that brought the Chinese communists to power in 1949 was one of the three greatest upheavals in modern world history. The first, the French Revolution (1789), destroyed the remnants of feudalism throughout western Europe and its leaders extolled the rights of the common people. The second, the Russian Revolution of 1917, charted a noncapitalist path to industrialization. Both events swept away old social classes and ruling elites. China's revolution joined these in remaking a major world society while restoring China's status as a major country. The communists built a strong government that made China the most experi-

mental nation on earth, veering from one innovative policy to another in an attempt to renovate Chinese life and resolve problems of underdevelopment. The People's Republic of China created a new model of economic development different from both Western-dominated capitalism, adopted by most poor nations, and the highly centralized Soviet communism. But the path was littered with conflict and repression. Furthermore, the Chinese, like all societies, were products of their history. Even under communist rule China remained partly an ancient empire and partly a modern nation, and its leaders often behaved much like the emperors of old in their autocratic exercise of power.

The Communist Triumph

The U.S. defeat of Japan in 1945 removed the common enemy of both of China's major political factions, Mao's communists and Chiang Kai-shek's nationalist government, sparking a fierce civil war between them for control of China. Chiang disdained Mao as an unpolished peasant with earthy language, while Mao despised Chiang, from a wealthy landlord family, for favoring the rich, yet both men shared some personality traits, such as patriotism, an autocratic style, and hunger for power. Chiang's 3.7-million-man army vastly outnumbered

Pacific Rim The economically dynamic Asian countries on the edge of the Pacific Basin: China, Japan, South Korea, Taiwan, and several Southeast Asian nations.

Pacific Century The possible shift of global economic power from Europe and North America to the Pacific Rim in the twenty-first century.

CHRONOLOGY		
China	**Japan**	**Korea and Taiwan**
1940 **1945–1949** Chinese civil war **1949** Chinese communist triumph	**1946–1952** U.S. occupation of Japan	**1950–1953** Korean War
1960 **1960** Sino-Soviet split **1966–1976** Great Proletarian Cultural Revolution **1978** Four Modernizations policy	**1960s–1989** Rapid economic growth	
1980		**1997** Asian financial collapse

the 900,000 communist troops. The United States lavished military aid on Chiang and provided planes and trucks to transport his soldiers in order to occupy as much Chinese territory as possible. The communists, aided by the Soviet Union (USSR), concentrated on north China and Manchuria. In trying to block Mao's forces, however, Chiang overstretched his supply lines. Chiang's Republic experienced, among other problems, a rapid decline in the value of Chinese currency that demoralized the population. The Chinese sought change, especially a less corrupt government, and many of them came to view the communist movement as a more honest alternative to Chiang's Nationalist Party.

In the villages that they controlled, the communists promoted a social revolution, known as the "turning over," by encouraging villagers to denounce local landlords, transferring land from richer to poorer peasants, replacing government-appointed leaders with elected village councils, and protecting battered wives. For example, encouraged to air their grievances by "speaking pains to recall pains" in village meetings, women warned abusive men to mend their ways or face punishment or arrest. Inevitably the release of pent-up rage against violent husbands or greedy landlords who mistreated tenants led to excesses, such as angry crowds beating them to death.

The military and political tide turned against the Republic. In 1948 Chiang's troops in Manchuria surrendered to the communists. To revive Chiang's prospects, the United States pressured him unsuccessfully to broaden his political base with democratic reforms. Some American leaders demanded that the United States send troops to help Chiang, but others concluded that his regime had lost too much popular support to win the conflict. Through 1949 the communists took the major cities of north China and pushed Chiang's army south. Finally Chiang fled to the island of Taiwan, along with thousands of troops and 2 million supporters. On Taiwan, with massive U.S. aid, the leaders of the relocated Republic of China developed a successful capitalist strategy for economic growth. Meanwhile, mainland China's history now moved in a direction very different from that of Chiang's Republic of China.

A New Economy and Government

The key question confronting the Chinese communists after 1949 was how to achieve rapid economic development in an overpopulated, battered country. Two decades of war had ruined the economy, leaving little capital for industrialization. Unlike Britain and France in the nineteenth century, China had no overseas empire to exploit for economic resources. The new leaders did not want loans and foreign investment that might reduce their independence and lead to a debt trap. Furthermore, they faced a powerful enemy: propelled by alarm at Mao's policies and anti-communist Cold War concerns, the United States launched an economic boycott to shut China off from international trade, refused diplomatic recognition, and surrounded China with military bases. Isolated, China created its own models of economic and political development.

Development Models Between 1949 and 1976 China followed two different models of economic development, each with its own priorities and consequences. The first, Stalinism, a system based on the Soviet model of central planning, heavy industry, a powerful bureaucracy, and a managerial system, dominated the early years (1949–1957) (see Chronology: China Since 1945). China received some Soviet aid in the 1950s, but otherwise the Chinese communists financed development before the late 1970s through self-reliance. This meant withdrawal from the global system. As in Japan in the late nineteenth century and the Soviet Union in the early twentieth, the state took the lead, emphasizing austerity and acquiring capital from the people by making them work hard for low wages, in hopes that future generations would live better. In the Stalinist years the communists abolished private ownership of business and industry and transferred land to poor peasants. Soon they began collectivizing the rural economy into cooperatives, in which peasants helped each other and shared tools. As in the Soviet Union, the emphasis on state directive fostered the rise of a new privileged elite in the government and in the ruling Communist Party, which cracked down on dissent.

By the late 1950s Mao, growing disenchanted with Stalinism, introduced a second model of development based on a unique synthesis of Marxism and Chinese thought, known as Maoism, that emphasized the mass mobilization of the population. Under Maoism, which was China's guiding ideology from 1957 to 1961 and then again from 1966 to 1976, the Chinese people were mobilized for development projects, such as building dams. Pest elimination also became a priority. For instance, everyone was issued fly swatters and asked to kill as many flies as possible in hopes of reducing disease. The communists also tried to reverse the ecological instability of recent centuries through massive tree-planting campaigns. However, Mao rejected the notion that China's fast-growing population was harming the environment.

Mao reorganized the rural economy into **communes**, large agricultural units that combined many families and villages into a common administrative system for pooling resources and labor. A commune could build and operate a factory, secondary school, and hospital, which would be impractical for a single village to have. The communes raised agricultural productivity, especially of grain crops such as rice and wheat, eliminated landlords, and promoted social and economic equality. Mao located industry in rural areas, thus keeping the peasants at home rather than fostering movement to cities, as happened in other countries. He held up a commune in the mountainous northwest as the model of self-reliance and revolutionary zeal; the commune claimed that, inspired by Mao's vision, it had increased agricultural production fivefold. Years later Chinese learned that the production figures had been inflated and that the commune had insufficient food.

The most radical Maoist policy was the **Great Leap Forward** (1958–1961), an ambitious attempt to industrialize China rapidly and end poverty through collective efforts. Farmers and workers were ordered to build small iron furnaces in their backyards, courtyards, and gardens and to spend their free time turning everything from cutlery to old bicycles into steel. The slogan "Achieve More, Better, Faster" swept through the nation. But the poorly conceived campaign, pushing the people too hard, nearly wrecked the economy and, along with disastrous weather, caused 30 million people to starve. One of Mao's critics in the Communist Party leadership charged: "Grains scattered on the ground, potato leaves withered; Strong young people have left to smelt iron, only children and old women reaped the crops; How can they pass the coming year?"[3] These failures undermined Mao's influence, bringing moderate policies in the early 1960s.

Chinese Politics As in the USSR, the Communist Party, led by Mao as chairman, dominated the political system; party members occupied all key positions in the government and military down to village leaders. Using the slogan "Politics Takes Command," the communists emphasized ideology, making political values pervasive. All Chinese were required to become members of political discussion groups, which met regularly in village or community centers. While people were supposedly free to voice their opinions, party activists monitored the discussions and reported dissenters. Political education was integrated into the schools, work units, and even leisure activities. Students often spent their school vacations working in factories or on farms. The party also sought to eradicate inequalities and to alter thought patterns and attitudes, emphasizing the interests of the group over those of the individual. To eliminate class distinctions, officials and intellectuals had to perform physical labor, such as

communes Large agricultural units introduced by Mao Zedong that combined many families and villages into a common system for pooling resources and labor.

Great Leap Forward Mao Zedong's ambitious attempt to industrialize China rapidly and end poverty through collective efforts.

Honoring Chairman Mao Since the beginning of communist rule in China in 1949, this giant portrait of Mao Zedong, the chairman of the Chinese Communist Party, has hung on the Gate of Heavenly Peace, the entrance to the Forbidden City of the Qing dynasty emperors, in the heart of Beijing. (Peter Guttman/Corbis)

laying bricks for house construction or spreading manure to fertilize farm fields, so that they would understand the experience of the workers and peasants.

Mao's system required massive social control, enabled by a vast police apparatus; millions suspected of opposing the communists were harassed, jailed, exiled, or killed. Even communist sympathizers, such as the outspoken feminist writer Ding Ling (1902–1986), were purged after falling out of official favor: in 1958 Ding was sent to a remote labor camp to raise chickens and was also imprisoned between 1970 and 1975. In exchange for accepting its policies, the state promised everyone the "five guarantees" of food, clothes, fuel, education, and a decent burial. But thousands of people, wanting more personal happiness than the system allowed, fled to British-ruled Hong Kong over the years.

Maoist China in the World

The communists restored China's status as a major world power (see Map 27.1), with only some setbacks, and remembering the domestic chaos between the 1830s and 1940s, pursued a foreign policy that maximized stability at home. Mao reasserted Chinese sovereignty in outlying areas of China and in 1950 sent armies to occupy Tibet, whose people, although conquered and incorporated into China by the Qing dynasty in the 1600s, were culturally and historically distinct from the

Chinese and had broken away from China in 1912. Most Tibetans, however, opposed Chinese rule, sparking periodic unrest. The Chinese suppression of a Tibetan revolt led the highest Tibetan Buddhist leader, the Dalai Lama (DAH-lie LAH-mah) (b. 1935), to flee to India in 1958. Devout Tibetans revered the Dalai Lama as both a spiritual and political leader, the reincarnation of previous Dalai Lamas and therefore someone to be worshiped. In exile the Dalai Lama became a defiant symbol of Tibetan resistance to Chinese rule, traveling the world to rally support for the Tibetan cause while promoting Buddhist ethics and world peace, for which he won the Nobel Peace Prize in 1989. China failed to reclaim another former Qing-ruled territory, Mongolia, which in 1924 had become a communist state allied to, and protected by, the USSR.

China faced major challenges in foreign affairs. In 1950 China, which supported the communist North Korean government installed in 1948, was drawn into the Korean War between the USSR-backed North Korea and United Nations forces led by the United States, sent to defend pro-U.S. South Korea. When the United Nations forces pushed the North Korean army toward China's border, despite Chinese warnings to stay away, and the U.S. commander, General Douglas MacArthur, talked recklessly of occupying North Korea and carrying the offensive across the Yalu River into China, the Chinese, feeling endangered, entered the conflict. Mao caught U.S. leaders by surprise by dispatching 300,000 troops into Korea, and the Chinese

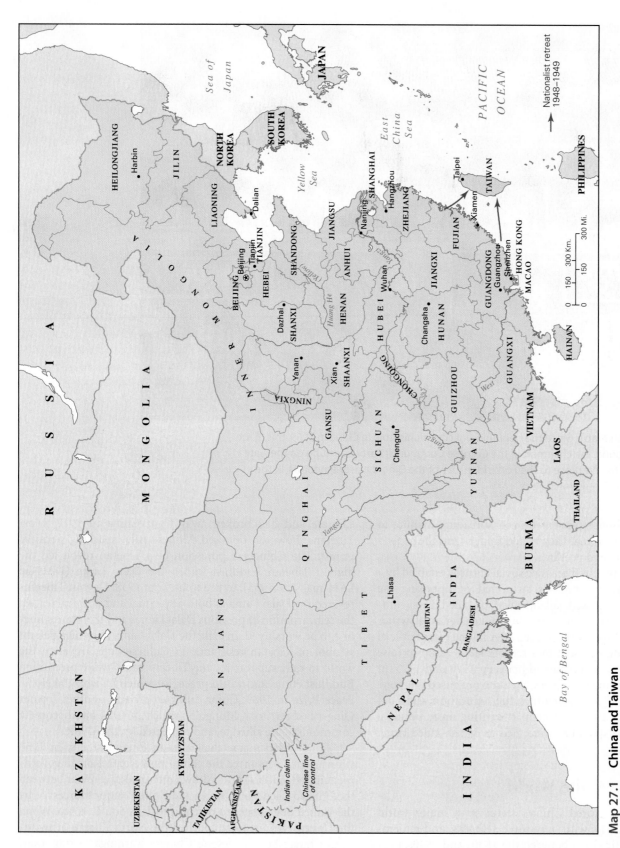

Map 27.1   China and Taiwan

China is a huge country, divided into many provinces, and occupies a large part of eastern Eurasia. In 1949 the government of the Republic of China, defeated by the Chinese communists, moved to the island of Taiwan, off China's Pacific coast.

forces pushed United Nations troops back south. The war produced huge casualties on both sides, including several hundred thousand Chinese, and reinforced the hostility and mutual fear between China and the United States. When the Korean War ended in a stalemate in 1953, the United States, seeking to halt communist expansion, signed a mutual defense treaty with Chiang Kai-shek's regime on Taiwan. The substantial U.S. forces stationed in Taiwan and South Korea joined the thousands of U.S. troops that had remained in Japan, Okinawa, and the Philippines after World War II, while the U.S. navy patrolled the waters off China, making for a formidable U.S. military presence in East Asia.

The Chinese communists felt encircled, and Mao used the paranoia to mobilize the population around his programs. The ability to achieve a stalemate in Korea with the powerful United States improved China's international position, but the United States continued to veto the Chinese communist effort to take China's United Nations seat from the Nationalist government in Taiwan. During the 1950s China, allied with the USSR, basically withdrew from the global system to consolidate the domestic revolution, maintaining limited trade with only a handful of Western nations. Meanwhile, many countries allied to the United States recognized the Republic of China, now based on Taiwan, as the official government of China.

China adapted to changing global politics. In the late 1950s tensions between China and the USSR grew. Chinese leaders did not share the Soviet view that what was good for the USSR was necessarily good for international communism. The Soviet policy of "peaceful coexistence" with the West enraged Mao, who labeled the United States "a paper tiger." Mao also opposed the 1956 decision of the Soviet leader, Nikita Khrushchev (KROOSH-chef), to reveal the excesses of Stalinist police-state rule in Russia, raising the issue of abuse of power by communist dictators. By 1960 the Sino-Soviet split was official; the USSR withdrew advisors and technicians, even the spare parts for the industries they had helped build. Accusing the Soviet leaders of deviation from true Marxism-Leninism, Chinese leaders painted a new world future: "On the debris of a dead imperialism, the victorious [socialist] people would create very swiftly a civilization thousands of times higher than the capitalist system and a truly beautiful future for themselves."[4] The Chinese built up their military strength, tested their first atomic bomb, and occasionally clashed with Soviet forces on their border. To counterbalance the power of the United States and the USSR, China sought allies and influence in Asia and Africa. Yet, despite fierce anti-U.S. and anti-Soviet rhetoric, Chinese leaders generally followed a cautious foreign policy.

During the 1970s Chinese foreign policy changed dramatically. The change was symbolized by U.S. president Richard Nixon's trip to Beijing in 1972, the first official contact between the two nations since 1949. The two nations shared a hostility toward the USSR; moreover, the bitter U.S. experience fighting communist forces in Vietnam and the gradual withdrawal of U.S. forces from that country had opened the door to foreign policy rethinking in both the United States and China. Chinese leaders perceived the United States as stepping back from

Asian military and political commitments, and hence as a diminishing threat. The United States now agreed to quit blocking Chinese membership in the United Nations and, in 1978, normalized diplomatic relations with China. Meanwhile, the Chinese developed better relations with non-communist nations in Southeast Asia and Africa.

Mao's Cultural Revolution

Mao was a complex figure. He was, for example, a self-proclaimed feminist who promoted women's rights but also a sexually promiscuous man who married several times and had many lovers, but who also seldom bathed or brushed his teeth. A poor public speaker with few close friends, he could nevertheless inspire millions to follow his lead. A poet and philosopher but also power hungry and ruthless, he made many enemies, even within the Communist Party leadership. Although many of his initiatives ultimately failed or resulted in misery for millions of people, he played a powerful role in modern world history, leading the communists to victory, reunifying China, focusing public attention on rural people, and placing his stamp on the world's most populous nation.

Mao's stamp was particularly strong when Maoism was China's guiding ideology. Dissatisfied with China's development and his eclipse by the early 1960s, in the mid-1960s Mao sought to regain his dominant status by resurrecting Maoism and offering a vision of a new society that comprised unselfish, politically conscious citizens. Maoism emphasized human will: people working together were capable of anything if they had confidence in their collective power. In Mao's vision of a disciplined society, individuals, inspired by the slogan "Serve the People," subordinated their own needs to the broader social order. His allies emphasized the cult of Mao and his revolutionary thoughts. Newspapers reported that, illuminated by Mao's ideas, factory workers discovered better techniques for galvanizing, the manager of a food store doubled his sales of watermelons, and farmers learned to judge exactly the right amount of manure to fertilize their plots. This campaign laid the foundation for a major social movement inspired by Mao's thoughts.

For a decade, between 1966 and 1976, massive turmoil generated by Mao convulsed and reshaped China like a whirlwind. The **Great Proletarian Cultural Revolution**, as it was called, was a radical movement that represented Mao's attempt to implant his vision, destroy his enemies, crush the stifling bureaucracy, and renew the revolution's vigor. The movement's major supporters, young workers and students known as **Red Guards**, roamed around cities and the countryside in groups, smashing temples and churches and attacking and arresting anti-Mao leaders. Mao's supporters created revolutionary

Great Proletarian Cultural Revolution A radical movement in China between 1966 and 1976 that represented Mao Zedong's attempt to implant his vision, destroy his enemies, crush the stifling bureaucracy, and renew the revolution's vigor.

Red Guards Young workers and students who were the major supporters of the Cultural Revolution in Mao's China.

擁護咱們老百姓自己的軍隊

Chinese Political Art This woodcut, carved during the Chinese civil war of the late 1940s, was typical of the political art made by the communists to rally popular support for their cause, a hallmark of Mao's era. Entitled "Support Our Common People's Own Army," the woodcut shows Chinese peasants working together with the communist military forces. (Woodcut by Ku Yuan, from Mei-shu, 1944)

sent to remote rural areas to experience peasant life. Anti-Mao officials, intellectuals, and people with upper-class backgrounds faced public criticism, followed by punishment if they failed to admit their political crimes. A Chinese journalist whose grandparents were capitalists, and hence identified as class enemies, remembered the attacks on her family: "Red Guards swarming all over the house and a great fire in our courtyard onto which were thrown my father's books, my grandparent's precious traditional furniture and my toys. The fire burned away everything."[6] Soon even Mao was dampening down the radical fervor.

Society, Gender, and Culture in Mao's China

Aiming to reshape Chinese society, the communist movement in many ways succeeded. Mao prodded everyone to get involved in political and economic activities. He also promoted a model of social equality, known as the **Iron Rice Bowl**, in which the people, especially in the villages, shared resources—food, draft animals, farm equipment—and the peasants enjoyed status and dignity. Maoism generally improved life for the poorer Chinese, especially in the thousands of villages. An emphasis on preventive medicine included the training of villagers as paramedics. These peasants, known as barefoot doctors, were given skills to address the everyday health care needs of their communities, such as distributing medication and setting broken bones. As a result, most Chinese now enjoyed decent health care where once famine and disease were dominant. Mass education raised literacy rates to the levels of those in industrialized nations. Peasants often appreciated the changes. In 1971 an elderly peasant told visiting Western scholars what he had gained: "Now we are free to work full-time, have a secure home, eat enough food, have complete medical care, receive education— and take our future in our hands."[7]

The communists also tried to overturn centuries-old, Confucian-influenced hierarchical relationships, including

committees, led by students, workers, and soldiers, to run cities, factories, and schools. Mao told them to destroy the party and government headquarters and that rebellion was justified. A Mao personality cult spread. The students carried copies of a little red book containing short quotations from Mao's writings, such as his claim that Marxism cannot be understood through books alone but also requires contact with the workers and peasants. One observer noted that "giant portraits of [Mao] now hung in the streets, busts were in every chamber, his books and photographs were everywhere on display."[5]

Online Study Center **Improve Your Grade**
Primary Source: "One Hundred Items for Destroying the Old and Establishing the New"

The turmoil affected everyone. The chaos of these years caused serious economic problems, disrupting industrial and agricultural production and closing most schools for two years. The upheaval also resulted in thousands killed, jailed, or removed from official positions, and millions of others were

Iron Rice Bowl A model of social equality in Mao's China in which the people, especially in the villages, shared resources and the peasants enjoyed status and dignity.

patriarchy, by raising the status of women. Mao praised women, who he said "held up half the sky," as a force in production. Two changes profoundly affected women's lives. First, a new marriage law in 1950 abolished arranged marriages, forbade men from taking concubines, and made divorce easier. Second, a land reform empowered women economically by expanding their property rights. Women now enjoyed legal equality with men and greater access to education. Consequently, women played a stronger public role, often leading local organizations, and women more often worked for wages. Yet few women held high national positions. Mao's last wife, Jiang Qing (chang ching) (1914–1991), a former film actress, wielded great power during the Cultural Revolution, but her radical policies made her unpopular. In 1976, after Mao's death, Jiang and her top party allies, the "Gang of Four," lost a power struggle and were imprisoned.

While many women no longer depended solely on men, they still faced obstacles. In conferences and periodicals, women debated the proper balance between housekeeping and paid work and whether they should devote their energies to the revolution as well as to their husbands and children. The rural areas remained more conservative than the cities in social matters. In general, however, communism changed the family system, often to the advantage of both women and men. Women activists worked to eliminate patriarchy, which they viewed as a relic of the past, and to build in its place a democratic family. An emphasis on love matches rather than arranged marriages fostered closer emotional ties between husbands, wives, and children, lessening male domination. Fathers spent more time with their children and their wives than had been common a generation earlier.

As with social patterns, the communists often undermined traditional beliefs and culture. Calling religion a bond enslaving people, Mao moved to control religious behavior and marginalize religious institutions such as Christian churches, Buddhist monasteries, and Islamic mosques. By the 1970s only a small minority of Chinese openly practiced religion. Only Buddhist, Christian, and Muslim leaders who cooperated with the state maintained their positions. Determined to use the arts as a weapon in the class struggle, Mao sought to break down elitism and to foster a "people's art" created by and for the common people. He wrote, "In the world today all culture, all literature and art belongs to definite political lines. Art for art's sake, art that stands above the class and party do not exist in reality."[8] Critics argued that art that strictly served revolutionary goals reduced it to political propaganda.

Government policies broadened popular participation in creating art, literature, and music. For example, during the Great Leap Forward, party activists went out to collect literature written by common people and to encourage peasants and workers to compose poetry and songs. In Shanghai alone 200,000 people produced 5 million poems. Peasants painted scenes of people at work, often in bright, cheerful colors conveying an optimistic tone. Part-time writers got a day off from the factory to work on literary projects. Everyone was urged to work hard for a better future and a new society. A 1958 poem proclaimed: "Labor is joy, how joyful it is, Bathed in sweat and

two hands full of mud. Like sweet rain, my sweat waters the land."[9]

The politicization of the arts reached its peak levels during the Cultural Revolution, when elitism came under fierce attack. Red Guards sang new songs in praise of change and Chairman Mao, such as "The East is red, the sun has risen. China has produced a Mao Zedong; He is the great savior of the people."[10] Opera and ballet became central for the new revolutionary art. Militant operas had a strong political message based on contemporary themes, such as the dignity of peasant life or Communist Party history. Rejecting Western-style ballet as decadent, dancers composed revolutionary ballets that integrated Chinese martial arts, such as kung fu, folk dances, and Russian ballet. For example, *The Red Detachment of Women* portrayed the experiences of a women's company of communist soldiers during the civil war against the Chiang's Republic.

The End of the Maoist Era

After Mao died in 1976, the Chinese took stock of Mao's legacy. The communists could claim many achievements. They had restored China to great power status and renewed the confidence of the people after thirteen decades of imperialistic exploitation and invasion by Western nations and Japan. China was no longer a doormat; it even had nuclear weapons. As they had for two millennia before the disasters of the nineteenth century, the Chinese once again envisioned themselves as the Middle Kingdom exercising influence in the world. The communists also took much of the sting out of poverty. Most Chinese, though enjoying little material surplus, could satisfy their basic food, housing, and clothing needs. During the 1940s impoverished Chinese had often had to resort to begging or prostitution to survive; by the 1970s few Chinese faced this dilemma. The economy in 1976 was healthier and more broadly based than in 1949, and food was more evenly distributed. Public health and literacy rates had risen substantially.

Mao's policies, however, had also resulted in failures and political repression. China may have gained control of its economic destiny but was still poor by world standards. Mao had discouraged free enterprise and individual initiative. On city streets few private cars interfered with the bicycles that most Chinese used to get to work or go shopping. Chinese wanted material benefits, such as better housing and more consumer goods, now rather than in a distant future. With few consumer luxuries or diversions available, life was dull. In addition, the fierce punishment of dissenters and the turmoil of the Great Leap Forward and Cultural Revolution had ruined numerous lives. Government coercion and corruption were also resented. The unfulfilled promises, and the chaos of the Cultural Revolution, disillusioned the youth. Bitter disagreements had ripped the Communist Party leadership apart. The Chinese often blamed Mao and his radicalism for the problems. Reformers in the party charged that, in his later years, Mao, isolated and clinging to unworkable utopian theories, had lost touch with common people's lives. Furthermore, the often erratic policies made people cynical, willing to give only passive cooperation to government policies and avoiding commitment to a particular line. Many Chinese were ready for change.

SECTION SUMMARY

- After Japan was defeated in World War II, Chinese communists and nationalists fought a civil war in which Mao Zedong's communists triumphed by appealing to people's frustration with the corruption of Chiang Kai-shek's nationalists.

- To develop its economy, China first employed Stalinism, which featured central planning dominated by a bureaucratic elite, and then shifted to Maoism, which emphasized mass mobilization of the people to industrialize and maximize output, but under Maoism millions starved to death and many suffered under political repression.

- China reasserted itself as a world power, reclaiming Tibet, becoming involved in the Korean War, ultimately splitting with the USSR, and reestablishing formal relations with the United States in the 1970s.

- Frustrated with China's development, Mao led a decade-long cultural revolution, a period of radical upheaval in which young Red Guards attempted to destroy Mao's enemies and obstacles to progress, which caused great economic problems and brought misery to many.

- Mao reshaped Chinese society, improving literacy rates and health care, especially for rural people, expanding the rights of women, opposing traditional religious institutions and elitism, and encouraging the people to produce their own literature and art.

- While Mao restored China as a world power and brought many out of poverty, after his death in 1976 many Chinese wanted to join the modern world and gain increased access to material benefits.

◆ Chinese Modernization

What factors explain the dramatic rise of Chinese economic power in the world since 1978?

With Mao gone, Deng Xiaoping (dung shee-yao-ping) (1904–1997), a longtime Communist Party leader who had often clashed with Mao, came to power in 1978 and changed China's direction. Deng and his allies rejected Mao's view of a self-sufficient, ideologically pure China outside the world economy, concluding that collectivized agriculture had failed to raise productivity enough to substantially improve rural living standards or finance a jump into the high technology that Deng believed China needed to modernize the economy enough to make China a major power. In 1978 Deng, portraying China as at a turning point in history, announced the policy of Four Modernizations: the development of agriculture,

industry, military, and science and technology to turn China into a powerful nation by 2000. After Deng's death his replacements generally followed his pragmatic policies, which transformed China into an economic powerhouse and reshaped its society.

Market Socialism

From 1978 to 1989 Chinese leaders pursued **market socialism**, a mix of free enterprise, economic liberalization, and state controls that produced economic dynamism. This pragmatic approach, unlike Mao's, was more concerned with economic results than socialist values. Twice purged for opposing Mao, Deng was fond of a Chinese proverb: "It doesn't matter whether a cat is black or white, only if it catches mice." Deng used the market to stimulate productivity. China reentered the world economy, but on its own terms, to obtain capital investment to spur manufacturing for the global market. Like Meiji Japan in the late 1800s, China began to import technology, foreign expertise, and capitalist ideas. Deng believed that China had reached a plateau; to move to the next levels required wider international participation. Hence, he improved ties with the United States, Japan, western Europe, and non-communist Southeast Asia. Dazzled by China's huge potential market of, as Western experts put it, 1 billion toothbrushes (for toothpaste) and 2 billion armpits (for deodorant), Western companies promoted increased trade.

Introducing capitalist ideas, such as offering workers material incentives rather than ideological slogans, Deng's reforms sparked dramatic changes. At first the government allowed small private enterprises, then it allowed larger ones, and ultimately both private and state-owned enterprises were competing with each other. In agriculture, Deng replaced Mao's communes with the contract system in which peasants could bid on and lease (but could not buy) land to work it privately. In many districts this free market led to soaring productivity and prosperity, with per capita income in rural areas rising four-fold in the first decade. Tapping a skilled, industrious, but cheap labor force, hundreds of Western and Asian companies set up manufacturing operations, producing goods such as shirts, underwear, and toys chiefly for export. China became a consumer society in the 1980s; even in small cities, shops stocked Japanese televisions and Western soft drinks. Over the next twenty-five years the economy quadrupled in size and foreign trade increased ten times over.

Deng also loosened political and cultural controls, arguing that liberation of thought and open-mindedness were essential for progress. Western popular culture, especially films, rock music, and discos, won a huge audience; books and magazines from around the world became available; and foreign travelers backpacked in remote areas. Chinese were even able to listen to popular music from Taiwan. The sentimental recordings of Taiwan's top female singer, Deng Lijun (deyn lee-choong), better

---

market socialism A Chinese economic program used between 1978 and 1989 that mixed free enterprise, economic liberalization, and state controls and that produced economic dynamism in China.

known to her millions of fans in Hong Kong, Japan, and Southeast Asia as Teresa Teng, were so widely played in Chinese homes and restaurants that people said that "the day belongs to Deng Xiaoping but the night belongs to Deng Lijun."[11] Intellectuals and artists enjoyed greater freedom; people long silenced or imprisoned were heard from again. The press was enlivened and the scope for public debate widened. Deng also increasingly tolerated religion, allowing Buddhist temples, Muslim mosques, and Christian churches to reopen.

Cultural figures, cowed during Mao's time, tested the limits of free expression. Novels and short stories revealed the depth of suffering during the Cultural Revolution. Writers reflected a widespread public cynicism about politics; popular writers developed massive audiences for stories daring to use sexual themes. Also demonstrating a new openness, Chinese-made films won international acclaim, while creative directors associated with semi-independent film studios skirmished with wary government censors, who decided whether films could be shown in China. Their films explored forbidden themes, portraying China as anything but a communist paradise. Rock musicians, especially Cui Jian (sway jen), a former trumpeter with the Beijing Symphony, became a major voice for alienated urban youth. Dressed in battered army fatigues and a coat style favored by Mao, Cui sang: "This guitar in my hands is like a knife. I want to cut at your hypocrisy till I see some truth." Cui's songs were indirect in their criticism, focusing more on bureaucratic corruption, social problems, and young people's frustrations than on national politics, but Chinese youth easily read between the lines for the hidden meanings. One fan commented that "Cui Jian says things we all feel, but cannot say."[12]

Reform and Repression

Although Chinese often applauded the ideological loosening and the growing economic options, the dramatic changes under Deng Xiaoping showed a dark underside in the later 1980s. Many districts had seen few benefits from the reorganization of rural life. Chinese authorities imposed one policy for the vast nation rather than allowing districts and villages to find a policy—stressing the individual, the collective, or both—that worked for them. Under Deng's market socialism, some villagers, because of their better land, local leadership positions, or entrepreneurial skills, benefited more than others, opening a gap between newly rich and poor villagers. Prices rose rapidly. A widely shared street poem charged that "Mao Zedong was bad, so bad, But if you had a dollar you knew what you had. Deng Xiaoping is fine, so fine, But a dollar's only worth a lousy dime."[13] Corruption increased as bureaucrats and Communist Party officials lined their own pockets.

Public dissension mirrored divisions at the top. Within the party, Stalinists and Maoists viewed economic liberalization as undermining one-party rule and the commitment to communism. The fall of communism in eastern Europe and the USSR in 1989 alarmed hardliners. But dissidents and some reformers, seeing strong controls as inhibiting initiative, pushed democracy as "the fifth modernization." In response, party leaders opposed to liberalization called for cracking down, arresting dissidents. The most famous dissident, the outspoken Wei Jingsheng (way ching-sheng) (b. 1950), a former Red Guard who became a democracy activist while working as an electrician at the Beijing Zoo, spent years in jail.

In 1989 the tensions in Deng's China reached a boiling point, generating massive protests and government repression of them. Thousands of protesters, led by university students and workers, took over downtown Beijing, calling for the resignation of the most unpopular hardline leaders, an end to government corruption, and a transition to a fully open, democratic system. The party hardliners, in alliance with Deng, purged the moderate party leaders and ordered the army to clear out the demonstrators in what became known as the Beijing Massacre. Sending in tanks, the army killed hundreds and arrested thousands, while millions around the world watched the violence on television. The courageous Beijing protesters had not only underestimated the government reaction but had also overestimated their popular support. Since many Chinese outside the cities, valuing stability more than vague promises of a better world, applauded the government crackdown, the protesters had also miscalculated the prospects of democracy in a country with an authoritarian political tradition.

Economic Change and Political Challenge

After the Beijing Massacre the communists modified market socialism into **market Leninism**, a policy whereby the Chinese state, obsessed with stability, asserted more power over society while also fostering an even stronger market orientation in the economy than had existed under market socialism. The communist leadership reestablished control in political, social, and cultural spheres, tolerating less dissent than they had in the 1980s, but the economy became further privatized. China now did not fit either the communist or the capitalist model. Eventually the party labeled the mixed system a socialist market economy. It benefited from the fact that, remembering the chaos of the Cultural Revolution and the 1989 unrest, Chinese often valued political stability over individual rights, especially at a time of overheated economic growth.

However, the control of the Leninist, or one-party, state was not absolute. In some local elections communist officials did permit competition between candidates, allowing nonparty members to run for office. Many dissenters were able to spread their message. For example, opponents of the environmentally damaging Three Gorges Dam project, constructed to control the Yangzi (yahng-zeh) River and provide electrical power, publicized their views, although they had little success in halting the expensive project, which forced several million people to move from their homes along the river. However, the Chinese state, dominated by the Communist Party and often

market Leninism A policy followed after the Beijing Massacre in 1989 whereby the Chinese communist state asserted more power over society while also fostering an even stronger market orientation in the economy than had existed under market socialism.

arbitrary in its actions, became warier of relaxing ideological controls and used the military and police to intimidate dissidents. Assertive political dissidents faced arrest, and public debate was dampened. China may execute more than 100,000 people a year, mostly criminals but including some accused of economic misbehavior or political opposition. Anxious to preserve national unity, China's leaders also suppressed dissent in Tibet and among Muslim Turkish groups in Xinjiang (shin-jee-yahng), in far western China. In both places people sought autonomy from China, greater religious freedom, and limits on Chinese immigration, which was overwhelming the local population.

After 1980, despite the ebb and flow of party domination, China enjoyed the fastest economic growth in the world, often 10 percent a year, abetted by a "get rich quick mentality" among many Chinese. Deng claimed that to get rich is glorious. Under Mao the Communist Party lionized Lei Feng, a soldier who loved everyone but himself and gladly served the people. Now they praised the rich, regardless of their motives or character. China's exports increased fifteenfold between 1980 and 2000. After 1989 the communist leadership sought popular support by offering consumer goods and wealth rather than political reform, providing shops with ample consumer goods and households with spending money. In the early days of reform people aspired to the "three bigs": bicycle, wristwatch, and sewing machine. By 2000 they wanted televisions, washing machines, and video recorders. As a result of the economic growth, the urban middle class grew rapidly. By 2005 China had already moved ahead of Germany into the number 3 position in the world economy, with the size of its economy trailing only the United States and Japan. Some experts have argued that the United States and China are the two countries that have most benefited from the mobility of capital and products with economic globalization. If the economy maintains the high annual growth rates experienced since the 1980s, China will have the world's largest economy by 2015.

Although the economic reforms beginning in 1990 have improved living standards for many Chinese, they have also produced numerous downsides. Economic dynamism has occurred largely in a few coastal provinces and special economic zones, where living standards approach those of China's more highly developed neighboring countries, Taiwan and South Korea. Towering skyscrapers and huge shopping malls with upscale shops dot the landscape of cities such as Shanghai and Shenzen. Elsewhere, however, conditions have often deteriorated. Unemployment grows dramatically as state enterprises close or become uncompetitive and inflation skyrockets. Although laws make it illegal to migrate to another district without government permission, millions of peasants seeking jobs or a less rustic life have nonetheless moved to cities, where they struggle. Another problem is that, as China has developed, the Chinese have become even greater users of world resources, such as oil and coal, and major polluters of the atmosphere. China has become the number two producer of greenhouse gases that cause global warming, although its output, about one-eighth of the world total, is only half that of the United States. Water supplies have become badly overstretched, and,

with private cars clogging the city streets where bicycles once dominated, smog blankets the cities. Land and energy grow more expensive.

Political and economic changes have influenced other areas of Chinese life. In the cities, the newly rich entrepreneurs—enjoying luxury cars, access to golf courses, and vacations abroad—live lives alien to most Chinese. By 2004, some 236,000 Chinese were millionaires. Even the middle class, chiefly working in business, can aspire to some of these benefits. With money concentrated in the private sector, teachers, professors, and doctors leave their low-paying state jobs to open businesses or join foreign corporations. Some village leaders use their power to amass wealth and power. The wealthy flaunt their affluence, and the poor resent it. Street songs in towns and villages have often mocked the powerful: "I'm a big official, so I eat and drink, and I've got the potbelly to prove it. Beer, spirits, rice wine, love potions—I drink it all."[14] By 2005 peasant protests against seizure of village land to build polluting factories, luxury housing, and golf courses had become frequent, numbering in the thousands and resulting in the arrests of protest leaders. Meanwhile, the shift to market forces leaves millions unable to afford medical care and schooling for their children. Thanks to the decline in health care, especially in rural areas, experts estimate that between half a million and 1.5 million Chinese have HIV or AIDS. Poorer Chinese, forgetting his failures, long fondly for Mao and the dismantled Iron Rice Bowl. Yet, despite reduced job security and social services, people are now freer than before to travel, change jobs, enjoy leisure, and even complain.

As the Chinese society and economy have rapidly changed, the Communist Party has faced problems Mao could never have anticipated. A Communist Party that once viewed itself as the protector of the working class and poor peasants welcomes wealthy businessmen and professionals into its ranks. Yet, after Deng's death in 1997, the party, formerly the surest path to success, split between hardliners and younger reform-minded leaders and lost legitimacy; it now needs to organize karaoke parties to recruit new members. Powerful provincial leaders whose first priority is economic growth increasingly ignore Beijing. Many Chinese now enjoy materially improved lives and suffer less interference than they had known under Mao. But the rapid economic growth raises questions as to whether Chinese leaders can resolve the increasing inequalities and spread wealth more equitably to check the growth of social tensions. Some pessimists forecast more conflicts between rich and poor Chinese, or civil war between rich and poor regions. Critics also worry that the Chinese economy might overheat and then collapse, taking down much of the world economy with it.

Social Change, Gender, and Culture

Given growing tensions and the rich-poor gap, the government struggles to maintain social stability. Popular attitudes favor stability. Chinese usually define human rights in terms of the right to property, food, and housing rather than the freedom of individuals to do as they like. One Chinese observer, a prominent woman journalist, argues that "ideals such as happiness and equality are luxuries for the poor. First they want clean water and electricity; then washing machines and fridges."[15] Popular participation in government and unfettered free speech are lower priorities for average Chinese.

Nonetheless, various developments undermine social stability. Economic growth and the quest for wealth have led to a rapid increase in crime and links between criminal groups and government officials. The close connection between government and business corruption, underworld activity, and financial success has led to Chinese talking about the "Five Colors," or surest roads to riches: Communist Party connections, prostitution, smuggling, illegal drug dealing, and criminal gangs. Mao's China had been one of world's safest countries, but after 1978 desperate people turned increasingly to crime as the way to get ahead; drug dealing became rampant once again, serving the growing number of people, especially youth, who used narcotics for escape. Maintaining Confucian and Maoist attitudes, Chinese often view wealth as corrupting and mistrust rich business interests.

The recent economic and social changes have offered women opportunities but also posed problems. Women's economic status has often improved, but many still face restricted gender expectations. The feminist journalist Xue Xinran (shoe shin-rahn) wrote that "Chinese women had always thought that their lives should be full of misery. Many had no idea what happiness was, other than having a son for the family"[16] (see Profile: Xue Xinran, a Chinese Voice for Women). Scholars consider the common stereotype of the long-suffering, submissive Chinese woman misleading, noting that modern Chinese women are often strong-willed and resourceful. However, rural women may feel more intimidated by men than urban women. In contrast to Mao's era, women now receive little support from government policies, which are aimed at economic growth, not gender equality. Rather than remaining in their villages, millions of rural women prefer to migrate to the cities for industrial and service jobs. They provide much of the labor force for the new factories that have helped turn China into an economic giant. Wherever they live, women commonly work long hours, and few women occupy high positions in the national government, Communist Party, top business enterprises, or in rural communities.

Women have also faced other new hardships. Since by the 1980s China already had 1 billion people, a fifth of humankind, Deng Xiaoping introduced a one-child-per-family policy to try to stabilize the population. Officials enforced the policy because they hoped to limit growth toward a maximum population of 1.4 billion in 2010. Critics of the one-child policy complained that children without siblings were pampered and self-centered. Furthermore, the policy encouraged and sometimes mandated abortion and, since traditional attitudes favoring sons remained, also resulted in widespread killing of female babies. With more boys than girls being born and raised, an imbalance in numbers between the sexes developed, resulting in a growing trade in the abduction and sale of women to desperate men unable to find wives.

Because of China's growing contacts with the larger world economy, Chinese society is affected by global entertainment and consumer culture. Western popular culture, which spread to China in the 1980s, has become a powerful force among youth. Cui Jian and other rock musicians who had participated in the Beijing student protest movement later resumed their musical careers, competing for a youth audience with heavy metal, punk, and rap musicians. Every city has discos and clubs offering Western music, and Chinese imitators of Anglo-American boy bands and girl groups have found a vast teen audience. In 2005 more than 8 million Chinese voted for three finalists in a hugely popular Chinese television program, *Super Girl,* a local version of the popular U.S. television program, *American Idol.* Television offers U.S. series dubbed in Chinese, such as *The X-Files* and *Baywatch*, and in Shanghai a theme park very similar to Disney World features a Wild West Town. Chinese consumers in many places indulge their desires as they are served by numerous McDonald's outlets (one near Mao's mausoleum), Hard Rock Cafes, Wal-Marts, and some 85,000 Avon agents selling American cosmetics and beauty products. Partly due to greater contact with the outside world, homosexuals, who faced discrimination under Mao, have been slowly coming out, especially in the cities, where gay bars are common, and even have hundreds of their own websites. But Western culture is not the only outside influence. South Korean popular culture and consumer products—music, clothing, television dramas, movies, cosmetics—became very fashionable among young Chinese in the early 2000s, and much of the conversion of millions of Chinese to evangelical Christianity is due to the thousands of South Korean Protestant missionaries in the country.

Those Chinese with enough money to afford satellite dishes, fax machines, and personal computers linked to the Internet have gained access to ideas around the world. More than 100 million Chinese are Internet users. To restrict the free flow of information and exposure to dissident writings, state officials have tried to crack down on cyberspace, passing laws restricting Internet use. They sometimes close down some of the thousands of Internet cafes and prevent local Internet providers from allowing access to banned websites. Western Internet providers seeking a larger role in Chinese cyberspace have faced criticism in the West for cooperation in these restrictions and sometimes allowing the government to identify dissidents. But websites and blogs—some 14 million are available to Chinese—proliferate rapidly, making monitoring difficult. The government sometimes shuts down newspapers and magazines whose reporting is too daring, but brave journalists and officials have risked punishment by openly criticizing micromanagement of the media. Another source of knowledge about Western ideas comes from the several hundred thousand Chinese, including the children of high officials, who have studied in Western universities.

Policies toward religion have been inconsistent. After temples and churches reopened in the 1980s, the government tolerated millions of Chinese turning to the faith of their ancestors: Buddhism, Christianity, Daoism, or Islam. But the government has cracked down on movements that are deemed a threat or that refuse to register and accept official restrictions. For instance, it has arrested leaders and members of the assertive, missionary *Falun Gong* meditation sect, a mix of

XUE XINRAN,
A CHINESE VOICE FOR WOMEN

Xue Xinran   The Chinese journalist, Xue Xinran, explored the lives of Chinese women on her radio program and in her writings.   (Courtesy, Asia Society, AustralAsia Centre)

In the 1980s Xue Xinran (shoe shin-rahn), known professionally as Xinran, began working for a radio network and went on to become one of China's most successful and innovative journalists. A radio call-in show that she launched in 1989 featured hundreds of poignant and haunting stories by women. The huge audience the show attracted and her sensitive handling of the callers made Xinran a role model and heroine for Chinese women. Her own life and career also revealed women's experiences in contemporary China.

Born in Beijing in 1958, Xinran had a difficult childhood that was complicated by the turmoil of the Cultural Revolution. Her mother came from a capitalist, property-owning family. But Xinran's grandfather, although he cooperated with the communists, lost his property and was imprisoned during the Cultural Revolution. Her mother joined the Communist Party and army at sixteen but was occasionally jailed or demoted in purges of those from capitalist class backgrounds. Xinran's father was a national expert in mechanics and computing but, like her mother, also from a once wealthy family. He too had been imprisoned. Xinran had been sent to live with a grandmother when she was one month old and seldom saw her parents during her childhood. Reflecting on her family, she wrote that, like many Chinese, her parents endured an unhappy marriage: "Did [my parents] love each other? I have never dared to ask." While working as an army administrator, Xinran married, had a son, PanPan, and later divorced.

Eventually she became a radio journalist. But she had to persuade the station to let her begin a nightly call-in program, *Words on the Night Breeze*. Since 1949 the media had been the mouthpiece of the Communist Party, ensuring that it spoke with one identical voice. However, Xinran said, "I was trying to open a little window, a tiny hole, so that people would allow their spirits to cry out and breathe after the gunpowder-laden atmosphere of the previous forty years." In starting her call-in program, the question that obsessed her was, What is woman's life really worth in a China where footbinding was a recent memory but women now lived and worked alongside men? Xinran's compassion and ability encouraged callers to talk freely about feelings. For eight groundbreaking years, women called in and discussed their lives, and Xinran was shocked by much of what they said. Broadcast all over China, the program offered an unflinching portrait of what it meant to be a woman in modern China, including the expectations of obedience to fathers, husbands, and sons. Women from every social status—daughters of wealthy families, wives of party officials, children of Cultural Revolution survivors, homeless street scavengers, isolated mountain villagers—called in stories, often heartbreaking tales of sexual abuse, gang rape, forced marriages, and enforced separation of families.

The stories Xinran heard did not fit the image promoted by the Communist Party of a happy, harmonious society. She told, for instance, of Jingyi and her boy friend, Gu Da,

university classmates who fell passionately in love but were sent by the government to work in different parts of the country. They had planned to eventually marry but lost touch during the chaos of the Cultural Revolution. For forty-five years Jingyi had first longed for and then searched for Gu Da. When they finally had a reunion in 1994, Jingyi was devastated to discover that Gu Da, despairing of ever seeing Jingyi again, had married another woman. Their saga provided a window on the disrupted personal and family lives common in China after 1949.

In Xinran's view, "When China started to open up [to the outside world], it was like a starving child devouring everything without much discrimination. But China's brain had not yet grown the cells to absorb truth and freedom." In 1997 the conflict between what Xinran knew and what she was permitted to say caused her to give up her career and leave for Britain, where she hoped to find a freer life and reach a global audience. In Britain, after mastering English, she first taught at the University of London and then became a columnist for a national newspaper, *The Guardian*. She published several nonfiction books based on the stories she learned in China. In *The Good Women of China: Hidden Voices* (2002), she opened a window revealing the lives of Chinese women to the outside world. Her reports revealed strong, resourceful characters who offered insights into China's past and present. Another book, *The Sky Burial* (2004), told the extraordinary story of an intrepid Chinese woman who spent thirty years searching rugged Tibet, a thousand miles from her home city, for her beloved husband, an army doctor who was reported killed. In 2002 Xinran married an Englishman, the literary agent Toby Eady. Every year she returns to China for visits and reporting.

THINKING ABOUT THE PROFILE

1. Why did Xinran achieve such fame in China?

2. What does her journalism tell us about the experiences of Chinese women?

Note: Quotations from Xue Xinran, *The Good Women of China: Hidden Voices* (New York: Anchor, 2002), pp. 126, 3, 227.

Daoist, Buddhist, and Christian influences, and has tried to close down rapidly proliferating Christian churches that have remained independent by not seeking government approval. While the Chinese remain a largely secular people, both Falun Gong and the independent churches have millions of followers who seek a deeper spiritual existence and sense of community.

China in the Global System

China's relations with the wider world have been colored by its historical experiences. In the nineteenth century this once powerful society suffered national humiliation as it lost wars to aggressive Western powers and Japan. Foreign gunboats patrolled China's rivers, and foreign interests controlled large swaths of Chinese territory. Years of civil war and Japanese invasion from the 1920s through the 1940s wrought devastation, but also left hope for a new future. Eventually Chinese saw their nation stand tall, strong and increasingly rich. In 1997 they celebrated the peaceful return of Hong Kong, which comprised several small islands and a peninsula on the southern coast, from British colonial control, which they saw as rectifying the loss of that territory during the Opium War of the mid-1800s. Hong Kong, a prosperous enclave whose towering skyscrapers, bustling shopping malls, and dynamic film industry made it a symbol of East Asian capitalism, was incorporated under the policy of "one nation, two systems." But critics charge that China's occasional interference in Hong Kong politics and its attempts to curb democracy have broken a pledge to respect the territory's special character and political freedoms. Nonetheless, a vocal pro-democracy movement in Hong Kong keeps these issues alive and can attract thousands of supporters to demonstrations. In 1999 Portugal also returned its small coastal colony of Macao, which it had first occupied in the 1500s, to Chinese control. Macao's economy is based on gambling casinos, a lucrative enterprise the once puritanical communists now seem happy to tolerate.

Since 1976 China has pursued a pragmatic foreign policy designed to win friends and trading partners but to also avoid entangling alliances. China has exercised regional influence by trading extensively with neighbors. It gradually improved relations with the United States and USSR, and it cultivated diplomatic ties with other nations but avoided close ties that might limit its options. It also became increasingly active in the world community, a far cry from the isolationism of Mao's era. China joined international organizations such as the World Trade Organization, which regulated global economic exchange. To enhance China's competitive stance, some 200 million children study English.

The post-Mao foreign policy enhanced national power while accepting the constraints imposed by the global system. By the twenty-first century China enjoyed tremendous influence in the world economy, importing vast amounts of capital and natural resources, such as Zambian copper and Venezuelan oil, while exporting industrial products of every kind. Taking advantage of a cheap but resourceful labor force, thousands of foreign investors have come from the West, Japan, Southeast Asia, South Korea, and even Taiwan, opening factories and ne-

gotiating joint ventures with Chinese firms. Meanwhile, China has supported the U.S. economy, becoming the major buyer of the treasury bonds that financed the growing U.S. national debt in the early 2000s. As the Japanese and Americans did in the later 1900s, Chinese enterprises have begun buying up companies based on manufacturing and natural resources in other nations. Thus China has become the world's most successful newly industrializing economy, buttressed by a vast resource base and a huge domestic market.

Yet China has met roadblocks in enhancing its global power, among them uncertain relations with its neighbors. The Chinese government, still claiming Taiwan as an integral part of China, continues to threaten that island with forced unification if the Republic of China on Taiwan, which has ruled the island since 1949 and enjoys a defense agreement with the United States, tries to declare a permanent break from China. Although economic and social links between China and Taiwan developed unofficially beginning in the 1980s, few in the island nation, which enjoys democracy and a much higher standard of living, want a merger with the mainland in the near future. Meanwhile, Chinese relations with Japan ebb and flow. The two nations need each other economically and have close economic ties—thousands of Japanese businessmen are based in China—but are also natural rivals, the Chinese remaining resentful of Japanese brutality during World War II and antagonistic to contemporary Japanese nationalism. In contrast to sporadic Chinese-Japanese tensions, China has improved political and economic relations with once bitter enemies such as South Korea and anti-communist countries such as Malaysia, the Philippines, and Australia. The leaders of these countries, seeing China as the future regional power, maintain friendly relations with China. In many of them, as well as in some African countries, large numbers of people are learning Chinese. In South Korea, for example, a close U.S. ally, as many people study Chinese as English. And some 90,000 foreign students study in China. Nonetheless, historical resentment of Japan and the West provides a strong foundation of Chinese nationalism, which sometimes provokes anti-Japan or anti-U.S. protest demonstrations. This resentment causes concern, for while by the early 2000s China only ranked fifth among the world's nations in defense spending, its neighbors have feared Chinese military power.

China's tremendous size, population, natural resources, military strength, national confidence, and sense of history have placed it in an unusual position of being a major global power while still having a much lower overall standard of living than that of North America, western Europe, Japan, and several industrializing Asian nations. Using such factors as literacy, life expectancy, and per capita income, the 2004 United Nations Human Development Report placed China only 94th out of 177 nations in overall quality of life. Nonetheless, China has been returning to its historical leadership as the Asian dragon and a major engine of the global economy. Experts debated whether either China or India might replace the United States as the major world power by 2050 or 2100. Some argued that India had some advantages over China, including democracy, a free press, and a sounder financial system, while others thought China had the better prospects, especially if the growing middle class fosters a more open political system, as happened in South Korea and Taiwan. Still others doubted that a decline of U.S. power was imminent. As during the long period of Chinese power and prosperity between 600 and 1800 C.E., China is once again a major force in world affairs.

SECTION SUMMARY

- Under Deng Xiaoping, China opened up to Western economic ideas and investment, gradually introducing private ownership and competition, as well as to political, religious, and cultural currents that had been suppressed under Mao.

- Although many supported Deng's reforms, they led to increasing corruption and a growing gap between rich and poor, especially in rural areas, and, in 1989, a violent suppression of prodemocracy dissidents in the Beijing Massacre.

- Under market Leninism, the Chinese state increased political and social control while continuing to privatize the economy, which grew briskly, though there was stagnation in many rural areas and environmental damage in others.

- The growth of China's economy has improved access to consumer goods but has also led to increased crime and drug use, and an effort to limit population has led to many abortions and the killing of female babies.

- China has become more open to Western culture, though its government has attempted to restrict the free flow of information.

- China has enjoyed a great recovery and return to world prominence in recent decades, though it still has uncertain relations with Taiwan and Japan, and its living standard remains much lower than many of its rivals.

◆ The Remaking of Japan

How did Japan rise from the ashes of defeat in World War II to become a global economic powerhouse?

Japan rose from the shambles of World War II to economic dynamism (see Map 27.2). In August 1945, Japan lay in ruins, its major cities largely destroyed by U.S. bombing and its economy ruined. Having no concept of military defeat or occupation, the Japanese people were psychologically devastated. Yet, within a decade the country had recovered from the disaster of World War II. After several decades of the highest economic growth rates in world history, Japan became one of the world's major economic powers, and by the 1980s it was challenging the United States for world economic leadership. A system stressing cooperation rather than individualism provided the basis for economic and social stability in an overcrowded land. But by the 1990s Japan was experiencing political and economic uncertainty.

Occupation and Recovery

The post–World War II occupation by the United States aided Japan's recovery. In the wake of defeat the Japanese people felt disoriented. The emperor, Hirohito (here-o-HEE-to) (1901–1989), still a revered figure, asked them to cooperate with the Allied occupation forces, and by and large they did. Japan was placed under a U.S.-dominated military administration, the Supreme Command of Allied Powers (SCAP), which was tasked with rebuilding rather than punishing Japan. The victorious World War II Allies also broke up Japan's empire. Japan lost Korea, Taiwan, and Manchuria, while the United States took control of the Ryukyu Islands, which were returned to Japan in the 1970s, and Micronesia. SCAP's mission was to demilitarize and democratize Japan, using the United States as the model, and to aid economic recovery. For their part, Japanese leaders hoped to win in peace what they had lost in war. SCAP dismantled the Japanese military, removed some civilian politicians, and tried and hanged seven wartime leaders as war criminals. Fearing that punishing the emperor, a member of an imperial family over 1,500 years old, would destabilize Japan, U.S. officials did not charge Emperor Hirohito with war crimes, but he was forced to renounce his godlike aura and become a more public figure. Scholars still debate his responsibility for Japanese wartime actions.

SCAP fostered political and social changes; some, including a thriving political democracy, took root. Sustaining democracy required a more egalitarian society in which once disadvantaged people shared in the economic progress. A new constitution guaranteed civil liberties and weakened the central government. It also had a unique feature: the document stated that, since they aspired to promote international peace and order, the Japanese people forever renounced war as the nation's sovereign right. The first democratic elections, held in 1946, involved various competing political parties. For the first time in Japanese history, all adult citizens, including women, could vote. Women gained status, including legal equality in society and marriage, but were only partly freed from the expectations of a patriarchal society. In education, new universities were opened, giving Japanese youth greater access than ever before to higher education. U.S. officials hoped to foster even greater political and social democratization, but, after the communist victory in China and the outbreak of the Korean War, the United States shifted its emphasis from restructuring Japanese society to integrating Japan into the anti-communist Western alliance, symbolized by the signing in 1951 of a formal U.S.-Japan peace treaty. U.S. military bases have remained in Japan ever since as part of a mutual defense treaty.

Under SCAP the economy gradually recovered, using the same sort of quasicapitalist system—a mix of government intervention and free markets—that Japan had had between the 1870s and the early 1930s. Land reform heavily subsidized the peasantry, making them strong government supporters and bringing unprecedented prosperity to the rural areas. SCAP also attempted to break up entrenched economic power, but these efforts were less successful; as before World War II, large industrial-commercial-banking combinations, or conglomer-

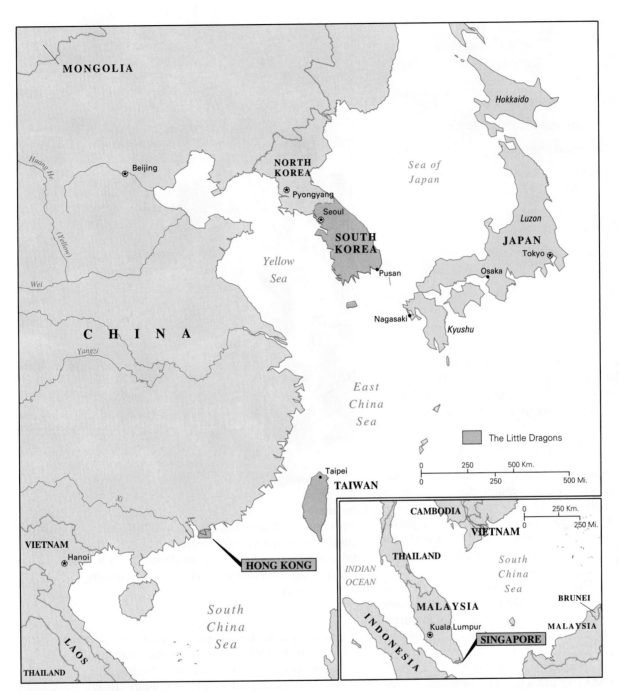

Map 27.2   Japan and the Little Dragons
Japan fostered the strongest Asian economy through the second half of the twentieth century, but in recent decades the Little Dragons—South Korea, Taiwan, Hong Kong, and Singapore—also have had rapid economic growth.

Online Study Center   **Improve Your Grade**   Interactive Map: Japan, 1800–1998

ates, still dominated business, especially manufacturing and foreign trade, making Japan more competitive in the world economy. But workers gained the right to unionize.

The policies implemented during the SCAP occupation, which officially ended in 1952, were most successful where U.S. and Japanese desires coincided or when the policies fit with the nation's traditions (see Chronology: Japan Since 1945). For

example, democratic government fit both criteria. The Japanese had enjoyed several decades of democracy, with competing political parties, before the Great Depression, and many Japanese longed for a return to this system, supported also by SCAP. Borrowing from abroad also fit with Japanese tradition. For several millennia the Japanese had been open to acquiring ideas, such as Buddhism, and technologies, such as textile manufacturing,

C H R O N O L O G Y
Japan Since 1945
1946–1952   SCAP occupation of Japan
1946   First postwar Japanese elections
1951   U.S.-Japan peace treaty
1960s–1989   Era of rapid Japanese economic growth
1989   Beginning of Japanese economic downturn
1993   Fragmentation of Liberal Democratic Party
1997   Asian financial collapse

Japanese Protest Political demonstrations are common in Japanese cities. During this protest in 2001, liberals and leftists criticized new middle-school textbooks, approved by the Education Ministry, that, the critics claimed, distorted history by emphasizing nationalist viewpoints and downplaying Japanese atrocities in World War II. (Getty Images)

from outside and adapting them to their own traditions. In the late 1940s they were again receptive to importing Western culture. With conditions stabilized, Japanese leaders embarked on a strategy of capitalizing on peace to strengthen the nation.

Politics in a One-Party Democracy

Despite stresses, Japan's democratic political system flourished. As in many western European countries, a variety of political parties, including socialists, communists, liberals, Buddhists, and rightwing nationalists, competed for parliamentary seats. But since the early 1950s one major party, the center-right Liberal Democratic Party (LDP), has dominated Japanese politics, applying generally conservative, probusiness, and pro-U.S. policies. The electoral system imposed by SCAP gave greater weight to rural voters, the conservative backbone of LDP support, rather than the more liberal urban voters. Prime ministers, usually LDP leaders, learned to negotiate with varied opposition parties as well as with the diverse factions within the LDP. Nonetheless, critics believe that a political system dominated by one party and a few wealthy kingpins, who face little criticism from a press and media largely owned by huge corporations, is at best a partial democracy.

However, the need to finance political careers and raise money for elections fostered political corruption. Powerful corporations and criminal gangs were leading financial contributors. Bribery scandals sometimes forced political leaders to resign. For example, Prime Minister Tanaka Kakuei (ta-NAH-ka KAH-koo-ay) (1918–1983), who rose from rural poverty to become one of the most powerful LDP kingpins, was arrested in 1976 and later convicted for accepting payments from the U.S.-based Lockheed Corporation. In 1993 the LDP fragmented in factional disputes, and various opposition parties gained support for several years. But in 2001 the LDP returned to power under a reform leader, though it faced challenges from opposition parties.

To protect its shores, Japanese leaders forged a military alliance with the United States, but the alliance brought Japan problems as well as benefits. Thanks to this alliance, which allowed U.S. bases in Japan, Japan's military spending remained meager compared to that of the United States and the USSR: under 1 percent of total spending on goods and services. This ability to devote more resources to the civilian economy was a major reason for Japan's rapid economic growth. While the Cold War superpowers invested in weapons and armies, Japan devoted its economic surplus largely to industrial development.

Despite these benefits of the military alliance with the United States, the Japanese debated the value of the treaties and bases. Leftist parties, labor unions, and militant student groups long opposed the U.S. military presence, which they viewed as neocolonialism. Japanese also feared that the U.S. military interventions in places such as Vietnam and Iraq made Japan a potential target for U.S. enemies. Remembering the horrors of World War II, especially the atomic bombings of Hiroshima and Nagasaki that killed some 200,000 Japanese, many Japanese favored pacifism and believed that Japan's economic strength protected them from attack. Student protests have periodically broken out against the U.S. military bases and defense umbrella. Yet, with U.S. support, Japan began increasing its military spending in the 1980s, and by 2001 it had the fourth largest military budget in the world, ahead of China. The decision of Japanese leaders in 2004 to send soldiers to support, in noncombat activities, the U.S. war effort in Iraq was widely unpopular in Japan and, to critics, violated the constitutional ban against engaging in war.

The Japanese Economy

Adapting capitalism to its own traditions, Japan has achieved phenomenal economic growth: its goods were in demand on every continent only a century after it opened to the outside world. Wartime destruction had required the rebuilding of basic industries using the latest innovations. Investing in new industries and high-tech fields, the Japanese became the world leaders in manufacturing products such as pianos, oil tankers, and automobiles, as well as electronics products such as watches, televisions, and cameras. As a result, from the 1960s through the 1980s Japan's annual growth rate was three times higher than that of other industrialized nations. Now an industrial giant possessing an advanced technology and distinctive economic and industrial structure, in 2000 Japan produced some 16 percent of the world's goods and services, half the U.S. percentage but twice that of third-place Germany.

Economic Growth What observers often called Japan's economic miracle was particularly impressive considering the country's lack of natural resources, including those that produce energy. Unlike the United States, western Europe, and China, Japan has few mineral resources, limited productive farmland, and no major rivers to produce hydroelectric power. Consequently, the Japanese must import minerals needed for industry, such as iron ore, tin, and copper. Oil obtained from Alaska, Southeast Asia, and the Middle East powers Japan's transportation.

The Japanese became known for innovative technologies and high-quality products. Among those technologies was its magnificent mass transit system, including the state-of-the-art bullet trains that whisked passengers around the country at 125 to 150 miles per hour and were always on time. The most advanced trains skimmed along the 225 miles between Tokyo and Kyoto in one hour. Some high-tech goods made in Japan found a large world market. Electronics manufacturers such as Sony, Atari, and Nintendo invented entertainment-oriented products, among them video and handheld game systems, that became part of life on every continent, especially for youth. In addition, millions of people, from Boston to Bogotá to Bombay, drove Toyotas, Hondas, and other Japanese-made cars.

By the 1980s the Japanese enjoyed living standards equal to those of most western Europeans. With unprecedented affluence, the Japanese became Western-style consumers; everyone now sought to own cars, televisions, washing machines, and air conditioners. The Japanese also enjoyed the world's highest average life expectancy: seventy-nine or eighty years. A more varied diet, including more meat and dairy products than their ancestors had, produced taller, healthier children. Western foods and beverages became popular and coffeehouses and bars dotted most streets in commercial and entertainment districts. Western fast-food outlets such as McDonald's, introduced in 1971, proved a great success. By 1994 McDonald's had over 1,000 restaurants in Japan, most of them hugely profitable, that served the same items popular in the West as well as dishes adapted to local taste, such as teriyaki burgers and Chinese fried rice. The rural areas now also shared in the prosperity, although life there remained harder than in the cities and most rural youth left their villages for the more exciting life of the cities. Furthermore, there was an underside to Japanese economic success. Many workers had to make do with part-time jobs offering few benefits, and a small but growing underclass of people had no permanent jobs or homes.

Japanese Capitalism Japan's capitalist economy has differed in fundamental ways from those of other industrial nations. It was a form of mercantilism, a cooperative relationship between government and big business that became known as **Japan, Inc.** (Japan Incorporated). Under this system, the national government and big business worked together to manage the economy. The government regulated business, setting overall guidelines, sponsoring research and development, and leasing the resulting products or technologies to private enterprise. Most Japanese businesses accepted the government guidelines because they took a longer-term view of profitability than was common among Western business leaders. But government-business cooperation occurred chiefly in international trade, the country's lifeblood, and it was made easier by the economic dominance of large Japanese conglomerates, most of which owned diverse enterprises such as factories, banks, and department stores. As in many other countries, the government aided Japanese businesses by erecting protectionist barriers and bureaucratic hurdles that impeded foreign businesses in the Japanese market.

Economic growth, which relies on a dedicated labor force, has generated new problems. As in the West, industrialization has fostered wealth but also harmed the environment. As cities grew, developers cleared farmland and forests. Pollution of rivers and bays wiped out coastal fishing. Smoggy air, produced by automobile exhaust mixing with pollutants from smokestacks, is so bad that city residents sometimes cover their noses and mouths with masks to avert respiratory difficulties. Thousands of people have died or been made ill by toxic waste dumped by factories. In addition to declining environmental health, many younger people resent the long hours and sacrifices expected of both white-collar and blue-collar employees in Japanese companies, especially since a high standard of living has already been achieved.

Japan, Inc. The cooperative relationship between government and big business that has existed in Japan after 1945.

Japan's business and factory life has played a role in Japanese success. The system takes advantage of Japanese cultural values, such as conformity, hard work, cooperation, thrift, and foresight, but has added new innovations. The 30 percent of workers employed in larger Japanese companies have often enjoyed lifetime job security and access to generous welfare benefits offered by their employer, such as health insurance, recreation, housing, and car loans. Some companies sponsor group tours abroad or own vacation retreats, in the mountains or at the seashore, that employees and their families can use. When a corporation has faced financial trouble, top managers usually accept responsibility for the problems, cutting their own pay rather than firing workers. Most workers remain with the same employer for life, though, by the 1980s, it became more common to change jobs. To encourage workers to feel a part of the corporate family, employers often gather the employees together to sing the company anthem each morning before they head for their workstations.

Japanese companies emphasize working in teams and "bottom-up" decision making through quality control circles and work groups, such as a factory team that installs a car engine; these groups decide how best to undertake their tasks and suggest improvements to management. Business offices tend to be organized around large tables, where white-collar employees work collaboratively, rather than around the small cubicles common in North America. Along with the worker participation in decisions, however, businesses and factories have also expected their employees to put company over personal interests, including regularly working overtime.

Japanese Society

Urbanization and affluence have contributed to social change. Sixty percent of Japanese now live in cities of over 100,000. With nearly 30 million people, Tokyo is the world's largest city. With car ownership so popular, Tokyo and other cities have become jammed with traffic. Some of Tokyo's legendary traffic jams take police several days to untangle. The city subways are convenient but overcrowded. Rush hour has evolved into "crush hour," with city employees equipped with padded poles pushing commuters into overflowing cars to enable subway train doors to close. Yet, despite Mafia-like organized crime syndicates, Japan's cities are the safest in the world; experts attribute low rates of violent crime in part to strict gun control.

The economy has changed men's lives, especially in the growing middle class. University-educated men typically want to become salaried white-collar office workers for major corporations. Japanese observers describe the **salaryman**, an urban middle-class male business employee who commits his energies and soul to the company, accepts assignments without complaint, and takes few vacations. The cover of a local book on the salaryman pictures a harried middle-aged man eying

the sundry items that define his work life: a computer, newspaper, lunch box, demanding boss, and subway strap. Many men working in white-collar jobs are also known as "7-11 husbands" because they leave for work at 7 A.M. and do not return until 11 P.M. After work they and their office mates socialize in restaurants, bars, and nightclubs while their wives take care of the home. In the 1980s one wife complained, "I don't know why Japanese men marry if they are never going to be home."[17]

Meanwhile, while earning more money, gaining legal protections, and enjoying greater freedom from traditional restraints, women still struggle for full social and economic equality in a hierarchical society obsessed with patriarchy and seniority, with older men dominating most institutions, including the family. Most women are expected to marry and then retire from the work force in their early twenties to raise children, even though they often remain in paid work. According to one young woman, when she and other women graduated from a top Japanese university, "our bright appearance [for the graduation ceremonies] in vividly colored kimonos [traditional robes] was deceiving. Deep in our hearts we knew that our opportunities to use our professional education would be few."[18] As single women often discovered they could support themselves, the average age of marriage for women rose from twenty-two in the 1950s to twenty-seven in the 1990s. Indeed, in recent years, many women have avoided marriage altogether, preferring to concentrate on their careers or leisure interests. Accordingly, marriage rates have declined, alarming politicians.

Despite the popular, contemporary image of the timid Japanese female, women have become more assertive than women in previous generations. Working against the patriarchal grain of society, feminist organizations and several prominent women's leaders have publicized women's issues, and working women have lobbied companies for equal treatment and pay. Some women have moved into middle management or prestige occupations, such as law, journalism, college teaching, and diplomacy. Yet, women also largely remain outside political and economic power, and only a few attain positions of political leadership. Women aspiring to gender equality admire activists such as Ichikawa Fusae (ee-CHEE-kah-wah foo-SIGH) (1893–1981), a former schoolteacher and journalist who had organized the women's suffrage movement in the 1920s and served in the parliament as a political independent for twenty-five years after World War II, campaigning for women's equality and human rights.

Family life has gradually changed. Although the traditional arranged marriage remains common, increasing numbers of men and women select their own spouse. Also reflecting a rise in personal freedom, more Japanese get married late or opt to end unhappy marriages in divorce, a rare decision before World War II. Studies have suggested that, while many wives are lonely and resentful with their husbands seldom home, the majority prefer spending their growing leisure time away from their husbands. In fact, husbands and wives generally lead separate social lives. Meanwhile, children in middle-class families do not expect to see much of their fathers

---

salaryman An Japanese urban middle-class male business employee who commits his energies and soul to the company, accepts assignments without complaint, and takes few vacations.

except on weekends. The decline of marriage has also had an impact on homosexuals, making it easier for them to find social acceptance. Japanese society has always tolerated homosexual behavior, but now more Japanese, especially homosexual professionals and creative people, have become open about their sexual orientation.

Urban housing remains cramped, and the elderly complain of neglect by their children, who have no room for them in their small homes. Birth control and abortion had been widely practiced in overcrowded Japan for centuries; the renewal of these practices after World War II, along with lower marriage rates, has enabled Japan to stabilize its population at 120 million for several decades. Yet declining birthrates also pose an economic dilemma. By 2000 Japan had a birthrate well below replacement standards and a rapidly aging population that placed a heavy burden on a shrinking work force but did not promote immigration to provide new workers. By 2005, foreigners, mostly Chinese and Koreans, numbered some 2 million in Japan, less than 2 percent of the total population. By contrast, foreigners accounted for 5 percent in Britain, 10 percent in Germany, 12 percent in the U.S., and 22 percent in Australia. Paying for benefits and services for the retired has imposed an increasing strain on those working. Despite laws banning discrimination, Japanese leaders have largely failed to elevate the status of or end prejudice against the *Burakumin*, a despised underclass for centuries, who number some 1 to 3 million people and traditionally did jobs considered unclean, such as leather-working.

Youth face their own kinds of pressures. The rigorous education system, which produces a well-trained workforce, is based on stiff examinations. Young people take exams to get into the better kindergartens, grade schools, and secondary schools. The entrance exam for the top universities is so rigorous it is known as "exam hell." Some students repeat the exams for several years before passing and gaining university admission. The Japanese school year is also longer than that in most other nations. These varied pressures, and the expectations of conforming to the values of mainstream society, have encouraged youth rebellion. Indifferent students, for example, sometimes drop out and join motorcycle gangs that roar along the highways by day and neighborhood streets by night, annoying middle-class families trying to sleep. University students have often supported leftwing political organizations that protest issues such as U.S. military bases or the destruction of farmland to build new airports or business developments (see Witness to the Past: A Japanese Generation Gap). Eventually, however, most young people return to the mainstream upon graduation from university and take jobs in the corporate or industrial world. Some who cannot conform emigrate to North America, Europe, or Brazil in search of a more free-spirited life.

Japanese Women Commuters   A female passenger boards a train compartment reserved for women in a subway station in Tokyo. Tokyo's subways are usually jammed with passengers and special cars allow women to travel without fear of possible sexual harassment.   (Getty Images)

A Japanese Generation Gap

The rapid pace of change since World War II has fostered growing generation gaps in many nations. In 1993 the Japanese essayist Yoshioka Shinobu (born in 1948) discussed the differences in perceptions between his "baby boomer" cohort born in the decade after 1945 and those Japanese of the next generation. Yoshioka's experiences reflected the exciting era of social experimentation during his teenage years in the 1960s. By contrast, young people in the 1970s faced a tighter economy and less official tolerance of radical ideas and organized political protests.

Whenever I hear someone mention Japan's baby boomers, ... I think back to a conversation I had ... [in] 1976 at a rock concert.... The band had the latest sound equipment, but its talent was no match for its technology. Bored, ... I struck up a conversation with two young girls.... They had run away from home ... because they were sick of school, and had come to Tokyo in search of adventure.... They had lied about their ages to get part-time jobs, were sharing a tiny apartment, and from time to time went out to concerts.... I told them I thought they must be having the time of their lives.

"Your generation had it good," one of the girls answered. "When you ran away from home, there was rock music, underground theater, demonstrations, all kinds of things—you could do whatever you wanted. Our generation has to walk a tightrope, ... and there's nothing to catch us if we fall. We lose our balance, we die. You guys might have walked a tightrope too, but you had a safety net below. If you didn't like it up on the rope, you could always dive down and let yourself be caught in midair. You could do whatever you wanted to."

She had hit home. So that's how we look in the eyes of someone ten years younger, I thought. My generation ... had an entirely different understanding of itself. [We] ... had many names ... : the baby boomers, the Beatles generation, the anti-Vietnam [War] generation.... [Our radical student movements] did much to discredit the established political system, but our generation was more than just a new political force. We began new trends in music, theater, art, and social customs ... that defied the existing structure of authority and social conventions. In those days, nothing was worse than a willingness to capitulate to the "system" and adopt its narrow conventions.

Consequently, we tried our hands at everything. Singers of traditional [music], who had put in years of hard work climbing the rigid, hierarchical ladder before they were allowed to perform publicly, suddenly found themselves displaced by our barely rehearsed bands and spontaneous concerts. Some put on plays in ... tents set up in vacant lots, ridiculing the empty and imitative formalism of Japan's commercial theater. Others ... took off nearly penniless to wander about in foreign countries—their adventureousness helped make travel abroad commonplace.

The two girls were saying that these experiences ... were only possible because we had a safety net underneath us.... The girls had a point. When [my] generation was growing up, the ... confusion of the early postwar years had given way to spectacular economic growth.... This ... engendered confidence in liberal politics and democratic government, and it also created a willingness to forgive the unruliness of the younger generation.... If we were arrested [in antiwar demonstrations] it did not worry us much.... The runaway girls told me that the age of such optimism was over.... Between my generation and the next, attitudes toward change took a 180-degree turn. For us, changes in society and the individual were exciting and intrinsically valuable. For the younger generation, however, change is frightening and the source of insecurity.

THINKING ABOUT THE READING

1. How did Yoshioka's generation contribute to change?
2. What does the essay tell us about Japan's connection to the wider world?

Source: Shinobu Yoshioka, "Talkin' 'bout My Generation," in Merry L. White and Sylvan Barnet, eds., *Comparing Cultures: Readings on Contemporary Japan for American Writers* (Boston: Bedford Books of St. Martin's Press, 1995), pp. 119–122. Reprinted with permission by Yoshioka Shinobu.

Culture and Thought

As they have done over the past two centuries, the Japanese have continued to blend traditional and modern cultures and beliefs, East and West. With old values and traditions under stress, Japanese have engaged in a debate about this blending and its effect on cultural identity. Artists and writers now ponder whether the historical process of synthesizing foreign and local ideas has been the nation's salvation or its bane. Some worry that Japan's adoption of foreign culture has imperiled its own distinctive culture. In 1993 a prominent writer agreed with this view: "We are up to our necks in Western culture. But we have planted a little seed. We are beginning to re-create ourselves."[19] Others contend that Japanese needed to become less inward and more global-minded, even encouraging immigration from other Asian countries that would make Japan a multicultural nation and offset the decline of young people in the population.

The questions about Japanese identity, as well as the problems facing Japanese society, are often analyzed in films that have achieved worldwide recognition. While the Japanese film industry, the world's third largest, produces escapist films, such as those portraying samurai warriors and gigantic city-wrecking monsters, that gain a large audience at home and abroad, it also makes thought-provoking masterpieces, especially grand historical epics and introspective psychological or sociological studies, that force audiences to reflect on Japanese life. One of the most skillful directors, Kurosawa Akira (kur-o-SAH-wa a-KEER-a) (1910–1998), became especially famous for films mixing a distinctive Japanese style and setting with a theme appealing to viewers in other cultures. *Rashomon* (1950), for example, deals with the relativity of truth by examining one event, the killing of a feudal lord and the violation of his wife by a bandit, through varied eyes, including the murdered lord, the wife, the bandit, and a woodcutter who witnessed the act. Another Kurosawa film, *Ikuru*, or "To Live" (1952), explores the meaning of life through the story of a Japanese bureaucrat dying of cancer who overcomes endless red tape to facilitate the building of a small neighborhood park.

The Japanese have the world's highest literacy rate (99.9 percent) and the largest numbers of newspaper readers, magazine subscribers, and bookstores per capita, which have fostered both popular and serious literature. Japan boasts several world-famous novelists, Kawabata Ysunori (ka-wa-BAH-ta yoo-suh-NOOR-ee) (1899–1972) being the first Japanese, in 1968, to receive the Nobel Prize for literature. Directly addressing Japanese identity, the writings of Mishima Yukio (me-SHE-mah YOO-kee-oh) (1925–1970) portray an effete, decadent "nation of shopkeepers" that need a return to the martial values of the Tokugawa period. His best novel concerns a disturbed young man torn, like Mishima himself, between old samurai and modern Westernized values. For Mishima, a conflicted homosexual and avid body builder, life became art; in 1970 he publicly committed suicide in samurai style in front of his private army to sacrifice himself for what he called the "old beautiful tradition of Japan, which is disappearing day by day."[20] His action shocked the Japanese, but his message died with him; the Japanese continued to develop a consumer society.

Continuity has long characterized Japanese popular culture. Every sport, art form, and religion that has appeared in the past 1,500 years in Japan still attracts practitioners or followers. For example, Japanese remain passionate about sumo wrestling, a sport, going back centuries, in which two large, paunchy Japanese men attempt to push each other out of a small ring. At the same time, change is also characteristically Japanese. While performances of kabuki or bunraku, theatrical forms that appeared in the 1600s, still attract devoted audiences, and young Japanese women preparing for marriage often master the even older tea ceremony, many more Japanese follow professional baseball teams; consume Japanese comics, or *manga* (mahn-gah), and animated films, or *anime*, that are popular worldwide; and flock to Japanese or Western films, discos, pinball palaces, and video-game arcades. Japanese also frequent nightclubs featuring a bewildering assortment of musical styles, including both local and imported versions of rock, jazz, reggae, country western, rap, and salsa. Modern Japanese, especially young people, have avidly adopted cultural forms from around the world.

Industrialization and urbanization have accelerated the declining influence of organized religion. Some Japanese remain deeply religious. Militant Buddhist groups claim several million followers, and various new religions based on Buddhist or Shinto traditions, or a mix of the two, have flourished by addressing material prosperity and family problems. Nonetheless, the contemporary Japanese are a largely secular people. In census questionnaires, while most Japanese described themselves as Buddhists, Shintoists, or both, less than 15 percent reported any formal religious affiliation by 2000. Japanese have become largely indifferent to religion except as an opportunity for a festival. Although Japan's Christian population is tiny, millions of non-Christians ardently celebrate Christmas as a commercial holiday, an opportunity to give and receive gifts, and Japanese department stores often feature elaborate Christmas displays, complete with Santa Claus and brightly-decorated Christmas trees.

The weak influence of organized religions and their moral systems has not resulted in social breakdown, however. Japanese remain among the world's most law-abiding, peaceful citizens, but morality now is mostly derived from the fear of bringing shame on the family or group rather than fear of retribution by gods or ancestors. The reluctance to disgrace the family suggests that Confucianism, the Chinese ethical system favoring family loyalty and social stability that was imported into Japan 1,400 years ago, remains an important foundation of Japanese thought. Yet the emphasis on conforming to the group and its rules has a downside. Criticizing the attitudes expressed by an old saying—"the nail that sticks up gets hammered down"—Japanese liberals have sought a less conformist society that would nourish rather than inhibit individual genius.

Japan in the Global System

The Japanese have had to readjust their views of the economy and international relations over the past several decades. Like their North American and European counterparts, Japanese companies have sought cheaper labor by setting up shop in Southeast Asia, South Korea, and China, a practice that has cost Japan jobs. In 1989 the Japanese economy went into a severe downturn, due in part to overvalued stocks that caused a crisis on the Tokyo Stock Exchange but also to global recession and competition from the newly industrializing nations of Southeast Asia, which produced consumer products similar to Japan's. Many Japanese investors went bankrupt, confidence was shaken, and more than 1 million workers were laid off. Only in the early 2000s did Japanese leaders, beginning to overcome political and bureaucratic inertia, introduce policies that fostered higher growth rates and renewed business confidence, but the recovery remained incomplete, the economy yet to regain the levels of the 1980s. As in the United States, Japanese corporations have reacted to foreign competition by slashing salaries and cutting benefits, modifying the business system that brought Japan prosperity for a half century.

While comfortable as an economic powerhouse, the Japanese remain reluctant to assert their political and military power in the world, remembering how the attempt to dominate eastern Asia brought them disaster during World War II. Japan's main concerns are the continued health of the world economy and continuing access to overseas resources and markets, the two pillars on which its prosperity has depended. In pursuing this goal, the Japanese people prefer that the country seek peaceful rather than military solutions to world problems. Japan has maintained a strategic alliance with its major trading partner, the United States, but the two nations have also remained keen economic rivals and have sometimes engaged in trade disputes. Japanese leaders have also worked to promote peaceful exchange with China and South Korea, two countries with long memories of Japanese imperialism during the first half of the twentieth century. Relations with China have been particularly strained, as the Chinese have demanded that Japan accept responsibility for World War II atrocities in China, such as the murder and injury of thousands of civilians known as the Rape of Nanjing, a Chinese city. Resurgent Japanese and Chinese nationalisms clash. As China and several other Asian nations rise economically, Japan faces more competition and the challenge of maintaining its position in the world economy.

SECTION SUMMARY

■ After World War II, a U.S.-led occupation of Japan (SCAP) worked to rebuild Japan's economy while demilitarizing the country and encouraging the return of democracy, much of which was successful; however, it was difficult to break up large business conglomerates.

■ The Liberal Democratic Party dominated Japanese politics for decades, with a brief break in the 1990s, and the presence of U.S. military bases within Japan was seen by some as neocolonialism but freed up resources to help fuel the economy.

■ Relying on innovation and collaboration between government and big business, Japan's economy has grown at a phenomenal rate, though it has caused environmental problems and great personal sacrifices on the part of workers.

■ Japan's cities have become increasingly congested, men are expected to devote all their energy to work, women struggle for equality and increasingly choose work over marriage, arranged marriages have become less common, and students face the pressure of an arduous education system.

■ Japanese have managed to blend their traditions with modern and foreign influences and have maintained a high degree of social order in spite of low participation in organized religion, but some criticize Japanese society as too conformist.

■ In the early 2000s, Japan's economy began to recover from a decade-long downturn, while in world politics, Japan has played an important role, though it has been hesitant to assert its power too forcefully.

◆ The Little Dragons in the Asian Resurgence

What policies led to the rise of the "Little Dragon" nations and their dynamic economies?

While China and Japan were rising to regional and global power, a few of their East Asian neighbors also achieved economic development. Known as the **Little Dragons** because their societies were strongly influenced by the region's dominant Chinese culture, these neighbors—South Korea, Taiwan, Singapore, and Hong Kong—built rapidly growing, industrializing economies. Except for Hong Kong, a British colony until 1997 and a bastion of free enterprise, these societies largely followed the Meiji Japan model of state-directed capitalism, which involved government intervention into otherwise free market economies. They were also inspired by Japan's resurgence after World War II, which depended on participation in the world economy. All the Little Dragons shared a Confucian cultural heritage, imported from China, that emphasized hard work, discipline, cooperation, and tolerance for authoritarian governments. They all achieved an export-oriented industrialization that dramatically raised incomes, reduced poverty, and forged high standards in health and education. For South Korea, however, this development came only after a brutal war that left a hostile, rigidly communist North Korea on the border. And Taiwan had to find its own path in the shadow of China. Singapore (see Chapter 31) and Hong Kong (now part of China) are city-states with largely Chinese populations.

The Korean War

The Korean War (1950–1953) was rooted in the Korean nationalism that, despite fierce repression, simmered during a half century of harsh Japanese colonial rule, which was imposed in 1910 (see Chapters 23 and 24). While introducing some economic modernization, the Japanese arrested or executed Korean nationalists, conscripted Korean women to serve Japanese soldiers, and relocated thousands of Korean workers to Japan. To maintain their rule, the Japanese manipulated the divisions within Korean society. Christians constituted one influential group that grew in numbers during the twentieth century. By the 1940s a fifth of Koreans had become Catholics or Protestants. Inspired by Soviet modernization, another group of Koreans had gravitated toward communism during colonial times, some escaping to the USSR to form a revolutionary movement. In contrast to these who imported ideas, a majority of Koreans maintained their adherence to Buddhism and Confucianism, regarding these traditional beliefs as central to Korean identity. Although Christians, communists, and traditionalists commonly hated Japanese rule and members of all

Little Dragons South Korea, Taiwan, Singapore, and Hong Kong, which were strongly influenced by Chinese culture and built rapidly growing, industrializing economies.

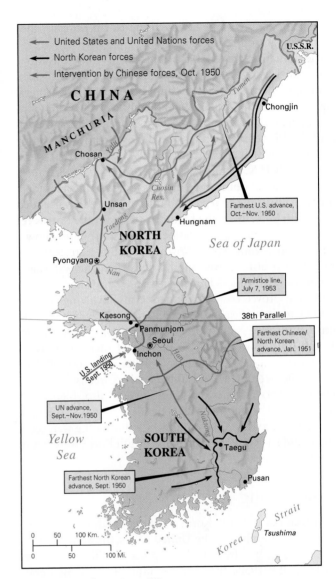

Map 27.3   The Korean War
In 1950, North Korean forces crossed the 38th parallel and invaded South Korea, but they were then pushed back north by United Nations forces led by the United States. The intervention of China in support of North Korea pushed the United Nations forces south and produced a military stalemate, preserving the border between North and South Korea at the 38th parallel.

groups worked underground to oppose it, they could not cooperate and no unified nationalist movement emerged.

Japan's crushing defeat by the United States in 1945 meant political liberation for Korea and a chance to reestablish the nation free of foreign interference. But the United States quickly occupied the southern half of the peninsula and the Soviet Union the north, bisecting Korea and making it a hostage to the Cold War. As the USSR and the United States imposed rival governments, unification quickly became impossible, alarming nationalists of all stripes. With Soviet help, in 1948 communists led by the ruthless Kim Il-Sung (KIM ill-soon) (1912–1994) formed a government in North Korea (see Chronology: The Little Dragons Since 1945). A clever strategist who was born into a Christian family and who had lived for years in the USSR, Kim quickly built a brutal communist system, eliminated his opponents, and reorganized rural society. But the impatient Kim disastrously overestimated the revolutionary potential of the south, where leftists often mistrusted Kim, and he also misjudged the Americans, who were determined to stop the spread of Soviet influence. The United States helped create and then supported a South Korean state headed by Rhee Syngman (REE SING-man) (1865–1965), better know in the West as Syngman Rhee. A longtime nationalist and politically conservative Christian from a powerful landlord family, Rhee had lived in exile in the United States for over two decades. Unpopular with the majority non-Christians, the autocratic, inflexible Rhee imprisoned or eliminated his opponents and sparked a rebellion by leftist movements supported by many factory workers and peasants, which United States troops helped crush. Although less repressive than Kim's North Korean regime, Rhee's South Korea held some 30,000 political prisoners.

These developments set the stage for the Korean War (see Map 27.3), a result of mixing revolution and nationalism into a Cold War–driven stew. Historians still debate the origins of this conflict, which shaped East Asian politics for half a century. Both Korean states, threatening to reunify Korea with military force, had initiated border skirmishes. In this highly charged context, North Korea, probably with tacit Soviet and perhaps Chinese approval, invaded the South in 1950. The United Nations, then dominated by Western nations, approved a request by the United States to lead a military intervention to support South Korea, thus turning a Korean crisis into a Cold War confrontation; the United States made the major commitment of troops, war materials, and funding to the United Nations force. U.S. president Harry Truman also secretly planned a strike on North Korea with atomic weapons if North Korea's ally, the USSR, entered the war. But while the Soviets gave military supplies and advice to the North Koreans, they sent no combat troops.

The initiative shifted back and forth. United Nations troops, aided by U.S. air power, quickly pushed the North Koreans back across the north-south border. But U.S. general Douglas MacArthur's (1880–1964) openly expressed aim to invade China and his decision to invade North Korea and push toward the Chinese border sparked a massive intervention by Chinese troops that drove back United Nations troops and turned a likely U.N. victory into a bitter stalemate. U.S. leaders had misjudged the Chinese willingness to fight and had underestimated Chinese military capabilities. When the war ended in 1953 with peace talks, the boundary between the Koreas remained in the same place it was before the war but was now a heavily fortified zone where North and South Korean troops glared at each other across the barbed wire. The war was a stalemate but both sides claimed victory.

The war proved costly in human terms, involving perhaps 1 million military dead and 1 or 2 million civilian Korean deaths. The United Nations forces suffered some 43,000 killed and over 100,000 wounded, 90 percent of them Americans. South Korean military casualties numbered over 100,000 dead and 160,000 wounded, and the North Koreans lost over 300,000 soldiers. Chinese casualties were also high, over 400,000 dead. The fighting also generated millions of Korean refugees who wandered the countryside during the war, seeking food and shelter. Both North and South Korea were left in economic shambles.

The Remaking of South Korea

The postwar rise of South Korea was nearly as dramatic as that of Japan. Closely allied to the United States, the South Korean governments ranged from highly repressive military dictatorships from the 1950s through the mid-1980s, to moderate semidemocracies in the later 1980s, and then to liberal democracies with free elections after the early 1990s. All regimes aimed at economic development. The dictator Park Chung Hee (1917–1979) argued in 1970, "My chief concern was economic revolution. One must eat and breathe before concerning himself with politics, social affairs, and culture."[21] The United States protected the South Korean regimes from any North Korean threats by permanently stationing troops and supplying generous economic and military aid. Five decades after the war, some 40,000 U.S. troops and more than one hundred U.S.-owned nuclear weapons remained in South Korea, reassuring some South Koreans and outraging others.

Mixing government intervention and free markets, South Korea has enjoyed enormous economic growth. The nation has become a key prong in the world economy, investing heavily in the Middle East, Southeast Asia, and Russia, often to secure oil supplies, while exporting automobiles and electronic products. By the mid-1990s South Korea had joined the ranks of advanced industrial nations, the first non-Western nation to make that transition since Japan in the late nineteenth century. It also moved into the top sixth of nations in the United Nations Human Development Index. Having acquired a standard of living South Koreans could only have dreamed of two decades earlier, with nearly full employment and universal literacy, by 2000 South Koreans enjoyed the highest rate of high-speed Internet access in the world: some 75 percent of households were wired, far more than in North America and Europe, and 35 percent of the population report that they play computer games online. The country became a high technology model. Prosperity reshaped society. Both boys and girls received free education through age twelve. South Korean women benefited from new job options, often in the professions and business. With more women in the work force and self-supporting, marriage rates declined and average births per woman fell dramatically from 6 in 1990 to 1.6 in 2005.

Economic growth has also fostered political change. Democracy movements had begun in the 1960s, but they often faced government repression. One dissident wrote that "bullets, nightsticks, and fists are not the only forms of violence. A nation with no expression of dissent is a nation in ruins."[22] Sometimes tensions exploded; in 1980 the dictatorship brutally crushed an uprising in a southern province that began when some five hundred people demonstrated, demanding an end of martial law; in response paratroopers landed and, using everything from bayonets to flamethrowers, began slaughtering the protesters and local people who got in their way. Hundreds of thousands of enraged people then drove the troops out of the city, only to face a much larger force, which shot their way into the city, killing over 2,000 people. Eventually political tensions diminished. During the later 1980s governments fostered more liberalization, tolerated a freer press, and made overtures toward former enemies in the USSR and China. By the early 1990s, four decades after the Korean War ended, the South Korean people had forced a change in direction. With the growth of the middle class and organized labor, democracy flowered, though it was sometimes sullied by political corruption. South Koreans boasted that the era when freedom and human rights were subordinated to economic growth and military security had ended, and took pride in the influence of their popular culture products in both China and Japan.

But while the country fostered economic dynamism, political participation, and personal freedom, and while it clearly outshined repressive North Korea in most key areas, problems arose. Many rural people and unskilled workers did not share in the prosperity, and factories expected long hours from poorly paid workers. Frustrated at their prospects, thousands of Koreans, many of them middle class, emigrated to the United States. Discontent also grew with the economic slowdown beginning in 1997. Furthermore, while South Koreans often welcomed the security provided by U.S. bases, others viewed the bases as an affront to Korean nationalism and demanded that they be removed. Koreans on both sides of the demilitarized zone yearned for reunification and an end to the peninsular cold war that resulted from the hot war. After years of hostility, and owing partly to South Korean efforts, which they called the "sunshine policy," to improve relations, North and South Korea finally achieved a wary peaceful coexistence. A dialogue begun in the later 1990s resulted in limited cross-border trade and allowed a few South Koreans to visit family

South Korean Economic Growth   One of South Korea's major, most diverse enterprises, the Hyundai Corporation, formed in 1976, engages in shipping, manufacturing, and trade, producing, among other products, chemicals, machinery, and information and telecommunications equipment. The ships in this company dry dock are being readied to carry Hyundai-made cars to distant markets around the world. (Tony Stone/Getty Images)

members in North Korea they had not seen since the early 1950s. Televised images of South Koreans tearfully embracing aging parents or siblings mesmerized the nation. In 2000 South Korean president Kim Dae-jung (kin day-chung) (b. 1925), a liberal reformer, visited North Korea, an event unthinkable a decade earlier. Yet national reconciliation still remains a dream rather than a reality, and South Koreans worry about North Korean military capabilities and its quest to build nuclear weapons.

Stalinism in North Korea

North Korea's leaders chose a completely different path from that taken by South Korea. The communist leader Kim Il-Sung's decision to reunite Korea with force, which led to the Korean War, proved a mistake that devastated the country, though North Korea quickly recovered with aid from China and the USSR. From 1948 until his death in 1994, Kim was the nation's president, head of the Communist Party, and commander of the armed forces. He also created a personality cult

around himself as the "Great Leader." North Koreans were taught that they owed everything—jobs, goods, schooling, food, military security—to Kim. To ensure loyalty and deflect blame for the regime's failures, Kim purged 70 percent of communist cadres and jailed or executed thousands of dissidents.

North Korea adopted a mix of Stalinism and Maoism to shape the economy and society. Soviet-style economic planning and central direction emphasized heavy industry and weapons at the expense of consumer goods. As a result, North Koreans did not enjoy the rising living standards of South Koreans. To inspire the population to work hard, Kim invented a political philosophy of self-reliance that was heavily influenced by Mao Zedong's policy of relying on a country's own strength and limiting contact with the world economy. North Korea benefited from a favorable industrial base built during Japanese colonial times, since it contained over three-quarters of Korea's factories and mines. For several decades the North Korean economy outshined its South Korean rivals. The huge military establishment, however, drained these resources as it concentrated on deterring enemies and intimidating South Korea.

Politically, North Korea stressed group loyalty, ultra-nationalism, and independence from foreign influence, following the model of Korea's hereditary Yi dynasty and Confucian bureaucracy of the early nineteenth century. A small government and military elite, isolated from the bleak existence of the peasantry and workers, enjoyed special privileges, living in comfortable apartments and having access to sufficient food. Fearing opposition, they controlled the people by using regimentation and restricting information. To monitor the activities and thoughts of the population, the government required each citizen to register at a public security office and urged people to spy on their families and neighbors, reporting those who questioned the government. To prevent people from hearing contrary views or unapproved culture, the only radios allowed were fixed to receive only the government station. Political prisoners and people caught trying to flee to China or South Korea faced long terms in harsh concentration camps or even execution.

By the 1990s the regime faced stresses that resulted in increasing international isolation. The economy declined rapidly, thanks to poor management, commodity shortages, and rigid policies. Satellite photos of the Korean peninsula at night revealed the stark differences in electrical power between a brilliantly lit South Korea and a completely dark North Korea. U.S. diplomatic pressure isolated the regime, discouraging foreign loans and investment and making North Korea totally reliant economically on the Soviet bloc. Various efforts to strike back, such as assassination attempts on South Korean leaders, earned North Korea a reputation as an unpredictable terrorist state, increasing its diplomatic isolation. When the Soviet bloc collapsed in 1989 and the USSR was dissolved in 1991, Russia and China demanded that North Korea pay cash for oil and other imports.

North Korea's problems increased after Kim Jong-Il (chong-ill) (b. 1942), known as the "Dear Leader" as well as for his reputation as a playboy, succeeded his deceased father in 1995. When the nation soon faced mass starvation, Kim requested and received food aid from South Korea and Japan, countries anxious to discourage desperation because it might spur North Korean military action. Eventually, as the food shortages continued, the United Nations also sent food, much of it supplied from the United States. Even with the aid many people died or were malnourished. Thousands of North Koreans fled to China to find food and work. Observers predicted the regime would collapse, but it avoided that fate. Thanks to isolation and tight information control, few North Koreans traveled abroad, studied foreign languages, met foreigners, or encountered foreign publications, films, and music. Having little knowledge of the outside world, even of prosperous South Korea, most North Koreans believed the state's propaganda. Meanwhile, a small dissident movement, risking harsh reprisals, smuggled in food from China and videotapes, books, and music from South Korea.

North Korea became a concern in both regional and world politics. By the late 1990s its military force was twice as large as South Korea's and apparently had a capability for building nuclear weapons. Experts disagreed as to whether they had

done so. But with both Koreas possessing lethal military forces, war became less likely. This perception encouraged the search for common ground in pursuing national unification. The economic disasters of the 1990s, especially food shortages, softened the North Korean position, and after 1998 South Korea actively sought better relations to reduce the threat from its dangerous northern neighbor and its unpredictable leader. North Korea's neighbors and the United States also sought diplomatic ways to eliminate the possibility of a conventional war or a nuclear confrontation.

Taiwan and China

The triumph of the Chinese communists on the mainland in 1949 led to the relocation of Chiang Kai-shek and his Nationalist government to the mountainous, subtropical Taiwan island, where he reestablished the Republic of China. Two governments claiming to represent China created a long-term diplomatic problem for the world community. Both the governments of the People's Republic on the mainland and of the Republic on Taiwan regarded the island as an integral part of China rather than a separate nation; this "one China policy" was endorsed by most of the world. Taiwan's people built a prosperous society but remained divided about the nation's future and its long-term relationship to China.

The Rise of Taiwan Taiwan had only become a part of Chinese territory in the seventeenth and eighteenth centuries, when the Qing dynasty claimed the island and Chinese from coastal provinces began settling the island in large numbers, relegating the small Malay-speaking native population to mountain districts. In 1910 Taiwan became a Japanese colony. Japan ruled Taiwan less harshly than it did Korea, financing industrialization that produced a higher standard of living than that known in mainland China. After World War II China reclaimed the island, but in 1947 local resentment of Chiang's heavy-handed regime, which ignored local customs, led to an island-wide uprising. Chiang dispatched 100,000 troops from the mainland, who killed 30,000 to 40,000 Taiwanese, including many local leaders, in quelling the unrest.

As Chiang's Republic of China collapsed in 1948–1949, the president and 2 million mainlanders moved to Taiwan, taking with them their government, the Nationalist Party, the remaining military forces, the priceless art collections of the national museum, and China's national treasury. These mainlanders and their descendants eventually constituted some 15 to 20 percent of the total island population, which numbered 23 million by 2005. The minority mainlanders dominated politics, the economy, and the military. The majority Taiwanese, although Chinese in culture and language, often considered the mainlanders colonizers. Chiang viewed Taiwan as a temporary refuge, since he hoped to reconquer the mainland and then return there. But after his death in 1972, many mainlanders (and their children) realized that, with a return to the mainland unlikely, Taiwan might be their permanent home. They then cultivated better relations with the Taiwanese.

Learning from their defeat in China, and using generous U.S. aid, the Republic's leaders promoted rapid industrial and agricultural growth and a more equitable distribution of wealth, implementing the land reform they had neglected on the mainland. With land ownership and access to credit facilities, the peasantry prospered. As in South Korea and Meiji Japan, the economy mixed capitalism and foreign investment with a strong government role, including extensive planning and sizeable state investment. Light industry and manufacturing eventually accounted for half of Taiwan's economic production and the bulk of exports, with electronics constituting the leading edge. Taiwan became the world's third largest producer, after the United States and Japan, of computer hardware. Between the early 1970s and the late 1990s it enjoyed more years of double-digit growth than any other nation. Taiwanese companies set up operations in Southeast Asia, China, Africa, and Latin America. By the 1980s the economic indicators far surpassed those on the mainland, including a per capita annual income of $8,000, 99 percent of households owning a color television, 92 percent literacy, and a life expectancy of seventy-five. In the late 1990s Taiwan businessmen built the world's tallest skyscraper, 1,667 feet high, in the capital city, Taipei. Rapid development, however, has brought severe problems, among them environmental destruction, traffic congestion, political corruption, and a severe economic slowdown in 1997. Concrete high-rise buildings increasingly displace the lush greenery of the mountains around Taipei.

Modernization has challenged Chinese values and traditions. The small roadside cafes selling noodle soup and meat dumplings, a beloved mainstay of local life for generations, often close, unable to compete with U.S. fast-food restaurants and convenience stores selling Coca-Cola, hamburgers, and ice cream. Rampant materialism concerns those who believe life should offer more than the quest for luxury goods and money. While Confucian values, such as the emphasis on hard work, have fostered the material success of the Little Dragons, some Taiwanese have worried that Confucian ethics, including respect for parents and concern for the community rather than the individual, are threatened. Agreeing with them, the Taiwan government has supported traditional Chinese culture and religion by mandating the teaching of Confucian ethics in the schools. Despite the modernization, traditional Chinese culture remains stronger in Taiwan than in the mainland. Over 90 percent of the people describe themselves as, like their ancestors, Buddhists, Daoists, Confucianists, or a mix of the three ancient traditions. Some 5 percent of Taiwan's people have adopted Christianity, and several million others are comfortable with secularism, only infrequently attending temples or churches.

Politics on Taiwan Like South Korea, Taiwan until the later 1980s followed the authoritarian Little Dragon political model. For several decades Chiang Kai-shek and his family controlled the island with a police state, which held numerous political prisoners. Favoring eventual reunification with the mainland whenever communist rule there ended, Chiang made it illegal to advocate making Taiwan per-

manently independent of China. Both the Nationalist leaders on Taiwan and the communists on the mainland believed in one China, of which Taiwan was one part. Both opposed those who advocated two separate Chinese nations. However, they disagreed on which party should rule this unified China. For four decades Chiang's political party, the Nationalists, ruled as the sole legal party, but in 1989, nudged by a growing middle class seeking liberalization, they permitted opposition candidates to run in elections. Gradually the regime recognized civil liberties, including the freedom of speech and press. The 2000 elections swept into office the Democratic Progressive Party (DPP), largely supported by the native Taiwanese; many party leaders, reflecting widespread Taiwanese opinion, advocated that Taiwan become a separate nation, a stance that angered both the Nationalist leaders on Taiwan and the communist leaders on the mainland. However, Taiwan's voters seemed less eager to confront China by 2005, when elections showed reduced support for the DPP.

China has remained Taiwan's permanent challenge. Fearing an invasion to forcibly annex the island, Taiwan lavishly funded its military, kept a large standing army, and bought the latest fighter jets and gunboats, at the same time maintaining a defense alliance with the United States and allowing U.S. bases. But in 1978 the United States recognized the People's Republic as China's only government, embraced the one-China policy, and withdrew diplomatic recognition from its longtime ally, the Republic of China on Taiwan. However, the United States has maintained a strong informal economic presence and repeatedly reaffirms a commitment to defend the island from attack. In the later 1980s Taiwan and China began informal talks about improving relations. As a result, informal trade between the two countries has grown substantially and many people from Taiwan have visited the mainland, to do business or look up relatives. However, doubts about whether China will move toward political liberalization and allow for free speech, competing parties, and democracy, as well as alarm at occasional Chinese military exercises being conducted near Taiwan, have precluded any serious negotiations on reunification. For several decades China's leaders have threatened military action to prevent any move by Taiwan for permanent independence. Such action would alarm Japan, which has close ties to Taiwan, and might draw in the United States because of its commitment to defend Taiwan. Thus Taiwan's political future remains an open question, fiercely debated by Taiwanese and their several competing political parties.

The Little Dragons in the Global System

The rise of the Pacific Rim, including China, Japan, and the Little Dragons, in the late twentieth century reshaped the global system. The quarter of the world's population living along the western edge of the Pacific Basin established policies that allowed them to outpace the West and the rest of the world in economic growth while maintaining political stability. A global economy that had been based on the tripod of the United States, western Europe, and Japan now has to accommodate China and the Little Dragons. In the Little Dragons, high annual economic growth rates helped them industrialize, with both the benefits and the problems that entailed. By the 1990s the Little Dragons had diversified into high technology, making computers and other electronics products and thereby posing an economic challenge to Japan and the West. Meiji Japan in the late 1800s had established the economic model by mixing capitalism and state investment with strong government authority. The Little Dragons successfully used that model to develop and compete with Japan and the West.

Some economic trends suggested that the Pacific Rim nations were becoming an Asian counterpart to the European Community, the free trade zone formed by western European nations, thus foreshadowing, some scholars argued, the Pacific Century, in which Asian nations would dominate the world economy. Many of the East and Southeast Asian nations forged closer economic cooperation, with Japan and China forming the hubs. But in 1997 an economic meltdown hit South Korea, Taiwan, Japan, and the industrializing economies of Southeast Asia. As businesses closed, unemployment soared. By the early 2000s South Korea and Taiwan had regained some of their dynamism but still faced challenges. The uncertainty in the Pacific Rim and the continuing global power of the United States suggested that a Pacific Century would not materialize in the near future, but China and Japan will undoubtedly play major roles in the years to come. Yet in many respects, East Asia had returned to its historical role as a key engine of the world economy.

SECTION SUMMARY

- After World War II, communist North Korea, assisted by the USSR and China, fought a war with South Korea, assisted by a U.S.-dominated United Nations force, that caused thousands of deaths and economic devastation and ended with the same border that existed at the start of the war.

- South Korean governments have grown more tolerant of internal dissent and more open to relations with former enemies such as communist North Korea and China, though their primary emphasis has been on economic growth.

- After the Korean War, North Korea recovered with support from the USSR and China and was ruled as a repressive communist dictatorship with a centrally planned economy whose shortcomings led to widespread food shortages in the 1990s.

- With the communists ruling mainland China, the nationalists took over Taiwan, which they ruled as a police state and turned into an economic powerhouse, but relations with mainland China have continued to be tense.

- China and the "Little Dragons" (Taiwan, South Korea, Singapore, and Hong Kong) grew rapidly in the late twentieth century, leading to predictions of a coming "Pacific Century," but a slowdown in the 1990s dampened such expectations.

◆ Chapter Summary

In the decades after World War II, East Asia experienced revolutionary upheavals and dramatic economic development that led to a resurgence of the region's influence in the world. The communist triumph in China began the process of change. After experimenting with a Soviet-style Stalinist development model, China's leader, Mao Zedong, imposed his own version of communism. Emphasizing collective efforts, political values, and mass mobilization, Mao reorganized the rural economy into communes. He also sparked the Cultural Revolution, which attacked the bureaucracy and those who opposed his political and economic vision but also created turmoil. After Mao's death, Deng Xiaoping led China in a new direction; his market socialism energized the economy but led to tensions and then repression. During the 1990s market Leninism continued the economic reforms, providing a basis for rapid growth. China became a world economic power, but the growing inequalities of wealth have threatened to destabilize the nation.

The experiences of Japan and the Little Dragons differed from those of China. After the World War II defeat and U.S. occupation of Japan, the nation rapidly rose to become an economic powerhouse, based on a system mixing political democracy and a form of capitalism in which government and business worked together. The Japanese rebuilt their industries and fostered new forms of business and production. But social change came slowly, leaving Japan hierarchical. The Little Dragon nations of South Korea and Taiwan achieved industrial growth and prosperity by borrowing the Japanese model and mixing free markets with government intervention, eventually fostering democracy, while North Korea chose Stalinism and isolation from the world. The dynamism of most East Asian nations suggests that they have recovered from the disasters they experienced from the mid-1800s to the mid-1900s as a result of Western imperialism, Japanese expansion, and war, but their overall role remains unclear for the twenty-first century.

Key Terms

Pacific Rim	Great Proletarian	market Leninism
Pacific Century	Cultural Revolution	Japan, Inc.
communes	Red Guards	salaryman
Great Leap Forward	Iron Rice Bowl	Little Dragons
	market socialism	

Suggested Reading

Books

Benson, Linda. *China Since 1949*. New York: Longman, 2002. Brief overview.

Cumings, Bruce. *Korea's Place in the Sun: A Modern History*. New York: W. W. Norton, 1997. A provocative and readable account emphasizing the years since World War II.

Dietrich, Craig. *People's China: A Brief History*, 3rd ed. New York: Oxford University Press, 1998. A fine study of China's Communist era.

Dreyer, June Teufel. *China's Political System: Modernization and Tradition*, 5th ed. New York: Longman, 2005. One of the best surveys of contemporary China.

Ebrey, Patricia Buckley, Anne Walthall, and James B. Palais. *East Asia: A Cultural, Social, and Political History*. Boston: Houghton Mifflin, 2006. A readable, comprehensive survey.

Gamer, Robert E., ed. *Understanding Contemporary China*, 2nd ed. Boulder, Colo.: Lynne Rienner, 2002. An excellent collection of essays on all aspects of Chinese society.

Kingston, Jeffrey. *Japan in Transformation, 1952–2000*. New York: Longman, 2001. A useful study of Japan's recent history.

McCargo, Duncan. *Contemporary Japan*, 2nd ed. New York: Palgrave, 2004. Provocative survey by a British scholar.

Reischauer, Edwin O., and Marius B. Jansen. *The Japanese Today: Change and Continuity*, 2nd ed., enlarged. Cambridge: Harvard University Press, 2004. A classic examination of Japanese society.

Schirokauer, Conrad, and Donald N. Clark. *Modern East Asia: A Brief History*. Belmont, Calif.: Wadsworth, 2004. Extensive coverage of China, Japan, and Korea in this era.

Schoppa, R. Keith. *Revolution and its Past: Identities and Change in Modern Chinese History*, 2nd ed. Upper Saddle River: Prentice Hall, 2006. Recent study offering an historical perspective.

Spence, Jonathan. *Mao Zedong*. New York: Viking, 1999. One of the best, most readable biographies of this major Chinese leader.

Stueck, William, ed. *The Korean War in World History*. Lexington: The University Press of Kentucky, 2004. A recent reassessment from multiple perspectives.

Tao Jie, et al., eds. *Holding Up Half the Sky: Chinese Women Past, Present, and Future*. New York: Feminist Press, 2004. Interesting essays on many aspects of women's lives in China today.

Terrill, Ross. *The New Chinese Empire*. New York: Basic Books, 2003. A readable recent study that places China's rise in historical context.

Yahuda, Michael. *The International Politics of the Asia-Pacific*, 2nd ed. New York: Routledge Curzon, 2004. Comprehensive study of the changing roles of China, Japan, Russia, and the U.S. in East Asia and the world.

Websites

Asian Studies (http://coombs.anu.edu.au/WWWVL-AsianStudies.html). A vast metasite maintained at Australian National University, with links to hundreds of sites.

China-Profile: Facts, Figures, and Analyses (http://www.china-profile.com). Offers useful information on China today.

East and Southeast Asia: An Annotated Directory of Internet Resources (http://newton.uor.edu/Departments&Programs/AsianStudies-Dept/asianam.html). A superb set of links, maintained at the University of Redlands.

Internet East Asian History Sourcebook (http://www.fordham.edu/halsall/eastasia/eastasiasbook.html). An invaluable collection of sources and links on China, Japan, and Korea from ancient to modern times.

Internet Guide to Chinese Studies (http://www.sino.uni-heidelberg.de/igcs/). An excellent collection of links, maintained at a German university.

CHAPTER **28**

Rebuilding Europe and Russia, Since 1945

CHAPTER OUTLINE
- Western Europe: Revival and Unity
- Western European Societies and Cultures
- Communism in the Soviet Union and Eastern Europe
- Communist Collapse: A New Russia and Europe

▥ **PROFILE**
Simone de Beauvoir, French Feminist and Philosopher

▥ **WITNESS TO THE PAST**
Restructuring Soviet Society

Online Study Center

This icon will direct you to interactive activities and study materials on the website: college.hmco.com/pic/lockard1e

Fall of the Berlin Wall In 1989, as communist governments collapsed in eastern Europe, peaceful protesters climbed on top of the Berlin Wall, which had already been decorated with graffiti. The wall, which divided communist East and democratic West Berlin, was soon torn down. (AP/Wide World Photos)

This [united] Europe must be born. And she will, when Spaniards say "our Chartres," Englishmen "our Cracow," Italians "our Copenhagen," and Germans "our Bruges." Then Europe will live.

SPANISH WRITER SALVADOR DE MADARIAGA, 1948[1]

J acques Delors (deh-LOW-er) faced a challenge. Born in 1925, this French banker's son turned socialist politician had lived through a tumultuous and divisive modern European history, including the Great Depression, World War II, and the Cold War. Now, after holding high economic positions in the French government, he had dedicated himself to building a united Europe. In 1985 he became president of the European Commission, established to further European political cooperation. His goal was to reconcile national loyalties with support for a united Europe. In December 1991, Delors convened the leaders of twelve European nations, already closely linked through a common economic market, in the Dutch city of Maastricht, full of historic buildings. Calling on all his formidable diplomatic skills and communicating his sense of mission, he prodded them to conclude a historic agreement for increased cooperation. The Maastricht meeting realized a dream of European unity that had been percolating among European visionaries, such as the Spanish writer quoted above, for decades. Now Europeans, chastened by centuries of conflict, seemed ready to subordinate national interests to a common good.

Delors asked the national leaders meeting at Maastricht to transform the economic and political alliance begun in the late 1940s and expanded in the 1950s into a more comprehensive union. This meeting on Europe's future took place in the same month that the Soviet Union (USSR) dissolved. With their biggest communist rival no longer a threat, European leaders hoped to link their countries to ensure a stable and peaceful future. They planned to invite some states formerly allied with the Soviet Union to join their union. In theory the new European Union, as the grouping was called, would stretch from the Atlantic to the western frontier of Russia, allowing people to cross borders between member states without passports and permitting trade goods to pass freely from country to country. A single currency, the *euro*, would also unite these states. Persuaded by Delors, conference leaders signed the Maastricht Treaty, and it was later ratified by voters in all member nations, though debates continued as new members joined. While facing bumps in the road, the European Union, given the centuries of European strife that was now fading, was nonetheless a huge achievement, for which Delors can claim some of the credit.

From 1945 until 1990 three themes dominated European history: (1) the Cold War shaped by the United States and the USSR, the world's rival superpowers, each with a political and military power vastly exceeding that of other nations; (2) the rebirth of western European wealth and power; and (3) the movement toward European unity represented by the Maastricht Treaty. After World War II, which had left most European countries in shambles, Europe became divided by the Cold War into mutually hostile political and military blocs. However, while eastern Europe came under Soviet domination in the later 1940s, enduring authoritarian communist governments and struggling economically, much of western Europe recovered its prosperity, ensuring freedom, peace, and the well-being of citizens. The trauma of two world wars had fostered a drive for unity by consensus of the nation-states involved rather than through military might. This movement accelerated after 1989, when the governments allied to the USSR collapsed and communism was largely abandoned, opening the way for a new, interconnected Europe that had to forge a new direction in a post–Cold War world in which the United States held the dominant power.

FOCUS QUESTIONS

1. What factors fostered the movement toward unity in western Europe?
2. How did the rise of welfare states transform western European societies?
3. What factors contributed to political crises in the Soviet Union and eastern Europe?
4. How did the demise of the communist system contribute to a new Europe?

◆ Western Europe: Revival and Unity

What factors fostered the movement toward unity in western Europe?

Western Europe emerged from the ashes of World War II economically and morally bankrupt, yet, made a rapid recovery with aid from the United States. Most western European societies reestablished working multiparty democracies that accorded personal freedom to their citizens. Beginning in 1947, however, Europe was split into two mutually hostile camps, western and eastern Europe, each with a different model of postwar reconstruction and rival military forces. Gradually West Germany, France, and Britain served as the core of a rebuilt, increasingly unified European community and were able to regain influence in the world. The combination of economic prosperity and new opportunities blunted the appeal of radicalism in western Europe.

Recovery from War

World War II had left western Europe devastated in the later 1940s. The war had cost some 50 million lives. Large-scale air raids had reduced major cities to rubble and destroyed bridges, tunnels, and roads; Europe's economic potential was cut by some 50 percent. Transportation, food, housing, and fuel were in short supply. The chaos of war and the redrawing of political boundaries after the war had displaced people from their home countries, including 10 million Germans who were forced to leave eastern Europe, where many had lived for generations, and move to Germany. Emotionally traumatized by the war and the atrocities that had been committed, Europeans also saw their prestige in tatters around the world. War crimes trials held by the victorious Allies in Nuremberg, Germany, in 1946 condemned Nazi leaders to death and declared crimes against humanity, especially genocide, indefensible. A Dutch thinker wrote that the old Europe was dead and beyond redemption. A fresh start was needed.

Economic growth provided the foundation for a new Europe. In 1947 the U.S. secretary of state, former general George Marshall (1880–1959), who had directed the U.S. army through World War II, proposed that, in order to achieve European stability and guarantee peace, the United States assist in restoring the economic health of the world, especially Europe. This initiative, the **Marshall Plan**, created a recovery program aimed at preventing communist expansion and spreading liberal economic principles, such as free markets. Recognizing that economic problems had helped spark World War II, between 1948 and 1952 the United States offered $13 billion in aid, about half going to Britain, France, and West Germany. In exchange, American business enjoyed greater

Marshall Plan   A recovery program proposed for western Europe by the United States that aimed to prevent communist expansion and to spread liberal economic principles.

C H R O N O L O G Y		
Western Europe	**Russia**	**Eastern Europe**
1940 **1946–1989** Cold War **1949** Formation of NATO **1957** European Common Market	**1955** Warsaw Pact	**1945–1948** Formation of communist governments
1960	**1979–1989** Soviet war in Afghanistan	
1980 **1991** Maastricht Treaty	**1991** Breakup of Soviet Union	**1989** End of communist governments

access to European markets. The Marshall Plan restored agricultural and industrial production while bolstering international trade. The rapid economic resurgence from 1948 to 1965, unmatched in world history except for Japan's recovery in the same years (see Chapter 27), also owed much to liberal democracy, modern production and managerial techniques, advances in science and technology, and changes in power generation, transportation, and agriculture.

The British leader Winston Churchill (1874–1965), who served twice as prime minister (1940–1945, 1951–1955), prophecied the new trends for Europe. First, speaking in the United States in 1946 with U.S. president Harry S Truman at his side, Churchill predicted the coming Cold War, warning that his wartime ally, the Soviet Union, was expansionist and required the concerted action of many nations to stop. In words that lived for years afterward, he said that "an iron curtain" had descended across Europe, dividing western Europe from eastern Europe and pro-Western, capitalist West Germany from communist East Germany. This Cold War division, however, as Churchill also predicted, helped stimulate a western European movement for cooperation. When eight hundred delegates met at the Hague, in Holland, in 1948, where they called for a democratic European economic union and the renunciation of national rivalry, Churchill urged them to "proclaim the mission and the design of a United Europe, where men and women of every country will think of being European as of belonging to their native land, and wherever they go in this wide domain they will truly feel 'Here I am at home'"[2] (see Chronology: Western Europe, 1945–1989). The Hague Congress proposed practical steps toward unity, such as creating a European assembly and a court of human rights, and generated what soon became the "European Movement."

The Remaking of European Nations

After the war, the western European governments and politics changed. Europeans made a commitment to sustain parliamentary democracy. This was true for both the republics and the surviving constitutional monarchies, including Belgium, Britain, the Netherlands, and the Scandinavian nations, where kings and queens remained symbols of their people but enjoyed little power. Four major states—France, Italy, West

C H R O N O L O G Y	
Western Europe, 1945–1989	
1946–1949	Greek civil war
1947–1989	Cold War
1947–1969	De Gaulle era in France
1948	Hague Congress on European unity
1948–1949	Berlin crisis
1948–1952	Marshall Plan
1949	Formation of NATO
1951	Formation of European Coal and Steel Community
1957	Formation of European Common Market
1969	West German ostpolitik policy

Germany, and Britain—were the most influential in postwar western Europe. Throughout Europe, new leaders and parties rose to power. Longtime dictators opposed to change were overthrown and replaced by democrats in Spain, Portugal, and Greece in the 1970s. The end of colonial empires, and the loss of revenues from them, also reshaped European politics.

New Politics New European political alignments emerged. Given the frequent conflicts between France and Germany in the past, political stability in western Europe depended on improved relations between these two nations, as well as on German recovery from war. Some leaders sought to reverse these old hostilities. Charles De Gaulle (1890–1970), the crusty general and proud nationalist who largely dominated French politics between 1947 and 1969, imagined France, as he put it, "like the princess in the fairy stories, as dedicated to an exalted and exceptional destiny."[3] But overcoming centuries of hatred, he made French-German reconciliation the cornerstone

Basque Terrorism The extremist Basque nationalist movement, the ETA, has waged a terrorist campaign against the Spanish government for decades. They have assassinated dozens of people and exploded bombs at government targets in cities and towns, resulting in the sort of destruction shown here after one attack. (AP/Wide World Photos)

of French policy. Similarly, the West German leader, Konrad Adenauer (ODD-en-HOUR) (1876–1967), sought a more co-operative relationship with France. Germany's reconciliation with France and its other neighbors was furthered in the 1960s by West German chancellor Willy Brandt (1913–1992), a fervent anti-Nazi who, in the 1930s, had moved to Norway and then Sweden to escape Adolph Hitler's government. Brandt accepted German responsibilities for the war and the new borders imposed after the war, which awarded a large chunk of German territory to Poland.

The improved French-German relationship also owed much to economic growth. Because of its sheer size and central location, West Germany's economy, which rapidly recovered in the 1950s and 1960s, lay at the heart of western European recovery. By 1960 West Germany, now firmly allied with France, accounted for a fifth of the world's trade in manufactured goods, surpassing Britain, which had been dominant in world trade in the 1800s.

New political parties and movements took shape. On the right, parties calling themselves Christian Democrats, which had been closely tied to the Catholic Church before World War II, freed themselves from clerical patronage. Still emphasizing Christian values and protecting the traditional family, these conservative parties either formed governments or led the opposition in a half dozen countries, including West Germany and Italy. But eventually some Christian Democratic leaders became corrupt: scandals arose especially in West Germany and Italy, and the parties had lost considerable support by the 1990s.

At the same time, parties on the left competed for support. Most influential, the social democratic parties, which favored generous welfare programs to provide a safety net for all citizens, acquired more clout than they had enjoyed in the prewar years. Social democratic governments came to power in several countries, including Britain and France, soon after the war and

moved toward state ownership of large industries such as steel and railroads. Eventually most of the social democratic parties, such as the British Labor Party, abandoned state ownership and economic planning for free markets. Meanwhile, the western European communist parties, with whom the social democrats had largely avoided cooperation, declined rapidly, maintaining a substantial following only in France, Italy, Portugal, and Spain. Seeking popular support in these democratic nations, they often embraced **Eurocommunism**, a form of communism in western Europe that embraced political democracy and free elections and that rejected Soviet domination. Despite the shift to Eurocommunism, however, the communist parties lost most of their support in the 1990s, often fragmenting into small feuding parties. By the 1980s a new political movement had had an impact, especially in West Germany. This movement, the **Greens**, rejected militarism and heavy industry and favored environmental protection over economic growth. Women such as Petra Kelly (1947–1992) were prominent in the West German Green Party leadership, helping it appeal to women voters and win seats in the West German parliament.

Western Europe was not immune to dissident movements and other forms of political unrest. For instance, a civil war raged in Greece between 1946 and 1949, where conservatives supporting the monarchy, aided by the United States, defeated revolutionaries who wanted to end the monarchy and establish a communist state. Elsewhere, the desire of ethnic minorities for their own nations spurred unrest, and sometimes terrorism by extremists. A chronic ethnic conflict embroiled Spain, where the Basque people, who live mostly in the north and speak a language completely different from Spanish, have long sought either autonomy within, or independence from, Spain. An underground Basque independence movement, known as ETA (for "Basque Homeland and Freedom"), has carried out assassinations, bombings, and other terrorist acts against peo-

---

Eurocommunism A form of communism in western Europe that embraced political democracy and free elections and that rejected Soviet domination.

Greens A political movement in western Europe that rejected militarism and heavy industry and favored environmental protection over economic growth.

ple linked to the Spanish government. Similarly, for decades in Northern Ireland, also known as Ulster, a territory that occupies a quarter of the island of Ireland but remains a part of Great Britain, the Catholic minority have sought freedom from British rule and the ability to merge the province with the largely Catholic Irish republic, while the majority Protestants have wanted to remain a British province. Over the past half century extremist Catholic and Protestant paramilitary groups have attacked each other and, at times, fought the British army, causing thousands of deaths, including those of many innocent civilians caught in the crossfire.

Dismantling European Empires In the thirty years after World War II, most European colonizers abandoned their efforts to quell nationalist movements in Asia and Africa and started to leave their colonial territories. For example, the British, whose empire had occupied an area 125 times larger than Great Britain, realized that imperial glory was only memory. In 1947 they bowed to the demands of Indian nationalists and recognized the independence of India, and they started a process of decolonization elsewhere as well. The Dutch, facing a determined nationalist resistance, reluctantly followed the British example and abandoned their lucrative colony, Indonesia, in 1950. By the mid-1960s the British had turned over most of their colonies in Africa, Asia, and the Caribbean to local leaders. By the 1990s they retained control of only a few tiny outposts, such as Gibraltar, a strategically valuable peninsula on the southern coast of Spain, and a few Caribbean, South Atlantic, and South Pacific islands. While postimperial Britain sought to balance a special relationship to the United States, forged in the fires of two world wars, with closer links to Europe, it also continued financial assistance and capital investment to many former colonies and maintained a more formal connection with them through the **British Commonwealth of Nations**. The Commonwealth, which the British established in 1931 and which comprised fifty-three states by 2000, provided a forum for the member states to cooperate politically and discuss issues of mutual interest.

By contrast to the British, the French and Portuguese only grudgingly recognized the inevitable. In the mid-1940s nationalist rebellions broke out in French-controlled Algeria and Vietnam, which France attempted to quell at the cost of much bloodshed. In his criticism of France's use of torture against rebels in Algeria, the French philosopher Jean-Paul Sartre, an outspoken opponent of colonialism, wrote: "We are sick, very sick. Feverish and prostrate, obsessed by old dreams of glory and the foreboding of its shame. France is struggling in the grip of a nightmare it is unable either to flee or to decipher."[4] In 1954, unable to defeat communist-led rebels, the French withdrew from Vietnam, and in 1962 they left Algeria, causing 800,000 European settlers, many embittered toward the French government for its withdrawal from Algeria, to flee to France.

British Commonwealth of Nations A forum, established by Britain in 1931, for discussing issues of mutual interest with its former colonies.

Although it retained a few small Caribbean, Pacific, and Indian Ocean islands and French Guiana, France, like Britain and the Netherlands, had to define its role in regard to its former colonies. Eventually France established close relations with most of its former colonies, including an enduring economic connection that critics considered a form of neocolonialism, or indirect domination, since French business interests and advisers remained prominent in these areas. Portugal wasted lives and wealth violently resisting decolonization against nationalist movements but, after democrats overthrew the longstanding fascist dictatorship, granted its African colonies independence in 1975.

Europe and NATO in the Cold War

Beginning in 1946, the Cold War, shaped by rivalry between the two superpowers, the United States and the USSR, influenced European politics and the various European nations' roles in the world. The USSR helped install communist governments in eastern Europe and East Germany. Meanwhile, the other superpower, the United States, assumed the burden for protecting western Europe militarily. In 1947 the U.S. president, Harry Truman (president 1945–1953), formed a policy, known as the **Truman Doctrine**, that asserted that the United States was the leader of the free world and was charged with defending countries, such as Greece and Turkey, that were threatened by communist movements or Soviet pressure.

Strong European and U.S. fears of possible Soviet attack led to the formation in 1949 of the North Atlantic Treaty Organization, commonly known as **NATO**, a military alliance that linked nine western European countries with the United States and Canada. NATO allowed coordination of defense policies against the USSR and the communist states allied with it, known as the **Soviet bloc**, to repulse any potential Soviet military attack across the "iron curtain" frontier. To discourage any Soviet expansion, permanent U.S. military bases were set up in NATO countries, especially West Germany. The Soviets responded in 1955 by forming the **Warsaw Pact**, a defense alliance that linked the communist-ruled eastern European countries with the USSR (see Map 28.1). By the 1980s senior officers in NATO and the Warsaw Pact had spent their careers preparing for a war that, partly because both sides possessed nuclear weapons and were reluctant to risk having their own territories destroyed, never came. Like Russians and Americans, western Europeans were alarmed by nuclear weapons, which could obliterate their cities in minutes, and worried that a nuclear conflict between

Truman Doctrine A policy formed in 1947 that asserted that the United States was the leader of the free world and was charged with protecting countries like Greece and Turkey from communism.

NATO (North Atlantic Treaty Organization) A military alliance, formed in 1949, that linked nine western European countries with the United States and Canada.

Soviet bloc The Soviet Union and the communist states allied with it.

Warsaw Pact A defense alliance formed in 1955 that linked the communist-ruled eastern European countries with the USSR.

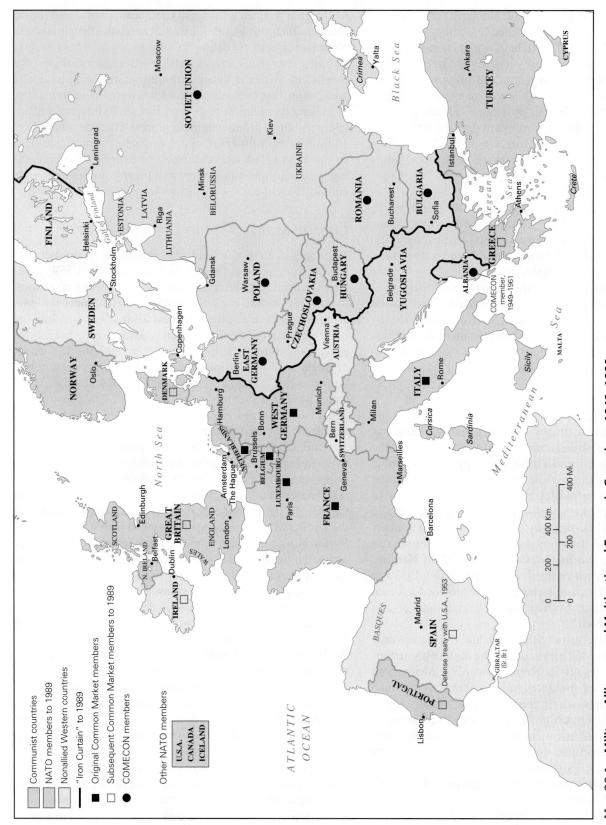

Map 28.1   Military Alliances and Multinational Economic Groupings, 1949–1989

Post–World War II Europe was divided by Cold War politics into communist and non-communist blocs. Most western European nations joined the NATO defense alliance. Western Europeans also cooperated in economic matters. By 1989 the Common Market had expanded from six to eleven members. The Soviet bloc counterpart, COMECON, had eight members.

the United States and the USSR would inevitably destroy Europe as well.

The Cold War and NATO were partly a response to the postwar division of Germany. Each of the four World War II allies—the United States, Britain, France, and the USSR—had an occupation zone in Germany and had also divided up the pre-1945 German capital, Berlin. In 1948 the three Western powers united their occupation zones. Angered by this move, the USSR blockaded Berlin to prevent supplies from reaching the city's Western-administered zone by land through Soviet-controlled East Germany. For a year the allies supplied the city by airlift to the Berlin airport; each day the allied cargo planes landed with 8,000 tons of food and fuel for 2 million Berliners. In 1949 the USSR stopped the blockade and allowed the creation of the Federal Republic of Germany, or West Germany, while forming its own allied government, the German Democratic Republic, or East Germany. By 1954 West Germany was fully sovereign and soon joined NATO.

In the 1960s, Cold War fears slackened in Europe as the danger of actual war faded, leading western Europeans to reappraise their policies toward both the United States and the Soviet bloc. Some Europeans, especially in Britain, were strong Atlanticists and promoted the U.S. alliance, while others emphasized what French president Charles De Gaulle called a "European Europe" and placed the United States at arm's length. Many Europeans grew to resent U.S. power and what they considered irresponsible U.S. foreign policies. Most Europeans opposed the American war in Vietnam, which American leaders justified as an effort to stop the spread of communism in Asia, as well as U.S. interventions to overthrow left-leaning governments in Latin America, such as Guatemala (1954) and Chile (1973). The West German chancellor Willy Brandt, a Social Democrat, began the rethinking of Cold War attitudes in 1969. Although Brandt was strongly anti-communist, his policy of **ostpolitik** ("eastern politics") sought a reconciliation between West and East Germany and an expanded western European dialogue with the USSR. This policy led to a thaw in West Germany's relations with the Soviet bloc and gave hope to eastern Europeans who wanted more freedom. Gradually western Europeans, by building their own military forces, became less reliant on U.S. power and played a larger role in NATO. Despite the differences between Europeans and Americans, however, the Western alliance and NATO remained strong because of mutual interests during the Cold War.

From Cooperation to European Community

As a result of wartime economic destruction, increasing U.S. political and economic power, and the costs of suppressing nationalism in the Western colonies, western Europe's role in the global economic system changed. Between 1800 and 1914 Europe had energized the world economy, supplying goods, services, capital, and people to the rest of the world. Between the

two world wars Europeans still owned enterprises all over the globe, including Indian tea plantations, Malayan rubber estates, African mines, and South American railroads. But during the 1940s Europeans lost influence to the United States. The Bretton Woods agreement on international monetary cooperation, negotiated by representatives of forty-four countries in 1944, reshaped the world economy by making the U.S. dollar, pegged to the price of gold, the staple currency of the Western nations.

Faced with declining economic influence in the world, Europeans concluded they had no choice but to cooperate with each other. In 1949 ten western European nations formed the Council of Europe, which sought to operate on the basis of a shared cultural heritage and democratic principles. In 1950 the Council produced the European Convention on Human Rights, the root of a Europe-wide justice system and court. But some leaders wanted more. The two most notable were Jean Monnet (MOAN-ay) (1888–1979), a French economist, financier, and former League of Nations official who was often called the "Father of United Europe," and French prime minister Robert Schuman (1886–1963), whose wartime service against the Nazis made him a strong proponent of French-German reconciliation; the two men wanted to make further war in Europe not only unthinkable but impossible. To encourage better economic coordination, they devised a plan for a European Coal and Steel Community (ECSC), which was finally formed with the signing of the Treaty of Paris in 1951. They hoped that the ECSC, which brought together six nations, including France and Germany, would be a first step to build a framework for unity and encourage peace in Europe. Indeed, the ECSC promoted European economic stabilization. But some European nations, including Britain, feared loss of economic independence and declined to join.

Building on the foundation of the ECSC, the Common Market, later known as the European Community (EC), was formed in 1957 with six members: France, Italy, West Germany, the Netherlands, Belgium, and Luxembourg. The new organization included a customs union to remove tariff barriers between members, thus opening frontiers to the free movement of capital and labor. The members also set a plan for preserving peace and liberty by pooling economic resources, and they called upon other Europeans to join in their efforts. Soon others did. The EC added Britain, Ireland, and Denmark in 1973.

The EC created unprecedented economic unity in the world's largest free trade zone, but it only slowly generated political unity. The founders, such as Monnet and Schuman, dreamed of a united Europe: societies that depend on one another, they reasoned, won't go to war. But European nationalism occasionally flared up. The EC weathered many disagreements as the member nations squabbled to get the best deal for their own farmers or businesses, and the British, an island people proud of their distinctive traditions and always wary of continental Europeans, periodically threatened to quit the grouping. Every member economy had to adapt to the laws of the marketplace, dumping uncompetitive industries. Some doubters, the "Euro-skeptics," believed cooperation had gone too far. Yet the EC greatly reduced old national tensions. The members eventually established an elected European Parliament, based in

---

ostpolitik ("eastern politics") A West German policy, promoted by Chancellor Willy Brandt, seeking a reconciliation between West and East Germany and an expanded dialogue with the USSR.

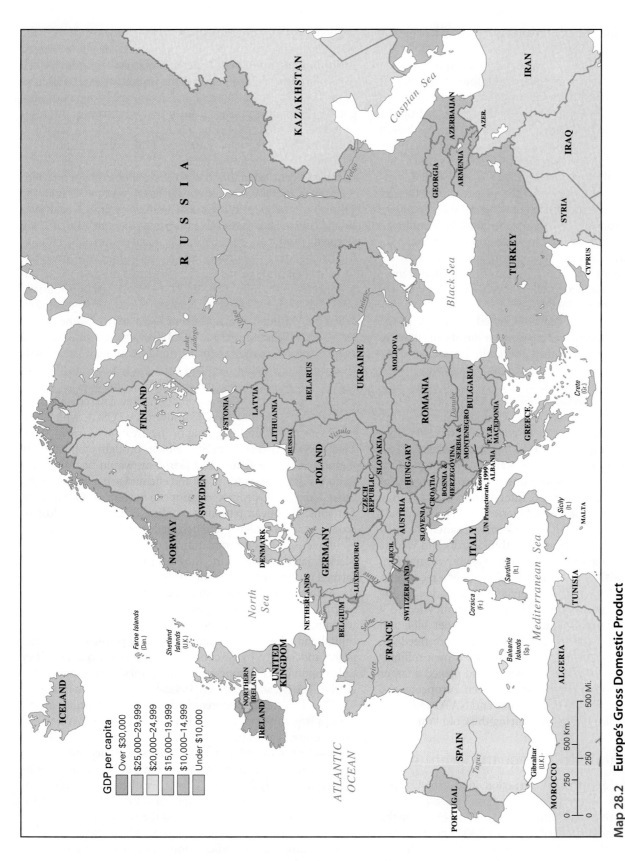

Map 28.2 Europe's Gross Domestic Product

The gross domestic product, or the official measure of the output of goods and services in a national economy, provides a good summary of a nation's economic production. In the early twenty-first century, Norway, Ireland, and Switzerland were the most productive European countries on a per capita basis, while former Soviet bloc nations had the weakest performance.

Brussels, Belgium, to discuss shared issues and to make policies that encouraged cooperation and standardization.

The European Community fostered unprecedented economic growth, creating a consumer society in western Europe (see Map 28.2). The prosperous 1960s spurred the rapid expansion of European and world trade. With higher wages, greater purchasing power, and more available consumer products, families bought automobiles, washing machines, refrigerators, and televisions. More people worked in the service sector and fewer in agriculture. The middle classes grew rapidly, while blue-collar workers shared middle-class aspirations. Consumer markets reached from Europe's sprawling cities into remote villages, transforming them. A journalist's description of an old French village in 1973 revealed the change: "The last horse trod its streets in 1968. The water mill closed down in 1952. The washing machine replaced the wash house—and broke up the community of women—in the 1960s."[5] Europeans invested in railroads using the latest technologies, high speed turnpikes to link peoples together, and mass transit—subways and commuter trains—to make city life more convenient. Yet prosperity did not eliminate all poverty or regional disparities. For example, industrialized northern Italy remained much wealthier than largely agricultural southern Italy.

Despite the growing cooperation and the successes it fostered, western Europe still faced mounting economic problems. Europeans were hurt by decisions by U.S. leaders that led to the dismantling of the Bretton Woods international monetary system. In 1971, with the U.S. economy undermined by the war in Vietnam, President Richard Nixon devalued the U.S. dollar, the staple currency of the Western nations, and ended its parity with gold. These moves destabilized world trade, triggering soaring prices and trade deficits. Then in 1973 European economies were brought to a standstill by a quadrupling of oil prices, followed by a short embargo on oil exports by the major oil-producing nations, which were angered by Western support of Israel. The frustrated motorists waiting in long lines at gas stations showed how vulnerable prosperity could be in the global system. Western Europe also faced the environmental problems common to all industrial societies, such as noxious air, toxic waste, and lakes and forests dying from acid rain, the apparent price of industrialization.

Cooperation also could not avert other economic problems deriving from global economic patterns. The end of cheap energy and growing competition from industrializing Asian nations and Japan hurt local European industries and workers. Factories built a century or more earlier, often decaying and inefficient, scaled back operations or closed, causing high unemployment in industrial cities such as Birmingham and Manchester in England. Jobless young people, living in bleak row houses or apartments and surviving on welfare payments, hung out on street corners, some turning to drugs or crime. By 1983 unemployment rates in western Europe had risen to 10 percent, posing a special problem to those just out of school, women, and immigrants. Some Europeans, blaming their problems on immigrant workers, especially the Arabs and Turks who competed with local people for jobs, sought to have immigration curbed. These feelings gave a boost to rightwing,

anti-immigrant parties. Capitalizing on the economic problems, free market conservatives often regained political power, and once in power, they penalized striking workers and weakened labor unions.

SECTION SUMMARY

- World War II devastated western Europe's population, infrastructure, and economy, but it enjoyed a remarkable period of growth, aided by extensive U.S. funding under the Marshall Plan.

- After World War II, Germany and France overcame centuries of mutual hatred, rightwing Christian Democrat parties competed with leftist social democrats, and the Greens agitated for environmental protection over economic growth.

- A wave of decolonization followed World War II, though the British Commonwealth maintained connections between Great Britain and its former colonies, and France, after struggling to maintain its colonies, maintained economic ties with its former holdings.

- The Cold War shaped European politics, with eastern Europe allied with the USSR and western Europe allied with the United States, but over time some European leaders distanced themselves from U.S. policies and advocated dialogue with the USSR.

- Having been surpassed economically by the United States, European countries joined together in the European Community, which became the world's largest free trade zone and led to increased prosperity; however, the 1970s brought hard times, and European unity sometimes threatened to give way.

 # Western European Societies and Cultures

How did the rise of welfare states transform western European societies?

In the ashes of World War II the wartime British prime minister, Winston Churchill, wrote, "What is Europe? A rubble heap, a charnel house, a breeding ground for pestilence and hate."[6] Seeing the need for change, western European nations embarked on various experiments to reshape their societies and improve the quality of life for all their citizens. The main experiment was the blending of capitalism and socialism. The economic boom from the late 1940s to the 1970s allowed most western European states, influenced by socialism, to construct welfare programs that fostered political stability, ensured public health, and eliminated poverty for most citizens. Gender relations, family life, and sexual attitudes were also reshaped, while musicians, philosophers, and churches addressed the changes of the times.

Social Democracy

The rise of western European **welfare states**, government systems that offer their citizens a range of state-subsidized health, education, and social service benefits, and the high quality of life they fostered, owed much to an influential political philosophy called social democracy. Social democracy derived from socialists in the early 1900s who favored evolutionary rather than revolutionary change, eventually promoting a mixing of liberal democracy, market economies, and a safety net for workers. Since 1945 social democratic parties have governed or been the dominant opposition in many Western countries. They have usually controlled the governments in the Scandinavian nations of Denmark, Finland, Norway, and Sweden and have often governed in several other nations, including Britain, France, and West Germany. They have also been influential in Australia, Canada, and especially New Zealand.

Welfare States   Since the 1940s social democracy has meant welfare programs, a mixed capitalist-socialist economy, a commitment to parliamentary democracy and civil liberties, support for labor unions, and the goal of moderating the extremes of wealth and poverty. As a result of these priorities, workers in northern and central Europe have gained more rights and protections than workers enjoy anywhere else in the world. In West Germany, for example, they received generous pensions and gained seats on the boards of directors of the enterprises that employ them. Whatever their occupation, Europeans have often valued leisure at the expense of work. Europeans boast that they work to live while Americans, who on average earn more, live to work. Surveys showed that less than half of Europeans considered it important to make lots of money. By the 1990s both white-collar and blue-collar Europeans worked fewer hours each year than their counterparts in the United States and Japan. The 35-hour workweek became the norm in France and West Germany. By 2000, the average German spent around 400 fewer hours a year on the job than the average American. Depending on the European society, the average paid vacation has averaged four to six weeks a year. During the most popular vacation month, August, the beach and mountain resorts are jammed, and, with their employees gone, stores often offer limited services. Social democracies remain free market economies, but capitalism is mixed with government regulation.

Citizens in nations influenced by social democracy have received generous taxpayer-funded benefits from the state. Europeans tend to define welfare not just as assistance to the poor, as Americans do, but as protections to ensure that everyone enjoys better living standards and opportunities. Free education through the university level (but with stiff university entrance exams) has helped people from working-class and farming backgrounds to move into the middle and upper classes. Generous unemployment insurance removes the pain of job loss. Governments also subsidize housing for the elderly, while inexpensive, widely available day care allows mothers to work outside the home for wages. Whether married or single, custodial parents receive child support payments from the welfare state. Adding to these benefits, extensive mass transit makes travel and commuting affordable for all. Meanwhile, socialized medicine, such as the British National Health Service, which opened in 1948, has removed the fear of serious illness, providing inexpensive prescription drugs and guaranteeing medical care to all. These benefits have greatly improved public health. Where Europeans had looked to the extended family for support in the early 1900s, now they expect the welfare state to care for the elderly and incapacitated. In addition, northern European nations have the most equitable distributions of income in the world and have nearly eliminated slums and real poverty.

The Scandinavian nations, poor a century ago, have claimed both the strongest social democratic governments and the world's most prosperous societies. Norway has achieved the highest standard of living in the Western world, thanks to North Sea oil and a generous welfare state. The annual Human Development Report, issued by the United Nations, ranked Norway and Sweden as having the highest quality of life in the world in 2004, followed by three other countries in which social democracy has been influential: Australia, Canada, and the Netherlands. In 2005 the Scandinavian nations were also ranked, along with countries such as Ireland, the Netherlands,

Swedish Father and Child   Swedes have been the most innovative Europeans in social policy, including adopting in 1975 a law requiring employers to grant parental leave. While women mainly take advantage of the law, some men, including this man with his child, take off the full allotted time.   (B.O. Olsson, photographer)

---

welfare states   Government systems that offer their citizens a range of state-subsidized health, education, and social service benefits; adopted by western European nations after World War II.

and Switzerland, as having the most press freedom in the world, with the least government interference in the free flow of information. Sweden has been Europe's most creative country in experimenting with social change. Women, youth, and even animals have more rights and protections there than elsewhere. Swedish citizens enjoy housing subsidies, free hospitalization, and a pension that pays two-thirds of their salary upon retirement. By providing child care in kindergartens and preschools, the Swedes attract women into the work force. While Sweden has achieved the world's most level playing field and lowest poverty rate, its services have not dampened economic growth. Indeed, after the 1970s, Sweden has often enjoyed the most dynamic economic growth in Europe. The other Scandinavian nations have also generally enjoyed strong economies.

Economic Challenges Although the welfare states help create political and social stability, when economic growth rates level off they cannot meet all the fresh demands placed on them. Funding the welfare programs has required high taxes, often half of a citizen's annual income, and worker protections make it hard for companies to fire workers, prompting companies to hire fewer people. Workers have enjoyed so much security that they have not needed to strive harder. Thus the shift from focusing on work to focusing on leisure has an economic cost. Furthermore, many people with modest incomes, especially immigrants, live in drab apartment blocks or houses, often far from potential jobs and the best schools.

Beginning in the 1980s the welfare states experienced more problems related to a downturn of the world economy and the resulting recession. For decades governments had paid for social services by borrowing against future exports, a strategy known as deficit spending. The falling export profits that resulted from the economic downturn thus placed the welfare systems under strain, forcing cutbacks in benefits, and also prompted nations to cut spending for military defense. To enhance their competitiveness, companies began downsizing, thus putting pressure on generous unemployment programs. In some countries, conservative parties gained power and began to modify the welfare systems. For example, in Britain, the government led by Prime Minister Margaret Thatcher (governed 1979–1990), a free market enthusiast, reduced health services, with the result that people had to wait longer to receive medical attention. But the conservative regimes did not dismantle welfare state institutions such as national health insurance, which remained hugely popular.

The economic problems, unlike those caused by the Great Depression of the 1930s, did not bring violence or political instability. While occasionally a political party with an anti-immigrant or anti–European Union platform has gained a following, extremist rightwing and ultranationalist forces have remained weak in most countries. For example, the French National Front, led by the paratrooper turned lawyer Jean-Marie Le Pen (b. 1928), won 10 percent of the national vote in 1986 with a platform calling for expulsion of Arab and African immigrants and secession from the European Community, but

since then Le Pen's appeal has faded. The welfare state, which allows even the unemployed to receive their basic necessities, provides stability because it diminishes workers' fear of job competition from immigrants. Hence, even most free market conservatives have accepted the broad framework of the welfare state, although they want to make it more efficient and cost-effective.

Social Activism, Reform, and Gender Relations

Western European societies changed dramatically in the decades since 1945. Although most people have seemed satisfied with their lives, occasional student and worker protests against capitalism and materialism have erupted. During the 1960s leftist activism was especially pervasive. Social movements helped spur new trends in other areas of life.

Social Protests and Movements A serious challenge to mainstream society came in 1968, when youth protests broke out in France that were aimed at the aging, autocratic president Charles De Gaulle, an antiquated university education system, and the unpopular U.S. war in Vietnam, France's former colony. Protest posters urged students to "be realistic—ask for the impossible." Soon university students went on strike, hundreds of them were beaten by police, protesters blocked traffic in parts of Paris, and activists fought pitched battles in the streets with police, who responded with teargas. As public sentiment shifted toward the protesters, industrial workers, demanding higher wages and more say in decision making, called a general strike, bringing some 10 million workers into the streets. Although De Gaulle outmaneuvered the protesters by rallying conservatives, raising workers' wages, and calling for a new national election, the protests begun in Paris soon spread to Italy and West Germany, where students resented conservative governments, staid bureaucracies, rigid university systems, and powerful business interests. Lacking strong public support, however, Europe's student protests soon fizzled; governments did not fall or need troops to restore order. However, De Gaulle resigned a year later after the public rejected, in a referendum, his proposals to reorganize the French government.

Europeans also dealt with social problems common to all industrialized nations, such as drug and alcohol abuse and high divorce rates. But European attitudes and responses to the problems were often different from those in other countries. In contrast to the United States, for example, which has harshly punished drug use and trafficking, by the 1980s western European legal systems generally treated drug use and minor drug sales as social and medical issues rather than criminal ones. Some European countries even decriminalized use of less dangerous drugs, such as marijuana. Other laws in Europe also differed from those elsewhere in the world. Europeans generally opposed and abolished capital punishment, and most European nations enacted strict gun control laws, often banning handguns. The scarcity of guns fostered low rates of violent crime.

Social Patterns Attitudes toward marriage and gender relations also shifted in Europe. After World War II, governments tried to revitalize traditional attitudes toward marriage and the family, such as the view that women were chiefly homemakers and that families should have many children. But in the 1960s and 1970s the changing attitudes toward sexual activity, often known as the sexual revolution, fostered in part by a general access to artificial means of birth control, began to undermine conventional practices. The contraceptive pill, which remained illegal in some Catholic countries until much later, gave women control over their reproduction and sexuality. The sexual revolution upset those with traditional values, such as the rural Spanish woman who ruefully observed the ease of pursuing sex outside of marriage: "If a boy wants to be alone with a girl there's no problem; they go off alone and whatever fires they have can burn."[7] Changing social attitudes also eliminated or moderated the social shame of divorce, extramarital sex, and unmarried cohabitation. All these activities, which had been around for centuries, now became open, a challenge to legal restrictions and cultural taboos. Although sex scandals involving politicians are not unknown, especially in Britain, in many countries political leaders have little fear of public criticism for openly having extramarital relationships or children out of wedlock. Pornography and obscenity laws were relaxed, allowing long banned work to be published, such as the racy 1920s novel *Lady Chatterly's Lover* by the British author D. H. Lawrence. British poet Philip Larkin satirized the times: "Sexual intercourse began, in nineteen sixty-three (Which was rather late for me)—Between the end of the *Chatterly* ban, And the Beatles' first LP."[8]

Inspired by feminist thinkers such as the French philosopher Simone de Beauvoir (bo-VWAHR) (see Profile: Simone de Beauvoir, French Feminist and Philosopher), women's movements grew in strength across Europe and, by the 1970s, pressed their agendas more effectively. An English women's group hoped that "a world freed from the economic, social and psychological bonds of patriarchy would be a world turned upside down, creating a human potential we can hardly dream of now,"[9] a change that might benefit both men and women. Feminists in general wanted legal divorce, easier access to birth control, the right to abortion, and reform of family laws to give wives more influence. Feminists had their most success in Protestant countries, which often adopted their agenda, such as legal abortion. In 1973 Denmark, which had legalized some limited abortions in the 1930s, became the first nation to allow abortion on request. The feminist movements also made headway in Catholic nations. Although Pope John Paul II (pope 1978–2005) reiterated the long-standing church ban on contraception, abortion, and divorce, many Catholics ignored the conservative teachings of their church on these matters. Whether dominated by Protestants or Catholics, governments wrestled with the abortion issue for years. During the 1970s and 1980s most Catholic nations, including Italy and Spain, followed the earlier examples of France, Britain, and Germany and, defying the Catholic Church, legalized both divorce and abortion.

The lives of both men and women were affected by the changes in work, politics, and family life that the women's movements helped foster. Men and women now shared the responsibility for financially supporting their families. By the 1980s women were half the work force in Sweden, a third in France and Italy, and a quarter in conservative Ireland. Women moved into the professions, business, and even politics, no longer male monopolies. At various times women headed governments in nations such as Britain, France, Iceland, and Norway. Even Ireland, where patriarchy remained strong, in 1991 elected its first woman president, social democrat Mary Robinson (b. 1944), who was an outspoken law professor, feminist, single parent, and supporter of homosexual rights. Women political activists made their voices heard. For instance, in 1976 two Northern Ireland mothers, Mairead Corrigan (b. 1944) and Betty Williams (b. 1943), jointly shared the Nobel Peace Prize for their efforts to bridge the Catholic-Protestant divide and bring peace to their troubled land. As they became wage earners, women became less dependent on men. Yet, some changes came slowly. So few women had been able to achieve high business and industry positions even in egalitarian Norway that, in 2006, Norway's social democratic government outraged corporate leaders by requiring that 40 percent of the board members of large private companies must be women.

As a result of less rigid gender roles, marriage patterns also gradually changed. In the 1970s the popular culture still held up the model of the married heterosexual couple, and even rock stars known for their live-in girlfriends, such as Mick Jagger of the Rolling Stones, a popular British group, married, surrounded by celebrities. Some celebrities, such as French rock star Johnny Halliday, apparently enjoyed weddings so much that they changed spouses frequently. But by the 1980s more men and women than before remained single. In 1998, 15 percent of women and men between twenty-five and twenty-nine years old in western Europe lived on their own. In Scandinavia and Germany, the singles accounted for between a quarter and a third of the adult population. Increasing personal independence and mobility fostered small nuclear families instead of the large extended families of old, especially in northern Europe. As unhappy couples no longer needed to stay married for economic survival, the rates of divorce around Europe more than doubled between 1960 and 1990.

Women increased their political power in part because they had won the right to vote and constituted a majority of the electorate. In some nations, such as Belgium, France, and Italy, female suffrage came only in 1945, as the ashes left by war discredited the old politics. Influenced by churches, until the 1970s women tended to be more conservative voters than men. But as once powerful institutions such as the military and church, whose leaderships were both dominated by men, declined in influence, more and more women voted for socialist and liberal parties supportive of the welfare state that guaranteed them and their children inexpensive health care and education.

Homosexuals also began to enjoy equal rights. Homosexual subcultures in Europe, especially in major cities such as Berlin and Paris, had been active since World War I. Organizing to change discriminatory laws and attitudes, reform movements

SIMONE DE BEAUVOIR, FRENCH FEMINIST AND PHILOSOPHER

Few thinkers have had more influence on the study of women and on contemporary women's movements than Simone de Beauvoir (1908–1986), the first systematic feminist philosopher and a prolific writer of novels, essays, and autobiographical works. She was born in Paris to a middle-class family. Her father, a lawyer, and a devout mother with very traditional values sent her to fashionable Roman Catholic girls' schools that taught her, she remembered, "the habit of obedience." She believed that God expected her "to be dutiful." Her classmates aimed at marriage rather than careers. But when World War I impoverished de Beauvoir's family, Simone was pushed toward a career. During her teens she battled her parents for more freedom to leave the house on her own and alarmed her parents by becoming an atheist.

Simone loved the liberating intellectual atmosphere at the Sorbonne in Paris, the most prestigious French university, but found that, to succeed in her studies there, she had to overcome gender stereotypes: "My upbringing had convinced me of my sex's intellectual inferiority. I flattered myself that I had a woman's heart and a man's brain." Graduating at the top of her class, she then supported herself, first as a high school teacher and then as a writer. De Beauvoir began a romantic and intellectual partnership with Jean Paul Sartre, later to become Europe's most acclaimed philosopher, whom she had met at the Sorbonne, and became a vital contributor to Sartre's ideas and books. The two maintained an intense free union, and their lifelong connection provided a model of an adult relationship between a man and woman without wedlock or exclusive commitment. Both had lovers on the side.

De Beauvoir's life reflected the transformation of a privileged woman into a feminist icon. By the late 1940s she was the most famous female intellectual of the day. Throughout her life she enjoyed the new opportunities gained by women as French society liberalized, offering women legal equality, educational opportunities, the vote, and diverse economic roles, but she also saw the limits to these freedoms. Sartre suggested she write about what difference being a woman had made in her life. The result was the pioneering 1,200-page study *The Second Sex* (1949), which challenged conventional thinking on women's issues, becoming perhaps the most influential book on women ever written. The study ranged through biology, history, mythology, sociol-

ogy, and Marxist and Freudian theory to conclude that all women were oppressed by the attitudes of society. It critically analyzed Western culture as dominated by males and argued that women are not born inferior but are made to view themselves as such. De Beauvoir showed how girls saw their future different from that of boys and had their choices, such as in careers, restricted. Men took themselves as the model: "There is an absolute human type, the masculine. He is the Absolute—she is the Other." In her view, marriage denied women's individuality, becoming a contract of subjugation rather than an equal partnership. Her writings greatly influenced the North American and European feminist movements. Later she addressed aging, including the way society dictated roles for the elderly.

Disillusioned by the slow pace of change in gender relations, in 1972 de Beauvoir became a feminist activist, acknowledging her solidarity with other women and arguing that they had to fight for an improvement in their social condition. She became president of the French League of Women's Rights and editor of journals that called attention to problems of violence, sexual assault, and lack of easily available contraception in Europe and the world. In 1976 she addressed the International Tribunal of Crimes against Women, noting, "You are gathered here to denounce the oppression to which women are subjected. Talk to the world, bring to light the shameful truths that half of humanity is trying to cover up." Admired by millions, de Beauvoir died in 1986 at age seventy-eight.

THINKING ABOUT THE PROFILE

1. How did de Beauvoir's personal life affect her ideas?

2. What were de Beauvoir's main arguments about how history and society shaped perceptions of gender?

Note: Quotations from Bonnie S. Anderson and Judith P. Zinsser, *A History of Their Own: Women in Europe from Prehistory to the Present*, vol. 2 (New York: Harper, 1988), pp. 204, 169, 422; and Bonnie G. Smith, *Changing Lives: Women in European History Since 1700* (Lexington, Mass.: D.C. Heath, 1989), p. 519.

Simone de Beauvoir and Jean Paul Sartre   The French feminist thinker Simone de Beauvoir and her partner, the philosopher Jean Paul Sartre, were frequent visitors to the cafés of European cities and influential participants in the lively intellectual life of post–World War II Europe. (Time Life Pictures/Getty Images)

began in Switzerland in the 1930s and, after World War II, in several other countries. Nonetheless, in the 1950s many governments continued to prosecute homosexuals, some of them respected figures in the arts, for consensual sexual activity. For example, in West Germny between 1953 and 1965 some 99,000 men were convicted, and frequently jailed, under still existing Nazi-era laws prohibiting homosexual activity. Laws opposing homosexual behavior began to be reformed or eliminated during the 1960s and 1970s, but combating prejudice took longer. Hence, in 1974 a conservative Christian Democrat leader in Italy, opposing social change, warned that "if divorce is allowed, it will be possible to have marriages between homosexuals, and perhaps your wife will run off with some pretty young girl."[10] As late as 1979 the West German government excluded homosexuals from legislation that paid compensation to minorities, such as Jews, that had been singled out for Nazi persecution. However, most societies developed more tolerant attitudes. Denmark recognized domestic partnerships for homosexuals in 1989. By 2001 most of northern Europe had such laws providing legal protection, and discrimination against homosexuals had ebbed. Several nations, including the Netherlands, Belgium, and Spain, legalized homosexual marriage in the early twenty-first century. Openly homosexual politicians, men and women, served as high government officials or political leaders in nations as socially different as the liberal Netherlands and conservative Ireland.

Immigration: Questions of Identity

Population movements had been a feature of western European history for centuries, but in the later twentieth century this pattern took a new turn as several million immigrants settled in various European countries as "guest workers." In response to economic growth that created labor shortages in northern Europe and Britain in the 1950s and 1960s, people from poorer southern Europe, especially Italians, Greeks, and Portuguese, migrated north in search of better jobs and pay. They were soon joined by Turks, Algerians, Moroccans, and people from West Africa and the Caribbean, who were fleeing even harsher poverty. Meanwhile, many Indians, Pakistanis, and Bangladeshis sought a better life in their former imperial power, Britain, while emigrants left the former Dutch colonies of Indonesia and Suriname (formerly Dutch Guiana) for the Netherlands. By 1974, 10 percent of the working population of France and West Germany were foreign-born. Middle Eastern immigrants worked in Scandinavia, Italy, and Spain.

The immigration reshaped European societies. By the early twenty-first century immigrants constituted 10 percent of the population of Germany, 6 percent in France, and 5 percent in Britain. Major European cities such as Paris, London, and Berlin took on an international flavor. By 2006 London's population was 40 percent nonwhite. Paris became a center of Arab and African culture, including a large recording industry churning out music by Arab and African musicians, often for export to their homelands. Islamic culture flourished in cities such as Hamburg (Germany) and Marseilles (France), where Arab- and Turkish-language radio stations had large audiences. As in North America, immigrants contributed much to European societies. For example, small neighborhood grocery stores run by Arabs served vital functions in French urban life. The Indian and Pakistani sundry goods and grocery shops and restaurants became features of English city life. Observers remarked that the favorite British food was now Indian curry, ironically a dish developed by mixing Asian and Portuguese cuisines, mostly spicy sauces poured over rice, in colonial India for British residents there that then spread widely around the world. People of Asian and African descent were elected to parliaments in countries such as Britain and the Netherlands..

The immigration also posed problems of absorption into European society, especially fostering tensions between whites and the nonwhite immigrants. Over the years, as Turks, Arabs, Africans, and Pakistanis arrived to do the low-paying jobs nobody else wanted and then settled down, they and even their local-born children faced discrimination and sometimes violent attack by rightwing youth gangs and others favoring their expulsion. For example, neo-Nazis in Germany sometimes set fire to immigrant apartment buildings, and young toughs in England boasted of "Paki-bashing," or beating up people from the Indian subcontinent. In response, many immigrants retreated into their own cultures. A British scholar of the Asian and West Indian settlers noted their preference for "the novels that document the idiocies of English social snobbery, the musical forms that sustain the separate immigrant lifestyles, the ghetto life that builds up defense-mechanisms."[11] However, while older immigrants often clung to the cultures and attitudes they brought from their Asian or Middle Eastern village, such as a husband's authority over his wife and the preference for arranged marriages, their children struggled to reconcile the contrasting expectations of their conservative parents and religious traditions with the materialistic, individualistic, secular societies of Europe.

Tensions between immigrants and local-born Europeans mounted further after 1989. Vanishing jobs put both the immigrants and the local people on the unemployment rolls or in competition for scarce work. Despite the economic problems, illegal immigration also increased. In 2001 perhaps 700,000 people fleeing extreme poverty or harsh repression illegally entered the European Union. Since the mid-1990s anti-immigrant (especially anti-Muslim) movements have emerged even in famously tolerant countries like Denmark and the Netherlands, especially after the terrorist attacks against the United States in 2001, which shocked Europeans. For their part, to express their alienation from European society, young people of Middle Eastern, South Asian, and African-Caribbean background have often turned to musical forms from their countries of origin, such as Algerian *rai* for Arabs and Jamaican dancehall and reggae for Afro-Caribbeans. Some immigrant youth have adapted African American rap to their needs, writing lyrics in their own languages. Hence, in France the Senegal-born M. C. Solaar achieved popularity for songs commenting on the lives of young people of African ancestry. Facing particular hostility since 2001, some Muslims, rejecting

Western culture as immoral and criticizing the Islam brought by their parents from North African, Turkish, or South Asian villages as corrupted by Sufi mysticism, have become more devout and rigidly orthodox than their parents. The most alienated Muslim youth, seeking a purpose in life, have turned to militant Islamic groups for direction.

Reshaping Cultures

Enriched by imports from cultures around the world, western Europeans enjoyed a resilient cultural life. The influence of mass culture from the United States became more widespread than before the war. American cigarettes, Coca-Cola, and chewing gum symbolized postwar fashions, while American films and music, especially jazz and rock, reshaped cultural horizons. African American jazz musicians often settled in Europe, especially in France and Scandinavia, in the 1950s and 1960s to escape racism at home; their music appealed especially to middle-aged, middle-class Europeans. North American and British cultural forms, such as popular music, that were linked by a common language tended to mix, prompting European governments to try to protect their languages and culture industries from the powerful Anglo-American challenge by, for instance, mandating how much foreign music could be played on government radio stations. Young people also enjoyed popular entertainments from outside of North America, such as Caribbean reggae music, Latin American dances, and Japanese animated films. Yet Europeans often treasured entertainers who reflected local culture, such as the waiflike French singer Edith Piaf (1915–1963), who was known for her sad, nostalgic songs of lost love and lost youth.

Rock music helped define youth cultures, allowing young people to embrace an exciting, edgy music that their parents often disliked. After rock emerged in the United States in the mid-1950s, it rapidly gained a huge following in Europe, where American rock stars such as Buddy Holly, Elvis Presley, and Chuck Berry enjoyed massive popularity. By the 1960s European musicians inspired by U.S. rock and blues, such as Francois Hardy in France and the Beatles and Rolling Stones in Britain, had reshaped the local music scenes. The Beatles, young working-class men from Liverpool, a cosmopolitan port city, matured as musicians while playing clubs in West Germany and became the symbols of youth culture for a decade. Beatlemania, as their impact was called, reached around the world. Rock became known as "yeah yeah" music in nations as different as Brazil and Malaysia, after the Beatles lyric "she loves you yeah yeah yeah." The music and fashion, such as clothing and hair length, of the Beatles and other rockers represented an assertion of youth identity. But eventually rock music introduced more personal reflection and social commentary, as reflected in such top-selling Beatles albums as *Revolver* (1966), which lambasted the taxman, greedy for revenues, and introduced Eleanor Rigby, a fictive woman who died alone, ignored by society. The Beatles 1967 album, *Sgt. Pepper's Lonely Hearts Club Band*, became the prototype of the concept album, with a linking theme, cross-cultural musical explorations (including use of Indian instruments), and provocative lyrics, influencing popular musicians around the world for decades after.

By the mid-1970s a new style of rock, called punk, appeared that expressed social protest. Although it gained a presence in North America and continental Europe, punk became especially influential in Britain, where working-class youth faced limited job options. The provocative songs of a leading British punk group, the Sex Pistols, deliberately insulted the monarchy and offended the deeper values of British society, much to the delight of their fans. As a leading punk magazine asserted: "[Punk] music is a perfect medium for shoving two fingers up at the establishment."[12] As punk's energy dissipated, it was replaced in the 1980s by escapist dance music. But punk provided a foundation for creative new forms of rock in the 1990s in Europe and North America.

Cultural forms from Asia and Africa also influenced European culture. For example, in Britain the popular **bhangra** music emerged from a blending of Indian folk songs with Caribbean reggae and Anglo-American styles, such as rock, hip hop, and disco. Using a mix of Indian and Western instruments, bhangra became a lively dance music, popular with both white and Indian youth in Britain. By the 1980s bhangra had spread to the Indian diaspora communities in continental Europe, North America, and the Caribbean, sustaining Indian identity and encouraging Indian youth to have fun. The music also developed an audience among young people in India and Pakistan. By the early 2000s bhangra's appeal had widened, becoming a truly world music.

Cultural life was influenced not only by the wave of cultural imports but also by local developments, especially political liberalism and a growing mass media such as television and cinema. These loosened conventional restraints and encouraged a wide variety of views. The creative cinema of France, Italy, and Sweden developed a global audience by depicting the humblest lives and psychological and social dilemmas common to people in a rapidly changing world. Literature also reflected political change. Writers known as postcolonialists sought to escape the world-view shaped by Western colonialism and dominance. For example, the India-born British writer Salman Rushdie (b. 1947), a Cambridge University–educated former actor and advertising copywriter from a Muslim family, confronted Western ethnocentrism. Remembering the prejudice he faced in British schools, Rushdie criticized Western society, especially the Western treatment of Asian peoples. At the same time, however, he challenged what he considered the antimodern sensibilities of Islamic culture. His books *Shame* (1983), a satire on Pakistan's history, and especially *The Satanic Verses* (1988), a critical look at Islamic history, created an uproar among conservative Muslims. Some Muslims, such as the rulers of Iran, issued death threats, forcing Rushdie to go into hiding and hire bodyguards.

bhangra A popular music that emerged in Britain from a blending of traditional folk songs brought by Indian immigrants with Caribbean reggae and Anglo-American styles, such as rock, hip hop, and disco.

Thought and Religion

Philosophy flourished, continuing a secularizing trend that had been strong in Europe for over a century. For several decades after World War II Europeans struggled to understand the horrors of that war, which seemed to contradict the emphasis on rational thought and tolerance that had been building in Europe since the Enlightenment of the seventeenth and eighteenth centuries. In seeking answers some turned to new philosophies while others struggled to reconcile religious faith and modern life.

Modern Philosophy **Existentialism**, a philosophy whose speculation on the nature of reality reflects disillusionment with Europe's violent history and doubt that objectivity is possible, and Marxism, which envisions a noncapitalist future for societies, became the most influential schools of secular thought. At the same time organized religion declined as churches struggled to remain relevant in an increasingly secular society.

The French philosopher Jean Paul Sartre (SAHRT) (1905–1980) and the French feminist thinker Simone de Beauvoir (1908–1986), his longtime partner, transformed existentialism from a little known Scandinavian and German approach into a philosophy with wide appeal. Sartre argued that women and men are defined by a reality that they tend to view as the work of fate or imposed by others. He advised people not to let others determine their lives. Rather, people must find their own meaning, whatever society's values. They cannot banish uncertainty about the world and their place in it, but they can overcome it. In his view, people must accept responsibility for their actions, and this should lead to political engagement to create a better society in which people have wider choices. Sartre himself became active in leftwing political movements, such as those promoting world peace and banning nuclear weapons. To ensure peace and freedom, he encouraged the movement toward European unity. Sartre provided a philosophy that every individual could act upon and that reached across political boundaries. During his life Sartre achieved fame unusual for a philosopher; when he died in 1980, thousands of people attended his funeral.

Meanwhile, like existentialism, other influential philosophies debated the nature of reality. Marxism fostered an understanding of social class and gender inequality, but as a political philosophy it lost many followers after the 1960s. In contrast to Marxism, which offers a certitude about truth and the workings of society, an approach called deconstruction, pursued by the Algeria-born Frenchman Jacques Derrida (DER-i-dah) (b. 1930), claimed that all rational thought could be taken apart and shown to be meaningless. Derrida questioned the entire Western philosophical tradition and the notion, still popular in Europe and North America, that Western civilization was superior to other cultures and occupied a special place in world history. Inspired by Derrida's questioning of accepted wisdom, by the 1990s literature and scholarship were influenced by the intellectual approach known as **postmodernism**, which contends that truth is not absolute but constructed by people according to their society's beliefs. For example, a society's notions of different male and female aptitudes or of the superiority of one literary work over another are not objective but merely subjective attitudes acquired by people as they grow up in that society. Even scholars, postmodernists argue, cannot completely escape the prejudices of their gender, social class, ethnicity, and culture. Other thinkers, among them many Marxists, rejected the postmodernist notion that truth is relative and objectivity impossible.

Christians, Jews, and Muslims While philosophy flourished, organized religious life went into decline. The horrors of World War II and postwar materialism had destroyed many people's faith. Churchgoing ceased to be the social convention it once was, leaving churches in many cities semideserted. Polls in the 1990s showed that, whereas some two-thirds of Americans had a moderate or strong religious faith, less than half of western Europeans did. While 40 percent of Americans regularly attended church, only 10 percent of western Europeans did. Scholars wrote of a "seasonal conformity," in which people attended church only at certain times such as Christmas or weddings. Meanwhile, conflicts between rival Christian churches, once a source of tension, lost their intensity. Protestants and Catholics no longer lived in separate worlds, and ecumenical cooperation among all church denominations increased. Formed in 1948, the World Council of Churches, based in Switzerland, brought together the main Protestant and Eastern Orthodox churches. Appalled by the Holocaust perpetrated by the Nazis against the Jews, Christian thinkers began acknowledging their faiths' relationship to Judaism by referring, for the first time in history, to Europe's *Judeo-Christian* heritage. Although the Jewish population in Europe decreased sharply because of the Holocaust and post–World War II emigration to Israel and the Americas, Jews remained a key religious minority there. Christians had also to deal with another faith: by 2000 immigration and conversions had made Islam the second largest religion in France, Belgium, and Spain after Roman Catholicism.

In northern Europe, Protestant churches struggled to maintain their influence in increasingly secular societies. Often churches paid a price for their close ties to the state. Governments often subsidized state churches, as in Scandinavia and Britain, and church-operated schools, as in West Germany, but many observers believed this government financial support only undermined religious devotion in societies where people increasingly found traditional values irrelevant. Churches funded partly by the state, these observers reasoned, did not need to actively solicit support from believers and so were un-

---

existentialism A philosophy, influential in post–World War II western Europe, whose speculation on the nature of reality reflects disillusionment with Europe's violent history and doubt that objectivity is possible.

postmodernism A European intellectual approach contending that truth is not absolute but constructed by people according to their society's beliefs.

able to generate religious passion among their members. A popular joke about a young British man joining the army, who wrote on his enlistment form "no religion" and was told, "We'll put you down as Church of England, then," reveals that state-supported churches often led to outward conformity or apathy rather than deep belief.

The Roman Catholic Church also had to address the changes in European societies. The Vatican remained conservative for a long time. But Pope John XXIII (pope 1958–1963) began a comprehensive reform with the convocations of church leaders known as the Second Vatican Council (1962–1965), or Vatican II. Vatican II launched the most radical church changes since the Council of Trent in the mid-1500s had responded to the Protestant Reformation. It officially ended the campaign against Protestantism sparked at Trent and reconciled the church with modernity and ecumenism while giving the laity greater responsibility in worship; it no longer required Latin in the liturgy, and it removed blame from the Jews for the death of Jesus. Even after Vatican II, however, many Catholics followed only the church teachings that met their own needs, widely ignoring, for example, the ban on artificial birth control, and some conservative Catholics turned to more traditionalist movements opposing Vatican II. Some Catholic women sought more influence in the church and advocated allowing women to become priests. In any case, every year fewer European and North American men and women entered Catholic religious vocations. Meanwhile, the church evangelized in Asia and Africa, and Asians, Africans, and Latin Americans made up a growing share of the priesthood and religious orders. As a result, Catholic churches in Europe and North America increasingly imported parish priests from countries such as Nigeria or Mexico, and some observers talked about a Third World rather than Western church of the future

Online Study Center **Improve Your Grade**
Primary Source: Vatican II: The Catholic Church Engages the Modern World

SECTION SUMMARY

- Western European governments have generally instituted the welfare state, a mix of capitalism and socialism in which citizens pay high taxes in exchange for an extensive safety net, including national health coverage, generous pensions, and workers' rights.

- In 1968, a wave of radical protest swept Europe, and over the decades European society was changed by the sexual revolution; increasing divorce rates; acceptance of birth control, abortion, and homosexuals; and rising numbers of women in the work force.

- The large numbers of immigrants, legal and illegal, who have come to western Europe seeking work have given many of its cities an international flair but have also led to tensions and problems with assimilation.

- Rock music, originally imported from the United States, became extremely popular among European youth, as

did punk, which expressed working-class frustrations, while other popular music showed Asian and African influences.

- Philosophies such as existentialism, which urged people to control their own lives, and postmodernism, which claimed that complete objectivity is impossible, became popular in postwar Europe.

- Organized religion became less influential in postwar Europe, while long-standing tensions among branches of Christianity faded, Roman Catholicism liberalized, and Muslims became a significant portion of the European population.

Communism in the Soviet Union and Eastern Europe

What factors contributed to political crises in the Soviet Union and eastern Europe?

Like western European countries, the Soviet Union changed after World War II. Western Europeans struggled for centuries to understand Russia. The British leader Winston Churchill called Russia a riddle wrapped in a mystery inside an enigma. For several generations during the Cold War the USSR was the major political, military, and ideological rival to the North American and western European nations. Americans and many Europeans feared the Soviet Union, while the Soviets feared U.S. ambitions and the military power of NATO, viewing themselves as more threatened than threatening. The USSR was the last great territorial empire and enjoyed substantial natural resources while maintaining a powerful state and a planned economy. But while the communists had modernized society, by the 1980s the Soviet system was showing signs of decay.

The Soviet State

The USSR emerged from World War II as the world's number two military and economic power, no mean achievement given the ravages of war in that land: 20 million killed, millions left homeless, cities blasted into rubble, the countryside laid waste. The trauma of that war helps explain the hostility toward the West: Russians resented the sacrifices they had been forced to make because of Germany's conflict with Britain and France. These experiences reinforced traditional Russian paranoia, fostered by two centuries of invasions by Germany or France, and led Russians to maintain a huge defense establishment and their power in eastern Europe, keeping the region as a buffer zone between them and western Europe. While the Soviet political system was rigid it was also subject to stresses that fostered some change over the decades.

CHRONOLOGY

The Soviet Union and Eastern Europe, 1945–1989

1945–1948	Formation of communist governments in eastern Europe
1948	Yugoslavia split from Soviet bloc
1953	Death of Stalin
1955	Formation of Warsaw Pact
1956	Khrushchev de-Stalinization policy
1956	Uprising in Hungary
1957	Launch of *Sputnik*
1960	Sino-Soviet split
1961	Building of Berlin Wall
1962	Cuban Missile Crisis
1968	Prague Spring in Czechoslovakia
1979–1989	Soviet war in Afghanistan
1980	Formation of Solidarity Trade Union in Poland
1985	Gorbachev new Soviet leader

Stalin's Russia   The USSR in the early postwar years reflected the policies of its leader, Josef Stalin (STAH-lin) (1879–1953). Stalin believed that, because of their key role in the victory over Nazism and the Russian occupation of eastern Europe, the Soviets could deal as equals with the West. He therefore left Soviet armies in eastern Europe and helped establish communist governments there. Stalin also kept control of the Baltic states of Estonia, Latvia, and Lithuania, formerly independent nations that the Soviets occupied in World War II. Thus was created the Soviet bloc of nations, divided from the West by an "iron curtain" of heavily fortified borders. In 1949 the USSR gained a key ally with the communist victory in China (see Chapter 27). By 1949 Soviet scientists, helped by information collected by spies in the United States, had built and tested an atomic bomb, enabling them to keep pace with the United States in the emerging arms race.

Stalin's years in power had been brutal for the Soviet people. The paranoid dictator, imagining potential enemies everywhere, maintained an iron grip on power. From the late 1920s through the early 1950s millions of Soviet citizens were exiled to Siberia, and hundreds of others, including top Communist Party officials and military officers Stalin suspected of disloyalty, were convicted of treason in show trials and then executed. After World War II the Communist Party maintained its tight rein on the arts, education, and science. For instance, party officials banned the poetry of Anna Akhmatova (uhk-MAH-tuh-vuh) (1888–1966), who had courageously recorded the agonies of Stalin's purge victims, and detained her in a filthy hospital; they also imprisoned scientists whose research questioned theories favored by party-approved scientists in fields such as plant genetics. Politics now shaped scientific research, resulting in flawed studies. Stalin's government also stepped up Russification, the effort to spread Russian language and culture in the non-Russian parts of the empire, especially Muslim Central Asia.

Post-Stalinist Russia   The death of Stalin, who had achieved God-like status in the USSR, in 1953 sparked dissidence and rethinking, which led to modest political change (see Chronology: The Soviet Union and Eastern Europe, 1945–1989). Stalin's demise had left a void. The Russian poet Evgeni Evtushenko remembered that "all Russia wept tears of grief—and perhaps tears of fear for the future."[13] Stalin's successor, Nikita Khrushchev (KROOSH-chef) (1894–1971), courageously began a process of de-Stalinization in 1956 with a secret speech to party leaders critical of Stalin's dictatorial ruling style and crimes, including the mass terror he had unleashed, which had resulted in millions of deaths. Khrushchev sought to cleanse communism of the brutal Stalinist stain in order to legitimize the communist system among the Soviet people and around the world. The speech circulated underground throughout the Soviet bloc, stirring up dissent in eastern Europe. In Poland workers went on strike, and hundreds died or were wounded when the government suppressed it with force. Twenty thousand Hungarians died in an abortive uprising against Soviet domination.

While it began a political thaw at home, de-Stalinization opened a split in the communist world that led eventually to China breaking its alliance with the USSR in 1960 and perhaps planted the seed for the unraveling of the Soviet Empire and system three decades later. Khrushchev promised that, under his leadership, the Soviet standard of living would eventually equal that of the United States. It never happened, but Khrushchev produced some achievements, especially in technology. In 1957 the USSR shocked the United States and the world by launching *Sputnik,* the first artificial satellite to orbit earth, and in 1961 cosmonaut Yuri Gagaran (guh-GAHR-un) (1934–1968) became the first man to fly aboard a rocket ship into earth orbit, returning to land a hero. In 1963, cosmonaut Valentina Tereshkova (tare-esh-KO-va) (b. 1937), the daughter of a tractor driver and textile mill worker, defied the then conventional wisdom about women's limited capabilities and became the first woman to fly in space. Along with these achievements of the Khrushchev era, however, came some old-style Soviet repressiveness: in 1957 Khrushchev prevented novelist Boris Pasternak (PAS-ter-NAK) (1890–1960) from publishing the novel *Dr. Zhivago,* a critical look at the Bolsheviks during the Russian Civil War (1918–1921) that had won a Nobel Prize in 1959 after being smuggled to the West.

In 1964 Krushchev was deposed, and a much more staunch repression returned under Leonid Brezhnev (1906–1982), a cautious bureaucrat who imposed a Stalinist system in which the state had a hand in everything. Russians still found subtle ways to express their discontent. As they had for centuries, even cautiously during Stalin's time, average Russians often addressed their political powerlessness with humor, passing jokes along to friends and relatives. In a popular Russian joke of the Brezhnev era, a man arrested for shouting "Brezhnev is an idiot" in Moscow's Red Square received fifteen days for hooliganism and fifteen years for revealing a state secret. Brezhnev led the country for the next two decades (1964–1982).

Under Brezhnev and his successors the Soviet state, run mostly in secret by a group of elderly, bureaucratic men, was intolerant of dissent, although less brutal than in Stalin's time. The secret police (KGB) monitored thought and behavior. Most citizens accepted domination by the Communist Party and Soviet bureaucracy as inevitable. Russians, having a long tradition of tolerating authoritarianism, learned how to survive its constraints, cooperating just enough with unpopular policies to avoid trouble. Active dissidence came from a few marginalized intellectuals and artists, who were often deprived of jobs and benefits. Some dissidents found themselves in the remote prison camps, known as the Gulags, of Siberia, where poorly fed inmates spent their regimented days in hard labor. Many died there.

Some of the intellectuals persecuted had made notable achievements. In 1970 the writer Alexander Solzhenitsyn (SOL-zhuh-NEET-sin) (b. 1918), a Red Army veteran imprisoned by Stalin in the Gulags for nine years, was forbidden to receive the Nobel Prize for literature. His novel, *One Day in the Life of Ivan Denisovich*, had exposed the harsh life in the labor camps. Another well-known dissident, Andrei Sakharov (SAH-kuh-rawf) (1921–1989), a physicist who had helped develop the first Soviet atomic bomb but became disillusioned with the government, was exiled to a remote city after championing human rights, democracy, and an end to the nuclear arms race. Sakharov won the Nobel Peace Prize in 1975 but was not allowed to attend the ceremonies. Milovan Djilas (JIL-ahs) (1911–1995), a Yugoslav communist leader turned dissident who criticized the communist governments in both his own country and the USSR, described the contrast between the two great political movements of modern Europe: "Fascism is a nightmare and madness; communism is force and taboo. Fascism is temporary, communism is an enduring way of life."[14]

The Soviet Economy

The Soviets had achieved notable successes, but they had also experienced severe economic problems. The Five-Year Plans introduced by Stalin beginning in 1928 had rapidly transformed the USSR from a backward to a fairly modern society. To encourage more economic progress in the postwar years, Soviet leaders had three tools: the Communist Party, the bureaucracy, and the military. By the 1980s, however, all three had proved inadequate to the task of directing a modern economy and society. The authoritarian party tolerated little dissent and fostered rigidity. The overcentralized bureaucracy often bungled

the planning and management. Officials planned the number of industrial products needed—from steel beams to dish pans—for five years ahead when they didn't know precisely how many they had produced five years earlier. Soviet bureaucrats were cautious, anxious to preserve their perks and power by not rocking the boat. The military, large but inefficient, was held together by brutal discipline, promoted incompetent officers, and wasted resources. In 1987 a West German college student deliberately exposed the flaws by piloting his small, single-engine plane unnoticed right through Soviet air security to land in Red Square, where he was arrested by astonished police.

Increasingly the economy struggled. The Soviets spent vast sums to achieve nuclear and military parity with the United States, devoting much of their budget to a massive defense establishment and heavy industry. The arms industry sucked money from other scientific and technological projects. Soviet factories were unable to supply consumer goods to meet growing demand. Some of the retail economy was illegal and carried out through the black market, where people often bought food and clothes from illegal vendors operating out of backrooms or on street corners. Worker absenteeism and indifference, caused by the practice of paying workers regardless of effort, made for inefficiency. Bored shop clerks often seemed annoyed to have their frequent tea breaks and gossip sessions interrupted by shoppers. The economy also took a blow from failure to innovate high technology. The Soviets completely missed the personal computer revolution sweeping the West beginning in the 1980s. By the 1990s few citizens or schools had yet acquired computers. Although better off than most people in Asia, Africa, or Latin America, most Soviet citizens lived well below North American and western European standards.

The environment also suffered. Industrial pollution led to dying forests and lakes, toxic farmland, and poisoned air. Diverting rivers for farming and power caused the Aral Sea, once nearly as large as North America's Lake Michigan, to practically dry up, and it also diminished the world's largest inland body of water, the Caspian Sea. In 1986 the nuclear power station at Chernobyl in the Ukraine exploded, causing numerous deaths and injuries, releasing radiation over a wide area of Europe, and revealing the Soviet Union's inadequate environmental protections.

When living standards rose in the 1950s, Soviet people turned optimistic about communism. One survey in the 1960s found that most Moscow university students expected to own a car and have a good life soon after graduating. Even U.S. intelligence analysts estimated in 1960 that the total Soviet production of goods and services would be three times higher than that of the United States by 2000. But the Soviet leaders and bureaucracy responded slowly to change and papered over problems. As disillusionment set in, by the 1970s fewer Soviet citizens believed in the communist future. The Soviet people joked cynically: "Under capitalism man exploits man; under communism it's the other way around." In a society that Soviet leaders claimed was classless, the contrast between the wealth of the party, government, and military elite and that of everyone else

Aral Sea As water from the rivers that supplied it was diverted for agriculture and industry, the Aral Sea in Soviet Central Asia lost over half its water between 1960 and 2000. This photo shows a stranded boat where rich lake fisheries once existed. (Courtesy, Internet Raytracing Competition)

was striking. Communism had fostered a favored elite that dissidents such as Djilas called a new class, people who enjoyed special privileges denied to average citizens, such as second homes in the countryside for weekend retreats. Social decay was also evident everywhere: drab working-class lives, rampant corruption and bribery, the shortage of goods, high rates of alcoholism, and demoralized youth seeking access to Western popular culture and consumer goods.

The Soviet Union in the Cold War

The Cold War ebbed and flowed. The tensions between the United States and the USSR reached a height in the late 1940s through late 1950s. During the Korean War (1950–1953), the Soviets supplied communist North Koreans fighting the South Koreans and the United States. The loss in lives in this war, few of them Russian, showed the disastrous consequences of superpower rivalry. Stalin's successors, less despotic than him, promoted a less aggressive policy, known as "peaceful coexistence," toward the West. From the late 1950s through late 1970s the tensions between the superpowers eased somewhat, even though Soviet-backed forces took control of North Vietnam in 1954 and Cuba joined the communist camp in 1959. However, there were also stumbling blocks to better relations. In 1961 the Soviet ally, East Germany, built a high, 27-mile-long wall around the part of Berlin administered by West Germany to prevent disenchanted East Germans from fleeing to the West. However, the wall also symbolized the fears, shared by all communist states, of exposing their people to what they viewed as the corrupting influence of Western culture and values. In 1962 a crisis caused by the secret placing of Soviet nuclear missiles in Cuba, ninety miles from Florida, and by the demand by the United States that the missiles be removed brought the two superpowers to the brink of nuclear war. The Soviets withdrew the missiles, easing tensions. The Soviets also

challenged the United States by helping arm the communist forces fighting U.S.-supported governments in South Vietnam, Laos, and the Philippines in the 1950s and 1960s, conflicts that drew in U.S. advisers and troops.

The Soviet role in the world reflected national interest rather than communist ideology alone. The Soviets generally subordinated the global crusade for communism to the normal pursuit of allies, security, and political influence. To gain allies, they supported nationalist and revolutionary movements in Asia, Africa, and Latin America, often supplying weapons and advice. On the whole, however, the Soviets followed pragmatic policies, usually sending military force into another country only when their direct interests were threatened. They could do nothing when China broke with the USSR in 1960 and became a rival for influence in international communism. Soviet and Chinese troops now watched each other warily along their common border. In contrast, seeing their own military security at stake, they tolerated no opposition to Soviet power in the east European satellites and intervened to protect their allied communist governments. Hence the Soviets moved quickly to use military force to suppress revolts in Poland and Hungary in the 1950s, liberalizing tendencies in Czechoslovakia in 1968, and dissident movements in Poland in the 1970s and 1980s. The **Brezhnev Doctrine** asserted Moscow's right to interfere in the satellites to protect communist governments and maintain the Soviet bloc.

Eventually, however, military interventions proved costly. For example, in 1979 Soviet armies invaded Afghanistan, on the southern border of the USSR, to prop up a pro-Soviet government. But in the 1980s, a rigidly anti-communist government in the United States, along with Arab nations and

---

Brezhnev Doctrine An assertion by Soviet leaders of Moscow's right to interfere in Soviet satellites to protect communist governments and the Soviet bloc.

Pakistan, actively aided the Afghan rebels, mostly militant Muslims, who were fighting the secular Afghan regime and the Soviet occupation. Ultimately Afghanistan, where the mountain and desert terrain made fighting difficult, proved a disaster for the USSR, costing 13,000 Russian lives and billions of dollars. Unable to subdue the opposition, the Soviets withdrew their forces in 1989. The Soviets' capacity to maintain empire was further undermined by economic problems, restless subject peoples, and the cost of supporting a huge military and its widespread commitments. These difficulties contributed to a major reassessment by Soviet leaders of the Soviet government and economy in the second half of the 1980s.

Soviet Society and Culture

Soviet society changed over the decades. After World War II population growth surged, from 180 million in 1950 to 275 million by the late 1980s. The Soviet people were far healthier, better paid, and more educated than their predecessors had been in 1917. Citizens enjoyed social services unimaginable fifty years earlier, such as free medical care, old-age pensions, maternity leaves, guaranteed jobs, paid vacations, and day-care centers. Most people were grateful to the state for providing such economic and physical security. In exchange for the security, however, people knew they had to accept state power and the subordination of individual rights. The benefits provided by the state, often termed "cradle to grave socialism," meant individuals were not responsible for their own lives. These conditions reshaped gender relations, religion, and ethnic relations while also fostering resistance that was expressed through new forms of literature and music.

Social Patterns and Religion The experiences of Soviet women reflected the provision of education and social services. While few women served in the Soviet hierarchy, most women were in the paid work force, in both low-end and highly skilled jobs. For example, among the highly skilled, some three-quarters of doctors were women. Young women in rural areas, where people made less money than city workers, often migrated to the cities in search of a better life. Worried that the floodtide of female migrants to cities would diminish the next generation of farmers, the state tried, with limited success, to discourage the migration. While rural women faced an especially hard life, often not having running water, indoor plumbing, central heating, or access to nearby shops, urban women also faced demoralizing challenges. In addition to their paid jobs, every day women of modest means stood in long lines in shops to buy food and necessities, took their kids to and from school, washed clothes and dishes in the bathroom sink, and often prepared meals in communal kitchens. Meanwhile, women increasingly divorced abusive husbands, and the state legalized abortion. As a result, the average family became smaller. Except in Central Asia the birthrate fell by nearly half between 1940 and the late 1970s. By the 1980s both the birthrate and life expectancy were falling rapidly. While officially promoting gender equality, the state also used the schools to perpetuate the Russian stereotype that women were weak and passionate while men were strong and rational. Sometimes feminist activists were harassed, arrested, or even deported.

In religious life, the state marginalized faith but did not eliminate it. Successive Soviet leaders promoted atheism and denounced Christianity as superstition, and the Russian Orthodox Church, for centuries a key focus of Russian life, became an informal agent of the state; the clergy, closely watched by the secret police, carefully avoided any suggestion of contesting the Communist Party. Still, Russians often attended church and nurtured their faith. In the 1980s, when the state became more tolerant, millions returned to the church, which performed mass baptisms and countless weddings. Several small Protestant sects fought official disapproval. Russia remained a largely secular society, and many Russians remained skeptical of or indifferent to organized religion.

Soviet social conditions and state policies also affected ethnic relations. Relations between ethnic Russians and the diverse ethnic minorities, ranging from Christian Armenians to Muslim Uzbeks, deteriorated, provoking discontent. Restless ethnic minorities chafed at political, economic, and cultural domination by ethnic Russians, who constituted only about half of the Soviet population by the 1980s. In Central Asian Soviet republics such as Kazakhstan and Uzbekistan, the newly built industrial cities attracted millions of ethnic Russian migrants, who monopolized most of the managerial and professional positions. Compared to neighboring regions of Asia, communism did bring relatively high living standards, such as better schools and health care, to Soviet Central Asia. But many Muslim peoples, such as the Uzbeks and Tajiks, resented the Russification of their cultures as Russian language and literatures displaced the local ones and Islamic practice waned. Central Asians were not alone in their disenchantment. The Baltic peoples (Lithuanians, Latvians, Estonians), forcibly annexed into the USSR during World War II, hated Russian domination and the policy that replaced local languages with Russian. Some Jews, who were scattered around the country, sought the freedom to openly practice their religion or to emigrate to Israel or North America.

Literature and Arts Soviet state policies forced cultural creativity largely underground. Intellectuals duplicated and exchanged copies of forbidden books and magazines in secret. Writers had to send their work abroad illegally to be published. Anti-Stalinist poets explored the breathing space between the official line and prison. Both imported and local versions of rock music became a major vehicle for presenting alternative ideas about life or criticizing the communist system. Soviet and east European authorities were often baffled by youth movements and the music they favored. Considering Western rock degenerate and immoral, the authorities subjected innovative musicians to restrictions, although few faced arrest. Russian Vladimir Vysotski (VLAD-eh-meer vih-SOT-skee) (1938–1980), an irreverent singer-songwriter-actor-poet on the fringe of official cultural life, provided a model for expressing political disenchantment without incurring arrest or exile, although he was harassed.

Soviet Rock Band For Soviet youth, rock music became a way of escaping the restrictions of Soviet life. This long-haired rocker from the 1980s wears a shirt with the communist symbol, the hammer and sickle, but the lyrics of rock bands often addressed the problems of Soviet life. (RIA-Novosti)

ceiving freedom as liberal democracy, rock musicians and their audience sought, as much as possible, to live beyond the police and the bureaucracy.

Eastern Europe in the Soviet System

Imposition of communist rule sealed the fate of eastern Europe for forty years. Soviet forces had stayed in the region after World War II, and during the late 1940s the Soviets installed communist governments in each eastern European nation, incorporating them into the Soviet bloc. Political parties were abolished, churches persecuted, and nationalistic leaders purged. In 1949 the communist nations formed COMECON (Council for Mutual Economic Assistance), which more closely integrated the Soviet and eastern European economies. communist rule brought some material improvements but also provoked opposition.

Communism fostered economic development, especially in Romania and Bulgaria, which had little industrialization before World War II. But many eastern Europeans, especially in the more industrialized Czechoslovakia, Poland, and East Germany, aspired to living standards closer to those in western Europe, dreaming of Western-style consumerism. To supply consumer goods and finance industrialization, the governments took out loans and built up huge debts. As in the USSR, increased industrial activity had environmental side effects: dirty air and toxic waste. Meanwhile, while the Soviets treated the satellite countries as neocolonies and exploited their resources, they also had to give them generous subsidies to maintain communist control.

Of all the eastern European communist nations, Yugoslavia followed the most independent path, breaking with the USSR entirely in 1948. communist control there owed little to the Soviets. In 1945 the Yugoslav Communist Party, led by Marshal Josip Broz Tito (TEE-toe) (1892–1980), who had been the widely popular leader of the local anti-Nazi resistance, won national elections. Tito wanted to avoid Soviet domination, arguing that small communist countries like Yugoslavia needed to remain independent of outside powers. Tito's Yugoslavia cooperated with the nonaligned nations while also maintaining friendly relations with the West. For several decades Tito's unique form of communism, which experimented with worker rather than manager control of factories, created enough prosperity and popular support to neutralize his nation's powerful ethnic divisions.

The refusal of eastern European populations to support Soviet domination fostered unrest. After the Soviets crushed protest demonstrations in Poland in the early 1950s, a Polish poet daringly wrote that life was not perfect: "They [the

Starting in the mid-1960s, Vysotski maintained a large cult following among the urban intelligentsia and other Russians for songs that exposed the Russian soul, extolled sex and liquor, and mocked Soviet corruption, hypocrisy, labor camps, and even politics: "But wait—let's have a smoke, better yet, let's drink to a time, when there will be no jails in Russia."[15] Cassette tapes of his concerts, performed without official approval before audiences in small theaters, enjoyed wide underground distribution. After his death from cancer, mourners made his grave a popular Moscow attraction, hundreds of people leaving flowers in his memory every month.

Young people wanted a liberalization of cultural expression. By the mid-1960s some young Russians were modeling themselves on the Anglo-American youth counterculture symbolized by "hippies," wearing jeans, bell-bottom pants, peace medallions, and miniskirts and listening to the Beatles or their Soviet clones. For Soviet youth, rock music, often spread by illicit cassettes, remained virtually the only escape from an oppressive society. Some 160,000 underground rock and jazz bands existed in the Soviet Union by the 1980s. Few musicians dared to challenge the system directly, but, like Vysotski before them, they explored the fringes, mocking the bureaucracy or the absurdity of Soviet life. Rather than seeking to change the Soviet government and its restrictions on individuals, or per-

communists] ran to us shouting, 'Under socialism, a cut finger doesn't hurt.' But they [the people] felt pain [and] lost faith."[16] Poland, with its strong Catholic allegiances, was the most restless satellite, with its workers demanding more public input into the government. The Poles were not the only anti-Soviet people in the region. In 1956 Hungarian leaders tried to break with rigid communism by reinstating private property, inviting non-communists into the government, and declaring the country neutral. A worker's council proclaimed that Hungarians wanted socialism that was adapted to Hungary's more liberal conditions. In response, a Soviet bloc force occupied Hungary and executed the anti-Soviet leaders. But even under the new pro-Soviet leaders, Hungary remained open to the West and was more tolerant of dissent than other Soviet satellites. While the other satellites followed the Soviet pattern of highly centralized bureaucracies, Hungary's blend of state influence and free markets, known as market socialism, created the most prosperous Soviet bloc economy. Hungarians called it "goulash communism," after their favorite dish, a mix of pasta and meat, and also because it provided abundant food.

Other disgruntled eastern Europeans also defied Soviet power. In Czechoslovakia in 1968 the reform-minded leader Alexander Dubček (DOOB-check) (1927–1993), during what was called the "Prague Spring," sought to shift to a more liberal "communism with a human face." Alarmed that the Czechs might start a dangerous trend, the Soviets sent Warsaw Pact troops into the country and replaced Dubcek and his supporters with repressive Soviet puppets. In Poland, the Soviets applied the Brezhnev Doctrine to suppress the independent Solidarity trade union, which openly challenged the communist system. The union was formed in 1980 when, in response to high food prices and growing economic inequality, shipyard workers led by Lech Walesa (leck wa-LEN-za) (b. 1943), an electrical engineer, went on strike. As food prices continued to increase, thousands of women took to the streets, shouting, "We're hungry!" The dissidents then formed Solidarity, which aimed at economic liberalization. The movement was banned after the government declared martial law. Nonetheless, even though illegal, Solidarity had 9.5 million members by 1981 and worked for political as well as economic goals. As one leader put it: "What we had in mind was not only bread, butter and sausage but also justice, democracy, truth, legality, human dignity, freedom of convicts, and the repair of the republic."[17]

With political avenues closed off, young east Europeans used culture, especially rock music, as a protest vehicle. The result was often further repression. Denouncing rock as a spiritually deadening art that must be eradicated, government leaders prohibited performances by the more daring rock bands. Some East German musicians, among them the leading singer-songwriter Wolf Biermann (b. 1936), also a poet and novelist, were forced into exile. Biermann considered himself a leftist but also promoted cultural liberalization and German reunification: "The German darkness descends over my spirit. It darkens overpowering in my song. It comes because I see my Germany so deeply torn."[18] Musicians soon learned how to express their political views obliquely. These attitudes set the stage for greater change at the end of the 1980s.

Soviet Decline and Reform

Soviet problems mounted, forcing a reappraisal of the political and economic system and the nation's place in the world. The USSR had steadily lost ground in world affairs to the United States and economic ground to Japan and West Germany. communist China went its own way in 1960 and became a bitter rival. The war in Afghanistan and the economic subsidizing of the east European satellites drained Soviet wealth. By the mid-1980s the USSR had few close remaining allies outside the Soviet bloc, which was restless. Soviet power in the world had always been mostly military, whereas the United States and its Western allies also had cultural, economic, technological, and even linguistic influence. All over the world people studied English or French, not Russian. Some observers found more power in rock music, videos, fast food, youth fashions, and news networks than in the Soviet Red Army. Young people from Bangkok to Buenos Aires avidly sought blue jeans and flocked to American adventure films; few of them knew or cared much about Soviet life. The Beatles, McDonald's, and the Cable News Network (CNN) were at least as crucial, some scholars concluded, in the West winning the Cold War as was U.S. military power. By the 1970s few Asian, African, or Latin American revolutionaries looked toward Moscow for inspiration.

This declining international influence, combined with spiraling social and economic problems and a stifling bureaucracy, ultimately led to the rise of younger, reform-minded Soviet leaders who introduced dramatic change. The thaw of the 1970s had given Soviet leaders more contact with the outside world and an appreciation of the growing technological gap between them and the West. The planned economy that had powered a largely peasant society into a superpower now seemed a severe drag. In 1985 Mikhail Gorbachev (GORE-beh-CHOF) (b. 1931) became Soviet leader. He realized the nation could not win an arms race because of the escalating costs of militarization. While hoping to preserve the basics of the Soviet system, he understood the need to liberalize the economy, decentralize decision making, and relax ideological controls. However, Gorbachev inherited a Communist Party that allowed no political competition and managed a planned economy, run from the top with little room for individual initiative. With such a rigid system, the Soviet leader concluded, the USSR could never match the United States as a superpower.

Gorbachev introduced a dazzling series of reforms to reenergize the Soviet Union. He developed closer relations with the West, abandoning the decades-long ideological struggle between communism and the liberal democracies. In 1987 the Treaty of Washington between the United States and the USSR lessened the threat of nuclear war by having both countries destroy their short- and long-range missiles. With his **glasnost** ("openness") policy, Gorbachev democratized the political system, including free elections, a real parliament that included non-communist parties, the release of most political

---

glasnost ("openness") The policy introduced in the Soviet Union by Mikhail Gorbachev to democratize the political system.

Restructuring Soviet Society

In 1987 Mikhail Gorbachev, the head of the Soviet Communist Party and government, published a book, *Perestroika,* outlining his policy of economic restructuring. His goal was to transform the inefficient, stagnant Soviet economy into one based on a decentralized market orientation similar to the market socialism of Hungary and China. The new policy gave greater autonomy to local government officials and factory managers and attempted to democratize the Communist Party itself. Causing a sensation, the book was ranked by some observers as the most important publication of the late twentieth century. By the early 1990s, with Gorbachev himself removed from office, the policy was eclipsed, but the book remained a testimony to the problems that led to the Soviet system's collapse. In this excerpt, Gorbachev defines perestroika.

Perestroika means overcoming the stagnation process, breaking down the braking mechanism, creating a dependable and effective mechanism for acceleration of social and economic progress and giving it dynamism.

Perestroika means initiative. It is the comprehensive development of democracy, socialist self-government, encouragement of initiative and creative endeavor, improved order and discipline, more glasnost (openness), criticism and self-criticism in all spheres of our society. It is utmost respect for the individual and consideration for personal dignity.

Perestroika is the all-round intensification of the Soviet economy, the revival and development of the principles of democratic centralism in running the national economy, the universal introduction of economic methods, the renunciation of management by injunction and by administration methods, and the overall encouragement of innovation and socialist enterprise.

Perestroika means a resolute shift to scientific methods, an ability to provide a solid scientific basis for every new initiative. It means the combination of the achievements of the scientific and technological revolution with a planned economy.

Perestroika means priority development of the social sphere aimed at ever better satisfaction of the Soviet people's requirements for good living and working conditions, for good rest and recreation, education and health care. It means unceasing concern for cultural and spiritual wealth, for the culture of every individual and society as a whole.

Perestroika means the elimination from society of the distortions of social ethics, the consistent implementation of the principles of social justice. It means the unity of words and deeds, rights and duties. It is the elevation of honest, highly-qualified labor, the overcoming of leveling tendencies in pay and consumerism.

This is how we see perestroika today. This is how we see our tasks, and the substance and content of our work for the forthcoming period. It is difficult now to say how long that period will take. Of course, it will be much more than two or three years. We are ready for serious, strenuous and tedious work to ensure that our country reaches new heights by the end of the twentieth century.

THINKING ABOUT THE READING

1. What did Gorbachev mean by perestroika?
2. What problems did the policy aim to solve?

Source: Mikhail Gorbachev, *Perestroika* (New York: HarperCollins, 1987), pp. 34–35. Copyright © 1987 by Mikhail Gorbachev. Reprinted by permission of HarperCollins Publishers.

---

prisoners, and deemphasis of the role of the Communist Party. Gorbachev also loosened state control of the media and the

CHRONOLOGY	
Europe, 1989–Present	
1989	End of communist regimes in eastern Europe
1990	Reunification of Germany
1991	Breakup of Soviet Union
1991–2000	Yeltsin era in Russia
1991–2000	Crises in Yugoslavia
1991	Signing of Maastricht Treaty
2004	Expansion of European Union into eastern Europe

arts and invited scholars to talk truthfully about the Soviet past. Furthermore, realizing the ruinous financial cost of maintaining the unpopular communist governments in eastern Europe, Gorbachev made clear he would not intervene to preserve them. They toppled or collapsed in 1989 (see Chronology: Europe, 1989–Present).

Admitting the faults of Soviet communism, Gorbachev also liberalized the economy, using market mechanisms in a policy known as **perestroika** ("restructuring") (see Witness to the Past: Restructuring Soviet Society). But the economic changes failed to take off. The intelligentsia wanted democratization, while the working classes preferred consumer goods, which did not come. Top bureaucrats, including the managers of state enterprises, proved resistant to changes that might threaten their role. Conservatives in the Communist Party and the secret police also opposed reforms that might undermine their power. Soon the Soviet system collapsed.

perestroika ("restructuring") Mikhail Gorbachev's policy to liberalize the Soviet economy using market mechanisms.

SECTION SUMMARY

- Under Stalin, the USSR ruthlessly suppressed dissent, while under Khruschev, it moderated somewhat and focused on competing with the United States economically and technologically; under Brezhnev, it became somewhat more repressive again.
- Although the Soviet economy grew under communism, it suffered from lack of innovation, inept planning, and an overemphasis on the military, and it created a privileged class of Communist Party and military insiders who lived much better than the common people.
- U.S.-USSR relations were strained by the Cuban Missile Crisis, the Berlin Wall, and Soviet support for communist Cuba and North Vietnam, but the USSR's foreign interventions were usually motivated by its national interest rather than a desire to spread communism.
- In exchange for limited freedom, Soviet citizens were offered extensive social services, but many non-Russians in Central Asia and the Baltics resented Russian domination and the devaluing of their own cultures, while Soviet youth turned to rock music to express their rebellion.
- Much of eastern Europe was effectively colonized by the USSR, though Yugoslavia pursued an independent communist course, and citizens of Poland, Hungary, and Czechoslovakia mounted periodic challenges to Soviet rule.
- With the USSR losing ground economically and culturally, Soviet leader Mikhail Gorbachev introduced reforms designed to democratize the USSR, to liberalize its economy, and to allow eastern European countries greater self-determination.

◆ Communist Collapse: A New Russia and Europe

How did the demise of the communist system contribute to a new Europe?

For four decades the Cold War and the iron curtain had provided the context for both western and eastern European politics. With the breakup of the communist bloc of nations in 1989 and the USSR in 1991, the political and economic face of Russia and the former Soviet territories, eastern Europe, and western Europe was reshaped. The collapse of these communist regions created hope but also uncertainties. Russia struggled to rebuild and to revive its power, but the capitalism introduced proved destabilizing. While Yugoslavia was torn apart by wars and Germany was reunited, Europeans had to redefine their identity. Western Europe pushed toward unification, seeking to include some of eastern Europe as well, but it still had to resolve the conflicting forces of nationalism and

cooperation. Most Europeans now chose governments through multiparty elections and pursued individual freedom. By the beginning of the twenty-first century, Europe, though no longer the world leader it had been for several centuries, still helped shape the age of globalization.

A New Russia and New Nations

A major development of twentieth-century history was the sudden collapse of the Soviet empire and communism in Europe. In 1985 there had been 5 million Soviet soldiers stationed from East Germany to Siberia's Pacific coast, symbolizing the reach of imperial Soviet power. Six years later the Soviet Union and its satellite nations had unraveled, without a shot being fired. Though the collapse was not a complete surprise, its pace was astonishing. While outside factors, including east European unrest and escalating U.S. defense spending that was hard for the Soviets to match, played a role in fostering the collapse, Soviet economic decline was probably the decisive cause. The result of the collapse was a Russia blending new ideas from the capitalist, democratic West with Soviet-era traditions.

Post-Soviet Russia The collapse showed the failure of the Soviet system, which was founded on Leninism or one-party rule and was strongly shaped by the political repression and centralized economy of Stalinism. Democratic governments and decentralized capitalism, dominant in North America, western Europe, and Japan, had adjusted better to global changes than the planned economies of communist states, and nationalist yearnings among non-Russians within the empire had sapped the foundation of empire. Mikhail Gorbachev's greatest contribution was to face up to the fact of failure. By 1991 Gorbachev, unable to control the forces unleashed, had lost his credibility and resigned as the Communist Party leader, and he was replaced by Boris Yeltsin (YELT-sin) (b. 1931), a communist bureaucrat turned reformer who had strong U.S. support. Yeltsin ended seven decades of communist rule by outlawing the Communist Party. Russians who welcomed the party's demise toppled statues of Lenin and restored czarist names to cities that had been renamed during the Soviet era. Leningrad, for example, once again became St. Petersburg.

Yeltsin acquiesced in the breakup of the USSR itself, a symbol of the nation's demise as a superpower, while maintaining the unity of the largest Soviet republic, Russia, which stretched from the Baltic Sea through ten time zones to the eastern tip of Siberia, only a few miles from Alaska (see Map 28.3). Glasnost had opened a Pandora's Box. Ethnic hatreds, long suppressed by military force or alleviated by the government-provided safety net, soon exploded to the surface. In 1991 all of the fourteen Soviet republics outside of Russia, from Lithuania and the Ukraine in the west to Kyrgyzstan in eastern Turkestan, declared their independence, sometimes under anti-Russian leaders. However, many of the former Soviet republics were now led by strongmen, former communist officials whose autocratic ruling style and intolerance of dissent resembled the old Soviet system.

Map 28.3　The Dissolution of the Soviet Union
In 1991 the leaders of Russia, who had abandoned communism, allowed the other fourteen republics to leave the Soviet Union, bringing an end to a vast federation that had endured for over seven decades. Even without the fourteen republics, Russia remained the world's largest nation in geographical size, stretching across ten time zones from the Pacific Ocean to the Baltic Sea.

Online Study Center　**Improve Your Grade**　Interactive Map: Russia and the Successor States

Most of the new states have struggled to achieve economic self-sufficiency and political stability. Some states have been engulfed in conflict between rival ethnic or nationalist groups or have fought each other over territorial claims, as did Christian Armenia and Muslim Azerbaijan. In three of the former Soviet republics—Georgia, Ukraine, and Kyrgyzstan—what observers called "colored revolutions" because their proponents symbolized their cause with a color, such as orange in the Ukraine, pro-democracy activists, with U.S. and western European encouragement, forced out dictatorial regimes. But the results of revolutions are usually unpredictable and those encouraged by foreign governments face a legitimacy problem. The new governments soon disappointed their supporters and it remained unclear whether the colored revolutions would lead to long-term political improvements. In Central Asia, inhabited largely by Muslims, some nominal and others devout in their faith, militant Muslims have launched insurgencies against the secular post-Soviet governments, seeking to replace them with Islamic states. Indeed, Islam gained support among the disenchanted and marginalized, especially jobless young men, in Central Asia. Islamic fervor has forced or prompted many women to don the headscarf or veil and to dress and be-

have modestly. Meanwhile, millions of ethnic Russians in the former Soviet republics faced resentment for their relative affluence and ties to the former colonizer. In Latvia, for example, the indigenous Lett people make up only half the population: Russians constitute a third. The Latvian government now requires everyone to learn the Latvian language, which was marginalized under Soviet rule.

Yeltsin had difficulty solving Russia's problems in the 1990s. Hoping to end economic stagnation, he took the advice of Russian free market enthusiasts and of U.S. advisers, who often knew little of Russian culture, and introduced a strategy known as "shock therapy": rapid conversion of the planned economy to market capitalism. This produced more consumer goods and a growing middle class but created other problems. Party officials converted the enterprises they managed into their own private companies, becoming Russia's new capitalists. Organized crime groups and a few well-placed former communists, known as **oligarchs**, amassed enough property and

oligarchs　Well-placed former communists who amassed enough wealth to gain control of major segments of the post–Soviet Russian economy.

wealth to gain control of major segments of the Russian economy. At the same time, Yeltsin faced secession movements within the Russian federation, especially in Chechnya, a largely Muslim Caucasus territory that Russia had annexed in the 1870s. In 1994 this oil-rich region declared independence. Although oil was also produced elsewhere in Russia, Yeltsin feared that recognizing Chechnya's independence would encourage other secession movements. Using military force, he therefore tried to crush the Chechen separatists, sucking the Red Army into a quagmire with thousands of casualties on both sides.

The economic pain of the Russian people was widespread. Millions of workers lost their jobs as inefficient, obsolete Soviet industries closed. More women than men lost their jobs, costing women income and social status. Some male leaders reemphasized the Soviet era ideal of men as soldiers and women as working mothers. Arguing that the communists had destroyed the family by encouraging women to work, conservatives advocated that women stay at home and tend to family obligations rather than taking jobs. With the end of free higher education, families preferred to devote their limited money for schooling on their sons. Some desperate women turned to prostitution for survival. Even when their enterprises did not close, factory workers, miners, and state employees, such as teachers, were often not paid for years. Yeltsin dismantled parts of the welfare state. As a result of reductions in health care, declining incomes, and the increasing tendency, especially among men, to escape worry through heavy drinking and illegal drug use, public health deteriorated and men's life expectancy dropped from sixty-four in 1990 to fifty-nine in 2002. By 1992 inflation was 2,500 percent, devastating people who lived on pensions and fixed incomes. According to a popular local joke, "All the good things the communists said about communism were false, but all the bad things they said about capitalism were true."

Russia Today In 2000, with the Russian economy near collapse and free markets discredited, Yeltsin resigned in disgrace and was replaced by Vladimir Putin (b. 1952), who ended shock therapy and changed the nation's direction. A former secret police colonel who kept a portrait of the modernizing eighteenth-century czar Peter the Great in his office, Putin supported capitalism and democratic reforms, including multiparty elections, but also pursued policies that were more authoritarian and nationalist than Yeltsin's. Political liberalism faded as Putin took control of much of the media, seizing or muffling opposition newspapers and television stations, and prosecuting some oligarchs for corruption. The state has also taken over many large private companies, turning the economy into a form of state capitalism not unlike Meiji Japan. Company managers profit while the public pays for losses. The economy made a modest recovery because of improved tax collection and higher prices for two leading Russian exports, oil and natural gas. Putin outmaneuvered rivals, including the discredited pro-U.S. free market advocates, the rebuilt communist Party, and extreme rightwing nationalists.

Putin brought back stability after fifteen years of turbulence, fostering a Russia that mixed the old autocratic government with a new, more outward-looking attitude. The Russian Orthodox Church, for centuries closely connected to Russian national identity and political power, regained some of the influence it had lost under communism. Within the church leadership, liberals promoted a tolerant and ecumenical view while conservatives largely denounced ecumenism. The extreme church conservatives supported anti-Semitic, anti-Muslim views and a return of the Russian monarchy. Yet, in many parts of Russia, Muslims—some 15 percent of the nation's population—and Christians have peacefully adapted to each other, living in harmony. Putin also sought good relations with Germany, France, the United States, and China. In Putin's Russia, however, the contrasts between rich and poor became stark. While elegantly dressed men and women in Moscow cavorted in fine restaurants and glitzy casinos, towns often went without heat and power. Corruption, poverty, unaccountability, weak legal institutions, and the festering war in Chechnya stifled development. Russia still had the world's third largest military budget, but it was only a fifth that of the United States. Polls showed that a majority of Russians preferred the communist years, especially under Leonid Brezhnev, to the new Russia, and many people expressed nostalgia for Stalin and Lenin. In surveying the post-Soviet era, a respected Russian historian harked back to Peter the Great and Catherine the Great, advising Russians, "Our future lies in openness to the entire world and in enlightenment."[19] It remained unclear whether Russia would follow that path.

The New Eastern Europe

The changes in the USSR resonated throughout eastern Europe. In the late 1980s the Soviet leader, Mikhail Gorbachev, who admired the Hungarian market socialism model, had begun promoting reform in eastern European countries, since the USSR could no longer afford to rescue their stagnant economies. When it became clear that the USSR was no longer willing to protect the corrupt, largely unpopular eastern European communist governments, they began to fall like dominoes. Democratic movements once underground surfaced. Hungary adopted a democratic system, Solidarity came to power in Poland, and East Germans voted with their feet by streaming across the border into West Germany, an exodus that led to the dismantling of the Berlin Wall. People around the world could watch on television as Berliners gleefully knocked down the Berlin Wall, the symbol of Cold War division, and carried off its bricks as souvenirs. Soon the East German regime and the other east European communist governments had collapsed or been overthrown. In Czechoslovakia, the playwright and former rock group lyricist, Václav Havel (vax-LAV hah-VEL) (b. 1936), who had been frequently arrested for his prodemocracy activities and whose hero was the eccentric American rock star Frank Zappa, was elected president after massive demonstrations forced the communist leaders to resign in a largely peaceful transfer of power known as the "Velvet Revolution." Havel announced, "Your government, my people, has been returned to you."[20]

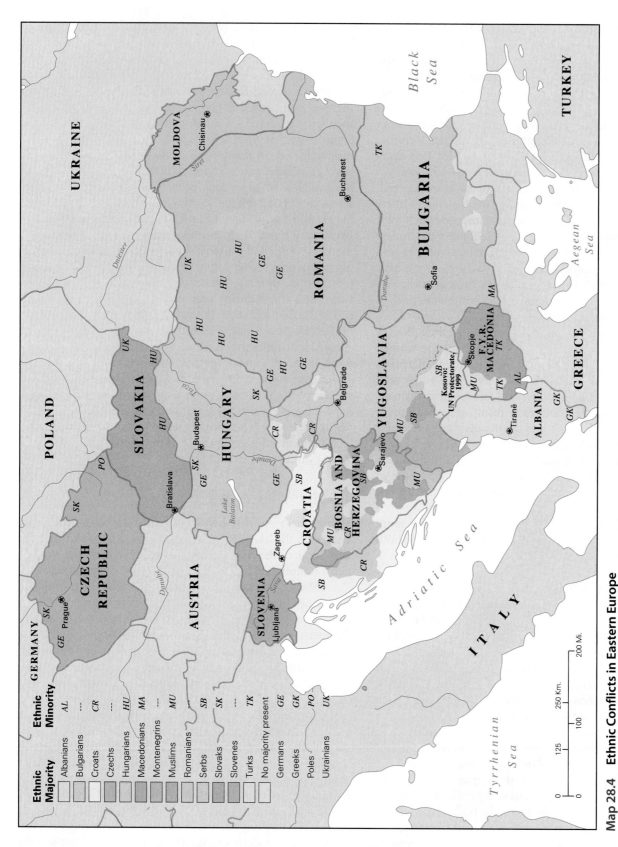

Map 28.4　Ethnic Conflicts in Eastern Europe
Many of the nations in central and eastern Europe contain substantial ethnic minorities, and tensions between various groups have often led to conflict. In Yugoslavia, the conflicts between the major ethnic groups—Serbs, Croats, Bosnian Muslims, and Albanians—led to violence and civil war at the end of the twentieth century.

Democratic or semidemocratic governments were installed, seeking to replace centralized planned economies with market forces. Allowed to elect their governments, east Europeans took up voting enthusiastically. Yet they also experienced the negatives of change, especially when reformers did not anticipate the results of their policies. As in the former Soviet Union, the end of communism uncorked ethnic hatreds and rivalries going back centuries. For example, Slovaks seceded from the Czechs, forming their own country, while Romanians repressed the large Hungarian minority. Several countries persecuted or avoided providing services, such as schools, to the Romany (Gypsies), and prejudice against Jews intensified.

The rapid move to capitalism, while providing abundant consumer goods, also proved destabilizing. Critics wrote of shock without therapy. Millions were thrown out of work as obsolete factories closed; western European or North American companies bought many of the remaining enterprises. Dazzled by the Western consumer goods just over the border, east Europeans may have misunderstood the risks that came with Western-style capitalism. Shops were full of attractive goods, but few people had the money to buy them. Only Poland and the Czech republic enjoyed robust economic growth. In addition, certain protections of the communist welfare system, such as free education, health care, and subsidized housing, were removed, causing misery. Finally, by 2000, salaries caught up with prices some places, but pockets of high unemployment remained and the rich-poor gap widened.

The political environment changed. Diverse political parties competed for power. Capitalizing on a widespread desire for rebuilding the social safety net, former Communist Party members who now called themselves reform communists, although their views resembled social democracy, won some national elections, especially in Poland and Hungary. They competed for power with free market advocates, pro-Western liberals, and rightwing nationalists. In a striking repudiation of the Soviet legacy, reform communists often supported joining the European Union and even the NATO military alliance. Anticommunists had few regrets of the changes since 1989, however jarring they were. For example, Adam Michnik, a leader of Polish Solidarity, reflecting on the struggles against communism, concluded that "without the slightest hesitation it is much better to live in a country that is democratic, prosperous and thus boring"[21] than in other types of countries.

The greatest instability came to Yugoslavia, a federation of states that self-destructed in bloody civil wars between ethnic groups (see Map 28.4). Created artificially for political convenience by diplomats after World War I, Yugoslavia contained antagonistic ethnic and religious groups. The largest, the nationalistic Orthodox Serbs, wanted to dominate the federation, while the Catholic Croats and Slovenians and the Bosnian and Albanian Muslims wanted independence for the regions they dominated. After the long-term federal leader, Tito, the product of a mixed Croat-Serb marriage whose autocratic policies limited dissent and kept the lid on ethnic hatreds, died in 1980, Yugoslavia became a seething cauldron of ethnic conflict.

The Velvet Revolution Protesters took to the streets in Prague, Czechoslovakia, to protest communist government and demand democracy. These protests, known as the Velvet Revolution for their peaceful nature, were led by Václav Havel, pictured on the poster carried by a protester. (Peter Turnley/Corbis)

The violence began in 1991, when the Serb-dominated Yugoslav army tried to stop two states, Slovenia and Croatia, from breaking away from the federation. In response, the United Nations sent in peacekeeping troops to secure their independence. In 1992 the Muslim majority in another Yugoslav state, Bosnia, declared independence, a move opposed by the minority Serbs and Croats in the state. Bosnian Serb militias, aided covertly by the largest Yugoslav state, Serbia, massacred thousands of Muslims, introducing a new term for genocide, "ethnic cleansing," and leading the United Nations to send more peacemakers. As the violence continued, U.S. air strikes under NATO auspices forced the Serbs to accept a peace treaty in 1995. The Bosnia conflict had killed 200,000 people and generated 4 million refugees. In 1999 violence returned when the Albanian majority in Kosovo, the southern region of Serbia, revolted and the Serbs responded with ferocity, prompting another NATO imposed settlement in 2000. Thousands of NATO troops remained in Bosnia and Kosovo, a symbol of eastern Europe's unresolved challenges.

Toward European Unity

Two themes have dominated western Europe in the years after 1989. One was the reunification of Germany. With the fall of communism and the Berlin Wall, the East German state collapsed and Germany was quickly reunified in 1990, but the financial costs proved burdensome and the results have satisfied neither West nor East Germans. Despite Germany's problems, Europeans have continued to move toward unity, a second theme. Yet, the movement has also faced setbacks.

The European Union The hasty German reunification disappointed its proponents. For many East Germans, merging with the prosperous West Germany promised access to a materially comfortable life they could only dream of before. But reunification cost billions and threw the German economy into a tailspin. Before reunification West Germany had enjoyed a long boom. A decade later, however, the reunified nation of 80 million people, suffering from Europe's slowest economic growth, was stuck in deep recession. Since Germany has western Europe's largest economy, the engine of the European Community, the German slump has dragged down the rest of Europe. Many workers in the former East Germany have lost jobs as obsolete factories have been closed or sold to West Germans, who often downsize the work force to make them more profitable. By 2004 the unemployment rate in the east was twice as high as in the west. Some disillusioned youth have turned to rightwing, often neo-Nazi, groups to express their anger. These extremist young people often favor local heavy metal rock groups whose songs promote hatred of foreigners and immigrants they see as taking jobs and maintaining alien cultures.

Worried by Germany's problems, western European leaders believed that hastening unification was the best strategy to stabilize post-communist Europe. The Maastricht Treaty, discussed in the chapter opener, which recognized a single currency, the euro, and a central bank, set a goal of achieving economic and monetary union by 2000. It required budgetary and wage restraint as a prelude to monetary union. The treaty pledged to promote balanced and sustainable economic progress by strengthening economic and social cohesion. By 2002, eleven of fifteen signers of the treaty had adopted the euro as their currency, an index of unity. European unity was also aided by other factors. Millions of Europeans were multilingual, moving easily between cultures, and young Europeans often studied in other European countries. The cosmopolitanism in turn influenced the arts. For instance, the popular Greek singer Nana Mouskeri (NA-na mouse-KUR-ee) gained a large international audience by recording in English, French, German, and Spanish. The Eurotunnel, which stretched ninety-four miles under the English Channel and made possible a three-hour train ride from London to Paris, symbolized the decline of both political and cultural borders.

The European Union (EU) doubled its membership from twelve nations in 1993 to twenty-five in 2004. In 1995 Sweden, Finland, and Austria joined, followed in 2004 by various eastern European nations, including the Czech Republic, Poland, and Hungary. The Danish prime minister told prospective new EU members: "In 1989 brave and visionary people brought about the collapse of the Berlin Wall. They could no longer tolerate the forced division of Europe. Today we are giving life to their hopes."[22] With the new members the EU became a bloc of nearly 400 million people encompassing most of Europe and enjoying a combined economic power equal to that of the United States. Some of the members, such as Sweden and Ireland, once one of Europe's poorest countries but now often known as the Celtic Tiger because its rapid growth resembled that of the "Little Tiger" nations of Southeast Asia (see

European Economic Power Business and political leaders from India and the European Union met in a summit in 2005 to increase trade relations, reflecting the growing economic power of both India and western Europe.
(AP/Wide World Photos)

Chapter 31), have continued to show steady economic growth. Conducting a quarter of the world's commerce, the EU became one of the three dominant economic forces in the world, along with the United States and Japan. Some observers spoke of a tripolar world led by the United States, the EU, and East Asia (especially China and Japan).

Challenges to Unity However, the European Union hit several major road bumps. Critics had long called the EU a faceless bureaucracy with innumerable rules that compromised national independence and threatened national traditions. Indeed, two of Europe's most prosperous nations, Norway and Switzerland, declined membership, fearing the loss of national identity and the cost of subsidizing poorer members. The EU leaders have been cautious in admitting those former Soviet bloc states that have weak economies and autocratic leaders. Turkey, a largely Muslim nation, has long sought membership, fostering a EU debate about how to define Europe and whether non-Christian nations have a role in it. This debate spilled over into the effort by European diplomats to prepare a constitution for the Union. Amid much controversy, the constitution proposed in 2004 rejected any mention of Europe's Christian heritage, a reflection of the changes affecting European societies during the twentieth century. But the voters in each member nation had to approve the document. In 2005 voters in two of the most pro-unity countries, France and the Netherlands, fearing loss of control to the EU bureaucracy, shocked EU leaders by rejecting the constitution. This rejection raised questions about the EU's future.

Increasing unity did not resolve, and may have contributed to, political, economic, and social problems caused by a changing global economy. The economic austerity policies of the 1990s unsettled welfare states and provoked government changes. Social democrats, who had governed eleven of the sixteen western European nations in the early 1990s, now jockeyed with centrists, free market conservatives, Greens, anti-immigrant nationalists, and the fading communists for power. Attempts to roll back social benefits sometimes set off massive protests and long strikes. While many Europeans preferred to maintain what they termed the social market economy, meaning the welfare state and an economic system that guaranteed generous leisure time, even at the cost of slower economic growth, both the German and French governments replaced the 35-hour workweek with the 40-hour workweek to increase their economic competitiveness. Yet, some large companies continued to downsize and cut or export jobs. In 2006 thousands in France rioted against loosening job protections. Some observers compared Europe's social market economies and their sluggish growth unfavorably with the dynamic U.S. economy and predicted Europe would continue to lose ground and sink into irrelevance. Others disagreed, noting that many European nations have nearly as high a per capita income as the U.S., less inequality, a greater commitment to sustainable development and quality of life for all, and, collectively, a larger Gross Development Product, the total production of goods and services.

Europeans also faced other challenges. By 2000 Europe, a century earlier overcrowded and the world's greatest exporter of people, had a declining population, due mainly to the world's lowest birthrate: 1.2 children per woman. Yet, concerned about a much higher birth rate among Muslims, Europeans became increasingly hostile to immigration from the Middle East. Tensions simmered and in 2005 rioting and vandalism by young Arab and African residents in France, many of them unemployed, caused much damage and raised the issues of what sort of integration of immigrants into European societies was possible. The European population decline also posed a long-term economic problem, since, with more people retiring from than entering the work force, younger workers had more responsibility for financing government services, such as pensions and health care, for the growing population of elderly. The problems contributed to widespread political disenchantment. By the early twenty-first century an anti-incumbent mood and strong anti-U.S. sentiments had taken hold, often causing voters to reject the governing parties. Anti-immigrant parties became more influential, even in the most tolerant nations, Denmark and the Netherlands. Thus Europeans still struggled to define their place in a changing world.

Europe and Russia in the Global System

With the end of the Cold War, Russia, western Europe, and the former Soviet bloc states searched for new roles in the world. Russia sought to maintain good relations with the EU, the United States, China, and the nearby Islamic nations, such as Iran, but also, like most nations, continued to act in its own self-interest. Sometimes this meant opposing U.S. or EU policies. NATO also needed to redefine its mission. By 2004 it had added many of the former Warsaw Pact nations, discomforting Russia. Western Europeans seemed more reluctant than Americans to devote vast sums to the military or to send their armed forces into combat. The crises in Yugoslavia showed European weakness, with the United States pressing NATO for intervention and then leading the effort to end the killing and restore order.

European relations with its military ally and main trading rival, the United States, became complicated. Various European nations, as part of a NATO commitment, sent troops to Afghanistan after the 2001 terrorist attacks on the United States and shared the goal of combating international terrorism. But most Europeans mistrusted the U.S. desire to invade oil-rich Iraq in 2003, believing it had little to do with fighting terrorism and fearing it would destabilize the Middle East. As a result, major European nations such as France and Germany criticized the U.S. invasion and occupation. Although their people strongly opposed the war, some close U.S. allies, such as Italy, Poland, and Spain, sent small token forces, but only Britain had a sizeable military presence in Iraq.

Europeans also disagreed on how best to respond to international terrorism, especially the threat posed by militant Islamic groups. The substantial Muslim immigrant populations in Europe complicated European nations' policies on the Middle East. By 2000, 19 million immigrants, including 13 million Muslims, made up 6 percent of the total EU population. Islamic militancy spread among some people of Arab or South Asian ancestry in Europe, especially among unemployed youth. The major terrorist network, Al Qaeda, had a presence in several nations. Indeed, some of the men who perpetrated the 2001 attacks on the United States had studied in Europe, especially in Germany, where they were recruited by Islamic militants. Deadly terrorist attacks on commuter trains in Madrid in 2004 and the London subway in 2005, which killed several hundred people, showed the potential for terrorist violence in Europe but also convinced many Europeans that Western military interventions in the Middle East might increase rather than diminish the terrorist threat. In 2006 shocked Europeans found how tense Muslim-Western relations had become when offensive cartoons insulting or satirizing the Islamic prophet Muhammad, published by a rightwing, anti-immigrant Danish newspaper to test the limits of press freedom and stimulate controversy, caused massive riots and demonstrations, often fomented by extremists, around the Muslim world, resulting in hundreds of deaths and attacks on Danish and other European embassies and business interests.

Europeans still played key roles in resolving world problems. Polls in the early 2000s showed that Europeans identified global warming as the major world problem. European nations took the lead in developing international treaties on issues such as climate change, biological and chemical weapons, international criminal courts, and genocide. U.S. opposition to these treaties built resentment. European workers also led movements against the economic globalization they saw as costing jobs and livelihoods. Saying the world is not for sale, French farmer José Bové set fire to a McDonald's outlet to protest against the large global corporations that often displace local enterprises, becoming a hero to those Europeans opposed to globalization and the institutions, such as the World Trade Organization (see Chapter 26), that promote it.

With the move, symbolized by the EU, toward closer political and economic integration, Europe became much more than a geographical expression and a collection of separate countries sharing certain cultural traditions and history. A few European leaders have even envisioned a political federation, or united states of Europe, but many hurdles would have to be overcome first. Europe is no longer the powerful colossus it had been in the nineteenth century, but its peoples are carving out a new place in the world.

SECTION SUMMARY

- The collapsing Soviet bloc and Soviet decay created problems for Gorbachev, and he was replaced by Boris Yeltsin, who allowed independence for all the non-Russian Soviet republics, some of which ended up with authoritarian governments, and pursued a rapid shift to capitalism.

- However, as a result of this "shock therapy," a small group of former Communist Party officials became extremely wealthy while most Russians suffered economically, and Yeltsin was replaced by the more authoritarian Vladimir

Putin, who brought back some stability and pursued good relations with Europe and the United States.

- With the fall of the USSR, formerly communist eastern Europe became more democratic, though many countries struggled economically and others suffered political upheaval, especially Yugoslavia, which experienced violent civil war and "ethnic cleansing."

- German reunification, celebrated at first, yielded mixed results, while the European Union grew to include twenty-five nations by 2004 but faced questions over whether to admit non-Christian nations and over what form its constitution should take.

- European nations struggled to navigate the evolving world economy, to deal with Islamic terrorism, and to work out relations with each other and with the United States, whose 2003 invasion of Iraq was generally unpopular in most countries.

Online Study Center ACE the Test

◆ Chapter Summary

Emerging shattered from World War II, western Europeans were determined to build a new Europe. Although the Cold War divided Europe, western Europeans rebuilt democracies and began a movement to foster unity. Sparked by French-German reconciliation, Europeans established institutions for economic cooperation. Eventually these became the European Union, which established a single currency and a European parliament. Stability also resulted from the rise of welfare states, which guaranteed all citizens fair access to housing, health care, and education. Social democratic parties took the lead in creating the safety net, but supporting it became more costly with growing economic problems and unemployment rates. Gradually family and gender relations changed, while millions of immigrants reshaped European societies.

The Soviet Union maintained a government and economy very different from those in western Europe. A powerful state dominated life and work. The Soviets installed communist governments in eastern Europe and brutally repressed opposition, but they failed to realize much economic dynamism and lost ground in the Cold War to a more powerful U.S.–western Europe alliance. By the 1980s the Soviet system and the Soviet bloc needed reform. Communism thus fostered modernization and improved living standards, but ethnic minorities were restless, the bureaucracy was stifling, and the economy remained stagnant. The unsettling reforms resulted in the collapse of communism and the dismantling of the Soviet Empire in 1991. Since then the former communist nations have struggled to introduce capitalism and liberal democracy. Meanwhile, by 2004 most of the European nations had joined the European Union, the world's third largest economic power. Germany struggled to make reunification work, Russia debated a new role in the world, and the European Union sought the appropriate mix of cooperation and national sovereignty.

 **Online Study Center** **Improve Your Grade** Flashcards

Key Terms

Marshall Plan	NATO	existentialism
Eurocommunism	Soviet bloc	postmodernism
Greens	Warsaw Pact	Brezhnev Doctrine
British Commonwealth of Nations	ostpolitik	glasnost
	welfare states	perestroika
Truman Doctrine	bhangra	oligarchs

Suggested Reading

Books

Bridenthal, Renate, et al., eds. *Becoming Visible: Women in European History,* 3rd ed. Boston: Houghton Mifflin, 1998. Offers readable essays.

Crockatt, Richard. *The Fifty Years War: The United States and the Soviet Union in World Politics, 1941–1991.* New York: Routledge, 1995. A detailed study of the Cold War and U.S.-Soviet relations.

Evtuhov, Catherine, et al. *A History of Russia: Peoples, Legends, Events, Forces.* Boston: Houghton Mifflin, 2004. A readable, up-to-date survey.

Gleason, Gregory. *The Central Asian States: Discovering Independence.* Boulder: Westview, 1997. A study of the peoples and modern history of Turkestan.

James, Harold. *Europe Reborn: A History, 1914–2000.* New York: Longman, 2003. A survey of the period.

McCormick, John. *Understanding the European Union: A Concise Introduction,* 3rd ed. New York: Palgrave Macmillan, 2005. A broadranging introduction to European integration.

Pagden, Anthony, ed. *The Idea of Europe: From Antiquity to the European Union.* New York: Cambridge University Press, 2002. An interesting collection of essays on European unity through the ages, including the contemporary era.

Rifkin, Jeremy. *The European Dream: How Europe's Vision of the Future is Quietly Eclipsing the American Dream.* New York: Tarcher/Penguin, 2004. A provocative, sympathetic examination by an American scholar.

Roskin, Michael G. *The Rebirth of Eastern Europe,* 4th ed. Englewood Cliffs: Prentice Hall, 2001. A provocative survey emphasizing politics and economics.

Ryback, Timothy W. *Rock Around the Bloc: A History of Rock Music in Eastern Europe and the Soviet Union.* New York: Oxford University Press, 1990. A fascinating examination of the role of rock music in the Communist bloc.

Smith, Bonnie G. *Changing Lives: Women in European History Since 1700.* Lexington, Mass.: D. C. Heath, 1989. A readable introduction with good coverage of the twentieth century.

Suny, Ronald Grigor. *The Soviet Experiment: Russia, the USSR, and the Successor States.* New York: Oxford University Press, 1998. An excellent overview of Soviet history and the aftermath.

Tipton, Frank B. and Robert Aldrich. *An Economic and Social History of Europe: From 1939 to the Present.* Baltimore: Johns Hopkins University, 1987. Accessible and comprehensive introduction.

Vinen, Richard. *A History in Fragments: Europe in the Twentieth Century.* Cambridge: Da Capo Press, 2000. A provocative, wide-ranging narrative by a British historian.

Wilkenson, James, and H. Stuart Hughes. *Contemporary Europe: A History,* 10th ed. Upper Saddle River, N.J.: Prentice-Hall, 2004. One of the best, most comprehensive general surveys.

Websites

EUROPA—Gateway to the European Union (http://europa.eu.int/index_en.htm). Provides information on many topics.

European Union in the US (http://www.eurunion.org/states/home/htm). Provides a wealth of data on the European Union.

Internet Resources on Russia and the CIS (http://www.ssees.ac.uk/russia.htm). A British site with a collection of links on many aspects of Russia and the Soviet Union.

Internet Modern History Sourcebook (http://www.fordham.edu/halsall/mod/modsbook.html). A very extensive online collection of historical documents and secondary materials.

Russian History Index: The World Wide Web Virtual Library (http://vlib.iue.it/hist-russia/Index.html). Contains useful essays and links on Russian history, society, and politics.

CHAPTER 29

The Americas and the Pacific Basin: New Roles in the Contemporary World, Since 1945

CHAPTER OUTLINE
- The United States as a Superpower
- The Changing Societies of North America and the Pacific Basin
- Political Change in Latin America and the Caribbean
- Changing Latin American and Caribbean Societies

■ PROFILE
Violeta Parra, Chilean New Song Pioneer

■ WITNESS TO THE PAST
Justifying Preemptive Strikes

A Naturalization Ceremony Seeking political freedom or economic opportunities, immigrants flock to the United States and many become citizens. At this ceremony, 800 residents, representing 88 countries, took the oath of citizenship in Columbus, Ohio, in April, 2005. (AP/Wide World Photos)

It's curious. Our generals listen to the [U.S.] Pentagon. They learn the ideology of National Security and commit all these crimes [against the Argentine people]. Then the same [American] people who gave us this gift come and ask, "How did these terrible things happen?"

PRESIDENT RAUL ALFONSIN OF ARGENTINA, 1984[1]

The women appeared one day in the historic Plaza de Mayo, adjacent to the presidential palace in downtown Buenos Aires, Argentina. It was 1977, and for several years the military regime running the country had been waging a bloody campaign to eliminate dissidents, killing or abducting some 30,000 people and arresting and torturing thousands more. Some of those targeted may have belonged to outlawed leftist groups, but many simply held progressive political ideas or were friends with regime critics. Initially only the feared secret police paid attention to the dozen or so frightened women who came once a week, standing in silent protest. Soon the women's ranks swelled to over a hundred at each weekly vigil, making them impossible to ignore. A year later the peaceful protesters numbered more than a thousand. Wearing kerchiefs on their heads and sensible flat shoes on their feet, the mothers and grandmothers pinned to their chests photographs of missing family members, victims of the state's terror. They all asked the same question: Where were their missing children, husbands, pregnant daughters, and grandchildren, some of them newborn infants?

The "Mothers and Grandmothers of the Plaza de Mayo," as they came to be known, dared to challenge one of Latin America's most brutal tyrannies. Whether rich, poor, or middle class, most were housewives taking to the street, as one put it, to fight the vicious armed forces, spineless politicians, complicit clergy, muzzled press, and co-opted labor unions, and to find their family members. Their courageous protest inspired others in Argentina and around the world with hope and moral outrage at repression by military forces. The gatherings continued weekly until 1983, when the regime fell and a civilian government could investigate the disappearances. Most of the women never learned the fates of their loved ones.

The protest by the Plaza de Mayo women illustrates how some Latin Americans addressed the authoritarian governments under which they lived, sometimes for decades, since World War II. Latin American countries often shifted back and forth between dictatorship and democracy, neither of which fostered widespread economic prosperity nor sustained stability amid the stark contrasts between rich and poor. Many Latin Americans also resented the United States, which, as Raul Alfonsin (b. 1927), the democratically elected Argentine president who replaced the military dictatorship, noted, often supported the Latin American military regimes and other despotic governments that repressed their people while welcoming U.S. investment.

The United States remained the hemisphere's dominant power during this period while gradually expanding its global influence. Wars in Korea and Vietnam were part of the U.S. effort to shape the global system while also opposing the expansion of communism. U.S. president Harry Truman (president 1945–1953) argued in 1947 that American political and business practices could only thrive at home if foreign countries also embraced similar practices. After World War II the United States became the global workshop and banker, preacher and teacher, umpire and policeman. It enjoyed unrivaled supremacy, a combination of military might, economic power, and political-ideological leadership that was contested only by the Soviet Union between 1946 and 1989. After 1989 the United States became the world's only remaining superpower. U.S. society increasingly differed from those of its North American neighbor, Canada, and the Pacific Basin countries of Australia and New Zealand. The three northernmost nations—Canada, Mexico, and the United States—shared a border and intertwined histories but had each developed different world-views and sometimes struggled to understand each other. Similar misperceptions often shaped relations between the English- and Spanish-speaking nations.

FOCUS QUESTIONS

1. How did the Cold War shape U.S. foreign policies?
2. How and why are the societies of the United States, Canada, and Australia similar to and different from each other?
3. Why have democracy and economic development proven to be difficult goals in Latin America?
4. How have Latin American and Caribbean cultures been dynamic?

◈ The United States as a Superpower

How did the Cold War shape U.S. foreign policies?

By virtue of its size, power, and wealth, the United States has played a major role in the world. The Americans helped Europe and Japan to regain their footing after World War II, espoused and often promoted human rights and freedom, have lavished aid on various allies or potential allies, and have provided leadership in a politically fragmented world. During the Cold War (1946–1989), U.S. policies were shaped by competition with the Soviet bloc for allies and strategic advantage, and these policies in turn influenced the world's perceptions of the United States (see Chronology: North America and the Pacific Basin, 1945–Present on page 904). Soviet domination of eastern Europe, the communist victory in China, and the Korean War all convinced Americans that communism was on the march. While millions of people around the world admired American democratic ideals, prosperity, and technological ingenuity, the U.S. drive to oppose communist expansion led to wars, interventions, support for often authoritarian allies, frequent neglect of human rights, and the globalization of capitalism that fostered widespread hostility toward the United States. After the Cold War, the United States and its allies faced new challenges, especially the rise of international terrorism.

The Postwar United States and the Cold War

World War II was a watershed for the United States, a rallying cry that forged Americans' vision of world politics. The war had accelerated political centralization and economic growth in the United States; at the same time, it had encouraged Americans to accept international involvements and thus promoted an activist foreign policy. By the later 1940s observers began referring to both the United States and the USSR as

CHRONOLOGY

	North America	Pacific Basin	Latin America and the Caribbean
1940	**1946–1989** Cold War **1950–1953** Korean War		**1959** Cuban Revolution
1960	**1963–1975** U.S. war in Vietnam	**1962–1990** Decolonization of Pacific islands **1973** End of "white Australia" policy	**1964–1985** Military government in Brazil **1973–1989** Military government in Chile
1980	**1994** Formation of NAFTA		
2000	**2001** Al Qaeda terrorist attacks in United States		

superpowers because of their unrivaled political, economic, and military might. The end of the war also placed the United States in the position of global powerbroker and policeman. As U.S.-Soviet rivalry increased, the two superpowers sought to outmaneuver each other and sometimes to block each other from gaining influence in other countries.

The American Century The victory over Nazism and Japanese militarism reinforced American confidence and sense of mission. In 1941, Henry Luce, the publisher of one of the most influential news magazines in the U.S., *Time*, declared that the twentieth century would be the American Century, and that Americans, citizens of the world's most powerful nation, must accept their duty and opportunity to exercise influence in the world, by whatever means they could. Luce believed that America's idealistic Bill of Rights, magnificent industrial products, and technological skills would be shared with all peoples. His view, while arrogant, reflected Americans' longtime belief in the exportability of their country's values and institutions, that their nation was the shining "City Upon a Hill," as a seventeenth-century colonist put it, and the world's model. But U.S.-style capitalism and democracy proved difficult to implant where they had no roots.

American leaders planned to take a leading role in the postwar world. In 1941, even before the nation entered World War II, a conference of influential Americans recommended a policy that emphasized strengthening U.S. economic influence around the globe. After the war the U.S. government pursued the strategy, rebuilding defeated Germany and Japan, establishing global financial networks, lavishing aid on western Europe to help stabilize it under democratic governments, and using U.S. military forces to protect U.S. allies in Asia. The United States also opposed radical nationalist movements, especially communist-led revolutionary groups, in Asia, Africa, and Latin America. In these ways, it took the lead in maintaining a global system in which it held the strongest position.

For several decades, as the U.S. economy soared, the notion of an American Century seemed realistic. Americans believed that they were destined to lead and inspire the world. But the economic superiority of the United States in the 1940s and 1950s was founded on unusual conditions, since many rival nations had been devastated by world war. Among the great powers, only the United States had not been bombed or financially drained, and therefore it was able to keep intact a modern industrial system. The United States alone could produce, on a large scale, the consumer goods needed by others. In 1950, it accounted for 27 percent of total world economic output. By supplying the world, Americans experienced an economic boom that lasted until the late 1960s and helped finance an activist U.S. foreign policy.

The United States became not just the supplier but also the engine of the world economy. Americans forged close trade links with Canada, western Europe, and Japan while sponsoring large-scale foreign aid programs and investment, especially in Asian and Latin American countries. Such foreign aid and investment benefited western European nations after World War II, helping to spark their economic renaissance and ensure their political stability. Other nations in East Asia, especially Japan, and some in Latin America also benefited from U.S. aid and investment. However, in these regions the aid and investment often supported cash crop agriculture and mining, reinforcing the economic dependence of developing nations on producing natural resources for the world economy and, as a result, promoting unbalanced economic growth. Later, U.S. investment developed light industry, especially textile factories, that utilized cheap labor in countries such as Mexico and Thailand. This investment and trade became very profitable for U.S. corporations. Asian, African, and Latin America countries became key U.S. markets, acquiring over a third of American exports by the 1990s. However, American consumption of ever more foreign imports, from Japanese cars to Middle Eastern oil, contributed to a chronic trade imbalance, as Americans

CHRONOLOGY

North America and the Pacific Basin, 1945–Present

1946–1989	Cold War
1947	Formation of CIA and National Security Council
1950–1953	Korean War
1954	U.S. Supreme Court invalidation of school segregation
1955	Sparking of Montgomery bus boycott by Rosa Parks
1960–1975	U.S. secret war in Laos
1962–1990	Decolonization of Pacific islands
1963	Assassination of U.S. president John F. Kennedy
1963–1975	U.S. war in Vietnam
1968	Assassination of Dr. Martin Luther King, Jr.
1969	Woodstock rock festival
1973	End of "white Australia" policy
1988	Canadian Multiculturalism Act
1991	Gulf War
1994	Formation of NAFTA
1999	Formation of Nunavut in northern Canada
2001	Al Qaeda terrorist attacks in United States
2003	U.S. invasion of Iraq

spent more for foreign products than they earned from exports. By 2005 imports were 57 percent larger than exports as Americans lived beyond their means and globalization led to outsourcing of manufacturing and jobs.

The Cold War The Cold War shaped U.S. foreign relations, especially with the USSR. American leaders saw the Soviet Union as pursuing global aggression and fostering political unrest. Although they had good reason to worry about the Soviet state, which was headed by a ruthless dictator, Joseph Stalin, and possessed formidable military might, U.S. leaders and intelligence analysts often overestimated the Soviet threat. George Kennan, the State Department official who constructed the anti-Soviet policy in the late 1940s and early 1950s, later admitted that the popular view held by Americans

of the USSR poised to attack the West was based more on imagination than on hard evidence. The Cold War produced an expectation of permanent conflict between two competing ideologies: communism and capitalist democracy. Given this assumption, the U.S. government became obsessed with secrecy and control. Two key U.S. institutions carrying out the anti-Soviet strategy, the Central Intelligence Agency (CIA) and the National Security Council, both established in 1947, operated in top secrecy, with little congressional oversight and ever larger budgets, reaching a total of $40 billion per year for all intelligence agencies by the 1980s. By the early 1950s the **domino theory**, which envisioned countries falling one by one to communism, became a mainstay of U.S. policy.

Anti-communism intensified within the United States after U.S. senator Joseph McCarthy (1909–1957), a hard-drinking former judge, and his allies charged, without offering proof, that communists had infiltrated the U.S. government and shaped foreign policy. During the early and mid-1950s a campaign, known as McCarthyism, to identify suspected communists in the government, the military, education, and the entertainment industry led to the firing or the blacklisting of not only a handful of secret communists but also of thousands of Americans who held leftwing or other unpopular political views, which were condemned as "un-American." (Blacklisting prevented people from working.) For example, high school teachers were fired for suggesting that, to better understand communism, their students read *The Communist Manifesto*, by Karl Marx, and university experts on Asia lost their positions for criticizing U.S. Asian policies. McCarthy called hundreds of people, from movie actors to State Department officials, before his Senate committee, where he questioned them about their political activities or the political views of their friends. In 1954 the U.S. Senate censured McCarthy for recklessly charging top military leaders with treason. To critics, McCarthy's investigation, which ruined many innocent people, was a witch-hunt that violated the Bill of Rights, a Cold War–driven hysteria that generated accusations against people who held largely harmless political opinions.

For much of the Cold War era, American leaders largely agreed on foreign policy goals. A broad consensus emerged around opposing the spread of communism and Soviet power. To pursue these goals, most American leaders favored an activist foreign policy, including the use of military power. However, U.S. leaders disagreed as to which approach was most effective in achieving the goals. Some leaders pursued **multilateralism**, an approach in which the United States sought a common front and a coordination of foreign policies with allies in western Europe, Japan, and Canada, avoiding activities that might enflame world opinion against the United States. In contrast, most policymakers, and the presidents they

domino theory A theory that envisioned countries falling one by one to communism and that became a mainstay of U.S. policy.

multilateralism A foreign policy in which the United States sought a common front and a coordination of foreign policies with allies in western Europe, Japan, and Canada, avoiding activities that might enflame world opinion against the United States.

served, favored **unilateralism**, a foreign policy in which the United States acted alone in its own perceived national interest even if key allies disapproved, as they did with the U.S. war in Vietnam. Unilateralism often led to support of repressive dictatorships allied to the United States, such as in the Philippines and the Congo. The Cold War–driven consensus stifled those who questioned the rationale, tactics, and cost of an activist policy. Ultimately the costly interventions abroad, especially the frustrating war in Vietnam, provoked a debate about the goals, operation, and impact of U.S. foreign policy. By the later 1960s, this debate had undermined the consensus and provoked increasing dissent within the nation.

The main U.S. strategy, known as **containment**, was aimed at preventing communists from gaining power, and the USSR from getting political influence, in other nations. Containment resulted in wars, as in Korea and later Vietnam, and to briefer interventions to shape governments, especially in countries that were gaining independence from Western colonialism or seeking to weaken Western economic domination. An influential, top secret government report, known as NSC-68, prepared by the National Security Council in 1950, provided the rationale for activist policies by painting a bleak picture of the USSR's search for world supremacy: "The issues that face us are momentous, involving the fulfillment or destruction not only of this [U.S.] Republic but of civilization itself."[2] NSC-68 sanctioned any tactics, including assassination, in the anticommunism struggle. It remained a key basis for U.S. military and intelligence policies abroad until the mid-1970s.

Rising U.S. Power   Containment policy led to a massive, expensive military buildup. NSC-68 had called for a huge defense budget and expansion of the nuclear weapons arsenal as a deterrent, to be paid for by tax increases and major reductions in social welfare spending. Security, the document argued, was to take precedence in the national budget, at the expense of all other priorities. The Soviets matched the U.S. military buildup, creating a constant escalation of military spending and ever more sophisticated weapons on both sides. Under a policy known in the United States as **Mutually Assured Destruction**, or MAD, the United States and the USSR used the fear of nuclear weapons to deter each other. Some historians believe that MAD prevented a direct military confrontation between the two rivals that might have sparked World War III. Americans reacted to the threat of nuclear war in the 1950s by often building bomb shelters in their basements or backyards and having schools hold mock air raid drills. During these drills millions of American students learned to "duck

and cover," jumping under their desks to protect themselves from a hypothetical nuclear attack.

Defense spending reshaped the U.S. economy. Despite the warning of U.S. president Dwight Eisenhower (g. 1953–1961), a chief commander during World War II, to guard against the growing influence on U.S. foreign and domestic policy of what he termed the military-industrial complex, an alliance of military leaders and weapons producers, defense became an enormous business. It employed a fifth of the U.S. industrial work force and a third of scientists and engineers by the 1960s, while costing U.S. taxpayers hundreds of billions a year. The United States also sold weapons to allied nations, among them despotic regimes, some of which, such as Argentina and Thailand, both ruled by military dictatorships, used the weapons against their own population or their neighbors; the United States also trained these regimes' military officers and police forces, who often used the tactics they learned to eliminate dissidents.

Between 1945 and 1975 U.S. power was unmatched in the world, and the United States maintained military bases on every inhabited continent and in dozens of countries around the world (see Map 29.1). Both the United States and the USSR intervened directly or indirectly in civil wars and revolutions to outflank the other. The United States employed military force, as in the long war in Vietnam and the invasion of the Dominican Republic in 1965, and covertly aided governments to suppress opposition or, as in Chile in 1973, helped overthrow governments considered unfriendly to U.S. economic or political interests, even if, as in Chile, these governments were democratic and had been freely elected. Some foreign observers applauded U.S. efforts to suppress leftwing governments and movements that might have favored the USSR or Communist China, while others were hostile to U.S. power and criticized the United States for superpower imperialism. The rivalry between the United States and the USSR persisted until the collapse of many communist regimes in 1989.

U.S. power, especially its economic leadership, was less dominant between the mid-1970s and the early 1990s. Reasons for this change included the rise of a rebuilt western Europe and Japan to economic power, the military strength of the USSR, the economic challenge from industrializing nations such as South Korea and China, and the damage done to the U.S. economy and prestige by the unsuccessful, widely unpopular war in Vietnam. Also a factor was the economic price Americans paid for global power. The increasing extension and cost of U.S. military commitments caused the nation's economic creativity to sag and industries to become obsolete as heavy defense spending diverted U.S. wealth away from the domestic economy. Over four decades the Cold War cost the U.S. government around $4 trillion, money that did not go to improving education and health care or meeting other needs. The growing U.S. defense budgets of the 1980s did help undermine the Soviet Union, which was unable to match the lavish spending on expensive weapons, such as unproven antimissile systems, but it also transformed the United States from a creditor nation into the world's largest debtor nation, leaving Americans with ballooning federal budget deficits. Only in the

unilateralism   A foreign policy in which the United States acted alone in its own perceived national interest even if key allies disapproved.

containment   The main U.S. strategy aimed at preventing communists from gaining power, and the USSR from getting political influence, in other nations during the Cold War.

Mutually Assured Destruction   A policy, known as MAD, in which the United States and the USSR used the fear of nuclear weapons to deter each other.

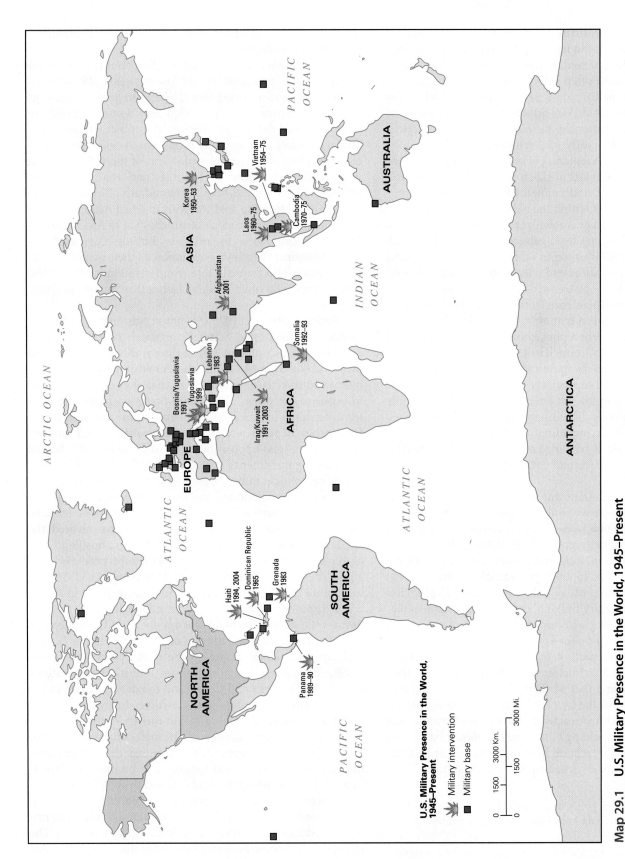

Map 29.1 U.S. Military Presence in the World, 1945–Present
As the major superpower, the United States maintained several dozen military bases outside of North America while engaging in military operations in Latin America, Africa, Asia, the Middle East, and Europe. This map shows some of the major U.S. bases and military conflicts.

Online Study Center **Improve Your Grade** Interactive Map: The Cold War

1990s, under President Bill Clinton (g. 1993–2001), did the U.S. government eliminate the budget deficits that had accelerated between the 1960s and the 1980s to pay for the Cold War.

Wars in Korea and Vietnam

In 1949 the Chinese communist victory in China, a country whose longtime government had been allied with and armed by the United States (see Chapter 27), escalated U.S. concern about the expansion of communism. communist expansion, and the U.S. determination to halt it, led to the Korean War. The decision to send U.S. troops to Korea, under the auspices of the newly formed United Nations, signaled the U.S. adoption of an interventionist foreign policy. The Korean War (1950–1953) was followed a decade later by a more massive U.S. intervention in another Asian society, Vietnam, which resulted in the longest war the United States had ever waged (1963–1975).

The Korean War was sparked when North Korea, ruled by a brutal communist regime allied to the USSR, invaded South Korea, a U.S. ally, with the goal of forcibly reunifying the Korean peninsula (see Chapter 27). The U.S. president, Harry S. Truman, viewed the North Korean invasion in the light of his World War II experience: as a second coming of Nazi aggression. The anti-communist mood in the United States, already inflamed by the communist victory in China, made it politically unthinkable for Truman not to oppose the North Korean thrust. Truman never consulted the U.S. Congress, which had the constitutional responsibility to declare war, and his approach to entering Korea thereafter made presidents supreme in decisions to go to war. Officially Korea was a police action under U.N. sponsorship rather than a war, a precedent that allowed future presidents to commit U.S. military forces without congressional approval. Scholars credit Truman's Korean intervention with contributing to the centralizing of power in the executive branch. Furthermore, the Soviet support of North Korea with arms and advice, and the intervention of the communist Chinese on the North Korean side,

deepened American fear of an expanding communism, especially in Asia. However, despite the 38,000 Americans killed and over 100,000 wounded, the war ended not in victory for the United States and the U.N. forces it led but in stalemate. For the first time since the War of 1812, the United States had failed to decisively win a major military conflict.

The U.S. intervention in Korea reflected not only Cold War anti-communism but also the desire of idealistic Americans to spread democracy and free market capitalism around the world. An American economic adviser to the South Korean government reported the hope of his more idealistic American colleagues that South Korea "will institute a whole series of necessary reforms which will so appeal to the North Koreans that their army will revolt, kill all the nasty communists, and create a lovely liberal democracy to the everlasting credit of the U.S.A.!"[3] North Korea, however, remained a rigid communist state and South Korea did not become a democracy until the 1980s, over three decades after the war.

The domino theory, which predicted a communist sweep through Southeast Asia, and the desire to maintain military credibility and keep valuable Southeast Asian resources, such as tin and tungsten, in friendly hands provided the rationale for financing the French effort to maintain colonial control (1946–1954) in Vietnam and, when that effort failed, increasing U.S. involvement, leading eventually to the U.S. military fighting Vietnamese communist forces armed by the USSR and China (see Chapter 31). Misunderstandings hurt the U.S. effort. Few U.S. leaders comprehended the historical and cultural factors, such as anti-Western nationalism and the examples of resistance to foreign invaders over the centuries, that sparked the Vietnamese communist movement they were fighting. As a growing communist-led insurgency, backed by North Vietnam, challenged a widely unpopular, U.S.- supported South Vietnamese government, the United States sent thousands of military advisers to South Vietnam.

By the mid-1960s, as the unpopular South Vietnamese regime lost ground and support, the U.S. president, Lyndon B. Johnson (g. 1963–1969), committed military forces and launched an intensive air war against targets in North and South Vietnam and later in neighboring Cambodia and Laos. U.S. troop totals topped off at 550,000 by 1967. The domino theory rhetoric often exaggerated the communist threat. In escalating the Vietnam conflict, Johnson asserted that "if we don't stop the [communists] in South Vietnam, tomorrow they will be in Hawaii and next week they will be in San Francisco,"[4] very unlikely scenarios given the limited Chinese and Vietnamese naval and air power. Between 1963 and 1975,

On Patrol in Vietnam   U.S. soldiers sought out National Liberation Front fighters and supporters in the villages, rice fields, and jungles of South Vietnam. They could not easily tell friend from foe and warily dealt with local people.   (Corbis)

2.5 million Americans served in Vietnam; 58,000 died and 300,000 were wounded there.

As support within the United States for the war ebbed with military stalemate and increasing casualties in what seemed a quagmire, Johnson's successor, President Richard Nixon (g. 1969–1973), gradually withdrew U.S. forces and negotiated a political settlement with North Vietnam. But a policy throughout the war of spending lavishly on both "guns and butter"— military and domestic needs—generated huge budget deficits and other economic problems with which the United States struggled from the later 1960s into the 1990s. The war in Vietnam ultimately cost U.S. taxpayers around $1 trillion. Furthermore, the lack of a military victory despite the high cost in lives made Americans temporarily wary of supporting other military interventions that might become Vietnam-like quagmires.

The United States and the Developing Nations

Decolonization, nationalism, the U.S.-Soviet struggle, and persistent poverty combined to make the Asian, African, and Latin American societies prone to crises, sometimes drawing in the United States. The United States often favored decolonization that presented opportunities to U.S. business; for example, it successfully pressured the Dutch to abandon Indonesia and the British to grant independence to most of their African colonies. However, it opposed independence for colonies, such as French-ruled Vietnam and Portuguese-ruled Mozambique, where communists or other leftists dominated the nationalist movements. After decolonization, Americans offered generous aid to friendly nations and to victims of famine or natural catastrophes. U.S. assistance also sparked the Green Revolution in agriculture, which led to improved food production in countries such as India, Mexico, and the Philippines. However, Cold War challenges often involved the United States in long-term confrontations with communist-led revolutions, as in China, Vietnam, and Cuba, and also sparked interventions to help U.S. allies suppress leftist insurgencies and to oppose left-leaning, though non-communist, governments, such as in Iran, Chile, and Guatemala. But some U.S.-installed or supported governments lacked widespread popular support or lost their credibility, often surviving only by repressing domestic opposition, sometimes killing thousands of their own citizens.

In some U.S. interventions, presidents dispatched troops to overturn a government or to support one side in a civil war or revolutionary situation. U.S. leaders used the threat of communism as the rationale for these actions, but some interventions removed democratic governments, as in Guatemala and Chile, or suppressed democratic movements. For example, President Lyndon Johnson, claiming that Americans would not permit another communist government alongside Fidel Castro's Cuba in the Western Hemisphere, dispatched 20,000 U.S. Marines into the Dominican Republic in 1965 to support a military government under attack by the democratically elected leaders they had recently overthrown. However,

Johnson had consulted no other Latin American governments, the Dominican communist movement was tiny, and the democratically elected leaders, while left-leaning, were noncommunist reformers who had wide popular support. Former Dominican president and the leader of the antimilitary movement, Juan Bosch (1909–2001), declared that "this was a democratic revolution smashed by the leading democracy in the world."[5]

In addition to military interventions, the United States also provided friendly governments or antileftist groups with weapons and other assistance. Instead of troops, presidents sent military advisers, intelligence agents, and funding. For example, the United States aided a pro-Western but often repressive government combating a leftist insurgency in El Salvador during the 1970s and 1980s. In Laos from 1960 to 1975, during what was known as the CIA's "secret war" because the U.S. role, while widely known in Southeast Asia, was kept hidden from Congress and the U.S. public, Americans recruited an army from among hill peoples to fight communist Laotian and North Vietnamese forces (see Chapter 31).

A final type of intervention involved covert destabilization, which involved American agents working underground to help undermine or spark the overthrow of governments seen as hostile to U.S. interests. Covert actions included hiring local people to spread misinformation about government policies, subsidizing opposition political parties, providing weapons to the military, and arranging for assassinations of government leaders. For example, U.S. clandestine activity, which undermined elected left-leaning democratic governments in Iran in the 1950s and Thailand and Chile in the 1970s, brought brutal dictatorships to all three countries. U.S. Secretary of State Henry Kissinger defended the U.S. encouragement of a military coup against the democratically elected, leftist Chilean government—a government that respected civil liberties—by explaining, "I don't see why we need to stand by and watch a country go communist due to the irresponsibility of its own people."[6] This attitude that the United States knows best what is in their interest has often infuriated people in other nations. Only in the mid-1970s, with congressional hearings on covert activities, did Americans learn of the U.S. role in Chile and other interventions. This awareness forced debate of the question, still unresolved today, of whether engaging in secret operations and foreign interventions unknown to the public is compatible with democracy and open, accountable government.

The United States in the Global System After 1989

The demise of the Soviet bloc in 1989 and the dissolution of the USSR in 1991 left the United States the dominant world power, although the European Union and the rising East Asian nations (especially China and Japan) also enjoyed great influence in the global system. But the lack of a rival superpower did not mean the end of challengers, among them international terrorists. The United States used its unsurpassed military and economic power to maintain a global presence and intervene in several countries, but Americans also paid a price in blood and treasure for activist foreign policies and global leadership, what some called the *Pax Americana* ("American Peace").

A New World Disorder

The United States now struggled to find a new role in a world characterized by what observers called a "New World Disorder" because of an outbreak of small, deadly conflicts. During the early 1990s, for example, President Bill Clinton (g. 1993–2001) sent a small number of U.S. troops, under United Nations auspices, to stabilize Somalia, a famine-racked northeast African state involved in a civil war. The intervention turned out badly, however, when the forces of a local warlord paraded the mutilated bodies of dead U.S. soldiers through the streets, forcing a U.S. withdrawal. In the aftermath, the reluctance to assert power in other turbulent states like Rwanda, Liberia, and Sierra Leone, all places where civilians were being slaughtered by the thousands, suggested that the United States lacked the political will to intervene to stop ethnic conflicts, genocides, or revolutions in small nations. However, working with European allies, Clinton sent U.S. forces to help end the deadly civil wars in the former Yugoslavia. Furthermore, the United States continued to try to resolve other foreign policy problems. For example, after being forced out of Vietnam in 1975, it refused diplomatic recognition and imposed a strict trade embargo against the communist-ruled country. However, in the 1990s the Clinton administration established diplomatic ties and lifted the embargo, which it viewed as punitive and counterproductive for U.S. business, forging better relations with Vietnam.

Cold War policies sometimes came back to haunt the United States. In the 1980s it had given military and financial aid to the Islamic rebels fighting Soviet troops and the pro-Soviet government in Afghanistan (see Chapter 30). Some of this aid went to Arab volunteers, among them the Saudi militant Osama bin Laden (b. 1957), who were fighting alongside the rebels. After the Soviets left Afghanistan in defeat in 1989, Muslim militants, the Taliban, defeated the other factions and took power. The Taliban imposed a rigid Islamic state and offered a base for Islamic groups to form into the global terrorist network known as Al Qaeda ("the Base"), which was led by bin Laden. Al Qaeda now plotted terrorist attacks against the United States, sometimes using leftover U.S. weapons (see Chapters 26 and 30). Further west, Iraq's ruthless dictator, Saddam Hussein, used weapons acquired from the United States, his ally against Iran in the 1980s, to threaten Iraq's neighbors and repress dissident groups. In 1991 the United States led a coalition of nations that pushed invading Iraqi forces out of Kuwait during the Gulf War and then later protected the Kurds in northern Iraq from Saddam's reprisals. The intervention in oil-rich Kuwait was part of a consistent U.S. policy over the decades to protect the flow of oil from the Middle East, especially the Persian Gulf, to the West.

9/11 and Its Aftermath

Americans had long been insulated from terrorist violence, including bombings and airplane hijackings. However, the terrorist attack launched by Al Qaeda on the World Trade Center in New York and the Pentagon in Washington, D.C., in September, 2001, which killed nearly 3,000 Americans, shocked the nation and led to a reshaping of both domestic and foreign policies. The new U.S. president, George W. Bush (b. 1946), introduced policies, such as preventive detention and monitoring of libraries, designed to prevent possible domestic terrorism but that critics believed went too far, infringing on civil liberties. By attacking buildings that symbolized often unpopular U.S. economic and military power to people around the world, the terrorists, young Muslim fanatics mostly from two close U.S. allies, Egypt and Saudi Arabia, hoped to capitalize on widespread anti-U.S. feelings. However, people in most countries, even if they disliked the United States and its power, deplored the bombings and the loss of innocent life.

The attacks prompted President Bush to declare a war on international terrorism using military force. But unlike the USSR during the Cold War, whose leaders had to be cautious, terrorist networks had no clear command structure or military resources and could not be influenced by diplomacy. With international support, the United States invaded Afghanistan to destroy Al Qaeda terrorist bases and displace the militant Islamic government that tolerated their presence. Bush announced a new doctrine of **preemptive war** that sanctioned unilateral military action against potential threats (see Witness to the Past: Justifying Preemptive Strikes), and he named Iraq, Iran, and North Korea as states at the core of an "axis of evil" that threatened their neighbors and world peace. The Bush doctrine advocated that the United States maintain overwhelming military superiority over all challengers. Critics perceived the Bush doctrine as a recipe for acquiring an American empire through military action, a violation, they charged, of international law and the United Nations charter.

The concern with international terrorism led to a resumption of unilateralist U.S. foreign policies, in which the United States acted without widespread international support. Rejecting opposition from the United Nations and key U.S. allies, among them Canada and Germany, in 2003 the Bush administration, claiming, based on faulty or manipulated intelligence, that Iraq possessed weapons of mass destruction and aided Al Qaeda, organized an invasion and occupation of Iraq, ending Saddam Hussein's brutal regime. But the U.S. forces found no weapons of mass destruction or evidence of a Saddam–Al Qaeda link; furthermore, the Bush administration had planned poorly for restoring stability in Iraq, a nation rich in oil but troubled by ethnic and religious divisions that threatened to explode into civil war and complicated U.S. attempts to foster democracy. A mounting insurgency by Iraqis and suicide bombings largely linked to foreign terrorists, who now flocked to Iraq to fight Americans, caused thousands of U.S. casualties and complicated political and economic reconstruction, making an early withdrawal of U.S. forces difficult. By 2006 basic services, such as electricity, and oil production had still not been restored to prewar levels and the streets in many

preemptive war A U.S. doctrine, triggered by the 2001 terrorist attacks, that sanctioned unilateral military action against potential threats.

Justifying Preemptive Strikes

In the wake of the shocking terrorist attacks on the United States in September 2001, the administration of President George W. Bush produced a document, the National Security Strategy of the United States, that restated the U.S. desire to spread democracy and capitalism while announcing that the United States would act preemptively, striking first, unilaterally if necessary, against any hostile states that the Bush administration believed might be planning to attack U.S. targets. Depending on the observer, the document either reflected or exploited Americans' fear of terrorist attacks. In 2003 Bush used the preemptive strike rationale to order a military invasion and occupation of Iraq, which he claimed had weapons of mass destruction. After Saddam's fall, Bush offered a new mission: fostering democracy in Iraq as an example for the Middle East. To critics, however, the failure to find such weapons, the faulty intelligence about them, and the huge financial and human costs of the resulting occupation for both Americans and Iraqis all suggested the dangers of a preemptive strategy. Furthermore, they argued, many presidents before Bush had claimed to promote democracy abroad but had rarely done so, especially when they used military force to install a pro-U.S. government in another country.

The great struggles of the twentieth century between liberty and totalitarianism ended with a decisive victory for the forces of freedom—and a single sustainable model for national success: freedom, democracy, and free enterprise. . . . Only nations that share a commitment to protecting basic human rights and guaranteeing political and economic freedom will be able to unleash the potential of their people and assure their future prosperity. . . . Today, the United States enjoys a position of unparalleled military strength and great economic and political influence. In keeping with our heritage and principles, we do not use our strength to press for unilateral advantage. We seek instead to create a balance of power that favors human freedom. . . . We will extend the peace by encouraging free and open societies on every continent.

Defending our Nation against its enemies is the first and fundamental commitment of the Federal Government. Today, that task has changed dramatically. Enemies in the past needed great armies and great industrial capabilities to endanger America. Now, shadowy networks of individuals can bring great chaos and suffering to our shores for less than it costs to purchase a single tank. Terrorists are organized to penetrate open societies and to turn the power of modern technologies against us. To defeat this threat we must make use of every tool in our arsenal. . . . The war against terrorists of global reach is a global enterprise of uncertain duration. . . . America will hold to account nations that are compromised by terror, including those who harbor terrorists—because the allies of terror are the enemies of civilization. . . . Our enemies have openly declared that they are seeking weapons of mass destruction. . . . The United States will not allow these efforts to succeed. . . . And, as a matter of common sense and self-defense, America will act against such emerging threats before they are fully formed. . . . We must be prepared to defeat our enemies' plans. History will judge harshly those who saw this coming danger but failed to act. In the new world we have entered, the only path to peace and security is the path of action. . . .

The struggle against global terrorism is different from any other war in our history. It will be fought on many fronts against a particularly elusive enemy over an extended period of time. . . . New deadly challenges have emerged from rogue states and terrorists. . . . Rogue regimes seek nuclear, biological, and chemical weapons. . . . We must be prepared to stop rogue states and their terrorist clients before they are able to threaten or use weapons of mass destruction against the United States and our allies. . . . The United States can no longer solely rely on a reactive posture as we have in the past. . . . We cannot let our enemies strike first. . . . We must adapt the concept of imminent threat to the capabilities and objectives of today's adversaries. . . . The greater the threat, the greater the risk of inaction—and the more compelling the case for taking anticipatory action to defend ourselves, even if uncertainty remains as to the time and place of the enemy's attack. To forestall or prevent such hostile acts by our adversaries, the United States will, if necessary, act preemptively.

THINKING ABOUT THE READING

1. How does the document reflect the tendency of U.S. leaders to claim a national goal of spreading U.S. political and economic models in the world?

2. What does the document offer as the rationale for preemptive actions?

*Source: The National Security Strategy of the United States (**http://www.whitehouse.gov/nsc/print/nssall.html**).*

regions remained unsafe, demoralizing Iraqis. The spiraling costs of the Iraq occupation and other expenses, combined with large tax cuts, ballooned U.S. budget deficits that could not be sustained long term without serious damage to the U.S. economy. The ever expanding appetite of Americans for oil contributed to the interventions in the Middle East and support for often corrupt, dictatorial regimes, and caused critics to charge that the Iraq war was also about oil. The Iraq war, unpopular in much of the world, charges that the U.S. tortured suspected terrorists, and the U.S. rejection of several international treaties, such as that on global warming, further alienated Western allies. Yet, the United States also earned praise for generous assistance to the victims of a catastrophic tidal wave in South and Southeast Asia in 2005.

Because of its unparalleled economic and military might, the United States had assumed heavy burdens, sending troops to Afghanistan, Iraq, and elsewhere while maintaining military bases in several dozen countries and islands around the world. While western Europeans and East Asians have generally concentrated on trade relations with other nations, Americans have attempted to balance trade and other nonterrorism issues with confronting the nations they perceive as dangerous. By 2004 the United States accounted for half of all military spending worldwide, spending as much on its military and weapons as all other nations combined, and it also accounted for about half of all arms sales to the world's nations. The United States plays a vital role in world governance through its diplomatic engagements, vast military deployments, and buttressing of the global economy, a fact appreciated by many nations because the cost is largely borne by U.S. taxpayers. As a result, while anti-U.S. sentiments grew steadily in the early twenty-first century, no coalition of nations has come together to oppose the U.S. role. However, the budget deficits that now pay for it, helping to double the national debt between 2000 and 2006, are only possible because Asian investors, especially the Chinese, Japanese, and South Koreans, finance around half of the debt and must eventually be repaid, giving these countries leverage with the United States in the future. Scholars debate whether the United States will retain its dominance in the years ahead or whether the growing burdens will overwhelm the economy and reduce U.S. power as other nations, perhaps China or India, surge ahead. Whatever the case, since the Romans two millennia ago, no other nation has been as dominant in military, economic, political, and social realms as the United States has been after 1990. This dominance has forced Americans to debate, as the Romans and, before them, the Athenians did, whether democracy and imperial power are consistent.

SECTION SUMMARY

■ For several decades after World War II, the United States enjoyed a period of economic growth and lavished economic aid on western Europe and Japan, where it helped those countries to recover, and later on developing nations, where it was not used as effectively.

■ During the Cold War, McCarthyism led to the persecution of many U.S. citizens for supposed communist sympathies, U.S. presidents aimed to contain the spread of communism through unilateral action, the two superpowers followed the Mutually Assured Destruction policy (which may have helped prevent a nuclear war), and defense spending became a key factor in the U.S. economy.

■ On the basis of the domino theory, which argued that if communism wasn't stopped it would take over the world, the United States adopted an interventionist foreign policy and fought communists in Korea and Vietnam, but neither war achieved U.S. goals and the Vietnam War severely crippled the U.S. economy.

■ During the Cold War, the United States opposed not only communist movements but also non-communist leftist movements in several countries, in many cases helping to replace them with brutal military dictatorships.

■ In response to the terrorist attacks of September 11, 2001, U.S. president George W. Bush proclaimed a policy of preemptive war and led the country to war in Afghanistan and then in Iraq, the second of which was fought despite United Nations disapproval and has been very controversial.

◆ The Changing Societies of North America and the Pacific Basin

How and why are the societies of the United States, Canada, and Australia similar to and different from each other?

In the years following World War II, the United States and Canada in North America and Australia and New Zealand in the southwestern corner of the Pacific Basin—all originally settled by people from the British Isles—shared a general prosperity, similar social patterns, and many cultural traditions, but they also played different roles in the world. Besides exercising more political, economic, and military power than these other nations, the United States had a stable democracy and a rapidly changing society. The United States, Canada, and Australia all attracted millions of immigrants from around the world, helping to globalize their cultures and link them more closely to other nations.

Prosperity, Technology, and Inequality in the United States

Living in the world's richest nation, many Americans benefited from a growing economy and widespread affluence. During the nation's most prosperous decade, the 1960s, the production of goods and services doubled, and per capita income rose by half. Many Americans moved into new automobile, aerospace, service, and information technology industries. By 2000 the United States accounted for a third of the world's total production of goods and services, over twice as much as second-place Japan, and enjoyed a median annual family income of over $40,000. As per capita producers of wealth, Americans exceeded everyone except the people of Luxembourg, Norway, and Switzerland. Americans also owned the majority of, and profited from, the giant multinational corporations, such as General Motors and Wal-Mart, that played ever larger roles in the globalizing world economy. However, there were downsides to this growth. With 6 percent of the world population, Americans also consumed around 40 percent of all the world's resources, such as oil and iron ore, and produced a large share of the chemicals, gases, and toxic wastes that pollute the atmosphere, alter the climate, and destroy the land. The United States lagged in environmental protection; a major world study in 2005 ranked the nation twenty-eighth in meeting sustainable environmental goals, well behind most of western Europe, Japan, Taiwan, and several developing nations, such as Chile and Malaysia. Americans also worked longer hours than any industrialized people except the Japanese.

The rise of high technology and the decline of smokestack industries, such as steel production, reshaped the economy and workplace. Americans celebrated innovations in medicine, space research, transportation, and particularly electronics. Space satellites greatly improved weather forecasting, communications, and intelligence gathering. Computers revolutionized life with their convenience and versatility, since these machines could, as *Time* magazine concluded, "send letters at the speed of light, diagnose a sick poodle [and] test recipes for beer."[7] By the twenty-first century Americans often carried with them pocket-sized devices, once the stuff of science fiction novels, that could make telephone calls, send text messages, play music, and access news and weather.

Beginning in the 1970s, a growing economy improved the lot of some people, especially those trained in the new technologies, but it hurt millions of others, including unskilled workers, younger workers, and children in single-parent households. As computers and robots increased efficiency, they also replaced many workers. In the 1980s, a third of industrial jobs disappeared. Industrialists won corporate bonuses for relocating factories and exporting jobs to Latin America or Asia, devastating factory-dependent American communities. By the early 2000s, although life for the majority of Americans remained comfortable compared to that in most other nations, unemployment for men was the highest it had been in five decades and millions of men and women had to work two jobs to support their families. Some economists referred to a "winner-take-all economy" that produced ever more millionaires—over 2 million of them by 2005—but also a struggling middle class and, at the bottom of the social ladder, more homeless people sleeping in city streets and parks. Except for the richest 1 percent of Americans, whose earnings skyrocketed, average incomes fell between 2001 and 2006. Yet, when surveyed, most Americans, often including people with modest incomes, identified themselves with the middle class and its aspirations rather than, as Europeans often did, with the working class.

In contrast to western Europe, Canada, Australia, and New Zealand, the United States never developed a comprehensive welfare state. As a result, despite federal government efforts at abolishing poverty, a widening gap separated the richest third and the poorest third of Americans. The inequality of wealth in the United States grew dramatically after 1980, and by 1997 the top 1 percent of the population owned 20 percent of all the wealth. By 2004, 12.5 percent of Americans lived below the poverty line, the highest poverty rate in the industrialized world. Today the gap between the richest 20 percent and the poorest 20 percent of Americans is three times wider than in Japan, the Netherlands, Sweden, or Germany, and millions of

Americans today have no health insurance, a striking contrast to western Europe and Canada, where social democratic policies prevail. A devastating hurricane that caused massive damage and flooding in the Gulf Coast in 2005, ruining New Orleans, rendering millions homeless, and killing several thousand people, starkly revealed the gap; most of the people who died or were only rescued days later were black and poor, unable to afford transportation out of the area. Partly because of the inequalities in wealth and health care, the United States ranked eighth—behind several European nations, Canada, and Australia—in overall quality of life in the 2004 United Nations Human Development Report.

Changes in the economy went hand in hand with the suburbanization of American life, deepening the inequalities. In the decades following World War II, families with young children wanted affordable housing. Millions of people sought a better life in suburbia, the bedroom communities on the edges of major cities. Suburbs, occupied typically by white Americans, built shopping malls, offered well-funded schools, and seemed immune from city violence. Governments supported the suburban trend by subsidizing real estate developers. William Leavitt, who built vast suburban tracts, known as Leavittown, around New York City, argued that no person who owned his or her own house and yard could be a communist because he or she was too busy keeping up, and working to pay for, his or her property. The two-car, multitelevision family became a common symbol of affluence. The automobile, increasingly affordable for the middle class, combined with government-funded freeway and highway construction, made long commutes from the suburbs to jobs in the central city possible. Later, as the jobs often moved to the suburbs, the city cores were increasingly dominated by the local-born poor, often nonwhite, or immigrants. Furthermore, increasing use of fossil fuels for gasoline, electricity, and heating caused pollution while clearing land for housing and business development harmed the environment.

American Political Life: Conservatism and Liberalism

Americans have tended to alternate between conservatism and liberalism in their political life, a pattern that continued in the decades after World War II. For most of these years, political conservatives, commonly allied with both big business groups favoring low taxes and opposed to government welfare programs and religious groups who disliked social and cultural liberalization, such as legal abortion and homosexual rights, dominated the presidency and often the United States Congress and the judiciary. Liberals played a key role in U.S. political life chiefly in the 1960s and, to a lesser extent, the 1990s; they were generally supported by labor unions and groups that sought social change and a stronger government safety net, such as women's and civil rights organizations. Each political philosophy was also reflected in society and culture.

The widespread desire for stability after the great Depression and a calamitous world war encouraged both a political and social conservatism throughout the 1950s. Prosperous, the middle and upper classes rarely questioned their government or the prevailing social arrangements. Americans who criticized U.S. foreign policy or favored radical social change faced harassment, expulsion from job or school, arrest, or grillings by congressional committees who accused them of being "un-American." Whatever their social class, more Americans than ever before married, producing a "baby boom" of children born in the years following the war. The mass media portrayed women as obsessed with bleaching their clothes a purer white and content in a world defined by kitchen, bedroom, babies, and home. Society expected homosexuals to remain deep in the closet, and those who did not faced taunting, beatings, or arrest. At the same time, the growing consumer economy emphasized pleasure and leisure time activities, such as cocktail parties, backyard barbecues, and baseball games. Like their parents, teenagers became consumers, creating a market for youth-oriented clothes and music.

American politics and society were reshaped again during the 1960s, becoming open to new ideas and lifestyles as liberalism became influential. The era saw many achievements, including the first people to walk on the moon and the idealism that created the Peace Corps, an agency that sent young Americans to help communities in developing nations, chiefly as teachers, health workers, and agricultural specialists. Presidents John F. Kennedy (g. 1961–1963) and Lyndon B. Johnson (g. 1963–1969) launched government programs to address poverty and racism. But the 1960s was also a decade of doubts, anger, and violence. Three national leaders were assassinated, including Kennedy, who was shot in the head while riding in a motorcade in 1963. The war in Vietnam, the civil rights movement for African Americans, and issues of environmental protection and women's empowerment divided the nation. The country's social fabric fragmented as pro-war "hawks" and anti-war "doves" competed for support. Riots and demonstrations punctuated the decade.

During the 1960s a large segment of young people, chiefly middle class, rebelled against the values of their parents and established society. The folksinger Bob Dylan (b. 1941), who had a very large following, sung: "Come, mothers and fathers, throughout the land, And don't criticize what you can't understand. Your sons and your daughters are beyond your command, Your old world is rapidly aging'. Please get out of the new one if you can't lend your hand, For the times, they are a-changing."[8] Some youth, especially high school and university students, worked to change society and politics, registering voters, holding "teach-ins" to discuss national issues, and going door to door to spread their cause. Other youth forged what they called a counterculture that often involved using illegal drugs, such as marijuana, and engaging in casual sex. Supporters of social change emblazoned the slogan "Make love, not war" on bumper stickers, posters, and buttons. The Summer of Love in 1967, during which young people from North America and elsewhere gathered in San Francisco to hear rock music and share comradery, and the Woodstock rock music festival of 1969, which attracted over 300,000 young people to a New York State farm field to hear some of the most popular rock

musicians, marked the zenith of both the youth counterculture and political activism.

In the 1970s, with the winding down of the war in Vietnam and widespread concern at the excesses of the decade, the nation returned to more conservative values and politics. With the exception of the 1990s, when the moderate Bill Clinton (g. 1993–2001) held the presidency, conservatives have maintained their dominance of American politics and the social agenda, including a vigorous campaign to punish illegal drug use. Religion has also remained a powerful force, with Americans being more likely to attend churches and profess strong Christian beliefs than Canadians or most Europeans. While many Protestants, Catholics, and Jews supported liberal causes, by the 1980s Christian conservatives, both Catholics and evangelical Protestants, became influential in politics and public life, helping elect political conservatives to office. Some experts attributed the rise of Christian conservatism to a rejection of the Enlightenment and its emphasis on reason and tolerance. In this view, believers sought certainty and timeless rules. Others pointed to the search for a personal spiritual experience to help people withstand the stresses of modern life. Many churches stressed membership in a supportive community of believers while others preached a philosophy of self-help. While Americans avidly consumed new technologies, such as cell phones and portable music players, polls showed that, because of religious conservatism, substantial numbers also mistrusted science, for example, rejecting scientific explanations for the origins of the universe and human evolution in favor of biblical accounts.

Observers found much to deplore and much to praise in U.S. politics. On the negative side, in contrast to the political activism of the 1960s, fewer Americans now participated in the democratic process, with barely half of eligible voters bothering to vote in presidential elections. Americans voted in lower numbers than people in other industrial democracies. Money from big corporations and other special interests increasingly played a major role in politics, fostering corruption and widespread political apathy. However, on the positive side, a free media exposed government corruption, including abuse of power by presidents. President Richard Nixon, facing impeachment, resigned in 1973 for sanctioning and then covering up illegal activities by his subordinates. The presidencies of both Ronald Reagan (g. 1983–1989) and Clinton were marred by congressional hearings examining their misdeeds. After the controversial, bitter 2000 and 2004 elections, Americans were sharply divided between the two major political parties and the divergent policies they supported.

American Society

American society was different from what it had been before World War II. For example, suburbanization influenced social patterns. Most suburbs lacked ethnic and cultural diversity and isolated residents from the stimulation, as well as the problems, of big city life. Suburban living also intensified the trend, begun before World War II, toward two-parent, single-breadwinner nuclear families that lived apart from other relatives. By moving people farther away from city jobs, it encouraged mothers to stay at home. From World War II to the mid-1960s the image, conveyed in the media and advertising, of the fashionably dressed, stay-at-home suburban housewife, smiling proudly as she served breakfast to her husband and children, remained ingrained in the culture, even as women increasingly found it necessary to undertake paid work, especially after 1960. Critics lambasted the conformity of life in the standardized suburban tract houses, which, according to a song from the 1950s, resembled "little boxes. There's a green one, a pink one, a blue one and a yellow one. And they're all made out of ticky-tacky, And they all look just the same."[9] Changing city life affected both ethnic and gender relations.

Ethnic Relations   The changing American society affected ethnic minorities, families, women, and men. Throughout the decades since World War II Americans addressed racial issues. As they had since the end of slavery, African Americans, over 10 percent of the population, continued to experience much higher rates of poverty than whites and faced various forms of discrimination. The southern states maintained strict racial segregation, forcing blacks to attend separate schools and to even use different public drinking fountains than whites. Racism and poverty often encouraged African Americans in northern industrial cities to concentrate in run-down inner-city neighborhoods, known as ghettos.

The civil rights movement, organized by African Americans in the 1950s, eventually forced courts, states, and the federal government to introduce reforms. For example, in 1954 the Supreme Court outlawed segregated schools. A year later, in Montgomery, Alabama, Rosa Parks (1913–2005), a seamstress and community activist, bravely refused to follow the local law

and give up her front seat on a bus to a white man, sparking a mass movement for change. A black minister, Reverend Martin Luther King, Jr. (1929–1968), led a bus boycott to protest her arrest and fine. Using the strategy of nonviolent resistance pioneered by Mohandas Gandhi in South Africa and India in the early twentieth century, King led a protest movement all over the South. While leading the 1963 March on Washington to demand equal rights for nonwhites, he presented his vision: "I have a dream. When we let freedom ring, all of God's children will be able to join hands and sing in the words of that old spiritual, 'Thank God almighty, we are free at last!'"[10] King's assassination by a white racist in 1968 shocked the nation, but by then the African American struggle for equal rights had inspired similar struggles by nonwhites elsewhere in the world, including black South Africans, Afro-Brazilians, and Australian Aborigines. Thanks to the efforts of King, Parks, and many others, African Americans gradually gained legal equality, and many became able to move into the middle and upper classes, although by the twenty-first century African Americans were still far more likely than whites to live in poverty, face unemployment, and be imprisoned.

Americans boasted that they lived in a "melting pot," a society where ethnic groups merged and lost their separate identity, which was often the case for people of European ancestry during the century before World War II. However, members of many ethnic groups, especially non-whites, often maintained their separate identities and cultures so that in the later twentieth century Americans faced an increasingly multiracial, multicultural society. By 2006 the U.S. population of 300 million, the third largest total in the world after China and India, was more diverse than ever, and over 10 percent were foreign-born. American life took on a cosmopolitan flavor as Latin American

Martin Luther King, Jr.   An Atlanta minister, Dr. Martin Luther King, Jr., led many peaceful demonstrations for African American civil rights. In this photo, Dr. King (center front, with his wife, Coretta Scott King, to his right) leads a 1963 March on Washington for Jobs and Freedom, attended by some 200,000 supporters.   (Corbis)

grocery stores, Asian restaurants, and African art galleries opened in communities throughout the country, and Spanish was widely spoken. Alaska and Hawaii, both with large non-white populations, became states in 1959, adding to the nation's diversity.

Ethnic groups grew through legal and illegal immigration. Millions of Latin Americans moved to the United States. By 2000 the Mexican American population alone numbered around 20 million and seemed poised to soon outnumber the 25 million African Americans. Several million Asians also relocated to the United States, especially from China, South Korea, India, and Southeast Asia. Immigrants also arrived from Europe, the Middle East, the Caribbean, and South Pacific islands, especially Samoans and Tongans. To survive, some immigrants, legal or illegal, have labored for meager wages in crowded sweatshops in big cities, where bosses often allow workers only one or two breaks during their shift and ignore city safety regulations. For example, Chinese sewed clothing in New York City and Mexicans did the same in Los Angeles. Immigration marginalized Native Americans even more than before. While many lived in cities, others remained isolated on reservations. Some of them joined movements to assert their rights, often seeking a return of lands seized by white settlers generations earlier, and a few tribes achieved prosperity by operating gambling casinos; however, most Native Americans remained poor.

Gender Relations Women's issues became more prominent than before in U.S. history. In the 1950s few women worked for high pay, colleges imposed strict quotas on female applicants, married women could not borrow money in their own names, there was no legal concept of sexual harassment, and men often joked of keeping women "barefoot and pregnant." By the early twenty-first century conditions had changed dramatically but it took a long struggle for gender equality. Beginning in the 1960s women often joined feminist movements demanding equal legal rights with men and improved economic status. In 1963 Betty Friedan's (1921–2006) passionate book, *The Feminine Mystique*, identified women's core problem as a stunting of their growth by a patriarchal society. Women often agreed with Friedan's message that housework was unfulfilling. With slogans such as "Sisterhood Is Powerful," women came together in groups, such as the National Organization for Women (NOW), founded by Friedan in 1966, to fight for expanded options and opportunities for girls and women. Thanks in part to feminists' efforts, the median income of women workers climbed from 62 to 70 percent of that of men, and the number of women with paid work more than doubled between 1960 and 2000. Women held governorships, served in Congress, and sat on the Supreme Court. By the twenty-first century more women than men finished secondary school and attended universities, some joining highly paid, traditionally male occupations such as law, university teaching, engineering, and medicine. While many young women rejected the feminist label by 2000, those that chose to pursue satisfying, well-paid careers, run for political office, and enjoy personal freedoms unimag-

inable to their great grandmothers owed their gains largely to the feminist movement and its male supporters. However, whether professionals or working class, most women with paid jobs struggled to juggle work with family and housekeeping responsibilities. One young mother of two complained in the 1990s that "it's like twenty-four hours a day you're working. My day never ends."[11] Sexual harassment, especially in the workplace, stalking, and rape remained serious problems.

Social and legal changes affected both women and men. Divorce became easier and more common; by the 1990s over half of all marriages ended in divorce. Single-parent households grew more frequent. Increasingly, as in Europe, men and women never married, often living with partners out of wedlock. Whatever their gender, Americans remained deeply divided on some women's issues, especially abortion, which was long common but illegal in the United States before being declared legal by the Supreme Court in 1973. Americans also disagreed about homosexuality. By the 1960s gay men and lesbians actively struggled to end harassment and legal discrimination, gaining greater acceptance in society. Yet the growing numbers who openly acknowledged their sexual identity still faced hostility. During the early twenty-first century Americans quarreled over allowing homosexuals to marry or establish legal partnerships, a pattern of acceptance common in Europe and Canada but opposed by many Christian churches in the United States.

American Popular Culture

Once importers of culture from Europe, Americans became the world's greatest exporters of popular culture products. U.S.-made films, television programs, books, magazines, and sports reached a global audience, and popular music had widespread influence. Various musical styles, including the Broadway musicals of songwriters such as Richard Rogers and Oscar Hammerstein, the blues of singer Billie Holiday and guitarist B. B. King, the jazz of saxophonist John Coltrane and trumpeter Miles Davis, and the country music of singer-songwriters Hank Williams and Dolly Parton spread far and wide.

But no music style had the power of rock, which in the 1950s and 1960s helped spark a cultural revolution, especially among youth, in the United States and gained a huge following abroad. The first exhilarating blasts of rock and roll, notably from the white singer Elvis Presley (1935–1977), whose suggestive, hip-swinging performances earned him the nickname "Elvis the Pelvis," and the inventive black guitarist Chuck Berry (b. 1926), defied the Eisenhower era's puritanical emphasis on social and political conformity, pleasing youth while often alarming adults. In the United States, and then throughout the world, rock music broke down social barriers by challenging sexual and racial taboos.

The first American popular music appealing across social class boundaries, rock was inspired by black music, chiefly rhythm-and-blues, but also by the country and gospel music of white southerners. Early rock made a powerful statement that young Americans were less divided by race than their parents. Rock became the heart of the youth movement of the 1960s, when albums by key rock musicians, such as the poetic

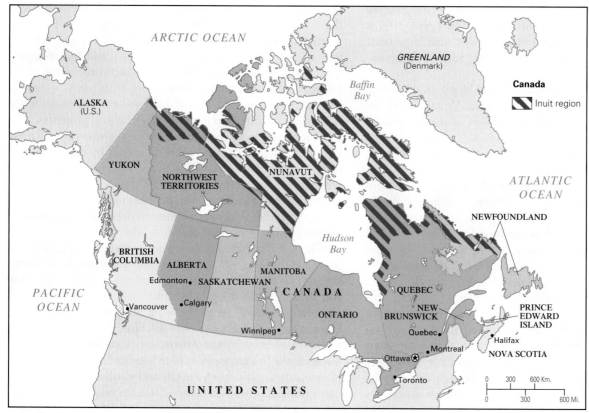

Map 29.2 Canada
The Canadian federation includes eleven provinces stretching from Newfoundland in the east to British Columbia and the Yukon in the west. In 1999 a large part of northern Canada, inhabited chiefly by the Inuit, became the self-governing region of Nunavut.

American singer-songwriter Bob Dylan and the British group the Beatles, seemed infused with messages that often shaped political awareness. After the 1960s rock lost its political edge but, evolving into forms such as punk, grunge, and heavy metal, remained at the heart of U.S. popular music.

The music created by African Americans, which has influenced all Americans and contributed to world culture, has also addressed problems of African American life. For example, the soul music in the 1960s, from artists like James Brown and Aretha Franklin, conveyed a message of black self-respect and unity parallel to the messages of the black pride movements of the era. In the 1980s and 1990s rap music emerged out of black ghettos to become the cutting-edge, politicized form of Western pop music. An eclectic mix of rock, soul, rhythm and blues, and Caribbean music, rap expresses the tensions of urban black youth yearning for independence, dignity, sex, and fun. The boastful, often angry tone highlights conflict between white and black, rich and poor, and male and female. Rap musicians have outraged segments of both white society and the black middle class, who fear the music threatens the social order. Musicians in nations around the world have adopted the rap style, often integrating it into their own traditions, but by the early twenty-first century rap's radical message was being watered down as it became mainstream in the United States and was embraced by more whites.

The Canadian Experience

Although they share cultural traditions and a democratic spirit with Americans, Canadians have remained proudly independent of their powerful southern neighbor while nurturing their political and social differences from Americans, such as by maintaining two official languages—English and French. Two parties, one liberal and one conservative, have dominated national elections, but, in contrast to the United States, smaller leftwing and rightwing parties also play key roles, often governing Canadian provinces. The Party Québécois (KAY-be-KWAH), for example, which supports French Canadian nationalism, has often won power in French-speaking Quebec, a province that contains a quarter of Canada's population, and periodically holds provincial votes, so far unsuccessful, on separating Quebec from Canada (see Map 29.2). In 1985 the federal parliament, hoping to preserve a united Canada, responded to French Canadians' resentments against Canada's English-speaking majority by recognizing Quebec as a distinct society within Canada and granting more autonomy to all the provinces. Canadians still debate how much power to allocate to the provinces and how much to the federal government.

Canadians, 33 million strong by 2005, cannot ignore their proximity to the United States, which has almost ten times

Canada's population and vastly more power in the world. Former prime minister Pierre Trudeau (troo-DOE) (g. 1968–1984), a French Canadian, complained that sharing a border with the United States was "like sleeping with an elephant. No matter how friendly or even-tempered the beast, one is affected by every twitch and grunt."[12] Most of Canada's people live within a hundred miles of the U.S. border and thus have easy access to the U.S. mass media and other cultural influences. Canada has also formed a major trading partnership with its southern neighbor. Americans own some 20 percent of the Canadian economy, prompting some Canadians to welcome U.S. investment as a spur to economic growth and others to resent U.S. domination. In 1994 the North American Free Trade Agreement (NAFTA) further bound the Canadian, Mexican, and U.S. economies. Yet, despite usually friendly U.S.-Canada relations, Canadians have often opposed U.S. foreign policies, including the wars in Vietnam and Iraq.

Despite occasional economic downturns, Canadians have enjoyed industrialization and prosperity, which in turn have fostered social stability. Agricultural, industrial, and natural resource exports have helped finance rising living standards; vast oil reserves have enriched western provinces. Canada has consistently ranked among the top five nations in the annual United Nations Human Development Index of quality of life. Unlike the more individualistic United States, over the years Canada, influenced by social democratic ideals, has built a strong social safety net for its citizens, including national health insurance. Also, like western Europeans, Canadians have generally been more liberal on social and economic issues than Americans. For example, in spite of strong opposition, Canadians have approved same-sex marriage, banned the death penalty, and, in some provinces, decriminalized marijuana use. As the society has become more secular, organized religion has had a declining influence in public life, in contrast to the United States. The secularizing trend has been especially notable in Quebec, where, a half century earlier, the Catholic Church had enjoyed great influence. By 2005 even openly homosexual politicians could gain popular support in Quebec and the province's birth rate, one of the world's highest in the 1940s, had fallen by over half to become one of the world's lowest.

Canadian society has become increasingly diverse. The nation has welcomed several million immigrants from all over the world, many from Asia and the Caribbean. In 2005 one of those Caribbean immigrants, Haitian-born Michaelle Jean, a television journalist in Quebec, became Canada's governor general, the nation's official head of state. Unlike Americans, who like to claim that they have become a "melting pot," the officially bilingual Canadians have adopted laws, especially the Multiculturalism Act of 1988, to allow ethnic minorities to maintain their cultures. But some Canadians, resenting the recognition of Portuguese Canadians or Chinese Canadians, have favored a melting pot of unhyphenated Canadians. Canadians have also recognized the rights of the indigenous Native Americans, known in Canada as the "First Nations," who have pressed land claims. To address the desire for autonomy of the Inuit, or Eskimo, people of the Arctic region, in 1999 the federal government transformed much

of northern Canada into the self-governing territory of Nunavut (NOO-nuh-voot), whose 27,000 people are mostly Inuit. Canadians are still in the process of determining, as the Quebec journalist Alain Dubuc put it, how much to think of themselves as English or French or Inuit Canadians and how much to live comfortably with multiple identities.

The Pacific Basin Societies

The diverse societies scattered around the Pacific Basin experienced major changes during this era as they adjusted to a new world. In the two largest, most populous countries, Australia and New Zealand, the majority population, descended from European, mainly British and Irish, settlers, had long identified with western European society, building economies that closely resembled those of the industrial West. But the rise of Asian economies, which fostered increased trade, prompted Australia and New Zealand to cultivate closer ties with East and Southeast Asian nations. Meanwhile, many Pacific islands once ruled by Britain, France, or New Zealand became independent nations navigating in a globalizing world.

Australia and New Zealand During this era Australia became one of the world's most affluent nations, known to its people as the "lucky country" because of its abundant resources and high living standards. Thanks in part to a comprehensive system of social welfare, health care, and education, Australians have forged a quality of life that placed the nation third after Norway and Sweden in the United Nations Human Development Report for 2004. However, the nation has also faced economic and social problems, among them a chronic high unemployment rate and areas of persisting poverty. Feminists complain that men dominate most institutions, including government, business, and churches, and that Australian women are less influential than women in most Western nations. Nonetheless, the efforts of women's organizations have forged considerable gender equity.

With 20 million people by 2005, Australia has become an increasingly diverse nation. In 1973 the federal government, seeking better relations with Asian nations and reflecting changing Australian social attitudes, abandoned restrictions on nonwhite, especially Asian, immigration—known as the "white Australia" policy—that had been in place since 1901. The shift to a policy based on skills rather than ethnicity stimulated immigration from Asia and the Middle East, and predominantly Asian neighborhoods developed in major cities. Newcomers from Europe also continued to arrive. For example, one of the major cities, Melbourne, boasted the world's largest Greek emigrant population. By 2001 nearly a quarter of Australia's people had been born abroad. Race relations improved as Aborigines, often poor and facing discrimination, gained some self-determination and land rights for their tribal territories. As a result, one group was able to block a dam project in the 1990s that threatened tribal land. Yet, those Aborigines living in cities, often in run-down neighborhoods, have struggled to find their place in the largely white-owned urban economy. Attacks on Arab immigrants by drunken

Lion Dance In recent decades, many Asians have settled in Australia. This Chinese lion's dance, in Melbourne's large Chinatown, celebrates the Chinese New Year. (Glenn Hunt/AAP)

white youth in Sydney in 2005 showed that racism had not been eliminated.

Changing global conditions have forced new economic thinking. With an economy based primarily on the export of natural and animal resources, such as minerals, wheat, beef, and wool, Australia needed secure outside markets. But the formation of the European Community and NAFTA threatened traditional markets in Europe and North America, raising questions about the nation's traditional link to Britain. In a 1995 referendum, 55 percent of Australians supported remaining a constitutional monarchy under the British queen. Yet, Britain was far away while Asia was, as Australians put it, the "near north." To secure markets and promote cooperation, Australians established closer trade links to nations in Southeast Asia, East Asia, and the Pacific islands. By 2000, Asian nations accounted for some 60 percent of Australia's export market. Australians saw themselves as suppliers and investors to the rising Asian and Pacific economies but also became consumers of Asian goods and investment.

Like Australians, New Zealanders had long cultivated their British heritage and depended on British patronage, but they now had to forge strategic and economic connections within the Asia-Pacific region. The nation's economy relied heavily on tourism and the export of agricultural products, mostly to Britain. Suffering from a stumbling economy and jolted by Britain's membership in the European Community, which diminished New Zealand's access to British markets, New Zealand cultivated especially close relations with the United States. However, these relations cooled after New Zealand refused to allow nuclear-armed U.S. ships to make visits to its ports. New Zealand then fostered economic cooperation with nearby Asian and Pacific countries, and by 2000 these countries accounted for one-third of the nation's trade.

New economic directions affected New Zealand's society. While experiencing rising unemployment, New Zealanders were supported by an elaborate social welfare system. Owing in part to expanded educational opportunities, women gained new economic roles and served in politics. In 1999 Helen Clark (b. 1950), a former university professor, became the nation's first female prime minister. Closer ties to the Pacific region also resulted in increased immigration from Asia and the Pacific islands. Like Australians, New Zealanders became more comfortable with ethnic diversity. The government recognized the land rights of, and worked to end discrimination against, the native Maori minority, who sought to maintain their Polynesian culture while adding modern economic skills.

The Pacific Islands While Australians and New Zealanders had long enjoyed independence, the decolonization of the Pacific islands, spurred by the United Nations, had to wait till the 1960s. Between 1962 and 1980 nine independent Pacific nations were formed in Polynesia and Melanesia, and in 1990 the United States gave up control of some of its Micronesian territories. The new states ranged from republics such as Fiji to kingdoms like Tonga to voluntary groupings such as the Federated States of Micronesia. Not all Pacific islanders, however, became independent. Some French-ruled islands, such as Tahiti and New Caledonia, became overseas departments of France, with representation in the French parliament, but many islanders still resented what they considered a disguised French colonialism. Most independent islands retained close ties to their former colonizer, as the Federated

States of Micronesia did with the United States. Whether nation or colony, islanders usually remained dependent on fishing, tourism, and the export of mineral and agricultural products, mostly to Japan, the United States, Australia, and New Zealand.

Islanders cooperated on common issues. They formed regional organizations to promote everything from duty-free trade to art festivals. Together the islanders fought high-technology fishing fleets from industrialized nations, especially Japan, that threatened their own low-technology fishing. To oppose nuclear weapons testing, and the radiation it created, they joined with Australia and New Zealand to declare the Pacific a nuclear-free zone. The international Law of the Sea Treaty gave the islands more control of adjacent sea beds, and hence their minerals. However, some problems affecting islands have defied solution. Thanks to rising sea levels, which threaten low-lying atolls and coastal plains, many islanders will have to relocate over the next century. The Tuvalo islands in the central Pacific, home to 11,000 people and on average only three feet above sea level, will be inundated by 2050.

The Pacific islanders have held on to some indigenous traditions while also adapting to social and political change. While most islanders have become Christian, some pre-Christian, precolonial customs have remained important. For example, Western Samoa, first ruled by Germany and then by New Zealand, has an elected parliament, adopted from the West, but clan chiefs still govern the villages, as they have for centuries. But certain forces have undermined traditional village life. Poverty has fostered migration to island cities, such as Suva in Fiji and Pago Pago in American Samoa, and emigration to Australia, New Zealand, Hawaii, and the mainland United States. By 2000 more Samoans and Cook Islanders lived abroad than at home, and thousands of Tongans lived in California. The money sent back by migrants has become a valuable source of income for their home islands. Some islands have also experienced ethnic or regional conflict as groups compete for political power and scarce land. For example, occasional military coups have rocked Fiji, resulting from tensions between the descendants of Indian immigrants, who comprise nearly half of the population, and the native Fijians. The Fijians fear that the Indians, should they gain power, would diminish the role of traditional Fijian chiefs and challenge tribal rights to land.

SECTION SUMMARY

■ On average, U.S. residents are among the wealthiest in the world, yet in recent decades many industrial jobs have been moved overseas and the gap between rich and poor has grown wider, with the former often living in suburbs and the latter left behind in inner cities.

■ In the 1950s, political conservatism dominated the United States and a large number of children were born; in the 1960s, liberalism was prominent, especially among the rebellious youth; and since the 1970s, conservatism has been generally dominant, though the country is sharply divided politically.

■ After 1945 more Americans lived in suburbs, African Americans gained legal rights through the civil rights movement, immigrants made America more diverse, women increasingly entered the work force, and gays and lesbians became more visible but still struggled for equal rights.

■ American culture became popular around the world, particularly music such as rock, which energized youth in the 1950s and 1960s, and rap, which initially expressed the radical political sentiments of African Americans but became watered down in the twenty-first century.

■ While Canada's culture and economy are strongly influenced by the United States, in many ways Canada resembles western Europe, with a strong social safety net and a more liberal attitude on social issues.

■ Australia and New Zealand have maintained their traditional ties with Britain but have also traded increasingly with their Southeast Asian neighbors, while many Pacific islands have gained independence from former colonizers but still face challenges such as rising sea levels, poverty, and ethnic conflict.

◆ Political Change in Latin America and the Caribbean

Why have democracy and economic development proven to be difficult goals in Latin America?

The Latin American and Caribbean peoples (see Map 29.3) had a different experience than North Americans and the Pacific Basin societies. Social inequality, economic underdevelopment, and the demands for change often created a pressure cooker, generating revolutionary and progressive political movements in impoverished villages and shantytowns. Sometimes leftists gained power, launching reforms, though only in Cuba did they remain in power for decades. A few Latin American countries and most small Caribbean islands enjoyed a consistent democratic tradition; elsewhere, however, military leaders or autocratic civilians often dominated governments. In most cases governments, whether democratic or dictatorial, proved unable to eliminate their nation's major problems.

Despotisms and Democracies

Latin American governments struggled to find the right mix of policies to raise living standards and expand political participation. Early in the century the Mexican Revolution, for example, challenged the inequities in society and wealth but later lost most of its revolutionary vigor and ultimately failed to resolve Mexico's problems. At other times paternalistic but authoritarian reformers mobilized workers and peasants for change, but they also failed to empower the mass of the population or significantly improve their lives.

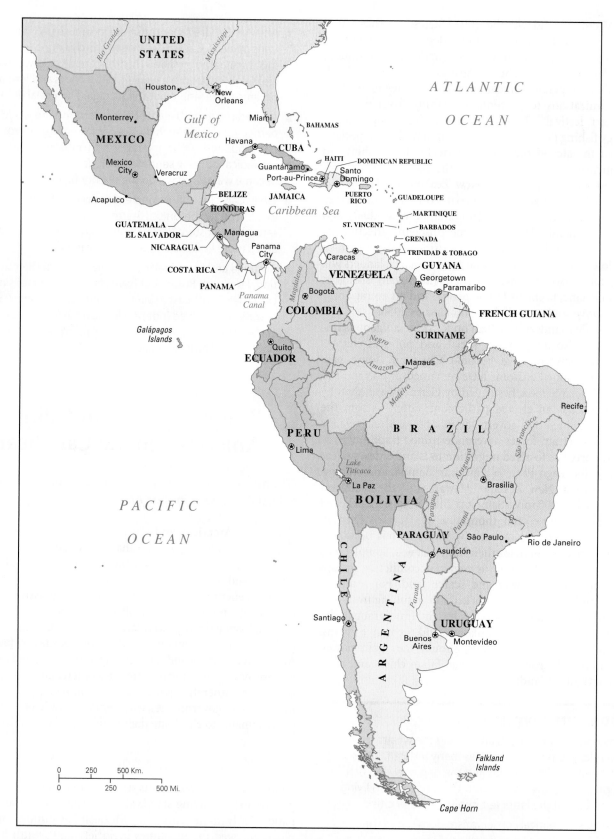

Map 29.3 Modern Latin America and the Caribbean

Latin America includes the nations of Central and South America and those Caribbean societies that are Spanish-speaking, including Cuba and the Dominican Republic. Brazil, Argentina, and Mexico are the largest Latin American nations. The peoples, mostly English or French speaking, of the small Caribbean islands also formed independent states.

The charismatic Juan Peron (puh-RONE) (1895–1974), a former army officer, admirer of the Italian fascist leader, Benito Mussolini, and hypnotic public speaker who was elected Argentina's president in 1946, was one of the major autocratic reformers (see Chronology: Latin America and the Caribbean, 1945–Present). Peron soon marginalized the legislature and crushed his opposition. With help from his hugely popular wife, Evita Peron (puh-RONE) (1919–1952), a radio and stage actress from a poor family and a proponent of social justice, the nationalistic Peron won the support of workers and the middle class by emphasizing industrialization and by having his government buy up banks, insurance companies, railroads, and shipping companies often owned by unpopular foreign interests. Meanwhile, Evita promoted women's issues, including voting rights. After Evita's death in 1952, Peron's popular support waned. Corruption, growing unemployment, inflation, strikes, and human rights abuses led to his overthrow in 1955. Peron returned to power briefly in 1973–1974, but otherwise the military ruled Argentina for most of the 1950s through early 1980s, often killing opponents. Yet Peron's followers sustained a Peronist movement with a working-class base that often governed the nation after the restoration of democracy in 1983.

Rightwing and leftwing forces, with vastly different goals, have jockeyed for power in Latin America. In the majority of countries from the 1950s through the late 1980s, rightwing military governments and despots ruled, suppressing labor unions, student protesters, and democracy activists to maintain stability. Some rightwing governments, especially in Central American countries such as El Salvador and Guatemala, organized informal armed units, known as death squads, to assassinate dissident peasants, liberal clergy, teachers, and journalists deemed threats to the regime. However, despite the repression, leftwing movements increased their strength. By 1979 the Sandinistas, a revolutionary movement led by Marxists, had mobilized enough popular support to defeat the dictatorship, in power since the 1920s, and gain control of Nicaragua. An even more radical movement, the Shining Path, emerged in Peru in 1970. The movement's leaders, half of them women, dismissed all other Latin American Marxists as sell-outs and mixed Maoist ideas with a call to emancipate the impoverished Indians of Peru. Their rebellion used terrorism to demoralize Peruvians and bring the country to its knees before finally being crushed in the early 1990s.

During the later 1980s, with rightwing authoritarian rule largely discredited because it was unable or unwilling to address mass poverty, many nations turned to democracy under centrist or moderate leftist leaders. But in most cases the free markets these democratic governments introduced were unable to resolve the severe problems or diminish social equalities, allowing both rightwing and extreme leftist forces to increase in strength. Some nations also faced racial and ethnic tensions. In particular, the large Indian communities in Bolivia, Peru, Colombia, Mexico, and Guatemala, often allied with the left, increasingly sought equal rights, a fairer share of the wealth, and recognition of their cultures, aspirations often opposed by whites. In 2005, for example, chronic resentment by Bolivia's Indian majority led to the

CHRONOLOGY

Latin America and the Caribbean, 1945–Present

1946–1955	Government of Juan Peron in Argentina
1954	CIA overthrow of Guatemalan government
1959	Triumph of Fidel Castro in Cuba
1962	Cuban missile crisis
1964–1985	Military government in Brazil
1973	Overthrow of Chilean government
1973–1989	Military government in Chile
1979–1989	Sandinista government in Nicaragua
1983	Restoration of Argentina's democracy
1990	U.S. invasion of Panama
1994	Formation of NAFTA
1998	Economic collapse in many nations
2000	Election of President Vicente Fox in Mexico
2002	Election of President Lula da Silva in Brazil

election, as president, of Evo Morales, a former small-town soccer player and trumpeter of humble origins who had led a movement of coca farmers fighting a white-dominated government and U.S. opposition to coca growing. At the ruins of an ancient temple, Morales took part in a spiritual ceremony steeped in the traditions of Tiwanaku, the state built by his Aymara Indian group that flourished centuries before the Incas. Walking barefoot up the pyramid steps, he donned a traditional tunic and cap and accepted a gold and silver baton from Aymara priests, then promised to "seek equality and justice" for the poor and do away with the vestiges of the Spanish colonial past.

By the later 1990s, as disillusionment with capitalism increased, the left was regaining the political initiative, working largely within a democratic context. Mobilizing workers and peasants, who had benefited little from the country's oil wealth, the former general Hugo Chavez was elected president of oil-rich Venezuela and introduced socialist policies that alienated the wealthy and middle class, who organized mass protests against his regime. However, these protests increased support for Chavez among poor Venezuelans, who supported his marginalization of the congress and control of the courts. Chavez called his policies the Bolivaran Revolution, linking them to the nineteenth-century, Venezuelan-born liberator. But the United States moved to isolate the dictatorial, pro-Cuba Chavez regime and support the opposition. During the early twenty-first century, voters, like those in Venezuela, who were desperate for more equitable economic and social policies also elected pragmatic leftist leaders in countries such as Argentina, Brazil, Chile, and Uruguay. These leaders often began the process, neglected by their cautious predecessors, of prosecuting the human rights violations that occurred years earlier under military rule. But whether imported economic ideas, whether from the left or the right, will work for Latin Americans remains to be seen.

The United States in Latin America

The United States has had a powerful economic and political presence in Latin America since the nineteenth century, and, as the world's major superpower, it had even more of an impact in the second half of the twentieth. Referring to longtime U.S. economic leverage over his country, a Nicaraguan leader critical of the United States claimed that his country's "function was to grow sugar, cocoa and coffee for the United States; we served the dessert at the imperialist dining table."[13] Not all Latin Americans took such a negative view, however. The U.S. role in the region was complex, with the country serving not only as the neighborhood bully at times—especially when it helped overturn governments—but also as a leading trading partner, a major source of investment capital, a supplier of military and economic assistance, and an inspiration to the region's democrats and free market enthusiasts. As a result, many Latin American leaders maintained close relations with various U.S. administrations and often supported U.S. foreign policies. U.S. popular culture, particularly films and music, has reached a huge audience, influencing local cultures. And several million people seeking a better life have moved to the United States legally or illegally. The United States gained favor in the region by transferring control over the Panama Canal, built by the United States in the early 1900s, to Panama in 1999; yet the agreement also allowed U.S. military bases to remain along the canal, a symbol of U.S. regional power.

The United States intervened in Latin American and Caribbean countries under the banner of anti-communism. These interventions aroused much local resentment, as was illustrated by the earliest intervention, in Guatemala in 1954. A force led by exiled Guatemalan military officers, covertly organized, armed, and trained by the U.S. Central Intelligence Agency (CIA), overthrew a democratically elected reformist government, led chiefly by liberals and socialists, that American leaders accused of being communist, an unsupported claim. The government had angered U.S. business interests, especially the powerful United Fruit Company, by implementing land reform and encouraging labor unions, whose leaders were chiefly leftists. The United Fruit Company controlled much of the Guatemalan economy, especially the banana plantations, and had close ties to officials in the Eisenhower administration. The removal of the democratic regime cheered both wealthy Guatemalans, especially large landowners, and U.S. corporations with investments in Guatemala, but the new Guatemalan leaders proved to be murderous tyrants.

Forming death squads, they killed over 200,000 Guatemalans, especially poor Indian peasants and workers, over the next three decades. By 1990, 90 percent of Guatemalans still lived in poverty, and one-third of them lacked adequate food.

The successful ousting of the Guatemalan government encouraged U.S. leaders to use their power elsewhere to further Cold War foreign policy objectives. Americans offered military assistance and advice to maintain friendly governments in power against the challenge of revolutionary movements in El Salvador, Honduras, and Colombia. As in Guatemala, the United States also used covert operations to help undermine or overthrow governments deemed too left-leaning, for example, in Brazil (1964), Chile (1973), and Nicaragua (1989). The American public was often unaware of the covert U.S. activities until years later. Sometimes the United States resorted to sending in U.S. military force, as in the Dominican Republic (1965) and Grenada (1982). Not all interventions were inspired by anti-communism. In 1990 U.S. troops invaded Panama to remove and arrest the dictator Manuel Noriega (b. 1940), a longtime U.S. ally and well-paid CIA informant who was also implicated in human rights abuses in Panama and in smuggling narcotics into the United States, and in 1994 U.S. troops were sent to Haiti, the Western Hemisphere's poorest country, in support of a reform government that had replaced a brutal dictatorship. U.S. troops have remained in Haiti promoting stability as leftwing and rightwing political forces intermittently battled for control, leaving Haitians poorer and more desperate.

The Mexican Experience

The Mexican Revolution in the early twentieth century had led to hopes of reducing social inequality, but the nation's leaders soon turned to emphasizing economic growth over uplifting the poor majority. As a result, even today, in a southern state where, nearly a century ago, the revolutionaries had promised to bring liberty and justice to the poor, peasant men, wearing traditional white cotton pants and shirt, still use a machete to cultivate their tiny plots of corn. Mexico's limited democracy offered regular elections and some civil liberties. But one party, the Party of Revolutionary Institutions, known as the PRI, controlled the elections and hence the government, often resorting to such electoral tricks as voter fraud. A coalition of factions ranging from left to right, the PRI was led by businessmen and bureaucrats. For decades its leaders fostered stability while deflecting challenges to their power monopoly. The PRI had typically either co-opted or arrested opponents, but in 1968 it shocked the nation by ordering police to open fire on a large demonstration, killing hundreds of university students and other protesters.

By the 1980s the PRI began to falter. Although leftist and rightwing parties struggled to overcome the PRI's vast power and wealth, they made some national gains. In the early 1990s a peasant revolt in a poor southern state, Chiapas, revealed starkly the PRI's failure to redress rural poverty. The election of a reformist, non-PRI president, Vicente Fox, a pro-U.S. free-market conservative, in 2000 ended the seven decades-long

PRI monopoly on federal power. However, Fox proved unable to foster much economic or social change. While the PRI lost some credibility, it still held power in many states and enjoyed a national power base. By 2005 a more open and pluralistic political system had emerged, with stronger leftist and rightwing parties contending with the PRI for support. Whether the democratic processes fostered by Fox, who failed to deliver on most of his promises but, unlike his predecessors, was not corrupt, can be consolidated and endure remained to be seen.

Mexico's economic system also gradually opened, but without diminishing poverty. For decades the PRI had mixed capitalism with a strong government role. However, the collapse of world oil prices in the 1980s damaged Mexico's development prospects, since Mexico's oil was the major foreign revenue source. In the late 1980s PRI leaders replaced protectionist policies with open markets. In 1994 the North American Free Trade Agreement (NAFTA) helped integrate the U.S. and Mexican economies, and many U.S.-owned factories opened on the Mexican side of the border that employed thousands of workers. The majority of these workers, however, have been poorly paid young women who are usually housed in crowded dormitories or flimsy shacks and often complain of harassment or assault by male workers or managers. Elsewhere Mexicans have lost jobs; peasant corn farmers, for example, unable to compete with highly subsidized U.S. farmers, have often been ruined. By 2000 half of the 100 million Mexicans lived on $4 a day or less, and the bottom 20 percent of Mexicans earned only 3.5 percent of the country's personal income. Even the urban middle class feels the economic pain as wages stagnate. In 1980 Mexico's economy was nearly four times larger than South Korea's; by 2005 a dynamic South Korea had pushed ahead of Mexico. In addition, Mexico's population quadrupled between 1940 and 2000, pressuring the nation's resources. Because of poverty and overpopulation, thousands of desperate Mexicans continue to cross the border to the United States each year, legally or illegally, in search of a better life.

Online Study Center Improve Your Grade
Primary Source: Free Trade and the Decline of Democracy

Revolutionary Cuba

In contrast to Mexico's mix of authoritarian and democratic politics, public ownership and capitalism, Cuba, led by Fidel Castro (b. 1927), built a society dominated by a powerful communist government. Castro, a onetime amateur baseball star nearly signed by a U.S. professional team who instead became a lawyer, came to power in 1959, the victor of a revolution against a repressive, corrupt dictator long supported by the United States. Although the son of a rich sugar planter, Castro allied with the Cuban Communist Party and promised to introduce radical change, prompting thousands of upper- and middle-class Cubans to flee to the nearby United States. In 1961 the United States moved to isolate and then overthrow his regime by organizing a military force composed of Cuban exiles that landed on a Cuban beach, known as the Bay of Pigs. But the invasion had been poorly planned and enjoyed little

popular support in Cuba. Castro's forces routed the invading exiles, a humiliation for the United States.

Needing a protector, Castro became a firm Soviet ally, thereby igniting even more opposition from an alarmed United States. The Cuba–USSR alliance soon precipitated a major crisis. In 1962 U.S. air surveillance of the island revealed Soviet ballistic missiles with a 2,000-mile range and capable of carrying nuclear warheads. The U.S. demand that the missiles be removed sparked what became known as the Cuban missile crisis, during which the United States imposed a naval blockade on Cuba and considered an invasion of the island. With the threat of nuclear confrontation looming, the Soviets backed down and removed the missiles, defusing the crisis. However, in the aftermath, the United States, hoping to bring down Castro's regime, imposed an economic boycott, strongly supported by Cuban exiles in the United States, that endured into the twenty-first century, cutting off Cuba from sources of trade and investment.

In the 1960s and 1970s Castro tried innovative socialist policies, often known as **Castroism**, to stimulate economic development in Cuba while also tightly controlling its population. Castro called capitalism "repugnant, filthy, gross, alienating because it causes war, hypocrisy and competition"[14]; yet his own policies generated little surplus food and few consumer goods. Despite valiant efforts, Cubans failed to diversify their sugar-based economy. Nonetheless, Castroism improved the material and social life of the working classes; the regime built schools and clinics, mounted literacy campaigns, and promoted equality for long-marginalized Afro-Cubans and women. In quality of life statistics, by the mid-1980s Cuba, with the lowest infant mortality and highest literacy rates and life expectancy, ranked well ahead of other Latin American nations. Cubans lived as long as North Americans and ten years longer than Mexicans and Brazilians. Cuba had nearly as many doctors per population as the United States and over twice as many as Mexico or Brazil. In addition, in contrast to some Latin American dictatorships, the Cuban government did not form death squads or sponsor murders of dissidents. However, it did attempt to control the Cuban people. Government agencies monitored citizens and their opinions, and Castro placed limits on free expression, jailing those who defied the ban. The jailed included brave writers, homosexuals, and those publicizing human rights violations and advocating free speech and elections. Seeking political freedom, better-paying jobs, or higher living standards, several hundred thousand Cubans have fled over the years, chiefly to the United States.

The Cuban Revolution, and the society it created, had international repercussions. Castro exchanged dependence on the United States for dependence on the USSR, which, to maintain the alliance, poured billions of dollars of aid into the country. With the collapse of the USSR in 1991, however, Castro lost his patron and benefactor. Since then Cuba has struggled. Because

---

Castroism Innovative socialist policies introduced by Fidel Castro to stimulate economic development in Cuba while tightly controlling its population.

Castro Addressing Crowd
A spellbinding orator, the Cuban leader, Fidel Castro, often recruits support for his government and policies by speaking at large rallies. (Corbis)

of the U.S. embargo, the country has few markets or sources of capital. The social welfare system has cracked, and the economy has crumbled despite efforts to introduce some market forces. Yet, frustrating his opponents, Castro remains in power. Critics of U.S. policy, including most U.S. allies, have argued that the U.S. embargo helps Castro by reinforcing strong anti-U.S. feelings and discrediting pro-U.S. dissidents. Remembering the history of U.S. domination from 1898 to 1959, many Cubans, while desiring a freer, more productive system, do not necessarily want the United States to determine their fate.

Brazil: Dictatorship and Democracy

While Mexico and Cuba, despite some successes, have disappointed those who hoped they would become development models for Latin America, few Latin American nations have had as much promise and experienced as many problems as Brazil. Occupying half of the South American continent, and with a population in 2005 of some 186 million, Brazil is Latin America's colossus and has its largest economy. From the mid-1940s to the mid-1960s the nation had a democratic government, which persisted for two decades despite increasing tensions between left and right and periodic economic crises. In 1961 Joao Goulart (jao joo-LART) (1918–1976), a populist reformer supported by leftist groups, assumed the presidency. Under his rule, the economy stumbled and efforts to organize the impoverished peasants and rural workers antagonized powerful landlords. Seeking to halt change and impose order, the military overthrew Goulart in 1964 and ruled Brazil for the next two decades under a harsh military dictatorship, which arrested some 40,000 citizens. Viewing Brazil as ripe for a communist takeover, the United States had encouraged the military coup. Brazilian industrialists, businessmen, planters, and affluent urbanites, fearing the nation faced turmoil, welcomed the change.

Between 1964 and 1985 authoritarian governments, headed by generals and supported by the United States, gave priority to economic growth and national security at the expense of social programs. Relying on brutal repression, the regimes imposed comprehensive censorship, outlawed political parties, and banned strikes and collective bargaining. Human rights abuses became rampant. Rightwing vigilante groups and death squads instilled terror, killing or torturing dissidents; one police squad assassinated over 1,000 people the government called "undesirables," among them labor leaders and shantytown residents. Death squads remained active into the 1980s, murdering up to 100 victims a month.

The generals imposed a capitalist economic model recommended by American advisers encouraging free markets and foreign investment. For a decade the economy boomed, eliciting foreign praise of the "Brazilian miracle" as annual growth rates averaged 10 percent between 1968 and 1974 and exports soared. The policies promoted a major shift in exports from natural resources, such as coffee, to manufactured goods. Industrialization relied heavily on foreign investment, technology, and markets. The United States and international lending agencies poured in $8 billion in aid. But the "miracle" depended on low wages and redistributing income upward to the rich and middle class, confirming the local saying that there is no justice for the poor. The top 10 percent of people enjoyed 75 percent of the income gain while half of all households lived below the poverty line. Less than half the labor force earned the minimum wage. While many people went barefoot and dressed in rags, Brazil made and exported shoes. Beginning in the 1960s, Brazilian governments encouraged land speculators and foreign corporations to open up the vast Amazon basin, the world's largest tropical rain forest and river system. The virgin forest was rapidly stripped for logging, farming, mining, and ranching, displacing many of the 200,000 Indians who lived off its resources.

By 1980 the "miracle" was fading as Brazil experienced an inflation rate of over 100 percent, a huge balance of payments deficit, a massive foreign debt, and sagging industrial production. Meanwhile, numerous sectors of society, including students, demanded democracy, and the Catholic Church criticized human rights violations and advocated for social justice. In 1985 the growing political liberalization climaxed with a return to democracy and the election of a civilian president. Under the successive democratic governments led by moderate reformers, however, many problems remained unresolved, since leaders feared that policies hurting big business might provoke a military coup. As economic problems increased, inflation soared to 2,500 percent by 1994. Responding to the gross inequality in rural land ownership, landless peasants seized land, but landowners hired gunmen to harass the militants. Social inequities such as school dropout rates, malnutrition, bankrupt public health services, homelessness, and debt slavery grew. Brazil maintained one of the world's most unequal income distributions: the wealthiest 1 percent of people earned the same percentage of national income as the poorest 50 percent. As a result, many Brazilians became disillusioned with democracy.

Although the economy revived in the later 1990s, Brazilians, wanting further reform, turned to the political left. In 2002 they gave leftist candidates 80 percent of the vote and elected as president socialist labor leader Luis Ignacio da Silva (b. 1944), known as Lula, a former metalworker and longtime dissident. While Lula has fostered faster economic growth, and some observers compare Brazil to dynamic Southeast Asian nations such as Malaysia, Singapore, and Thailand, peasant and worker groups believe Lula's economic policies go too far in pleasing financial interests and international lenders. Despite the booming economy, by 2006 corruption scandals threatened to bring down the regime. Whatever their political fortunes, Brazilians have often shared an optimistic outlook because of the nation's size and economic potential, reflected in the saying that "God is a Brazilian." But a perennial local joke reflects cynicism: "Brazil, Country of the Future, but the future never comes."[15]

Chile: Reform and Repression

While Cubans sought to escape underdevelopment through revolution, Chileans, like Brazilians, tried a succession of strategies, from reform to dictatorship to democracy. Chileans enjoyed a long tradition of elected democratic governments sustained by a large middle class, high rates of literacy and urbanization, and mass-based political parties. Nonetheless, a wealthy elite of businessmen, military officers, and landowners held political power and suppressed labor unrest. Despite a growing manufacturing sector, Chile depended on the export of minerals, especially copper. By the 1960s it was divided politically between the right, center, and left, and a stagnant economy widened the gap between rich and poor. Two-thirds of Chileans earned under $200 a year.

Chile shifted direction with the 1970 elections. Six liberal, socialist, and communist parties united in a left-leaning coalition, the Popular Unity, that was supported largely by small businessmen, the urban working class, and peasants. Their winning presidential candidate, Salvador Allende (ah-YEN-dee) (1908–1973), who had developed compassion for the poor while working as a medical doctor, promised a "Chilean road" to socialism, with red wine and meat pies, through constitutional means in a parliamentary democracy. His regime took over, and paid compensation to, banks and a copper industry that had been dominated by powerful U.S. corporations. Land reform broke up underutilized ranches and divided the land among the peasant residents. Allende's government supported the labor unions and provided the urban shantytowns with health clinics and better schools. Both employment and economic production reached the highest levels in Chilean history. The Popular Unity was also committed to the creation of a Chilean cultural renaissance. Imported magazines, recordings, and films from abroad, especially from the United States, had become popular in Chile, particularly among the middle class, marginalizing Chilean-produced cultural products. According to a pro-Allende cultural organization, "Our folklore, our history, our customs, our way of living and thinking are being strangled [by] the uncontrolled invasion [of the U.S. media and popular culture]."[16]

Democracy flourished and Allende enjoyed growing popularity, but the Popular Unity government also generated opposition. The rapid reforms produced shortages of luxury goods, fostering middle-class resentment. Allende's opponents controlled the mass media and judiciary and dominated the congress. At the same time, the U.S. president, Richard Nixon, worried about Allende's friendship with Cuba's Fidel Castro and feared that Allende's socialism without revolution could become a model for Latin America, threatening U.S. power and economic interests. The United States also mounted an international economic embargo on Chilean exports. The CIA undertook a disinformation campaign, such as spreading untrue rumors that Allende planned to conscript women into the military, cooperated in assassinating pro-Allende military officers, and organized strikes to paralyze the economy.

In 1973 a military coup supported by the United States overthrew Allende, who died while defending the presidential palace from an assault. The military imposed a brutal military dictatorship led by General Agusto Pinochet (ah-GOOS-toh pin-oh-CHET) (b. 1915). Pinochet launched a reign of terror, arresting some 150,000 Allende supporters and detaining and routinely torturing hundreds of political prisoners for years. The regime murdered thousands of dissidents, sometimes in front of other prisoners held in the national stadium, and buried the victims in unmarked mass graves. Thousands of Chileans fled the country. The junta forbade labor unions and strikes, prohibited free speech and political parties, restored nationalized U.S. property, and engaged in public burnings of books and records produced by leftist Chileans. Advised by U.S. economists, Pinochet shifted to a free enterprise economy, similar to military-ruled Brazil's, that generated growth and moderate middle-class prosperity purchased at the cost of a monumental foreign debt and environmental degradation. But little of this wealth trickled down to the poor, whose living standards deteriorated. By the later 1980s, unemployment had skyrocketed to 30 percent of Chileans, and some 60 percent of people were poor. Two observers wrote that Pinochet's Chile "remained a dual society of winners and losers. The rich, roaring through traffic in their expensive sedans, seemed to mock those left behind, trapped in fuming buses."[17]

However, a severe economic crisis that undermined the regime's legitimacy led to a return to a civilian-led liberal democracy. Escalating social tensions and political protests prompted the junta to hold an election and restore democracy in 1989. The resulting center-left governments struggled to maintain middle-class prosperity while promoting a more equitable distribution of wealth. They retained free enterprise while making additions to health, housing, education, and social spending. These policies chipped away at poverty. The population living in poverty has been reduced by half and unemployment has plummeted. Tax increases and increased welfare have not stifled the annual economic growth of about 10 percent. Chile has become the most prosperous Latin American economy, enjoying a stable democratic system. Chilean and U.S. officials have discussed the possibility of Chile joining NAFTA. Yet, many Chileans remain bitter toward the United States for having once helped install and perpetuate a brutal military regime.

SECTION SUMMARY

- In Latin America, rightwing and leftwing movements competed for power; rightwing movements were dominant from the 1950s through the 1980s, and moderates and leftists such as Venezuela's Hugo Chavez gained more power in the 1990s.

- Many Latin Americans resented U.S. interference in their economies and support for the overthrow of leftist governments, while others welcomed the U.S. example of democracy and free trade.

- The Mexican Revolution led to decades of single-party rule that failed to significantly help the poor, and a reformist president elected in 2000 also failed to improve their lot. Many Mexicans illegally crossed the U.S. border in search of a better life.

- Under Castro, communist Cuba has attempted to control its people but has also provided excellent medical care and education; however, the withdrawal of aid from the USSR in 1991 and the U.S. embargo have left its economy struggling.

- Under a brutal U.S.-supported military dictatorship, Brazil enjoyed a period of impressive growth but then experienced extreme inflation and increasing gaps between rich and poor; democracy returned in the mid-1980s, and the economy recovered in the late 1990s.

- Alarmed by the popularity of a democratically elected leftist government in Chile, the United States supported a 1973 coup there as well as the brutal military dictatorship that resulted, which rewarded the wealthy and further impoverished the poor, and which was replaced by a democratic government in 1989.

Changing Latin American and Caribbean Societies

How have Latin American and Caribbean cultures been dynamic?

The societies of Latin America and the Caribbean, while facing daunting economic problems, have had social and cultural patterns different from those of North America and the Pacific Basin. Rather than balanced economic growth, Latin American and Caribbean nations have often emphasized export of traditional natural resources such as oil, sugar, coffee, bananas, wool, and copper. The Spanish-speaking nations, Portuguese-speaking Brazil, and the English- and French-speaking Caribbean societies, being derived from varied mixes of peoples and traditions, often have little in common with each other. But the regions' peoples have fostered dynamic cultural forms that have found international popularity.

Latin American Economies

Although often enjoying economic growth, no Latin American nations have achieved the level of prosperity found in the industrialized West. Latin Americans forged rising literacy rates, lowered infant mortality rates, and more people than ever now own televisions, even in poor neighborhoods. Nonetheless, the world price for most of their natural resource exports usually has declined every year, leaving less money for economic development. Most countries have experienced little growth in per capita income or productivity. To pay the bills and import luxury items, governments have taken out loans, eventually owing billions to international lenders. Rapidly expanding populations, growing at 3 percent a year, add to the social burden and cause environmental problems. Governments have tried to satisfy land hunger, mineral prospecting, and timber exploitation by treating indigenous peoples and the rain forests they inhabit as expendable resources.

As Brazil, Chile, and Mexico demonstrated, Latin America has also suffered severe income inequality. By 2000 the top 10 percent of the population earned half of all income, and 70 percent of the people lived in poverty. The rich have often evaded taxes, leaving states with little money for building schools and clinics. The small elite class drives Rolls Royces, while the poor lack bus service. In Brazil half of the people have had no access to doctors even while Rio de Janeiro has become the world's plastic surgery capital, with hundreds of cosmetic surgeons catering to wealthy Brazilians and foreigners. In Caracas, Venezuela's capital, one shopping mall that serves the affluent boasts 450 stores, an amusement park, two movie theaters, and a McDonald's. But any customers coming from a slum of open sewers and tin shacks, perched a few miles away on unstable hillsides, would have to pay half a day's wage for a Big Mac. To survive, poor peasants in some nations, especially after the decline of world coffee prices pushed coffee growers out of jobs, have often turned to growing coca and opium for making

U.S. Factory in Mexico Since the 1980s growing numbers of U.S. companies have relocated industrial operations to Mexico, building many factories along the Rio Grande River that separates Mexico from Texas. In this factory, in Matamoros, Mexico, the mostly female labor force makes toys for the U.S. market. (Keith Dannemiller/Corbis)

cocaine and heroin. But the drug trade, largely to the U.S. market, fosters political turbulence and government corruption and profits only a few drug kingpins.

Agriculture has remained a mainstay of most Latin American economies. Landholding is usually concentrated in a small group of aristocratic families and multinational corporations, such as the U.S.-based United Fruit Company. By the 1990s, 60 percent of all agricultural land was held in large estates and farmed inefficiently, contributing to food shortages and malnutrition. Modern agriculture requires large investments for machinery, fertilizers, pesticides, and fuel, but growing beans and corn to feed hungry peasants supplies inadequate revenue. As a result, vast tracks of rain forests and land that once grew food crops have been transformed into ranches, which often raise beef cattle for fast-food outlets in North America and Europe. Latin America remains a food importer, mostly from North America, and malnutrition causes half of all child deaths. In Peru's major city, Lima, hundreds of poor children, known as "fruit birds," desperately compete with stray dogs for spoiled fruit. In Mexico, beef cattle consume more food than the poorest quarter of people.

Life in rural areas has often been marked by hardship. A Brazilian novel captured the hopelessness of the rural workers in the drought-tortured northeast, where, in the 1980s, life expectancy was thirty years, eighty-five children died each hour, and only two-thirds of children attended school. The herder Fabiano understands that everything prevents his escape from endless poverty: "If he could only put something aside for a few months, he would be able to get his head up. Oh, he had made plans, but that was all foolishness. Ground creepers were never meant to climb. Once the beans had been eaten and the ears of corn gnawed, there was no place to go but to the boss's cash drawer [for a loan]."[18]

Unemployment and unprofitable farms have generated migration from rural areas to cities; by 2000 the region had become the world's most urbanized, with 75 percent of people living in cities and towns. The migrants fill cities with surplus people living in festering shantytowns and working as shoeshine boys, cigarette vendors, car washers, or in other poorly paid work. Half the urban population lack adequate water, housing, sanitation, and social services. But economic growth has also fostered growing middle classes, which have become a third of the population in Argentina, Chile, and Uruguay and a fifth in Brazil and Mexico.

Beginning in the 1980s many Latin American nations, hoping to emulate the success of the United States, adopted **neoliberalism**, an economic model, encouraged by the United States, that promoted free markets, privatization, and Western investment. The model generated growth for a decade, but more people than ever remained stuck in poverty. The neoliberal model failed to curb government corruption, install honest judicial systems, foster labor-intensive industries, or reduce the power of rich elites or dependence on foreign loans and investment. Free markets have often meant a few people enjoyed fabulous wealth while most people remained poor. The nation that most ardently adopted neoliberalism, Argentina, saw its economy collapse in 1998; unemployment soared and, by 2001, half of the people lived in poverty. The economy only revived after Argentineans elected pragmatic leftists into power in 2003. Since then the economy has grown by 9 percent a year and, in 2006, the nation paid back the money still owed to the International Monetary Fund, a rare occurrence in the world

neoliberalism An economic model encouraged by the United States in the developing world that promoted free markets, privatization, and Western investment.

and a symbol of recovery as well as of a turn to a more state-oriented economy and a paternalistic style of governing by President Nestor Kirchner, a Peronist. But although neoliberalism lost credibility, no other economic model, such as Cuban communism or Allende's socialism with democracy, had widespread support or a record of success in Latin America.

Latin America: Society and Religion

Political and economic change has modified social arrangements, especially in gender relations and family life. Although men dominate the governments, militaries, businesses, and the Catholic Church, women's struggles have managed to reduce gender inequality. Once considered helpless and groomed as girls to be a wife and mother, many women now go out to paid work, some fighting for recognition in male-dominated trades. Millions of women have earned money selling clothing, handicrafts, and food in small markets or from street stalls. Factories relocating from North America attract young women, who are preferred to men because they accept lower wages and have been raised to obey. As women have entered the work force, family life has undergone strains. By the 1990s far fewer people married, especially among the poor. But divorce, banned by the Catholic Church, has remained difficult or impossible in some nations, and men still enjoy a double standard in sexual behavior, with men's extramarital affairs being tolerated while women's are condemned. Although abortion is illegal everywhere in the region, Latin America has one of the world's highest abortion rates. Gay men and lesbians also struggle for acceptance. Homosexuality remains illegal in many nations, including Castro's Cuba, although Brazil and Costa Rica have fostered more tolerant climates.

As gender expectations have changed, women have become more active in politics. Between 1945 and 1961 women gained the right to vote. In 1974 Isabel Peron (b. 1931) of Argentina, a former dancer who married Juan Peron after Evita's death, succeeded her late husband to become the region's first woman president, but she was ousted in a military coup in 1976. In 1990 Violeta Chamorro (vee-oh-LET-ah cha-MOR-roe) (b. 1919), a newspaper publisher, was elected president of Nicaragua, and she served until 1996. In 2006 Chileans showed a willingness to expand their political horizons by electing as president the pediatrician turned socialist politician Michelle Bachelet (BAH-she-let), a divorced mother of three and avowed agnostic whose father was murdered while she and her mother were jailed and tortured during the Pinochet years. Leading the victorious center-left coalition, Bachelet struck a blow for gender equity by filling half of her cabinet positions with women, including the key defense and economy ministries. Men have often resented women's empowerment, and dictatorships have singled out women activists, such as Bachelet's mother, for torture. During military rule in Argentina, Brazil, and Chile, women political prisoners were kept naked and often raped. For instance, Doris Tijereno Haslam (b. 1943), an early member of the leftist Sandinista movement in Nicaragua who fought as a guerrilla commander, was twice arrested and badly tortured by the corrupt dictatorship of General Anastasio Somoza Debayle

(1923–1967). After the Sandinista victory in 1979 she headed the national police and served in the congress. Women fought back against discrimination and violence, as in Mexico, where the feminist movement challenged inequitable laws and social practices. In 1974 the Mexican legislature passed a law, similar to one proposed but never approved in the United States, guaranteeing women equal rights for jobs, salaries, and legal standing. In countries such as Argentina, Brazil, and Uruguay, liberal women's groups have made loosening the anti-abortion laws a top priority and have gained more public support for their cause.

Another traditional foundation for Latin American society, religion, also was subject to change. In the 1960s progressive Latin American Roman Catholics developed **liberation theology**, a movement to make Catholicism more relevant to contemporary society and address the plight of the poor. Priests favoring liberation theology, especially in Brazil, cooperated with Marxist and liberal groups in working for social justice until the Vatican prohibited the movement in the 1980s. On the whole, the Roman Catholic hierarchy remained conservative. While fewer Catholics attended church services, popular Catholicism still centered on fiestas, pilgrimages, and the family altar. Protestantism, chiefly evangelical or pentecostal, grew rapidly with increased missionary efforts, attracting converts with its participatory, emotional services. By the 1990s Protestants numbered nearly 20 percent of the population in Guatemala and 8 percent in Brazil and Chile. But their active evangelization, which often targeted Catholics, caused resentment among Catholic leaders. Nonetheless, the religious landscape of Latin America looked very different and was more diverse in 2000 than it had been a century earlier.

Brazilian Society

Latin America's largest nation, Brazil, has reflected both the region's social changes and its continuities during the era. Over the decades urbanization, population growth, industrialization, and the ebb and flow of politics have introduced new influences, yet long-standing social patterns have also persisted.

Between 1920 and 1980 urban population grew from about a quarter to three-fifths of Brazilians. Migrants jammed into shantytowns surrounding the central cities, such as the notorious hillside shacks of Rio de Janeiro. Poverty remained pervasive. By the 1980s three-fifths of breadwinners averaged under $100 per year in income, three-fourths of Brazilians were malnourished, a third of adults had tuberculosis, a quarter of the population suffered from parasitic diseases, and millions of abandoned or runaway children wandered city streets, living by their wits. Yet, despite the street people, the shantytowns were also well organized, led by community activists and filled with hard-working residents proud of their communities and seeking a better future for their children.

---

liberation theology   A Latin American movement that developed in the 1960s to make Catholicism more relevant to contemporary society and to address the plight of the poor.

Although Brazilians have increasingly tolerated racial and cultural diversity, race remains a central social category. Like the United States, Brazil has never become a true racial "melting pot." Afro-Brazilians often condemn what they view as a racist society steeped in prejudice and having a wide gap in racial income. Race has often correlated with social status: whites dominate the top brackets, blacks the bottom, and mixed-descent Brazilians fall in between. The flexible Brazilian concept of race, however, differs from the biological concept that North Americans have. Dark-skinned people can aspire to social mobility by earning a good income since, as a popular local saying claimed, "money lightens." Furthermore, Afro-Brazilian culture has had a growing influence, and many whites have embraced aspects of black culture. For example, over a third of Brazilians, often devout Catholics, have adopted or been influenced by one of the Afro-Brazilian faiths, formed decades ago, that link a West African god or other African traditions with a Roman Catholic saint and ceremonies.

For Brazil, as for most nations, professional sports have become a popular entertainment and diversion from social problems. For instance, European football, or soccer, has been hugely popular in Brazil, as in most of Latin America, for decades, uniting Brazilians of all social backgrounds. From the late 1950s to late 1970s the storied career, fluid play, and magnetic personality of the superstar Pele (b. 1940), from a poor Afro-Brazilian family, did much to spread the popularity of soccer in the world. Brazilians are proud of the international success of their national team, which won the World Cup championships five times between 1958 and 2002 by employing a creative, teamwork-oriented strategy, known as "samba football," that Brazilians have identified with the national spirit. A playwright noted how his countrymen obsessively suspend their daily lives during the World Cup, which is held every four years: "The nation pauses, all of it. Robbers don't rob, ghosts don't haunt, no crimes, no embezzlements, no deaths, no adulteries."[19]

Latin American Cultures

Latin America has fostered creative cultural forms that have reached a global audience. The mass media have both shaped and reflected the prevailing cultures. Inexpensive transistor radios became widely available, and by the 1980s thousands of radio stations had sprouted all over the region. While most stations were privately owned, governments frequently sought to control their content. In 1950 television came to the main cities, eventually spreading widely. Immensely popular local television soap operas dominated prime time viewing, with those from Brazil and Mexico enjoying the widest popularity. They also gained a large market around the world.

Literature has also flourished, with writers often criticizing or describing social conditions and government failures. For instance, the popular Brazilian novelist Jorge Amado (HOR-hay ah-MAH-do) (1912–2001) blended fantasy, realism, and political commitment in ways that provided insight into life in his home region, Brazil's impoverished northeast. Former journalist Gabriel García Márquez (MAHR-kez) (b. 1928), a Nobel Prize–winning Colombian novelist, developed an international audience for imaginative books full of what literary scholars called "magic realism," the representation of possible events as if they were wonders and impossible events as commonplace. His most famous work, *One Hundred Years of Solitude* (1970), charts the history of a Colombian house, the family who live in it, and the town where it was located, through wars, changing politics, and economic crises.

Some writers tested the tolerance of governments for works critical of those holding power. For example, in Chile, the greatest epic poem of the leftist writer and former diplomat Pablo Neruda (neh-ROO-da) (1904–1973), *General Song*, published in 1950, portrays the history of the entire hemisphere, showing an innocent pre-Columbian America cruelly awakened by Spanish conquest. The poem romanticizes the Incas, extolls the liberators who ended Spanish rule, castigates foreign capitalists (often from the United States), who are depicted as exploiters, and identifies an emerging mass struggle to establish an America truly governed by and for the people rather than the rich. In 1971 Neruda won the Nobel Prize for literature, cheering his admirers around the hemisphere and distressing those who viewed him and his radical views as a threat to Latin American society.

Other art forms also developed a social consciousness. For instance, the Brazilian New Cinema movement, launched in 1955, tried to replace the influence of Hollywood films with films that reflected Brazilian life. One of the movement's finest films, *Black Orpheus* (1959), which gained an international following, employed a soundtrack of local popular music to examine the annual pre-Lenten Carnival in Rio de Janeiro's shantytowns and the extremes of wealth and poverty revealed in the different ways rich and poor celebrated Carnival.

Like other peoples, Latin Americans have mixed local cultural traditions with imported influences, but the local forms have often proved more inspiring. For example, a musical style known as **New Song**, based chiefly on local folk music and closely tied to progressive politics and protest, gained popularity in a half-dozen countries in the 1960s and 1970s, becoming especially influential in Chile. Seeking an alternative to the Anglo-American popular culture favored by elite Chileans, Chilean musicians have used indigenous Andean instruments and tunes. During the later 1960s Chilean New Song pioneers such as Violeta Parra and Victor Jara (HAR-a) wrote or collected songs that addressed problems of Chilean society such as poverty and inequality. Parra (1918–1967) served as the bridge between the older generation of folk musicians and the younger generation of singer-songwriters (see Profile: Violeta Parra, Chilean New Song Pioneer). Her protégé Jara put his goal of using music to promote his political goals in song: "I don't sing for the love of singing, Or to show off my voice, But for the statements, Made by my honest guitar."[20]

New Song A Latin American musical movement based chiefly on local folk music and closely tied to progressive politics and protest; became popular in the 1960s and 1970s, especially in Chile.

Violeta Parra, Chilean New Song Pioneer

Violeta Parra An influential Chilean musician, folklorist, and artist, Violeta Parra is credited with founding the folk-music-oriented New Song movement, influencing many musicians in Chile and throughout Latin America. (Archivo, La Fundacion Violetta Parra)

Born in 1918 to a poor schoolteaching family, Violeta Parra was the key figure in the early development of New Song, a Chilean music based chiefly on local folk music, and a multitalented artist in many mediums, including poetry, filmmaking, tapestry, and painting. Despite her lower-middle-class background, the unconventional Parra lived and dressed like a peasant, wearing her hair long and almost uncombed. Restless and unsuited for marriage, she struggled to find the best outlet for her talents while supporting herself and her two children, Isabel and Angel (AHN-hell). After working as a commercial entertainer, she began collecting, writing, and singing folk music in the 1940s and eventually collected over 3,000 songs. She had clear musical goals: "Every artist must aspire to unite his/her work in a direct contact with the public. I am content to work with the people close to me, whom I can feel, touch, talk and incorporate into my soul." Yet, unlike her protégés, such as Victor Jara, who was deeply engaged in leftwing movements, she never became directly active in politics.

In the early 1950s Parra began Chile's first folk music radio program and recorded her debut album, with simple guitar-accompanied arrangements. She also taught briefly at a southern Chilean university. Parra and her children introduced Andean and African American folk music to Chile after a four-year sojourn in Paris, France, where they encountered musicians from various countries. Settling with her children in Chile's capital city, Santiago, she enjoyed cooking huge pots of beans for the young Chileans who gathered around her to drink wine, discuss Chilean affairs, and exchange songs and stories. A café the Parras opened in Santiago became a meeting place for performers and other Chileans interested in New Song and leftist politics. Parra greatly influenced younger urban musicians, who began learning from her how to play traditional Andean instruments while collecting or writing their own songs, and she provided a role model for other Latin American musicians. As Cuba's top New Song musician, Silvio Rodriguez, claimed: "Violeta is fundamental. Nothing would have been as it is had it not been for Violeta."

Parra's songs displayed two essential elements of later New Song: a base in folk music and concern with Chile's social, economic, and political problems. In "Look How They Tell Us About Freedom," she critiqued the Catholic Church establishment and her nation's ills: look how the nation's religious and political leaders brag about freedom, she sang, when they are actually keeping it from us; they boast about tranquility as their power tortures us. Her music attacked such issues as the brutality of the police, the inequalities of capitalism, the exploitation of Indians, and chronic conflict between Latin American governments. At the same time, her songs retained an intense, highly personal, and contemporary mood, which was both Chilean and universal.

Besides being held in contempt by the Chilean elite for her unconventional life and antiestablishment sympathies, Parra was plagued by poverty and increasing personal problems, including depression. Even her closest friends found her strong, often unpredictable personality difficult, and younger musicians began gravitating to Victor Jara and other New Song figures. Her later songs took on a more philosophical spirit. On her last album in 1966 she recorded her famous farewell, "Gracias a la Vida" (I Give Thanks to Life), a prayerlike expression of gratitude for the richness of life: "I am grateful for the life that has benefited me so much; It has given me both laughter and tears; because of this I can differentiate happiness from sadness; everybody's song is my own song." Not overtly political, the song reflected her identification with the common people and became the underground anthem of many Latin Americans living under dictatorships. As Parra's depression deepened, she committed suicide in 1967. But her career had built a bridge between an older, peasant-based folk tradition and the developing interest of younger musicians. She may have gone, but New Song flowered in Chile and around Latin America.

THINKING ABOUT THE PROFILE

1. Why did her peers consider Parra fundamental to the evolution of New Song in Latin America?

2. How did Parra's life reflect Chilean social and political conditions?

Notes: Quotations from *Studies in Latin American Popular Culture,* 2 (1983), pp. 177–178, and 5 (1986), p. 117; and Nancy E. Morris, *Canto Porque es Necesario Cantar: The New Song Movement in Chile, 1973–1983* (Albuquerque: Latin American Institute, University of New Mexico, Research Paper Series No. 16, July 1984), p. 6.

Because of its leftwing connections, New Song was vulnerable to changing political conditions. In 1970 Chilean New Song musicians had joined the electoral campaign of the leftist Popular Unity coalition, which sought to unseat a centrist administration. After the coalition's leader, Salvador Allende, won the presidency, he encouraged the media to pay more attention to New Song and less to popular music from the United States. For their part, New Song musicians promoted the new government's programs, such as land reform, and some toured abroad to foster foreign support for Allende's government. In 1973, the Chilean military seized power and arrested, executed, or deported most of the New Song musicians while making it illegal to play or listen to New Song. Before thousands of other detainees held in the national stadium, soldiers publicly cut off Victor Jara's fingers, which he had used to play his guitar, and then executed him, symbolizing the death of free expression in Chile and the government's fear of the power of popular culture.

Caribbean Societies and Cultures

With diverse populations of blacks, whites, and Asians, the Caribbean islands, like Latin America, offered an environment for creative cultural development, especially in religion and music. Jamaica, where slavery and colonialism had fostered a blending of African and European traditions, proved particularly fertile soil. **Rastafarianism**, a religion mixing Christian, African, and local influences, arose in Jamaica in 1930 and attracted urban slum dwellers and the rural poor by preaching a return of black people to Africa. The believers revered the emperor Ras Tafari of Ethiopia, the sole unconquered, uncolonized African state in 1930. Its followers, known as Rastas, adopted distinctive practices, including smoking ganja, an illegal drug, and sporting dreadlock hair, that outraged Jamaica's social and economic elite. The return to Africa became more a spiritual than a physical quest and was mixed with black nationalism. As a movement of the black poor, Rastafarianism became identified in Jamaica and other Caribbean islands with radical groups seeking to redistribute wealth.

The most influential popular music to come out of the Caribbean had similar mixed origins. In the 1960s Jamaican musicians created **reggae**, a style blending North American rhythm and blues with Afro-Jamaican traditions and marked by a distinctive beat maintained by the bass guitar. The songs of reggae musicians, who were often Rastas, promoted social justice, economic equality, and the freedom of people, especially Rastas, to live as they liked without interference by the police. The international popularity of reggae owed much

---

Rastafarianism A religion from Jamaica that arose in 1930 and that mixed Christian, African, and local influences; Rastafarianism attracted urban slum dwellers and the rural poor by preaching a return of black people to Africa.

reggae A popular music style that began in the 1960s and that blended North American rhythm and blues with Afro-Jamaican traditions; reggae is marked by a distinctive beat maintained by the bass guitar.

to Bob Marley (1945–1981), a Rasta, and his group, the Wailers. Marley became the first international superstar from a developing nation. His perceptions were shaped by the status of black people in Jamaica and the wider world, in particular the degrading conditions of the nonwhite poor. His explosive performances and provocative lyrics offered clear messages: "Slave driver, the table is turned; Catch a fire, you gonna get burned."[21] As New Song musicians did in Chile, Marley and other reggae musicians became involved in politics, and many musicians supported socialist Michael Manley (1924–1997), whose antibusiness policies as prime minister (1972–1978) prompted economically crippling sanctions by the United States that caused the Jamaican people hardship. After Marley's death from cancer in 1981, many reggae musicians watered down their message, leaving raunchy party music to dominate the Caribbean music scenes.

Latin America and the Caribbean in the Global System

The peoples of Latin America and the Caribbean, who remained major suppliers of natural resources to the world but also lived in the shadow of the United States, forged closer relations with one another. Over the years various leaders sought to increase regional economic cooperation. Commerce between Latin American nations, frequently joined in trade pacts, more than doubled between 1988 and 1994. For example, the Southern Cone Common Market, formed in 1996, included six South American nations with over 200 million people. Similarly, Caribbean countries cooperated in the Caribbean Community and Common Market, formed in 1973. Latin and North American leaders periodically met in summits to bolster hemispheric solidarity and enhance cooperation on immigration, tariff reduction, suppression of the illegal drug trade, and other issues, but these proved more symbolic than substantive. Some U.S.-Latin American issues remain contested. For instance, while people in the United States have blamed Latin American drug cartels for smuggling illegal drugs into the United States, Latin Americans have often resented the U.S. interventions and economic impositions they consider "Yankee imperialism." Latin American and Caribbean leaders have also feared being pushed aside in a world economy dominated by North American, European and, increasingly, Asian nations.

Globalization influenced Latin Americans and their economies. Asian nations, especially China, Japan, Taiwan, and South Korea, captured a growing share of Latin America's traditional overseas markets while also investing in Latin America and the Caribbean. In a globalized economy, a hiccup in Tokyo or New York caused a stomach ache in Ecuador or El Salvador. Since most Latin American and Caribbean economies followed the track of the U.S. economy, they were particularly vulnerable to change in the United States. When the 2001 terrorist attacks in the United States diverted U.S. attention to the Middle East, the sudden U.S. disinterest in Latin America and its problems sparked a regional economic downturn that reduced demand for Latin American exports. The economic gains made in the mid-1990s slipped away, and the fifth of Latin America's 500 million people who lived in extreme poverty by 2000 faced an even grimmer future. Only a few nations, such as Brazil and Chile, had much hope of improving their status in the global system. Although U.S. exports to Latin America nearly matched those to Europe, by 2006 relations between the United States and Latin America were at their lowest point since the Cold War.

Buffeted by political changes and economic crises, Latin Americans search for their identity and role in a world dominated by other societies. Calling on leaders to recognize the needs of all the people, regardless of class, ethnicity, and gender, and for both North and Latin Americans to find common ground with each other, the salsa music star and lawyer Ruben Blades (blayds), who splits his time between his native Panama and the United States, ponders the hemisphere's destiny in song: "I'm searching for America and I fear I won't find her. Those who fear truth have hidden her. While there is no justice there can be no peace. If the dream of one is the dream of all let's break the chains and begin to walk. I'm calling you, America, our future awaits us, help me to find her."[22]

SECTION SUMMARY

- Latin American economies have been marked by over-dependence on natural resources, extreme inequality of income, agriculture that deemphasizes production of foodstuffs for domestic consumption, increasing urbanization, and failed experiments with free trade.

- Though men continue to dominate Latin American society, more women have entered the work force, and several have become national leaders, while liberation theology, a Catholic movement addressing the plight of the poor, became popular for awhile but was outlawed by the Vatican and Protestantism gained a following.

- Brazil, Latin America's largest nation, became increasingly urban and suffered widespread poverty, with a racial divide between lighter- and darker-skinned people, but Brazilians have found escape from their problems through popular sports such as soccer.

- Latin American culture has flourished, with writers employing magic realism to explore their region's experience, others airing political views through poetry and music, and many preferring to use local traditions and forms rather than foreign ones.

- In the Caribbean, the Jamaican religion of Rastafarianism promoted redistribution of wealth and a closely related musical form, reggae, that frequently included calls for social justice and freedom from police interference.

- Latin American and Caribbean nations forged closer relations, signed several trade pacts, and shared an uneasy economic relationship with the United States, while Asian nations also became important competitors with and investors in their economies.

Online Study Center ACE the Test

◆ Chapter Summary

Having emerged from World War II as the dominant superpower, the United States soon engaged in a Cold War with the Soviet Union. The U.S. campaign to contain communism fostered the growth of a powerful military and a strong government. During the Cold War the United States lavished aid and investment on its allies and the developing nations and intervened in many nations, including some in Latin America and the Caribbean, to counter revolutionary movements or overthrow left-leaning governments. While the U.S. economy flourished for decades, American society and culture rapidly changed, as ethnic minorities and women struggled for equal rights. Although shaped, like the United States, by massive immigration from Europe, especially Britain, the societies of Canada, Australia, and New Zealand have more liberal attitudes on social issues and, unlike the United States, have extensive social welfare systems.

Latin American and Caribbean experiences differ from those in the United States and Canada and the Pacific Basin. Military dictatorships dominated many Latin American nations for decades. Most nations struggled to implement and sustain democracy, which became prevalent in the 1990s, and to find the right economic mix to foster economic development. Many people have remained in dire poverty. Women and nonwhites have worked to improve their status, with only modest success. The Latin American and Caribbean peoples have also fostered dynamic cultural forms, from innovative literatures to popular musical forms, that have often expressed protest and have gained worldwide audiences.

Online Study Center Improve Your Grade Flashcards

Key Terms

domino theory	Mutually Assured	neoliberalism
multilateralism	Destruction	liberation theology
unilateralism	preemptive war	New Song
containment	Castroism	Rastafarianism
		reggae

Suggested Reading

Books

Brown, D. Clayton. *Globalization and America Since 1945.* Wilmington, Del.: Scholarly Resources, 2003. A brief but useful study of the U.S. role in a globalizing world.

Chafe, William H. *The Unfinished Journey: America Since World War II,* 5th ed. New York: Oxford University Press, 2003. An outstanding, readable survey of the era.

Clayton, Lawrence A., and Michael L. Conniff. *A History of Modern Latin America,* 2nd ed. Belmont, Calif.: Wadsworth, 2005. A readable general history, with much on the contemporary era.

DePalma, Anthony. *Here: A Biography of the New American Continent*. New York: PublicAffairs, 2001. A U.S. jounalist's account of contemporary Canada, Mexico, and the United States.

Green, Duncan. *Faces of Latin America*. London: Latin American Bureau, 1991. An entertaining and provocative examination of Latin America's people and their vibrant cultures.

Hillman, Richard S., ed. *Understanding Contemporary Latin America*, 3rd ed. Boulder: Lynne Rienner, 2005. A valuable collection of essays.

Isserman, Maurice, and Michael Kazin. *America Divided: The Civil War of the 1960s*. New York: Oxford University Press, 2000. Comprehensive history of this important era in U.S. history.

Kinzer, Stephen. *Overthrow: America's Century of Regime Change from Hawaii to Iraq*. New York: Times Books, 2006. A critical examination of U.S. interventions and forced regime changes abroad over the past century.

Page, Joseph A. *The Brazilians*. Reading, M.A.: Addison-Wesley, 1995. Readable examination of Brazilian society and culture.

Paterson, Thomas, et al. *American Foreign Relations*, 6th ed. Boston: Houghton Mifflin, 2004. A readable survey with much on this era.

Rosen, Ruth. *The World Split Open: How the Modern Women's Movement Changed America*. New York: Viking, 2000. One of the best studies of the women's movement in the U.S. since World War II.

Schaller, Michael, et al. *Present Tense: The United States Since 1945*. Boston: Houghton Mifflin, 2004. An up-to-date and informative survey.

Skidmore, Thomas E., and Peter H. Smith. *Modern Latin America*, 6th ed. New York: Oxford University Press, 2004. An excellent introduction to the recent history of the region and its nations.

Terrill, Ross. *The Australians*. New York: Touchstone, 1988. Readable introduction to Australian history and society.

Thompson, Roger C. *The Pacific Basin Since 1945*, 2nd ed. New York: Longman, 2001. An Australian scholar's broad examination of the East Asian, Pacific, Latin American, and North American societies and their relations.

Winn, Peter. *Americas: The Changing Face of Latin America and the Caribbean*, 3rd ed. Berkeley: University of California Press, 2006. A sweeping, highly readable examination of the region and its peoples.

Websites

WWW-VL: History: United States (http://vlib.iue.it/history/USA/).   A virtual library, maintained at the University of Kansas, that contains links to hundreds of sites.

Internet Modern History Sourcebook (http://www.fordham.edu/halsall/mod/modsbook.html).   Extensive online collection of historical documents and secondary materials.

Internet Resources for Latin America (http://lib.nmsu.edu/subject/bord/laguia/).   This outstanding site, from New Mexico State University, provides information and links.

Latin American Network Information Center (http://lanic.utexas.edu/).   Very useful site on contemporary Latin America, maintained at the University of Texas.

U.S. Diplomatic History Resources Index (http://faculty.tamu-commerce.edu/sarantakes/stuff.html).   An index of sources on U.S. foreign policy.

CHAPTER 30

The Middle East, Sub-Saharan Africa, and New Conflicts in the Contemporary World, 1945–Present

Online Study Center

This icon will direct you to interactive activities and study materials on the website: college.hmco.com/pic/lockard1e

Modern vs. Traditional Wearing traditional clothing, including veils and head scarves, Egyptian women walk through downtown Cairo in 1998 in front of billboards promoting popular entertainers. The scene illustrates the encounter between Islamic customs and modern ideas in many Middle Eastern nations. (AP/Wide World Photos)

I saw the Berlin Wall fall, [Nelson] Mandela walk free. I saw a dream whose time has come change my history—so keep on dreaming. In the best of times and in the worst of times gotta keep looking at the skyline, not at the hole in the road.

"YOUR TIME WILL COME" BY SOUTH AFRICAN POP GROUP SAVUKA, 1993[1]

The Nigerian writer Chinua Achebe (ah-CHAY-bay) (b. 1930) dissected the underside of African politics in a controversial 1987 blockbuster novel, *Anthills of the Savannah*, about a military dictatorship like the one he had experienced in his own country. *Anthills* portrays the problems faced by average people in Nigeria and throughout much of Africa and the Islamic world, mercilessly depicting the immorality, vanity, and destructiveness of dictatorship. Achebe did not have to look far for examples: the Nigerian military leaders who overthrew a civilian government in 1983 had first arrested people whose corruption was well known, a popular move, but then proceeded to jail anyone, including journalists, who questioned the regime's own economic mismanagement and human rights abuses. Achebe's satire on moral bankruptcy forewarns of the dangers of unaccountable, repressive power. Just as the black and white musicians in the South African pop group, Savuka, could sing of dreams changing history and a new era beginning with the end of white minority rule, Achebe also offered a powerful message about the need for people to hope for, and struggle to attain, a better life.

The political and economic realities of contemporary Africa and the Middle East are reflected in these regions' arts and literature. The candid Achebe has argued that the artist and society cannot be separated. He and other writers, musicians, and artists have used their art to spur political and social change. Achebe claims that no novel is ever politically neutral because even saying nothing about politics is a political statement that says everything is OK. *Anthills* argued eloquently that, in Achebe's view, everything is not OK. Like various other creative people, Achebe, who has specialized in urban satires attacking corruption, social injustice, the pretensions of politicians, and the destabilization brought by the West, has had to live in exile from intolerant governments.

Despite achievements in many areas of life, the problems vividly described by Achebe for Nigeria—corruption, economic stagnation, combustible social tensions, and failed promises of democracy—have applied to most other nations in sub-Saharan Africa and the Middle East. The triumph of nationalism and the resulting decolonization had reshaped Africa and the Middle East. Between 1945 and 1975 country after country became independent or escaped from Western political domination. In contrast to various East Asian, Southeast Asian, and

935

Latin American nations, however, African and Middle Eastern nations have often struggled just to survive. While innovative in areas such as music, literature, and other forms of culture, few of the nations have successfully resolved their social and economic problems. For some nations, Islam has become a rallying cry to assert political interests and preserve cultures. To serve their own ends, global superpowers have manipulated governments and intervened to shape the regions.

FOCUS QUESTIONS

1. How have Arab-Israeli tensions and oil shaped contemporary Middle Eastern politics?
2. What roles has Islam played in the contemporary Middle East?
3. What were the main political consequences of decolonization in sub-Saharan Africa?
4. What new economic, social, and cultural patterns have emerged in Africa?

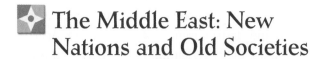

The Middle East: New Nations and Old Societies

How have Arab-Israeli tensions and oil shaped contemporary Middle Eastern politics?

Few world regions have witnessed more turbulence in the past half century than the Middle East, the predominantly Muslim nations stretching from Morocco eastward across North Africa and western Asia to Turkey, Iran, and Afghanistan. The major ethnic group, the Arabs, have dominated most of these nations, but Turks, Iranians, Kurds, and Israeli Jews also influence the region. After World War II the Middle Eastern societies ended Western colonization and asserted their own political interests, often under modernizing leaders. But within these societies, dictatorial governments have proliferated and chronic political instability has been common. Centuries old hostilities between Sunni and Shi'a Muslims simmer. Meanwhile, the Persian Gulf area, which contains much of the world's oil reserves, has made the Middle East crucial to the global system.

The Reshaping of the Middle East

In the decade after World War II nationalist governments in the Middle East replaced most of the remaining colonial regimes. The French abandoned control of Morocco, Tunisia, Lebanon, and Syria while the Italians left Libya. However, Muslim guerrillas fought 500,000 French troops for eight years to bring independence to Algeria, which had a large European settler population. Some 250,000 Algerians died in the conflict. Seeing no clear end to the struggle, the French granted independence in 1962 (see Chronology: The Middle East, 1945–Present). Some Middle Eastern nations, such as Egypt and Morocco, had a long history of national identity and thus unity, but many were fragile states. For example, after World

War I the British had formed the new, artificial states of Iraq, Jordan, and Palestine with arbitrary boundaries, while Afghanistan, Turkey, Lebanon, and Syria included diverse and often feuding ethnic and religious groups.

Iran and Turkey, which had never been colonized, sought influential roles in the region and built formidable military forces. Both also abused their citizens' human rights, arresting dissidents and restricting ethnic minorities. Iran shifted from a secular, pro-Western royal government to a militant Islamic government. By contrast, Turkey, led largely by secular politicians and generals, looked increasingly westward, joining NATO (the North Atlantic Treaty Organization), hosting U.S. military bases, developing democratic institutions, and applying for membership in the European Union. But Turkey's governments, while generally promoting a modern version of women's rights, have also suppressed the culture and language of the largest ethnic minority, the Kurds, who chiefly live in southeastern Turkey, and, although the nation's 70 million people are largely Muslim, have limited political activity by groups favoring an Islamic state.

After decolonization the hopes for development throughout the Middle East were soon dashed as vested economic interests, such as large landowners, and most of the Muslim clergy opposed significant social and economic changes. Many people remained mired in illiteracy, poverty, and disease. Freewheeling and enduring multi-party democracy has been hard to establish or maintain but some have made the effort. Turkey shifted from military-dominated to democratically elected governments by the 1980s, but the military remained powerful and strict internal security laws resulted in the imprisonment of several thousand people for political offenses. Lebanese could choose between many competing warlord or religious-based parties, and a new constitution in 2002 allowed both men and women in the small Persian Gulf kingdom of Bahrain (BAH-rain) to elect a parliament with considerable power. In the early twenty-first century the Moroccan king, Muhammad VI, who claims descent from the prophet Muhammad,

CHRONOLOGY

	The Middle East		Sub-Saharan Africa
1940	**1948** Formation of Israel		**1948** Apartheid in South Africa
	1954–1962 Algerian Revolution		**1957–1965** African decolonization
1960	**1967** Arab-Israeli Six-Day War		**1975** Independence for Portuguese colonies
	1973 OPEC oil embargo		
	1979 Islamic revolution in Iran		
1990	**2003** United States invasion of Iraq		**1994** Black majority rule in South Africa

used a tolerant interpretation of Islam to try and modernize his nation, granting new rights to women and strengthening civil liberties and the role of an elected parliament. But in

CHRONOLOGY

The Middle East, 1945–Present

1948	Formation of Israel
1948–1949	First Arab-Israeli War
1951	Nationalist government in Iran
1952–1970	Nasser presidency in Egypt
1953	CIA overthrow of Iranian government
1954–1962	Algerian Revolution
1956	Suez crisis
1960	Formation of OPEC
1967	Arab-Israeli Six-Day War
1973	Arab-Israeli (Yom Kippur) War
1973	OPEC oil embargo
1978	Egypt-Israel peace treaty
1979	Islamic revolution in Iran
1979–1989	Soviet war in Afghanistan
1980–1988	Iran-Iraq War
1987	Beginning of Palestinian Intifada
1996–2001	Taliban government in Afghanistan
1993	Limited Palestinian self-government
2000	Renewed Israeli-Palestinian conflict
2001	U.S. invasion of Afghanistan
2003	U.S. invasion and occupation of Iraq

most countries elections were rigged, parliaments were weak, or governments made it hard for opposition candidates to run. Furthermore, the United States and the Soviet Union, attracted by the region's oil and strategic location along vital waterways, including the Persian Gulf and Suez Canal, soon filled the power vacuum created by decolonization. To become more influential in the world, Arabs talked about uniting across political borders, but pan-Arab nationalism, based more on Arabs' shared cultural and linguistic background than political interests, was never able to overcome political rivalries and meddling by the superpowers. Divided by rival Muslim sects and differing outlooks toward the West, Arabs floundered in their quest for unity. In addition, a number of post-1945 challenges have made the Middle East a highly combustible region subject to strains.

Arab Nationalism and Egypt

Confrontation between Arab nationalism and the world's superpowers, especially during the 1960s and 1970s, was acute in Egypt, a former British protectorate and the most populous Arab country, with 77 million people by 2005. In 1952 a charismatic Egyptian leader, General Gamal Abdul Nasser (NAS-uhr) (1918–1970), led a military coup that ended the corrupt pro-British monarchy. Although he was raised lower middle class in the cosmopolitan city of Alexandria, Nasser's frequent visits to his parents' impoverished farming village had sparked his sympathy for the poor and his resentment of rich landlords. Like many Egyptians, he also despised the British who dominated Egypt and the Egyptian leaders who collaborated with them. As a radical student and then army officer with a commanding personality, he had demonstrated a flare for politics and developed a vision of a new Egypt, free of Western domination and social inequality.

As Egypt's president, Nasser, a modernizer, preached socialism and unity, promising to improve the lives of the impoverished masses and to implement land reform, ideas that made him a hero in the Arab world. To generate power and improve flood control, Nasser's regime used Soviet aid to build the massive Aswan High Dam along the Nile, completed in 1970. But his nonaligned foreign policy antagonized a United States obsessed by the Cold War rivalry with the Soviet Union. Nasser's support of pan-Arab nationalism generated wars. Accusing the West of "imperialist methods, habits of blood-sucking and usurping rights, and interference in other countries,"[2] in 1956 Nasser's government took over ownership of the British-operated Suez Canal, a key artery of world commerce that was built through Egypt in the nineteenth century to allow ships to move between the Mediterranean and Red Seas. To Egyptians foreign ownership of the canal had symbolized their subjugation to foreign powers. To Europeans, the canal was the lifeline that moved oil and resources to the West from Asia. To protect that link Britain, France, and Israel sent in military forces to reclaim the canal from Egyptian troops, but diplomatic opposition by the United States, which disliked Nasser but feared regional instability, and the pro-Egypt Soviet Union forced their withdrawal. By standing up to the West, Nasser became an even greater Arab hero and a leader of the movement among developing nations for nonalignment, or neutrality, between the two rival superpowers. However, the Israeli defeat of Egypt and its allies in a brief 1967 war humiliated Nasser. Furthermore, although Nasser had introduced social and economic reforms, they fostered little economic development and gave Egypt no economic or military strength in the world.

Nasser's successors followed pragmatic, pro-U.S. policies and in 1978 signed a peace treaty with Israel brokered by the U.S. president, Jimmy Carter. But a shift to capitalism and heavy U.S. aid largely has failed to improve living conditions. Egypt's leaders reversed Nasser's land reform and dismantled the socialist economy, allowing a few well-connected capitalists to acquire state property and become fabulously rich while the poorest became even poorer. In the capital city, Cairo, the contrast between the glittering rich neighborhoods, featuring luxury apartments and mansions surrounded by high walls, and the poor, overcrowded neighborhoods, where the most desperate families live in huts on top of ramshackle apartment buildings, has grown more dramatic. Millions of Egyptians have sought work in oil-rich Arab nations. With little oil and few resources other than the fertile lands along the Nile, Egypt suffers from high malnutrition and unemployment, low rates of literacy and public health, and a huge national debt. While liberals seek more democracy, Islamic militants, feeding on these frustrations, challenge the secular but corrupt, repressive government. In 2005 other candidates were able to run against the long-entrenched president but were hampered in campaigning; Islamic parties won many parliamentary seats but the major liberal opposition leader was arrested after the election.

Israel in Middle Eastern Politics

The conflict between Israel and the Arabs, especially the Palestinians, became the Middle East's most insurmountable problem, sustaining tensions for over half a century. Under the influence of Zionism and its dream of a homeland for a long persecuted people, Jews had been emigrating from Europe to Palestine since the late 1800s, building cities and forming productive socialist farming settlements. The growing Jewish presence, however, especially the buying of land, triggered

occasional conflicts with the Palestinian Arab majority. Then the Nazis' murder of 6 million Jews during World War II spurred a more militant Zionism and Jewish desire for a homeland free of oppression, setting the stage for the birth of Israel. But the new nation never established a secure position or fostered allies within the region.

The Birth of Israel Israel emerged in a climate of violence. In the late 1940s Jewish refugees, traumatized by the Holocaust, poured into Palestine from post–World War II Europe. Moderate Jewish leaders negotiated with the British, sympathetic to the Zionist cause, for a peaceful transfer of power to them in Palestine. Meanwhile, Zionist extremists, impatient with negotiations, practiced "gun diplomacy," using terrorism, such as bombings and assassinations, against the British, Arabs, and moderate Jews. At the same time, Arabs, opposed to an Israeli state at their expense, resorted to violent attacks on Jews. Unable to maintain order, Britain abandoned the territory, referring the Palestine question to the new United Nations, then dominated by Western nations. As the British withdrew in 1948, Jewish leaders proclaimed the establishment of the state of Israel, based on the Zionist claim that Jews had a right to form their own sovereign state. By establishing a multiparty parliamentary democracy and seeking to rebuild shattered Jewish lives, the Israelis gained the strong support of Western nations and especially the United States, which pumped in several billion dollars a year in aid for the next five decades.

The establishment of a Jewish state in Palestine led to full-scale war in 1948–1949 between Israel and its Arab neighbors, to whom Israel was a white settler state and a symbol of Western colonialism (see Map 30.1). As Palestinian Arabs fled the fighting and continued terrorism against them by Jewish extremists, or heeded the calls of opportunistic Arab leaders to leave, Israelis occupied their farms and houses. The Israelis won the war against the disorganized Arabs and expelled 85 percent of the Palestinian Arabs from Israel. Palestinian refugees settled in overcrowded, squalid refugee camps in Egypt, Lebanon, Jordan, and Syria. While some Palestinian exiles became a prosperous middle class throughout the Middle East, most remained in the camps, nursing their hatred of Israel. They supported the Palestine Liberation Organization (PLO), a coalition of Arab nationalist, Muslim, and Christian groups led by Yasser Arafat (YA-sir AR-uh-fat) (1929–2004), an engineer and journalist from a wealthy Jerusalem family who was educated at Egypt's Cairo University. Arafat's pragmatic style united factions. However, neither the Western nations nor Israel officially recognized or would negotiate with the PLO until the 1990s, prompting it to resort to terrorism against Israel, such as by attacking public buses and rural settlements.

Israel remained in a state of confrontation with its Arab neighbors and the PLO. The Palestinians remaining in Israel participated in democratic politics but were disproportionally poor and often saw themselves as second-class citizens. Meanwhile, thousands of Jewish immigrants arrived, many from Middle Eastern countries where they had faced discrimination or retribution. The immigration intensified the divisions in

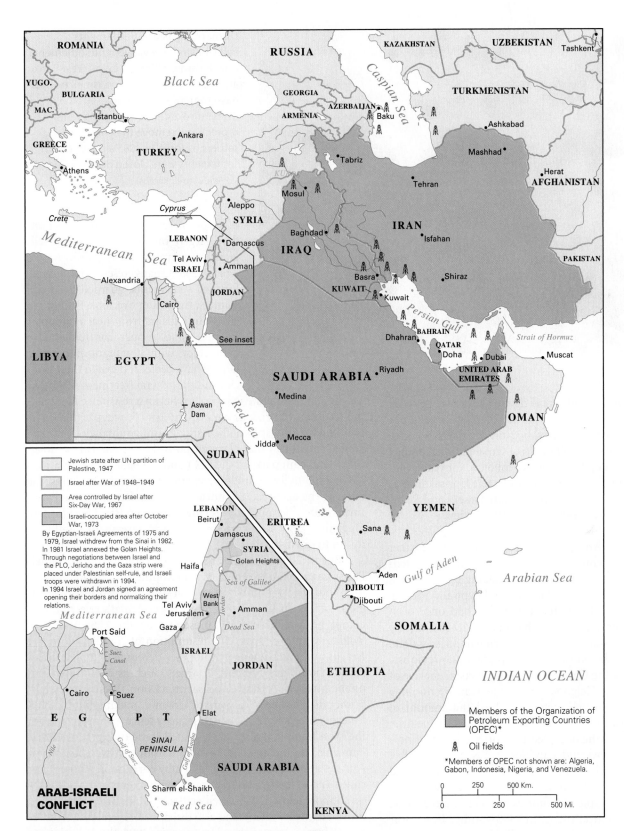

Map 30.1　Middle East Oil and the Arab-Israeli Conflict

Several Middle Eastern nations, including Saudi Arabia, Iran, Iraq, Libya, and the small Persian Gulf states, are rich in oil and active members of OPEC. Israel, founded in 1948, and the neighboring Arab countries of Egypt, Jordan, and Syria have been in chronic conflict that has resulted in four wars. Israel's victory in the 1967 war allowed it to take control of Gaza, the West Bank, and the Golan Heights.

Dismantling Israeli Settlements
Palestinians have viewed the settlements built by ardent Zionists in the West Bank and Gaza as a provocation. Israeli troops have sometimes been ordered to dismantle settlements, expensive to protect, and remove the enraged settlers by force. In 2005 all the Israeli settlements were closed down in Gaza. (AP/Wide World Photos)

Israeli society between secular and devout Jews and between Jews from Europe and those from the Middle East. Israelis, obsessed now with military security, became well armed, especially by the United States. Half of Israel's total national budget went to the military. A cycle of violence followed for years, with a PLO attack on Israelis followed by an Israeli reprisal such as the bombing of a refugee camp in Lebanon. Israelis and Palestinians could seldom comprehend each other's views.

Israel and the Arabs Since 1967

An Arab-Israeli War in 1967 further complicated regional politics, heightening conflict and reshaping Israeli society. Responding to an ill-advised attack led by Egypt and Jordan, Israel gained control of new territories that had once been part of Palestine: the West Bank, that part of Jordan on the western side of the Jordan River; the eastern half of Jerusalem, filled with both Jewish and Islamic holy places and previously governed by Jordan; the Gaza Strip, a small coastal enclave of Egypt; and the Golan Heights, a Syrian plateau overlooking northeast Israel. The Israeli victory doubled the amount of land controlled by Israel, but this land incorporated a large Arab population. Israel and the occupied territories combined now contained 3 million Jews and 2 million Arabs, a combustible situation. By 2005 Israel and the occupied territories contained some 5 million Jews and 4 million Arabs. Israel treated the Palestinians in the occupied territories as a colonized people, allowing them no political rights. In 1973 another Israeli war with Egypt and Syria proved costly to all sides.

Increasing Israeli control over the Palestinians in the occupied territories exacerbated the conflict. Although many Israelis wanted to trade occupied land for a permanent peace settlement, others hoped to permanently annex the occupied lands as part of biblical Israel. Ultranationalist Israelis, with government support, began claiming and settling on Arab land, creating an-

other problem: thousands of Jewish settlers, largely militant Zionists and religious conservatives, living amid hostile Arabs. Palestinians resent the heavily fortified settlements, guarded by Israeli soldiers, that often overlook Palestinian cities and villages from nearby hilltops. Because Israel proper has remained a democracy with a vibrant free press, Israelis have heatedly debated these policies and the general treatment of Arabs.

In 1987 desperate Palestinians began a resistance known as the **Intifada** (Uprising) against the Israeli occupation. However, the turmoil spawned a rising Islamic militancy in the occupied territories that alarmed both the secular Fatah movement, the main party in the PLO, and the Israelis. Negotiations led in 1993 to limited self-government under the PLO in some parts of the occupied territories, the basis for a possible Palestinian state, and a peace agreement between Israel and Jordan. Optimists hoped a permanent peace agreement might be found to satisfy both sides.

But in 2000 violence erupted again, returning the Israel-Palestine problem to center stage in Middle Eastern politics. Political blunders—a provocative visit to a disputed Muslim religious site by an Israeli leader and Yasser Arafat's rejection of a comprehensive peace deal presented by the U.S. president, William Clinton—sparked a resumption of conflict. Moderate Israelis and Palestinians lost hope as demoralizing Palestinian suicide bombings of civilian targets, such as restaurants and public buses, and Israeli reprisal attacks on Palestinian neighborhoods renewed fifty years of violence, making life insecure for everyone. Israel built a high security fence separating it from the West Bank that also incorporated some occupied territory, enraging Palestinians. Yet, in 2005 tensions eased. After Yasser Arafat's death, Fatah, bogged down by corruption, chose a less controversial leader and the Israeli government, with wide public support, closed the Israeli settlements in Gaza, which had proven costly to defend and also disbanded several illegal settlements in the West Bank. However, in 2006 the Palestinians, tired of Fatah's ineffective regime, gave the militant Islamic Hamas movement a majority of seats in the Palestinian parliament, alarming Israelis since Hamas had sponsored terrorist

---

Intifada ("Uprising") A resistance begun in 1987 by Palestinians against the Israeli occupation.

attacks and refused to recognize Israel's right to exist. Hamas owed its victory in part to its longtime social welfare activities and to hundreds of conservative Muslim women wearing head scarves who campaigned door to door for the party; six of them won seats, including the mother of three Hamas militants killed fighting Israelis. The future of Israeli-Palestinian relations remained uncertain. With only a third of the world's 14 million Jews living in Israel, the Zionist dream of a Greater Israel stretching from the Mediterranean coast through the West Bank to the Jordan River is fading. Nonetheless, with conflicting visions of how Israelis and Palestinians might coexist, no basis for ensuring long-term peace has yet emerged.

Online Study Center **Improve Your Grade**
Primary Source: Arab and Israeli Soccer Players Discuss Ethnic Relations in Israel, 2000

Islamic Revolution in Iran

Rich in oil and strategically located along the Persian Gulf, Iran, once known as Persia, had been buffeted between rival European nations for a century. Outside interference in Iranian affairs continued after World War II, when internal politics revolved around a conflict between the young king, Shah Mohammed Pahlavi (pah-LAH-vee) (1919–1980), and nationalist reformers opposed to foreign domination. In 1951 nationalists came to power, reducing the shah to a ceremonial role; because Iran had been receiving little of the revenue from the British-dominated oil industry, the nationalists also took ownership of that industry. In response Britain and its ally, the United States, which considered the nationalists to be sympathetic to communism and the USSR, cut off aid and launched a boycott to close oil markets, bringing Iran to near bankruptcy and fostering unrest. In 1953, American CIA agents secretly organized opposition among military leaders and paid disgruntled Iranians to riot against the nationalist government, undermining their authority. In the turmoil, royalists overthrew the nationalist government, imprisoned its leaders, and restored the unpopular shah to power, embittering many Iranians. Shah Pahlavi, a ruthless, pleasure-loving man who dreamed of restoring Persia as a great power and making Iran as industrialized as France, allied himself with the strongest superpower, the United States, and allowed U.S. companies to control the oil industry.

Along with the modernization, the shah's three and a half decades of rule also brought a huge military force built with oil revenues and political repression. What the shah termed his "white revolution," which promoted a market economy and women's rights while enlarging the middle class, was admired in the West but failed to improve living standards for most Iranians. While a corrupt elite siphoned off most of the money earmarked for development, including generous U.S. aid, and the royal family lived extravagantly, 60 percent of peasants remained landless. Seeing no future in the villages, people flocked to the cities, which became choked in traffic and smog. The population of Tehran, the capital, increased fivefold between 1945 and 1977. To increase national pride and attract Western tourists, the shah spent billions to renovate the splendid palaces and tombs of Persepolis, a city built for Persian kings 2,400 years ago, but few Iranians had the money to visit the city.

The shah's policies and the persisting inequalities fostered unrest. The absolute monarchy tolerated little dissent and the shah's secret police eliminated opposition. Political prisoners numbered in the thousands. The Iranian poetess Faruq Farrukhzad (fuh-ROOK fuh-ROOK-sad) wrote of how the intellectuals, cowed into submission by the shah, lost their voice, retreating into "swamps of alcohol [while] the verminous mice gnawed through the pages of gilded books, stacked in ancient closets."[3] Conservative Shi'ite leaders opposed the modernization, such as the unveiled women and crowded bars, which they viewed as Westernization and a threat to Muslim religion and culture. Then in 1979 the economy slumped. Strikes and protests forced the shah into exile in the United States and turned the United States and Iran into bitter foes.

With the shah's departure, an Islamic revolution began to reshape Iran. While some Shi'ite thinkers discouraged the clergy from political activism, others promoted clerical involvement in governing an Islamic state. The latter's views prevailed when militant Shi'ite clerics, led by the long exiled Ayatollah Ruhollah Khomeini (roo-HOLE-ah KOH-may-nee) (1902–1989), took power, eliminated leftists and moderate nationalists, and overturned the shah's modernization. Khomeini had long criticized the shah's secular policies, urging that they be replaced by the Islamic Shari'a, which devout Muslims considered the law of God. As Iran became an Islamic state, thousands of Iranians fled abroad, many settling in the United States. Among the new restrictions, women were forced to wear veils and prohibited from socializing with men from outside their families. The regime restricted personal freedoms, as reflected in a popular joke: "We used to drink in public and pray in private. Now we pray in public and drink in private." Like the shah, the clerics ruled by terror, suppressed ethnic minorities, such as the Kurds in the northwest, and executed opponents.

The Iranian Revolution fostered opposition from outside. The United States became bitterly opposed after Islamic militants, led by women students, seized the U.S. Embassy in Tehran in 1979 and held it and the U.S. diplomats for one year. The militants hated the United States for its long support of the shah. Iran's Arab neighbors, who had always feared Iran's territorial size, large population (68 million in 2005), military strength, and regional ambitions, were also alarmed. Now they had to worry about Islamic militancy aimed at their more secular governments. The tensions were fueled by centuries of animosity between the mostly Sunni Arabs and the mostly Shi'ite Iranians. An Iranian program to develop nuclear power and, many international observers believed, nuclear weapons also concerned the international community.

Eventually Iranian politics changed as the nation mixed theocracy with the trappings of democracy. A more open electoral process allowed opposition parties to win seats in parliament. Beginning in 1997, reformers gained a share of power. This, however, fostered a power struggle between moderate reformers, many of them clerics, and the hardline clerics who controlled the judicial and electoral systems. With the economy floundering, the reformers sought closer ties to the outside world, democratization, and a loosening of harsh laws but found the United States unwilling to improve relations. Young people, resenting clerical leadership and Islamic laws, often supported reform. By the early 2000s, people increasingly challenged restrictions on personal behavior. For example, young women, often unveiled or wearing fashionable head scarves, began socializing again with men. But the hardliners maintained overall political power, banning reformist newspapers and disqualifying reformist political candidates. At home the hardliners were distressed when Shirin Ebadi (shih-RIN ee-BOD-ee) (b. 1947), a feminist Iranian lawyer and human rights activist, won the Nobel Peace Prize in 2003 for bravely challenging the clerical leadership and favoring a reformist Islam. Ebadi contended that Iran would only have the rule of law when women enjoyed the same rights as men under the law. But in 2005 Iranians lost faith in the ineffective reformist leaders and elected a hardline, anti-reform president who pledged to increase the nation's nuclear capabilities and restore conservative values. One of his first acts was to ban Western music from radio and television.

Iraq and Regional Conflicts

Iraq proved a major source of regional instability. In 1958 the Iraqi army overthrew an unpopular monarchy and began over four decades of ruthless military dictatorships that crushed all opposition. These governments also fostered secular policies and some economic development, making Iraq one of the most prosperous Arab societies by the 1980s. These regimes were usually led by members of the **Ba'ath** ("Renaissance") Party, which favored socialism and Arab nationalism and strongly opposed Israel. Representing the Sunni minority of 20 percent, the Ba'ath ruled a nation with a restless Arab Shi'ite majority, located mostly in the south, and a disaffected Kurdish minority in the north. A rival Ba'ath group ran Syria. In 1979 Saddam Hussein (b. 1937), a landless peasant's son and army officer, took power in Iraq and proved even more brutal than his predecessors.

Alarmed by the Iranian Revolution, and hated by Ayatollah Khomeini, who considered Saddam's secular regime godless, in 1980 Saddam launched a war against Iran, using poison gas against Iranian soldiers, but he was unable to achieve victory. The war drew in outsiders because it threatened Persian Gulf shipping lanes and hence the world supply of oil. For example, the United States, with its vested interest in Iraq's oil—the world's second largest proven reserves—and hostility toward Iran, sided with Iraq, attacking Iranian shipping and arming Saddam's military. As the casualties mounted, both Iran and Iraq drafted teenagers to fight. The costs of war were staggering: over 260,000 Iranian and 100,000 Iraqi dead and grave damage to the Iraqi economy, including major destruction in Iraq's main port, Basra.

When the war ended in 1988 with no victor, Saddam's actions fostered regional tension. The United States government viewed Saddam as a useful strategic ally and continued providing him with weapons. But Iraqi leaders had long claimed that Kuwait, a British protectorate until 1961 that sits atop oil riches and blocks Iraq from enjoying greater access to the Persian Gulf, should be part of Iraq. In 1991 Iraq invaded prosperous Kuwait, ruled by an Arab royal family. The United States, worried that oil-rich Saudi Arabia might be next, formed a coalition and launched the Persian Gulf War (1991), which drove Iraqis from Kuwait and killed perhaps 30,000 Iraqi soldiers. The war restored Americans' faith in their military, undermined by the bitter defeat in Vietnam in 1975, but the euphoria proved short-lived. Saddam remained in power, persecuting dissidents and slaughtering Shi'ites and Kurds who rebelled, with U.S. encouragement, after the Gulf War defeat. At least 30,000 Shi'ites and many thousands of Kurds died from the fighting. But Saddam's war-making capabilities had been badly damaged and the U.S. and U.N. eventually gave the Kurds in the north some military and police protection, freeing them from Iraqi power and allowing them to set up a government with democratic trappings in their region; and sanctions imposed by the United Nations to restrict Iraq's foreign income and hence ability to buy weapons undermined Iraq's economy. Because of these sanctions and Saddam's economic mismanagement, the Iraqi people, who numbered 26 million by 2005, struggled to acquire food and medical supplies, and thousands died from the resulting shortages.

Saudi Arabia, Oil, and the World

The Persian Gulf War pointed up the close connection between Saudi Arabia, a kingdom built on the twin pillars of conservative Islam and oil, and the outside world, especially the United States, which had military bases and a strong economic stake in the kingdom. Comprising mostly bleak desert, Saudi Arabia possesses the world's largest known oil reserves. Beginning in the 1940s the nation's leaders used oil revenues to fund modernization projects, building highways, hospitals, and universities. By the 1980s the Saudis had achieved health and literacy rates that were high by the standards of Africa and the rest of the Middle East. Glittering shopping malls, which offered the latest Western fashions and electronic gadgets, have served affluent urbanites, who reach the malls in luxury cars often driven by chauffeurs. Yet, outside the cities, poor Saudis often still travel by camel and sleep in tents.

Despite the modernization, Saudi political and social life has remained conservative, with the royal family exercising power and living extravagantly while tolerating corruption and quashing dissent. They have used their power to maintain traditional customs and social patterns. Indeed, the country became a laboratory for the clash between modern institutions (like television) and a highly puritanical, patriarchal Islamic culture. With the acquiescence of the Saudi royal family, the Wahhabis, followers of the most rigid form of Islam, maintain a stranglehold on Islamic thought and practice and on religious education in the kingdom's schools. Wahhabis are hostile

---

Ba'ath ("Renaissance") A political party in the Middle East that favored socialism and Arab nationalism and strongly opposed Israel.

Oil Wealth Saudi Arabia contains the world's largest oil operations, mostly located on or near the Persian Gulf. A Saudi worker overlooks one of the nation's many refineries, which produces the oil exports that have brought the nation wealth. (Bill Strode/Woodfin Camp & Associates)

to Western and often any modern ideas; they believe, for example, that women should stay at home and be controlled by men. Hence, although some educated women wish to enjoy freedom, thanks to Wahhabi-influenced laws they still cannot legally drive or work alongside men. Armed with canes, a special police force patrols the streets and markets, including the city malls, to punish women for violating the strict dress codes, which require them to be covered head to foot. In the 1990s the religious police prevented unveiled female students from fleeing a school dormitory fire, causing dozens of the girls to burn to death. The Shi'ite minority, despised by the Wahhabis, have enjoyed few rights. These conflicts have fostered tensions. Saudi and Western critics believe that what they see as the narrow Islam taught in Saudi schools promotes extremism and anti-Western feeling.

Saudi Arabia's policies have strongly influenced world oil prices and availability. The kingdom was the major player in the formation in 1960 of **OPEC** (Organization of Petroleum Exporting Countries), a cartel designed to give the producers more power over the price of oil and leverage over consuming nations. OPEC's members range from Middle Eastern nations such as Algeria, Iran, and the United Arab Emirates to more distant countries such as Mexico, Nigeria, and Indonesia. In 1973 OPEC members, angry at Western support of Israel, reduced the world oil supply to raise prices, badly discomforting industrialized nations by causing long lines at gasoline stations. After the embargo ended the world price remained high, enriching

OPEC members. High prices also forced the U.S. and western Europe to find ways to conserve fuel, such as by designing more fuel-efficient cars. But in the 1980s reduced oil consumption broke OPEC's power and prices plummeted, damaging the economies of most OPEC members.

Saudi Arabia remained the world's largest exporter of oil, ensuring political support and profits from industrialized nations but not guaranteeing Saudi prosperity. Indeed, by the 1990s the Saudi economy had soured. Between 1980 and 2000 income levels fell by two-thirds, resulting in the cutting of government welfare benefits and climbing unemployment. Meanwhile, members of the royal family spent money lavishly and often violated Wahhabi restrictions with their high living abroad, cavorting in the nightclubs of Beirut and the casinos of Europe. Resentment of the royal family increased, as did dislike of the royal family's U.S. allies. Many Saudis oppose the U.S. military bases on Saudi soil, which symbolize U.S. support for the royal family and materialistic interest in the kingdom's oil. Seeing little future for themselves, frustrated young people often drink alcohol and have mixed-gender parties behind closed doors. In contrast, others have embraced militant Islam, a few joining terrorist groups such as Al Qaeda. Most of the young men who hijacked four U.S. airliners and crashed them into the Pentagon and World Trade Center in 2001 were Saudis, often well educated and from middle-class families. The Al Qaeda leader, Osama bin Laden (b. 1957), a militant Wahhabi from a large, wealthy Saudi family, had long raged against the presence of U.S. military bases in Saudi Arabia. Yet, Saudis also have been among the biggest investors in the U.S. and European economies, and many Saudis have studied in the West. Thanks to oil, Saudi Arabia and the industrialized nations,

---

OPEC (Organization of Petroleum Exporting Countries) A cartel formed in 1960 to give producers more power over the price of oil and leverage with the consuming nations.

especially the United States, have remained close allies despite vastly different social and political systems.

SECTION SUMMARY

- After World War II, nationalist governments replaced many colonial regimes in the Middle East, but the region has failed to develop many working multiparty democracies.

- Egyptian leader General Gamal Abdul Nasser became a hero when he threw off British influence, seized control of the Suez Canal, and pursued socialist policies, but neither Nasser nor his pro-American successors brought prosperity to Egypt.

- Traumatized by the Holocaust, many Jews moved to Palestine after World War II and established the state of Israel, which led to a war between Jews and Arabs, a mass exodus of Palestinians into refugee camps, and enduring tensions.

- After the 1967 Arab-Israeli War, Israel occupied lands with a large Arab population and severely limited their freedom, and, while Israelis debated how to achieve peace, Palestinians became increasingly militant in their opposition.

- After nationalists overthrew the Iranian shah, the United States helped organize a coup that returned him to power and he ruled ruthlessly until 1979, when he was overthrown by Islamic fundamentalists.

- From 1958 on, Iraq was ruled by ruthless military dictatorships dominated by the Sunni minority, and in 1979 Saddam Hussein came to power, launched a costly war against Iran, and then was attacked by the United States after invading Kuwait.

- Saudi Arabia grew extremely wealthy from oil sales, but many citizens have remained poor, and Saudi society is dominated by extremely conservative religious leaders, some of whose followers resent the close relationship the Saudi royal family has forged with the United States.

Change and Conflict in the Middle East

What roles has Islam played in the contemporary Middle East?

In 1979 the Islamic world celebrated thirteen centuries of Islamic history. For most of those centuries Muslims had made brilliant contributions to the world, fostering extensive trade networks, accommodating and introducing scientific knowledge, and founding powerful empires. By the nineteenth century, however, the European powers increasingly reconfigured the political and economic life of these societies, though the longer history and older traditions of Islam remained relevant into the present. Islamic societies also experienced social and cultural change. And new conflicts resulting from foreign interventions, Islamic militancy, and international terrorism unsettled the Middle East and world politics, reshaping the region's role in the global system.

Religion, Ethnicity, and Conflict

In parts of the Middle East ethnic and religious hostilities have fostered long-term conflict. In Lebanon, for example, a series of political crises and then a long civil war resulted from rivalry between a dozen rival factions, Christian and Muslim, for control of the small state and its resources. In this deeply fragmented land, a national government existed largely only in name during the 1970s and 1980s. Lebanon's main city, Beirut, once a prosperous, freewheeling mecca for trade, entertainment, and tourism, was devastated by factional fighting. Supporting various factions, Israel, Syria, and the United States were all sucked into the chronic conflict. Syria stationed troops in the north and east, and Israel did the same in the south. In the 1980s the United States intervened on behalf of a weak national government led by the largest, most pro-Western Christian faction. U.S. warships shelled areas around Beirut dominated by opposition, especially Shi'ite, factions while U.S. Marines secured the Beirut airport. The disastrous U.S. mission resulted in some five hundred U.S. deaths from suicide bombers and the holding of U.S. hostages. The intervention also made the United States a focus of Arab rage. In the 1990s the fighting ebbed, and Lebanon regained some stability but little national unity.

Elsewhere, in the Sudan, a huge country linking the Middle East and sub-Saharan Africa, the Arab Muslim-dominated government, which imposed an Islamic state, used military force to control the rebellious African Christians and animists in the south; this conflict resulted in 2 million deaths. In 2005 the two sides agreed to end the conflict, but by then the Arab-controlled Sudan government faced a rebellion in Darfur, an impoverished western region where African Muslim farmers competed for scarce land with Arab pastoralists. To regain control the government launched, with the aid of local Arab militias, a genocide against the Africans. Thousands of people died from military assaults on their villages or from disease and starvation after they fled, many into neighboring Chad.

Another longtime ethnic conflict concerned Kurds, a large ethnic group—over 20 million strong—inhabiting mountain districts in Iran, Iraq, Syria, and Turkey. Although deeply divided by clan and factional rivalries, Kurds had long sought either their own nation or self-government within their countries of residence. This desire brought them into constant conflict with central governments. Kurdish rebel groups were especially active in eastern Turkey, where the Turkish government, hoping to build a national identity based on Turkish identity and language, repressed Kurdish culture and language, banning Kurdish books, newspapers, and records. Kurds were also restless in oil-rich northern Iraq, where the dictator, Saddam Hussein, made Kurds a special target of his repression, launching military operations, including air raids and poison gas attacks, against Kurdish villages.

Gender Relations

Gender relations and family life have changed relatively little in the Middle Eastern societies. Although women have been elected prime ministers in the predominantly Muslim nations of Bangladesh, Pakistan, Indonesia, and Turkey, no Arab or Iranian women have reached this goal. In a few nations also, notably Turkey, Iraq, and Lebanon, urban women have expanded their economic opportunities by running businesses and entering the professions. But compared to women in the rest of the world, most Middle Eastern women remained in the home, often secluded from the outside world, with their lives as daughters, wives, and mothers controlled by the men of their families.

Male and female reformers have challenged women's subservient status for centuries, and a full-fledged feminist movement emerged in Egypt in the 1920s. Muslim liberals advocated improving women's lives through education, hence empowering them to change society. Turkey, Tunisia, and Iraq adopted Western-influenced family laws allowing civil marriages and divorce and according women rights in divorce and child custody. Blaming patriarchal cultural traditions rather than Islam for restrictions, some women activists argued that the Quran supported women's rights. Some women used such arguments to fight against controlling parents and spouses and to expand their options. But conservative Muslims opposed these liberal laws and prevented their enactment in other Middle Eastern societies. Devout women often opposed secular feminism, arguing that women were best protected by strict Islamic law, but this conservatism did not necessarily make them reluctant to become leaders and activists. For instance, Zainab Al-Ghazali (1917–2005) in Egypt founded an organization that built mosques, trained female preachers, and promoted an active women's role in public life; her staunch support of Islamic values upset not only liberal feminists but also Egypt's modernizing President Nasser, who had her jailed and tortured. The conflict between liberals and conservatives, modernizers and traditionalists, often resulted in gender role confusion, as an Egyptian writer noted: "Our mothers understood their situation. We, however, are lost. We do not know whether or not we still belong to the harem, whether love is forbidden or permitted."[4]

Liberal and conservative Muslims disagree on women's dress. Liberals sympathetic to modernization and feminism often see the veil as a symbol of female subjugation. Many women, especially from the urban middle and upper classes, have adopted Western dress. On the other hand, traditionalists have praised the veil as a part of female modesty. Since the 1960s, in secular nations such as Turkey and Egypt, women influenced by revivalist Islam have sparked political debates by lobbying to wear the veil or the less restrictive head scarf as a symbol of piety. This has been a major issue in Turkey, where the secular government, wary of Islamic militancy, has banned head scarves from schools. A young Egyptian reflected the views of many religious women who reject liberal views when she claimed that "being totally covered saves me from the approaches of men and hungry looks. I feel more free, purer,

and more respectable."[5] Many independent-minded, well-educated Muslim women have not wanted to uncritically adopt Western ways. For instance, the liberal Moroccan sociologist and Quranic scholar Fatema Mernissi, a frequent visitor to the West who credited her illiterate grandmother's advice to travel with stimulating her curiosity about the world, argued that Western women face their own version of the veil through their obsession with physical appearance, which, she believed, limited their ability to compete with men for power: "I thank you, Allah, for sparing me the tyranny of the 'size six harem.' I am so happy that the conservative male elite [in the Middle East] does not know about it. Imagine the [Muslim] fundamentalists switching from the veil to forcing women to fit size 6."[6]

Attitudes toward homosexuality have generally become more repressive. For centuries Muslim societies often tolerated, although did not approve, homosexual activity, and writings sympathetically exploring homosexual experiences circulated widely. By the late nineteenth century this changed, forcing homosexuals into the closet. However, by the 1990s the taboo began to slowly diminish, at least in some cities. The strict gender segregation in countries such as Saudi Arabia, where people spend most of their time, and enjoy emotional bonds, with other people of the same sex and where touching and hand holding between friends of the same sex has been common for centuries, actually makes it easier for homosexual couples to escape notice. Yet, in many countries homosexual behavior, when discovered, frequently results in jail terms or even more severe punishments.

Religion and Culture

The clash between tradition and modernity in the Middle East has provided a fertile environment for creativity in religion, music, and literature. Islam has remained at the heart of Middle Eastern life, but, despite its message of peace, social justice, and community, it has often proved more divisive than unifying (see Map 30.2). Age-old divisions such as those between Sunni and Shi'a, liberal and conservative, secular and devout, Sufi and anti-Sufi, remain powerful, especially in western Asia. While many Middle Easterners have adopted a more conservative brand of Islam, musicians and writers often resist the trend toward puritanical practices and beliefs.

Varieties of Islam Antimodern, usually puritanical militants known as **Islamists**, who seek an Islamic state and are bitter rivals of secular Muslims, became increasingly influential, especially in Egypt, Algeria, Turkey, and Iran. Anti-Western revivalist groups such as the Muslim Brotherhood, founded in Egypt after World War I, spread around the region. The writings of the Iranian Ali Shariati (SHAR-ee-AH-tee) (1933–1977), educated in France but a critic of the West, influenced Shi'ites. He castigated Western democracy as

---

Islamists Antimodern, usually puritanical Islamic militants who seek an Islamic state.

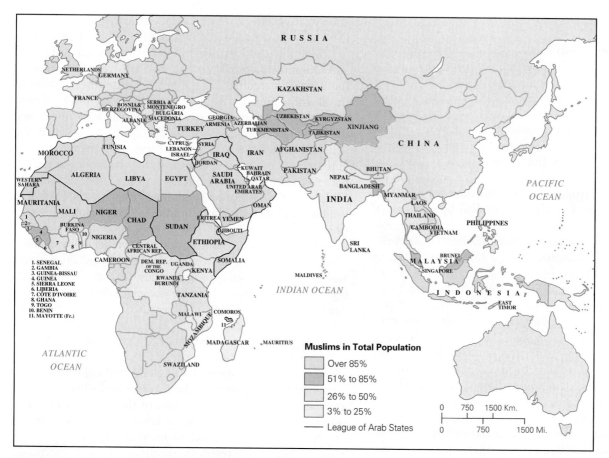

Map 30.2   The Islamic World
The Islamic world includes not only the Middle East—Western Asia and North Africa—but also countries with Muslim majorities in sub-Saharan Africa, Central Asia, and South and Southeast Asia. In addition, Muslims live in most other Eastern Hemisphere nations and in the Americas.

Online Study Center **Improve Your Grade** Interactive Map: Modern Islam, 2002

subverted by the power of money but also blamed Islamic tradition for reducing women to, as he put it, the level of a washing machine. Egyptian writer Sayyid Qutb (SIGH-eed ka-TOOB) (1906–1966) sparked political Sunni Islam and redefined *jihad* ("struggle") as violent opposition to the West rather than, as most Muslim thinkers had taught for centuries, personal struggle to maintain faith. Qutb lived in the United States for two years; he found Americans friendly but was appalled by the racism directed toward black Americans, as well as by the hedonism, such as heavy drinking and casual male-female romance, that he witnessed. Returning to Egypt, Qutb promoted an Islamic state and joined the militant Muslim Brotherhood. Inspired by thinkers like Qutb, the most extreme Islamists, known as *jihadists,* formed organizations that plotted violence against Muslims and non-Muslims they considered obstacles to imposing their rigid version of Islam.

While most people have rejected extremist groups, disillusionment with governments that repress opposition groups, dissatisfaction with lack of material improvement, and resentment of Western influence and world power have prompted a growing turn to Islam for moral support. When elections are allowed, Islamic groups with their large followings tend to tri-

umph over secular parties, as happened in Iraq, Egypt, and Palestine in 2005, a reason why pro-Western modernists often fear democracy. In a troubled world the Islamic revival satisfies for millions a need for personal solace, a yearning for tradition, and a dream of a just political system as propounded by the earliest Muslims. During the past several decades Islamic influence has grown. For example, Islamic dress and practice became more common in Egypt after war losses to Israel, as well as in Iraq after the U.S. invasion of 2003, which overthrew Saddam Hussein and the secular Ba'athist government. These upheavals allowed local religious leaders to assert power. Shi'ite activists in Iraq have closed bars and harassed unveiled women, while Sunni militants attack followers of Sufi mysticism, which they view as heresy. Islamists in Algeria, Egypt, and Saudi Arabia have mounted movements aimed initially at challenging their governments; eventually, frustrated at home, they have become linked to international terrorist groups.

Music and Literature While Islamic militants have condemned music, dance, and other pleasures, many people—both the secular and the devout—have been fans of popular culture, especially popular music. While popular music has provided entertainment, the musicians often hope to encourage national unity or shape society, usually in a more liberal direction. Some musicians, among them the Egyptian singer Oum Kulthum (oom KAL-thoom) (1904–1975), have symbolized Arab people's feelings. Attracting a region-wide following with her emotional songs of abandonment and love, Kulthum dominated Middle Eastern popular music from the 1940s through the 1960s. At her height she was one of the two most popular figures among the Arabs all over the region, the other being her friend, Egypt's president Nasser. Her concerts attracted huge crowds and her recordings were always on the radio and in films. Popular music was also a unifying force that created a sense of community. Hence, the songs of peace and coexistence sung by hugely popular Lebanese singer Fairuz (fie-ROOZ) were sometimes credited with being the major symbol of hope in that turbulent, civil war–plagued land. Similarly Israelis revered Yemen-born Shoshana Damari (1923–2006), whose optimistic songs encouraged Israeli unity by extolling the nation and its military forces.

In religiously dogmatic or ethnically divided states, popular music has sometimes stirred controversy. The Islamic government of Iran, opposed to women performing in public, tried to silence all female singers, including especially the vocalist and film star Googoosh (GOO-goosh), whose melancholic Westernized pop music had a huge audience in Iran during the 1960s and 1970s. The clerics destroyed all the recordings, posters, and films they could locate, turning Googoosh into a popular symbol of opposition to clerical rule. Some music, such as the *arabesk* pop music of Turkey, which is rooted in the experiences of migrants to Istanbul from the country's largely Arabic- and Kurdish-speaking southeast, has derived from powerless subgroups. One observer noted that "arabesk describes a decaying city in which poverty-stricken migrant workers are exploited and abused, and calls on its listeners to pour another glass of wine and curse fate and the world."[7]

Some popular music styles blend Arab and foreign forms while addressing social problems. For example, the **rai** ("opinion") pop music of Algeria is based on local Bedouin chants, Spanish flamenco, French café songs, Egyptian pop, and other influences, and its improvised lyrics often deal with forbidden themes of sex and alcohol. By the 1970s synthesizers, drum machines, and electric guitars were added to the exciting mix. Rai holds great appeal to urban working-class youth in North Africa and to the offspring of Arab immigrants in France, but it is anathema to puritanical Islamic militants in Algeria, who have frequently forced singers into exile or even assassinated them. Rai musicians often move their base to Paris.

Middle Eastern writers have used their literature to express ideas forbidden in politics and religion. For instance, the novels of the Egyptian Naguib Mahfuz (nah-GEEB mah-FOOZ) (b. 1911), a merchant's son turned government official and

Arab Art   The large monument of Revolution, in Baghdad, sculpted by a major modern Iraqi artist, Jawad Salim (1920–1961), occupies a central place in the city. Commissioned in 1958 after the overthrow of the monarchy, it celebrates the Iraqi struggle for justice and freedom and often provided a motif for Iraqi poets. (Monument to Revolution, Liberation Square, Baghdad. Artist: Jawad Salim)

journalist, have addressed social problems, such as poverty, and questioned conservative religious values and blind faith, which he believes keep individuals from realizing their full potential. Many of his writings have been banned in Egypt and other Islamic nations. But Mahfuz, strongly influenced by both Western and Arab writers, has achieved worldwide renown and in 1988 became the first Arab writer to win a Nobel Prize for literature. Iranian writers have often been anticlerical and have attacked religious hypocrisy. They have also risked punishment by satirizing the failings of governments and business. One famous Iranian novel recommended opportunism for career success: "Try to establish connections with the holders of high offices. Agree with everybody, no matter what his opinion is."[8]

---

rai ("opinion")   A pop music of Algeria based on local Bedouin chants, Spanish flamenco, French café songs, Egyptian pop, and other influences and featuring improvised lyrics that often deal with forbidden themes of sex and alcohol.

Turmoil in Afghanistan

Violence and extreme militant Islamic movements emerged in Afghanistan, fostering instability there for three decades. Afghanistan's diverse Muslim ethnic groups, further subdivided into rival tribes, have little sense of national unity in this landlocked land of harsh deserts and rugged mountains. From the early 1800s until 1978 kings from the largest ethnic group, the Pashtuns, loosely governed the territory. Some Afghan leaders advocated modernization, triggering revolts by conservative tribes. In 1978 pro-communist generals seized power, forged close ties with the Soviet Union, and introduced radical social and economic reforms that challenged Islamic traditions. They implemented land reform, promoted women's education, and replaced Islamic law with a secular family law giving women more rights.

When conservative Islamic rebels, known as **mujahidin** ("holy warriors"), rebelled against the pro-Soviet regime, the Soviet Union invaded in 1979 to protect the regime, launching decades of turbulence. The mujahidin, while poorly armed and divided, won small victories against the 150,000 Soviet troops. Both sides resorted to ruthless brutality, attacking civilians suspected of aiding or supporting the enemy. Indiscriminate Soviet air attacks on the rebels created 5 million refugees and turned the population against the Soviet occupation. The United States, Pakistan, and Arab nations sent military and financial aid to the rebels, especially to extremist Pashtun factions, and Islamic volunteers such as the wealthy Saudi Osama bin Laden (b. 1957), a trained engineer turned Islamic militant. By the mid-1980s Afghanistan had become an unwinnable quagmire for the Soviet forces, which withdrew in 1989, a defeat which led to the ending of Soviet communism and the dismantling of the Soviet Empire. The pro-Soviet government collapsed, and rival mujahidin groups fought for control. With the USSR gone and the civil war over, the West offered little help to reconstruct the ruined country.

Afghanistan soon returned to global attention. As conflict between rival militias continued, a group of Pashtun religious students known as the **Taliban** ("Students"), many educated in Pakistan, organized a military force to impose order and stamp out what they considered immoral behavior, such as rape and drinking, among the tribal factions fighting each other to control the post-Soviet government. The Taliban conquered much of the Pashtun south and then seized the capital, Kabul, in 1996. Eventually they extended their influence into the north, where ethnic factions continued to resist the Taliban. The puritanical Taliban reversed the modernization of the pro-Soviet regime and introduced an especially harsh form of Islamic rule. Women in the capital, Kabul, who once wore jeans and T-shirts and attended universities, were now required to wear long black robes and stay at home. Education for women was banned and alcohol disappeared from stores. The Taliban banned pleasures such as music as sinful and executed people for even minor infractions. Under the Taliban the streets were safe but life offered no joy. Reflecting their intolerance and disdain for Afghanistan's pre-Islamic past, the Taliban also destroyed spectacular monumental Buddhas carved into a mountainside over a millennium ago, outraging the world.

International terrorist groups with a jihadist agenda and hatred for the West, especially for the United States, and for the Saudi royal family, began to form around Arab volunteers who had come originally to fight for the mujahidin cause and then, often facing jail in their own countries as radicals, remained. The Saudi Osama bin Laden became the leader and chief financial backer of the largest international terrorist group, Al Qaeda. Bin Laden called on Muslims to take up arms against the United States and other Western regimes, whom he called "crusaders" after those Christian knights who invaded the Middle East and fought Muslims during the Intermediate Era: "Tell the Muslims everywhere that the vanguards of the warriors who are fighting the enemies of Islam belong to them."[9] In the late 1990s these Islamic terrorist groups made Taliban-controlled Afghanistan their base, building camps to train more terrorists.

Islamic Militancy, Terrorism, and Western Interventions

The rise of international terrorism linked to Islamist groups and chiefly targeting Americans and Europeans soon resulted in a renewal of superpower intervention. After the Al Qaeda attacks on the United States in September 2001, the United States, with widespread world support, sent military forces into Taliban-ruled Afghanistan. Soon the United States and its allies among local anti-Taliban, mostly non-Pashtun groups, had displaced the Taliban, destroyed the Al Qaeda bases, and installed a fragile pro-Western government. Many Afghans and most Muslims outside Afghanistan, even in conservative Iran and Saudi Arabia, applauded the demise of the Taliban, but instability ensued in Afghanistan: tribal warlords controlled large territories; the major Taliban and Al Qaeda leaders, including bin Laden, evaded the U.S. troops and went into hiding; and the United States and western Europe struggled to foster development and support a fledgling democracy in a poor, largely tribal land. By 2005 a Taliban-led insurgency against the pro-Western regime was growing in strength.

The Afghan war was followed by a larger conflict in Iraq. Charging that Iraq's dictator, Saddam Hussein, had weapons of mass destruction and was linked to Al Qaeda, the U.S. president George W. Bush, supported chiefly by Britain, ordered an invasion and occupation of Iraq in 2003 without support from the United Nations, many Western allies, and regional allies such as Turkey and Egypt. Massive looting followed the quick U.S. victory, as museums, ancient historical sites, power plants,

---

mujahidin ("holy warriors") Conservative Islamic rebels who rebelled against the pro-Soviet regime in Afghanistan in the 1970s and 1980s.

Taliban ("Students") A group of Pashtun religious students who organized a military force in the 1980s to fight what they considered immorality and corruption and to impose order in Afghanistan.

armories, and communications networks were plundered. U.S. credibility suffered after the Americans found no nuclear, biological, or chemical weapons or any Saddam–Al Qaeda links. Nor had the Americans adequately planned for the problems of the postwar reconstruction. While the Bush administration shifted its goal to fostering democracy, U.S. forces struggled to contain factional divisions and restore basic services, such as electricity and clean water, to Saddam-era levels. They also struggled to maintain order against a persistent resistance movement, supported by many Sunnis, and to defend against terrifying suicide bombings by newly arrived foreign jihadis linked to Al Qaeda. Bush also failed to convince critics around the world that the Iraq conflict did not distract from the global campaign against international terrorism. Many Iraqis, especially Shi'ites and Kurds, had hated Saddam's bloody regime and welcomed his demise, but Iraqis, remembering British colonization after World War I, also often resented yet another Western occupation and feared potential U.S. control of their oil industry. While Arab liberals often hoped democracy would flower in Iraq and throughout the region, the occupation of an oil-rich Arab country, at a high cost in U.S. and Iraqi casualties, tied down the U.S. military and intensified anti-U.S. feeling around the world, probably increasing support for Islamic militancy in the Muslim world generally.

The Middle East in the Global System

The Middle East has been subject to explosive forces, some of them linked to changes in the global system. By the late twentieth century, observers in the region argued that much of the Middle East had adjusted poorly to a rapidly changing world, lagging behind much of Asia and Latin America in development. For example, a Lebanese novelist wrote that the dictatorial Arab regimes succeeded in depriving people not only of dignity but also of air: the opportunity to discuss problems freely. In 2002 various Arab thinkers issued an Arab Human Development Report that outlined the economic and social failures of the Arab world, including the marginalization of women and the limited development in health and education (see Witness to the Past: Assessing Arab Development). Debate is also fostered by regional cable networks, such as Qatar-based Al Jazeera, that spread awareness of political and social developments while promoting a modern image, such as using unveiled female news anchors. Furthermore, in some countries urban people have access to the Internet, often at cafés, and go online to access foreign news, shop, or arrange dates. Arab and Turkish chat rooms and blogs abound. Religious and political groups also use the web to recruit support, among them Al Qaeda and the Iraqi insurgents.

The region's economic record has been checkered. By 2005 the Middle East had the world's highest unemployment rate, 13.2 percent and, except for sub-Saharan Africa, the slowest economic growth and lowest productivity. Only Turkey has fostered much industrialization and high economic growth rates. Nations with oil, such as Algeria, Iran, and Libya, have remained dangerously dependent on oil revenues for economic survival. Oil wealth often leads to political corruption, reduces the willingness of autocratic leaders to heed calls for democracy, and sometimes funds Islamist and terrorist groups, but several small Persian Gulf states have used their oil wealth to become centers of global commerce. For example, Dubai (doo-BUY) has become one of the world's most modern cities, with luxury hotels, futuristic architecture, the world's largest artificial port, and thousands of businessmen and workers from all over the world. The continuing Western and Japanese appetite and growing need of industrializing nations such as China and India for oil ensures that the profits will flow to oil-rich nations for years to come. However, Middle Eastern nations that are without oil and so must rely mostly on agriculture have struggled to build modern economies with limited resources.

Middle Easterners increasingly have hoped to preserve revered traditional patterns while finding ways to harmonize them with the realities of the modern world. Past and present, tradition and modernity, have been all jumbled in the contemporary Middle East. An Egyptian novelist wrote that a Cairo resident has a split personality: "Half of him believes, prays, fasts and makes the pilgrimage [to Mecca]. The other half renders his values void in banks and courts and in the streets, the cinemas, perhaps even at home among his family before the television set."[10] The recent history of the Middle East, like that of India and sub-Saharan Africa, has challenged the widespread notion that contact with the modern world automatically erodes all traditional cultures and steers people inevitably toward Western models. Older patterns of life and thought, including Islam, have persisted in much of the region. Observers disagree whether this constitutes a major barrier to progress or gives the people an anchor to deal with the destabilizing, often undesirable effects of change.

Islamic militancy has become a major factor in the Middle East, tapping a strand of unease with Western ideas. Many Muslims have not looked to the West for inspiration, rejecting what they see as the materialistic, hedonistic values of Western culture. As an example of such militancy, the Iranian Revolution of 1979 began the first successful attempt by an Islamic country to become totally independent of Western political, economic, social, and cultural influence. Iranians and Arabs have often agreed with the Indian Muslim poet Muhammad Iqbal (ik-BALL) (1873–1938), who wrote in 1927: "Against Europe I protest, And the attraction of the West: Woe for Europe and her charm, Swift to capture and disarm! Earth awaits rebuilding; rise! Out of slumber deep, Arise!"[11] Militancy has emerged around the Islamic world as a challenge to capitalism, secularism, failed governments, and Western-style democracy. Other Muslims, however, have feared Islamic militancy, which has not delivered a better material life in the main country controlled by Islamists, Iran. Middle Eastern reformists have sought greater economic development, political freedom, and rights for women. The hopes of modernist Muslims were expressed by an influential liberal reformer, Reza Aslan, born in Iran and living in the United States, who argued that a Reformation has begun among believers to cleanse Islam of what he termed the "false idols" of bigotry and fanaticism and return the faith to its roots as an egalitarian social reform movement.

Assessing Arab Development

Under the auspices of the United Nations Development Programme, a group of Arab scholars and opinion makers from the twenty-two member states of the Arab League, a regional organization, met to consider the Arab condition. In 2002 they issued the first of four planned reports that offered both a description of the Arab condition and a prescription for change. Hailed by Arab and non-Arab observers as a pathbreaking effort by Arabs to foster a debate on the inadequacies of Arab development and local barriers to progress, the first document reported great strides in many areas but also unsolved problems. This excerpt is from the Executive Summary.

The Arab Human Development Report 2002 . . . places people squarely at the [center] of development in all its dimensions: economic, social, civil, political, and cultural. It provides a neutral forum to measure progress and deficits, propose strategies to policymakers, and draw attention to country problems that can benefit from regional solutions. It is guided by the conviction that solid analysis can contribute to the many efforts underway to mobilize the region's rich human potential. There has been considerable progress in laying the foundations for health, habitat, and education. Two notable achievements are the enormous quantitative expansion in educating the young and a conspicuous improvement in fighting death. For example, life expectancy has increased by 15 years over the last three decades, and infant mortality rates have dropped by two-thirds. Moreover, the region's growth has been "pro-poor": there is much less dire poverty (defined as an income of less than a dollar a day) than in any other developing region.

But there have been warning signs as well. Over the past twenty years, growth in per capita income was the lowest in the world except in sub-Saharan Africa. . . . If such trends continue [into] the future, it will take the average Arab citizen 140 years to double his or her income. . . . The decline in productivity has been accompanied by deterioration in real wages, which has accentuated poverty. It is evident that . . . Arab countries have not developed as quickly or as fully as other comparable regions. . . . The Arab region is richer than it is developed, . . . hobbled by a . . . poverty of capabilities and . . . opportunities.

These have their roots in three deficits: freedom, women's empowerment, and knowledge. Growth alone will neither bridge these gaps nor set the region on the road to sustainable development.

The way forward involves tackling human capabilities and knowledge. It also involves promoting systems of good governance, those that promote, support and sustain human well-bring, based on expanding human capabilities, choices, opportunities and freedoms, . . . especially for the poorest and most marginalized members of society. The empowerment of women must be addressed throughout. . . .

[The Report concludes that] People in most Arab countries live longer than the world average life expectancy of 67. However, disease and disability reduce life expectancy by between five and 11 years. Arab women have lower life expectancy than the world average. . . . Arab countries have made tangible progress in improving literacy: . . . female literacy rates tripled since 1970. Yet 65 million adults are illiterate, almost two-thirds of them women. . . . One out of every five Arabs lives on less than $2 per day. . . . Arab countries had the lowest freedom score [in the world] in the late 1990s. . . . [Utilization] of Arab women's capabilities through political and economic participation remains the lowest in the world. . . . Serious knowledge deficits include weak systems of scientific research and development.

The Arab world is at a crossroads. The fundamental choice is whether its trajectory will remain marked by inertia, as reflected in much of the present institutional context, and by ineffective policies that have produced the substantial development challenges facing the region; or whether prospects for an Arab renaissance, anchored in human development will be actively pursued.

THINKING ABOUT THE READING

1. How have Arabs done in promoting freedom, women's empowerment, and knowledge?

2. What does the report consider the major improvements and the major failures and challenges of the Arab nations?

Source: *Arab Human Development Report 2002: Creating Opportunities for Future Generations* (UNDP, 2002), available online at http://www.rbas. undp.org/ahdr/press_kits2002/PRExecSummary.pdf. Reprinted with permission of the United Nations Development Program (UNDP).

Interventions by outside powers, such as the United States, reflect the global importance of the Middle East, especially its oil wealth and its strategic location among key waterways of world trade. Until cost-effective alternative power sources become common, all industrial economies need access to Middle Eastern oil, without which modern lifestyles would come to a screeching halt. The desires of some leaders within the region and some leaders outside to control the oil flow have led to wars. The world community will not tolerate anything that threatens the movement of oil tankers through the Persian Gulf. While U.S. leaders hope democracy will spread, many experts worry that instability in Iraq might spill over to its neighbors, unsettling the entire region. Furthermore, few conflicts or persistent problems, including the Arab-Israel conflict, seem resolvable anytime soon. These challenges make the Middle East a focus of world attention and, some fear, a potential tinderbox.

SECTION SUMMARY

- For several decades, Lebanon was mired in civil war among a variety of factions supported by foreign governments, including the United States; in the Sudan, Arab Muslims fought with African Christians and launched a genocide against African Muslims; and the Kurds came into conflict with the governments of several Middle Eastern countries.

- Although some Middle Eastern women have attained greater freedom and adopted Western dress, many remain in the home and wear a veil, which some argue protects them from predatory men.

- Middle Eastern societies have been divided between Islamists and secular Muslims, and musicians and writers, popular among the people, have raised the ire of religious conservatives.

- In Afghanistan, U.S.-supported Islamic rebels and Soviet-assisted communists fought for a decade until the Soviets withdrew, after which the Taliban, led by extremely conservative, repressive Muslims, took over much of the country and allowed terrorist groups such as Al Qaeda to base themselves there.

- After Al Qaeda's September 2001 attack on the United States, a U.S.-led invasion overthrew the Taliban and set up a weak pro-Western government, and in 2003 the United States invaded Iraq, generating massive looting and persistent, violent opposition, even by Iraqis who hated life under Saddam Hussein.

- Middle Eastern societies have been torn between those who feel they have failed to adapt to the modern world and those who champion tradition and urge rejection of the modern, Western values, while the region has remained extremely important to outside powers, such as the United States, because of its oil reserves.

◈ Political Change in Sub-Saharan Africa

What were the main political consequences of decolonization in sub-Saharan Africa?

As in the Middle East, the rise of nationalism and the consequent wave of decolonization in Africa reduced Western political influence, reshaping societies and politics. Between 1957 and 1975 the colonial era ended in sub-Saharan Africa (see Chronology: Sub-Saharan Africa, 1945–Present). Countries became politically independent as the British, French, Belgians, and eventually the Portuguese came to terms with rising nationalist activity. In the early 1960s, as optimistic Africans celebrated their freedom and formed governments, some observers proclaimed that this was Africa's Age of Glam-

CHRONOLOGY

Sub-Saharan Africa, 1945–Present

1948	Introduction of apartheid in South Africa
1949	First mass-based political party in Gold Coast
1952–1960	Mau Mau uprising in Kenya
1957	Independence for Ghana
1957–1975	African decolonization
1961	Assassination of Patrice Lumumba in Congo
1965–1980	White government in Southern Rhodesia
1967–1970	Nigerian Civil War
1975	Independence for Portuguese colonies
1991–1994	Civil war in Somalia
1994	Genocide in Rwanda
1994	Nelson Mandela first black president of South Africa
1998	End of Mobuto era in Congo

our. The times were electric with change, and hopes for a better future were high. But with the end of colonial domination institutions had to be built anew. The years since 1960 have been, in many respects, the most momentous and rapid time of change in all of Africa's history, though they have often been destabilizing. Africans still struggle to find the right mix of policies to resolve their problems.

Nationalism and Decolonization

Rising nationalism sparked decolonization. Between the late nineteenth century and the 1950s the European colonial powers did little to encourage national feeling among Africans and maintained control through divide and rule of the different ethnic groups. In most colonies nationalists had to struggle to overcome the ethnic complexities imposed by colonialism, especially the drawing of boundaries to include rival groups in the same country. For example, each of the major Nigerian ethnic groups—the Hausa, Yoruba, and Igbo (Ibo)—had little in common with each other and formed their own nationalist organizations, a challenge to those Nigerians who wanted to build a united front. Independence often came peacefully after negotiations between nationalist leaders and European rulers. Sometimes, however, independence came only after bitter struggles and violence by nationalists willing to fight against long odds.

Nationalist Movements The increasing problems posed for Western colonizers often encouraged them to transfer power peacefully. World War II had undermined Western credibility in the European colonies. As in World War I, Europeans slaughtered both one another and the Africans they drafted or recruited to fight in North Africa, Asia, and Europe. The drafting and casualties caused Africans to feel revulsion against the Western powers and their pretensions of superiority, represented by the British official in Nigeria who argued that the "barbarism" of the Nigerians required the maintenance of what he called the British "civilizing mission" into the far future. The British and French claimed to be fighting for freedom and democracy, but Africans noticed that these values were seldom applied in the colonies. With Western vulnerability obvious, nationalist leaders negotiated for reforms in the 1940s. After the war the British encouraged African hopes by granting independence to India and Burma, and they also began to introduce local government in some African colonies. Yet most colonial governments did little to prepare their societies for true political and economic independence.

The first change came in the British Gold Coast. In 1948 small farmers boycotted European businesses that were suspected of profiteering at their expense. The growing tensions led to riots in the towns. A rising leader in the Gold Coast, Kwame Nkrumah (KWAH-mee nn-KROO-muh) (1909–1972), who had graduated from both British and American universities, became convinced that only socialism could save Africa. In 1949 he organized a political party, the first real mass organization in Africa, but he was soon arrested by the British, who viewed Nkrumah as a dangerous subversive and leftist. Because of the continued unrest, however, the British allowed an election in 1951 for a legislative council, and Nkrumah's party won a huge majority. After negotiations, in 1957 the Gold Coast became independent and was renamed Ghana, after the first great West African kingdom over a millennium earlier. Nkrumah became the nation's first prime minister and the hero of Africa, proclaiming that Africans must become masters of their own destiny. He also preached **pan-Africanism**, the dream that all Africans would cooperate to eventually form some sort of united states of the continent.

The anticolonial dam had now burst, and it was impossible to stem the tide. By 1963 all the British colonies in West Africa had become independent, largely through a combination of peaceful negotiations and strikes by workers. By contrast, the French at first failed to recognize change. Having no plans to abandon their empire, they fought brutal but unsuccessful wars in the 1950s to keep Vietnam and Algeria from leaving the colonial fold. But they finally realized that a peaceful transition might better serve their long-term aims of maintaining economic influence. France gave its colonies the option of voting for a complete break or for autonomy within a French community of closely connected nations. Initially only the West African colony of Guinea opted to expel the French completely, prompting the French to withdraw all economic aid from Guinea. Later the French colonies became fully independent, though they usually maintained close political and economic ties to France.

Violence and Revolution Whereas peaceful power transfers worked in some colonies, such as in British and French West Africa, widespread violence preceded or accompanied independence in others. For example, many British settlers had migrated to Kenya after both World War I and World War II, taking land from the Africans to establish farms. In 1952 many Gikuyu, Kenya's largest ethnic group, which had suffered the most land losses, began an eight-year uprising against British rule, known as the **Mau Mau Rebellion**, during which they attacked British farmers and officials. The British sent thousands of troops to Kenya and committed atrocities against pro–Mau Mau villages, ultimately killing 10,000 Gikuyu and detaining 90,000 others in harsh prison camps, where many died from disease or mistreatment. Finally, realizing the futility of their cause, the British released from prison the leading nationalist leader, Jomo Kenyatta (ken-YAH-tuh) (ca. 1889–1978), a former herd boy who had studied anthropology in Britain. Negotiations resulted in Kenyan independence in 1963, and Kenyatta became the first freely elected prime minister. Britain also granted independence to its other East African colonies, Uganda and Tanzania. In Kenya white settlers who had strongly opposed political rights for the African majority often remained, sometimes serving in the Kenyan government.

Violence also engulfed the Belgian Congo, a vast, natural resource-rich territory containing some two hundred ethnic groups. The Belgians had failed to foster an educated leadership class, encourage national consciousness, or build adequate paved roads, bridges, and telephone systems. At independence the Congo had only a few university graduates. The only Congolese leader with any national following, the widely admired and left-leaning visionary Patrice Lumumba (loo-MOOM-buh) (1925–1961), a former post office clerk and brewery director, opposed the economic domination of Belgian business and mining interests. In 1959 riots broke out in Congolese cities, forcing the Belgians to announce the colony's first free elections, which were won by Lumumba's party. As the Belgians left and Lumumba took power, some Congolese troops mutinied and attacked whites. Taking advantage of the chaos, Belgian-supported leaders in the mineral-rich Katanga region who opposed Lumumba and wanted power announced their secession from the country. The United Nations sent in a peacekeeping force that restored order in the Congo. But Katanga leaders, with the complicity of Belgium and the United States, who feared that Lumumba favored the Soviet Union, abducted and murdered him in 1961. Both Belgium and the United States supported the Congo's new leader, General Joseph Mobuto (mo-BOO-to), who became a dictator. In 1971 Mobuto, who had given his country a new name, Zaire, also changed his name to Mobuto Sese Seko, "Mobuto the All Powerful." He introduced a new ideology—Mobutoism—that required his people to sing his

pan-Africanism The dream that all Africans would cooperate to eventually form some sort of united states of the continent.

Mau Mau Rebellion An eight-year uprising in the 1950s by the Gikuyu people in Kenya against British rule.

Mau Mau During the 1950s Africans in Kenya, especially the Gikuyu, rebelled against British colonial rule. The British responded by detaining some 90,000 suspected rebels and sympathizers in concentration camps such as this, where many died. (Hulton-Deutch Collection/Corbis)

praises every day at the workplace and in schools, and he ordered them to replace European names and values with African ones, including exchanging Western clothes, such as ties, for traditional garb. Wearing a tie became an act of political resistance for men.

Portugal, ruled by a fascist dictator, had been reluctant to give up its African colonial empire. Revolts had broken out in its three colonies—Angola, Guinea-Bissau, and Mozambique—in the early 1960s, but the Portuguese launched military campaigns to crush them. Angola's liberation movement was divided into three rival factions based on the country's major ethnic groupings. Marxists led the major liberation movements in Mozambique and Guinea Bissau. The visionary Amilcar Cabral (AH-mill-CAR kah-BRAHL) (1924–1973), a university-educated agronomist who founded and led the Guinea-Bissau movement, emphasized educating the people to empower them, telling his followers: "Learn from life, people, books, the experiences of others, never stop learning."[12] Portuguese agents assassinated Cabral in 1973. In 1974, however, Portugal's war-weary army ended the dictatorship in Portugal. The new democratic, socialist-led government granted the colonies their independence in 1975. However, in Angola, the nationalist factions fought each other for dominance for the next two decades and Mozambique's revolutionary government faced a long insurgency supported by white-ruled South Africa.

The British colonies of the Rhodesias and Nyasaland in southern Africa, all containing white settlers who bitterly resisted efforts at political and social equality for Africans, were among the last African colonies to gain independence under black majority rule. As African nationalists launched largely nonviolent resistance campaigns in the colonies, the British feared the growing costs of suppressing the resistance. In 1963 they granted independence to Zambia (Northern Rhodesia) and Malawi (formerly Nyasaland), both of which only had small white minorities. But the large white settler population in Southern Rhodesia declared independence from Britain in 1965 and installed a white racist government that imposed stricter racial segregation and prohibited political activity by nonwhites. Africans in Southern Rhodesia took up arms against the white settler government in two rival Marxist-led liberation movements. By 1980 the African resistance was so strong that the United States and Britain pressured the white government to allow elections, which were won by Robert Mugabe (moo-GAH-bee) (b. 1924), a former political prisoner who had transformed his guerrilla movement into a party. The country became independent as Zimbabwe.

Political Change and Conflict

A West African scholar called *nation* "a magical word meant to exorcise ethnic quarrels and antagonisms—and as such very precious"[13]; but, as he conceded, the magic usually failed to overcome disunity. New African nations typically experienced political and economic challenges that fostered instability: coups, prolonged civil wars, and recurring famines (see Map 30.3). Several million refugees fled the fighting, repression, and hunger, and corruption and ethnic divisions made dictatorship more common than democracy. During the 1990s various countries crumbled into brutal anarchy that resulted in the deaths of thousands. Several countries have seen governments dominated by one ethnic or religious group wage chronic warfare against other ethnic or religious groups.

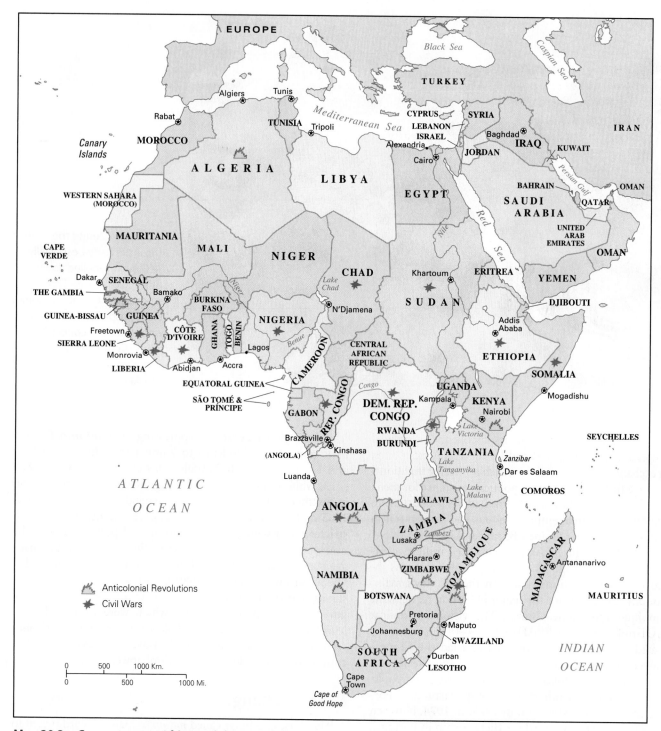

Map 30.3   Contemporary Africa and the Middle East
Sub-Saharan and North Africa contain over forty nations. Six sub-Saharan African nations and Algeria
in North Africa experienced anticolonial revolutions, and a dozen sub-Saharan nations have been
racked by civil wars since independence.

***Democracy and
Dictatorship***
Although the new nations typically started as parliamentary democracies, only a few sustained democratic systems. Rule by the military or by one dominant party has been more common. Militaries have often been the only groups that can govern effectively, since they have a shared ideology of leadership, good internal communications, and a tradition of discipline.

Military officers, however, enjoying a privileged existence, are also often out of touch with the population; used to giving orders, they have ruled with a heavy hand and often looted treasuries. Civilian leaders have often favored one-party states because, they argue, such parties can minimize ethnic divisions by incorporating all the ethnic groups. While some of these one-party states, such as in the Congo (Zaire), have been despotisms, others have been relatively open, even allowing some democratic choice among candidates for office. Some nations, such as Nigeria and Ghana, shifted back and forth between authoritarian military dictatorships and ineffective, corrupt civilian governments. Not all the despotic governments have brutally mistreated their own people, but some have become major violators of civil liberties and human rights. For example, during the 1970s in Uganda, then ruled by Idi Amin (EE-dee AH-meen) (1925–2004), a poorly educated former amateur boxing champion who rose to become a general, some 300,000 people suspected of opposing Amin were killed, and thousands more were jailed or fled into exile.

Western-style democracy has had little chance to flower in these artificial, multiethnic countries created by a colonialism that generally intensified ethnic hostilities. These countries typically have a tiny middle class and numerous poor people. And, given the deteriorating economic conditions of the past thirty years, governments have had little money to spend on containing ethnic tensions or for building schools, hospitals, and roads. Furthermore, the nationalist leaders and parties that have governed the new nations have often lost their credibility and mass support after a few years. For instance, Ghana's Kwame Nkrumah, once Africa's greatest hero, was overthrown for economic mismanagement and an autocratic governing style and died in exile.

African leaders have been a mixed lot. Some have been highly respected, farsighted visionaries, such as Tanzania's Julius Nyerere (NEE-ya-RARE-y) (g. 1962–1985) and Mozambique's Samora Machel (g. 1975–1986), and pragmatic problem solvers, such as South Africa's first black president, Nelson Mandela. While not all their initiatives have succeeded, they have used political office largely to improve society rather than enrich themselves. Others have disappointed or brutalized their people. Some, such as the Congo (Zaire) dictator Mobuto (g. 1965–1997) and the Nigerian military dictator Sani Abacha (g. 1993–1998), have been ruthless crooks, arresting or murdering opponents and plundering the public treasury to amass multibillion-dollar fortunes. When Abacha, hopped up on Viagra, died of a heart attack while he engaged in an orgy with prostitutes, few Nigerians lamented. Whether dictators or not, leaders have too often been reluctant to give up their power: even when their credibility has ended, they have rigged elections or had compliant parliaments declare them presidents for life.

Political instability, conflict, and social unrest have grown as people have struggled for their share of the dwindling pie. The blatant corruption, conspicuous consumption, and smuggling in government and the business sector have increased inequalities and deepened public frustrations. Sub-Saharan Africa has the world's highest rate of income inequality. In some countries, government officials have become known as "Mr. 10 Percent," a reference to the share of public budgets they grab. East Africans chastise the **wabenzi**—"people who

drive a Mercedes Benz"—a privileged urban class of politicians, high bureaucrats, professionals, military officers, and businessmen who manipulate their connections to amass wealth. Political, military, and business elites have often squandered scarce resources on importing luxuries, such as fancy cars and hard liquor, signs of the continuing hold of Western taste and consumer goods.

On the other hand, in some societies relations between governments and the governed have improved, offering wider participation in politics. New grassroots and other nongovernmental organizations have worked for issues such as human rights and the environment. Ordinary people, especially women, have demanded and sometimes gained greater responsibility for improving their lives. For example, by 2000 some 25,000 local women's groups in Kenya had pushed for improved rights and other issues of interest to women, such as environmental protection. The Kenyan women's rights and environmental activist, Wangari Maathai (wan-GAHR-ee MAH-thai), won the Nobel Peace Prize in 2005 (see Chapter 26). Since few Africans can afford health insurance, in countries such as Senegal poor people have come together to form small mutual health organizations, negotiating with local clinics to get an affordable group rate for health care. Strong support from women voters helped Liberian economist Ellen Johnson-Sirleaf (b. 1939), a Harvard-trained banker and former United Nations official admired by Liberians as tender but also tough, become the first woman president in Africa in 2005, as the country sought to recover from a long civil war and then a corrupt dictatorship. But she faced a monumental challenge to bring progress and stability to a maimed nation with no piped water or electric grid and few functioning schools and hospitals.

Political Violence The combination of artificial boundaries, weak national identity, and economic collapse has produced chronic turmoil in several African nations, resulting in what one discouraged African observer called the dark night of bloodshed and death. For example, Liberia and Sierra Leone, once among the more stable countries, disintegrated in the 1990s as ethnic-based rebel groups challenged their country's government for power. In both countries thousands fled the slaughter and the maiming of civilians, causing larger African nations like Nigeria to send in troops to bring stability. In drought-plagued Somalia, when longtime military rule collapsed in 1991, the country divided into regions ruled by feuding Somali clans with their own armies. As the Somali economy disintegrated, causing thousands to starve to death, the United Nations dispatched a humanitarian mission. But some Americans in the United Nations force were killed and the United Nations withdrew in 1994, unable to achieve a unified government. While the fighting lessened, Somalia remained a country in name only, controlled by warlords.

Sometimes hatreds have led to genocide, killing directed at eliminating a particular group. This happened in the small, impoverished, and densely populated state of Rwanda, most of whose population belonged to the majority Hutu and minority Tutsi ethnic groups. The German and then the Belgian colonizers had ruled through Tutsi kings. Soon after independence, the

---

wabenzi ("people who drive a Mercedes Benz") A privileged urban class in Africa of politicians, high bureaucrats, professionals, military officers, and businessmen who manipulate their connections to amass wealth.

Hutu rebelled against the Tutsi-dominated government, slaughtering thousands of Tutsi and forcing others out of the country. Those Tutsi who remained faced discrimination and repression. In 1994 the extremist Hutu government in Rwanda began a genocide against the remaining Tutsi and moderate Hutus, murdering over 500,000 people. Tutsi exiles based in Uganda then invaded Rwanda, forcing the Hutu leadership and its followers into the neighboring Congo. Over 2 million Hutu fled. The new Tutsi-led government continued to face militant Hutu resistance groups based in the Congo, leading to Rwandan military incursions into the Congo.

Nigeria: Hopes and Frustrations

The hopes and frustrations of contemporary Africa are mirrored in Nigeria, which in 2005 was home to some 130 million people, about a fifth of Africa's total population. Nigeria's ethnic diversity and natural wealth have been both a blessing and a curse. Like many African countries, Nigeria contains an extraordinary variety of ethnic groups, languages, religions, artistic traditions, and even ecologies. While some 250 ethnic groups live in Nigeria, about two-thirds of the people belong to the Hausa-Fulani, Igbo (Ibo), or Yoruba groups. Nigeria's oil wealth has brought income—80 percent of the nation's total revenues—but has also corrupted politics and increased social inequality.

Nigeria's history has frequently been punctuated by coups, countercoups, riots, political assassinations, and civil war rooted in regional and ethnic rivalries. Between 1967 and 1970 Nigeria endured a bloody civil war to prevent the secession of the Igbo-dominated and oil-rich southeast region. The religious divide between Christians, who dominate the south, and Muslims, who control the northern states, has also complicated politics. Following a Muslim revival among the Hausa-Fulani, northern states have often imposed strict Islamic law, antagonizing non-Muslims. Several Muslim women were sentenced to death by stoning for adultery while the men involved were not punished, causing an outcry in Nigeria and around the world. Sometimes severe Christian-Muslim fighting has broken out for control of religiously mixed cities or districts, causing the death of hundreds of people. The numerous destabilizing factors have often led to corrupt military rule, which brought stability by suppressing opposition but pushed the people hard, alternating with periods of corrupt civilian democracy, which increased political freedom but often caused ineffective government.

The Nigerian oil industry, while creating some prosperity, has also made Nigeria dependent on oil exports and spawned political and economic problems. A few politicians, bureaucrats, and businessmen have monopolized oil profits, fostering corruption, sometimes outright plunder of public wealth, and the inequitable wealth distribution resented by many Nigerians. By 2005 the top 20 percent of Nigerians received 56 percent of all the country's wealth while the bottom 20 percent got only 4.4 percent. People living in the southern districts producing the oil see few jobs or other benefits and watch sullenly as pipelines through their villages move oil to the coastal ports, from where tankers carry most of the oil to consumers in Europe and North America. Their sporadic protests, including sabotage of the oil pipelines, have been met with military force; protest leaders are accused of treason and sometimes executed. Disenchanted Nigerians refer to a "republic of the privileged and rich" and a "moneytocracy." Oil money created high expectations in the 1970s, but the economic boom turned to bust in the 1980s when world oil prices collapsed, increasing economic hardship and social unrest and forcing the nation to take on massive foreign debt to pay its bills. Nigeria's per capita income declined by three-quarters between 1980 and 1993.

In addition to the ethnic divisions and economic inequality, the debate about whether Nigeria should seek to adopt Western political, economic, and cultural models or attempt to retain its own indigenous traditions has never abated. The Nigerian writer Mabel Segun (SAY-goon) beautifully expressed the cultural dilemma in her poem "Conflict":

> Here we stand, Infants overblown, Poised between two civilizations [Europe and Africa], Finding the balance irksome, Itching for something to happen, To tip us one way or the other. Groping in the dark for a helping hand, And finding none. I'm tired of hanging in the middle way—But where can I go.[14]

The New South Africa

Another large country, South Africa, experienced conflict and inequality for over three centuries. From World War II to the early 1990s South Africa remained the last bastion of institutionalized white racism on a continent where white rule had once been widespread. The white population, some 15 percent of the total and divided between an Afrikaner majority (descendants of Dutch settlers) and an English minority, ruled the black majority (74 percent) and the Indians (2 percent) and mixed-descent Coloreds (9 percent). Aided by a ruthless police security system, the result was a nearly unparalleled cruelty, a chilling juxtaposition of comfort for whites and despair for blacks. Before things rapidly changed in the 1990s, the authoritarian government rendered public protest of any type dangerous.

Apartheid Society South African racial inequality and white supremacy, in place for several centuries, became more systematic after 1948, when Afrikaner nationalists won the white-only elections and declared full independence from Britain. A top nationalist leader claimed: "We [whites] need [Africans] because they work for us but they can never claim political rights. Not now, nor in the future."[15] Their new policy, **apartheid** (uh-PAHRT-ate) ("separate development"), set up a police state to enforce racial separation and passed laws requiring all Africans to carry ID ("pass") cards specifying the locations where they could legally reside or visit.

---

apartheid ("separate development") A South African policy to set up a police state to enforce racial separation.

Interracial marriage and sexual relations were also outlawed. The lives of nonwhites were controlled to a degree inconceivable in most other countries.

Apartheid expanded segregation to include designated residential areas, schools, recreational facilities, and public accommodations. Urban black men were commonly housed in crowded dormitories near the mines or factories where they worked or, often with their families, in shantytown suburbs of major cities, from where they commuted to their jobs. While white families usually lived comfortably in well-furnished apartments or houses with spacious yards and swimming pools, a typical house in Soweto, a dusty African suburb of Johannesburg, was bleak, with the residents using candles or gas lamps for lighting. Only a quarter of the Soweto houses had running water and perhaps fifteen in one hundred enjoyed electricity. Demoralized blacks, especially men, found escape in alcohol, frequenting the informal bars that dotted African urban neighborhoods.

Apartheid also created what white leaders called tribal homelands, known as **bantustans**, rural reservations where black Africans were required to live if they were not needed in the modern economy. The system allocated whites 87 percent of the nation's land and nonwhites the other 13 percent. Every year thousands of Africans were forcibly resettled to the impoverished bantustans, which contained too little fertile land and too few jobs and services, such as hospitals and secondary schools. Infant mortality rates in the bantustans were among the world's highest. Under this system black families were fractured as men and women were recruited on annual contracts for jobs outside the bantustans. Even if a husband and wife were both recruited for jobs in the same city, they could not legally visit each other if their ID cards restricted each of them to a different city neighborhood.

Rich in strategic minerals such as gold, diamonds, uranium, platinum, and chrome, South Africa became the most industrialized nation on the continent. But the wealth and its benefits were monopolized by the white minority. While whites enjoyed one of the world's highest standards of living, with access to well-funded schools and medical centers, Africans and also the Colored and Indian minorities enjoyed few benefits from the system. Spending on health, literacy, and education was imbalanced. Whites controlled over two-thirds of the nation's wealth and personal disposable income. By 1994 the ratio of average black to white incomes stood at 1:10, the most inequitable income distribution in the world. African unemployment reached 33 percent. Nonetheless, because of the country's mineral wealth and extensive foreign investment, the South African government enjoyed the open or tacit support of several powerful industrialized countries, including the United States, Britain, and Japan, who feared that unrest or black majority rule might threaten their billions in investments and access to lucrative resources.

bantustans Rural reservations in South Africa where black Africans under apartheid were required to live if they were not needed in the modern economy.

Despite the repression, Africans resisted and often paid a price for their defiance. South African leaders forged the world's leading police state, with the world's highest rate of execution and brutal treatment of dissidents. Among the victims was Stephen Biko (1946–1977), a former medical student who led an organization that encouraged black pride and self-reliance. Biko was beaten to death in police custody. Hundreds of Africans were arrested each day for "pass law" violations and held for a few days or weeks before being released. For example, a mineworker might be arrested for visiting his wife who was a live-in maid in a white household a few miles away. The police violently repressed protests and imprisoned thousands of dissidents, including numerous children, often without trial. Death squads of off-duty policemen sometimes assassinated black leaders, such as Victoria Mxenge (ma-SEN-gee), a lawyer who defended anti-apartheid activists. Defying the government, strikes, work interruptions, and sabotage became common. Resistance was often subtle, too; Nobel prize–winning white South African novelist Nadine Gordimer (b. 1923), a longtime critic of apartheid, described in her novel, *Something Out There*, how even domestic servants in white households could protest and assert their dignity in nonverbal ways:

> Every household in the fine suburb had several black servants—a shifting population of pretty young housemaids whose long red nails and pertness not only asserted the indignity of being undiscovered fashion models but kept hoisted a cocky guerrilla pride against servitude to whites.[16]

The African National Congress (ANC), long a voice for nonviolent resistance, emerged as the major opposition organization. The ANC remained multiracial, with some whites, Coloreds, and Indians serving in its leadership. In 1955, despairing of peaceful protest, a more militant ANC leadership had framed its inclusive vision in the Freedom Charter: "South Africa belongs to all who live in it, black and white."[17] But the ANC was declared illegal and government repression forced it underground, where it adopted a policy of violent resistance and trained young South Africans in exile how to use weapons. Several of its main leaders, including Nelson Mandela (man-DEL-uh) (b. 1918), spent as many as thirty years in prison for their political activities (see Profile: Nelson and Winnie Mandela, South African Freedom Fighters). Women, among them Mandela's wife, Winnie Mandela, played an influential role in the ANC, often, like the men, facing arrest and mistreatment.

Postapartheid Society Ultimately, moderation and realism in both the ANC and the ruling National Party brought a more just and democratic society. International isolation, economic troubles, the increasing incompatibility between apartheid's restrictions and a need for more highly skilled black workers, and growing black unrest forced the government to relax apartheid and release Mandela from prison. The two parties agreed on a new constitution requiring "one man, one vote." In 1994 an amazed

NELSON AND WINNIE MANDELA, SOUTH AFRICAN FREEDOM FIGHTERS

Courageous symbols of unbroken black determination, Nelson Mandela (b. 1918) and Winnie Mandela (b. 1934) made a mark on history in the struggle against apartheid, South Africa's policy of rigid racial separation, despite severe white supremacist repression. The inspirational Mandelas represented African ambitions for several generations.

Nelson Mandela was born in the Transkei reserve near South Africa's southeast coast, the son of a Xhosa (KHO-sa) chief. His middle name, Rolihlahla (ROH-lee-la-la), meant "troublemaker." Mandela was groomed to succeed his father as chief, but, after years of hearing stories about the valor of his ancestors in war, he wanted to help with the freedom struggle. After attending a Methodist school and then earning a B.A. from the only college for black South Africans, he qualified as a lawyer and opened the country's first black legal practice. He also joined the African National Congress (ANC), which had, for half a century, followed a policy of promoting education for blacks and cautiously criticizing rather than confronting the government. Mandela and his young colleagues transformed the ANC into an activist mass movement. In 1958 he married Winnie Madikizela (MAH-dee-kee-ZEH-la), a Xhosa nurse, but they had only a short life together before political repression separated them.

The white government tolerated little opposition. In 1960, after police opened fire on 20,000 peaceful black protesters, killing 69 of them (including women and children), the government banned the ANC and arrested black leaders. The ANC then became an underground movement committed to violence. In 1964, found guilty of sabotage and treason, Mandela was sentenced to life in prison. In his stirring statement to the court, Mandela articulated his goals: "During my lifetime I have dedicated myself to this struggle of the African people. I have fought against [both] white and black domination. I have cherished the ideal of a democratic and free society in which all persons live together in harmony and with equal opportunities. It is an ideal for which I am prepared to die."

Mandela spent most of the next three decades in the notorious Robben Island prison off Cape Town, where he was joined by dozens of other ANC leaders and members. He turned the prison experience into an ANC school, leading political discussions and studying other freedom fighters, such as Mohandas Gandhi and Jawaharlal Nehru in India. Over the years Mandela grew into an international hero. During his imprisonment, although jailed for a short time herself and then confined to a remote settlement, Winnie Mandela kept her husband's flame burning, gaining an international reputation as a freedom fighter. Returning to Johannesburg in 1985, Winnie campaigned ceaselessly for black rights and her husband's release, earning a reputation for courage and skill in negotiating a male-dominated society.

In 1990, after secret negotiations, a realistic new South African president, F. W. de Klerk, legalized the ANC and released Nelson Mandela from prison. In 1993 Nelson Mandela and de Klerk shared a Nobel Peace Prize. In 1994 the first all-race elections made Nelson Mandela the first black president of South Africa. At his inauguration, he told the people: "Out of the experience of an extraordinary human disaster that lasted too long must be born a society of which all humanity will be proud. Let there be justice [and] peace for all. We must act together as a united people, for the birth of a new world. God bless Africa!"

Forgiving and pragmatic, Mandela remained popular with most South Africans, white and black. His moderate, accommodationist style reassured whites but also disappointed some impatient blacks. Meanwhile his marriage to Winnie became strained, in part because of her controversial activities, legal problems, and political ambitions. Her popularity declined after 1988 when bodyguards she hired to protect her from

world saw white supremacy come to an end in the first all-race elections in South African history, which installed Mandela as president and gave the ANC two-thirds of the seats in Parliament.

The ANC government enjoyed massive goodwill but has also faced daunting challenges in healing a deeply fragmented society while restoring the pride and spirits of African communities destabilized by apartheid. Mandela worked to find the right mix of racial reconciliation and major changes to benefit the disadvantaged black majority. In 1999 Mandela left office, a still popular figure, and the ANC retained power in free elections. It improved services, such as electricity and water, in black communities, raised black living standards, and created opportunities for Africans, fostering a growing black upper and middle class. Yet millions of other blacks have felt neglected, wanting better land and services and complaining about corruption and mismanagement at the local level. Crime has rapidly increased, violent protests have broken out, and black unemployment has remained high, prompting some blacks to leave the ANC and join opposition parties, some of them also having many white supporters. South Africa has one of the world's highest rates of HIV/AIDS, with some 5 million South Africans infected. Nonetheless, given the long history of repression and fear, the rapid transition to multiparty democracy has been impressive. South Africa has become the model of progress for sub-Saharan Africa, and people all over the continent hope that the nation succeeds in healing racial wounds while spreading the benefits of its wealth to all its citizens.

Nelson Mandela A symbol of black South African aspirations for nearly thirty years in prison, Mandela led the African National Congress after his release and, in 1994, was elected the nation's first black president. (Corbis)

black and white foes were implicated in the kidnapping and murder of a black youth; Winnie herself was convicted of involvement in the kidnapping, but her sentence was commuted. In 1996 Nelson and Winnie Mandela divorced. Winnie remained active in the ANC, supporting a militant faction that mistrusted Nelson's conciliatory policy of bringing white and black South Africans together. Nelson later married Grace Machel, the widow of the respected Mozambique president Samora Machel, who had been killed in an airplane crash.

In 1991, at the age of eighty-one, Mandela voluntarily retired from politics and moved to his native village. In his autobiography, he wrote, "I have walked a long road to freedom. I have tried not to falter, I have made missteps along the way. After climbing a great hill, one only finds that there are many more hills to climb. With freedom come responsibilities. I dare not linger, for my long walk is not yet ended." The long walk taken by Nelson and Winnie Mandela changed history.

THINKING ABOUT THE PROFILE

1. Why did the Mandelas become international symbols of the freedom struggle?
2. How did the Mandelas change history?

Note: Quotations from Kevin Shillington, *History of Africa*, rev. ed. (New York: St. Martin's, 1995), p. 405; and Nelson Mandela, *Long Walk to Freedom: The Autobiography of Nelson Mandela* (Boston: Little, Brown, 1996), pp. 620, 625.

SECTION SUMMARY

- European colonial rulers had played rival ethnic groups in Africa against each other, but after World War II, pressures for independence became stronger and Ghana, under the leadership of Kwame Nkrumah, became the first colony to achieve independence.

- Most British colonies attained independence through peaceful means, but Kenya's transition was long and violent, as was that of the Belgian Congo, Angola, Guinea-Bissau, Mozambique, and Zimbabwe.

- After independence, many African nations were ruled by military dictatorships or corrupt civilians, many nationalist leaders lost favor over time, the gap between rich and poor widened, and some nations experienced ongoing violence, disorder, and genocide.

- Nigeria, home to rival ethnic and religious groups, has experienced civil war, coups, and corrupt military rule, and while its oil reserves have brought wealth to the elite, they have hardly benefited the poor, and dependence on them led to economic problems in the 1980s.

- Under apartheid, a white minority in South Africa viciously suppressed the black majority with laws restricting their political, economic, and physical freedom, but the African National Congress, led by Nelson Mandela, resisted fiercely and ultimately won control of the government in 1994.

Changing African Economies, Societies, and Cultures

What new economic, social, and cultural patterns have emerged in Africa?

In the decades since the 1960s, for many sub-Saharan African nations, achieving economic development and true independence has seemed a desperate struggle rather than an exhilarating challenge. African nations have tried various strategies to generate development to benefit the majority of people, but no strategy has proved effective over the long term. Economic problems have proliferated. But Africans have created new social and cultural forms to aid them in dealing with their political and economic problems.

Economic Change and Underdevelopment

Africa has experienced severe economic problems. As during colonial times, Africans have mostly supplied agricultural and mineral resources, such as cocoa and copper, to the global economy, but this has not brought widespread wealth. For example, in Kenya, small farmers encouraged to abandon subsistence food growing and take up tobacco planting found that their new crops brought in little money, required cutting down adjacent forests, and leached nutrients from the soil. In 2004 one of the farmers, Jane Chacha, who still lived in the same two-room, mud-and-thatch house she and her husband built fifteen years earlier, complained that "this is a hopeless dream. Growing tobacco has been nothing but trouble."[18]

Only a few countries have enjoyed consistently robust economic growth, been able to escape reliance on producing one or two resources, or substantially raised living standards. With a few exceptions, nations have fostered economic growth but little economic development that benefits the majority of people. Sub-Saharan Africa contained nineteen of the world's twenty poorest countries in 2004. With over 670 million people (almost 13 percent of the world population) by 2004, this region accounts for only 1 percent of the world's production of goods and services, about the same as one of the smallest European nations, Belgium, with 10 million people. Most sub-Saharan African countries have annual per capita incomes of under $1,000 per year, and some are under $500. Half of the people live in poverty, earning less than $1 per day, the highest rate of poverty in the world. Sub-Saharan Africa has also had the world's highest infant mortality rates and lowest literacy rates and average life expectancies.

The economic doldrums have been linked to other problems. The region's economies have generally grown by 1 to 2 percent a year, but its population increase is the world's highest, over 3 percent. Since 10 to 15 percent of babies die before their first birthday, parents have had an incentive to have many children to provide for old-age security. At current rates the population will double to 1.3 billion by 2025, but new jobs, classrooms, and food supplies will not keep pace. Only a few nations have enjoyed self-sufficiency in food production; most require food imports from Europe and North America. Women grow the bulk of the food, but the male farmers growing cash crops for export receive most of the government aid. Millions of Africans, perhaps a third of them children, are chronically malnourished, and as a result often have permanent brain damage. Several million children die each year from hunger-related ailments. Severe drought and the drying up of water sources is a chronic problem in many regions, resulting in numerous deaths from dehydration or starvation or in migration in search of a better life. Less than half of school-age children attend school, while millions of others work in the labor force. Many rural schools lack toilets for girls, discouraging their attendance. As a result, some 25 million girls receive no elementary education. Poverty means scraping by, physically and mentally exhausted by the struggle for survival. Many people face joblessness; for example, half of Kenya's secondary school graduates could not find paid work in the 1990s.

To achieve economic development, Africans have sought viable economic strategies. What scholars term "neocolonial capitalism," because it involved close economic ties to the Western nations and free markets of some sort, became the most common development model. The countries following this model favored the cash crops and minerals that had dominated the colonial economy, often at the expense of food production, and welcomed western European and U.S. investment and economic advice. Westerners, especially British and French, have managed or owned a substantial portion of the economies.

A few countries prospered with this strategy, at least for a awhile, but the political consequences were often negative. Ivory Coast (or Côte d'Ivoire) and Kenya were among the most hospitable to a Western presence, and in the 1960s and 1970s this policy paid off with high rates of growth and rising incomes. Ivory Coast remained a major exporter of coffee and cocoa, while Kenya, with world famous game parks, lived from tourism and the export of coffee, tea, and minerals. By the mid-1980s both had per capita incomes about double the African average. That success came at some cost, however. For example, the Ivory Coast timber industry rapidly cut down the once verdant rain forest, causing less rain. In addition, close relations with France resulted in more French living there by the 1990s than during colonial times, and the French and other non-Ivoreans owned most of the economy. But the successes also proved short-lived. Both countries eventually became one-party states that, while stable, grew despotic. Well-placed leaders plundered the economies. While the glittering major cities, Abidjan and Nairobi, had fancy restaurants, boutiques, and nightclubs, some rural people faced starvation. By the late 1990s, as world prices for coffee and cocoa collapsed, the economies experienced increasing stress, protesters demanded more democracy, the delicate ecologies became dangerously unbalanced, and crime rates soared. Economic development became a fading memory. By the early 2000s Ivory Coast was engulfed in civil war, while Kenyans had forced out a dictator and elected a reformist government that has failed to fulfill its promises to end corruption and maintain press freedom.

The most disastrous example of neocolonial capitalism was the Democratic Republic of the Congo (known as Zaire between 1971 and 1997). A huge country, with 60 million people, Congo enjoys a strategic location in the center of Africa, rich mineral resources, and good land. But it became Africa's biggest failure. Over the years the United States and Belgium poured billions of investment and aid into the Congo to keep President Mobuto Sese Seko in power. To the Congolese, however, Mobuto was unforgivingly corrupt, looting the treasury and foreign aid to amass a huge personal fortune—some 4 to 5 billion dollars—while repressing his opponents. Mobuto built palaces for himself all over the country and in Europe and hired top chefs from France to prepare his food, meanwhile spending little money on schools, roads, telephones, and hospitals. As a result of neglect, the Congo suffered one of the world's highest infant mortality rates, limited health care, and widespread malnutrition. In 1998 a long-festering rebellion gained strength, forcing Mobuto into exile, where he died. Rebels took over, but they have done little to foster democracy or development. The Congo was soon fragmented in civil war and interethnic fighting, and rebel groups controlled large sections of the sprawling country. Nearly 4 million Congolese died from the fighting and its side effect, the collapse of medical care, between 1998 and 2004, causing a humanitarian crisis.

The most recent showcases for economic success have been Ghana and Botswana. Once a symbol of failure, Ghana has made steady progress. For several decades after Kwame Nkrumah lost power the country had experienced a roller coaster of corrupt civilian governments interspersed with military regimes. In the 1990s the leaders gradually strengthened democracy and adopted certain policies of the Asian Little Dragons, such as Taiwan and South Korea, by mixing capitalism and socialism. Ghana became increasingly prosperous: by 2000 it enjoyed one of the continent's highest annual per capital incomes, $1,600, and a life expectancy of fifty-seven. Investment in schools resulted in one of Africa's most educated populations. Beginning as a failure like Ghana, Botswana, when it gained independence in 1966, exported nothing, was one of the world's poorest countries, and had an annual per capita income of $35. Gradually, however, using ethnic traditions as a foundation, Botswanans carved out a successful democracy; the economy, health care, education, and protection of resources all steadily improved, despite deadly droughts. By 2000 Botswanans had fostered living standards higher than those of most African and many Middle Eastern, Asian, and Latin American societies, boasting an annual per capita income of over $3,000, an economy growing by 11 percent a year, and a literacy rate of 70 percent. Unfortunately, the AIDs epidemic, which hit Botswana particularly hard, rapidly undermined economic and health gains.

African Socialisms

To foster development, some African nationalists have pursued revolutionary or reformist strategies. They have concluded that the political and economic institutions inherited from colonialism, such as large Western-owned businesses and plantations, could not spark economic development, since they were implanted to transfer wealth and resources to the West rather than to benefit Africans. After independence more wealth still flowed out of Africa than into it, and the disparity has increased every year. The radicals argued that, to empower Africans, it was necessary to reduce the colonial state to ashes and replace it with something entirely new.

Various social revolutionary regimes emerged from the long wars of liberation against entrenched colonial or white minority governments. Some Africans looked toward communist-ruled China or the USSR for inspiration. Marxist revolutionary governments came to power in Angola and Mozambique after the Portuguese left, but they struggled to implement socialism. To counter these governments, the white-ruled South African state sponsored opposition guerrilla movements, aided by a U.S. government wanting to overturn Marxist regimes, that kept these countries in civil war for several decades. During Angola's long civil war, over 1.5 million people died. Leaders on both sides exploited natural resources for their own gain. While the war eventually ended, Angola, blessed with coffee, oil, diamonds, and other minerals but plagued with corruption, still struggled to foster development. The civil war in Mozambique, one of the world's poorest nations, resulted in 1 million deaths and 5 million refugees. Since its war came to an end in 1992, the pragmatic Marxist leaders introduced free multiparty elections and liberalized the economy, raising the per capita income to $1,200.

One social revolutionary state, Zimbabwe, the former British colony of Southern Rhodesia, at first became Africa's biggest success story. The Marxist-influenced government, led by the liberation hero Robert Mugabe, a schoolteacher turned lawyer, proved pragmatic for over a decade, respecting democratic processes and human rights, encouraging the white minority to stay, and trying to raise living standards and opportunities for black Zimbabweans. The country became one of the few food-exporting nations on the continent. Zimbabwe eventually faced severe problems, however, including tensions between rival African ethnic groups. Continuing white ownership of the best farmland produced resentment among land-hungry blacks. During the 1990s Mugabe, succumbing to the allure of power and wealth, became more dictatorial and used land disputes to divide the nation. As his support among both whites and Africans waned, he rigged elections, harassed or jailed his opponents, and ordered the seizure of white-owned farms. By 2005 commercial agriculture had collapsed, the country was gripped by drought, life expectancy had dropped sharply, and Mugabe's police had demolished the homes and shops of poor blacks who favored the opposition, driving them out of the cities. The nation, once one of Africa's most promising, veered toward catastrophe.

Another African nation, Tanzania, experimented with a socialism compatible with African traditions, especially cooperation and mutual sharing of resources. Under its visionary president, Julius Nyerere (1922–1999), Tanzania opted for "African socialism," based on local traditions, which reorganized agriculture into cooperative villages and devoted resources to education and social services, with the goal of achieving local and national self-sufficiency. Nyerere encouraged some democracy in his one-party state by holding regular elections and allowing multiple candidates—all members of the ruling party—to run for each office or parliamentary seat. Nyerere's emphasis on building and funding schools and clinics improved literacy to 68 percent and health to well above African norms.

But Nyerere's dreams were dashed as the government became overly bureaucratic, the planning proved inadequate, and people often lost enthusiasm for socialism. Because Tanzania imported few luxury goods, life was austere compared to that available to affluent city residents in neighboring capitalist Kenya. Peasants often preferred their small family farms and individual effort to the collective villages they were encouraged, or forced, to join. As the economy slumped, Tanzania had to take more foreign loans. Tanzania's African socialism had produced as many failures as successes, and Nyerere, still admired by his people, retired in 1985, one of the few founding African leaders to voluntarily give up power. Nyerere's successors dismantled much of the socialist structure, promoted free enterprise, welcomed foreign investment and loans, and fostered a multiparty system and respect for civil liberties. Yet life for most Tanzanians has improved little, malnutrition has become widespread, and Tanzania remains a poor nation.

Cities, Families, and Gender Relations

Modern Africa has seen rapid social change. Since the 1940s, more people have lived in cosmopolitan cities where traditional and modern attitudes meet, mix, and clash. Cities have grown rapidly. However difficult, city life offers more variety—jobs, department stores, movie theaters, nightclubs—than village life and so attracts rural people. While some older, precolonial cities have remained centers of trade and tourism, they have been largely eclipsed as economic centers and the seats of government by the cities that developed under colonial auspices, such as Nairobi (Kenya), Lagos (Nigeria), and Dakar (Senegal), which have grown nearly 5 percent a year since 1980. Between 1965 and 2000 the percentage of sub-Saharan Africans living in urban areas doubled, from 14 to 30 percent. But people concentrate in one or two key cities for each country. Hence, Abidjan in Ivory Coast and Luanda in Angola each contain a quarter of their country's population. With their modern office towers, theaters, and shopping centers, cities have become the centers for political and economic power as well as for cultural creativity and social change.

Cities have grown so fast that services such as buses, water, power, police, schools, and health centers cannot meet the needs of their populations. These problems are exemplified by Nigeria's largest city, Lagos, which grew from less than a million in 1965 to a megalopolis of some 10 million by 2000. A journalist described the urban chaos:

> Lagos is a vast laboratory of helter-skelter expansion, a fount of confusion and frenzy. A tiny minority of people live extremely well, in villas or plush apartments, and they go to work in gleaming skyscrapers that sit awkwardly next to traditional marketplaces. A vastly larger number of people live in appalling slums, where open sewers may run under disintegrating floorboards. The traffic jam, or "go-slow," is a fact of life. Much of the everyday commerce occurs in this city through the windows of cars, trucks, and other vehicles.[19]

Social changes have been numerous. Interethnic mixing, even marriage, has become more common. Neighborhoods have developed their own slang, hairstyles, music, dance, art, and poetry. They forge their own institutions such as bars, churches, football (soccer) leagues, labor unions, women's clubs, and student movements. Many of these are voluntary associations that help migrants adjust by creating a new community to replace the village left behind. Small traders set up shop along the sidewalks, hawking everything from food and drinks to cheap clothes, religious items, and music cassettes. Sports has become a major activity. Various African nations have enjoyed international football success, and Ethiopians and Kenyans have dominated long-distance running in the Olympic Games. Africans have also played in the U.S. National Basketball Association and the National Football League.

The family, while remaining the primary social unit, has also changed. The extended family of the villages declined in the cities and was often replaced by the smaller nuclear family. Individualism increasingly challenged the communalism of the village tradition, where marriages were largely arranged by elders. In the cities, young people often arrange their own marriages, and love has become a major criterion for selecting a spouse. Traditionally village men had an economic incentive to take more than one wife, since women did most of the routine farm work, especially the planting, weeding, and harvesting of food crops that ensured family survival and gave rural women economic status. With no farming option, however, urban women have lost economic status and men no longer need several wives. Men enjoy more educational opportunities than women and hence dominate the remunerative wage labor in business and transportation. Sometimes governments erected barriers against women in the economy. Hence, President Mobuto in the Congo stressed an authoritarian male model and discouraged women from seeking paid work, and in the 1980s Nigeria's military regime blamed market women for high prices, raiding their stalls and beating them.

Gender roles have changed as women have become more independent and a growing number served in governments and parliaments. Indeed, sub-Saharan Africa ranks ahead of the rest of the developing world in the percentage of women (16 percent) in legislative positions. While women are educationally disadvantaged compared to men, some women use their skills to good advantage, achieving such positions as politicians, professors, lawyers, and company heads. For example, the Kenyan Grace Ogot (OH-got) (b. 1930) served in parliament while writing short stories in which her heroines confronted traditional values and change. Women have formed groups to work for society's improvement. For instance, the Nigerian Eka Esu-Williams (b. 1950), the daughter of a midwife, earned a Ph.D. in Immunology and pursued an academic career before forming Women Against AIDS in Africa in 1988, with the goal of educating and empowering women, more likely than men to get HIV, through workshops, schools, and support schools. Some women have become teachers, nurses, and secretaries, but these are poorly paid occupations. Women are usually left with self-employment in low-wage activity, such as the small-scale trade of hawking goods and keeping stalls in city markets, a female near monopoly for centuries; domestic work as maids, cooks, or nannies; or hairdressing. Women have formed organizations for work, savings, or worship. Meanwhile, many men spend long hours commuting to and from work and socializing with their friends after work in bars or at club meetings. Although homosexuals face severe intolerance in many African countries, homosexuality has been more open in South Africa, where the courts legalized homosexual marriage in 2005.

African Cultural Expression

Africans have reconstructed their cultures in creative ways. In the popular arts, especially music and literature, imported ideas are combined with African culture. Africans believe they have much to offer world culture. As the Senegalese writer and president Leopold Senghor (sah-GAWR) (1906–2001) has asked, "Who else would teach rhythm to the world that has died of machines and cannons?"[20]

Popular Music Urbanization, the growth of mass media, and the mixing of ethnic groups and outside influences have all created a fertile ground for mixed popular music styles that have reflected social, economic, and political realities. Exciting new musical genres have emerged as both male and female musicians have sought to make sense of their changing social identities, world-views, and lives. Miriam Makeba (muh-KAY-ba) (b. 1932), the South African jazz and pop singer forced by the apartheid government to spend

decades in exile, described her mission as follows: "I live to sing about what I see and know. I don't sing politics, I sing truth."[21]

Popular music has become a creative blending of local and imported influences. As one Ghanaian musician remarked: "In the 'new music' coming out of Africa, the rich spontaneity and color of African life are magnified a hundred times."[22] The new forms of musical expression have reflected the presence of hundreds of distinctive cultures in this vast region. The rise of varied African-based popular music styles has helped Africans adjust to change while affirming their spirit in the face of external influences and internal failures. For instance the *juju* music of the Nigerian Yoruba reflects Yoruba traditions and values while mixing local and Western instruments, such as electric guitars. Through the Africanization of musical ideas and technology coming from abroad, Africans have confronted the powerful influences emanating from the industrialized nations.

Musicians have been groping for a new Africa that can resolve its problems while successfully blending the old and the new, the indigenous and the foreign. African popular musicians also reach an international audience, performing and selling recordings around the world. Perhaps the greatest African superstar, the Senegalese Youssou N'Dour (YOO-soo en-DOOR) (b. 1959), travels all over the world and does collaborations with leading Western musicians. Yet, he remains true to his roots, living in Dakar and following his tolerant Sufi Muslim faith. Some musicians are highly political. The Nigerian Fela Kuti (1938–1997), whose music mixed jazz, soul, rock, and Yoruba traditions, used his songs as a weapon to attack the Nigerian government and its Western sponsors, and faced frequent arrest and beatings for his protests. Like Bob Marley, Bob Dylan, and Chile's Victor Jara, Fela gained worldwide fame for his use of music to attack injustice and influence politics. Women also used music to express their views. For instance, Oumou Sangare of Mali

African Cultural Expression Africans have developed diverse and vibrant popular music, often by mixing Western and local traditions. In Nigeria, juju music, played by bands such as Captain Jidi Oyo and his Yankee System in this 1982 photo, has been popular among the Yoruba people.
(Courtesy, Christopher Waterman, UCLA)

had a massive hit with her account of a young woman torn between pleasing her parents and her loved one.

A particularly influential African pop music developed in the Belgian Congo in the 1950s and spread rapidly. Congolese (Zairean) pop music, known widely as **soukous** ("to shake"), was shaped by dance rhythms from Cuba and Brazil, musical forms that were themselves African in origin. Soukous depends heavily on the guitar, imported from the West, as well as on traditional African songs and melodies. Congolese musicians, unable to make a living or speak freely in their troubled homeland, have often sought their fortunes in other African countries or Europe, hence enlivening the musical culture of other nations. Soukous became a major dance music throughout Africa and among African immigrants in Europe.

Literature As with popular musicians, writers have produced distinctive literatures by combining old traditions with new influences to comment on modern society. African literature has questioned the status quo, asserted African identity, and attempted to influence political change and economic development. Major figures have often written in English or French to better develop an international reputation. For example, the Nigerian Wole Soyinka (WOE-lay shaw-YING-kuh) (b. 1934), a Yoruba poet, playwright, novelist, and sometime filmmaker who won the 1986 Nobel Prize for literature, has mixed Yoruba mysticism with criticisms of Western capitalism, racism, and cultural imperialism and of African failures, including the brutalities of Nigerian political life. A former political prisoner, Soyinka has denounced repressive African leaders, including Nigeria's, with as much venom as he attacks Western imperialists, chastising "Nigeria's self-engorgement at the banquet of highway robberies, public executions, public floggings and other institutionalized sadisms, casual cruelties, wanton destruction."[23] The powerful criticism of governments offered by Soyinka and his Nigerian colleague Chinua Achebe, discussed in the chapter opening vignette, has often forced both men to live in exile. Not all African writers accept Soyinka's and Achebe's highly critical view of African politics.

Writers and artists have also tried to find authentic African perspectives. **Negritude** is a literary and philosophical movement to forge distinctively African views that first developed in the 1930s. The Senegalese writer and later the first president of his country after independence, Leopold Senghor, a former professor of classics in France, was a major negritude voice, attempting to balance the Western stress on rational thought with African approaches to knowledge, such as mysticism and animism, long disdained by Europeans as superstition. To Senghor, Africans needed to assert, rather than feel inferior about, their black skins and cultural traditions. Negritude influenced French artists and writers, and the philosopher Jean Paul Sartre praised the approach as a key weapon against all forms of oppression.

One of the best-known writers in Francophone West Africa, Ousmane Sembene (OOS-man sem-BEN-ee) (b. 1923) of Senegal, was influenced more by Marxism than negritude. Drafted into the French army during World War II, Sembene, the son of a poor fisherman, fought in Italy and Germany. After the war he worked in France as a dockworker and became a leader of the dockworkers' union, and his first novel portrayed the stevedore's hard life. Eventually Sembene returned to Senegal. His writings, often set in the colonial period, show African resistance to Western domination and social inequality. Sympathizing with exploited people, his work also attacks Senegal's privileged elite, including greedy businessmen and government officials. Sembene also made films that gained international acclaim. Like his writings, some of the films satirize corrupt African bureaucrats and illustrate the struggle of the poor for breathing room in a system in which the rich exploit the poor.

English-language literature has also flourished in South Africa and East Africa. For example, Kenyan Ngugi Wa Thiongo (en-GOO-gee wah thee-AHN-go) (b. 1938), a former journalist turned university professor who did his graduate studies in England, has written several novels that explore the relationship between colonialism and social fragmentation, showing Gikuyu society struggling to retain its identity, culture, and traditions while adjusting to the modern world. Ngugi's heroes are alienated figures drifting back and forth between African and Western traditions. Once a devout Christian, Ngugi later rejected Christianity, which he viewed as a legacy of colonialism. His 1979 novel, *Petals of Blood*, portrays a Kenya struggling to free itself from neocolonialism but also beset with corruption. His attacks on the privileged local elite allied with Western exploitation earned Ngugi several terms in Kenyan jails and later forced him into exile.

Religious Change

Africans have maintained a triple religious heritage: animism/polytheism, Islam, and Christianity. All these faiths have many followers, although the older animism has lost influence, and the relations between the traditions are not always easy. With their links to wider worlds, Christianity and Islam are also globalizing influences, spreading Western or Middle Eastern political, social, and economic ideas. Africans often view religions in both theoretical and practical terms, refusing to divorce metaphysical speculation from everyday life. They adopt views that help them survive the changes of modern times, rejecting old ideas and adding new ones as needed. Religion has remained in constant flux.

Christianity became Africa's largest religion, attracting some 250 to 300 million followers by 2000, both the fervent and the nominal in faith. Some countries, such as Congo, South Africa, and Uganda, became largely Christian. Africans are prominent in the world leadership of the Anglican and Catholic churches. Christianity has proven a powerful force for social change. Many Christian churches prevent their followers from practicing traditional customs. Believers often favor the liberation of women, and mission schools have educated many African leaders, influencing their world-views. A growing num-

---

soukous ("to shake") A Congolese popular music that was shaped by dance rhythms from Cuba and Brazil.

negritude A literary and philosophical movement to forge distinctively African views.

ber of independent churches, some blending African traditions into worship and theology, have no ties to the older Western-based denominations. By promising to help members acquire wealth and happiness, some African churches have enjoyed spectacular growth, which has enabled them to build big urban churches that attract thousands of congregants each Sunday. In a reversal of historical patterns, several Nigerian churches even send missionaries to revitalize Christianity in the West, establishing branches in Europe and North America. Yet many other Africans have viewed Christianity as connected to Western imperialism. According to a popular nationalist saying: "When the missionaries came the Africans had the land and the Christians had the Bible. They taught us to pray with our eyes closed. When we opened them they had the land and we had the Bible."[24]

Over 200 million black Africans follow Islam. About a fourth of all sub-Saharan countries have Muslim majorities. Some revivalist and Wahhabi movements have gained influence, especially in northern Nigeria, where some states have imposed Islamic law, sparking deadly clashes with Christian minorities. Muslim-Christian clashes in Nigeria caused by Muslim outrage at cartoons published in Denmark in 2005 that mocked the prophet Muhammad left over one hundred people dead. But most Muslims and Christians remain moderate and inclusive. While politicians use religion as a wedge issue, and Christian-Muslim clashes have occurred in countries such as Ivory Coast, tolerance has more often marked relations among Christians, Muslims, and animists. Among the Yoruba, for example, members of each group mix easily and even intermarry. Ethnicity often divides people more than religion.

Africa in the Global System

African developments have occurred in a global context. During the Cold War, some African countries, especially their elites, benefited from the international rivalry between the USSR and the United States. It gained them aid but also fostered manipulation on the part of the superpowers. Countries such as Congo and Angola often became pawns in the Cold War, with the superpowers helping to support or remove leaders. But with the Cold War over, the Western world has largely ignored Africa, providing it with little aid and investment. Furthermore, the wealth gap between African countries and the Western industrialized nations has grown even wider than during colonial times. Today the gap between the richest Western nations and the poorest African countries is around 400 to 1.

Global conditions have often proven counterproductive for Africans. Only when the world economy boomed in the 1950s and 1960s did African economies show steady growth. Since the 1970s, however, as the world economy soured and the world prices for many African exports collapsed, African economic growth rates steadily dropped. Western experts have encouraged a policy known as "structural adjustment," in which international lenders, such as the International Monetary Fund (IMF) and the World Bank, loan nations money on the condition that these nations open their economies to private investment and, to balance national budgets, reduce government spending for health, education, and farmers. The result-

ing hardship on average people—from eliminating money for poor children to attend the village primary school to closing the local office that aids small farmers—increases unrest and resentment both of governments and of the Western nations that control the IMF and World Bank. This private investment also promotes a shift away from traditional farming, which mostly involves shifting cultivation and produces little food surplus, to modern agriculture, which is much more productive. But modern agriculture, with its reliance on tractors, chemical fertilizers, and new seeds, entails a large environmental and social cost: marginal land poorly suited to farming is often turned into desert, and small farmers, both men and women, do not have the means to buy the modern supplies.

To obtain the goods—cars, fashionable clothes, electronic gadgets—desired by the politically powerful urban middle and upper classes, African nations have taken out loans to pay for them. By 1998, as a percentage of total output, African countries had the largest foreign debts in the world: $230 billion. At the same time, the world prices for most of Africa's exports, such as coffee, cotton, and tobacco from Tanzania and cocoa from Ghana, have steadily dropped since the 1960s. Some exports now bring in a third of what they once did, leaving ever larger revenue gaps. And small farmers, such as the cotton growers in Mali, cannot compete with highly subsidized Western farmers and the tariff barriers erected in Europe, North America, and Japan against food and fiber imports from Africa. Increasingly desperate, countries such as Guinea-Bissau and Somalia have agreed to allow dangerous toxic waste, such as deadly but unwanted chemicals produced in the West, to be buried on their land in exchange for cash.

Africa's economic problems have had diverse roots. Some resulted from colonialism, which imposed economic policies that caused severe environmental destruction, such as desertification and deforestation, while incorporating the people into the world economy as specialized producers of minerals or cash crops for export rather than food farmers. Hence, Zambia relies on exploiting copper (87 percent of exports), Uganda coffee (72 percent), Malawi tobacco (72 percent), and Nigeria oil (95 percent). Nations have remained vulnerable to drops in world commodity prices for their exports. The colonial regimes also often failed to build roads, schools, and clinics. Since independence, bad policy decisions, poor leadership, corruption, unstable politics, and misguided advice from Western experts have also contributed to the economic crisis. In addition, the rapid spread of HIV/AIDS has ravaged African nations, killing and affecting millions (see Chapter 26). In some nations a third of the population has the HIV virus.

But although falling behind much of Asia and Latin America economically, Africans have had both successes and failures. Using foreign aid and their own resources, they have made rapid strides in literacy, social and medical services, including active birth control campaigns, and road construction. Some nations, such as South Africa and Uganda, have a feisty free press. Africans have also attempted to work together to resolve problems. The African Union, formed in 2000 with 54 members, has sent peacekeeping troops into violence-torn countries such as Sudan. But finding the right mix of African and Western ideas to promote economic progress, political stability, and democratic decision making has proved difficult. By the 1990s Africans had grown skeptical about the usefulness of Western models of development, which often depend on expensive high technology, and were also disillusioned with centralized governments controlling economic activity. Many nations have moved toward more democratic systems and private enterprise. However, political leadership has often failed to root out corruption, restructure existing institutions, and foster food production. Millions still live in poverty. Africa suffers a particularly acute "brain drain" as academics, students, and professionals, seeking a better life, move to Europe or North America.

African history is not only an authentic, dynamic saga of indigenous African development but also part of a larger global process. Over the past half century Western influence has remained strong, including outside manipulation of governments, economic power, and cultural and religious life. Hence, Africans have not enjoyed complete control of their destiny. The Ghanaian historian Jacob Ajayi (a-JAH-yee) laid out the challenge: "The vision of a new [African] society will need to be developed out of the African historical experience. The African is not yet master of his own fate, but neither is he completely at the mercy of fate."[25]

SECTION SUMMARY

- African countries have struggled economically, with many being forced to import food and others, like the Congo, to enter into neocolonial relationships with Western powers, but Ghana and Botswana have managed to significantly improve their economies.

- Marxist revolutionary governments, which appealed to many Africans who wanted to erase the colonial legacy, came to power in Angola and Mozambique, both of which then entered into long civil wars, as well as in Zimbabwe.

- African cities have grown rapidly and often lack necessary services, individualism has grown more common, and women have lost some of the economic value they had in agricultural villages, though some have become successful professionals.

- African musicians, writers, and artists have drawn on local traditions as well as influences from the West to create original forms, such as soukous, as well as works that criticize both Western encroachment and homegrown corruption.

- While animism has grown less influential in Africa, Christianity is the most popular religion and has undermined traditions and been seen by some as connected to Western imperialism, while Islam is followed by 200 million Africans.

- The economic gap between Africa and the industrialized West continues to grow larger, and Western attempts to help Africa through the IMF and the World Bank often include requirements that harm the environment and the poor and inspire resentment, as do tariffs against African imports and the enduring colonial legacy.

Online Study Center   ACE the Test

◆ Chapter Summary

The Middle East and sub-Saharan Africa have shared certain experiences, including decolonization, mass poverty, reliance on exporting natural resources, political instability, and intervention by Western powers. Yet, while Islam had adherents in both regions, the societies and cultures of Africans and Middle Easterners have remained quite different.

The Middle East was reshaped by diverse developments since 1945. Arab nationalism, especially strong in Egypt, generated conflict with the West and with Israel, which became the major Arab enemy. The Arab-Israel conflict greatly destabilized the region, while ethnic and religious divisions fostered violent struggles within nations. Islam proved most potent as a revolutionary political force in Iran, long a battleground for international rivalries over its oil supplies. The Middle East, especially the Persian Gulf region, provided much of the world's oil, fostering wealth but also global attention as world consumption increased. Oil-rich Saudi Arabia forged an alliance with the United States. Most Middle Eastern societies remained conservative but also fostered cultural creativity. The rivalry between militants and secular Muslims has provided a major cleavage in many countries.

By the 1970s the long colonized African nations had achieved independence under nationalist leaders. But the hopes for a better life were soon dashed. Artificially created multiethnic nations have found it difficult to sustain democracy, and dictatorial governments have often gained power. Most nations have remained dependent on exporting one or two resources. Ambitious development plans have given way to economic stagnation and, as commodity prices fall, increasing poverty. Neither capitalism nor socialism has proved able to both stimulate growth and raise living standards for Africa's majority. But South Africa was finally transformed from a racist state to a multiracial democracy. Societies urbanized, redefined family life and gender roles, and created new music and literature. Africans still search for the right mix of imported ideas and local traditions to create better lives.

Online Study Center   Improve Your Grade Flashcards

Key Terms

Intifida	mujahidin	wabenzi
Ba'ath	Taliban	apartheid
OPEC	pan-Africanism	bantustans
Islamists	Mau Mau	soukous
rai	Rebellion	negritude

Suggested Reading

Books

Anderson, Roy R., et al. *Politics and Change in the Middle East: Sources of Conflict and Accommodation*, 7th ed. Upper Saddle River, N.J.: Prentice-Hall, 2003. An introductory survey of politics and economies.

Bates, Daniel G., and Amal Rassam. *Peoples and Cultures of the Middle East*, 2nd ed. Upper Saddle River, N.J.: Prentice-Hall, 2001. A readable introduction to the social and cultural patterns of the region.

Clark, Nancy L. and William H. Worger. *South Africa: The Rise and Fall of Apartheid.* New York: Longman, 2004. A brief survey with documents.

Cleveland, William L. *A History of the Modern Middle East*, 3rd ed. Boulder, Colo.: Westview, 2004. A political overview of the region during this era.

Cooper, Frederick. *Africa Since 1940: The Past of the Present.* New York: Cambridge University Press, 2002. A brief overview of contemporary history.

Danielson, Virginia. *The Voice of Egypt: Umm Kulthum, Arabic Song, and Egyptian Society in the Twentieth Century.* Chicago: University of Chicago Press, 1997. A fascinating view of modern Egypt through the life and work of the Arab world's most famous pop singer.

Davidson, Basil. *The Black Man's Burden: Africa and the Curse of the Nation State.* New York: Times Books, 1992. Reflections on modern Africa and its challenges by an influential historian.

Esposito, John L. *Islam: The Straight Path,* 3rd ed. revised. New York: Oxford University Press, 2005. Detailed examination of modern Islam.

Gerges, Fawaz A. *The Far Enemy: Why Jihad Went Global.* New York: Cambridge University Press, 2005. A gripping account of the rise of Islamism, Al Qaeda, and terrorism by a Lebanon-born, U. S.-based scholar.

Gerner, Deborah J. and Jillian Schwedler, eds. *Understanding the Contemporary Middle East,* 2nd ed. Boulder: Lynne Rienner, 2003. Useful collection of essays on varied aspects of the Middle East today.

Gordon, April A., and Donald L. Gordon, eds. *Understanding Contemporary Africa,* 3rd ed. Boulder, Colo.: Lynne Rienner, 2001. An excellent collection of essays on aspects of Africa.

Keddie, Nikki R. *Modern Iran: Roots and Results of Revolution.* New Haven: Yale University Press, 2003. Updating and revision of a major study.

Martin, Phyllis M., and Patrick O'Meara, eds. *Africa,* 3rd ed. Bloomington: Indiana University Press, 1995. Essays on African history, politics, culture, and economies.

Nugent, Paul. *Africa Since Independence: A Comparative History.* New York: Palgrave Macmillan, 2004. A recent, detailed survey.

Smith, Charles D. *Palestine and the Arab-Israeli Conflict: A History with Documents*, 5th ed. Boston: Bedford/St. Martin's, 2004. A comprehensive, balanced survey.

Tenaille, Frank. *Music Is the Weapon of the Future: Fifty Years of African Popular Music.* Chicago: Lawrence Hill, 2000. A recent overview of varied African pop musicians and musical styles.

Websites

Africa South of the Sahara
(http://www-sul.stanford.edu/depts/ssrg/africa/guide.html). A valuable gateway for links on many topics in African studies.

African Studies Internet Resources
(http://www.columbia.edu/cu/lweb/indiv/). Provides valuable links to relevant websites on contemporary Africa.

Arab Human Development Reports
(http://www.un.org/Pubs). The general United Nations site contains links to the reports, issued annually beginning in 2002 and available online, that assess the successes and challenges facing the Arab nations.

History of the Middle East Database
(http://www.nmhschool.org/tthornton/mehistorydatabase/mideastindex.htm). A useful site on history, politics, and culture.

Internet African History Sourcebook
(http://www.fordham.edu/halsall/africa/africasbook.html). Contains useful information and documentary material on Africa.

Internet Islamic History Sourcebook
(http://www.fordham.edu/halsall/islam/islamsbook.html). A comprehensive examination of Islamic societies and their long history, with useful links and source materials.

CHAPTER 31

South Asia, Southeast Asia, and Global Connections, 1945–Present

CHAPTER OUTLINE

- The Reshaping of South Asia
- South Asian Politics and Societies
- Revolution, War, and Reconstruction in Indochina
- New Nations in Southeast Asia
- Tigers, Politics, and Changing Southeast Asian Societies

■ **PROFILE**
Raj Kapoor, Bollywood Film Star

■ **WITNESS TO THE PAST**
A Thai Poet's Plea for the Environment

Online Study Center

This icon will direct you to interactive activities and study materials on the website: college.hmco.com/pic/lockard1e

Commuting to Work Vietnam has largely recovered from its decades of war and has experienced increasing economic growth. These women in Hanoi are commuting to work by bicycle. (Mary Cross)

This music sings the struggle of [humanity]. This music is my life. This is the revolution we have begun. But the revolution is only a means to attain freedom, and freedom is only a means to enrich the happiness and nobility of human life.

HAZIL, THE INDONESIAN REVOLUTIONARY NATIONALIST IN MOCHTAR LUBIS'S
NOVEL *A ROAD WITH NO END* (1952)[1]

In 1950 a small, idealistic group of leading Indonesian writers published a moving declaration promoting universal human dignity: "We [Indonesians] are the heirs to the culture of the whole world, a culture which is ours to extend and develop in our own way [by] the discarding of old and outmoded values and their replacement by new ones. Our fundamental quest is [helping] humanity."[2] These writers hoped that Indonesia could combine the most humane ideas of East and West to become a beacon to the world, open to all cultures and showing respect for the common people. The writers' beliefs had been shaped by their familiarity with Western Enlightenment intellectual traditions, including the ideals of democracy, free thought, and tolerance, and also by the Indonesian Revolution against the repressive colonial Dutch, a nationalist struggle, waged in the name of political freedom, that raged between 1945 and 1950 and had finally led to Indonesian independence. While delighted with independence, the writers warned against the dangers of a narrow nationalism that devalued other cultures.

The writers had been inspired by the irreverent Sumatran poet Chairul Anwar (CHAI-roll ON-war) (1922–1949), who believed the revolution had destroyed the old colonial society and opened up the possibility of building a new, open society. A true bohemian who was undisciplined in his personal life, Anwar had risen from poverty—his family was too poor to send him to secondary school—to master the Dutch, English, Spanish, and French languages. Influenced both by Western books and by an Indonesian sensibility, Anwar excited Indonesian writers with his pathbreaking poems that stretched the possibilities of the Indonesian language. But Anwar had died when just twenty-seven years old, sapped by his appetite for the pleasures of the flesh, and his death left it to others, among them the liberal Sumatran novelist and journalist Mochtar Lubis (MOKE-tar LOO-bis) (b. 1920), whose work is quoted above, to carry on the campaign. Their goal, as expressed in the 1950 writers' declaration, was to create a new society by blending widely admired ideas from abroad with Indonesian ideas, to foster change while also preserving continuity.

The declaration's noble aspirations and recognition of Indonesia's connection to the wider world reflected a new sense of possibility as walls of colonialism were being knocked down. But the writers' idealism was soon dashed by the realities of the early post–World War II years. While Indonesians, like other Southeast Asians, longed for human dignity, other, more immediate goals took precedence, including securing independence, building a new nation, and addressing problems of poverty and underdevelopment. The cosmopolitan values of Anwar, Lubis, and their colleagues even came to seem quaint and contrary to the dominant nationalist agenda. But despite false starts and conflicts, over the following decades Indonesians and other nations of South and Southeast Asia sought, and sometimes found, answers to their challenges while increasing their links to global networks.

The societies of South and Southeast Asia, which changed dramatically without destroying tradition, offer striking contrasts with the wider world as well as with each other. Except for East Asia, this is the most densely populated part of the world: well over 1.5 billion people live in the lands stretching eastward from Pakistan and India to Indonesia and the Philippines. It is also a very diverse area, containing a wide array of languages, ethnic groups, religions, world-views, governments, and levels of economic development. Some nations have experienced destabilizing conflict; others have achieved widespread prosperity. This region of contrasts between wealth and poverty, development and underdevelopment, has played an important role in the world for over four millennia and continues to be one of the cornerstones of the world economy.

FOCUS QUESTIONS

1. What factors led to the political division of South Asia?
2. What have been the major achievements and disappointments of the South Asian nations?
3. What were the causes and consequences of the wars in Indochina?
4. How did decolonization shape the new Southeast Asian nations?
5. What role do the Southeast Asian nations play in the global system?

 # The Reshaping of South Asia

What factors led to the political division of South Asia?

World War II undermined British colonial control and led to independence for the peoples of South Asia. The British, economically drained by the war and realizing that continued control of India would come only at a great cost in wealth and perhaps lives, handed power over to local leaders. The first prime minister of independent India, Jawaharlal Nehru (NAY-roo) (1889–1964), told his people: "A moment comes, which comes rarely in history, when we step from the old to the new, when an age ends and when the soul of a nation, long suppressed, finds utterance."[3] Yet Nehru's idealism about India's independence was tempered by the realities of the challenges ahead. India's long struggle for independence, marked by the nonviolent philosophy of Mohandas Gandhi (1868–1948), had ironically ended with Gandhi assassinated

and British India divided into several separate, often hostile countries, predominantly Hindu India and largely Muslim Pakistan. Two other major South Asian nations also gained independence: mostly Buddhist Sri Lanka and, in the 1970s, largely Muslim Bangladesh. Each of the four nations had its achievements and failures, but the geographically largest and most populous, India, has been the regional colossus and a major player in world affairs.

Decolonization and Partition

The religious divisions of South Asia undermined regional unity. During World War II relations between the British and the mainly Hindu leadership of the Indian National Congress ruptured (see Chapter 25). Taking advantage of this rupture, and fearing domination by the much larger Hindu community in India, the Muslim League pressed its case with the British for a separate Muslim nation, to be called Pakistan. After the war ended, negotiations to bring the Congress and the Muslim

CHRONOLOGY

	South Asia	Southeast Asia
1940	**1947** Independence for India and Pakistan **1948–1964** Nehru era in India	**1945–1950** Indonesian Revolution **1946–1954** First Indochina War **1948** Independence of Burma
1950		
1960		**1963–1975** U.S.-Vietnamese War **1966–1998** New Order in Indonesia
1970	**1971** Formation of Bangladesh	**1975** Communist victories in Vietnam, Cambodia, Laos
1980	**1984** Assassination of Indira Ghandi	
1990		**1997** Asian economic crisis

League together in a common vision broke down in 1946. As the tension increased, rioting broke out, and Muslims and Hindus began murdering each other, pulling victims from buses, shops, and homes. In Calcutta alone 5,000 people died. The rioting undermined any pretence of Hindu-Muslim unity, and the Muslim leader, Mohammed Ali Jinnah (1876–1948), announced that if India were not divided it would be destroyed. The rioting spread into the Ganges Valley and the Punjab. The Congress leaders and British officials now realized that some sort of partition was inevitable. In 1947 British negotiators reached an agreement with Congress and Muslim League leaders to create two independent nations, India and a Pakistan formed out of the Muslim majority areas of eastern Bengal and the northwestern provinces along the Indus River (see Chronology: South Asia, 1945–Present).

The two nations emerged in hopefulness. In a speech to his new nation, India, Prime Minister Nehru proclaimed: "Long years ago we made a tryst with destiny, and now the time comes when we shall redeem our pledge. At the stroke of the midnight hour, when the world sleeps, India will awake to life and freedom."[4] A similar mood of renewal struck people in Pakistan. But the euphoria in both new nations proved short-lived as a bloodbath ensued. Muslims and Hindus had often lived side by side, but partition sparked hatreds between local members of the majority faith, who felt empowered, and religious minorities, who feared discrimination. As violence flared, thousands of Hindus and Sikhs fled Pakistan for India, and thousands of Muslims fled India for Pakistan. Altogether some 5 million refugees crossed the India–West Pakistan border, and a million crossed the India–East Pakistan border. Religious extremists sometimes attacked whole villages or whole trainloads of refugees. About half a million refugees died from the religious violence.

The sixty-eight-year-old Mohandas Gandhi, who remarked that from his youth he had dreamed of communal unity, labored to stop the killing. Moving into the Muslim quarter of

CHRONOLOGY

	South Asia, 1945–Present
1947	Independence for India and Pakistan
1948	Assassination of Mohandas Gandhi
1948	Sri Lankan independence
1950	Indian republic
1948–1964	Nehru era in India
1959	Sri Lanka's Sirimavo Bandaranaike first woman prime minister
1962	India-China border war
1971	Formation of Bangladesh
1975–1977	State of emergency under Indira Gandhi
1984	Assassination of Indira Gandhi
1988–1990	First Benazir Bhutto government in Pakistan
1993–1996	Second Benazir Bhutto government
1999	Military government led by Pervez Musharraf

Delhi, he toured refugee camps without escort, read aloud from the scriptures of all religions, including Islam's holiest book, the Quran, and confronted Hindu mobs attacking mosques. Finally, in desperation, and hoping to send a message to everyone in India and Pakistan, Gandhi, who weighed only 113 pounds, began a fast until all the violence in the city had stopped or he died. He quickly fell ill, but Gandhi's effort worked, allowing him to break off his fast. After the violence subsided, a substantial Muslim and Sikh minority remained in India and a Hindu and Sikh minority in Pakistan. But partition had been shattering. A Muslim poet spoke for many disillusioned people: "This is not that long looked-for break of the day. Where did that fine breeze blow from—where has it fled?"[5] Furthermore, Gandhi's support for Muslim victims of Hindu violence outraged Hindu extremists, who regarded Gandhi as a traitor to Hinduism. In January 1948, one of them gunned down Gandhi as he walked to a meeting, shocking the whole country.

Despite its bloody start, India was built on a solid political foundation. Britain bequeathed the basis for parliamentary democracy, a trained civil service, a good communications system, and an educated if Westernized elite committed to modernization. India became a republic with a constitution based on the British model, led by a prime minister chosen by the majority party in an elected parliament. However, given its huge ethnic, religious, and linguistic diversity (fourteen major languages and hundreds of minor languages), India has had difficulty building national unity. To accommodate the many religious minorities, regions, and diverse cultures, India adopted a federal system, with elected state governments, and was officially secular with complete separation of religion and state. Kashmir (CASH-mere), a mountainous Himalayan state

on the India-Pakistan border, presented a long-term problem because it had a Muslim majority but a Hindu ruler who opted to join India. Kashmir has remained a source of constant tension and sometimes war between India and Pakistan.

The new Pakistan confronted numerous problems. It was an artificial country, with two wings separated by a thousand miles of India. The nation's founding leader, Jinnah, died soon after independence, and his successor was assassinated. Before independence Muslims had been overrepresented in the British Indian military, and the army now played a stronger role in Pakistan's politics than in India's. The loss of top civilian leaders, lack of a balanced economic base, massive poverty, and geographical division made Pakistan more vulnerable than India to political instability and military rule. Pakistan and India quarreled over issues from water use to trade to ownership of Kashmir.

India During the Nehru Years

India's first prime minister, Nehru, a close associate of Gandhi and the son of a respected early Indian nationalist, dominated Indian politics for a decade and a half (1948–1964). A gifted speaker and brilliant thinker, Nehru was supported by the middle class, who saw him as the builder of a modern India, and by the mass of the people because he identified himself with issues of concern to the poor. The majority of Indians lived in overcrowded, unhealthy urban slums or dusty villages that lacked electricity and running water. Nehru promised to raise living standards and address the nation's overwhelming poverty. He believed firmly in democracy, emphasizing consent rather than coercion. While India lagged behind communist-ruled China in

Muslims Leaving India for Pakistan During Partition As India and Pakistan split into two new nations in 1947, millions of Muslims and Hindus fled their homes to escape violence. This photo shows displaced Muslims, carrying a few meager belongings, jamming a train headed from India to Pakistan. (Wide World Photos)

economic development, it nevertheless preserved a system of personal freedom. Believing in peaceful coexistence with neighbors and renouncing military aggression, Nehru became a major figure on the world stage, helping found the Non-Aligned Movement of nations, such as Egypt and Indonesia, unwilling to commit to either the U.S. or Soviet camps in the Cold War. Hoping to prevent a nuclear conflict between the superpowers, Nehru led the Congress Party to three smashing electoral victories.

Nehru's policies derived from his complex ideals. Although the British-educated lawyer admired Western politics, literature, and economic dynamism, he also respected India's cultural heritage. Nehru talked of India's moral strength, which, he believed, sanctioned his leadership of the non-aligned countries. Yet he opposed any narrow understanding of tradition and religion. Raised a Hindu, Nehru was nevertheless a secularist who believed that Congress should represent all religions and social groups and promote justice for all. Although himself a high-caste brahman, he distrusted the influence of the Hindu priests. Perhaps Nehru's greatest contributions came in addressing social problems. He shared Gandhi's opposition to restrictions imposed by the caste system and fought gender inequalities. In 1955, after years of struggle, Nehru convinced parliament to approve new laws on untouchability and women's rights that provided penalties for discrimination. The lowest-ranking social group, untouchables, acquired special quotas in government services and universities, while Hindu women gained equal legal rights with men, including the right to divorce, property rights, and equal inheritance. To discourage child marriage, Nehru set a minimum marriage age at eighteen for males and fifteen for females. But the laws, which challenged centuries of tradition, were often ignored, especially in rural areas.

Nehru's government built the framework for productive economic change. Nehru introduced a planning system to foster modern technology and mixed capitalism and socialism, private capital and a strong state sector. He left established industries in private hands but set up public ventures to, for example, build power plants and dams, which doubled power production, and irrigation canals, which increased agricultural yields by 25 percent. In the 1960s the Green Revolution, agricultural innovation marked by the introduction of new high-yield wheat and rice, fostered a dramatic rise in food production. Nehru employed five-year plans to make India independent of foreign suppliers for power, steel, basic commodities, and food. By the 1970s India was one of the world's ten most industrialized nations and nearly self-sufficient in food.

But the Nehru record was mixed. Some of his policies proved failures. Government control of the private sector through regulations gave bureaucrats great power, fostered corruption, and shackled private enterprise. Nehru failed to cultivate good relations with Pakistan or with China, and in 1962 Chinese troops humiliated Indian forces during a border dispute. Nehru also failed to recognize that a rapidly growing population, which rose from 389 million in 1941 to 434 million in 1961, would undermine most of India's economic gains. In addition, he only belatedly endorsed family planning, and the government built schools and universities but failed to substantially raise literacy rates. Yet, when Nehru died in 1964, millions mourned the end of an idealistic era that had earned India respect in the world. Furthermore, Congress had no leader of comparable stature to follow Nehru.

Nehru Opening a New Dam
As prime minister, Jawaharlal Nehru tried to build a modern India, devoting scarce financial resources to improving the economic infrastructure. In this photo, Nehru opens a new dam, which will generate power for commerce and industry. (Corbis)

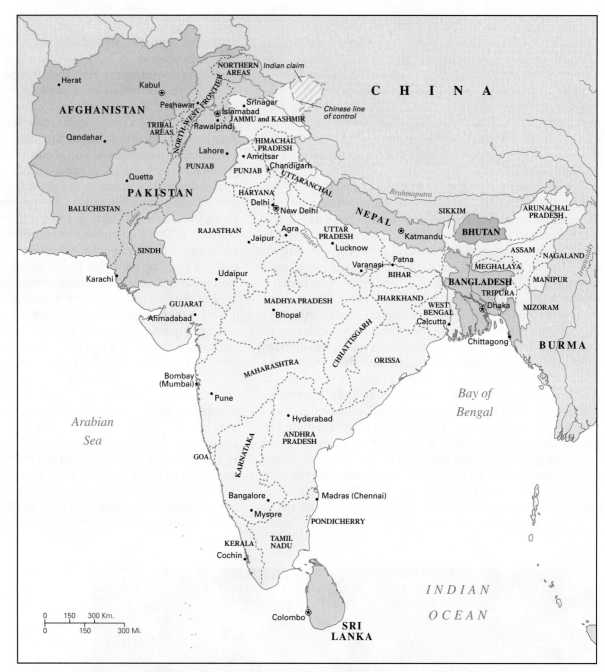

Map 31.1 Modern South Asia
India, predominantly Hindu, is the largest South Asian nation and separates the two densely populated Islamic nations of Bangladesh and Pakistan. Buddhists are the majority in Sri Lanka, just off India's southeast coast. The small kingdoms of Bhutan and Nepal are located in the Himalayan mountain range.

Online Study Center *Improve Your Grade* Interactive Map: The Partition of India, 1947

The Making of Pakistan and Bangladesh

Pakistan faced greater challenges than did India. Jinnah had pledged to make the nation happy and prosperous, but the leaders who followed him had only limited success, in part because of differences, and sometimes tensions, between ethnic groups who shared an Islamic faith but often little else. From the beginning tensions flared between the nationalistic Bengalis, who dominated the east, and the Punjabis and Sindhis, who dominated the west. The two regions, although strongly Islamic, dif-

fered in language, culture, and outlook. The factionalized Pakistani parliament, whose members chiefly represented regions and ethnic groups rather than rival ideologies, proved unworkable, providing an excuse for military leaders to take over the government in 1958. By 1969 dissatisfaction with military dictatorship led to riots, prompting martial law.

At the end of the 1960s ethnic tensions came to a boil, eventually fracturing Pakistan into two nations, Pakistan and Bangladesh (Bengali Nation) (see Map 31.1). The Bengalis in East Pakistan had felt they did not get a fair share of the nation's resources and political power. After the **Awami League**, a Bengali nationalist party, won a majority of East Pakistan's seats in national elections, in early 1971 Pakistani troops arrested the party leader, Sheikh Mujiber Rahman (shake MOO-jee-bur RAH-mun) (1920–1975), in the middle of the night. Then, hoping to crush Awami League support, troops opened fire on university dormitories and Hindu homes, causing hundreds of casualties.

Inspired by Sheikh Mujiber, who asked his supporters to carry the message of independence to every rice field and mango grove in the country, the Awami League then declared independence. In response, troops from West Pakistan poured into East Pakistan, terrorizing the Bengali population with massacres, arson, and the raping of thousands of women. At least half a million Bengalis died at Pakistani hands. The civil war caused 10 million desperate, starving Bengali refugees to flee to India. World opinion turned against Pakistan. India appealed for world support of East Pakistan, armed the Bengali guerrillas, and, after an ill-advised Pakistani attack on Indian airfields, declared war and sent troops into both West and East Pakistan, rapidly gaining the upper hand. Fearful of India, Pakistan had long cultivated an alliance with China and the United States, both of which supplied it with military aid. The United States, where the administration of President Richard Nixon ignored the massive killing of Bengalis, and China threatened to intervene on behalf of Pakistan, but Soviet backing of India discouraged such a move. By the end of 1971 Pakistani troops in Bengal had surrendered to Indian forces, and the Awami League, led by Sheikh Mujibur, established a new nation, Bangladesh, in what had been East Pakistan.

The Indira Gandhi Era

Nehru had not only led India but had also fostered a family political dynasty. With the sudden death of Nehru's respected successor in 1966, the Congress selected Nehru's daughter, Indira Gandhi (1917–1984), to be the nation's first woman prime minister. She had worked closely with her father while her husband (no relation to Mohandas Gandhi) served in parliament. A shrewd campaigner, Mrs. Gandhi enjoyed a decade and a half in power. When her support waned in the 1967 elections, she responded aggressively with policies to win back the poor. Her status was elevated by India's smashing military victory over archenemy Pakistan. But Mrs. Gandhi's war triumph and mounting domestic problems also fostered her use of increasingly harsh policies, which often made matters worse. Powerful vested interests ignored her reforms, the economy faltered, and many Indians turned against the Congress.

Indian democracy faltered. In 1975 Gandhi declared a state of emergency, suspending civil rights, closing state governments, and jailing some 10,000 opposition leaders and dissidents. One arrested leader complained that those who were in jail should be out while those who were out should be in. While her actions were condemned, however, some of her policies

improved the economy. Meanwhile, her youngest son, Sanjay Gandhi (1946–1980), launched a controversial birth control campaign to forcibly sterilize any man with more than three children and implemented a slum-clearance program that forced thousands out of sidewalk shanties. Both programs became deeply unpopular. In 1977 Indira lifted the emergency and announced general elections. After thirty years in power, the Congress Party, and with it Indira Gandhi, was voted out of office and replaced by an uneasy coalition of diverse parties that included Hindu nationalists who wanted to end the secular approach of the Congress. But the coalition government solved few problems, and in 1980 it collapsed.

Indira Gandhi and the Congress returned to power in the 1980 elections, restoring the Nehru dynasty. But they also faced new problems. Nearly half the electorate had stayed away, disenchanted with cynical politics, and Mrs. Gandhi faced growing unemployment and unrest. In 1980 Sanjay Gandhi died in a plane crash, and Indira Gandhi elevated her eldest son Rajiv (1944–1991), an apolitical airline pilot, as her heir apparent. Violence in the Punjab, India's richest state, which had a heavy Sikh population, provoked Mrs. Gandhi's final crisis. The growing political consciousness of the Sikhs, whose religion mixes Hindu and Muslim ideas, had led to a desire for statehood. In 1983 armed Sikh extremists occupied the Golden Temple at Amritsar (uhm-RIT-suhr), the holiest shrine in the Sikh religion, and turned it into a fortress. They called for an independent Sikh homeland and murdered those, including moderate Sikhs, who opposed them. In 1984 the Indian army stormed the Golden Temple against fierce resistance. When the fighting ended, the temple was reduced to rubble and over a thousand militants and soldiers lay dead.

Violence had returned to Indian political life. The destruction of their holiest temple shocked the Sikhs and led to the shooting death of Indira Gandhi by two of her Sikh bodyguards. The assassination in turn generated rioting and attacks on Sikhs. Hindu mobs roamed Delhi, burning Sikh shops and killing Sikhs, often by pouring gasoline over them and setting them ablaze. The dead numbered in the thousands. Rajiv Gandhi, succeeding his mother at only forty years old, proved ineffective. In 1991, while campaigning in the southern city of Madras, he was blown up by a young Sri Lankan woman handing him flowers. The suicide bomber, who had the bomb hidden in her clothing, opposed India's support of the Sri Lankan government in its war against the secessionist group to which she belonged. Yet despite this tumult, India remained a functioning democracy and a thriving nation.

SECTION SUMMARY

■ After World War II, when majority Muslim Pakistan broke off from majority Hindu India, widespread religious violence broke out and a dispute over the territory of Kashmir set the stage for continued tension between the two countries.

■ Nehru attempted to expand the rights of women and, through a mix of capitalism and socialism, vastly

Awami League A Bengali nationalist party that began the move for independence from West Pakistan.

increased India's industrial and agricultural output, but the population expanded at a dangerously rapid rate and not all policies were successful.

■ East and West Pakistan were divided along ethnic lines, and a military crackdown on a Bengali nationalist party led to a bloody civil war in which India intervened on behalf of East Pakistan, which then became a separate country, Bangladesh.

■ Nehru's daughter, Indira Gandhi, was prime minister for over a decade, but she treated her opposition harshly and was assassinated in the midst of clashes between Hindus and Sikhs, and her son and successor, Rajiv Gandhi, was also assassinated.

South Asian Politics and Societies

What have been the major achievements and disappointments of the South Asian nations?

South Asian societies changed beginning in the 1970s, each forging its own political role in the region. With a little over 1 billion people by 2005 and 65 percent of the land in the subcontinent, the Republic of India rose to regional dominance. Indian governments began to liberalize the economy, stimulating growth. At the same time, growing Hindu nationalism has challenged the domination of India's Congress Party, threatening its secular vision. Meanwhile, India's neighbors in South Asia have struggled to achieve stability and economic development. Both Pakistan and Sri Lanka have experienced persistent ethnic violence, while India and Pakistan remain on bitter terms, building up military forces and nuclear weapons to use against the other. Whatever the political tensions that divide them, however, they also share some life patterns. In each South Asian nation ancient customs exist side by side with modern machines and ways of living; some of them, such as democratic forms, are imports from outside.

Indian Politics

When India celebrated its fiftieth jubilee of independence in 1997, the nation's president reminded his people that India's challenge was to achieve economic growth with social justice. That goal remains elusive; India has been unable to mount the sort of concerted attack on mass poverty found in China. However, Indians can boast that, in politics, their country has maintained one of the few working multiparty democracies outside the industrialized nation-states, one that fosters lively political debate and forces candidates to appeal to voters. An Indian novelist described the rhetoric of political campaigns leading up to elections: "The speeches were crammed with promises of every shape and size: promises of new schools,

clean water, health care, land for landless peasants, powerful laws to punish any discrimination."[6] While such grandiose promises usually proved difficult to fulfill, millions of people voted in these elections, and changes in state and federal governments have regularly occurred.

India rejected the revolutionary path of China, instead promoting civil liberties and constitutional democracy. However, scholars debate how that democracy has shaped India. To some observers, for example, democracy fosters national unity by providing a flexible system for accommodating the differing interests of the diverse population. Others, however, argue that democracy has intensified differences between groups. Certainly, tensions between Hindus and Muslims and between high-caste and low-caste Hindus, manipulated by opportunistic politicians, have complicated political life. There are also differences over how real the effects of democracy are in the presence of powerful economic and political elites. While voting is said to give the poor an opportunity to put pressure on elites, elites are seen as manipulating the democratic system to preserve their privileges. Some say that democracy has become only a safety valve for popular frustration, creating the illusion of mass participation that prevents a frontal attack on caste and class inequalities. Yet, lower caste voters do make their voice heard, sometimes forcing officials to meet their needs, such as by paving the pathways in their neighborhoods.

The Congress Party has remained nationally influential for over five decades but has had to contend with rivals. On the left, several communist parties dominate politics in West Bengal in the northeast and Kerala in the southwest, repeatedly winning elections by promoting modernization and support for the poor within a democratic framework. On the right, several Hindu nationalist parties have opposed the secular Congress, but with limited success until the 1990s. In the southern Indian states various parties representing regional interests gradually gained strength, generally dominating state governments and becoming part of federal coalitions. These regional parties, often led by stars of the local film industries, have worked to protect local languages while preserving English, the only common language understood by educated people around the country, as a national language. All of India's parties have suffered from corruption, elected officials and the bureaucrats they hire often seeing public service as a way to enrich themselves.

Since 1989 Indian politics has become more pluralistic. The Congress lost several elections to coalitions that included Hindu nationalists. The major Hindu nationalist party, the **Bharatha Janata** (BJP), gained influence in north India with a platform of hostility to Muslims and of state support for Hindu issues, such as having schools teach Indian history in accordance with Hindu traditions and religious writings. The BJP slogan, "One Nation, One People, One Culture," confronts the Gandhi-Nehru vision of a tolerant multicultural state. By the late 1990s India suffered from rising political corruption, violent secessionist movements in border regions, caste conflict, religious hostilities, and fragmentation into several rival political factions. In 2002 major Hindu-Muslim violence broke

Bharatha Janata (BJP) The major Hindu nationalist party in India.

out again, leaving over a thousand people dead and over 100,000 terrified Muslims, burned out of their cities, huddled in tent camps. In 2004 the Congress, led by Rajiv Gandhi's Italian-born, sari-wearing widow, Sonia Gandhi (b. 1946), a Roman Catholic who met Rajiv when both were students in England, capitalized on disenchantment among the poor and Muslims and, allied with leftist parties, unexpectedly defeated the ruling BJP-led coalition and formed a new government committed to secularism and economic growth. A Pakistan-born Sikh economist, Manmohan Singh, became the first non-Hindu prime minister. Furthermore, a free press monitors politics. In 2005 an investigation of corruption by a television station forced several members of parliament to resign, indicating the continued vibrancy of Indian democracy.

Indian Economic Growth

India has struggled to resolve problems inherited from colonial times: economic backwardness, skyrocketing population growth, and crushing poverty for the majority. Nehru had sought to end ignorance, poverty, and inequality of opportunity. While his dream has not yet been realized, Indians can boast of many gains, especially after India changed directions economically in the 1970s. For example, in 1956 India had to import vital foodstuffs and manufactured goods. By the late 1970s it was a net exporter of grain and by 2000 was making and exporting its own cars, computers, and aircraft.

After 1991 Indian leaders dismantled the socialist sector of the economy built by Nehru while sparking economic revival. Reform, deregulation, and liberalization contributed to an economic growth rate of 6 to 7 percent a year by the late 1990s. Several cities, especially Bangalore and Bombay, became high-tech centers closely linked to global communications. Hundreds of North American and European companies, taking advantage of a growing, educated Indian middle class, especially university graduates fluent in English, have moved information and technical service jobs, such as call-in customer service and computer programming, from North America and Europe to India. India's boom has even prompted thousands of highly educated Indians living in North America and Europe to return to India and join its high-tech sector. These returnees—30,000 technology professionals in 2004 and 2005 alone—often move into spacious, newly built California-style suburbs with names like Ozone and Lake Vista. Even greater progress has been made in agriculture. Since 1947 India has doubled food production, thanks largely to the Green Revolution of improved seeds and fertilizers. The nation now grows enough wheat and rice to feed the entire population, but persisting social, economic, and regional inequalities have prevented equitable distribution of the food.

In spite of the economic revival, many Indians have yet to enjoy its fruits. Compared to China, Malaysia, and South Korea, India's economy has been less able to deliver a better life to the mass of the population. More than half of Indians still live below the poverty line, and 40 percent lack an adequate diet. While China nears universal literacy, only half of Indians can read and write. Meanwhile population growth eats away at

the national resources. Every year 30 million Indians are born. By 2050 India will have 1.5 billion people, more than China and four times more than the United States. Ironically, success in doubling life expectancy contributes to overpopulation, which causes overcrowded cities, a lack of pure drinking water and adequate sanitation, and insufficient primary health care. India has half as many physicians per population and over twice as much infant mortality as China; Chinese live twelve years longer than Indians. Millions of Indians sleep on city sidewalks for lack of money and housing. While affluent Indians increasingly buy fancy imported cars to drive along newly built highways, many commuters ride on the roofs of jammed buses and trains. Yet, most quality-of-life indices place India ahead of most African nations.

The stark contrasts between the modern and traditional sectors of the economy have produced development amid underdevelopment and raised questions as to who benefits from the changes. The "haves" can afford to pay for services that strapped governments cannot provide: good schools, clean water, decent health care, efficient transport. Despite increased agricultural productivity, per capita calory consumption remains well below world averages. Ambitious birth control campaigns enjoy success in cities but less in the countryside. The Green Revolution has increased output but mostly benefits the big landowners, who can afford the large investments in tractors and fertilizers. Successive Indian governments have been unable or unwilling to challenge vested interests such as the powerful landlords. Meanwhile, poor peasants, unable to make a living from their small farms, fall further behind. Half the rural population has become landless. Poverty fosters growing urban crime and rural banditry, especially in several densely populated northern states. The population below the official poverty line lacks purchasing power to sustain local industry. Economic growth and poverty ravage the environment as cities encroach on farmland and people cut down trees for firewood. As in China, poor peasants protest, often violently, the taking of their land for building factories, often foreign-owned, and highways. The Chipko forest conservation movement, based on traditional and Gandhian principles and led mostly by women, is one of many groups working to protect the environment. A Chipko leader, the globetrotting Sunderlal Bahugana (SUN-dur-LOLL ba-hoo-GAH-na), stresses the place of people in the larger web of nature. The Congress-led government pledged to spend more on rural health care and education.

Indian Cities, Gender Patterns, and Cultures

In his will, India's first prime minister, Jawaharlal Nehru, asked that his ashes be scattered in the Ganges River, not because of the river's traditional religious significance to Hindus but because it symbolized to him India's millennia-old culture, ever changing and yet ever same. Such a pattern has indeed characterized India's society and culture. Ancient traditions such as caste, gender stereotypes, and family practices have persisted but have also been modified, especially in the cities, and Indians make religion both central to their lives and a source of conflict.

Indians have also used literature, film, and other cultural forms to examine their society and place in the world.

The contrast between the villages, where 80 percent of Indians live, and the often modern cities remains stark. Unlike in the villages, in the cities the growing urban middle class—many millions strong by 2006—enjoy recreations and technologies, from golf to video games, that are available to the affluent around the world. As young people move around the country, often on the new national highway system, they identify less with their home region and more with India, becoming cosmopolitan. Whether they live in the Punjab, Calcutta, or Bangalore, educated urban young people often like the same music and buy the same consumer goods, a homogenization that conservatives see as a threat to local cultures. Practices that ensure strict divisions between castes, such as avoiding physical contact or sharing food, are harder to maintain in cities than in villages. City people often still pay attention to caste, but their approach to preserving it is different. For instance, high-caste families often place classified ads in national newspapers seeking marriage partners from similar backgrounds for their children, as in this example: "Suitable Brahman bride for handsome Brahman boy completing Ph.D. (Physics). Write with biodata, photograph, horoscope."[7] Caste remains much more firmly rooted in the villages. At the bottom of the caste system, the untouchables, some 20 percent of India's population, still live difficult lives, especially in the villages, even though government assistance and laws to improve their status have enabled some low-caste people to enter high-status occupations or succeed in politics. The grooves of tradition run deep, particularly in the rural areas, and changes can bring demoralization and disorientation as well as satisfaction.

However, in some regions, especially in cities, families have changed. Modern life has hastened the breakup of the traditional joint families, where parents lived in large compounds with their married and unmarried children and grandchildren; some Indians now live in smaller, nuclear families. New forms of employment, which can cause family members to move to other districts or countries, have undermined family cohesion. A traditional preference for male babies, however, has continued, and the ratio of females to males in the population has even declined. Today the ability of technology to determine the sex of a fetus has led many Indians who want male children to terminate pregnancies. Experts worry that a population that is becoming predominantly male will experience increasing social problems.

Nehru had believed that India could progress only if women played a full part in the nation. In response to such concerns, new laws banned once widespread customs such as polygamy, child marriage, and sati. Female literacy has risen, from 1 percent in 1901 to 27 percent in 2000, though it is still only half the male rate. But some changing customs have penalized women. For example, the practice of requiring new brides to provide generous dowries to their in-laws, once restricted to higher castes, has become common in all castes. As a result, especially in rural areas, reports have increased of families banishing, injuring, or killing young brides whose own families failed to supply the promised dowries. Notions of women's rights, common in cities, are less known in villages. In some towns the police harass unmarried couples in public parks for public displays of affection.

Some women have experienced more changes than others. Many Indian women have benefited from education, even becoming forceful leaders in such fields as journalism, business, trade unions, the arts, and government. Women have even been elected to parliament and serve as chief ministers of states, especially in south India. Outside the big cities, however, women have remained largely bound by tradition, expected to demonstrate submission, obedience, and absolute dedication to their husband. Women's organizations affiliated with the Hindu nationalist BJP downplay patriarchy, emphasizing women as mothers producing sons and portraying Muslim men as a threat to Hindu women. But an antipatriarchy women's movement, growing for a century, has become more active since the 1970s, suggesting that women's issues will remain on the nation's agenda. For instance, the Self-Employed Women's Association, founded by Ela Bhatt in 1972, has provided low-cost credit and literacy training to some of the poorest city women, the ragpickers and sidewalk vendors. By 2004 AIDS grew rapidly as a health problem, a result largely of women being forced into prostitution to serve the sexual needs of increasingly mobile male workers such as long-haul truckers. HIV infection has spread largely along the transportation networks.

Religion, like society, has changed, becoming intertwined with politics. As it has for millennia, religion still plays a key role in Indian life. Although Hindus form a large majority, India's population also includes 120 million Muslims, over 20 million Sikhs, and nearly 20 million Christians. Religious differences have become politicized. Some upper-caste Hindus, for instance, particularly in the BJP, have used the notion of a Hindu nation to marginalize Muslims and low-caste Hindus. Civil unrest involving violent attacks on Muslims by militant Hindu nationalists, often fundamentalists who interpret the ancient Hindu religious texts, or Vedas, literally, has caused political crises. Sometimes Muslims have initiated the violence. For instance, in 2006 Muslims protesting Danish cartoons offensive to Muslims rioted and attacked Hindu and Western targets. Tensions are fueled by mass poverty among all the religious groups. Yet, despite the tensions, Muslims occupy high positions in India's government, business, and the professions and play a key role in cultural expression, such as films and music. India's most famous modern artist, Tyeb Mehta (b. 1925), is a Shi'ite Muslim whose works, much of which address the Hindu-Muslim divide, sell all over the world.

Indians have also eagerly embraced modern cultural forms to express ideas. While Indian-born novelists such as Arundhati Roy (AH-roon-DAH-tee roy) and Salman Rushdie have achieved worldwide fame, a more popular cultural form in contemporary India has been film. India has built the world's largest film industry; it makes about a thousand movies a year, and many also find a huge audience among both Indian emigrants and non-Indians in Southeast Asia, Africa, Europe, and the Caribbean. The Bombay film industry, known as **"Bollywood,"** has become India's largest (see Profile: Raj Kapoor, Bollywood

---

Bollywood The Bombay film industry.

RAJ KAPOOR,
BOLLYWOOD FILM STAR

Raj Kapoor As the most influential male lead and director in Indian films, Kapoor could attract the top actresses to star in his films. He made many films with Nargis, the two of them shown here in a 1948 musical, "Barsaat." (Dinodia Picture Agency)

Raj Kapoor (1924–1988) was a true pioneer: the first real superstar of Indian film, an accomplished actor, director, producer, and all-round showman. Kapoor skillfully combined music, melodrama, and spectacle to create a cinema with huge popular, even international, appeal, especially among the poor. He was born in Peshawar, the son of one of India's most distinguished stage and film actors, Prithviraj Kapoor, among whose hundreds of roles was that of Alexander the Great. The family settled in Bombay in 1929, when the Hindi-language film industry was in a formative stage (Hindi is the major language spoken in north India). At age twenty-two Kapoor entered an arranged marriage to Krishnaji. Although he had romances with actresses, the marriage endured and the couple had five children.

Handsome and vigorous, with a talent for comedy, music, and self-promotion, the young Kapoor formed his own film company in 1948 with hopes of appealing to the common person. Over the next three decades he starred in or oversaw dozens of films, many of them commercially successful. Kapoor's greatest success came during the Nehru years from the late 1940s to mid-1960s, when Indians were optimistic and looked outward. His films, often subtitled in local languages, brought him celebrity all over South Asia and in Southeast Asia, East Africa, the Middle East, the Caribbean, and the Soviet Union. He was largely responsible for the recognition of Indian cinema in the world. Songs from his films were sung or hummed on streets of cities and small towns thousands of miles from India. He and his female costars became popular pin-ups in the bazaars of the Arab world and folk heroes in the Soviet lands. Kapoor, like Nehru, believed that an Indian could be international, enjoying foreign products and influences, while also remaining deeply Indian. A song from his film *The Gentleman Cheat* in 1955 reflected the hero's transnational identity: "The shoes I'm wearing are made in Japan, My trousers fashioned in England. The red cap on my head is Russian. In spite of it all my heart is Indian."

Kapoor believed that some of his films achieved international success because "the young people of those countries saw in the films their own sufferings, the strivings to achieve, and their own triumph over a world in chaos." Fans saw in his characters youth, optimism about life, and revolt against authority, the little man straddling the great divides of wealth and poverty, city and village, sophistication and innocence. For example, in *The Vagabond* (1951) he portrays a rebellious youth and petty thief growing up on the streets, both daring and vulnerable, charming and reckless, surviving by his wits.

The themes of Kapoor's films often touched on social problems or politics and were filled with humanism and sensitivity. They cried out against destitution and unequal wealth, offering underdog heroes who were poor but also happy. These themes permeated some of his most popular films, such as *The Vagabond*, which broke box office records in the USSR and the Middle East, where it was dubbed into Arabic, Persian, and Turkish. An ardent fan of American comedians, especially Charlie Chaplin, Kapoor, like Chaplin, often portrayed a deglamorized tramp, the little man at odds with the world and hiding his pain behind a smiling face, a figure he thought "had a greater identity with the common man."

Kapoor's romanticism was evident in his sympathetic treatment of women. The heroine, often played by the actress Nargis (NAR-ghis) (1929–1981), a Muslim whose mother was a famed singer, was always a central player in his films. Sometimes Kapoor's films presented women as strong and without flaws, as was his character's love interest, Nargis, in *The Vagabond;* at other times women were victims, exploited and tormented by religion and tradition. Kapoor argued, "We eulogize womankind as the embodiment of motherhood but we always give our women the worst treatment. They are burnt alive [in sati], treated as slaves [by men]." Yet, in spite of his concern for the sexual exploitation of women, Kapoor's films presented sensuous actresses and opened the way to more sexually explicit scenes, shocking social conservatives.

Kapoor's career faded in the 1970s, when his style of romantic hero became old-fashioned. The newer films focused on the angry young man, often a gangster, and turned away from Kapoor's adoring treatment of women. At the time of his death in 1988 he was making a film exploring the taboo subject of love across the India-Pakistan border, between a Hindu and a Muslim. His sons, all actors, tried to keep his banner alive, but Bollywood moved in new directions, centering stories on men and their challenges rather than balancing strong male-female roles as Kapoor had done.

THINKING ABOUT THE PROFILE

1. Why is Kapoor often credited with spreading Indian film to other countries?

2. What social viewpoints were expressed in his films?

Note: Quotations from Sumita S. Chakravarty, *National Identity in Indian Popular Cinema, 1947–1987* (Austin: University of Texas Press, 1993), pp. 138, 203; and Malti Sahai, "Raj Kapoor and the Indianization of Charlie Chaplin," *East-West Film Journal,* 2/1 (December, 1987), p. 64.

Film Star), churning out films in the major north Indian language, Hindi, but companies in other regions of India make films in local languages, such as Tamil in southeast India. Many films, especially musicals, have portrayed a fantasy world that enables viewers to forget the problem-filled real world. As one fan explains: "I love to sit in the dark and dream about what I can never possibly have. I can listen to the music, learn all the songs and forget about my troubles."[8] Religious divisions are muted in Bollywood, and the leading directors, writers, and stars often come from Muslim backgrounds. Because of their super-star status, film stars are often able to move into state and federal politics. For example, voters in southern India have long favored stars of the local film industry as state leaders. By the 1980s that trend had even spread to parts of north India.

Islamic Politics and Societies

South Asia's two densely populated Muslim countries, Pakistan and Bangladesh, have struggled to develop and to maintain stability. Both countries are divided between secular and devout Muslims, have alternated between military dictatorships and elected civilian governments, and have generally conservative cultures.

Pakistan Containing 150 million people, over 95 percent of them Sunni Muslims, Pakistan has had difficulty transforming its diverse ethnic and tribal groups into a politically stable, unified nation. The most long-lasting civilian leader, Zulkifar Ali Bhutto (zool-KEE-far AH-lee BOO-toe) (r. 1971–1977), a lawyer educated at top universities in Britain and California, came to power with great ambitions. Although from a wealthy landowning family, he pursued socialist policies unpopular with the wealthy. Accusing him of corruption, the army took power and later executed Bhutto. The Soviet occupation of Afghanistan in 1979 and the Pakistan-supported Islamic resistance to the Soviets that followed (see Chapter 30) distracted Pakistanis from their unpopular military regime and brought more U.S. military aid to Pakistan.

Pakistani politics has remained turbulent. In 1986 Bhutto's daughter, Benazir Bhutto (BEN-ah-ZEER BOO-toe) (b. 1953), a graduate of Britain's Oxford University, put together a movement to challenge the military regime. As unrest increased in 1988, Benazir Bhutto became prime minister and later became the first head of a modern Asian government to give birth to a child while in office. She was respected abroad but struggled to govern effectively. Accused of abuse of power, she was dismissed in 1990. The civilian who replaced her tried to strengthen Islamic practices. Benazir Bhutto returned to power after the 1993 elections but failed to resolve critical problems, including growing fighting between ethnic factions and attacks by militant Sunnis on the small Shi'a Muslim and Christian minorities. In 1996 she was once again removed.

In 1999 the military took over, installing as president Indian-born General Pervez Musharraf (per-VEZ moo-SHAR-uff) (b. 1943), whose family had fled to Pakistan during the partition of India in 1947. He faced the same challenge as his predecessors: to halt factional violence, punish corruption, collect taxes from

the wealthy, restore economic growth, and balance the demands of both militant and secular Muslims. Although Musharraf allied with the United States after the 2001 terrorist attacks on the United States and the resulting U.S. invasion of Afghanistan, many Pakistanis prefer closer ties with the Middle East and resent the U.S. and the West, in part because the United States, while seeking Pakistani help in the war on international terrorism, is reluctant to remove high tariff barriers against Pakistani textiles, a major export that accounts for nearly half of all manufacturing jobs. Pakistanis make everything from shirts to sheets for Western companies, and experts argue that an expansion of this work might relieve the high unemployment rate and hence reduce the appeal of extremist Islam for desperate young men.

Pakistani society and culture have remained conservative. Pakistan's founding leader, Jinnah, a cosmopolitan British-educated lawyer, had favored more rights for women, arguing that it was a crime that most Pakistani women were shut up within the four walls of the house as prisoners. But national leaders who shared this view were reluctant to challenge the strong opposition to women's rights, especially in rural areas. In 1979 an Islamizing military government pushed through discriminatory laws that made women who were raped guilty of adultery, a serious offense. Women enjoyed far fewer legal rights than men and were more commonly jailed or punished than men for adultery. Women's groups who courageously protested in the streets were attacked by military force, prompting the feminist poet Saeeda Gazdar (SIGH-ee-da GAZ-dar) to write: "The flags of mourning were flapping, the hand-maidens had rebelled. Those two hundred women who came out on the streets, were surrounded on all sides, besieged by armed force, [repressed by] the enemies of truth, the murderers of love."[9] By the 1990s things had changed little: only 10 percent of adult women were employed outside the home, and fewer than 20 percent were literate. The United Nations ranked Pakistan near the bottom of nations in women's equality. In some districts Islamic militants succeeded in restricting women from voting or from attending school with males.

Serious problems persist in Pakistan. It remains a land of villages dominated by large, politically influential landowners. Life expectancy for Pakistanis improved from forty-three to sixty years between 1960 and 1997, but 40 percent of children in that period suffered from malnutrition. The attempts by Islamic leaders to prohibit the broadcasting of music by popular singers, especially women such as London-based Nazia Hassan, set off an ongoing debate about the role of Westernized popular culture and women entertainers.

Bangladesh Even more so than Pakistan, Bangladesh, overcrowded with 125 million people, has encountered barriers to development. Mostly flat plains, the land is prone to devastating hurricanes, floods, tornados, and famine. The nation's founder, Sheik Mujiber Rahman, had hoped that the nation he envisioned—secular, democratic, and socialist—would rapidly progress, but, after tightening his power, he was assassinated by the military. None of the succession of governments after him, whether military or civilian, has had much success in resolving problems, and all have suffered from corruption. Several leaders have been assassinated. After 1991 democracy became the main pattern, and the two largest parties have been led by women. The conservative Islamic and procapitalist Khaleda Zia (ZEE-uh) (b. 1945), the widow of an assassinated leader, heads one party while the left-leaning Sheikh Hasina Wajed (shake ha-SEE-nah WAH-jed) (b. 1947), the daughter of the assassinated Sheik Mujibur Rahman, the nation's first prime minister, leads the Awami League. Sheikh Hasina herself escaped an assassination attempt in 2004. The two women, bitter rivals, have alternated as the nation's prime minister.

Despite political turbulence, however, Bangladesh has had more success than Pakistan. The nation has been a pioneer among developing nations in programs to eliminate poverty and now provides some formal education to 60 percent of its children. The Grameen Bank, which loans small amounts of money, particularly to poor women for starting a village business, has helped millions of people, earning world attention (see Chapter 26). A visionary activist, Fazle Hasan Abed, launched a movement to improve rural life through forming cooperatives. But the nation's per capita income remains $120 per year (35 cents per day), and only 35 percent of adults are literate. Nearly half the population live below the official poverty line. Conflict and instability continue to plague the country.

As in Pakistan, social and cultural issues have divided Bangladesh. Unlike Pakistan, Bangladesh is officially a secular state and has a large Hindu minority (16 percent). Although over the centuries the Bengalis incorporated Hindu and Buddhist influences as well as Sufi mysticism into their version of Islam, making them tolerant of opposing views, militant Muslim political movements seeking an Islamic state gained strength in the 1990s, heightening divisions among Muslims. The militants, allied with Khaleda Zia's party, succeeded in restricting women's rights. For example, public universities implemented a regulation to require women students to return to their dormitories by sunset in order to, as they put it, protect the women's chastity. Islamic militants also pressured the government to prosecute feminist writers such as the medical doctor turned novelist Taslima Nasreen (b. 1962). Nasreen criticized religion and a conservative culture for holding Bengali women back and argued that the basic division in the world was not between religions but between those favoring modern, rational values and those steeped in irrational, blind faith. Muslim militants condemned Nasreen's writing as blasphemy against Islam, a capital offense. Nasreen fled into exile in Europe to escape death threats.

Sri Lanka and Its Conflicts

Sri Lanka, an island nation of 20 million people, shares problems of ethnic conflict and poverty with its South Asian neighbors but, like India, has generally maintained a democracy. In 1948 the leaders of the majority ethnic group, the Sinhalese, some 75 percent of the population and mostly Theravada Buddhists, negotiated independence from Britain and inherited a colonial economy based on rubber and tea plantations. Laws passed by the Sinhalese-dominated government that discriminated against the language and culture of the major ethnic minority, the Tamils, mostly Hindus, generated fighting between the two groups. A Tamil community had existed in northern Sri Lanka for hundreds of years but many Sri Lankan Tamils descended from immigrants who were recruited from India in the nineteenth century to work on British coffee, tea, and rubber planations.

In 1959 Sirimavo Bandaranaike (sree-MAH-vo BAN-dar-an-EYE-kee) (1916–2004), the Sinhalese widow of an assassinated leader, led her party to victory and became the world's first woman prime minister. Her enemies derided her as a "kitchen woman," someone who knew all about cooking but nothing about running a country, yet she proved to be a strong leader and dominated her nation's politics in the 1960s and 1970s. Although she implemented socialist policies aimed at remedying problems of the poor, she faced resistance from a communist-led rebellion among poor Sinhalese.

Sinhalese-dominated Sri Lankan governments promoted Sinhalese nationalism; they also sponsored textile and electronics manufacturing to reduce dependence on cash crop exports. While socialist policies discouraged free enterprise, they fostered the highest literacy rates (85 percent) and, by providing rice and free medical care to the poor, the longest life span (sixty-nine) in South Asia. These policies benefited all of the nation's ethnic groups.

In 1983 a section of the Tamil minority seeking independence for their northern and eastern region began a rebellion that has kept the island in a constant state of tension. The assassination of top political leaders and communal fighting became common. In 1994 Chandrika Kumaratunga (CHAN-dree-ka koo-MAHR-a-TOON-ga) (b. 1945), the University of Paris–educated daughter of Sirimavo Bandaranaike, led her left-leaning, chiefly Sinhalese party to victory and became Sri Lanka's second woman leader. She sought both military victory over the Tamils and political peace but achieved neither, narrowly escaping an assassination attempt in 2000. Nearly 60,000 people, many innocent civilians, have died in twenty years of violence between Tamils and Sinhalese. The violence split the Buddhist clergy between those advocating peace and tolerance and those demanding defeat of the Hindu Tamils, whom they view as a threat to Buddhism. Although national reconciliation has proven elusive, the Sinhalese and moderate Tamils continue to practice democratic politics.

South Asia in the Global System

Since 1945 South Asian nations have grown in geopolitical and economic stature. Although Nehru strode the world stage as a major leader of the nonaligned nations, seeking a middle ground between the United States and the USSR, his successors lacked his international influence. However, in the past decade India has become a center of advanced technology, importing high-tech and service jobs from the West, and one of the most industrialized nations outside of Europe and North America, exporting heavy machinery, steel, and autos while producing abundant consumer goods for local consumption. Some Indian employees, such as those providing telephone technical support to users of U.S.-made computers, receive training in mastering an American or Australian accent to facilitate rapport. Every year Indian universities turn out thousands of talented engineers and computer scientists who have built up homegrown industries and have also helped staff the high-tech "silicon valleys" of North America and Europe. Several Indian universities have gained international reputations for producing top-flight scientists and engineers. By the early twenty-first century experts debated whether India or China might eventually compete for world economic leadership with the United States, whose multidimensional power Indian leaders admired. Some pointed to India's large number of English-speakers, solid financial system, and vibrant democracy as advantages. However, critics argued, the nation's boom has added few jobs and to become a world power India, like China, needed to contain social tensions and find ways to better share the wealth and reduce rural poverty.

South Asian technology and ingenuity have led to scientific achievements. In 1975 the Indian government launched into orbit its first satellite, named after Aryabhata (OUR-ya-BAH-ta), a major Indian scientist and mathematician who lived over fifteen hundred years ago. In 1998 India openly tested its first nuclear bomb. But these achievements have also triggered India-Pakistan rivalries. In response to the regional arms race with India, Pakistan developed nuclear weapons. Since the late 1990s the weapons experts of many nations and international organizations have worried about Pakistan's nuclear abilities, since Islamic militants, some with possible links to global terrorist networks, have influence in Pakistan's military and play a key role in local and national politics. In 2004 a top Pakistani nuclear scientist admitted to selling nuclear secrets to other nations.

Global and regional politics have intensified Indian-Pakistani rivalries. After U.S. president George W. Bush, in the wake of the 2001 terrorist attacks on the United States, justified preemptive military attacks against potential threats and ordered U.S. forces into Afghanistan and Iraq, some Indians, adapting that justification to their own ends, wondered why India should not preemptively attack Pakistan: "If the United States can fly its bombs 10,000 miles to hit terrorist bases [in Afghanistan], why should India wait to knock out Pakistan's [military] bases?"[10] But while India-Pakistan relations have remained combustible, after 2000 Indian and Pakistani leaders promoted a thaw in relations, visiting each others' countries and giving hope that tensions might diminish. The thaw fostered cross-border visits and sports competitions.

South Asians have also made a distinctive contribution to world politics. Although maintaining traditional social patterns and cultural viewpoints, the four major South Asian nations, all democracies some or most of the time, have been led by women at various times, a striking difference from the preference for male leaders elsewhere in the world. Indeed, both Sri Lanka and Bangladesh elected two different women prime ministers. Hence, while women remain disadvantaged, they have enjoyed more high-level political power than in other nations. The political power of a few women is just part of the great complexity of this region.

SECTION SUMMARY

- India's multiparty democracy has endured despite religious and caste tensions, and the Congress Party has been consistently influential, though communist parties have often governed in the northeast and south and Hindu nationalists have gained strength since 1989.

- Despite great advances in agricultural and industrial production, India still suffers from extensive poverty, and its rapidly growing population is likely to perpetuate this problem.

- While caste distinctions have remained strong in villages, they have broken down somewhat in cities; women have advanced in education and opportunity, though they are still less educated than men; and religion continues to be a source of tension.

- Pakistan has alternated between civilian and military governments and has been slow to grant women equal rights, while Bangladesh has combated poverty in spite of great challenges and has generally accepted religious minorities, though militant Muslim groups have gained influence in recent years.

- Since it became independent, Sri Lanka has been a democracy; it elected the world's first woman prime minister, and it has nurtured a well-educated, long-lived population, but since 1983 the minority Tamils have fought for independence from majority Sinhalese.

- India has produced talented engineers and computer scientists and made advances in technology, although its nuclear weaponry has prompted Pakistan to also develop nuclear arms and thus raised the worry of nuclear weapons in the hands of Islamic terrorists.

- Though women's rights are not universal in South Asia, more South Asian women have achieved positions of great power than in other areas of the world.

Revolution, War, and Reconstruction in Indochina

What were the causes and consequences of the wars in Indochina?

From the 1940s through the 1970s, the peoples of the Southeast Asia region that the French called Indochina—Vietnam, Cambodia, and Laos—experienced the most wrenching violence as two powerful Western nations—France and the United States—attempted to roll back revolutionary nationalism. The end of World War II and the rise of the Cold War set the stage

Indochina, 1945–Present

1945	Formation of Viet Minh government in Vietnam
1946–1954	First Indochina War
1953	Independence of Laos, Cambodia
1963	Assassination of South Vietnam president Ngo Dinh Diem
1961–1975	U.S.-Vietnamese War
1964	Gulf of Tonkin incident
1968	Tet Offensive
1970	Overthrow of Prince Sihanouk in Cambodia
1975	Communist victories in Vietnam, Cambodia, Laos
1978	Vietnamese invasion of Cambodia

for two successive struggles with global implications. During the first struggle, known as the First Indochina War (1946–1954), the French attempted to maintain their colonial control of Vietnam against communist-led opposition, a conflict that eventually ended in French defeat (see Chronology: Indochina, 1945–Present). The second and more destructive war, in which the United States and its Vietnamese allies waged an ultimately unsuccessful fight against communist-led Vietnamese forces, also dragged in the peoples of neighboring Cambodia and Laos. When the fighting ended, all the societies involved had to rebuild their economies and the lives shattered by the turmoil.

Vietnamese Nationalism and the First Indochina War

For Vietnam, the first decade after World War II included an anticolonial revolution. In 1945 the Japanese army in southern Vietnam had surrendered to British forces, who moved into the major southern city, Saigon, and then prepared the ground for a French return to power. Meanwhile the Viet Minh, a communist-led anti-Japanese guerrilla force that, armed and trained partly by the United States during the war, had occupied much of rural northern and central Vietnam during the Japanese occupation, captured the capital of colonial Vietnam, the northern city of Hanoi, and in 1945, before the French could reassert their power, declared the end of French colonialism. Although it only controlled the northern part of the country, the Viet Minh–led government, headed by Ho Chi Minh, became the first non-French regime in Vietnam in over eighty years. In his address to a half-million jubilant Vietnamese who

gathered in Hanoi's main square, Ho quoted the U.S. Declaration of Independence and added: "It means: All the peoples on earth are equal from birth, all the peoples have a right to live and to be happy and free."[11] In northern Vietnam the Mandate of Heaven, an ancient concept that gave legitimacy to Vietnamese emperors, had now passed to the Viet Minh. Both French and American observers on the scene noted that the majority of Vietnamese supported the Viet Minh.

However, Vietnamese independence faced formidable roadblocks. The French, desperate to retain their empire in Southeast Asia especially because of its rubber, rice, and tungsten, quickly regrouped and reoccupied southern Vietnam. Meanwhile, the Republic of China sent its troops to disarm the remaining Japanese soldiers in northern Vietnam. This provocative move made the Vietnamese fear a permanent presence by their traditional enemy, China. Using earthy language, Ho told his followers he had to patiently negotiate with the French because it was better for the Vietnamese to sniff French manure for a while than to eat China's all their lives. The United States, influenced by Cold War thinking and an ally of both France and republican China, was alarmed at Ho Chi Minh's association with the USSR and communism. Worried about growing communist movements in Asia, the United States had shifted from supporting the Viet Minh as an anti-Japanese ally during World War II to opposing all left-wing nationalists, including Ho and the Viet Minh.

Vietnam remained tense. The French, refusing to accept Ho's government, had Vietnamese allies among anti-communist Catholics and pro-Western nationalists. Ho negotiated with the French for recognition of Vietnamese independence in the north. The French did arrange for Chinese troops to withdraw but refused to give up their claims to northern Vietnam. Ho also appealed to the U.S. president, Harry Truman, for U.S. political and economic support for Vietnam's independence but received no answer. French leaders, in control of the south, were determined to regain domination of all of Vietnam. In 1946 Ho warned a French diplomat that a war would be costly and unwinnable: "You will kill ten of my men while we will kill one of yours, but you will be the ones who will end up exhausted."[12] When the French ended peaceful negotiations, the Viet Minh had to secure their nation's independence through a brutal war with France.

During the First Indochina War from 1946 to 1954 the French attempted, with massive U.S. economic and military aid, to maintain their colonial grip. Sending in a large military force, the French pushed the Viet Minh out of the northern cities, but the brutal French tactics alienated the civilian population. In the rural areas they controlled the Viet Minh won peasant support and new recruits by transferring land to poor villagers. The French could not overcome an outgunned but determined Viet Minh with a nationalist message. As his forces became bogged down in what observers called a "quicksand war," a French general complained that fighting the Viet Minh was "like ridding a dog of its fleas. We can pick them, drown them, and poison them, but they will be back in a few days."[13] After a major military defeat in 1954, when Viet Minh forces, still led by Ho, overwhelmed a key French base in the mountains and took thousands of French prisoners, the French abandoned their efforts and went home.

Two Vietnams

The peace agreements negotiated at a conference in Geneva, Switzerland, in 1954 divided the country into two Vietnams. But while northern and southern Vietnamese spoke different dialects and often had different customs, few Vietnamese wanted separate nations. The agreements left the Viet Minh in control of North Vietnam and provided that elections be held in 1956 to determine whether the South Vietnamese wanted to join with the North in a unified country. Ignoring the Geneva agreements, which it had not signed, the United States quickly filled the political vacuum left by the French departure and helped install Ngo Dinh Diem (no dinh dee-EM) (1901–1963), an anti-communist who had been a longtime resident in the United States, as president of South Vietnam. With U.S. support Diem refused to hold reunification elections. U.S. president Dwight Eisenhower later admitted that the elections had to be prevented since Ho would have won 80 percent of the vote in a free election throughout the country. Like their American allies, some Vietnamese opposed communist ideology.

Ho's North Vietnam and Diem's South Vietnam differed dramatically. Ho's government built a disciplined state that addressed the inequalities of the colonial period. Land reform redistributed land from powerful landlords to poor peasants. However, the government's authoritarian style and socialist policies prompted nearly a million anti-communist North Vietnamese, mostly middle class or members of the Catholic minority, to move to South Vietnam, where President Diem, an ardent Catholic from a wealthy, landholding mandarin family, established a government based in Saigon. The United States poured economic and military aid into South Vietnam and, to stabilize Diem's increasingly unpopular regime, sent military advisers to aid the South Vietnamese army. The rigid Diem alienated peasants by opposing most land reform.

Soon the political dynamics changed. By the late 1950s, dissidents in South Vietnam, including former Viet Minh soldiers, had formed a communist-led revolutionary movement, the **National Liberation Front** (NLF), often known as the Viet Cong. Armed by North Vietnam, the insurgency in South Vietnam grew and engulfed many districts, and the Diem government responded with repression, murdering or imprisoning thousands of suspected rebels and other opponents. Adding to the anti-Diem mood, Buddhists resented the government's pro-Catholic policies, and nationalists generally viewed Diem as an American puppet. Meanwhile, the NLF spread their influence in rural areas, often assassinating government officials.

By the early 1960s the NLF, now aided by North Vietnamese troops, controlled large sections of South Vietnam, and thousands more American troops, still called military advisers, assisted Diem's army, becoming more involved in combat. In 1963 U.S. leaders, judging Diem ineffective, sanctioned his overthrow by his own military officers, who killed him. As the situation deteriorated after Diem's death, U.S. concerns about a possible Communist sweep through Southeast Asia provided the rationale for U.S. action. The stage was set for what Americans called the Vietnam War (1963–1975) and what many Vietnamese termed the American War.

The American-Vietnamese War

By the mid-1960s the United States had escalated the conflict into a full-scale military commitment (see Map 31.2). U.S. president Lyndon Johnson's (g. 1963–1969) excuse was an alleged North Vietnamese attack on a U.S. ship in the Gulf of Tonkin in 1964, which probably never occurred. When Johnson said in 1965, "I want to leave the footprints of America there [Indochina]. We can turn the Mekong into [an economically developed] Tennessee Valley,"[14] he was reflecting a long-time American sense of mission to change the world and spread American values, especially democracy and capitalism. However, Johnson and other U.S. leaders, civilian and military, had little understanding of the nationalism and spirited opposition to foreign occupation that had shaped Vietnam, a country with many historical reasons for mistrusting foreign powers—whether Chinese, French, or American—on "civilizing" missions.

Soon the war intensified, drawing in a larger U.S. presence and more North Vietnamese forces and expanding the violence across the country. In 1965 Johnson ordered an air war against targets in both South and North Vietnam and a massive intervention of ground troops, peaking at 550,000 Americans by 1968. Meanwhile, Diem was succeeded by a series of military regimes that never achieved credibility with the majority of South Vietnamese. Military supplies and thousands of North Vietnamese troops regularly moved south through the mountains of eastern Laos and Cambodia, along what came to be known as the Ho Chi Minh Trail.

Despite their technological superiority, U.S. forces struggled to find effective strategies to overcome advantages enjoyed by the communists. U.S. policies often ignored South Vietnamese leaders and the consequences of U.S. military actions for the people. Since the South Vietnamese army, largely conscripts, suffered from low morale and high desertion and casualty rates, Americans did much of the fighting. U.S. strategists viewed Vietnam chiefly in military terms: they measured success by counting the enemy dead and creating free fire zones, areas where civilians were ordered to evacuate so that U.S. forces could attack any people remaining as the enemy. Such policies made it hard for the United States to win the "hearts and minds" of the South Vietnamese and diminish widespread local support for the NLF. Vietnam also became the most heavily bombed nation in history, as the United States dropped on that country nearly triple the total bomb tonnage

National Liberation Front (NLF) Often known as the Viet Cong, a communist-led revolutionary movement in South Vietnam that resisted American intervention in the American-Vietnamese War.

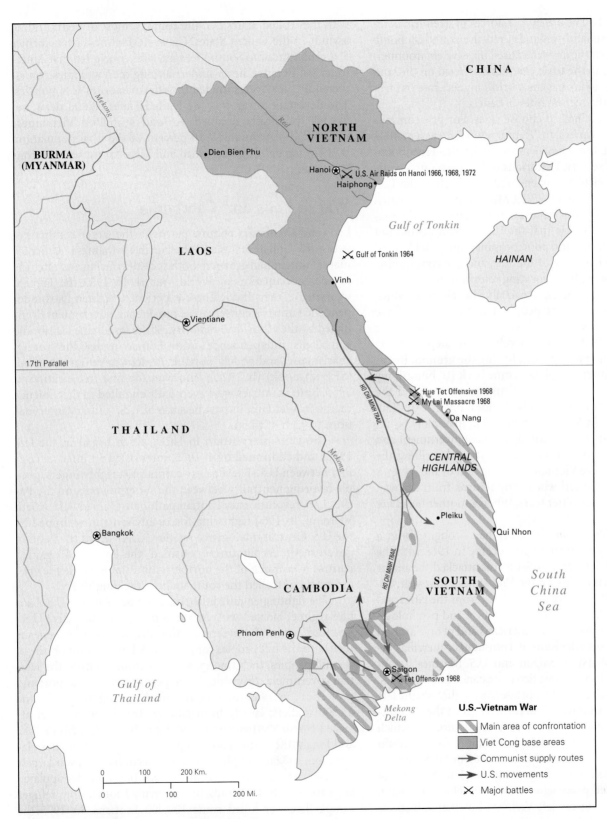

CHINA

NORTH VIETNAM

Dien Bien Phu

Hanoi ⊛ ✕ U.S. Air Raids on Hanoi 1966, 1968, 1972
Haiphong

BURMA (MYANMAR)

LAOS

Gulf of Tonkin

✕ Gulf of Tonkin 1964

Vinh

HAINAN

⊛ Vientiane

17th Parallel

HO CHI MINH TRAIL

✕ Hue Tet Offensive 1968
✕ My Lai Massacre 1968
• Da Nang

THAILAND

Mekong

CENTRAL HIGHLANDS

• Pleiku

• Qui Nhon

⊛ Bangkok

HO CHI MINH TRAIL

CAMBODIA

SOUTH VIETNAM

South China Sea

Phnom Penh ⊛

Gulf of Thailand

⊛ Saigon
✕ Tet Offensive 1968

Mekong Delta

U.S.–Vietnam War

▨ Main area of confrontation
▓ Viet Cong base areas
→ Communist supply routes
➜ U.S. movements
✕ Major battles

0   100   200 Km.
0   100   200 Mi.

Map 31.2   The U.S.-Vietnamese War

From the early 1960s until 1975 South Vietnam, aided by thousands of U.S. troops and air power, resisted a communist-led insurgency aided by North Vietnam, which sent troops and supplies down the Ho Chi Minh Trail through Laos and Cambodia.

used in World War II. The use by U.S. forces of chemical defoliants to clear forests and wetlands, and the countless bomb craters resulting from the air war, caused massive environmental damage. Thanks to the toxic chemicals sprayed on the land and water, Vietnam today has the world's highest rate of birth defects and one of the highest rates of cancer.

South Vietnamese had to choose sides. For pro-communist Vietnamese, the American-Vietnamese War was a continuation of the First Indochina War to expel the French and rebuild a damaged society. Historians of Vietnam often argue that a communist victory was ensured, even before the U.S. military intervention, when the Viet Minh humbled the hated French colonizers and thus gained a popularity with the majority of Vietnamese people that the United States could not overcome. Furthermore, for poor peasants, inequitable land ownership was the key issue of the war, and the communists gained peasant support by advocating reform to help landless peasants. Some U.S. policies, especially the air war, which killed thousands of innocent people, backfired. One of the thousands of women who fought for the NLF reported: "The first days I felt ill at ease—marching in step, lobbing grenades, taking aim with my rifle, hitting the ground. But as soon as I saw the American planes come back [to bomb], my timidity left me."[15] Other South Vietnamese supported the pro-U.S. government or rejected both sides. Pham Duy (fam do-ee), a folksinger in South Vietnam who, like many South Vietnamese, disliked both the corrupt Saigon government and the often ruthless communists, wrote a song describing the war's impact on average Vietnamese: "The rain of the leaves is the tears of joy, Of the girl whose boy returns from the war. The rain on the leaves is bitter tears, When a mother hears her son is no more."[16]

By 1967 the U.S. military strategy had brought about a military stalemate, but a turning point came in 1968 with the **Tet Offensive**, in which communist forces attacked the major South Vietnamese cities during the Vietnamese new year. Although the communists were pushed back from the cities and suffered high casualties, Tet proved a political and psychological setback for the United States. Americans and people around the world watched on television as communist guerrillas attacked the U.S. embassy in Saigon and U.S. Marines fought their way, block by block, against fierce resistance into key cities.

Tet caused Americans to reappraise the conflict. By the late 1960s a majority of Americans had turned against the commitment to a seemingly endless war, a quagmire in which American soldiers were being killed or injured for uncertain goals. Even the death of Ho Chi Minh in 1969 did not alter the situation. The United States began a gradual withdrawal of troops and negotiated peace agreements with North Vietnam. In 1973 U.S. ground forces left Vietnam but maintained air support. By 1975 the NLF and North Vietnam had defeated the South Vietnamese forces and reunified the country under communist leadership. As communist forces marched into Saigon, more than 70,000 South Vietnamese who had worked with the United States fled the country, most of them finding asylum in the United States. General Maxwell Taylor, former U.S. ambassador to South Vietnam, later concluded that Americans lost because, never understanding the Vietnamese on either side, they overestimated the effectiveness of U.S. policies. The devastating war cost the United States 58,000 dead and 519,000 physically disabled. Around 4 million Vietnamese were killed or wounded—10 percent of the total population. By 1975 the fighting had ended and Vietnam turned to reconstruction.

War in Laos and Cambodia

Laos and Cambodia became pawns in the larger conflict between the United States and the North Vietnamese. Anticolonial sentiment had grown in both societies during and after the Japanese occupation of World War II. In 1953 the French, wearying of their Indochinese experience, granted Laos independence under a conservative, pro-French government dominated by the ethnic Lao majority. At the same time Cambodia gained its independence from France under the young, charismatic, and widely popular Prince Norodom Sihanouk (SEE-uh-nook) (b. 1922), who won the first free election in 1955. Both countries were eventually engulfed in the violence raging in Vietnam, in part because of U.S. military interventions in each of them.

The U.S. intervention in Laos, which began in the late 1950s and continued until 1975, intensified an internal conflict between U.S.-backed anti-communist rightwingers, people favoring neutrality between the superpowers, and the **Pathet Lao**, revolutionary Laotian nationalists allied with North Vietnam. In 1960 rightwing forces advised and equipped by the U.S. Central Intelligence Agency (CIA) seized the Laotian government. As fighting intensified, the Pathet Lao gained control over much of the northern mountains, while the government controlled the south and the Mekong Valley.

The fighting engulfed the entire nation. The pro-U.S. Laotian regime, bloated with corruption, had an ineffective U.S.-financed army. To overcome this disadvantage, Americans turned to the hill peoples for recruits. A large faction of one of the hill peoples, the Hmong, sought autonomy from the Laotian government. Promising them permanent U.S. support and protection, in 1960 the CIA recruited a secret army of some 45,000 soldiers, largely from among Hmong people, that attacked North Vietnamese forces along the Ho Chi Minh Trail and fought the Pathet Lao. Ten percent of the Hmong population, some 30,000 people, died during a conflict that was largely unknown to the American public. U.S. bombing depopulated large areas of the highlands, forcing many Laotians into refugee camps. The war killed some 100,000 Laotians. In 1975 the Pathet Lao took full control of a war-weary Laos. Thousands of anti-communist Laotians fled into Thailand, many later moving to the United States and other Western nations.

Tet Offensive Communist attacks on major South Vietnamese cities in 1968, a turning point in the American-Vietnamese War.

Pathet Lao Revolutionary Laotian nationalists allied with North Vietnam during the American-Vietnamese War.

Like Laos, Cambodia also became part of the Indochina conflict. Its first president, the multitalented Prince Sihanouk, ruled as a benevolent autocrat while also writing sentimental popular songs, playing the saxophone, directing films, and publicizing his political views in foreign newspapers. Sihanouk diplomatically maintained Cambodian independence and peace. But during the 1960s both the Vietnamese communists, whose forces roamed the border area, and the United States, whose war planes bombed communist positions in Cambodian territory, violated Cambodian neutrality. Sihanouk faced other problems as well. The **Khmer Rouge** (kmahr roozh) ("Red Khmers"), a communist insurgent group seeking to overthrow the government and led by alienated intellectuals educated in French universities, built a small support base of impoverished peasants. In addition, although Sihanouk remained popular among the majority of peasants, military officers and big businessmen resented his dictatorial rule and desired to share in the U.S. money and arms flowing into neighboring South Vietnam, Laos, and Thailand.

In 1970 Sihanouk was overthrown by U.S.-backed generals and civilians, beginning a tragic era in Cambodian history. With Sihanouk in exile, U.S. and South Vietnamese forces soon invaded eastern Cambodia in search of Vietnamese communist bases, and the resulting instability created an opening for the Khmer Rouge to recruit mass support. The pro-U.S. government lacked legitimacy and became increasingly dependent on U.S. aid for virtually all supplies, and the ineffective Cambodian army suffered from corruption and low morale. Meanwhile, to attack the Khmer Rouge, U.S. planes launched an intensive, terrifying air assault through the heart of Cambodia's agricultural area, where most of the population lived. The bombing killed thousands of innocent civilians. Rice production declined by almost half, raising the possibility of massive starvation. Amid the destruction, the Khmer Rouge rapidly enlarged its forces, recruiting from among the displaced and shell-shocked peasantry. From 1970 through 1975 between 750,000 and 1 million Cambodians, mostly civilians, perished from the conflict between the Khmer Rouge, who were brutal toward their enemies, and the U.S.-backed government. In 1975 the Khmer Rouge seized the capital, Phnom Penh.

Conflict and Reconstruction in Indochina

After years of war and destruction, Vietnam, Laos, and Cambodia began to rebuild and deal with lingering tensions resulting from the bitter divisions. The challenge was daunting. In the largest nation, Vietnam, socialist policies failed to revitalize the economy, and the reunification of North and South Vietnam proved harsh. Because of mismanaged political and economic policies, natural disasters, a long U.S. economic embargo, and the devastation of the war, between 1978 and 1985 half a million refugees, known as "boat people," risked

their lives to escape Vietnam in rickety boats, becoming easy targets for pirates. After spending months or years in crowded refugee camps in Southeast Asia, most of the refugees were resettled in North America, Australia, or France.

In the 1980s the Vietnamese government recognized its failures and introduced market-oriented reforms similar to those in China favoring private enterprise and foreign investment. These reforms increased productivity, fostered some prosperity in the cities, and ended the refugee flow. Emphasis on education more than doubled the 1945 literacy rates to 85 percent of adults. But the shift from rigid socialism also widened economic inequality, leaving most farmers living just above the poverty line. Vietnamese debated the appropriate balance between socialist and free market policies to resolve the rural problems. Politically, Vietnam, like China, remained an authoritarian one-party state, with little democracy, but restrictions on cultural expression loosened. Several former soldiers became rock or disco stars, and many writers addressed contemporary problems and the war's legacy in fiction. For example, "The General Retires," a short story by a former North Vietnamese soldier, caused a sensation by depicting the despair of an old soldier contemplating the emptiness of the new society.

After victory in the long struggle to end foreign domination, the communists expanded ties to the West and the world economy. By the late 1990s, the United States and Vietnam had resumed diplomatic relations, and U.S. president Bill Clinton lifted the U.S. economic embargo. Bustling Saigon, now renamed Ho Chi Minh City, has enjoyed especially dynamic economic growth and prosperity. Consumers in the United States now buy shrimp and underwear imported from Vietnam while many Americans, including former soldiers and Vietnamese refugees, visit Vietnam. Hundreds of American veterans operate businesses or social service agencies in Vietnam, sometimes in partnership with former communist soldiers. Still, the ruling communists have to satisfy the expectations of the 80 million Vietnamese struggling to overcome the devastation wrought by decades of war.

Like the Vietnamese, Laotians also needed to deal with the divisions and destruction caused by the war. Many Laotians fled into exile to escape retribution or hard times, among them 300,000 Hmongs who settled in the United States. Since the 1980s Laotian leaders have sought warmer relations with neighboring Thailand and China as well as with the United States, but these relations have not fostered a more open society or energized the economy. Rigid communists still dominate the one-party state. While several cities and districts have vibrant economies, attracting Western tourists, most Laotians remain poor. Looking across the Mekong at the busy freeways, neon lights, and high-rise buildings on the Thailand side, Laotians often suspect that capitalist, democratic Thailand offers a more successful model of development.

Cambodia has faced a far more difficult challenge than Vietnam and Laos, because war was followed by fierce repression. Agriculture had been badly disrupted by war, raising the specter of widespread starvation. When the communist Khmer Rouge, hardened by years of brutal war, achieved power in 1975, they

Khmer Rouge ("Red Khmers") A communist insurgent group seeking to overthrow the government in Cambodia during the 1960s and 1970s.

Honoring Ho Chi Minh These schoolgirls, dressed in traditional clothing and parading before Ho Chi Minh's mausoleum in Hanoi, are part of an annual festival to honor the leading figure of Vietnamese communism. (AP/Wide World Photos)

Khmer Rouge to the Thailand border. The Vietnamese invasion liberated the Cambodian people from tyranny and installed a less brutal communist government. But military conflict continued for years as a Khmer Rouge–dominated resistance, subsidized chiefly by China and the United States, which both wanted to weaken Vietnam by forcing it to spend money in Cambodia, controlled some sections of the country. Cambodia proved to be for Vietnam what Vietnam had been for the United States, an endless sinkhole of conflict that drained scarce wealth and complicated Vietnam's relations with the West.

In the early 1990s a coalition government was formed under United Nations sponsorship that brought about change. The Khmer Rouge, which refused to take part, splintered and collapsed as a movement. While the resulting peace was welcomed by all, the government remained repressive and corrupt. The ruling party tolerated some opposition but controlled the voting. Sihanouk returned from exile to become king but had little power and served largely as a symbol of Cambodia's link to its past. Life for many Cambodians remained grim as they faced everything from the high price of fuel to poor education, problems that have spurred some people to organize in support of more democracy and attention to social problems. Nevertheless, the new government has transformed Cambodia, while still haunted by past horrors, from a traumatized to a functioning society, kept afloat largely by Western tourism and aid.

turned on the urban population with a fury, driving everyone into the rural areas to farm. The Khmer Rouge's radical vision of a propertyless, classless peasant society, combined with their violence against those believed to dissent or resist, led to the flight of thousands of refugees into neighboring countries and what survivors called the "killing fields": the Khmer Rouge executed thousands of victims in death camps and shot or starved many others, including both common people such as peasants and taxi drivers and Westernized and educated people such as doctors and artists. Ultimately the Khmer Rouge and their brutal leader, Pol Pot (1925–1998), in their attempt to create a new communist society, were responsible for the death of 1 to 2 million Cambodians. Perhaps 500,000 were executed and the rest died from illness, hunger, and overwork, sparking comparisons with Nazi Germany.

The situation changed in 1978, leading to a new government. The Vietnamese, alarmed at Khmer Rouge territorial claims and the murder of thousands of ethnic Vietnamese in Cambodia, allied with an exile army of disaffected former Khmer Rouge, invaded Cambodia, and rapidly pushed the

SECTION SUMMARY

■ After World War II, the communist Viet Minh, led by Ho Chi Minh, took partial control of Vietnam and declared independence, but the U.S.-supported French fought back in the First Indochina War, which ended in frustration for the French.

■ Instead of allowing an election to determine the future of South Vietnam, the United States installed Diem as president but he was opposed by the communist National Liberation Front, setting the stage for the Vietnam War.

■ Using a questionable attack as a pretext, the United States went to war to rid Vietnam of communism, but despite vastly superior resources, the United States and its allies in South Vietnam could not triumph over the communists, who gained control of Vietnam two years after the U.S. pulled out its ground forces.

■ In Laos the United States recruited Hmong hill people to fight the Pathet Lao revolutionaries, who took control of the country in 1975, while in Cambodia the United States bombed areas occupied by North Vietnamese and supported a weak, dependent government, which was overthrown in 1975 by the Khmer Rouge.

■ Vietnam struggled after the war, but in the 1980s it opened up its economy and by the 1990s had reestablished ties with the rest of the world, including the United States.

■ Many Laotians fled into exile, while the communist-dominated government has opened somewhat to the world economy, and Cambodia endured vicious repression under the Khmer Rouge, who continued to wreak havoc even after a Vietnamese invasion pushed them out of power.

CHRONOLOGY

Non-Communist Southeast Asia, 1945–Present

1945–1950	Indonesian Revolution
1948	Independence of Burma
1963	Formation of Malaysia
1965	Secession of Singapore from Malaysia
1965–1966	Turmoil in Indonesia
1966–1998	New Order in Indonesia
1997	Economic crisis in Southeast Asia

New Nations in Southeast Asia

How did decolonization shape the new Southeast Asian nations?

In addition to the Indochinese countries, the nationalist thrust for independence from colonialism produced other new nations in Southeast Asia in the aftermath of World War II (see Map 31.3). But the euphoria of independence proved short-lived, and the building of states capable of improving the lives of their people had only just begun. Indonesia, the Philippines, Burma, and the other new nations, while often facing violent unrest, avoided the destructive warfare rocking Indochina but also had to overcome economic underdevelopment, promote national unity in ethnically divided societies, and deal with opposition to the new ruling groups. The years between 1945 and 1975 were marked by economic progress, but also by conflict and dictatorships. The leaders also had to forge new relationships with the former colonial powers and the new superpowers of a Cold War world—the United States and the Soviet Union—as well as with nearby China.

Indonesia: The Quest for Freedom and Unity

Indonesian independence came through struggle. The violent resistance to Dutch colonialism of the late 1940s, known as the Indonesian Revolution, was a bitter conflict in which the Dutch used massive violence to suppress the Indonesian nationalists, who fought back. In a short story about the brutal battle to control the east Javanese city of Surabaya, a nationalist writer noted that, for the revolutionary soldiers, "everything blurred: the future and their heart-breaking struggle. They

only knew that they had to murder to drive out the enemy and stop him trampling their liberated land. They killed [the Dutch soldiers] with great determination, spirit and hunger."[17] The United States, fearing regional instability, pressured the Dutch to grant independence in 1950 (see Chronology: Non-communist Southeast Asia, 1945–Present).

Indonesia still faced the challenge of fostering a unified nation. Given the diversity of islands, peoples, and cultures, Indonesian leaders became obsessed with creating national unity and identity. Their national slogan, however, "unity in diversity," expressed more a goal than a solid reality. During the 1950s and early 1960s Indonesia was led by the charismatic but increasingly authoritarian president Sukarno (soo-KAHR-no) (1902–1970), the son of a Javanese aristocrat and a Balinese mother and an inspirational nationalist. A spell-binding orator who was able to rally popular support and bring different factions together, Sukarno worked to create national solidarity and unite a huge nation in which villagers on remote islands and cosmopolitan city dwellers on Java knew little about each other.

Despite his efforts, however, Sukarno proved unable to maintain stability. The multiparty parliamentary system he headed in the 1950s became divisive. Regionalism grew as outer islanders resented domination by the Javanese, who constituted over half of Indonesia's population and, many outer islanders believed, were favored by Sukarno. Sukarno's nationalistic but poorly implemented economic policies contributed to a severe economic crisis by the early 1960s and deepened divisions between communist, Islamic, and military forces. A pro-communist Javanese novelist described the economic failures of the Sukarno years: "Jakarta [the capital city] reveals a grandiose display with no relationship to reality. Great plans, enormous immorality. [There are] no screws, no nuts, no bolts, no valves, and no washers for the machinery we do have."[18]

By 1965 Indonesia had become a country of explosive social and political pressures and was experiencing its greatest crisis as an independent nation. After a failed attempt by a small military faction with communist sympathies to seize power, a group of discontented generals arrested Sukarno, took power,

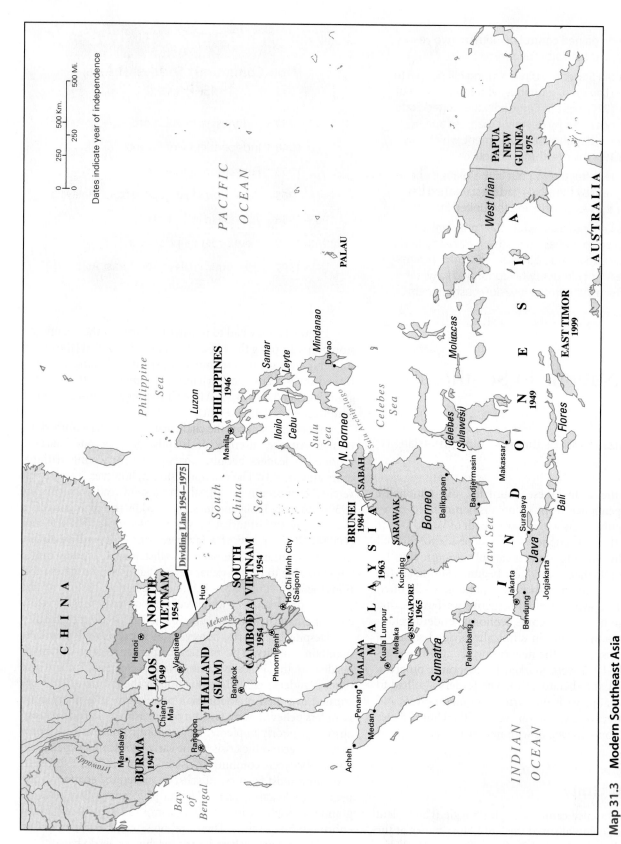

Map 31.3 Modern Southeast Asia

Indonesia, covering thousands of islands, is the largest, most populous Southeast Asian nation. Southeast Asia also includes four other island nations (including the Philippines and Singapore), five nations on the mainland, and Malaysia, which sprawls from the Malay Peninsula to northern Borneo.

and launched a brutal campaign to eliminate all leftists, especially those affiliated with the large communist Party, which had built up its influence among poor peasants in Java. The resulting bloodbath, led by the army and Muslim groups, killed perhaps half a million Indonesians, including communists and members of the large, unpopular Chinese minority. Most communist leaders were killed or arrested; thousands of leftists were held in remote prison camps for years. Sukarno died in disgrace in 1970.

Making the Philippine and Malaysian Nations

The Philippines and Malaysia both became independent but troubled nations. In the sixteenth century the Philippines had been one of the first Southeast Asian societies to be colonized by a Western country, Spain. At the end of the nineteenth century, the United States replaced Spanish rule with its own. In the nineteenth century the British had colonized Malaya, on the Malay Peninsula, and also dominated the northern Borneo territories of Sabah (North Borneo) and Sarawak. The Americans and British both exploited their colonies' natural resources—cash crops and minerals—for export. However, the two ruling powers also treated the colonized people less harshly than the French did the Vietnamese or the Dutch the Indonesians. As a result, anti-Western nationalism in the Philippines, Malaysia, and British Borneo before World War II was weaker and less violent than in Vietnam and Indonesia.

The Philippines achieved independence from the United States on July 4, 1946, though the two countries remained bound by close political and economic links. The new nation soon faced problems sustaining democracy. A small group of landowners, industrialists, and businessmen who had prospered under U.S. rule manipulated elected governments to preserve their political and economic power and to protect U.S. economic interests. Free elections involved so much violence, bribery, and fraud that disillusioned Filipinos spoke of them as decided by "guns, goons, and gold."

Furthermore, nationalists often believed that continuing U.S. influence hindered the creation of a truly independent Filipino identity and culture. Several major U.S. military bases near Manila symbolized this influence, and the popular U.S. films, television programs, music, comics, and books helped to spread it. A prominent Filipina scholar wrote that her people "sing of White Christmases and of Manhattan. Their stereos reverberate with the American Top 40."[19] Outside influences—first Spanish and then American—on Filipino culture were often superficial, but Filipinos have struggled to create a clear national identity out of the diverse mosaic of local languages and regions.

Economic inequality and social divisions have fueled conflict. A Filipino poet portrayed the gap between the rich and poor: "[For the affluent] there's pleasure and distraction, fiesta and dancing, night-long, day-long; who dares whisper that thousands have no roofs above their heads; that hunger stalks the town."[20] The Communist-led Huk Rebellion from 1948 to 1954 capitalized on discontent among the rural poor. Only heavy U.S. assistance to the government suppressed the rebellion. In the 1970s the communist New Peoples Army (NPA) controlled many rural districts. Like the Huks, the NPA's promise of radical social and economic change attracted support from rural tenant farmers and urban slum dwellers. Religious differences have also led to conflict. While most Filipinos became Christian in Spanish times, the southern islands have large Muslim populations, who have often resented political domination by and favoritism toward Christians. As a result, several Muslim groups have taken up arms to fight for autonomy. In 1972 President Ferdinand Marcos (1917–1989) used the restoration of law and order as an excuse to suspend democracy, and from 1972 until 1986 he ruled as a dictator, resolving few problems.

Compared with the Philippines, governments proved more stable in Malaya after independence. After World War II the British sought to dampen political unrest in Malaya as communist-led insurgents kept the colony on edge for a decade. In 1957, with the insurgency crushed, Malaya became independent as a federation of states under a government led by the main Malay party, **UMNO** (United Malays National Organization). However, the predominantly Chinese city-state of Singapore, a major trading center and military base, remained outside the federation as a British colony. In Malaya the majority ethnic group, the Malays, nearly all Muslim, dominated politics, but the Chinese, a third of the population, were granted liberal citizenship rights and maintained strong economic power. British leaders, seeing their colonial role in Singapore as well as in two northern Borneo states they controlled, Sabah and Sarawak, as burdensome, suggested joining them with Malaya in a larger federation, to be called Malaysia. This new, geographically divided Malaysia was formed in 1963.

In the years that followed Malaysia struggled to create national unity out of deep regional and ethnic divisions. Singapore withdrew from Malaysia in 1965 and became an independent nation. Given the need to reduce political tensions, sustain rapid economic growth, and preserve stability, the leaders of the key ethnic groups in Malaya—Malays, Chinese, and Indians—cooperated through political parties that allied in an UMNO-dominated ruling coalition, but below the surface ethnic tensions simmered. Street fighting between Chinese and Malays following the heated 1969 election led to a nationwide state of emergency. After 1970 Malay-dominated governments pursued policies designed to reshape Malaysia's society and economy.

Diversity and Dictatorship in Thailand and Burma

Thailand and Burma also struggled to create national unity and stability. Although historical rivals, the two countries have shared certain patterns. The majority ethnic groups, the Thais and the Burmans, are both Theravada Buddhists who assert authority over a variety of ethnic minorities, including various hill tribes, Muslim peoples, and immigrant trading communities,

UMNO (United Malays National Organization) The main Malay political party in Malaysia.

largely Chinese and Indians. Both countries also have experienced insurgencies by disaffected ethnic, religious, or political factions. However, while Burma had been an often restless British colony since the mid-1800s, Thailand (once known as Siam) was the only major Southeast Asian country to avoid colonization. As a result, Thais have had more control over their government, economy, and culture than other Southeast Asians have enjoyed.

In Thailand, leaders sought to build a national culture based on Thai cultural values, including reverence for Buddhism and the monarchy, which had little formal power but symbolized the nation. Thai culture promotes respect for those in authority and values social harmony. However, this conservatism has also fostered authoritarian governments and bureaucratic inertia. Ethnic and religious diversity has also posed political problems. Various communist and Islamic insurgent groups operated during the 1960s and 1970s in ethnic minority regions. Partly because of this unrest, Thailand's political history after 1945 was characterized by long periods of military rule, often corrupt and oppressive, followed by short-lived democratically elected or semidemocratic governments.

Not until the 1970s would a true mass politics develop in Thailand, as opposition movements challenged the long-entrenched military regime. Opposition gained sway in part from Thais' resentment of the United States, which supported the military regime and had military bases and some 50,000 troops in the country. The presence of free-spending American soldiers created a false prosperity while also posing a challenge to Buddhist morality. Staunch Buddhists were outraged by the sleazy bars, gaudy nightclubs, and brothels that often exploited poor Thai women and that served the Americans but also attracted eager Thai men.

In 1973 antigovernment feelings boiled over and the military regime was overthrown following student-led mass demonstrations that involved several hundred thousand people. The military strongman was forced to flee the country, having lost public support after his troops arrested protest leaders and killed or wounded over a thousand demonstrators. The collapse of military rule opened a brief era of political liberalization. For the first time in Thai history, democracy and debate flourished. The civilian government tolerated these activities, yet it proved fragile and unable to resolve major problems. Meanwhile, rightwing military officers and bureaucrats became alarmed at challenges to their power and privileges, and Thai society became increasingly polarized between liberals and conservatives. Finally, in 1976, bloody clashes between leftist students and rightwing youth gangs led to a military coup and martial law, which resulted in the killing or wounding of hundreds and the arrest of thousands of students and their supporters. The return of military power reestablished order, but the massacres discredited the military.

To the west of Thailand, Burma emerged from the Japanese occupation devastated, with whole cities blasted into rubble by Allied bombing. After the war the British returned to reestablish their colonial control. However, facing a well-armed Burmese nationalist army and weary of conflict, they elected to negotiate independence with the charismatic nationalist leader Aung San (1915–1947). In 1948 the British left Burma, but newly elected Prime Minister Aung San was assassinated by a political rival. He was replaced by his longtime colleague, U Nu (1907–1995), an idealistic Buddhist who, like Aung San, supported democracy. Soon key ethnic minorities, fearful of domination by the majority Burmans, each declared their secession from Burma and organized armies. For the next four decades the central government rarely controlled more than half the nation's territory as the ethnic armies and communist insurgents fought each other and the Burmese army. To fund their armies the insurgents often relied on revenues from growing and exporting opium.

In 1962 the army deposed U Nu and seized control. Skeptical of democracy for a fragmented nation, military rulers suspended civil liberties, imposed censorship, and devoted most government revenue to the military. The military took over industries, banks, and commerce, and discouraged foreign investment. However, by the 1980s, as a result of the military keeping a tight control of the government and economy, economic stagnation and political repression had fostered dissent and the various secession movements continued, only to be largely suppressed in the 1990s.

SECTION SUMMARY

■ After a difficult fight for independence from the Dutch, Indonesia's wildly diverse population struggled to attain unity under Sukarno, but different groups became more divided and a group of generals cracked down harshly on leftists and removed Sukarno from power.

■ After attaining independence, the Philippines remained strongly influenced by the United States and struggled with economic inequality and a Muslim insurgency, while Malaysia experienced intermittent tensions between the politically dominant Malays and the economically strong Chinese.

■ Thailand alternated between long periods of military rule and short periods of democratic or semidemocratic rule, while Burma endured decades of factional fighting and, since 1962, brutal military domination.

 # Tigers, Politics, and Changing Southeast Asian Societies

What role do the Southeast Asian nations play in the global system?

Southeast Asia changed dramatically after 1975, mixing influences from the past and from the wider world. The fast pace of change has reshaped societies and cultures in both cities and villages. Some nations have developed economically. Indonesia, Malaysia, Singapore, and Thailand, enjoying lively market economies geared to world commerce, have gained reputations as "tigers" because of their economic dynamism. At the same time, governments play a major role in stimulating economies and often have become authoritarian in an effort to ensure social stability.

The Resurgence of Southeast Asia

After the mid-1970s a shift of economic direction allowed several Southeast Asians to develop and play a greater role in the world economy. On the eve of this shift, in 1976, Indonesia, Burma, and Thailand were under military rule, a dictator governed in the Philippines, and only Malaysia and Singapore had at least partial democracies. Few of the countries had achieved impressive economic growth. But in the years to follow, and especially after 1980, the pace of change accelerated in every area of life. Leaders, inspired by the example of Japan's industrialization in the late nineteenth century and encouraging their people to "Look East," mixed capitalism and activist government to spur economic growth and industrialization. Local entrepreneurs of Chinese ancestry provided much of the initiative and capital for economic expansion. By the 1990s experts talked about a vibrant Pacific Rim that included the "tiger" nations as well as Japan, China, Taiwan, and South Korea (see Chapter 27). Some forecast a Pacific Century in which these nations would lead the world economically and increase their political strength.

Economic growth contributed to social and political change. Migrants crowding into cities brushed elbows with other peoples, encouraging cultural mixing. More schools were built, helping foster larger middle classes that sought more political influence. Yet, while nations were slowly being built in both institutions and people's minds, governments often abused their powers, squashing dissent and repressing personal liberties. There were also drawbacks to economic growth: industrial activity and the expansion of agriculture, mining, and logging caused widespread environmental destruction.

To promote economic growth and political stability, Southeast Asian countries began cooperating as never before. Founded in 1967 by Malaysia, Indonesia, Thailand, Singapore, and the Philippines, **ASEAN** (Association of Southeast Asian Nations) was a regional economic and political organization aimed at fostering economic exchange among the non-Communist Southeast Asian nations and coordinating opposition to Communist Vietnam. However, ASEAN's priorities shifted after the end of the wars in Indochina in 1975. As Vietnam, Cambodia, Laos, Burma, and the tiny, oil-rich state of Brunei, on Borneo, became members, ASEAN emerged as the world's fourth largest trading bloc. It also provided a forum for the various nations to work out their differences and deal with the wider world. In the early twenty-first century ASEAN, wanting regional stability, cultivated closer relations with the dominant East Asian nations, China and Japan.

Still, challenges demanded solutions. By 2000 there were some 550 million Southeast Asians, a huge increase over the 20 to 25 million four centuries earlier. Population growth outstripped economic growth, placing a greater burden on limited resources such as food and water, especially in the Philippines, Indonesia, and Vietnam. The impact of these conditions sometimes resulted in riots or even full-blown insurgencies. But despite occasional eruptions of violence and political upheavals, the destructive wars of the earlier years were not repeated. In some cases, dictatorships were eventually replaced by more open regimes.

In 1997 most Southeast Asian countries faced a severe economic crisis, part of a broader collapse among Asian and world economies. The widespread dislocations called into question the prospect of a forthcoming Pacific Century. The reasons for the troubles included poorly regulated banking systems, overconfident investments, and government favoritism toward well-placed business interests. The dislocations hit all social classes. By the early 2000s, however, as the crisis eventually bottomed out, several countries began to put their economies back on a rapid growth track.

Indonesia: New Order and Islamic Society

The colossus of Southeast Asia, Indonesia, with a rapidly growing population of 230 million that includes more than seven hundred ethnic groups, struggled to preserve political stability while developing economically. Between 1966 and 1998 the government, known as the **New Order**, headed by general-turned-president Suharto (b. 1921), a Javanese former soldier first in the Dutch colonial and then in the nationalist army, mixed military and civilian leadership to maintain law and order. For instance, Suharto used force to repress regional opposition to his Javanese-dominated central government, as in East Timor, a small, former Portuguese colony where the mostly Christian population sought independence, and in north Sumatra, where the fiercely Islamic Achehnese have sought independence for decades. However, although it limited political opposition, the New Order improved Indonesia's economic position and encouraged the rise of an educated urban middle class and a vibrant popular culture shaped by creative musicians, writers, artists, and filmmakers. Per capita income, life expectancy, and adult literacy increased, aided by an annual economic growth rate of nearly 5 percent by the 1990s, though a third of the population remained desperately poor, earning less than a dollar a day.

Yet, for all the economic productivity, the New Order also started some negative trends. During these years Indonesia became economically dependent on exporting oil, which represented 80 percent of foreign earnings. When the decline of world oil prices in the 1980s reduced funds for the national

---

ASEAN (Association of Southeast Asian Nations) A regional economic and political organization formed in 1967 to promote cooperation among the noncommunist Southeast Asian nations; eventually became a major trading bloc.

New Order The Indonesian government headed by President Suharto from 1966 to 1998, which mixed military and civilian leadership.

budget, Indonesia was forced to accumulate an enormous foreign debt. Adding to the problems, the rapid development of mining, forestry, and cash crop agriculture took a toll on the environment. Rain forests were clear-cut so rapidly for timber and to open space for plantations that forest fires became common, polluting the air and creating a thick, unhealthy haze every year that spread into neighboring nations. Furthermore, income disparities between classes and regions widened while political and business corruption became a major problem. One Indonesian fiction writer criticized a society in which government officials and predatory businessmen solicited bribes and grabbed public funds for themselves: "Indonesia, Land of Robbers. My true homeland stiff with thieves. In the future, I shall plunder while my wife shall seize."[21] Thanks to such corruption, the wealthy frolicked in nightclubs, casinos, and golf courses built across the street from slums or on land appropriated from powerless villages. Suharto, the son of poor peasants, became one of the world's most corrupt leaders, and he and his family acquired over $15 billion in assets from their business enterprises, which received government favoritism, and from access to public coffers.

Many Indonesians disliked the New Order. For some, Islam provided the chief vehicle for opposition. Some 87 percent of Indonesians are either devout or nominal Muslims, but few have supported militant Islamist movements like those in the Middle East and Pakistan. Suharto discouraged such Islamic radicalism as a threat to national unity in a country that also includes Christians and Hindus. However, devout Muslims have often opposed the government's secular policies and have desired a more Islamic approach to social, cultural, and legal matters. Muslim conservatives denounce gambling casinos, racy magazines and films, and scantily-clad female pop singers. At the same time, a progressive, democratic strand of Indonesian Islamic thought has favored liberal social and political reform. The Muslim liberals tap into the traditional Javanese emphasis on harmony, consensus, and tolerance that was incorporated into Indonesian, especially Javanese, Islam; they thus offer a stark contrast to the more dogmatic Islam common in countries such as Pakistan and Saudi Arabia. But, whether conservative or liberal, Muslims have blamed the government for poor living standards and massive corruption. Poets, novelists, musicians, and theater groups also addressed the New Order's problems.

By the 1990s Indonesian society was suffering from increasing class tensions, insecurities, student protests, and labor unrest, all of which set the stage for dramatic changes. When the economy collapsed, throwing millions out of work and raising prices for essential goods, riots throughout the country resulted to Suharto's resignation in 1998. With the longtime strongman gone, the country fell into turmoil, and protests and ethnic clashes proliferated. Many civilians, particularly among the urban middle class, wanted to strengthen democracy, and in 1999 free elections were held. Later, Megawati Soekarnoputri (MEH-ga-WHA-tee soo-KAR-no-POO-tri), the daughter of Indonesia's first president, Sukarno, became Indonesia's first woman president. Like her father, Megawati followed secular, nationalist policies but also showed little faith

in grassroots democracy and resolved few problems. By 2004 popular support for her regime had ebbed and she was defeated for reelection by a Javanese general.

The end of Suharto's New Order, and the disorderly democracy that replaced it, brought unprecedented freedom of the press and speech but also new problems. Removing New Order restrictions allowed long-simmering ethnic hostilities to reemerge. East Timor, for example, which had endured a long, unpopular occupation by Indonesia, finally achieved independence, but only after thousands of its people were killed by Indonesian troops and pro-Indonesian Timorese militias. Conflicts in Indonesia between Muslims and Christians and continuing regional rebellions, especially in Acheh, resulted in numerous deaths. Islamic militants capitalized on the instability to recruit support. Terrorist attacks in Indonesia, especially the bombing of popular tourist venues on Bali in 2003 and 2005, added to the growing tensions, raising questions about the long-term viability of Indonesian democracy. Complicating the political problems, in 2005 over 100,000 Indonesians perished from earthquakes and a deadly tidal wave, or tsunami, that destroyed cities and washed away coastal villages on Sumatra. Efforts to recover from these major setbacks further undermined the economy.

Politics and Society in the Philippines

Like Indonesia, the Philippines, a nation of 85 million people, also experienced political turbulence and social instability. In economic development the Philippines lagged well behind the most prosperous nations in Southeast Asia. During the fourteen years that Ferdinand Marcos ruled the nation as a dictator, economic conditions worsened, rural poverty became more widespread, the population grew rapidly, and political opposition was limited by the murder or detention of dissidents, censorship, and rigged elections. The dictator and his family and cronies looted the country for their own benefit, amassing billions. The government built high walls along city freeways so that affluent motorists would not have to view slums along the route. In the capital, Manila, a tiny minority lived in palatial homes surrounded by high walls topped with bits of broken glass and barbed wire, and with gates manned by armed guards. Across the street from the glittering pavilions of Manila's Cultural Center, whose landscaped gardens were a gaudy monument to Marcos splendor, homeless families slept in bushes. The majority of rural families were landless, and child malnutrition increased. A Filipino novelist described the unchanging rural society and its poverty, with villagers eking out a living on unproductive land: "Nothing in the countryside had changed, not the thatched houses, not the ragged vegetation, not the stolid people. Changeless land, burning sun."[22] To find work and escape poverty, Filipinos often migrated, temporarily or permanently, to other Asian nations, the United States, or the Middle East. Some 10 million Filipinos lived abroad by 2006, many being women who worked as nurses, maids, or entertainers. About 2,500 Filipinos leave the country every day for overseas work.

The failures of the Marcos years led to massive public protests in 1986 that brought down Marcos and restored

People's Power Demonstration in the Philippines In 1986 the simmering opposition to the dictatorial government of Ferdinand Marcos reached a boiling point, resulting in massive demonstrations in Manila. Under the banner of "people's power," businesspeople, professionals, housewives, soldiers, students, and cultural figures rallied to topple the regime. (Corbis)

democracy. The opposition had rallied around U.S.-educated Corazon Aquino (ah-KEE-no) (b. 1933), a descendant of a Chinese immigrant, whose popular politician husband had been assassinated by Marcos henchmen. In a spectacular nonviolent revolution under the banner of "people's power," street demonstrations involving students, workers, businessmen, housewives, and clergy demanded justice and freedom. Marcos and his family fled into exile in the United States, which had long supported his regime. As Marcos and his family escaped by helicopter, thousands of demonstrators who broke into the presidential palace found that the dictator's wife, Imelda Marcos, a former beauty queen, had acquired thousands of pairs of shoes and vast stores of undergarments, symbolizing the Marcos's waste of public resources. Mrs. Aquino became president and reestablished democracy.

Yet the hopes that the nation could resolve its problems proved illusory and politics remained turbulent. The government, while open to dissenting voices, was, as had been true since independence, dominated by the wealthiest Filipinos, mostly members of the hundred or so landowning families who were favored during U.S. colonial rule; members of these families have held some two-thirds of seats in Congress. Mrs. Aquino, herself a member of one of these families, voluntarily left office at the end of her term in 1992. Her successors had rocky presidencies; one of these men, a former film star with a reputation for heavy drinking, gambling, and womanizing, was impeached for corruption and vote-rigging. In 2001 another woman, Gloria Macapagal-Arroyo (b. 1947), a Ph.D. in economics and the daughter of a former president, became president but also faced allegations of corruption. She was reelected in 2005 but faced constant challenges questioning her legitimacy. Two decades after the overthrow of Marcos the public seems disillusioned with the results. Many Filipinos also resented the continuing close ties to, and influence from, the United States. A best-selling pop song reflected the opposition to what nationalists considered U.S. neocolonialism: "You just want my natural resources, And then you leave me poor and in misery. American Junk, Get it out of my bloodstream. Got to get back to who I am."[23]

Post-Marcos governments had successes and failures. Democracy returned, a free press flourished, and the economy improved after 1990, yet much of the economic growth was eaten up by the region's fastest population growth, since Filipinos maintained their preference for large families. And none of the governments successfully addressed poverty or seemed willing to curb the activities of influential companies exploiting marine, mineral, and timber resources, often harming the environment. A local Catholic priest noted how economic exploitation and environmental destruction have remained characteristic for decades: "A plunder economy, that's the post World War II Philippine history: plunder of seas, plunder of mines, plunder of forests."[24] Differences in access to health care, welfare, and related services continued to reflect the great gaps in income between social classes and regions.

Politics and Society in Thailand and Burma

Since the 1970s the contrasts between prosperous Thailand and stagnant Burma, both countries with histories and cultures very different from those of Indonesia and the Philippines, have been striking. In the early 1950s both nations had economies of similar size and growth rates, but the gap between them has become vast, with Thais enjoying the most success. Both nations have had a long history of military dictatorship, but only the Thais, finding the repressive atmosphere chilling, made a transition to more open government.

By the 1980s Thailand had turned away from military dictatorship and developed a semidemocratic system combining

A Thai Poet's Plea for Saving the Environment

Angkhan Kalayanaphong (AHN-kan KALL-a-YAWN-a-fong), born in 1926, the most popular poet in Thailand for decades, also gained fame as an accomplished graphic artist and painter. His poems often addressed social, Buddhist, and environmental themes. In his long poem, "Bangkok-Thailand," he examines Thailand and its problems in the 1970s and 1980s. The author pulls no punches in condemning Thai society for neglecting its heritage; he skewers politicians, government institutions, big business, and the entertainment industry. In this section, Angkhan pleads for Thais to save the forest environment being destroyed by commercial logging.

Oh, I do not imagine the forest like that
So deep, so beautiful, everything so special.
It pertains to dreams that are beyond truth. . . .
Dense woods in dense forests; slowly
The rays of half a day mix with the night.
Strange atmosphere causing admiration.
Loneliness up to the clouds, stillness and beauty.
Rays of gold play upon, penetrate the tree-tops
rays displayed in stripes, the brightness of the sun.
I stretch out my hand drawing down clouds mixing them
  with brandy.
This is supreme happiness. . . .
The lofty trees do not think of reward for the scent of their
  blossoms. . . .

Men kill the wood because they venerate money as in all
  the world. . . .
The lofty trees contribute much to morals.
They should be infinitely lauded for it.
The trace of the ax kills. Blood runs in streams. . . .
You, trees, give the flattering pollen attended by scents.
You make the sacrifice again and again.
Do you ever respond angrily? You have accepted your fate
  which is contemptuous of all that is beautiful.
But troublesome are the murderers, the doers of future sins.
Greedy after money, they are blind to divine work.
Their hearts are black to large extent, instead of being
  honest and upright.
They have no breeding, are lawless. . . .
Thailand in particular is in a very bad way.
Because of their [commercial] value parks are 'purified,'
  i.e., destroyed.
Man's blood is depraved, cursed and base.
His ancestors are swine and dogs. It is madness to say they
  are Thai.

THINKING ABOUT THE READING

1. What qualities does the poet attribute to the forest?

2. What motives does he attribute to the loggers and businessmen who exploit the forest environment?

Source: Klaus Wenk, *Thai Literature: An Introduction* (Bangkok: White Lotus, 1995), pp. 95–98. Copyright © 1995 Klaus Wenk. Reprinted with permission of the publisher, White Lotus Co., Ltd.

---

traditions of order and hierarchy, symbolized by the monarchy, with notions of representative, accountable government. While most successful political candidates came from wealthy families, often of Chinese ancestry, the rapidly expanding urban middle class generally supported an expansion of democracy that would give them more influence. A new constitution adopted in 1997 guaranteed civil liberties and reformed the electoral system. A lively free press emerged.

Thailand has generally enjoyed high rates of economic growth since the 1970s. Despite a growing manufacturing sector, the export of commodities such as rice, rubber, tin, and timber remains significant. Although the Chinese minority, some 10 percent of the population, controls much of the wealth, Thais enjoy high per capita incomes and standards of public health by Asian standards. Indeed, hoping to save money, thousands of people from North America and Europe come to Thailand each year for medical treatment. Yet perhaps a quarter of Thais are very poor, especially in rural areas. The economic "miracle," as some have called it, has, in many respects, been built on the backs of women and children, many from rural districts, who work in urban factories, the service sector, and the sex industry. Millions of Thai women have identified with

the songs of popular singer Pompuang Duangjian (POM-poo-ahn DWONG-chen) (1961–1992), herself the product of a poor village, that often deal with the harshness of the lives of poor female migrants to the city, where they encounter predatory men: "So lousy poor, I just have to risk my luck. Dozing on the bus, this guy starts chatting me up. Say's he'll get me a good job, now he's feeling me up."[25] Pompuang herself had only two years of primary school education and worked as a sugar-cane cutter before starting a music career. With much of her money stolen by lovers, managers, and promoters, she died at age thirty-one unable to afford treatment for a blood disorder.

Problems besides widespread poverty and sexual exploitation also challenge Thais. The economic collapse of 1997 that affected much of Asia also threw many Thais out of work. The rapidly growing, overcrowded capital, Bangkok, is one of the most polluted cities in Asia, drenched in toxic matter from factories and automobiles despite efforts by local environmental groups to clean up the air. The nation's once abundant rain forests disappear at a rapid rate, a fact lamented by Thai musicians and poets (see Witness to the Past: A Thai Poet's Plea for Saving the Environment). Health issues have arisen too: the

AIDs rate skyrockets. Yet, despite their problems, Thais have reason for optimism. The people possess a talent for political compromise, and Buddhism teaches moderation, tolerance, respect for nature, and a belief in the worth of the individual. Thais have the basis for a democratic spirit, a more equitable distribution of wealth, and an environmental ethic.

Whatever Thailand's problems, they seem dwarfed by Burma's. Under Burma's harsh, corrupt military regime, few outside the ruling group have prospered despite the country's valuable natural resources of timber, oil, gems, and rice. By the 1980s Burma was ranked by the United Nations as one of the world's ten poorest nations. Sparked by economic decline and political repression, mass protests in 1988, led by students and Buddhist monks, demanded civil liberties. These protests ended, however, when soldiers killed hundreds and jailed thousands of demonstrators. The regime increased its repression. In 1990 Burma (now renamed Myanmar (myahn-MAH), under international pressure, allowed elections, though with restrictions. Taking advantage of the elections, and while most of its leaders were in jail, the opposition quickly organized and won a landslide victory. Aung San Suu Kyi (AWNG sahn soo CHEE) (b. 1945), daughter of the founding president and an eloquent orator, returned from a long exile in England to lead the democratic forces. But the military refused to hand over power, put Aung San Suu Kyi under house arrest, and rounded up hundreds of opposition supporters. Refusing to compromise in exchange for the regime ending her house arrest, Aung San Suu Kyi said that she did not consider herself a martyr because other Burmese had suffered much more than she had. A courageous symbol of principled leadership, she won the Nobel Peace Prize in 1991 for her role in Burmese politics.

Today the military regime remains in power and still detains opposition leaders, including Aung San Suu Kyi. The generals cleverly manipulate politics while slightly relaxing their grip. Although many Burmese still dream of democracy, and illicit cassettes of protest music and opposition messages are exchanged from hand to hand, others have accommodated themselves to military rule, valuing stability and worried about a possible civil war. To expand the economy and thus increase its own revenues, the government began welcoming foreign investment. Western, Japanese, and Southeast Asian corporations invest in Burma, especially in the timber and oil industries, diminishing the willingness of other countries to punish Burma for gross human rights violations.

Diversity and Prosperity in Malaysia and Singapore

Of all the Southeast Asian nations, Malaysia and Singapore, both open to the world as they have been for centuries, have achieved the most political stability and economic progress. The two nations, once joined in the same federation, have shared a similar mix of ethnic groups, though while Malays constitute slightly over half, Chinese a third, and Indians a tenth of the Malaysian population, around three-quarters of Singaporeans are Chinese. Both countries maintain democratic

forms, but the ruling parties restrict the ability of opposition political groups to compete in elections on a level playing field and sometimes arrest or harass opposition leaders. After 1970 Malaysia has remained politically stable by maintaining a limited democracy and holding regular elections in which the ruling, modernizing Malay-led coalition of parties controls the voting and most of the media. The Chinese-dominated ruling party in Singapore has used similar strategies to maintain its hold on power. Since the print and broadcast media are controlled by the government or their allies in both nations, dissidents use the Internet to spread their views on their societies. Both countries have successfully diversified their economies and thus stimulated economic development, and they have also raised living standards and spread the wealth.

In Malaysia religion has remained vital, including in politics, which has often divided the Muslim majority from the Christian, Hindu, Buddhist, and animist minority. Conflict also occurs within religious traditions. For instance, Islamic movements with dogmatic, sometimes militant views have gained support among some young Malays, especially rural migrants to the city, who are alienated by a Westernized, materialistic society and looking for an anchor of certainty in an uncertain world. These movements, which discourage contact with non-Muslims, encourage women to dress modestly, and sometimes reject modern technology or products, often alarm secular Malays and non-Muslims who view the movements as taking Malaysia backward. In response, Malay women's rights groups use Islamic arguments to oppose restrictions favored by conservatives. They find some support among the numerous women holding high government positions. Hence, Sisters in Islam, founded in the 1980s by the politically well-connected academic, Zainab Anwar, espouses an Islam supporting freedom, justice, and equality and fights strict interpretations of Muslim family law. At the other extreme, aimless Malay youth mock the conventions of mainstream society, wearing long hair and listening to heavy metal music.

Supported by abundant natural resources, such as oil and tin, economic diversification, and entrepreneurial talent, Malaysia has become a highly successful developing nation, surpassing European nations like Portugal and Hungary in national wealth. High annual growth rates have enabled Malaysia to achieve a relatively high per capita income and to build light industry that employs cheap labor to make shoes, toys, and other consumer goods for export. Many of these workers are women; half of Malaysian women work for wages. The manufacturing sector has continued to grow rapidly: Malaysians even build their own automobiles. Timber and oil have become valuable export commodities. Malaysia recovered rapidly from the 1997 Asian economic collapse by imposing more government controls on the economy, ignoring Western economic advice. But economic growth comes at the price of toxic waste problems, severe deforestation, and air pollution.

Economic growth in Malaysia corresponds to social change. Violence between Chinese and Malays in 1969 resulted in the New Economic Policy; aimed at redistributing more wealth to Malays, it has fostered a substantial Malay middle class. Others also benefited from the prosperity. By the 1980s

Kuala Lumpur Dominated by new skyscrapers, including some of the world's tallest buildings, and a spectacular mosque, the Malaysian capital city, Kuala Lumpur, has become a prosperous center for Asian commerce and industry. Modern buildings gradually replace the older shophouses built decades ago. Yet, poor shantytowns have also grown apace to house the poor. (Corbis)

televisions, stereos, and videocassette recorders became nearly universal in the cities and increasingly common in the rural areas. Official poverty rates dropped from some 50 percent in 1970 to around 20 percent by 2000. As in other Asian nations and Latin America, many young women labor in electronics and textile factories. Nevertheless, the gap between rich and poor remains and may have widened. In the bustling capital city, Kuala Lumpur, jammed freeways, glittering malls, and high-rise luxury condominiums contrast with shantytown squatter settlements and countless shabbily dressed street hawkers hoping to sell enough of their cheap wares to buy a meal.

Restricted to a tiny island, Singapore, despite few resources, has done even better than Malaysia economically and has become among the world's most prosperous nations. The numerical and political predominance of Chinese, the descendants of immigrants during the past two centuries, makes Singapore unique in Southeast Asia. The Singapore government has mixed freewheeling economic policies with an autocratic leadership that tightly controls the 5 million people and limits dissent. Singapore is run like a giant corporation, efficient and ruthless. People pay a stiff fine if caught spitting, littering, or even tossing used chewing gum on the street. Yet it is also one of the healthiest societies, enjoying, for example, the world's lowest rate of infant mortality. Singapore has devoted more of its national budget to education than other nations, and everyone studies English in school. The city has become a hub of light industry, high technology, and computer networking, in the vanguard of the information revolution. Businesspeople and professionals from around the world have flocked to this globalized city, just as they had flocked to the Straits of Melaka trading states of Srivijaya and Melaka centuries ago.

Southeast Asia in the Global System

Although Southeast Asians still export the natural resources they did in colonial times, some nations have seen major economic growth through industrialization and exploitation of other resources. The gold, pepper, and spices of earlier centuries have been largely replaced by oil, timber, rubber, rice, tin, sugar, and palm oil. With these exports the region's role in the world has also changed, fostering some of the fastest-growing economies in the world. Malaysia, Thailand, Singapore, and, to some extent, Indonesia and Vietnam have become major recipients of foreign investment. Meanwhile, workers produce manufactured goods like shoes, clothing, computer chips, and sports equipment for European and North American markets. To overcome underdevelopment, several countries elsewhere in Asia, Africa, and Latin America borrow economic models from the Southeast Asian "tigers." By the early twenty-first century the Southeast Asian nations were shifting their focus from the United States to China, which they viewed as the rising world power with which they must cooperate for regional stability.

Southeast Asians have also influenced politics worldwide. The Indonesian Revolution against the Dutch, for instance, had electrifying global effects because it forced a major colonial power to abandon its control while giving hope to colonized Africans. Similarly, Vietnamese communists under Ho Chi Minh, in their ultimately successful fifty-year fight against French colonialism, Japanese occupation, and then U.S. intervention, stimulated a wave of revolutionary efforts, from Nicaragua to Mozambique, to overthrow Western domination. The Vietnamese struggle for independence also inspired student activists in Europe and North America; a few of the more radical shouted slogans in praise of the Vietnamese communist leader, Ho Chi Minh, while protesting against war and inequality in the 1960s. Women have long played an influential role in Southeast Asia, and the political leaders Megawati Soekarnoputri in Indonesia, Corazon Aquino in the Philippines, and Aung San Suu Kyi in Burma have become inspirations to women worldwide.

Engagement with the outside world has shaped modern Southeast Asia. Global influences and economic development have increasingly modified lives. For example, the resident of an upscale suburb of Kuala Lumpur, Bangkok, or Manila, connected through her home computer to the information superhighway and working in a high-rise, air-conditioned office reached by driving a late-model sports car along the crowded freeways, has a way of life vastly different from that of the peasant villager whose life revolves around traditional society. The modern cities feature malls, supermarkets, boutiques, Hard Rock Cafes, and Planet Hollywoods. Even rural areas, while maintaining age-old traditions, have become more connected to wider networks by televisions, outboard motors, motor scooters, and telephones.

Yet change has often been superficial. In poor city neighborhoods restaurants may have compact disc players and cold beer, but they also feature traditional music and dance and serve up fiery hot curries. For every youngster who joins the fan club for a Western or local pop star, another identifies with an Islamic, Buddhist, or Christian organization, sometimes a militant one. Many people find themselves perched uneasily between the cooperative village values of the past and the competitive, materialistic modern world.

SECTION SUMMARY

- Beginning the late 1970s, Southeast Asia experienced rapid economic growth through a Japanese-style mix of capitalism and active government involvement, though a severe economic crisis hit the region in 1997.

- Under Suharto, the Indonesian New Order government repressed regional opposition and improved the economy, but Suharto was extravagantly corrupt and was forced to resign in 1997 amid widespread unrest and economic collapse.

- Under Marcos, the Philippines was divided between the very rich and the poor; Marcos was forced out after massive protests, and the democratically elected governments that followed were more open to dissent but still dominated by the wealthy.

- Since the 1980s, Thailand has developed a semidemocratic system and has grown economically, though it has endured widespread poverty and sexual exploitation, while Burma has been burdened with a corrupt regime that has failed to take advantage of ample natural resources and stifled its opposition.

- Malaysia has taken advantage of abundant natural resources to become highly successful, surpassing some European nations in wealth, while Singapore, with fewer resources, has been even more successful through a combination of economic freedom and political restriction.

- With their rapidly growing economies, the Southeast Asian "tigers" have inspired developing nations around the world, and while most of the region has joined the modern world, tradition thrives in them as well.

  *Online Study Center* **ACE the Test**

✦ Chapter Summary

After decolonization, the societies of southern Asia struggled to shape their futures. The traumas of World War II made a return to the imperial patterns of old impossible. Since Hindu and Muslim leaders could not agree on a formula for unity after independence, British India fragmented into two rival nations, predominantly Hindu India and mostly Muslim Pakistan. Under Nehru, India adopted democratic practices and modernizing policies. Indians generally sustained multiparty democracy, raised the legal status of untouchables and women, achieved a dramatic rise in food production, industrialized, and fostered high-technology enterprises. But they failed to transform rural society, distribute the fruits of economic growth equitably, and eradicate Hindu-Muslim conflict. Muslim-dominated Pakistan divided when Bangladesh broke away, and both Pakistan and Bangladesh have had difficulty maintaining democracy and generating economic development. India and Pakistan, both armed with nuclear weapons, have remained hostile neighbors.

Like South Asians, Southeast Asians also regained the independence they had lost under Western colonialism. Vietnamese communists led by Ho Chi Minh launched a revolutionary war that eventually forced the French to leave, giving the communists control of North Vietnam. The United States, influenced by Cold War thinking, supported anti-communist South Vietnam and, in response to a growing communist insurgency, sent American troops to South Vietnam. But the United States withdrew in 1975, unable to triumph over a determined foe. The conflict caused several million casualties and major environmental damage. With the war over, Vietnam, Cambodia, and Laos, all under communist control, struggled for reconstruction. The rest of Southeast Asia also faced challenges after achieving independence. Some, such as Indonesia and Malaysia, worked to build national unity in a complex mosaic of peoples and cultures. Burma, Thailand, and the Philippines experienced chronic unrest that often led to military or civilian dictatorships. But eventually Malaysia, Singapore, Thailand, and Indonesia achieved rapid economic growth, supplying natural resources and manufactured goods to the world.

Online Study Center **Improve Your Grade** Flashcards

Key Terms

Awami League	Tet Offensive	UMNO
Bharatha Janata	Pathet Lao	ASEAN
Bollywood	Khmer Rouge	New Order
National Liberation Front (NLF)		

Suggested Reading

Books

Abinales, Patricio N. and Donna J. Amoroso. *State and Society in the Philippines.* Lanham, M.D.: Rowman and Littlefield, 2005. Readable recent study with much on recent politics.

Beeson, Mark, ed. *Contemporary Southeast Asia: Regional Dynamics, National Differences.* New York: Palgrave Macmillan, 2004. Essays on varied topics.

Brown, Judith M. *Nehru.* New York: Longman, 1999. A readable biography of an important Asian leader.

Ganguly, Sumit, ed. *South Asia.* New York: New York University Press, 2006. Recent essays on the South Asian countries.

Ganguly, Sumit and Neal DeVotta, eds. *Understanding Contempoary India.* Boulder: Lynne Rienner, 2003. Accessible collection covering most aspects of Indian society.

Harrison, Selig S., et al., eds. *India and Pakistan: The First Fifty Years.* New York: Cambridge University Press, 1999. An excellent collection of essays covering many topics.

Karnow, Stanley. *Vietnam: A History,* 2nd ed. New York: Penguin, 1997. One of the better introductions to modern history and the American-Vietnamese War.

Kingsbury, Damien. *South-East Asia: A Political Profile,* 2nd ed. New York: Oxford University Press, 2005. An up-to-date, comprehensive survey by an Australian scholar.

Lockard, Craig A. *"Dance of Life": Popular Music and Politics in Southeast Asia.* Honolulu: University of Hawaii Press, 1998. An examination of politics and societies through popular culture.

Marlay, Ross, and Clark Neher. *Patriots and Tyrants: Ten Asian Leaders.* Lanham, Md.: Rowman and Littlefield, 1999. Sketches of Asian nationalists, such as Gandhi, Nehru, Ho, and Sukarno.

Neher, Clark D. *Southeast Asia: Crossroads of the World,* 2nd ed. DeKalb: Center for Southeast Asian Studies, Northern Illinois University, 2004. A general, readable introduction to cultures and politics.

Olson, James S., and Randy Roberts. *Where the Domino Fell: America and Vietnam, 1945–1995,* 4th ed. St. James, N.Y.: Brandywine, 2004. An outstanding survey with an emphasis on U.S. policies and actions.

Stein, Burton. *A History of India.* Malden, M.A.: Blackwell, 1998. A detailed history with good coverage of the contemporary era.

Varshney, Ashutosh. *Ethnic Conflict and Civic Life: Hindus and Muslims in India,* 2nd ed. New Haven, C.T.: Yale University Press, 2003. A key study of Hindu-Muslim relations in three cities, including peacemaking and violence.

Vickers, Adrian. *A History of Modern Indonesia.* New York: Cambridge University Press, 2005. Quirky but fascinating study.

Websites

Asian Studies: WWW Virtual Library (http://coombs.anu.edu.au/WWWVL-AsianStudies.html). A vast metasite maintained at Australian National University, with links to hundreds of sites.

East and Southeast Asia: An Annotated Directory of Internet Resources (http://newton.uor.edu/Departments&Programs/AsianStudies-Dept/). A superb set of links on Southeast Asia, maintained at the University of Redlands.

Internet Indian History Sourcebook (http://www.fordham.edu/halsall/india/indiasbook.html). An invaluable collection of sources and links on India from ancient to modern times.

Virtual Library: South Asia (http://www.columbia.edu/cu/libraries/indiv/area/sarai/). A major site maintained by Columbia University.

WWW Southeast Asia Guide (http://www.library.wisc.edu/guides/SEAsia/). An easy-to-use site.

The Contemporary World, Since 1945

The world has changed dramatically since 1945. Some observers have described these years as the most revolutionary age in history, reshaping whole ways of life and worldviews. All regions of the world, opening to ideas and products from everywhere, have become, as some experts put it, part of a global village or global system. The Indonesian thinker Soedjatmoko (so-jat-MOH-ko), summing up the era's trends, described a world of collapsing "national boundaries and horrifying destructive power, expanding technological capacity and instant communication [in which] we live in imperfect intimacy with all our fellow human beings."[1] This interconnected and rapidly changing global society, and the people who shape it, have produced both great good and indescribable horrors.

The contemporary world has become a global unity within a larger diversity. Globalization has fostered or intensified networks of exchange and communication: international trade pacts and electronic fund transfers, jet-speed travel and fax machines. These networks link distant societies. Yet, even as they have become more closely linked, nations have not been able to work together to meet the challenges facing humanity, such as poverty and environmental distress. No clear international consensus has emerged on maintaining strong local cultures in the face of global influences, correcting the widening gap between rich and poor nations, and achieving a better balance between environmental preservation and economic development. Solving these problems requires complex strategies and the joint efforts of many nations. Ensuring a brighter future also requires examining how the patterns of the past and the trends of the present may shape the years to come.

GLOBALIZATION AND CULTURES

Over recent centuries the world's people have built a human web, or networked society—a global system that today encompasses most of the world's 6.5 billion people. All these terms imply transnational connections and the institutions that foster them, such as the World Bank, the Internet, and religious missionaries. Around the world people speak, with fear or enthusiasm, of globalization. Some observers see the trend as dangerous folly, others as a boon, and still others have mixed feelings. In recent decades, people have experienced global influences not only by, for some, frequent travel abroad but because these influences have reshaped the cities, towns, and villages where they live. The interaction between global influences and local traditions, such as religion and music, has become a force in the world, helping to shape cultures.

Globalization and Its Impacts

The roots of globalization go deep into the past. During the first millennium of the Common Era trade networks such as the Silk Road, which linked China and Europe across Central Asia and the Middle East, and the spread of religions such as Buddhism, Christianity, and Islam, connected distant societies. A thousand years ago an Eastern Hemisphere–wide economy based in Asia and anchored by Chinese and Indian manufacturing and Islamic trade networks represented an early form of globalization. The links between the hemispheres forged after 1492, during which Europeans competed with each other and with Asians for a share of the growing trade in raw materials, expanded the reach of this economy. In the nineteenth century the Industrial Revolution, which produced desirable trade goods, and European imperialism, which led to the Western colonization of large parts of the world, extended the connections even further, aided by technological innovations such as steamships and trans-oceanic cables.

The integration of commerce and financial services today is more developed than ever before. As the global system has become increasingly linked, societies have become more dependent on each other for everything from consumer goods and entertainments to fuels and technological innovations. For example, all over the world people consume Chinese textiles, U.S. films, Persian Gulf oil, Indian yoga, and Japanese electronics. Videoconferencing allows business partners in Los Angeles, Berlin, and Hong Kong to confer instantaneously with one another. During the early twenty-first century the world's most powerful nation, the United States, has become increasingly reliant on Asian nations, especially China, to finance its skyrocketing national debt. The debt has grown in part because of a costly U.S. military engagement in Iraq and an increasing economic imbalance as Americans import more from abroad than they export. Such interdependence, as well as the reach of political, cultural, and social events across distances, has had an increasing impact in a shrinking world. This reality was demonstrated in 2005 when some faraway African societies were affected indirectly by Hurricane Katrina, which devastated the Gulf Coast of the United States, disrupting the export of corn from the U.S. Midwest through the port of New Orleans. Japan, a major consumer of that corn, then turned to South Africa for supplies, which deprived people in Malawi of South African corn, causing widespread starvation in Malawi. Yet, while globalization affects every country to some degree, the great bulk of world trade and financial flow and activity is concentrated in, and has the largest impact on, the peoples of three huge interlinked blocs: North America, Europe, and a group of Asian nations stretching from Japan to India.

Furthermore, many observers believe that globalization is unmanageable. U.S. journalist Thomas Friedman writes:

Globalization isn't a choice. It's a reality, and no one is in charge. You keep looking for someone to complain to, to take the heat off your markets. Well guess what, there's no one on the other end of the phone. The global market today is an electronic herd of anonymous stock, bond and currency traders sitting behind computer screens. Sure, this is unfair [but] there's nobody to call.[2]

If governments are often somewhat powerless in the face of global economic trends, they need to adapt by educating their citizens, especially their young people, for a new, more competitive world. Various Asian nations, such as India, Taiwan, and Singapore, have adapted to these changes more rapidly than North American and European nations, pouring money into education, science, and high technology. The Western nations that have successfully adjusted to globalization are mainly those, especially in Scandinavia, that have combined open markets with strong societal and environmental protections.

This impersonal globalization, operating independent of governments, has had major impacts on societies, politics, economies, cultures, and environments. Whether they are seen as positive or negative consequences depends on the observer. For example, some Western free market enthusiasts celebrate a new global order in which everybody on the planet is in the same economy, offering entrepreneurs unparalleled opportunities for profit. But graffiti by disillusioned Poles in the 1990s took a different view, complaining that when Poland abandoned communism it asked for democracy but ended up with the bond market and domination by transnational corporations. Scholars and others energetically debate the value and scope of globalization (see Historical Controversy: Globalization: For and Against).

Global forces, symbolized by advertising for foreign-made goods and satellites miles up in the sky relaying information around the world, interact with local cultures, raising questions about national and local identity. As a result, local traditions and products sometimes get replaced, and imported and local cultures blend. An example of blending comes from France, where, with its large Arab immigrant population, Arab entrepreneurs have prospered by selling fast-food hamburgers and pizza prepared according to Muslim requirements and adapted to Arab taste. People around the world consume global products, from fast food to fashionable footwear to action films, but still enjoy cultural traditions that are distinctly local and popular with earlier generations. Examples include the unique Thai style of boxing in which combatants can attack with both hands and feet, sumo wrestling in Japan, and the African-influenced martial arts of Brazil.

To adapt and flourish in an interconnected world, people have had to become aware of international conditions. In North America, activists seeking to fight inequality or preserve the environment have urged people to think globally but act locally. Thinking globally, for example, would include understanding how rapid deforestation in the tropics—especially in the Amazon and Congo Basins, where rain forests recycle vast amounts of water into the air—diminishes rainfall around the world. Acting locally, Brazilian environmental and citizens' groups work to save their rain forests, while environmentally conscious North Americans and Europeans support organizations, businesses, and political leaders committed to improving the global environment. Others wonder, however, if this is

enough, arguing that, since the world is so interlinked, people must think and act both globally and locally—to embrace both a global citizenship and a local citizenship. But, despite greatly increased travel and migration, only a small minority of people have become true citizens of the world, comfortable everywhere. Few people have gone as far toward an ecumenical view as Australian Aboriginal writer Colin Johnson, who both embraced Hinduism, imported from India, and dedicated his first novel to the Jamaican reggae star Bob Marley and his Rastafarian faith. Moreover, world government remains a distant prospect at the beginning of the twenty-first century.

Cultural Imperialism: The Globalization of Culture

The inequitable relationship between the dominant West and the developing nations has compelled observers to examine global change. Arising from this effort has been the concept of cultural imperialism, in which the economic and political power of Western nations, especially the United States, enables their cultural products to spread widely. Some African writers have called this pattern a "cultural bomb" because, they believe, Western products and entertainments destroy local cultures. In this view, the developed countries export popular music, disco dancing, skimpy women's clothing, and sex-drenched films and publications reflecting these countries' own values and experiences. Other societies adopt these products, which modify or suffocate their own traditions. For instance, big budget Hollywood films attract large audiences while local films, made on small budgets, cannot compete, and the local film industries often die as a result. To survive, local filmmakers adopt the formulas used by successful Hollywood filmmakers: sex and violence. Critics of Western power argue that cultural exchange has been common throughout history but in the modern world has become largely a one-way street, leading to domination by Western, especially Anglo-American, culture.

Popular culture produced in the United States, entertaining but also challenging to traditional values, has emerged as the closest thing available to a global entertainment. The Monroe Doctrine—the early-nineteenth-century declaration by Congress that the United States would interfere in Latin American political developments—has now become, in the view of certain wags, the "Marilyn Monroe Doctrine," after the famous American actress who, for many non-Americans, symbolized U.S. culture in the 1950s. Other examples of American cultural influence were popular U.S. television programs, such as the drama series *Dallas*, the racy *Desperate Housewives,* and *The Muppet Show,* a variety show, which have been broadcast in dozens of nations.

Some American icons, from basketball star Michael Jordan to McDonald's, have become symbols of a new global modernity and capitalism. In 1989 two young East Germans crossed the Berlin Wall and discovered their first McDonald's restaurant. One of them remembered, "It was all so modern, the windows were so amazing. I felt like a lost convict who'd just spent twenty-five years in prison. I was in a state of shock."[3] Not even the Chinese, with one of the world's most admired cuisines, were immune to the appeal of modern U.S. marketing techniques and convenience for harried urbanites.

Globalization: For and Against

The first pictures taken from the moon in 1969, which showed the earth as a blue oasis in the middle of nowhere, made clear that humans share a single home. The pictures also suggested that this home is shared by an interlinked future. Different kinds of networks have increasingly connected peoples across distance and borders, and globalization—the interconnections between societies, the rise in cross-border exchanges, and the creation of one world—has become a major subject of debate. Often used vaguely and inconsistently, the concept became a metaphor to explain capitalism spreading throughout the world. But to many observers, the concept has deeper meanings, describing a process that both unites and divides, creates winners and losers, and brings both new possibilities and new risks. The debates on globalization cut across political leanings and national divisions.

THE PROBLEM

Globalization inspires passionate support and bitter opposition, generating immense discussion and disagreement. The debate focuses on four questions: When did globalization begin? What are the arguments in favor of it? What are some of the major opposing views? Is the trend leading the world into a troubled era of increasing conflict or greater cooperation?

THE DEBATE

The first question, the roots of globalization, remains disputed. Some scholars argue that its origins lie deep in the past, going back to the interconnections that slowly enveloped people from the dawn of cities and states. The German historians Jurgen Osterhammel and Niels Petersson, for example, trace it back a millennium or two to the silk trade between China and the Mediterranean region, the sea trade between the Middle East and India, and the caravans crossing the deserts of Africa, all activities that moved people, ideas, artwork, natural resources, goods, and coins. By contrast, Robbie Robertson, an Australian, argues that history changed dramatically only five hundred years ago, when the gradual linking of the world by European voyages of discovery transformed societies and economic activities. Still other scholars trace it no further back than the mid-nineteenth century, pointing to the first permanent transoceanic telegraph cable in 1866, global social movements such as feminism, and global regulatory bodies such as the Universal Postal Union. Some other writers claim that globalization did not affect most of humanity until the 1960s or later. Whatever the roots, by 2000 a global system defined by market capitalism, over two hundred nation-states, some four hundred international organizations, and 40,000 transnational corporations, existed with no central authority.

On the second and third questions, whether the effects are positive or negative, the debate has raged for years. Among the benefits attributed to globalization are higher living standards and the worldwide sharing of culture. British sociologist John Giddens identifies a worldwide trend toward democracy and intellectual freedom. Walter Anderson praises the opening of societies to one another, as reflected in communications satellites and the fiber-optic submarine cable system winding its way around the world. As a result, he notes, the Inuit people living in northern Alaska watch twenty-eight channels of satellite television, take courses through the Internet, and stay in touch with their families by cell phones. Free market enthusiasts, such as Indian-born, U.S.-based economist Jagdish Bhagwati, stress the fostering of economic freedom. Opposing antiglobalization movements as the misguided enemy of progress, all these thinkers complain that newspapers and television reports focus more on shuttered textile factories, as jobs move overseas, than on the African child at the computer. Bhagwati claims that when properly governed, globalization becomes a powerful force for social good, bringing prosperity to underdeveloped nations, reducing child labor, increasing literacy, and helping women by creating jobs that increase their income and status. Another enthusiast, Thomas Friedman, considers globalization the principal trend of the post–Cold War world, symbolized by the Lexus, a Japanese-made luxury car sold around the world. Yet, he argues, people often prefer to hold on to meaningful traditions, symbolized by the olive tree often found at the center of an Arab village, rather than embrace new ideas. The world, he argues, has gotten flat, and this level playing field has allowed over two billion Chinese, Indians, and Russians to contemplate eventually owning a car, house, refrigerator, and toaster, increasing competition and raising the demand for the world's resources dramatically.

The contrary views on globalization stress negative consequences. These consequences include a concentration of economic power, more poverty, and less cultural diversity. The challengers of economic globalization argue that powerful governments and multinational corporations bully the marketplace, control politics, and stack the deck in their favor. Walter LaFeber shows how U.S. basketball star Michael Jordan, whose games were broadcast all over the world, became an international phenomenon of great commercial appeal, benefiting the international corporations who used Jordan to create a demand for their expensive products, such as sneakers, often at the expense of local manufacturers making the same product. To LaFeber, the terrorist attacks on the United States, especially the World Trade Center in New York in 2001, must also be understood in the context of the growing opposition to globalization around the world as the rich become richer and the poor become poorer. Joseph Stiglitz, an ardent fan of capitalism and former World Bank official, believes that globalization can be positive but that misguided policies and the economic power of industrial nations have made free trade unfair for developing nations. Looking at other aspects of globalization, Cynthia

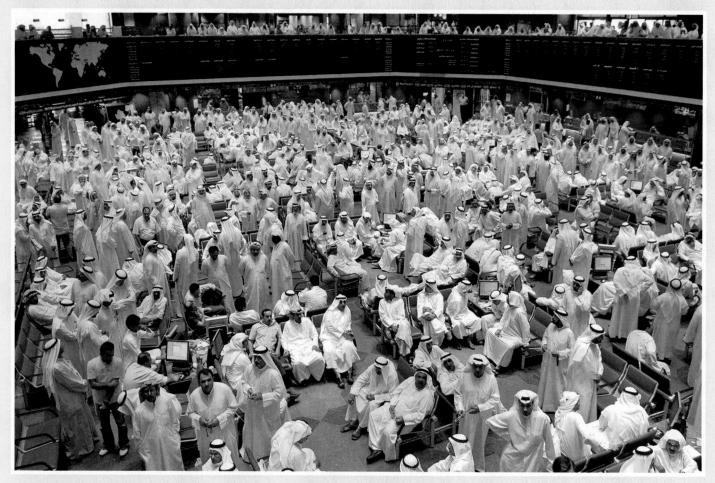

Kuwaiti Stock Exchange Capitalism has spread widely in the world, and with it financial institutions such as investment banks and stock exchanges. The oil-rich, politically stable Persian Gulf sultanate of Kuwait has one of the most active stock exchanges. (Corbis)

Enloe explores the often negative effects of tourism and U.S. military bases on women, who, enjoying fewer economic options than men, often need to sell their bodies to male tourists and soldiers to survive. James Mittelman argues that, experienced from below, globalization fosters the loss of local political control as power shifts upward and also a devaluation of a society's cultural achievements as foreign cultural products, such as music and films, become influential. All of these globalizing trends spur angry resistance, reflected in antiglobalization movements.

Experts also disagree about the fourth question, where globalization is taking the world. Some predict a growing divide both between and within societies. Benjamin Barber, for example, analyzes the conflict between consumerist capitalism (what he calls McWorld, after McDonald's) and tribalism or religious fundamentalism (what he terms jihad, after Islamic militants). Barber dislikes both trends: the dull homogeneity of McWorld, in which everyone, moved by capitalism and advertising, has the same tastes and ideas; and the balkanized world of jihad in which rival cultures, convinced of their own superior values and disdainful of others, struggle for dominance. Other scholars also predict tensions. John Giddens argues that the globalization of

information, symbolized by the World Wide Web, that puts people in touch with others who think differently will promote a more cosmopolitan world-view respecting cultural differences but will also generate a backlash among narrow nationalists and religious fundamentalists who see only one path to truth. Preventing conflict between the factions and lessening the growing divide between rich and poor nations require cooperation between nations. Bhagwati, for example, supports managed rather than unfettered globalization, with world leaders discussing how to foster equality as well as growth. Taking a different approach, Mittelman doubts that globalization can be managed and calls for people around the world, rather than leaders and governments, to work together to decentralize political and economic power to build a future of greater equity.

EVALUATING THE DEBATE

The globalization discussion, much more than an academic debate, is a disagreement about profound transformations in the world and about what ethical and institutional principles should be applied to better organize human affairs for a brighter future. Some authors engaged in the debate have proposed catchy ideas, such as the Lexus and the olive tree, jihad and Mc-World, but the reality of globalization is usually more complex. Both proponents and opponents make convincing points about the consequences of globalization; the truth may lie somewhere between. Globalization may indeed bring great benefits, at least to a section of the world's people. The free flow of ideas inspires some people to demand more political rights or social inequality, while many young women working long hours for low wages in foreign-owned factories may often prefer that life to the dead end of rural poverty. But improving the lives of those who do not benefit, as even globalization proponents Bhagwati and Friedman concede, will probably require action such as land reform to help poor peasants, more funding for schools, and stiffer environmental and worker protection laws to smooth the impacts on societies, cultures, and environments. Yet, the relations between business interests and their political supporters prompting globalization and the antiglobalization activists, often from worker or peasant backgrounds, remain tense. Local, national, regional, and global forces are intermingling in new and complex ways that may necessitate not just actions to remedy inequalities but also new ways of thinking.

THINKING ABOUT THE CONTROVERSY

1. When did globalization begin?
2. What are the positive arguments for globalization?
3. What main points do opponents make?

EXPLORING THE CONTROVERSY

Among the key historical studies are Robbie Robertson, *The Three Waves of Globalization: A History of a Developing Global Consciousness* (New York: Zed Books, 2003), and Jurgen Osterhammel and Niels P. Petersson, *Globalization: A Short History* (Princeton: Princeton University Press, 2005). Some of the major proponents are John Giddens, *Runaway World: How Globalization Is Reshaping Our Lives* (London: Routledge, 2000); Walter Truett Anderson, *All Connected Now: Life in the First Global Civilization* (Boulder, Colo.: Westview Press, 2001); Jagdish Bhagwati, *In Defense of Globalization* (New York: Oxford University Press, 2004); and Thomas L. Friedman, *The Lexus and the Olive Tree: Understanding Globalization* (New York: Anchor, 2000) and *The World Is Flat: A Brief History of the Twenty-First Century* (New York: Farrar, Straus, and Giroux, 2005). Writers questioning the benefits include Walter LaFeber, *Michael Jordan and the New Global Capitalism*, new and expanded ed. (New York: W. W. Norton, 2002); Joseph E. Stiglitz, *Globalization and Its Discontents* (New York: W. W. Norton, 1993); Cynthia Enloe, *Bananas, Beaches and Bases: Making Feminist Sense of International Politics*, updated ed. (Berkeley: University of California Press, 2001); and James H. Mittelman, *The Globalization Syndrome: Transformation and Resistance* (Princeton: Princeton University Press, 2000). For one view of future trends, see Benjamin R. Barber, *Jihad vs. McWorld* (New York: Times Books, 1995). On globalization generally, see David Held, ed., *A globalizing World? Culture, Economics, Politics* (New York: Routledge, 2000); Robert K. Schaeffer, *Understanding Globalization: The Social Consequences of Political, Economic, and Environmental Change* (Lanham, M.D.: Rowman and Littlefield, 1997); and Manfred B. Steger, *Globalization: A Very Short Introduction* (New York: Oxford University Press, 2003).

In 1993 a famous roast duck restaurant in China's capital, Beijing, sent its management staff to study the McDonald's operation in British-ruled Hong Kong and then introduced its customers to "roast duck fast food." The restaurant also faced a challenge from the growing number of McDonald's franchises in Beijing. Yet, Chinese restaurants flourish around the world.

Still, popular American entertainments often face opposition. Governments, from the Islamic clerics running Iran to the more democratic leaders of India, have attempted to halt or control the influx of what they consider destabilizing, immoral pop culture. In 1995 an Islamic political party in Pakistan even demanded, unsuccessfully, that the United States turn over to them American pop stars Madonna and Michael Jackson so that they could be placed on trial as "cultural terrorists" destroying humanity. In 2005, representatives of many nations, meeting under the auspices of the United Nations cultural organization, agreed that all nations had the right to restrict cultural imports, outraging American political and entertainment leaders. To maintain their cultural traditions and boost local artists many nations have mandated, as Portugal did in 2006, that a set percentage of music on radio and television must be locally made.

Forming New World Cultures

Whatever the real scope of cultural imperialism, a new world culture appears to be on the rise. The world is becoming one vast network of relationships as ideas, people, and goods move between its different regions. Similar cultural forms, often Anglo-American in origin, develop across national boundaries, transcending any one territory, society, or tradition. Yet the rising world culture is not uniform. No total homogenization of expression and meaning has occurred.

Anglo-American cultural forms are not the only ones to reach a global audience. Mexican and Brazilian soap operas, Indian (Bollywood) films, Nigerian novels, Arab, African, and Caribbean pop music, and Japanese comics and electronic games have been popular all over the globe. For example, thanks in part to the popularity of Jamaican singer/songwriter Bob Marley, reggae music spread around the world, as one observer marveled in the 1980s:

In Papeete, Tahiti, the buses all have speakers the size of foot lockers, making them moving sound systems. Their routes are jumping with the rhythms of [reggae groups] Steel Pulse, Black Uhuru, and Bob Marley. Four thousand miles away in Tokyo, there is a reggae night spot called Club 69, where local youth wear dreadlocks and dance to the beats of the Wailers. Africa has its own reggae styles and hundreds of bands.[4]

The cultural traffic flow is not one way. In North America, western Europe, and Australia, people take up Indian yoga, Chinese *tai qi*, and other Asian spiritual disciplines; patronize Thai, Indian, Chinese, and Japanese restaurants; enjoy Brazilian and African pop music; learn Latin American dances; and master Asian martial arts, such as karate and judo. Even classical musicians in the West have embraced foreign influences. For instance, in 1998 the Chinese cellist Yo Yo Ma, born in Paris

and later a U.S. resident, founded the Silk Road Ensemble, which brings together Western, East Asian, and Middle Eastern musicians to tour the world playing music that mixes the instruments and traditions of both East and West.

The meeting of global and local cultures fosters hybridization, the blending of two cultures, a process that can be either enriching or impoverishing. Record stores in Western cities set aside some of their display space to sell a hybrid form called "world music," popular music originating largely outside of the West that mixes Western influences with local and other traditions. Some experts contend that world music reflects Western cultural imperialism, since Western influence—rock beats and electric instruments, for example—are often strong, and Anglo-American rock stars such as Peter Gabriel, Paul Simon, and Sting have promoted and sometimes appropriated some of the music. Yet world music has introduced Western and global audiences to a rich variety of sounds, often rooted in Asian, African, Caribbean, and Latin American traditions. While reshaping music for a global market, world music has also given Asian, African, and Latin American musicians a larger audience. Just like Western pop stars, some world musicians such as the Brazilian singer-songwriter Caetano Veloso, the Indian film diva Asha Bhosle (the most recorded artist in history: 20,000 songs in over a dozen languages), and the Senegalese Youssou N'Dour, the descendant of griots, who mixes guitars with West African talking drums, perform around the world.

INEQUALITY AND DEVELOPMENT

Globalization, resulting from interconnections transcending the boundaries of nations, benefits some people but not all equally. The gap between rich and poor nations, and rich and poor people within nations, has grown and remains one of the world's major problems. In 1960 the richest fifth of the world's population had a total income thirty times the poorest fifth; by 2000 the ratio had more than doubled. The former Soviet leader Mikhail Gorbachev, a keen student of world affairs, has asked: "Will the whole world turn into one big Brazil, into countries with complete inequality and [gated communities] for the rich elite?"[5] International and national leaders have addressed the challenges of development, considering a more equitable sharing of the world's diminishing resources.

The North-South Gap

With the changes in the global system since World War II, nations on every continent have improved their living standards, lowered poverty rates, and increased their stake in the global economy, which has more than quintupled in size since 1950. The average per capita income in the world grew 2.6 times in the same period, to some $5,000 per year. But the rising tide of the world economy has not lifted all ships, leaving some nations, especially in the southern lands near or below the equator, poor relative to the northern countries. The economies of these nations, known as underdeveloped nations, have stagnated or enjoyed only very modest growth, leaving the majority of their people in poverty. Over 1 billion people live in extreme poverty, with an income of less than $1 per day. Using a popular term for an underdeveloped nation, Jamaican reggae star Pato Banton reflected on the harshness of poverty in a 1989 song, "Third World Country":

> In a Third World country, the plants are green, it's a beautiful scene. Seems like a nice place for human beings. But there's people on the streets, no shoes on their feet. They gotta hustle to get a little food to eat. Things shouldn't be this way.[6]

The gap between the richest and poorest countries, often known as the North-South gap, has widened steadily (see map). For instance, the difference in average per capita incomes between industrialized and nonindustrialized nations grew from 2:1 in 1850 to 10:1 in 1950 to 30:1 by 2000. Today the industrialized North contains a quarter of the world's population but accounts for over three-quarters of its production of goods and services. Poor nations from Haiti to Sierra Leone have experienced civil war or insurgency as rival factions fight to control their limited resources and revenues.

The growing North-South gap has many aspects all documented in dry statistics that, however, represent real people. The disparity in consumption is striking. For example, while Americans, 5 percent of the world's population, consume 40 percent of the world's resources, people in a Bolivian valley consume few resources and experience an impoverished material life. According to a study of the valley: "In a man's lifetime, he will buy one suit, one white shirt, perhaps a hat and a pair of rubber boots. The only things which have to be purchased in the market are a small radio-record player, the batteries to run it, plaster religious figures, a bicycle, and some cutlery."[7] Food consumption also differs dramatically. On average, North Americans consume twice as many calories each day as Haitians and Bangladeshis. While overeating contributes to widespread obesity in industrialized nations, a sixth of the world's people are chronically malnourished, often suffering permanent brain damage because of it, and lack access to clean water. Fifteen million children die each year from hunger-related ailments.

There are also other indicators of difference in wealth. The 10 percent of people who live in the most industrialized nations consume two-thirds of the world's energy. Literacy rates range from a low of 14 percent in Niger, in West Africa, to a high of 99 percent in some twenty wealthy countries. Life expectancy ranges from a high of eighty in Japan to a low of thirty-seven in Sierra Leone, in West Africa. Over 60 percent of the world's poorest people are women, who often struggle to compete with men for resources or are often prevented by local custom from working outside the home.

Challenges of Development

Of course, the experiences of the Asian, African, and Latin American nations involve more than the bleak story of poverty and underdevelopment. Life expectancy worldwide has grown by nearly half and infant mortality has dropped by two-thirds since 1955. Some Asian and Latin American nations have achieved literacy rates comparable to those of some European nations. The number of countries the United Nations considers to have "high human development" grew from sixteen to fifty-five between 1960 and 2004. The rapidly industrializing nations of East and Southeast Asia have led the way: Singapore and South Korea achieved similar world economic rankings with such European nations as Italy, Greece, and Portugal. Several Latin American nations, Caribbean islands, and small oil-rich Persian Gulf states joined the top development category. Many rising nations—such as Malaysia, Thailand, India, and Brazil—formed a growing group of Newly Industrializing Countries (NICs) which, since the 1960s, have enjoyed high economic growth rates. Malaysia, for example, has dramatically reduced poverty rates, while India and Singapore have become centers of high technology. Nor is technological innovation restricted to the well educated. In India, for example, creative farmers have made their work easier by inventing cotton-stripping machines and modifying motorcycles into tractors.

While some countries are on the rise, however, others struggle to spur economic growth that benefits all the population. Valiant efforts have failed to substantially raise living standards or create wealth for everyone. For instance, in much of Latin America the wealthiest 20 percent have enjoyed huge income increases while the poorest 40 percent have lost income. Capitalism supported by Western investment has helped a few countries, especially those that combine strong governments with social and economic reform, as in South Korea, Malaysia, and Thailand. But reliance on free markets and Western investment has often failed to sustain development. Little of the trickle down of wealth from the rich to the poor, predicted by Western economists who favor free enterprise, has occurred. Instead, the result has often been trickle out: the loss of a country's wealth to multinational corporations and international banks. Throughout the Contemporary Era, for example, more wealth has flowed out of Africa and Latin America in the form of resources and profits than has flowed in through aid and investment.

At the same time, alternatives to capitalism have not necessarily brought improvement.Communist and other social revolutionary countries have experienced severe problems. Some of these countries, such as Fidel Castro's Cuba and Mao Zedong's China, did a good job of delivering education and health care but were unable to create much wealth. Some communist countries, such as Angola and Vietnam, also sometimes faced civil wars and trade embargoes imposed by the West that drained their economies. Since in most cases neither capitalism nor socialism by itself proved the answer, most communist regimes eventually introduced economic liberalization, such as allowing private companies and Western investment while still maintaining strong, centralized governments. Since adopting this model after the end of the Maoist era, China, for example, has generated the world's most rapid economic growth; in recent years Vietnam has tried to follow the same path. However, economic liberalization that dismantles government services has deprived millions of Chinese and Vietnamese, especially peasants, of the free education and health care they enjoyed under socialism, fostering unrest. The formula of mixing capitalism and socialism has worked well in much of East and

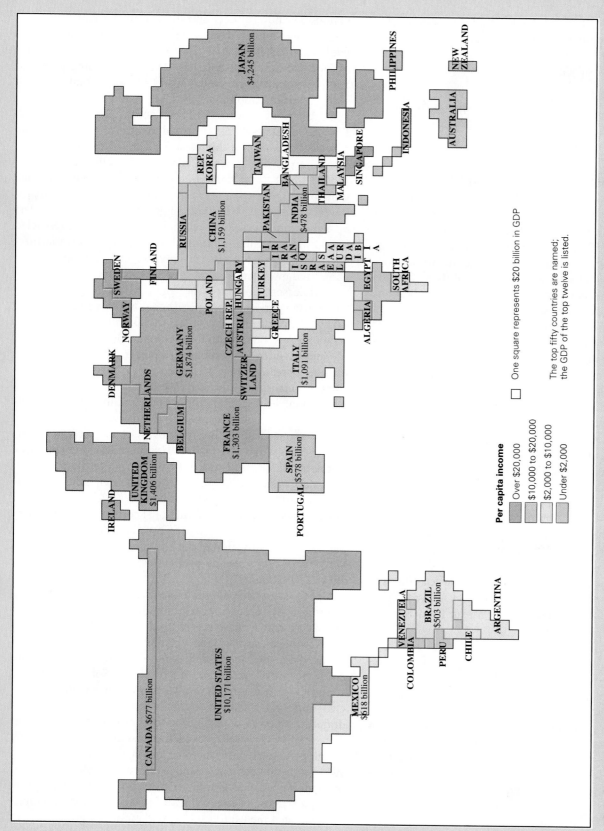

Global Distribution of Wealth The countries of North America, northern Europe, and Japan have the most wealth and the world's highest per capita incomes, averaging over $20,000 per year. At the other extreme, many people in South America and most people in the poor countries of sub-Saharan Africa, South Asia, and the Middle East earn under $2,000 per year.

Per capita income

- Over $20,000
- $10,000 to $20,000
- $2,000 to $10,000
- Under $2,000

☐ One square represents $20 billion in GDP

The top fifty countries are named; the GDP of the top twelve is listed.

Southeast Asia. In these regions, a dynamic, largely unfettered private sector has evolved along with government investment, planning, land reform, investment in education, and other public policies to benefit the common people.

Envisioning a New World Order

The challenge of development is only a part of a larger contemporary question: how societies, working together, can forge a new, more equitable world order. The old world order, built in the nineteenth century when powerful Western nations conquered much of Asia and Africa, was one in which a few rich nations politically and economically dominated most of the others. Even after World War II, decolonization, and the rise of revolutionary states such as China, a few nations, mostly in the West and East Asia, still held disproportionate power and influence. The United States has played the key role and borne the major costs in managing the global system through military alliances (such as NATO), trade pacts (such as GATT), and international organizations (such as the World Bank). However, since the 1960s experts and, often, leaders of underdeveloped nations have argued that fostering widespread economic development also requires addressing the inequalities within the global system, including adjusting power relations between the North and South, and spurring cooperation on international issues. The United Nations has been one major attempt at global cooperation but has had a mixed record.

The current world order contains many problems. The tensions resulting from governments unable significantly to raise living standards for the majority, to deal successfully with mounting social and economic problems, or to sustain hope for a better future have often led to political instability: coups, rebellions, and interventions by foreign powers. Conflicts in one nation then often spill over into neighboring nations, complicating international relations. Furthermore, people have experienced feelings of powerlessness in a world dominated by the governments, businesses, armies, and cultural influences of a few industrialized nations and the impersonal force of global markets. Leaders in the West have also expressed doubts about globalization. French president Jacques Chirac (g. 1995–present), for example, is suspicious of globalization, arguing that democracies "must tame it, accommodate it, humanize it, civilize it."[8]

The prospect of fostering a more equitable sharing of world resources raises questions about the availability of resources. Experts worry that the world's resources and environment could not support a Western standard of living for all the world. If every Chinese, Indian, Egyptian, and Peruvian, they argue, consumed the same products and calories as Americans, Swedes, or Japanese, world resources would quickly diminish. For all 6.5 billion people in today's world to live at a western European standard of living would require a 140-fold increase in the consumption of resources and energy. Present oil supplies would run out in one or two decades, assuming the oil could be pumped and refined into petroleum that fast. Furthermore, the world population is growing rapidly—4.4 people born every second—, and most of the growth is occurring in the developing nations, putting even more pressure on diminishing resources.

China's recent economic success shows the challenges ahead. By the early twenty-first century a China rushing toward development had become a huge consumer of the world's industrial, agricultural, and natural resources, energizing global trade but causing shortages elsewhere. For example, world oil prices have soared since 2000 in part because of China's increasing energy appetite as Chinese switch from bicycles to cars. If the Chinese consumed as much oil per capita as Americans their demand would exceed the present world production. By 2006 the Chinese consumed nearly twice as much meat and more than twice as much steel as Americans. China's living standards remain far below those of Japan and South Korea. Should they rise to that level, however, in the next decade or two, China will import vastly more resources than it does today, further stressing supplies. Assuming China does not experience a revolution, civil war, or economic collapse, all of which are possible, experts expect it to have the world's largest economy by 2035 or 2040, eclipsing the United States. As occurred in the industrializing West earlier, rapid Chinese development, including the growing use of polluting fossil fuels, has also led to environmental degradation, including dangerous air pollution. People in nations once poor but becoming developed, such as China and India, do not believe that the industrialized Western peoples have any more right to consume the world's resources than they do, and they want their fair share.

Resolving problems of underdevelopment, and the poverty it brings, requires change within individual countries, such as implementing land reform, curbing corruption, and reducing bureaucratic obstacles to enterprise. Many experts have advocated "bottom up" development that involves peasants, workers, and women, rather than bureaucratic elites, in decision making. Such decisions would include shaping policies that provide families with adequate economic security, hence reducing the desire among parents for many children to ensure their support in old age. The Grameen Bank in Bangladesh, which loans money to poor women, is an outstanding example of such a "bottom up" policy. The visionary Tanzanian leader Julius Nyerere argued that people cannot be developed by outsiders but must develop themselves, using their own efforts and visions to improve their lives. Self-development, however, requires more social and economic equality within societies so that the wealth can be shared more equitably.

International cooperation is hobbled because the leaders of rich and poor nations often disagree on how to address global inequality. For economic and strategic reasons, Western nations want to protect their access to and heavy consumption of resources such as oil and copper and also worry about trade competition from Newly Industrializing Nations. In democratic nations these leaders have had to answer to voters, who fear compromising their own prosperity. Beginning in the 1970s various conferences and movements have debated modifying the world economic order by, for example, stabilizing world prices for natural resource exports, which chiefly come from developing nations, so that governments could better anticipate annual revenues. Responding to a worldwide campaign to help poor nations, in 2005 the industrialized nations canceled the burdensome debts of the poorest nations. Yet critics wondered whether poor nations with corrupt, often dictatorial, governments would use increased revenues or aid wisely. Furthermore, several Western nations, including the United States, Britain, and France, have often opposed efforts to build a new economic order because such an order could threaten their powerful position in the world economy and transfer wealth to poor nations.

SUSTAINABLE ENVIRONMENTS

The decades since the mid-twentieth century were unusual for the intensity of environmental deterioration and the centrality of human effort in sparking it. The industrialized nations especially had become used to rapid economic growth and were dependent on abundant cheap energy and fresh water, needs that led to environmental destruction on an unparalleled scale. By the dawn of the twenty-first century the challenge of a changing environment became obvious. On every continent, but especially in Eurasia and North America, gas-guzzling vehicles, smoky factories, coal-fired power plants, and large farming operations produce large amounts of carbon dioxide and other pollutants, contributing to rising average temperatures that scientists call global warming. This climate change, if it continues, may have a greater impact—possibly catastrophic—on human life than any conventional war or other destructive human activities. Problems such as global warming raise the question of whether in the long term the natural environment can maintain itself and support plant, animal, and human life—a pattern known as sustainability.

Societies and Environmental Change

Experts have wondered whether the world's resources—minerals, wild plants, food crops, fresh water—could sustain present living standards on a long-term basis. For the past several decades scientists have been alarmed at the human consumption of natural resources faster than nature can replenish them. A major scientific study in the 1990s concluded that a devastating environmental crash would occur during the twenty-first century as resources become exhausted, forests disappear, plant and animal species die off, a warming climate makes certain regions uninhabitable, and pollution increases.

Human activity has altered environments since prehistory, sometimes with catastrophic results. Environmental collapse triggered by agricultural practices or deforestation helped undermine the Mesopotamians, Romans, and Maya, among others. But modern industrial societies and rapidly growing populations encroach on their natural settings even more heavily than did earlier societies. In the twentieth century people used more energy than had been used in all previous history. Between the 1890s and the 1990s the world economy grew fourteen times larger, industrial output twenty times, energy use fourteen times, carbon dioxide emissions seventeen times, water use nine times, and marine fish catches thirty-five times. These increases contributed to, among other pressing problems, air and water pollution, disposal of hazardous waste, declining genetic diversity in crops, and a mass extinction of plant and animal species. With their heavy economic production and consumption, people today are borrowing from tomorrow.

The atmosphere faces particular dangers, including a measurable warming. Earth's climate changed little, with only minor fluctuations, between the last Ice Age, which ended 10,000 years ago, and the end of the eighteenth century, when the Industrial Revolution began in Europe, but it has been changing fast over the past two centuries. The global temperature rose by one degree during the twentieth century. Since 1985, the world has experienced the highest average annual temperatures on record and unprecedented droughts. Scientists

Protesting Global Warming People in societies around the world became alarmed at the increasing environmental damage brought by modern economic activity and exploitation of resources. This demonstration by environmental activists concerned with global warming, a potentially dangerous trend caused by burning fossil fuels such as coal that produces more carbon dioxide, took place in Turkey. (AP/Wide World Photos)

now largely agree that global warming has been increasing, although they debate its causes and dangers. Without major efforts to curb warming, scientists forecast a rise of somewhere between an alarming 2.5 and a catastrophic 10.4 degrees by 2100, which, if it happens, will change human life dramatically. Referring to the enclosed buildings where warm-weather plants are raised in cold climates, scientists speak of a Greenhouse Effect, the overheating of earth from human-made pollutants. The main culprits are gases such as carbon dioxide, chlorofluorocarbons, and methane that accumulate in the atmosphere and trap heat. The amount of heat-trapping carbon dioxide in the atmosphere increased by a third between 1900 and 2000, mostly from burning coal and oil. The greenhouse gases come largely from factory smokestacks, coal-fired power plants, and gasoline-powered vehicle exhausts. The most industrialized nation, the United States, has become the major producer, accounting for some 25 percent of the carbon dioxide and up to 50 percent of the other polluting chemicals. Europe, Russia, Japan, and China produce much of the rest. Some pollutants also destroy the ozone layer, a gaseous region in the upper atmosphere that protects humans from the cancer-causing ultraviolet rays of the sun. Scientists discovered that the ozone depletion rate in the 1990s was twice as fast as was thought a decade earlier.

In the pessimistic scenarios, the consequences of rising temperatures for many of the world's peoples are devastating. Earth gets baked, rich farmland turns to desert, and forests wilt. Fresh water, already scarce, becomes even harder to find as lakes and streams dry up. Rising ocean temperatures damage fisheries and kill most protective coral reefs while also increasing the intensity of hurricanes, making them more often like the catastrophic storm that devastated New Orleans and the U.S. Gulf Coast in 2005. Tropical and subtropical nations find agriculture and life generally more difficult. In North America farming becomes tougher in the southern United States, though more productive in a warming Canada. As the ice on Greenland melts, pouring fresh water into the North Atlantic, the warming Gulf Stream may shift southward and bring harsher winters to Europe and eastern North America.

Some peoples might face even more daunting challenges. Global warming has reduced the ice covering the Arctic Ocean by half in recent years while thawing the adjacent land; these developments diminish the habitat for cold-adapted animals, such as polar bears, and threaten the livelihood and settlements of Arctic peoples. At the other end of the world, the West Antarctic ice shelf holds a vast amount of water and in some places has already begun to melt. If this trend accelerates, it will raise sea levels enough over the next two centuries to cover much low-lying coastal land. This will have disastrous consequences for regions such as the U.S. Gulf Coast and Florida, the Low Countries of northwest Europe, Bangladesh and eastern India, and small island nations already now barely above sea level, including Tonga, Tuvalu, the Bahamas, and the Maldives.

Environmental Issues and Movements

The environmental challenges, such as diminishing resources, global warming, and deforestation, reinforce the scientific concept, first popularized in the 1970s, of global ecology—of the world, including human societies, as a complex web in which all living things interact with each other and their surroundings. From earliest times, societies have had complex relations with the environment, including interdependence with it. The Industrial Revolution, which has reshaped the world over the past two centuries, often for the better, came at great costs to the environment. Yet the world's leaders cannot agree on ways to better balance economic growth, which all nations desire, with environmental protection.

The exploitation of the earth's resources for human benefit, which has accelerated since 1945, has undermined sustainability. While soil, forests, and fisheries are renewable resources if properly managed, which they often were not in the past century, mineral resources such as oil and copper cannot be replaced once used up. Oil experts disagree as to when all known recoverable oil reserves will become exhausted. Optimists think oil supplies will be adequate for 30 or 40 years before declining and becoming scarce well before the century ends. Pessimists, noting the increased demand by countries such as China and India, believe all easily exploitable sources will be gone within two or three decades, causing conflict as nations scramble for oil supplies. Anticipating future resource and energy shortages, experts have for years recommended that industrial nations conserve oil by reducing dependence on it as the main fuel while developing renewable energy resources, such as solar, tidal, and wind power. Some nations have turned toward building more nuclear power plants, which are expensive and potentially dangerous but do less damage to the climate than burning fossil fuels. So far a few developing nations and some European countries have shown the most commitment to conservation and developing renewable energies.

Scientific conclusions about global warming and the need to reduce dependence on oil have often challenged powerful economic interests and upset governments that favor economic growth and worry about economic competition from rival nations. For example, since the 1970s U.S. presidents and Congress, fearing possible negative effects on U.S. business, have often opposed environmental agreements, such as the Kyoto treaty of 1997, which was an effort, supported by most of the world's nations, to begin reducing greenhouse gases, as well as a European proposal seeking a 15 percent alternative energy use by 2010 (versus 1 percent today). Leaders of a few other powerful nations, including Japan, Russia, Britain, and China, have also been reluctant to cooperate with the world community on environmental issues. In 2005, 150 nations met in Montreal, Canada, and reaffirmed their commitment to the Kyoto treaty. To sustain environmental health, a Canadian statesman has argued, requires a "revolution in [our] thinking as basic as the one introduced by Copernicus who [in the 1500s] first pointed out that the earth was not the center of the universe."[9]

An environmental movement began in the West in the late nineteenth century, eventually sparking similar movements around the world. Yet environmental awareness grew slowly. In the 1940s, the American environmentalist Aldo Leopold called for an ethic that treats the land with respect because all life belongs to a community of interdependent relationships: "Land is a fountain of energy flowing through a circuit of soils, plants, and animals, a sustained circuit, like a slowly augmented revolving fund of life."[10] Such ideas did not gain a large following. By the 1970s, however, views had changed; organizations such as Greenpeace, Earth First!, and the Rainforest Action Network pressed for a global commitment to stop environmental destruction. In 1992 a United Nations–sponsored global conference in Rio de Janeiro issued a proclamation urging sustainable development: "Human beings are entitled to a healthy and productive life in harmony with nature."[11] But the realities of modern politics, national rivalries, and fierce economic competition continue to make such a change difficult.

GLOBAL PASTS AND FUTURES

The study of history helps us understand today's news and views as they are reported in daily newspapers, broadcast on radio and television, and disseminated on the World Wide Web. Historians often describe their work as involving a dialogue between past, present, and future. A few years ago French scientist René Dubos argued: "The past is not dead history. It is living material out of which makes the present and builds the future."[12] Current global problems have their roots in the patterns of world history: the rise of cities, states, and organized religions; the expansion of trade and capitalism to global dimensions; the unprecedented mastery and altering of nature represented by the scientific, industrial, and technological revolutions; the proliferation of competitive, unequal nations; and the myriad of social, economic, political, and cultural connections between peoples encompassed in the expanding global system. While seeking to understand how the past shaped the present, historians also speculate on how current trends may shape the future.

Understanding the Global Past

World historians offer several ways of understanding the world of yesterday, today, and tomorrow. One view is that contacts and collisions between different societies produce change. Whether through peaceful exchange or warfare or perhaps both, when societies encounter other societies they are exposed to different customs and ideas. For millennia after the transition to agriculture most of those contacts were with nearby peoples, but around two thousand years ago, thanks to advances in transportation and growing economies, increasingly mobile peoples began to encounter others much further away, laying the roots for a global system to emerge after 1450. Historians also emphasize continuity, the persistence of social, cultural, political, and religious ideas and patterns, as well as change, the transformations in ways of life, work, and thought. Continuities are common. For example, many Christians, Muslims, Jews, Buddhists, and Hindus still look at the world through the prism of traditional religious values forged millennia ago and still meaningful today. Hence, in 2004 over 400,000 Christian missionaries—many from countries like Nigeria, the Philippines, and South Korea—were spreading the gospel around the world, at an annual cost of some $11 billion. Islam increased its following from 400 million people in 1960 to 1.3 billion by 2004. Yet changes, too, are everywhere. Thus most people, among them the devout followers of the old religions, also engage in activities, face challenges, and use forms of transportation and communication nonexistent a few generations ago. As a result, missionaries and clerics often use radio, television, and the Internet to spread their message. Another insight offered by global historians is that great transitions, such as the agricultural and industrial revolutions or, more recently, the rise of high technology, can turn history in new directions. Hence, thousands of years ago farming largely displaced hunting and gathering, two centuries ago industry transformed the world economy, and today instant communication and information bring distant peoples closer together. For instance, youngsters in Wisconsin can watch Australian-rules football matches from Melbourne on cable television while fans of Chinese rock and rap groups can hear their music on websites accessible from around the world.

As an example of the contacts and collisions that foster change, some scholars explain the changes of the past five hundred years in terms of the larger world's exposure and accommodation to the West, which led in turn to the political, economic, and military triumph of the West and often the adoption of its values and institutions. As a result of the spread of Western cultural influences, market economies, economic consumption practices, and individualistic values, they see a growing standardization of the world's societies. Many people welcome this standardization as a sign of progress, while others perceive it as a threat to local traditions. Still others consider the claim that societies and cultures are standardizing inaccurate, seeing instead a real increase in differences, especially the growing gap between rich and poor nations. In fact, living standards in the world have not been standardized. While people in the rich countries usually own several expensive electrical appliances, from washing machines to plasma televisions, millions of people in the poor nations do not even have electricity. Still, thanks to contacts between distant societies, the Western value of materialistic indulgence has became common, even if often out of reach for the poorest half of the world's people.

The experiences of most societies over the past half century reveal a mix of change and continuity. For example, Western ideas have gained even greater influence in the world since 1945 than they had before. People in different lands have adopted Western ideas of government, such as constitutions and elections, although not necessarily the substance of democracy, along with Western-rooted ideologies and faiths: capitalism, socialism, nationalism, and Christianity. Western pop culture, from rock music to soft drinks and blue jeans, has spread widely, leading to the "Coca-Colazation" of the world stemming from Western economic power, including advertising. Yet influences from the West are usually strongest in large cities and penetrate less deeply into the villages in Africa, Asia, and the Middle East, where traditional ways reflect continuity with the past. As a result, city youth in Malaysia or Tanzania may follow the latest recordings from Western pop stars, but these recordings may be unknown to their rural counterparts. Yet the urban youth may also share with rural youth traditional views about family and faith, and rural youth may, like their city counterparts, own motorcycles, boom boxes, and cell phones that make their lives different from those of their parents.

As a result of the transition to globalizing technology, culture, and commerce, the contacts between societies and their interdependence have vastly increased since 1945. In different ways nuclear weapons, multinational corporations, earth-circling satellites, World Cup soccer, and cable news networks draw people together, willingly or not. Imperialists once claimed proudly that "the sun never set on the British Empire." By the 1990s observers noted that "the sun never sets on McDonald's." Closer contact, of course, does not necessarily mean friendly relations and a less dangerous world; it can also bring collisions. Guided missiles and planes carrying bombs can reach 10,000 miles from their base. Over the past several decades over 60,000 Americans have died fighting in Vietnam, Afghanistan, and Iraq in support of U.S. efforts to reshape distant nations. On the other side, terrorist plots hatched in Afghanistan by Islamic militants who blame the United States for Middle Eastern problems killed Americans in New York City and Washington, D.C., in 2001. Some of the terrorists involved in planning or carrying out those and other attacks were once secular Muslims who went to Europe or the United States for college and, culturally disoriented and resentful of Western policies, became Islamic militants and then joined a terrorist organization with global reach and access to high technology such as satellite phones, computers, and the Internet. Experts also speak of cyberspace terrorism, in which political or religious extremists advertise their violent goals and deeds on websites. The same technologies that allow people to instantly access and share information around the world also allows governments to spy on citizens and criminals to use cyberspace for their own purposes. Meanwhile, hackers can live anywhere and disrupt computer operations all over the world. Technology also threatens governments. In 2005 the search engine company, Google, made available a program, Google Earth, that can be freely downloaded and allows a user anywhere to see aerial and satellite photos of any location in the world. Governments from Algeria to India to Russia protested unsuccessfully that this violated their laws and revealed data, such as the layout of military bases, that they did not want available to the general public.

The contacts, changes, and transitions since 1945 have created a global village, a single community of exchange and interaction. In some regions, such as Southeast Asia, even remote villages have become part of this global village. By the 1960s, for example, people living in the once isolated interior of the island of Borneo, divided between Indonesia and Malaysia, could access the outside world through battery-powered transistor radios and cassette players, and also by means of visiting traders, Christian missionaries, and government officials. Borneo's interior people also often left their remote villages to find work at logging camps, oil wells, or plantations as their rain forest environment and small farms rapidly disappeared, destroyed by international timber and mining operations that cut forests and stripped land to procure resources to ship to distant countries. As once remote peoples, like those in the Borneo interior, are brought into the global system, and ethnic minorities are incorporated into nations, they find it harder to maintain their cultures and languages. Half of all languages are in danger of dying out over the next several decades and less than one percent of languages are used on the Internet.

Towards the Future

Women and men created the present world from the materials of the past and are now laying the foundation for the future. As a Belgian scholar wrote a few years ago, "We cannot predict the future, but we can prepare it."[13] But this raises the questions of what kind of future. In 1974 the American economic historian Robert Heilbroner, asking what promise the future holds, doubted the permanence of modern industrial society and even democracy in the face of population explosion, environmental degradation, resource depletion, militarization, and the increasing economic desperation of people in the poorest countries. His question remains highly relevant in the early twenty-first century. For example, as industrialization spreads to other nations, the world requires more use of fossil fuels, which spurs more global warming. Heilbroner drew a gloomy picture of the future. He believed most people are not willing to sacrifice for the good of future generations. Like him, other experts often despair. The world's long history of war, inequality, and exploitation, even when seemingly offset by progress, does not foster optimism. Indeed, some respected experts predict human extinction if people do not adopt more sustainable ways, and scientific studies are more frequently pessimistic than optimistic about the future. Worried tht we face environment collapse, one study concludes: "Our generation is the first to be faced with decisions that will determine whether the earth our children inherit will be habitable."[14]

Yet, since World War II humanity has produced many green shoots of hope. Western Europe moved rapidly to political and economic unity, defusing centuries of conflict. Eastern Europeans and Russians overturned dogmatic communist regimes, ending the long Cold War between the superpowers. The Scandinavian nations, a hundred years ago among the poorest European societies, have virtually eliminated poverty, achieving the world's highest quality of life. Several Asian nations rapidly developed, dramatically improving living standards and national wealth. A century ago desperately poor, China has become not only able to feed and clothe its huge population but also to export industrial products to the world. Thanks in part to global efforts, black majority rule came to South Africa. Over two dozen nations, including some in Asia, Latin America, and the Caribbean, have elected women presidents or prime ministers, and women, making their voices heard, have increasingly gained more power over their lives in many countries. Despite some notable conflicts, wars have become less common than before. Unlike the Cold War years

International Women's Day 2005 Women around the world became more willing to assert their rights. Activists from diverse Indian nongovernmental organizations interested in women's rights marched in New Delhi, India's capital, in 2005 to mark International Women's Day. (AP/Wide World Photos)

between 1946 and 1992, when fighting between and within nations was frequent, between 1992 and 2005 the number of wars with over 1,000 battle deaths a year declined by 80 percent.

Hopeful developments have also resulted from international cooperation. A large majority of nations have signed agreements to ban weapons of mass destruction, punish genocide, and reduce gases contributing to global warming. Drastic reductions in the arms race have diminished the threat of nuclear war. United Nations agencies have improved lives for children and women in many countries and spurred cooperation on environmental issues. Local nongovernmental organizations, often with international connections, have also become active, working for the rights of women, children, workers, and peasants and for a healthier environment. Human rights groups with chapters around the world have

worked courageously to promote civil liberties and the release of political prisoners. Encouraged by environmental activists abroad, brave tribal groups in tropical rain forests have resisted the logging and mining destroying their habitats. Not least in its effects, the growing information superhighway now instantly links millions of office or home computers with people, libraries, and other information sources around the world.

A history not only of cruelty and exploitation but also of compassion and sacrifice provides hope in navigating troubled times. Remembering when people behaved magnificently may foster inspiration to answer the challenges. The contemporary age offers ample examples of inspiring people: democracy activists such as Nelson Mandela, Vaclav Havel, Mohandas Gandhi, and Aung San Suu Kyi; social activists such as Wangari Maathai, Dr. Martin Luther King, Jr., Shirin Ebadi, and Mukhtaran Bibi; cultural figures such as Wole Soyinka, Violeta Parra, Simone de Beauvoir, and Cui Jian; and figures who have built links between societies such as Jean Monnet, Bono, and the Dalai Lama. Historians sometimes view the past as a stream with banks. The stream is filled with people killing, bullying, enslaving, and doing other things historians usually record, while on the banks, unnoticed, women and men build homes, raise children, tend farms, settle disputes, sing songs, whittle statues, trade with their neighbors, and chat with travelers from other lands. Historians often ignore the banks for the stream, but what happens on the banks may be more reassuring.

Some observers, believing that cultural differences will increasingly drive international politics, forecast a clash of civilizations, such as between the Christian West and Islam, which are seen as irreconcilably opposed in world-views. But simplistic formulas miss the complexity of the global order. None of the great religions and the cultures that they shaped are monolithic, the divisions among Christians or Muslims, Westerners or Middle Easterners, being as great as their differences with other traditions. No cultures or religions have a monopoly on values such as peace, justice, charity, tolerance, public discussion, and goodwill. In any case, nations generally shape their foreign policies according to their national interests rather than ideology. Wars over resources, such as oil and water, some observers claim, are more likely to occur than wars over cultural differences. Other observers doubt that, whatever the tensions, any titanic military struggle like the two world wars of the twentieth century is inevitable; they expect that the world will cooperate on major issues and tolerate different concepts of economics, government, God, morality, and society for years to come. Furthermore, thanks to the many available information sources people can become informed about why past societies, such as the Mesopotamians and Maya, destroyed their environments and collapsed, and how countries blundered into wars or failed to develop cooperative relations with their neighbors that maintained peace. These insights, if acquired, may help people today to avoid repeating the mistakes of the past and construct a better future.

Four centuries ago, the English playwright William Shakespeare wrote that the past is prologue to the present. The study of world history allows us to ask questions about the global future because we understand the changing patterns of the global past, including the building of societies, their interactions through networks, and the great transitions that reshaped humanity. These have led to an increasingly connected world in the past 1,500 years. The contemporary age has been marked by a complex mix of dividing and unifying forces, unique societies differing greatly in standards of living but linked into a global system of exchange. People today cannot yet know with certainty where the path will lead, but they can help build it. Nineteenth-century British novelist Lewis Carroll (1832–1898) suggested a way of looking at the problem in his novel *Through the Looking Glass*, about Alice in Wonderland. Lost and perplexed in Wonderland, Alice asked the Cheshire Cat: "Would you tell me, please, which way I ought to go from here?" The enigmatic cat pondered the query for a few moments and then replied: "That depends a great deal on where you want to get to."[15] Societies, working together, must chart that course into the future.

SUGGESTED READING

BOOKS

Baylis, John, et al., eds. *The Globalization of World Politics: An Introduction to International Relations*, 3rd ed. New York: Oxford University Press, 2004. Essays on world politics by British scholars.

Brown, Lester. *Plan B 2.0: Rescuing a Planet Under Stress and a Civilizaion in Trouble*. New York: W. W. Norton, 2006. A survey of the world's environmental and resource challenges and some possible solutions.

Hannerz, Ulf. *Transnational Connections: Culture, People, Places*. New York: Routledge, 1996. Interesting essays on cultures and networks in the age of globalization by a Swedish scholar.

Held, David, ed. *A Globalizing World? Culture, Economics, Politics*. New York: Routledge, 2000. An excellent collection of essays and readings on various aspects of globalization, compiled by British scholars.

Hobsbawm, Eric. *On the Edge of the New Century*. New York: The New Press, 1999. Thoughts on the past, present, and future by a British historian.

Kennedy, Paul. *Preparing for the Twenty-First Century*. New York: Random House, 1993. A study of how population, technology, and the environment shaped the contemporary world and various regions.

Mayor, Federico, and Jerome Bindé. *The World Ahead: Our Future in the Making*. New York: Zed Books, 2001. A comprehensive study, prepared by European scholars for the United Nations, of political, economic, social, cultural, and environmental trends.

Mazrui, Ali. *Cultural Forces in World Politics*. London: Heinemann, 1990. A challenging examination of world-views and patterns by a distinguished African scholar.

Newland, Kathleen, and Kamala Chandrakirana Soedjatmoko, eds. *Transforming Humanity: The Visionary Writings of Soedjatmoko*. West Hartford, Conn.: Kumarian Press, 1994. Thoughtful essays on development, violence, religion, and other issues in the contemporary world by an influential Indonesian thinker.

Pieterse, Jan Nederveen, ed. *Global Futures: Shaping Globalization*. London: Zed Books, 2000. Provocative essays on world trends by scholars from around the world.

Sachs, Jeffrey. *The End of Poverty: Economic Possibilities for Our Time*. New York: Penguin, 2005. Controversial but stimulating discussion of global poverty issues.

Seager, Joni. *The Penguin Atlas of Women in the World*, revised and updated. New York: Penguin, 2003. Creative, indispensable examination of women around the world.

Sen, Amartya. *Identity and Violence: The Illusion of Destiny*. New York: W. W. Norton, 2006. Provocative critique by an India-born economist of the clash of civilizations idea.

Smith, Dan, and Ane Braein. *Penguin State of the World Atlas*, 7th ed. New York: Penguin, 2003. The latest edition of an invaluable map-based reference providing an overview of world conditions.

State of the World. New York: W. W. Norton. Informative annual surveys of the world's environmental health that are published annually by the Worldwatch Institute in Washington, D.C.

Taylor, Timothy D. *Global Pop: World Music, World Markets*. New York: Routledge, 1997. A fine study of the world music industry and major musicians.

WEBSITES

Global Problems and the Culture of Capitalism (http://faculty.plattsburgh.edu/richard.robbins/legacy/). An outstanding site, aimed at undergraduates, with a wealth of resources on many topics.

Globalization Guide (http://www.globalisationguide.org). A useful collection of essays and links.

The Globalization Website (http://www.sociology.emory.edu/globalization/). A very useful site with many resources and essays related to globalization.

United Nations (http://www.un.org). The pathway to the websites of the many United Nations agencies, operations, and ongoing projects.

The WWW Virtual Library (http://vlib.org). The homepage of a vast and indispensable British-based network of links on many topics and issues.

GLOSSARY

The glossary for *Societies, Networks, and Transitions: A Global History* is for the complete text, Chapters 1 through 31.

absolutism A system of strong monarchial authority in which all power is placed in a supreme authority, a king or queen. *(p. 445)*

Achaemenid The ruling family of the Classical Persian Empire (ca. 550–450 B.C.E.). *(p. 146)*

Age of Revolution The period from the 1770s through the 1840s when revolutions rocked North America, Europe, the Caribbean, and Latin America. *(p. 566)*

Ahura Mazda (the "Wise Lord") The one god of **Zoroastrianism**. *(p. 150)*

Aksum A literate, urban state that appeared in northern Ethiopia before the Common Era and grew into an empire and a crossroads for trade. *(p. 231)*

Allah To Muslims the one and only, all-powerful God. *(p. 274)*

animism The belief that all creatures as well as inanimate objects and natural phenomena have souls and can influence human well-being. *(p.15)*

apartheid ("separate development") A South African policy to set up a police state to enforce racial separation; lasted from 1948 to 1994. *(p. 956)*

Arianism A heretical Christian sect that arose in the fourth century C.E. that taught that Jesus was not divine but rather an exceptional human being. *(p. 218)*

Aryans Indo-European-speaking nomadic pastoralists who migrated from Iran into northwest India between 1600 and 1400 B.C.E. (see **pastoral nomadism**). *(p. 47)*

asceticism A system of austere religious practices, such as intense prayer, that was used to strengthen spiritual life and seek a deeper understanding of god; began to be used in the Christian church in the fifth and sixth centuries C.E. *(p. 218)*

ASEAN (Association of Southeast Asian Nations) A regional economic and political organization formed in 1967 to promote cooperation among the non-Communist Southeast Asian nations; eventually became a major trading bloc. *(p. 993)*

Atlantic System A large network that arose with the trans-Atlantic slave trade; the network spanned western and Central Africa, the east coast and southern region of English North America, the Caribbean Basin, and the northern and eastern coastal zones of South America. *(p. 473)*

audiencias Judicial tribunals with administrative functions that served as subdivisions of viceroyalties in Spanish America. *(p. 500)*

australopithecines Early **hominids** living in eastern and southern Africa 3 to 4 million years ago. *(p. 9)*

Awami League A Bengali nationalist party that began the move from independence from West Pakistan. *(p. 975)*

Ba'ath ("Renaissance") A political party in the Middle East that favored socialism and Arab nationalism and strongly opposed Israel. *(p. 942)*

Bahai An offshoot of Persian Shi'ism that was founded in 1867; Bahai preached universal peace, the unity of all religions, and service to others. *(p. 649)*

Balfour Declaration A letter from the British foreign minister to Zionist leaders in 1917 that gave British support for the establishment of Palestine as a national home for the Jewish people. *(p. 776)*

Bantu Sub-Saharan African peoples who developed a cultural tradition based on farming and iron metallurgy, which they spread widely through great migrations. *(p. 67)*

bantustans Rural reservations in South Africa where black Africans under apartheid were required to live if they were not needed in the modern economy. *(p. 957)*

baroque An extravagant and, to many, shocking European artistic movement of the 1600s that encouraged release from restraints of thought and expression. *(p. 451)*

Bedouins Tent-dwelling nomadic Arab pastoralists of the seventh century C.E. who wandered in search of oases, grazing lands, or trade caravans to raid (see **pastoral nomadism**). *(p. 270)*

benefices In **medieval** Europe, grants of land from lord to **vassal**. *(p. 391)*

Bhagavad Gita ("Lord's Song") A poem in the *Mahabharata* that is the most treasured piece of ancient Hindu literature. *(p. 51)*

bhakti Devotional worship of a personal Hindu god. *(p. 363)*

bhangra A popular music that emerged in Britain from a blending of traditional folk songs brought by Indian immigrants with Caribbean reggae and Anglo-American styles, such as rock, hip hop, and disco. *(p. 881)*

Bharatha Janata (BJP) The major Hindu nationalist party in India. *(p. 976)*

Black Hole of Calcutta A crowded jail in India where over a hundred British prisoners of a hostile Bengali ruler died from suffocation and dehydration in 1757. This event precipitated the beginning of British use of force in India. *(p. 660)*

Black Legend The Spanish reputation for brutality toward Native Americans, including the repression of native religions, execution of rebels, and forced labor. *(p. 502)*

bodhisattva ("One who has the essence of Buddhahood") A loving and ever compassionate "saint" who has postponed his or her own attainment of **nirvana** to help others find salvation through liberation from birth and rebirth (see **Buddhism, Mahayana**). *(p. 186)*

Boers Dutch farming settlers in South Africa in the eighteenth century. *(p. 470)*

Bollywood The Bombay film industry in India. *(p. 978)*

Bolsheviks The most radical of Russia's antigovernment groups in the early twentieth century, who embraced a dogmatic form of Marxism. *(p. 722)*

bourgeoisie The urban-based, mostly commercial, middle class that arose with **capitalism** in the Early Modern Era. *(p. 435)*

Brahman The Universal Soul, or Absolute Reality, that Hindus believe fills all space and time. *(p. 176)*

Brahmanas Commentaries on the **Vedas** that emphasize the role of priests (**brahmans**). *(p. 52)*

brahmans The priests, the highest-ranking caste in Hindu society. *(p. 50)*

Brezhnev Doctrine In the late twentieth century, an assertion by Soviet leaders of Moscow's right to interfere in Soviet satellites to protect Communist governments and the Soviet bloc. *(p. 886)*

British Commonwealth of Nations A forum, established by Britain in 1931, for discussing issues of mutual interest with its former colonies. *(p. 871)*

Buddhism A major world religion based on the teachings of the Buddha that emphasized putting an end to desire and being compassionate to all creatures. *(p. 178)*

Bunraku The puppet theater of Tokugawa Japan. *(p. 543)*

Burakumin ("Hamlet people") A despised Japanese subgroup who traditionally were restricted to poor neighborhoods and performed jobs considered unclean and undignified. *(p. 706)*

Bushido ("Way of the Warrior") An idealized ethic for the Japanese **samurai**. *(p. 322)*

caliphate An imperial state headed by an Islamic ruler, the caliph, considered the designated successor of the Prophet in civil affairs. *(p. 274)*

calligraphy The artful writing of words. *(p. 286)*

calypso A song style in Trinidad that often featured lyrics addressing daily life and topical subjects. *(p. 621)*

can vuong ("Aid-the-king") Rebel groups who waged guerrilla warfare for fifteen years against the French occupation of Vietnam. *(p. 675)*

capitalism An economic system in which property, exchange, and the means of production are privately owned. *(p. 430)*

caste system The four-tiered Hindu social system comprising hereditary social classes that restrict the occupation of their members and their relations with members of other castes. *(p. 50)*

Castroism Innovative socialist policies introduced by Fidel Castro to stimulate economic development in Cuba while tightly controlling its population. *(p. 923)*

caudillos Latin American military strongmen who acquired and maintained power through force between the early nineteenth and mid-twentieth centuries. *(p. 616)*

Centuriate Assembly A Roman legislative body made up of soldiers. *(p. 203)*

Chavín The earliest-known Andean urban society. *(p. 102)*

chinampas Artificial islands built along lakeshores of the central valley of Mexico and used by the Aztecs for growing food. *(p. 349)*

Chinoiserie An eighteenth- and nineteenth-century Western vogue for artistic products of China such as painting, ceramics, lacquer ware, and decorative furniture. *(p. 688)*

chivalry The rigid code of behavior, including a sense of duty and honor, of **medieval** European knights. *(p. 391)*

Clovis A Native American culture dating back some 11,500 to 13,500 years. *(p. 96)*

Co-hong A nineteenth-century Chinese merchant's guild that had a monopoly on Guangzhou's trade with the West. *(p. 688)*

Cold War A conflict lasting from 1946 to 1989 in which the United States and the USSR competed for allies and engaged in occasional warfare against their rivals' allies rather than against each other directly. *(p. 807)*

colonialism Government by one society over another society. *(p. 474)*

Columbian Exchange The transportation of diseases, animals, and plants from one hemisphere to another that resulted from European exploration and conquest between 1492 and 1750. *(p. 499)*

commercial capitalism The economic system in which most capital was invested in commercial enterprises such as trading companies, including the world's first joint-stock companies. *(p. 435)*

communes Large agricultural units introduced in China by Mao Zedong that combined many families and villages into a common system for pooling resources and labor. *(p. 838)*

Confucianism A Chinese philosophy based on the ideas of Confucius (ca. 551–479 B.C.E.) that emphasized the correct relations among people; became the dominant philosophy of East Asia for two millennia. *(p. 122)*

conquistadors The leaders of Spanish soldiers engaged in armed conquest in the Americas. *(p. 495)*

consuls Two **patrician** men, elected by the **Centuriate Assembly** each year, who had executive power in the Roman Republic. *(p. 203)*

containment The main U.S. strategy aimed at preventing Communists from gaining power, and the USSR from getting political influence, in other nations during the **Cold War.** *(p. 905)*

Coptic Church A branch of Christianity, based on **Monophysite** ideas, that had become influential in Egypt and became dominant in Nubia between the fourth and sixth centuries C.E. *(p. 231)*

Cossacks Tough adventurers and soldiers from southern Russia who were descendants of Russians, Poles, and Lithuanians fleeing serfdom, slavery, or jail. *(p. 484)*

Counter Reformation A movement to confront Protestantism and crush dissidents within the Catholic Church (see **Protestants, Reformation**). *(p. 441)*

courtly love A standard of polite relationships between knights and ladies that arose in the 1100s in **medieval** Europe. Courtly love was celebrated in song by wandering troubadours. *(p. 394)*

creoles People of Iberian ancestry who were born in Latin America. *(p. 500)*

Cro-Magnons The first modern, tool-using humans in Europe. *(p. 13)*

cubism An early-twentieth-century form of painting that rejected visual reality and emphasized instead geometric shapes and forms that often suggested movement. *(p. 735)*

cultivation system An agricultural policy imposed by the Dutch in Java that forced Javanese farmers to grow sugar on rice land. *(p. 672)*

cultural relativism The notion that societies are diverse and unique, embodying different standards of correct behavior. *(p. xxxi)*

cuneiform ("wedge-shape") A Latin term used to describe the writing system invented by the Sumerians. *(p. 36)*

Cynicism A Hellenistic philosophy, made famous by the philosopher Diogenes (fourth century B.C.E.), that emphasized living a radically simple life, shunning material things and all pretense, and remaining true to one's fundamental values (see **Hellenism**). *(p. 169)*

daimyo ("Great name") Large landowning territorial magnates who monopolized local power in Japan beginning during the Ashikaga period (1338–1568). *(p. 324)*

Daoism A Chinese philosophy that emphasized adaptation to nature; arose in the late Zhou era. *(p. 125)*

Dar al-Islam ("Abode of Islam") The Islamic world stretching from Morocco to Indonesia and joined by both a common faith and trade; arose between the eighth and the seventeenth centuries. *(p. 289)*

Darkest Africa Those areas of the African continent least known to Europeans but, in European eyes, awaiting to be "opened" to the "light of Western civilization." *(p. 465)*

deism Belief in a benevolent God who designed the universe but does not intercede in its affairs. *(p. 454)*

Delian League A defensive league organized by Greek cities in the fifth century B.C.E. to defeat the Persians. *(p. 161)*

desertification The transformation of once productive land into useless desert. *(pp. 65 and 823)*

devaraja ("God-king") The title used by Indianized Southeast Asian rulers, who wished to be seen as a reincarnated Buddha or **Shiva** worthy of cult worship. *(p. 370)*

development Growth in a variety of economic areas that benefits the majority of people; the opposite of **monoculture.** *(p. 507)*

direct rule A method of ruling colonies whereby a largely European colonial administration supervised all activity, even down to the local level, and native chiefs or kings were reduced to symbolic roles (see **colonialism**). *(p. 641)*

dominion A country that has autonomy but owes allegiance to the British crown; developed in the early twentieth century. *(p. 623)*

domino theory A theory that envisioned countries falling one by one to communism and that became a mainstay of U.S. policy during the **Cold War.** *(p. 904)*

Dravidian A language family whose speakers are the great majority of the population in southern India. *(p. 45)*

dreamtime In Aboriginal Australian mythology, the distant past when the spiritual ancestors gave order and form to the universe at the world's creation. *(p. 248)*

Dust Bowl Parts of the U.S. Midwest and Southwest during the 1930s where disappearing topsoil and severe drought threw agriculture badly out of balance. *(p. 733)*

dyarchy A form of dual government that began in Japan during the Nara period (710–784) whereby one powerful family ruled the country while the emperor held mostly symbolic power. *(p. 317)*

dynastic cycle The Chinese view of their political history, which focuses on dynasties of ruling families. *(p. 88)*

empiricism An approach that stresses experience and the testing of propositions rather than reason alone in acquiring knowledge. *(p. 454)*

enclosure Arising in Early Modern Europe, the pattern in which landlords fenced off common lands once used by the public for grazing livestock and collecting firewood. *(p. 455)*

encomienda ("Entrustment") The Crown's grant to a colonial Spaniard in Latin America of a certain number of Indians from whom he extracted tribute. *(p. 507)*

Enlightenment A philosophical movement based on science and reason that began in Europe in the late seventeenth century and continued through the eighteenth century. *(p. 453)*

Estado Novo ("New State") A fascist-influenced and modernizing dictatorship in Brazil led by Getulio Vargas between 1930 and 1945. *(p. 777)*

ethnocentrism Viewing others narrowly through the lenses of one's own society and its values. *(p. xxx)*

Eurocommunism A form of communism in western Europe in the later twentieth century that embraced political democracy and free elections and that rejected Soviet domination. *(p. 870)*

excommunicate To expel a person from the Roman Catholic church and its sacraments. *(p. 396)*

existentialism A philosophy, influential in post–World War II western Europe, whose speculation on the nature of reality reflects disillusionment with Europe's violent history and doubt that objectivity is possible. *(p. 882)*

extraterritoriality Freedom from local laws for foreign subjects. *(p. 690)*

fascism A twentieth-century ideology that typically involved extreme **nationalism,** hatred of ethnic minorities, ruthless repression of opposition groups, violent anticommunism, and authoritarian government. (*p. 735*)

feminism A philosophy that became strong in the twentieth century promoting political, social, and economic equality for women with men. (*p. 602*)

Fertile Crescent A large semicircular fertile region that included the valleys of the Tigris and Euphrates Rivers stretching northwest from the Persian Gulf, the eastern shores of the Mediterranean Sea, and, to some scholars, the banks of the Nile River in North Africa. (*p. 31*)

feudalism A political arrangement characterized by a weak central monarchy that ruled over smaller states or influential families that were largely autonomous but owed service obligations to the monarch; prevailed in **medieval** Europe. (*p. 390*)

fief In **medieval** Europe, the thing granted in a feudal contract, usually land (see **feudalism**). (*p. 391*)

filial piety The Confucian rule that children should respect and obey their parents (see **Confucianism**). (*p. 123*)

First World A later-twentieth-century term for the industrialized democracies of western Europe, North America, Australia-New Zealand, and Japan. (*p. 806*)

Fourth World A later-twentieth-century term for the poorest societies, with very small economies and few exploitable resources. (*p. 806*)

gauchos Cowboys in Argentina and Uruguay who worked on large ranches and were skilled horsemen and fighters. (*p. 616*)

Geez The classical Amharic written language of Ethiopia, a mixture of African and Semitic influences. (*p. 232*)

geomancy Known in Chinese as *feng shui* ("wind and water"), a system for determining the auspicious settings of human dwellings and graves that emerged in ancient times. (*p. 137*)

Ghana The first known major Sudanic state, formed by the Soninke people of the middle Niger valley around 500 C.E. (see **Sudan**). (*p. 235*)

glasnost ("openness") The policy introduced in the Soviet Union by Mikhail Gorbachev in the 1980s to democratize the political system. (*p. 889*)

global village A later-twentieth-century term for an interconnected world community in which all people, regardless of their nationality, share a common fate. (*p. 824*)

globalization A pattern in which economic, political, and cultural processes reach beyond **nation-state** boundaries. (*p. 813*)

Great Depression A collapse of the world economy that lasted in varying degrees of severity through the 1930s. (*p. 728*)

Great Leap Forward Mao Zedong's ambitious attempt in the later 1950s to industrialize China rapidly and end poverty through collective efforts. (*p. 838*)

Great Proletarian Cultural Revolution A radical movement in China between 1966 and 1976 that represented Mao Zedong's attempt to implant his vision, destroy his enemies, crush the stifling bureaucracy, and renew the revolution's vigor. (*p. 841*)

Green Revolution A later-twentieth-century term for increased agricultural output through the use of new high-yield seeds and mechanized farming. (*p. 816*)

Greens A twentieth-century political movement in western Europe that rejected militarism and heavy industry and favored environmental protection over economic growth. (*p. 870*)

griots A respected class of oral historians and musicians in West Africa who memorized and recited the history of the group, emphasizing the deeds of leaders. (*p. 236*)

guerrilla warfare An unconventional military strategy of avoiding full-scale direct confrontations in favor of small-scale skirmishes. (*p. 809*)

guilds In **medieval** Europe, collective fraternal organizations of craftsmen and merchants designed to protect the economic interests of their members. (*p. 392*)

Gulags Russian shorthand for harsh forced-labor camps in Siberia. (*p. 727*)

gunboat diplomacy The Western countries' use of superior firepower to impose their will on local populations and governments in the nineteenth century. (*p. 695*)

haciendas Vast ranches in Spanish America. (*p. 507*)

hadith The remembered words and deeds of Muhammad, revered by many Muslims as a source of belief. (*p. 272*)

haiku The seventeen-syllable poem that proved an excellent vehicle for discussing the passage of time and the change of seasons in Early Modern Japan. (*p. 544*)

haj The Muslim pilgrimage to the holy city of Mecca to worship with multitudes of other believers from around the world. (*p. 275*)

Harappan Name given to the **city-states** and the widespread Bronze Age culture they shared that were centered in the Indus River Valley and nearby rivers in northwest India between 2200 and 1800 B.C.E. (*p. 42*)

Hellenism A widespread culture flourishing between 359 and 100 B.C.E. that combined western Asian (mainly Persian) and Greek (Hellenic) characteristics. (*p. 164*)

hieroglyphics The ancient Egyptian writing system, which evolved from pictograms into stylized pictures expressing ideas. (*p. 59*)

highlife An urban-based West African musical style mixing Christian hymns, West Indian calypso, and African dance rhythms. (*p. 770*)

hijra The emigration of Muslims from Mecca to Medina in 622. (*p. 273*)

Hispanization The process by which, over nearly three centuries of Spanish colonial rule beginning in 1565, the Catholic religion and Spanish culture were imposed on the Philippine people. (*p. 529*)

history The study of the past that looks at all of human life, thought, and behavior and that includes both a record and an interpretation of events, people, and the societies they developed. (*p. xxvi*)

historical revision Changing understanding of the past. (*p. xxvi*)

Holocaust The Nazis' deliberate murder of Jews and Romany (Gypsies), one of the worst genocides in world history. (*p. 741*)

Holy Inquisition A church court created in 1231 in **medieval** Europe to investigate and eliminate heresy; inquisitions continued into the 1600s. (*p. 396*)

hominids A family including humans and their immediate ancestors. (*p. 8*)

Homo erectus ("Erect human") A **hominid** that emerged in East Africa probably between 1.8 and 2.2 million years ago. (*p. 9*)

Homo habilis ("Handy human") A direct ancestor of humans, so named because of its increased brain size and ability to make and use simple stone tools for hunting and gathering. (*p. 9*)

Homo sapiens ("Thinking human") A **hominid** who evolved around 400,000 or 500,000 years ago and from whom anatomically modern humans (*Homo sapiens sapiens*) evolved around 100,000 years ago. (*p. 10*)

horticulture The growing of crops with simple methods and tools. (*p. 18*)

humanism The name for the European **Renaissance** philosophy, which emphasized humanity, worldly concerns, and reason rather than religious ideals. (*p. 409*)

ideology A coherent, widely shared system of ideas about the nature of the social, political, and economic realm. (*p. 583*)

imperialism The control or domination, direct or indirect, of one state or people over another. (*p. 474*)

impressionism A European artistic movement of the late nineteenth century that sought to express the immediate impression aroused by momentary scenes that were bathed in light and color. (*p. 604*)

Indianization The process by which Indian ideas spread into and influenced many Southeast Asian societies; a mixing of Indian with indigenous ideas. (*p. 193*)

Indios ("Indies peoples") The Filipinos at the bottom of the Spanish colonial social structure, who faced many legal restrictions. (*p. 531*)

indirect rule A method of ruling colonies whereby districts were administered by traditional (native) leaders, who had considerable local power but were subject to European officials (see **colonialism**). (*p. 641*)

Indo-Aryan synthesis The fusion of **Aryan** and **Dravidian** cultures in India over many centuries. (*p. 50*)

Indo-Europeans Various tribes who all spoke related languages that derived from some original common tongue and who eventually settled Europe, Iran, and northern India. (*p. 27*)

Industrial Revolution A dramatic transformation in the production and transportation of goods that transformed western Europe from the 1770s to the 1870s. (*p. 577*)

international settlements Special zones in major Chinese cities set aside for foreigners in the later nineteenth century where no Chinese were allowed; arose as a result of China's defeat in the Opium and Arrow Wars. *(p. 690)*

Intifada ("Uprising") A resistance begun in 1987 by Palestinians against the Israeli occupation of Gaza and the West Bank. *(p. 940)*

Iron Rice Bowl A model of social equality in Mao's China in which the people, especially in the villages, shared resources and the peasants enjoyed status and dignity. *(p. 842)*

Islamic revivalism Arab movements beginning in the eighteenth century that sought to purify Islamic practices by reviving what their supporters considered to be a purer vision of Islamic society. *(p. 651)*

Islamists Antimodern, usually puritanical Islamic militants who seek an Islamic state. *(p. 945)*

Jacobins A radical faction in the French Revolution that believed civil rights had to be set aside in a crisis; the Jacobins executed thousands of French citizens. *(p. 570)*

Jainism An Indian religion that believes that life in all forms must be protected because everything, including animals, insects, plants, sticks, and stones, has a separate soul and is alive; arose in 500 B.C.E. as an alternative to Hinduism. *(p. 177)*

janissaries ("new troops") Well-armed, highly disciplined, and generally effective elite military corps of infantrymen in the Ottoman Empire. *(p. 476)*

Japan, Inc. The cooperative relationship between government and big business that has existed in Japan after 1945. *(p. 853)*

Jiangxi Soviet A revolutionary base, established in 1927 in south-central China, where Mao Zedong organized a guerrilla force to fight the Guomindang. *(p. 757)*

jihad Effort by a Muslim to live as God intended; a spiritual, moral, and intellectual struggle to enhance personal faith and follow the **Quran.** *(p. 275)*

Jomon The earliest documented culture in Japan, known for the ropelike design on its pottery. *(p. 94)*

Ka'ba A huge sacred cube-shaped stone in the city of Mecca to which people made annual pilgrimages. *(p. 271)*

Kabuki The all-male and racy drama that became the favored entertainment of the urban population in Tokugawa Japan. *(p. 543)*

kana A Japanese phonetic script developed in the Heian period (794–1184) that consisted of some forty-seven syllabic signs derived from Chinese characters. *(p. 318)*

Khmer Rouge ("Red Khmers") A Communist insurgent group that sought to overthrow the government in Cambodia during the 1960s through the mid-1990s. *(p. 987)*

kibbutz A Jewish collective farm in twentieth-century Palestine that stressed the sharing of wealth. *(p. 654)*

knights In **medieval** Europe, armored military retainers on horseback who swore allegiance to their lord. *(p. 391)*

kotow The tribute-bearers' act of prostrating themselves before the Chinese emperor. *(p. 315)*

kshatriyas Warriors and landowners headed by the rajas in the Hindu **caste system.** *(p. 50)*

Kushans An Indo-European people from Central Asia who conquered much of northwest India and western parts of the Ganges Basin and constructed an empire (50–250 C.E.) that also encompassed Afghanistan and parts of Central Asia. *(p. 184)*

laager A defensive arrangement of wagons in a circle. Used by the Boers in South Africa in the eighteenth and nineteenth centuries to guard against attacks by native Africans. *(p. 638)*

laissez faire Restriction of government interference in the marketplace, such as laws regulating business and profits. *(p. 581)*

Lamaism The Tibetan form of **Buddhism,** characterized by the centrality of monks (*lamas*) and huge monasteries. *(p. 364)*

Lapita The ancient western Pacific culture that stretched some 2,500 miles from just northeast of New Guinea to Samoa. *(p. 93)*

Legalism A Chinese philosophy that advocated harsh control of people by the state; became the dominant philosophy during the Qin dynasty (221–207 B.C.E.) and was later tempered by **Confucianism.** *(p. 125)*

Leninism A political system imposed by Lenin (1870–1924) in which one party holds a monopoly on power, excluding other parties from participation. Used in the Soviet Union from 1917 to the later 1980s. *(p. 726)*

liberalism An ideology of the Modern Era, based on **Enlightenment** ideas, that favored emancipating the individual from all restraints, whether governmental, economic, or religious. *(p. 586)*

liberation theology A Latin American movement that developed in the 1960s in Latin America to make Catholicism more relevant to contemporary society and to address the plight of the poor. *(p. 928)*

lingua franca A language widely used as a common tongue among diverse groups with different languages. *(p. 766)*

Little Dragons South Korea, Taiwan, Singapore, and Hong Kong, which were strongly influenced by Chinese culture and built rapidly growing, industrializing economies in the twentieth century. *(p. 858)*

loess The dust blown in from the Mongolian deserts that enriched the soils of northern China. *(p. 83)*

Long March An epic journey, full of hardship, in which Mao Zedong's Red Army fought their way 6,000 miles on foot and horseback through eleven Chinese provinces in the mid-1930s to establish a safe base of operation. *(p. 757)*

Luddites Antiindustrialization activists in Britain who destroyed machines in a mass protest against the effects of mechanization (see **Industrial Revolution**). *(p. 579)*

ma'at Ancient Egyptian term for justice, the correct order of things. *(p. 60)*

madrasas Religious boarding schools found all over the Muslim world. *(p. 278)*

Magna Carta ("Great Charter") An agreement signed by King John of England in 1215 that limited the feudal rights of the English king and his officials while protecting the rights of the church, lords, and merchants. *(p. 397)*

Mahabharata ("Great Bharata") An **Aryan** epic and the world's longest poem. *(p. 48)*

Mahayana ("the Greater Vehicle to salvation") One of the two main branches of **Buddhism;** a more popularized form of Buddhist belief and practice than **Theravada.** Mahayana Buddhism tended to make Buddha into a god and also developed the notion of the **bodhisattva.** *(p. 186)*

mandarins Educated men who staffed the imperial Chinese bureaucracy from the Han dynasty until the early twentieth century. *(p. 130)*

Mandate of Heaven A Chinese belief from ancient times that rulers had the support of the supernatural realm as long as conditions were good, but rebellion was justified when they were not. *(p. 88)*

Mande Diverse Sudanic peoples who spoke closely related languages, shared many customs, and dominated the western Niger River Basin and adjacent areas of West Africa (see **Sudan**). *(p. 235)*

Manicheanism A blend of **Zoroastrianism, Buddhism,** and Christianity, founded by Mani (216–277 C.E.), that emphasized a continuing struggle between the equal forces of light and dark. *(p. 224)*

Manifest Destiny Americans' conviction that their country's institutions and culture, regarded as unmatched, gave them a God-given right to take over the land. *(p. 607)*

manorialism The **medieval** European system of autonomous, nearly self-sufficient agricultural estates. *(p. 391)*

mansa ("King") Mande term used by the Malinke people to refer to the ruler of the Mali Empire (1234–1550). *(p. 331)*

Maoism An ideology promoted by Mao Zedong that mixed ideas from Chinese tradition with Marxist-Leninist ideas from the Soviet Union. *(p. 759)*

Marathas A loosely knit confederacy led by Hindu warriors from west-central India; one of several groups that challenged British domination after the decline of the Mughals. *(p. 659)*

market Leninism A policy followed after the Beijing Massacre in 1989 whereby the Chinese Communist state asserted more power over society while also fostering an even stronger market orientation in the economy than had existed under **market socialism.** *(p. 845)*

market socialism A Chinese economic program used between 1978 and 1989 that mixed free enterprise, economic liberalization, and state controls and that produced economic dynamism in China. *(p. 844)*

maroons Slaves who escaped from plantations and set up African-type societies in the interior of several American colonies. *(p. 511)*

Marshall Plan A recovery program proposed for western Europe by the United States that aimed to prevent Communist expansion and to spread liberal economic principles. (p. 868)

Marxism-Leninism The basis for Soviet communism, a mix of **socialism** (collective ownership of the economy) and **Leninism.** (p. 726)

matrilineal kinship A pattern of kinship that traces descent and inheritance through the female line. (p. 15)

Mau Mau Rebellion An eight-year uprising in the 1950s by the Gikuyu people in Kenya against British rule. (p. 952)

May Fourth Movement A radical nationalist resurgence in China in 1919 that opposed **imperialism** and the ineffective, warlord-controlled Chinese government. (p. 755)

Maya The most long-lasting and widespread of the classical Mesoamerican societies, who occupied the Yucatan Peninsula and northern Central America for almost 2,000 years. (p. 237)

medieval A term first used in the 1400s by Italian historians to describe the centuries between the classical Romans and their own time. (p. 383)

Meiji Restoration A revolution against the Tokugawa shogunate in Japan in 1867–1868, carried out in the name of the Meiji emperor; led to the successful modernization of Japan. (p. 704)

mercantilism An economic approach that emerged in Early Modern Europe based on a government policy of building a nation's wealth by expanding its reserves of precious metals. (p. 436)

Meroitic A cursive script developed in the Classical Era by the Kushites in Nubia that can be read only partly today. (p. 231)

Mesoamerica The region stretching from central Mexico southeast into northern Central America. (p. 99)

Mesolithic The Middle Stone Age, which began around 15,000 years ago as the glaciers from the final Ice Age began to recede. (p. 14)

messianism The Hebrew belief that their God, Yahweh, had given them a special mission in the world. (p. 74)

mestizos Groups in Latin America that blended white and Indian ancestry. (p. 500)

metaphysics The broad field of philosophy that studies the most general concepts and categories underlying ourselves and the world around us. (p. 157)

Metis People in Canada of mixed French and Indian descent. (p. 505)

Middle Passage The slave's journey by ship from Africa to the Americas. (p. 472)

millet The nationality system through which the Ottomans allowed the leaders of religious and ethnic minorities to administer their own communities. (p. 295)

Mithraism A Hellenistic cult that worshiped Mithra, a Persian deity associated with the sun; had some influence on Christianity. (p. 169)

Moche A prosperous, powerful state that formed along the northern Peruvian coast from 200 B.C.E. to 700 C.E. (p. 243)

modernism A Western cultural trend that openly broke with **romanticism** and other traditions by embracing progress and welcoming the future. (p. 603)

monasticism The pursuit of a religious life of penance, prayer, and meditation, either alone or in a community of other seekers. (p. 179)

monoculture An economy dependent on the production and export of one chief commodity. (p. 507)

Monophysites A heretical sect in the fourth century C.E. that argued that Jesus had a single divine nature rather than both a divine and a human form. (p. 222)

monotheism The belief in a single, all-powerful god. (p. 60)

Moros The Spanish term for the Muslim peoples of the southern Philippines. (p. 529)

mound building The construction of huge earthen mounds, often with temples on top, by some peoples in the Americas from ancient times to the fifteenth century C.E. (p. 97)

mujahidin ("Holy warriors") Conservative Islamic rebels who rebelled against the pro-Soviet regime in Afghanistan in the 1970s and 1980s. (p. 948)

mulattos Groups in Latin America that blend African ancestry with white and Indian ancestry. (p. 500)

multilateralism In the twentieth and twenty-first centuries, a foreign policy in which the United States sought a common front and a coordination of foreign policies with allies in western Europe, Japan, and Canada, avoiding activities that might enflame world opinion against the United States. (p. 904)

multinational corporations Giant business enterprises that operate all over the world; multinationals have gained a leading role in the global marketplace. (p. 814)

Muslim Brotherhood An Egyptian religious movement founded in 1928 that expressed popular Arab reaction to **Westernization.** (p. 776)

Mutually Assured Destruction A policy, known as MAD, in which the United States and the USSR used the fear of nuclear weapons to deter each other during the **Cold War.** (p. 905)

Nam Tien ("Drive to the South") A long process beginning in the tenth century in which some Vietnamese left the over-crowded north to migrate southward along the coast of Vietnam. (p. 378)

National Liberation Front (NLF) Often known as the Viet Cong, a Communist-led revolutionary movement in South Vietnam that resisted American intervention in the American-Vietnamese War. (p. 984)

nationalism A primary loyalty to, and identity with, a nation bound by a common culture, government, and shared territory. (p. 583)

nation-states Politically centralized countries with defined territorial boundaries. (p. 584)

NATO (North Atlantic Treaty Organization) A military alliance, formed in 1949, that linked nine western European countries with the United States and Canada. (p. 871)

Neanderthals Hominids who were probably descended from *Homo erectus* populations in Europe and who later spread into western and Central Asia. (p. 13)

negritude A twentieth-century literary and philosophical movement to forge distinctively African views. (p. 964)

neo-Confucianism A form of **Confucianism** arising in China during the Song period (960–1279) that incorporated many Buddhist and Daoist metaphysical ideas (see **Buddhism, Daoism**). (p. 308)

neoliberalism An economic model encouraged by the United States in the developing world that promoted free markets, privatization, and Western investment. (p. 927)

Neolithic The New Stone Age, which began between 10,000 and 11,500 years ago with the transition to simple farming. (p. 14)

Nestorians A heretical Christian sect in the fourth century C.E. that believed that the divine and human natures of Jesus were independent of each other. (p. 222)

networks Arrangements or collections of links between different societies, such as the routes over which traders, goods, diplomats, armies, ideas, and information travel. (p. xxxi)

New Culture Movement A movement of Chinese intellectuals started in 1915 that sought to wash away the discredited past and sprout a literary revival. (p. 754)

New Deal A new U.S. government program of liberal reform within a democratic framework introduced by President Franklin Roosevelt to alleviate suffering caused by the **Great Depression.** (p. 734)

New Economic Policy (NEP) Lenin's pragmatic approach to economic development, which mixed **capitalism** and **socialism.** (p. 726)

New Order The Indonesian government headed by President Suharto from 1966 to 1998, which mixed military and civilian leadership. (p. 993)

New Song A Latin American musical movement based chiefly on local folk music and closely tied to progressive politics and protest; became popular in the 1960s and 1970s, especially in Chile. (p. 929)

Nicene Creed A set of beliefs, prepared by the council at Nicaea in 325 C.E., that became the official doctrine of the early Christian church. (p. 218)

Nilotes Ironworking pastoralists from the eastern **Sudan** who settled in East Africa in the classical era and there had frequent interactions with the **Bantus** (see **pastoral nomadism**). (p. 236)

nirvana ("the blowing out") A kind of everlasting peace or end of suffering achieved through perfection of wisdom and compassion (see **Buddhism**). (p.179)

Noh Japanese plays that use stylized gestures and spectacular masks; began in the fourteenth century C.E. (p. 323)

nonviolent resistance Noncooperation with unjust laws and peaceful confrontation with illegitimate authority, pursued by Mohandas Gandhi in India. (p. 762)

nuclear weapons Explosive devices that owe their destructive power to the energy released by either splitting or fusing atoms. (*p. 809*)

nuxu A secret form of writing developed by some Chinese women to share their experiences, possibly beginning as early as the Han period. (*p. 131*)

oligarchs Well-placed former Communists who amassed enough wealth to gain control of major segments of the post-Soviet Russian economy. (*p. 892*)

oligarchy Rule by a small group of wealthy leaders. (*p. 153*)

Olmecs The earliest urban society in Mesoamerica. (*p. 101*)

OPEC (Organization of Petroleum Exporting Countries) A cartel formed in 1960 to give producers more power over the price of oil and leverage with the consuming nations. (*p. 943*)

oral traditions Verbal testimonies concerning the past; the major form of oral literature in cultures without writing. (*p. 339*)

Orientalism An eighteenth- and nineteenth-century scholarly interest among British officials in India that prompted some to rediscover the Hindu classical age. (*p. 664*)

ostpolitik ("Eastern politics") A West German policy, promoted by Chancellor Willy Brandt, that sought a reconciliation between West and East Germany and an expanded dialogue with the USSR. (*p. 873*)

Pacific Century The possible shift of global economic power from Europe and North America to the **Pacific Rim** in the twenty-first century. (*p. 836*)

Pacific Rim The economically dynamic Asian countries on the western edge of the Pacific Basin: China, Japan, South Korea, Taiwan, and several Southeast Asian nations. (*p. 836*)

Paleolithic The Old Stone Age, which began 100,000 years ago with the first modern humans and lasted for many millennia. (*p. 14*)

pan-Africanism The dream, originating in the early twentieth century, that all Africans would cooperate to eventually form some sort of united states of the continent. (*p. 952*)

pariahs The large group of outcasts or untouchables below the official Hindu castes. (*p. 50*)

parliamentary democracy Government by representatives elected by the people. (*p. 586*)

pastoral nomadism An economy based on breeding, rearing, and harvesting livestock. (*p. 26*)

Pathet Lao Revolutionary Laotian nationalists allied with North Vietnam during the American-Vietnamese War. (*p. 986*)

patriarchy A system in which men largely control women and children and shape ideas about appropriate gender behavior. (*p. 35*)

patricians The aristocratic upper class who controlled the Roman Senate. (*p. 203*)

Paulistas Portuguese slavers from the southern Brazilian settlement at Sao Paulo. (*p. 497*)

Pax Romana ("Roman Peace") The period of peace and prosperity in Roman history from the reign of Augustus through that of Emperor Marcus Aurelius in 180 C.E. (*p. 207*)

Peloponnesian War A long war between Athens and Sparta and their respective allies in 431–404 B.C.E. that resulted in the defeat of Athens. (*p. 162*)

people's war An unconventional struggle that combined military action and political recruitment, formulated by Mao Zedong in China. (*p. 758*)

Perestroika ("Restructuring") Mikhail Gorbachev's policy to liberalize the Soviet economy using market mechanisms. (*p. 890*)

periodization Dividing long periods of historical time into smaller segments such as "the ancient world" or "modern history." (*p. xxx*)

pharaohs Rulers of ancient Egypt. (*p. 58*)

philosophes The intellectuals who fostered the French **Enlightenment.** (*p. 455*)

pidgin English The form of broken English that developed in Africa during the colonial era. (*p. 770*)

plantation zone A group of societies with economies that relied on enslaved African labor; the plantation zone stretched from Virginia and Kentucky southward through the West Indies and the east coast of Central America to central Brazil and the Pacific coast of Colombia. (*p. 507*)

plebeians The commoner class in Rome. (*p. 203*)

plural society A medley of peoples who mix but do not blend, instead maintaining their own cultures, religions, languages, and customs. (*p. 674*)

polis A **city-state** in Classical Greece; each polis embraced nearby rural areas, whose agricultural surplus then helped support the urban population. (*p. 152*)

polyandry Marriage of a woman to several husbands. (*p. 360*)

polytheism A belief in many spirits or deities. (*p. 15*)

postmodernism A European intellectual approach contending that truth is not absolute but constructed by people according to their society's beliefs. (*p. 882*)

preemptive war A U.S. doctrine, triggered by the 2001 terrorist attacks, that sanctioned unilateral military action against potential threats (see **terrorism, unilateralism**). (*p. 909*)

proletariat The industrial working class. (*p. 588*)

protectionism Use of trade barriers to shield local industries from foreign competition. (*p. 605*)

Protestants Groups that broke completely with the Roman Catholic Church as the result of the **Reformation.** (*p. 439*)

purdah The Indian Muslim custom of secluding women. (*p. 369*)

qi In Chinese thought, the energizing force pervading the universe. (*p. 309*)

Quetzalcoatl The feathered serpent, a symbol that goes back deep in Mesoamerican history. (*p. 343*)

quipus Differently colored knotted strings used by the Incas to record commercial dealings, property ownerships, and census data. (*p. 352*)

Quran ("Recitation") Islam's holiest book; contains the official version of Muhammad's revelations, and to believers is the inspired word of God. (*p. 272*)

racism A set of beliefs, practices, and institutions based on devaluing groups that are supposedly biologically different. (*p. 471*)

rai ("opinion") A twentieth-century pop music of Algeria based on local Bedouin chants, Spanish flamenco, French café songs, Egyptian pop, and other influences and featuring improvised lyrics that often deal with forbidden themes of sex and alcohol. (*p. 947*)

Rajputs ("King's sons") An Indian warrior caste formed by earlier Central Asian invaders who adopted Hinduism. (*p. 359*)

Ramadan The thirty days of annual fasting when Muslims abstain from eating, drinking, and sex during daylight hours, to demonstrate sacrifice for their faith and understand the hunger of the poor. (*p. 275*)

Rastafarianism A religion from Jamaica that arose in 1930 and that mixed Christian, African, and local influences; Rastafarianism attracted urban slum dwellers and the rural poor by preaching a return of black people to Africa. (*p. 931*)

Red Guards Young workers and students who were the major supporters of the **Great Proletarian Cultural Revolution** in Mao's China. (*p. 841*)

Reformation The movement to reform Christianity that was begun by Martin Luther in the sixteenth century. (*p. 437*)

reggae A popular music style that began in Jamaica in the 1960s and that blended North American rhythm and blues with Afro-Jamaican traditions; reggae is marked by a distinctive beat maintained by the bass guitar. (*p. 931*)

Renaissance ("Rebirth") A dramatic flowering in arts and learning that began in the Italian city-states around 1350 and spread through Europe through the 1500s. (*p. 409*)

Romance languages Languages that derive from Latin, such as French, Italian, and Spanish. (*p. 215*)

romanticism A philosophical, literary, artistic, and musical movement that questioned the **Enlightenment's** rationalist values and instead glorified emotions, individual imagination, and heroism. (*p. 603*)

Russification A czarist policy in the nineteenth century that promoted Russian language and culture for non-Russian peoples; created resentment among many Muslims in Central Asia and the Caucasus. (*p. 711*)

salaryman A Japanese urban middle-class male business employee who commits his energies and soul to the company, accepts assignments without complaint, and takes few vacations. (*p. 854*)

samba A Brazilian popular music and dance that arose in the early twentieth century. (*p. 621*)

samurai ("One who serves") A member of the Japanese warrior class, which gained power between the twelfth and fourteenth centuries and continued until the nineteenth. *(p. 322)*

Sanskrit The classical language of north India, originally both written and spoken but now reserved for religious and literary writing. *(p. 48)*

satrap ("Protector of the kingdom") An official in the Classical Persian Empire (ca. 550–450 B.C.E.) who ruled according to established laws and procedures and paid a fixed amount of taxes to the emperor each year. *(p. 149)*

scholar-gentry A Chinese social class of learned officeholders and landowners that arose in the Han dynasty and continued until the early twentieth century. *(p. 130)*

Scientific Revolution An era of rapid European advance in knowledge, particularly in mathematics and astronomy, that occurred between 1600 and 1750. *(p. 392)*

Second World A later-twentieth-century term for the Communist nations, led by the USSR and China. *(p. 806)*

sepoys Mercenary soldiers recruited among the warrior and peasant castes by the British in India. *(p. 661)*

serfs In **medieval** Europe, peasants legally bound to their lord and tied to the land through generations. *(p. 392)*

sericulture Silk making, which arose in ancient China. *(p. 132)*

shamans Specialists in communicating with or manipulating the supernatural realm. *(p. 15)*

Shari'a The Islamic legal code for the regulation of social, economic, and religious life. *(p. 278)*

Shi'a The branch of Islam that emphasizes the religious leaders descended from Muhammad through his son-in-law, Ali, whom they believe was the rightful successor to the Prophet. *(p. 280)*

Shinto ("Way of the gods") The ancient animistic Japanese cult that emphasized closeness to nature; enjoyed a rich mythology that included many deities (see **animism**). *(p. 142)*

Shiva The Hindu god of destruction and of fertility and the harvest. *(p. 45)*

shogun ("Barbarian-subduing generalissimo") In effect a Japanese military dictator who controlled the country in the name of the emperor; the first shogun took power in 1185, and the last one fell in 1868. *(p. 322)*

Sikhs ("Disciples") Members of an Indian religion founded in the Early Modern Era that adopted elements from both Hinduism and Islam, including mysticism. *(p. 522)*

Silk Road A lively caravan route through Central Asia that linked China with India, the Middle East, and southern Europe that began during the Han dynasty (207 B.C.E.–221 C.E.) and continued for many centuries. *(p. 129)*

simony In **medieval** Europe, a practice whereby wealthy families paid to have their sons appointed bishops. *(p. 396)*

Sinicization The process by which Central Asian invaders maintained continuity with China's past by adopting Chinese culture. *(p. 126)*

Slavophiles Nineteenth-century Russians who emphasized Russia's unique culture and rejected Western models. *(p. 712)*

socialism An ideology arising in nineteenth-century Europe offering a vision of social equality and the common, or public, ownership of economic institutions such as factories. *(p. 587)*

socialist realism Literary and artistic works that depicted life from a revolutionary perspective, a style first introduced in Stalin's Russia. *(p. 727)*

societies Broad groups of people that have common traditions, institutions, and organized patterns of relationships with each other. *(p. xxxi)*

Socratic Method A method of asking people leading questions to help them examine the truth of their ideas; introduced by the Greek philosopher Socrates (469–399 B.C.E.). *(p. 156)*

Sophists Thinkers in Classical Greece (fifth century B.C.E.) who emphasized skepticism and the belief that there is no ultimate truth. *(p. 156)*

soukous ("to shake") A Congolese popular music of the later twentieth century that was shaped by dance rhythms from Cuba and Brazil. *(p. 964)*

Soviet bloc In the twentieth century, the Soviet Union and the communist states allied with it. *(p. 871)*

soviets Local action councils formed by Russian radicals before the 1917 Russian Revolution that enlisted workers and soldiers to fight the factory owners and military officers. *(p. 724)*

sphere of interest An area in which one great power assumes exclusive responsibility for maintaining peace and attempts to monopolize the area's resources. *(p. 610)*

Stalinism Joseph Stalin's system of government, which included state ownership of all property, such as lands and businesses, a planned economy, and one-man rule. *(p. 726)*

state capitalism An economic system in which the state takes a leading role in supporting business and industrial enterprises; introduced by the Meiji government in Japan. *(p. 705)*

steppes The plains of Central Asia. *(p. 46)*

Stoicism A Hellenistic philosophy begun by Zeno in the third century B.C.E. that emphasized the importance of cooperating with and accepting nature, as well as the unity and equality of all people (see **Hellenism**). *(p. 169)*

Sudan A grassland region stretching along the southern fringe of the Sahara Desert from the western tip of Africa to the Nile valley. *(p. 64)*

sudras The mostly poorer farmers, farm workers, and menial laborers in the Hindu **caste system.** *(p. 50)*

suffragettes Women who press for the same voting rights as men. *(p. 602)*

Sufism A mystical approach and practice within Islam that emphasized personal spiritual experience. *(p. 284)*

sultan A Muslim ruler of only one country. *(p. 278)*

Sunni The main branch of Islam comprising those who accept the practices of the Prophet and the historical succession of caliphs. *(p. 280)*

Swahili Name for a distinctive people, culture, and language, a mix of **Bantu,** Arab, and Islamic influences, that developed during the Intermediate Era on the East African coast. *(p. 336)*

Taliban ("Students") A group of Pashtun religious students who organized a military force in the 1980s to fight what they considered immorality and corruption and to impose order in Afghanistan. *(p. 948)*

Tantrism An approach within both **Buddhism** and Hinduism that worshiped the female essence of the universe; developed in the Intermediate Era. *(p. 363)*

Teotihuacan ("the City of the Gods") The largest city in the Americas and the capital of an empire in central Mexico during Classical times. *(p. 241)*

terrorism Small-scale but violent attacks aimed at undermining a government or demoralizing a population. *(p. 830)*

Tet Offensive Communist attacks on major South Vietnamese cities in 1968, a turning point in the American-Vietnamese War. *(p. 986)*

The Analects The book of the sayings of Confucius (ca. 551–479 B.C.E.), collected by his disciples and published a century or two after his death (see **Confucianism**). *(p. 123)*

Theosophy A nineteenth-century North American and European movement that blended Hindu thought with Western spiritualist and scientific ideas. *(p. 665)*

Theravada ("Teachings of the Elders") One of the two main branches of **Buddhism,** the other being **Mahayana,** that arose just before the Common Era. Theravada remained closer to the Buddha's original vision. *(p. 185)*

Third Industrial Revolution The creation since 1945 of unprecedented scientific knowledge of new technologies more powerful than any invented before. *(p. 815)*

Third World A later-twentieth-century term for the societies in Asia, Africa, Latin America, and the Caribbean, which were shaped by mass poverty and a legacy of colonization or neocolonialism. *(p. 806)*

trade diaspora Merchants from the same city or country who live permanently in foreign cities or countries. *(p. 163)*

transitions Passages, changes, events, or movements that reshape societies and regions. *(p. xxxi)*

trekking The migrations of **Boer** settlers in cattle-drawn wagons into the interior of South Africa whenever they wanted to flee government restraints. *(p. 470)*

tribes Associations of clans that traced descent from a common ancestor. *(p. 27)*

tribunes Roman men elected to represent **plebeian** interests in the **Centuriate Assembly.** *(p. 203)*

Truman Doctrine A policy formed in 1947 that asserted that the United States was the leader of the free world and was charged with protecting countries like Greece and Turkey from communism. *(p. 871)*

tyrant Someone who ruled a Greek **polis** outside the law, not necessarily a brutal ruler. *(p. 154)*

ukiyo-e Colorful Japanese woodblock prints that celebrated the life of the "floating world," the urban entertainment districts of Tokogawa Japan. *(p. 543)*

umma The community of Muslim believers united around God's message. *(p. 273)*

UMNO United Malays National Organization, the main Malay political party in Malaysia. *(p. 991)*

unilateralism In the twentieth and twenty-first centuries, a foreign policy in which the United States acted alone in its own perceived national interest even if key allies disapproved. *(p. 905)*

Upanishads Ancient Indian philosophical writings that speculated on the ultimate truth about the creation of life. *(p. 52)*

Urdu A language developed in Mughal India that mixed Hindi, Arabic, and Persian and was written in the Persian script. *(p. 519)*

usury The practice of loaning money at interest; considered a sin in **medieval** Europe, although necessary to commerce. *(p. 393)*

vaisyas The merchants and artisans in the Hindu **caste system.** *(p. 50)*

Vajrayana ("Thunderbolt") A form of **Buddhism** that featured female saviors and the human attainment of magical powers; developed in the Intermediate Era and became the main form of Buddhism in Nepal and Tibet. *(p. 363)*

vassal In **medieval** Europe, a subordinate person who owed service to a lord. *(p. 390)*

Vedanta ("Completion of the **Vedas**") A school of Classical Indian thought that offered Hindus mystical experience and a belief in the underlying unity of all reality. *(p. 177)*

Vedas The **Aryans'** "books of knowledge," the principal source of religious belief for Hindus: a vast collection of sacred hymns to the gods and thoughts about religion, philosophy, and magic. *(p. 47)*

Viet Minh The Vietnamese Independence League, a coalition of anti-French groups established by Ho Chi Minh in 1941 that waged war against both the French and the Japanese. *(p. 766)*

voyageurs French explorers and trappers in North America. *(p. 498)*

Wabenzi ("People who drive a Mercedes Benz") A privileged urban class in Africa since the mid-twentieth century of politicians, high bureaucrats, professionals, military officers, and businessmen who manipulate their connections to amass wealth. *(p. 955)*

Wahhabism A militant Islamic revivalist movement founded in Arabia in the eighteenth century. *(p. 651)*

warlords Local political leaders with their own armies. *(p. 754)*

Warsaw Pact A defense alliance formed in 1955 that linked the Communist-ruled eastern European countries with the USSR. *(p. 871)*

wayang kulit Javanese shadow puppet play, developed during the Intermediate Era, based on Hindu epics like the *Ramayana* and local Javanese content. *(p. 375)*

welfare states Government systems that offer their citizens a range of state-subsidized health, education, and social service benefits; adopted by western European nations after World War II. *(p. 876)*

Westernization A deliberate attempt to spread Western culture and ideas. *(p. 664)*

Yijing The Book of Changes, an ancient Chinese collection of sixty-four mystic hexagrams and commentaries upon them that was used to predict future events. *(p. 90)*

Young Turks A modernizing group in Ottoman Turkey that promoted a national identity and that gained power in the early twentieth century. *(p. 647)*

zaibatsu The most powerful Japanese corporations that dominated the national economy beginning during the Meiji regime and maintained an especially close relationship to the government. *(p. 705)*

zamindars Mughal revenue collectors that the British turned into landlords who were given the rights to buy and sell land. *(p. 665)*

Zen A form of Japanese **Buddhism** that emerged in the Intermediate Era; called the meditation sect because it emphasizes individual practice and discipline, self-control, self-understanding, and intuition. *(p. 323)*

ziggurat A stepped, pyramidal-shaped temple building in Sumerian cities, seen as the home of the chief god of the city. *(p. 34)*

Zionism A movement arising in late nineteenth century Europe that sought a Jewish homeland. *(p. 585)*

Zoroastrianism A monotheistic religion founded by the Persian Zoroaster that later became the state religion of Persia. Its notion of one god opposed by the Devil may have influenced Judaism and later Christianity (see **monotheism**). *(p. 150)*

NOTES

Preface

1. Geoffrey Barraclough, *Main Trends in History* (New York: Holmes and Meier, 1979), p. 153.

Introducing World History

1. P. L. Hartley, quoted in David Lowenthal, *The Past is a Foreign Country* (Cambridge: Cambridge University Press, 1985), p. xvi.

Chapter 15 Global Connections and the Remaking of Europe, 1450–1750

1. From "The Tempest," *The Riverside Shakespeare*, 2nd ed. (Boston: Houghton Mifflin, 1997), p. 1684.
2. Quoted in Edith Simon, *The Reformation* (New York: Time-Life Books, 1966), p. 74.
3. Franciscan friar Toribio de Montolinia, quoted in Marvin Lunenfeld, ed., *1492: Discovery, Invasion, Encounter: Sources and Interpretations* (Lexington, Mass.: D.C. Heath, 1991), p. 214.
4. Quoted in Carlo M. Cipolla, *Before the Industrial Revolution: European Society and Economy, 1000–1700*, 2nd ed. (New York: W.W. Norton, 1980), p. 270.
5. Quoted in Miriam Beard, *History of the Businessman* (New York: Macmillan, 1938), p. 239–240.
6. Quoted in H. O. Taylor, *Thought and Expression in the Sixteenth Century*, vol. 1 (New York: Macmillan, 1920), p. 175.
7. Quoted in Charles Blitzer, *Age of Kings* (New York: Time-Life Books, 1967), p. 11.
8. From "Hamlet," The Riverside Shakespeare, 2nd ed. (Boston: Houghton Mifflin, 1997), p. 1204.
9. Quoted in James Krokar et al., *Rhetoric and Civilization*, vol. 2 (Littleton, Mass.: Copley, 1988), p. 620.
10. Quoted in Frederic Delouche et al., *Illustrated History of Europe* (New York: Barnes and Noble, 2001), p. 244.
11. Quoted in *What Life Was Like During the Age of Reason* (Alexandria, Va.: Time-Life Books, 1999), p. 18.
12. P. P. Shafirov, quoted in Paul Dukes, *The Making of Russian Absolutism, 1613–1801*, 2nd ed. (New York: Longman, 1990), p. 77.
13. Quoted in Blitzer, *Age of Kings*, p. 119.
14. From Hobbes, *The Leviathan*, Chapter 13 (**oregonstate.edu/instruct/ph1302/texts/ hobbes/leviathan-c.html**)
15. Quoted in Martin Oliver, *History of Philosophy* (New York: Metro Books, 1997), p. 73.
16. Quoted in Norman Davies, *Europe: A History* (New York: Harper, 1996), p. 599.
17. Quoted in John M. Hobson, *The Eastern Origins of Western Civilisation* (Cambridge: Cambridge University Press, 2004), p. 194.
18. From Dena Goodman and Kathleen Wellman, eds., *The Enlightenment* (Boston: Houghton Mifflin, 2004), p. 167.
19. The quotes are from Christopher Hill, *The World Turned Upside Down: Radical ideas During the English Revolution* (Hammondsworth, England: Penguin, 1975), p. 107; and Delouche, *Illustrated History of Europe*, p. 247.
20. Quoted in Simon, *Reformation*, p. 30.
21. Quoted in Diarmaid MacCulloch, *The Reformation: A History* (New York: Penguin, 2005), p. 609
22. Quoted in Robert Wallace, *Rise of Russia* (New York: Time-Life Books, 1967), p. 140.

Chapter 16 New Challenges for Africa and the Islamic World, 1450–1750

1. Quoted in Ali Mazrui, *The Africans: A Triple Heritage* (Boston: Little, Brown, 1986), p. 11.
2. Quoted in Basil Davidson, ed., *African Civilization Revisited* (Trenton, N.J.: African World Press, 1991), p. 118.
3. Quoted in Robert W. July, *A History of the African People*, 5th ed. (Prospect Heights, Ill: Waveland, 1998), p. 74.
4. Quoted in Basil Davidson, *Africa in History* (New York: Touchstone, 1995), pp. 176–177.
5. Andre Alvares de Almada, quoted in George E. Brooks, *Landlords and Strangers: Ecology, Society, and Trade in Western Africa, 1000–1630* (Boulder, Colo.: Westview Press, 1993), p. 267.
6. Quoted in Derek Nourse and Thomas Spear, *The Swahili: Reconstructing the History and Language of an African Society, 800–1500* (Philadelphia: University of Pennsylvania Press, 1985), p. 82.
7. Quoted in Michael Pearson, *The Indian Ocean* (New York: Routledge, 2003), p. 119.
8. From Roland Oliver and Caroline Oliver, eds., *Africa in the Days of Exploration* (Englewood Cliffs, N.J.: Prentice-Hall, 1965), p. 111.
9. From Basil Davidson, ed., *The African Past: Chronicles from Antiquity to Modern Times* (New York: Grosset and Dunlap, 1964), p. 136.
10. Quoted in Kevin Shillington, *History of Africa*, rev. ed. (New York: St. Martin's, 1995), p. 216.
11. Malcolm Cowley and Daniel Mannix, "The Middle Passage," in David Northrup, ed., *The Atlantic Slave Trade* (Lexington, Mass.: D.C. Heath, 1994), pp. 99, 101.
12. Quoted in Charles Johnson and Patricia Smith, *Africans in America: America's Journey Through Slavery* (New York: Harcourt Brace, 1998), p. 79.
13. Quoted in R. A. Houston, "Colonies, Enterprise, and Wealth: The Economies of Europe and the Wider World in the Seventeenth Century," in Euan Cameron, ed., *Early Modern Europe: An Oxford History* (New York: Oxford University Press, 1999), p. 165.
14. Quoted in Winthrop D. Jordan, "Slavery: Its Development in Colonial America," in Mildred Bain and Ervin Lewis, eds., *From Freedom to Freedom: African Roots in American Soil* (New York: Random House, 1977), p. 166.
15. Quoted in Halil Inalcik, *The Ottoman Empire: The Classical Age, 1300–1600* (London: Phoenix Press, 2000), p. 41.
16. Quoted in Arthur Goldschmidt, Jr., *A Concise History of the Middle East*, 4th ed. revised and updated (Boulder, Colo.: Westview Press, 1991), p. 129.
17. Quoted in Andrew Wheatcroft, *The Ottomans* (New York: Viking, 1993), p. 89.
18. Ibrahim Pecevi, quoted in Philip Mansel, *Constantinople: City of the World's Desire, 1453–1924* (New York: St. Martin's, 1995), p. 171.
19. Quoted in Inalcik, *Ottoman Empire*, p. 189.
20. From John J. Saunders, ed., *The Muslim World on the Eve of Europe's Expansion* (Englewood Cliffs, N.J.: Prentice-Hall, 1966), p. 35.
21. Quoted in Francis Robinson, *The Cultural Atlas of the Islamic World Since 1500* (London: Stonehenge, 1987), p. 49.
22. Quoted in Willem Floor, "The Dutch and the Persian Silk Trade," in Charles Melville, ed., *Safavid Persia: The History and Politics of an Islamic Society* (London: I.B. Taurus, 1996), p. 325.

Chapter 17 Americans, Europeans, Africans, and New Societies in the Americas, 1450–1750

1. Quoted in Michael C. Meyer and William L. Sherman, *The Course of Mexican History*, 2nd ed. (New York: Oxford University Press, 1983), p. 86.
2. From Lewis Hanke, ed., *History of Latin American Civilization: Sources and Interpretations*, vol. 1 (Boston: Little, Brown and Company, 1973), p. 64.
3. Quoted in Oliver Cox, "The Rise of Modern Race Relations," in William Barclay et al., eds., *Racial Conflict, Discrimination, and Power* (New York: AMS Press, 1976), p. 91.
4. Quoted in Herman J. Viola, "Seeds of Change," in Herman J. Viola and Carolyn Margolis, eds., *Seeds of Change: A Quincentennial Commemoration* (Washington, D.C.: Smithsonian Institution Press, 1991), p. 13.
5. Quoted in L. S. Stavrianos, *Lifelines from Our Past: A New World History*, rev. ed. (Armonk, N.Y.: M.E. Sharpe, 1997), p. 96.
6. Alonso de Zuazo, quoted in Kathleen Deagan and Jose Maria Cruxent, *Columbus's Outpost Among the Tainos: Spain and America at La Isabela, 1493–1498* (New

Haven, Conn.: Yale University Press, 2002), p. 210.

7. Magá Lahen Hurao, quoted in Geoffrey C. Gunn, *First Globalization: The Eurasian Exchange* (Lanham, Md.: Rowman and Littlefield, 2003), p. 194.

8. Quoted in Jane MacLaren Walsh and Yoko Sugiura, "The Demise of the Fifth Sun," in Viola and Margolis, *Seeds of Change*, p. 41.

9. Louis Le Golif, quoted in David Cordingly, ed., *Pirates: Terror on the High Seas* (North Dighton, United Kingdom: JG Press, 1998), p. 37.

10. Quoted in Noble David Cook, *Born to Die: Disease and New World Conquest, 1492–1650* (Cambridge: Cambridge University Press, 1998), p. vi.

11. From Hanke, *History of Latin American Civilization*, p. 388.

12. Quoted in Jonathan C. Brown, *Latin America: A Social History of the Colonial Period* (Belmont, Calif.: Wadsworth, 2000), p. 146.

13. Fray Diego Duran, quoted in Rolena Adorno, "The Indigenous Ethnographer: The 'Indio Ladino' as Historian and Cultural Mediation," in Stuart B. Schwartz, ed., *Implicit Understandings* (New York: Cambridge University Press, 1994), p. 397.

14. Quoted in Felipe Fernandez-Armesto, *Millennium: A History of the Last Thousand Years* (New York: Scribner's, 1995), p. 300.

15. Quoted in Marysa Navarro and Virginia Sanchez-Korrol, "Latin America and the Caribbean," in *Restoring Women to History* (Bloomington, Ind.: Organization of American Historians, 1988), p. 23.

16. Gonzalo Fernandez de Oviedo, quoted in L. S. Stavrianos, *Global Rift: The Third World Comes of Age* (New York: William Morrow, 1981), p. 83.

17. Guzman Poma de Ayala, quoted in Brown, *Latin America*, p. 183.

18. Quoted in Robert Heilbroner and Aaron Singer, *The Economic Transformation of America, 1600 to the Present*, 3rd ed. (Fort Worth, Tex.: Harcourt Brace, 1994), p. 68.

19. Quoted in David Freeman Hawke, *Everyday Life in Early America* (New York: Harper and Row, 1988), p. 120.

20. Quoted in Salvador de Madariaga, *The Rise of the Spanish American Empire* (New York: Macmillan, 1947), pp. 90–91.

21. From Fray Toribio Motolinia, "The Ten Plagues of New Spain," in John Francis Bannon, ed., *Indian Labor in the Spanish Indies* (Boston: D.C. Heath, 1966), p. 45.

22. Quoted in Stuart B. Schwartz, "Brazil," in Seymour Drescher and Stanley L. Engerman, eds., *A Historical Guide to World Slavery* (New York: Oxford University Press, 1998), p. 101.

23. Gonzalez de Cellorigo, quoted in Jonathan Williams, *Money: A History* (New York: St. Martin's, 1997), p. 162.

Chapter 18 South Asia, Southeast Asia, and East Asia: Triumphs and Challenges, 1450–1750

1. Quoted in Anthony Reid, "Early Southeast Asian Categorizations of Europeans," in Stuart B. Schwartz, ed., *Implicit Understandings* (Cambridge: Cambridge University Press, 1994), p. 275.

2. Quoted in Om Prakash, *European Commercial Enterprise in Pre-Colonial India* (New York: Cambridge University Press, 1998), p. 4.

3. Quoted in Francis Robinson, *The Cultural Atlas of the Islamic World Since 1500* (London: Stonehenge, 1992), p. 39.

4. The quotes are from Rhoads Murphey, *A History of Asia*, 4th ed. (New York: Longman, 2002), p. 185; and Michael Edwardes, *A History of India* (New York: Farrar, Straus and Cudahy, 1961), p. 191.

5. Quoted in Edwardes, p. 190.

6. Quoted in John E. Wills, Jr., *1688: A Global History* (New York: W.W. Norton, 2001), p. 276.

7. Quoted in Geoffrey C. Gunn, *First Globalization: The Eurasian Exchange* (Lanham, Md.: Rowman and Littlefield, 2003), p. 214.

8. Quoted in Klaus Wenk, *Thai Literature: An Introduction* (Bangkok: White Lotus, 1995), pp. 14–16.

9. Joost Schouten, quoted in Michael Smithies, *Descriptions of Old Siam* (Kuala Lumpur: Oxford University Press, 1995), p. 19.

10. Quoted in Nicholas Tarling, "Mercantilism and Missionaries: Impact and Accommodation," in Colin Mackerras, ed., *Eastern Asia: An Introductory History*, 3rd ed. (Frenches Forest, NSW, Australia: Longmans, 2000), p. 115.

11. Quoted in David Joel Steinberg, *The Philippines: A Singular and a Plural Place*, 3rd ed. (Boulder: Westview, 1994), p. 82.

12. Pedro Chirino, quoted in Carolyn Brewer, "From Animist 'Priestess' to Catholic Priest: The Re/gendering of Religious Roles in the Philippines, 1521–1685," in Barbara Watson Andaya, ed., *Other Pasts: Women, Gender and History in Early Modern Southeast Asia* (Honolulu: Center for Southeast Asian Studies, University of Hawaii at Manoa, 2000), p. 69.

13. The quotes are from Felipe Fernandez-Armesto, *Millennium: A History of the Last Thousand Years* (New York: Scribner's, 1995), p. 324; and Alisa Zainu'ddin, *A Short History of Indonesia* (Sydney: Cassell Australia, 1968), p. 88.

14. Thomas Stamford Raffles, quoted in Anthony Reid, *Southeast Asia in the Age of Commerce, 1450–1680*, vol. 1 (New Haven, Conn.: Yale University Press, 1993), p. 164.

15. Quoted in Jonathan S. Spence, *Emperor of China: Self-Portrait of Kang-Hsi* (New York: Vintage, 1975), p. 29.

16. Quoted in Richard J. Smith, *China's Cultural Heritage: The Ch'ing Dynasty, 1644–1913* (Boulder, Colo.: Westview Press, 1983), p. 210.

17. Quoted in Francesca Bray, "Towards a Critical History of non-Western Technology," in Timothy Brook and Gregory Blue, eds., *China and Historical Capitalism* (New York: Cambridge University Press, 1999), p. 184.

18. Quoted in John A. Harrison, *The Chinese Empire* (New York: Harcourt Brace Jovanovich, 1972), p. 335.

19. Jean-Baptiste DuHalde, quoted in Carolyn Blunden and Mark Elvin, *The Cultural Atlas of China* (Alexandria, Va.: Stonehenge, 1991), p. 144.

20. Quoted in Spence, *Emperor of China*, pp. 72–73.

21. Quoted in Joanna Waley-Cohen, *The Sextants of Beijing: Global Currents in Chinese History* (New York: W.W. Norton, 1999), p. 55.

22. Matsuo Basho, quoted in Noel F. Busch, *The Horizon Concise History of Japan* (New York: American Heritage, 1972), p. 64.

23. Quoted in Ronald P. Toby, "The 'Indiraness' of Iberia and Changing Japanese Iconographies of Other," in Schwartz, *Implicit Understandings*, p. 326.

24. Quoted in Edward Seidensticker, *Japan* (New York: Time Inc., 1961), p. 58.

25. Yamaga Soko, quoted in Conrad Totman, *A History of Japan* (Oxford: Blackwell, 2000), p. 221.

26. Quoted in Mikiso Hane, *Modern Japan: A Historical Survey*, 2nd ed. (Boulder, Colo.: Westview Press, 1992), p. 36.

27. Chikamatsu Monzaemon, quoted in *What Life Was Like Among Samurai and Shoguns* (Alexandria, Va.: Time-Life Books, 1999), p. 118.

28. The haiku are from Conrad Schirokauer, *A Brief History of Chinese and Japanese Civilizations*, 2nd ed. (San Diego: Harcourt Brace Jovanovich, 1989), p. 373; and Harold G. Henderson, *An Introduction to Haiku: An Anthology of Poets from Basho to Shiki* (Garden City, N.Y.: Doubleday Anchor, 1958), p. 40.

Societies, Networks, Transitions: Connecting the Early Modern World, 1450–1750

1. Francisco Lopez de Gomara, quoted in Roger Schlesinger, *In the Wake of Columbus: The Impact of the New World on Europe, 1492–1650* (Wheeling, Ill.: Harlan Davidson, 1996), p. 23.

2. Quoted in Peter J. Hugill, *World Trade Since 1431: Geography, Technology, and Capitalism* (Baltimore: Johns Hopkins University Press, 1993), p. vii.

3. Quoted in Roger Savory, *Iran Under the Safavids* (Cambridge: Cambridge University Press, 1980), p. 205.

4. Quoted in Gregory Blue, "China and Western Social Thought in the Modern Period," in Timothy Brook and Gregory Blue, eds., *China and Historical Capitalism* (New York: Cambridge University Press, 1999), p. 64.

5. Quoted in Kenneth Chase, *Firearms: A Global History to 1700* (New York: Cambridge University Press, 2003), p. 2.

6. Quoted in Patricia Risso, *Merchants and Faith: Muslim Commerce and Culture in the Indian Ocean* (Boulder, Colo.: Westview Press, 1995), p. 96.

7. Quoted in Robert B. Marks, *The Origins of the Modern World: A Global and Ecological*

Narrative (Lanham, Md.: Rowman and Littlefield, 2002), p. 81.

8. Quoted in Christine Dobbin, *Asian Entrepreneurial Minorities: Conjoint Communities in the Making of the World-Economy, 1750–1940* (Richmond, United Kingdom: Curzon, 1996), p. 23.

9. Quoted in J. Donald Hughes, "Biodiversity in World History," in Hughes, ed., *The Face of the Earth: Environment and World History* (Armonk, N.Y.: M.E. Sharpe, 2000), p. 31.

10. Quoted in H. William Skinner, *Chinese Society in Thailand: An Analytical History* (Ithaca, N.Y.: Cornell University Press, 1957), p. 8.

11. Balthasar Barreira, quoted in George E. Brooks, *Landlords and Strangers: Ecology, Society, and Trade in Western Africa, 1000–1630* (Boulder, Colo.: Westview Press, 1983), p. 306.

12. Quoted in Annemarie Schimmel, *The Empire of the Great Mughals: History, Art, and Culture* (New Delhi: Oxford University Press, 2005), p. 113.

13. Quoted in Susan Mann, *Precious Records: Women in China's Long Eighteenth Century* (Stanford, Calif.: Stanford University Press, 1997), p. 108.

14. Quoted in Schimmel, *Empire of Great Mughals*, p. 130.

15. Juan Gimes de Sepulveda, in Marvin Lunenfeld, ed., *1492: Discovery, Invasion, Encounter: Sources and Interpretations* (Lexington, Mass.: D.C. Heath, 1991), pp. 219–220.

Chapter 19 Modern Transitions: Revolutions, Industries, Ideologies, Empires, 1750–1914

1. Quoted in Eric Hobsbawm, *The Age of Revolution, 1789–1848* (New York: New American Library, 1962), p. 44.

2. From Charles Dickens, *A Tale of Two Cities* (New York: Bantam, 1989), p. 1.

3. From David A. Hollinger and Charles Capper, eds., *The American Intellectual Tradition: A Sourcebook,* vol. 1, 2nd ed. (New York: Oxford University Press, 1993), p. 131.

4. Quoted in William Appleman Williams, *America Confronts a Revolutionary World, 1775–1976* (New York: William Morrow, 1976), pp. 15, 25.

5. Quoted in Peter N. Stearns, *Life and Society in the West: The Modern Centuries* (San Diego: Harcourt Brace Jovanovich, 1988), p. 164.

6. Quoted in Eric Hobsbawm, *Workers: World of Labor* (New York: Pantheon), p. 34.

7. Quoted in Michael Elliott-Bateman et al., *Revolt to Revolution: Studies in the 19th and 20th Century European Experience* (Manchester, England: Manchester University Press, 1974), p. 87.

8. Jose San Martin, quoted in Edwin Early, *The History Atlas of South America* (New York: Macmillan, 1998), p. 76.

9. Quoted in Carlos Fuentes, *The Buried Mirror: Reflections on Spain and the New World* (New York: Houghton Mifflin, 1992), p. 252.

10. Quoted in E. Bradford Burns and Julie A. Charlip, *Latin America: A Concise Interpretive History*, 7th ed. (Upper Saddle River, N.J.: Prentice-Hall, 2002), p. 75.

11. Quoted in John R. Gillis, *A World of Their Own Making: Myth, Ritual, and the Quest for Family Values* (New York: Basic Books, 1996), p. 65.

12. Quoted in Fernand Braudel, *The Perspective of the World: Civilization and Capitalism, 15th–18th Century* (New York: Harper and Row, 1984), p. 553.

13. Quoted in Peter Gay, *Age of Enlightenment* (New York: Time, Inc., 1966), pp. 105–106.

14. Quoted in Peter Hall, *Cities in Civilization* (New York: Fromm International, 1998), p. 310.

15. Quoted in Oliver Zimmer, *A Contested Nation: History, Memory and Nationalism in Switzerland, 1761–1891* (Cambridge: Cambridge University Press, 2003), p. 119.

16. Quoted in W. Raymond Duncan et al., *World Politics in the 21st Century*, 2nd ed. (New York: Longman, 2004), p. 311.

17. Quoted in Patrick Galvin, *Irish Songs of Resistance* (New York: Folklore Press, n.d.), p. 84.

18. Quoted in S. C. Burchell, *The Age of Progress* (New York: Time, Inc., 1966), p. 120.

19. Quoted in Reginald Nettel, *Sing a Song of England: A Social History of Traditional Song* (London: Phoenix House, 1969), p. 183.

20. Quoted in Robert A. Huttenback, *The British Imperial Experience* (New York: Harper and Row, 1966), p. 101.

21. Hillaire Beloc, quoted in Eric Hobsbawm, *The Age of Empire, 1875–1914* (New York: Vintage, 1987), p. 20.

22. Quoted in John Steele Gordon, *A Thread Across the Ocean: The Heroic Story of the Transatlantic Cable* (New York: Perennial, 2003), p. 215.

23. Quoted in Winnifred Baumgart, *Imperialism: The Idea and Reality of British and French Colonial Expansion, 1880–1914* (New York: Oxford University Press, 1986), p. 88.

24. Quoted in L. S. Stavrianos, *Global Reach: The Third World Comes of Age* (New York: William Morrow, 1981), p. 263.

25. Quoted in Baumgart, *Imperialism*, p. 52.

Chapter 20 Changing Societies in Europe, the Americas, and Oceania, 1750–1914

1. *Nostromo* (Garden City, N.Y.: Doubleday, Page, and Company, 1924), p. 77.

2. The Kume quotes are from Donald Keene, *Modern Japanese Diaries: The Japanese at Home and Abroad as Revealed Through Their Diaries* (New York: Columbia University Press, 1998), pp. 90–115.

3. Quoted in Frederic Delouche et al., *Illustrated History of Europe* (New York: Barnes and Noble, 2001), p. 312.

4. Quoted in Louise A. Tilly and Joan W. Scott, *Women, Work and Family* (New York: Holt, Rinehart and Winston, 1978), p. 64.

5. Quoted in Dorothy Marshall, *Industrial England, 1771–1851* (New York: Charles Scribner's, 1973), p. 135.

6. Quoted in T. W. C. Blanning, "The Commercialization and Sacralization of European Culture in the Nineteenth Century," in T. W. C. Blanning, ed., *The Oxford Illustrated History of Modern Europe* (Oxford: Oxford University Press, 1996), p. 147.

7. The quotes are from Alexis De Tocqueville, *Democracy in America and Two Essays on America* (New York: Penguin, 2003), pp. xxv, xxxiii.

8. Quoted in James Chase and Caleb Carr, *America Invulnerable: The Quest for Absolute Security from 1812 to Star Wars* (New York: Summit, 1988), p. 46.

9. From Peter Blood-Patterson, *Rise Up Singing* (Bethlehem, Pa.: Sing Out Publications, 1988), p. 246.

10. Quoted in Walter L. Williams, "American Imperialism and the Indians," in Frederick E. Hoxie, ed., *Indians in American History: An Introduction* (Arlington Heights, Ill.: Harlan Davidson, 1988), p. 233.

11. Quoted in Gabriel Kolko, *Main Currents in Modern American History* (New York: Pantheon, 1984), p. 47.

12. Quoted in Simon Serfaty, *The Elusive Enemy: American Foreign Policy Since World War II* (Boston: Little, Brown, 1972), p. 13.

13. Quoted in William Appleman Williams, *The Contours of American History* (Chicago: Quadrangle, 1966), p. 284.

14. Quoted in Robert Heilbroner and Aaron Singer, *The Economic Transformation of America, 1600 to the Present*, 3rd ed. (Fort Worth, Tex.: Harcourt Brace, 1994), p. 163.

15. The quotes are in Juliet Haines Mofford, ed., *Talkin' Union: The American Labor Movement* (Carlisle, Mass.: Discovery Enterprises, 1997), pp. 12, 24.

16. From Mark Van Doren, ed., *The Portable Walt Whitman* (New York: Penguin, 1973), p. 210.

17. Quoted in Lloyd Gardner, *Safe for Democracy: The Anglo-American Response to Revolution, 1913–1923* (New York: Oxford University Press, 1984), p. 26.

18. From Mariano Azuela's novel *The Flies*, quoted in Lesley Byrd Simpson, *Many Mexicos*, 4th ed. rev. (Berkeley: University of California Press, 1967), p. 298.

19. Quoted in Stanley J. Stein and Barbara H. Stein, *The Colonial Heritage of Latin America: Essays on Economic Dependence in Perspective* (New York: Oxford University Press, 1970), p. 151.

20. Quoted in E. Bradford Burns, *Latin America: A Concise Interpretive History*, 5th ed. (Englewood Cliffs, N.J.: Prentice-Hall, 1990), p. 213.

21. Quoted in Michael C. Meyer and William L. Sherman, *The Course of Mexican History*, 2nd ed. (New York: Oxford University Press, 1983), p. 416.

22. Quoted in Lloyd Braithwaite, "The Problem of Cultural Integration in Trinidad," in David Lowenthal and Lambors Comitas, eds., *Consequences of Class and Color: West Indian Perspectives* (Garden City, N.Y.: Anchor, 1973), p. 248.

23. General Leonard Wood, quoted in Saul Landau, *The Dangerous Doctrine: National Security and U.S. Foreign Policy* (Boulder, Colo.: Westview Press, 1988), pp. 80–81.
24. Quoted in Louis Hartz, *The Founding of New Societies* (New York: Harcourt, Brace and World, 1964), p. 248.
25. Quoted in Donald Denoon and Philippa Mein-Smith, *A History of Australia, New Zealand and the Pacific* (Malden, Mass.: Blackwell, 2000), p. 210.

Chapter 21 Africa, the Middle East, and Imperialism, 1750–1914

1. Quoted in Edmund Burke III, *Prelude to Protectorate in Morocco: Precolonial Protest and Resistance, 1860–1912* (Chicago: University of Chicago Press, 1976), p. xi.
2. Quoted in Alan Palmer, *The Decline and Fall of the Ottoman Empire* (New York: Barnes and Noble, 1992), p. 58.
3. Quoted in John Iliffe, "Tanzania Under German and British Rule," in B. A. Ogot, ed., *Zamani: A Survey of East African History*, new ed. (Nairobi: Longman Kenya, 1974), p. 301.
4. Quoted in Kevin Shillington, *History of Africa*, rev. ed. (New York: St. Martin's, 1995), p. 296.
5. Muhammad Bello, quoted in Robert W. July, *A History of the African People*, 5th ed. (Prospect Heights, Ill.: Waveland, 1998), p. 191.
6. Francois Coillard, quoted in John Iliffe, *Africans: The History of a Continent* (New York: Cambridge University Press, 1995), p. 208.
7. Quoted in Basil Davidson, *Africa in History: Themes and Outlines*, rev. ed. (New York: Touchstone, 1991), p. 272.
8. Quoted in Tom Hopkinson, *South Africa* (New York: Time Inc., 1964), p. 93.
9. The lyrics are in David B. Coplan, *In Township Tonite: South Africa's Black City Music and Theater* (London: Longman, 1985), pp. 44–45.
10. Quoted in Iliffe, *Africans*, pp. 200–201.
11. H. H. Johnston, quoted in M. E. Chamberlain, *The Scramble for Africa* (Harlow, U.K.: Longman, 1974), p. 96.
12. Nnamdi Azikiwe, quoted in Minton F. Goldman, "Political Change in a Multi-National Setting," in David Schmitt, ed., *Dynamics of the Third World: Political and Social Change* (Cambridge: Winthrop, 1974), p. 172.
13. Rev. J. B. Murphy, quoted in Shillington, *History of Africa*, pp. 333–334.
14. Quoted in Dennis Austin, *Politics in Ghana* (London: Oxford University Press, 1964), p. 275.
15. Quoted in Leroy Vail, "The Political Economy of East-Central Africa," in David Birmingham and Phyllis M. Martin, eds., *History of Central Africa*, vol. 2 (New York: Longman, 1983), p. 233.
16. Quoted in Andrew Wheatcroft, *The Ottomans* (New York: Viking, 1993), p. 146.
17. Quoted in Halil Inalcik, "Turkey," in Robert E. Ward and Dankwart A. Rostow, eds., *Political Modernization in Japan and Turkey* (Princeton: Princeton University Press, 1964), pp. 57–58.
18. Quoted in Afaf Lufti al-Sayyid Marsot, *Egypt in the Reign of Muhammad Ali* (New York: Cambridge University Press, 1994), p. 28.
19. Quoted in Yahya Armajani and Thomas M. Ricks, *Middle East: Past and Present*, 2nd ed. (Englewood Cliffs, N.J.: Prentice-Hall, 1986), p. 221.
20. Quoted in Charles Issawi, *The Middle East Economy: Decline and Recovery* (Princeton: Markus Wiener, 1995), p. 126.
21. Gertrude Bell, quoted in Emory C. Bogle, *The Modern Middle East: From Imperialism to Freedom, 1800–1958* (Upper Saddle River, N.J.: Prentice-Hall, 1996), p. 103.
22. Quoted in Eric R. Wolf, *Peasant Wars of the Twentieth Century* (New York: Harper and Row, 1969), p. 209.
23. The quotes are from Akram Fouad Khater, ed., *Sources in the History of the Modern Middle East* (Boston: Houghton Mifflin, 2004), p. 75; Wiebke Walther, *Women in Islam* (Princeton: Markus Wiener, 1993), p. 221.
24. Quoted in Burke, *Prelude to Protectorate*, p. 38.
25. From Khater, *Sources*, p. 34.

Chapter 22 South Asia, Southeast Asia, and Colonization, 1750–1914

1. From Huynh Sanh Thong, *An Anthology of Vietnamese Poems from the Eleventh Through the Twentieth Centuries* (New Haven, Conn.: Yale University Press, 1996), p. 88.
2. The poem excerpts are in Helen B. Lamb, *Vietnam's Will to Live: Resistance to Foreign Aggression from Early Times Through the Nineteenth Century* (New York: Monthly Review Press, 1972), pp. 134, 152.
3. Quoted in Sinharaja Tammita-Delgoda, *A Traveller's History of India*, 2nd ed. (New York: Interlink, 1999), p. 154.
4. The quotes are in Burton Stein, *A History of India* (Malden, Mass.: Blackwell, 1998), pp. 265–266.
5. Charles Metcalfe, quoted in David Ludden, *An Agrarian History of South Asia* (New York: Cambridge University Press, 1999), p. 161.
6. Quoted in Tammita-Delgoda, *Traveller's History*, p. 167.
7. Quoted in ibid., p. 173.
8. Quoted in Judith M. Brown, *Modern India: The Origins of an Asian Democracy*, 2nd ed. (New York: Oxford University Press, 1994), p. 134.
9. Dadabhai Naoroji and R.C. Dutt, quoted in Ainslee T. Embree, *India's Search for National Identity* (New York: Alfred A. Knopf, 1972), pp. 48–49.
10. Quoted in Clark D. Moore and David Eldridge, ed., *India Yesterday and Today* (New York: Bantam, 1970), pp. 154–155.
11. The quotes are in Francis Robinson, *The Cultural Atlas of the Islamic World Since 1500* (Oxford: Stonehenge, 1992), pp. 148–149.
12. From Rabindranath Tagore, *Gitanjali: A Collection of Indian Songs* (New York: Macmillan, 1973), pp. 49–50.
13. Quoted in John McLane, ed., *The Political Awakening of India* (Englewood Cliffs, N.J.: Prentice-Hall, 1970), p. 46.
14. Douwes Dekker, from Harry J. Benda and John A. Larkin, eds., *The World of Southeast Asia: Selected Historical Readings* (New York: Harper and Row, 1967), p. 127.
15. Quoted in Truong Buu Lam, *Resistance, Rebellion, Revolution: Popular Movements in Vietnamese History* (Singapore: Institute of Southeast Asian Studies, 1984), p. 11.
16. From Huynh, *Anthology of Vietnamese Poems*, p. 214.
17. The quotes are in Lamb, *Vietnam's Will to Live*, p. 229; Truong Buu Lam, *Patterns of Vietnamese Response to Foreign Intervention, 1858–1900*, Monograph Series No. 11, Southeast Asia Studies (New Haven, Conn.: Yale University Press, 1967), p. 8.
18. Quoted in David Joel Steinberg, 3rd ed., *The Philippines: A Singular and Plural Place* (Boulder, Colo.: Westview Press, 1994), p. 64.
19. The quotes are in Teodoro A. Agoncillo, *A Short History of the Philippines* (New York: Mentor, 1969), p. 93; and Mina Roces, "Reflections on Gender and Kinship in the Philippine Revolution, 1896–1898," in Florentino Rodao and Felice Noelle Rodriguez, eds., *The Philippine Revolution of 1896: Ordinary Lives in Extraordinary Times* (Manila: Ateneo de Manila University Press, 2001), p. 34.
20. Quoted in David Joel Steinberg et al., *In Search of Southeast Asia: A Modern History*, rev. ed. (Honolulu: University of Hawaii Press, 1987), p. 274.
21. Quoted in Daniel B. Schirmer, *Republic or Empire: American Resistance to the Philippine War* (Cambridge: Schenkman, 1972), p. 237.
22. The quotes are in David Howard Bain, *Sitting in Darkness: Americans in the Philippines* (Baltimore: Penguin, 1986), p. 2; and Gary R. Hess, *Vietnam and United States: Origins and Legacy of War* (Boston: Twayne, 1990), p. 25.
23. Quoted in Ngo Vinh Long, *Before the Revolution: The Vietnamese Peasants Under the French* (New York: Columbia University Press, 1991), p. v.
24. Tran Tu Binh, *The Red Earth: A Vietnamese Memoir of Life on a Colonial Rubber Plantation*, translated by John Spragens, Jr. (Athens, Ohio: Center for International Studies, Ohio University, 1985), p. 26.
25. Raden Ajoe Mangkoedimedjo, quoted in Norman Owen et al., *The Emergence of Modern Southeast Asia: A New History* (Honolulu: University of Hawaii Press, 2005), p. 197.

Chapter 23 East Asia and the Russian Empire Face New Challenges, 1750–1914

1. Quoted in Frederic Wakeman, Jr., *Strangers at the Gate: Social Disorder in South China, 1839–1861* (Berkeley: University of California Press, 1966), p. 126.
2. Quoted in Jonathan D. Spence, *The Search for Modern China*, 2nd ed. (New York: W.W. Norton, 1999), p. 148.

3. Quoted in Derk Bodde, *Chin"s Cultural Tradition: What and Whither?* (New York: Holt, Rinehart and Winston, 1957), pp. 62–63.

4. Chu Tsun, quoted in Hsin-Pao Chang, *Commissioner Lin and the Opium War* (New York: W.W. Norton, 1970), p. 89.

5. Quoted in Mark Borthwick, *Pacific Century: The Emergence of Modern East Asia* (Boulder, Colo.: Westview Press, 1992), p. 97.

6. The quotes are from Franz Schurmann and Orville Schell, eds., *Imperial China* (New York: Vintage Books, 1967), p. 146; and Ssu-Yu Teng and John K. Fairbank, eds., *China's Response to the West: A Documentary Survey, 1839–1923* (New York: Atheneum, 1963), p. 26.

7. Quoted in Jean Chesneaux et al., *China: From the Opium Wars to the 1911 Revolution* (New York: Pantheon, 1976), p. 123.

8. S. Wells Williams, quoted in John A. Harrison, *China Since 1800* (New York: Harcourt, Brace and World, 1967), p. 42.

9. Hsu Tung, quoted in Joseph R. Levenson, *Confucian China and Its Modern Fate: A Trilogy* (Berkeley: University of California Press, 1968), p. 105.

10. Quoted in Earl Swisher, "Chinese Intellectuals and the Western Impact, 1838–1900," *Comparative Studies in Society and History*, 1 (October, 1958), p. 35.

11. Wang Pengyun, from Cyril Birch, ed., *Anthology of Chinese Literature* (New York: Grove Press, 1972), p. 294.

12. Quoted in Lloyd Gardner, *Safe for Democracy: The Anglo-American Response to Revolution, 1913–1923* (New York: Oxford University Press, 1984), p. 318.

13. Quoted in Ono Kazuko, *Chinese Women in a Century of Revolution* (Stanford, Calif.: Stanford University Press, 1989), p. 30.

14. Quoted in Jonathan D. Spence, *The Gate of Heavenly Peace: The Chinese and Their Revolution, 1895–1980* (New York: Viking, 1981), p. 52.

15. Otsuki Gentaku, quoted in Mikiso Hane, *Modern Japan: A Historical Survey*, 2nd ed. (Boulder, Colo.: Westview Press, 1992), p. 59.

16. Quoted in Patricia Fister, "Female *Bunjin*: The Life of Poet-Painter Ema Saiko," in Gail Lee Bernstein, ed., *Recreating Japanese Women, 1600–1945* (Berkeley: University of California Press, 1991), p. 109.

17. Quoted in Matthi Ferrer, *Hokusai* (New York: Barnes and Noble, 2002), p. 9.

18. Yanagawa Seigan, quoted in H. D. Hartoonian, *Toward Restoration: The Growth of Political Consciousness in Tokugawa Japan* (Berkeley: University of California Press, 1970), pp. 1–2.

19. Quoted in Paul Varley, *Japanese Culture*, 4th ed. (Honolulu: University of Hawaii Press, 2000), p. 238.

20. Quoted in Kenneth B. Pyle, *The Making of Modern Japan*, 2nd ed. (Lexington, Mass.: D.C. Heath, 1996), p. 101.

21. Fukuzawa Yukichi, quoted in Mikiso Hane, *Peasants, Rebels, and Outcasts: The Underside of Modern Japan* (New York: Pantheon, 1982), p. 33.

22. Quoted in Conrad Totman, *A History of Japan* (Malden, Mass.: Blackwell, 2000), p. 341.

23. The quotes are from Varley, *Japanese Culture*, p. 272.

24. Ch'oe Ik-hyon, quoted in Bruce Cumings, *Korea's Place in the Sun: A Modern History* (New York: W.W. Norton, 1997), pp. 146–147.

25. Quoted in L. S. Stavrianos, *Global Rift: The Third World Comes of Age* (New York: William Morrow, 1981), p. 344.

Chapter 24 World Wars, European Revolutions, and Global Depression, 1914–1945

1. Quoted in Anne Applebaum, *Gulag: A History* (New York: Doubleday, 2003), p. 3.

2. Quoted in S. L. Marshall, *World War I* (Boston: Houghton Mifflin, 1987), p. 53.

3. Quoted in Sir Michael Howard, "Europe 1914," in Robert Cowley, ed., *The Great War: Perspectives on the First World War* (New York: Random House, 2003), p. 3.

4. David Lloyd George, quoted in Holger H. Herwig, ed., *The Outbreak of World War I*, 6th ed. (Boston: Houghton Mifflin, 1997), p. 12.

5. The quotes are in Michael J. Lyons, *World War I: A Short History*, 2nd ed. (Upper Saddle River, N.J.: Prentice-Hall, 2000), p. 195; and Ian Barnes and Robert Hudson, *The History Atlas of Europe: From Tribal Societies to a New European Unity* (New York: Macmillan, 1998), p. 131.

6. From L. S. Stavrianos, ed., *The Epic of Modern Man: A Collection of Readings* (Englewood Cliffs, N.J.: Prentice-Hall, 1966), p. 354.

7. Quoted in A. J. Nicholls, *Weimar and the Rise of Hitler*, 2nd ed. (New York: St. Martin's, 1979), p. 11.

8. Quoted in Piers Brendon, *Dark Valley: A Panorama of the 1930s* (New York: Alfred A. Knopf, 2000), p. 6.

9. Quoted in L. S. Stavrianos, *Global Rift: The Third World Comes of Age* (New York: William Morrow, 1981), p. 499.

10. Quoted in Brendon, *Dark Valley*, p. 493.

11. Quoted in Kenneth B. Pyle, *The Making of Modern Japan*, 2nd ed. (Lexington, Mass.: D.C. Heath, 1996), p. 173.

12. Senator William Borah, quoted in William Appleman Williams, *American-Russian Relations, 1781–1947* (New York: Rinehart, 1952), p. 164.

13. *The Great Gatsby* (New York: Scribner's, 1925), p. 182.

14. Paul Reynaud, quoted in Brendon, *Dark Valley*, pp. 153–154.

15. Quoted in Robert Heilbroner and Aaron Singer, *The Economic Transformation of America, 1600 to the Present* (Fort Worth: Harcourt Brace, 1994), p. 289.

16. From Harold Leventhal and Marjorie Guthrie, eds., *The Woody Guthrie Songbook* (New York: Grosset and Dunlap, 1976), pp. 180–181.

17. Maurice Sachs, quoted in Brendon, *Dark Valley*, p. 168.

18. Quoted in Felix Gilbert with David Clay Large, *The End of the European Era, 1890 to the Present*, 4th ed. (New York: W.W. Norton, 1991), p. 263.

19. Quoted in Harold James, *Europe Reborn: A History, 1914–2000* (New York: Longman, 2003), p. 139.

20. Quoted in Martin Kitchen, *A World in Flames: A Short History of the Second World War in Europe and Asia, 1939–1945* (London: Longman, 1990), p. vi.

21. Quoted in Stephen J. Lee, *European Dictatorships, 1918–1945*, 2nd ed. (London: Routledge, 2000), p. 207.

22. Quoted in George Donelson Moss, *America in the Twentieth Century*, 4th ed. (Upper Saddle River, N.J.: Prentice-Hall, 2000), p. 257.

23. The quotes are in James L. McClain, *Japan: A Modern History* (New York: W.W. Norton, 2002), p. 515.

Chapter 25 Imperialism and Nationalism in Asia, Africa, and Latin America, 1914–1945

1. Quoted in James C. Scott, *The Moral Economy of the Peasant: Rebellion and Subsistence in Southeast Asia* (New Haven: Yale University Press, 1976), p. 236.

2. Quoted in James W. Trullinger, *Village at War: An Account of Conflict in Vietnam* (Stanford, Calif.: Stanford University Press, 1994), p. 18.

3. Dick Spottswood, liner notes to the album *Calypsos from Trinidad: Politics, Intrigue and Violence in the 1930s* (Arhoolie 7004, 1991).

4. Quoted in Lester Langley, *Central America: The Real Stakes: Understanding Central America Before It's Too Late* (New York: Dorsey, 1985), p. 23.

5. Kenneth Wherry of Nebraska, quoted in John Brooks, *The Great Leap: The Past Twenty-five Years in America* (New York: Harper and Row, 1966), p. 327.

6. Quoted in *A Pictorial Biography of Luxun* (Beijing: Peoples Fine Arts Publishing House, n.d.), p. 157.

7. "Report on an Investigation of the Peasant Movement in Hunan," in *Selected Works of Mao Tse-Tung*, vol. 1 (Peking: Foreign Languages Press, 1965), p. 28.

8. Quoted in Stephen Uhalley, Jr., *Mao Tse-Tung: A Critical Biography* (New York: New Viewpoints, 1975), p. 55.

9. Quoted in John Meskill, "History of China," in John Meskill, ed., *An Introduction to Chinese Civilization* (Lexington, MA: D.C. Heath, 1973), p. 302.

10. Quoted in Sinharaja Tammita-Delgoda, *A Traveller's History of India*, 2nd ed. (New York: Interlink, 1999), p. 189.

11. From Clark D. Moore and David Eldridge, eds., *India Yesterday and Today* (New York: Bantam, 1970), p. 174.

12. Quoted in Martin Deming Lewis, ed., *Gandhi: Maker of Modern India?* (Lexington, Mass.: D.C. Heath, 1965), p. xii.

13. Quoted in Hermann Kulke and Dietmar Rothermund, *History of India*, 3rd ed. (New York: Routledge, 1998), pp. 135–136.

14. Sir T.P. Sapru, quoted in Judith M. Brown, *Modern India: The Origins of an Asian Democracy*, 2nd ed. (New York: Oxford University Press, 1994), p. 280.

15. "Phan Boi Chau's Prison Reflections, 1914," in Robert J. McMahon, ed., *Major Problems in the History of the Vietnam War: Documents and Essays* (Lexington, Mass.: D.C. Heath, 1990), p. 32.

16. Hoai Thanh, quoted in David Marr, "Vietnamese Historical Reassessment, 1900–1944," in Anthony Reid and David Marr, eds., *Perceptions of the Past in Southeast Asia* (Singapore: Heinemann, 1979), pp. 337–338.

17. Sitor Situmorang, quoted in Harry Aveling, ed., *From Surabaya to Armageddon: Indonesian Short Stories* (Singapore: Heinemann, 1976), p. vii.

18. Obafemi Awolowo, quoted in Chester L. Hunt and Lewis Walker, *Ethnic Dynamics: Patterns of Intergroup Relations in Various Societies*, 2nd ed. (Holmes Beach, Fla: Learning Publications, 1979), p. 277.

19. Quoted in Veit Erlmann, *African Stars: Studies in Black South African Performance* (Chicago: University of Chicago Press, 1991), pp. 95–96.

20. Quoted in Charles Hamm, "'The Constant Companion of Man': Separate Development, Radio Bantu and Music," *Popular Music*, 10/2 (May, 1991), p. 161.

21. Quoted in Hans Kohn, *A History of Nationalism in the East* (New York: Harcourt, 1929), p. 257.

22. The quotes are from Akram Fouad Khater, ed., *Sources in the History of the Modern Middle East* (Boston: Houghton Mifflin, 2004), pp. 167, 176.

23. Severino Fama, quoted in Robert M. Levine, *The History of Brazil* (New York: Palgrave, 1999), p. 107.

24. From Frederick B. Pike, ed., *Latin American History: Select Problems. Identity, Integration, and Nationhood* (New York: Harcourt, Brace and World, 1969), p. 319.

Societies, Networks, Transitions: Global Imbalances in the Modern World, 1750–1945

1. From Jim Zwick, ed., *Mark Twain's Weapons of Satire: Anti-Imperialist Writings on the Philippine-American War* (Syracuse, N.Y.: Syracuse University Press, 1992), pp. 3–5.

2. Quoted in L. S. Stavrianos, *Lifelines from Our Past: A New World History*, rev. ed. (Armonk, N.Y.: M.E. Sharpe, 1997), p. 114.

3. Rev. Sydney Smith, quoted in Frederic Delouche et al., *Illustrated History of Europe: A Unique Portrait of Europe's Common People* (New York: Barnes and Noble, 2001), p. 289.

4. Senator Albert Beveridge of Indiana, quoted in Henry Allen, *What It Felt Like Living in the American Century* (New York: Pantheon, 2000), p. 7.

5. Quoted in Benjamin Schwartz, *In Search of Wealth and Power: Yen Fu and the West* (New York: Harper Torchbooks, 1964), p. 29.

6. Quoted in Scott B. Cook, *Colonial Encounters in the Age of High Imperialism* (New York: Longman, 1996), p. 100.

7. From Clark D. Moore and David Eldridge, eds., *India Yesterday and Today* (New York: Bantam, 1970), p. 170.

8. Quoted in John A. Harrison, *China Since 1800* (New York: Harcourt, Brace and World, 1967), p. 161.

9. Quoted in Ranajit Guha, *History at the Limit of World-History* (New York: Columbia University Press, 2002), p. 91.

10. International Congress of the League Against Imperialism and Colonial Oppression, quoted in Clive Ponting, *The Twentieth Century: A World History* (New York: Henry Holt, 1998), p. 197.

11. Quoted in Richard H. Robbins, *Global Problems and the Culture of Capitalism* (Boston: Allyn and Bacon, 1999), p. 90.

12. Quoted in "Introduction," in Walter D. Wyman and Clifton B. Kroeber, eds., *The Frontier in Perspective* (Madison: University of Wisconsin Press, 1965), p. xviii.

13. Quoted in Pamela Scully, "Race and Ethnicity in Women's and Gender History in Global Perspective," in Bonnie G. Smith, ed., *Women's History in Global Perspective*, vol. 1 (Urbana: University of Illinois Press, 2004), p. 207.

14. Quoted in Ng Bickleen Fong, *The Chinese in New Zealand* (Hong Kong: Hong Kong University Press, 1959), p. 96.

15. Quoted in J. R. McNeill and William H. McNeill, *The Human Web: A Bird's-Eye View of World History* (New York: W.W. Norton, 2003), p. 217.

16. Quoted in Daniel R. Headrick, *The Tentacles of Progress: Technology Transfer in the Age of Imperialism, 1850–1940* (New York: Oxford University Press, 1988), p. 127.

17. Quoted in L. S. Stavrianos, "The Global Redistribution of Man," in Franklin D. Scott, ed., *World Migration in Modern Times* (Englewood Cliffs, N.J.: Prentice-Hall, 1968), p. 170.

18. Quoted in Daniel R. Headrick, *The Tools of Empire: Technology and European Imperialism in the Nineteenth Century* (New York: Oxford University Press, 1981), p. 116.

19. Quoted in Gordon Rohlehr, *Calypso and Society in Pre-Independence Trinidad* (Port of Spain: Gordon Rohlehr, 1990), pp. 80–81.

Chapter 26 The Remaking of the Global System, Since 1945

1. Quoted in Adrian Boot and Chris Salewicz with Rita Marley as Senior Editor, *Bob Marley: Songs of Freedom* (London:Bloomsbury, 1995), p. 278.

2. Quoted in Sean Dolan, *Bob Marley* (Philadelphia: Chelsea House, 1997), p. 113.

3. Frantz Fanon, *The Wretched of the Earth* (New York: Grove, 1968), pp. 97–98.

4. Quoted in Goran Hyden, *Beyond Ujamaa in Tanzania: Underdevelopment and an Uncaptured Peasantry* (Berkeley: University of California Press, 1980), p. 202.

5. Quoted in Jennifer Seymour Whitaker, *How Can Africa Survive?* (New York: Harper and Row, 1988), p. 13.

6. Mohammed Mossadeq, quoted in Michael H. Hunt, *The World Transformed, 1945 to the Present* (Boston: Bedford/St. Martin's, 2004), p. 283.

7. The quotes are in Choi Chatterjee et al., *The 20th Century: A Retrospective* (Boulder, Colo.: Westview Press, 2002), pp. 153, 306.

8. Dalai Lama, *My Land and My People* (New York: Warner Books, 1997), p. x.

9. Quoted in Peter Singer, "Navigating the Ethics of Globalization," *Chronicle of Higher Education*, October 11, 2002, p. B8.

10. Quoted in J. Donald Hughes, *An Environmental History of the World: Mankind's Changing Role in the Community of Life* (New York: Routledge, 2002), p. 206.

11. Quoted in Miriam Ching Louie, "Life on the Line," *The New Internationalist* (http://www.newint.org/issue302/sweat. html).

12. Walter Rodney, *How Europe Underdeveloped Africa* (London: Bogle-L'Ouverture, 1972), p. 162.

13. Quoted in Clive Ponting, *The Twentieth Century: A World History* (New York: Henry Holt and Company, 1998), p. 545.

14. Quoted in Hunt, *World Transformed*, p. 428.

15. Quoted in Eric Hobsbawm, *The Age of Extremes: A History of the World, 1914–1991* (New York: Pantheon, 1994), p. 365.

16. A. G. Hopkins, "Globalization: An Agenda for Historians," in Hopkins, ed., *Globalization in World History* (New York: W.W. Norton, 2002), p. 11.

17. From Hazel Johnson and Henry Bernstein, eds., *Third World Lives of Struggle* (London: Heinemann Educational, 1982), p. 173.

18. J. R. McLeod, "The Seamless Web: Media and Power in the Post-Modern Global Village," *Journal of Popular Culture*, 15/2 (Fall 1991), p. 69.

19. Quoted in Timothy D. Taylor, *Global Pop: World Music, World Markets* (New York: Routledge, 1997), p. 158.

20. Quoted in Chatterjee et al., *20th Century*, p. 222.

21. Quoted in David Reynolds, *One World Divisible: A Global History Since 1945* (New York: W.W. Norton, 2000), p. 491.

22. Quoted in Hunt, *World Transformed*, p. 409.

23. Quoted in Tariq Ali, *The Clash of Fundamentalisms: Crusades, Jihads and Modernity* (London: Verso, 2003), p. 280.

24. Michael Sturmer, quoted in Hobsbawm, *Age of Extremes*, p. 558.

Chapter 27 East Asian Resurgence, 1945–Present

1. Quoted in Jerome Chen, *Mao and the Chinese Revolution* (New York: Oxford University Press, 1967), p. 6.

2. The quotes are from Ross Terrill, *Mao: A Biography* (New York: Harper, 1980), p. 198.

3. Peng Dehuai, quoted in Craig Dietrich, *People's China: A Brief History*, 3rd ed. (New York: Oxford University Press, 1998), p. 130.

4. Quoted in Jonathan D. Spence, *The Search for Modern China*, 2nd ed. (New York: W.W. Norton, 1999), p. 558.

5. Quoted in Maurice Meisner, *Mao's China and After: A History of the People's*

Republic, 3rd ed. (New York: The Free Press, 1999), p. 281.

6. Xue Xinran, *The Good Women of China: Hidden Voices* (New York: Anchor, 2002), p. 175.

7. Quoted in the Committee of Concerned Asian Scholars, *China! Inside the Peoples Republic* (New York: Bantam, 1972), p. 34.

8. From Timothy Cheek, *Mao Zedong and China's Revolutions: A Brief History with Documents* (Boston: Bedford/St. Martin's, 2002), p. 116.

9. Quoted in Hu Kai-Yu, *The Chinese Literary Scene: A Writer's Visit to the People's Republic* (New York: Vintage, 1975), p. 227.

10. Quoted in Orville Schell, *Discos and Democracy: China in the Throes of Reform* (New York: Anchor, 1989), p. 101.

11. Quoted in June Teufel Dreyer, *China's Political System: Modernization and Tradition* (New York: Paragon House, 1993), p. 345.

12. The quotes are in Andrew F. Jones, *Like a Knife: Ideology and Genre in Contemporary Chinese Popular Music* (Ithaca, N.Y.: East Asia Program, Cornell University, 1992), pp. 97, 148.

13. Quoted in Orville Schell, *Mandate of Heaven: A New Generation of Entrepreneurs, Dissidents, Bohemians, and Technocrats Lays Claim to China's Future* (New York: Simon and Schuster, 1994), p. 35.

14. Quoted in R. Keith Schoppa, *Revolution and Its Past: Identities and Change in Modern Chinese History* (Upper Saddle River, N.J.: Prentice-Hall, 2002), p. 433.

15. Xue Xinran, author Interview in *Random House: Reading Group for the Good Women of China* (http://www.randomhouse.co.uk/offthepage/guide.htm?command=Search&db=catalog/mai).

16. Ibid.

17. Quoted in James L. McClain, *Japan: A Modern History* (New York: W.W. Norton, 2002), p. 585.

18. Misuzu Hanikara, from Richard H. Minear, ed., *Through Japanese Eyes*, vol. 2 (New York: Praeger, 1974), p. 88.

19. Kenzaburo Oe, quoted in Patrick Smith, *Japan: A Reinterpretation* (New York: Pantheon, 1997), p. 238.

20. Quoted in Mikiso Hane, *Modern Japan: A Historical Survey*, 2nd ed. (Boulder, Colo.: Westview Press, 1992), p. 371.

21. Quoted in Frank Gibney, *The Pacific Century: America and Asia in a Changing World* (New York: Charles Scribner's, 1992), p. 231.

22. Cho Se-hui, quoted in Bruce Cumings, *Korea's Place in the Sun: A Modern History* (New York: W.W. Norton, 1997), p. 337.

Chapter 28 Rebuilding Europe and Russia, Since 1945

1. Quoted in Norman Davies, *Europe: A History* (New York: Harper, 1998), p. 1066.

2. Quoted in ibid.

3. Quoted in Felix Gilbert with David Clay Large, *The End of the European Era, 1890 to the Present*, 4th ed. (New York: W.W. Norton, 1991), p. 429.

4. Quoted in Harold James, *Europe Reborn: A History, 1914–2000* (New York: Longman, 2001), p. 248.

5. Quoted in Robert O. Paxton, *Europe in the Twentieth Century* (New York: Harcourt Brace Jovanovich, 1973), p. 576.

6. Quoted in Davies, *Europe*, p. 1065.

7. Quoted in Bonnie G. Smith, *Changing Lives: Women in European History Since 1700* (Lexington, Mass.: D.C. Heath, 1989), p. 509.

8. Quoted in Richard Vinen, *A History in Fragments: Europe in the Twentieth Century* (New York: Da Capo, 2000), p. 370.

9. Quoted in Bonnie S. Anderson and Judith P. Zinsser, *A History of Their Own: Women in Europe from Prehistory to the Present*, vol. 2 (New York: Harper Perennial, 1988), p. 334.

10. Amintore Fanfani, quoted in Vinen, *History in Fragments*, p. 493.

11. Gordon Lewis, quoted in Chester L. Hunt and Lewis Walker, *Ethnic Dynamics: Patterns of Intergroup Relations in Various Societies*, 2nd ed. (Holmes Beach, Fla.: Learning Publications, 1979), p. 316.

12. *Sniffin' Glue*, quoted in Peter Wicke, *Rock Music: Culture, Aesthetics and Sociology* (New York: Cambridge University Press, 1990), p. 148.

13. Quoted in Ronald Grigor Suny, *The Soviet Experiment: Russia, the USSR, and the Successor States* (New York: Oxford University Press, 1998), p. 387.

14. Quoted in James, *Europe Reborn*, p. 279.

15. Quoted in Timothy W. Ryback, *Rock Around the Bloc: A History of Rock Music in Eastern Europe and the Soviet Union* (New York: Oxford University Press, 1990), p. 35.

16. Quoted in Davies, *Europe*, p. 1102.

17. Quoted in James, *Europe Reborn*, p. 300.

18. Quoted in Elaine Mensh and Harry Mensh, *Behind the Scenes in Two Worlds* (New York: International Publishers, 1978), p. 313.

19. Dmitry Likhachev, quoted in Catherine Evtuhov et al., *A History of Russia: Peoples, Legends, Events, Forces* (Boston: Houghton Mifflin, 2004), p. 819.

20. Quoted in James Wilkenson and H. Stuart Hughes, *Contemporary Europe: A History*, 10th ed. (Upper Saddle River, N.J.: Prentice-Hall, 2004), p. 559.

21. Quoted in Vinen, *History in Fragments*, p. 520.

22. Quoted in Wilkenson and Hughes, *Contemporary Europe*, p. 590.

Chapter 29 The Americas and the Pacific Basin: New Roles in the Contemporary World, Since 1945

1. Quoted in James D. Cockcroft, *Latin America: History, Politics, and U.S. Policy*, 2nd ed. (Chicago: Nelson-Hall, 1996), p. 567.

2. Quoted in Marilyn B. Young, *The Vietnam Wars, 1945–1990* (New York: HarperCollins, 1991), p. 25.

3. Quoted in James Matray, *The Reluctant Crusade: American Foreign Policy in Korea, 1941–1950* (Honolulu: University of Hawaii Press, 1985), p. 3.

4. Quoted in L. S. Stavrianos, *Global Rift: The Third World Comes of Age* (New York: William Morrow, 1981), p. 712.

5. Quoted in Walter LaFeber, *America, Russia and the Cold War: 1945–1992*, 7th ed. (New York: McGraw-Hill, 1993), p. 248.

6. Quoted in Cockcroft, *Latin America*, p. 531.

7. Quoted in Walter LaFeber et al., *The American Century: A History of the United States Since 1941*, 5th ed. (Boston: McGraw-Hill, 1998), p. 519.

8. From Peter Blood-Patterson, ed., *Rise Up Singing* (Bethlehem, Pa.: Sing Out Publications, 1988), p. 219.

9. Folksinger Malvina Reynolds, quoted in Richard O. Davies, "The Ambivalent Heritage: The City in Modern America," in James T. Patterson, ed., *Paths to the Present: Interpretive Essays on American Society Since 1930* (Minneapolis: Burgess, 1975), p. 163.

10. Quoted in George Donelson Moss, *America in the Twentieth Century*, 4th ed. (Upper Saddle River, N.J.: Prentice-Hall, 2000), p. 409.

11. Quoted in James T. Patterson, *America Since 1941: A History*, 2nd ed. (Fort Worth, Tex.: Harcourt, 2000), p. 254.

12. Quoted in Wayne C. Thompson, *Canada 1997* (Harpers Ferry, Va.: Stryker-Post, 1997), p. 1.

13. Jaime Wheelock, quoted in Kyle Longley, *In the Eagle's Shadow: The United States and Latin America* (Wheeling, Ill.: Harlan Davidson, 2002), p. 291.

14. Quoted in Sebastian Balfour, *Castro*, 2nd ed. (New York: Longman, 1995), p. 167.

15. The quotes are in Thomas E. Skidmore and Peter H. Smith, *Modern Latin America*, 4th ed. (New York: Oxford University Press, 1997), p. 147; Joseph A. Page, *The Brazilians* (Reading, Mass.: Addison-Wesley, 1995), p. 5.

16. Quoted in David J. Morris, *We Must Make Haste—Slowly: The Process of Revolution in Chile* (New York: Vintage, 1973), pp. 270–271.

17. Pamela Constable and Arturo Valenzuela, *A Nation of Enemies: Chile Under Pinochet* (New York: W.W. Norton, 1991), p. 38.

18. Graciliano Ramos, *Barren Lives*, quoted in E. Bradford Burns, *Latin America: A Concise Interpretive History*, 5th ed. (Englewood Cliffs, N.J.: Prentice-Hall, 1990), p. 231.

19. Nelson Rodrigues, quoted in Warren Hoge, "A Whole Nation More Agitated than Spike Lee," *New York Times*, June 5, 1994, p. A1.

20. From Jara's song "Manifiesto." ("Manifesto"). The song and the translation can be found on Jara's album *Manifiesto: Chile September 1973* (XTRA 1143, 1974).

21. See Marley's album *Catch a Fire* (Island ILPS 9241, 1973).

22. Quoted in Jan Fairley, "New Song: Music and Politics in Latin America," in Francis Hanly and Tim May, eds., *Rhythms of the World* (London: BBC Books, 1989), p. 90.

Chapter 30 The Middle East, Sub-Saharan Africa, and New Conflicts in the Contemporary World, 1945–Present

1. See Savuka's album *Heat, Dust and Dreams* (EMI 9777-7-98795, 1993).

2. Quoted in Ian J. Bickerton and Carla L. Klausner, *A Concise History of the Arab-Israeli Conflict*, 2nd ed. (Englewood Cliffs, N.J.: Prentice-Hall, 1995), p. 131.

3. Quoted in James Alban Bill, *The Politics of Iran: Groups, Classes and Modernization* (Columbus, Ohio: Charles E. Merrill, 1972), pp. 76–77.

4. Latifa az-Zayyat, quoted in Wiebke Walther, *Women in Islam from Medieval to Modern Times* (Princeton: Markus Wiener, 1993), p. 235.

5. Quoted in Daniel Bates and Amal Rassam, *Peoples and Cultures of the Middle East*, 2nd ed. (Upper Saddle River, N.J.: Prentice-Hall, 2001), p. 235.

6. Fatema Mernissi, *Scheherazade Goes West: Different Cultures, Different Harems* (New York: Washington Square Press, 2001), p. 219.

7. Martin Stokes, *The Arabesk Debate: Music and Musicians in Modern Turkey* (Oxford: Clarendon Press, 1992), p. 1.

8. Sadiq Hidayat, in *Hajji Aqa*, quoted in Bill, *Politics of Iran*, p. 105.

9. From Akram Fouad Khater, ed., *Sources in the History of the Modern Middle East* (Boston: Houghton Mifflin, 2004), p. 362.

10. Naguib Mahfuz, quoted in Bates and Rassam, *Peoples and Cultures*, p. 199.

11. Quoted in Frances Robinson, *The Cultural Atlas of the Islamic World Since 1500* (Alexandria, Va.: Stonehenge, 1982), p. 158.

12. Quoted in Basil Davidson, *The People's Cause: A History of Guerrillas in Africa* (Burnt Mill, U.K.: Longman, 1981), p. 165.

13. A. Toure, quoted in Bill Freund, *The Making of Contemporary Africa: The Development of African Society Since 1800* (Bloomington: Indiana University Press, 1984), p. 192.

14. From James E. Miller et al., eds., *Black African Voices* (Glenview: Scott Foresman, 1970), p. 322.

15. Prime Minister John Vorster in 1968, quoted in L. S. Stavrianos, *Global Rift: The Third World Comes of Age* (New York: William Morrow, 1981), p. 759.

16. Quoted in Jean Comaroff, *Body of Power, Spirit of Resistance: The Culture and History of a South African People* (Chicago: University of Chicago Press, 1985), p. vi.

17. Quoted in Gwendolen Carter, "The Republic of South Africa: White Political Control Within the African Continent," in Phyllis Martin and Patrick O'Meara, eds., *Africa*, 2nd ed. (Bloomington: Indiana University Press, 1986), p. 353.

18. Quoted in Joe Asila, "No Cash in This Crop," in Wayne Edge, ed., *Global Studies: Africa*, 2nd ed. (Guilford, Conn.: Dushkin, 2006), p. 285.

19. Sanford Unger, *Africa: The People and Politics of an Emerging Continent* (New York: Simon and Schuster, 1985), pp. 131–132.

20. Quoted in Richard A. Fredland, *Understanding Africa: A Political Economy Perspective* (Chicago: Burnham, 2001), p. 139.

21. Quoted in John Follain, "Only the First Step for 'Mama Africa,'" *New Straits Times*, February 23, 1990.

22. Kenneth Goldstein and Saka Acquaye, Liner notes to Acquaye's album *Voices of Africa: High-Life and Other Popular Music* (Nonesuch 72026, n.d.).

23. Quoted in Tejumola Olaniyan, "Narrativizing Postcoloniality: Responsibilities," *Public Culture*, 5/1 (Fall 1992), p. 47.

24. Quoted in Chinweizu, *The West and the Rest of Us: White Predators, Black Slavers, and the African Elite* (New York: Vintage, 1975), p. 1.

25. Quoted in Jennifer Seymour Whitaker, *How Can Africa Survive?* (New York: Harper and Row, 1988), p. 197.

Chapter 31 South Asia, Southeast Asia, and Global Connections, 1945–Present

1. Mochtar Lubis, *Road with No End*, translated by Anthony Johns from 1952 Indonesian edition (Chicago: Henry Regnery, 1968), p. 9.

2. Quoted in Anthony Johns, "Introduction," in Lubis, *Road with No End*, p. 4.

3. Quoted in John R. McLane, ed., *The Political Awakening of India* (Englewood Cliffs, N.J.: Prentice-Hall, 1970), p. 178.

4. Quoted in B. N. Pandey, *The Break-up of British India* (New York: St. Martin's, 1969), p. 209.

5. Faiz Ahmed Faiz, quoted in Sugata Bose and Ayesha Jalal, *Modern South Asia: History, Culture, Political Economy* (New York: Routledge, 1998), p. 200.

6. Rohinton Mistry, *A Fine Balance* (London: Faber, 1996), p. 143.

7. Quoted in Susan Bayly, *Caste, Society and Politics in India from the Eighteenth Century to the Modern Age* (New York: Cambridge University Press, 1999), p. 315.

8. Quoted in Jeremy Marre and Hannah Charlton, *Beats of the Heart: Popular Music of the World* (New York: Pantheon, 1985), p. 150.

9. Quoted in Bose and Jalal, *Modern South Asia*, p. 232.

10. Quoted in Stanley Wolpert, *A New History of India*, 7th ed. (New York: Oxford University Press, 2004), p. 462.

11. Quoted in William J. Duiker, *Ho Chi Minh: A Life* (New York: Hyperion, 2000), p. 323.

12. Quoted in George Donelson Moss, *Vietnam: An American Ordeal*, 4th ed. (Upper Saddle River, N.J.: Prentice-Hall, 2002), p. 40.

13. Jacques Philippe Leclerc, quoted in James S. Olson and Randy Roberts, *Where the Domino Fell: America and Vietnam, 1945–1995*, 3rd ed. (St. James, N.Y.: Brandywine, 1999), p. 28.

14. Quoted in Thomas G. Paterson et al., *American Foreign Policy: A History Since 1900*, 3rd ed. rev. (Lexington, Mass.: D.C. Heath, 1991), p. 553.

15. Anh Vien, quoted in Arleen Eisen Bergman, *Women of Vietnam*, rev. ed. (San Francisco: Peoples Press, 1975), p. 123.

16. Quoted in Neil L. Jamieson, *Understanding Vietnam* (Berkeley: University of California Press, 1993), p. 290.

17. From Idrus, "Surabaya," in Harry Aveling, ed., *From Surabaya to Armageddon: Indonesian Short Stories* (Singapore: Heinemann, 1976), p. 13.

18. From Pramoedya Ananta Toer, "Letter to a Friend in the Country," in Aveling, *From Surabaya*, p. 72.

19. Doreen Fernandez, "Mass Culture and Cultural Policy: The Philippine Experience," *Philippine Studies*, 37 (4th Quarter, 1980), p. 492.

20. "The Kingdom of Mammon," in Amado V. Hernandez, *Rice Grains: Selected Poems* (New York: International Publishers, 1966), p. 31.

21. From Taufiq Ismail's story "Stop Thief!" in David M. E. Roskies, ed., *Black Clouds over the Isle of Gods and Other Modern Indonesian Short Stories* (Armonk, N.Y.: M.E. Sharpe, 1997), p. 97.

22. F. Sionel Jose, quoted in David G. Timberman, *A Changeless Land: Continuity and Change in Philippine Politics* (New York: M.E. Sharpe, 1991), p. xi.

23. "American Junk," by the Apo Hiking Society, quoted in Craig A. Lockard, *Dance of Life: Popular Music and Politics in Southeast Asia* (Honolulu: University of Hawai'i Press, 1998), p. 156.

24. Quoted in Robin Broad and John Cavanaugh, *Plundering Paradise: The Struggle for the Environment in the Philippines* (Berkeley: University of California Press, 1993), p. xvii.

25. Quoted in Pasuk Phongpaichit and Chris Baker, *Thailand: Economy and Politics* (Kuala Lumpur: Oxford University Press, 1995), pp. 413–415.

Societies, Networks, Transitions: The Contemporary World, Since 1945

1. Kathleen Newland and Kamala Chandrakirana Soedjatmoko, eds., *Transforming Humanity: The Visionary Writings of Soedjatmoko* (West Hartford, Conn.: Kumarian Press, 1994), pp. 186–187.

2. Quoted in Jan Pronk, "Globalization": A Developmental Approach," in Jan Nederveen Pieterse, ed., *Global Futures: Shaping Globalization* (London: Zed Books, 2000), p. 46.

3. Daphne Berdahl, quoted in James L. Watson, ed., *Golden Arches East: McDonald's in East Asia* (Stanford, Calif.: Stanford University Press, 1997), p. xvii.

4. Billy Bergman, *Hot Sauces: Latin and Caribbean Pop* (New York: Quill, 1985), p. 18.

5. Quoted in Hans-Peter Martin and Harald Schumann, *The Global Trap: Globalization and the Assault on Democracy and Prosperity* (New York: Zed Books, 1996), p. 163.

6. From Banton's album, *Visions of the World* (IRSD-82003, 1989).

7. Frank Cajka, quoted in Peter Worsley, *The Three Worlds: Culture and World Development* (Chicago: University of Chicago Press, 1984), p. xi.

8. Quoted in Robbie Robertson, *The Three Waves of Globalization: A History of a Developing Global Consciousness* (New York: Zed Books, 2003), p. 263.

9. Lester Pearson, quoted in Lester R. Brown, *World Without Borders* (New York: Vintage, 1972), p. ix.

10. Aldo Leopold, *A Sand County Almanac* (New York: Ballantine, 1966), p. 253.

11. Quoted in J. Donald Hughes, *An Environmental History of the World: Humankind's Changing Role in the Community of Life* (New York: Routledge, 2001), p. 230.

12. Rene Dubos, *So Human an Animal* (New York: Scribner's, 1968), p. 270.

13. Ilya Prigogine, quoted in Federico Mayor and Jerome Bindé, *The World Ahead: Our Future in the Making* (New York: Zed Books, 2001), p. 1.

14. Lester Brown et al., "A World at Risk," in *State of the World 1989* (New York: W.W. Norton, 1989), p. 20.

15. Lewis Carroll, "Alice's Adventures in Wonderland," in *The Complete Works of Lewis Carroll* (New York: Modern Library), pp. 71–72.

INDEX

Communist triumph in, 836–837; Cultural Revolution in, 841–842; decline of religion in, 828; economic and political change in, 845–846; end of Maoist era, 843–844; environmental destruction in, 822; fascism in, 736; in global system, 813, 849–850; information flow in, 829; lack of freedom and, 806; Maoism in the world, 839–841, 1007; market economy in, 814, 834(illus.), 844–845, 890; modernization in, 844–850; United Nations and, 811; new economy and government in, 837–839; one-child policy in, 821; population growth in, 821; reform and repression in, 845; refugees from, 825; social services in, 818; society, gender and culture in, 842–843, 846–949; Soviet Union and, 837, 841, 884, 886, 889; Taiwan and, 863; Korean War and, 907; United States and, 911, 1001; India and, 973, 977; World Conference on Women (1995), 830; oil needs of, 949, 1011; Pakistan and, 975; Southeast Asia and, 999; development in, 1009; economic power of, 1009; McDonald's restaurants in, 1002, 1006; pollution in, 1011

China, Republic of, 757, 758, 837, 840(map), 841, 849, 862. See also Chiang Kai-shek; Taiwan; civil war in, 698, 758–759, 810, 835, 836–837; Sun Yat-sen and, 696, 697, 698, 755; Vietnam and, 983

Chinese calendar, xxix

Chinese explorers (Zheng He), 491, 539

Chinese immigrants, 693, 791; in Australia, 596(illus.), 625, 918(illus.); in Caribbean area, 619; in United States, 609, 613; in Hawaii, 615; in Malaya, 768, 997; railroads and, 613; in Singapore, 673–674, 680, 794(illus.), 991, 998; in Southeast Asia, 680, 793, 991, 993; in Thailand, 996

Chinese language, 849

Chinese merchants (traders), 532, 549, 550, 553, 692–693; intermarriage of, 558; in Philippines, 529, 530–531 and illus.; in Southeast Asia, 555, 680, 752; European trade and, 688, 689

Chinese Nationalist Party. See Guomindang party (China)

Chinese Revolution, 696–698, 836

Chinese writing, 529

Chinoiserie (Chinese artistic products), 688

Chipko tree protection movement (India), 823, 977

Chirac, Jacques (French leader), 1009

Chirot, Daniel (historian), 787–788

Chishtiya (Sufi movement), 522

Chivalry: Japanese bushido, 543

Chocolate, 716, 790. See also Cocoa (cacao)

Cholera, 604, 634, 650, 825

Chongqing, China, 758

Choson Korea, 541, 703

Christian calendar, xxix

Christian Church, 547. See also Catholic Church; Protestantism; specific sect; capitalism and, 435; doctrine of, 430; Greek Orthodox, 603, 646; Russian Orthodox, 712, 727, 887, 893; in Europe, 882–883; conservatives in, 913

Christian Democrats (Europe), 870, 880

Christianity (Christians): crusading tradition of, 433; Enlightenment and, 454; in Africa, 465, 466, 467, 473, 964–965; in Ottoman Empire, 476, 477; in Safavid Persia, 481, 482; Spanish explorers and, 491; Native Americans and, 495, 500, 502, 507; African American culture and, 512; progress and, 550; rivalry with Islam, 433, 529; slaves and, 574; socialism and, 587; in Japan, 543, 597; Afro-Brazilians and, 620; in West Africa, 632; in South Africa, 640, 644; Arab, 646, 650, 654; in China, 691, 695(illus.), 847, 849; decline of, in Europe, 729; humanitarian groups, 811; global dominance of, 826(map), 827; fundamentalist, 828; militancy of, 828; Korean, 858; in Europe, 897; in Pacific islands, 919; in Philippines, 991; in India, 978; in Pakistan, 980; in East Timor, 993; spread of, 1001

Christian missionaries, 559, 828, 1012. See also Catholic missionaries; Jesuits; in Safavid Persia, 481; in North America, 498, 505; in Americas, 493, 499, 503; in China, 539, 688, 690, 691, 692, 695; in Japan, 542; in Melaka, 529; in Siam, 528; in South Asia, 524; Native Americans and, 558; in Pacific region, 625; Protestant, 614, 631, 650, 928; in Africa, 631, 633, 641, 642; in Persia, 649; in Southeast Asia, 676; in Vietnam, 657; colonial education and, 681; in India, 664, 665, 669; in Korea, 703, 708; colonialism and, 789; abolition and, 793

Christian-Muslim hostility, 1014; in Ottoman expansion, 443, 477; in Africa, 965; in Middle East, 944; in Nigeria, 956; in Indonesia, 994

Christina (Sweden), 456

Chulalongkorn (Siamese ruler), 676

Chumash people, of California, 502

Churches (buildings): Ethiopian, 465; Hagia Sofia, 478

Churchill, Winston, 741, 869, 875, 883; at Yalta, 745

Church of England (Anglicanism), 439, 440(map), 441, 449, 603, 883, 964

Cinnamon trade, 524. See also Spice trade

Cinque, Joseph (rebel slave), 473

Cities and towns. See also Urbanization: African, 461, 464, 640; Aztec, 495; Chinese, 538; in colonial Latin America, 507; Eurasian polycentrism in, 548; growth of, in Europe, 431, 456, 599-600; Japanese, 543, 700, 705; industrialization and, 581; in United States, 613; Safavid Persia, 481; in colonial Southeast Asia, 681; colonial, 752; Chinese revolution in, 754; African nationalism and, 769; global population increase in, 819, 821; suburbanization, in United States, 912, 913–914; Latin American growth, 927; Brazilian shantytowns, 817(illus.), 928; growth of, in Africa, 962; in India, 977–978; in Southeast Asia, 998(illus.), 999; Western pop culture in, 1013

Citizenship: women excluded from, 571; Ottoman reform and, 647; denied to German Jews, 738; naturalization ceremony, 900(illus.); global, 1002

City-states: Aztec, 490; Maya, 490; East African, 462(map), 464, 469; Hausa (West Africa), 462(map), 463, 474, 555, 633–634, 641

Civil disobedience, Indian nationalism and, 760, 762

"Civilizing mission" of French colonials, 593, 642, 674, 786, 789

Civil liberties, 1014. See also Human rights; in Europe, 573; in United States, 731, 743; European fascism and, 737, 738; terrorist threat and, 832; in Taiwan, 863

Civil rights movement (United States), 913, 914 and illus.

Civil service examinations, 685; in China, 535, 537, 539

Civil war: in Switzerland, 441; English, 449, 455; African slave trade and, 468; in Ethiopia, 470; Inca, 496; in Southeast Asia, 531; in Japan, 541–542, 549, 704; in Latin America, 615; in Mexico, 617; in United States, 611, 631, 785; in colonial Africa, 634, 636, 642; in Persia, 649; in Sri Lanka, 663; in Vietnam, 674; in China, 698, 758–759; in Russia, 724–725 and map, 884; in Spain, 738–739, 785, 795; in Palestine, 776; in China, 801, 810, 835, 836–837, 849; in Angola, 806, 961; population pressures and, 821; in Nigeria, 810, 956; in Greece, 870; in Yugoslavia, 891, 894(map), 895, 909; in Somalia and Yugoslavia, 909; in Lebanon, 944; in Liberia, 955; in Afghanistan, 948; in Africa, 954(map); in Congo, 961; in Ivory Coast, 960; in Pakistan, 975

Ci Xi (Chinese empress), 694, 696

Clans, Zulu, 638. See also Chiefs (chiefdoms)

Clark, Helen (New Zealand leader), 918

Classical Era, xxx

Climate (climate change; weather), 556. See also Drought; China and, 846; global warming, 811, 818, 822–823, 898, 1010–1011; industrialization and, 1013; Little Ice Age, 430–431, 491, 498

Clinton, William ("Bill"), 907; Somalia and, 909; conservatives and, 913; Arab-Israeli conflict and, 940; Vietnam and, 987

Clive, Robert (British India), 660, 661(illus.)

Clocks, 549, 559; European, 453

Cloth and clothing: See also Textiles (textile industry); African cotton, 463, 474; Chinese, 536; in colonial Latin America, 502; European, 430, 467, 555; Indian, 525; Javanese batik, 528, 532, 553, 776; Turkish modernization and, 774; for Islamic women, 934(illus.), 943, 945

Clove plantations, 631. See also Spice trade

CNN (Cable News Network), 829, 889

Coal and coal mining, 551; in Britain, 578(map), 579, 582–583; in Europe, 580; pollution from, 604, 1011; in United States, 613

Coca (cocaine), 500, 813, 921, 926

"Coca-Colazation," 1012. See also Westernization

Cocoa (cacao), 819; in colonial Africa, 643, 769, 787; chocolate, 716, 790; in Africa, 960, 965

Codex (book), Aztec, 496(illus.)

Coffee, 434, 507, 511, 556; in Africa, 640, 960, 965; Bach cantata on, 451; in Brazil, 510,

827, 978–980; Japanese, 856–857; Brazilian, 929; cultural imperialism in, 1002

Finance, 1001; Great Depression and, 732; Indian merchants and, 520

Financial institutions, 814. *See also* Banks and banking

Finland, 584; Russia and, 709; independence of, 721; in European Union, 896

Firearms. *See* Guns (gunpowder weapons)

First Indochina War (1946–1954), 983–984, 986

First Nations, 493, 498, 917. *See also* Native Americans

First World, concept of, 806

Fishing (fishermen), 433, 498, 558; by Native Americans, 489, 492; off Newfoundland, 491; Aboriginal Australians, 625; decline in world harvest, 821; in Pacific islands, 919

Fitzgerald, F. Scott, 732

Five-Year Plans: Soviet Union, 726, 727, 885; India, 973

Flamethrowers, 719

Flanders (Flemish), 505; capitalism in, 435; Catholicism in, 443; paintings, 438 *and illus.*

"Floating World" in Japan, 543, 700

Floods (flooding): in Iraq, 650; in China, 691; deforestation and, 823; from hurricanes, 912

Florida, United States and, 609

Flowers in the Mirror (Li), 685, 688

Folk songs (folk music): Burmese, 675; Indian *bhangra*, 827, 881; in 1960s, 913; Chilean, 929–931 *and illus.*; Vietnamese, 986

Folk traditions: African, 512

Food crops. *See* Cash crops; *specific foods*

Food (diet): in Columbian exchange, 431, 500, 501, 556–557; scurvy (vitamin C deficiency), 493; sugar in, 508; Indian curry, in Britain, 880; in Japan, 853; North-South disparity in, 1007

Food production: African self-sufficiency, 960

Football (soccer), 796; in Brazil, 929

Footbinding, in China, 536, 754; movement against, 685, 696

Forbidden City (Beijing), 835, 839*(illus.)*

Forced labor. *See also* Slavery (slaves); in colonial Latin America, 507; indentured, 503, 668, 693; gulags (prison camps), 712, 722, 726–727; in colonies, 750–751; Native Americans and, 493, 503*(illus.)*, 507

Ford, Henry, 613

Ford Motor Company, 728, 815

Foreign investment, 817; in Asia, 814; British, 590, 618, 957; in China, 806, 849; American, 903; in Taiwan, 863; in Brazil, 924; in South Africa, 957; in Burma, 997; in Southeast Asia, 999; capitalism and, 1007

Foreign policy, United States: Cold War, 808, 873, 902, 904–905, 922; Muslim terrorism and, 831

Forests: *See also* Deforestation; Brazilian, 924; rain forests, 822, 924, 927, 960, 994; tree-planting campaigns, 818, 822–823, 838, 977

Fortifications: British, in India, 525; Ottoman, 477; Portuguese, in South Asia, 524; in Spanish missions, 502

Fossil fuels, pollution from, 912. *See also* Oil and oil industry; global warming and, 1010 *and illus.*, 1011, 1013

"Four Freedoms" (Roosevelt), 734

Fourteen Points (Wilson), 721

Fourth World, concept of, 806

Fox, Vicente (Mexico), 922–923

France, 449, 738. *See also under* French; centralization in, 433; Huguenots in, 443; absolutism in, 445, 455; Enlightenment salons in, 454*(illus.)*, 455; overseas trade of, 434, 506*(map)*; exploration by, 553; American Reovlution and, 568; chronology (1789–1815), 567; Napoleonic Era, 571–573 *and map*, 575; nationalism in, 584; Paris Commune and, 588–589; revolution in, 566, 569–571, 605, 785; alliances of, 591; industrialization in, 580, 590; women's rights in, 602; women textile workers in, 601; Mexico and, 617; invasion of Egypt by, 629–630; colony in India, 659; Egypt and, 648; China and, 690, 691*(map)*, 696, 711; Crimean War and, 711; Russian elite and, 709; in World War I, 716, 717–721 *and map*, 750; Russian civil war and, 724, 725*(map)*; League of Nations and, 722; in World War II, 739, 740*(map)*, 741, 744, 789; Lebanon and, 650, 772; global economy and, 785; in world-system theory, 787; Ottoman partition and, 771, 772, 773*(map)*; mercantilism in, 436; monarchy in, 445; atomic weapons of, 810; globalization and, 813; Ottoman alliance with, 475; postwar reconstruction of, 868; reconciliation with Germany, 869–870; rivalry with England, 525, 549; European Community and, 873, 897; Le Pen's National Front in, 877; workweek in, 876, 897; trade with Siam, 528; Suez crisis and (1956), 938; Africa and, 960; warfare of, 444–445; Arab immigrants in, 1002

Franciscan missions, in Americas, 502

Franco, Francisco (Spanish fascist), 739

Frank, Andre Gunder (historian), 550, 551, 787

Franklin, Aretha (American singer), 916

Franklin, Benjamin, 568, 569, 791

Franz Ferdinand, Archduke, 719

Frederick II, the Great (Prussia), 450, 456

Free blacks, 512, 577; African colonies of, 632; in United States, 611

Freedom, Locke and, 454–455

Freedom of religion, 444, 449, 503, 521. *See also* Religious tolerance

Freedom of speech, 570; Iroquois, 498

Free market (free trade), 732, 745, 817, 830, 907. *See also* Capitalism; laissez faire and, 581; Latin America and, 615, 618; British, in China, 688, 790, 806; British in Egypt, 648; British and, 590, 791; British India, 661; United States and, 605, 695; Chinese agriculture and, 844; European, 868–869, 876; in Britain, 870, 877; in Latin America, 921; in Africa, 960; globalization of, 1002, 1003; development and, 1007

Freetown, Sierra Leone, 632

Free World, concept of, 808

French Canadians, 623, 916, 917. *See also* Quebec

French colonies (French Empire), 488, 547, 753. *See also* Vietnam, French rule of; in Caribbean, 497, 509; in North America, 497, 498 *and map*, 499, 503–505; Atlantic system and, 513; in India, 520*(map)*, 525, 526; in

Africa, 634–635 *and map*, 636, 637, 641, 642, 769; in 1913, 592*(map)*, 717, 784; "civilizing mission" of, 593, 674, 786, 789, 952; in Pacific region, 625, 918; in Southeast Asia, 527*(map)*, 676, 765; in West Africa, 789, 814; in Algeria, 650, 803, 806, 871, 936; French Guiana, 778*(map)*, 805, 871; decolonization and, 803, 804*(map)*, 806

French East India Company, 525

French exploration, 432*(map)*; of Canada, 493; North America, 498

French impressionism, 604, 701

French language, 445; in Canada, 504, 622, 623, 916; in colonial Africa, 642; in Africa, 805

French legal codes, 571, 622, 647, 648

French Revolution (1789), 566, 584, 605, 785, 836; ending old regime in, 569–570; legacy of, 571; struggle for France and, 570–571

French Southeast Asia, 527, 676, 765. *See also* Vietnam, as French colony

Freud, Sigmund, 735

Friedan, Betty (American feminist), 915

Friedman, Thomas (historian), 1001–1002, 1003, 1005

Fugger, Jacob (German banker), 435

Fuggers of Germany, 435, 441, 555

Fujian (Chinese province), 539

Fukuda Hideko (Japanese feminist), 706

Fukuzawa Yukichi (Japanese Westernizer), 702

Fulani jihad, 633–634, 651. *See also* Hausa-Fulani

Fulani people of West Africa, 459–460

Fundamentalist Christianity, 828

Fundamentalist religions, 812, 1004

Fur trade, 553, 612; beaver, in North America, 498; in Canada, 504, 623; in Alaska, 625; Russian, 484, 540, 711

Futabatei Shimei (Japanese novelist), 706

Gabriel, Peter (musician), 1006

Gadsden Purchase, by United States, 608*(map)*

Gaelic language, 449

Gagaran, Yuri (Soviet cosmonaut), 884

Galileo Galilei, 453, 559

Galleons (ships), 434, 533

Gallipoli, World War I in, 720

Gama, Vasco da (Portuguese explorer), 467, 469, 524

Gamelan music (Indonesia), 681

Ganda people of Buganda, 465

Gandhi, Indira (India), 975

Gandhi, Mohandas K., 760–762 *and illus.*, 764, 784, 803, 1014; assassination of, 761, 972; caste system and, 763, 973; Hindu-Muslim violence and, 971–972; nonviolent resistance and, 668, 760, 762, 914, 970; on Western civilization, 594

Gandhi, Rajiv (India), 975, 977

Gandhi, Sanjay (India), 975

Gandhi, Sonia (India), 977

Ganges River (India), 977

Gang of Four (China), 843

Gao of Sudanic Africa, 460

García Márquez, Gabriel, 929

Garibaldi, Giuseppi (Italian nationalist), 584, 784

958; Chilean, 925, 926; Iranian, 941; Islamic women's clothing and, 945; African urban, 965; Indian, 972, 978; Malay, 997–998; Southeast Asian, 993

Middle East, 645. *See also specific country;* use of term, xxviii; African slaves in, 466; chronology (1500–1750), 475; Islam in, 460; chronology (1805–1882), 631; European colonialism in, 630, 721; World War I in, 720; chronology (1914–1945), 772; chronology (1922–1979), 751; remaking of, 771–776; African slave trade in, 793; terrorists in, 831; trade networks of, 526; foreign workers in, 824, 825; immigrants in Europe from, 880, 897; Western military interventions in, 898

Middle East (1945–present), 936–950; Arab-Israeli conflict, 938, 939(*map*), 940–941; Arab nationalism and Egypt, 937–938; assessing Arab development, 950; change and conflict in, 944–950; chronology, 937; gender relations in, 945; in the global system, 949–950; Iraq and regional conflicts, 942, 948–949; Islamic militancy, 948–949; Islamic Revolution in Iran, 941–942; nationalism in, 935–936; oil in, 939(*map*), 943 *and illus.;* religion, ethnicity and conflict in, 944; religion and culture in, 945–947; reshaping of, 936–937; Saudi Arabia and the world, 942–944; turmoil in Afghanistan, 948; Pakistani ties to, 980

Middle Passage, 472–473 *and illus.*

"Middle Way," 734. *See also* Social democrats

Midlands, Great Britain, 578

Midway, Battle of (1942), 744

Migrations (population movement), 547. *See also* Immigrations; Refugees; deportation of French Acadians, 503–504; hybrid groups and, 557–558; Indian relocations, 498, 609–610; westward, in United States, 609; labor, in colonial Africa, 643; Boers, in South Africa, 638, 639 *and illus.;* Armenian, 647; Jewish to Palestine, 654; of Arabs, to Americas, 650; African American, 732; in Great Depression, 733; in Europe, 738; from colonies, 751; Chinese, 758; frontiers and, 791; African slavery and, 791, 793; Asian and European (1750–1940), 792(*map*); feminization of, 819; global flows, 823–824; rural-to-urban, in China, 846; Latin Americans to United States, 915; from Pacific islands, 919; rural-to-urban, in Latin America, 927

Militant Islam. *See* Islamic militancy; Jihad

Military. *See also* Armed forces; Navy; War (warfare); Weapons and military technology; French, 445; Buganda (Africa), 465; Ottoman Janissaries, 476–477, 479, 647; Aztec, 487, 489; Dutch colonial, 531, 555; English, in India, 526; European expansion and, 547–548; Japanese, 541, 704, 706, 707–708, 738, 745, 757, 853; in Latin America, 616; European, in colonial Africa, 634; Islamic, in Africa, 633 *and illus.;* Mandika, 637; Zulu, 638; in British India, 661, 665; Ottoman Empire, 476–477, 478–479; Chinese, 687, 690, 694, 835; in World War I, 715, 717; Korean, 701; Nazi German, 741; and Chinese Maoism, 759; Mexican, 779;

British, in Iraq, 775; Russian expansion and, 711, 893; Safavid Persia, 481; decolonialization and, 803; Sikh, in India, 523; social revolution and, 806; Taiwanese, 863; North Korean, 861, 862; Soviet buildup, 885, 886, 889, 905; Wahhabis, 652; power of, in Middle East, 936; in Suez crisis (1956), 938; Israeli, 940 *and illus.;* African government and, 954; Portuguese, in Africa, 953

Military, United States, 677, 732, 911. *See also* Armed forces, United States; in Mexico, 610; interventions by, 614, 621; in World War II, 743; Cold War buildup, 808, 810, 905; end of Cold War and, 812; in East Asia, 841; bases, in Japan, 850, 852; bases, in South Korea, 860; bases, in Taiwan, 863; Islamic terrorism and, 831; Korean War and, 907; interventions by, 908, 922; worldwide (1945–present), 906(*map*); in Lebanon, 944; in Saudi Arabia, 943–944; Persian Gulf War (1991), 942; in Laos and Cambodia, 986–987; bases, in Philippines, 991; in Afghanistan, 980, 1013; in Iraq, 949, 1001, 1013; in Vietnam War, 986, 1013; women and, 1004

Military dictatorship (military rule): in Africa, 954–955; in Burma, 992, 997; in Chile, 925–926; of Indonesia, 989, 991; in Latin America, 901–902, 921; in Pakistan, 972, 974, 980; in Thailand, 992; United States' arms sales to, 905

Military-industrial complex, 905

Mill, John Stuart (Scottish philosopher), 586

Mindanao, Philippines, 529

Mindon (Burmese ruler), 676

Miners' Union (Britain), 582

Ming dynasty (China), 533, 534–535

Mining and minerals, 553, 1011. *See also* Coal; Gold; Iron and steel industry; *specific metals;* in colonial Bolivia, 505; diamond, in Africa, 636, 639; in Latin America, 616, 618; in Australia, 625, 626; in colonial Africa, 643; in South Africa, 640, 770, 957; in developing nations, 903

Minorities. *See* Ethnic minorities; *specific minorities*

Mirabai (Indian woman poet), 522

Mishima, Yukio (Japanese writer), 857

Missionaries. *See* Catholic missionaries; Christian missionaries; Jesuits; Muslim, 828; Protestant, 505, 559, 614, 631, 650, 847, 928

Mississippian culture, 490

Mississippi River, 553; African American music of, 614; French exploration of, 498; as United States border, 607

Mitsui corporation, 705 *and illus.*

Mittelman, James (historian), 1004

Mixed cultures (mixed-descent people): *See also* Mestizos; Mulattos; in African slave trade, 474; in Americas, 488, 500, 555, 557–558; Eurasian, 532, 533; in Latin America, 574, 598, 616, 619; Metis, in Canada, 505, 623; in South Africa, 470; in United States, 609, 611; coloreds, in South Africa, 638

Mlimu (African animist spirit), 636

Mobutuism in Zaire (Congo), 952–953

Mobutu Sese Seko, 952–953, 955, 961

Moctezuma II (Aztec ruler), 495

Modern Era, xxx

Modernization, 603–604, 827; in Ottoman Empire, 647; in Brazil, 779; in Burma, 676; in China, 694, 695, 698, 755, 844; in Egypt, 647–648 *and illus.,* 934(*illus.*), 937; Islam and, 652–654, 669, 945; in Japan, 591, 686, 696, 700, 702–703; of Korea, 858; in Meiji Japan, 704–707 *and map,* 784; in Russia, 709 *and illus.;* in Siam, 676; in Taiwan, 863; of Turkey, 774 *and illus.,* 783; in Middle East, 774–775, 949; world-system concept and, 786–788; in Saudi Arabia, 942; opposition to, in Iran, 941; in Afghanistan, 948; in India, 973, 976; capitalism and, 1002

Moldavia, 646

Moluccas. *See* Maluku (Moluccas)

Mombasa (East African city-state), 467, 469

Monarchy. *See* Kingship (emperors; monarchy)

Monasteries and monks: Buddhist, 528, 815(*illus.*)

Monet, Claude (French painter), 604

Monetary system, 555. *See also* Currency; American metals in, 435; Bretton Woods, 745, 873, 875; European, 896

Mongkut (Siamese ruler), 676

Mongolia (Mongolian Empire), 534(*map*), 535, 540; breakup of, 483; weaponry of, 549; China and, 687, 698; Communism in, 808; Soviet alliance with, 839

Moniz, Donha Felipa (wife of Columbus), 491

Monma Chiyo (Japanese lesbian), 730

Monnet, Jean (French economist), 873, 1014

Monoculture, 507, 509. *See also* Cash crops

Monogamy, in China, 755

Monomotapa (East Africa), 462(*map*), 470

Monopoly, 590. *See also* Big business; political, in Mexico, 922–923

Monopoly trade, 436, 447, 531, 581; British, in China, 690; Indian salt trade, 762

Monotheism, Islam and, 460, 519

Monroe, James, 610

Monroe Doctrine, 610, 1002

Monsoons, 526, 667; India and, 659

Montaigne, Michel Eyquem de (French writer), 439

Montenegrins, 894(*map*)

Montesquieu, Baron de, 455, 503, 568, 586

Montessori, Maria (Italian educator), 602

Montreal, 498, 504

Morales, Evo (Bolivian leader), 921

Morality: changing standards of, xxx–xxxi; Protestant, 441; Buddhist, 992

More, Thomas (English writer), 439

Morelos, José Maria (Mexico), 577

Morgan, Henry (English pirate), 497

Morgan, J. P. (American financier), 613

Morocco, 434, 461, 547, 548, 650; expansion of, 483; labor migration from, 825; monarchy in, 936–937

Moronobu (Japanese artist), 543, 544(*illus.*)

Moros (Philippine Muslims), 529

Moses (Hebrews), 606

Moshoeshoe (Sotho leader), 638

Mosques: in Africa, 463(*illus.*); in India, 523; in Ottoman Empire, 478–479 *and illus.;* in Kuala Lumpur, 998(*illus.*)

Mossi people of Niger Basin, 461

Mothers and Grandmothers of the Plaza de Mayo (Argentina), 901

China, 696; French colonial, 785; in Siam, 528; in Africa, 960, 961
Schools for girls. *See* Women, education of
The Scholars (Wu), 537
Schuman, Robert (French leader), 873
Science, 430, 549. *See also* Computers; High technology; Mathematics; Technology; astronomy, 437–438, 453, 540, 549; Chinese, 534; European, 451, 604; Locke's empiricism and, 454, 455; industry and, 581; Islam and, 654; physics, 602, 604, 735, 789; in British India, 789; of Renaissance Europe, 437–438; western, in China, 754, 755; industrialization and, 816; Christian conservatives and, 828, 913; in India, 982; global warming and, 1011
Scientific Revolution, in Europe, 453
Scotland (Scots), 556; Presbyterianism in, 441, 449; in colonial America, 503; English and, 571
Script: *See also* Writing; Persian, 519; Egyptian hieroglyphs, 629
Seclusion of women (purdah), 670; in Africa, 461; in India, 522; in Middle East, 945; in Safavid Persia, 481, 482; in Saudi Arabia, 943; veiling and, 652, 943, 945
Seclusion policy: in Japan, 699, 702; in Korea, 703
Second Vatican Council (1962–1965), 883
Second World, concept of, 806
Secret police: Argentine, 901; Iranian, 941; Soviet, 727, 885, 890
Secularism, 430, 438, 454
Secularization: in Mexico, 617; in Europe, 603; in United States, 606; in Ottoman Empire, 647; Indian nationalism and, 763; in Egypt, 775; of Turkey, 774; Christian opposition to, 828; in Soviet Union, 887; in Canada, 917
Security Council (United Nations), 810–811
Segun, Mabel (Nigerian writer), 956
Self-determination (self-government). *See also* Independence; Nationalism; Locke on, 454; United States' civil war and, 611; nationalism and, 658, 667, 784; after World War I, 717, 721, 765; in Vietnam, 766; in Egypt, 775; United Nations and, 810; Palestinian, 940; Kurds and, 944
Self-Employed Women's Association (India), 978
Self-help organizations, 644, 819
Self-sufficiency, 507; in Russia, 446; in Ottoman Empire, 477; in Latin America, 618; colonization and loss of, 674; in colonial Africa, 643; in Indian villages, 664, 763; of Qing China, 686–687; in former Soviet Union, 892; in Africa, 960; in Tanzania, 962
Sembene, Ousmane (Senegalese writer), 964
Seminole Indians, 610
Sen, Amartya (Indian economist), 817
Senate (United States), 904
Seneca Falls, Women's Rights Convention in, 614
Senegal, 558; as French colony, 636, 641, 789; women's work in, 819; health care in, 955; literature of, 964; peanut exports of, 643, 789
Senegambia region, 459, 474; slave trade in, 471
Senghor, Leopold (Senegal), 964
Sephardic Jews, 555

Sepoy warriors, in British India, 661, 663, 665
September 11 (2001) terrorist attacks, 831, 897, 909, 943, 948, 1013
Serbia (Serbs), 475, 559, 894(*map*); independence of, 646; World War I and, 716, 719; ethnic cleansing and, 810, 895
Serfs (serfdom), 430, 435. *See also* Peasants; Russian, 445, 709, 711; emancipation of, 711, 722
Serra, Junipero (missionary), 502
Service industries, 816
Seward, William, American expansionist, 610
Sewerage and sanitation, 604, 821
Sex Pistols (British punk group), 881
Sexuality. *See also* Homosexuality; Prostitution; in Europe, 456; Filipino, 558; harassment of slave women, 511; industrialization and, 601; sexual revolution, 878
Sexually-transmitted diseases, 499, 556, 625. *See also* AIDS/HIV
Shaarawi, Huda (Egyptian feminist), 775–776
Shadow puppet drama (Indonesia), 767
Shahs, of Persia (Iran), 483, 649, 774–775, 941
Shaka Zulu, 638
Shakespeare, William, 429, 438–439, 1014
Shamans: African, 474; Muslims and, 651; Pueblo Indian, 500
Shamyl (Chechen leader), 711
Shandong Peninsula (China), 695, 754–755; Japanese in, 698
Shanghai, 690, 755, 821, 846, 847
Sharecropping, 611, 619. *See also* Tenant farmers
Shar'ia (Islamic law): modernity and, 652, 653; in Nigeria, 956; in Iran, 941, 942
Shariati, Ali (Iranian writer), 945–946
Shawnee Indians, 622
Sheep raising, in Australia and New Zealand, 625, 626, 716
Sheffield, industrialization in, 580(*illus.*)
Shellshock, in World War I, 719
Shen, Michael Alphonsus (Chinese traveler), 539
Shi'a Islam (Shi'ism), 559; in Safavid Persia, 480, 482, 483; Sunni rivalry with, 481, 483, 484, 828, 942, 946, 980; in Iraq, 650, 654, 775, 942, 946, 949; in Persia (Iran), 649, 774, 941; Aga Khan IV and, 811; *Hezbollah* movement and, 831; in Saudi Arabia, 943; in Lebanon, 944
Shifting cultivation, in Africa, 965
Shining Path (Peru), 921
Shinobu Yoshioka (Japanese essayist), 856
Shinto religion, in Japan, 541, 857
Shipbuilding, 433
Ships and shipping (merchant marine): *See also* Navy (warships); Ottoman, 475–476; slave trade, 471, 472–473 *and illus.*; Dutch, 531; Indian Ocean trade and, 517, 524; major routes, 592(*map*); Suez Canal and, 648; in China, 689(*illus.*); German submarine attacks on, 720; canal construction and, 795; Spanish galleons, 434, 533; steamships, 579, 590, 593, 690, 702, 783, 795
Shiva (Hindu god), 522
Shock therapy, in Russia, 892
Shoguns, in Japan, 541, 544, 699, 702. *See also specific shogunate*

Shona kingdom (East Africa), 464, 470, 636
Shrines, Aztec, 502
Siam. *See* Thailand (Siam)
Siberia, 558; Russia and, 688, 690, 702, 710(*map*), 791; prison camps in, 712, 722, 726–727, 884, 885; Russians in, 446, 483, 534(*map*), 540
Sidqi az-Zahawi, Jamil (Iraqi poet), 652
Siege weapons, 549
Sierra Club, 823
Sierra Leone, 474, 632, 637, 909; colleges in, 642; ethnic conflict in, 955; life expectancy in, 1007
Siglienza y Gongora, Carlos de (Mexican scholar), 501
Sikhs, 522–523, 659, 662; nationalism of, 975; partition of India and, 971, 972; in India, 978
Silesia, coal in, 580
Silk industry and trade: Chinese, 505, 534, 542, 543, 553, 689, 693; Indian, 525
Silk Road Ensemble, 1006
Silk Road trade, 480, 483, 484, 1001
Silver: Japanese, 543; as medium of exchange, 689
Silver, from Americas, 434, 436, 496, 499, 500, 513, 520, 553, 555; Bolivian, 618; in China, 505, 533, 538, 550
Simon, Paul (singer-songwriter), 1006
Sinan, Pasha, 477, 478–479
Singapore, 752, 858, 990(*map*), 992; Chinese in, 673, 680, 794(*illus.*), 991, 998; Indian immigrants in, 668; English language in, 829; independence of, 991; globalization and, 813, 1002; economic growth in, 851(*map*), 1007; prosperity in, 997, 998; high technology in, 1007
Singh, Manmohan (Indian leader), 977
Singh, Ranjit (Marathas), 659, 662
Sinhalese: Buddhism and, 663; in Sri Lanka, 663, 981
Sinn Fein (Ireland), 586
Sino-Japanese War (1894-1895), 695–696, 706
Sisal fiber, 507
Sisters in Islam (Malaysia), 997
Skin color, racism and, 471, 473, 512, 558. *See also* Racism; in United States, 611–612, 619; in Brazil, 619; color bars in Africa, 640, 642
Skyscrapers, in East Asia, 863, 998(*illus.*)
The Sky Burial (Xue), 848
Slave revolts, 473, 512, 631; in Haiti, 574–575
Slavery, abolition of, 610, 611, 785; in Brazil, 616; in France, 570; in United States, 569
Slavery, African, 466, 556; in colonial Brazil, 505; in colonial North America, 503, 509; disease and, 499; intermarriage and, 557; maroon societies, 512; in plantation zone, 434, 488, 507–509, 510–512 *and illus.*, 550; women as, 510–511 *and illus.*
Slavery (slaves). *See also* Slavery, African; British industrialization and, 578; in China, 535; in colonial Brazil, 497; Dutch and, 531; indentured labor, 503, 668, 693; in Islam, 653; Native Americans as, 471, 493, 494, 503(*illus.*); in Nicaragua, 621; Protestant missionaries and, 559; resistance by, 459, 510–511; revolts by, in Americas, 574, 631; in United States, 605, 606

Japan, 541, 542, 543; African Muslim, 633 (illus.); Zulu, 638; Marathas, 659; Nepalese Gurkhas, 663
Warsaw Pact, 871, 889, 897
Warships. See Navy (warships)
War (warfare): See also Civil wars; Cold War; Guerrilla warfare; World Wars; specific wars; religion and, 443; in Europe, 444–445, 550; Pacific Islander, 494; Spanish conquistadors, 495–496 and illus.; in Bengal, 526; gunpowder and, 549; Maori, in New Zealand, 626; preemptive war doctrine, 909, 910, 982; post-Cold War decline in, 1013–1014
Washington, D.C., 606, 1013; King's March on (1963), 914 and illus.
Washington, George, 568
Watt, James (English inventor), 579
Wealth and wealthy, 434, 593. See also Income inequality; in Latin America, 574; in United States, 613, 614, 912; world economy and, 790; in Brazil, 924, 925; in Chile, 925, 926
Wealth gap: in Latin America, 618; Britain and India, 668; colonial, 752; distribution of, 814; in China, 846; in Russia, 893; in Egypt, 938; in Nigeria, 956; in India, 977; in Philippines, 991; in Malaysia, 998; global, 1008(map), 1012
Weapons and military technology, 795. See also Artillery; Bombs and bombing; Cannon; Guns; Nuclear weapons; Africa Oyo, 463; Native American, 491; of Safavid Persia, 481; shipboard, 434; Spanish conquistador, 487, 495, 496(illus.); swords, 495, 531, 542, 549; Aztec, 489–490; Western, and Islam, 653; European, 433, 444–445, 467, 479, 518, 529, 550, 553, 634, 652, 690, 784; French colonial, 637; Zulu spears, 638; Japanese, 702; in World War I, 717, 719, 720; Nazi Germany, 738; United States' sales of, 812, 905, 911; Soviet aid to revolutionaries, 803; biological weapons, 811; Cold War buildup, 810, 852; landmines, 809, 811; chemical, in Vietnam War, 986
Weapons of mass destruction, 809. See also Nuclear weapons; search for, in Iraq, 909, 910, 948
Weather. See Climate (climate change; weather)
The Wealth of Nations (Smith), 580–581
Weaving, women and, 680. See also Textiles (textile industry)
Wei Jingsheng (Chinese dissident), 845
Weimar Republic (Germany), 729; war reparations and, 728, 734, 737
Welfare states, 589, 912; in Europe, 807, 814, 875, 876–877, 897; end of, in eastern Europe, 895; end of, in Russia, 893; Japan as, 854; New Zealand as, 807, 918
Well of Loneliness (Hall), 729
Wells, Ida B. (anti-lynching activist), 612
Wesley, John (founder of Methodists), 603
West Africa: See also specific country; cash crop plantations in, 633; European colonialism in, 630, 637, 805; European trade with, 460, 464, 465–466, 555; freed slaves in, 632; Ashante people of, 636, 644, 784; gold from, 433–434; hybrid social groups in, 558; Islam in, 633; World War I and, 750; music of,

769–770; nationalism in, 769, 952; French in, 789, 814, 952; literature of, 964; Portuguese exploration of, 466, 467; slave trade and, 459, 471, 510, 549; Sudan, 460–461, 555; women traders in, 558
West Bank, 939(map), 940 and illus.
Western Asia, 776; as Near East, xxviii
Western civilization, xxvii
Western colonization, 1001. See also Western imperialism
Western Europe, 549. See also specific countries; advantages of, 550; food sources in, 556; love marriage in, 601; immigrants to United States from, 613; Islam and, 645; colonization, 658; Ottoman Empire and, 480; political fragmentation of, 433; technological advances in, 453, 480; world economy and, 553
Western Europe (1945–present), 785, 868–883. See also European Union; chronology, 869; from cooperation to European Community, 873–875 and map; cultural reshaping in, 881; humanitarian groups in, 811; immigrant labor in, 824; immigration and identity in, 880–881; NATO and Cold War in, 871–873 and map; China and, 844; politics in remaking of, 869–871; recovery from war in, 807, 868–869, 903; revolutions and, 806; social democracy in, 876–877; social reform and gender relations in, 877–880; societies and cultures, 875–883; thought and religion in, 882–883; United States and, 808, 812; welfare states in, 814, 876–877; Canada and, 917; oil embargo (1973) and, 943; Africa and, 960; unity in, 1013
Western Hemisphere. See Americas, the (New World)
Western imperialism (Western domination), 802, 806. See also Colonialism; Imperialism; specific empire; industrialization and, 590–591; resurgence of, 590–594; in Asia, 657–658; China and, 835, 843; Christianity and, 965; revolutions against, 999
Westernization (Western culture), 734–735, 795, 827; in British India, 663–664, 667, 669; in China, 691, 692, 694, 844, 847; in Siam, 676; Japanese expansion and, 702, 706–707 and map; in Russia, 446, 712; of Turkey, 774 and illus.; in global system, 785, 789; Islam and, 775–776, 828, 945, 946; in Japan, 852; Derrida's deconstruction of, 882; opposition to, in Iran, 941; in Middle East, 949; in Africa, 966; global standardization and, 1012
Western nations: See also Western Europe; United States; specific nations; environmental destruction in, 822; immigrant labor in, 824; Asian "Little Dragons" and, 864; resource consumption of, 821, 1009; cultural imperialism of, 1002, 1006
Western Samoa, 919
Western trade, with China, 688, 689
West Germany, 873, 893, 896; economic growth of, 807, 812; European Community and, 873; foreign workers in, 880; France and, 869–870; homosexuality in, 880; postwar reconstruction of, 868; as welfare state, 876; church-operated schools in, 882
West Indies. See Caribbean region
Westphalia, Treaty of (1648), 444

Whale hunting, 625
What Is to Be Done (Lenin), 723
Wheat: in Argentina, 752; in Canada, 623, 716; government subsidies for, 817
Wheatley, Phyllis (African slave poet), 631
White collar workers, 583
"White man's burden," 593, 667, 677
White Russians, 724, 725(map)
White supremacy: See also Racism; in South Africa, 470, 638, 640, 770, 956–957
Whitman, Walt (American poet), 614
Wilde, Oscar (Irish writer), 601
Wilhelm II, Kaiser (Germany), 719, 721
William and Mary (England), 449
William I, Kaiser (Germany), 584
William of Orange, 443, 449
Williams, Betty (Irish activist), 878
Williams, Hank (musician), 915
Williams, Henry (Jamaican slave), 631
Wilson, Woodrow, 615, 722, 732; World War I and, 720; Fourteen Points of, 721; Russian Communism and, 724; Mexico and, 753
Windmills, 555; in Caribbean, 508(illus.)
Wine: in Algeria, 650; in Vietnam, 751
"Winner-take-all" economy, 912
Winthrop, John (Puritan leader), 503, 569
Witches, torture of, 456
Wolf, Eric (historian), 550
Wollstonecraft, Mary, 571, 602
Wolof people of Senegal, 636
Women: See also Childbearing; Feminism; Gender; Marriage; Women's rights; in African politics, 461–462, 463; Arawak, 490(illus.); in Japan, 543; in American Revolution, 568; in markets, 531; in Mexican Revolution, 617 and illus.; in Mughal India, 519–520, 522, 523; African colonialism and, 643–644; "new women" in India, 670; Islamic modernization and, 652; Ottoman, 477, 480; sati (widow burning) and, 519, 558; in Siam, 528; as slaves, 510–511 and illus., 512; in Southeast Asia, 528; in Spanish Americas, 500–501, 502–503; Chinese footbinding of, 536, 685, 696, 754; Vietnamese poets, 674; in Philippines' revolution, 677; birth control and, 819, 821; development and, 819; in Japan, 729–731; AIDS and, 825; Russian economic woes and, 893; in suburban United States, 914; protests by, 901; Islamic modernization and, 934(illus.), 943; Palestinian Muslim, 941; poverty of, worldwide, 1007
Women, education of: in Europe, 454; in Indonesia, 681, 682; in China, 536, 558–559, 688, 754; in Egypt, 653; in Korea, 703; in Japan, 543, 700, 854; in Russia, 712; reduced fertility and, 821; in Saudi Arabia, 943; in India, 978
Women, seclusion of (purdah), 670; in Africa, 461; in India, 522; in Middle East, 945; in Safavid Persia, 481, 482; in Saudi Arabia, 943; veiling and, 652, 943, 945
Women, work of, 729. See also Market women; in textile industry, 474, 502, 528, 532, 553, 601, 606, 612(illus.), 613, 680, 693, 705; in colonial Africa, 643–644, 790; market women, 643–644, 680, 769, 790, 928, 963; in World War II, 743; in Africa, 769, 963;